FIELDING'S
CARIBBEAN

Other Fielding Titles

Fielding's Australia
Fielding's Bahamas
Fielding's Belgium
Fielding's Bermuda
Fielding's Brazil
Fielding's Britain
Fielding's Budget Europe
Fielding's Caribbean
Fielding's Europe
Fielding's Far East
Fielding's Guide to Freewheeling RV Adventures
Fielding's Guide to the World's Most Dangerous Places
Fielding's Guide to the World's Great Voyages
Fielding's Guide to Kenya's Best Hotels, Lodges & Homestays
Fielding's Guide to the World's Most Romantic Places
Fielding's Hawaii
Fielding's Holland
Fielding's Italy
Fielding's London Agenda
Fielding's Los Angeles Agenda
Fielding's Malaysia
Fielding's Mexico
Fielding's New York Agenda
Fielding's New Zealand
Fielding's Paris Agenda
Fielding's Portugal
Fielding's Scandinavia
Fielding's Southern Vietnam on Two Wheels
Fielding's Southeast Asia
Fielding's Spain
Fielding's Vacation Places Rated
Fielding's Vietnam
Fielding's Worldwide Cruises

FIELDING'S CARIBBEAN

The most in-depth and savvy guide to the islands

Fielding Worldwide, Inc.

308 South Catalina Avenue

Redondo Beach, California 90277 U.S.A.

FIELDING WORLDWIDE INC.

PUBLISHER AND CEO	**Robert Young Pelton**
PUBLISHING DIRECTOR	**Paul T. Snapp**
ELECTRONIC PUBLISHING DIRECTOR	**Larry E. Hart**
PUBLIC RELATIONS DIRECTOR	**Beverly Riess**
ACCOUNT SERVICES MANAGER	**Christy Harp**
DATABASE PUBLISHING MANAGER	**John Guillebeaux**

EDITORS

Linda Charlton   **Kathy Knoles**

PRODUCTION

Gini Martin   **Chris Snyder**
Craig South   **Janice Whitby**

Joyce Wiswell

COVER DESIGNED BY	**Digital Artists, Inc.**
COVER PHOTOGRAPHERS — Front Cover	**Mark Lewis & Donald Nausbaum/Tony Stone Images**
Back Cover	**Julie Houck/Westlight**
INSIDE PHOTOS	**Carol Lee, Benford Associates, Grenada Tourist Office, Karen Weiner, Escalera Associates, Robinson, Yesavich & Pepperdine, Inc., Saba Tourist Office, Trombone Associates, Corel Professional Photos**

Inquiries should be addressed to: Fielding Worldwide, Inc., 308 South Catalina Ave., Redondo Beach, California 90277 U.S.A., ☎ *(310) 372-4474*, Facsimile *(310) 376-8064*, 8:30 a.m.–5:30 p.m. Pacific Standard Time.

ISBN 1-56952-029-1

Library of Congress Catalog Card Number

94-068330

Printed in the United States of America

Letter from the Publisher

The Caribbean can be a daunting place when it comes to choosing the perfect island getaway. Our focus is making sure you get the best experience for your time and money. To assist you we have created handy comparison tables for accommodations and restaurants complete with best buy and highest rated listings so you can get the most for your money. You'll also find the intros tighter and with a definite accent on the romantic and adventurous. Loyal readers will be pleasantly surprised to find the entire book rewritten and with every listing checked for accuracy just before presstime (March 1995). This means there is no other guide as up-to-date, as useful or as accurate as *Fielding's Guide to the Caribbean.*

Author Joyce Wiswell faced with the task of covering and reviewing hundreds of "tropical getaways on white sandy beaches" brings a youthful enthusiasm along with a true love of the Caribbean to this book. She has tackled the daunting task of giving the reader a balanced overview of the region as well as highlighting the unique personality of each island. In these 1000 plus pages you will find the famous, the hidden and the overlooked all rated and reviewed in our new easy-to-use format. Supporting her efforts have been the staff and researchers at Fielding Worldwide who have done an impressive job of gathering, checking, sorting and compiling over 1500 attractions, hotels and restaurants. Special thanks to our staff for making it all come together. If it helps you find that one perfect place for your once-a-year getaway then we have done our job.

Today, the concept of independent travel has never been bigger. Our policy of *brutal honesty* and a highly personal point of view has never changed; it just seems the travel world has caught up with us.

Enjoy your Caribbean adventure.

RYP

Robert Young Pelton
Publisher and CEO
Fielding Worldwide, Inc.

Fielding Rating Icons

The Fielding Rating Icons are highly personal and awarded to help the besieged traveler choose from among the dizzying array of activities, attractions, hotels, restaurants and sights. The awarding of an icon denotes unusual or exceptional qualities in the relevant category.

RATINGS							
Fielding Award	Author Selection	Money Saver	Expensive	Quality	Warning	Danger	Inexpensive
Spacious	Cramped	Mild Disapproval					

CULTURAL							
Museum/ Art	Interesting Architecture	History	Book Reference	Artistically Important	Musically Interesting	Cultural Archeology	Crafts
Theatre	Festivals						

SIGHTS							
Picturesque	Great Scenery	Market	Beaches/ Resorts	Cultural	Fortress	Castles	Church

WHERE TO STAY							
Simple	Luxurious	Cottage	Bed & Breakfast	Scenic	Business	Honeymoon	Chateau

TRAVEL TIPS							
Arrival/ Departure	By Air	By Water	By Train	By Car	Bus/Local Transit	Barge	River Boat
Calendar	Itinerary	Compass	Kids				

ACTIVITIES

Downhill Skiing	X–country Skiing	Water Sports	Sailing
Scuba Diving	Snorkeling/ Diving	Deep-sea Fishing	Freshwater Fishing
Swimming	Hiking	Walking	Relaxing
Golf	Tennis	Horseback Riding	General Sports
Cycling	Workout		

SPECIAL INTEREST

Nightlife	Singles	Romantic	Nude Beaches
Lecture	Spectacular Cuisine	Wine Tasting	Shopping
Cafe Stops	Gardening	Pro Sports	Mystery

A NOTE TO OUR READERS:

If you have had an extraordinary, mediocre or horrific experience we want to hear about it. If something has changed since we have gone to press, let us know. Those business owners who flood us with shameless self promotion under the guise of reader's letters will be noted and reviewed more rigorously next time. If you would like to send information for review in next year's edition send it to:

Fielding's Caribbean
308 South Catalina Avenue
Redondo Beach, CA 90277
FAX: (310) 376-8064

TABLE OF CONTENTS

LIST OF MAPS

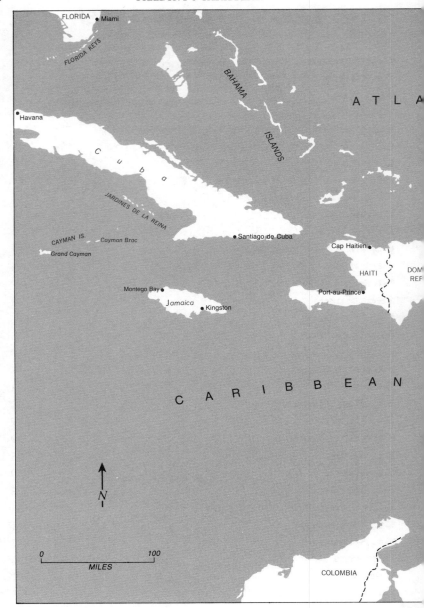

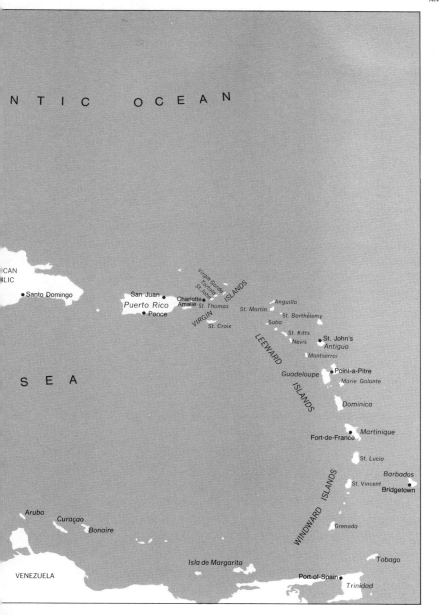

TO OUR READERS

So you've dived Grand Cayman, done Club Med to death, and dived three years straight in a row in Bonaire. You've taken enough Caribbean cruises to sleep through a package tour, and you've had it with the hidden surcharges on your not-all inclusive bill. Maybe you've heard about one too many pirate-and-lassie theme nights in the lizard lounge of your Aruban resort, and if you meet one more American tourist in bermuda shorts and white socks, you think you'll throw up.

Hold on—this newly written, up-to-the minute Caribbean guide has been written just for you— the cutting-edge traveler who yearns for the untried-but-true tropical experiences, the independent adventurer who thrills at the idea of discovering little traversed trails, secluded waterfalls, and pristine dive sites whose locations are known only by local masters. This guide is for the Caribbean tourist who wants to intimately *experience* the rainforest, not just have it explained, who wants to pit his or her own physical, emotional and psychological limits against the challenges of the tropics. Of course, we at Fielding are firm believers of finding that perfect beach (even that perfect bar) and vegging out like a cucumber, but we also believe tourism in the 90s is all about finding new things, new places, new risks to try out. And that's what our guide for 1995 is all about.

For instance, ever think about kayaking like an Arawak Indian in the Virgin Islands, following the trail of the original natives? How about mountain climbing around a still boiling volcano or bicycling through the hills of the French-styled Guadeloupe? Commandeering Argentine horses around mountain trails in Jamaica? How about picking an island in the Grenadines and sailing your own charter to four uninhabited ones? These are the adventures we at Fielding cherish, and you'll find all the ways, means, and how-not-to's clearly delineated in our guide. In order to bring you fully realized descriptions of the regions' best dive sites, we've collected the opinions of experts on every single island; to bring you the finest treks available, we've even done many ourselves. But we don't know *everything*—the best way to use this book is to let it inspire you and then take you further. If you end up with adventures we don't even know about, make sure you write to us.

At Fielding we also believe in experiencing, no matter what our budget, the best in lodging and food. In this edition, you'll find the latest information—updated days before printing—about accommodations in several categories, from beach resorts and hotels to self-catering villas to intimate inns and even cheap digs. When you have the money, there's nothing finer than a luxurious tropical resort where everything you've ever imagined (including your own private island) can be arranged, but the Caribbean is not only for the rich and famous. In the section called "Caribbean Planner" you'll find numerous ways to save money without ever feeling a pinch. And as for dining, we have included not only the best places to eat, but the finest island delicacies to ferret out. Some of our best meals have been in out-of-the-way places most folks have never heard about, cooked by smiling native ladies who put true love in their cooking.

In order to use this book in the most efficient way, you can read the introductions to each island chapter and peruse the section called "Treks." This will give you a tantalizing introduction to the possible pleasures on each island; from there you can investigate sections called "People," "Where to Stay," and "Where to Eat."

Before you take off, make sure you have read the chapter upfront called "Caribbean Planner" which will help you make travel and lodging reservations to your best advantage. The chapter "Caribbean Culture" will prepare you to enter into the life and soul of each island.

How do we end the introduction to a book that is brimming ear to ear with advice? Of course, we could warn you about the tropical sun, or tell you about drinking water, or give you tips about how to avoid a bout with the tropical trots. But we have a little piece of advice we think is much more important. We at Fielding have heard (and have actually tested thoroughly) that the only book worth reading on a Caribbean vacation is the trashiest, steamiest novel you can find because you can flit in and out of the pages without ever losing the plot.

FIELDING'S BEST VALUE ACCOMMODATIONS

Rating	Accommodation	City	Island
★★★	Fountain Beach	Road Bay	Anguilla
★★★	Hawksbill Beach Hotel	St. John's	Antigua
★★★	Aruba Palm Beach	Oranjestad	Aruba
★★★	Discovery Bay Hotel	St. Peter	Barbados
★★★★	The K Club	Codrington	Barbuda
★★★	Sand Dollar Beach Club	Kralendijk	Bonaire
★★★	Mango Bay Resort	North Sound	British Virgin Islands
★★★	Pan-Cayman House	Georgetown	Cayman Islands
★★★★	Curacao Caribbean Hotel	Willemstad	Curaçao
★★★	Sans Souci Manor	Bagatelle	Dominica
★★★★	Hotel Rio Taino	Puerto Plata	Dominican Republic
★★★★	Rex Grenadian	St. George's	Grenada
★★★	Plantation Ste. Marthe	Pointe-a-Pitre	Guadaloupe
★★★	Braco Village Resort	Kingston	Jamaica
★★★★	Meridien Martinique	Fort-de-France	Martinique
★★★	Villas of Montserrat	Plymouth	Montserrat
★★★	Mt. Nevis Hotel	Charlestown	Nevis
★★★	Mayaguez Hilton	West Coast	Puerto Rico
★★★	Captain's Quarters	The Bottom	Saba
★★★	Tropical Hotel	Gustavia	St. Barthélémy
★★★	Hilty House Inn	Christiansted	St. Croix
★★★	Old Gin House	Oranjestad	Sint Eustatius
★★★	Cinnamon Bay Campground	Coral Bay	St. John
★★★	White House	Basseterre	St. Kitts
★★★	Marigot Bay Resort	Castries	St. Lucia
★★★	Grand Case Beach Club	Philipsburg	St. Martin
★★★	Hotel 1829	Charlotte Amalie	St. Thomas
★★★★	Young Island Resort	Kingston	St. Vincent
★★★★	Asa Wright Nature Center	Port of Spain	Trinidad
★★★	Turtle Beach Hotel	Plymouth	Tobago
★★★	Windmills Plantation	Cockburn Town	Turks & Caicos

CARIBBEAN PLANNER

By Air

Numerous airlines fly to the Caribbean, and depending on your point of departure and destination, you may be able to fly direct nonstop. San Juan, Puerto Rico serves as a major hub for all Caribbean destinations, and American Airlines has greatly expanded its Caribbean terminal in recent years to accommodate the enormous influx of passengers. If your island destination is small, you may have to supplement an international flight on a major carrier with a smaller bumper-plane flight, or even a ferry ride, if the island is private. Most islands have their own national carrier (although the planes might be quite small), which transports passengers between neighboring islands.

Among the major airlines offering U.S.-Caribbean connections are: Aeromexico, Air Jamaica, ALM, American, American Eagle, Avensa, Avianca, British West Indian Airlines (BWIA), Cayman Airways, Continental, Delta, Dominicana, Lacsa, LanChile, Mexicana, Northwest, TACA, TWA, United, USAir, and Viasa.

Your first task, after picking your destination and date of travel, is to choose your class of airfare—first class, business class, cash (economy or tourist class), excursion or discount, and standby. Be on the lookout for numerous promotional fares and fares available from bucket shops, or wholesalers who offer tickets at discounts provided certain date requirements are met. Fares are usually lower during low season (mid-April-mid-December) and considerable discounts can be obtained by purchasing tickets far in advance. On the other hand, be on the lookout for last-minute deals offered by wholesalers who need to sell off their pool of tickets.

All flights must be reconfirmed 48 hours before departure, both ways. There have been reported cases of travelers losing their confirmation on their way home just for failing to confirm appropriately.

Smoking is allowed on most nonstop flights between the U.S. and international destinations (the exceptions are Northwest and USAir, which do not allow smoking). Federal law bans smoking on all U.S. flights within the U.S. and its territories that are less than six hours.

Luggage requirements during high season are more strictly enforced than at other times, when the plane is likely not to be full. On major international carriers, passengers are usually allowed to carry one bag on board that fits under the seat or in the overhead bin; two bags may be checked as cargo. Airlines differ in the weight and size of luggage, so make sure you check before packing. In general, a checked bag cannot exceed 62 inches or 70 pounds. You may have to pay an extra fee for sporting gear or oversized equipment. Inter-island flights may have even tighter restrictions on baggage. Label your luggage clearly, and make sure any color coded tags that mark your destination are properly marked and attached.

Chartered flights often have requirements that travelers do not take notice of until it is too late. Often extra charges are assessed if you change the date of your travel, or your ticket may not even be valid if you change the date. In the case of nonrefundable tickets, your best bet is to buy cancellation insurance to protect you in case you need to change the flight. Charter operators have been known to fail, so do investigate the company's history before forking out any large amount of money. For more information, contact **Jax Fax** *(397 Post Rd., Darien, CT 06820;* ☎ *(203) 655-8746; FAX (203) 655-6257.*

Last-minute travel clubs provide a wealth of information on bargains and cheap tickets. You don't even have to travel at the last minute in some cases. Membership is usually required at an annual fee, though a few clubs offer free membership.Among the most active are **Vacations to Go** ☎ *(713) 974-2121;* **FLY ASAP** ☎ *(800) -FLY-ASAP.*

One of the cheapest ways to fly is as a representative for courier services. Passengers can receive discounted or free tickets if they accept the task of delivering a package or letter to an agency at the intended destination. Usually the courier must return within a specified time limit (most often a week) and is only allowed to travel with hand luggage. Applications must be filled out in advance, and the best tickets are usually available on the shortest advance notice. For more information, get a hold of the book: *Air Courier Bargains*

($14.95, $2.50 shipping and handling), by Kelly Monaghan *(The Intrepid Traveler, P.O. Box 438, New York, NY 10034; ☎ (212) 569-1081).*

For more information on travel to individual islands, see "Arrival and Departure" in the directory at the end of each chapter.

By Sea

Cruising the Caribbean islands in large ocean-going vessels is one of the most popular ways to visit the region. Various itineraries, covering different regions, are available, allowing you to visit a maximum number of destinations in the shortest amount of time. Passengers can choose to visit individual islands on shore excursions, which are not included in the fixed cruise rate. Often cruiseliners hire special guides who are familiar with the region, give lectures and often present slide shows of each island to prepare you for your excursion.

The price of cruises depends greatly on the kind of ship you choose, as well as the size and location of your cabin. Do acquire as much information as you can prior to booking a cabin. Charts issued by the **Cruise Lines Association** *(CLIA, 500 Fifth Avenue, Suite 1407, New York, NY 10110; ☎ (212) 921-0066, FAX (212) 921-0549)* can give you detailed information regarding ship layout and facilities and are available at the CLIA-affiliated travel agencies.

Giant cruiseliners aren't the only way to sail the Caribbean seas. Fabulous day cruises (or even week-long cruises) on an enormous array of vessels from Hobie Cats to schooners can be chartered, either through your hotel or through the local marina. Picnic trips are especially fun, where you are deposited on an island in the morning and picked up in the afternoon. You can even hitch a ride on the mail ferry on some islands or talk a fisherman into taking you out to sea while he gathers his day's catch. Some socially ambitious travelers even hang out at marinas to flirt with the millionaire yachties who dock at port; many a free round-the-world cruise has been obtained in this fashion; the island of St. Barts is especially good for this. For more information about local conditions, see under the "Sports" section of each individual island.

For the best information about cruising the Caribbean, see *Fielding's Worldwide Cruises* guide, by Anne Campbell.

By Land

Once you get to your island of choice, how to get around will be the task upmost in your mind. One of the advantages of staying at an all-inclusive resort is that any need to tool around the island looking for more diversion will be sorely reduced by the wealth of activities at your resort. Packaged tours also simplify the issue of land transportation; included in the package usually are airport transfers and sightseeing tours. If you are traveling on your own, however, you may be tempted to rent a car. In some cases, if you stay at less expensive accommodations, you may need a car to get to a beach.

Most islands have numerous car rental agencies, which will deliver vehicles to the airport or directly to your hotel. Many airports have agencies at the exit for international flights. Most companies prefer credit cards for payment, and the minimum age required to rent the car differs from agency to agency. (In general, it's best to stick with American-based agencies like Budget, Avis, and Hertz, in case of billing mistakes, etc.) To rent a car in the Caribbean, you will most always need to show your U.S. driver's license; in a few cases you will need to have an International Driver's Permit, especially on islands where the street signs are not in English. (International licenses can be obtained from your nearest American Automobile Association—check your local directory.)

Driving conditions differ drastically from island to island. On numerous islands, driving is on the left side of the street, which can be hazardous if you are not used to it. Roads on some islands are disastrously narrow and wind dangerously around the sides of mountains. On wealthier islands, roads can be highly modern and paved. On some islands, it simply isn't safe to drive at night due to the ever-presence of crime. Do check with the island's consulate or tourist board for other warnings you should heed.

Some islands have excellent bus systems, including special ones to favorite beaches; on other islands, bus transport is so crowded and dangerous that tourists are well advised to forego it. Taxis are omnipresent and special ones can be hired by your hotel, usually significantly more expensive than ones you hail yourself in the street. Most taxi drivers are relatively honest; islands have different ways of regulating rates, but usually the driver is required to carry an updated list of fees. Sometimes special rates can be negotiated for extended service; if you are planning to take a taxi to an out-of-the-way restaurant, do arrange for the driver to pick you up when you are finished. Many taxi drivers in the Caribbean are also schooled as guides and can be charmingly loquacious about the island's charms. Some travelers have even reported that their taxi driver became their best friend and took them to sights they never would have found on their own.

For more information about land travel, see "Getting Around" in the directory at the back of each island chapter.

Lodging

Lodging in the Caribbean runs from the fabulous to the primitive, from the $10,000 fantasy island to a tent pitched on a beach. Some of the most exclusive hideaways in the world are to be found in the Caribbean, as well as all-inclusive resorts, where every one of your needs, from entertainment to sports to dining and sunbathing, can be completely fulfilled. Although you can play havoc with your gold card in some top-class hotels, you can also find extremely affordable accommodations, from large moderately priced hotels to charming small inns. On many islands you can stay at bed-and-breakfast guesthouses where the lodging is run by congenial locals who love to share their life stories with you. For those who are looking for more privacy, there are numerous opportunities to rent villas and apartments with kitchen facilities; some, rented in the absence of the owner, often come with their own maid and chef. In addition to information provided here, you will find detailed listings of different types of accommodations in each island chapter.

It's important to choose and reserve a room well in advance of your trip, particularly during high season when the best rooms go fast and many fine hotels (and small ones) are completely booked. Most hotels expect you to arrive before 5 p.m., so if you are planning to be later, do inform them. Many times hotels will provide transfers from the airport; check to see if it is included in your rate.

It's essential to find out what meal plan your hotel rate includes. Options are the European Plan (EP with no meals), Continental Plan (CP with Continental breakfast), Breakfast Plan (BP, with full breakfast), Modified American Plan (MAP, with two meals), Full American Plan (FAP, with three meals), or All-Inclusive (with three meals, all facilities and drinks unless otherwise noted). In order to pick the plan that's best for you, consider how important eating out at different restaurants is to you, whether you enjoy eating at a big or small restaurant, etc. Many hotels insist on the Modified American Plan during high season, but sometimes it is possible to exchange dinners for lunch. Do arrive at your hotel with the deposit receipt in hand, in the case of mistakes or problems. Hidden surcharges should also be investigated (see below under the "Secrets of Surcharges.") In some cases, you will be charged for sports equipment and perhaps beach chairs.

If you plan to lounge around in your room, the location and view of the apartment may be very important to you. There's nothing like having a sit-on balcony where you can take breakfast overlooking the ocean in the morning, but you will pay prettily for the privilege. Decide whether you want to stay on the leeward side of the island (calm water, good for snorkeling) or the windward side (rough, high waves, good for surfing). Also, find out whether the lodging is walking distance to the beach. Inquire if the hotel has a free shuttle to the nearest one. If not, you will have to either hire a taxi or rent a car to get around.

On many islands, cooling trade winds (encouraged by ceiling fans) make air-conditioning superfluous, but if you like to take naps in the afternoon, air-conditioning can help to cool the midday heat down. Second-floor rooms usually have the best ventilation, in particular corner ones which can take advantage of cross currents. Do make sure that if you open the windows, there are screens in place. Mosquitoes can ruin an otherwise paradisiacal vacation.

Anyone traveling on a budget should definitely book a room during off-season (mid-April to mid-December) since gloriously low rates can be discovered at some of the finest lodgings in the entire region.

(For more information on All-Inclusives and alternative accommodations, see "Ten Ways to Save Money" below.)

Fielding's Choice Hotels in the Caribbean

NUDE BEACHES

Hedonism II (Negril, Jamaica)

Couples (Ocho Rios, Jamaica)

Sandals Royal Caribbean (Montego Bay, Jamaica)

Grand Lido Negril (Negril, Jamaica)

Jamaica-Jamaica (Runaway Bay, Jamaica)

DIVING

Club Med Turkoise (Providenciales, Turks & Caicos)

Spanish Bay Reef All-Inclusive Dive Resort (Grand Cayman)

GOLF

Sandals Royal Caribbean (Montego Bay, Jamaica)

Sandals Dunn's River (Ocho Rios, Jamaica)

Playa Naco Golf and Tennis Resort (Dominican Republic)

Jamaica-Jamaica (Runaway Bay, Jamaica)

Sandals St. Lucia (St. Lucia)

SPA/FITNESS

Swept Away (Negril)

San Souci Lido (Ocho Rios, Jamaica)

Le Sport (St. Lucia)

LaSource (Grenada)

Jalousie Plantation (St.Lucia)

Radisson Ciboney Spa/Villa/Beach Resort (Ocho Rios, Jamaica)

SHOPPING

Le Flamboyant (Phillipsburg, St. Maarten)

Almond Beach Club (Barbados)

FREE WEDDINGS

Boscobel Beach Hotel (Jamaica)

Couples (Jamaica)

Grand Lido Negril (Jamaica)

Hedonism II (Jamaica)

Jamaica-Jamaica Hotel (Jamaica)

San Souci Lido (Jamaica)

SPECIAL HONEYMOON PACKAGES

Aruba Royal Resort (Aruba)

Bolongo Beach resort (St. Thomas)

Casa del Campo (Dominican Republic)

Cinnamon Reef(Anguilla)

Cormorant Beach Club (St. Croix)

Francois Plantation (St. Barts)

Harbour Village (Bonaire)

Long Bay Beach Resort (Tortola)

Turtle Cove (Provo, Turks & Caicos)

Secret Harbour (Grenada)

FAMILY

Club Med St. Lucia (St. Lucia)

Club Med Punta Cana (Dominican Republic)

Franklin D. Resort (Runaway Bay, Jamaica)

Boscobel Beach (Ocho RIos, Jamaica)

Packing the Suitcase

One look at the fashion advertisements in a magazine like *Caribbean Travel & Life* will give you an idea of how to dress on an island. The first rule is cool; the second rule is comfort; and the third rule is chic (depending on where you stay and what restaurants you haunt.) On an island like Martinique, even the hotel maids will treat you differently if you are fashionably attired, but on Saba, no one really cares what you wear (in fact you could easily become overdressed) and on some private islands, if you're the only guests, you can practically go around nude.

Generally, however, daytime dress revolves around cotton slacks or shorts for men, and shorts or sundresses for women. Some protection should always be brought for the sun, whether it is a good pair of sunglasses, a light coverup for your arms, or a wide-brimmed hat. During the winter, men will enjoy wearing a jacket and open-neck shirt at night, particularly if you are dining in romantic inns or elegant gourmet restaurants where the service is first class. Many of the more expensive eateries boast strong air-conditioning, which can be a shock to your system if you've been out in the sun all day. Women will want a sweater in the evenings or a light shawl. Singles who are cruising nightclubs or staying at singles-only resorts should probably dress to kill, but couples can get away with anything that's casually chic. In most countries (but especially poor ones), you should leave all expensive jewelry at home.

Synthetic and nylon just don't make it in the tropics since they tend to stick to your skin. Do collect a wardrobe of lightweight cottons—if you can wash it out yourself and hang it up to dry, all the better. Some hotels will accept ironing, but don't count on it, particularly if you need it at the last minute. Dry cleaning is an iffy proposition on most islands.

Swimsuits come in all shapes and sizes (as do bodies), and you should wear whatever makes you feel most comfortable. "Sexy," however, is hardly against the law in the Caribbean, but you should follow the local scene as to when to go topless. (Throughout this book, names of accepted beaches for nude bathing are clearly delineated.) In many islands, however, most locals do not want to see tourists walking around the city or anywhere other than the beach in their swimsuits. Despite the tropical largesse, there does exist a certain formality, particularly in the British dependencies, which should be respected. Generally, respect the local customs and the locals will respect you.

Your choice of shoes can make or break your vacation. Don't bring along your entire shoe closet, but a few well-chosen pairs can go a long way. Sturdy walking shoes or open-toe sandals with substantial soles are good for city sightseeing; hiking boots are a must for mountain climbing; jogging shoes can be used for multi-purposes, and one pair of dress shoes will get you through the evening. Cowboy boots tend to be too hot, not to mention bulky to pack. Cheap beach slippers can usually be picked up on the island.

Purses and wallets can become a problem in the Caribbean. You don't want to attract attention by carrying a huge purse, nor do you want to carry a lot of money around on you at one time. Purses and wallets should never be left unattended at the beach, so your best bet is to buy a tiny plastic necklace bag that carries your funny money (maybe a few dollars for snacks). Leave your room key at the reception of your hotel and lock up your passport, tickets, and other money in the hotel safe.) On excursions in the city, it may behoove you to carry money in a body wallet that attaches inside your clothes. Expensive cameras should be carried in inexpensive cases, the tattier the better; never walk around with a bag that advertises the make of your camera. On wealthier islands, such as Aruba and St. Martin, you may not have to walk around like a secret agent, but the advice is helpful in poorer countries, like Jamaica and the Dominican Republic, where difficult economic conditions have driven some to crime. As a tourist, no matter how "cool" you think you look, your status as a foreign tourist is clearly obvious to any local who is used to picking out potential victims. Just the fact that you are looking admiringly at the scenery targets you as a tourist.

Don't despair if you think you have no clothes for a Caribbean vacation. One of the joys of traveling through these islands is that if you packed the wrong clothes, there are many opportunities to buy new ones. Island designers are now finding their land legs and are producing beautiful fashions out of hand-painted silks, tie-dyed, and silk-screened batiks. Check the "What to Buy" section in each island chapter for suggestions of trendy boutiques. Colors are fantastically bright, styles are sensual and flowing. Unfortunately, some travelers discover that these beautiful tropical fashions do not work so well back home in more northern climes, except for Tropical Dress-Up nights. As such, you might control some of your more passionate impulses to buy the entire store out.

Packing light should be your prime goal before you leave home. You can always save space in your suitcase if you ask your hotel in advance if your room comes equipped with a hairdryer (many first-class ones do, and others provide one upon request). If you need an electric shaver, check in advance if you need to bring along an adapter plug or an electrical transformer. To simplify matters, some people on a Caribbean vacation just decide to let their wet hair dry in the sun and their beards grow long till they get home. (The latter is especially good if you've gone on a rugged expedition and want to impress your friends back home in the office.) In the directory of each island, you can find more information about electrical appliances under "Current."

More and more airlines are becoming tighter in their overweight restrictions on baggage and carry-on items; remember, you may want to buy clothes, gifts, etc., during your vacation and will need some extra space (and weight) in your luggage. Most airlines will not accept luggage that measures more than 62 inches (width plus length plus height), and most will not accept more than two bags. Carry-on pieces must fit under your seat or in the overhead bin (remember this before you lug home some oversized piece of artwork.) Finally, if you are flying between islands on very small planes, check with the airline about the luggage restriction (it may be smaller than on major carriers). In addition, some private islands have no porters, and you are sure to find none if you are traveling by ferry.

FIELDING'S RULE FOR PACKING:

Put in everything you think you'll need and then take out one-half of it. Women should take out two-thirds.

Money Managing

When traveling in the Caribbean, it's best to take a combination of cash (American dollars), credit cards and traveler's checks, depending how you plan to pay for your expenses. The gift of prepaid package tours is that you don't have to carry around a lot of money (which cuts down on the chance of having your money stolen). Most top-class hotels and resorts accept major credit cards, but in smaller restaurants and shops and some budget hotels, you are better off paying in cash or the local currency. U.S. dollars are generally accepted on most islands, and unlike European countries, paying in American dollars often wracks up a substantial discount for you. If you can avoid exchanging money, you will save time as well, since you will have to find a way to exchange the money back into your own currency when you leave.

Before purchasing traveler's checks, investigate how well the local currency is doing in relation to the American dollar. If the U.S. dollar is dropping, you are better off buying traveler's checks in the currency of the country you are visiting. Some currencies are subject to inflationary leaps and dips, while others float nicely with the U.S. dollar. Best rates can be found at exchange houses and at banks. Beware of the ringing phrase "black market." Especially in poor countries like the Dominican Republic, do your best to avoid exchanging money on the street with strangers who approach you (the most charming ones are often the most nefarious). Numerous scams are played out on tourists in this way; some innocent travelers fork over their dollars never to see them again; others are suddenly surrounded by a group of scam artists who then rob the tourist of all his valuables.

Credit cards are the easiest way to travel through the Caribbean, but which is the best one to pack in your wallet? Statistics have shown that vendors throughout the Caribbean readily accept Visa and Mastercard at more than 40,000 locations. American Express is accepted by the mega-merchants, that is, those accounting for at least 95 percent of the region's charge volume. (Because American Express charges merchants a fee significantly higher than the competition, only the largest and most upscale business can afford to accept it). If you plan to get cash from an ATM (Automated Teller Machine) with your credit card, you're better off using VISA, which is accepted at more ATMs in the Caribbean (415) than either Mastercard or American Express. Do note that if you use MasterCard or Visa, the transaction is considered an interest-bearing loan and you will be charged a transaction fee.

To exchange American dollars into local currency, the best places to go are banks and bank-operated exchange booths at the airport. Less favorable rates are usually found at hotels, stores and privately run exchange houses. It's best to arrive in the country with a small amount of local currency to avoid having to wait in a long line at the airport exchange house. (That way, you hire a taxi and get to your hotel to relax as soon as possible.) To receive foreign currency by mail, contact **Thomas Cook Currency** *(511 Madison Avenue, New York, NY 10022;* ☎ *(212) 757-6915.)*

The proliferation of ATM (automated teller machines) allows travelers to obtain immediate cash through such international networks as Cirrus and Plus. Your own bank card can be used at ATMs in the Caribbean to withdraw funds from your checking account, as well as obtain cash-advances from your credit card. Each card has special limits (both in time and amount of money), so check all the rules of your particular cards. Transaction charges are applied to your checking account back home and can often be higher than you are used to at home. Do verify from your bank or credit card whether ATM machines are maintained on the island you will be visiting.

Holders of American Express cards are eligible to apply for their Express Cash program, which allows you to withdraw cash and/or traveler's checks from a worldwide network of 57,000 American Express dispensers and participating bank ATMs. Enrollment is required, and takes about two weeks to process. On a basic card, you are allowed to withdraw $1000 for a seven-day period, more if your card is gold or platinum. Each cash transaction costs a minimum fee of $2.50, maximum $10.00, and a one percent fee for traveler's checks, except for the platinum card. American Express card holders can also cash personal checks for up to $1000 in a seven-day period in U.S. territory (21 days abroad). Of this sum, $200 can be in cash, the rest in traveler's checks (gold and platinum cards can receive more).

There are many ways to receive money from home. Anyone (cardholder or not) can make use of the American Express MoneyGram for up to $10,000.

The sender needs only to go to an American Express officer, pay up to $1000 with a credit card and anything over that in cash, and phone a transaction number to your recipient, who presents the ID and reference number to the nearest Moneygram agent. Although the service is American Express, the only credit cards you can use in this transaction are MasterCard, Visa, and Discover.

Western Union offices also wire money abroad. The sender must take either cash or a check to the nearest office (phone orders can be done with a credit card). Recipients in the Caribbean can pick up the cash in minutes if sent from the U.S. or Canada; fees are generally 5–10 percent of the total. For more information on available locations, ☎ *(800) 325-6000.*

Documents

All Caribbean islands described in this guide require some form of documentation and ID when passing through customs. Some require a fully valid passport; others accept proof of citizenship in the form of a birth certificate and photo ID; sometimes even a passport that's been out of date for five years is acceptable. (You will find specific information in the Directory section of each chapter, under the heading "Documents.") Do note that a driver's license alone does not prove birth of citizenship. Most often, a return or ongoing ticket is required to show your intent as well as proof of accommodations. Do arrive on the island with some receipt or confirmation of your hotel lodgings. In some cases, even proof of sufficient funds for the duration of your stay is required.

In some cases, tourist cards issued by the government are required on certain islands. These may be obtained at the airline when you purchase your ticket, the consulate, government tourist office, or travel agent; in some cases, you can buy it on arrival at the Immigration Office at the airport. For students, businesspersons, and longer stays, visas are generally required, issuable from consulates.

Customs and Duties

Upon arrival from all Caribbean destinations except Puerto Rico, all U.S. citizens must make declarations of all purchases to the U.S. Customs Official. (Travelers to Puerto Rico do not pass through customs and there is no duty assessed on purchases.)

The duty-free allowances in various regions are:

$1200 for the U.S. Virgin Islands

$600 for Antigua (and Barbuda), Aruba, Barbados, Belize, Bonaire, British Virgin Islands, Curaçao, Dominica, Dominican Republic, Grenada, Jamaica, Montserrat, Saba, St. Eustatius, St. Kitts, Nevis, St. Lucia, St.Maarten, St. Vincent, The Grenadines, Trinidad and Tobago.

$400 for Anguilla, the Cayman Islands, Guadeloupe, Martinique, St. Barthélémy, St. Martin and Venezuela.

If you stay on an island for less than 48 hours or if you've been outside the U.S. within 30 days of your current trip, you can only bring back $25 worth of duty-free goods (except in Puerto Rico, where there is no limit). This $25 allowance includes 10 cigars, 50 cigarettes and 4 ounces of perfume or liquor. In countries with a $400–$600 allowance also add 200 cigarettes (one carton), 100 cigars (not Cuban) and one liter of liquor or wine (for those over 21). The $1200 allowance includes 1000 cigarettes (five cartons); 100 cigars (not Cuban, and five liters of liquor or wine (for those over 21).

On all purchases over the allowance, a flat 10 percent duty is assessed on the first $1000 worth of merchandise. Do remember to register any expensive equipment or jewelry you take with you on your trip to avoid paying unnecessary duty. These items can be registered with the U.S. Customs before departure. Except for gifts under $50 sent directly to the recipient (or those shipped from Puerto Rico), all items shipped home are considered dutiable.

Among these items which are duty-free are antiques (at least 100 years old); some island arts and crafts, and those items sold in specified duty-free shops (many available in shops at the airport and in duty-free shopping zones). Always obtain some certification or receipt that guarantees the item bought is duty-free and save these slips for your customs check in the U.S. (For more information, see the "The Low-Down on Duty-Free" below.)

Do note well that some goods, such as plants, animals, illegal drugs, or endangered species are not permitted to be imported into the United States.

For further information, you can obtain publications from the **U.S. Customs Service** (*P.O. Box 7404, Washington D.C.20044*). To receive tape-recorded messages by phone, ☎ *(202) 927-2095.*

Insurance

Many different kinds of insurance are available to protect you and your valuables during your Caribbean vacation. Your first step should be to talk to your insurance broker to determine what your present policy covers, in case of medical emergency, theft, death, property damage (yours and theirs), and personal liability while driving. Do look into service provided by your credit card because there may be a special program which awards you insurance every time you use the credit card. Special travel insurance can cover such things as baggage and personal effects, flight insurance in case of accidental injury or death, personal accident and sickness while traveling, and automobile collision for protections against collision, theft, property damage, and liability in foreign countries. In countries where the driving is on the left side of the road and/or where conditions and drivers are dangerous, it would be advisable to take out collision insurance through the car rental agency. Also consider joining a reputable automobile club, the largest being the **American Automobile Association** *(1000 AAA Drive; Heathrow, FL 32746-5063;* ☎ *407-444-7000).* As for excursions or overnight expeditions, particularly in rugged conditions, do check to see if you are guaranteed a refund if you must cancel the trip (due to illness or unforeseen circumstance). It's also important to determine whether you can purchase bad weather insurance, as you might have to pay for an expensive airline ticket only to find out that the weather has totally precluded your active involvement in the excursion. It is possible to obtain a combination of all the above policies, especially if you are working through a reliable broker. On the other hand, it's up to you to calculate the risk of these conditions happening in relation to the cost of the insurance.

Kid Travel

Kids do well in the Caribbean, particularly at all-inclusive resorts where they can be mesmerized by a variety of activities while their parents wile away the afternoon on their own private beach. These days, hotels are outdoing each other with children's activities, from circus schools to kayaking programs to arts and crafts classes using the special folklore techniques of the islands.Many hotels allow children under 12 (and sometimes 16) to stay free in their parent's room (verify the cut-off age when you book and don't try to cheat— they may ask for a birth certificate or will look at the passport). Villa rentals are often a smart way for families to save money (especially those with kitchens where you can cook your own food). In picking an island for families, however, it is best to choose an English-oriented one, unless you are intent on your child learning a new language (often a frustrating experience for a short vacation). Also, take care in choosing a babysitter who can communicate well enough in English, since a lonely child can soon become hysterical without appropriate reassurances.

Special airfares can be obtained for children depending on your departure and arrival points. In some instances, if the child is under two and sits on your lap, without occupying a seat, the fare is 10 percent of the accompanying adult's fare. (Sometimes the child can fly free.) Children ages 2-11 pay half to two-thirds of the adult fare. Before booking a fare, check to see if the airline provides services such as special kid meals and freestanding bassinets (for those sitting in the bulkhead where there is more leg room). The best information and advice can be obtained from the annual February/March issue of *Family Travel Times* (contact: **Travel With Your Children**, *45 W. 18th Street, New York, NY 10011;* ☎ *(212) 206-0688).*

Grandparents should not hesitate to plan a trip with their grandchildren. International and domestic tours are available, specifically designed for the grandparent/grandchild pairing. For more information contact **Grand Travel** *(6900 Wisconsin Ave., Suite 706, Chevy Chase, MD 20815;* ☎ *(301) 986-0790 or (800) 247-7651).* Another organization **Rascals in Paradise** *(650 5th Street, Suite 505, San Francisco, CA 94107;* ☎ *(415) 978-9800 or (800) 872-7225)* also offers family-oriented programs.

All children, including infants, are required to travel abroad with a passport.

Student Travel

A number of valuable discounts are available for students. Most concerns can be answered by **Council Travel**, a subsidiary of the Council on International Educational Exchange (CIEE), *205 E. 42nd Street, New York, NYU 10017;* ☎ *(212) 661-1450*, which can provide advice on bargain travelling, study programs, work permits and insurance. The organization can issue you an International Student Identity Card (ISIC) or $16 to those students with legitimate credentials. Ask them to send you a copy of their magazine *Student Travels* ($1 for postage), which delineates all the Council's services and CIEE's programs and publications.

Single Travel

Financially speaking, singles are somewhat at a disadvantage in the travel industry since two people sharing a double room always save money. All-inclusive resorts like the Club Meds and some scuba packages sometimes pair up guests upon request. Socially, however, singles are at a great advantage, since they are more prone to become befriended by locals (attractive and otherwise), and native islanders tend to look on all single tourists as highly eligible (at least temporarily). Do protect your valuables extra-carefully if you are alone and be cautious about accepting to transport goods (probably contraband) for locals back to the States. It goes without saying that women traveling alone should not go off to secluded coves or caves with anyone they do not know well. And be cautious of anyone who becomes your "immediate friend."

For those who can't stand the thought of traveling alone, a novel service is being offered by **Travel Companion** and its owner Jens Jurgen *(P.O. Box P-833, Amityville, NY 11701;* ☎ *(516) 454-0880)* who actually pairs up strangers (same sex or opposite) to travel together. In a type of "Dating Game" process, applicants fill out their preferences for destination, type of companion, money issues, etc., and then receive a list of potential partners. Although Jurgen's listings are extensive, the risk of making a tragic choice is high (well, at least in our picky opinion, it is), so you should always talk to your traveling companion (and meet him or her in person) before you ever leave home. To list your name in Jurgen's files for a six-month period will run you $36–$66. Send $4 to receive a small copy of his newsletter filled with lots of travel tips for single travelers and 300-400 names of singles looking for a suitable companion—like you. Some people should have a great time, but just don't say we didn't warn you.

Senior Travel

Seniors should never travel without researching every single discount they are entitled to receive. With some savvy planning, you could reap hundreds of dollars in savings, combined with traveling off-season. Your first task should be to write for more information from the **National Council of Senior Citizens**; *1331 F St., NW, Washington, D.C. 20004;* ☎ *(202)347-8800.* A membership to this nonprofit organization runs $12 per person/ per couple; in return you receive a monthly newsletter which includes invaluable travel tips. You may even find some significant hotel and auto rental discount coupons.

Chartered trips and package tours are often offered through senior clubs, and certain cruises are especially designed for older citizens. For information about all-inclusive tours and cruises for seniors 60 years and older, contact **SAGA International Holidays**, *222 Berkeley St., Boston, MA 02116; toll-free* ☎ *(800) 343-0273* in the U.S.

For other ideas and sound advice, write for your copy of "101 Tips for the Mature Traveler" available from **Grand Circle Travel**, *347 Congress St., Suite 3A, Boston, MA 02210;* ☎ *(617)350-7500 or toll free (800) 248-3737* in the U.S. This agency also provides escorted tours and cruises for seniors.

When to Go: Parties to Sports

Islanders know how to throw a party, and festivals full of song and dance occur year-round in the Caribbean. On some islands, there are even more festivals during the off-season, which serves to attract visitors who are keen for off-season bargains. Although Carnival is generally celebrated as the advent of Lent, it can happen anytime in the Caribbean, even during the summer. Throughout the year individual islands celebrate their own arts and crafts traditions, as well as various other religious and folklore celebrations. Sports competitions happen according to the high season for that sport, attracting athletes and fishermen from all over the world. (Singles should note these events as prime times to visit and the chance for meeting someone "tall and tan and young and handsome" soars sky-high.) For more information, check under "When to Go" in the directory of each individual island.

CARNIVAL

Guadeloupe (January-Lent)

Bonaire (February)

Puerto Rico (February)

St. Lucia (February)

St. Maarten(February)

Aruba (mid-late February)

Martinique (for six weeks starting after New Year's)

Trinidad (Monday and Tuesday preceding Ash Wednesday)

St. Thomas (After Easter, sometime in April).

Curaçao (late January-early February)

Cayman Islands (May) St. John (July)

Antigua (July

Anguilla (early August)

Turks & Caicos (late August)

CULTURAL FESTIVALS

Barbados' Hole Town Festival (February 17)

St. Martin Food Festival (May)

Tobago Heritage Festival (July)

Barbados' Crop-Over Festival (August)

St. Bart's Cayman Islands Pirate Week (late October)

MUSIC

Barbados' Caribbean Jazz Festival (May)

Aruba's Jazz and Latin Music Festival (June)

Puerto Rico's Festival Pablo Casals (June)

Dominican Republic's Merengue Festival (10 days in July)

Jamaica's Reggae Sunsplash Music Festival (August)

Statia/America Day (St. Eustatius) Puerto Rico's Hatillo Festival of the Masks (December)

SPORTS

Grenada's New Years Fiesta Yacht Race

Antigua's Tennis Week (January)

Jamaica's Classic Golf Tournament (January)

Curaçao Regatta (March)

Antigua's Windsurfing Week (April)

British Virgin Islands Spring Regatta (April)

U.S. Virgin Islands International Rolex Spring Regatta (April)

Anguilla's Boat Racing Day (May 30)

Aruba's High-Winds Pro-Am Windsurfing Tournament (June)

U.S. and British Virgin Islands' Hook In and Hold On Boardsailing Regatta (June and July)

Grenada's Carriacou Regatta (end of July)

Martinique's Tour des Yoles Rondes (yawl race) (early August)

Virgin Islands Open Atlantic Blue Marlin Tournament (August)

Bonaire's Sailing Regatta (October)

Barbados' International Road Race Series (December)

Secret Tips for Caribbean Survival

(What you don't know will cost you).

The Low-Down on Duty-Free Shopping

Duty-free is a word that makes some travelers' blood tingle, and it's true—in the Caribbean, spectacular deals can be made on liquor, crystal, china, linen and jewelry. European imports, from Gucci to Fendi to Chanel, and Dior, can be had for a fraction of their cost back in the native label land. However, duty-free shopping is not as easy as it sounds, and many people have grave misconceptions about it. In order to survive the Caribbean shopping challenge, you need some advance information, reams of patience and a sure eye for quality.

Simply, duty-free means that merchants are not required to pay import taxes on certain items that they transport into the country; consequently, they can pass the savings directly onto the customer. In this way, many Caribbean dealers bypass the middleman element and act as both direct importer and retailer. As a result, they are able to sell you those same items at 30-40 percent discount less than prices found stateside.

The Bahamas is the king of duty-free islands, where you can find the lowest prices for the largest selection of high-quality goods. (Do see the *Fielding's Bahamas* guide.) Long known as the mecca of the Caribbean, the U.S. Virgin Islands comes in a close second, having been declared a duty-free port over 300 years ago. In fact, when the three Virgin Islands—St. John, St. Croix and St. Thomas, were sold to the U.S. in 1917, the negotiation required the islands to remain duty-free to protect the businessmen living there. As a consequence, you will find no sales tax on any of the islands, and shoppers get an added bonus: U.S. Citizens may bring home $1200 worth of goods purchased duty-free—two to three times the amount allowed on any other Caribbean island (As well, if you go over that amount in the USVI, you need only pay a 5 percent charge as opposed to the customary 10 percent charge on other islands.) And there's more: American citizens can ship home an additional $100 worth of duty-free goods daily. So count that up— if you stay 10 days in the USVI (and that's about 3 days per island), you can spend up to $2200 on duty-free goods.

Even islands which are not officially duty-free often have duty-free shops at the airport or in specially designated stores such as **Pointe Seraphine** on St. Lucia, and **La Zona Franca** in Santo Domingo in the Dominican Republic

Islands that do not have duty-free privileges have found other ways to offer impressive discounts in imported goods. Through a process called "in-bond," imported goods are stored in bonded warehouses and treated as though they had never entered the country. Since no duty is charged on them, a 25-35 percent discount of U.S. prices can be maintained without loss to the vendor. In such cases, goods are often delivered directly to the client at the airport upon departure or to the cruiseliner on the day of departure.

When shoppers see the amazing array of French perfumes, Dutch porcelain, and Swiss crystal, all caution can easily be thrown to the wind, but there are certain warnings that should be well heeded. First of all, don't be misled into thinking that all duty-free items are bargains. Unless you do your homework and know prices back home, you may think you are getting a great deal, but retail pricing scams do exist, and some vendors may give a 50 percent discount on an item that was already marked 100 percent more than the customary price—yes, just to fool you harried tourists. Furthermore, if you don't know a Fendi from a Ferrari, you may even be fooled into thinking that a knock-off is actually an original, but this is a trend that is happening all over the world.

To avoid falling victim to Caribbean shopping scams, arm yourself with a pen and paper. That is, take some time before you leave home and collect average prices of luxury items you might be interested in buying. (It's easy enough to stop by your favorite department store.) You may well be surprised to find that some seeming bargains on electronic equipment in particular are no bargain at all, and unless you obtain the appropriate warranties (always check before you buy), you may get royally ripped off. For example, an Olympus Stylus Zoom 35-70mm camera sells for $180 in New York but is a whopping $240 on Jamaica. As such, you're probably best buying camera equipment and stereos back home at discount stores.

A good rule of thumb is to buy the goods of whatever mother country is associated with the island. In general, imports from the mother country are not usually taxed. For example, on the French islands of Guadeloupe, Martinique, St. Martin, and St. Barts, the best products to head for are undoubtedly French perfumes, crystal and cosmetics—at prices considerably lower than in France. On British dependencies of Anguilla, Antigua, Montserrat, Nevis, St. Kitts, Grenada, St. Lucia and St. Vincent, it's best to purchase English-made products such as fine bone china and woolens.

There are some official safeguards employed by islands to protect the consumer from getting cheated. Both the USVI and the Bahamas have established duty-free control boards. On St. Thomas, a Retailers Association requires its member stores to provide a 30-day, money-back guarantee on all items. You can tell whether a store belongs to the association by the "Shop with Confidence" sticker that is proudly displayed in the window. You'll feel much safer shopping in these stores, but always hold onto your receipt and check the merchandise carefully before returning home. The cost of sending the item back from the States may well not be worth it.

A special system exists in all Caribbean nations (except the French West Indies, Cuba and Venezuela), which allows many native arts and crafts produced in the island to be brought into the U.S. without a duty charge. Such products as wood carvings from Jamaica, silk-screened fabrics from St. Lucia, and hand-painted batiks from St. Kitts all fall under the category.

If you have any further questions regarding general custom and duty-free laws, contact the **U.S. Customs Service**, *Information, Room 210, 6 World Trade Center, New York, NY 10048;* ☎ *(212) 466-5550.*

The Secrets of Surcharges

One of the biggest shocks on a Caribbean vacation comes when your final bill is presented, and the total has no relationship to the room rate that you thought you were booked. Suddenly the bill sports charges you've never heard of: government, tax, long-distance phone fee, service charges, and maybe even an energy surcharge. And when you finally recover and make it to the airport, you're hit with one last charge—the departure tax—right when you spent your last guilder, peso, or Caribbean dollar in the duty-free shop.

The antidote to such shocks is preparation and advance information. The following is a summary of what to look for.

Hotels on all islands charge a government tax, which ranges from 5-10 percent of the bill. In most cases, hotels add an extra 10-15 percent service charge. The general custom is to divide this among the staff, but more often than not, it isn't. Do not feel obliged to tip extra if the service charge is included.

Energy surcharges added to your bill help to defray the costs of electricity on islands where the fee can be exorbitant. Usually, guests are not informed of the surcharge until they check out, so do ask in advance. In Aruba, the energy surcharge is often added to the bill in a per diem rate (about $3 per room per night) or as a percentage of the overall tax and service charge (normally about one percent). These charges usually are never quoted in a brochure or told to you over the phone when you are booking the room.

Most islands in the Caribbean charge a departure tax on outward-bound American travelers. Puerto Rico doesn't charge one, and the U.S. Virgins Islands only recently began to do so. Each island determines its own tax, according to the mode of transport (sea or air), destination (local or international), and age (child or adult). Guadeloupe and Martinique charge no tax.

Telephone surcharges can raise the amount of your bill to unbelievable levels. Sometimes a flat rate is charged for local calls (10-75 cents), but international calls may run you double or triple the amount, including operator assistance. It's best to go to the local telephone company to make calls or use an international calling card, such as AT&T, Sprint, or MCI, and use the pay phone. The term "long distance" can also be defined in highly unexpected ways. For example, according to telephone districts, the French St. Martin is considered long-distance from Sint Maarten, the Dutch side of the same island.

In the Caribbean, restaurants often include a service charge onto your bill as a matter of course. Do check your bill carefully before leaving another 15 percent for the service.

Even all-inclusives have hidden charges. They are subject to the same government taxes as normal lodgings, and these charges are often not included in the quoted price. Service charges are also often left out of the quoted price (normally ten percent of the bill) and costly activities like golf and scuba diving. The word "ultra inclusive" these days is being used by such resorts as the Sandals chain to refer to fixed rates that include these activities.

Unseen charges can appear on a final cruise bill as well. The port tax is levied on the cruise ship by an island for docking privileges. The charges, assessed according to the size of the ship and the number of passengers, is divided by the passengers and averages about $57 (depending on the length of the cruise). Cruises rarely include the cost of land excursions and special watersports activities, and you may find yourself paying a bundle to have a short sightseeing tour. For example, snorkeling during a Carnival cruise, will cost you an added $22 per person; scuba about $50. On Costa Cruise Lines, a tour of an island, like St. John, would run you about $32 per adult. Take three of them, and a couple would add an extra $198 to their final bill.

Perhaps the best extra charge on a cruise will be gratuities royally expected of passengers, since cruising is one of the most service-intensive forms of travel available. From the maitre d' to the bartender, from the cabin steward to the waiter, cruise personnel depend on tips to supplement their income. These charges are never included in the quoted price, (except for Seabourne Cruise Line), one of the most luxurious plying the Caribbean, which collects a service charge upfront and forbids the staff from accepting more tips. Guidelines for tipping can be obtained from most cruise lines and, indeed, passengers are usually presented with a summary. On the average, the cabin steward receives $3 per day per person; $1.50 per person per day to the bus-person and wine steward. The laundry service, bartenders, and deck stewards also expect gratuities. A couple could add $150 per week to their bill.

Except for the most luxurious, elite cruises, alcohol is usually never included, and most items are outrageously expensive. Although soft drinks and juices are included in the price, if you drink them by the pool or at the bar, you are usually charged for them.

In short, never be embarrassed or shy to ask about hidden charges on your bill—way in advance, if possible. You will be a lot happier during and after your vacation if you know exactly how to budget your money and exactly what you will be expected to pay.

Ten Ways to Save Money

Saving money on a Caribbean vacation takes a little know-how and some advance planning, but it's not at all difficult. In fact, saving money can be so subtle you may not even feel the pain of sacrifice. In fact, most extra charges on a trip can be easily avoided or circumscribed with the following advice:

1) CHOOSE A CHEAP ISLAND

It's embarrassing for some countries to admit it, but they are cheaper than others. Cheap usually goes along with unpopular, but that's not always the case. **Santo Domingo** in the Dominican Republic is one of the most inexpensive destinations in the Caribbean. The most elegant hotel in the city, the hotel Santo Domingo, runs about $142 per night, for a double, including taxes and service charges. A night for two, in the heart of the colonial zone, can run about $60 a couple at the 16th -century **Hostál Nicolás Nade**. Food for two can run about $20–40 a day. **Saba** is another cheap island. No one dresses up, there are no expensive restaurants, and socializing is done over a beer in a simple cafe.

2. LIVE THE VILLA LIFE

Groups of four or more can wrack up real bargains by renting villas. Imagine paying $45 per day per person for eight people at a 4 bedroom/3 bath villa with pool on St. Martin from mid-April-mid-December. (**Shamrock**, available through *Heart of the Caribbean Ltd.;* ☎ *800-231-5303.* Villas that come with their own kitchens can add to savings. Most villas in Jamaica and Barbados come with their own cook; on other islands, a reasonable surcharge will get you great (and inexpensive) island cooking. Even if you don't want to cook in every meal, eating breakfast at home and packing your lunch for a picnic on the beach can make a substantial improvement in your available funds.

3. HOUSE SWAP

Ever imagine that a Caribbean family might want your home during the winter season? Home exchanges are arranged through such organizations as **Intervac** ☎ *(800) 756-4663* and **Vacation Exchange Club** ☎ *(800) 638-3841.* These companies publish a directory which lists potential interested parties; the edition comes out three or four times a year. Preparation for the exchange should start a year in advance. The only costs involved include a nominal fee ($45–$60) to list your home, phone calls and postage for contacting potential exchangers and arranging the exchange. You should, of course, carefully interview the potential party so you can avoid any theft or damage to your home.

4. RIDE ON A PACKAGE DEAL

Tour operators who buy airfare and accommodations in bulk at substantial discounts often get a combined air/hotel rate for less than what you would get on your own. (See all-inclusive resorts below). The **Caribbean Travel Service** *(☎ (800) 962-2080)* specializes in finding the best package deals to the Caribbean, Bahamas and Bermuda and guarantees the lowest price.

5. MINE THE OFF-SEASON

If you're sweltering in Manhattan or Malibu during July and August, the last place you may want to travel to is a Caribbean island, with no air-conditioning and balmy temperatures in the 80s. But summertime is actually one of the best times to visit the islands. Soft, breezy tradewinds keep temperatures at a comfortable level; savings of 10-40 percent off winter hotel rates keeps your wallet humming. Add to that abandoned beaches and fewer people—and you have a paradise in the making.

Summer discounts (which embraces low season, usually mid-April through mid-December) include bargains on yacht charters that add-on extra days at sea to family-style resorts where kids can often come for free. Villas often reduce their prices, and sometimes even throw in a complimentary meal or the use of a van. All-inclusive resorts often lower their rates for the same amenities. Among the biggest all-inclusive discounts is **Le Sport** (St. Lucia) at 20 percent savings; **Pineapple Beach Club** (Antigua) with 19 percent savings; **Boca Chica Beach Resort** (Dominican Republic) at 20 percent savings; and **Jack Tar Village Royal** (St. Kitts) at 20 percent.

Summertime in the Caribbean is often filled with festivals and celebrations, designed especially to attract the tourist trade. Some of the best regattas and races are held during this period

Honeymoon packages are especially geared for the June, July and August wedding. Summertime activities at resorts also include special programs for kids, which include arts and crafts classes, nature walks, mini-tennis, watersports and movies. At the **Club Med Punta Cana**, there is even a circus school program for children. Computer classes are offered along with field trips, a petting zoo, pool tournaments and watersports for children at **Jamaica's Boscobel Beach Resort**. At the **Hyatt Regency Cerromar** and **Hyatt Dorado Beach Hotel** in Puerto Rico, there is a special camp for children 3 to 15 (year round) and another one for teens 13–17 (year-round). Flying trapeze lessons are held for kids 2–11 at the **Club Med in St. Lucia**. At the **Stouffer Grand Beach Resort** in St. Thomas, kids can enjoy a beach crunch, water olympics, magic shows, treasure hunts, swim lessons, movies, carnival, pizza parties and nature hikes.

Superb sailing bargains off-season are also available, if you know where to look. **Huntley Yacht Vacations** ☎ *(800) 322-9224* offers an 8-day cruise of the British Virgin Islands on a 71-foot Motoryacht, fully crewed (8 passengers) for $10,400 (a 25 percent savings from high-season). **Journeys by Sea** ☎ *(800) 825-3632* offers a 14-day cruise of the British and U.S. Virgin Islands on a 42-ft. Endeavour bareboat (6 passengers) for $1950 (58 percent savings). **Blue Water Cruises** *(☎ (800) 524-2020, FAX (800) 825-5956)* offers power and sail yachts from 40 ft. to 200 ft. at all-inclusive prices from $1250 per person for 8 days and 7 nights. Price includes watersports equipment, meals, beverages, crew and full service. Summer savings from 10–20 percent.

BEST DISCOUNTED HOTELS OFF-SEASON

Cinnamon Reef (Anguilla): 40 percent

Hyatt Regency Aruba Resort (Aruba): 37 percent

Royal Pavilion (Barbados):48 percent

Hyatt Regency Grand Cayman (Caymans): 35 percent

San Souci (Jamaica) 44 percent

Hermitage (Nevis): 43 percent

Le Toint (St. Barts): 39 percent

l'Habitation (St. Martin): 39 percent

Gallows Point Resort (St. John): 50 percent

Palm Island (St. Vincent): 35 percent

6. BOOK AN ALL-INCLUSIVE

The biggest marketing craze in the Caribbean islands these days is the all-inclusive resort. Club Med is celebrating its 27th anniversary as a trendsetter in North America and the famous Sandals resorts are approaching the fifteenth year of their Caribbean invasion. Dozens of competitors are now competing with these giants in a mad rush to attract clients. The truth is, however, not all all-inclusives were created equal, and what is an all-inclusive on one island may be a semi-inclusive on another. Advertising these days is highly misleading, and before you make any decisions, it's important to clarify all the terms of your contract.

Generally, "all-inclusive" means that you pay one price for a package deal.Most are located on a beach because free watersports is usually part of the package. Suites are often standard and some resorts even offer private villas. Sometimes there is little rate differential between a standard and deluxe so it's worth asking for an upgrade.

The all-inclusive vacation actually started with the French-born Club Med in 1950 who thought the idea of offering all meals, sports, and a spartan room would attract clients who did not want to keep pulling out their wallet every time they wanted to do, eat, or drink something. Their first wave of guests even helped to cook meals and wash dishes. Drinks were "paid" for by beads that were strung up as bracelets, and all other incidentals were signed for. In the late 1970s, a Jamaican entrepreneur imitated the Club Med style with Negril Beach Village, using shark's teeth for beads. Out of this was invented a couples-only retreat called Couples in Ocho Rios, the first all-inclusive to include drinks as part of the fixed rate. The chain Super-Clubs developed out of this initial idea, which now includes six properties in Jamaica, plus one in Cuba. The idea was definitely upgraded by another Jamaican entrepreneur, who created the Sandals chain of resorts, adding fitness centers, watersports programs, and swim-up bars., as well as a variety of specialty restaurants. He also instituted a special "Island Hopping" program which allows travelers to move from Antigua to St. Lucia to Barbados. One of the best little exchanges is between the Sandals on St. Lucia and Antigua, which can be done in a day trip.

The best selection of all-inclusives is on Jamaica—nearly 24 resorts (nearly one-third of all hotel properties). While such programs attract tourists, local restaurateurs and vendors have complained that such clients tend to be so happy with the multi-pleasures of their accommodations that they never leave the premises. In recent years, the Jamaican Tourist Board is boosting the marketing of the Inns of Jamaica, which are trying to survive in the face of such king-like lodgings, and often provide a more relaxing escape from the hubbub of touristic socializing.

In recent years, excellent all-inclusives can be found on Antigua, St. Lucia, Barbados, and even Cuba (the Club Varadero). Twenty-five all-inclusives have taken root in the Dominican Republic. Familiar names, like Wyndham, have entered the market—such as the Wyndham Morgan Bay Resort in St. Lucia and the Heywoods in Barbados.

These days some hotels which are not all-inclusives are now offering special all-inclusive wings, such as the Bolongo Bay Resort in St. Thomas and the Paradise Island Resort and Casino in the Bahamas. And all-inclusives need not be for the extravagantly wealthy. A new "Lido" class of more moderately priced all-inclusive packages are being offered by the formerly upscale San Souci resort in Ocho Rios in

Jamaica. These days many Club Meds are moderately priced and the Jack Tar Villages in St. Kitts, the Dominican Republic, and Jamaica are impressively reasonable. Other good buys for the money include the Pineapple Resorts in Anguilla and Antigua and Club Fortuna and Forte Nassau Beach Hotel in the Bahamas.

Are You a Good Candidate for an All-Inclusive?

Who shouldn't go to an all-inclusive? If you plan to spend your vacation simply shuttling from the beach to your bed, you're better off in an intimate inn. If you want to fan out over the island and sightsee and shop, you won't get your full value out of an all-inclusive. If you don't like socializing, or in some cases, a big dose of sensual overkill, you'll come away from an all-inclusive moaning. Furthermore, if you don't like where you are, you have signed up for a nonrefundable vacation, and you will eventually feel like a prisoner. And there are certain general guidelines you should always follow: couples should never go to a Sandals; families should never go to Hedonism II or a Club Med targeted for singles and couples.

On the other hand, if you like to eat and drink a lot, you may find good savings in an all-inclusive package. At some resorts, like the Club Meds, there are simply fantastic buffets, the likes of which you have never seen before (imagine eating as many lobsters as you want at one sitting; ditto on the desserts). Other resorts have a slew of specialty restaurants, and take great pride in serious French or Italian meals with excellent service, aperitifs, and good wine. Sport lovers can indulge in their most expensive fantasies—like all-day scuba or golf for no extra fee—the savings will be significant. If you're on a honeymoon, the all-inclusive package can help you to feel pampered without ever having to think twice about money. At some resorts, you can purchase an entire wedding package that includes the fee for a minister, documents, champagne, flowers, and a special dinner. Lately, many all-inclusives have started to include sightseeing tours in the package and excursions.

The most elite all-inclusives have their own private islands, such as Petit St. Vincent in the Grenadines. Jumby Bay, off Antigua, also has its own island, with 38 exquisitely furnished rooms and an international-class kitchen. At Ciboney in Jamaica, the four-diamond resort offers a personal attendant to guests who cooks their breakfast and serves it at their own villa pool.

The final trick in choosing an all-inclusive is to determine your most compelling interest. Scuba divers should head for package deals close to excellent diving sites and which have included diving in the package. If you envision yourself needing several cocktails a day, make sure drinks are included in the package. If you don't plan to spend much time in your room, don't choose to upgrade to a suite.

With all the competition now among all-inclusives, you can ferret out good bargains. For example, Club Med's "Wild Card" program offers savings of up to $150-$300 per person if you are willing to book two weeks in advance and don't mind not knowing which club you will be sent to until one week within departure. A special program for families offered by Club Med, with similar requirements, is called "Family Dream Vacations."

7. ALTERATIVE ACCOMMODATIONS

Campgrounds, inns, bed and breakfasts, and guesthouses generally offer big savings over traditional hotels. For the outdoorsman, they offer more exciting environments as well. On some islands you can pitch tents in the national park or along the beach, but you should always inquire at the local tourist office about what is legally permitted. Tobago and Trinidad have some of the most charming bed and breakfasts in the Caribbean, at times the most preferred lodging available for the congeniality and hospitality of the host/chef.

8. DON'T PAY FOR KIDS

More and more resorts are offering "kids-stay-free" programs, including discounted meals for tots. At the Forte Nassau Beach Hotel, kids under 12 can share their parent's room for free. Other kid-for-free resorts are the Hyatts on Aruba, Casa de Campo in the Dominican Republic; Trelawney hotel and Boscobel Beach Resort in Jamaica, Stouffer Grand Beach Resort and Sapphire Beach Resort on St. Thomas. During August each year, Bonaire celebrates Family Month with island-wide family activities and discounts on airfare, lodging and dining. For more information, contact the Bonaire Tourist Board.

9. BOOK A BARGAIN CRUISE

With so many competing cruiseliners plying the waters of the Caribbean, there's bound to be a few unbooked berths. Best bargains can be had from cruise discounters who buy space in bulk from cruise lines at deeply reduced prices and pass the savings to their clients. Discounters, however, rarely give you as much information as normal travel agents, and you may not get your first choice in date or destination. Consumer fraud is also a risk if your contact is by mail and phone. Before doing business, check out the firm with the **Cruise Line International Association** (☎ *212-921-0066*), as well as the Better Business Bureau, where the business is located. Pay with a credit card and if the trip sounds too good to be true, it probably is.

10. LAST-MINUTE DISCOUNTS

Advanced booking doesn't always get you the best rate. Short-notice vacation clubs, which charge a $20-48 membership fee, have hotlines and published updated lists of available trips. Another technique is to call the hotel of your choice two weeks in advance, ask what's available, and ask for a discount.

FIELDING'S RULE:

If you don't ask for a discount, you will probably never get one.

Telephone Trauma

Most islands in the Caribbean do have relatively efficient telephone systems, although some remote islands have none. You will not always find a phone in your room, so if that is a problem, make sure you ask before you book the hotel. Most restaurants, hotel lobbies, post offices and special street booths have public telephones.

Even if your room has a phone, it's the worst place to make a call. Hidden surcharges will send the bill sky-high (see "Secrets of Surcharges" above). You will always save money if you go to the local Cable & Wireless company where you can purchase a credit card to make phone calls. Don't be tempted by the convenience of that phone sitting by your bedside unless you don't care about money.

For making long-distance calls, it is also possible to use your own credit card related to your long-distance carrier at home. Before you leave, check what services that carrier can provide you. Two new long distance services are giving the corporate giants of AT&T, Sprint, and MCI some competition. Global Telemedia's Enhanced Value Card is a prepaid long-distance phone card. Callers simply dial a number to access the service. When the time has run out, users can punch in their credit card number to buy more time. Currently, it can be used in Puerto Rico, the USVI, Barbados, the Bahamas, Bermuda, the Dominican Republic, Trinidad, Tobago, and the Cayman Islands. Codes for Jamaica, Aruba and Antigua are soon to follow. (For more information ☎ *(615) 588-3692.*

An ATN (American Travel Network) phone card charges you a flat fee of 17.5 cents a minute for calls within the U.S.—including Puerto Rico and the USVI. Rates from other Caribbean Islands are higher, although generally still lower than the competition's. The card is free and there are no minimum calling requirements or surcharges. Callers are billed monthly. For more information ☎ *(800) 477-9692.*

More and more common are public pay phones which take American Express, MasterCard, and Visa credit cards. AT&T's Language Line Service (☎ *800-752-6096)* provides interpretive services for telephone calls in Spanish, French and other languages.

Local Calls

The number of digits in telephone numbers vary throughout the Caribbean; there are variations sometimes on the same island, between old and new numbers. Instructions for calling from the U.S. to an island, and from the island to numbers abroad differ from island to island. Generally, those islands in the 809 area code follow the same procedures, but codes for islands differ from one island to another. You should always check with the operator before calling another Caribbean island from your destination.

From the U.S.

Numbers in the Caribbean within the area code 809 may be called direct, by dialing 1 + 809 + local number.

Numbers outside the 809 area code must be called as follows: dial 011 (international access code) + island country code + city code (if applicable) + local number.

To the U.S.

When calling from a region within the 809 area code, dial 1 + area code + local number.

When calling from a location outside the 809 area code, dial the international access code (check with the operator) + U.S. country code + area code + local number.

Between Islands

When dialing within the same 809 area code, dial 1 + local number.

When calling from a location within the 809 area code to a location outside the 809 area, dial 011 (international access code) + country code + city code (if applicable) + local number.

When calling from a number outside the 809 area code to one within the 809 area, dial the international access code + 1 + 809 + local number.

Health Precautions

In general the Caribbean promotes good health and well-being more than perhaps any other region in the world.Steady sunshine, clean air, unpolluted seas should bring a traveler home feeling invigorated and renewed. In general, there are few health risks associated with any of the islands represented here, although the U.S. State Department has issued warnings about malaria in the Dominican Republic, especially along the border with Haiti. For up-to-the-minute reports, do call the Centers for Disease Control's International Travelers' Hotline; ☎ *(404) 332-4559* to receive a menu of existing conditions at your destination. You will need a touch-tone phone.

Perhaps the most obvious risk is overexposure to the sun. In the haste to have a relaxing time at the beach, it's easy to forget that skin more used to northern climes burns at a faster rate under near-equatorial rays. Do use a very strong sunscreen your first few days, limit your sun exposure to fifteen-minute sessions, and drinks lots of liquids. Judging the amount of sun you can take by how your skin looks in the moment is a very bad technique; sunburns usually don't appear until hours later—when it's too late. For serious sunburns, do not hesitate to consult with the physician on call at your hotel; local remedies are usually very good and often sold over the counter.

Great care should be taken when swimming, diving, or snorkeling in the Caribbean. Undertows and currents can be extremely rough, especially on the windward side of the islands, and can suddenly pull you under or far out to sea. Do try to swim only near a lifeguard, and if there is none, ask a companion to spot for you. The advice and admonishments of dive instructors and other watersports instructors, who are usually experts in their field and know their regions well, should be absolutely followed. Many a vacation has been ruined or worse, lives even lost, because their directions went unheeded. Sharks do swim in Caribbean waters, but they do not normally come near shore. Special caution should be taken with jellyfish, the Portuguese man-of-war, sea urchins, and eels—all of which sting, bite, or scratch if you touch them. In an attempt to see the beautiful coral reefs up close, many a diver and snorkeler has been severely scratched.

In each island chapter under "Medical Emergencies" in the directory of each chapter, you will find the names, addresses and telephone numbers of hospitals in the region. In general, any serious emergencies are best flown out of the island immediately; you will always find better medical care back home. If you are presently taking medication, make sure you have plenty (even an extra dose, should you lose your suitcase), and even take along an extra copy of your prescription. Any inoculations (required or otherwise) can be listed on a special inoculation card, signed by the administering physician, and carried with your passport and visa. It's not a bad idea to carry your own sterile syringes (disposable ones are available at local pharmacies) in case you will need an injection. Do not count on finding these supplies at your destination.

Any sexually active traveler should always carry a supply of condoms to offset the risk of being infected by the AIDS virus. Condoms made in the United States are far superior to anything you would find on any Caribbean island.

Drug Busts

Drugs—selling, possessing, using them—is illegal in the Caribbean, but you wouldn't know it at times. Depending how you dress, your age, and your level of "hipness," you may find yourself approached repeatedly by "vendors" hawking anything from the local weed (in Jamaica it's called *ganja*) to harder stuff on more sophisticated island scenes like Montserrat and Mystique. In Jamaica officials claim that marijuana is only grown wild in the highlands, but ask a local and he or she may show you their own personal patch in their backyard. Unlike other third-world countries, few tales of imprisonment for possession have come out of the Caribbean, but extreme caution, nevertheless, should always be taken. Under no circumstances should you transport any illegal drugs through customs; U.S. customs officials are trained to spot offenders immediately, and lately officials have been using highly trained beagle dogs to sniff out contraband in luggage.

Deciphering the Language

You say Ca-rib-BE-an and I say Ca-RIB-bee-an. The polls are still out on what's correct, but most islanders say Ca-rib-BE-an, or at least whatever it is that you don't say. The truth is, although even the authors of this guide have been haughtily corrected, it doesn't really matter so long as you can get to your hotel. The official language of islands often have to do with their last conqueror—you'll find Spanish, French, British-inflected English, Dutch, and Papiamento (a combination of all of the above), as well as a delightful array of local *patois* (or dialects) spoken by both cityfolk and those who live in the backcountry. Most people will be surprised to find English the official language on a number of islands: the U.S. Virgin islands, the British Virgin Islands, Turks& Caicos, Puerto Rico, Montserrat, Antigua, and Anguilla. And even on those islands where the official language is French or Spanish, many people in tourism (especially at top-class hotels) speak English. The poorer a country is, however, and the less developed the touristic infrastructure, the fewer people you will find who speak English. In such cases, it's wise to bring a phrase book with you and/or bone up on the language before you come. If you are participating in rigorous trekking expeditions or scuba diving sojourns, do investigate ahead of time whether your instructor or guide speaks good English. It's really really hard on the old nervous system to be in high-risk situations when you can't understand the pigeon-English instructions of your group leader.

In all situations, whenever you speak to an islander, speak slowly (but do not shout), even if his or her official language is English. Most Americans don't stop to think that their own accent might sound terribly convoluted to a foreigner who is used to hearing English with a native lilt or to one who has learned English informally.

Weather Disasters

Hurricanes are a fact of life in the Caribbean—some big, some small. The region is still recovering from the disastrous havoc wreaked by Hurricane Hugo in 1989. Officials on many islands simply don't possess the equipment to adequately warn locals of impending weather crises; imagine the even skimpier news that will trickle down to you as a tourist. That means you, as a traveler, must take full responsibility for scoping out brewing tropical conditions before you come, by reading the daily newspapers and even calling the National Weather Bureau in Washington, D.C. to determine the possibility of inclement weather in your destination. (For current weather conditions in the U.S. and abroad, plus the local time and other travel tips, call the Weather Channel Connection ☎ *(900) WEATHER*; 95 cents per minute) from a touch-tone phone. This information is absolutely essential if you plan to scuba dive, snorkel, sail, or windsurf, because the conditions of the water will determine the safety (and even feasibility) of your excursion. While traveling, do your best to acquire stateside newspapers that will give you more extensive coverage of the weather.

The rainy season in the Caribbean usually coincides with fall, several months before the start of high season in mid-December. Even then, showers are usually brief and interchanged with sunshine. Some intrepid folks just choose to remain on the beach, enjoy the cool rain, then let the returning hot sun dry them off. Don't do this, of course, in strongly inclement weather or electrical storms. Locals are usually savvy in reading the "character" of a shower so listen and seriously heed their advice.

In general, however, Caribbean weather is why travelers come to the Caribbean. Imagine a perfect day somewhere verging on the edge of summer, but without oppressive heat and often a cool trade breeze, and you will know the weather almost all year round in the region. Temperatures average between 78-85 degrees F, with lowest lows dipping to 65 degrees F, and highs struggling to peak at 95 degrees F. The hottest time of the day is always at noon, but that's the time you head straight for an air-conditioned shop or restaurant. Beaches are nearly always cooled by breezes, windward sides of an island in particular. If you're planning to do any climbing, start out at (or before) dawn or in the late afternoon to avoid getting caught by the midday sun.

Cool mountainous areas are always a wonderful escape from the heat, and many exist on the islands. The only islands that don't have a peak to their name are the Caymans, Bonaire, Curaçao, and Aruba. Saba is nearly all mountain, and the Dominican Republic has numerous rugged peaks.

CARIBBEAN CULTURE

Caribbean art is made of many colors, many materials, and many native techniques. Centuries of input from numerous continents have created a heady blend of traditions, old and new. A renaissance of Caribbean arts in the 1940s is still being felt today, as the newest generations of islanders look back to their roots for inspiration. The following is a summary of the best arts—visual, musical, literary and culinary—the Caribbean can offer.

Music

Barbados

Barbados' middle name is percussion, and the "boob-a-tuk" thump of the large log drum gave its name to traveling minstrel bands back in the 1800s. By the middle of the last century, the Barbadian (or Bajan) tuk band was performing at picnics called village meets, combining the pale whisper of the fife with the hearty drum beat. Today, tuk bands still perform at village meets held on the weekend, on holidays, and at the Crop Over Festival held in July. Special arrangements could even be made to have a tuk band play at one's wedding. The beat takes its inspiration from British regimental bands, propelled by a rapid, pulsating cadence overlaid on an African drum base. Tuk bands almost reach evangelical proportions as they move from village to village, gathering fans who jump up and down and dance wildly to the music.

Behavior can get wild as men put on dresses and others dress up as donkeys or bears.

Curaçao

Rumba meets the Irish jig in Curaçao's most popular dance called the tumba. As a grass-roots version of Venezuela's rumba, tumba also draws on the influence of the European colonizers to create this provocative dance rhythm. If you visit a local Curaçao dance party, you're sure to hear the beat. The best time to hear it is during the pre-Lent Carnival festivities, when the Tumba Festival brings competing musicians together from all over the island. The winning song is then played all year. One of the most important tumba groups playing locally (ask about) is Nos Antiyas.

Dominican Republic

Before merengue hit the world music charts, as popular today as salsa and samba, the spicy Latin Caribbean beat had been born and raised in the Dominican Republic. The saxophone and the accordion lend their special timbres to the mix, enlivened by the two-headed *tambora* (bass drum) and *guiros* (bottle gourds). The bassline is plucked in by the African-based *marimbula*, a large string instrument. The result is a kind of blazing Latin polka, with its distinctive beat called *cinquillo*. Among the top masters of merengue are Johnny Vetura, who was popular in the 60s, trumpeter Wilfrido Vargas, who also sings, and Sergio Vargas. It was thanks to Ventura that the merengue band was streamlined into a dance form. The original stiff-legged choreography was allegedly created for a wounded general, incorporating the Spanish two-step and the rumba. However, the fast, tightly performed merengue is unique in that it allows enormous room for individual spontaneous expression. As in samba, the upper waist is kept quiet while all the action happens down below. In Santo Domingo, merengue blares out of glitzy hotel ballrooms as well as the simplest dives—all night long. Best clubs are the El Yarey Bar at the Sheraton, Guacaa Taina, a subterranean disco with stalactites and stalagmites, and Bella Blue Disco, the city's trendiest disco. The place to catch great merengue jams in Santo Domingo is at Avenida George Washington, known as the Malecón, at nightfall, where the area turns into a party. You can practically hear a different merengue from each door, blaring away in competition. Big splashy Las Vegas-type reviews can also be found at the top-class hotels. Country fiestas always have great merengue bands. During the Merengue Festival in Santo Domingo (10 days in July), you can hear the best music the island has to offer.

Guadeloupe

Carnival in Guadeloupe is taken over by the supercharged rhythms of *zouk*, a beat born in the French West Indies, later transported to the top Parisian dance clubs by fine Caribbean performers. The use of the Afro-Caribbean *tambout*, a bamboo percussion instrument, roots the beat in ancient forms, extending to biguine, choval bwa, Creole mazurkas, and other French Antillean folk forms. But zouk is really a marriage between studio techniques and tradition. Among the top groups have been the internationally known Kassav; other great performers are Zouk Machine, Lazair, Jocelyne Bernard, and Gazoline. To hear zouk on the island, tune into local radio stations, or frequent the local nightclubs. There's even a zouk DJ ensconced at the supermarket Mammoth. The Festival des Arts de la Guadeloupe presents numerous live bands. Debs Records in Pointe-a-Pitre has a good selection of the latest hits.

Jamaica

Reggae is the ghetto child of Jamaica—its heart, its soul, its inspiration. Its origins lie in ancient forms, such as *mento*, a modernized version of the old slave songs deeply rooted in spirituality. During the 1960s, ska and rock-steady intermingled with rock and American soul, giving a certain persistent but soulful edge to Afro-Caribbean rhythms. Inspired by Rastafarian idealism and pro-black movements, reggae became a mouthpiece for protest at the same time bringing a powerful message of love and peace. Bob Marley and the Wailers were not the first local group to play reggae, but they were undoubtedly the most influential; today Marley is beloved as a national hero, and in many quarters has reached the status of guru and spiritual saint. His son Ziggy and his wife Rita are also stars in their own right now. Jimmy Cliff is another reggae great, responsible for bringing reggae into the chic dance-halls of America. The new form "righteous reggae" refers to a a type of lyric that preaches the Rastafarian message of love, peace and black liberation. Dance-hall reggae and dub are two forms which have been inspired by the proliferation of rap music. There are so many record shops in Kingston that you won't have any trouble taking home a superb island collection. IRIE-FM, the radio station, plays reggae 24 hours. You can also hear it blaring away constantly in nightclubs and resorts, particularly in Kingston and Negril. The Reggae Sunsplash Festival, held in August, is known throughout the world for its spectacular array of stars.

Montserrat

Soca was born in the arms of the great Montserrat musician Mighty Arrow when he married calypso with soul. Mighty Arrow is known as the Father of Soca, and it was he who coined the word, a blending of the words soul and calypso. Today it is one of the most popular beats in the Caribbean. A major hit, "Hot Hot Hot" was heard in clubs and air waves throughout the Caribbean. Montserrat's main station Radio Antilles generously plays Mighty Arrow's hits as well as the work of other artists. Fine souvenir recordings can be bought from Arrow's Manshop in Plymouth.

Puerto Rico

The fiery blend of mambo, rumba, conga, cha-cha and other Latin sounds come together in the irresistible beat of *salsa*. Puerto Rico's version arrived via Cuba, where the intoxicating drums of the Santeria cult had intermingled with big band brass. Romantic melodies usually sung by a dancing trio are backed by a drum ensemble that demands a master leader, such as Tito Puente, who excels on the timbales. Cow bells, claves, maracas, congos, and guiros combine to produce a kitchen sink background to a piano, bass and horn section. The basic three-step of the dance is quite erotic, and in the hands of fine dancers can be entirely provocative. These days new salsa is being enlivened by its flirtation with jazz and rock; among the biggest names to look for are Frankie Ruiz, Bobby Valentin, Santiago and others. The finest singer, without question, remains Celia Cruz now the grand dame of the genre.

St. Croix

The U.S. Virgin Islands is now the arena for an old traditional music form that's been rejuvenated by a wild sense of percussion. The form is *quelbe*, also known as scratch music because of the corrugated gourds the bands scrape for percussion. In the olden days, quelbe was performed on a banjo, fife, and long bass instrument made from automobile exhaust pipes. Local St. Croix bands such as Blink & the Roadmaster and Stanley & the Ten Sleepless Knights do their best to preserve the original forms, while groups such as Native Rhythm have infused the beat with electronic instruments to sound more modern. Weekend church festivities always find a quelbe band in high gear, and good groups can be heard in Frederiksted clubs, as well as the Calabash Club in Christiansted.

Trinidad

The Caribbean Renaissance of music, it might be said, could be singularly owed to Trinidad. Since the beginning of this century, the West Indian form called King Calypso has shaken the walls of Trinidad. The original name was *kaiso*, an African word in the language of Hausa, rooted in the traditions of verbal sparring *(picong)* and folklore story-telling. In the 1930s, not only wit but severe political satire entered the lyrics, and some musicians were even arrested for criticizing the government. Calypso finally found its way north to great success in the United States. Today's calypso intermingles French-Caribbean cadence music with East Indian melodies and Motown soul. Lyrics are still controversial and opinionated, with topics ranging from apartheid to family squabbles. Mighty Sparrow is Trinidad's most famous promoter, a prolific songwriter of over 500 songs.

The king of Trinidadian musical instruments is the steel drum, or pan, which can play anything from calypso to Mozart. It's a humbly born instrument, originating when poor musicians in the 1930s created makeshift instruments out of hub caps, paint buckets, and pots and pans. With the advent of oil refining, musicians appropriated oil drums and found them incredibly versatile, able to be fine-tuned and tempered. Pans come in various ranges, including bass, cell-pan, guitar-pan, and ping-pong. The concave drums with raised notes are struck and stroked with padded drumsticks. Steel drums can be purchased at Lincoln Enterprises in Woodbrook. Some of the top bands (some with over 200 members who can't even read music) are the Renegades, Neal and Massy All-Stars, and Invaders.

If you get out to the countryside, you're bound to hear the gentler Spanish-influenced folk songs called *parang*. *Cuatros* (four-stringed guitars) join maraas, violins, and mandolins to express a tender melody not unlike Spanish carols. The best place to catch the real thing is in the village of Lopinot in the Arouca Valley, where the tradition survives with great tenacity.

The best time to hear steel bands and all kinds of Trinidadian music, is during the island's biennial Steelband Festival, usually held in October in Port of Spain. Carnival is also a fantastic time to hear all sorts of Trinidadian beats. The biggest festivals are at Soca village near Port of Spain harbor, where half a dozen orchestras perform for over 25,000 revelers. Mas' Camp Pub in the Woodbruck district of Port of Spain has the flavor of Carnival year-round with live music Friday and Saturday nights. Check with your hotel and neighboring ones for local performances during the weekend.

Visual Arts

Jamaica

Jamaica's visual art ranks among the most important in the Caribbean islands. Jamaica's art world enjoys a vast variety of forms and styles, from avant-garde to primitive to Neo-Expressionist, although all Jamaican artists tend to strive to find a national point of view. The late Edna Manlet, called the "Mother of Jamaican Art," spawned a movement during the 30s that radically challenged the limits of "acceptable" art by introducing visions of colonial rebellion and native passion. A group of native artists actually banded together under Manley (Ralph Campbell, Albert Huie and Alvin Marriott, among them) and called themselves the Institute Group (they had forced Kingston's Institute of Jamaica to give them a show). Intuitive art followed in the next generation, which created a truly national form, mixing elements of naiveté. The early intuitive painter Mallica "Kapo" Reynolds became known for intensely spiritual expressions. Sculptors David Miller Senior and his son David Miller used African and Jamaican themes heavily in their work. Other fine painters are Carl Abrahams and Sidney McLaren.

Crafts

Puerto Rico

Local crafts in Puerto Rico reach very high standards among Caribbean artistry, but none higher than the *santos*, hand-carved and painted wooden statues that depict saints and other religious figures. The technique did not originate here, but Puerto Rico remains one of the few islands where the craft is thriving. It was originally brought to the New World by Christian missionaries; today local carvers have added their own individual expressions. Some of the best carvers, called *santeros*, are Pedro Pablo Inaldi and Domingo Orta of Ponce. Enter a Puerto Rican home and you are sure to find at least one santos, if not scores of them reverentially placed around the room.

Also famous in Puerto Rico are colorful masks from Ponce and Loiza, worn during island festivals. They originated in medieval Spain when masqueraders would try to scare the villagefolk with terrifying masks. Today in Puerto Rico, an African flavor is apparent in the masks. Masks made in Loiza tend to be made of coconut shells and painted with off-centered faces in bright colors. Masks made in Ponce are styled in papier-mache and come in the shape of multi-horned devils and animals. Mask fanatics should definitely attend the three big mask festivals: Ponce Festival in February, the Festival of Loiza Aldea in July, and the Dia de las Mascaras in December in Hatillo.

Saba

Saban lacework is a delicate artwork that can find no peers in the Caribbean. Each village and family has developed its own unique style. Dating back centuries, the drawn threadwork, called Spanish Work, was brought to the island a century ago by the daughter of a prominent island family, having learned the technique in a Venezuelan convent school. As she passed it on to her fellow islanders, they became so skilled that they won international contests. Today you can buy the lace in such forms as tablecloths, napkins and handkerchiefs. Most families sell their wares from their porch (Saba is a very informal island); you can also pick up excellent items in the impromptu craft market that always meets the ferry. Other lace stores include the Island Craft

Shop and Saban Tropical Arts in Windwardside, the Saba Artisan Foundation in the Bottom, and Hell's Gate Community Center.

Bahamas

Look in any direction in the Bahamas and you're sure to see straw. In the 1720s, the governor's wife introduced plait palm-fronding after seeing it in Bermuda. Through the years, weavers, especially women, honed the craft of making baskets, using the silver top of the thatch palm. The first artistic baskets were hawked to tourists at vegetable and fruit stands as early as 1860. Today weavers craft bags, baskets, mats, dolls, hats and other items out of straw. The best can be found at the International Bazaar in Freeport and at Market Plaza in Nassau. Excellent bargains can be found at the straw market. You'll get the best price by efficient and persistent haggling.

Cuisine

Guadeloupe

Dining reaches gourmet proportions in Guadeloupe, where French elan merges with African resourcefulness to create the island's Creole cuisine. African techniques and ingredients are combined with pungent East Indian spices to create a rich aromatic melange that could be considered as haute as Cordon Bleu. In the hands of some native chefs, dishes like *accras* (salt codfish fritters), *crabes farcis* (spicy stuffed crabs), *boudin* (blood sausage), and *colombos* (curries) reach artistic excellence. Creole chefs, usually women, often develop their trade at the feet of their mothers and the loving care they put into the food can veritably be tasted. During the month of August, the Fete des Cuisinieres honors these talented culinary artists with a parade awash with colorful costumes and lavish gold jewelry. A five-hour banquet follows the parade, open to a limited guest list.

(For more information on island cuisine, see under "Where to Eat" in the individual chapters. Jamaica, in particular, has a long and hefty tradition of eating. For more information on the history of each island, see "History" in each island chapter.

Best Bars

Every Caribbean island boasts its star bar. For elegant dining, you go to a restaurant; for fried shrimp you can go to a seaside shack. But to meet the local salt of the earth or hobnob with ex-pats, celebs in disguise, and government ministers on their day off, you go to a Caribbean bar. It may take you your entire vacation time to find just the right one, on the right beach, overlooking just the right view, but whatever effort you put into the task will be worth it. Some bars, Club Med style, are strewn with snapshots of previous clients, some have walls littered with calling cards. The best concoct a heady mix of colorful clients and fine local brew, but when the sun, surf and sand is perfect, all you really need in this lay-back-and guzzle region is a bartender, a stool, a cold beer and you.

Bar Numero Uno: Rick's Cafe

Negril, Jamaica

Opened in 1974 by American Richard Hershman who transformed a private villa into an outdoor eatery and bar, Rick's Cafe is perched on the precarious edge of a cliff. With a few rum punches tucked under your belt, it's not hard to imagine yourself plunging head first over the 25-foot cliff; in fact some daring clients actually do dive intentionally into the aquamarine sea from the lower 10-ft. lip. Rick's specialty is the fresh tropical fruit daiquiri. You'll be joined at sunset by over 200 people clamoring for the same spectacular view. The tall, tan and handsome are in full supply here, in fact if *you* aren't, you might feel self-conscious gawking.

Le Select

St. Barts

Despite the name on this hoity-toity island, Le Select is about as unselective as possible when it comes to admitting clientele. Which is exactly why it's beloved by locals, Americans and French tourists alike, attracting everyone from construction workers to cruise day-trippers to sexy French tourists in black spandex tights and high heels. In 1987 even the King and Queen of Sweden graced the outdoor courtyard with its hodgepodge of furniture and walls littered with yellowed newspaper clippings. The bar started 40 years ago when St. Bart's capital Gustavia didn't even have a bar or a restaurant. Best chow is the Le Select cheeseburger, washed down with a Carib beer or a *'tipunch* (rum with cane syrup and a few licks of lime juice). Views run from motorbikes gunning the corner to a fabulous spread of the harbor. Sound runs from reggae to zouk.

Bomba's Shack

Tortola, BVI

Bomba's shack is one of the weirdest bars in the world, closer to a bombed-out shack with its haphazard walls and mismatched floorboards and a floor full of sand. You can leave a pair of sunglasses on the wall or take one; you'll also find lots of calling cards, parts of automobiles, shoes, and even photographs of previous Bomba parties where everyone looks, if not, bombed out, at least smashed to high heaven. Mushroom tea is a favorite on the menu, but the real risk-takers order the Bomba Punch, a blend of passionfruit, guava, banana, pineapple, papaya and orange juice mixed with homemade rum—a secret recipe from the ancestors. Local bands jam on Wednesday-Sunday. The best chow is the all-you-can-eat barbecue steamed in grape leaves. Best time to come is at the full moon, for the famous Full Moon Parties.

Cheri's Cafe

Sint Maarten

Owner American expat Cheri Batson just wanted a humble little open-air joint in Cinnamon Grove Shopping Center for one night of Superbowl. But the idea got out of hand and burgeoned into a bar that's sprouted a long pair of legs. The TV screens are still there, the roofs still have no walls, but the present staff of 80 today serves 400 meals a night. It's the place to hear the hottest music on the island, from hip house to calypso to American rock and reggae. Dancing is de rigeur. Frozen strawberry daiquiris are killers.

Charlie's Bar

San Nicholas, Aruba

Brassieres hang on the walls at Charlie's along with baseball caps, license plates, matchbooks, shoes, and miscellaneous refuse of the past half-century of clients. Dutch owner Charlie Brouns helped defend this part of San Nicholas from German U-boat invasions during World War II; today his son commandeers the bar, but the old geezer behind the counter is Guus (with two u's), who will tell you whaling tales from the old days of Aruba. Dutch divers crowd in next to American tourists and even Aruban locals who chow down on the fresh catch of the day and a cold Heineken.

Foxy's Tamarind Bar

Jost Van Dyke, BVI

The island has only 100 residents, but the bar overlooking one of the prettiest beaches of the island has been around for 27 years. The owner named Foxy is a born entertainer, song and shtick man, who loves entertaining. Guests get calypsos written about them, and on Thursday-Saturday, a live band reigns. Other nights, the latest canned Caribbean music blares away. A real "the way it was" bar, it's got sand on the floor, a counter weary from all the sunburnt elbows that have leaned on it, and flying fish sandwiches you have to hold down to eat. The specialty is Painkiller Punch, sold in plain plastic glasses, for $3 each. New Year's Eve shouldn't be celebrated anywhere else but here.

John Moore Bar

Barbados

John Moore looks like every other rum shack in the Caribbean—at first, that is. The more you settle into your chair, a time lapse overtakes you and you feel like you're growing into the ages-old bar stool. Opened in 1958, it instantly attracted the tourist trade, since the location was ideal (sandwiched between the main highway and a perfect western beach) and the congeniality was superb. The famed dish served here is fried fish, to the accompaniment of a jukebox that blares calypso and reggae.

ANGUILLA

Anguilla is about 35 miles square with excellent beaches and great diving.

Long, flat and skinny, Anguilla looks like an anchovy—indeed the name in Italian means "eel," a nickname reportedly bestowed on the island by Christopher Columbus when he cruised past in 1493. Today imbued with a British gentility, the island is a model of peace, quiet and pristine beauty; poets fall over themselves trying to describe the three blues of sea, sky and horizon. With no casinos, cinema, duty-free shopping, museums, or golf courses, there's not much to do in Anguilla but surrender to nature; celebs like Robert De Niro and Princess Stephanie of Monaco find it quite easy. A dry climate has always rendered Anguilla the least populous of the British Crown Colonies in the Eastern Caribbean, but the swell of tourists in the last decade (17,000 in 1982 to 93,000 in 1992), has turned the economy from its former sea orientation to tourism. And yet, even though everyone wants to buy land here, no one seems able to, since the tight control of property and its very inaccessibility has saved Anguilla from the kind of overdevelopment that's nearly drowned nearby St. Martin. The result is an island where the beaches are still clean, the brew is still local, and the local scratch bands haven't succumbed to pretension. In short, an island to love.

Sometimes called the South Beach of the Caribbean, Anguilla boasts a remarkable clarity of light which throws a sparkling glow over everything. Even at peak season, it's easy to find secluded strands perfect for walking, snoozing, snuggling, or snorkeling There are offshore reef and water sports galore, with fish pots and lobster traps and handcrafted racing boats boasting designer driftwood and exotic walls made of conch shells. Underwater is a Fujichrome spectacular of corals and fish. The landscape buzzes with wildlife—diving pelicans, mischievous frigate birds, and noisy tropical birds. Everywhere you'll see hummingbirds feasting on flowering hibiscus and your breakfast table might even be visited by bananaquits, a little yellow bird with an unabashed appetite. There's even one local residence where snowy egrets stroll through the backyard.

Bird's Eye View

This 16-by- 3- 1/2 mile island is scrubby, flat and often dusty. It rises from the Anguilla Bank 180 feet below sea level to only 213 feet above at its highest point. A frequent location for some of the most luxurious fashion shoots in the world, Anguilla boasts more than 33 brilliantly white beaches and no real city; instead the island is dotted with small villages. Refreshing wind rustles through the golden meadows full of towering savannah grass and migrating birds alight on serene ponds and around the picturesque bay. With the advent of spring, Anguilla bursts into flame with flamboyant trees shading gingerbread houses and hanging over seaside cliffs.

Anguilla's main road starts at West End, a village in the southwest and runs to The Quarter, a small settlement in the center of the island. The same road connects to island harbour.Turn-offs will take you to isolated beaches and fishing villages. The Department of Tourism is located in The Valley, at the center of the island. Nearby is Wallblake Airport. The port of entry is at Sandy Ground at Road Bay, on the north coast.

Anguilla

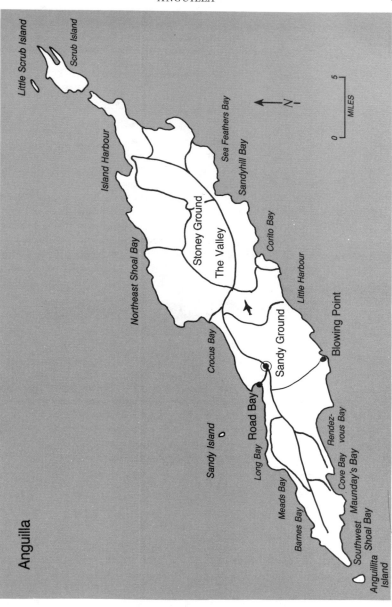

Little Scrub Island

Scrub Island

Island Harbour

Sea Feathers Bay

Sandyhill Bay

Stoney Ground

The Valley

Corito Bay

Northeast Shoal Bay

Little Harbour

Crocus Bay

Sandy Ground

Blowing Point

Sandy Island

Long Bay

Road Bay

Rendez-
vous Bay

Meads Bay

Cove Bay

Maunday's Bay

Barnes Bay

Southwest
Shoal Bay

Anguillita
Island

N

0 5

MILES

People

The natives of Anguilla are polite, proud and friendly. Nearly everywhere else in the Caribbean, natives seem sleepy; here they are wide awake and look you straight in the eye. Industrious and hardworking, many toil at several jobs, taking pride in their work and helping each other out during hurricanes and drought. (Many native-borns actually work abroad and send money home). Since Anguilla never had a big plantocracy, the shadow of slavery doesn't hover; hence, there are few racial tensions and little class pretension. Anguilla is the sort of place where both the British governor and the hotel clerk ride their bikes to work. Anguillian goats, who never seem to know when to get out of the way of oncoming traffic, seem to hold the real power here. Most natives are boat racing fanatics; in fact, Anguilla is the only British isle in the Caribbean where cricket is *not* the number one sport.

Fielding Tip:

It's considered rude to meet anyone without the prerequisite greeting: a gentle good morning or good afternoon, or more informally "okay" or "awrigh" (meaning, "hello-how- are-you-everything okay-allright?"

History

Long before the Europeans arrived in the Caribbean, Arawak Indians inhabited Anguilla's hot and dusty scrubland. Over the past ten years, some 40,000 Amerindian artifacts have been uncovered by the Anguilla Archaeological and Historical Society from some 50 sites, indicating Anguilla may have been an important ceremonial site, even a pilgrimage, for this native American tribe. By the time the English settled in the 1650s, the Arawaks had vanished—probably decimated by European conquistadors and marauding pirates. When the dry climate foiled all British attempts at farming, their former slaves divided up the land, cultivated pigeon peas and corn, and then finally turned to the sea, building and trading sloops and schooners and fishing in rich waters. In the late 60s, the British forced Anguilla into an uncomfortable tri-island alliance when the Associated State of St. Kitts-Nevis-Anguilla was signed into law. The single act stimulated a determined, if not exactly violent, rebellion, which found Anguillians marching a coffin around the island, burning the Government House, and sending its 12 policemen packing.World headlines roared with news of "The Eel that Squeeled" (sic) as the Brits sent in paratroopers, only to be met on the shore by cheering Anguillians singing the British national anthem and waving Union Jacks. Finally the Brits succumbed and gave Anguilla what it really wanted—a benevolent overlord who took the pains to build a badly needed phone system, a new pier and roads.Today Anguilla is a happy British dependent with its own elected governing body.

Beaches

Windsurfing and sailing are readily available at many Anguilla hotels.

Rendezvous Bay, one of the island's most spectacular strands, is two miles of pure sand dunes facing the rolling hills of St. Martin. Good for long, lonely walks, the beach is studded with pretty seashells and monstrous-shaped driftwood as well as coconuts that have dropped from the palm trees that shade the strand. **Shoal Bay**, on the western tip, boasts an expansive sweep and silvery glow. The sea is full of iridescent fish who beg for snorkelers. **Savannah Beach**, rife with palms, is where you go when you are looking for unadulterated privacy. **Captain's Bay**, tucked on the island's northeast edge, offers good treks past a field of wild frangipani; from here you get an excellent view of crashing waves among the coral reefs. A climb across the karst takes you to **Windward Point** on the easternmost tip. **Limestone** is good for a snooze or quiet reading time. **Crocus or Little Bay**, home to the boat races, is best for snorkeling; here you'll find lobster, turtles and huge shoals of fishes, armies of sergeant majors, butterflyfish, iridescent blue doctorfish, grunts, squirrelfish, and *wrasses*. **Cove Bay's** white strands are terribly secluded except for fishing boas. Maunday's Bay Home is home to **Cap Juluca**, the luxurious resort, and sports some of the largest seagrape trees on the island. **Sandy Ground** on Road Bay, is a must-see village of picturesque proportions, located between the big salt pond and the island's commercial and yacht harbor on Road Bay.

Dive Sites

Two large reefs lie off the northwest and west coasts, directly behind each other; here you'll find massive coral formations that reach right to the surface of the water. The variety of coral is stunning—from star coral and clower coral to sea fans and large elkhorn and staghorn. The reefs are rich with marine life, and it will be a cinch to glimpse such species as angelfishes, torpedo-headed wrasses, damselfishes, trumpetfishes, and tiny metallic squids, among others. Centuries ago, these reefs spelled deep danger for seagoing vessels; as such, there are at least two dozen shipwrecks which have been discovered near Sandy, Scrub, and Dog islands, as well as off the south coast and the northern reefs. Sometimes humpback and sperm whales, which migrate northward from the Caribbean in March and April (and on their return in September and October) can be spotted off the island's coast.

Treks

Before starting on any trek, pick up a topographical map from the Land and Survey Department which shows some footpaths and tracks and especially designed for hikers. (The department, along with the Anguilla Tourist Office, is located in a group of government buildings midway between the Valley and the airport.) East of Island Harbor are some rough dirt roads that can be hiked to **Captain's Bay**, a secluded, most romantic beach bracketed by limestone cliffs. Another road leads to **Windward Point**, where untamed vegetation and a rough seascape of breaking ocean waves makes for a spectacular view. Porpoises and dolphins are often sighted here midway between Sandy ground and The Valley; to get there take a paved road that veers north from the main highway to where the Government House, the official residence of the governor, is located. Directly east of the house, you'll discover two footpaths that lead to the **Cavanah Cave**, a former phosphate mine, and **Kartouche Cave**, which is rife with bats. The hike from the main road only takes about twenty minutes, but you'll need a local to guide you since the paths have now been overgrown by vegetation. You may even miss the entrance to the Kartouche Cave since a large tree has now sprouted in its entrance. Do carry lighting as the caves are very dark. Bird-watchers will particularly enjoy **Caul's Pond**, a large gathering of brackish water that attracts huge flocks of black-necked stilts and white-checked pintain ducks at sunset. Great white herons, belted kingfishers, and the endangered peregrine falcon have also been sighted. An easy walk can be taken down the flat, gravelly north shore of the pond to get the best view of the birds. On the south side of the island, in the direction of Savannah Bay, the main road follows the edge of **East End Pond**, another fine bird-watching area known for its two types of egrets and a variety of warblers.

What Else to See

Anguilla's gorgeous natural beach scene overshadows any other man-made sights, so spend most of your extra time either slung out in local bars or discovering new beaches. In the afternoon, do catch the local fishermen spilling their sacks of spiny lobster on the sand for prospective buyers. For the most spectacular view, cross the crest of the little hill on the final stretch of the Shoal Bay road and look toward the horizon, particularly at sunset.

The Fountain, near Shoal Bay, is the island's only natural spring, today considered a site of ceremonial pilgrimage after archaeologists discovered numerous 2000-year-old petroglyphs of an Arawak god.The large-dome shaped cavern stands on a ridge 70 feet above sea level. A steel ladder was added many years ago for easier access to the cave, whose entrance is quite small, allowing in very little natural light.

Island Harbour is a disarmingly charming fishing village peopled with descendants of the marauding Irish mixed with African slaves. That means green eyes and chocolate skin—a devastating combination, and with a lively spirit to match. Don't miss catching the strains of local bands at Smitty's bar.

Scilly Cat, only two minutes by boat from the island's harbor, is a wonder of coral, sand and exotic vegetation. You can spend the whole day there plying a variety of water sports and chowing down on native-style barbecue. Don't miss **Gorgeous Scilly Cay** restaurant, an island tradition, where you can hear the best local bands.

Johnno, the famous beach bar at Sandy Ground, is the place to be on Sunday, when the entire island turns out for a rock-out party. It's usually a local's scene, but visitors are welcome to join in the maddening calypso and reggae beat.

Fielding Tip:

Learn the language of land directions in Anguilla, inspired by the winds. East is "up." West is "down." And both north and south are "over."

City Celebrations

Festival

Various locations, The Valley.

To celebrate Emancipation Day, or "August Monday" when the slaves were freed, Anguillans throw a week-long party each year that begins the first week of August. Festivities include boat races—the island's national sport—cultural events and general acts of merriment.

Historical Sites

Wallblake House ★★★

Crossroads, The Valley, ☎ *(809) 497-2405.*

This plantation house, circa 1787, can be toured only by appointment, but even if you just get to see the outside, it's worth a look. Great tales of intrigue, murder, a French invasion and dysfunctional family history surround the place, which is now owned by the Catholic Church. While you're here, check out the newer church next door with its open-air side walls. The best time to come is Saturday mornings in the winter, when local artisans display their works on the grounds.

Sports

The sea is king, when it comes to sports in Anguilla. Sailboat-racing is a mania, sometimes merely the excuse for riotous beachside parties and barbecues. (Look for them on New Year's Day, Anguilla Day and Easter, as well as spontaneously.) There are also excellent scuba, sailing, and snorkeling possibilities. Most hotels have some kind of activities program; the best will always be connected with the largest resorts. Some of the top hotels have numerous courts. Free playing time is available at the Scouts Headquarters (For more information, call the Anguilla Drugstore ☎ *2738.*

Tamariain Water Sports

P.O. Box 247, The Valley., Anguilla, West Indies

The island's only full-service PADI (Professional Association of Diving Instructors) dive facility offers dives to a variety of underwater sites, as well as a course that takes beginners on one open-water dive ($80). They also offer Sunfish sailboats for rent and host water-skiing excursions.

Where to Stay

Highest Rated Hotels in Anguilla

★★★★★ **Malliouhana Beach Hotel**

★★★★ **Cap Juluca**

★★★★ **Cinnamon Reef Beach Club**

★★★★ **La Sirena**

★★★ **Carimar Beach Club**

★★★ **Casablanca Resort**

★★★ **Coccoloba**

★★★ **Cove Castles Villa Resort**

★★★ **Fountain Beach**

★★★ **Frangipani Beach Club**

Most Exclusive Hotels in Anguilla

★★★	**Casablanca Resort**	$350–$1100
★★★	**Cove Castles Villa Resort**	$350–$990
★★★	**Pineapple Beach Club**	$270–$660
★★★★	**Cinnamon Reef Beach Club**	$155–$330
★★★★	**La Sirena**	$100–$280

Fielding's Best Value Hotels in Anguilla

★★★★	**Cinnamon Reef Beach Club**	$155–$330
★★★★	**La Sirena**	$100–$280
★★★	**Cove Castles Villa Resort**	$350–$990
★★★★★	**Cap Juluca**	$275–$2085
★★★★★	**Malliouhana Beach Hotel**	$240–$810

In Anguilla you can sleep stinking rich (like the luscious five-bedroom villa at the Cap Juluca) or "rough" it in a bed and breakfast for under $100. The latest trend is to stay in newly built cottages and villas designed to reflect the island's all-seasonal lifestyle, particularly good for return visitors who already know the island. For bed and breakfast digs (usually located along or near the main road of the island) contact the tourist offices in Anguilla and New York. Best bargains are found in the summer when you can wrack up to 60 percent discounts. If you have no car, choose lodgings near and in Sandy Ground, Shoal Bay, and Island Harbour, since restaurants and shops will be within walking distance. Most hotels, except for the cheapest, usually have air-conditioning, phones, TVs and private baths. Crime has been considered so nonexistent that some hotels actually boast they have no locks on the door. If you haven't evolved to such transcendental levels of trust, do inquire before you book yourself in.

Hotels and Resorts

Paradise Cove, Anguilla's newest luxury property, located in the cove on the western end of the island, is sporting a new restaurant for breakfast and light meals, and an expanded children's playground, making the 14 fully furnished suites fully adaptable for families. La Sirena Hotel, overlooking Meads Bay, has added a fifth villa—three-bedrooms that can comfortably accommodate six adults or a large family. New athletic and entertainment facilities have been added to Cap Jaluca, and a 32-foot speedboat is now available for excursions. A putting green on the southern shore of Maundays Bay Lagoon was installed as was an English-regulation croquet court.

Arawak Beach Resort $100–$300 ★★★

P.O. Box 98, The Valley, Island Harbour, ☎ (800) 553-4939, (809) 497-4888.
Single: $100–$300. Double: $300.

Located on the site of an ancient Arawak Indian village, this newer resort consists of two-story villas furnished with Amerindian replicas. Lots of interesting touches here: A small museum exhibits artifacts found on the site; the courtyard is planted with traditional island crops like cotton and papaya; and the watersports include canoe rentals. No smoking throughout, and though you can bring your own, no liquor is served. 14 rooms. Credit Cards: V, MC, A.

Cap Juluca $275–$2085 ★★★★

Maunday's Bay, ☎ (800) 323- 139, (809) 497-6666.
Single: $275–$2085. Double: $275–$2085.

It doesn't get much better than here at Cap Juluca, the epitome of resort living at its swankest. Guest rooms, housed in whitewashed villas, are exquisitely decorated and boast giant walk-in closets, walnut louvered doors and windows and huge patios. Breakfast is served by two maids; when you return from dinner, you'll find they left flickering candles when they turned down the beds. The imaginatively landscaped grounds include scenic lagoons, two restaurants, three tennis courts and the gorgeous beach. Worth every precious cent! 91 rooms. Credit Cards: V, MC, A.

Casablanca Resort $350–$1100 ★★★

P.O. Box 444, The Valley, Rendezvous Bay West, ☎ *(800) 231-1945, (809) 497-6999.*
Single: $350–$1100. Double: $350–$1100.

This Moorish-influenced, pink and green resort is a rather incongruous sight on this laid-back island, but if you like pizazz, Casablanca delivers. The $20-million, 200-acre resort boasts three miles of beach, two lit tennis courts, complimentary watersports, a 1200-square-foot pool, games room, library, three restaurants and such special touches as hand-carved and hand-painted mosaics created by Moroccan artisans. Beach wing rooms have the best views, but the garden rooms are bigger and have more luxurious baths. By far Anguilla's grandest resort. 88 rooms. Credit Cards: V, MC, A.

Cinnamon Reef Beach Club $155–$330 ★★★★

Little Harbour, ☎ *(800) 223-1108, (809) 497-2727.*
Single: $155–$330. Double: $155–$330.

Pleasantly informal is the atmosphere at this intimate 40-acre resort. Accommodations are in whitewashed villas set on the beach or perched on a bluff; each has living and dining rooms, a raised bedroom, patio complete with hammock, and tiled sunken showers (no baths). For recreation, there's a huge pool (40 by 60 feet), three tennis courts and all kinds of complimentary watersports. Located on Anguilla's southern coast, this excellent resort's only downfall is its relatively small beach, though its calm waters make for great windsurfing. Rooms include a Continental Breakfast. 22 rooms. Credit Cards: V, MC, A.

Coccoloba $225–$425 ★★★

Barnes Bay, ☎ *(800) 982-7729, (809) 497-6871.*
Single: $225–$425. Double: $225–$425.

A true tropical hideaway, chic Coccoloba is nestled on a rocky headland between two picture-perfect beaches. Most guest rooms are in cottages on a bluff above the beach, though seven units are housed in a beachside villa. All have sea views, but some are better than others. Each room is done in traditional West Indian decor, with bright Caribbean colors, marble baths and individual, though not secluded, patios. All watersports are free, and extras like complimentary soft drinks on the beach and high tea daily keep you pampered. 51 rooms. Credit Cards: V, MC, A.

Frangipani Beach Club $195–$1200 ★★★

Meads Bay, ☎ *(800) 892-4564, (809) 497-6442.*
Single: $195–$555. Double: $250–$1200.

This newer enclave of Spanish-style pink stucco and red-tile roof villas offers one- to three-bedroom suites on gorgeous Meads Bay Beach. All units have air conditioning, full kitchens, natural rattan furnishings and a patio or balcony; some boast Jacuzzis as well. The restaurant is open only for breakfast and lunch. Watersports cost extra. 21 rooms. Credit Cards: A.

Malliouhana Beach Hotel $240–$810 ★★★★★

Meads Bay, ☎ *(800) 835- 796, (809) 497-6111.*
Single: $240–$780. Double: $240–$810.

Every little detail is in place at this impeccable resort, set atop a cliff overlooking two beaches. Guest rooms are spacious and nicely decorated with high-quality rattan furniture, Haitian art, marble baths with oversized tubs and patios or balconies. There are four tennis courts, three pools, all watersports and an open-air exercise pavilion with lovely ocean views to keep you motivated. But gorgeous as this spot is—and it is lovely—the staff can be a bit cool, and the overall atmosphere a bit snooty and reserved. 53 rooms.

Mariners, The   **$115–$535**   ★★★

Sandy Ground, ☎ *(800) 848-7938, (809) 497-2671.*
Single: $115–$190. Double: $115–$535.
A true West Indian-style resort, complete with gingerbread cottages and hand-crafted lattice. Accommodations have pitched ceilings, Haitian wicker furniture painted in pastels, and modest bathrooms. The nicer cottages boast living rooms and well-equipped kitchenettes. Be warned that not all units have air conditioning. This all-inclusive resort is situated at the far end of Anguilla's busiest beach, near a deep-water port. True couch potatoes can rent a TV and VCR for an added fee. Service is friendly but sometimes lacking. 25 rooms. Credit Cards: V, MC, A.

Pineapple Beach Club   **$270–$660**   ★★★

Rendezvous Bay, ☎ *(800) 345-0356, (809) 497-6061.*
Single: $270–$565. Double: $355–$660.
A solid choice for those watching their pocketbooks, this cozy, all-inclusive resort is set on Anguilla's southernmost tip. One-story bungalows set around a central courtyard opening to a beautiful beach, have a distinctive West Indian style, with wide verandas, trellises and whimsical gingerbread trim. Rooms are nicely done in mahogany furnishings, hand-crafted linens and ceiling fans in lieu of air conditioning. Formerly the Anguilla Great House, this pleasant spot offers complimentary watersports. 27 rooms. Credit Cards: V, MC, A.

Rendezvous Bay Hotel   **$90–$240**   ★★

Rendezvous Bay, ☎ *(800) 274-4893, (809) 497-6549.*
Single: $90–$240. Double: $90–$240.
Set among 60 acres of coconut trees, this is the island's first resort, and though it draws a lot of repeat customers, it does show its age. Not a bad choice for the price, though, with the lovely beach making up for a lack of amenities—no pool, for example. The original rooms are simple and lack air conditioning, while the newer villas have spacious one-bedroom suites and air; some also have kitchenettes. There are two lighted tennis courts, a game and TV room and, best of all, an elaborate electric train setup in the lounge. Decent value, and pleasantly informal. 47 rooms. Credit Cards: V, MC.

Apartments and Condominiums

Independent-minded folks with time on their hands will enjoy the villa life in Anguilla, though there are drawbacks. Some staples might need to be bought in neighboring St. Martin/Sint Maarten. In general, prices will be much higher than at home. Check yearly for new listings since new properties are always being built.

Carimar Beach Club   **$130–$630**   ★★★

Meads Bay, ☎ *(800) 235-8667, (809) 497-6881.*
Single: $130–$630. Double: $250–$630.

These comfortable one- and two-bedroom apartments (and one three-bedroom) are owned as condominiums and rented out when the owners aren't using them. The villas are Mediterranean style and nicely done with wicker and rattan furniture, TVs, full kitchens, large living rooms, dining areas and balconies or patios. Most offer only partial views of the magnificent beach. The tropical grounds include two tennis courts but no pool. There's no restaurant or bar on-site, but the complex is within walking distance of Malliouhana and Coccoloba. 23 rooms. Credit Cards: V, MC, A.

Cove Castles Villa Resort $350–$990   ★★★

Shoal Bay West, ☎ *(800) 348-4716, (809) 497-6801.*
Single: $350–$590. Double: $350–$990.
This ultra-modern apartment resort may take some getting used to at first, with its futuristic white structures a somewhat jarring site. Accommodations are in eight 2 bedroom beach houses and four 3 bedroom villas. All have two baths, cable TV, a well-stocked and very modern kitchen, living and dining rooms, skylights, nice furnishings and a covered beachfront veranda. There's a restaurant and bar on the premises, and unlike other apartment complexes, limited room service. The beach is fantastic. 12 rooms. Credit Cards: A.

Easy Corner Villas $90–$295   ★★★

Road Bay, ☎ *(800) 223-9815, (809) 497-6433.*
Single: $90–$295. Double: $90–$295.
Families are prevalent at this complex of one- to three-bedroom apartments with combination living and dining areas, full kitchens and a patio; only three are air-conditioned. A restaurant and coffee shop are located on-site, and daily maid service is available for an extra fee. Located on a bluff overlooking Road Bay, this simple spot represents good value for the price. 15 rooms. Credit Cards: V, MC, A.

La Sirena $100–$280   ★★★★

Meads Bay, ☎ *(800) 331-9358, (809) 497-6827.*
Single: $100–$160. Double: $1200.
Accommodations at this pleasant property are in two- and three-bedroom apartments in Mediterranean-style white stucco buildings. Units are nicely done with rattan furnishings, ceiling fans and Caribbean pastels. There are two pools on-site, plus a formal restaurant and a casual poolside cafe. The beach is a two-minute walk. Not the most exciting place around, but good value for the rates. 24 rooms. Credit Cards: V, MC, A.

Paradise Cove $310–$425   ★★★

P.O. Box 135, The Cove, Anguilla, ☎ *(809) 497-3559, FAX: (809) 497-2559, in the U.S. (800) 553-4939, FAX: (516) 261-9606.*
Single: $310–$310. Double: $425–$425.

An intimate and romantic hideaway nestled among palm trees and lush tropical gardens just five minutes walk from beautiful Cove Beach. Centrally air-conditioned one and two bedroom elegantly furnished units with private bathrooms and fully equipped kitchens, telephones and private laundry facilities. Cable TV on request. Olympic pool, spacious Jacuzzis, kiddie pool. Pool bar, boutique, watersports, island tours. Private cooks available. Credit Cards: V, MC, A.

Sea Grape Beach Club Villas   **$180–$450**   ★★

Meads Bay, ☎ *(800) 223-9815, (809) 497-6433.*
Single: $180–$450. Double: $280–$450.
These modern two-bedroom condominiums are very nicely appointed; each has three bathrooms, ultra-large closets and private decks with sweeping ocean views. They're especially suited for those who like to spread out—each unit encompasses some 2000 square feet. The grounds include a restaurant, bar, watersports (for a fee) and two tennis courts. 10 rooms. Credit Cards: V, MC, A.

Shoal Bay Villas   **$147–$385**   ★★★

P.O. Box 81, North Coast, North Coast, ☎ *(800) 722-7045, (809) 497-2051.*
Single: $147–$385. Double: $147–$385.
Contemporary villa-style condominiums located on the beach west of Island Harbour. The one- and two-bedroom units have kitchenettes and painted rattan furniture, but no air conditioning. The palm-studded beach is a tropical dream, and there's a restaurant and bar on-site with occasional live music. No children in the winter. 13 rooms. Credit Cards: V, MC, A.

Inns

The lifestyle is breezier and more casual at Anguilla's handful of inns; management is often more attentive. Travelers young in spirit and weak on wallet should also check out the small properties in "Budget Bunks."

Ferryboat Inn   **$70–$225**   ★★

Blowing Point, ☎ *(809) 497-6613.*
Single: $70–$125. Double: $85–$225.
This family-owned and operated inn, near the ferry dock and beach, is a solid choice for those on a budget. Accommodations are comfortable and simple, consisting of one- and two-bedroom suites that are not air conditioned and a two-bedroom beach house that is; all have full kitchens. There's a bar and restaurant on-site, and the views at night of neighboring St. Martin are enchanting. 7 rooms. Credit Cards: V, MC, A.

Fountain Beach   **$100–$365**   ★★★

Shoal Bay, ☎ *(800) 523-7505, (809) 497-3491.*
Single: $100–$280. Double: $285–$365.
Set on a scrumptious beach along the rural north coast, this secluded resort appeals to those who like privacy. Accommodations are in oversized studios and one- and two-bedroom suites with Caribbean antique artwork, colorful rattan and wicker furniture, large marble baths and full kitchens. The grounds include two tennis courts and a pool. Decent digs for the rates. 10 rooms. Credit Cards: V, MC, A.

Inter-Island Hotel   **$35–$135**   ★★

Lower South Hill, ☎ *(809) 497-6259.*
Single: $35–$40. Double: $55–$135.
This small villa-style guest house, located near Sandy Ground, is a quarter mile from the beach, but at these rates, who's complaining? Rooms are simple but very clean and comfortable with ceiling fans (no air conditioning) and tiny bathrooms; one- and two-bedroom suites are also available. Not much in the way of amenities, but

an excellent choice for those who really can't afford Anguilla to begin with. 14 rooms. Credit Cards: V, A.

Low Cost Lodging

You'll find best bargains on lodging anytime during low season (mid-April-December). During high season, the cheapest small hotel will bed two (no meals) for about $50, but you're risking seediness. In this very low-cost range, you'll find either cotlike beds and shared bathrooms in guest houses, or basic furnishings in no-atmosphere edifices. Don't even think about being near a beach, though Lloyd's (below) is but a downhill stroll to the sea.

Where to Eat

Highest Rated Restaurants in Anguilla

★★★★★ **Pimms**

★★★★ **Hibernia**

★★★★ **Malliouhana Hotel Restaurant**

★★★★ **Palm Court**

★★★ **Barrel's Stay**

★★★ **Ferryboat Inn**

★★★ **Koak Keel**

★★★ **Lucy's Harbour View**

★★★ **Mango's**

★★★ **Old House**

Most Exclusive Restaurants in Anguilla

★★★★	**Malliouhana Hotel Restaurant**	$30–$40
★★★	**Mango's**	$20–$35
★★★★	**Hibernia**	$20–$30
★★★★	**Palm Court**	$20–$26
★★★	**Roy's**	$14–$30

Fielding's Best Value Restaurants in Anguilla

★★★	**Koak Keel**	$8–$40
★★★	**Paradise Cafe**	$10–$27
★★★	**Lucy's Harbour View**	$15–$30
★★★★	**Palm Court**	$20–$26
★★★	**Ferryboat Inn**	$7–$26

When Anguilla was discovered in the mid-80s by the cream of Carib connoisseurs, the taste for lobster exploded. Fishermen now go further and further from shore to catch the island's prized marine treasure. It's usually readily available except during the brief hibernating and spawning season, which coincides with the slow tourist season of early summer. Most restaurants keep an ample supply of both crayfish and lobster in live pots offshore. At the **Palm Court Restaurant** at the Cinnamon Reef Resort, two different lobsters are true competitors: simply grilled in a delicate essence of cilantro and a unique lobster salad with plantains and baby artichokes in a peanut dressing. No matter where you're lodged, alternate your meals between tony French elegance found at the island's most expensive resorts, like Cap Jaluca, and budget creole cooked by talented locals at primitive-looking shacks. Local chefs do wonders also with red snapper, whelk and conch. For meateaters, a favorite is Island Mutton Stew with native vegetables. West Indian dishes are prepared superbly here, especially pumpkin soup. Don't miss the island's traditional brew—Perry's Soda Pop.

Barrel's Stay   **$$$**

Road Bay, ☎ (809) 497-2831.
French cuisine.
Lunch: 11:00 a.m.–3:00 p.m., entrees $8–$30.
Dinner: 6:30 p.m.–9:30 p.m., entrees $8–$30.
The name becomes obvious when you see this spot fashioned from old rum barrels and disassembled barrel stays. Tasty seafood and meat entrees dressed in creative sauces are served outside on a terrace. Some say the food is overpriced, but the French wines are reasonable. Credit Cards: V, MC, A.

Ferryboat Inn   **$$$**   ★ ★ ★

Cul de Sac Rd., ☎ (809) 497-6613.
Latin American cuisine.
Lunch: 12:00 a.m.–2:30 p.m., entrees $7–$26.
Dinner: 7:00 p.m.–10:00 p.m., entrees $7–$26.

Set on the beach near the Blowing Point Ferry Pier, this tres romantic spot specializes in French/Caribbean dishes. Wonderful soups like French onion and black bean; lobster thermidor is the house favorite. The Ferryboat is especially inviting at night, with the flickering lights of weaving an enchanting spell. Credit Cards: V, MC, A.

Hibernia   **$$$**

Island Harbour, ☎ (809) 497-4290.
Seafood cuisine.
Lunch: 12:00 a.m.–2:00 p.m., entrees $17–$30.
Dinner: 7:00 p.m.–9:00 p.m., entrees $20–$30.
There are just 10 tables at this lovely spot, set in a West Indian-style cottage with a wide porch, on the island's northeast corner. Specialties include grilled and smoked seafood, creatively enhanced with fresh local ingredients. They whip up their own breads and ice cream daily. Closed September and October. Closed: Mon. Credit Cards: V, MC, A.

Koak Keel **$$$** ★ ★ ★

The Valley, ☎ *(809) 497-2930.*
Latin American cuisine.
Lunch: 11:00 a.m.–2:00 p.m., entrees $6–$28.
Dinner: 7:00 p.m.–11:00 p.m., entrees $8–$40.

Situated in a beautifully restored plantation great house from the 18th century, with service as gracious as the surroundings. Fresh breads and roast meats are prepared in a large rock oven, and the lobster crepes are to die for. A neat spot to try "EuroCaribe" cuisine. Credit Cards: V, MC, A.

Lucy's Harbour View **$$$** ★ ★ ★

South Hill, ☎ *(809) 497-6253.*
Latin American cuisine.
Lunch: 11:30 a.m.–3:30 p.m., entrees $8–$16.
Dinner: 7:00 p.m.–10:00 p.m., entrees $15–$30.

Like the name implies, diners enjoy wonderful views from this casual cafe set high on a steep hill overlooking Sandy Ground. The menu focuses on fresh vegetables and lobster and fish dishes. Whole red snapper and pumpkin soup are house specialties. Closed: Sun. Credit Cards: V, MC, A.

Malliouhana Hotel Restaurant **$$$** ★ ★ ★ ★

Meads Bay, ☎ *(809) 497-6111.*
French cuisine.
Lunch: 12:30 p.m.–3:30 p.m., entrees $11–$30.
Dinner: 7:00 p.m.–10:30 p.m., entrees $30–$40.

Set in an open-air pavilion on a rocky promontory overlooking the sea, the feel here is wonderfully elegant, with gracious service, fine china and crystal and gourmet goodies. Famed French chef Michel Rostang created the menu and occasionally whips up the dishes himself. It'd be easy to make an entire meal of the imaginative hors d'oeuvres, but save room for the catch of the day. The wine cellar stocks some 25,000 bottles, most priced in the $25.00–$35.00 range. Credit Cards: V, MC, A.

Mango's **$$$** ★ ★ ★

Barnes Bay, ☎ *(809) 497-6491.*
American cuisine.
Dinner: 6:30 p.m.–9:00 p.m., entrees $20–$35.

Make reservations far in advance to get into this hot spot, which has two seatings for dinner, at 6:30 and 8:30. They use the freshest ingredients, grill-cook meat and fish, offer up some tasty vegetarian selections, make their own bread, desserts and ice cream daily—and best of all, do it all with an absolute minimum of calories. You'd never know by the taste that you're actually eating healthy food! Closed: Tue. Credit Cards: V, MC, A.

Old House **$$$** ★ ★ ★

George Hill, ☎ *(809) 497-2228.*
Latin American cuisine.
Lunch: 11:30 a.m.–2:30 p.m., entrees $7–$13.
Dinner: 6:30 p.m.–10:30 p.m., entrees $16–$20.

Yes, this eatery really is situated in an old house, set on a hill near the airport. West Indian specialties include conch and local lamb; the fruit pancakes keep the locals coming. Credit Cards: V, MC, DC, A.

Palm Court $$$ ★★★★

Cinnamon Reef Resort, ☎ *(809) 497-2727.*
Latin American cuisine.
Lunch: 12:00 a.m.–2:30 p.m., entrees $12–$18.
Dinner: 7:00 p.m.–9:30 p.m., entrees $20–$26.

Haitian furniture, colorful murals and huge picture windows overlooking the sea make this place special. The nouvelle Caribbean food is good too, with items like grouper encased in toasted pumpkin seeds or banana rum sauce. Lunch is more casual, with good salads, soups and sandwiches. Save room for the mango puffs in caramel sauce. Credit Cards: V, MC, A.

Paradise Cafe $$$ ★★★

Shoal Bay West, ☎ *(809) 497-6010.*
Indian cuisine.
Lunch: 12:00 a.m.–2:30 p.m., entrees $8–$14.
Dinner: 7:00 p.m.–9:30 p.m., entrees $10–$27.

Ocean breezes set many windchimes tinkling, a nice backdrop to tasty dishes with unique French and Asian influences. Try the West Indian bouillabaisse, individual pizzas or the catch of the day. Reservations are suggested; for better or worse, the rich and famous have discovered this spot. Closed in September. Credit Cards: V, MC, A.

Pimms $$$ ★★★★★

Cap Juluca Hotel, Maunday's Bay, ☎ *(809) 497-6666.*
French cuisine.
Dinner: 7:00 p.m.–10:00 p.m., entrees $20–$35.

One of the finest restaurants in all the Caribbean, located in the wonderful resort of Cap Juluca. Candlelit tables overlook the gorgeous beach, and the Continental-style cuisine, spiced with West Indian accents, is fabulous. Try the local lobster or grouper. Dress up for this spot, and don't even think about getting in without reservations. Credit Cards: V, MC, A.

Riviera Bar & Restaurant $$$ ★★

Road Bay, ☎ *(809) 497-2833.*
French cuisine.
Lunch: 11:00 a.m.–3:00 p.m., entrees $6–$16.
Dinner: 6:00 p.m.–9:30 p.m., entrees $20–$35.

This bistro on the beach compliments its French and Creole dishes with distinctive Asian accents—oysters sauteed in sake and soy sauce, for instance. There's occasional live music at this casual site, and the daily happy hour, 6:00–7:00 p.m., is happening. Credit Cards: D, V, MC, A.

Roy's $$$ ★★★

Crocus Bay, ☎ *(809) 497-2470.*
English cuisine.
Lunch: 12:00 a.m.–2:00 p.m., entrees $4–$16.
Dinner: 6:00 p.m.–9:00 p.m., entrees $14–$30.

Two British expatriots set up this little slice of their home land, and they got it right, all the way down to the English beers (thankfully served cold) and dart board. Dine al fresco on the veranda, with nice sea views, on fish and chips and Caribbean favorites like barbecued chicken and lobster Creole. Closed: Mon. Credit Cards: V, MC.

Where to Shop

There is little to speak of, in terms of shopping; most of the young female locals head for the trendy shops of St. Martin to dress themselves. Anything of value is to be found in the top-of-the-crop resorts and hotels. One of the most renowned local artists is **Courtney Deonish** (imported from Barbados), whose impressive carvings are sold at the airport.

For local crafts try **Elsie's in Stoney Ground** for embroidery and crochet, and the Anguilla Craft Shop, also in Stoney Ground, for straw artisanry, jams, jellies and local shellwork.

The latest craze on Anguilla are tiny wooden house plaques painted by **Lucia Butler**, sometimes known as the Caribbean's Grandma Moses. On layered pieces of wood she paints whimsical pastels and ornate gingerbread details of typical West Indian cottages. Houses of different sizes range from $18–$45 at the **Arts and Crafts Center** or at the artist's home studio (☎ *809-497-4259* for an appointment).

Anguilla Directory

ARRIVAL AND DEPARTURE

American Airlines offers direct service from the U.S. to San Juan, Puerto Rico, where you can change to American Eagle for the one-hour hop to Antigua. There are two American Eagle flights daily. You can also fly American or Continental to Dutch Sint Maarten's Juliana Airport, where connections to Anguilla can be found on WINAIR or LIAT. For about the same fee ($25 one way), Anguilla's own **Tyden Air** (☎ *800-842-0261* or *809-497-2719*) makes the 5-minute flight offering "Immediate Pickup" service that saves passengers baggage handling, all check-in procedures, and waiting. During high season (mid-December to mid-April), the Sint Maarten/Anguilla fare on Tyden is raised to $45, due to the chaos at Juliana, but the return trip remains $25. You can also take a taxi from Juliana Airport to Marigot on the French side (about $10) and catch one of the Anguilla power boats ($9) departing every 30–40 minutes for the 15-minute ride. If returning by boat with a lot of luggage, ask the French immigration officials in Marigot to call you a cab; the taxi stand is but a ten-minute walk away.

Upon leaving the island by air, all travelers are charged a $10 departure tax.

CLIMATE

Anguilla has one of the driest climates in the region—a bane to farmers, but a boon to tourists. As a result, vegetation is short and sparse, with few palm trees. With the lowest average annual rainfall in the Leeward Islands, Anguilla receives only 30-45 inches annually. Hurricane season is intense.

CURRENT

Most outlets are 110 AC, as in the U.S.

DOCUMENTS

Visitors must show ID with a photo, preferably a passport, and an on-going ticket. Departure tax is $6 at the airport and $2 at the ferry port.

GETTING AROUND

You'll need a car or open-air jeep called a mini-moke to visit more than one beach; hitchhiking is safe and accepted. Taxis are readily available at both Wallblake Airport and Blowing Point dock. You won't find any rental car agencies there; a taxi can deliver you there. Good local agencies are **Triple K** (representing Hertz), ☎ *809-497-2934*, **Maurice Connors** ☎ *809-497-6410*;, and **Roy Rogers Rental** ☎ *809-497-6290*, Fax *809-497-3345*. Note well that driving is on the left and you must obtain a local driver's license from your rental agency. If you're game to cycle, try **Boo's Cycle Rental**.

The island bus service begins from a roadside stop a few steps from the pier at Blowing Point.

LANGUAGE

The official language is English spoken with a West Indian lilt.

MEDICAL EMERGENCIES

For serious problems, head for a hospital in Puerto Rico. The small hospital at Crocus Bay is usually overflowing with natives.

MONEY

Official currency is the Eastern Caribbean dollar (EC), usually marked by "$" sign in stores and restaurants. Before you shell out any dough, however, make sure the price is not referring to American dollars. Traveler's checks, personal checks (sometimes, with picture ID), and American dollars are also readily accepted.

TELEPHONE

From North America to Anguilla, dial *809* (area code) + *497* (country code) + local number (4 digits). Faxes are widely used by hotels and other businesses. To save money when calling home from Anguilla, go to the Cable & Wireless office and buy a phone card. Before leaving home, check with your own telephone service to see how you can most cheaply call home using your own special card.

TIME

Anguilla is on Atlantic standard time, one hour ahead of Eastern standard time in winter (that means 1 p.m. in New York, 2 p.m. in Anguilla). During the summer, it's the same time.

TIPPING AND TAXES

Service charges (10–15 percent) and an 8 percent government tax are usually included in hotel bills; 10 percent on all food and beverage tabs. Some establishments charge a fee for credit cards. Waiters and waitresses appreciate tips, but don't expect any. If a young boy carries your bag at the airport, one dollar per bag will put a smile on his face. More often, your taxi driver will tote them.

TOURIST INFORMATION

Contact the Anguilla Tourist Office ☎ *800-553-4939*. Before you go, you can get an updated list of rates for accommodations and a map. Better maps are available in local stores.

WHEN TO GO

The Miller Genuine Draft Moonsplash Tour in January is a well-attended music festival. Anguilla Day is celebrated by a huge boat race on May 30. The Queen's Birthday is feted by celebrations in the month of June. The Anguilla National Summer Festival takes place on August 4–12. The Christmas Fair at the Governor's Residence takes place in December. On holidays and during Carnival, the whole island turns out to bet on spectacular boat races. Carnival itself, in the month of August, is celebrated with early morning dancing, beachside barbecues and special pageants.

ANGUILLA HOTELS	RMS	RATES	PHONE	FAX
Road Bay				
★★★★★ Cap Juluca	91	$275–$2085	(800) 323-0139	(809) 497-6617
★★★★★ Malliouhana Beach Hotel	53	$240–$810	(800) 835-0796	(809) 497-6011
★★★★ Cinnamon Reef Beach Club	22	$155–$330	(800) 223-1108	(809) 497-3727
★★★★ La Sirena	24	$100–$280	(800) 331-9358	(809) 497-6827
★★★ Carimar Beach Club	23	$130–$630	(800) 235-8667	(809) 497-6071
★★★ Casablanca Resort	88	$350–$1100	(800) 231-1945	(809) 497-6899
★★★ Coccoloba	51	$225–$425	(800) 982-7729	(809) 497-6332
★★★ Cove Castles Villa Resort	12	$350–$990	(800) 348-4716	(809) 497-6051

ANGUILLA HOTELS	RMS	RATES	PHONE	FAX
★★★ Fountain Beach	10	$100–$365	(800) 523-7505	(809) 497-3493
★★★ Frangipani Beach Club	21	$195–$1200	(800) 892-4564	(809) 497-6440
★★★ Pineapple Beach Club	27	$270–$660	(800) 345-0356	(809) 497-6019
★★ Arawak Beach Resort	14	$100–$300	(800) 553-4939	(809) 497-4898
★★ Easy Corner Villas	15	$90–$295	(800) 223-9815	(809) 497-6410
★★ Mariners, The	25	$115–$535	(800) 848-7938	(809) 497-2901
★★ Rendezvous Bay Hotel	47	$90–$240	(800) 274-4893	(809) 497-6026
★★ Shoal Bay Villas	13	$147–$385	(800) 722-7045	(809) 497-3631
★ Ferryboat Inn	7	$70–$225	(809) 497-6613	(809) 497-6713
★ Inter-Island Hotel	14	$35–$135	(809) 497-6259	(809) 497-5381
★ Sea Grape Beach Club Villas	10	$180–$450	(800) 223-9815	(809) 497-6410

ANGUILLA RESTAURANTS	LOCATION	PHONE	ENTREE
Road Bay			
American			
★★★ Mango's	Road Bay	(809) 497-6491	$20–$35••
English			
★★★ Roy's	Road Bay	(809) 497-2470	$4–$30
French			
★★★★★ Pimms	Maunday's Bay	(809) 497-6666	$20–$35••
★★★★ Malliouhana Hotel Restaurant	Road Bay	(809) 497-6111	$11–$40
★★★ Barrel's Stay	Road Bay	(809) 497-2831	$8–$30
★★ Riviera Bar & Restaurant	Road Bay	(809) 497-2833	$6–$35
Indian			
★★★ Paradise Cafe	Road Bay	(809) 497-6010	$8–$27
Latin American			
★★★★ Palm Court	Road Bay	(809) 497-2727	$12–$26
★★★ Ferryboat Inn	Road Bay	(809) 497-6613	$7–$26
★★★ Koak Keel	Road Bay	(809) 497-2930	$6–$40
★★★ Lucy's Harbour View	Road Bay	(809) 497-6253	$8–$30
★★★ Old House	Road Bay	(809) 497-2228	$7–$20

ANGUILLA RESTAURANTS	LOCATION	PHONE	ENTREE

Seafood

★★★★ Hibernia	Road Bay	(809) 497-4290	$17–$30

Note: • Lunch Only

•• Dinner Only

ANTIGUA

Antigua is a snorkeler's paradise with plenty of barrier reefs, wrecks and caves.

Antigua starts with an A—a letter that could be easily used to spell either attitude or adventure. Formerly a British Colony, Antigua comes wrapped with a British frostiness that finds its way into the cool, distant smiles of waiters, hotel clerks, and even shopkeepers. But, with nary a day of rain, and miles and miles of glorious beaches (365, claim the tourist office), the island still boasts enough attributes of paradise to keep American, Canadian, British and German millionaires heading for the super-deluxe resorts on its southern and western shores. Today, the island also attracts a broader base of tourists, and can accommodate all budgets, from the backpacker to the honeymooner, the latter always looking to save money at no sacrifice of romance. Color and music explode in August when Carnival comes to the streets of Antigua, filling the air with calypso competitions, steel bands and fanciful costumes. Since flying is the easiest way to reach the Caribbean—some airlines fly direct—Antigua is the best place to start a Caribbean vacation; from here, you can always charter a sailboat and fan out to neighboring islands. In fact, during the last weeks of April (or beginning of May), when international yachting fans congregate for Antigua's annual Sailing Week—the premier nautical event in the Caribbean—some hearty travelers actually chuck their flight ticket home and hitch a ride on one of the many colorful sailboats bobbing in the harbor.

Bird's Eye View

Sprawling over about 108 square miles, Antigua is the largest, most developed, and most visited of the Leeward Islands. Together with Barbuda and Redonda, an uninhabited rocky inlet, it forms the independent nation of Antigua and Barbuda, within the Commonwealth of Nations. To the south lies the French island of Guadeloupe; to the southwest lies the British dependency of Montserrat, and to the west, the island of Nevis. The capital is St. John's, with a population of about 36,000. The island of Antigua itself is divided into six parishes. Travelling through the island, you will be able to discern clearly the variety of regions as you pass from the hilly ranges in the southwest to the almost desertlike cacti in the northeast to the enormous bush and woodland in the interior. **Boggy Peak**, its highest elevation, rises to 1330 feet. There are 365 talcum-soft white beaches fringed with palm trees, among the most beautiful in the West Indies.

History

The Siboney Stone people were the first to graze the terrain of Antigua with settlements dating back to 2400 BC. Arawaks lived on the islands between AD35 and 1100. Columbus discovered the island on his second voyage in 1493, naming it Santa Maria de la Antigua. The absence of freshwater springs persuaded French and Spanish colonists to sail on, and by 1632, the

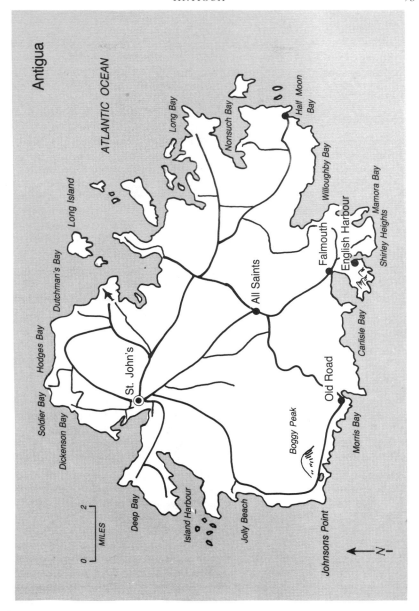

English had successfully established coloniz;tion. Apart from a brief French invasion in 1666, the three islands of Antigua, Barbuda and Redonda have all remained British. The first large sugar estates were established in Antigua by Sir Christopher Codrington in 1674, who convinced the natives on Barbuda to raise provisions for the plantations (a village in Barbuda bears his name). As production increased forests were cleared for cultivation and African slaves were imported by the boatloads. (Today many Antiguans trace the lack of rainfall to this early forest devastation.) A vicious cycle of drought led eventually to barren lands, testimony of which can be seen in the ruined towers of sugarcane throughout the island. Abolition arrived in 1834, but the former slaves found they could barely subsist due to a lack of surplus farming and an economy that was based on agriculture and not manufacturing. Poor labor conditions and growing violence led to the organization of unions in 1939. A strong political Labor Party emerged seven years later, catapulting Antiguans into the twentieth century. During World War II, Antigua was selected as a military base and American servicemen arrived in droves. Until 1959, Antigua was administered as part of the Leeward Islands, until attaining associated status with full self-internal government in 1967.

Since 1990 scandal and accusations of corruption have rocked the Antiguan government, including misuse of public funds and a series of arson attacks and murders investigated by Scotland Yard. In 1990 the governments of Antigua and Barbuda became embroiled in a scandal where they were accused of being involved in the sale of weapons to the Medellin cartel of drug traffickers in Colombia.

Today Antigua maintains strong links with the U.S., having actively assisted in the U.S. military intervention in Grenada in 1983. Since 1982, both Antigua and Barbuda have intensified their program of foreign relations and have agreed that the People's Republic of China could open an embassy. In 1990 it opened relations with the USSR and in April 1983 with the Ukraine. Today both islands are constitutional monarchies, with executive power invested in the British sovereign and exercised by the Governor-General, who is appointed on the advice of the Antiguan Prime Minister.

Since the sugarcane industry fell off completely in 1972, tourism has monopolized the economy. In recent years, touristic activities have undergone a tremendous expansion, bringing the number of tourists who visit yearly to nearly half a million (half of which are cruise passengers).

People

As of a 1992 census, 64,000 people live in Antigua, most of them of African descent, although there is a small minority of English, Portuguese, Lebanese, and Syrian. On first glimpse, the natives of Antigua may seem formal and distant, but once you crack the facade of formality, a warm, generous character surfaces. Because Antigua has an excellent harbor and easy access to the outside world, its people are quite used to traveling and are well aware of current events. The relative stability of the democracy has been reflected in the nature of the people, who are considered among the leaders in the Caribbean family. About one-third of all Antiguans live in or around the capital of St. John's, on the northwest coast. The remainder are spread evenly throughout the island, in over 40 small towns and villages. Most own some kind of property, even if it is just a small shack in the countryside. Today the population stands at about 80,000, some 85 percent who are of African descent.

To delve more deeply into the Antiguan character, read Jamaica Kinkaid's devastating profile of the island and its people called *A Small Place* (1988).

Beaches

You could spend several lifetimes exploring the 365 beaches in Antigua. Beyond West Bay's Seven Mile Beach, the nearest beach to St. John's is Fort James, not conducive to swimming because of its milky film and rough waters. Nevertheless, on weekends, it gets very crowded. Further out is Dickenson Bay, with numerous hotels along the strand section off the beach. On the peninsula west of St. John's, past the Ramada Royal Antiguan Hotel, are several picturesque beaches. **Galley Bay**, past Five Islands, is secluded and pristine, especially popular with joggers at sunset. A spectacular beach is **Galleon**, near English Harbour, though you'll need a car or taxi to get there. One of the most beautiful in the Caribbean is **Shoal Beach**, famous for its uninterrupted stretch of silvery powder. The four **Hawksbill** beaches at the end of the peninsula are attractive crescent shapes (one is a nudist beach). **Dark Wood Beach**, on the road from St. John's to Old Round around the southwest coast, is quite pleasant, with a bar and overpriced restaurant.

Dive Sites

Magnificent shoals and coral reefs dot the shoreline of Antigua, in crystal-clear waters perfect for snorkelers. Nearly always sea life can be found in very shallow water, at sites no more than 60 feet in depth. Small, neon-like fish such as blue tang parrotfishes, and wrasse are profuse, as are staghorn and elkhorn corals. The occasional turtle, stingray, and eagle ray are sighted, along with the even rarer dolphin. An underwater park has been recently marked to include part of **Cades Reef**, a two and a half mile reef about one mile from **Cades Bay** on the leeward coast. Visibility ranges from 80 to 150 feet. Here, staghorn coral abound, and you can always tell the nature of a site by its descriptive name—Big Sponge, Snapper Ledge, and Eel Run. The most advanced divers head for **Sunken Rock**, which drops to a depth of 122 feet. Along the drop-off swim stingrays, barracudas, and the occasional dolphin. Overhanging corals form a cleft through which divers may swim, making one feel as if a cave has been entered. Beyond the coral formation, in shallower waters, marine life such as blue and brown chrimis, sergeant majors, and parrotfish can be seen. Antigua and Barbuda have just recently become known for their wreck sites. Six wrecks lie close to Antigua's shores—the most popular is the *Andes*, a three-masted, fully rigged merchant vessel that went down in 1905. It's found today south of **St. John's Harbor** by Deep Bay in only 20 feet of water. Treasure is known to still be intact, and a diver, Mel Fisher, retains a fifteen-year contract with the island's government for salvaging. If you plan to snorkel in Barbuda, bring your own dive equipment, since there is no dive shop, but snorkeling equipment can be rented. (For more information, see the chapter on Barbuda.) Diving is most easily done from a chartered boat hired in Antigua that comes equipped with scuba gear and a decompressor.

Treks

Antigua is a crisscross maze of tracks, footpaths and dirt roads. The Historical and Archaeological Society organizes group hikes once a month (inquire at the Antigua Museum in St. John's or through the Tourist Board.) An exciting day trip can be taken to **Long Island**, home of the famous **Jumby Bay** resort), north of Parlam Harbour. Flat and dry, the island is densely wooded and ponds attract an enormous number of exotic birds, from egrets to white-cheeked pintails, to laughing gulls. Nature trails and bike paths wander through the forests, beside the mangroves, and down the beaches. A visit to **Pasture Bay**, on the north side of the island, may render a rare glimpse of the hawksbill turtle that nests on the beach from May to December. (The hawksbill shell is used to make tortoiseshell, but such products are confiscated by the U.S. government upon arrival in the States.) The northeastern corner of **Long Island** has an archaeological site that boasts floor flints over 7000 years old—dating back to the time when Antigua and its surrounding islands were merely one great landmass during the last ice age. The island can be visited on day trips by booking for lunch at Jumby Bay; the resort's ferry will pick you up from the Beachcomber jetty, north of the international airport.

Great Bird Island is another paradise for birdwatchers. This tiny uninhabited islet with its own beach and limestone cliffs provides nesting grounds for the red-billed tropicbird. Make the short climb from the beach to the top of the cliffs to see the graceful birds have a great time gliding on the wind currents blowing in from the Atlantic. From April to September, you can also sight laughing gulls, and sometimes purple martins, as well as terns and brown noodies. It's easy to find a boat operator in Antigua who offers daily trips to Bird Island by yacht and catamaran; a picnic lunch is usually included, along with snorkeling equipment. Be on the lookout in the surrounding reefs for lobsters and eagle rays.

The remnants of a volcano are found at **Green Castle Hill**, southwest of St. John's and just east of Jennings. The rock formations here, which rise to 595 feet, are thought by some to be megaliths of a prehistoric civilization. A spectacular three-way view of the island awaits anyone with the skill to climb the not-so-easy hill (about a one hour trek).The trail starts at the brick factory.

Many short hikes can be taken through the secondary forest located at **Wallings Woodland**, on the north slopes of Signal Hill. Treks that last no longer than an hour can be made between **Old Road and Falmouth**, with pleasant stops for picnics, swimming and snorkeling. Hikers will need to get a topographical map from the tourist board, and dress appropriately for thorny bushes and spiny plants (long pants are best). A trail that ends up at the gorgeous **Rendezvous Bay** beach starts at Old Road, bearing southeast to the top of the cliff along **Fishers Hill**, continuing east over **Mt. Carmel** to **Farley Bay**, another exquisite beach, then continuing east for about a half-hour over **Tucks Point** to **Rendezvous**. Snorkeling is excellent right in front of the beach.

Bats Cave, a cavern found on the north side of English harbour, is exactly as it sounds—hundreds of bats hang upside down from the ceiling. Local legend says that the cave actually goes under the sea as far as Guadeloupe. (Permission must be obtained from the Medical School to visit.) To arrive at the cave, take a footpath east of the Medical School.

A nature walk has been designated on developed footpaths that wind around the hills from English harbour to Shirley Heights. The trail begins at the **Galleon Beach Hotel** gate (look for the sign that says "To the Lookout" and is designated by white tape on tree branches. You'll pass through swampy areas (dress appropriately) and continue through amazing landscapes strewn with extraterrestrial-type boulders. It finally meanders through forest on the way to the signal station at the peak. Before you go, obtain a brochure from the **Carib Marina** (outside the Nelson's Dockyard) or from the National Parks Authority, which describes the flora on the trail.

What Else to See

Although St. John's, the capital of Antigua, looks a bit tatty these days, there are areas being developed for tourism and worthy of a stroll, particularly **Redcliffe Quay**, a picturesque district full of historical buildings and now duty-free stores, souvenir shops and new restaurants. Cruise ship passengers tend to crowd into **Heritage Quay**, off the harbor, where there is also a casino and a big-screen TV satellite.

If you're looking for a cool interior to escape from the sun, dip into the city's **Anglican Cathedral**, rebuilt several times due to earthquakes. No matter where you stand in St. John's, you can see the twin towers. The present building was rebuilt in 1843.

Fascinating weekly lectures are given at the **Museum of Marine and Living Art**, where you can view exhibits of sea shells, shipwrecks and even pre-Columbian history. A tour of the English Harbour is a must if you have any sort of naval fetish. The area has been designated as a national park. The best view of the harbor is from **Limey's Bar**. Take the footpath that leads round the bay to **Fort Berkeley** for a great view that you'll share with grazing goats. Nearby, the future King William IV spent his nights at **Clarence House** when he served in the Navy during the 1780s. Overlooking the English Harbour, at Shirley Heights, are the ruins of 18th-century fortifications. It's best to go on Sundays when the steel bands play at the bar on the lookout point called the Battery. Prepare yourself for very loud music.

Best View:

Even Antiguans still flock to the top of the Shirley Heights installations to view the fabulous sunsets. You can see the English and Falmouth Harbours in the foreground and the hills and coast of Antigua in the distance. On a clear day you can see as far as Redonda, Montserrat and Guadeloupe.

City Celebrations

Carnival

Various locations, ☎ *(809) 462- 194.*
What began some 20 years ago as a celebration to welcome Queen Elizabeth II has become a full-fledged annual festival with 11 days of art shows, parades and partying. The main event is "Juve," when some 400 locals dance behind steel and brass bands. Held in late July and early August, you can pick up a full program once on the island.

Sailing Week   ★★★★

English Harbour.
The Caribbean's premiere yachting event is now in its 27th year. Some 200 boats from 25 countries pour into English Harbour for five races, and there's lots going on for landlubbers as well—food vendors, beach dancing and above all, lots of partying (and lots of cops to keep things from getting out of hand). For $30 you can dress up and attend Lord Nelson's Ball at the Admiral's Inn, but those in the know say it's a bit too stuffy compared to the unabashed goings-on elsewhere. Held the last week of April.

Historical Sites

Nelson's Dockyard National Park   ★★★★★

Nelson's Dockyard, English Harbour, ☎ *(809) 460-1005.*
Hours Open: 8:00 a.m.–6:00 p.m.
This pretty spot is the only Georgian-style naval dockyard left in the world. It has a rich history as home base for the British fleet during the Napoleonic Wars and was used by Admirals Nelson and Hood. The area includes colonial naval buildings, nice beaches, ancient archeological sites and lots of nature trails. Short dockyard tours, nature walks of varying length and boat cruises are offered daily. Check out the

Admiral's House, a lovely inn and museum of colonial history, then have a drink at their popular bar. Children under 16 admitted to the park for free. General admission: $2.60.

St. John's Cathedral

Newgate Street and Church Lane, St. John's, ☎ *(809) 461- 82.*
This Anglican cathedral has a sorrowful history. Originally built of wood in 1683, it was replaced by a stone building in 1745, then destroyed by an earthquake in 1843. Replaced in 1847, it was once again heavily damaged by earthquake in 1973. Restoration continues as funds are available. The figures of St. John the Baptist and St. John the Divine were taken from a French ship in the early 19th century, and the iron railing entrance dates back to 1789. Free admission.

Museums and Exhibits

Dow's Hill Interpretation Center

Near Shirley Heights, English Harbour.
Hours Open: 9:00 a.m.–5:00 p.m.
The multimedia presentations of the island's six periods of history, from Amerindians to slavery to independence, are unique to the Caribbean. Bring your camera, as the views from the observation platforms are spectacular. $2 for kids under 16. General admission: $4.00.

Museum of Antigua and Barbuda   ★★

Church and Market Street, St. John's, ☎ *(809) 462-1469.*
Hours Open: 8:00 a.m.–4:00 p.m.
Mainly intended for the island's children but worth a look if you're in the neighborhood, this small museum spotlights Antigua's geological and political past. Some interesting exhibits include a life-size Arawak house, a wattle and daub house, models of sugar plantations and Arawak and pre-Columbian artifacts. There's also a decent giftless selling local arts and crafts, books and historic artwork. Donation Requested.

Tours

Jolly Roger

Redcliff Quay, English Harbour, ☎ *(809) 462-2064.*
This is the largest sailing ship in local waters—108 feet long—and a great way to spend the day. A "pirate" crew will have you walking the plank, dancing the limbo, eating, drinking, and in general making merry as you sail the seas. Lunch, cocktail and dinner cruises. Prices vary.

Sports

The **Antigua Sailing Week** is a major Caribbean event, held at the end of April-beginning of May.

All you have to do is head for the English Harbour to meet some of the hundreds of yachties who cruise in from all over the world. Most hotels now arrange day-sailing excursions. Numerous dive facilities are located along **Dickenson Bay**, and certification courses are available. The watersports concession located there can also reserve a deep-sea fishing expedition. Windsurfing is generally best accomplished on the eastern shores; regattas are regularly planned so ask about. Most of the big hotels have tennis courts, and many visitors return for the Antigua Tennis Week in late April or May. Rates for balls and rackets are exorbitant. Golfers will find an18-hole course at the **Great Valley Course**, near St. John's. Horseback riding can be arranged through your hotel, as there are several stables and resorts with their own horses and equipment. The southeast countryside is rife with trails and a great half-day trek can be made to **Monks Hill**. Also attractive is the ride around **Half Moon Bay** that circles around Mannings and overlooks Soldier Point on the Atlantic.

Golf

Two locations, English Harbour.
Hours Open: 8:00 a.m.–6:00 p.m.
The island has only two golf courses, so it won't be hard to make your choice. At **Half Moon Bay Hotel** (☎ *460-4300*) there are nine holes (2410 yards, par 34), with more challenging conditions at **Cedar Valley Golf Club** (☎ *462-0161*). Their 18-hole, par-70 course has some lovely views of the north coast. Green fees are $30 and cart rental is an additional $30.

Watersports

Long Bay Hotel, Long Bay, ☎ *(809) 463-2005.*
If it involves getting wet, they have it here at the Long Bay Hotel, where nonguests can rent equipment for scuba (experienced only), snorkeling, sailing, etc. They also offer snorkel trips (four minimum) to a few small islands, though conditions are great just off the beach, thanks to Long Bay's double reef. Also check out **Shorty's** (☎ *462-6066*) where they have all kinds of watersports and glass-bottom excursions; and **Halycon Cove Watersports** (☎ *462-0256*), where you can water ski. Both are at Dickenson Bay.

Windsurf Shop

Lord Nelson Beach Hotel, Dutchman's Bay, ☎ *(809) 462-3094.*
Here's your chance to try this ever-popular sport; they guarantee you'll be whisking around on your own after $50 and a two-hour lesson. (And in case you mess up, they have radio-assisted rescues.)

Where to Stay

Highest Rated Hotels in Antigua

★★★★★ **Curtain Bluff**

★★★★★ **Jumby Bay**

★★★★ **Copper and Lumber Store**

★★★ **Admiral's Inn**

★★★ **Blue Waters Beach Hotel**

★★★ **Club Antigua**

★★★ **Galley Bay**

★★★ **Half Moon Bay Club**

★★★ **Hawksbill Beach Hotel**

★★★ **Hodges Bay Club Resort**

Most Exclusive Hotels in Antigua

★★★★★ **Jumby Bay**	$650–$980
★★★ **St. James Club**	$250–$655
★★★ **Galley Bay**	$210–$520
★★★ **Trade Winds Hotel**	$194–$250
★★★ **Siboney Beach Club**	$135–$275

Fielding's Best Value Hotels in Antigua

★★★ **Hawksbill Beach Hotel**	$130–$375
★★★ **Trade Winds Hotel**	$194–$250
★★★ **Club Antigua**	$170–$325
★★★ **Blue Waters Beach Hotel**	$125–$290
★★★ **Hodges Bay Club Resort**	$99–$147

Antigua offers an enormous array of resorts, hotels and self-catering accommodations, including those on close-by Barbuda (see "Barbuda"). Construction is a constant reality, but conservation groups are taking the issue in hand to preserve the coastline. Most properties focus around St. John's, along the coast to the west, and to the north in clockwise direction to the airport. There are also options near English Harbour and Falmouth Harbour in the southeast. Some hotels do close in September and October to spruce up for winter. If you arrive on the island without a reservation, the tourist office will help you book a room. Most hotels don't have air-conditioning, though the combination of ceiling fans and swift breezes keep things cool.

Hotels and Resorts

Hotel rooms run from the gloriously luxurious ($500 and up at Jumby Bay) to so-called inexpensive hostelry rooms (about $75 at Admiral's Inn), which are pleasantly simple. Jumby Bay, now open year-round, was voted the Caribbean's number-two best all-inclusive resort by the *Caribbean Travel and Life* readership—a private island resort two miles off Antigua's northeastern coast. It's now open year-round. The upscale Half-Moon Bay Club on the southeast coast has gone all-inclusive, and the Long Bay Hotel has been refurbished. Hawksbill Beach Resort, a long-time favorite for its four superb beaches, has added new beachfront cottages. Sandals Antigua was voted number-three for all-inclusive resorts in the *Caribbean Travel and Life* reader's poll.

Antigua Sugar Mill Inn $55–$105   ★

Coolidge, English Harbour, ☎ *(809) 462-3044.*
Single: $55–$95. Double: $65–$105.
Because it is the closest hotel to the airport, this spot does a big business with overnight guests on their way to hither and yon. Rooms are simple but do have air conditioning, and there's a pool, restaurant, bar and historic stone sugar mill with an observation tower on-site. The beach is nearly a mile away, which helps explain the very reasonable prices. 24 rooms. Credit Cards: V, MC, DC, A.

Barrymore Hotel $53–$75   ★

Old Fort Road, English Harbour, ☎ *(809) 462-1055.*
Single: $53–$61. Double: $68–$75.
Lots of business travelers stay at this low-frills hotel, which consists of very basic rooms with motel-like furnishings; only some have air conditioning. The grounds are quite nice, though, and there's a pool and restaurant on-site. The beach is a mile away. 36 rooms. Credit Cards: V, MC, DC, A.

Blue Heron Beach Hotel $63–$140   ★

Johnson's Point Beach, English Harbour, ☎ *(809) 462-8564.*
Single: $63–$120. Double: $63–$140.
This very basic and somewhat rundown beach hotel appeals mainly to Europeans on a budget. The best units are right on the beach and have balconies; all are simply furnished with wood and formica. Watersports are free, and there's a nice beach bar. Nothing quaint or especially charming here, but the rates keep 'em coming. 40 rooms. Credit Cards: V, MC, A.

Blue Waters Beach Hotel   **$125–$290**   ★ ★ ★

Soldier Bay, English Harbour, ☎ *(800) 372-1323, (809) 462- 292.*
Single: $125–$255. Double: $145–$290.

Lots of repeat visitors, mainly Europeans, flock to this classic island property. The setting is its greatest asset—14 acres of meticulously manicured gardens and a small palm-fringed beach that, while pretty, is not great for swimming. Accommodations are set along the beach and have air conditioning, pastel-colored rattan furniture, and a small patio or balcony. Villas offer two or three bedrooms with kitchens, living and dining rooms, and Jacuzzis. Afternoon tea is an especially nice ritual, but the overall service sometimes lags. 67 rooms. Credit Cards: V, MC, A.

Club Antigua   **$170–$325**   ★ ★ ★

Jolly Beach, English Harbour, ☎ *(800) 777-1250, (809) 462- 68.*
Single: $170–$225. Double: $225–$325.

This all-inclusive resort, set on 38 acres with a half-mile beach, hums with action and attracts mainly young people who don't mind the busy beach—lined with vendors hawking everything from jewelry to joints—and noisy nightlife. Lots to do here, including four restaurants, five bars, a slot casino, happening disco, all watersports, eight tennis courts and, for the kids (and their parents), a supervised children's club. The cheapest rooms, called minimums, are just so and quite small; the other classes are larger and worth the extra bucks. 472 rooms. Credit Cards: V, MC, A.

Curtain Bluff   **$330–$600**   ★ ★ ★ ★ ★

Morris Bay, English Harbour, ☎ *(809) 462-8400.*
Single: $330–$500. Double: $430–$600.

Antigua's most famous resort has earned its reputation for lavish accommodations and excellent service. Extras like fresh flowers daily, bidets and plush robes accent the spotless rooms and suites. The best bets are the bluffside split-level apartments, which offer up great views from two balconies. The all-inclusive rates include all watersports—even scuba—drinks, tennis, fitness center and putting green. The only thing missing is a pool. This is one of the Caribbean's prettiest settings, but the atmosphere can be a bit too refined for laid-back types. 62 rooms. Credit Cards: A.

Galley Bay   **$210–$520**   ★ ★ ★

Five Islands, English Harbour, ☎ *(809) 462- 302.*
Single: $210–$440. Double: $330–$520.

This all-inclusive resort is set on 40 lovely acres adjacent to a bird sanctuary. Accommodations are on the beach in Polynesian thatched huts and modern cottages; all lack air conditioning but do have coffee makers, robes and hair dryers. The best rooms are built around a salt pond and coconut grove; request these "Ganguin Village" units. The beach is great and the hotel offers most watersports as well as one tennis court, a restaurant, bar and the very popular afternoon tea. This spot is popular with Europeans who aren't looking for much of a nightlife. 30 rooms. Credit Cards: V, MC, A.

Halcyon Cove Beach Resort   **$110–$475**   ★ ★

Halcyon Cove, Dickenson Bay, ☎ *(800) 255-5859, (809) 462- 256.*
Single: $110–$210. Double: $110–$475.

Lots of group tours from the U.S. and Europe congregate at this busy spot, made even more crowded by the many cruise passengers who spend the day at its excellent beach. The expansive complex includes several restaurants, four bars and a nightclub, a casino, and extensive watersports including scuba, water skiing and glass-bottom boat rides. Rooms are just adequate with standard furnishings and air conditioning; only the beachside units have TVs, and many rooms lack views. Not great, but the rates are reasonable. 135 rooms. Credit Cards: V, MC, A.

Half Moon Bay Club $245–$325 ★★★

Half Moon Bay, English Harbour, ☎ *(809) 460-4300.*
Single: $245–$285. Double: $285–$325.
A decent all-inclusive beach resort, located next to the Mills Reef Club on a nice beach. Suites are luxurious if a bit worn, and there's no air conditioning. In addition to the usual watersports there is an excellent windsurfing school, nine holes of golf and five tennis courts. 100 rooms. Credit Cards: V, MC, DC, A.

Hawksbill Beach Hotel $130–$375 ★★★

Five Islands, English Harbour, ☎ *(809) 462-1515.*
Single: $130–$310. Double: $165–$375.
This lively spot is frequented by Europeans and young babyboomer couples. The atmosphere is nicely informal, and restaurant prices are quite reasonable. Accommodations are in West Indian-style cottages near the beach with nice lawns; all have tropical decor, pleasant furnishings and modern baths. There's also a Colonial-style Great House with three bedrooms and a kitchenette. The 37 acres include an old sugar mill that has been transformed into a boutique, tennis, watersports and four beaches, one where you can shuck your bathing suit. 88 rooms. Credit Cards: V, MC, DC, A.

Jumby Bay $650–$980 ★★★★★

Jumby Bay Island, English Harbour, ☎ *(800) 421-9016, (809) 462-6000.*
Single: $650–$980. Double: $650–$980.
Situated on its own 300-acre private island, this glorious Mediterranean-style all-inclusive resort attracts mature, affluent travelers who like everything just so. The original former home, some 230 years old, is now the main Great House with a lounge, library, games room and restaurant. Accommodations are in circular bungalows and cottages, all spacious with separate sitting areas and expensive furnishings, though no phone, air conditioning or TV. Most guests get around the expansive grounds on bikes, and yachters pull in for dinner. Heavenly! 50 rooms. Credit Cards: V, MC, A.

Long Bay Hotel $155–$370 ★★

Long Bay, English Harbour, ☎ *(809) 463-2005.*
Single: $155–$290. Double: $255–$370.
This intimate resort, run by the Lafaurie family, is set far out on Antigua's northeast coast. Guest rooms, situated in motel-style wings, are large but simple; the cottage units, with gabled ceilings, nice artwork and small but fully equipped kitchens, are nicer. For recreation, there's one tennis court, free watersports (scuba costs extra), a library and games room. This is an authentic Caribbean retreat—not some corpo-

ration's idea of one. Lots of American families are attracted by the warm and friendly service. 26 rooms. Credit Cards: V, MC, A.

Pineapple Beach $305–$425 ★★★

Long Bay, English Harbour, ☎ *(800) 345- 271, (809) 463-2006.*
Single: $305–$425. Double: $305–$425.

This all-inclusive resort flanks a beautiful beach, but bring your written confirmation notice, as they have a distressing tendency to overbook. A good spot for those who want all-inclusive amenities without sacrificing an arm or leg. Accommodations front the ocean and are of average size with wicker furniture, local artwork, large balconies and Mexican tile floors. This place teems with action, with folks running from tennis to volleyball to croquet to the casino, which has only one-armed bandits. 130 rooms. Credit Cards: V, MC, A.

Royal Antiguan $115–$165 ★★★

Deep Bay, English Harbour, ☎ *(800) 228-9898, (809) 462-3733.*
Single: $115. Double: $165.

Owned by Ramada, this ugly high-rise is the island's most American-like resort and has yet to meet its full potential. It does a bang-up business, though, by offering modern conveniences like direct-dial phones, TV and air conditioning. Set on 150 acres, there's a lot to keep visitors occupied, including a full casino, enormous pool with swim-up bar, lots of tennis and watersports and a supervised children's program. It's a few minutes' walk to the beach, which is frequented by local artists displaying their wares. 282 rooms. Credit Cards: V, MC, DC, A.

Runaway Beach $65–$280 ★★

Runaway Bay, English Harbour, ☎ *(809) 462-1318.*
Single: $65–$85. Double: $65–$280.

This small resort puts up its guests in cottages perched on a mile-long, reef-protected beach. The lower units sacrifice views for air conditioning and kitchenettes; the upper units have sleeping lofts and ceiling fans instead. The beach gets crowded when cruise ships are in port. Service can be slow and indifferent, but rates are reasonable. 33 rooms. Credit Cards: V, MC, DC, A.

Sandals Antigua ★★

Dickenson Bay, ☎ *(800) 726-3257, (809) 462- 267.*
Rack rate Per Week: $3190–$4375.

Only heterosexual couples are allowed at this all-inclusive resort, set on a small, lively beach lined with palms and local vendors. Most accommodations are in motel-like units that are small but adequate; the 17 rooms in rondovals are better. There's tons going on here, and the staff will cheerfully badger you to participate—this is not the spot for discreet liaisons. Most of the couples are young, and many are honeymooning. One week's minimum stay costs $3190–$4375 per couple. 207 rooms. Credit Cards: V, MC, A.

St. James Club $250–$655 ★★★

Marmora Bay, English Harbour, ☎ *(800) 274- 8, (809) 460-5000.*
Single: $250–$600. Double: $305–$655.

Set on 40 lush acres, this very nice resort does not necessarily live up to its reputation as a playground for the rich and famous, and chances are slight you'll actually see tennis pro Martina Navratilova. Nevertheless, this is a great spot, with two pretty beaches, an attractive European-style casino, tony boutiques and a lively disco. Rooms are beautifully furnished, and the two-bedroom villas are wonderful. Guests can choose from watersports, horseback riding, working out in the gym, playing tennis or frolicking in three pools. Nice! 178 rooms. Credit Cards: V, MC, DC, A.

Apartments and Condominiums

Self-catering units are available throughout the island, but many complain that staples in St. John's are expensive and not worth the trouble to discover and buy. (Truth is, eating out in Antigua can be just as expensive, or more). If you're still interested, options range from simply furnished studio apartments to glorious homes rented by the owner. Booking is generally through the unit itself. Do be wary of booking units from abroad before you actually see what you have rented: Surprises can include thin walls which give no privacy and strangely built rooms with little beach view. One general booker for several different complexes is **La Cure Villas** *(11661 San Vincente Blvd., Los Angeles, CA 90049.)*

Antigua Village $100–$475   ★ ★
Dickenson Bay, ☎ (809) 462-2931.
Single: $100–$475. Double: $100–$475.
This rambling complex of red-roof condominiums is located on a peninsula along a busy beach. Choose from spacious studios or one- and two-bedroom units, all with kitchenettes, bright tropical decor, air conditioning and daily maid service; only a few have TVs. Watersports are free, and there's a restaurant, bar and minimarket on-site. A reliable spot, but nothing too exciting. 100 rooms. Credit Cards: V, MC.

Barrymore Beach Club $75–$240   ★ ★
Runaway Bay, English Harbour, ☎ (800) 542-2779, (809) 462-4101.
Single: $75–$105. Double: $120–$240.
This recently renovated beachfront complex consists of hotel rooms and one- and two-bedroom apartments with kitchenettes but no air conditioning. There's also a three-bedroom villa for rent with its own pool. There's a restaurant and bar on-site, but not much else to get excited about. 36 rooms. Credit Cards: V, MC, A.

Galleon Beach Club $130–$365   ★
Freeman's Bay, English Harbour, ☎ (809) 460-1024.
Single: $130–$365. Double: $130–$365.
This is a time-share complex of cottages scattered about the beach or a steep hillside. Accommodations are in one-bedroom suites or two-bedroom cottages; all have rattan furnishings, living and dining areas and kitchenettes, but lack air conditioning, TVs and phones. There's a good Italian restaurant on the premises. Maintenance and housekeeping can be sloppy. 36 rooms. Credit Cards: V, MC, A.

Hodges Bay Club Resort $99–$147   ★ ★ ★
Hodges Bay, English Harbour, ☎ (809) 462-2300.
Single: $99–$115. Double: $124–$147.
Located in an exclusive residential neighborhood, this recently renovated complex has picturesque beachfront villas with one or two bedrooms, air conditioning, full kitchens and nice views off the balconies. The beach is excellent for snorkeling, and

day trips are offered to Prickley Pear Island, one mile offshore. There's a bar and restaurant on-site, as well as a pool, two tennis courts and free watersports. 26 rooms. Credit Cards: V, MC, A.

Marina Bay Beach Hotel $80–$255 ★ ★

Corbinsons Point, Dickenson Bay, ☎ *(800) 273-6510, (809) 462-3254.*
Single: $80–$125. Double: $130–$255.

A pleasantly basic spot, with spacious and bright studios and one- and two-bedroom villas. All have air conditioning, cable TV, full kitchens and Italian-tiled baths. Located on a public beach with watersports available. There's no restaurant on-site, but several within an easy walk. 27 rooms. Credit Cards: V, DC, A.

Siboney Beach Club $135–$275 ★ ★ ★

Dickenson Bay, ☎ *(800) 533- 234, (809) 462- 806.*
Single: $135–$275. Double: $135–$275.

This three-story apartment building, enhanced by lots of greenery, is near a good but busy beach. The one-bedroom suites are nicely furnished with rattan, kitchenettes and ceiling fans; there's also a maid to tidy things up and limited room service. There's entertainment most nights at the bar, and extensive watersports including excursions via catamaran or glass-bottom boat. The service is very friendly at this well-run spot. 12 rooms. Credit Cards: V, MC, DC, A.

Trade Winds Hotel $194–$250 ★ ★ ★

Dickenson Bay, ☎ *(809) 462-1223.*
Single: $194–$250. Double: $194–$250.

This all-suite hotel is located above Dickenson Bay with great ocean views. The beach is nearly a mile away, but the management will take you to and fro. There's a small pool on-site, as well as a restaurant and piano bar. Accommodations, in Spanish-style villas, are decent. Lots of Europeans like this spot. 41 rooms. Credit Cards: V, MC, DC, A.

Yepton Beach Resort $115–$500 ★ ★

Deep Bay, English Harbour, ☎ *(800) 361-4621, (800) 462-2520.*
Single: $115–$500. Double: $115–$500.

This condominium resort consists of Mediterranean-style white stucco buildings with nice views of the beach and lagoon. All units have air conditioning and kitchenettes and include studios with Murphy beds or one- and two-bedroom apartments. All line the excellent beach. There's a restaurant and bar with live music three nights a week, with lots of other eating choices within walking distance. All-inclusive plans are offered on request. 38 rooms. Credit Cards: V, MC, A.

Inns

Most inns on Antigua are expensive, but they provide a charming ambiance and down-home hospitality. The most authentically historical is **Admiral's Inn**, set in an 18th century building, overlooking the harbor; here you might find billionaire yachties sipping drinks with grungy sailors in the breezy patio bar. Windsurfers who don't mind the basic furnishings like to congregate at the **Lord Nelson Club**. The **Inn at English Harbour**, near Galleon Beach, tends to best capture the seaside hominess most travelers seek in an inn.

Admiral's Inn $79–$149   ★★★

Villa Olga, English Harbour, *(809) 460-1027.*
Single: $79–$149. Double: $79–$149.

Housed in a Georgian brick building dating back to 1788, this intimate inn has a
nautical theme and is loaded with charm. Rooms are small but very nice with beam
ceilings and antiques; some have air conditioning and patios. This spot is a tourist
attraction in its own right, so can get crowded with folks coming through to take a
look. Management transports guests to two nearby beaches. A great spot if you
don't mind sacrificing resort amenities for a quaint, distinctive atmosphere. Credit
Cards: V, MC, A.

Copper and Lumber Store $85–$325   ★★★★

English Harbour, *(809) 460-1058.*
Single: $85–$195. Double: $175–$325.

This very charming and also very modern inn is housed in a restored Georgian warehouse, dating back to 1780, which overlooks the marina at English Harbour. Studios and duplex suites have authentic or reproduction 18th-century furnishings,
canopy beds, brass chandeliers and hand-stenciled floors. The charm extends to the
bathrooms, which boast mahogany-paneled showers. No air conditioning, but ceiling fans provide a breeze. There's no beach or pool but guests are whisked via ferry
to nearby Galleon Beach. A wonderful spot, but also a busy tourist attraction. 38
rooms. Credit Cards: V, MC, A.

Inn at English Harbour $135–$445   ★★

English Harbour, *(809) 460-1014.*
Single: $135–$295. Double: $185–$445.

Set on ten acres of beach and hillside overlooking colorful Nelson's Dockyard, this
small inn has rooms in cottage-style buildings on the beach or atop a hill. All are
nicely done with island-style rush rugs, wicker and modern furniture and ceiling
fans. There are two restaurants and bars, and free watersports. The clientele is
mostly English. 28 rooms. Credit Cards: CB, V, MC, DC, A.

Lord Nelson Beach Hotel $60–$100   ★★

Dutchman's Bay, English Harbour, *(809) 462-3094.*
Single: $60–$77. Double: $70–$100.

This family-run inn, small and informal, could use a renovation to bring it fully into
the 1990s. Rooms are simple but at least have balconies, and there's a restaurant
and bar on-site. Basic watersports are offered, and this spot is loved by windsurfers.
Located on a rather isolated spot on the northeast coast, there's virtually nothing
within walking distance, so you'll need a rental car. 16 rooms. Credit Cards: V, MC, A.

Low Cost Lodging

Finding a budget room on Antigua is not impossible. A good source is *A Guide to
Small Hotels and Guest Homes*, provided by the Tourist Office (ask them for one). Of
course, no money pays for no ambiance; most low-cost lodgings are in modern, stucco
buildings with only basic furnishings. A location beachside will be rare. As such, you'll
probably have to throw the extra bucks into renting a car.

Where to Eat

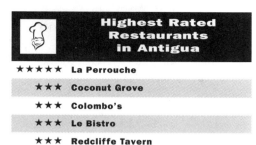

Highest Rated Restaurants in Antigua

★★★★★ La Perrouche
★★★ Coconut Grove
★★★ Colombo's
★★★ Le Bistro
★★★ Redcliffe Tavern

Most Exclusive Restaurants in Antigua

★★★★★ La Perrouche	$18–$35
★★★ Chez Pascal	$22–$29
★★ The Wardroom and Pub	$18–$30
★★★ Coconut Grove	$15–$30
★★ Lobster Pot	$15–$25

Fielding's Best Value Restaurants in Antigua

★★★ Colombo's	$22–$32
★★★ Le Cap Horn	$13–$20
★★★ Warri Pier	$7–$40
★★ Brother B's	$6–$15
★★★ Redcliffe Tavern	$10–$20

Antigua has rarely suffered for the lack of good restaurants, but new additions are always cropping up. Prices for a top-class dinner aren't cheap; expect to fork over at least $95 for two in the most expensive places. Spices, influenced by East Indian and creole cooking, are liberally added and tend to run on the hot side. Look for specialties like banana and cinnamon pancakes with Antiguan rum syrup, sea urchin flan, and lump crabmeat with avocado and lemon grass.

For steel bands and a barbecue on Sundays, reserve first and then head to **Shirley Heights Lookout**, housed in a restored 18th century fort with a memorable view of Nelson's Dockyard and English Harbour.

Admiral's Inn   **$$$**

Nelson's Dockyard, English Harbour, ☎ *(809) 460-1027.*
American cuisine. Specialties: Pumpkin soup, red snapper.
Lunch: 12:00 a.m.–2:30 p.m., entrees $10–$25.
Dinner: 7:00 p.m.–9:30 p.m., entrees $10–$25.

Like the Copper and Lumber Store Hotel alongside it, the Admiral's Inn is so long on atmosphere and history, the food doesn't have to be good to be worth a visit. But thankfully, that is not the case here, especially for a silky pumpkin soup. Some never get as far as the restaurant, preferring to stay in the dark bar or sit under the old trees outdoors, looking out at the convoys of ships in the harbor. Those so inclined can eat here three times a day, and breakfast, served daily from 7:30 to 10:00 a.m., is a terrific deal. Closed September through mid-October. Associated Hotel: Admiral's Inn. Reservations recommended. Credit Cards: V, MC, A.

Big Banana Holding Co.   **$$$**

Redcliffe Quay, St. John's, ☎ *(809) 462-2621.*
Italian cuisine. Specialties: Pizza, conch salad.
Lunch: 12:00 a.m.–4:00 p.m., entrees $6–$30.
Dinner: 4:00 p.m.–12:00 p.m., entrees $6–$30.

A lot of locals and tourists homesick for pizza flock here at all hours. The pies in question are rather pricey and not very exciting, but the location, in the interesting and trendy Redcliffe Quay shopping center, helps. All in all it's considered very proper to sit under the whirring fans and just sip a cool tropical drink (these are bright, frothy and potent). Salads, seafood dishes and fruit plates are also available. Closed: Sun. Credit Cards: V, MC, DC, A.

Brother B's   **$$**   ★★

Long Street, St. John's,
Indian cuisine. Specialties: Pepperpot soup and fungi, pelleau, bull's foot soup.
Lunch: entrees $6–$15.
Dinner: entrees $6–$15.

A not-to-be missed touch of local color, Brother B's in Soul Alley (near the Museum) is the place to be to experience a taste of real Antiguan culture, hear the live buzz of other diners amiably feasting on local West Indian eats and freshly squeezed juices, and to tap to the beat of a hired band at noon. Credit Cards: Not Accepted.

Calypso   **$$$**

Redcliffe Street, St. John's, ☎ *(809) 462-1965.*
International cuisine. Specialties: Pumpkin soup, baked chicken with cornmeal.
Lunch: 10:00 a.m.–4:00 p.m., entrees $8–$25.

This open-air, lunch-only spot jumps weekdays, and is an accessible, friendly location to try West Indian specialties. These often include fresh seafood, sauteed or prepared in batter. Homey stews and soups with pumpkin or okra satisfy; the less adventurous can chow down on burgers and sandwiches. Closed: Sun. Credit Cards: Not Accepted. Credit Cards: V, MC, DC, A.

Chez Pascal $$$ ★★★

4 Tanner Street, St. John's, ☎ *(809) 462-3232.*
French cuisine. Specialties: Bisque de langouste, croustade de fruits de mer.
Dinner: 6:30 p.m.–10:00 p.m., entrees $22–$29.
Lyon-born Pascal Milliat, previously the chef de cuisine at La Sammana, the swank five-star resort on St. Martin, owns and toils in the kitchen of this, his own chez with the ever-pleasant assistance of his spouse, Florence, who seats patrons. Dishes are classic French with a twist of "Antiguaise" sprinkled hither and yon. Vichyssoise is a popular starter. Closed: Sun. Reservations recommended. Credit Cards: V, MC, DC, A.

Coconut Grove $$$ ★★★

Dickenson Bay, St. John's, ☎ *(809) 462-1538.*
International cuisine. Specialties: Grilled local lobster, chilled gazpacho.
Lunch: 11:30 a.m.–3:00 p.m., entrees $15–$30.
Dinner: 6:30 p.m.–10:00 p.m., entrees $15–$30.
A simple beachfront spot surrounded by tall coconut palms swaying in the breeze, this eatery is a choice spot for privacy, moonlight and a nicely grilled lobster caught fresh that day. Chicken, hearty chops, tangy soups and salads are also on offer. Associated Hotel: Siboney Beach Club. Reservations required. Credit Cards: V, MC, DC, A.

Colombo's $$$ ★★★

Galleon Beach, English Harbour, ☎ *(809) 463-1452.*
Italian cuisine. Specialties: Veal Scaloppine, carpaccio.
Lunch: 12:30 p.m.–2:30 p.m., entrees $22–$32.
Dinner: 7:00 p.m.–10:00 p.m., entrees $22–$32.
Only in the Caribbean can one eat spaghetti Bolognese or carpaccio in a fancy, thatched-roof hut and dance to a reggae band on the beach. But everything here is scrupulously good and the service is amiable. There are daily specials and a variety of wines. Associated Hotel: Galleon Beach Club. Reservations required. Credit Cards: V, MC, DC, A.

G & T Pizza $$ ★★

East Falmouth Harbor, Falmouth Harbour,
Italian cuisine. Specialties: Pizza, salads.
Lunch: 12:00 a.m.–4:30 p.m., entrees $7–$19.
Dinner: 4:30 p.m.–10:30 p.m., entrees $7–$19.
Blend in with the seafaring crowd at this popular restaurant on the waterfront at the Antigua Yacht Club in Falmouth Harbour that serves tasty pizzas and salads for under $20. Seating is on informal picnic tables framed by palm trees, and day or night, entertainment is provided by sailboats and motorcraft on the oceanfront. G&T stays open until midnight for drinks, and there's a happy hour from 5-6 p.m. Closed: Tue. Reservations recommended. Credit Cards: V, MC, A.

Hemingway's $$ ★★

St. Mary's Street, St. John's, ☎ *(809) 462-2763.*
International cuisine. Specialties: Lobster soup, tropical chicken with fruit salsa.
Lunch: 11:30 a.m.–4:30 p.m., entrees $7–$15.

Dinner: 4:30 p.m.–10:00 p.m., entrees $7–$15.

Not very far from the sea in the traditional West Indian town of St. John's is this tropical Victorian house with a restaurant on the second floor. There's a lot of activity and people-watching opportunities on the porch, where frothy tropical drinks can be sipped. Nibble on lobster, salads, burgers and spicy chicken. Vegetarian specialties are also available. Closed: Mon. Credit Cards: Not Accepted.

La Perrouche $$$ ★★★★★

Falmouth Harbour, ☎ *(809) 460-3040.*
International cuisine. Specialties: Whitefish with polenta, lobster with Bordelaise sauce.
Dinner: 6:00 p.m.–10:00 p.m., entrees $18–$35.

This charmer is an ideal splurge restaurant, one of a handful on the island that boasts native French or French-trained chefs. The artist in question at this bloom-bedecked outdoor establishment is David Wallach, who served a stint at L'Esperance. Together with partner Mona Frisell, he creates a culinary palette of tropical colors and tastes each evening. Wallach imports a special whitefish chosen for its delicacy, and local lobster is used as a sauce ingredient. Desserts involve a small orchard of exotic fruits, including sweet "black" pineapple. Well-chosen wine list. Closed: Sun. Reservations required. Credit Cards: V, MC, A.

Le Bistro $$$ ★★★

Hodges Bay, St. John's, ☎ *(809) 462-3881.*
French cuisine. Specialties: Red snapper baked in foil, seafood in puff pastry.
Dinner: 6:30 p.m.–10:30 p.m., entrees $22–$26.

Le Bistro, on the island's north shore, caters to residents with expensive villas in the area, but anyone with a fancy for fine cuisine can repair here for classic French dishes prepared with care. Lobster and red snapper are usually available, and made with cream, white wine and fresh herb sauces. The dining room is attractive and plant-filled. Closed: Mon. Reservations required. Credit Cards: V, MC, A.

Le Cap Horn $$$ ★★★

Falmouth Harbour, ☎ *(809) 460-3336.*
French cuisine. Specialties: Seafood, pizzas, steak.
Lunch: 12:00 a.m.–6:30 p.m., entrees $10–$13.
Dinner: 6:30 p.m.–11:00 p.m., entrees $13–$20.

A highly recommended Italian and French restaurant in a verdant outdoor setting en route to Nelson's Dockyard. Snacks, wood-fired pizza or more substantial meat dishes are available for decent prices. Dine early or late on the porch on daily specials for under $20. Reservations recommended. Credit Cards: V, MC, A.

Lemon Tree $$$ ★★

Long and Church Streets, St. John's, ☎ *(809) 462-1969.*
International cuisine. Specialties: Cajun garlic shrimp, burritos.
Lunch: 10:00 a.m.–4:00 p.m., entrees $15–$25.
Dinner: 4:00 p.m.–11:00 p.m., entrees $15–$25.

The atmosphere here is very South Seas, with a lot of wicker and wooden blinds, good for a cool-off drink or meal after a visit to the Museum of Antigua and Barbuda nearby. Graze Caribbean-style from a long menu of finger foods, Tex-Mex items and the usual lobster and chicken dishes, which vary in quality. Unfortunately, with a cruise crowd in attendance, service can be rushed. Good for music in the evening. Credit Cards: V, MC, DC, A.

Lobster Pot $$$ ★★

Runaway Bay, St. John's, ☎ *(809) 462-2856.*
Seafood cuisine. Specialties: Chicken in coconut milk and curry, fresh fish.
Lunch: entrees $7–$12.
Dinner: entrees $15–$25.
Even picky diners will find something to their liking at this airy eatery in Runaway Bay that does creative things with chicken and lobster at prices that won't leave you breathless. The substantial menu runs the gamut from hearty breakfasts to leafy salads, sandwiches and fresh local fish and shellfish. Commune with nature at tables on the seaside veranda; come early for these or reserve a seat. Associated Hotel: Runaway Beach Club. Reservations recommended. Credit Cards: V, MC, DC.

Redcliffe Tavern $$ ★★★

Redcliffe Quay Street, St. John's, ☎ *(809) 461-4557.*
Italian cuisine. Specialties: Barbecued chicken, pasta, fresh local seafood.
Lunch: 8:00 a.m.–3:00 p.m., entrees $7–$20.
Dinner: 3:00 p.m.–7:30 p.m., entrees $10–$20.
Begin or end a shopping tour at the charming Redcliffe Quay complex in St. John's harbor with lunch or dinner or a snack at the Redcliffe Tavern. It's one of a handful of vintage structures that have been restored for commercial usage. Once an old warehouse, the Tavern sports antique hardware for decor, and the Wheatstone serves good burgers or barbecue or pastas and freshly caught lobster. Architecture buffs and Anglophiles should find the surroundings especially appealing. Closed: Sun. Credit Cards: V, MC, A.

Shirley Heights Lookout $$$ ★★

Shirley Heights, English Harbour, ☎ *(809) 463-1785.*
Seafood cuisine. Specialties: Pumpkin soup, lobster with lime sauce.
Lunch: 9:00 a.m.–4:00 p.m., entrees $15–$26.
Dinner: 4:00 p.m.–10:00 p.m., entrees $15–$26.
Something festive is always happening in this two-story pub-restaurant amidst the ruins of Fort Shirley—especially on Sunday, when there's dancing and live bands that play for free from mid-afternoon on. Barbecued meats at decent prices accompany the tunes, and the views behind the Lookout are superb. The rest of the week, eat in peace upstairs or downstairs for breakfast, lunch or dinner. The second-floor dining room is a very intimate trysting spot. Credit Cards: V, MC, AE.

The Wardroom and Pub $$$ ★★

Nelson's Dockyard, English Harbour, ☎ *(809) 460-1058.*
International cuisine. Specialties: West African groundnut soup, shepherd's pie.
Lunch: 11:30 a.m.–4:30 p.m., entrees $8–$25.
Dinner: 6:00 p.m.–11:00 p.m., entrees $18–$30.
Old Antigua hands will be pleased with the new face given the 18th-century Copper and Lumber Store Hotel in Nelson's Dockyard. Others should come at least once to savor the atmosphere and eat remarkably fine food at remarkably high prices, especially at dinner in the Wardroom on the ground floor. But American-style or English lunches and cool drinks are within most everyone's reach at the hotel's pub.

Associated Hotel: Copper and Lumber Store. Closed: Wed. Reservations recommended. Credit Cards: V, MC, A.

Warri Pier   **$$$**   ★ ★ ★

Dickenson Bay, St. John's, ☎ *(809) 462-0256.*
International cuisine. Specialties: Seafood linguine, marlin.
Lunch: 12:00 a.m.–6:00 p.m., entrees $7–$35.
Dinner: 6:00 p.m.–10:00 p.m., entrees $7–$40.

Dine on marlin— *warri* is the local name—on a private pier belonging to the Halcyon Cove Beach Resort. This is a lovely setting poised high above the sand like a great wooden bird on the northern edge of Dickinson Bay, about a mile and a half from the airport. Undoubtedly, it's an excellent perch from which to observe the setting sun. Light meals of chunky fruit salads or burgers and seafood soups are substantial at lunch. Dinner gets somewhat fancier with grilled lobster and the like and luscious desserts. Associated Hotel: Halcyon Cove Beach Resort. Reservations recommended. Credit Cards: V, MC, A.

Where to Shop

Redcliffe Quay and **Heritage Quay** now compete for tourist shoppers (though if you want to avoid the cruise crowd, park yourself at Redcliffe).The best shops are clustered on **St. Mary's Street** or **High Street** in St. John's. Duty-free items are omnipresent, and there are also some special Antiguan crafts such as rum, silk-screened fabrics, native straw work, and curios made from shells. Hot new clothing stores have also sprung up or expanded in the last year. Check easy-to-wear cotton and cotton/lycra styles for men, women and children at BAE stores in Redcliffe Quay. Also in Redcliffe Quay is the chic Debra Moises boutique, which carries husband-and-wife-designed sensations in flowing gauze and one-of-a-kind hair accessories (carried by Bergdorf's and Saks in Manhattan). For some strange reason, some shops in Antigua close on Thursday at noon.

Do check out the Saturday fruit and vegetable market at the West Bus Station. You can also find a good selection of local handicrafts.

Antigua Directory

ARRIVAL AND DEPARTURE

BWIA has daily flights from Miami and New York. American Airlines also flies from Baltimore, Washington, D.C., Miami, Puerto Rico, and

New Orleans. Air Canada flies from Toronto. Continental Airlines now operates six times a week from Newark, New Jersey (every day but Tuesday, with one stop in St. Maarten).

The V.C. Bird airport, just 4-1/2 miles from St. John's, receives all air traffic. LIAT and American Airlines operate frequent air service to neighboring islands, such as Anguilla, Barbados, Barbuda, Dominica, Martinique, Grenada, Jamaica, Montserrat, Nevis, Guadeloupe, Trinidad, St. Croix, St. Kitts, St. Lucia, St. Maarten, St. Thomas, St. Vincent, Puerto Rico, and Tortola. Carib Aviation also arranges charters (for 5-9 passengers), which often works out much cheaper than a regular airline. They are located at the **V.C. Bird Airport**; ☎ *462-3147*; after office hours ☎ *461-1650*. Consider a day trip to Montserrat, which is only an 18-minute flight away.

The departure tax is U.S.$12.

CLIMATE

The Antiguan climate is probably the best in the Caribbean, with so little rainfall that water shortage sometimes becomes a problem. Any rainfall is usually restricted to brief heavy showers. Constant sea breezes and trade winds keep the air fresh and the temperatures hovering around 81 degrees F, except in the hot season (May-November), when temperatures can rise to 93 degrees F. The mean annual rainfall of 40 inches is slight for the region.

DOCUMENTS

U.S. and Canadian citizens must show proof of citizenship (passport, birth certificate, or voter's registration) plus a photo ID, and an ongoing or return ticket.

ELECTRICITY

The majority of hotels use 110 volts, 60 cycles, same as the U.S. Some shaver outlets are 110-volt. Hotels generally have adapters.

GETTING AROUND

The best guides in Antigua are generally taxi drivers. Or stop by the taxi rank on St. Mary's Street. Buses don't go to the airport, or to very few beaches. Look for one outside Dew's or Bryson's supermarket. Do barter for a price beforehand since there are no meters. And make sure you are both talking about the same dollars (Antiguan or American).

Buses tend to leave only when there seems to be enough riders.

Hitchhiking during the day seems fashionable and safe.

Car rental agencies are numerous. Some hotels have their own rental car services. Others found at the airport include **Titi Car Rental** ☎ *809-460-1452*; and **Jonas Rent-A-Car** ☎ *809-462-3760*. If you plan to drive, do be careful since Antiguan roads are notorious for potholes, crumbling shoulders, and bad signs. Antiguan drivers are about as courteous as French ones, so drive defensively.

If you want to rent a car, you must purchase a license (about US $12), valid for three months by showing your own valid license to the agency.

Motorcycles and mountain bikes are probably the easiest way to see the island. Try **Ivor's** at English Harbour or **Sun Cycles** in Hodges (for bikes only).

LANGUAGE

English is the official language, though the special Antiguan lilt may make some words indistinguishable.

MEDICAL EMERGENCIES

Holberton Hospital, on the outskirts of St. John's, is a 220-bed hospital. Serious medical emergencies are usually flown off the island to Miami. Do ask if you hotel has a doctor on call.

MONEY

The official currency is the Eastern Caribbean dollar (known as Bee Wee or EC). You get the best exchange rates at banks. Most establishments will accept American and Canadian dollars. Credit cards and traveler's checks are accepted at top hotels and many shops and eateries.

TELEPHONE

From the U.S., dial 809.

TIME

Atlantic standard time.

TIPPING AND TAXES

Most hotels and restaurants add a 10 percent service charge. When not included, tip 10–15 percent for waiters, $1 per room per day for maids, and 50 cents per bag for bellhops. Tip taxi drivers 10 percent.

TOURIST INFORMATION

The official tourist office is located on Long Street in St. John's. You can also find information centers at the airport, at the ship terminal in St. John's and at Heritage Quay. For more information call ☎ *462-0480; FAX 462-2483.* In the U.S. call ☎ *(212) 541-4117.*

WHEN TO GO

Men's Tennis Week, a professional and amateur tournament is held in January.

Women's Tennis Week, a professional and amateur tournament, is held in early April. Race Week, a week of boat races between sailors from all over the Caribbean, is held in late April. The Queen's Birthday is celebrated in June. Carnival is held during the week before the first Monday of August. Independence Day is November 1. Independence Week Half Marathon is held in early November. Christmas and Boxing Day is December 2 and 26.

ANTIGUA HOTELS	RMS	RATES	PHONE	FAX
St. John's				
★★★★★ Curtain Bluff	62	$330–$600	(809) 462-8400	
★★★★★ Jumby Bay	50	$650–$980	(800) 421-9016	
★★★★ Copper and Lumber Store	38	$85–$325	(809) 460-1058	(809) 460-1529
★★★ Admiral's Inn		$79–$149	(809) 460-1027	(809) 774-8010
★★★ Blue Waters Beach Hotel	67	$125–$290	(800) 372-1323	
★★★ Club Antigua	472	$170–$325	(800) 777-1250	
★★★ Galley Bay	30	$210–$520	(809) 462-0302	
★★★ Half Moon Bay Club	100	$245–$325	(809) 460-4300	
★★★ Hawksbill Beach Hotel	88	$130–$375	(809) 462-1515	
★★★ Hodges Bay Club Resort	26	$99–$147	(809) 462-2300	
★★★ Pineapple Beach	130	$305–$425	(800) 345-0271	
★★★ Royal Antiguan	282	$115–$165	(800) 228-9898	
★★★ Siboney Beach Club	12	$135–$275	(800) 533-0234	
★★★ St. James Club	178	$250–$655	(800) 274-0008	
★★★ Trade Winds Hotel	41	$194–$250	(809) 462-1223	
★★ Antigua Village	100	$100–$475	(809) 462-2931	
★★ Barrymore Beach Club	36	$75–$240	(800) 542-2779	
★★ Halcyon Cove Beach Resort	135	$110–$475	(800) 255-5859	
★★ Inn at English Harbour	28	$135–$445	(809) 460-1014	
★★ Long Bay Hotel	26	$155–$370	(809) 463-2005	
★★ Lord Nelson's Beach Hotel	16	$60–$100	(809) 462-3094	
★★ Marina Bay Beach Hotel	27	$80–$255	(800) 273-6510	
★★ Runaway Beach	33	$65–$280	(809) 462-1318	
★★ Sandals Antigua	207		(800) 726-3257	
★★ Yepton Beach Resort	38	$115–$500	(800) 361-4621	
★ Antigua Sugar Mill Inn	24	$55–$105	(809) 462-3044	
★ Barrymore Hotel	36	$53–$75	(809) 462-1055	
★ Blue Heron Beach Hotel	40	$63–$140	(809) 462-8564	
★ Galleon Beach Club	36	$130–$365	(809) 460-1024	

ANTIGUA RESTAURANTS	LOCATION	PHONE	ENTREE
St. John's			
American			
★★ Admiral's Inn	English Harbour	(809) 460-1027	$10–$25
French			
★★★ Chez Pascal	St. John's	(809) 462-3232	$22–$29••
★★★ Le Bistro	St. John's	(809) 462-3881	$22–$26••
★★★ Le Cap Horn	Falmouth Harbour	(809) 460-3336	$10–$20
Indian			
★★ Brother B's	St. John's		$6–$15
International			
★★★★★ La Perrouche	Falmouth Harbour	(809) 460-3040	$18–$35••
★★★ Coconut Grove	St. John's	(809) 462-1538	$15–$30
★★★ Warri Pier	St. John's	(809) 462-0256	$7–$40
★★ Calypso	St. John's	(809) 462-1965	$8–$25•
★★ Hemingway's	St. John's	(809) 462-2763	$7–$15
★★ Lemon Tree	St. John's	(809) 462-1969	$15–$25
★★ The Wardroom and Pub	English Harbour	(809) 460-1058	$8–$30
Italian			
★★★ Colombo's	English Harbour	(809) 463-1452	$22–$32
★★★ Redcliffe Tavern	St. John's	(809) 461-4557	$7–$20
★★ Big Banana Holding Co.	St. John's	(809) 462-2621	$6–$30
★★ G & T Pizza	Falmouth Harbour		$7–$19
Seafood			
★★ Lobster Pot	St. John's	(809) 462-2856	$7–$25
★★ Shirley Heights Lookout	English Harbour	(809) 463-1785	$15–$26

Note: • Lunch Only

       •• Dinner Only

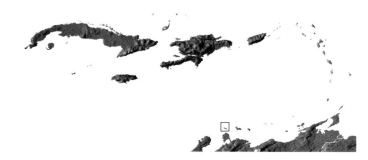

ARUBA

Wind-bent divi-divi (watpana) trees are a common sight on Aruba.

With the highest percent of repeat visitors in the Caribbean, there is something definitely addictive about Aruba. Something habit-forming *had* to inspire *Bon Appetit* readers to elect the smallest, but most developed of the ABC Islands, their all-time favorite destination in the Caribbean. Sure, there are nice beaches, dry sunny weather, and cool breezes, but how do you explain honeymooners who return *18 years in a row* to the same hotel? Only fifty years ago, Lago Oil workers, Dutch seamen and Norwegian whalers prowled the streets and busted up barrooms; today those besotted sailors have been replaced by half a million sunburned tourists a year, who seem to thrive on the big resorts, the ten casinos, the hundred restaurants, and what seems to be the zillion duty-free shops. Simply, Aruba has raised the island packaged vacation to a strange, but wonderful art. If you stay at a big all-inclusive resort in Aruba, you can sleep, surf, sun, soak, wine, dine and shop without ever leaving the property.

Aruba is not exactly a pretty island, unless you've got a yen for tough scrubby land with lots of cacti. What it does have are temperate blue waters that give way to nearly every watersport imaginable—from parasailing and game fishing to jet skis, snorkeling and scuba. Because of the constant trade winds, windsurfing has become the number one sport, particularly during the end of May and the beginning of June, when the never-say-die converge for the annual Aruba Hi-Winds Pro-Am Windsurfing Competition. Even during the year, the die-hard surfers are a sight to behold, as they make their daily pilgrimage to the beach, en masse across LG. Smith Boulevard, their sails held high over tight gleaming muscles.

Bird's Eye View

The smallest of the ABC islands, Aruba lies 16 miles off the northeast coast of Venezuela, about a four-hour plane ride from New York. Sprawling over 74.5 square miles, the twenty-mile-long island looks like a slab of ham pointing northwest to southeast toward South America. Like Bonaire and Curaçao, its sister islands, Aruba has scant vegetation, yet its outback, called *cunucu*, is a soul-stirring landscape. As the paved road gives way to gravel and finally to coral dust, a stark and arid terrain appears, punctuated by upended boulders, mauve dunes, crashing waves and an array of scrubby Aruban vegetation, from cacti *(kadushi)* tomnesquite *(kwihi)* and the wind-bent divi-divi trees *(dwatapana)*.Tiny bright red flowers called fioritas provide one of the few splashes of color. On the northwesternmost tip, at Kudarebe, the sand dunes make for excellent warm-weather sledding.

Dutch-gabled and pastel-pretty, Oranjestad, the capital, called Playa, is a dazzling yellow brick town. Shops line the main shopping street of Nassaustraat and Wilhelminastraat. About 7500 hotels rooms stretch along the five-mile strand of pure white sand on Palm Beach and in the smaller Eagle Beach and Druif Bay (both south of Palm, near Oranjestad). During the year, over 540,000 tourists add to the native population of a mere 71,000.

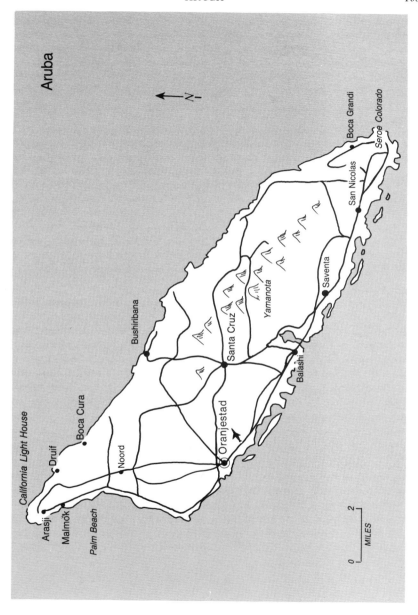

History

When Spanish explorers arrived in the 15th century, the Caiquetios, a tribe of Arawaks, may have already been living on Aruba for over 4500 years, having migrated there from their ancestral homes in Venezuela. The Spanish exiled most of them in 1513, though more immigration occurred around 1640, when the Dutch permitted the Indian population to live a free—if difficult—life in Aruba. Though the last full-blooded natives died out in 1862, remains of their villages, workshops and cemeteries can be glimpsed throughout the Aruban countryside. Many place names still retain their Indian origins, such as Arashi, Daimari, Jamanota, and perhaps the name Aruba itself, which some think is Arawak for "guide." Even the faces of modern Arubans—with their high cheekbones and tawny complexions—strongly reflect their native ancestry.

After being discovered by the Spanish explorer Alonso de Ojeda in 1499, Aruba was deemed useless along with its sister island Bonaire and Curaçao, and ignored for years. After the Spanish shipped off the resident male Indians to work the salt mines of Hispaniola, they began a limited colonization, turning the dusty mote into a large ranch and introducing horses, donkeys, sheep, dogs, goats, pigs, cats and chickens. In 1636, the Dutch took over and continued ranching. The English and the Spanish duked it out briefly from 1792-1816, though the Dutch remained in control. Aloe cultivation and gold mining became important industries

In 1824 a lowly goat herd discovered the first gleaming nuggets of gold and started a tropical gold rush. Smelters were built and miners flooded the island. When the going got rough, major smelters shut down in 1914, but today there are those who still find a singular nugget. The real gold of Aruba became aloe vera, brought over from North America via Jamaica in the mid-19th century, a hardy succulent that adapted well to the climate. By 1900 Aruba had become the largest exporter of aloe vera, earning itself the nickname of Island of Aloe, for producing over 90 percent of the world's supply. Today every Aruban home boasts its own small crop, using it as a natural laxative and wound-healer.

In 1924, oil refining arrived, ushering in an unprecedented era of prosperity. By 1985 the oil boom had bust, and the country's biggest employer Exxon went home, leaving the country its worst crisis, with 60 percent of the foreign exchange lost, 70 percent of the harbor space empty, and 40 percent of the population unemployed. In 1986, Aruba separated from its sister islands of the Netherlands Antilles (Curaçao, Bonaire, Sint Maarten, Saba and Statia), but still remained part of the Dutch Kingdom. This was a move favored by Arubans, but the time couldn't have been less favorable. It forced the island to totally depend on tourism. Government guarantees were given to the Hyatt, Sheraton and Holiday Inns—a plucky move that worked. Today tourism is Aruba's biggest industry, employing about half the population.

People

Expect to find some Dutch customs and windmills on Aruba.

Arubans have legendary smiles and sunny dispositions—character traits tailor-made for tourism. In fact, Arubans are sometimes so helpful that they fight among themselves over who gets to help you. Acts of kindness are considered a way of life. Sociopsychologists have attributed this collective congeniality to several historical factors, including the relative absence of slavery and the benign Dutch intervention. Even the government has shown itself to be enlightened, and there seem to be no overt inequalities in service. As such, Arubans have a high standard of living, often earning as much as visiting tourists, so there is little resentment over spending habits (the downside of this is that nothing is cheap). About three-quarters of the people living full-time on the island are native-born. Racial intermingling has also had a long history here, starting with the Indian base, and adding 16th-century Spaniards, 17th-century Dutch, 18th-century Portuguese and French Huguenots and 19th-century African and Italian gold diggers, not to mention Americana oil technicians in the 20th century. The majority of Arubans are Roman Catholic.

Beaches

Several yachts and catamarans offer cruises along Aruba's coast.

Of the three ABC Islands, Aruba is considered to have the most beautiful beaches. All are open to the public free of charge. Do avoid swimming on the east side because the surf can get dangerously rough. **Palm Beach**, considered by some to be one of the ten best beaches in the world, is the hub of Aruban beachlife—interpret that as *crowded*—but it is also excellent for swimming and other watersports. **Fishermen's Hut**, north of the hotel strip, is the favorite hangout of the windsurfing crowd. Here you'll see a lovely view of neon sailboats bobbing madly in the wind. **Rodger Beach** is notable for its lovely palm trees, and **Baby Lagoon** on the west is unusually calm. A truly wondrous wide stretch of strand, **Manchebo Beach** seems to magically inspire women to fling their tops off. Other good beaches are **Bachelor's Beach** and **Boca Grandi** in the east, which is good for windsurfing.

Dive Sites

Interesting coral reefs surround Aruba, and a few fascinating ships have wrecked off its shores. Most underwater activities are conducted on the leeward side, where the waters are calmer, offering both shallow and deep water options. Some walls drop to 100 feet or more. Snorkelers will appreciate the area between **Druif Beach** and **Arashi**, where the waters are the most gentle. At Arashi Beach, within swimming distance of shore, there is situated a reef of elkhorn on the sandy bottom in 20-40 feet of water. The best visibility can be found at **Baby Lagoon**, on the southeast tip. Only experienced divers should head for the windward side of the island; though there are many small bays *(bocas)*, the water is usually very choppy and the currents impossibly strong except for the most able of swimmers. Snorkelers and divers both can enjoy two wrecks. The *Pedernales*, a World War II oil tanker, lies near the Holiday Inn in a mere 20-40 feet of water. The *Antilla*, a German cargo ship wrecked by the Germans at the beginning of the last world war, rests in 60 feet at Malmok. The wreck is full of small basket sponges, gorgonians, and other formations. Most of the dive operators are located on the leeward coast in the neighborhood of Palm and Eagle Beaches.

Treks

Aruba has not designated any marked hiking trails, but many tracks lead off the main road. The Aruba Tourism Authority can suggest many excursions to hikers and those interested in birds, animals and plant life, led by well-studied naturalists; the best is Julio Maduro at **Corvalu Tours** (*☎ 297-8-21149*).

Cacti, scruffy foliage, huge boulders, caves and dust comprise Aruba's interior.

Do take the time to head for the outback in Aruba, called the *cunucu*. The best view of Aruba is from the 541-ft.-high hill, **Hooiberg**, which takes a hardy trekker to conquer (though some early-morning joggers have been spotted puffing up it). Northeast of Hooiberg, at Ayo and Casibari, you'll discover enormous rocks, the size of buildings which boast Amerindian drawings.

At the Fontein Cave and Guadariki Cave in the San Nicholas area, you can also see the reddish mystic marks that are the last remnants of Aruba's first inhabitants.

Arikok National Park contains many of the islands' numerous species of trees, including rare lignum vitae and brazilwood. A restored adobe house on the premises dates back 200 years, showing the history of frontier life. Bird-watchers will particularly enjoy Bubali Pond, a man-made site from processed sewage that creates a haven for black cormorants, stilts, sandpipers, bank swallows, wood storks and ospreys. **Frenchman's Pass**, a winding, tree-shaded byway north of the lagoon, is also a raucous residence for green parrots in the wee hours.

Bubali Pond, on the north side of Eagle Beach at Pos Chikito, is a bird sanctuary. The pond, filled with fish, now attracts a huge variety of birds, with flocks arriving at sunset creating a spectacular vignette. Pelicans arrive in swarms as do black olivaceous cormorants, who perch on rocks letting their spread wings dry. Great egrets with long, spiny black legs also fly in profuse numbers.

The Haystack, the popular name for the conical Hoiberg which stands almost in the center of the island, is a curious volcanic formation covered with dry forests of kibrahacha, or yellow poui, white manjack, and other flowering trees together with a huge assortment of cacti. A flight of several hundred steps leads to the peak (541 feet) where, on a clear day, you can see all the way to Venezuela. On the south side, the Canashito area is full of caves that contain Arawak petroglyphs. In this area you'll find huge boulders strewn about, and weathered into bizarre shapes that seem to suggest magical forces. **Ayó**, northeast of Hooiberg, has been called the Stonehenge of Aruba, where rare burrowing owls have burrowed into holes they have dug under boulders. East of Ayó, a trail leads through a handsome plantation to the coast at Andicuri Bay, a good site for a picnic.

Interesting trails can be found south of Spanish Lagoon, at Mangl Halto (the name means "tall mangroves"). There's a lovely beach here; trails from the main road run north and south to the lagoon and bird refuge and to the ruins of the Balashi gold mine, leftover from Aruba's gold rush days in 1898.

What Else to See

On the jagged, windy northern coast, the **Natural Bridge**, the largest in the Caribbean and Aruba's most natural formation after the beaches, is one of the island's biggest attractions. Every bus and jeep stops here, so expect crowds. Honeymooners like to pose for photos as the waves surround the gaping coral bridge. The culturally starved can head for a trio of small but fascinating museums. The **Archaeology Museum** features artifacts from the island's Indian past. The **Numismatic Museum** showcases more than 30,000 coins from all over the world, including the rare jotin from 1798. (Brazil should have taken notice how the governor of the Netherlands Antilles Johan R. Lauffer solved a coin shortage at the time by cutting one coin into four pies; the word *jotin* is taken from the French *guillotine*.) The **Historical Museum** is housed in the island's oldest building, **Fort Zoutman**, built in 1796 by the Dutch. It's also the site of the weekly **Bonbini Festival**, held every Tuesday evening, featuring local music, dance, crafts and food.

BEST VIEW:

Schooner Harbor is a great photo op for its colorfully docked sailboats and open market where fishermen and boatpeople hawks their wares in open-stall markets.

City Celebrations

Carnival

Various locales around Aruba, Oranjestad.

This yearly party starts two weeks before Lent (usually in February). Don't miss the Grand Parade, held on the Sunday before Lent. Other festivities include street dancing and the crowning of the Carnival Queen.

Jazz and Latin Music Festival

Various venues, Oranjestad.

This yearly festival, begun in 1988 and run under the auspices of the Aruba Tourism Authority, is a local favorite. Held every June, it attracts some big names.

Historical Sites

Fort Zoutman

Off Lloyd G. Smith Blvd., Oranjestad.

Behind the government buildings. The fort, built in 1796, is the island's oldest building. The Willem III tower was added in 1868 and served as a lighthouse for decades. On the grounds is Museo Arubano, a historical museum in an 18th-century home that displays relics and artifacts found around Aruba.

Museums and Exhibits

Aruba Archeology Museum

Zoutmanstraat 1, Oranjestad.

Artifacts from the precolonial period—including some skeletons 2000 years old—are on exhibit at this small museum. Its founder, Martin Bloom, conducts interesting island tours (see "Special Tours/Excursions"). Free admission.

De Man Shell Collection

18 Morgensten St., Oranjestad.

The De Mans are proud owners of one of the world's largest private shell collections. Call ahead and if they're free, they'll let you check it out.

Numismatic Museum   ★★

Irausquin Plein 2A, Oranjestad.

Located in the Ministry of Culture building. More than 3000 pieces of coins and currency from 400 countries from the private collection of J.M. Odor. Free admission.

Tours

Atlantis Submarines

Seaport Village Marina, Oranjestad.
Hours Open: 10:00 a.m.–3:00 p.m.

Not for the claustrophobic, but a great excursion for everyone else in a modern submarine that goes as deep as 150 feet below the sea to observe coral and fish along the Barcadera Reef. Trips depart every hour on the hour, and reservations are essential. The fee is $48 for adults, $34 under 16; children under four not permitted.

De Palm Tours

L.G. Smith Blvd. 142, Oranjestad.

If it involves showing tourists around Aruba, they're happy to oblige at De Palm. On- and off-road excursions start at $49.95 and include lunch and snorkeling;

three-hour treks for hikers cost $25; deep-sea fishing starts at $220; horseback rides are $30 for two hours. They also do boat tours and snorkel excursions, with prices starting at $22.50.

Martin Booster Tracking

Diamontbergweg 40, San Nicolas.

Martin Booster, an archeologist who founded the Archeology Museum, personally conducts these interesting tours that explore the island's pre-Columbian roots. Via jeep, he'll take you far into the interior and regale you with tales of Aruba past and present. The tour generally departs at 8:30 a.m. and goes until 3:30 p.m.; the $40 price includes lunch.

Sports

Aruba's temperate blue waters give way to nearly every watersport—from parasailing to game fishing to jet skis, snorkeling and scuba, but the number one sport here is windsurfing. Consistent year-round winds and shallow flat waters make it one of the top sailboard destinations in the world, particularly good for beginners and intermediates. For 300 days of the year, guaranteed winds blow up to 20 knots. The prime location is **Fisherman's Huts**, north of the Holiday Inn on Palm Beach. For those not up to high winds yet, quieter waters are available farther south on Palm beach, where there is also equipment and instructors. The most advanced head for **Bachelor's Beach**. During the end of May and the beginning of June, the hail-and-hearty converge here from around the world for the annual **Aruba Hi-Winds Pro-Am Windsurfing Competition**. Aruba is a haven for all watersports, but golf and tennis find lots of takers. Companies dedicated to well-organized sports activities can be found in major hotel lobbies. Scuba diving is probably Aruba's best kept secret, and nowadays, many operators offer one-tank dives so you will have time for all your other pleasures. (For more information, see "Dive Sites" above.) Sport-fishing is big on the island, and half and full-day charters can be arranged through one's hotel or directly from local operators. Less than a mile from shore, the sea is rich with kingfish, tuna, bonito, wahoo, and blue and white marlin. Boat excursions for picnics and sightseeing are available on catamarans and glass-bottom vessels for viewing the corals—check with your hotel. Though yachting is not a big pastime here yet, there is a nautical club at the mouth of the Spanish Lagoon. Horseback riding is available daily on trails throughout the countryside, on paso fino horses imported from South

America; the mounts of these finely trained horses are known for an unbelievably comfortable ride.

Aruba Golf Club

Golfweg 82, San Nicolas.

This desertlike course has nine holes and lots of sand traps and goats to keep things interesting. It is located on the island's southeastern part, and open only to members on Saturday and Sunday. Greens fees are $7.50 for nine holes, $10 if you want to go around twice. Hopefully, a long-awaited 18-hole championship course will open this year along the west end; inquire at your hotel.

Aruba Sail Cart

Bushire 23, Oranjestad.
Hours Open: 10:00 a.m.–7:00 p.m.

Can't quite get the hang of windsurfing? This goofy sport is easy to learn instead. You'll be whisking about in no time on special carts equipped with a windsurf-type sail—fun! Costs about $15 for a half-hour.

Rancho El Paso

44 Washington, Oranjestad.

Here's the spot to come for trail rides on beautiful paso fino horses.

Red Sail Sports

Seaport Marketplace, Oranjestad.

The island's largest selection of watersport rentals, including scuba instructions and packages. One-tank dives start at $30.

Windsurfing

Various locales around Aruba, Oranjestad.

Windsurf rentals are available at most major hotels, or try: **Pelican Watersports** (☎ *297-8-2300)*; **Windsurfing Aruba** (☎ *297-8-33472)*; **Roger's Windsurf Palace** (☎ *297-8-21918)*; or **Red Sail Sports** (☎ *297-8-24500)*, among others.

Where to Stay

Highest Rated Hotels in Aruba

★★★★ Aruba Marriott Resort

★★★★ Aruba Sonesta Hotel

★★★★ Hyatt Regency Aruba

★★★ Americana Aruba Hotel

★★★ Amsterdam Manor Beach

★★★ Aruba Hilton Int'l Hotel

★★★ Aruba Palm Beach

★★★ Costa Linda Beach Resort

★★★ Divi Aruba Beach Resort

★★★ La Cabana Beach Resort

Most Exclusive Hotels in Aruba

★★★	Aruba Hilton Int'l Hotel	$125–$880
★★★	Playa Linda Beach Resort	$115–$605
★★★	Aruba Marriott Resort	$156–$450
★★★★	Hyatt Regency Aruba	$205–$300
★★★	Americana Aruba Hotel	$175–$185

Fielding's Best Value Hotels in Aruba

★★★	Amsterdam Manor Beach	$90–$140
★★★	Divi Aruba Beach Resort	$135–$195
★★★★	Hyatt Regency Aruba	$205–$300
★★★	La Cabana Beach Resort	$95–$640
★★★	Costa Linda Beach Resort	$270–$430

What you get on Aruba are either hi-rise, glitz-and-glitter beach resorts, low-rise garden-like resorts, or time-share apartments and condominiums. The number of rooms available in Aruba has skyrocketed in recent years, probably shooting beyond 8000 by 1995. Most of the hotels are situated on L.G. Smith Boulevard, west of Oranjestad. Moderate-priced accommodations with good quality are hard to find, families sometimes suffer in Aruba unless they go in for apartments or time-shares. Whatever you do, don't arrive in Aruba without a reservation, especially during high season (mid-December-mid-April). In any case, you must give the name of your hotel to the immigration officer when you arrive. Condominiums give you the option of cooking your own meals, but are usually housed in modern, unattractive buildings. If you want a bargain, go off season and save up to 45 percent. You can also take advantage of packages offered by some hotels.

Gambling is a major attraction on Aruba and there are many casinos.

Hotels and Resorts

If you have a taste for the Vegas life, stay in one of Aruba's many top-class resorts that will serve your every need; between the health club, the casino, the lagoon-style pool, and the full deck of restaurants, you'll never have to leave the premises. High-rises, of course, give you a better view of the sea; low-rises seem more intimate and are usually planted around fabulous gardens. Some hotels, like the Sonesta, offer some of the best shopping malls on the island.

Americana Aruba Hotel   **$175–$185**   ★ ★ ★

J.E. Irausquin Blvd. 83, Palm Beach, ☎ *(800) 447-7642, 297-8-64500.*
Single: $175–$185. Double: $175–$185.
Situated directly on Palm Beach with its own full casino, this well-managed property consisting of twin high-rise towers is a busy spot, with lots going on and a social

hostess to see that it stays that way. Most guests are from the U.S. and Canada. Accommodations are decent if not spectacular, with air conditioning, bamboo and wood furniture, cable TV and hair dryers; some overlook the "fantasy" swimming pool with waterfalls and spas. A great spot for kids with special supervised activities, though not exactly teeming with island flavor. 419 rooms. Credit Cards: V, MC, A.

Aruba Beach Club $130–$290 ★★

J.E. Irausquin Blvd. 51-53, Palm Beach, ☎ *(800) 445-8667, 297-8-23000.*
Single: $130–$290. Double: $130–$290.
This time-share resort is on the sea at Druif Beach, and shares facilities with the Casa Del Mar Beach Resort, including three restaurants, three pools, three bars and four tennis courts. Accommodations are decent enough with air conditioning, cable TV, kitchens and balconies. The atmosphere is casual and lively. 131 rooms. Credit Cards: V, MC, DC, A.

Aruba Hilton Int'l Hotel $125–$880

J.E. Irausquin Blvd. 77, Palm Beach, ☎ *(800) 445-8667, 297-8-64466.*
Single: $125–$880. Double: $125–$880.
Hilton has taken over this former Concorde Hotel and $20 million later, has turned it into a decent and efficient operation. Accommodations are in a high-rise and nicely decorated with all the modern touches; all balconies have full ocean views. The grounds include a new watersports center, two pools (one for kids), very nice public spaces, a health club, two tennis courts and a full casino. Splurge on the VIP floors if your budget allows; the extra bucks buy a hair dryer, minibar and more space to move around. 479 rooms. Credit Cards: V, MC, DC, A.

Aruba Marriott Resort $156–$450

L.G. Smith Blvd., Palm Beach, ☎ *(800) 223-6388.*
Single: $156–$450. Double: $156–$450.
Opening in May 1995, the new Marriott promises to be a smashing full-service resort, with a magnificent pool, huge casino, spiffy health spa, tennis and all the usual watersports. Lots of bars, restaurants and shopping on-site to keep visitors happy, though as with all these mega-resorts, genuine island atmosphere is scarce. 413 rooms.

Aruba Palm Beach $115–$255

J.E. Irausquin Blvd. 79, Palm Beach, ☎ *(800) 345-2782, 297-8-63900.*
Single: $115–$255. Double: $115–$255.
This eight-story Moorish-style beachfront hotel is set amid exquisitely landscaped tropical grounds. Rooms are spacious and come with all the usual amenities, though their balconies are quite small, and not all have an ocean view. Walk-in closets are a nice touch. They offer all the expected recreational diversions, from tennis to watersports. A choice spot. 200 rooms. Credit Cards: V, MC, DC, A.

Aruba Sonesta Hotel $115–$530

L.G. Smith Blvd. 82, Oranjestad, ☎ *(800) 766-3782, 297-8-36389.*
Single: $115–$530. Double: $115–$530.
No beach, but boats depart every 20 minutes to a private island seven minutes away where all sorts of watersports await. Located in the heart of Oranjestad in the Seaport Village complex, which offers some 85 shops and restaurants. After entering

through an impressive atrium lobby, guests are brought to their very nice rooms, which have all the usual amenities plus minibars and tiny balconies. The children's program is free and highly rated, and the casino is huge and happening. A great spot, but only for those who don't mind being well off the beach. 299 rooms. Credit Cards: V, MC, DC, A.

Best Western Bucuti $115–$235   ★★

J.E. Irausquin Blvd., Eagle Beach, ☎ *(800) 528-1234, 297-8-31100.*
Single: $115–$235. Double: $115–$235.
This casual lowrise has very nice accommodations with sitting areas, sofa beds, microwave ovens, refrigerators, TVs and pleasant furnishings. It shares facilities with the adjacent Best Western Manchebo Beach Resort, with all the usual watersports, tennis, pools and casino. The beach is large and wide, and Aruba's only sanctioned topless spot. 63 rooms. Credit Cards: V, MC, A.

Best Western Manchebo $100–$180   ★★

L.G. South Blvd. 55, Palm Beach, ☎ *(800) 528-1234, 297-8-23444.*
Single: $100–$180. Double: $115–$180.
This sprawling lowrise, located on one of Aruba's best beaches, has guest rooms that are comfortable if unexciting; each has a refrigerator, which is always welcome. It's a sister property to the adjacent Best Western Bucuti, and between the two, guests are kept busy with all the typical resort amenities. Lots of Europeans like this spot. 71 rooms. Credit Cards: V, MC, DC, A.

Best Western Talk of The Town $85–$215   ★★

L.G. Smith Blvd. 2, Oranjestad, ☎ *(800) 528-1234, 297-8-82380.*
Single: $85–$215. Double: $95–$215.
This lowrise motel near the airport has traditional guest rooms, some with microwaves and refrigerators, as well as apartments of one or two bedrooms and full kitchens. There's a good restaurant and two pools on-site; beach lovers are transported to a nicer beach than the one across a busy street. A good choice for budget travelers, as the service is quite caring. 63 rooms. Credit Cards: V, MC, DC, A.

Bushiri Beach Hotel $230–$330   ★★

L.G. Smith Blvd. 35, Oranjestad, ☎ *(800) 462-6868, 297-8-25216.*
Single: $230–$330. Double: $230–$330.
Aruba's first all-inclusive resort is physically nondescript, but excellent service (this is a training school for budding hoteliers) makes up for the lack of atmosphere. There's tons to do—watersports, gambling classes, sightseeing excursions, tennis, sailing—and lots of young people frequent this busy property. Rates are quite reasonable since everything is included—including all you can possibly drink, and then some. Parents can stash their kids in the supervised programs. 150 rooms. Credit Cards: V, MC, A.

Divi Aruba Beach Resort $135–$195   ★★★

J.E. Irausquin Blvd. 47, Palm Beach, ☎ *(800) 223-6725, 297-8-23300.*
Single: $135–$195. Double: $135–$195.
Located on glorious Druif Beach, this popular lowrise is nicely casual and very friendly. Standard accommodations are in motel-like wings and feature tile floors, ceiling fans (as well as air), and small balconies. Concrete casitas offer more privacy.

Other rooms front the ocean and have tiled patios and larger bathrooms, while the newer Divi Dos rooms include refrigerators and Jacuzzis. Lots of honeymooners at this spot, which comes highly recommended more for the excellent beach than for the property itself. 202 rooms. Credit Cards: V, MC, DC, A.

Holiday Inn Aruba $121–$170   ★★

J.E. Irausquin Blvd. 230, Palm Beach, *(800) 465-4329, 297-8-63600.*
Single: $121–$170. Double: $121–$170.

It's a Holiday Inn, after all, so don't come looking for anything special. Rooms are acceptable but could really use a refurbishing; on the other hand, the outdoor gardens are quite nice. There's lots to keep you occupied, including watersports, six tennis courts, horseback riding, a large pool, health center and, of course, the ubiquitous casino. 600 rooms. Credit Cards: V, MC, DC, A.

Hyatt Regency Aruba $205–$300   ★★★★

J.E. Irausquin Blvd. 85, Palm Beach, *(800) 233-1234, 297-8-61234.*
Single: $205–$300. Double: $205–$300.

Set on 12 acres fronting Palm Beach, this sprawling high-rise resort is known for its famous pool, a giant, multi-level swimming hole with waterslides, waterfalls and all sorts of bells and whistles. Rooms are all the same size (the view determines the price) with Southwestern decor, oversized baths and loads of amenities, though the balconies are disappointingly tiny. The grounds are lush and lovely with all the usual sporting diversions, a pretty lagoon dotted with black swans and lots of eateries. Grand, glorious and Aruba's best. 360 rooms. Credit Cards: CB, V, MC, DC, A.

La Cabana Beach Resort $95–$640   ★★★

J.E. Irausquin Blvd. 250, Eagle Beach, *(800) 835-7193, 297-8-79000.*
Single: $95–$640. Double: $95–$640.

All accommodations are suites at this beachfront resort located five minutes from Oranjestad. Choose from studios or apartments with up to three bedrooms; all have full kitchens, whirlpools, hair dryers, and private balconies. Besides having the most rooms in Aruba, the hotel also boasts the biggest pool and biggest casino. One of the three pools has a 120-foot waterslide; another has a waterfall. The Club Cabana Nana ($80 per week) keeps kids out of the way. There's always something happening at this very fun and well-serviced resort. 803 rooms. Credit Cards: V, MC, DC, A.

Tamarijn Aruba Resort $145–$190   ★★

J.E. Irasquin Blvd. 41, Palm Beach, ☎ *297-8-24150.*
Single: $145. Double: $190.

This all-inclusive resort is a sister property to the Aruba Divi Beach Resort, with golf carts whisking guests to and fro. The Dutch-style architecture consists of two-story townhouse-style units with the typical furnishings and amenities inside. The grounds include two tennis courts, restaurants and bars and watersports. Guests can get free admittance and transport to the Alhambra Casino. Lots of honeymooners here. 236 rooms. Credit Cards: CB, V, MC, A.

Apartments and Condominiums

Families and couples will find the best bargains in this section. Some complexes even throw in a rental car; if you don't plan on driving, make sure you are near an accessible bus route. Some of the most inexpensive deals can be found in the Malmok district.

Amsterdam Manor Beach $90–$140 ★★★

Eagle Beach, ☎ *297-8-31492.*
Single: $90–$140. Double: $90–$140.

This complex is marked by its authentic Dutch style, with gabled roofs and inner courtyards, though it desperately needs some landscaping. Accommodations range from studios to two-bedroom apartments, all with pinewood furniture and full kitchens. The nice pool is set right on the road and lacks privacy. Eagle Beach is across the street, and guests can arrange watersports at various nearby properties. Not a top choice, but decent enough for the price. Lots of Europeans here. 72 rooms. Credit Cards: V, MC, DC, A.

Caribbean Palm Village $85–$290 ★★

Palm Beach Road, Noord Village, ☎ *297-8-62700.*
Single: $85–$256. Double: $85–$290.

Located a mile from Palm Beach, this low-rise apartment complex is off the beach and away from shops and restaurants, so you'll be using the rental car that's included with the rates. Accommodations are in suites with two baths, living and dining areas and kitchens, and very nicely decorated. There's a decent Italian restaurant on-site, plus two pools and supervised programs for the kiddies. 170 rooms. Credit Cards: V, MC, DC, A.

Casa del Mar Beach Resort $135–$400 ★★

J.E. Irausquin Blvd. 53, Palm Beach, ☎ *297-8-23000.*
Single: $135–$400. Double: $135–$400.

This time-share resort has two-bedroom suites both on the beach and offshore, all with full kitchens. A social hostess keeps kids busy for parents who want some time alone. Facilities are shared with the Aruba Beach Club and include three restaurants, three bars, three pools, four tennis courts, watersports and a fitness center. 147 rooms. Credit Cards: V, MC, DC, A.

Playa Linda Beach Resort $115–$605 ★★★

J.E. Irausquin Blvd. 87, Palm Beach, ☎ *(800) 346-7084, 297-8-61000.*
Single: $115–$605. Double: $115–$605.

This time-share complex has a great location on a great beach. Accommodations are in studios and one- and two-bedroom apartments, tropically decorated and with modern kitchens and private verandas. There's an open-air restaurant, beach bar, snack bar, health club with masseuse on call and a neat swimming pool complete with falls and whirlpools. Each week they throw a cocktail party for guests. 194 rooms. Credit Cards: V, MC, DC, A.

Inns

Though small and decidedly not luxurious, inns offer the comfort of genuine, intimate hospitality and an owner/manager that really cares about your well-being.

Low Cost Lodging

If you stay in one of the following properties, you won't want to spend a lot of time in your room, but who wants to in Aruba anyway? Furnishings are basic, facilities are clean. Most are situated in Malmok, at the northwestern tip of Palm Beach.

Where to Eat

Highest Rated Restaurants in Aruba

★★★★ Chez Mathilde

★★★★ Papiamento

★★★★ Valentino's

★★★ Bali

★★★ Bon Appetit

★★★ Brisas del Mar

★★★ Charlie's Bar

★★★ Die Olde Molen

★★★ La Dolce Vita

★★★ Mi Cushina

Most Exclusive Restaurants in Aruba

★★★★ Papiamento	$20–$33
★★★ Die Olde Molen	$15–$30
★★★★ Valentino's	$16–$26
★★★ Talk of the Town	$18–$20
★★★ Steamboat	$15–$15

Fielding's Best Value Restaurants in Aruba

★★★ La Dolce Vita	$11–$32
★★★ Bon Appetit	$14–$28
★★★★ Papiamento	$20–$33
★★★ Charlie's Bar	$7–$22
★★★★ Chez Mathilde	$19–$33

With more than 100 international restaurants, Aruba is becoming a Disneyland of cuisines. French, German, American, Swiss, Spanish—all are at your fingertips in Aruba. Plentiful supplies of Dutch cheese have inspired *keshi yena*—a stewed chicken-or-meat stuffed Gouda cheese pocket. From Indonesia, a former Dutch colony, came the lavish *rijsttafel* (rice table), an array of savory meat and vegetable dishes served with rice. From Spain, via nearby Venezuela, comes the delicious caramel dessert *flan quesillo.* You can, however, also eat strictly Aruban specialties, such as *sopi di yuana*—iguana soup—which tastes strangely like mom's chicken soup. *Funchi* (cornmeal bread) and *pan bati* (Aruban griddle bread made with cornmeal) are Amerindian specialties that accompany every Aruban meal. At the atmospheric Papiamento mi Cushina in Cura Cabai owned by native Wijke Maduro, a ten-minute drive from Oranjestad, you can go true Aruban—with specialties like *keri keri* (finely minced fried shark) or *bestia chiquita stoba* (stewed lamb served with delicious freshly baked pan bati.) Other local delights worth trying include *pastechi* (cheese or meet-filled turnovers), wild hare stew, and *carbito* stew, a traditional seasoned feast of goat meat.When you get tired of exotica, head for the hotel coffee shops for American-style grub.

Arubans enjoy the people to people contact tourism has brought them.

Bali **$$** ★ ★ ★

Lloyd G. Smith Boulevard, #11, Oranjestad, ☎ *011-297-8-20680.*
Asian cuisine. Specialties: Indonesian Rijstaffel.
Lunch: 12:00 a.m.–3:30 p.m., prix fixe $10–$20.
Dinner: 6:00 p.m.–11:00 p.m., prix fixe $10–$20.
Feast on almost 20 different Indonesian specialties while bobbing gently on the sea in this intricately decorated houseboat in Schooner Harbour. In what could be

Aruba's most exotic dining experience, servers present dishes of varying intensity (but nothing is overly spicy), including *nasi goreng* or *bami goreng*, rice and noodles with egg, peas, chicken or beef. Lighter meals are also served, including Western-style sandwiches. No lunch is served on Saturday. Reservations recommended. Credit Cards: V, MC, A.

Bon Appetit $$$ ★★★

Palm Beach 29, Palm Beach, ☎ 011-297-8-65241.
Seafood cuisine. Specialties: Keshi yena, pan bati.
Dinner: 6:00 p.m.–11:00 p.m., entrees $14–$28.

A very warm and welcoming restaurant in an informal setting, with lots of tile and desert flora, Bon Appetit serves traditional Aruban dishes like *keshi yena* (Edam cheese stuffed with meat), *pan bati* (cornmeal johnnycakes) and a plate-busting, juicy prime rib. It's popular with locals, but also convenient to tourists, as it is within close proximity to the hotel strip in Palm Beach. Catch up with the latest news in the folksy bar before dinner. The restaurant is closed in September. Closed: Sun. Reservations recommended. Credit Cards: V, MC, DC, A.

Boonoonoonoos $$$ ★★

Wilhelminastraat 18A, Oranjestad, ☎ 011-297-8-31888.
Latin American cuisine. Specialties: Ajaka (chicken in banana leaves), Jamaican jerk ribs.
Lunch: 12:00 a.m.–5:00 p.m., entrees $5–$13.
Dinner: 5:30 p.m.–10:30 p.m., entrees $13–$33.

No, the eyes do not deceive, there really are four pairs of oo's in the name of this downtown restaurant, which means "extraordinary" in Jamaican patois. Located in a restored colonial home that's been brightly splashed with paint, cuisine covers the Caribbean in a large nutshell as conceived by Austrian chefs Kurt and Jacky Biermann. Signature dishes include Jamaican jerk ribs and a silky pumpkin cream soup; hungry diners will be more than satisfied with the Carib Combo platter, groaning with eight or nine dishes representing several Caribbean islands. No lunch is served on Sunday. Reservations recommended. Credit Cards: V, MC, DC, A.

Brisas del Mar $$$ ★★★

Savaneta 22A, East Oranjestad, ☎ 011-297-8-47718.
Seafood cuisine. Specialties: Broiled lobster, catch of the day.
Lunch: 12:00 a.m.–2:30 p.m., prix fixe $10–$30.
Dinner: 6:30 p.m.–9:30 p.m., prix fixe $10–$30.

Bustling and jammed with locals, especially on music-filled weekends, Brisas del Mar is about 20 minutes away from downtown Oranjestad, but well worth the trek for spanking fresh seafood and some of the finest local dishes on the island. Reservations at this folksy beach shack are required because there are only 10 or so tables. A recurring special is a flavorful fish stew, loaded with whatever's fresh, in a tasty broth. Groups can order the Aruban special, a potpourri of lightly fried fish cakes, spiced minced shark, hot relishes, plenty of rice and corn pancakes. Reservations required. Credit Cards: V, MC, A.

Buccaneer Restaurant $$ ★★

Gasparito 11-C, East Oranjestad, ☎ 011-297-8-66172.
Seafood cuisine.

Dinner: 5:30 p.m.–10:00 p.m., entrees $7–$23.
Well-prepared and moderately-priced seafood satisfies crowds of diners who come back again and again to this aquarium-laden, cozy restaurant located just a short jog from the large hotel strip in Noord. If you don't want to eat, there's a popular bar, and plenty of swimming marine life to gaze at. European-style meat dishes are also available for seafood-hating companions. No lunch is served on Mondays. Closed: Sun. Credit Cards: D, V, MC, DC, A.

Chalet Suisse $$$ ★★

J.E. Irausquin Boulevard, Palm Beach,
International cuisine. Specialties: Dutch pea soup, veal in cream sauce.
Dinner: 6:00 p.m.–10:30 p.m., entrees $15–$30.
For a change of pace, enjoy Old European specialties in a wood-panelled dining room that's a cool, comfortable spot protecting diners from the glare of the sun outside. Homey and rib-sticking dishes like Dutch split pea soup, veal and steak offer few surprises, but are exceptionally well prepared. Closed: Sun. Reservations recommended. Credit Cards: V, MC, DC, A.

Charlie's Bar $$ ★★★

Main Street 56, San Nicolas, ☎ *011-297-8-45086.*
American cuisine. Specialties: Grilled shrimp, churrasco.
Lunch: 12:00 a.m.–4:00 p.m., entrees $7–$18.
Dinner: 4:00 p.m.–9:30 p.m., entrees $7–$22.
You too can become a part of history by hanging a hankie or old tennis shoe to join the hundreds of other artifacts on the ceiling of this 50-plus-year-old bar. It's located in the once-thriving ghost town of San Nicolas, former headquarters of The Standard Oil Company. Charlie's served as a watering hole for workers (no women were allowed then) and it now overflows with tourists seeking a cold brew (or something stiffer) and a simple lunch or dinner of fresh seafood or steak. Overseeing all this activity is Guus Dancker, who has manned the circular bar for more than 40 years. Closed: Sun. Credit Cards: Not Accepted.

Chez Mathilde $$$ ★★★★

Havenstraat 23, Oranjestad, ☎ *011-297-8-34968.*
French cuisine.
Lunch: 11:30 a.m.–2:30 p.m., entrees $16–$25.
Dinner: 6:00 p.m.–11:00 p.m., entrees $19–$33.
Every Caribbean island must have a bastion of haute cuisine, and this elegant and intimate beauty in a 19th-century town house is IT in Aruba. Dishes are prepared in the classic French style by a Dutch chef, including thick and juicy lamb or veal chops, pate, bouillabaisse, tournedos with peppercorns and lobster thermidor. The romantic setting comes complete with candlelight, fine tableware and classical music. No lunch is served on Sunday. Reservations required. Credit Cards: D, V, MC, DC, A.

Die Olde Molen $$$ ★★★

J.E. Irausquin Boulevard, Palm Beach,
International cuisine.
Dinner: 6:00 p.m.–10:30 p.m., entrees $15–$30.

Until the brisk winds that blow on the islands constantly threatened to ruin them, this authentic Dutch windmill among the high-rise hotels in Palm Beach sported real sails. Reassembled from an 1800s-era mill that was shipped over from the old country, this tourist attraction is now a restaurant serving international food with Aruban touches. Shrimp is often featured, prepared in a savory cheese sauce, as is pepper steak and liqueured ice cream desserts. Worth a visit for the aesthetic value. Closed: Sun. Credit Cards: V, MC, DC, A.

La Dolce Vita $$$ ★★★

Palm Beach 29, Oranjestad, ☎ *011-297-8-65241.*
Italian cuisine. Specialties: Veal, snapper.
Dinner: 6:00 p.m.–11:00 p.m., entrees $11–$32.

Life is truly sweet here, especially for weary shoppers hoofing it down the fashionable Caya Betico Croes, where this well-known Italian restaurant is located. After several hours perusing the almost duty-free jewelry and clothing shops, snag a table (after reserving ahead) in this refurbished private home for veal and red snapper prepared in different ways, or pastas and authentic Italian desserts and coffee drinks. Closed: Wed. Reservations recommended. Credit Cards: D, V, MC, A.

La Paloma $$$ ★★

Noord 39, Noord, ☎ *011-297-8-62770.*
Italian cuisine. Specialties: Conch stew with pan bati, caesar salad, red snapper.
Dinner: 6:00 p.m.–11:00 p.m., entrees $13–$28.

A nice place to take the family for American-style Italian food, La Paloma is always full of patrons who like the huge menu chock full of pasta with red sauces and huge steaks, the brisk service and old-fashioned decor (chianti bottles!). The restaurant is housed in a low-rise building in the Noord area. If you want peace and quiet, this place isn't it. The bar is a popular watering hole. Closed: Tue. Reservations recommended. Credit Cards: V, MC, A.

Mi Cushina $$$ ★★★

Noord Cura Cabai 24, San Nicolas, ☎ *011-297-8-48335.*
Latin American cuisine. Specialties: Bestia chiquito stoba, pan bati.
Lunch: 12:00 a.m.–2:00 p.m., entrees $12–$24.
Dinner: 6:00 p.m.–10:00 p.m., entrees $12–$24.

There are a handful of charming small restaurants serving home-style Aruban cuisine, which is not readily available outside of the islands; one of the best is Mi Cushina, or owner Wijke Maduro's "kitchen" and family museum. Occasionally, Maduro serves iguana soup or goat stew, but usually there is fresh fish like grouper or shark served lightly fried in cake form or minced with tangy sauce. A specialty is *bestia chiquito stoba*, or lamb stew in a Creole sauce. Entrees are reasonably priced because of the hearty portions, which include some of the best pan bati on the island. Closed: Tue. Reservations recommended. Credit Cards: V, MC, DC, A.

Old Cunucu House $$$ ★★★

Palm Beach 150, Palm Beach, ☎ *011-297-8-61666.*
International cuisine. Specialties: Pan fried conch, cornmeal, pan bati.
Dinner: 6:00 p.m.–10:00 p.m., entrees $14–$27.

Experience the Aruba of bygone days in this 1920s-style dwelling with a restaurant whose name means "old country" house. Tasty seafood is featured, as well as New York steaks and a few Aruban specialties. The atmosphere here is very relaxed and informal, amidst modern high-rise hotels that dwarf it. Even if you don't come to eat, there's a rustic bar with live and local entertainment on weekends. Closed: Sun. Reservations recommended. Credit Cards: V, MC, DC, A.

Papiamento   **$$$**   ★ ★ ★ ★

Washington 61, Noord, ☎ *011-297-8-64544.*
Latin American cuisine. Specialties: Meat or fish cooked on hot marble, clay pot seafood.
Dinner: 6:00 p.m.–11:00 p.m., entrees $20–$33.
This is possibly one of Aruba's "don't miss" experiences if only for the exquisite sur-
roundings. Dining here is like being invited to a gracious private home—which this
is. Lenie and Eduardo Ellis design their own handwritten menus, garnish their Con-
tinental dishes with fresh garden herbs, and have decorated the various dining areas
with distinctive plantings and antiques. You can dine by the pool or request a single
honeymoon table. Perennial favorites are available on the ever-changing menu. Res-
ervations required. Credit Cards: V, MC, A.

Steamboat   **$$**   ★ ★ ★

Lloyd G. Smith, Oranjestad, ☎ *011-297-8-66700.*
International cuisine. Specialties: Buffet Brunch.
Lunch: 12:00 a.m.–5:00 p.m., entrees $7–$10.
Dinner: 5:30 p.m.–11:00 p.m., prix fixe $15.
One of Aruba's best bargains is this buffet foodery in a shopping center near all the
hotel action. Steamboat serves a large breakfast or brunch for under $8, and large
sandwiches are available for lunch. Dinner is another all-you-can eat buffet that
draws crowds (understandably) for $15 per person. Credit Cards: V, MC, A.

Talk of the Town   **$$$**   ★ ★ ★

L.G. Smith Boulevard 2, Oranjestad, ☎ *011-297-8-23380.*
American cuisine. Specialties: Prime rib, steaks.
Dinner: 5:30 p.m.–11:00 p.m., entrees $18–$20.
This is an excellent stop for people with big appetites, with superb beefsteaks and
prime rib feasts on Saturday nights for under $20. Located near the airport in a Best
Western resort of the same name that resembles a Spanish hacienda, it's a surpris-
ingly nice spot for quiet, intimate, candlelit dinners, and possibly the only restaurant
in the Caribbean that's been awarded membership in the prestigious Chaine de
Rotisseurs culinary society. Associated Hotel: Talk of the Town Resort. Closed:
Mon. Reservations recommended. Credit Cards: V, MC, DC, A.

Valentino's   **$$$**   ★ ★ ★ ★

Palm Beach Road, Noord, ☎ *011-297-8-64777.*
Italian cuisine. Specialties: Mozzarella in carozza, penne del pastor.
Dinner: 6:00 p.m.–11:00 p.m., entrees $16–$26.
Arubans like to come here to celebrate special occasions along with residents and
guests at the chic Caribbean Palm Village Resort in Noord. The reason is delicious
pastas—especially fettucini with salmon—intimate tables and gracious, friendly service. Before dining, patrons can unwind with drinks, then ascend to the second-

story courtyard restaurant overlooking the pool and cooled by evening breezes. Associated Hotel: Caribbean Palm Village. Closed: Sun. Reservations required. Credit Cards: V, MC, DC, A.

Where to Shop

Oranjestad, the capital, is a shopper's haven. Shops line the main shopping streets of Nassaustraat and Wilhelminastraat, selling mostly duty-free products (minus the eight percent duty), such as liquor, jewelry, electronics, crystal, china, perfumes and designer fashions. Shopping malls—**Holland Aruba Mall**, **Seaport Village Mall** and the **Strada Complex**—make for one-stop shopping while **Harbour Town** and **Port of Call Marketplace** cater to the cruise crowd. The best free-port shopping can be found at **Caya G. F. Betico Croes**.

Aruba Directory

ARRIVAL AND DEPARTURE

American Airlines flies nonstop to Aruba from New York's JFK Airport and Miami daily. The flight takes about 4-1/2 hours from NYC. American also flies nonstop. If you book recommended accommodations and flights at the same time through American, you can receive substantial discounts. You can also save money by reserving your flight 14 days in advance, as well as flying Monday through Thursday. ALM also flies to Aruba six days a week from Miami. The Venezuela airline VIASA flies three times a week from Houston. Aruba's national carrier Air Aruba flies from Newark, Baltimore and Miami. Air Canada offers flights from Toronto or Montreal to either Miami or New York, and then transfer to American or ALM.

The departure tax is $10.

CLIMATE

Dry and sunny, Aruba boasts average temperatures of 83 degrees F, though trade winds make the heat seem gentler. Mosquitoes get frisky in July and August, when it is less windy.

DOCUMENTS

U.S. and Canadian citizens need to show some proof of citizenship—birth certificate, passport, or voter's registration plus a photo ID; driver's license is not accepted. You must also show an ongoing or return ticket.

ELECTRICITY

Current runs at 110 volts, 60 cycles, as in the U.S.

GETTING AROUND

Taxis are plentiful, but the lack of meters requires firm negotiations with the driver before you take off. Drivers often know the city as well as private guides. Ask your hotel to recommend one. A dispatch office is also located at **Alhambra Bazaar and Caino** ☎ *(809) 297-8-21604*. You can also flag down taxis from the street. Rates are fixed (no meters) but you should confirm the price before you set off. All Aruban taxi drivers are specially trained guides; an hour's tour will run about $30.

Cars are easily rented on the island; you will need a valid U.S. or Canadian driver's license to rent a car; different agencies have various age requirements. You will save money if you rent from a local agency rather than from one of the well-known agencies. Among the best are **Hedwina Car Rental** ☎ *8-26442* and **Optima** ☎ *8-36263*. Avis, Budget and Hertz are all available at the airport.

Scooters are the best vehicle to toot around the island and are the most economical. You'll save money renting for two days or longer. **Ron's** ☎ *8-62090* and **George's** ☎ *8-25975* will deliver to the airport.

Inexpensive buses run hourly between the beach hotels and Oranjestad. The main terminal is located in South Zoutmanstraat, next to Fort Zoutman. A free Shopping Tour Bus departs hourly beginning at 9:15 a.m.–3:15 p.m., starting at the Holiday Inn and making stops at all the major hotels on the way toward Oranjestad.

LANGUAGE

Arubans are pleasantly multilingual. The official language is Dutch; also spoken is English, Spanish, Portuguese and the local dialect called Papiamento.

MEDICAL EMERGENCIES

Horacio Oduber Hospital ☎ *24300* is a modern facility near Eagle Beach, with an efficient staff. Ask your hotel about doctors and dentists on call.

MONEY

The official currency is the Aruban florin (also called the guilder), written as Af or Afl. American dollars are accepted at most establishments, but it might be cheaper to pay in florins.

TELEPHONE

To call Aruba from the U.S., dial ☎ *011+297+8* followed by the 5-digit number. Forget calling home from your hotel—surcharges can hike the price of an overseas call to exorbitant levels. Instead, head for SETAR, the local company, with several locations in Oranjestad and near the high-rise hotels in Palm Beach. From here, you can make phone calls using a card you purchase, and also send and receive faxes.

TIME

Aruba is on Atlantic Standard Time, year round.

TIPPING AND TAXES

Aruban custom is to charge 10–15 percent service charge and 5 percent government tax. The total of these two charges (fifteen percent) is usually written into the "tax" slot on credit cards. If you want to give more for service, feel free but it is not expected.Hotels add 11 percent service charge.

TOURIST INFORMATION

Aruba Tourism Authority, *A. Shuttestraat 2, Oranjestad, Aruba, N.A.* ☎ *011+297/82-3777*, FAX *83-4702*. From the U.S. call ☎ *(800) 862-7822.*

WHEN TO GO

New Year is celebrated with an explosion of fireworks set off by the hotels and serenaded by strolling musicians and singers. Carnival is a blowout event, which starts two weeks before Lent, and culminates with a Grand Parade on the Sunday preceding Lent. National Anthem and Flag Day on March 18 is celebrated by displays of national dancing and folklore. A weekly Bonbini show in the courtyard of the Fort Zoutman museum on Tuesdays 6:30 p.m.–10:30 p.m. also presents island folklore, song, and dance. The International Theatre Festival is an annual event; contact the tourist board for exact dates.

ARUBA HOTELS		RMS	RATES	PHONE	FAX
Oranjestad					
★★★★	Aruba Marriott Resort	413	$156–$450	(800) 223-6388	
★★★★	Aruba Sonesta Hotel	299	$115–$530	(800) 766-3782	
★★★★	Hyatt Regency Aruba	360	$205–$300	(800) 233-1234	
★★★	Americana Aruba Hotel	419	$175–$185	(800) 447-7642	
★★★	Amsterdam Manor Beach	72	$90–$140	297-8-31492	297-8-71463
★★★	Aruba Hilton Int'l Hotel	479	$125–$880	(800) 445-8667	
★★★	Aruba Palm Beach	200	$115–$255	(800) 345-2782	
★★★	Costa Linda Beach Resort	155	$270–$430	(800) 346-7084	
★★★	Divi Aruba Beach Resort	202	$135–$195	(800) 223-6725	
★★★	La Cabana Beach Resort	803	$95–$640	(800) 835-7193	
★★★	Playa Linda Beach Resort	194	$115–$605	(800) 346-7084	
★★	Aruba Beach Club	131	$130–$290	(800) 445-8667	
★★	Best Western Bucuti	63	$115–$235	(800) 528-1234	
★★	Best Western Manchebo	71	$100–$180	(800) 528-1234	

ARUBA HOTELS		RMS	RATES	PHONE	FAX
★★	Best Western Talk of The Town	63	$85–$215	(800) 528-1234	
★★	Bushiri Beach Hotel	150	$230–$330	(800) 462-6868	
★★	Caribbean Palm Village	170	$85–$290	297-8-62700	297-8-62380
★★	Casa del Mar Beach Resort	147	$135–$400	297-8-23000	297-8-26557
★★	Dutch Village	97	$145–$415	(800) 367-3484	
★★	Holiday Inn Aruba	600	$121–$170	(800) 465-4329	
★★	Mill Resort	102	$105–$550	297-8-67700	
★★	Tamarijn Aruba Resort	236	$145–$190	297-8-24150	

ARUBA RESTAURANTS		LOCATION	PHONE	ENTREE

Oranjestad

		American		
★★★	Charlie's Bar	San Nicolas	011-297-8-45086	$7–$22
★★★	Talk of the Town	Oranjestad	011-297-8-23380	$••18–$20
		Asian		
★★★	Bali	Oranjestad	011-297-8-20680	$10–$20
		French		
★★★★	Chez Mathilde	Oranjestad	011-297-8-34968	$16–$33
		International		
★★★	Die Olde Molen	Palm Beach		$••15–$30
★★★	Old Cunucu House	Palm Beach	011-297-8-61666	$••14–$27
★★★	Steamboat	Oranjestad	011-297-8-66700	$7–$15
★★	Chalet Suisse	Palm Beach		$15–$30••
		Italian		
★★★★	Valentino's	Noord	011-297-8-64777	$16–$26••
★★★	La Dolce Vita	Oranjestad	011-297-8-65241	$11–$32••
★★	La Paloma	Noord	011-297-8-62770	$13–$28••
		Latin American		
★★★★	Papiamento	Noord	011-297-8-64544	$20–$33••
★★★	Mi Cushina	San Nicolas	011-297-8-48335	$12–$24
★★	Boonoonoonoos	Oranjestad	011-297-8-31888	$5–$33

ARUBA RESTAURANTS	LOCATION	PHONE	ENTREE
Seafood			
★★★ **Bon Appetit**	Palm Beach	011-297-8-65241	$14–$28••
★★★ **Brisas del Mar**	East Oranjestad	011-297-8-47718	$10–$30
★★ **Buccaneer Restaurant**	East Oranjestad	011-297-8-66172	$7–$23••
Note: • Lunch Only			
•• Dinner Only			

BARBADOS

Large numbers of sailboats are available for charter in Barbados.

Three centuries ago, Barbados was called the "Brightest Jewel in the English Crowne," and today, this tiny coral island still gleams, not just as a "veddy British" trinket, but as a Caribbean treasure in its own right. After a long struggle to balance itself politically after declaring independence from Britain thirty years ago, Barbados is now returning to a celebration of its own Bajan culture, interlacing the passion for cricket and afternoon teas with the more boisterous native traditions of rum, calypso and Rastafarianism. In 1993, the Human Development Report of the United Nations placed Barbados first among all developing nations in the world—the third year in a row—and tourists can't help but feel blessed by the efficiency of service, the top-class cuisine, and the general enthusiasm of spirit. Long one of the most cosmopolitan and sophisticated islands in the Caribbean, Barbados is looking even spiffier these days as a building boom creates new hotels and restaurants by the dozens. Spearheaded by the Pemberton Resorts' new **Royal Westmoreland Golf and Country Club**, the construction of golf facilities, including an international school and six multi-million-dollar courses, will rank Barbados among the top destinations for golf in the world. Carnival and the annual Crop Over festival are the times when Barbados truly hangs loose, but those interested in getting away from it all can still find a wild and rugged Barbados tucked in the backcountry. A new Concorde charter service will allow travelers to reach Barbados in less the flight time normally required and will reap hundreds of saved dollars in an 8 day/7 night package at one of 15 luxury hotels on the island.

Bird's Eye View

A pear-shaped coral island that stretches 21 miles north and 14 miles east to west, Barbados is the most easterly of the complex of West Indies islands—a series of stepping stones that arch from South Florida to South America. Spanning a total of 166 square miles, Barbados boasts a remarkably varied topography—in an hour you can pass through the lush rainforest of St. Thomas, the rugged rocky coast of St. Joseph, and the gentle sloping capped hills of St. Andrew. The northernmost parish of St. Lucy is where the Caribbean and the Atlantic coast meet. Because Barbados is the first land hit by the westerly trade winds traversing the Atlantic, the air is fresh and invigorating, so much so that in the 19th century the island became known as the "sanitarium of the West Indies" because boatloads of Brits came to air out their vaporous lungs. Perhaps the good air explains the longevity of Barbadians, who on the average, live well into their seventies.

History

When the Portuguese explorer Pedro a Campos discovered Barbados in the 17th century, he found the island totally uninhabited. As the sailor took

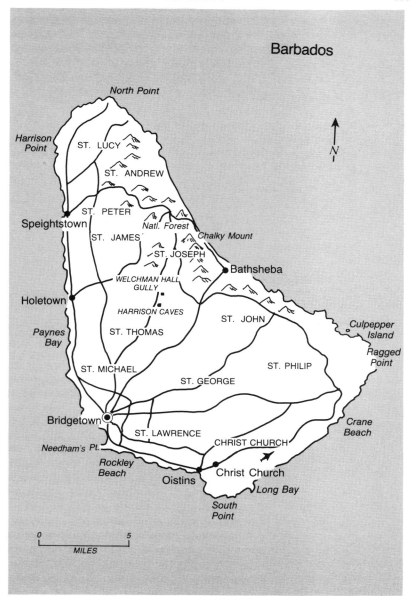

Barbados

in the lush tropical surroundings, he spotted fig trees with clumps of bushy roots hanging from branches that resembled beards. From that came the name Barbados, which in Portuguese means "the bearded ones." Long before the first European contact, Arawak Indians were said to be living on the island, but they were long gone by the time of the first British expedition in 1625. Two years later, eighty British settlers under the leadership of Captain John Powell settled at Jamestown (later renamed Holetown). Soon, conditions proved highly favorable for tobacco, cotton and sugarcane production, and thousands of African and European slaves were shipped over to till the fields. A strong fortress system (26 forts along 21 miles of coast) kept the island from invasion, and Barbados became the only island in the Caribbean to be under uninterrupted British rule for over three centuries. In 1937, economic problems caused by the fluctuating price of sugar led to demonstrations in Bridgetown, which resulted in the establishment of a British Royal Commonwealth to the West Indies—a gesture which proved instrumental in bringing about social and political reform, including universal adult suffrage in 1951. Fifteen years later, Barbados received its full sovereignty.

Today Barbados is a British Commonwealth nation with a parliamentary system of government headed by an appointed governor-general and an elected Prime Minister. British influence extends to the courts, laws, language and place names.

People

Barbados is still a place where stately women carry umbrellas with pride, children peer from shutters, and men slam down dominoes on rickety tables. About 80 percent of the native population hail from African origin, another 15 percent are of mixed blood. Although Europeans represent only about 5 percent of the total population, a strong sense of British tradition still pervades, including a profound commitment to education (the island boasts a whopping literacy rate of 99 percent). Schoolchildren descended from slaves were taught to think of Barbados as Little England, and even in the most inland roads, you'll see children dressed in the mandatory school uniforms (pressed shirt and ties for both sexes), all color coded in true British fashion. So strong is the Brit lifestyle here the afternoon tea is still habitually enjoyed, and passions for cricket and polo run deep. Along esplanades and streets, however, you might see locals playing *warri*, a traditional bead game from West Africa.

Driving around aimlessly is a way of life in Barbados—there's even a word for it: "buttin' 'bout." In fact, the best thing to do in Barbados is to throw away your map because asking and receiving directions can often be the prelude to new friendships or a spontaneous game of road tennis. If you really want to delve into the soul of Barbados, pick up a copy of the highly acclaimed novel *In the Castle of My Skin* by George Lamming.

One sad note: due to high unemployment, U.S. advisories have warned about purse-snatching, sexual crime and armed robbery. Avoid flashing jewelry and keep an eye on wallets and packs carried on the back.

Beaches

All beaches in Barbados are open to the public, even those abutting the high-priced hotels; local law requires that access to the beaches be open, either through the road or through the hotel's entrance. A beautiful drive through sugarcane fields will take you to the rugged, surf-pounding beaches of the east coast (North Point, Cove Bay, and Archer's Bay), but most people prefer the calmer western beaches called the **Gold Coast** (Paradise Beach, Paynes Bay, and Sandy Lane Bay, Treasure Beach, Gibbs Bay, Heywoods Beach, Rockley, and Bentson Beach). The water most everywhere stays a comfortable few degrees below body temperature. The most secluded and charming hotel beach is behind the **Coconut Creek Club**, in St. James. **Mulins Bay**, just south of Speightstown, is a particularly pleasant nonhotel beach with a good restaurant-bar and a free outdoor shower. Parking is in the lot across the road. The most dramatic beach is most likely **Batsheba**, on the rugged northeast side, where foamy waves pound the shores with huge salt sprays. Here you'll see lots of old Barbadian families taking their weekend and holiday escapes.

Dive Sites

Coral reefs surround the coast of Barbados; there is both an outer reef good for divers and an inner reef, which snorkelers make good use of. In general, however, the sites are best for beginning divers. The barrier reefs must be reached by boat, about a quarter-mile to three-quarter miles from shore. The western formations are unique, starting at a plateau of about 50 feet, dropping to a valley of 80 feet, and rising again to 60-80 feet and dropping again to another valley at 90 feet. Marine life includes moray eels, parrotfishes, squid, blue chubs and turtles, among others There are several shipwrecks, and clear visibility allows excellent possibilities for photography. The best areas for snokeling lie on western shores, where reefs can be found in 20-30 feet of water; these sites can be reached from shore by swimming.

Treks

Barbados also offers a number of wild and cultivated habitats that are fascinating places for retreat when the sun and surf get too much. As elsewhere in the tropics, the best and coolest hours for serious hikes are from dawn to ten o'clock in the morning and from four to six in the afternoon. The **Barbados National Trust** organizes free morning hikes starting at 6 a.m. for residents, which has become an islandwide passion; visitors are welcome and it is a wonderful way to meet and converse with islanders. As many as 300 people congregate for the treks, which are divided into various levels of expertise—you're sure to find one that fits your feet.(Each hike is approximately five miles long and lasts three hours—come appropriately dressed (good hiking shoes and sunhat) and it's not a bad idea to bring your own waterbottle. Different trails are covered each week, check the local newspapers and visitor's guides for the schedule.

Near the beach of Bathsheba are the **Andromeda Gardens**, worth a stop if you have any interest in viewing the island's native vegetation set in lovingly designed gardens. For an enjoyable and instructive self-guided walk, visit the

Barbados Wildlife Reserve, where you can view indigenous animals in their natural habitat. The 54-acre **Flower Forest** also has self-guided walks that take you through all the trees, flowers and plants of the island. A half-day excursion can also be taken through **Welchman Hall Gully**, especially in the late afternoon, to see tropical flora. A trip down under can be had via electric carts through the **Harrison Caves**.

BEST VIEW:

If you drive to a tiny village called Pie Corner, go past a horse farm, and then through a cow pasture to Cove Bay, you'll find a 50-ft cliff, where you can look out onto Paul's Point, a chalky chunk of natural sculpture that resembles the Winged Victory of Samothrace. The view is considered to be most beautiful on the island.

Warning: Don't swim near coral, where the dreaded sea urchins lie. If you do, head straightaway for the local pharmacy and buy candle grease, which you melt over your palms and knees to leach out the stinging spines.

What Else to See

Barbadian history and culture still lives vibrantly in the art and architecture of the island. Most visitors only visit the capital, **Bridgetown**, for shopping forays, but there are a few sights for which you might consider sacrificing precious time at the beach. **The Careenage**, a haven for the old clipper ships, still exudes an air of intrigue, although these days it has lost some of its former glory. Cars usually whiz by **Trafalgar Square**, but the stained glass windows of the **Public Building** represent the crowned heads of England, and are worth a quick look. The monument, dedicated to Admiral Horatio Nelson, celebrates his contributions to the island. It's rare to find Jewish houses of worship in the Caribbean, but the synagogue on Synagogue Lane is one of the oldest in the Western Hemisphere, erected on the site of an even older synagogue established by Brazilian Jews. From here, you could take a taxi to visit the garrison Savannah, especially if a cricket game or horse race is in full force.

Speightstown, on the west coast, has retained much of its colonial look and flavor. Two-story shops with Georgian-style galleries propped up by two-by-four pillars line the narrow street., Just to roam the sidewalks clogged with food vendors is an education in the vast variety of exotic tropical fruits that are available on the island.

An interesting excursion is to take a tram through **Harrison's Cave**, home of geologic formations of crystallized limestone. Streams, pools and waterfalls—one of them 40 feet high—cause slow but steady erosion of the rock.

Anyone interested in antiques should visit a few plantation houses, some of which date back to the 17th century. **Drax Hall** is considered the oldest plantation house on the island, and many of the bedrooms and parlor of **Sunbury Plantation** actually look as if someone is still living there. **St. Nicholas Abbey** boasts an owner Lt. Col. Stephen Cave, who will prove a true living legend if you corner him into conversation. To round out the history lesson, visit the **Barbados Museum**, which houses a fine collection of Barbadian furnishings, fine art and artifacts from the early days. (The Barbados Heritage Passport, a package program, was recently expanded to 15 of the most outstanding cultural sites on the island (plantations, gardens, museums, mills, etc.). Run by the Barbados National Trust, the package offers entrance to all sites for $35, a 50 percent discount from regular admission prices.)

BEST VIEW:

Grenade Hall, a restored 19th century signal station, surrounded by a user-friendly tropical forest, offers the most spectacular panorama of the island.

Historical Sites
Bridgetown

Francia Plantation ★★★

Highway X, St. George, ☎ *(809) 429- 474.*
Hours Open: 10:00 a.m.–4:00 p.m.
This family house, still home to descendants of the original owner, provides an authentic look at old Barbados. Also worth checking out is the Sunbury Plantation Home in St. Philip *(☎ 423-6270),* a 300-year-old home filled with fine antiques. General admission: $4.00.

Gun Hill Signal Station ★★

Highway 4, St. George, ☎ *(809) 429-1358.*
Hours Open: 9:00 a.m.–5:00 p.m.
This 1818 signal station was used by the British Army. Even if you're not into such things, the views from atop the highland are worth the trip. General admission: $4.00.

Old Synagogue ★★★

Synagogue Lane, Bridgetown, ☎ *(809) 426-5792.*
Hours Open: 9:00 a.m.–4:00 p.m.
Built by Jews from Brazil in 1654, the synagogue is the second-oldest in North America. It was partially destroyed by hurricane and rebuilt to its present state in 1833. The grounds include a cemetery, still used today, with graves of early Jewish settlers from as far back as the 1630s. Free admission.

Morgan Lewis Sugar Windmill

Highway 2, St. Andrew, ☎ *(809) 426-2421.*
Hours Open: 9:00 a.m.–5:00 p.m.
This historic spot provides a fine example of the windmills used to process sugarcane in the 17th-19th centuries. Nice views of the "Scotland District." General admission: $2.50.

St. Nicholas Abbey ★★★

Cherry Tree Hill, St. Peter, ☎ *(809) 422-8725.*
Hours Open: 10:00 a.m.–3:30 p.m.
This is Barbados' oldest structure, dating back to 1650, though it was actually an abbey only in the mind of a former owner, who dubbed it so in the 1800s. Two hundred acres of sugarcane surround the Jacobean-style great house of wood and stone. General admission: $2.50.

Museums and Exhibits

Barbados Museum ★★★★

St. Ann's Garrison, St. Michael, ☎ *(809) 427- 201.*
Hours Open: 9:00 a.m.–5:00 p.m.
This unusually fine museum, housed in a former military prison, traces the island's history from prehistoric times to the present. Good exhibits on natural history, West Indian maps and arts and the slave trade. The grounds also include a decent gift shop and an excellent cafe. General admission: $5.00.

Parks and Gardens
Bridgetown

Welchman Hall Gully ★★★

Highway 2, St. Thomas, ☎ *(809) 438-6671.*
Hours Open: 9:00 a.m.–5:00 p.m.
A peaceful oasis owned by the Barbados National Trust, with acres of labeled trees and flowers, and possibly even a green monkey. The breadfruit trees are said to be descended from seeds brought by Captain Bligh. General admission: $5.00.

St. Peter

Andromeda Gardens ★★★

Bathsheba, St. Joseph, ☎ *(809) 433-9261.*
Hours Open: 9:00 a.m.–5:00 p.m.
This unique spot encompasses eight acres of gardens set into oceanfront cliffs. The emphasis is on unusual plants from around the world, and they have those aplenty, plus hundreds of orchids, hibiscus and palm varieties—plus a babbling brook winding throughout. General admission: $5.00.

Farley Hill ★★★★

Farley Hill, St. Peter.
Hours Open: 8:30 a.m.–6:00 p.m.
Very rugged grounds and the ruins of a once-grand plantation house mark this picturesque national park. General admission: $2.00.

Flower Forest ★★★

Highway 2, St. Joseph, ☎ *(809) 433-8152.*

Hours Open: 9:00 a.m.–5:00 p.m.
Set on an old sugar plantation in the scenic Scotland District, this park encompasses eight acres of flowering trees and shrubs. Great views of Mt. Hillaby, too. General admission: $6.00.

Tours
Bridgetown

Atlantis Submarines Barbados   ★★★★★

McGregor Street, Bridgetown, ☎ *(809) 436-8929.*
Hours Open: 9:00 a.m.–6:00 p.m.
The perfect way to see the world below, without getting wet, is aboard an Atlantis submarine, which takes its passengers in air-conditioned comfort some 150 feet beneath the water's surface. The two-hour tour includes the sighting of a shipwreck. Recommended for everyone but the claustrophobic. General admission: $70.00.

Harrison's Cave   ★★★★★

Highway 2, St. Thomas, ☎ *(809) 438-6640.*
Hours Open: 9:00 a.m.–4:00 p.m.
This is the island's biggest tourist attraction, and rightfully so, as these limestone caverns are unique to the Caribbean. Better yet, it's all tastefully done with discreet lighting that preserves the feel of the place. Don a hard hat (more for drama than necessity) and ride an electric tram through the immense caverns, which come complete with waterfalls and streams. Reservations are recommended. General admission: $8.00.

Jolly Roger Cruises   ★★★★

Shallow Draft, Bridgetown, ☎ *(809) 436-2149.*
Lots of options for multihour cruises, including the Bajan Queen, a Mississippi riverboat replica that is the largest cruise ship of its kind and the only one offering sit-down dining. There are also two very fun pirate frigate replicas that offer snorkel trips and general merrymaking. Prices start at $52.50 and include transport from your hotel.

St. Peter

Animal Flower Cave   ★★★

Highway 1B, North Point, ☎ *(809) 439-8797.*
Hours Open: 9:00 a.m.–4:00 p.m.
The cavern takes its name from the small sea anemones that prettily open their tentacles, but don't expect to see too many nowadays. General admission: $1.50.

Barbados Wildlife Preserve   ★★★★

Highway 1, St. Peter, ☎ *(809) 422-8826.*
Hours Open: 10:00 a.m.–5:00 p.m.
This walk-through preserve, essentially a monkey sanctuary run by the Barbados Primate Research Center, features free-roaming land turtles, peacocks, parrots—even a kangaroo. They also have good exhibits on the island's natural history and an interesting walk-in aviary. General admission: $10.00.

Where the Rum Comes From   ★★★★

Pick up from your hotel, St. Peter.

The wonderful world of rum is the focus of this tour, held each Wednesday from 12:00–2:15 p.m. You'll tour Cockspur, manufacturers of Barbadian rum for more than 200 years, then sip the potable and groove to a steel band while supping on a buffet meal. General admission: $28.00.

Sports

Barbados is a perfect island for surf and turf sports. Hiking, as sponsored by the Barbados National Trust and the Duke of Edinburgh's Award Scheme, has nearly become a national pastime on Sunday mornings from January-May when group treks are arranged, according to skill and endurance. (For more information, see "Treks" above.) Horseback riders can enjoy a variety of trails through tropical forests; one spectacular ride is the 3-4 hour tour of the Villa Nova Plantation, which includes a hearty lunch. Tennis courts can be found at most of the major hotels, and there are usually facilities for night-playing.

Conditions for all watersports in Barbados rank among the finest in the Caribbean, especially windsurfing, which takes advantage of the sturdy trade winds between November and May and the shallow offshore reef off Silver Sands. Deep-sea fishermen have raved about the variety of barracuda, sailfish, marlin and wahoo. Resort certification in scuba can be arranged through **Sandy Beach Watersports**; do check out their most recent scuba-holiday packages. Snorkeling is also favorable, especially in **Folkstone Underwater Park**, where visibility can range up to 100 feet most of the year.

Pemberton Resort's new **Royal Westmoreland Golf and Country Club**, is presently building a $30 million dollar, 27-hole course over 500 acres in the hills overlooking the two adjacent Pemberton hotels—Royal Pavilion and Glitter Bay. Sandy Lane also updated their course and opened an international golfing school in 1993. The Barbados government has approved five more courses on the island's south coast.

Bridgetown

Dive Shop, The

Aquatic Gap, St. Michael, ☎ *(809) 426-9947.*
Hours Open: 8:30 a.m.–4:30 p.m.
They offer great scuba excursions to colorful reefs and wrecks, with prices starting at $40 per one-tank dive. Beginners can take a resort course for $50, and deep-sea fishers can arrange a charter for $300 per boat per half-day.

Christ Church

Barbados Windsurfing Club

Silver Sands Hotel, Christ Church, ☎ *(809) 428-6001.*

Rent a windboard for $20 an hour, $40 per half day, or partake in a lesson to learn this challenging sport.

Fun Seekers, Inc.

78 Old Chancery Lane, Christ Church, ☎ *(809) 435-9171.*

You can rent motorbikes or bicycles here, or better yet, partake of a cruise aboard the 44-foot Limbo Lady. Lunch cruises cost $50 and include snorkeling; sunset sails are $40. They'll pick you up at your hotel if need be.

St. Peter

Caribbean International Riding

Auburn, St. Joseph, ☎ *(809) 433-1453.*
Hours Open: 7:30 a.m.–6:00 p.m.

Trail rides on handsome horses range from a 75-minute jaunt ($28) to a three-hour tour of the historic Villa Nova Plantation, complete with lunch, for $88.

Heywoods Golf Course

St. Peter, ☎ *(809) 422-4900.*

Only guests of the Almond Beach Village can golf at this nine-hole, par-three course. Fees are $35, and if the mood suits you, you can go around twice without paying for the privilege.

Sandy Lane Golf Course

Sandy Lane Hotel, St. James, ☎ *(809) 432-1311.*

This is the island's best, an 18-hole championship course with a famed 7th hole that has an elevated tee and wonderful views. Greens fees are $120 for $18 holes, $90 for nine.

Where to Stay

Highest Rated Hotels in Barbados

★★★★★ **Glitter Bay**

★★★★★ **Royal Pavilion**

★★★★★ **Sandy Lane Hotel**

★★★★ **Barbados Hilton**

★★★★ **Cobblers Cove Hotel**

★★★★ **Coral Reef Club**

★★★★ **Marriott's Sam Lord's**

★★★★ **Sandals Barbados**

★★★★ **Sandpiper Inn**

★★★ **Almond Beach Club**

Most Exclusive Hotels in Barbados

★★★★★ **Sandy Lane Hotel**	$500–$955
★★★ **Tamarind Cove Hotel**	$280–$640
★★★ **Colony Club Hotel**	$271–$480
★★★ **Haywoods Wyndham**	$185–$535
★★★ **Almond Beach Club**	$259–$395

Fielding's Best Value Hotels in Barbados

★★★ **Casuarina Beach Club**	$80–$165
★★★★ **Barbados Hilton**	$149–$201
★★ **Sea Breeze Beach Hotel**	$45–$245
★★ **Sand Acres Beach Club**	$75–$125
★★ **Sandridge Beach Hotel**	$60–$195

Accommodations in Barbados range from the fabulously chic (villas with private pools, sprawling resorts, beachfront mansions built like a fort) to inexpensive rooms in simple hotels with basic amenities. Since brochures don't always do justice (or too much justice!) to properties, do your best to learn everything you can before making a reservation. If you're seeking high fashion, **St. James Beach** is where you'll want to roost; lesser budgets should try the studio apartments in Hastings and Worthing in the south. The best bargains for the best price are small inns run intimately by live-in managers; look for these in "The Inns" section. Unfortunately prices during high season soar skyward due to the high demand, but great bargains can be found in off-season.

For easy booking, take advantage (or ask your travel agent to) of a central reservation service operated by the Barbados Hotel Association; first call toll-free ☎ *800-462-2526* or *800-GO-BAJAN.*

Hotels and Resorts

Barbados' hotels are among the poshest in the Caribbean and resorts like the Royal Pavilion, and Sandy Lane compete with the world's best while Treasure Beach perhaps boasts the most repeat visitors. Like everything else in Barbados, many hotels have been renovated in recent years to gleaming effect. The **Coral Reef Club** and the **Sandpiper Inn** have gotten facelifts. The Moorish-style **Tamarind Cove** has added new suites, shops, and a classy seafood restaurant. The first all-inclusive resort, once called Pineapple Beach Club, now the **Almond Beach Club**, features one of the best authentic Bajan restaurants, **Enid's**, as well as upgraded fitness facilities and an "All-inclusive Plus" program.

A new **Concorde** charter service package now offers a two-hour flight from JFK Airport on a Concorde and an 8 day/7-night package in one of 15 luxury hotels. Prices range from $2800–$5500. For more information call ETM Travel Group at ☎ *203-454-0090,* or toll-free *(800) 992-7700.* This is a fine (and easy!) deal for honeymooners since most of the finer resort hotels also offer on-staff consultation for wedding arrangements.

Bridgetown

Barbados Hilton   **$149–$201**   ★★★★

Needhams Point, St. Michael, ☎ *(800) 445-8667, (809) 426- 200.*
Single: $149–$184. Double: $161–$201.

A good, safe choice—but don't expect a lot of Caribbean flavor at this hotel. Surrounded by nice beaches and near an oil refinery that sometimes produces pungent odors, this spot has all the modern conveniences you'd expect from a Hilton—plus lots of conventioneers running around in name tags. The pool is excellent but for unknown reasons closes at 6:00 p.m. There's a health club and tennis courts on site, as well as an old British Fort for exploring. Accommodations are fine and the service is professional. 184 rooms. Credit Cards: V, MC.

Coconut Creek Club Hotel   **$240–$350**   ★★★

St. James Street, Bridgetown, ☎ *(800) 462-2566, (809) 432- 803.*
Single: $240–$310. Double: $280–$350.

Set amid beautifully landscaped grounds, this very private resort attracts lots of European celebrities. Accommodations, in Spanish-style cottages, are small but very clean and chic, with tropical decor, air conditioning, and walk-in closets. They sit on a low bluff overlooking two quite secluded beaches that almost disappear during high tide. Somehow, Coconut Creek manages to be both informal and sophisticated, and the service is outstanding. 53 rooms. Credit Cards: V, MC, A.

Colony Club Hotel   **$271–$480**   ★ ★ ★

St. James Street, Bridgetown, ☎ (800) 466-2526, (809) 422-2335.
Single: $271–$371. Double: $300–$480.

A simple but gracious resort lining one of Barbados' best beaches, Colony Club puts guests up in Mediterranean-style bungalows with private patios and the usual amenities. TVs can be rented for those who can't go without. Watersports are complimentary, as is the shuttle that runs guests into town. A nice, quiet spot that appeals mainly to travelers from England. 76 rooms. Credit Cards: V, MC, A.

Ginger Bay Beach Club   **$80–$205**   ★ ★ ★

Crane, St. Philip, ☎ (800) 466-2526, (809) 423-5810.
Single: $80–$205. Double: $80–$205.

Situated on a small bluff overlooking one of Barbados' best beaches, Ginger Bay is a lovely property, but its remote location is not for everyone. All accommodations are in spacious one-bedroom suites with kitchens, modern baths and canopied king beds. They open onto private terraces complete with hammocks—a nice touch. The beach is reached via a staircase though a cave. Except for a pool and tennis court, there's not much happening here, but beach lovers are kept happy. 16 rooms. Credit Cards: V, MC, DC, A.

Grand Barbados Beach   **$125–$605**   ★ ★ ★

Aquatic Gap, St. Michael, ☎ (800) 466-2526, (809) 426- 890.
Single: $125–$605. Double: $135–$605.

Set on Carlisle Bay, one mile from Bridgetown, this sophisticated hotel does big business with leisure as well as business travelers, who like the full-service amenities lacking at many other island resorts. Guest rooms are small but modern and come equipped with the usual creature comforts, including air and satellite TV. The pool is too small if everyone decides to partake, but the beach is nice and surprisingly quiet given its near-city locale. All watersports are free, including sailing. The long pier adds atmosphere. 133 rooms. Credit Cards: V, MC, DC, A.

Marriott's Sam Lord's   **$110–$225**   ★ ★ ★ ★

St. Philip, ☎ (800) 228-9290, (809) 423-5918.
Single: $110–$225. Double: $110–$225.

Marriott's Sam Lord's Castle takes its name from the 1820 great house built by Samuel Hall Lord, known as the "Regency Rascal" for his penchant for tricking ships to his jagged shore, then looting the smashed cargo. Today's resort is set among 72 acres with formal gardens and all the resort amenities you'd expect from a fine Marriott property. Accommodations are quite varied; choose a cottage if budget permits. All runs smoothly, but the overabundance of conventioneers can leave individual travelers feeling forgotten and overwhelmed. 234 rooms. Credit Cards: V, MC, DC, A.

Sandals Barbados   **$105–$335**   ★ ★ ★ ★

Black Rock, St. Michael, ☎ *(800) 726-3257, (809) 424- 888.*
Single: $105–$235. Double: $125–$335.

A complete overhaul has left Sandals looking shiny and spiffy. This all-inclusive resort, open only to heterosexual couples, provides all meals, drinks and recreational diversions in one price. The activity is there for the taking—those who would rather leave it may be happier at a less-organized resort. Everything you'd ever want to do is there for the asking, and guests work frantically to earn a tiny pair of sandals to show what good sports they are. Lots of honeymooners. 178 rooms. Credit Cards: V, MC, A.

Christ Church

Benston Windsurfing Hotel   **$50–$70**   ★

Maxwell, Christ Church, ☎ *(809) 428-9095.*
Single: $50–$70. Double: $55–$70.

You know the windsurfing's gotta be good if an entire (albeit small) hotel is dedicated to it. Those staying at this basic property are devoted to the sport, and, as such, are generally young and lively. Accommodations are spacious but bare-bones; everyone's always out zipping along the surf, anyway. They'll teach you how to do it, but most who come here are already pretty darn good. 15 rooms. Credit Cards: V, MC, DC, A.

Caribbee Beach Hotel   **$60–$105**   ★ ★

Hastings, Christ Church, ☎ *(800) 466-2526, (809) 436-6232.*
Single: $60–$90. Double: $65–$105.

There's no beach at this beach hotel, just the ocean slamming into a seawall. Oh well . . . the rates are low, though they probably should be even lower. Rooms are air-conditioned and furnished in basic motel style. The absence of both a beach and a pool make other budget properties a better choice. 55 rooms. Credit Cards: V, MC, DC, A.

Divi Southwinds Resort   **$115–$245**   ★ ★

St. Lawrence Gap, Christ Church, ☎ *(800) 367-3484, (809) 428-8076.*
Single: $115–$245. Double: $115–$245.

Set on 20 acres, this resort partially lines the beach, though most of the complex is inland. Accommodations, in white stucco buildings, are mostly suites with full kitchens, living areas, air conditioning and attractive tropical furnishings. For fun, there are two tennis courts, two pools and a private beach. Lots of entertainment attracts a clientele of mostly young families. 160 rooms. Credit Cards: V, MC, DC, A.

Southern Palms   **$69–$265**   ★ ★ ★

St. Lawrence Gap, Christ Church, ☎ *(800) 466-2526, (809) 428-7171.*
Single: $69–$265. Double: $94–$265.

Set on six acres surrounding an old plantation-style manor house, Southern Palms attracts a fun-loving set. The resort sprawls with a variety of buildings of different influence, including Italian, Spanish and West Indian styles. Lots of organized activities keep guests busy, from miniature golf tournaments to steel band dances. All the usual watersports are free, and accommodations are pleasant. 92 rooms. Credit Cards: V, MC, DC, A.

St. Peter

Almond Beach Club   **$259–$395**   ★★★

Vauxhall, St. James, ☎ *(809) 432-7840.*
Single: $259–$295. Double: $305–$395.
This all-inclusive resort is refreshingly free of pressure to join in activities, but if you're game, there's a slew of stuff going on, from island tours to shopping trips to watersports. Half the accommodations are in one-bedroom suites with island decor. The grounds include three pools, tennis and squash, and lots of dining options. The beach is narrow and not great for swimming, but better ones are close by. 147 rooms. Credit Cards: V, MC, DC, A.

Barbados Beach Village   **$100–$335**   ★★

Fitt's Village, St. James, ☎ *(800) 462-2426, (809) 425-1440.*
Single: $100–$335. Double: $110–$335.
Set on a sandy beach, this complex includes a mix of standard rooms and deluxe units with living areas, kitchens and separate bedrooms; all have motel-like furnishings, air conditioning and high ceilings. Typical resort recreational diversions are offered, though maintenance and service can be shoddy. 88 rooms. Credit Cards: V, MC, DC, A.

Buccaneer Bay Hotel   **$90–$330**   ★★★

Paynes Bay, St. James, ☎ *(809) 432-7981.*
Single: $90–$200. Double: $200–$330.
Set on one of the best beaches on the west coast, this small hotel has large air-conditioned rooms with refrigerators, toasters and tea kettles, plus TV sets on request. The pool has a swim-up bar but other diversions, such as watersports, are lacking, though they can be arranged nearby. 29 rooms. Credit Cards: V, MC, A.

Cobblers Cove Hotel   **$135–$625**   ★★★★

Road View, St. Peter, ☎ *(800) 223-6510, (809) 422-2291.*
Single: $135–$625. Double: $135–$625.
Built on the site of a former British fort, this lovely and intimate all-suite hotel keeps guests pampered, earning its reputation as one of the island's finest resorts. Suites are nicely decorated and come with kitchenettes. The lush tropical grounds include a tennis court, pool and nice beach. If you're up for splurging, book the Camelot Suite, fit for a king with marble floors, its own small pool and a spiral staircase leading to a private sundeck. 39 rooms. Credit Cards: MC.

Coral Reef Club   **$74–$250**   ★★★★

St. James Beach, St. James, ☎ *(800) 525-4800, (809) 422-2372.*
Single: $74–$134. Double: $117–$250.
Small cottages with spacious accommodations are scattered about the nicely landscaped grounds here at Coral Reef, one of Barbados' best bets. Flawlessly run by the O'Hara family—which does indeed give a damn—the grounds are lushly maintained and the beach is terrific, attracting a loyal following. All rooms come equipped with refrigerators, hair dryers, a small library of paperbacks and air condi-

tioning. Most watersports are free, and tennis courts are a short stroll away. 71 rooms. Credit Cards: V, MC, A.

Discovery Bay Hotel   **$120–$375**   ★★★

Holetown, St. James, ☎ *(800) 466-2526, (809) 432-1301.*
Single: $120–$375. Double: $170–$375.

This plantation-style hotel, set on four tropical acres, consists of two-story structures around an attractive courtyard. Accommodations are spacious and modern, though the air conditioning doesn't always keep up. There's also a three-bedroom villa for those who don't mind splurging. The grounds include watersports (most free), two tennis courts, a pool and a windsurfing school. The welcome drink you receive on arrival portends the excellent, friendly service. A good choice in the price range. 85 rooms. Credit Cards: V, MC, A.

Glitter Bay   **$200–$325**   ★★★★★

Porter's, St. James, ☎ *(800) 283-8666, (809) 422-4111.*
Single: $200–$325. Double: $200–$325.

This refined beachfront resort, which sports an impressive Great House as its centerpiece, is top-drawer in every aspect. All accommodations are in suites set among beautifully landscaped grounds, and include air conditioning, marble baths, bidets, kitchenettes, living rooms and great views. The large free-form pool comes complete with waterfall, and the two tennis courts are in top condition. All watersports are complimentary, and guests can partake of the facilities at the Royal Pavilion next door. Luxury all the way! 81 rooms. Credit Cards: V, MC, DC, A.

Haywoods Wyndham   **$185–$535**   ★★★

Highway 1, St. Peter, ☎ *(800) 822-4200, (809) 422-4900.*
Single: $185–$535. Double: $185–$535.

Located on the island's west coast on 32 tropically landscaped acres, Haywoods consists of seven buildings of various architectural influence. Reviews are mixed: some say it's grand, others say it's a legend only in its own mind. All agree that the service could use improvement, but that the wealth of recreational activities—free use of the nine-hole golf course, air-conditioned squash, three pools, five lighted tennis courts, great beach—helps take out the sting. Judge for yourself. 288 rooms. Credit Cards: V, MC, DC, A.

King's Beach Hotel   **$105–$245**   ★★

Road View, St. Peter, ☎ *(800) 466-2526, (809) 422-1690.*
Single: $105–$245. Double: $105–$245.

This Spanish-style beachfront hotel does a good business with families, with a playground and kid's club wooing the younger set. Guest rooms are air-conditioned and sport TVs and minibars as well as floor-to-ceiling windows affording great views. All the usual watersports, plus a pool and tennis court, round out the action. 57 rooms. Credit Cards: V, MC, A.

Royal Pavilion   **$235–$330**   ★★★★★

Porters, St. James, ☎ *(800) 283-8666, (809) 422-5555.*
Single: $235–$330. Double: $235–$330.

This elegant Mediterranean-style enclave is Barbados' best, with gorgeous grounds and excellent accommodations, all in junior suites with marble floors, lovely furnishings and lots of perks. Virtually all have ocean views. Use of the two lighted tennis courts and watersports is complimentary, as are afternoon tea and occasional evening cocktails. The beach is fine. Guests can use facilities at the neighboring Glitter Bay, which is a bit more informal. Those opting for the Royal Pavilion are indeed treated like royalty. Wonderful! 75 rooms. Credit Cards: V, MC, DC, A.

Sandpiper Inn $110–$445   ★ ★ ★ ★

St. James Beach, St. James, ☎ *(800) 223-1108, (809) 422-2251.*
Single: $110–$141. Double: $285–$445.
There's a real island feel to this charming hotel, set right on the beach among coconut trees. Accommodations are in suites with kitchens, one or two bedrooms, air conditioning and nice local artwork. Two lighted tennis courts, a pool and free watersports (except skiing, which costs extra) round out the picture. 45 rooms. Credit Cards: V, MC, A.

Sandy Lane Hotel $500–$955   ★ ★ ★ ★ ★

St. James, ☎ *(800) 223-6800, (809) 432-1311.*
Single: $500–$955. Double: $500–$955.
Luxury doesn't come cheap here, but it's worth every hard-earned cent to retreat to Sandy Lane, one of the island's best choices. A recent refurbishment has put this place back on top, and all is impeccable. Accommodations are lovely with antique and local-style furnishings and lots of extras. There are all the usual watersports and complimentary golf on 18 holes. Lots of old money and Britains here, and while the service befits the rates, the atmosphere can be a tad snooty. Casual types will be happier (and spend lots less) elsewhere. 121 rooms. Credit Cards: V, MC, DC, A.

Tamarind Cove Hotel $280–$640   ★ ★ ★

St. James, ☎ *(800) 466-2526, (809) 422-1726.*
Single: $280–$490. Double: $320–$640.
Classic Spanish architecture marks this romantic beachfront resort, which is nestled among coconut trees and coral sands. Guest rooms and suites are very nice; the newer suites have Roman tubs and bidets. Three pools, once complete with waterfall, enhance the grounds. All watersports are free, including sailing and skiing. There's lots of nightlife here, including a Barbadian revue and boisterous barbecues. 116 rooms. Credit Cards: V, MC, A.

Treasure Beach Hotel $155–$445   ★ ★ ★

Paynes Bay, St. James, ☎ *(800) 466-2526, (809) 432-1346.*
Single: $155–$445. Double: $155–$445.
This small hotel is set on a nice coral beach, but its small grounds and tiny pool are definite drawbacks. Nevertheless, the hotel has a very loyal following and lots of repeat visitors. Accommodations are in suites (but lack kitchens) and are very nicely done with tropical art and furnishings; toasters and kettles are available on request. Request a unit on an upper floor for more privacy. 26 rooms. Credit Cards: V, MC, DC, A.

Apartments and Condominiums

Noting the uneven supply and demand for Barbados accommodations, local businessmen have turned to building apartments and renovating private homes that suit many different lifestyles. Depending on your budget, you can choose to stay in a private home worthy of an exiled contessa or in a small, inexpensive apartment. A three-bedroom property on the west coast, on the beach but without sultanic amenities, could run $1500-$3000 a week in high season; $950-$2000 off season. Many homes come with built-in household help who often act quite proprietary. If you do your own cooking, stock the larder with provisions form **Eddie's and Jordan's**, supermarkets located in Speightstown. They offer nearly everything you're used to along with interesting local products like a fiery hot yellow sauce, which makes a great gift to take home.

Christ Church

Casuarina Beach Club $80–$165 ★★★

St. Lawrence Gap, Christ Church, ☎ *(809) 428-3600.*
Single: $80–$165. Double: $80–$165.
Set on seven acres of tropical palms and shrubs, this family hotel has air-conditioned studios and apartments of one or two bedrooms, all with kitchenettes and spiffy accessories. Resort-style amenities include two tennis courts, squash, an Olympic-size pool, a few bars and a restaurant. Nice beach, too. 129 rooms. Credit Cards: V, MC, A.

Club Rockley Barbados $180–$535 ★★

Worthing, Christ Church, ☎ *(800) 462-2526, (809) 435-4880.*
Single: $180–$535. Double: $180–$535.
This condominium resort consists of modest townhouses set along the fairway of a nine-hole golf course, in a predominantly residential neighborhood. Units come with one or two bedrooms, kitchens, air conditioning and uninspired decor. The grounds are extensive, with seven pools, five tennis courts, lawn games and two air-conditioned squash courts. A shuttle runs guests to a private beach club every half hour when the usual water diversions are available, included in the all-inclusive package. 108 rooms. Credit Cards: V, MC, DC, A.

Half Moon Beach Hotel $75–$215 ★★

St. Lawrence Gap, Christ Church, ☎ *(800) 466-2526, (809) 428-7131.*
Single: $75–$215. Double: $90–$215.
Set on tropical Dover Beach, this small complex consists of one- and two-bedroom apartments with kitchens and modern furnishings. There's a pool and restaurant on-site, but not much else, though the friendly staff and reasonable rates make Half Moon worth a look if you're on a budget. 36 rooms. Credit Cards: V, MC, A.

Sand Acres Beach Club $75–$125 ★★

Maxwell Coast Road, Christ Church, ☎ *(800) 466-2526, (809) 428-7141.*
Single: $75–$125. Double: $75–$125.
Accommodations at this beachfront property are in studios or one-bedroom apartments with kitchens. The grounds include a simple restaurant, standard pool and a beach bar, as well as one tennis court and watersports for an additional fee. The beach is nice, but service can be harried. 37 rooms. Credit Cards: V, MC, A.

Sea Breeze Beach Hotel $45–$245 ★★

Maxwell Coast Road, Christ Church, ☎ *(800) 822-7223, (809) 428-2825.*
Single: $45–$245. Double: $50–$245.

Located on two secluded beaches, this apartment complex has air-conditioned studios with kitchenettes and balconies overlooking gardens or the beach. There are also three 2 bedroom units for those who need the space. Two restaurants and a pool complete the scene. 60 rooms. Credit Cards: V, MC, DC, A.

Sea Foam Haciendas   **$70–$93**   ★★

Worthing, Christ Church, ☎ *(800) 822-7223, (809) 435-7380.*
Single: $70–$93. Double: $70–$93.
Very comfortable two-bedroom apartments with kitchens, living/dining areas, air conditioning and full maid service. Many sport nice ocean views, and watersports are available. No restaurant on site, but several nearby. 12 rooms. Credit Cards: V, MC.

Woodville Beach Apartments   **$47–$129**   ★★★

Hastings, Christ Church, ☎ *(800) 466-2526, (809) 435-9211.*
Single: $47–$129. Double: $47–$129.
Accommodations at this oceanfront complex range from studios to one- and two-bedroom units, each with full but tiny kitchens, though only some have air conditioning. They are rather spartan, but clean and comfortable. The beach is quite rocky and recommended only for strong swimmers; better bathing is found at Rockley Beach, a five-minute walk. 28 rooms. Credit Cards: Not Accepted.

Yellow Bird Apartments   **$55–$105**   ★

St. Lawrence Bay, Christ Church, ☎ *(809) 435-8444.*
Single: $55–$105. Double: $65–$105.
Situated across the street from the bay and a small beach, this apartment complex offers air-conditioned studios with full kitchens and ocean-view balconies. There's a poolside bar and restaurant, but little else in the way of extras. 21 rooms. Credit Cards: V, MC, A.

St. Peter

Asta Apartment Hotel   **$50–$235**   ★★

Palm Beach, Hastings, ☎ *(800) 466-2526, (809) 427-2541.*
Single: $50–$235. Double: $50–$235.
Studios and apartments of one and two bedrooms offer guests the option of cooking in to save money. (There's also a restaurant on-site and several within walking distance when you tire of your own fare.) There's a pool on the grounds but little else, as reflected in the rates. One nice extra: the maid does the dishes. 60 rooms. Credit Cards: V, MC, A.

Beachcomber Apartments   **$80–$300**   ★★

Paynes Bay, St. James, ☎ *(809) 432- 489.*
Single: $80–$195. Double: $155–$300.
Basic apartments are air-conditioned and come in studios or one- or two-bedroom configurations. Though they call themselves luxury apartments that may be stretching it. No pool or restaurant on-site, but the beach is nice and maid service is available. 9 rooms. Credit Cards: V, MC.

Sandridge Beach Hotel   **$60–$195**   ★★

Roadview, St. Peter, ☎ *(800) 466-2526, (809) 422-2361.*
Single: $60–$195. Double: $70–$195.

This apartment hotel has studios and one-bedroom units with air conditioning, kitchenettes and TV rentals. There's a pool and restaurant, plus complimentary watersports, including free glass-bottom boat rides. A good choice for families. 52 rooms. Credit Cards: V, MC, A.

Settler's Beach Hotel   **$555–$705**   ★★★

Holetown, St. James, ☎ *(800) 466-2526, (809) 422-3052.*
Single: $555–$705. Double: $555–$705.

Accommodations are in bi-level townhouses or cottages, each with large living/dining areas, kitchens, two bedrooms and spacious terraces; all are sunny and colorfully decorated. The lush grounds include a small pool, access to two tennis courts and a restaurant. Kids under 18 stay free, so expect to see lots of families. 22 rooms. Credit Cards: V, MC, A.

Sugar Cane Club   **$40–$85**   ★★

Maynards, St. Peter, ☎ *(809) 422-5046.*
Single: $40–$85. Double: $40–$85.

Located in a remote region on a hilltop overlooking the Caribbean, the small hotel offers studios and apartments with modern touches like air conditioning and color TV. There's a bar and restaurant on-site, as well as a pool, sauna and putting green. Nothing too exciting, but at those rates, it doesn't have to be. 23 rooms. Credit Cards: V, MC, DC, A.

Inns

The best inns in Barbados offer an intimate, relaxing escape from the bustle of top-class resorts and package deals. The most attractive are housed in buildings that date back to the 18th and 19th century. Furnishings are more often than not simple, but views, like those from the **Kingsley Club**, sometimes rate as stupendous. **Bagshot House's** charm is its down-home congeniality, while **Sugar Cane Club** is best if you're seeking total peace and quiet.

Bridgetown

Island Inn   **$130–$230**   ★★★

Aquatic Gap, St. Michael, ☎ *(800) 743-4276, (809) 436-6393.*
Single: $130–$170. Double: $180–$230.

This intimate all-inclusive resort, housed in an 1804 former rum store for the British Regiment, has lovely guest rooms for those who like modern luxury (all rooms are air-conditioned, for example) combined with historic charm. Accommodations are situated around a picturesque courtyard with gurgling fountains, and include Persian rugs, limestone brick walls and white rattan furniture. The all-inclusive rates include such extras as picnic baskets and a two-hour cruise. Nice! 23 rooms. Credit Cards: V, MC, DC, A.

Christ Church

Ocean View Hotel   **$34–$71**   ★★★

Hastings, Christ Church, ☎ *(809) 427-7871.*
Single: $34–$44. Double: $55–$71.

Don't be put off by the faded exterior along a busy street; the Ocean View's considerable charms lie within. This is Barbados' oldest hotel, dating back to 1898, and if you don't mind forgoing modern conveniences, a stay here will live on in your memory. Guest rooms are individually decorated with a decidedly funky slant, with lots of genuine antiques mixing with the merely old. Tropical flowers add to the ambience. This special spot is not for everyone, but well loved by those who appreciate its unique flair. 35 rooms. Credit Cards: V, MC, A.

Seaview Hotel   **$95–$305**   ★★

Hastings Main Road, Christ Church, ☎ *(809) 426-1450.*
Single: $95–$305. Double: $95–$305.

Housed in a historic building from 1776, the Seaview is one of Barbados' oldest hotels. Rooms are air-conditioned and decorated in a faux-Georgian style that meshes nicely with the high ceilings and shuttered windows. The grounds include a small pool, tennis and squash. A bit overpriced for what you get. 25 rooms. Credit Cards: V, MC, A.

St. Peter

Kingsley Club   **$85–$106**   ★★

St. Joseph, ☎ *(809) 433-9422.*
Single: $85–$97. Double: $89–$106.

This remote and peaceful spot appeals to Barbadians and those who savor a true island experience. Rooms in the historic house are simple but clean, and the views are spectacular. It's best not to attempt the very strong surf, although the beach is glorious. 7 rooms. Credit Cards: V, MC, A.

Low Cost Lodging
Christ Church

Fairholme   **$35–$65**   ★

Maxwell, Christ Church, ☎ *(809) 428-9425.*
Single: $35–$65. Double: $35–$65.

A combination of hotel and apartment complex, the Fairholme consists of a converted plantation house that holds standard guest rooms and 20 Spanish-style studio apartments with air conditioning. There's a restaurant, bar and pool, but little else. Still, it's hard to beat the rates. 31 rooms. Credit Cards: Not Accepted.

Where to Eat

Highest Rated Restaurants in Barbados

★★★★ **Bagatelle Great House**

★★★★ **Carambola**

★★★★ **David's Place**

★★★★ **Ile de France**

★★★★ **La Cage aux Folles**

★★★★ **Pisces**

★★★★ **Raffles Old Towne**

★★★★ **The Fathoms**

★★★ **Brown Sugar**

★★★ **Josef's**

Most Exclusive Restaurants in Barbados

★★★ **Josef's**	$25–$40
★★★ **La Maison**	$23–$40
★★★ **Reid's**	$21–$40
★★★★ **Carambola**	$20–$40
★★★★ **Pisces**	$15–$30

Fielding's Best Value Restaurants in Barbados

★★★ **Reid's**	$21–$40
★★★ **Josef's**	$25–$40
★★★★ **Bagatelle Great House**	$30–$35
★★★★ **Carambola**	$20–$40
★★★ **Brown Sugar**	$10–$25

Barbados' restaurants are world-class, and can hold their own against any international cuisine.

Bajan cooking blends the ethnic influences of the British colonists, the Arawak Indians in residence on the island at the time of their arrival, and the African slaves imported between 1640 and 1807.

Flying fish—boiled, baked, stewed, fried, steamed or stuffed—is the island specialty, available on many menus. One of the hotspots is **La Maison**, tucked inside an old coral-stone Bajan house where the red snapper marinated in herbs and honey is reportedly sublime.

Wine bars and tapas are now the rage in Barbados. Tapas fanatics should head for the **Waterfront Café** in a restored coral-limestone warehouse on Bridgetown's inner harbor, where the young and gorgeous chow down on "fish-melts" (batter-fried flying fish roe) and lime squash while listening to great jazz. Lunch is also good since the view of the bay is spectacular.

Among the most romantic spots are **Carambola**, on the west coast (do catch the sunset) and **The Mews** on the Gold Coast, where you can dine on the patio under a starry sky or inside the white stucco house brimming with tropical plants. Even more romantic is **Reid's**, a St. Peter restaurant with open sides that overlook manicured gardens filled with fountains and singing tree frogs called *coquis*.

Do stop by the supermarket and check out the huge variety of island spices. You'll also discover nine different brands of *mauby*, the local sugar-and-tree bark drink. Hot sauce addicts can choose from at least 12 different brands of local brew made from scotch-bonnet peppers, mustard, garlic, scallions and spices; visitors have been known to chug home a gallon or two.

Bridgetown

Bagatelle Great House	**$$$**	★ ★ ★ ★

Highway 2A, St. Thomas Parish, ☎ *(809) 421-6767.*
French cuisine.
Dinner: 7:00 p.m.–9:30 p.m., entrees $30–$35.

Diners too timid to experience the vibrant street scene on the Baxter Road, an open-air market in the heart of Bridgetown where vendors cook fish on hot fires, come to Bagatelle Great House, which duplicates this method with whatever's fresh that day. The restaurant is located within the former residence of the first governor of Barbados, and this is probably one of the island's more elegant dining experiences, with stellar service—though the food is less distinguished than the surroundings. Guests can eat downstairs or on a small terrace one flight above. Closed: Sun. Reservations required. Credit Cards: V, MC, A.

Brown Sugar	**$$$**	★ ★ ★

Aquatic Gap, St. Michael Parish, ☎ *(809) 426-7684.*
Latin American cuisine. Specialties: Flying fish, Creole orange chicken.
Lunch: 12:00 a.m.–2:30 p.m., prix fixe $14–$25.
Dinner: 6:00 p.m.–9:45 p.m., entrees $10–$25.

One of the better values on the islands, and a lovely one to boot, is this lush, terraced, tropical-style restaurant located a few miles south of Bridgetown. Smart businesspeople and others in the know dine here at lunch on weekdays when a West Indian buffet is available for $14.00. There are various soups, salads and stews to choose from, including pepper pot. Other offerings include flying fish, jerk chicken and pork and luscious desserts. Dinner is more of a Continental affair, with international touches added to local ingredients, like the popular Creole orange chicken. Reservations recommended. Credit Cards: V, MC, DC, A.

Carib Beach Bar $$ ★★
Sandy Beach, Worthing,
International cuisine. Specialties: Fish fry, barbecue.
Lunch: 11:30 a.m.–3:00 p.m., entrees $6–$16.
Dinner: 3:00 p.m.–10:00 p.m., entrees $6–$16.
One of a string of economical beach bars that pop up on several locations around the islands, Carib is right on the sand at Sandy Beach, offering fish sandwiches and fresh seafood in a comfortable upstairs restaurant, and potent rum punches in the lower-level bar. Better yet are the Wednesday night fish fries and Friday barbecue buffet, which both start at 7:30 p.m. and cost around $10 for a substantial amount of food. A happening place that stays open fairly late. The restaurant closes at 7:30 on Sundays. Credit Cards: V, MC.

Chicken Barn, The $ ★★
Highway 7, Worthing,
American cuisine. Specialties: Fried chicken.
Lunch: 10:00 a.m.–3:30 p.m., entrees $3–$11.
Dinner: 3:30 p.m.–10:30 p.m., entrees $3–$11.
The Chicken Barn is a convenient quick lunch stop that serves fried chicken and decent burgers for a little over $1. In fact, the Barn is one of a group of inexpensive faster food establishments on Highway 7 not far from Sandy Beach in the town of Worthing, a great place for budget-minded travelers. You can also get salads and fish and chips for under $4. Closed: Sun. Credit Cards: Not Accepted.

Josef's $$$ ★★★
Waverly House, St. Lawrence Gap, ☎ (809) 435-6541.
International cuisine. Specialties: Toast skagen, dolphin meuniere.
Lunch: 12:00 a.m.–2:30 p.m., entrees $10–$13.
Dinner: 6:30 p.m.–9:30 p.m., entrees $25–$40.
Although Austrian chef and restaurateur extraordinaire Josef Schwaiger sold his well-loved namesake restaurant to open two other fashionable spots, the flame has passed splendidly to Swedish chef Nils Ryman. Ryman has kept Josef's more stellar creations on the mostly seafood menu, including the sublime dolphin meuniere, but has added some fine dishes of his own, namely a smorrebrod of shrimp with dill mayonnaise. It might be difficult to snag a dinner reservation, but a weekday lunch is a viable option for a smoked fish or chef's salad. No lunch served on weekends. Reservations required. Credit Cards: V, MC, A.

Waterfront Cafe $$$ ★★
The Careenage, Bridgetown, ☎ (809) 431-0303.

International cuisine.
Lunch: 10:00 a.m.–2:00 p.m., entrees $8–$25.
Dinner: 2:00 p.m.–10:00 p.m., entrees $8–$30.
The Waterfront Cafe is an inexpensive cool-off eatery on the Careenage, a small inlet for light craft. It serves Bajan-inspired quick meals like pepper pot soup, a copious appetizer platter and flying fish interspersed with familiar burgers and English pub food. There's music every evening, usually jazz, and a relaxed bar scene. Seating is either outdoors facing the water or in the dining room. Closed: Sun. Reservations recommended. Credit Cards: V, MC, A.

Christ Church

Da Luciano's   **$$$**   ★★
Staten, Christ Church, ☎ *(809) 437-7544.*
Italian cuisine.
Dinner: 6:30 p.m.–10:30 p.m., entrees $19–$33.
A lot of care goes into the presentation and preparation of the Italian food served here in a handsome old home, Staten, a historical landmark near a white sand beach popular with locals. Starters include a mixed seafood platter and antipasto, and main courses and pastas are hearty and often infused with plenty of garlic. Reservations recommended. Credit Cards: V, MC.

David's Place   **$$$**   ★★★★
St. Lawrence Main Road, Christ Church, ☎ *(809) 435-6550.*
Latin American cuisine. Specialties: Baxter Street fried chicken.
Lunch: 11:00 a.m.–3:00 p.m., entrees $9–$13.
Dinner: 6:00 p.m.–10:00 p.m., entrees $14–$30.
Wear loose clothing to eat this delicious Bajan food in a pretty cottage beside St. Lawrence Bay, where every table has an ocean view. A spicy fried chicken named in honor of the Baxter Street food vendors is a specialty, as is pepperpot and pumpkin soup. Huge helpings of rice and peas, cheese bread, potatoes and vegetables come with all the entrees, but you can't stop there. Make room for fantastic desserts like coconut cream pie if you can—you won't regret it. Reservations recommended. Credit Cards: V, MC, A.

Ile de France   **$$$**   ★★★★
Hastings, Christ Church, ☎ *(809) 435-6869.*
French cuisine. Specialties: Foie gras.
Dinner: 6:30 p.m.–10:00 p.m., entrees $18–$38.
An innovative French restaurant located on the lush grounds of one of Barbados' traditional hotels, the Windsor Arms, Ile de France brings Gallic intensity to its slower-paced, old-fashioned surroundings. Many classic dishes are represented, including a definitive foie gras and ballotine de canard (one of the owners is from Toulouse), escargots de Bourgogne, and crepes flambeed at tableside. The atmosphere is sublime and unobtrusive, with candlelight, subtle lighting and music. Associated Hotel: Windsor Arms Hotel. Closed: Mon. Reservations required. Credit Cards: V, MC.

Pisces   **$$$**   ★★★★
St. Lawrence Gap, Christ Church, ☎ *(809) 435-6564.*

Seafood cuisine. Specialties: Red snapper caribe.
Dinner: 6:00 p.m.–10:00 p.m., entrees $15–$30.

Flowers, greenery, an oceanfront table and an impeccable reputation for fresh seafood draws visitors to Pisces again and again. Red snapper caribe with tomatoes and shrimp is an ongoing special, although it may be difficult to choose an entree from the long and varied menu that invariably includes the catch of the day served any style, with a butter sauce or with Jamaican jerk seasonings. There's a refreshing gazpacho and a few meat, chicken and vegetarian dishes. Reservations required. Credit Cards: V, MC, A.

T.G.I. Boomers $$ ★★

St. Lawrence Gap, Christ Church, ☎ (809) 428-8439.
International cuisine. Specialties: Flying fish.
Lunch: 11:30 a.m.–6:00 p.m., entrees $4–$11.
Dinner: 6:00 p.m.–10:00 p.m., entrees $11–$17.

This very welcome (for variety and bargain prices) bar-restaurant near Rockley Beach serves three meals a day, including an all-American breakfast of bacon and eggs, french toast or an omelette (with coffee and juice) for $6.50. At lunch, burgers, deli and fish sandwiches and vegetarian dishes are offered for under $10. Dinner plates of steak or seafood are garnished with vegetables, rice or potatoes and soup or salad. It also serves the needs of party types and barhoppers with daiquiris and other blender drinks at the bar, which stays open until midnight. Credit Cards: V, MC, A.

Witch Doctor $$$ ★★

St. Lawrence Gap, Christ Church, ☎ (809) 435-6581.
Latin American cuisine. Specialties: Pumpkin soup.
Dinner: 6:15 p.m.–9:45 p.m., entrees $13–$30.

You'll think you're on another island when dining at this wild jungle-themed dining room serving spicy, innovative and traditional island cuisine. If the decor doesn't get to you, the good food will satisfy, including creamy pumpkin soup, seafood cocktail marinated in lime and flying fish. Reservations recommended. Credit Cards: V, MC, A.

St. Peter

Atlantis Hotel $$$ ★★

Bathsheba, St. James Parish, ☎ (809) 433-9445.
Latin American cuisine. Specialties: Pepper pot stew, flying fish.
Lunch: 12:00 a.m.–3:00 p.m., prix fixe $12–$17.
Dinner: 7:00 p.m.–9:00 p.m., prix fixe $15–$17.

You might go without a full meal for a week after the enormous Sunday brunch at the Atlantis Hotel, a traditional hostelry with a breathtaking sea vista. Although this dining room operated by owner Enid Maxwell serves set lunches and dinners at very reasonable prices, Sunday is when everyone (including tour groups) blows in. The tables groan with authentic "Bajan" specialties, including pepper pot stew (assorted meats in a rich broth, simmered for days), breadfruit, flying fish and rice and peas. If lines are overwhelming, try the Edgewater Hotel dining room nearby *(☎ 433-9902)*. Associated Hotel: Atlantis Hotel. Reservations required. Credit Cards: A.

Carambola **$$$** ★★★★

Derricks, St. James Parish, ☎ *(809) 432-0832.*
French cuisine.
Dinner: 6:30 p.m.–9:30 p.m., entrees $20–$40.

This old favorite is still wowing a select group who ooh and aah over the spicy Thai-French cuisine (a unique combination) served in a cliffside dining room, with the sea lapping 10 feet below. Carambola is located in a converted old home north of Bridgetown in St. James Parish, where chef Paul Owens and owner Robin Walcott have prepared and planned such delights as green or red curry chicken or filet of dolphin with dijon mustard sauce. It's too bad that only dinner is served, because the view is spectacular. Closed: Sun. Reservations required. Credit Cards: V, MC, A.

Koko's **$$$** ★★★

Prospect House, St. James Parish, ☎ *(809) 424-4557.*
Latin American cuisine. Specialties: Pepper pot soup, seafood.
Dinner: 6:30 p.m.–10:00 p.m., entrees $12–$22.

The chef here is a talented saucier, creating a symphony of flavors that accentuate the freshly caught shellfish and game garnishing the colorful plates. The beach setting is pretty, with tables set on the patio of a traditional Bajan house on the west coast of the island. The food is largely island-style, with pepper pot soup often on hand, as well as lightly fried shellfish cakes in a tangy citrus and mayonnaise sauce. Closed: Mon. Reservations recommended. Credit Cards: V, MC.

La Cage aux Folles **$$$** ★★★★

Summerland Great House, St. James Parish, ☎ *(809) 424-2424.*
International cuisine. Specialties: Sesame prawn pate, orange peel chicken.
Dinner: 7:00 p.m.–10:30 p.m., entrees $25–$38.

There aren't any showgirls with feathered plumes anywhere in sight at this eclectic Asian-Caribbean restaurant. The setting, in the Summerland Great House, a restored plantation, is entertainment enough. The food, luckily, plays a stellar role, with Chinese crispy duck, sesame prawn pate and orange peel chicken as predominant examples. There's a balcony for cocktails and a view of lush gardens, and an intimate antique-filled room for private parties within. Owners are experienced restaurateurs with establishments in London. Closed: Tue. Reservations required. Credit Cards: V, MC.

La Maison **$$$** ★★★

Balmore House, St. James Parish, ☎ *(809) 432-1156.*
Seafood cuisine.
Dinner: 6:30 p.m.–10:00 p.m., entrees $23–$40.

Comfortably positioned in yet another Great House on the St. James coast (will they ever run out of them?), La Maison has been wowing visitors and residents alike since it opened in the early 1990s with sophisticated, French-inspired seafood. Dining here is likened to a posh beach camp-out, with tables set out on the sand under a tent or indoors in a courtyard exposed to ocean breezes and views. The ever-changing menu may feature salmon with cream sauce, marinated flying fish and rich ice cream or chocolate desserts. Closed: Mon. Reservations required. Credit Cards: V, MC.

Raffles Old Towne $$$ ★★★★

1st Street, St. James Parish, ☎ *(809) 432-6557.*
International cuisine. Specialties: Curries.
Dinner: 7:00 p.m.–10:00 p.m., entrees $25–$35.
Named after the Raffles Hotel in Singapore and inspired by British colonial exploits
abroad, this highly regarded restaurant employs a big-game hunter theme in an intimate room close to the ocean in Holetown. Naturally, there are curries and chutneys, blackened fish and chicken, and a full-course dinner for $40. Raffles rates
three "knives and forks" (the highest culinary honor) from the Barbados Tourism
Authority. Reservations required. Credit Cards: V, MC, DC, A.

Reid's $$$ ★★★

Derricks, St. James Parish,
International cuisine. Specialties: Lobster.
Dinner: 7:00 p.m.–10:00 p.m., entrees $21–$40.
Fresh fish, lobster and escargots in white wine and garlic are served to diners at this
plantation building south of Holetown. Reservations should be made a few days in
advance to enjoy manicured garden views, gurgling fountains and a well-chosen
wine list. Closed: Mon. Reservations required. Credit Cards: V, MC, A.

The Fathoms $$$ ★★★★

Paynes Bay, St. James Parish, ☎ *(809) 432-2568.*
International cuisine. Specialties: Lobster, octopus.
Lunch: 11:00 a.m.–3:00 p.m., entrees $6–$8.
Dinner: 6:30 p.m.–10:00 p.m., entrees $15–$29.
Daring seafood dishes are the hallmark of this ocean-view, red-roofed spot on
Paynes Bay, near Holetown. You can stick with a grilled lobster, stuffed crab or
catch of the day, but octopus and sea eggs (white sea urchins' roe, prepared deviled
or breaded) are sometimes on the menu. At night it's romantic with candlelight and
crashing waves for sound effects; other times it's Bajan casual. Besides seafood, there
are burgers, salads and pork crepes. With less than 25 tables in the dining area, make
reservations well in advance. Reservations recommended. Credit Cards: V, MC, A.

The Mews $$$ ★★★

Second Street, St. James Parish, ☎ *(809) 432-1122.*
Seafood cuisine. Specialties: Fresh fish.
Dinner: 7:00 p.m.–10:00 p.m., entrees $20–$30.
This is one of two new restaurants opened by award-winning chef Josef Schwaiger,
who sold his popular Josef's in St. Lawrence Gap. It's already very successful among
his many admirers and assorted fish fanciers (Josef's specialty) who like to dine in a
trellised garden on paupiettes of snapper and a sublime lime mousse. Before or after
dinner, walk across the street to **Nico's Champagne and Wine Bar**, ☎ *(809) 432-*
0832 for some bubbly or chablis by the glass. Closed: Sun. Reservations required.
Credit Cards: V, MC, A.

Where to Shop

Even the shopping scene in Barbados has been recently spruced up, with the addition of more stores to an already bulging array of specialty boutiques, departments stores and resort-wear shops spread throughout the island. Even the beach peddlers have new kiosks. At the newly renovated cruise terminal (probably the best in the Caribbean), you can stroll through an attractive indoor shopping and entertainment arcade lined with 20 duty-free shops, crafts boutiques and restaurants—all designed to resemble a West Indian town with gingerbread cottages in pastel colors. Cruise passengers (and other foreign tourists) can choose among jewelry, liquor, china, electronics, perfume and leather goods, all duty-free for U.S. citizens (with savings of up to 40 percent off U.S. prices). There are also shops of Barbadian woodcarvings and fine art galleries as well as clothing and souvenir boutiques. Here you can also find a tourist information center, car and bike rentals, automated teller machines, florists, dive shops and a communications center with fax and phones.

Most resort hotels have a bevy of boutiques at their entrance or on premises, but prices are usually marked way up; you pay for the convenience (the Hilton and Sandy Lane do have interesting stock, however). If you're looking for department stores (and impressive ones for an island), head for downtown (especially **Da Costas Mall** with over 50 stores), but branches can usually be found in resort communities as well as at **Holetown** and **Speightstown**, where you also find specialty boutiques of top quality and resort-wear shops. On the west coast, there is the **Sunset Crest** shopping mall.

Perhaps the most outstanding Bajan art you can take home is **pottery**. Native potters use clay from the area, eschewing cheap souvenir figurines and instead fashioning the traditional shapes used in Bajan kitchens, such as the monkey pot that actually makes water taste better since it can be stored at the proper temperature. The ramshackle town of **Chalky Mount**, high on a cliff overlooking Barbados' northeastern St. Andrew parish is considered to be the epicenter of Bajan folk art. Here, every home has a potter's wheel and fathers pass down the craft techniques to their sons, a tradition that dates back 300 years. Best pottery can be found at **Chalky Mount Potter** ☎ *(809-422-9619)* and also at **Springer's Pottery** ☎ *(809-422-9682).*

Other local crafts include black-coral jewelry, attractive wall-hangings made from dried grasses and flowers, and straw mats, baskets and bags. Leatherwork is just beginning to find its place among Bajan craft art.

Barbados Directory

ARRIVAL

American Airlines, Air Canada and BWIA are the principal carriers to Barbados, flying from New York, Toronto, Miami and San Juan to Grantley Adams Airport. Good connections can be made with other Caribbean islands, especially British Airways, which has good deals between Antigua, St. Lucia, Barbados and Trinidad. It's best to buy ongoing tickets ahead of time as Barbados agents add a 20 percent service tax. Reserve months in advance for the Christmas season and during the Crop Over festival in August. A departure tax, payable at the airport upon leaving, is $US $12.50.

CLIMATE

Constant northeast trade winds keep temperatures between 75-85 degrees F year round. The wet season, from June to November, is more humid that at any other time; September and October are the rainiest months. Weather can change quickly—in a cross trip on the island from west to east, you can start out with sunny skies and end up in a raging storm. Rainfall varies from 50 inches on the coast to 75 inches in the higher interior.

CRUISES

Cruiseships dock at the Deep Water Harbour's pier. Most folks on a limited time schedule head for Pelican Village to do some shopping. You can easily catch a taxi waiting at the dock. (The walk can get long and hot!) If you want to catch a smaller ship or sailboat to another island, hang around the port here and see who you can meet; ships are arriving all the time on their way to other islands.

DOCUMENTS

U.S.and Canadian citizens need to show proof of citizenship (passport, birth certificate, or voter's registration card, along with a government-issued photo ID, like a driver's license). Also required is an ongoing or return ticket.There is a departure tax of U.S. $12.50.

ELECTRICITY

The current is 100 volts, 50 cycles, as in the U.S., though the speed is somewhat slower. Hotels with 220 volts usually provide adapters.

GETTING AROUND

From the airport it's a good hour's drive to the part of the west coast where many (but not all) of the best hotels and houses to let are located.You can rent a car at the airport, but only local agencies are available.

Since the road from the airport is a bit hairy, visitors are better off taking a taxi to the hotel, and then renting a car from there. If you rent a car, you'll need your own license, plus a driver's permit issued at the airport by the police or your rental agency for a $5 fee. Take the insurance ($5 a day) if you're not sure you are already covered. Do note that driving is on the left.

The most highly recommended car-rental agency is **National Car Rental**, Bush Hall, Main Road, St. Michael; ☎ *809-426-0603*. Cars will be delivered to a location anywhere on the island.

Also try **P&S Car Rentals** (☎ *809-424-2052 or 424-2907*), Pleasant View, Cave Hill, St. Michael; **Sunny Isle Motors**, ☎ *809-435-7979*. In general, roads are well paved and locations well marked.

Taxi drivers are no longer naive on Barbados and know their way around know-nothing tourists. Do ask your concierge or hotel management how much a particular trip should cost before you get in the taxi; otherwise you could get bilked.

Public buses are reliable and safe, but unbearably crowded at rush hours (8:30 a.m.–9:30 a.m. and 3:30–6:00 p.m.). The route that runs down the south and west coast is an inexpensive way to see the island.

GUIDES

Although the more independent traveler prefers to rent his own car and toddle around on his own, hotels can arrange a personal guide for you if you want to see more of the island. Excellent service is offered by **Sally Shearn's VIP Tour Service** ☎ *809-429-4617*.

LANGUAGE

English is the official language, spoken with a pronounced island lilt.

MEDICAL EMERGENCIES

Top-class hotels usually have a doctor on call. Queen Elizabeth Hospital, located on Martinsdale Road in Bridgetown, is the preeminent training hospital in the Caribbean.

MONEY

The official currency is the Barbados dollar, worth about 50 cents in American currency. Most stores will accept American dollars and traveler's checks. However, to get your best rate, it's better to exchange your American dollars for Bajan ones at a bank.

TELEPHONE

Area code is 809.

TIPPING AND TAXES

Most hotels and restaurants add a 10 percent service charge. Feel free to tip extra if the service is especially fine.

TOURIST INFORMATION

The tourist office is located in the Harbour Industrial Park near the Deep Water Harbour in Bridgetown. You'll also find information posts at the airport and at the cruise ship pier at the Deep Water Harbour. They are only open weekdays. From the U.S. call ☎ *(213) 380-2198*.

WATER

Water is safe to drink in Barbados, pumped from an underground source in the island's coral reefs.

WHEN TO GO

Crop Over Festival in July and August is an islandwide celebration of Barbadian arts, food, music and dance, which harks back to the 19th century when the last of the year's sugarcane crop was feted. Three weeks of competitions, festivities, feasts, and fairs celebrate the culture and history of the island. Kaddoment Day, a national holiday held on August 1, is the culmination of the Crop Over Festival, with costumes, music, street dancing and fireworks. The Holetown Festival in February, commemorating the first settlement in 1627, is celebrated by a big street party, as is the Oistins Fish Festival at Easter. In November the National Independence Festival of Creative Arts (NIFCA) usually sponsors an annual month-long celebration of Barbadian talent competitions in art, music, song and dance. In July, the Sir Garfield Sobers International School's Cricket Tournament, named after a famous Barbadian cricketer, has become an international event, attracting worldwide participation.

Every Sunday year-round traditional Sunday hikes are cosponsored by various charities, encouraging participants to walk at their own pace. Walks start at 6 a.m. and 3:30 p.m. Call the **Barbados National Trust** ☎ *(809) 428-5889*. On Sundays in January, **Barbados Horticultural Society's Open Garden Program** presents local gardeners displaying their gardens from 2 p.m.–6 p.m. For more information, call ☎ *809-428-5889*. On Wednesday afternoons, January-April, **Barbados National Trust Open House Program** invites visitors to browse through the private homes of architectural and historical importance to the island.

The period between Christmas and Easter is the most popular time for tourists, though the British summer is busier than it used to be.

BARBADOS HOTELS	RMS	RATES	PHONE	FAX
Bridgetown				
★★★★ **Barbados Hilton**	184	$149–$201	(800) 445-8667	
★★★★ **Marriott's Sam Lord's**	234	$110–$225	(800) 228-9290	
★★★★ **Sandals Barbados**	178	$105–$335	(800) 726-3257	
★★★ **Coconut Creek Club Hotel**	53	$240–$350	(800) 462-2566	
★★★ **Colony Club Hotel**	76	$271–$480	(800) 466-2526	

BARBADOS HOTELS		RMS	RATES	PHONE	FAX
★★★	Crane Beach Hotel	18	$105–$300	(800) 466-2526	
★★★	Ginger Bay Beach Club	16	$80–$205	(800) 466-2526	
★★★	Grand Barbados Beach	133	$125–$605	(800) 466-2526	
★★★	Island Inn	23	$130–$230	(800) 743-4276	

Christ Church

★★★	Casuarina Beach Club	129	$80–$165	(809) 428-3600	
★★★	Ocean View Hotel	35	$34–$71	(809) 427-7871	
★★★	Sandy Beach	89	$100–$175	(800) 462-2526	
★★★	Southern Palms	92	$69–$265	(800) 466-2526	
★★★	Woodville Beach Apart-mens	28	$47–$129	(800) 466-2526	
★★	Caribbee Beach Hotel	55	$60–$105	(800) 466-2526	
★★	Club Rockley Barbados	108	$180–$535	(800) 462-2526	
★★	Divi Southwinds Resort	160	$115–$245	(800) 367-3484	
★★	Half Moon Beach Hotel	36	$75–$215	(800) 466-2526	
★★	Sand Acres Beach Club	37	$75–$125	(800) 466-2526	
★★	Sea Breeze Beach Hotel	60	$45–$245	(800) 822-7223	
★★	Sea Foam Haciendas	12	$70–$93	(800) 822-7223	
★★	Seaview Hotel	25	$95–$305	(809) 426-1450	
★	Benston Windsurfing Hotel	15	$50–$70	(809) 428-9095	
★	Fairholme	31	$35–$65	(809) 428-9425	
★	Yellow Bird Apartments	21	$55–$105	(809) 435-8444	

St. Peter

★★★★★	Glitter Bay	81	$200–$325	(800) 283-8666	
★★★★★	Royal Pavilion	75	$235–$330	(800) 283-8666	
★★★★★	Sandy Lane Hotel	121	$500–$955	(800) 223-6800	
★★★★	Cobblers Cove Hotel	39	$135–$625	(800) 223-6510	
★★★★	Coral Reef Club	71	$74–$250	(800) 525-4800	
★★★★	Sandpiper Inn	45	$110–$445	(800) 223-1108	
★★★	Almond Beach Club	147	$259–$395	(809) 432-7840	
★★★	Buccaneer Bay Hotel	29	$90–$330	(809) 432-7981	
★★★	Discovery Bay Hotel	85	$120–$375	(800) 466-2526	

BARBADOS HOTELS	RMS	RATES	PHONE	FAX
★★★ Haywoods Wyndham	288	$185–$535	(800) 822-4200	
★★★ Settler's Beach Hotel	22	$555–$705	(800) 466-2526	
★★★ Tamarind Cove Hotel	116	$280–$640	(800) 466-2526	
★★★ Treasure Beach Hotel	26	$155–$445	(800) 466-2526	
★★ Asta Apartment Hotel	60	$50–$235	(800) 466-2526	(809) 426-9566
★★ Barbados Beach Village	88	$100–$335	(800) 462-2426	
★★ Beachcomber Apartments	9	$80–$300	(809) 432-0489	(809) 432-2824
★★ King's Beach Hotel	57	$105–$245	(800) 466-2526	
★★ Kingsley Club	7	$85–$106	(809) 433-9422	
★★ Sandridge Beach Hotel	52	$60–$195	(800) 466-2526	
★★ Sugar Cane Club	23	$40–$85	(809) 422-5046	

BARBADOS RESTAURANTS	LOCATION	PHONE	ENTREE

Bridgetown

American			
★★ Chicken Barn, The	Worthing		$3–$11
French			
★★★★ Bagatelle Great House	St. Thomas Parish	(809) 421-6767	$30–$35••
International			
★★★ Josef's	St. Lawrence Gap	(809) 435-6541	$10–$40
★★ Carib Beach Bar	Worthing		$6–$16
★★ Waterfront Cafe	Bridgetown	(809) 431-0303	$8–$30
Latin American			
★★★ Brown Sugar	St. Michael Parish	(809) 426-7684	$14–$25

Christ Church

French			
★★★★ Ile de France	Christ Church	(809) 435-6869	$18–$38••
International			
★★ T.G.I. Boomers	Christ Church	(809) 428-8439	$4–$17
Italian			
★★ Da Luciano's	Christ Church	(809) 437-7544	$19–$33••

BARBADOS RESTAURANTS	LOCATION	PHONE	ENTREE
Latin American			
★★★★ David's Place	Christ Church	(809) 435-6550	$9–$30
★★ Witch Doctor	Christ Church	(809) 435-6581	$13–$30••
Seafood			
★★★★ Pisces	Christ Church	(809) 435-6564	$15–$30••

St. Peter

	LOCATION	PHONE	ENTREE
French			
★★★★ Carambola	St. James Parish	(809) 432-0832	$20–$40••
International			
★★★★ La Cage aux Folles	St. James Parish	(809) 424-2424	$25–$38••
★★★★ Raffles Old Towne	St. James Parish	(809) 432-6557	$25–$35••
★★★★ The Fathoms	St. James Parish	(809) 432-2568	$6–$29
★★★ Reid's	St. James Parish		$21–$40••
Latin American			
★★★ Koko's	St. James Parish	(809) 424-4557	$12–$22••
★★ Atlantis Hotel	St. James Parish	(809) 433-9445	$12–$17
Seafood			
★★★ La Maison	St. James Parish	(809) 432-1156	$23–$40••
★★★ The Mews	St. James Parish	(809) 432-1122	$20–$30••

Note:　• Lunch Only

•• Dinner Only

BARBUDA

Barbuda offers soft white sand, gorgeous sea views and a relaxed lifestyle.

Barbuda is not a "Wow" island. It's flat and featureless, with about as much excitement as a bird-watcher could take. Who's it for, then? The *totally* rich and reclusive. For years, only one resort, Coco Point, dominated the island, until fashion mogul Mariuccia Mandelli, alias Krizia of Milan, chose tiny Barbuda for her personal Eden. Club K, Krizia's $30 million-dollar dream resort, today totally reflects her taste, at the same time capturing the evanescent sense of space and breeze that defines the island. Any entertainment and sports activities are dependent on these two resorts, where you will feel as close to being on a deserted island-cum-butler as you can get. If the first-class attention gets you down or the top-notch cuisine starts to get boring, a boatman can always deposit you, a picnic basket, and a two-radio signal in hand, on the isolated beach at Spanish Point. Leave the cellular phones at home.

Bird's Eye View

Barbuda lies 30 miles north of Antigua, some 68 square miles of flat, coral terrain. Only about 1500 people live here, the majority in the town of Codrington on the edge of the lagoon. An impressive frigate bird colony is located in the mangroves of the Condrington lagoon, where hundreds of birds mate between August and December. The River Road runs from Codrington to Palmetto Point, about three miles, past Cocoa Point, and on to Spanish Point, a half-mile-finger of land that divides the Caribbean from the Atlantic.

People

The natives of Barbuda are unusually tall, a trait they have inherited from their descendants in the Corramante tribe in Africa. The population stands at about 1500 and most people live in Codrington, the only village on the island, located on the edge of the lagoon.

Beaches and Other Natural Wonders

Lush, tropical vegetation is all but nonexistent on Barbuda's coral rock terrain, but beaches are generally glorious. The Wa'Omoni Beach Park is the hub of beach activities, perfect for a day trip, where you can barbecue freshly caught lobster on the beach and visit the Frigate Bird Sanctuary. Here, you can actually witness the miracle of seeing birds, the *fregata magnificicens*

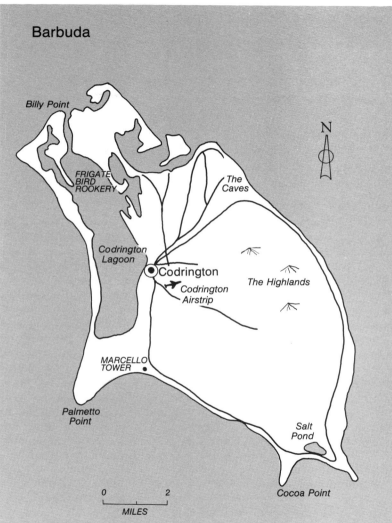

Barbuda

Billy Point

*FRIGATE
BIRD
ROOKERY*

*The
Caves*

N

*Codrington
Lagoon*

◉ Codrington

The Highlands

*Codrington
Airstrip*

*MARCELLO
TOWER* ●

*Palmetto
Point*

*Salt
Pond*

0   2

MILES

Cocoa Point

(frigate birds), hatch their eggs deep within the mangrove bushes. Ask your hotel to arrange a tour, which can only be accomplished in a small motorboat. Bird-watchers will also be delighted with numerous sightings of tropical mockingbirds, pelicans and herons, plus about 150 more species throughout the island. Other sights include a fascinating system of caves in the northeast where Indian carvings have been found, and River Fort, a martello tower on the south coast.

Treks

Barbados, in general, is an unspoiled wilderness waiting to be discovered by those who need few amenities and are able to make spontaneous adjustments in schedule. Treks and guided tours are difficult to arrange ahead of time, and the best-laid plans tend to go awry at the last minute. The island has no paved roads, only dirt tracks over which only jeeps survive, and none are marked. Having a map in hand is absolutely necessary; one, by B.S. Dyde, clearly shows trails and all the main attractions. Horses and guides are available, but do inquire in advance at the tourist office in Antigua, or through your hotel. The best way to visit Barbuda is on a day-flight from Antigua, on a LIAT flight, with guide, driver and sightseeing itinerary planned well in advance. Thorny bush requires good hiking boots and long pants; bring your own water because the climate is very hot and dry.

A spectacular sight, especially during the mating season from late May to December, is the Man of War island—a large brackish estuary on the west coast which is home to literally thousands of frigate birds who crowd onto tiny bushes. During their courtship rituals, the males spread their expansive wings and puff up their red throat pouches as they glide above the flapping females below on the bush. Local boatmen readily take visitors in rowboats the short ride from the jetty west of town to the middle part of the lagoon. The birds seem to ignore visitors and, for some reason, allow themselves to be photographed at very close range.

From Codrington, take the Highland Road about three miles directly east to the Highlands on the east side of the island—here you will find a panoramic view and the ruins of Highland House, built in the early 18th century by the Codrington family. About five miles inland from town is the Darby Sink Cave, about 70 feet deep, with a sinkhole full of lush vegetation. The descent down is not hard, although the path does drop severely at one point.

The rocky, uninhabited island of Redonda, is best reached by boat from Montserrat, where boat operators offer daily excursions. Landing is made through surf onto rocks near the southwest tip of the leeward side. Once ashore, you must climb a steep, rocky cleft to reach the island's few acres of flat terrain. The island is home to a small black iguana, burrowing owl and boobies.

Tours

Frigate Bird Sanctuary   ★ ★ ★

North End, Codrington Lagoon.
Reached only via small boat, this pristine spot is one of the world's largest bird sanctuaries and the spot where fregata magnificens (frigate birds) brood their eggs in mangrove bushes. These impressive birds have eight-foot wingspans and soar to 2000 feet. Mating season, September to February, is the best time to come; chicks hatch from December to March and remain in the nest for up to eight months. Also look out for pelicans, warblers, snipes, ibis, herons, kingfishers, tropical mockingbirds and cormorants.

Sports

All sports activities are arranged through the two resorts on the island. Your only problem will be what to choose. You might consider hanging around the dock of the K Club and hitching a ride on one of the many schooners which dock regularly.

Where to Stay

★★★★ **Coco Point Lodge**

★★★★ **The K Club**

★★ **Palmetto Beach Hotel**

| ★★★★ **Coco Point Lodge** | $455–$1000 |
| ★★★★ **The K Club** | $900–$2700 |

Fielding's Best Value Hotels in Barbuda

| ★★★★ **The K Club** | $900–$2700 |
| ★★ **Palmetto Beach Hotel** | $181–$352 |

You basically have two choices in Barbuda: extravagantly expensive resorts or a bed in a local home. There is one self-catering unit, but it is extremely basic.

Hotels and Resorts

The two resorts on Barbuda give you the kind of beach experience you will never forget. **Coco Point Lodge** is situated on one of the most fabulous beaches in the Caribbean, and the K Club, created in loving detail by the Italian designer Krizia, is where the haughtiest of the haute couture go to be reborn. If you stay at any of these places, make sure your bank account can withstand the beating.

Coco Point Lodge   **$455–$1000**   ★★★★

> *Coco Point,* ☎ *(809) 462-3816.*
> *Single: $455–$905. Double: $555–$1000.*
> This secluded resort is for those who really do want to get away from it all, and don't mind the lack of bells and whistles at more commercial properties. Set on one of the Caribbean's most glorious beaches, Coco Point accommodates guests in ranch-style villas that are comfortably though simply furnished. The all-inclusive rates include everything from soup to nuts (and drinks), but there's very little action

at night—people come here to relax, not party. The athletic-minded will find two tennis courts and all watersports. Unwind! 34 rooms. Credit Cards: Not Accepted.

Palmetto Beach Hotel $181–$352 ★★

Patmetto's Peninsula, ☎ *(809) 460- 326.*
Single: $181–$352. Double: $181–$352.

Located on the island's southwestern side, this small hotel offers an alternative to Barbuda's two other much pricier resorts. Guest rooms are air-conditioned and have separate living areas; the nine cottages offer more privacy but rely on sea breezes for cooling. A pool, tennis court and watersports round out the activities, and two restaurants keep guests sated. 35 rooms. Credit Cards: V, MC, A.

The K Club $900–$2700 ★★★★

Coco Point, ☎ *(809) 460- 300.*
Single: $900–$2000. Double: $900–$2700.

Most everything is perfect at this stylish enclave of white cottages set on a spectacular beach. Accommodations are spacious and beautifully decorated by owner Krizia, the Italian fashion designer, who oversaw every detail of development, down to the cotton lounging robes in each room. The all-inclusive rates include wonderful meals and all activities, but splendid as everything is, it's still overpriced. Those who can afford the ultimate escape won't be disappointed, though service is not always up to par and management is on a revolving-door basis. Amenities: golf, tennis. 27 rooms. Credit Cards: V, MC, DC, A.

Apartments and Condominiums

There is one lone apartment complex on the island, but furnishings are extremely casual; it's best to have a camper's enthusiasm. If you plan to do your own cooking, bring as many staples from home as possible—prices run high in Antigua. You can always bargain with fishermen bringing in their daily catch of fresh fish and lobster.

Inns

There's only one "inn" on the island, but the condition of rooms is often iffy. It's also a long hot haul from the middle of town.

Low Cost Lodging

Visitors have been known to bargain for a room in local homes. The best way is to come in person to make the contact. Hot water is not always guaranteed and you will probably have to share the bathroom.

Where to Eat

Restaurants at the two resorts are considered spectacular. If you're staying there, meals are included in the all-inclusive rate. The K-Club specializes in Mediterranean cuisine.

Where to Shop

Forget Codrington for anything worth taking home; the boutiques at both resorts carry the traditional Caribbean trinkets and sportswear. Even Antigua's airport won't offer up much, so you might arrange a stop in St. John's before flying home the same day.

Barbuda Directory

ARRIVAL

LIAT ☎ *809-462-0701* makes the 15-minute flight from Antigua's V.C. Bird Airport to Barbuda's Codrington Airport in two daily runs (morning and afternoon). There is also a another private airport, the Coco Point Airstrip, at Coco Point Lodge, 8 miles from Codrington.

CLIMATE

Average temperatures hover around 75–85 degrees F. year-round.

DOCUMENTS

U.S. and Canadian citizens need to present a valid passport (or original birth certificate and photo ID), plus an ongoing ticket. British citizens need to show a valid passport.

ELECTRICITY

Most of the island uses 220 volts AC/60 cycles. Some hotels in the Hodges Bay area run on 110 volts AC/60 cycles. Do check your hotel's conditions before you come.

GETTING AROUND

Taxis are omnipresent outside major hotels and the airport. However, jeeps are the best way to zip about the island; most people prefer small Suzuki four-wheel drives. You'll need an Antiguan driver's license (available for purchase when you rent a vehicle). Negotiate like crazy for a good price.

Both Coco Point Lodge and K Club can arrange a day tour of the island. Profit Burton, a private guide, usually meets visitors at the airport and will design personal tours for you in his minivan.

LANGUAGE

The official language is English.

MEDICAL EMERGENCIES

Don't get sick in Barbuda or you'll have to fly to Puerto Rico or Miami. Make sure you bring your own medicines if you have a chronic condition. Some basic care can be found at the small Springview Hospital, funded by a New York not-for-profit organization.

MONEY

Official currency is the Eastern Caribbean dollar, but most establishment welcome American dollars. Exchange houses are hard to find here; exchange before you come.

TELEPHONE

Area code is *809*. Phone service is limited. Make sure you bring your own calling card from home to save money on long-distance calls.

TIPPING AND TAXES

Most hotels add a ten percent service charge; tip extra if the service is especially nice.

TOURIST INFORMATION

Antigua and Barbuda Tourist Office Box 363, Long St., Antigua, W.I., ☎ *809-462-0480* or *809-462-2105*, FAX *809-462-2483*. In the U.S. ☎ *(212) 541-4170*.

WATER

Officially, you can drink tap water, but most visitors feel safer downing the bottled variety.

WHEN TO GO

See the calendar in the "When to Go" section of Antigua.

BARBUDA HOTELS	RMS	RATES	PHONE	FAX
Codrington				
★★★★ Coco Point Lodge	34	$455–$1000	(809) 462-3816	
★★★★ The K Club	27	$900–$2700	(809) 460-0300	(809) 460-0305
★★ Palmetto Beach Hotel	35	$181–$352	(809) 460-0326	

BONAIRE

Bonaire has one of the largest flamingo colonies in the world. The birds build their mud nests in the salt pans.

Once sleepy Bonaire, the B in the ABC islands of the Netherlands Antilles, is now being battered by jackhammers and chainsaws. In the last three years, a building boom has hit this tiny Dutch isle like a hurricane from which it may never recover. Once the scuba diver's rough-but-ready paradise—in the 1980s, it was *the* place to dive—Bonaire is finally moving into the modern age, and if you've been gone for a few years, the change will be startling. For the first time in Kralendijk, the island's capital, there are traffic jams, big yellow cranes, and parking that's becoming a chore. Two new shopping malls— pretty pink and mellow yellow—adorn the harborside, with two more slated soon for production. A recent cleanup campaign called "Tene Boneiru Limpi" (Keep Bonaire Clean) got rid of debris in the countryside and the project has become an islandwide contest. Unfortunately, illegal drugs have infiltrated the country, and petty crime, mostly theft of rental cars (particularly 4-wheel drives) is on the rise. Still, more and more cruise liners are docking in port, and Americans continue to lead the pack of dive fanatics, with Europeans closing the gap of annual visitors. Despite the modernization, new buildings are being designed to tastefully reflect the native colonial Dutch style, and the dive sites, thanks to the die-hard diving ecologists who first "founded" the island, have kept the blue waters pure and the dive sites pristine. These days, Bonaire is being touted as the place to go, even if you *don't* dive (though, to take full advantage of the island's vast underwater treasures, including 86 offshore dive sites, at least one of you in the couple should be obliged to dive!)

Bird's Eye View

Bonaire is the "B" in the ABC Islands that includes Aruba and Curaçao, and the second largest of the five islands that make up the Netherlands Antilles. Fifty miles north of Venezuela, it sprawls over 112 square miles in a shape that resembles a boomerang. With a population of a mere 11,000, it rates as the most sparsely populated island in the Caribbean. The island itself is formed from the tip of a 24-mile-long (three-mile wide) volcanic ridge that pokes out of the sea, buffeted on the windward side by tradewinds blowing from the northeast. In contrast, the leeward side embraces a protected harbor surrounded by calm waters.The diversity in typography throughout the island is startling—from the northern green hills of the Washington-Slagbaai National Park to the flat, almost desertlike terrain of the south. The highest ridge is the 790-ft. **Brandaris Peak** located in the park. Gritty, rocky beaches stretch around the island, though calmer conditions on the leeward side attract the most divers; most of the island's development is here. The scenic, seahugging road north of the main hotel has been recently closed to make way for the development of private homes in the area, though it has been replaced by a stunning new road that rises up from a scenic view and then travels inland through Bonaire's stark stubby *kunucu* countryside.

Bonaire's uninhabited kid sister, **Klein Bonaire**, all 1500 square acres, is tucked into the curve of the main island, just one-half mile offshore and pro-

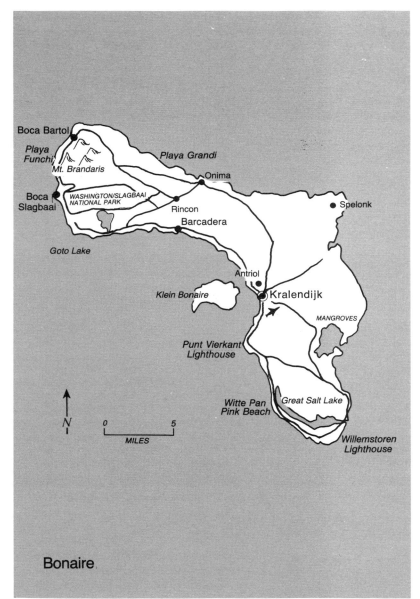

Boca Bartol
Playa Funchi
Mt. Brandaris
Playa Grandi
Onima
Boca Slagbaai
WASHINGTON/SLAGBAAI NATIONAL PARK
Rincon
Barcadera
Spelonk
Goto Lake
Antriol
Klein Bonaire
Kralendijk
MANGROVES
Punt Vierkant Lighthouse
Witte Pan Pink Beach
Great Salt Lake
Willemstoren Lighthouse
N
0   5
MILES

Bonaire

tected from wind and waves. Both islands receive little rainfall, which accounts for the desertlike vegetation, such as cacti, divi-divi trees and other desert succulents, that dot the landscape. The entire coast of both Bonaire and Klein Bonaire are lined with coral reefs, which inspired ecologically committed legislators to protect all the reefs within the marine park.

The Dutch-influenced capital city of **Kralendijk** stretches along a wide, sheltered cove with boutiques, restaurants, bars and government offices occupying most of the buildings. Both to the north and south of this small city are resort developments that serve all kinds of tourists.

History

Antilles International Salt Company has reactivated Bonaire's salt mines.

Ever since the Spanish explorer Amerigo Vespucci discovered Bonaire in 1499, entrepreneurs have been toying with how to exploit it. Failing to discover gold on the island, the Spanish turned to extracting salt from the seas, stripping the forests of hardwoods and dyewoods, and hunting wild goats and sheep. Neither the Dutch, who arrived in 1623, or the British, who took control in the early 19th century, could discover any successful ventures. A U.S. merchant named Joseph Foulke, to whom the British leased the land in

1810, also failed to make good. When the Dutch returned six years later, they ventured into shipbuilding, brickmaking and stock raising with little success. In recent years, many of Bonaire's natives were forced to find work off-island in the oil refineries of Venezuela, Curaçao and Aruba. As news of Bonaire's natural wonders became disseminated by the emigration, tourists began to trickle onto the island: fishermen who gloried in the abundance of marine life and untouched coral reefs and bird-watchers who were astounded by the glorious flocks of pink flamingos at Goto Meer and Pekel Meer. But it wasn't until the first scuba divers arrived around 1962, when there were only two major hotels, that the island began to discover where its real treasures lay—right underwater.

Beaches

Brilliant white is the color of most beaches in Bonaire, but most are gritty and full of coral. Hence, they are not really suitable for long strolls. Beaches on the leeward coast tend to run narrow. All the major hotels are located on beaches (managements have tried to beef up the sand there) but some of the best ones are along the southern coast, like the clothes-optional Sorobon or Boca Cai on Lac Bay, full of mangroves at the north end of the bay. At Playa Chiquito, the surf is treacherously strong (too dangerous for swimming), but the strand is good for sunbathing, though there are few places for shade. Pink Beach, south of Kraldendijk, is good for swimming but gritty for strolling. Snorkelers head for Playa Funchi, but the absence of facilities has left the beach in smelly disrepair. Lots of tour boats end up in Boca Slagbaai where you can see flocks of flamingos dipping their long legs in the water. Do stop there if you have just trekked through the National Park.

Dive Sites

Diving is the king sport on Bonaire. Drop-off is very near the shore on both islands, a factor that both snorkelers and divers have found endearing. **The Bonaire Marine Park**, surrounding the island, is now managed by STINA-

PA, an acronym for the Netherlands Antilles National Foundation, which supports biological projects and studies essential to Bonaire's preservation. Such acts of preservation keep diving conditions on Bonaire comparable to those in the Red Sea, in terms of the vertical reef face near shore and the desertlike environment. Stringent laws passed in 1971 ban spearfishing and the removal of any marine life from Bonaire's waters. You're also requested not to feed the fish (it only makes them more aggressive), touch coral or any underwater life), not drop litter, and not kick up sand with your fins which can harm coral. Advanced buoyancy courses are available to teach divers how to remain horizontal along the reef. In order to scuba, all divers must have a valid "admission" ticket to the marine park, a modest $10 fee that includes a small green disk affixed to your gear. All island dive operators and the park headquarters at Karpata are able to issue marine park dive permits.

There are 86 dive sites around Bonaire and Klein Bonaire. The easily accessible shore dive sites are clearly marked with yellow stones by the road. Most all sites can be reached by car. A relaxing warmup dive can be found at **Habitat's Baby Dock** (boats aren't allowed to dock here). At *La Machaca*, a wreck site here, you'll find yellowtail snappers and large neon-colored parrotfish and foureye butterflyfish. A five-foot tarpon called Charlie is said to hang out here. At **Kelin Bonaire**, depths reach to 70 feet along the scalloped reef, where large forests of black coral sway with the current; barracudas are sighted here as well as black durgons swimming through gorgonians and mountainous star coral. On the far north side of Bonaire's west coast is the site called **Country Garden**, known for its huge splashes of colorful coral and sponges, damselfish no bigger than a finger, small spotted drums and lizardfish. **Peter Hughes Dive Bonaire**, the most popular, if not world-famous dive show, has docks right off the beach, and also provides mesh for bags for your gear, which you can dunk right into rinse tanks and hang on a peg to dry. One of the most famous wrecks is the *Hilma Hooker*, drug-carrying freighter that was confiscated and sunk in 1984. The site is about 250 feet offshore, so you need to make a swim through Gorgonians and mountainous star coral before reaching there. A sand channel is reached after a 60-ft. drop, where scores of black margates, mahogany snappers, and yellowtail snappers can be seen. The hull of the 1027-ton freighter can actually be entered. One of the most unusual dive sites on Bonaire is the **night dive** at the town pier in the capital of Kralendijk. Thirty feet below the darkened undersides of boats docked at the pier is a rich invertebrate life on pillars and lots of marine creatures seeking safety—or dinner—in the sponges and corals and ties and shoes. Be careful—you can't just surface anywhere, and you must follow your boat's flashing green strobe first. Otherwise you could bang your head on the pier's underside or become a scuba sandwich between the shifting weight of freighters and small boats. Another great night dive is off **Bonaire**

Undersea Adventures' dock, where lobsters and three-foot-long barracudas can be glimpsed.

Treks

Some Bonaire tours include the huts where salt mine slaves lived.

Washington-Slagbaii National Park is a must-see in Bonaire—no matter how much time you spend under water, you won't have had the full Bonaire experience without trekking through at least some of the park. Once a plantation producing aloe, charcoal and goats, it was privately held until the end of the 1960s, when the owner finally sold it to the Netherlands Antilles government with the express wish that it stay in its natural state. Today, it has grown to about 13,400 acres. Visitors enter through a simple gate, with a $3 fee for adults. There are three routes mapped through the park: yellow arrows mark the 22-mile circuitous route along the Caribbean coast; green marks a shorter 15-mile route, and a dotted green marks the hiking trails of the Brandaris Peak. In the park you'll find secluded beaches, brilliantly hued parrots, large iguanas, huge flocks of flamingos, and magnificent dive and scuba opportunities. One of the best places to view birds is **Salina Mathijs**, a salt flat which is home to greater flamingos from October to January, located immediately past the park entrance. Nearby **Playa Chiquita** has a creamy white sand beach, good for picnics, but extremely treacherous for swimming because of strong currents. **Salina Slagbaai**, on the west side of the park, is also excellent for picnics, and much better for swimming. From January to July, it is also a feeding ground for greater flamingos. About two miles west of the Goto Meer, at Nukove, you'll find excellent beaches for swimming, hidden caves, and some of the island's best snorkeling sites. Don't forget to bring a picnic if you come here.

Caves on land are the best attraction on Bonaire, next to the myriad of underwater coves in the sea. Along the coast, there are at least 40 caves that have been discovered in the last ten years. At Barcadera, on the west coast, steps lead down to the **Cueva Barcadera**, whose water basin at the entrance was allegedly used to attract wild goats into captivity. You should be an experienced cave-explorer before entering the small entrance, and you should carry your own lights. Most of the exploration will by necessity be done on hands and knees, so wear gloves and knee pads.

The **Pekel Meer Lagoon**, a 135-acre **flamingo sanctuary** and breeding ground, is located in the southern part of the island. It attracts more than 10,000 flamingos. Access to the refuge is by car, but because the flamingos are sensitive to noise, visitors must walk quietly along the edge of the lagoon where they can get close enough for a glimpse. Bring along a telephoto lens or powerful binoculars.

What Else to See

Visitors to Bonaire come to revel in the natural sights, but the small capital of Kralendijk deserves a perusal, recently spruced up by well-supported restoration projects. Traversing the town is easy since there are only two main roads. The **fish market** is always a hoot, located today near the Hotel Rochaline, and historical buffs will find interesting **Indian artifacts** at the Instituo Folklore Bonaire. Guides will want to drag you out to see the slave huts on the southwestern coast, which is only interesting if you like imagining how two grown men could fit into the tiny hovels. Whatever you do underwater, don't miss visiting the Washington/Slagbaai National Park, in the northwest of the island (see "Treks" above).

Museums and Exhibits

Instituto Folklore Bonaire

Ministry of Education, Kralendijk.

If you happen to be in the neighborhood (don't bother otherwise), drop in for a look at local artifacts and musical instruments from the pre-Columbian days. The cramped and poor exhibits prevent this small museum from reaching its potential.

Parks and Gardens

Bonaire Marine Park

The entire coastline.

To keep its world-famous reefs intact, this government-run park, which includes the entire coastline of Bonaire and neighboring Klein Bonaire, has enacted strict rules for snorkelers and divers. You may not step on or collect the coral, and anchors are forbidden—patrolling marine police see that the rules are enforced. The undersea world includes some 80 species of colorful coral and 270 species of fish. The Visitors Center offers up brochures, slide shows and lectures. The $10 fee allows for one calendar year of diving.

Washington/Slagbaai National Park   ★ ★ ★ ★ ★

Northwest Territory.
Hours Open: 8:00 a.m.–5:00 p.m.

This 13,500-acre national park, dedicated to preserving the island's natural landscape, is well worth a visit. Opt for the short route (15 miles and marked with green arrows) or the longer version (22 miles and yellow arrows); if you're driving, a four-wheel drive is essential for navigating the dirt roads. Once a plantation of divi-divi trees and aloe plants, the park has been a wildlife sanctuary since 1967, with additional acreage added in 1978. The roads take you past dramatic seascapes, freshwater lakes and lowland forest that is home to 130 species of birds (bring your binoculars) and a few mammals like donkeys and goats. There's a small museum at the gatehouse; just past it colorful flamingos roost on a salt pond from October to January. Plan on at least a few hours in this special spot. General admission: $3.00.

Tours

Bonaire Sightseeing Tours   ★ ★ ★

Kralendijk.

If you prefer exploring Bonaire in the hands of professional guides, they'll take care of you. Excursions, via jeep or minivan, are offered to the northern coast, the low-lying south or Washington/Slagbaai National Park. Prices range from $12 to $45.

Cruises   ★ ★ ★ ★

Various locales.

A few hours' excursion on the sea is always a wonderful way to unwind. A few companies offer such jaunts. The Bonaire Dream, a glass-bottom boat, lets you see underwater life without getting wet; catch it at the Harbour Village Marina. Sunset and snorkel cruises are offered by the *Woodwind* (*599-7-607055*). Don't forget the sunscreen!

Sports

Diving, of course, is the king sport on Bonaire (for more information, see under "Dive Sites" above). Recently, however, boardsailing and **windsurfing** have also become the rage in Bonaire. Head for the windward coast of Bonaire, where the trade winds from the Guinea-Bissau end their transatlantic blow in Lac Bay. This is Jibe City, a four-sq.-mile lagoon where the trade winds blow at 12-35 knots year round. Beginners can feel assured by water that only reaches waist high and the steady onshore winds mean no one ever worries about being blown out to sea. The company Wind Surfing Bonaire now stocks 50 state-of-the-art BIC boards with carbon masts, new Aerotech sails with Windsurfing Hawaii, and Chinook booms—all rigged and ready to launch.

For more information: **Windsurfing Bonaire**, *P.O. Box 301,Bonaire;* ☎ *599-7-5363* or *800-748-8733, rentals $25 per hour; $40 per half day lesson $20 plus board.*

Sailing has enjoyed a 15-year tradition in Bonaire, with a major regatta race held in October. These days it's an islandwide party. The tourist office can supply more details. For longer expeditions, hang out at the marina at Harbour Village and negotiate with crews. Your hotel can also arrange water-skiing. Full and half-day charters for **fishing**, complete with all the provisions, are available through hotels. The offshore fishing grounds beyond the Marine Park are abundant with wahoo, mackerel, tuna, barracuda, swordfish, and many others. Boating of all types can be seen from the harbor at Kralendijk, and many offer day trips to Klein Bonaire for lunch and snorkeling. The **Bonaire Sailing Regatta** attracts sailors from all over the Caribbean to compete in various categories, including yachts, sailfish, dinghies, windsurfers, hobie cats, fishing sloops and others.

Horseback riding can be arranged by your hotel through **Rini's Stables**.

A few tennis courts are located at major resorts, including the Sunset Beach Hotel, Harbour Village, Divi Flamingo Beach and the Sand Dollar.

Deep-Sea Fishing

Various locales.

This outfit will take you out for a half- or full day of fishing. **Piscatur Charles** (☎ *599-7-8774)* offers reef fish excursions aboard a 15-foot skiff.

Scuba Diving

Various locations.

Bonaire's rich reefs make for excellent diving; in fact, it's considered one of the top three spots in the world for scuba. Many outfits offer lessons, equipment rentals and excursions. Best known is **Captain Don's Habitat Dive Center** *(Kaya Gobernador N. Deprot,* ☎ *599-7-8290),* a PADI five-star training facility. Also check out: **Dive I and Dive II** *(Divi Flamingo Beach Resort,* ☎ *599-7-8285);* **Bonaire Scuba Center** *(Black Durgon Inn,* ☎ *599-7-8978);* **Sand Dollar Dive and Photo** *(Sand Dollar Condominiums,* ☎ *599-7-5252);* **Neil Watson's Bonaire Undersea Adventures** *(Coral Regency Resort,* ☎ *599-7-5580);* **Great Adventures Bonaire** *(Harbour Village Beach Resort,* ☎ *599-7-7500);* and **Bruce Bowker's Carib Inn Dive Center** *(Carib Inn, 599-7-8819).* Personalized tours for twosomes are offered by **Dee Scarr's Touch the Sea** *(*☎ *599-7-8529).*

Windsurfing Bonaire

Great Southern Travel & Adventures, Kralendijk, ☎ *(800) 748-8733.*

This is a great spot for both beginners and experts. Lessons start at $20 an hour, and they'll even pick you up at your hotel.

Where to Stay

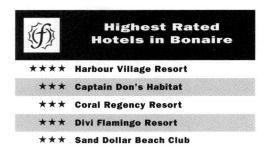

Highest Rated Hotels in Bonaire

★★★★	Harbour Village Resort
★★★	Captain Don's Habitat
★★★	Coral Regency Resort
★★★	Divi Flamingo Resort
★★★	Sand Dollar Beach Club

Most Exclusive Hotels in Bonaire

★★★★	Harbour Village Resort	$170–$400
★★★	Captain Don's Habitat	$150–$245

Fielding's Best Value Hotels in Bonaire

★★★	Sand Dollar Beach Club	$160–$350
★★★★	Harbour Village Resort	$170–$400
★★★	Coral Regency Resort	$150–$230
★★★	Divi Flamingo Resort	$85–$140

Bonaire's accommodations are geared for divers, the serious kind who need casual, but efficient service delivered with an amiable hospitality. Some serious divers who know the area well tend to stay in condominiums, apartments or crowd into the more casual guest homes. A new phase in Bonaire's development was marked by the recent opening of the Harbor Village Beach resort, a paradise of lush landscaping that acts as a haven for wealthy Venezuelans, Europeans and Americans. In the last several years Bonaire has seen a minor explosion of affordable apartments, inns and guesthouses.

Hotels and Resorts

All hotels face the sea. All you need to do is choose whether you want to stay in town or in the countryside. Perhaps the liveliest hotel is **Captain Don's Habitat**, due to the wildcat personality of its owner, Don Stewart, who has been rumored to shoot a mosquito with a pistol. **Divi Flamingo Beach Hotel** has the best restaurants, the Chibi-Chibi and the Calabase Terrace, plus a casino that draws crowds. **Sorobon Beach Resort** is infamous for its clientele who like to take advantage of the nearby "clothes optional" beach.

Captain Don's Habitat $150–$245 ★★★

Kralendijk, ☎ (800) 327-6709, 599.
Single: $150–$245. Double: $150–$245.

The clientele at this casual spot is mostly scuba divers and the facilities cater to them well, with instruction, seven boats and an underwater photo shop. Landlubbers are kept happy, too, in two-bedroom cottages with kitchens or oceanfront rooms or villas. The beach is tiny, but the pool is nice, and kids are kept busy in supervised activities during high season. The atmosphere here is informal and fun, especially when Captain Don stops by to spin tall tales. 43 rooms. Credit Cards: V, MC.

Divi Flamingo Resort $85–$140 ★★★

J.A. Abraham Blvd., Kralendijk, ☎ (800) 367-3484, 599.
Single: $85–$140. Double: $85–$140.

Despite the need for at least a fresh coat of paint, the Divi remains a popular choice due to its friendly staff and lively atmosphere. The original buildings housed German prisoners of war during World War II, but from that dubious start the resort has grown into a pleasant and fun spot. Accommodations are merely adequate and desperately in need of a redo, but the grounds are nice with tennis (including a resident pro), extensive dive facilities (with special programs for the handicapped), casino and lots of after-dark entertainment. 145 rooms. Credit Cards: V, MC, DC, A.

Harbour Village Resort $170–$400 ★★★★

Kaya Gobernador Debrot 71, Kralendijk, ☎ (800) 424- 4, 599.
Single: $170–$400. Double: $170–$400.

Catering to divers, this Iberian village-style complex offers both traditional guest rooms and condos with kitchens; all are spacious, nicely decorated and have air conditioning. The beach is wide by Bonaire standards, and the diving facilities are choice. There's also a spiffy fitness center, a pool and traditional watersports free of charge. The grounds are quite pretty and the digs luxurious, but maintenance is sometimes lacking. 72 rooms. Credit Cards: V, MC, DC, A.

Sunset Beach Hotel $80–$140 ★★

Kaya Gobrenador Debrot 75, Kralendijk, ☎ 599.
Single: $80–$140. Double: $80–$140.

Located on one of the better beaches, the Sunset's accommodations are, unfortunately, set far inland, so ocean views are scarce. Rooms are quite plain, but do offer such extras as coffee makers, refrigerators and air conditioning. The extensive grounds, which could use more landscaping to reach their potential, include two tennis courts, a good dive center and a small pool. The friendly staff can't make up for the fact that this place is screaming for renovation. 145 rooms. Credit Cards: V, MC, DC, A.

Apartments and Condominiums

One and two-bedroom apartments are often chosen by visitors to Bonaire who want to save a little money, but you may empty your wallet anyway if you stock up on staples in Bonaire; the prices can be exorbitant. In most cases, you may need a car. For more information about housekeeping units, contact **Hugo Gerharts** *(Kralendijk, Bonaire, N.A.;* ☎ *011-599-7-8300)* or **Harbourstown Real Estate** *(Kaya Grandi 62, P.O. Box 311;* ☎ *011-599-7-5539, FAX 599-7-5081).*

Buddy Dive Resort   **$80–$165**   ★★

Kaya Gobernador Debrot, Kralendijk, ☎ *(800) 359- 747, 599.*
Single: $80–$165. Double: $80–$165.

Accommodations vary from small apartments with no air conditioning to newer and more spacious units with air conditioning and kitchens. Primarily serving divers, this no-frills complex provides clean towels daily, but maid service only once a week. There's a pool and bar, but no restaurant. A decent choice for those who don't mind fending for themselves and are seeking budget quarters. 30 rooms. Credit Cards: V, MC, DC, A.

Coral Regency Resort   **$150–$230**   ★★★

Kaya Gobernador Debrot 90, Kralendijk, ☎ *(800) 327-8150, 599.*
Single: $150–$210. Double: $150–$230.

This time-share resort (beware of hard sells) puts up guests in studios and one- and two-bedroom suites in two-story buildings arranged around a free-form pool. Units are attractive with large sitting areas, air conditioning and full kitchens. There's a recreation center and dive shop, as well as a bar and restaurant—but no beach to speak of. 28 rooms. Credit Cards: V, MC, DC, A.

Sorobon Beach Resort   **$110–$165**   ★★

Lac Bay, ☎ *599.*
Single: $110–$165. Double: $110–$165.

Bonaire's only "naturalist" resort means that clothes are optional—and many guests take advantage of this fact. Accommodations are in cabinlike structures and consist of one-bedroom units with small kitchens and simple furnishings. The grounds include a small family-style restaurant, bar and private beach—the better to bare all on. The remote location also assures privacy, and a daily shuttle into town assures diversion. A nice, simple spot for the carefree set who don't mind forgoing air conditioning. 20 rooms. Credit Cards: V, MC.

Sunset Oceanfront Apartments   **$60–$190**   ★★

P.O. Box 333, Kralendijk, ☎ *599.*
Single: $60–$190. Double: $130–$190.

This small apartment complex is across the street from the ocean, but a half-mile from the beach. Accommodations are in one- and two-bedroom apartments that overlook the sea; each has a small kitchen, contemporary furnishings and air conditioning only in the bedrooms. There's a small pool on-site, but little else in the way of extras. Restaurants and a casino are within an easy walk. 12 rooms. Credit Cards: V, MC, DC, A.

Inns

These are inns dedicated to serving the committed diver. Furnishings are usually very basic and require a no-nonsense attitude. **Sunset Inn** probably has the best location for walking to the city's restaurants and shops.

Carib Inn   **$64–$124**   ★★

J.A. Abraham Blvd., Kralendijk, ☎ *599.*
Single: $64–$124. Double: $64–$124.

This intimate scuba resort, founded by American diver Bruce Bowker, attracts those who love the sport and are seeking simple lodgings without a lot of extras. Seven of the nine units have their own kitchen; all are air-conditioned and were recently redone. There's a pool but not much else; you'll have to cook in or walk to a nearby restaurant to be sated. Bowker runs a pleasant inn, with lots of repeat guests, so reserve early. The dive center is excellent. 9 rooms. Credit Cards: V, MC, A.

Sunset Inn   **$60–$105**   ★

Kaya C.E.B. Hellmund 29, Kralendijk, ☎ *599.*
Single: $60–$105. Double: $60–$105.

Located within walking distance of a few dive centers, the back-to-basics Sunset has air-conditioned rooms with kitchenettes and coffee makers, though not much else. Its central location makes exploring Kralendijk on foot easy. 7 rooms. Credit Cards: V, MC, A.

Low Cost Lodging

To save money in Bonaire, travel with several people and share the cost of an apartment or condominium. The tourist board can also supply names of private homes that will rent out individual rooms. Also, try to travel during low season (mid-April through mid-December), when rates are slashed.

Where to Eat

Highest Rated Restaurants in Bonaire

★★★★	Classic Eatery
★★★	Chibi-Chibi
★★★	China Garden
★★★	Den Laman
★★★	Green Parrot
★★★	Mona Lisa
★★★	Raffles
★★★	Red Pelican
★★★	Richard's Waterfront
★★★	Toys Grand Cafe

Most Exclusive Restaurants in Bonaire

★★★	Red Pelican	$20–$35
★★★	Chibi-Chibi	$15–$26
★★★★	Classic Eatery	$15–$25
★★★	Mona Lisa	$15–$23
★★★	Den Laman	$11–$22

Fielding's Best Value Restaurants in Bonaire

★★★	Red Pelican	$20–$35
★★★	Mona Lisa	$15–$23
★★★	Den Laman	$11–$22
★★★	Richard's Waterfront	$13–$28
★★★	China Garden	$5–$24

Bonaire is a fish-eating culture; practically everything else has to be shipped in. Perhaps that's one of the reasons costs can run high. A few hotels, like the Divi Flamingo Beach Hotel and Harbour Village, have good restaurants, but most diners head for the city of **Kralendijk** when the hour to feast arrives. Among native specialties are local fish like wahoo, dolphin (not the Flipper kind), and conch, fungi (a thick pudding made from cornmeal), goat stew, and a fine array of Dutch cheeses. Indonesian cuisine adds a little exotica to the local fare; especially good is the new **Toy's Grand Café**, which serves Indonesian delicacies in a funky retro atmosphere. For a real change of pace, head for the base of the customs pier, and indulge in schnitzel and fries while enjoying the bay view at a cute little eatery called **'t Ankertje** ("little anchor" in Dutch). Some of the best hamburgers on the island are found at **The Green Parrot** at the Sand Dollar Resort.

Beefeater   **$$$**   ★★
Kaya Grandi 12,
American cuisine. Specialties: Steaks, scampi, homemade ice cream.
Dinner: 6:30 p.m.–11:30 p.m., entrees $15–$25.
In the center of town is this restored, authentic Bonaireian town home, very intimate, serving rather dear beef and seafood dishes, as well as vegetarian cuisine. But the surroundings are lovely, with a courtyard view. It's nice to see how old Bonaire might have looked. Desserts are homemade and utilize local fruit. Closed: Sun. Reservations recommended. Credit Cards: V, MC, A.

Chibi-Chibi   **$$$**   ★★★
J.A. Abraham Boulevard, ☎ *(599) 7-8285.*
International cuisine. Specialties: Antillean onion soup, fettuccini flamingo.
Dinner: 6:00 p.m.–10:00 p.m., entrees $15–$26.
Like the tropical bird that is its namesake, the Chibi-Chibi is positioned prettily on stilts, and for an experience like none other, the sea below is lit at night so diners can espy the vivid marine life below their tables. (Not surprisingly, you must reserve in advance.) Cuisine is familiar to American tastes, with fresh fish available, but local specialties are also on hand, including *keshi yena*, a whole Edam cheese stuffed with chicken and spices. Associated Hotel: Divi Flamingo Beach Hotel. Reservations recommended. Credit Cards: V, MC, DC, A.

China Garden   **$$**   ★★★
Kaya Grandi 47, ☎ *(599) 7-8480.*
Chinese cuisine. Specialties: Goat Chinese-style, lobster in black bean sauce.
Lunch: 11:30 a.m.–2:00 p.m., entrees $5–$24.
Dinner: 4:00 p.m.–10:00 p.m., entrees $5–$24.
Housed in a grand restored home downtown, this popular restaurant is possibly the best Chinese eatery from a handful of choices. In typical island hodgepodge style, the China Garden combines Cantonese specialties with local favorites like goat, with a few American sandwiches thrown in. Everything is generously portioned, so you get what you pay for and then some. All sweet-and-sour and black-bean sauced

dishes are recommended, and the seafood is fresh. Closed: Tue. Reservations recommended. Credit Cards: V, MC, A.

Classic Eatery $$$ ★★★★

1 Kaya L.D. Gerharts 4, ☎ *(599) 7-8003.*
International cuisine. Specialties: Fresh fish, duck a l'orange, sweet red pepper soup.
Lunch: 9:00 a.m.–4:00 p.m., entrees $5–$15.
Dinner: 4:00 p.m.–11:00 p.m., entrees $15–$25.
This is a French salon in the true sense of the word—without the snob factor. Because it's such a small restaurant (less than 10 tables), everyone gets individualized attention. The classic French menu, with some innovative touches, always includes duck a l'orange and a soup of roasted sweet red peppers. If you don't want to eat, stop by for a drink at the enormous mahogany bar where the local arts community holds court regularly. Closed: Sun. Reservations recommended. Credit Cards: V, MC.

Den Laman $$$ ★★★

Kaya Gobernador,
Seafood cuisine. Specialties: Red snapper Creole, conch flamingo, kingfish.
Dinner: 6:00 p.m.–11:00 p.m., entrees $11–$22.
Seafood doesn't get much fresher or better prepared on the island than in this indoor-outdoor restaurant. Red snapper lightly grilled or prepared Creole style is a best bet and is usually available. Decor is piscatorial, with a huge aquarium providing a running conversation piece; it can be fun for kids. Closed September. Closed: Tue. Credit Cards: V, MC, A.

Green Parrot $$ ★★★

Kaya Gobernador, ☎ *(599) 7-5454.*
International cuisine. Specialties: Onion string appetizer, barbecue.
Lunch: 11:30 a.m.–3:00 p.m., entrees $5–$10.
Dinner: 4:30 p.m.–10:00 p.m., entrees $10–$20.
Homesick Americans will like this jumping place, which has frothy and fruity margaritas, juicy burgers, barbecue and, familiar to habitues of the Tony Roma's chain, an onion string loaf. The view is great at sunset since it is situated on a hotel pier that is open to the breezes. It's a good place to grab a reasonably priced lunch when coming from or going to the airport, which is only a few miles away. There is a buffet on Sunday with barbecued meats and lively entertainment. Associated Hotel: Sand Dollar Condominiums. Reservations recommended. Credit Cards: V, MC, A.

Kilumba $$ ★★

Kaya L.D. Gerharts, ☎ *(599) 7-5019.*
Seafood cuisine. Specialties: Stewed goat, catch of the day.
Lunch: entrees $8–$15.
Dinner: entrees $8–$15.
Bonaireians like this seafood-Creole spot north of town, named after an African sea god. Why? Because the atmosphere at the bar is mellow, and everyone knows everyone else; a good place to schmooze. Goat stew is recommended at lunch, and in the evenings, usually quite busy, fish dinners are given the spotlight. Credit Cards: Not Accepted.

Mona Lisa $$$ ★★★

Kaya Grandi 15, ☎ *(599) 7-8718.*
International cuisine. Specialties: Pork tenderloin sate with peanut sauce, wahoo.
Lunch: 12:00 a.m.–2:00 p.m., entrees $12–$23.
Dinner: 6:00 p.m.–10:00 p.m., entrees $15–$23.
Absorb some local color in this popular bar and restaurant, where the Dutch-born chef personally oversees each table. The Mona Lisa's bar, decorated with a profusion of hometown knickknacks, is a riot of activity. Copious snacks are served there until very late. The pretty restaurant wears a more demure face, with a diverse menu of Indonesian, Dutch and French favorites. An ongoing special is pork sate (tenderloin marinated with garlic, sesame oil, soy and other spices) served with peanut sauce, but a popular French onion soup is always available. Closed: Sat, Sun. Reservations recommended. Credit Cards: V, MC, A.

Raffles $$$ ★★★

Kaya C.E.B. Hellmund 5, ☎ *(599) 7-8617.*
International cuisine. Specialties: Seafood platter Caribe, salmon cascade.
Dinner: 6:30 p.m.–10:00 p.m., entrees $11–$25.
Bonaire has a number of old homesteads, but Raffles, with a red London phone booth as its landmark and mascot, roosts in one of the oldest of the old. Patrons have more than a hope for an intimate conversation in the indoor dining room, along with Caribbean entrees, French-style desserts and soft jazz playing. There's also a terrace for people watching. *Pescado de mariscos,* a Latin bouillabaisse, is usually available; also chicken and steaks. Make room for the mousse made with two kinds of chocolate. Reservations recommended. Credit Cards: V, MC, A.

Red Pelican $$$ ★★★

Kaminda Sorobon 64, Lac Bay, ☎ *(599) 7-8198.*
Seafood cuisine. Specialties: Seafood stew, marinated fish salad.
Lunch: 12:00 a.m.–2:00 p.m., entrees $4–$6.
Dinner: 7:00 p.m.–10:00 p.m., entrees $20–$35.
A sophisticated, intimate spot, the Red Pelican is very close to being the toniest restaurant on the isle, with a location a little ways off the tourist track, on the windward coast in Lac Bay. Decor is island-tropical and cuisine is International. Expect herring, stews and chicken dishes. Associated Hotel: Lac Bay Resort. Closed: Sun. Reservations recommended. Credit Cards: V, MC, A.

Rendez-Vous Restaurant $$$ ★★

3 Kaya L.D. Gerharts, ☎ *(599) 7-8454.*
International cuisine. Specialties: Chicken apricot, keshi yena.
Dinner: 6:00 p.m.–10:30 p.m., entrees $14–$26.
The livin' is easy at this midtown eatery which, like most on the island, has two dining areas—indoor and out. But wherever you sit, it's cozy, and a loaf of home-baked bread gets things off to a nice start. Local dishes are well represented, and *keshi yena* (Edam cheese stuffed with meat) is prepared picadillo style, with raisins. Otherwise, there's always good seafood, with a daily special, and vegetarians needn't feel slighted. Good fruit desserts, patisserie and espresso. Closed: Sun. Reservations recommended. Credit Cards: V, MC, A.

Richard's Waterfront   **$$$** ★★★

60 J.A. Abraham Boulevard, ☎ *(599) 7-5263.*
Seafood cuisine. Specialties: Conch al Ajillo, grilled wahoo, seafood soup.
Dinner: 6:30 p.m.–10:30 p.m., entrees $13–$28.

The food is usually stellar at this friendly waterfront charmer, especially when attentive owner Richard Beady, from Boston, is around to check on things. The daily special, on a blackboard, regularly features fresh fish of the day; wahoo is recommended. There won't be many surprises, like extra hot pepper in the popular fish soup, which is a favored starter. Both conch and shrimp are often prepared with garlic-butter sauce. The bar is a favorite with locals and others, especially at sunset, for all the usual reasons. Closed: Mon. Reservations recommended. Credit Cards: V, MC, A.

Toys Grand Cafe   **$$$** ★★★

J.A. Abraham Boulevard, ☎ *(599) 7-6666.*
International cuisine. Specialties: Snails in blue-cheese sauce, nasi goreng.
Lunch: 11:30 a.m.–2:00 p.m., entrees $5–$15.
Dinner: 5:00 p.m.–10:00 p.m., entrees $10–$23.

Someone with a touch of whimsy created this eclectic restaurant on the main drag in Kralendijk. The walls are covered with familiar figures from the cartoon and entertainment worlds. Not grand in cuisine, but in concept; it's mostly fun. Not really for kids (maybe grown up ones), as the interesting and creative menu is peppered with Indonesian favorites, meats and shellfish with vivid sauces. At certain times of the day, a few meals are available at a substantial discount. Credit Cards: Not Accepted. Credit Cards: V, MC.

Zeezicht Restaurant   **$$$** ★★

Kaya Corsow 10, ☎ *(599) 7-8434.*
Seafood cuisine. Specialties: Ceviche, local snails in hot sauce, seafood soup.
Lunch: 9:00 a.m.–4:00 p.m., entrees $5–$9.
Dinner: 4:00 p.m.–11:00 p.m., entrees $9–$25.

See the zee (sea) at this waterfront eatery with a front porch at the water's edge. A good American breakfast is served from 9 a.m., and lunch is usually local fish and conch sandwiches, which are recommended. There are Indonesian specialties, including a mini-rijstaffel for those who can't handle the usual 16-dish feast. Whether eating inside or out, there is something for everyone here, food and ambience-wise. Service can be slow at peak times. Credit Cards: V, MC, A.

Where to Shop

Shopping in Bonaire is for the bored spouse who doesn't like diving. You can, however, find some bargains, up to 50 percent, on gemstone jewelry, ceramics, liquor and tobacco. Most stores will accept American cash, credit cards and traveler's checks, but make sure prices are quoted in U.S. dollars. An easy stroll down Kaya Grandi in Kralendijk will take you past most of the interesting shops. Locally wrought jewelry and batiks from Indonesia are a little extra special at **Ki Bo Ke Pakus** in the Divi Flamingo Beach Resort 7 Casino. Dutch cheeses can be found at **Littman's Gifts** next door to Littman's Jewelers, a long-time establishment.

Bonaire Directory

ARRIVAL AND DEPARTURE

ALM offers nonstop flights to Bonaire from Atlanta (twice a week) and from Miami (once a week). Air Aruba also has a direct flight from Newark, New Jersey three times a week (these flights first touch down in Aruba before flying onto Bonaire). American Airlines flies daily to Curaçao from Miami, allowing passengers to make immediate transfers to Bonaire, usually on ALM, which makes 4–5 daily nonstop flights to Bonaire from Curaçao. A plus for flying on American Airlines is that you can sometimes receive a discount if you book your hotel at the same time you make your flight reservation.

The departure tax is $10. There is also an inter-island departure tax of $5.65.

CLIMATE

Temperatures average 82 degrees F and vary only 6 degrees between summer and winter. Water temperatures range from 76–80 F. Bonaire gets less than 20 inches of rainfall per year. Bonaire is below the Hurricane Belt and is rarely bombarded by storms or heavy seas.

DOCUMENTS

U.S. and Canadian citizens need show only proof of citizenship (passport, original or notarized birth certificate or voter's registration with photo ID), and an ongoing or return ticket.

ELECTRICITY

Current runs 127 volts, 50 cycles. American appliance will work slower; best to bring an adapter.

GETTING AROUND

Expect to take a taxi from the airport to your hotel—about $10. Rates are established by the government, and most honest drivers will show the list of prices if you ask. Do note that rates are higher (25 percent) after 8 p.m., and from 11 p.m.–6 a.m. (50 percent).

Driving in Bonaire is on the right side of the road. Unless you are an experienced driver, tooting around Bonaire in a scooter or moped can be dangerous since roads are often strewn with rocks or full of holes. The best way to see the Washington National Park is in a Jeep, van, or automobile. To rent a car, you will need to show a valid U.S., British, or Canadian driver's license.

Budget, Avis and Dollar Rent a Car all have booths at the airport.

LANGUAGE

Papiamento is the unofficial island language, Dutch the official. English is almost unilaterally spoken. Spanish is also well known.

MEDICAL EMERGENCIES

St. Francis Hospital in Kralendijk ☎ *8900* is run by well-trained doctors who studied in the Netherlands. Divers will be happy to know it comes equipped with a decompression chamber.

MONEY

Official currency is the Netherlands Antilles florin or guilder, written as NAf or Afl. Most establishments list prices in guilders, but will accept dollars (giving change in guilders). U.S. dollars and traveler's checks are accepted everywhere.

TELEPHONE

From the U.S. dial 011 (international code), plus 5997 (country code), plus the 4-digit local number. Few lodgings have room phones, so most people head down to the Landsradio office in Kralendijk. The airport also has telephones.

TIME

Bonaire is on Atlantic Standard time.

TIPPING AND TAXES

Most hotels and restaurants add a 10–15 percent service charge. The government also requires hotels to add a $4.10-per-person daily room tax. Feel free to tip more for especially good service.

TOURIST INFORMATION

The Tourism Corporation of Bonaire is located at *12 Kaya Simon Bolivia*; ☎ *8322* or *8649*, FAX *8408*, weekdays only. Or from the U.S. call Tourism Bonaire ☎ *(800) 826-6247*.

WATER

Tap water is safe to drink since it comes from distilled seawater.

WHEN TO GO

Carnival takes place in February. Coronation Day is April 30. St. John's Day is June 24. St. Peter's Day is celebrated in Rincon on June 28. Bonaire Day is September 6. Annual Sailing Regatta are a series of races celebrated with a festive air in mid-October.

BONAIRE HOTELS	RMS	RATES	PHONE	FAX
Kralendijk				
★★★★ **Harbour Village Resort**	72	$170–$400	(800) 424-0004	
★★★ **Captain Don's Habitat**	43	$150–$245	(800) 327-6709	

BONAIRE HOTELS		RMS	RATES	PHONE	FAX
★★★	Coral Regency Resort	28	$150–$230	(800) 327-8150	599-7-5680
★★★	Divi Flamingo Resort	145	$85–$140	(800) 367-3484	
★★★	Sand Dollar Beach Club	73	$160–$350	(800) 288-4773	599-7-8760
★★	Buddy Dive Resort	30	$80–$165	(800) 359-0747	
★★	Carib Inn	9	$64–$124	599	
★★	Sorobon Beach Resort	20	$110–$165	599	
★★	Sunset Beach Hotel	145	$80–$140	599	
★★	Sunset Oceanfront Apartments	12	$60–$190	599	
★	Sunset Inn	7	$60–$105	599	

BONAIRE RESTAURANTS		LOCATION	PHONE	ENTREE
Kralendijk				
American				
★★	Beefeater	Kralendijk		$15–$25••
Chinese				
★★★	China Garden	Kralendijk	(599) 7-8480	$5–$24
International				
★★★★	Classic Eatery	Kralendijk	(599) 7-8003	$5–$25
★★★	Chibi-Chibi	Kralendijk	(599) 7-8285	$15–$26••
★★★	Green Parrot	Kralendijk	(599) 7-5454	$5–$20
★★★	Mona Lisa	Kralendijk	(599) 7-8718	$12–$23
★★★	Raffles	Kralendijk	(599) 7-8617	$11–$25••
★★★	Toys Grand Cafe	Kralendijk	(599) 7-6666	$5–$23
★★	Rendez-Vous Restaurant	Kralendijk	(599) 7-8454	$14–$26••
Seafood				
★★★	Den Laman	Kralendijk		$11–$22••
★★★	Red Pelican	Lac Bay	(599) 7-8198	$4–$35
★★★	Richard's Waterfront	Kralendijk	(599) 7-5263	$13–$28••
★★	Kilumba	Kralendijk	(599) 7-5019	$8–$15
★★	Zeezicht Restaurant	Kralendijk	(599) 7-8434	$5–$25

Note: • Lunch Only

•• Dinner Only

BRITISH VIRGIN ISLANDS

Boats and kayaks are available for rent on BVI.

BVI refer to themselves as Nature's Little Secrets. The country has never sought nor desired mass tourism, preferring to let the discerning traveler discover it. The quiet, unassuming attitude is felt the moment you step off the plane, reflected in the gentle nature of the people and the laid-back way of life. The *dolce far ninete* (nothing-to-do) philosophy reigns in the BVI, and those who require high-rise resort amenities, late-night bars and other externally generated entertainment should not even buy a ticket. Even at The Baths, BVI's most famous beach on its second largest island, Virgin Gorda, there are no bustling beach cafes, souvenir shops, or crowds.What BVI does have are miles and miles of nearly deserted, uninterrupted beaches, tiny coral coves perfect for diving, and even a few islands where the only place to stay is a luxurious private home that can rent for up to $8000 a day. For more reasonable budgets, a full week on the water in the BVI, sailing from island to island, under the direction of a well-trained captain, can run under $450 per person summer and fall. Essentially, the compactness of the BVI, the purity of the waters and the accessibility of facilities offer an unparalleled opportunity to experience as many different dive, snorkeling and trekking sites as possible in the shortest amount of time.

Bird's Eye View

More than 40 islands, rocks and cays make up the complex called the British Virgin Islands, the most important being Tortola, Virgin Gorda, Beef Island, Anegada and Jost van Dyke. Lying 60 miles east of Puerto Rico and directly northeast of St. John, the islands harbor a population of only about 12,000 people stretched over 16 inhabited islands. From nearly any advantage point, the view is that of seemingly endless tropical islands stretching off into the horizon. The appearances of these islands range from sloping mountains cloaked with verdant green growth to scrub and cactus-covered hills layered with massive rounded boulders. Long stretches of palm-shaded beaches border much of the island's perimeters. Offshore rough-hewn rock formations poke their heads out of the water, providing perches for seabirds.

Tortola, the capital and largest island, is a good base for exploring the archipelago. The coastline snakes in and out, providing a wealth of anchorages and long, fine beaches. Hills angle up to a rocky spine, running the length of the island. On the moist north side of the island (exposed to the Atlantic), vegetation takes the form of a jungle, with aromatic flowering bushes.The highest point is the 1740-ft. Mount Sage, a rainforest that is part of the BVI National Trust. The north side retains the air of old Tortola, with its quaint inns, rustic bars and isolated beaches.The island's West Indian roots can be seen in Road Town, where pastel-colored wood shops line Main Street and local chefs add Caribbean flavor to dishes like conch fritters and shrimp creole. Here, on the arid southern coast, facing the Sir Francis Drake Channel, one finds the stark beauty of foothills decorated with cactus and scrub bush. Protected year-long from the brunt of the trade winds, this is perfect sailing territory, considered among the best in the world. Although the ocean is

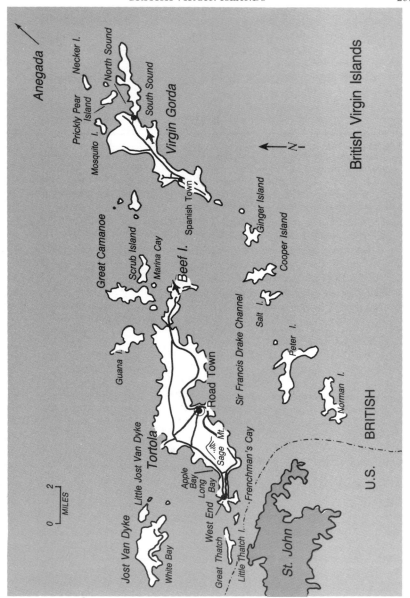

British Virgin Islands

calm for much of the year, certain bays are famous worldwide among surfers for the fine waves during January and February.

History

The Virgin Islands were discovered by Christopher Columbus on his second voyage in 1493. Fascinated by the exquisite natural beauty of the islands, he named them *Las Once Mil Virgines* (the 11,000 Virgins) in honor of St. Ursula and her followers. The truth is, Columbus was the not the first human to set forth on the island. Prior to the European invasion, these islands had been populated by successive waves of Indian tribes migrating north from the Orinoco region of South America. Unfortunately, the arrival of the Europeans spelled the end of the native population; within a generation, there was not a trace of them. The occupation of the island by the Spanish and other Europeans followed a pattern similar to that of other Caribbean islands. For two centuries, control of the island was passed from one country to another while the islands remained mostly uninhabited. Many of those who balked at directly challenging the Spanish chose instead the path of piracy and pirateering, the most famous of whom were Sir John Hawkins, Henry Morgan, Jost Van Dyke and Edward Teach, better known as Blackbeard. These islands provided a secluded and safe anchorage for these brigands. Even today the legacy of piracy survives in the names of many islands and in the ever-persistent legends of buried treasure. Control of the Virgin Islands finally equalized with the Danish taking control of the western islands, now known as the U.S. Virgin Islands, while the British controlled the eastern set—so-named the British Virgin Islands. In fact, Tortola (BVI) is separated from St. John (USV) by less than two miles. From the 1700s to the mid-1800s, a plantation economy supported these islands. The remnants of the sugar industry can still be seen in the ruins of sugar mills hidden in the bush. In 1967, the BVI became a self-governing member of the British Commonwealth.

People

The people of the British Virgin Islands have an extraordinarily friendly reputation and will naturally extend you greetings as you stroll down the street. In fact, an islander can become quite hurt if you don't return the greeting. At the same time, Gordians and Tortolans are said to be somewhat retiring and not exactly prone to inviting travelers into their homes. Those who live in the interior mountains definitely tend to by shyer, but their life-style is also comparatively less pressured by touristic demands; these are older people in the mountain communities who still ride donkeys, make their own charcoal and harbor age-old superstitions about *duppies* or spirits. As tourism blossomed due to the efforts of established black families as well as spunky individuals, some of the island's women have become renowned for their cooking skills, in particular Mrs. V. Thomas who was decorated by the Queen of England for her guava jelly and mango chutney. As construction demands rise, traditional island occupations, like stonemasonry and gardening, have begun returning, and sailors in the old school of sloops are finding another kind of work in more progressive boating. Because of the generous economic assistance received from Great Britain, islanders enjoy a considerable enthusiasm for, and strong identification with, their mother country.

TORTOLA

Twelve by three miles wide, Tortola is home to three-fourths of the residents of the BVI. It's a refreshingly unaffected combination of the young and new, a reflection of a refined and contemporary approach to West Indian culture. Years of British rule have given Tortola a well-educated and worldly population, one largely unaffected by tourism. Nevertheless, most of the hotels are located here, about a dozen around Road Town. There are a couple of places to stay near Wickam's Cay I and II, on the southeast shore, and on the northwest shore at Apple Bay. In general, the crime rate is low and many residents seldom lock their doors, but it's not suggested a tourist follow their habit.

Beaches

The finest beaches and bays are located on the north side of Tortola. At the **West End**, where the majority of hotels are situated, are the Pirate's Pub and the Pusser's Pub; **Smuggler's Cove** to the north is an exquisite crescent-shaped strand. **Long Bay** and **Apple Bay** are notable, the latter is where surfers find their biggest waves (check out Bomba's Surfside shack made out of driftwood). **Cane Garden Bay** has a gently curving beach and is a popular anchorage. Good beaches are also located around **Beef Island**, the site of Tortola's airport, including the extremely dramatic **Josiah's Bay** and **Elizabeth Beach**. Outstanding, powdery beaches can be found on all the islands of the BVI. Snorkelers and divers can take full advantage of the crystal clear waters.

Dive Sites

Fascinating dive sites are almost second nature in Tortola; there are over 60 charted ones. Many are located around the numerous off-lying islands and rock structures. Marine life is outstanding, with healthy coral reefs and many larger sea animals, including turtles, spotted eagle rays and the occasional manta ray. Owing to the geological formation, depths seldom exceed 90 feet, because the entire island chain rests on top of a vast plateau. To reach deep waters, you must travel a great distance. Dive conditions are excellent year-round, In summer, water reaches 80 degrees F, in winter 76 degrees F. On an average day, underwater visibility runs 60–100 feet. Among the best dives are *RMS Hone*, a 250-ft. ship that sunk in a hurricane off Salt Island in 1867. **Painted Walls** features a series of canyons culminating in a massive vertical walled pass, with every imaginable color of invertebrate. **Alice in Wonderland** is one of the finest coral reefs in the area. **Rainbow Canyon** is a beautiful shallow reef, just about 25–40 feet deep, with undercut corals, beds of garden eels and lots of tropicals.

Treks

Sage Mountain National Park is a 92-acre reserve on Tortola, where reforestation projects have been underway for the last two decades. It's situated on peaks that form a volcanic backbone down the center of Tortola, boasting the highest elevation—1780 ft—in both the British and U.S. Virgin Islands. Two trails, well developed, wind through terrain that resembles rainforest, with hanging vines and prickly ferns as well as a variety of hard- and softwood trees. The trails are neatly graveled and marked with directional signs; some plants are clearly labeled as well. To see a panoramic view, take the unsurfaced road to a parking area and the park entrance. You'll need at least a half-day to fully experience the park.

Norman Island, across from Drake Channel is all deserted except for a few wild animals and seabirds. There are some old ruins, a salt pond that attracts a huge variety of birds, and several footpaths. A thirty-minute hike will take you to **Spy Glass Hill**, up a steep hill from where you can get a spectacular view. It's said that buccaneers and nefarious pirates used this lookout to spy on Spanish treasure ships; rumor has it the island is still used as a drug smuggling base, so watch where you point your camera. Snorkelers will find the island's partially submerged caves exciting to explore.

What Else to See

The best sights in the British Virgin Islands have to do with sun, surf and beach; anything else should be left for a rainy or hazy day. The Tourist Office can arrange a visit to **Road Town's Folk Museum** or the **rum factory**. Do consider taking a frog-jumper's flight or quick cruise to one of the surrounding islands—you can make it back the same day. Most people come back from **Cooper Island** raving about the beauty, and if you get tired of the beach you can always trek through some fascinating trails. **Anegada**, reached best by small plane from Tortola's Beef Island, can also turn into a memorable day excursion, mostly for divers.

Museums and Exhibits

British Virgin Islands Folk Museum   ★★★

Main Street, Road Town.
Hours Open: 10:00 a.m.–4:00 p.m.

Housed in a traditional West Indian building, this museum showcases artifacts from Arawak Indians and the island's plantation and slave eras. There are also some interesting relics salvaged from the wreck of the *RMS Rhone*, a British mail ship that sank off Salt Island in 1867. Free admission.

Parks and Gardens

J.R. O'Neal Botanical Gardens   ★★★

Station Avenue, Road Town, ☎ *(809) 494-4557.*
Hours Open: 8:00 a.m.–4:00 p.m.

Indigenous and exotic plants are beautifully showcased at this four-acre garden, which includes an herb garden and hothouses for orchids and ferns. Free admission.

Mount Sage National Park   ★★★★

Ridge Road, West End.

Located on the peak of a volcanic mountain, this 92-acre national park protects the remains of a primeval rain forest—most, alas, was cut down over the years. A graveled path will take you to the top, some 1780 feet up, the highest elevation in the British and U.S. Virgin Islands. A nice day trip. Free admission.

Tours

Travel Plan Tours   ★★★

Waterfront Plaza, Road Town, ☎ *(809) 494-2872.*
Island tours take about 2.5 hours and include all the hot spots. $50 per person.

Sports

Why bother with other sports when the sea treasures are as spectacular as they are on these islands? Don't even think about golf (there isn't a course), but there are tennis courts at some hotels. Horseback riding can be arranged through your hotel. Bare-boating (self-crew yacht chartering) is one of the biggest pastimes here, or you can charter a boat that comes equipped with a crew. Navigation is not difficult and the weather is usually so clear you can't get lost. (Do note that bareboaters aren't allowed to travel to Anegada because of the dangerous route through the reef.) If you're not an educated sailor, think about taking a few classes at the **Nick Trotter Sailing School** at the **Bitter End Yacht Club, North Sound** ☎ *494-2745*. The best centers for fishing are Salt Island, Anegada, Jost Van Dyke, West End, Tortola, and Peter Island. Bird-watchers should have a blast on Virgin Gorda and Guana Island, off Tortola.

Boardsailing B.V.I.

Long Look, West End, ☎ *(809) 495-2447.*
Learn the popular sport of windsurfing for $20 for a one-hour lesson. Boards can be rented for $155 a week. On Virgin Gorda, the **Nick Trotter Sailing School** at the Bitter End Resort *(*☎ *809-872-2392)* offers courses and rentals.

Boating

Road Town, ☎ *(809) 494-2331.*
At the Moorings Resort, you can rent all manner of sailing yachts, from bareboat (no crew) to the works, with a skipper, cook and crew. Try Virgin Island Sailing, also in Road Town, for charters. Call from the States: ☎ *800-233-7936.*

Deep-Sea Fishing

Various locations.
Sport fishers can arrange a charter or join a scheduled excursion. **Captain Dale** *(*☎ *809-495-5225)* arranges trips out of Virgin Gorda.

Scuba Diving

Various locations.
Several outfits will teach you the ropes and take you to the best underwater sports. On Tortola: **Baskin in the Sun** *(*☎ *809-494-5854)* and **Underwater Safaris** *(*☎ *809-494-3235)*. On Virgin Gorda, try **Kilbrides Underwater Tours** at the Bitter End Resort *(*☎ *809-495-9638)*; two-tank dives cost $80–$90.

Shadow's Ranch

Todman's Estate, Road Town, ☎ *(809) 494-2262.*

Hop aboard a horse and venture along the beach or up to Mount Sage National Park. Prices start at $25 per hour.

Where to Stay

Highest Rated Hotels in British Virgin Islands

★★★★★	Guana Island
★★★★★	Necker Island
★★★★★	Peter Island Resort
★★★★	Biras Creek Hotel
★★★★	Drake's Anchorage
★★★★	Little Dix Bay Hotel
★★★	Bitter End Yacht Club
★★★	Long Bay Beach Hotel
★★★	Mango Bay Resort
★★★	Olde Yard Inn

Most Exclusive Hotels in British Virgin Islands

★★★★	Little Dix Bay Hotel	$225–$1000
★★★★	Guana Island	$485–$635
★★★★	Drake's Anchorage	$223–$600
★★★	Sugar Mill Hotel	$115–$320
★★★	Treasure Isle Hotel	$85–$230

Fielding's Best Value Hotels in British Virgin Islands

★★★	Prospect Reef Resort	$91–$279
★★	Fort Burt Hotel	$60–$95
★★★	Olde Yard Inn	$85–$180
★★★★★	Peter Island Resort	$195–$3900
★★★★	Biras Creek Hotel	$340–$840

Accommodations in the British Virgin Islands are the antithesis of the big-island resort; for the most part, they are intimate and casual and reflect the style of the owner/management, usually husband-and-wife teams. The tiny isles of the BVI are rarely overrun with tourists during the peak season, but those travelers seeking maximum solitude will want a copy of *Intimate Inns & Villas*. The colorful booklet lists more than two dozen small properties on the islands of Virgin Gorda, Tortola Anegada, and Jost Van Dyke. Copies are available from the **British Virgin Islands Tourist Board** in NY (☎ *800-835-8530*).

Wherever you stay, check your final bills; many a tourist here have been charged for snorkeling gear that they had already returned. Also remember that ordering from the minibar will spell instant death to your wallet: a six-pack of Jamaican beer, a couple of bottles of mineral water, and a couple of colas ran someone we know about $75. Also check your credit charges after you've been home for several months—you might have had your number stolen.

Hotels and Resorts

Most of the hotels in the BVI are located in Tortola, situated around Road Town (one grand exception is the exquisite Little Dix on Virgin Gorda). However, room rates seem to be competitive with big resort hotels, with no real relation to quality. The premier property is **Long Bay**, which acts as the social hub of the island. The only thing marring its beachfront is the heavy presence of coral, which can be dangerous to unsuspecting bathers. Staying on Tortola will save you (hopefully) from some of the disasters that hit other islets, like power losses and low water supplies. At all hotels, the lifestyle is casual outdoors. Do note that outside of beaches, skimpy attire tends to offend residents.

Long Bay Beach Hotel $55–$295   ★★★

Road Town, ☎ *(800) 729-9599, (809) 495-4252.*
Single: $55–$265. Double: $110–$295.

Situated on a 50-acre estate that slopes down to a powdery mile-long beach, Long Bay offers a variety of accommodations, ranging from standard guest rooms to villas of two to five bedrooms, some with their own private pool. Some units are located along a hillside, others are right on the beach. Active types are kept happy with a pitch-and-putt golf course, pool and tennis. The restaurant, housed in an old sugar mill, offers live music most nights. Villa dwellers can arrange to have a chef prepare a private dinner. 80 rooms. Credit Cards: V, MC, A.

Prospect Reef Resort $91–$279   ★★★

Road Town, ☎ *(800) 356-8937, (809) 494-3311.*
Single: $91–$270. Double: $91–$279.

Set on lush grounds overlooking a channel (but lacking a beach of note), the choices here range from standard guest rooms to studios to villas and townhouses with kitchenettes; only some have air conditioning. Lots going on, including six tennis courts, a par-three golf course and a health club with pampering treatments. Several pools include one that is junior-Olympic sized and another that contains saltwater. Sailboats can be rented at the small harbor. Those with difficulty walking should note that there are lots of steep stairs and climbs. 131 rooms. Credit Cards: V, MC, A.

Sugar Mill Hotel   **$115–$320**   ★★★

Road Town, ☎ (800) 462-8834, (809) 495-4355.
Single: $115–$320. Double: $125–$320.
The dining room is housed in a 350-year-old sugar mill and rum distillery, hence the name. All is quite nice at this garden estate, with accommodations in simple cottages scattered about a hillside. Furnishings are basic but adequate; some have kitchens but none have air. There's a small pool for those who don't want to cross the street to get to the beach. Owned by an American couple who used to write about travel and food, so you know they know what they're doing. Great meals! 21 rooms. Credit Cards: V, MC, A.

Treasure Isle Hotel   **$85–$230**   ★★★

Road Town, ☎ (800) 334-2435, (809) 494-2501.
Single: $85–$220. Double: $95–$230.
All the air-conditioned rooms at this pretty resort overlook the harbor and marina, and include tropical art and pleasant rattan furniture. Situated on 15 acres of hillside, the grounds include a festive free-form pool, a full dive facility, and water sports for an extra fee. Management is friendly, and guests here are kept happy. Lots of evening entertainment for the partying set. 43 rooms. Credit Cards: V, MC, A.

Village Cay Marina Hotel   **$115–$330**   ★★

Road Town, ☎ (809) 494-2771.
Single: $115–$330. Double: $115–$330.
This small hotel is located downtown in the Village Cay Marina Complex. Rooms are air conditioned and have cathedral ceilings, Oriental rugs, cable TV with VCRs and hair dryers. There's a restaurant and bar on site, as well as a small pool and watersports. The clientele is largely comprised of yachtsmen, and there's lots to do within walking distance. 19 rooms. Credit Cards: V, MC, A.

Apartments and Condominiums

Yacht owners and vacationers prepared to settle for a long stay take advantage of the lovely private homes rented by owners during high season. Apartments and cottages also offer the opportunity for independent living, especially if you want to do your own cooking. Bring your best staples from home since prices on Tortola run high. Several townhouse units along the southeast shore are excellent for romantic sunset viewing, and in some villas, maid service is included (**Fort Recovery Estates**). Tortola's premier villa rental is **Shannon House**, built into a hill, and boasting a network of romantic trails, large boulders, and luscious gardens; the kicker is the split-level pool with a water slide that plunges into the sea off a cliff. If you're just looking for a place to store your luggage before you head out to the beach, the cottages at **Over the Hill** will serve nicely. For luxury rentals, contact **McLaughlin Anderson Vacation** at ☎ *800-537-6246* or *809-776-0635.*

Admiralty Estate Resort   **$110–$275**   ★★

Road Town, ☎ (809) 494- 14.
Single: $110–$275. Double: $110–$275.

Perched on a hillside, this condominium hotel has one- and two-bedroom units that are attractively furnished and include air conditioning, full kitchens, living and dining areas and balconies with a view. There's a restaurant on-site with limited room service available, and nightly entertainment in the pool bar. Four tennis courts and a pool complete the picture. 30 rooms. Credit Cards: V, MC, A.

Fort Recovery Estates $125–$295   ★★

Road Town, ☎ *(800) 367-8455, (809) 495-4467.*
Single: $125–$295. Double: $200–$295.

The fieldstone tower is about all that remains of this 17th-century fort, today a small enclave of attractive villas with full kitchens and air-conditioned bedrooms. Larger parties can rent a four-bedroom, three-bathroom house. The small beach makes for good swimming and watersports, or unwind in a yoga class. Daily maid service keeps things looking fresh. The grounds are nice and bright, with lots of colorful flowers scattered about. 10 rooms. Credit Cards: V, MC, A.

Frenchman's Cay Resort $107–$270   ★★

West End, Road Town, ☎ *(800) 235-4077, (809) 495-4844.*
Single: $107–$185. Double: $113–$270.

Set on its own small cay and connected via bridge to Tortola, this luxury enclave of villas has nice views of the channel and neighboring islands. One- and two-bedroom villas include a full kitchen, ceiling fans (no air conditioning), and island art. The small beach is good for snorkeling, but rocks make wading difficult. There's also a small pool, hammocks meant for snoozing, a tennis court and an open-air restaurant. A nice, quiet spot. 9 rooms. Credit Cards: V, MC, A.

Nanny Cay Resort $50–$195   ★★

Nanny Cay Marina, Road Town, ☎ *(809) 494-2512.*
Single: $50–$80. Double: $85–$195.

Set on a private 25-acre inlet on Sir Francis Drake Channel, Nanny Cay houses guests in studio apartments with kitchenettes, West Indian decor and air conditioning. Lots of yachtsmen come here, lured by the 180-slip marina. Extras include two restaurants and bars, a pool and tennis. Service can be uneven. 42 rooms. Credit Cards: V, MC, A.

Rockview Holiday Homes $100–$755   ★★

Road Town, ☎ *(800) 621-1270, (809) 494-2550.*
Single: $100–$755. Double: $100–$755.

This informal villa complex is set in lush tropical gardens. Accommodations range from one- to five-bedroom villas situated on a hillside or overlooking the beach, all with full kitchens. Some even have their own pool. Maid service is available, and you can hire a chef if you're not up for cooking. 20 rooms. Credit Cards: V, MC, A.

Inns

Since everything in the BVI practically resembles an inn, the following properties are more notable for their management, usually run by owners, who like to get involved in their client's vacations. The best is **Sugar Mill Estate**, which also serves fine meals in surroundings that will make you want to stay longer than planned. **Fort Burt** offers the most stunning view, situated as it is on a hill on the southwestern tip of Road Town (the downside is that you have to hike that hill to get anywhere). If you want to meet yacht owners, they tend to hang out at the bar at the **Cane Garden Beach Hotel**.

Moorings-Mariner Inn   **$80–$165**   ★ ★

Road Town, ☎ (800) 535-7289, (809) 494-2331.
Single: $80–$150. Double: $90–$165.
It's a yachting crowd here, dahling, but the hospitality is still warm, friendly and blessedly informal. Facing the busy marina and within walking distance of shops and restaurants, this small hotel houses guests in lanai-style rooms with island decor and kitchenettes, but no air conditioning (sea breezes do the job). Landlubbers are kept happy with a pool and tennis court, but may feel out of place among all the seafaring folk. A good dive center rounds out the scene. 40 rooms. Credit Cards: V, MC, A.

Sebastian's on the Beach   **$75–$190**   ★

Little Apple Bay, Road Town, ☎ (800) 336-4870, (809) 495-4212.
Single: $75–$180. Double: $85–$190.
Set on its own beach, this small hotel is split in two by a road; request a room on the beach side for obvious reasons, but ask that it not be one of the rear units, as they have no view. Just two rooms have air conditioning; the rest make do with ceiling fans. The beach is fine for swimming, a good thing since there's no pool. There's a bar and restaurant, plus a fun weekly barbecue. 26 rooms. Credit Cards: V, MC, A.

Low Cost Lodging

Budget accommodations are now available here, usually in a good location that won't require a car. **Sea View**, a popular local restaurant, merely added rooms (with a view) and studios to its property. Campers who don't need much more than a bed and hangers should head for the **Jolly Roger** Inn or **Harbour View Guest House** (the latter has a simple kitchenette).

Where to Eat

Highest Rated Restaurants in British Virgin Islands

★★★★ **Biras Creek**

★★★★ **Brandywine Bay**

★★★★ **Capriccio di Mare**

★★★★ **Skyworld**

★★★★ **The Tradewinds Restaurant**

★★★★ **The Upstairs**

★★★ **Mrs. Scatliffe's**

★★★ **Olde Yarde Inn**

★★★ **Pirate's Pub & Grill**

★★★ **Pusser's Leverick Bay**

Most Exclusive Restaurants in British Virgin Islands

★★★★	**Biras Creek**	$40–$40
★★★★	**Skyworld**	$23–$40
★★★	**The Apple**	$15–$35
★★★	**Olde Yarde Inn**	$18–$30
★★★	**Teacher Ilma's**	$18–$25

Fielding's Best Value Restaurants in British Virgin Islands

★★★★	**Biras Creek**	$40–$40
★★★	**Olde Yarde Inn**	$18–$30
★★★	**Virgin Queen**	$8–$16
★★★	**Teacher Ilma's**	$18–$25
★★★	**Pusser's Leverick Bay**	$13–$24

Excellent West Indian cuisine is available throughout Tortola; however, prices here are extravagant and can even give New York prices a run for the money, though the casual settings often belie the reality of the final bill. To save time, you'll probably want to stay around **Road Town**, where the majority of restaurants are located, but an excursion out to Sugar Mill on the northwest coast can end up a spectacular experience; even though the owners are American ex-pats, they've been highly acclaimed for their curried banana soup and cold rum soufflés. One of the best views, overlooking the town, can be had at **Skyworld** on the Ridge Road.

Resort food is not to be sniffed at on BVI, and some of the best dining can be found at both Virgin Gorda's **Bitter End Yacht Club** and **Biras Creek**, where diners will have breathtaking views. The menu at the **Peter Island Resort** changes every day, a combination of West Indian delicacies and Continental favorites. For home-cooked meals and a big, generous heart, head for **Mrs. Scatlife's**, east of Sugar Mill at Carrot Bay, whose owner might serenade you with gospel music after dinner. English pub food can be had at **Pussers**, with locations in both Tortola and Virgin Gorda; while you're there, don't miss downing a Painkiller, made from Pusser's Rum, a local product, orange and pineapple juice, and coconut creme. Reservations at most popular restaurants are essential, especially at the smaller ones which can book up fast.

Bing's Drop Inn   **$$**   ★ ★

Fat Hog's Bay, East End, ☎ *(809) 495-2627.*
Indian cuisine. Specialties: Conch fritters, fish stew.
Dinner: 6:30 p.m.–12:00 p.m., entrees $10–$20.
Do drop in to Bing's—and you'll probably make a local friend or two. Tasty homestyle conch fritters and fish stew are specialties and more elaborate lobster, chicken and steak dishes are served as well. Come to dance and kibitz here after a meal elsewhere; it's a very unpressured environment that stays open for snacks and drinks until midnight. Closed: Mon. Reservations recommended. Credit Cards: V, MC, A.

Brandywine Bay   **$$$**   ★ ★ ★ ★

Sir Francis Drake Highway, West End, ☎ *(809) 495-2301.*
Italian cuisine. Specialties: Homemade mozzarella, beef and lobster carpaccio, tiramisu.
Dinner: 6:30 p.m.–9:00 p.m., entrees $20–$28.
For a special occasion, drive out a little east of Road Town to this hillside spot owned by Cele and David Pugliese for Tuscan food that's very widely praised. Whether it's local fish simply grilled with homegrown fresh herbs or an elaborately sauced roast duckling, everything is superb. Dining is on the terrace outside the once-private home that overlooks the Sir Francis Drake Channel. Hostess Cele will personally describe each entree on the menu while David prepares and arranges everything picture-perfectly (he's a former fashion photographer). Closed August-October. Closed: Sun. Reservations recommended. Credit Cards: V, MC, A.

Capriccio di Mare   **$$**   ★ ★ ★ ★

Waterfront Drive, West End, ☎ *(809) 494-5369.*
Italian cuisine. Specialties: Pastries, pasta and pizza, frozen granite.

Lunch: 11:30 a.m.–4:00 p.m., entrees $8–$15.
Dinner: 4:00 p.m.–9:00 p.m., entrees $8–$15.
This new arrival is a welcome taste treat for seafood-dominated Tortola. A little sister operation to the popular Brandywine Bay, a bastion of cucina fiorentina, Capriccio di Mare is an informal Italian cafe—a place to sit and sip espresso or cappuccino and nibble pastries or sandwiches on foccacia bread. Pizzas with a choice of vegetable or meat toppings are also available, as well as pastas. Closed: Sun. Credit Cards: Not Accepted. Credit Cards: D, V, MC, A.

Chopsticks $$ ★★
Wickham's Cay, ☎ *(809) 494-3616.*
Asian cuisine.
Lunch: entrees $10–$20.
Dinner: entrees $10–$20.
When you have a yen for Japanese (no pun intended), Chinese and other Asian (crossbred with West Indian) foods, and it's after 10 p.m., where you gonna go? Chopsticks, a cool spot with a veranda situated across from the Cable and Wireless office in Wickham Cay (you can also call mamma), has a good reputation for local fish and conch. All dishes are available for takeout. Open from 7:30 a.m. until late; hours vary. Credit Cards: V, MC, A.

Mrs. Scatliffe's $ ★★★
Carrot Bay, West End, ☎ *(809) 495-4556.*
Indian cuisine. Specialties: Pot roast, chicken or pork, spicy papaya soup.
The former chef of the well-regarded Sugar Mill, a native Tortolian, operates this West-Indian restaurant on the deck of her home, a pastel-colored building with a tin-roof in Carrot Bay. Diners come for the set meal of four courses, which are prepared with fruits and vegetables from her own garden. Popular starters are fresh fruit daiquiris, followed by soup, home-baked bread, chicken in a coconut shell or curried goat, and more of that fresh fruit in her imaginative ice cream desserts. Entertainment follows, usually, a family sing-out. Credit Cards: Not Accepted.

Pusser's Landing $$$ ★★
Sopers Hole, ☎ *(809) 495-4554.*
International cuisine. Specialties: Beef Wellington, guava chicken, nightly dessert specials.
Lunch: 11:00 a.m.–3:00 p.m., entrees $5–$9.
Dinner: 6:00 p.m.–10:00 p.m., entrees $13–$25.
Diners can look out to the lights of St. Thomas from this waterfront restaurant in Tortola's West End, a fancier link in the Pusser's chain, serving black bean soup, West Indian ribs, roasted half-chicken in guava sauce and the signature Pusser's dishes, Beef Wellington with Bearnaise sauce and mud pie for dessert. Special events include dancing under the stars to a live band on Saturdays and all-you-can-eat shrimp dinners on Tuesday nights for $17.95. Credit Cards: D, V, MC, A.

Pusser's Outpost and Pub $$$ ★★
Main Street, ☎ *(809) 494-4199.*
International cuisine. Specialties: Beef Wellington, lobster club sandwich, mud pie.
Lunch: 11:00 a.m.–3:00 p.m., entrees $7–$9.
Dinner: 5:00 p.m.–10:00 p.m., entrees $15–$25.

Enjoy varied international cuisine with the yachting set in this second link in the Pusser's (local rum) chain of eateries. The two-story establishment has a downstairs pub where the namesake libation can be quaffed, accompanied by sandwiches and snacks amid a boisterous atmosphere. Escape upstairs later to the Outpost for Beef Wellington prepared with choice cuts of beef tenderloin, mushroom duxelle and homemade pastry, served with Bearnaise sauce. Later, if you have room, down Pusser's famous mud pie, dessert-style or in a rum-Irish cream concoction. Reservations recommended. Credit Cards: V, MC, A.

Skyworld $$$ ★★★★

Ridge Road, West End, ☎ *(809) 494-3567.*
International cuisine.
Lunch: 10:00 a.m.–5:30 p.m., entrees $7–$13.
Dinner: 6:30 p.m.–10:00 p.m., entrees $23–$40.
A perfect remembrance of a Tortola visit is dining or having a drink before sunset and watching a technicolor movie in the sky at this dining room perched some 1000 feet above sea level. You can partake from chef George Petcoff's international menu of veal with capers, beautifully grilled local fish, passion fruit sorbets or less elaborate conch fritters or french fries and onion rings. At lunch enjoy the view from a different perspective with a sandwich on home-baked bread while casting an eagle eye on neighboring islands in the distance. Closed in September. Reservations recommended. Credit Cards: V, MC, A.

Spaghetti Junction $$$ ★★

Waterfront Drive, West End, ☎ *(809) 494-4880.*
Italian cuisine. Specialties: Chilled roasted eggplant and plum tomatoes, veal scaloppine.
Dinner: 6:00 p.m.–10:00 p.m., entrees $10–$25.
You can get spaghetti and other pastas in this cute joint located upstairs in a small blue building, built back a little ways from the sea in Road Town. Formerly a bar that overlooked the water, it is now separated from the ocean by new roads and office buildings—all in the name of progress. Yachties and others like it for its infectious grooves. The caesar salad, served with sun-dried tomatoes, isn't bad, either. Daily chalkboard specials and desserts. Closed: Sun. Reservations recommended. Credit Cards: Not Accepted.

Sugar Mill $$$ ★★★

Apple Bay, West End, ☎ *(809) 495-4355.*
International cuisine.
Lunch: 12:00 a.m.–2:00 p.m., entrees $6–$12.
Dinner: 7:00 p.m.–8:30 p.m., prix fixe $18–$28.
Bon Appetit columnists Jefferson and Jinx Morgan spent a lot of years cooking and writing about food and wine before they decided to buy a 300-year-old sugar mill in Apple Bay, converting it to a world-class inn and restaurant. The Morgans have wisely kept their menu small, allowing them to concentrate on the details of each dish, which usually includes a cold fruit soup and fresh fish in banana leaves with herbs from the Mill's own garden. Leave room for a scrumptious banana bread pudding with rum sauce when it's available. Associated Hotel: Sugar Mill Estate. Reservations recommended. Credit Cards: V, MC, A.

The Apple   **$$$**   ★ ★ ★

Zion Hill Road, ☎ *(809) 495-4437.*
Indian cuisine. Specialties: Whelks in garlic butter.
Dinner: 6:30 p.m.–9:00 p.m., entrees $15–$35.

An enterprising and talented Tortolian, Liston Molyneux, has opened a restaurant
in his home in Little Apple Bay, on Zion Hill, preparing local dishes like uncom-
monly served whelks (a type of snail), and the more familiar conch. Lunches are var-
ied and include curried chicken rotis (West Indian burritos), or crepes. An
interesting Sunday barbecue of West Indian treats is also offered from 7–9 p.m.
Closed in September. Closed: Mon. Reservations recommended. Credit Cards: V, MC,
A.

The Fish Trap   **$$$**   ★ ★ ★

Columbus Centre, ☎ *(809) 494-3626.*
Seafood cuisine. Specialties: Prawns provencale, prime rib, teriyaki chicken.
Lunch: 11:30 a.m.–3:00 p.m., entrees $8–$14.
Dinner: 6:30 p.m.–8:00 p.m., entrees $14–$25.

An informal, open-air terrace restaurant in Wickham's Cay that always has some
good-value meals happening, the Fishtrap features barbecues on Saturdays and Sundays, prime rib on Sundays and local fish, shellfish, teriyaki chicken and other
hearty, honest food the rest of the week. Closed: Sun. Reservations required. Credit
Cards: V, MC, A.

The Upstairs   **$$$**   ★ ★ ★ ★

West End, ☎ *(809) 494-2228.*
International cuisine. Specialties: Filet mignon, roast duck.
Lunch: 12:00 a.m.–2:00 p.m., entrees $10–$16.
Dinner: 6:00 p.m.–8:30 p.m., entrees $16–$27.

An intimate dining room with lovely views of the harbor, The Upstairs has received
kudos from the likes of *Gourmet* magazine. The star of the Prospect Reef Resort,
which is built on a coral reef, the restaurant offers simple but exceptionally well-pre-
pared (and pricey) meals like local lobster served grilled as an entree or gratine as an
appetizer. Service is attentive and gracious. Ask for a window table for stargazing.
Associated Hotel: Prospect Reef Hotel. Reservations required. Credit Cards: V, MC, A.

Virgin Queen   **$$**   ★ ★ ★

Fleming Street, ☎ *(809) 494-2310.*
English cuisine. Specialties: Queen's pizza, shepherd's pie, bangers and mash.
Lunch: 12:00 a.m.–2:00 p.m., entrees $7–$12.
Dinner: 6:00 p.m.–9:00 p.m., entrees $8–$16.

The Queen's pizza has been nominated for best in the islands, but it's also great finger food for sailors and other active types who like to quaff a few, throw darts at a
board and shoot the breeze. There's a TV for background noise to go with the
other fare offered—mostly English pub and West Indian food like bangers and
mash, saltfish and shepherd's pie. Closed: Sun. Credit Cards: Not Accepted.

Where to Shop

In Road Town, the shopping hub is located on Main Street, starting at the **Sir Olva Georges Plaza**. Unfortunately there is no duty-free shopping, and you must sift through imported goods from Great Britain to find any bargains. **Pusser's Rum** (the "official drink of the British Royal Navy"), is one of the big island buys, available at the company store on Main Street. An aromatic excursion to the **Sunny Caribee and Spice Company** won't be time wasted, especially if you want to pick from the best selection of Caribbean spices and handicrafts on the island. Do stop next door at the **Sunny Caribee Gallery**, which features fine artwork by islanders as well as handpainted furniture and wood carvings. If you need to supplant your vacation wardrobe, there are several boutiques including **Sea Urchin** in the Abbot Building, and **Kids in De Sun**, also in the Abbot Building, which specializes in tropical attire for children.

RESORT ISLANDS NEAR TORTOLA

It will take an extra effort to get to these resorts (private ferry, boat taxi, or private plane), but all you need do is ask the management when you make the reservation. What you get in return are resorts that take full advantage of the natural surroundings; sometimes you won't even have a phone, TV or road to remind you of civilization. Best nature walks (though strenuous) are found at the **Guana Island Club**, north of Tortola's east end, which has been designated as a nature sanctuary. The luxury property is the **Peter Island Resort and Yacht Harbour**, which attracts wealthy yacht-owners to its attractive pool and tennis courts, as well as families who can take advantage of the two-bedroom villas.

Anegada

Only 290 people live on Anegada, mostly in the community called The Settlement. They share this 7-mile curve of coral with some very large iguanas and about 16 flamingos that were released into the ponds in 1992. Hawksbill and green turtles nest along the northshore. The fishing here is excellent and enough vessels have crashed against the craggy coral reefs to make wreck diving a spectacular sport. Even snorkelers can find deep satisfaction exploring caverns and ledges just off the shore in the coral reefs, where they will see shoals of neon-colored fish, nurse sharks, rays, turtles, and barracudas. Lobloy Bay, has a small beach bar and sun shelters. Over the years Anegadians have been the victims of several development schemes which have left them suspicious, not to mention poorer, but they remain friendly to the selected tourists who risk the small planes to arrive. Although there is no regular boat ferry, day trips to the island are available. (Do note that only qualified crew are allowed to navigate the route to Anegada because of the dangerous reef system.)

Where to Stay

Hotels and Resorts

Anegada Reef Hotel $130–$230   ★ ★

Setting Point, ☎ *(809) 495-8002.*
Single: $130–$170. Double: $165–$230.
Located in a rural setting on rural Anegada, this small hotel appeals to those who truly want to get away from it all, and don't mind a lack of amenities and extras. Accommodations are very simple, but clean and comfortable, and the family that runs the place goes out of their way to please. The hotel owns its own fishing boat for deep-sea excursions. The rates are a bit high for what you get, but lots of people come again and again, lured by the laid-back tranquility of this spot. Three meals a

day are included with room rate. 16 rooms. Credit Cards: Not Accepted. Credit Cards: V, MC.

Where to Eat

Anegada Reef Hotel   **$$$**   ★★

Setting Point, ☎ *(809) 495-8002.*
International cuisine. Specialties: Lobster.
Lunch: 8:30 a.m.–4:00 p.m., entrees $17–$30.
Dinner: 4:00 p.m.–9:30 p.m., entrees $17–$30.

Visions of lobster barbecuing on the beach at this low-key resort (the only one on Anegada) draw day-trippers to experience a very informal (if pricey) crustacean feast served on picnic tables. Sides usually include caesar salad and garlic bread. To dine here, reserve by 4 p.m., and if you are flying in, the hotel will meet you with a private bus. Associated Hotel: Anegada Reef Hotel. Reservations required. Credit Cards: Not Accepted. Credit Cards: V, MC.

Del's Restaurant and Bar   **$$**   ★★

The Settlement, ☎ *(809) 495-8014.*
Seafood cuisine. Specialties: Cracked conch.
Lunch: 12:00 a.m.–3:00 p.m., entrees $7–$10.
Dinner: 7:30 p.m.–12:00 p.m., entrees $10–$20.

Del's is one of a small number of beach bars and restaurants serving local food on this tiny coral atoll with only one hotel, a campground and lots of beautiful sand. Naturally, it's West Indian, rounded out with sandwiches and seafood served three times a day. It's a great way to start or end a day trip to Anegada, which can be reached by air or boat. Credit Cards: V, MC.

Guana Island

Where to Stay

Guana Island   **$485–$635**   ★★★★★

Guana Island, ☎ *(800) 544-8262, (809) 494-2354.*
Single: $485–$585. Double: $485–$635.

Situated on an 850-acre island, this hideaway resort was formerly a sugar cane plantation and is now a nature sanctuary. Accommodations are in white stone cottages arranged along a hilltop with smashing views of neighboring islands. Groups of 30 can rent the entire island—the perfect spot for a family reunion of jet-setters. Great hiking and bird watching, as well as tennis and watersports. Tranquil and lovely. 15 rooms. Credit Cards: Not Accepted.

Jost Van Dyke

Jost Van Dyke (pronounced "yost") is that perfect island for Robinson Crusoe fans who want to get away from it all. No markets, no electricity, though there are some spiffy bars and restaurants where you can meet international yacht owners who cruise up in their multimillion-dollar schooners. **White Bay**

Beach is most easily reached by boat and has a beautiful sandy beach, small hotel, and restaurant. **Sandy Cay**, an uninhabited islet off Jost Van Dyke, boasts a lovely white stretch of sand...and nothing else.Windsurfing and snorkeling are considered excellent. The BVI have established camp grounds on Jost Van Dyke—about fifteen campsites, with a small restaurant, or snack bar and grocery. The camp is directly next to the ferry landing, a fortunate choice since the islands have no taxis or cars for hire. Bring your own bedding and cooking supplies; a few erected tents are available, but most are bare sites. Write ahead to reserve a space, because the idea has caught on with great popularity lately. Each campsite has its own prices. For more information, write the British Virgin Islands Tourist Board.

Where to Stay

Hotels and Resorts

Sandcastle $225–$295 ★

White Bay, ☎ *(809) 771-1611.*
Single: $225–$295. Double: $240–$295.
This tiny resort consists of four octagonal cottages set among tropical gardens. This place is not for everyone—there's no electricity and just limited hot water—but those who don't mind roughing it love the peace and serenity. Dinner by candlelight is a romantic affair. 4 rooms. Credit Cards: V, MC.

Apartments and Condominiums

Sandy Ground Estates ★★

P.O. Box 594, West End, Tortola, White Bay, ☎ *(809) 494-3391.*
Rack rate Per Week: $780–$1200.
This tropical isolated retreat consists of eight houses with simple, casual furnishings and full kitchens. Each house looks different and is individually furnished. Arrange to have your refrigerator stocked prior to arrival. Rates are $740 to $1200 for a week; the larger houses sleep eight. 8 rooms. Credit Cards: V, MC.

Where to Eat

Abe's By The Sea $$$ ★★

Little Harbour, ☎ *(809) 495-9329.*
Seafood cuisine. Specialties: Fresh lobster with lime and butter sauce, pig roast.
Lunch: 11:30 a.m.–3:00 p.m., entrees $8–$25.
Dinner: 7:00 p.m.–9:30 p.m., entrees $12–$30.
Abe's is a swinging place to try fresh fish, lobster and conch on a waterfront terrace in Jost Van Dyke's Little Harbour. Bright coral and fish nets decorate this popular hangout for yachtspeople and tourists who drop in morning, noon and night. An American breakfast with sausage, ham, bacon and eggs and juice is a good buy for $5. Lunches and dinners are substantial and served with rice and peas, coleslaw or green salad and corn on the cob; sandwiches are also available. There's a traditional pig roast Wednesdays. Reservations recommended. Credit Cards: V, MC.

Club Paradise $$$ ★★

Great Harbour, ☎ *(809) 495-9267.*
Seafood cuisine. Specialties: Sauteed grouper, flying fish sandwich.

Lunch: 11:00 a.m.–3:00 p.m., entrees $4–$8.

Dinner: 7:00 p.m.–10:00 p.m., entrees $15–$25.

There are many nice touches that make this simple open-air restaurant in Great Harbour a good place to alight. There's a delicious Barbados-style flying fish sandwich available for lunch for $5, served on home-baked bread. At dinner, patrons can pick a lobster from the tank. On Wednesdays there's a pig roast, and live entertainment is a regular feature. Cheeseburgers on that fresh bread, a whole cornish hen with honey-glazed carrots and garlic and sauteed grouper can also be enjoyed here on a regular basis. Reservations recommended. Credit Cards: V, MC, A.

Foxy's Tamarind $$$

Great Harbour, ☎ (809) 495-9258.

American cuisine. Specialties: Filet mignon, rotis, painkiller punch.

Lunch: 12:00 a.m.–2:30 p.m., entrees $6–$9.

Dinner: 6:30 p.m.–9:00 p.m., entrees $15–$30.

Don't expect luxury at this famous beach bar presided over by the magical Philicianno "Foxy" Callwood—only unabashed camaraderie and excellent grilled meat and seafood. An institution for close to 30 years, Foxy's Tamarind Bar draws an amazing yachting crowd for New Years' Eve, overwhelming Great Harbour with an overflow of boats and frenzied folks. The rest of the year it's calypso, reggae or soca (soul and calypso) music with burgers, rotis and killer rum punches. Foxy's is open from 9 a.m. until closing time, which varies. Credit Cards: V, MC.

Sandcastle $$$

☎ (809) 775-5262.

International cuisine. Specialties: Boneless chicken breast, New York steak, fresh fish.

Lunch: 11:00 a.m.–3:30 p.m., prix fixe $18–$25.

Dinner: 7:30 p.m.–11:00 p.m., prix fixe $30–$35.

Arrive in your own boat or arrange to be picked up by the Sandcastle's private motor launch from Tortola to dine simply and by candlelight (there's no electricity). The five-course prix fixe meal includes a basket of fresh bread, soup, a garden salad, an entree (depending on what's fresh) and dessert. Reservations have to made by 4 p.m. for dinner, and patrons usually call from a VHF radio to relay their meal choices with Chef Bill, who caters to special dietary needs. Seafood and shellfish choices are seasonal, but there's usually chicken breast and steak. Associated Hotel: Sandcastle Hotel. Reservations required. Credit Cards: V, MC.

Mosquito Island

Privately owned by Drake's Anchorage resort, Mosquito Island has dropdead views over North Sound to Virgin Gorda and Prickly Pear. The only way to get here is by boat. If you've got the dough, why not rent the whole island and let your friends come over. The beach at South Bay is extremely pleasant, dotted with huge boulders and quiet sandy coves.

Where to Stay

Drake's Anchorage   **$223–$600**   ★ ★ ★ ★

Mosquito Island, ☎ (800) 624-6651, (809) 494-2254.
Single: $223–$600. Double: $316–$600.

Located on a private island just off Virgin Gorda, this resort has four beaches, with one just big enough for a snuggling couple. Accommodations are in three separate cottages lining a narrow beach and feature Haitian art, red-tile floors and modern baths; ceiling fans keep things cool. There are also two luxurious villas set off a bit. Three excellent restaurants give guests dining choices, and all the usual watersports are available. A lovely, peaceful spot that guests hate to leave. 12 rooms. Credit Cards: V, MC, A.

Necker Island

Got $10,000 per day to spend on a Caribbean vacation? (Hey, meals included!) The hefty price tag at the incredible Necker Island includes everything, even the whole private island, which accommodates one group of up to 24 people at a time. Upon landing in St. Thomas, you're whisked away by helicopter to a tiny land mass—74 lush green acres covered with brilliantly red bougainvillea atop of which is a Bali-like tropical mansion that has brought oo's and aah's to the lips of Princess Diana, Steven Spielberg, Oprah Winfrey, Robert Redford, etc. Created by British entrepreneur Richard Branson of Virgin Atlantic Airways and Virgin Records, the open-air house sports a living room with a 360-degree view of the sea. There are two guesthouses, besides the main 10-bedroom, 8-bathroom house, several fresh water pools, and a cheerful staff who can cook for you or assist you in cooking your own. In the main house, the 24-foot long dining table is bordered by 22 chairs, complete with beautiful settings, elegant place mats, gleaming silvers, etc. Food is luscious, endless and irresistible, everything from non-stop desserts to the potpourri of freshly caught fish. Activities are endless, from tennis, snorkeling, waterskiing, swimming, banana boating, windsurfing, power boating, hiking, to just lazing about on the beach.

Where to Stay

Apartments and Condominiums

Necker Island   ★ ★ ★ ★ ★

Necker Island, ☎ (800) 225-4255, (809) 494-4492.
Rack rate Per Day: $5500–$10900.

Got $5500 burning a hole in your pocket? Need room to spread out? Try this private house—mansion is more like it—on its own 74-acre estate. The hilltop house has 10 bedrooms, six with their own bath, a Jacuzzi in the master bedroom, and its own pool, tennis court and watersports. The rates (which only start at $5500 and go all the way up to $10,900—per day) include three maids, two gardeners, a couple to cook your meals and a boatman to whisk you off to neighboring islands. Who says money can't buy happiness? Credit Cards: Not Accepted.

Peter Island

Where to Stay

Hotels and Resorts

Peter Island Resort   **$195–$3900**   ★★★★★

Peter Island, ☎ *(800) 346-4451, (809) 494-2561.*
Single: $195–$480. Double: $195–$3900.

Located on its own private island south of Tortola, this smashing resort shuttles guests over by boat or helicopter. Everything is quite luxurious, and the beaches are to die for. Accommodations are beautifully done and include standard guest rooms and villas with two to four bedrooms. The extensive grounds (the resort takes up about half of the 1800-acre island) include a gorgeous free-form pool, four tennis courts with a pro, a yachting marina and extensive trails for walking or mountain biking. The food is great and the service impeccable. Bravo! 50 rooms. Credit Cards: V, MC, DC, A.

Where to Eat

The Tradewinds Restaurant   **$$$**   ★★★★

Peter Island, ☎ *(809) 494-2561.*
International cuisine. Specialties: Tortola seafood soup, crab-stuffed island chicken.
Dinner: 7:00 p.m.–9:00 p.m., entrees $18–$36.

Glide onto the Peter Island ferry (after reservations are made, of course) for a short ride to this beautiful private island and its attached resort. The Tradewinds, the island's main dining room, is known for expensive but five-star gourmet dinners served year-round. A memorable meal consists of an appetizer of grilled honey-glazed quail, followed by Caribbean pepperpot soup, caesar salad, lemon-poached shrimp with shrimp mousse, and strawberries Romanoff. Afterwards, dance with your partner under a starlit sky. Associated Hotel: Peter Island Resort. Reservations required. Credit Cards: V, MC, A.

Salt Island

What to See

Parks and Gardens

Rhone National Marine Park   ★★★★★

Salt Island, Salt Island.
One of the Caribbean's best diving spots, the underwater scenes in the movie *The Deep* were filmed here. The chief attraction is the wreck of the *RMS Rhone*, a 310-foot British steamer that sank in a hurricane in 1867. Pieces of the boat rest from 20 to 80 feet deep, and make for fascinating viewing.

Virgin Gorda

Huge boulders form a natural swimming pool and underwater caves known as The Baths of Virgin Gorda.

The most chic resorts of the BVI are located on Virgin Gorda, an eight-square-mile slab of scrub and cactus whose shape some say resembles a "fat virgin"—hence its name. Notwithstanding a brief gold rush in the 17th century, the idyllic island lay undiscovered until Laurence Rockefeller cruised the bay and decided to build his Little Dix Bay Hotel. Boats from Tortola regularly dock at the southern settlement of Spanish Town, where most of the 1500 islanders live. The best beaches lay south of Spanish Town, and in the extreme southeast you can find ruins of an old 19th-century copper mine. The road to the north of the island passes through Savannah Bay and Pond Bay before reaching Virgin Gorda's second town, Gun Creek. Below is North Sound, where two fine resorts are located.

The big attraction on Virgin Gorda is a spectacular series of massive granite boulders, the Baths, whose jumbled piles are backed by coconut palms. The stones, made of a granite that is not common to the Caribbean, are thought to have been carried there by glacial movement during the Ice Age. "Having nothing to do" is one of the major pastimes here, but if you say you're bored while staying at Little Dix Bay, they will scurry you off along the coast to a secluded beach, deposit you with drinking water, a picnic and an umbrella, and pick you up later.

Arrival

Most folks take the easy route and take a frog-jumper's flight with American Eagle or Sunair. Boats can also be chartered from Road Town, Tortola, or from St. Thomas in the USVI. Nothing seems to run on schedule here, which is okay, because there's no place to rush to.

Treks and Beaches

Virgin Gorda looks like two different islands north to south. The northern tip is mountainous, while the south is flat, with boulders blocking every curve. Everything above a thousand feet on Virgin Gorda is considered a national park. You'll find a self-guided trail at the 265-acre park at the forested peak near the island's center; it leads to an observation point. The lookout is the end of a paved road leading to Little Dix Bay resort. The first place most people head to are **The Baths**, where snorkeling, in the limpid pools created by the pattern of the huge boulders, is considered to be superb. (These days you may have to fight for space among the many cruise passengers who alight here; do ask your hotel what their arrival schedule is.) Some hearty souls actually climb the island's tallest mount, the 1370-ft. **Gorda Peak**; the trail boasts some unusual flora, including tropical orchids. Great treks can be made through **Devil's Bay National Park**; a fifteen-minute trail through a natural garden of native vegetation and massive boulders will take you to a fine secluded beach. Other beaches noted for their beauty include **Trunk Bay**, wide and sandy and reachable by boat or along a rough path from Spring Bay, a sandy beach north of Yacht Harbour. There is also **Mahoe Bay**, at Mango Bay Resort, with its gently curving beach and vivid blue water.

The greatest adventure in Virgin Gorda is to just get on a boat and explore the numerous other islands, like **Necker**, **Mosquito**, **Jost Van Dyke**, and **Anega-** **da**. You'll usually find at least one resort on these islands, where you can have a fabulous lunch.

City Celebrations

Virgin Gorda Tours Association ★★★

Fischers Cove Beach Hotel, South Sound, ☎ *(809) 495-5252.*
Want to see the island but lack your own wheels? They'll shuttle you about, taking in all the high points, for $50. Two tours are offered daily; call for a schedule.

Parks and Gardens

Virgin Gorda Peak ★★★★

South Sound.
The "peak" in the name rises some 1500 feet, making it the island's highest point. This 265-acre preserve is home to indigenous and exotic plants and has been reforested with mahogany trees. Hike to the top, then catch your breath at the observation tower, though foliage obscures the view.

Tours

The Baths

Lee Road, South Sound.

Gigantic house-size boulders strewn about have formed saltwater grottoes and small pools great for snorkeling. This is by far the island's most-visited spot, so come early in the morning or late in the afternoon to avoid the crowds.

Sports

Beyond a tennis court at the Little Dix Bay resort, all other sports take advantage of the glorious seas. Most hotels will arrange diving, sailing expeditions, and deep-sea fishing; you can also find agencies at the Yacht Harbour or negotiate directly with crew members lolling about. At **Kilbrides Underwater Tours**, you can speed out to underwater caves, wrecks and coral forests in two 42-foot dive boats under the able direction of Bert Kilbride, considered a true pro in the area. Certification courses run about $60 and you can even get a video made of your dive. If you are interested in chartering a yacht, there are a couple of agencies beside the Little Dix Bay Resort. Both one-day trips and longer excursions can be arranged.

Where to Stay

There are fabulous resorts here, as well as other options, from inns to bargain alternatives that should be scoped out in person.

Hotels and Resorts

Little Dix Bay still remains the premier luxury resort, with enough activities to keep you exhausted. Special packages throughout the year are well worth taking advantage of. **Biras Creek** comes in a close second, an 150-acre estate that even houses a bird sanctuary. The beach at Leverick Bay Hotel can often seem overrun by cruise passengers.

Biras Creek Hotel   **$340–$840**

North Sound, ☎ (800) 223-1108, (809) 494-3555.
Single: $340–$670. Double: $340–$840.

Located on a 150-acre estate and accessible only by boat, all accommodations at this tropical retreat are in suites with pleasant decor and, best of all, open-walled private showers. The beach is rather grassy, so most guests opt for sunning at the pool. Surrounded by water on three sides, this is a true escape, and guests are appropriately pampered. The rates include all watersports and tennis on two courts. The restaurant is highly regarded. 33 rooms. Credit Cards: V, MC, A.

Bitter End Yacht Club   **$295–$405**

North Sound, ☎ (800) 872-2392, (809) 494-2746.
Single: $295–$405. Double: $295–$405.

This lively yacht club and cottage colony houses guests in hillside or beachfront villas with tropical decor and small porches. Visitors can also opt to stay in eight Freedom sailboats. There's lots going on at all times; those seeking an island hideaway will be happier elsewhere. All kinds of watersports are for the taking, and the sailing school is highly touted as among the Caribbean's best. A fun spot for both sailors and landlubbers. 94 rooms. Credit Cards: V, MC, DC, A.

Fischer's Cove Beach $95–$270

North Sound, ☎ *(800) 621-1270, (809) 495-5252.*
Single: $95–$270. Double: $105–$270.
This cottage enclave overlooks St. Thomas Bay. Accommodations are in stone cottages with one or two bedrooms and a kitchenette. The property includes two bars and two restaurants, but little else in the way of diversions. Great local food. 20 rooms. Credit Cards: V, MC, A.

Little Dix Bay Hotel $225–$1000

Little Dix Bay, North Sound, ☎ *(800) 928-3000, (809) 495-5555.*
Single: $225–$755. Double: $225–$1000.
Lots of couples at this luxury resort, which was completely redone in late 1993. Set on a private bay on a 500-acre estate, Little Dix has a lovely crescent beach, formal gardens, seven tennis courts and a fleet of boats to take you to the beach of your choice. Accommodations are in wood cottages with tropical decor; about half have air conditioning. The service is so good you'll be spoiled for life, but some consider this spot a tad pretentious. 98 rooms. Credit Cards: V, MC, DC, A.

Apartments and Condominiums

Self-catering cottages and villas are available, though you should probably bring most staples from home. **Guavaberry-Spring Bay Vacation Homes** is close to the Baths, one of the island's main attractions.

Guavaberry Spring Bay $90–$195

North Sound, ☎ *(809) 495-5227.*
Single: $90–$195. Double: $90–$195.
Unique hexagonal or round cottages, perched on stilts, are simply furnished with one or two bedrooms, a sitting room, modern bath and kitchen. Great views of Sir Francis Drake's Passage and neighboring islands. The helpful management will shuttle you about, but you'll still want a car for mobility. This nice spot is enhanced by the friendly service. 16 rooms. Credit Cards: Not Accepted.

Leverick Bay Resort $96–$255

North Sound, ☎ *(800) 848-7081, (809) 495-7421.*
Single: $96–$120. Double: $96–$255.
A hillside villa complex with standard guest rooms, two-bedroom condos and one- to four-bedroom villas with kitchens. There's an outdoor pool and 44-slip marina, as well as tennis, a dive shop, beauty salon and restaurant. The resort gets crowded with day-trippers when cruise ships are in port. 16 rooms. Credit Cards: V, MC, A.

Inns

There's only one inn on the island, managed by the owner. The style is casual, the furnishings nothing to write home about. You'll have close contact with the other guests.

Olde Yard Inn $85–$180

The Valley, ☎ *(800) 633-7411, (809) 495-5544.*
Single: $85–$180. Double: $100–$180.
Situated in a garden setting overlooking Handsome Bay, this charming inn puts guests up in two-story buildings (great views from the upper floors) with simple island furniture, tile floors and roomy baths. Four rooms are air-conditioned. A reading and film library keeps visitors contented, and the staff happily accommo-

dates those with special interests, arranging sea sails and the like. The restaurant draws raves. 14 rooms. Credit Cards: V, MC, A.

Low Cost Lodging

Best bargains can be found after the winter season (starting in April-November). If you're game, take a day trip to the island and ask about for any rooms in private homes. Groups of travelers can also rent houses and bring down the per-person rate.

Where to Eat

For such a tiny island, the cuisine on Virgin Gorda can run to the superb, especially at the **Little Dix Bay Hotel** (the stupendous views from the dining terrace don't hurt either). At the **Biras Creek** hotel, dining is highly romantic, perched high on the hilltop, and the wine list is considered to be one of the best in the Caribbean. The best place to have Sunday brunch is **Pusser's Pub**, at Leverick Bay, on North Sound (good place for American-style hamburgers as well).

Biras Creek   **$$$**   ★★★★

☎ *(809) 494-3555.*
International cuisine. Specialties: Half lobster any style, stilton with port.
Dinner: 7:30 p.m.–9:00 p.m., prix fixe $40.
Dine in a stone "castle keep" with all-encompassing views of the Caribbean and Atlantic from the airy and luxurious main dining room of the tony Biras Creek Resort. The four-course, prix-fixe dinner menu changes each evening, but fresh half-lobster served grilled or poached with lemon or garlic butter is always available if requested by 4 p.m., for an extra $5. The well-chosen menus combine local specialties like conch with spicy mango chutney or pumpkin soup with rum. For a "veddy" English touch, stilton and port arrive shortly after dessert. Associated Hotel: Biras Creek Estate. Reservations required. Credit Cards: V, MC, A.

Chez Michelle   **$$$**   ★★

The Valley, ☎ *(809) 495-5510.*
International cuisine. Specialties: Lobster remy, pastas.
Dinner: 6:30 p.m.–9:30 p.m., entrees $16–$28.
An intimate Gallic spot amidst the surf and turf, Chez Michelle provides cozy, candlelit surroundings in a West Indian house near the Yacht Harbour. The specialty is local lobster, flambeed in cognac and served with a delicately rich mushroom sauce. Fresh pastas made in-house are justifiably popular, as is the rack of lamb. Reservations recommended. Credit Cards: V, MC.

Olde Yarde Inn   **$$$**   ★★★

The Valley, ☎ *(809) 495-5544.*
International cuisine. Specialties: Seafood delight, fresh fish, grilled lamb chops.
Dinner: 6:30 p.m.–8:30 p.m., entrees $18–$30.
The ambience is lovely at this garden restaurant in the Olde Yarde Inn, and the French-Continental food enhances the experience. Inn guests and others can dine here all day, starting with a breakfast menu that commences at 8 a.m. But the real draw is dinner, where classics like escargot with garlic butter or caesar salad for two can be paired with local fish of the day, or Caribbean lobster with lemon butter

sauce. Desserts are all homemade and change frequently. Associated Hotel: Olde Yarde Inn. Reservations recommended. Credit Cards: V, MC, A.

Pirate's Pub & Grill   **$**

Saba Rock,
American cuisine. Specialties: Barbecue, sandwiches, dessert drinks.
Lunch: 12:00 a.m.–4:00 p.m., entrees $5–$7.
Dinner: 4:00 p.m.–8:00 p.m., entrees $5–$7.
It can get wild and woolly here some nights when the booze flows, but this informal pub is (relatively) kind to the pocketbook, serving a small menu of hefty sandwiches, ribs and chicken with all the trimmings for under $10, although a side order of potato salad at $2.50 is a tad much. Patrons are expected to drink their desserts here, downing such delights as raspberry pound cake and strawberry short cake blended at the bar. Entertainment is in the form of darts, or impromptu jam sessions with whomever washes up on the beach. Credit Cards: V, MC, A.

Pusser's Leverick Bay   **$$$**

Leverick Bay, ☎ (809) 495-7369.
American cuisine. Specialties: Filet of beef Wellington, mud pie.
Lunch: 11:30 a.m.–4:30 p.m., entrees $6–$10.
Dinner: 6:00 p.m.–10:00 p.m., entrees $13–$24.
The Virgin Gorda branch of the popular Pusser's chain is located in a boisterously colored Victorian house, where familiar and tasty stateside favorites like nachos with guacamole and jalapeño pepper and cheddar fries are served with drinks. The chain's filet of beef Wellington is a specialty, served with fresh mushrooms and encased in pastry. There's also lobster, and pasta with vegetables. Desserts are huge and sweet, like mud pie with mocha ice cream and cookie crust, or the Mud Head, a chocolate and Pusser's rum concoction with gooey cream on top. Credit Cards: V, MC, A.

Teacher Ilma's   **$$$**   ★ ★ ★

The Valley, ☎ (809) 495-5355.
Latin American cuisine. Specialties: Calalloo, grouper.
Lunch: 11:00 a.m.–1:30 p.m., entrees $3–$10.
Dinner: 7:00 p.m.–9:30 p.m., prix fixe $18–$25.
Teacher Ilma is Mrs. Ilma O'Neal, a veteran schoolmistress and now kitchen doyenne serving full-course dinners each night and lighter repasts at lunch. Located in her own home at Princess Quarters, Teacher presents genuine island favorites like conch, callaloo soup and roast pork to an appreciative culinary audience. Desserts might include pies and cakes made with exotic local fruits and nuts. Closed: Sun. Reservations required. Credit Cards: Not Accepted.

The Bath and Turtle Pub   **$$$**

The Yacht Harbour, ☎ (809) 495-5239.
International cuisine. Specialties: Fried shrimp in coconut batter, specialty pizzas.
Lunch: 11:30 a.m.–5:00 p.m., entrees $7–$15.
Dinner: 6:30 p.m.–9:30 p.m., entrees $11–$30.
A convivial bar-tavern, The Bath and Turtle has two happy hours a day, one mid-morning, and another one before sundown. Drinks are usually fruity and tropical, accompanied by good pizzas (Mexican crabmeat, veggie and special of the day), a

West Indian chicken sandwich with spicy local seasonings, filet mignon, lobster and burgers. The location is fine too, next to a shopping center and the local lending library. The Pub is open for breakfast from 8 a.m. and usually stays open until 9 p.m. Reservations recommended. Credit Cards: V, MC, A.

The Crab Hole   **$$**   ★★★
South Valley, ☎ *(809) 495-5307.*
Latin American cuisine. Specialties: Calalloo soup, stewed goat, rotis.
Lunch: 11:00 a.m.–3:00 p.m., entrees $6–$12.
Dinner: 6:30 p.m.–9:00 p.m., entrees $10–$15.
One of a growing handful of West Indian restaurants in Virgin Gorda, The Crab Hole draws locals who come to chow down on home-cooking, island style, be it callaloo (local spinach) soup, spicy chicken curried rotis or plantains and rice and peas. There's lively entertainment as well on Friday and Saturday nights. Reservations recommended. Credit Cards: Not Accepted.

Where to Shop

The British Virgin Islands don't give American citizens the same duty-free break as do the U.S. Virgin Islands. There's not much to rave about here in terms of quality. Boutiques at Little Dix Bay and the Bitter End resorts carry the proverbial casual wear and souvenir merchandise. Along the Yacht Harbour you'll find another bevy of shops, including a few handicraft stores. Most of the work is imported from other islands, though you can find interesting buys on homemade preserves and spices.

British Virgin Islands Directory

ARRIVAL AND DEPARTURE

Travel to and from Tortola and the BVI requires an extra step. There is no airport in the country big enough to handle large jets, so most visitors transfer in San Juan, St. Thomas, or St. Maarten and arrive via a smaller island hopper (which should give you the idea to include those other stops in your itinerary.) American Eagle makes seven flights a day from San Juan to Beef Island/Tortola. In the U.S., call ☎ *800-433-7300.* Sunaire also has daily service to Tortola from St. Thomas and St. Croix. LIAT flies from Antigua, St. Kitts, St. Maarten, St. Thomas and San Juan, but the planes are very small and they are rarely on time. The departure tax per airline passenger is $5.

St. Thomas can also be reached by boat from Tortola, a 45-minute trip on public ferry. You can buy tickets from several companies, including **Smith's Ferry Service** ☎ *809-494-4495* and **Native Son** ☎ *809-495-4617*. The departure tax for sea passengers is $4.

Because government regulation forbids anyone to rent a car at the airport, taxis are omnipresent whenever a plane arrives. Your hotel can also arrange for a taxi to meet you.

CLIMATE

Little rain falls on this nearly-perfect temperate island, with temperatures hovering between 75 degrees F and 85 degrees F year-round. The constant trade winds keep the humidity low. Even during the rainy season, rain usually arrives in 10-minute bursts which stop as fast they start.

CRUISES

B.V.I. has become a ready port of call for many cruiseliners. Many stop at Tortola and bring passengers aboard on small ships.

DOCUMENTS

Customs officials prefer visitors bring passports, but will accept proof of citizenship (birth certificate, voter's registration card, plus a photo ID). Travelers must also show an ongoing or return ticket. Departure tax by air is $5; by sea $4.

ELECTRICITY

Current runs 110 volts, 60 cycles, as in the U.S.

GETTING AROUND

Private ferry service between Caneel Bay and Little Dix Bay is provided by the island resorts three times a week. Or your concierge can arrange a private water taxi—a fast twin-engined outboard catamaran for $275 one way. Public ferries are also available. They run Thursday and Sunday, between Cruz Bay and Spanish Town on Virgin Gorda. Call Transportation Services on St. Thomas, for information (☎ *776-6282l*, $22 one way). A passport is required for travel between the American and British Virgin Islands.

Public ferries also make the 45-minute voyage from St. Thomas (Charlotte Amalie) to Road Town and West End on Tortola. Companies providing this service include **Smith's Ferry Service** ☎ *809-494-4495* and **Native Son** ☎ *809-495-4617*.

Transportation on Virgin Gorda is mainly by boat, often in the form of one of Little Dix's handy Boston Whalers.

Pick up a copy of the BVI "Welcome Tourist Guide," which gives an extensive list of yachts, sloops, trimarans, and Carib runabouts that may be charted on Tortola and Virgin Gorda. Prices per day range from U.S. $60 to U.S $19,000 per week.

Car rental prices can be exorbitant during high season because the demand is so high. As such, it's best to reserve a car before you arrive.

Rates seems to change daily, so verify any last-minute adjustments at least two days before your expected pickup. Narrow dirt roads which are often not well lighted require sturdy wheels like gurghels or jeeps. To rent a car, you must obtain a BVI license by presenting your valid hometown driver's license and shelling out $10. Though there are numerous local agencies, the best security is to stay with U.S.-based agencies which can verify mistakes in billing, etc. Among the best are **Avis** ☎ *809-494-3322*, **National** ☎ *809-494-3197*, **Hertz** ☎ *809-495-4405* or toll-free *800-654-3001* in the U.S.

LANGUAGE

British English is spoken with a West Indian accent.

MEDICAL EMERGENCIES

The Peebles Hospital, Porter Road, Road Town; ☎ *809-494-3497* is a fully functioning facility with lab and x-ray machines. Hotels usually have a list of doctors on-call in Tortola.

MONEY

The American dollar is used exclusively.

TELEPHONE

To reach B.V.I. from the U.S., dial *809* (area code) + *49* (country code) + local number.Area code is *809*.

TIME

Atlantic Standard Time throughout the year.

TIPPING

Hotels customarily add a 10–15 percent service charge to the bill; feel free to tip more for special service. Waiters and taxi drivers both expect to be tipped 10–15 percent.

TOURIST INFORMATION

The **British Virgin Islands Tourist Board** on Tortola is located in the *Joseph Josiah Smith Social Security Building, Waterfront Dr., Road Town;* ☎ *43134*, FAX *43866*. Few hotels have phones in the room, so do ask in advance if you need one. Calls can be made with phone cards purchased from the Cable & Wireless company. In the U.S. call ☎ *(800) 538-8530*.

WHEN TO GO

The BVI Summer Festival in August is one of the island's biggest events, which includes two weeks of festivities, song, dance, and parades. Also in August, fish enthusiasts can also attend the International Marlin Tournament at the Birch Creek resort. In November hop a ferry to Virgin Gorda's Bitter End Yacht Club when the Pro-Am Regatta sets sail. The annual Spring Regatta is a Caribbean-wide yacht race, featuring outdoor music and street fairs. For a schedule, call ☎ *800-835-8530* in the U.S. Easter is celebrated by a three-day festival in Virgin Gorda.

BRITISH VIRGIN ISLANDS HOTELS	RMS	RATES	PHONE	FAX
Anegada				
Setting Point				
★★ Anegada Reef Hotel	16	$130–$230	(809) 495-8002	(809) 495-9362
Guana Island				
★★★★★ Guana Island	15	$485–$635	(800) 544-8262	(809) 495-2900
Jost Van Dyke				
White Bay				
★★ Sandy Ground Estates	8		(809) 494-3391	(809) 495-9379
★ Sandcastle	4	$225–$295	(809) 771-1611	(809) 775-5262
Mosquito Island				
★★★★ Drake's Anchorage	12	$223–$600	(800) 624-6651	(617) 959-5147
Necker Island				
★★★★★ Necker Island			(800) 225-4255	
Peter Island				
★★★★★ Peter Island Resort	50	$195–$3900	(800) 346-4451	(809) 949-2313
Tortola				
Road Town				
★★★ Long Bay Beach Hotel	80	$55–$295	(800) 729-9599	(914) 833-3318
★★★ Prospect Reef Resort	131	$91–$279	(800) 356-8937	
★★★ Sugar Mill Hotel	21	$115–$320	(800) 462-8834	
★★★ Treasure Isle Hotel	43	$85–$230	(800) 334-2435	(809) 494-2507
★★ Admiralty Estate Resort	30	$110–$275	(809) 494-0014	
★★ Fort Burt Hotel	8	$60–$95	(809) 494-2587	(809) 494-2002
★★ Fort Recovery Estates	10	$125–$295	(800) 367-8455	(809) 495-4036
★★ Frenchman's Cay Resort	9	$107–$270	(800) 235-4077	
★★ Moorings-Mariner Inn	40	$80–$165	(800) 535-7289	(809) 494-2226
★★ Nanny Cay Resort	42	$50–$195	(809) 494-2512	(809) 494-0555
★★ Rockview Holiday Homes	20	$100–$755	(800) 621-1270	
★★ Village Cay Marina Hotel	19	$115–$330	(809) 494-2771	
★ Sebastian's on the Beach	26	$75–$190	(800) 336-4870	(809) 495-4466

BRITISH VIRGIN ISLANDS HOTELS	RMS	RATES	PHONE	FAX

Virgin Gorda

North Sound

		RMS	RATES	PHONE	FAX
★★★★	Biras Creek Hotel	33	$340–$840	(800) 223-1108	(809) 494-3557
★★★★	Little Dix Bay Hotel	98	$225–$1000	(800) 928-3000	(214) 871-5444
★★★	Bitter End Yacht Club	94	$295–$405	(800) 872-2392	(809) 494-2745
★★★	Mango Bay Resort	8	$105–$320	(800) 223-6510	(809) 495-5674
★★★	Olde Yard Inn	14	$85–$180	(800) 633-7411	(809) 495-5986
★★	Fischer's Cove Beach	20	$95–$270	(800) 621-1270	
★★	Guavaberry Spring Bay	16	$90–$195	(809) 495-5227	
★★	Leverick Bay Resort	16	$96–$255	(800) 848-7081	(809) 495-7363

BRITISH VIRGIN ISLANDS RESTAURANTS	LOCATION	PHONE	ENTREE

Anegada

Setting Point

International

		LOCATION	PHONE	ENTREE
★★	Anegada Reef Hotel	Setting Point	(809) 495-8002	$17–$30

Seafood

		LOCATION	PHONE	ENTREE
★★	Del's Restaurant and Bar	Setting Point	(809) 495-8014	$7–$20

Jost Van Dyke

White Bay

American

		LOCATION	PHONE	ENTREE
★★	Foxy's Tamarind	White Bay	(809) 495-9258	$6–$30

International

		LOCATION	PHONE	ENTREE
★★	Sandcastle	White Bay	(809) 775-5262	$18–$35

Seafood

		LOCATION	PHONE	ENTREE
★★	Abe's By The Sea	White Bay	(809) 495-9329	$8–$30
★★	Club Paradise	White Bay	(809) 495-9267	$4–$25

Peter Island

International

		LOCATION	PHONE	ENTREE
★★★★	The Tradewinds Restaurant	Peter Island	(809) 494-2561	$18–$36••

BRITISH VIRGIN ISLANDS RESTAURANTS	LOCATION	PHONE	ENTREE
Tortola			

Road Town

	Asian			
★★ Chopsticks	Road Town	(809) 494-3616	$10–$20

	English			
★★★ Virgin Queen	Road Town	(809) 494-2310	$7–$16

	Indian			
★★★ Mrs. Scatliffe's	West End	(809) 495-4556	$0–$0•
★★★ The Apple	Road Town	(809) 495-4437	$15–$35••
★★ Bing's Drop Inn	East End	(809) 495-2627	$10–$20••

	International			
★★★★ Skyworld	West End	(809) 494-3567	$7–$40
★★★★ The Upstairs	West End	(809) 494-2228	$10–$27
★★★ Sugar Mill	West End	(809) 495-4355	$6–$28
★★ Pusser's Landing	Road Town	(809) 495-4554	$5–$25
★★ Pusser's Outpost and Pub	Road Town	(809) 494-4199	$7–$25

	Italian			
★★★★ Brandywine Bay	West End	(809) 495-2301	$20–$28••
★★★★ Capriccio di Mare	West End	(809) 494-5369	$8–$15
★★ Spaghetti Junction	West End	(809) 494-4880	$10–$25••

	Seafood			
★★★ The Fish Trap	Road Town	(809) 494-3626	$8–$25

Virgin Gorda

North Sound

	American			
★★★ Pirate's Pub & Grill	North Sound		$5–$7
★★★ Pusser's Leverick Bay	North Sound	(809) 495-7369	$6–$24

	International			
★★★★ Biras Creek	North Sound	(809) 494-3555	$40–$40••
★★★ Olde Yarde Inn	North Sound	(809) 495-5544	$18–$30••
★★★ The Bath and Turtle Pub	North Sound	(809) 495-5239	$7–$30

BRITISH VIRGIN ISLANDS RESTAURANTS	LOCATION	PHONE	ENTREE
★★ Chez Michelle	North Sound	(809) 495-5510	$16–$28••
Latin American			
★★★ Teacher Ilma's	North Sound	(809) 495-5355	$3–$25
★★★ The Crab Hole	North Sound	(809) 495-5307	$6–$15

Note: • Lunch Only

•• Dinner Only

CAYMAN ISLANDS

The 12,000 green turtles at Cayman Turtle Farm on Grand Cayman range in size from two ounces to 400 pounds.

Cayman Islands is a scuba Eden. Due south of Florida and Cuba, the three small Cayman islands were eclipsed for centuries by Jamaica (180 miles to the southeast), but have today zoomed into world-class status as divers, snorkelers, saltwater anglers, and beach-loving layabouts learn to love the high standard of living (20 percent higher than in the U.S.), the low crime rate, and the ingratiating good manners. The islands also draw travelers who need little nightlife and revel in the ease, peace and thriftiness of renting a condo by the beach. Reports of the Caymans having the best dive sites in the world have attracted over 75,000 scubaniks a year (out of the 400,000 tourists who visit annually); the Cayman walls, particularly in the north, are said to rank next to Australia's Great Barrier Reef and the Red Sea in the excellence and accessibility of their sites. Money does seem to find its way here. *The Firm*, Hollywood's recent Tom Cruise movie about money-laundering on the Caymans brought the Caymans a newfound publicity, at the same time erroneously suggesting an island lacking in moral conscience. What *is* conspicuously absent here are the traditional Caribbean straw-hat markets and open-air produce stands; instead expensive Italian sandals have replaced the traditional bare feet, and native vendors have been usurped by sophisticated ex-pats who run the trendy boutiques. Still, the simple life can still bleed through on the Caymans, when the town's rooster is heard daily crowing from the veranda of the Old Courts Building at dawn.

Bird's Eye View

Grand Cayman, 22 miles long and eight miles wide, is the principal island of a complex which includes Cayman Brac and Little Cayman. About an hour's flight from Miami, Grand Cayman covers 76 square miles of land mass, though half of that is swamp. About 89 miles to the northeast of Grand Cayman lies Cayman Brac (the name means "bluff" in Gaellic), a limestone bluff rising from sea level to a height of 140 feet. Five miles west of Cayman Brac, the mile-wide Little Cayman lives up to its name, with a land mass of a mere 10 square miles. The capital of the islands is Georgetown, on the west side of Grand Cayman. No rivers cross the islands, but the vegetation is lush and tropical, dotted with coconut trees, thatch palm, Australian pine and seagrape.

West Bay Beach is the hub of tourism in Grand Cayman, an exquisite strand that gently curves around the western shore. Here, you'll find most of the resorts and hotels. An enormous coral reef surrounds North Sound, a massive bay in the west. Sting Ray City is the shallow habitat of two dozen western Atlantic stingrays whom Caymanian divers have fed and tamed to eat out of their hands.

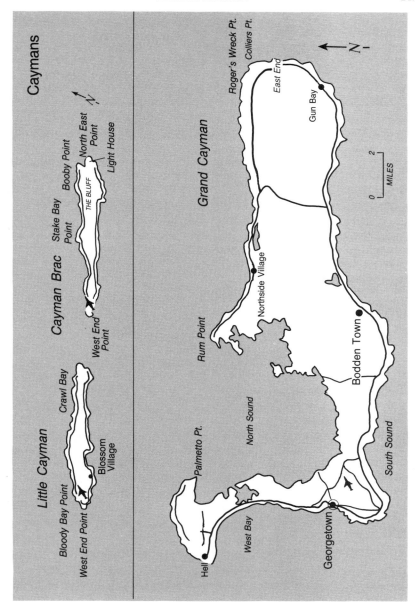

Caymans

Little Cayman

Bloody Bay Point
West End Point
Crawl Bay
Blossom Village

Cayman Brac

Stake Bay Point
Booby Point
THE BLUFF
North East Point
Light House
West End Point

N

Grand Cayman

Roger's Wreck Pt.
Colliers Pt.
East End
Gun Bay
Northside Village
Rum Point
Bodden Town
North Sound
Palmetto Pt.
Hell
West Bay
Georgetown
South Sound

N

0   2
MILES

History

Columbus discovered the Caymans in 1503 and dubbed them *Las Tortugas* for the enormous numbers of tortoises which would provide sustenance to English, Dutch and French sailors for centuries. (Las Tortugas somehow evolved into Los Caimanes, the Spanish name for a kind of tropical American crocodile). For a good 150 years after being sited, the Caymans were almost entirely avoided. They were remote, perilous to approach by sea, and their interiors were inhospitable—swampy and mosquito-infested in Grand Cayman, and hard and scrubby on Little Cayman and Cayman Brac. Among the few creatures which did thrive here were crocodiles, called *caymanas* in the language of the Carib Indians. For a time the critters shared the island with such buccaneers as Sir Henry Morgan and Edward Teach (the original Blackbeard) who hid out in the islands while preying on Spanish and French ships. (Cayman history abounds with stories of sunken treasure and tales of derring-do.) The abundance of meaty sea turtles made the islands a convenient provisioning stop, but by most accounts, the first real settlers didn't arrive until 1655 when deserters from Oliver Cromwell's army abandoned their platoon in Jamaica as the English were taking it from the Spanish. In 1670, Spain ceded both Jamaica and the Caymans to Great Britain. A century later, Grand Cayman had 933 residents, most of whom were slaves. After emancipation by Britain in 1835, the island became home to many other freed slaves; their descendants gradually becoming part of the families of the island, paving the way for the harmony that still exists today.

Just 33 years ago Jamaica chose independence but the Caymans stayed on a British Crown Colony. The first tourists started to arrive in the Caymans during the 1950s while the roads were still bad, the insects voluminous, and the electrical supply iffy. Legislation creating tax-investment havens in 1966 favored offshore banking and trust companies whose executives began seeing vacation promise in the islands. A tourist board, established in 1966, began strictly supervising hotel inspections, which has succeeded in raising and maintaining a high standard of service. About half-a million people visit the Cayman Islands each year.

People

Nearly all the 30,000 Caymanians live on Grand Cayman, a fourth of them in George Town. About 1650 live on Cayman Brac and a mere 50 on Little Cayman. Their ancestry is an ethnic mix from 50 countries, including Jamaica, the U.S., and the U.K.The lilting brogue is a leftover from British seafarers centuries ago. The utter lack of racial tension on the island stems from the fact that neither sugar plantations or long-term slavery was part of the island's history, and the mixing of races seems to have been more fluid here than on other islands. In 1841, an observer noted that Caymanians were "strictly honest and industrious," and that even the wealthy were prone to walk around without shoes on. Today the simple life still seems to prevail, though Caymanians enjoy the highest standard of living in the Caribbean. There is little serious crime. And if the Caymans are short on native culture, locals make up for it for being congenial and tolerant.

Today lots of offshore investors park their money here because taxes and fees are few and client's identities are usually shielded by law. So profitable are the ventures that there are more than 50 banks and $435 million in assets here. Though the recent movie *The Firm* and its plot about money-laundering in the Caymans almost smudged the reputation of the island, locals insist such a scam can't happen here. They claim that anyone trying to deposit lots of U.S. cash would raise eyebrows among local officials.

Beaches

The beaches of the Caymans can be described in a few short words—powder-fine white strands with a handful of birds. **Seven Mile Beach** is considered one of the most fantastic beaches in the Caribbean, marked by a beautiful crescent shape and clear turquoise blue waters. Public buses operate hourly down the strand. North of the Holiday Inn, where most of the watersports facilities are based, is a public beach with small cabanas and tables and chairs. Most memorable sunsets can be seen from the beach at **Rum Point**, at the northeastern tip of North Sound, a sleepy little community of private homes and condos. **Little Cayman** is known for its long white beaches with nary a footprint to mar their beauty. For some reason, locals don't use the beaches much for sunbathing or swimming, so most of the strands are exquisitely private and not crowded.

Dive Sites

Grand Cayman's greatest treasures are underwater, and luckily, all fish and marine life are protected under Grand Cayman's strictly enforced marine park regulations. Grand Cayman's **West Wall**, directly off Seven Mile Beach, is a model of scuba finesse, with over five major dive sites. Another 50 sites are located along the **North Wall**, **South Wall** and **East End**. All major sites are equipped with environmental moorings to avoid anchor damage. The West Wall is by far the easiest and most comfortable for diving. Sea conditions vary from glassy calm to gentle ripples caused by a whisper of the wind. The drop-off is less than one mile offshore—making it easily accessible. Water ranges from 80 degrees in winter to 83 degrees in summer. Underwater visibility averages 100 feet. Among dives are **Big Tunnels**, a series of eight or more coral canyons, many of which are bordered by walls that rise 50–60 feet. **Bonnie's Arch** is one of the island's most distinctive and beautiful coral formations, where a magnificent coral bridge forms an archway that runs 45-70 feet. **Northwest Point** is the most challenging dive at the northern tip of the island, always boasting a current that varies from slight to strong and a cascading wall that acts as the drop-off; its marine life is exceptionally beautiful. **Soto's Central** is the most fascinating shallow reef—a labyrinth of coral grottoes, tunnels, caves and canyons in 35-45 feet deep water.

Cayman Brac's **marine parks** are located on the north coast between Buccanneer's Inn and White Bay and on the south coast from Brac Reef to Beach Point and from Jennifer Bay and Deep Well. Spot Bay on the northeast and small shoreside strips at Dennis Point and Salt Water Point on the southwest coast are replenishment zones. On the north coast, where waters are calmer, wall formations are close enough for diving from shore. This area also has excellent snorkeling. On the south shore, diving by boat is required because the water is too rough. Walls, about 300 feet from shore, give way to a series of canyons formed by long fingers of coral reaching 75 feet deep and more. Mixed in with sponges will be elkhorn coral, staghorn, brain, and others. There are two fully equipped dive centers on the island, both offering underwater photography and certification courses.

Little Cayman is surrounded by extensive reefs and excellent walls. On the northern coast, the marine park stretches three miles around Bloody Bay from Spot Bay to Grape Tree Bay. Jackson's Point and Bloody Bay Wall begin at 20 feet and plunge down a sheer escarpment. A fantastic sight are the numerous pink and blue lacy sponges that cling to the huge black coral trees in depths of 60-100 feet.

FIELDING'S CHOICE:

Sting Ray City, the world-famous dive site, in North Sound, is less than an hour's catamaran ride from the Hyatt Regency's dock. The surprise is that you can actually scuba and snorkel with a large family of sting rays, who, years ago, learned to bump a diver's mask so the diver would drop his bag of squid. Those who have done it have been scared out of their minds but have come back glowing.

Treks

Grand Cayman was made for hiking; nearly any beach or road is suitable for walking, with the exception of the primary roads around towns and resorts. Bird-watching is especially fine around the tracks circling lagoons and mangroves maintained by the government's Mosquito Research and Control Unit. Do obtain an excellent map from the Lands and Survey Department, which show the bird migrations around the various wetlands. Cayman Brac's and Little Cayman's dirt roads prove to be especially good trekking. Do dress appropriately—you'll need good hiking boots to protect your heels from the jagged limestone, sunhat and sunscreen. Do always carry your own water supply.

On the North Shore, certain trails have not been well maintained but they are accessible from the Queens highway and lead to scenic hikes along the rocky cliffs overlooking the north shore. These cliffs, reaching about 40 feet high, contain the metal caymanite, which is used in popular jewelry. Some trails lead inland and are excellent for bird-watching and for scoping out the rare Cayman iguana—a highly endangered lizard. Also seen here may be the rare spotted agouti, known locally as the Cayman rabbit, which was once hunted for its meat and is now a household pet.

The flat roads and light traffic on **Cayman Brac** make for excellent trekking. You can walk the main road north to almost the entire length of the island, passing many of the coastal settlements. The most fascinating route is the newer east-west road down the center of The Bluff, over which nary a car can be seen. From here there are dozens of footpaths which intersect with the highway. The Brac is honeycombed with caves, many of them yet unexplored. Legends have long purported that treasures lay hidden in many of them. Do be careful when hiking, because dense vegetation often hides the entrances to caves. As such, there is even the danger of falling into a well-obscured opening.

On Little Cayman, there are two trails starting from the airstrip on the western coast, each running about a mile. One leads to West End Point and the other, called the Nature Trail, crosses to Spot Bay on the northern shore.

What Else to See

There is little to dazzle the eye in regards to historical settings in Grand Cayman, but a jaunt around George Town should include a trip to the **Cayman Islands National Museum**, on the waterfront at Hog St. Bay, where you can view some 2000 artifacts about the island's history. If you get bored, the little library on Edward Street stocks English novels and magazines. To see more of Grand Cayman, you might consider renting a bike, motorbike, or even a car. You can start out driving along Seven Mile Beach, past the residence of the island's governor and onto the West Bay. A stop at **Hell**, a formation of jagged burnt charcoal-colored rocks called iron-shore, has spawned a cottage industry of products imbued with "hell" themes. There is even a post office nearby where you postmark letters "from Hell." At the **Cayman Turtle Farm**, you can watch reptiles being hatched and raised (28,000 yearlings released into the sea last year) and scour the gift shop for turtle paraphernalia. Along the **South Sound Road**, you'll drive past some of the most attractive old wooden houses on the island. Bat fanatics can stop at their own **Bat Cave** (take the dirt road off the main road, to Bodden Town, heading east). A cliff overhanging the sea houses numerous caves, just beware where you walk. At the **Cayman Islands National Botanic Park**, you can hike over a 1 1/2-mile marked trail. The *Submarine Atlantis* at George Town Harbour—

considered the stretch limo of the Caribbean—makes a sightseeing dive on a sophisticated vessel by a Creole pilot whose assistant entertains as you browse 100 feet down, among puffers, parrot fish and the reef life.

City Celebrations

Pirates' Week ★★★★★

Various locations, Georgetown, ☎ *(809)949-5078.*
To celebrate its history as a pirate haunt, this island-wide festival, held in late October, brings out the buccaneer in locals. There are costume parades, fishing tournaments, treasure hunts and the ever-popular kidnapping of the governor. Lots of ho-ho-hoing, and more than a few bottles of rum.

Museums and Exhibits
Cayman Brac

Brac Museum ★★

Stake Bay.
Hours Open: 9:00 a.m.–4:00 p.m.
This small museum exhibits local antiques and relics from shipwrecks. Free admission.

Grand Cayman

Cayman Islands National Museum ★★

Harbour Drive, Georgetown, ☎ *(809)949-8368.*
Hours Open: 9:00 a.m.–5:00 p.m.
Housed in an 1833 West Indian building on the waterfront—which in previous incarnations was a jail, courthouse and dance hall—this museum exhibits more than 2000 items detailing the history of the islands and its peoples. Students & Seniors $2.50. General admission: $5.00.

Treasure Museum ★★★

West Bay Road, Georgetown, ☎ *(809)947-5033.*
Hours Open: 9:00 a.m.–5:00 p.m.
This small museum specializes in recovered artifacts from shipwrecks, with lots of pieces from the Maravillas, a Spanish galleon that sank in 1656. Among the exhibits are a seven-pound gold bar, dioramas of the islands' seafaring history and an animated Blackbeard the Pirate, who regales visitors with long-ago tales that may or may not be true. General admission: $5.00.

Tours

Atlantic Submarines Cayman ★★★★★

Goring Avenue, Georgetown, ☎ *(809)949-7700.*
Not for the claustrophobic but memorable for everyone else, this modern submarine seats 46 people in air-conditioned comfort. It travels along the Cayman Wall at depths of up to 90 feet, giving non-divers a taste of the fascinating underwater sights. Night dives are especially recommended. Prices range from $79–$90; half that for kids under 12 (children under four are not permitted). Atlantis also operates two research subs that go as deep as 800 feet and carry just two passengers at a time. This trip costs $275 per person; a highlight is the wreck of the cargo ship *Kirk Pride*.

Cayman Turtle Farm ★★★

West Bay, Georgetown, ☎ *(809)949-3893.*
Hours Open: 8:30 a.m.–5:00 p.m.

The island's most-visited tourist attraction houses more than 12,000 green turtles, from hatchlings to giant specimens weighing 400 pounds. It's the world's only green sea turtle farm, and while it supplies turtle meat to local restaurants, it also strives to replenish their numbers in the wild. You can taste turtle dishes at the cafe, but skip the gift shop, as U. S. citizens can't import anything made of these endangered critters. Children 6–10 are half price and under 6 are free. General admission: $5.00.

Sting Ray City ★★★★★

North Sound.

Some two miles off the northwest tip and 12 feet down live several dozen stingrays that await handouts from divers and snorkelers. They are relatively tame, but beware of their stinger tails! One of the Caribbean's most popular dive sites.

Sports

Watersports are the bread and butter—or is that the fish and crabcake?—of the Caymanian experience. Scuba is king, and there are three dive shops that have the capability of serving 75,000 divers annually. (For more information, see above under "Dive Sites"). The less athletically inclined should definitely take a cruise on the island's famous submarine, the 28-passenger *Atlantis* (☎ *949-7700*), which dives up to 150 feet both day and night. Also consider a glass-bottom boat trip—contact the Holiday Inn for information. Deep-sea fishing has caught on with a great passion in recent years. Blue marlin, bluefin and yellowfin tuna, wahoo, dolphin, tarpon, groupers, snappers, barracuda, and the occasional shark are all potential catch. The prime fishing season runs from November-March, but fishing year-round remains good. In June, there is a Million Dollar Month sport-fishing competition, with a one-million-dollar prize (where *do* they get that money?) awarded to the angler who breaks the current world record for Atlantic blue marlin (the odds are probably harder than the New York Lottery). On Grand Cayman, Sunfish and Hobie Cats can be rented as well as 60-ft. catamarans chartered with crew. Seven-Mile Beach receives the most cruises. North Sound, Spots Bay, and Hub Bay have all proved safe for anchors, but boats must first register at the Port Authority in George Town if they want to come ashore. A yacht race is held annually in the spring for locals and visitors. Some hotels and condo complexes have tennis and there is an unusual 18-hole golf course called the Links. You can also do as the British bankers do—take in cricket, or polo, with all the gusto of an ex-pat.

Deep-Sea Fishing

Various locations, Georgetown.
Several outfits offer charters and excursions for deep-sea, reef, bone and fly fishers: **Crosby Ebanks** *(☎ 809-947-4049)*, **Capt. Eugene's Watersports** *(☎ 809-949-3099)*; **Charter Boat Headquarters** *(☎ 809-947-4340)*, and **Island Girl** *(☎ 809-947-3029)*. Serious fishermen and women should plan to visit Grand Cayman in June, when the Million Dollar Month fishing tournament is held, featuring international competitors and cash prizes. *For details, contact Box 878, West Wind Building, Grand Cayman.*

Golf

Two locations, Georgetown.
The island's newest course is the Links at Safehaven *(☎ 809-947-4155)*, a par-71, 6519-yard championship course designed by Roy Case. Duffers can also tee off at Britannia, designed by Jack Nicklaus, which includes a nine-hole regulation course, an 18-hole executive course, and a Cayman course, in which special short-distance balls are used. Green fees are $25–$50; ☎ *(809) 949-8020.*

Scuba Diving

Various locations, Cayman Islands.
Chances are excellent that your hotel will have its own dive center, or check out one of the following: Grand Cayman: **Dive Cayman BVI** *(☎ 809-947-5133)*, **Parrot's Landing** *(☎ 800-448-0428 or 809-949-7884)*, **Quabbin Dives** *(☎ 800-238-6712 or 809-949-5597)*, **Sunset Divers** *(☎ 809-949-7111)*, **Bob Soto's** *(☎ 809-947-4631)*, **Don Foster's** *(☎ 809-949-5679)* and **Red Sail Sports** *(☎ 809-949-8745)*. Cayman Brac: **Divi Tiara** *(☎ 809-948-1316)* and **Brac Aquatics** *(☎ 809-858-7429)*. Little Cayman: **Southern Cross Club** *(☎ 809-948-1099)*. Prices are generally about $40 for a single-tank dive; $55 for two tanks.

Windsurfing

Various locations, Georgetown.
Chances are good your hotel can set you up for windsurfing, but if it lacks facilities, try **Cayman Windsurf** *(☎ 809-947-7492)* or **Sailboards Caribbean** *(☎ 809-949-1068)*.

Where to Stay

Highest Rated Hotels in Cayman Islands

★★★★★	Clarion Grand Pavilion
★★★★★	West Indian Club
★★★★	Beach Club Hotel
★★★★	Hyatt Regency Grand Cayman
★★★★	Little Cayman Beach
★★★★	Radisson Resort
★★★★	Spanish Bay Reef North Wall
★★★★	Treasure Island Resort
★★★	Ambassadors Inn
★★★	Caribbean Club

Most Exclusive Hotels in Cayman Islands

★★★	Holiday Inn Grand Cayman	$238–$832
★★★★★	West Indian Club	$130–$365
★★★	Harbour Heights	$190–$295
★★★	Indies Suites	$160–$290
★★★★	Treasure Island Resort	$160–$275

Fielding's Best Value Hotels in Cayman Islands

★★★	Pan-Cayman House	$150–$370
★★★	Caribbean Club	$160–$425
★★★★	Hyatt Regency Grand Cayman	$180–$500
★★★	Indies Suites	$160–$290
★★★	Ambassadors Inn	$60–$80

About half of the 3000 rooms in the Cayman Islands are situated not in hotels but in rental condos, which look like sitting ducks, almost none higher than a palm tree, as regulated by law. A good book to get is the *Rates and Facts* booklet put out by the tourist board. The chain establishments on Grand Cayman's Seven Mile Beach are big and well equipped with restaurants and recreational facilities. Most folks like to settle into one of the hotels or condos on West Bay because it is easy to walk up and down the strip for meals, shopping, etc. without ever needing a car. If you want to avoid the hustle of George Town and Seven Mile Beach, stay on the north side or east side. Many prefer the flexibility of renting a one to three bedroom apartment with a fully equipped kitchen and daily maid service.

Hotels and Resorts

The big chain hotels, like **Holiday Inn**, **Radisson** and **Ramada**, give good service here and particularly lean toward providing package tours, some specifically for divers. The **Hyatt Regency**, luxurious and lushly landscaped, is known for being the hub of lively social activities, especially at night and has the island's only golf course. (Hyatt's private villas come with their own pool, Jacuzzi and cabaña.) The **Spanish Bay Reef**, the first all-inclusive property on Grand Cayman, rates as the island's most secluded—a true dive hotel. **Pirates Point Resort** is run by a Cordon-Bleu educated-chef.The Beach Club Colony should be avoided if you don't care for your personal beach space to be invaded by loads of cruise passengers.

Cayman Brac

Brac Reef Beach Resort　　　　**$106–$147**　　　　★

West End Point, ☎ (800)327-3835, (809)948-7323.
Single: $106–$147. Double: $106–$147.
Divers like this casual hotel and its all-inclusive package rates that include all drinks, transportation from the airport and three buffet meals daily. Dive packages are available at additional cost. The rooms are basic but at least air cooled. There's a pool and tennis court to keep nondivers occupied. 40 rooms. Credit Cards: V, MC, A.

Divi Tiara Beach Resort　　　　**$95–$200**　　　　★★

West End Point, ☎ (800)948-1553, (809)948-7553.
Single: $95–$185. Double: $100–$200.
Set on a fine beach, this pleasant hotel appeals to those who want to avoid crowds. Rooms are typical but do offer air conditioning and were recently redone; a few have Jacuzzis to boot. There's a pool and tennis court, and most meals are served buffet-style. Good service. The dive center is excellent. 58 rooms. Credit Cards: V, MC, A.

Little Cayman

Little Cayman Beach　　　　**$118–$137**　　　　★★★★

Blossom Village, ☎ (809)948-1033.
Single: $118. Double: $128–$137.
This resort, opened in 1993,has a nice sandy beach off a reef-protected bay. Air-conditioned guest rooms are a cut above the competition on the island and attractively furnished. Guests keep busy diving (they have an excellent shop), hanging out

by the pool, riding bikes, or playing pickup volleyball games. The bar and restaurant are good and popular with locals. 32 rooms. Credit Cards: V, MC, A.

Southern Cross Club $125–$285   ★★
Crawl Bay, ☎ *(800)899-2582, (809)948-3255.*
Single: $125–$185. Double: $215–$285.
This 1950s cottage resort sits on a pretty beach. Rooms are basic and rely on ceiling fans to keep things cool. The rates include three family-style meals a day and watersports. Most who come are into deep-sea fishing, with the hotel arranging excursions. The bar attracts lots of tale-swapping fishermen and women. 10 rooms. Credit Cards: Not Accepted.

Grand Cayman

Beach Club Hotel $125–$265   ★★★★
Seven Mile Beach, West Bay, ☎ *(800)223-6510, (809)949-8100.*
Single: $125–$240. Double: $125–$265.
Dating back to the 1960s (making it one of the island's oldest resorts), the Beach Club resembles a colonial plantation villa. Accommodations are strung along the beach and include standard and unexciting guest rooms and villas. Watersports cost extra, and there's a great dive shop on-site. Lots of cruise passengers converge here when their ship is in port, so don't expect tranquility. 41 rooms. Credit Cards: V, MC, DC, A.

Clarion Grand Pavilion $155–$455   ★★★★★
West Bay Road, West Bay, ☎ *(809)947-5656.*
Single: $155–$455. Double: $155–$455.
This spot reopened in January 1994 after extensive refurbishing. Accommodations are tasteful and well appointed, and all have air conditioning and such extras as a trouser press (do you really need creases in the Caribbean?) and hair dryers. There's a pool and fitness center, and parents can stash the kids in supervised programs all year round. 90 rooms. Credit Cards: V, MC, DC, A.

Holiday Inn Grand Cayman $238–$832   ★★★
Seven Mile Beach, West Bay, ☎ *(800)465-4329, (809)947-4444.*
Single: $238–$298. Double: $238–$832.
Lots of action at this busy hotel. Guest rooms are air-conditioned and nicely done, though only some boast views. There's a dive shop, twice-weekly barbecues by the pool and all sorts of watersports. A favorite spot to while away the day for cruise passengers. Not a lot of island flavor—this is, after all, a Holiday Inn—but dependable lodgings. 212 rooms. Credit Cards: V, MC, DC, A.

Hyatt Regency Grand Cayman $180–$500   ★★★★

Seven Mile Beach, West Bay, ☎ *(800)233-1234, (809)949-1234.*
Single: $180–$400. Double: $225–$500.
This is a world-class resort all the way, and definitely Grand Cayman's finest resort. Accommodations are in British Colonial-style buildings surrounding a central courtyard, and are simply fabulous, with expensive furnishings, original art, air conditioning (of course) and Italian marble baths. Landscaping is lush, and guests can choose from four pools, four tennis courts, a dive shop, all watersports and 18 holes

of golf designed by Jack Nicklaus. Lots of bars and lounges, including one seen in *The Firm*. Elegant!236 rooms. Credit Cards: V, MC, A.

Radisson Resort $165–$390 ★★★★

Seven Mile Beach, West Bay, ☎ (800)333-3333, (809)949-88.
Single: $165–$240. Double: $165–$390.

Set on a scenic spread of beach, the Radisson is a five-story hotel with comfortable and contemporary guest rooms. A very nice deck houses a pool, bar and Jacuzzi set among potted plants. All the usual watersports, plus a dive shop and health club, keep guests busy, and the disco hops once the sun goes down. A truly pleasant spot, with lots of elegant touches. 315 rooms. Credit Cards: V, MC, DC, A.

Sleep Inn $90–$0 ★★

Seven Mile Beach, West Bay, ☎ (800)627-5337, (809)949-9111.
Single: $90–$185. Double: $997.

This modern hotel, set right on the beach, has air-conditioned guest rooms with all the typical amenities. Eight suites have kitchenettes. The grounds are basic, with just a pool and Jacuzzi for recreation, but watersports can be found nearby. 116 rooms. Credit Cards: CB, V, MC, DC, A.

Spanish Bay Reef North Wall $160–$218 ★★★★

West Bay Road, West Bay, ☎ (800)223-6510, (809)949-3765.
Single: $160–$218. Double: $160–$218.

Situated on a private coral reef on the island's isolated northwest tip, this all-inclusive resort houses guests in air-conditioned rooms with Caribbean decor. Popular with divers, it offers good facilities for scuba, as well as other watersports and the typical resort pool. The rates include all meals and activities. The atmosphere is nicely casual, but service is not always up to par. 50 rooms. Credit Cards: V, MC, DC, A.

Sunset House $90–$190 ★★

South of GeorgeTown, ☎ (800)854-4767, (809)949-7111.
Single: $90–$185. Double: $95–$190.

Great diving and snorkeling right offshore, but there's no beach to speak of at this casual hotel that dates back to the late 1950s. Accommodations are in standard guest rooms and two efficiencies; all are nicely done and air-cooled. Two pools help make up for the lack of beach, and there's a full-service dive shop, with a fleet of six boats, on-site. A really nice spot. 59 rooms. Credit Cards: V, MC, A.

Treasure Island Resort $160–$275 ★★★★

Seven Mile Beach, West Bay, ☎ (800)327-8777, (809)949-7777.
Single: $160–$195. Double: $160–$275.

One of the island's largest resorts, this former Ramada fronts the beach and situates its guest rooms around a courtyard with two pools, a Jacuzzi and a gurgling waterfall. Accommodations are larger than usual and nicely done with minibars and sitting areas. There's live music in the nightclub six nights a week, and by day lots to keep busy with, including two tennis courts, a dive shop and all watersports. A good choice for those who like a lot of action. 280 rooms. Credit Cards: V, MC, A.

Apartments and Condominiums

Lots of visitors who come to Caymans come for rough and rugged adventure underwater, so they're used to taking care of themselves. More and more self-catering accommodations are appearing every year. The downside is that if you plan to cook for yourself, food costs are extremely high; this year at least the markets seemed to be getting better stocked. Amid the action on Seven Mile Beach, a short walk from restaurants and a supermarket, are **Pan Cayman** in the Caribbean Club; here you'll find a better beach and a lot more peace and quiet. Golfers congregate in the **Britannia Villas**, which is part of the Hyatt complex, at the golf course. The **Indies Suites** are a good bargain for travelers who spend most of their time underwater and shut their eyes the minute their head hits the pillow (one plus is the free breakfast).

Grand Cayman

Beachcomber Condos   **$190–$395**   ★

Seven Mile Beach, West Bay, ☎ (800)327-8777, (809)947-4470.
Single: $190–$395. Double: $190–$395.

This condo complex has two-bedroom, two-bath units with air conditioning, fully equipped kitchens and a balcony or patio with ocean views. Several units have dens that can convert into a third bedroom if needed. There's a pool on-site, and maid service is available, but you'll have to dine elsewhere. 19 rooms. Credit Cards: V, MC.

Caribbean Club   **$160–$425**   ★★★

Seven Mile Beach, P. O. Box 30499, West Bay, ☎ (800)327-8777, (809)947-4099.
Single: $160–$280. Double: $160–$425.

This colony of villas includes one- and two-bedroom units (only six are actually on the beach) in a secluded atmosphere. The pink cottages are air-conditioned and include large living/dining areas, full kitchens and attractive, comfortable decor. The restaurant is popular with visitors as well as locals. There's a tennis court, but no pool. No kids under 11 during the winter season. 18 rooms. Credit Cards: V, MC, A.

Cayman Kai Resort   **$140–$220**   ★★

North Side, East of Rum Plantation, West Bay, ☎ (800)223-5427, (809)947-9055.
Single: $140–$215. Double: $150–$220.

Situated in a 20-acre grove along the secluded north shore beach, this secluded resort houses guests in one- and two-bedroom lodges and villas, all with kitchens but only some with air conditioning. The beach is not great for swimming, but the snorkeling is great. The property caters primarily to divers, but is a bit more formal than the island's other dive resorts. A restaurant, bar and three tennis courts keep nondivers occupied. 20 rooms. Credit Cards: V, MC, A.

Christopher Columbus Apts   **$190–$390**   ★★

Seven Mile Beach, West Bay, ☎ (809)947-4354.
Single: $190–$390. Double: $190–$390.

Popular with families, this condominium resort offers individually decorated two-bedroom, two-bath units with air conditioning, small but complete kitchens and light, tropical furnishings. As expected, the penthouse units are by far the nicest (and most expensive). No restaurant or bar, so guests congregate at the pool, tennis courts and sandy beach. 28 rooms. Credit Cards: V, MC, A.

Colonial Club   **$230–$500**   ★

West Bay Road, West Side, ☎ *(809)947-4660.*
Single: $230–$455. Double: $255–$500.
Built in the Bermudian style with a pink and white exterior, this condo complex has comfortable two- and three-bedroom units with central air, complete kitchens and maid service. Located on an especially nice stretch of beach, extras include a pool and lighted tennis court. No restaurant on-site, so you'll have to cook in or venture out. 15 rooms. Credit Cards: V, MC, A.

Discovery Point Club   **$145–$315**   ★★

Seven Mile Road, West Bay, ☎ *(809)947-4724.*
Single: $145–$285. Double: $145–$315.
Located on Seven Mile Beach, this well-appointed resort offers one- and two-bedroom condos with all the modern conveniences, including air and full kitchens. There are also studios sans cooking facilities. A pretty pool and two tennis courts are on-site, but no restaurant or bar. 45 rooms. Credit Cards: V, MC, A.

George Town Villas   **$165–$420**   ★

Seven Mile Beach, West Bay, ☎ *(809)949-5172.*
Single: $165–$405. Double: $165–$420.
A condominium community with two-bedroom units that come equipped with two baths, full kitchens, air conditioning, living and dining areas and washer/dryers. There's a pool and tennis court, and shopping and restaurants are nearby. 54 rooms.
Credit Cards: V, MC, A.

Grand Bay Club   **$120–$310**   ★★★

Seven Mile Beach, West Bay, ☎ *(809)947-4728.*
Single: $120–$195. Double: $120–$310.
All units at this modern complex are suites, ranging from studios that lack kitchens to one- and two-bedroom units with cooking facilities. Maids keep things tidy. The site includes a large pool, Jacuzzi and tennis. No restaurant, but there are many within a walk. 21 rooms. Credit Cards: V, MC, A.

Grapetree/Cocoplum Condos   **$135–$280**   ★★

Georgetown, ☎ *(800)635-4824, (809)949-5640.*
Single: $135–$280. Double: $135–$280.
Situated in a secluded area of Seven Mile Beach—though the beach here is not the greatest—this condo complex includes one- to three-bedroom units with all the usual amenities, as well as daily maid service. Watersports are available nearby, and the grounds include a tennis court and two pools. No restaurant, though. 50 rooms. Credit Cards: V, MC, A.

Harbour Heights   **$190–$295**   ★★★

Seven Mile Beach, West Bay, ☎ *(800)327-8777, (809)947-4295.*
Single: $190–$280. Double: $190–$295.
This three-story condominium overlooks the pool and seafront along Seven Mile Beach. Two-bedroom suites are attractive, with living/dining areas, complete kitchens, air conditioning and balconies. The grounds are nicely landscaped, and the beach is good for swimmers. Restaurants are nearby. 46 rooms. Credit Cards: Not Accepted. Credit Cards: V, MC, A.

Indies Suites $160–$290   ★★★

West Bay Road, West Bay, ☎ (800)654-3130, (809)947-5025.
Single: $160–$290. Double: $160–$290.

This very comfortable and attractive hotel houses guests in nicely furnished suites
with full-size kitchens. The complimentary Continental breakfast is a nice touch.
There's no restaurant, but guests can grab snacks at the pool bar. The beach is
across the street, a liability when so many similar properties lie directly on the sand.
Nevertheless, this is a good choice. 40 rooms. Credit Cards: V, MC, A.

Island Pine Villas $110–$225   ★

Seven Mile Beach, West Bay, ☎ (800)223-9815, (809)949-6586.
Single: $110–$220. Double: $110–$225.

This two-story condo complex is within walking distance of shops and restaurants.
Units are quite comfortable, with one or two bedrooms, air conditioning, kitchenettes and patios or balconies. No pool or restaurant, but a good value nonetheless.
40 rooms. Credit Cards: V, MC, DC, A.

Lacovia Condominiums $200–$285   ★★★

Seven Mile Beach, West Bay, ☎ (800)223-9815, (809)949-7599.
Single: $200–$285. Double: $200–$285.

Stylish and tasteful, this condo complex surrounds a free-form pool and clubhouse
with sauna and games. Units have one to three bedrooms with separate living/din-
ing areas, full kitchens and Spanish-style balconies; most also boast oversized tubs.
Maids tidy up daily. The grounds include nice landscaping, and there's a tennis
court for working up a sweat. 45 rooms. Credit Cards: A.

London House $235–$750   ★★★

West Bay Beach, West Bay, ☎ (800)423-4095, (809)947-4060.
Single: $235–$290. Double: $235–$750.

This mission-style complex has well-maintained accommodations and a pool, watersports and maid service to round out the picture. Units have one or two bedrooms
and kitchenettes. Ceiling fans supplement the air conditioning. The beach is nice
and quiet, happily not frequented by cruise ship passengers. 21 rooms. Credit Cards:
V, MC, A.

Morrit's Tortuga Club $145–$440

East End, ☎ (800)447- 309, (809)947-7449.
Single: $145–$380. Double: $130–$440.

This plantation-style condo complex is situated on eight beachfront acres near some
of Grand Cayman's best diving sites. Three-story buildings house comfortable one-
and two-bedroom units with full kitchens. Built on the site of the former Tortuga
Club, today's resort is a far cry from that hideaway spot, but it remains popular with
divers. In addition to a pool, there's a decent restaurant and both windsurfing and
diving schools. 85 rooms. Credit Cards: V, MC, A.

Pan-Cayman House $150–$370   ★★★

Seven Mile Beach, West Bay, ☎ (800)248-5115, (809)947-4002.
Single: $150–$370. Double: $150–$370.

A popular apartment complex with 10 units ranging from two to three bedrooms, all with two baths, air conditioning, full kitchens and maid service. Great views from the private balconies or patios. 10 rooms. Credit Cards: Not Accepted. Credit Cards: V, MC.

Plantana $180–$425   ★ ★

Seven Mile Beach, West Bay, ☎ *(809)947-4430.*
Single: $180–$425. Double: $180–$425.
One- and two-bedroom condominiums are arranged on three floors, with the ones higher up offering the best views. All are individually decorated and have full kitchens and screened balconies or patios; most also have washer/dryers. A pool supplements the sea for splashing about. One of the nicer condo complexes on the island. 49 rooms. Credit Cards: V, MC, A.

Plantation Village Resort $145–$405   ★

Seven Mile Beach, West Bay, ☎ *(800)822-8903, (809)949-4199.*
Single: $145–$405. Double: $145–$405.
Set on four acres of Seven Mile Beach, this condo complex has individually decorated two- and three-bedroom units with two baths, complete kitchens, central air and screened lanais. Maids pick up daily. There are two pools, a Jacuzzi, a tennis court and a playground for the kids. Lots of families here. 70 rooms. Credit Cards: V, MC, A.

Silver Sands $200–$235   ★ ★

West Bay Road, Seven Mile Beach, West Bay, ☎ *(800)327-8777, (809)949-3343.*
Single: $200–$235. Double: $200–$235.
Set amid tropical gardens, this casual complex has air-conditioned two-bedroom units with all the modern amenities. There's a nice resort feel to this place with its extra-large pool, gazebo, two tennis courts and nearby watersports. 42 rooms. Credit Cards: V, MC, A.

Tarquynn Manor $143–$395   ★ ★

Seven Mile Beach, West Bay, ☎ *(800)223-9815, (809)947-5060.*
Single: $143–$395. Double: $230–$395.
At least one bedroom in these two- or three-bedroom units fronts the beach. The modern units have air conditioning, kitchens and patios or balconies. A concierge handles special requests. There's an outdoor pool and games room to keep kids occupied. 20 rooms. Credit Cards: V, MC.

Victoria House $165–$395   ★ ★

Seven Mile Beach, West Bay, ☎ *(800)327-8777, (809)947-4233.*
Single: $165–$380. Double: $175–$395.
These Caribbean-style apartments front the ocean and are far from the madding tourist crowds. Units are air-conditioned and come in a variety of configurations, from studios to penthouses. All are comfortable with tropical styling and have full kitchens. There's no pool on-site, but watersports are available nearby, and there is one tennis court. Sea turtles frequent the quiet beach in the mornings. 26 rooms. Credit Cards: V, MC, A.

Villas Pappagallo $160–$284   ★ ★

Seven Mile Beach, West Bay, ☎ *(800)232-1034, (809)949-8098.*

Single: $160–$284. Double: $180–$284.

Located on a private, secluded beach on the northwest shore, this complex consists of Mediterranean-style villas, all with air conditioning, kitchenettes and balconies. Lots to do here, including two tennis courts, a pool and noshing at the Italian restaurant. You'll have to travel a half-mile for watersports. 40 rooms. Credit Cards: V, MC, A.

Villas of the Galleon $200–$430   ★★

West Bay Beach, West Bay, ☎ (809)947-4433.
Single: $200–$430. Double: $200–$430.

Facing a private beach, this condo complex offers units with one or two bedrooms, all with air conditioning, modern kitchen, small baths and balconies; maids tidy up daily but take Sundays off. Most folks here are staying for a long time. Request an upper floor unit for the best sea views. 75 rooms. Credit Cards: V, MC, A.

West Indian Club $130–$365   ★★★★★

West Bay Beach, West Bay, ☎ (809)947-5255.
Single: $130–$365. Double: $130–$365.

These two-story beachfront apartments are situated near the center of famed Seven Mile Beach. The well-appointed one- and two-bedroom units have full kitchens, terraces and air conditioning only in the bedrooms. A maid keeps things looking fresh, and you can hire a cook for a custom-made meal. 6 rooms. Credit Cards: V, MC, A.

Inns

These are basically scuba-devoted inns, low on luxury, but high on congeniality. Seaview hotels attracts a very young crowd.

Little Cayman

Pirates Point Resort $140–$405   ★

Pirates Point, ☎ (809)948-1010.
Single: $140–$200. Double: $255–$405.

Most accommodations at this pleasant inn are in air-conditioned rooms with private baths; there are also four cottages overlooking the sea. The best reason to come, however, is mealtime: owner Gladys Howard is a graduate of Paris' Cordon Bleu, and judging from the food, she passed with flying colors. A friendly, peaceful spot. 10 rooms. Credit Cards: V, MC.

Sam McCoy's Lodge $105–$185   ★★

Crawl Bay, ☎ (800)626- 496, (809)948-4526.
Single: $105–$185. Double: $105–$185.

Only some rooms at this very informal spot have their own bath. The food's great though, with casual meals taken with Sam, his family and fellow guests. The rates include three squares a day and transportation to and from the airport. 6 rooms. Credit Cards: Not Accepted.

Grand Cayman

Seaview Hotel $65–$105   ★★

Near GeorgeTown, ☎ (809)949-8804.
Single: $65–$105. Double: $65–$105.

Opened in 1952, this is the oldest operating hotel on the island. Rooms are air-conditioned and have private baths. Guests can splash in the outdoor pool or head for the beach, where a dive center and watersports are offered. The piano lounge is a pleasant spot by night. 15 rooms. Credit Cards: V, MC, A.

Low Cost Lodging

One way to save money in the Caymans is to cram a lot of people into a multi-bedroom apartment. But individuals can find single rooms for rent in guest houses (don't hesitate to ask the tourist board). The nightclub keeps things hopping at **Windjammer Hotel**, where rooms are also air-conditioned and come with kitchenettes. Diving is the main topic of conversation at these lodgings, especially at the **Ambassadors Inn**, which attracts the diehards.

Grand Cayman

Ambassadors Inn   **$60–$80**   ★ ★ ★

South Church Street, ☎ *(800)648-7748, (809)949-7577.*
Single: $60–$70. Double: $70–$80.
Located a mile from George Town and some 200 yards and across the street from the beach, this casual spot appeals to divers on a budget. Rooms are basic but do offer air conditioning and private baths. There's a pool on-site. 18 rooms. Credit Cards: V, MC, A.

Windjammer Hotel   **$100–$155**   ★

West Bay Road, West Bay, ☎ *(809)947-4608.*
Single: $100–$155. Double: $100–$155.
Located at the Cayman Falls Shopping Plaza, across from Seven Mile Beach, this small hotel offers air-conditioned rooms with kitchenettes. There are two restaurants, a bar and a nightclub, and this place does do a good after-dark trade. 12 rooms. Credit Cards: V, MC, A.

Where to Eat

	Highest Rated Restaurants in Cayman Islands	
★★★★★	Lantana's	
★★★★★	Ottmar's Restaurant	

	Most Exclusive Restaurants in Cayman Islands	
★★	Pirate's Point Resort	$25–$35
★★	Grand Old House	$20–$34
★★	Lobster Pot	$15–$28
★★	Ristorante Pappagallo	$14–$25
★★★★★	Ottmar's Restaurant	$12–$25

	Fielding's Best Value Restaurants in Cayman Islands	
★★	Pirate's Point Resort	$25–$35
★★	Lobster Pot	$15–$28
★★	Almond Tree, The	$14–$22
★★	Grand Old House	$20–$34
★★★	Crow's Nest	$12–$19

Although most of the food is imported on this dry, scrubby island, the Caymans took top honors in the first annual Caribbean Culinary Competition in 1993. However, prices, in general, tend to be highly inflated in regards to quality (one plus is that portions tend to be enormous). Of course, fresh fish is the basis of most menus; the biggest Caymanian specialty is turtle in all its varied forms (turtles on the Cayman Islands are specifically bred for food). The best time to eat lobster is from August through January. Chef Tell, the TV cooking celeb, has his own restaurant on St. Church Street called **Chef Tell's Grand House**, which specializes in both German delicacies as well as tropical delights like spicy fried coconut shrimp and deep-fried grouper in a minted yogurt-and-curry sauce. (Reservations are required and be prepared to spend between $15–$31 for a main course). **Hemingway's** in the Hyatt Regency on West Bay Rd. is considered to serve the best seafood around. For ambiance, try the **Ristorante Pappagallo**, set on a 14-acre bird sanctuary and housed in an elegant thatch and reed Polynesian tribal lodge—the Italian chefs do wonder with tropical products. Risk-takers should try the blackened alligator tail at **Benjamin's Roof** at Coconut Place, off West Bay Rd. The best bargain bet is to splurge at lunch at the better restaurants and save almost 50 percent off dinner prices. Reservations are usually necessary. Supermarkets are more expensive than in the U.S. but now feature salad bars and prepared salads for about $4 per pound—perfect for picnics or eating in. Try **Kirks**, **Foster's Food Fair**, and **Hurley's**, all located along Seven Mile Beach. Or make breakfast your main meal at the enormous all-you-can-eat buffet at the Holiday Inn for under $10. Also, don't miss the all-you-can-eat buffets of fajitas and seafood as listed in the Friday *Cayman Compass* publications, available everywhere.

Cayman Brac

Edd's Place $$$ ★★

West End, ☎ (809) 948-1208.
Asian cuisine.
Lunch: 7:00 a.m.– 4:00 p.m., entrees $6–$15.
Dinner: 4:00 p.m.– 11:00 p.m., entrees $10–$25.

A nice change from resort cookery on Cayman Brac is this restaurant and bar that's open early for breakfast and later on serves Chinese food and local favorites. If you phone the management, they'll arrange to pick you up, as there is no bus service, and taxis are expensive. Reservations recommended. Credit Cards: V, MC.

Little Cayman

Pirate's Point Resort $$$ ★★★

☎ (809) 948-4210.
International cuisine.
Lunch: entrees $25–$35.
Dinner: entrees $25–$35.

Owner Gladys Howard, trained at Paris' Cordon Bleu, whips up wonderful seafood dishes supplemented by lots of local fruits and vegetables. You can try to recreate some of her dishes back home by buying one of her cookbooks. Associated Hotel: Pirate's Point Resort. Reservations required. Credit Cards: Not Accepted.

Grand Cayman

Almond Tree, The $$$ ★★★

North Church Street, ☎ (809) 949-2893.
Seafood cuisine. Specialties: Callaloo, conch, turtle steak.
Dinner: 5:30 p.m.–10:00 p.m., entrees $14–$22.

An informal and reliable restaurant located just north of George Town, the Almond Tree is a good place to try turtle steak, which is unavailable stateside. More sensitive diners will find all types of seafood, including conch, lobster, filets and a popular all-

you-can-eat main course extravaganza for under $15 on Wednesdays and Fridays.
It's lit up dramatically at night with tiki torches. Closed: Tue. Reservations recommended. Credit Cards: V, MC, A.

Benjamin's Roof $$$ ★★

Coconut Place, ☎ *(809) 947-4080.*
International cuisine. Specialties: Lobster bisque, cajun shrimp.
Dinner: 3:00 p.m.–10:00 p.m., entrees $12–$30.
Greenery abounds in this cool spot in the Coconut Place retail center with a bar dispensing strong libations, a pianist in the corner and spicy blackened-cajun style fish and seafood, with barbecued ribs, lamb and pastas to round out the menu. Desserts are also notable for their richness. Reservations required. Credit Cards: V, MC, A.

Corita's Copper Kettle II $$ ★★

Eastern Avenue, ☎ *(809) 949-5475.*
Latin American cuisine. Specialties: Conch, callaloo.
Lunch: entrees $10–$15.
Busy office workers grab a Jamaican-style breakfast and come back for lunch at this spic-and-span diner located in George Town. Simple, island-style fare includes conch and lobster burgers and local spinach soup. Hot peppers are sprinkled liberally here and there, so beware. Credit Cards: V, MC, A.

Cracked Conch $$$ ★★★

Selkirk's Street Plaza, ☎ *(809) 947-5217.*
Seafood cuisine. Specialties: Cracked conch, conch fritters, key lime pie.
Lunch: 11:30 a.m.– 3:00 p.m., entrees $6–$15.
Dinner: 6:00 p.m.– 10:00 p.m., entrees $10–$25.
Not a place for intimate conversation, the noisy Cracked Conch serves lots of seafood in dim, rather stark surroundings. But the food, especially conch, served lightly fried, is smashing. Burgers, soups and other fast meals are also available, and all meals are prepared for takeout. Reservations recommended. Credit Cards: V, MC, A.

Crow's Nest $$$ ★★★

South Sound, ☎ *(809) 949-9366.*
Latin American cuisine. Specialties: Lobster, conch.
Lunch: 11:30 a.m.–2:00 p.m., entrees $5–$8.
Dinner: 5:30 p.m.–10:00 p.m., entrees $12–$19.
Romance is in the air at this exquisite little eatery on the south point of the island, where diners eat with the ocean waves lapping behind them. Wonderful for a star-filled evening meal or view lunch, the Crow's Nest offers tasty, usually spicy dishes like chicken with hot pepper sauce, coconut fried shrimp and key lime pie. It's hard to believe that George Town is only four miles away. Reservations required. Credit Cards: V, MC, A.

Garden Loggia Cafe $$$ ★★

West Bay Road, ☎ *(809) 949-1234.*
International cuisine. Specialties: Roast suckling pig, lobster.
Lunch: entrees $9–$16.
Dinner: entrees $16–$34.
This top-rated indoor-outdoor cafe facing an elegant expanse of greenery is noted for Sunday buffets replete with champagne and roast suckling pig, and a Friday

night all-you-can-eat seafood spread. Otherwise, the bill of fare usually includes jerk chicken and seafood. Associated Hotel: Hyatt Regency. Reservations required. Credit Cards: V, MC, A.

Grand Old House $$$

Petra Plantation, ☎ *(809) 949-9333.*
International cuisine. Specialties: Grouper.
Lunch: 11:45 a.m.–2:30 p.m., entrees $13–$32.
Dinner: 6:00 p.m.–10:30 p.m., entrees $20–$34.

This lovely gingerbread house in George Town is owned by jolly, red-cheeked TV celebrity Chef Tell Erhardt, who also labors in the kitchen. Cuisine is savory and often deep-fried, but good for a splurge. Erhardt uses herbs, curries and sauces liberally, but with a sure hand, as befits the island's number-one caterer. German specialties are also offered from time to time, reflecting the chef's heritage. Expect spaetzle and sauerkraut interspersed with local delicacies. Closed May through October. Closed: Sun. Reservations required. Credit Cards: V, MC, A.

Hemingway's $$$

West Bay Road, ☎ *(809) 949-1234.*
International cuisine. Specialties: Jerk chicken, lobster.
Lunch: 11:30 a.m.–2:30 p.m., entrees $17–$23.
Dinner: 6:00 p.m.–10:00 p.m., entrees $17–$23.

Spectacular Seven Mile Beach looms blue in front of diners supping at this, the Hyatt Regency Grand Cayman's luxury dining room. The chefs here create nouvelle Caribbean dishes utilizing local fish, turtle steak and chicken, accompanied by lightly zingy herb and citrus sauces. Cocktails are creative and service is attentive. Associated Hotel: Hyatt Regency. Reservations required. Credit Cards: V, MC, A.

Hog Sty Bay Cafe $$$ ★★

North Church Street, ☎ *(809) 949-6163.*
English cuisine.
Lunch: 11:30 a.m.–5:30 p.m., entrees $5–$12.
Dinner: 6:00 p.m.–10:00 p.m., entrees $12–$19.

A good, casual American-English style pub, the Hog Sty Bay Cafe in George Town Harbor is a relaxing perch for burgers and sandwiches or fish and chips. It's hard to miss the brightly painted bungalow that hums inside with a crowd of regulars who also like to come for the swoony sunset views and happy hour drinks. Breakfast is also served, with all the usual offerings plus Mexican-style eggs for added zing. Reservations required. Credit Cards: V, MC, A.

Lantana's $$$

West Bay Road, ☎ *(809) 947-5595.*
Mexican cuisine. Specialties: Conch fritters with ancho chile mayonnaise.
Dinner: 5:30 p.m.–10:00 p.m., entrees $20–$34.

Lantana's is one of the island's most prestigious dining establishments, due to its creative New Mexican-style food. Most dishes are prepared with flair by an Austrian chef, Alfred Schrock, who understands how well West Indian culinary treats blend with dessert hot sauces and condiments. Witness his lightly fried conch fritters with ancho chile mayonnaise and Santa Fe cilantro pesto pasta with seafood. A Viennese tarte tatin is scrumptious. Surroundings recall Santa Fe's Coyote Cafe. Associated Hotel: The Caribbean Club. Reservations required. Credit Cards: D, V, MC, A.

Lobster Pot $$$ ★★
North Church Street, ☎ *(809) 949-2736.*
Seafood cuisine. Specialties: Lobster, turtle soup.
Lunch: 11:30 a.m.–2:30 p.m., entrees $10–$25.
Dinner: 5:00 p.m.– 10:00 p.m., entrees $15–$28.
When the Hog Sty Bay Cafe is busy, this upper-level pub facing West Bay fits the bill. The Lobster Pot manages an intimate atmosphere despite its popularity and the tendency of servers to rush diners through their meals. Nevertheless, the food is good, encompassing lobster, salads and frozen tropical drinks. There's a dart board, natch, for diversion. Closed: Sun. Reservations required. Credit Cards: D, V, MC, A.

Ottmar's Restaurant $$$ ★★★★★
West Bay Road,
International cuisine. Specialties: Fresh fish, rijstaffel.
Dinner: 6:00 p.m.–10:00 p.m., entrees $12–$25.
Another excellent dining room run by an Austrian expatriate, Ottmar's in the Clarion Grand Hotel proffers classical-French cuisine like bouillabaisse and then turns around and offers a Dutch-Javanese *rijstaffel* (a spicy feast of 16 courses surrounded by steamed rice). The room is elegant and spacious, and conversations are carried on unheard by diners at neighboring tables. Associated Hotel: Clarion Grand Pavilion. Closed: Sun. Reservations required. Credit Cards: V, MC, A.

Ristorante Pappagallo $$$ ★★
Palmetto Drive, ☎ *(809) 949-1119.*
Italian cuisine.
Dinner: 6:00 p.m.–10:30 p.m., entrees $14–$25.
Northern Italian cuisine is served in a series of thatched-roof huts facing a lagoon, surrounded by palm trees and wooden bridges. Despite the overwhelming atmosphere and chattering macaws in cages for background music, the food is reasonably good, with veal and seafood predominating. Even if you don't come to eat, it's a good spot for a cocktail. Reservations required. Credit Cards: V, MC, A.

The Wharf $$$ ★★
West Bay Road, ☎ *(809) 949-2231.*
Latin American cuisine. Specialties: Seafood.
Lunch: 12:00 a.m.–2:30 p.m., entrees $21–$30.
Dinner: 6:00 p.m.–10:00 p.m., entrees $21–$30.
The ultimate West Indian dining experience is a seafood supper on the waterfront at the Wharf, which is justly famous for its sublime conch chowder. Chef Tony Egger likes to pair fresh local seafare with Caribbean touches, including a seafood medley baked with a papaya sauce. Calypso bands like to play here, and there's a popular bar attached. Reservations recommended. Credit Cards: D, V, MC.

Verandah Restaurant, The $$$ ★
West Bay Road, ☎ *(809) 947-4444.*
American cuisine. Specialties: Breakfast buffet.
Lunch: 6:00 a.m.– 4:00 p.m., entrees $6–$15.
Dinner: 6:00 p.m.– 9:00 p.m., entrees $18–$32.

The only reason this restaurant in the Holiday Inn is mentioned is because it serves up a bountiful all-you-can-eat breakfast for $10, a great buy in bargain-starved Grand Cayman. This morning feast could easily get you through the rest of the day. Associated Hotel: Holiday Inn Grand Cayman. Reservations recommended. Credit Cards: V, MC, A.

Where to Shop

You wouldn't go to Grand Cayman just to shop, but George Town does boast charming shops that offer the high-end designer luxury items; the bait is the duty-free status which makes imported crystal, china, French perfumes and British woolen goods seem a sometime-bargain. Casual resort wear in stylish designs can be found at **Mango Mames**, in Coconut Place on West Bay Road. For an unusual buy, take home some genuine gold pieces-of-eight and other ancient coins and artifacts recovered from pirate ships and turned into jewelry. The **Jewelry Centre** on Fort Street stocks the most complete collection of loose and set diamonds, as well as black coral (imported) and caymanite.

Cayman Islands Directory

ARRIVAL AND DEPARTURE

Grand Cayman is serviced by Cayman Airways (☎ *800-422-9626)* from Miami, Tampa, Atlanta and Houston; by American Airlines ☎ *800-433-7300* from Miami and Raleigh-Durham, by USAir ☎ *800-428-4322* from Baltimore-Washington, and by Northwest Airlines ☎ *800-447-4747* from Detroit, Minneapolis, and Memphis via Miami. Cayman Airways is also the only airline that services Little Cayman and Cayman Brac.

A taxi from the airport to central Seven Mile Beach is $8–$12, Seven Mile Beach to George is about $8, taxi rates are set by law.

CLIMATE

With an average temperature of 79 degrees, the Caymans are pleasant year-round. High season runs from mid-December to mid-April, but July and August when waters are clearest, are the prime times for diving.

DOCUMENTS

U.S. and Canadian citizens may show either a valid passport or proof of citizenship (voter registration or birth certificate with photo ID) and an ongoing or return ticket.

ELECTRICITY

The current runs 110 volt, 60-cycles, as in the United States.

GETTING AROUND

Taxis are omnipresent whenever a plane arrives, and rates are officially fixed.Since the islands are small and flat, bicycling and walking are pleasant alternatives to walking. Autos, are nevertheless, easy to rent. Major U.S. firms are here as well as local ones, like **Just Jeeps** ☎ *949-7263*. Motorcycles and motorscooters are for hire at **Soto's** ☎ *947-4652*.

Driving is on the left side of the street.

LANGUAGE

English is the main tongue, though the accent is a highly musical melange of Irish, Welsh, Scottish and West Indian lilts.

MEDICAL EMERGENCIES

George Town Hospital ☎ *949-8600* is the only facility on Grand Cayman, located on Hospital Road. Cayman Brac has an 18-bed facility called Faith Hospital ☎ *948-2243*.

MONEY

The official currency is the Cayman Islands dollar, unique to the islands. Most tourist establishments accept U.S. dollars and credit cards. Local banks will cash traveler's checks. Do keep track which dollars (American or Cayman) are being quoted on menus, etc. If quoted in Cayman dollars, the price will look a lot cheaper than it actually is.

TELEPHONE

Area code is 809. International calls can be made 24 hours a day. Local calls now use 7 digits (as opposed to 5 digits in the past).

TIME

Eastern Standard time all year long, with no change during the northern shift to Daylight Savings.

TIPPING AND TAXES

Service charges are not standardized among hotel establishments and can range from 5 percent at condos to 15 percent at top hotels. Always check your bill before adding your own tips. Taxi drivers generally don't expect tips unless you've exhausted them with huge trunks. Bellboys expect 50 cents per bag.

TOURIST INFORMATION

The **Cayman Islands Department of Tourism** is located in the Harbour Centre in George Town ☎ *949-0623*.Tourist information booths can also be found at the pier and at the airport. In the U.S. call ☎ *(213) 738-1968* or *(212) 682-5582.*

TOURS

Half-day guided sightseeing tours (Turtle Farm, Hell, Governor's Residence, George Town) average $30 per person a half-day; a tour to the caves and blowhole sites on the eastern end is $45 per person; full-day tours including lunch and stops at all island sites average $65 per person. None include swimstops. An all-day snorkel trip with lunch averages $50 per person; a one-tank offshore dive is $30-$35, with all equipment, $35–40. **Evco Tours** *(☎ 809-949-2118)* offers six-hour tours around the island, as does **Greyline** *(☎ 809-949-2791)* and **Reids** *(☎ 809-949-6311).*

WHEN TO GO

Pirates Week Festival in October is celebrated with parades, songs, contests and games; even businessmen arrive at the office dressed in costume. Million Dollar Month brings anglers from all over the world to compete in one of the world's biggest big-fish contests. Batabano, the weekend before Easter, is the island's cultural carnival weekend. Queen Elizabeth's birthday in mid-June is celebrated with a full-dress uniform parade, marching band and 21-gun salute.

CAYMAN ISLANDS HOTELS	RMS	RATES	PHONE	FAX
Cayman Brac				
West End Point				
★★ **Divi Tiara Beach Resort**	58	$95–$200	(800) 948-1553	(809) 948-1316
★ **Brac Reef Beach Resort**	40	$106–$147	(800) 327-3835	(813) 323-8827
Grand Cayman				
Georgetown				
★★★★★ **Clarion Grand Pavilion**	90	$155–$455	(809) 947-5656	
★★★★★ **West Indian Club**	6	$130–$365	(809) 947-5255	
★★★★ **Beach Club Hotel**	41	$125–$265	(800) 223-6510	(809) 947-5167
★★★★ **Hyatt Regency Grand Cayman**	236	$180–$500	(800) 233-1234	(809) 949-1234
★★★★ **Radisson Resort**	315	$165–$390	(800) 333-3333	(809) 949-0288
★★★★ **Spanish Bay Reef North Wall**	50	$160–$218	(800) 223-6510	(809) 949-1842
★★★★ **Treasure Island Resort**	280	$160–$275	(800) 327-8777	(809) 949-8489
★★★ **Ambassadors Inn**	18	$60–$80	(800) 648-7748	(809) 949-7050

CAYMAN ISLANDS HOTELS		RMS	RATES	PHONE	FAX
★★★	Caribbean Club	18	$160–$425	(800) 327-8777	(809) 947-4443
★★★	Grand Bay Club	21	$120–$310	(809) 947-4728	(809) 947-5681
★★★	Harbour Heights	46	$190–$295	(800) 327-8777	(809) 947-4522
★★★	Holiday Inn Grand Cayman	212	$238–$832	(800) 465-4329	(809) 947-4213
★★★	Indies Suites	40	$160–$290	(800) 654-3130	(809) 947-5024
★★★	Lacovia Condominiums	45	$200–$285	(800) 223-9815	(809) 949-0172
★★★	London House	21	$235–$750	(800) 423-4095	(809) 947-4087
★★★	Morrit's Tortuga Club	85	$145–$440	(800) 447-0309	(809) 947-7669
★★★	Pan-Cayman House	10	$150–$370	(800) 248-5115	(809) 947-4002
★★	Cayman Kai Resort	20	$140–$220	(800) 223-5427	(809) 947-9102
★★	Christopher Columbus Apts	28	$190–$390	(809) 947-4354	(809) 947-5062
★★	Discovery Point Club	45	$145–$315	(809) 947-4724	(809) 947-5051
★★	Grapetree/Cocoplum Condos	50	$135–$280	(800) 635-4824	
★★	Plantana	49	$180–$425	(809) 947-4430	(809) 947-5076
★★	Seaview Hotel	15	$65–$105	(809) 949-8804	(809) 949-8507
★★	Silver Sands	42	$200–$235	(800) 327-8777	(809) 949-1223
★★	Sleep Inn	116	$90	(800) 627-5337	(809) 949-6699
★★	Sunset House	59	$90–$190	(800) 854-4767	(809) 949-7101
★★	Tarquynn Manor	20	$143–$395	(800) 223-9815	(809) 947-5060
★★	Victoria House	26	$165–$395	(800) 327-8777	(809) 947-5320
★★	Villas Pappagallo	40	$160–$284	(800) 232-1034	(809) 947-7054
★★	Villas of the Galleon	75	$200–$430	(809) 947-4433	
★	Beachcomber Condos	19	$190–$395	(800) 327-8777	(809) 947-5019
★	Colonial Club	15	$230–$500	(809) 947-4660	(809) 947-4839
★	George Town Villas	54	$165–$420	(809) 949-5172	(809) 947-0256
★	Island Pine Villas	40	$110–$225	(800) 223-9815	(809) 949-0428
★	Plantation Village Resort	70	$145–$405	(800) 822-8903	(809) 949-0646
★	Windjammer Hotel	12	$100–$155	(809) 947-4608	(809) 947-4391

CAYMAN ISLANDS HOTELS	RMS	RATES	PHONE	FAX

Little Cayman

Crawl Bay

		RMS	RATES	PHONE	FAX
★★★★	Little Cayman Beach	32	$118–$137	(809) 948-1033	(809) 948-1040
★★	Sam McCoy's Lodge	6	$105–$185	(800) 626-0496	
★★	Southern Cross Club	10	$125–$285	(800) 899-2582	
★	Pirates Point Resort	10	$140–$405	(809) 948-1010	(809) 948-1011

CAYMAN ISLANDS RESTAURANTS	LOCATION	PHONE	ENTREE

Cayman Brac

West End Point

Asian

		LOCATION	PHONE	ENTREE
★★	Edd's Place	West End Point	(809) 948-1208	$6–$25

Grand Cayman

Georgetown

American

		LOCATION	PHONE	ENTREE
★	Verandah Restaurant, The	Georgetown	(809) 947-4444	$6–$32

English

★★	Hog Sty Bay Cafe	Georgetown	(809) 949-6163	$5–$19

International

★★★★★	Hemingway's	Georgetown	(809) 949-1234	$17–$23
★★★★★	Ottmar's Restaurant	Georgetown		$12–$25••
★★	Garden Loggia Cafe	Georgetown	(809) 949-1234	$9–$34
★★	Grand Old House	Georgetown	(809) 949-9333	$13–$34
★	Benjamin's Roof	Georgetown	(809) 947-4080	$12–$30••

Italian

★★	Ristorante Pappagallo	Georgetown	(809) 949-1119	$14–$25••

Latin American

★★★	Crow's Nest	Georgetown	(809) 949-9366	$5–$19
★★	Corita's Copper Kettle II	Georgetown	(809) 949-5475	$10–$15•
★★	The Wharf	Georgetown	(809) 949-2231	$21–$30

CAYMAN ISLANDS RESTAURANTS	LOCATION	PHONE	ENTREE
Mexican			
★★★★★ **Lantana's**	Georgetown	(809) 947-5595	$20–$34••
Seafood			
★★ **Almond Tree, The**	Georgetown	(809) 949-2893	$14–$22••
★★ **Cracked Conch**	Georgetown	(809) 947-5217	$6–$25
★★ **Lobster Pot**	Georgetown	(809) 949-2736	$10–$28

Little Cayman

Crawl Bay

International			
★★ **Pirate's Point Resort**	Crawl Bay	(809) 948-4210	$25–$35
Note: • Lunch Only			
•• Dinner Only			

CURAÇAO

Willemstad, capital of Curacao features Dutch-inspired architecture.

The "C" in the ABC Islands (part of the five-island Netherlands Antilles federation), Curaçao is an excellent choice when one half of the traveling couple dives and the other one doesn't. Beaches here are small and intimate; you can get cable TV for hours, and the bustling harbor, expensive stores, excellent restaurants, and lively casinos of the Dutch-inspired capital of Willemstad could tempt even a devoted diver to take off his wet suit.

The fact that Curaçao is such an excellent dive spot is one of the Caribbean's deepest guarded secrets. Because most hard-core divers naturally gravitate toward the diving mecca of Bonaire, Curaçao has become a poor relation when it comes to enticing divers from the U.S., but in truth, Curaçao attracts many Dutch recreational divers who might spend up to three weeks underwater. In fact, these Dutch scubaniks are rough-and-ready divers who love to wear "Sea Hunt" suits and go where no diver has gone before. With visibility from 60–150 feet and water temps 70-85 degrees F, the island offers a wide range of sites at every skill; and eco-sensitive divers, especially, will appreciate the permanent moorings of the 12-mile long **National Underwater Park**, where spearfishing is prohibited and the fish are just beginning to get used to the divers. No one should leave Curaçao, however, without a vigorous trek through **Christoffel Park**, where cactuses grow over ten feet tall and iguanas scurry underfoot before they are made into a delicious soup the whole island adores.

Bird's Eye View

At 171 square miles, Curaçao rates as the largest of the five islands in the Netherlands Antilles. Shaped like the arched wings of a great heron, it is located 35 miles north of the coast of Venezuela (which explains why it was long a tourist haven for Venezuelans before the rest of the world discovered it). The entrance of the harbor splits the main downtown area of Willemstad into two. Downtown, which is well developed and recently renovated, is the hub of Curaçao shopping and its vibrant colors and pastel-house facades are true picture ops. The contrast between the bustling Dutch-cobbled pastel fronts of Willemstad and the countryside is stark; once you leave the capital, the landscape takes on the color of brown and russet, studded with three-pronged cactuses, spiny-leafed aloes, and divi-divi trees. You can still see Dutch windmills pumping water to irrigate the arid fields. Since the island receives very little rainfall, much of its landscape looks like the Sonoran Deserts of the American Southwest. Continuing past East Point of Curaçao you will get to the tiny island of Klein Curaçao ("Klein" is little in Dutch.) There are two sides to the island, windward and leeward.

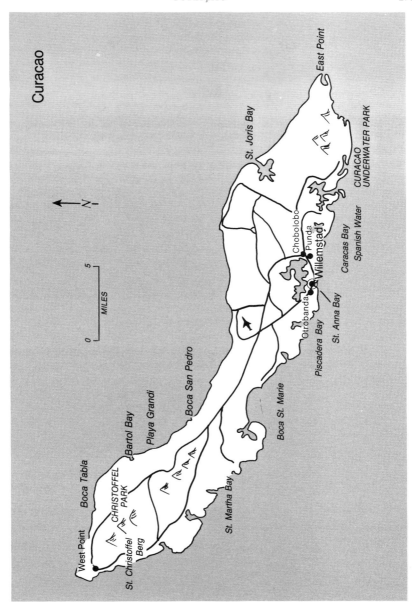

Curacao

History

Long before Alonso de Ojeda set foot on the island in 1499, Arawak tribes—from the clan of the Caquetios called Curaçaos—were inhabiting the island. After Ojeda marked his claim, a Spanish settlement followed in 1527. A hundred years later, the Spanish unceremoniously left the island, leaving it in the hands of Holland, which deemed it a possession of the Dutch West Indies Company. The island's natural harbors and strategic location in the Caribbean inspired predatory interest among the French and British, who continually tried to send the Dutch packing, with little success. In 1642, a young Dutchman named Peter Stuyvesant became governor of the island, a mere three years before he took over governorship of the Dutch colony of New Amsterdam, today known as New York. During Dutch rule, the island was divided up into plantations. Not all were devoted to agriculture; some of the estates were utilized for salt mining. In 1863 emancipation freed the slaves. The island made waves on the international scene until oil was discovered in Venezuela, and the Royal Dutch Shell Company, impressed with Curaçao's fine harbor potential, erected the world's largest oil refinery there. The industry lasted well into this century, attracting laborers from many nations who have created the melting pot that makes up Curacao's population today.

Today Curaçao is part of the kingdom of the Netherlands. The other Dutch territories-Bonaire, Saba, St. Eustatius, and St. Martin—are administered through Willemstad, the capital of the Netherlands Antilles.

People

Curaçao is one of the few islands in the Caribbean where the annual income averages $5000 or more (most people on other islands scrape by on $1500 or less). The Shell Refinery remains an important element in the island's economy. In addition, Curaçao has obtained the reputation as an international banking center, with hundreds of millions of dollars passing through businesses that only have a phone and P.O. box number. Today there are 79 nationalities represented on the island, from Dutch, English, Spanish and Portuguese, to Chinese, East Indian, and Venezuelan. About 80 percent of the population are Roman Catholics; the Jewish population totals today about 600. Rabbi Aaron L. Peller remains the head of the Mikve Israel-Synagogue, which is thought to be the oldest in continuance in the Western Hemisphere, since Jews from Spain and Portugal, via Brazil, were among the earliest settlers on the island.

Beaches

Good beaches are hard to come by in Curaçao. The northwestern coast should be avoided by swimmers since it is too rough, though the west has some calm bays good for swimming and snorkeling. Many of the beaches are private and charge a fee, but in return you get changing facilities, clean stretches, and snackbars. Public beaches are notoriously unkempt. Avoid the beach near Willemstad (at the Avila Beach Hotel); it's artificial, gritty, and too dense for good snorkeling. **Santa Barbara**, located at the mouth of Spanish Water Bay, is popular with locals and has full services. The Curaçao Yacht Club is close by. On the northwest side, **Boca St. Martha**, where the Coral Cliff Resort is located, exudes a certain peacefulness and the bay is gorgeous. **Knip**, further up the coast, rates as one of the best on the island, with its large, sandy stretch; on weekends it can get crowded and noisy with music. **Playa Forti**, on the western tip, has dark sand and is good for swimming.

Klein Curaçao, a small, uninhabited island off East Point, makes a nifty day-excursion; many charter boats and dive operators offer packages with lunch included.

Dive Sites

Curaçao is sitting on some of the best dive sites in the Caribbean and never bothered to tell anybody. Until recent years, the island just didn't have the operators and boats necessary for quality diving. Even today there are really only about two dive operators with the boats that can deliver trips more in-depth other than the learn-to-dive program (they are the **Lion's Den Center** and **Peter Hughes' Princess Divers**, at the **Curaçao Princess Beach and Casino Resort**). Stretching roughly from town to the East Point of the island are 15 different dive sites, primarily wall dives. The last five dives before East Point are straight vertical walls, starting in 20-40 feet of water and plunging down. The walls are draped with black corals, sponges and typical marine life. Heading west is a different system, where the walls are actually slopes (about 45 degrees). Around Klein Bonaire, the leeward side has pretty good diving with moderate walls and basic shallow stuff. The west side, buffeted by trade winds, is one of the nicest walls in the Caribbean—reports say the amount of marine life is staggering. Whales are often seen in the channel crossing. Gigantic corals and sponges off **Boca St. Martha** are truly remarkable; one rare sponge, as large as a king-size mattress, has been reputed to have survived 800 years. Sunk in 1977 close to the Willemstad Harbor, the *Superior Produce* is considered one of the best wreck dives.

Curaçao Seaquarium has a new section, "Animal Encounters," where divers ($50) and snorkelers ($30) can enter a large pool where they can feed lemon, reef and nurse sharks through mesh fencing. Set in between the "Stingray Encounter" and the "Shark Encounter" is an underwater observatory with large glass portholes so nondivers can share the excitement.

For more information on Princess Divers, contact **Peter Hughes Diving** at *6851 Yumuri Street, Suite 10, Coral Gables FL 33146;* ☎ *800-9-DANCER* or *305-669-9391* or *305-669-9475* (fax).

Treks

The **Christoffel National Park** is rife with opportunities for hiking and climbing. Forty minutes from Willemstad, the 4000-acre park offers three routes through its terrain for cars, but to see the wildlife it's best to take the well-marked walking trails. Hikers will see Indian rock paintings and caves that are home to some of the bats that help pollinate the island's cactus plants. The rail to the summit takes about three hours round trip from the park headquarters at the Savonet plantation house, or about an hour and a half from the car park, on Zorgvlied Trail. The Savonet Route offers an introduction to the flora of Curaçao, including plants and trees. It starts at the visitor's center and meanders east, then north, leading to bat-infested caves and petroglyphs. At the old plantation house is now ensconced a new **Museum of Natural and Cultural History**. The **Zorgvlied Route** (green markings) takes about 90 minutes and makes a winding circuit through the north area of the park, returning along the eastern flank of Mount Christoffel, crossing the footpath that goes to the summit. The **Zevenbergen Route** circles the southwest area of the park, passing over hills and leading to spectacular lookouts. Two rare species of orchids are found only here. The **Christoffel Trail**, marked by red, leads also to panoramic views and is excellent for bird-watching. If you drive to the base of the mountain instead of starting the hike at the visitor's center, you'll cut an hour off the three-hour hike. Near the top of the mountain, the track steepens deeply and rain can make it dangerously slippery. Hikers must use hands and feet to proceed to the peak. If you visit in the morning, you will be treated to orioles, troupials and yellow breasted sugar birds being fed at the plantation house. Parrots blown in from Bonaire by a recent hurricane are now situated in the breeding park. The park is open 8 a.m.–4 p.m. Monday to Saturday and from 6 a.m.–3 p.m. Sunday. The entrance fee is $9. A guide to accompany you on foot or in their own vehicle costs about $14 more. A guidebook, purchased at the headquarters, might help lone travelers.

On the leeward side of the island there are numerous coves with beaches suitable for swimming which can be reached only on foot or via dirt roads suitable for hiking. In the north, the dirt road and tracks lead to wild desolate landscapes where strong waves crash dramatically against the rocky shores.

FIELDING'S CHOICE:

With over 150–200 deer on the island, Christoffel National Park now offers a new deer-watching program. Sessions are held in the afternoon 4 p.m.-6:30 p.m., with small groups led by guides (maximum of eight people) on a ten-minute walk to the observation tower for a presentation and to await the deer. Call for reservations. Located on the highest point of the island, the park also offers unusual walking trails which takes you past fascinating flora, Indian caves and wildlife. A museum on the grounds features an exhibit on the geology of the island.

What Else to See

Willemstad is a port ready-made for cruise passengers. Shopping is the best in the Caribbean and most of the sightseeing can be seen within a six-block radius. The city is cut in half by Santa Anna Bay. On one side is the Punda, and the other side the Otrabanda (literally, "the other side"). The Punda is the touristic side, with its numerous boutiques, restaurants and marketplaces. The Otrabanda is more residential, the heart of the local Curaçao life.

To cross from one side to the other, you can either 1) ride the free ferry; 2) drive or take a taxi over the Juliana Bridge; 3) walk across the Queen Emma Pontoon bridge.

One of the most fantastic views of Willemstad can be had standing on the Otrabanda side, looking back at the pastel-colored face of the other side, where spiffy rows of townhouses and gabled roofs attest to the Dutch heritage. The **Queen Emma Bridge**, beloved by the natives and affectionately called the Lady, is a 700-ft. floating bridge, the creation on the American consul Leonard Burlington Smoth, who made a small fortune off the tolls. Today's there's no fee. Further north is the 1625-ft.-long **Queen Juliana Bridge**; the view from here is terrific, especially at sunset when the various colors of the dying sun turn the sea into a colorful palette.

The **floating market on the Punda side** is a must first stop. Early mornings Venezuela schooners park and unload their dazzling loads of fresh fruits, vegetables and freshly caught fish. The best time to see the arrivals is 6:30 a.m., but traffic bears up all day.

The **Mikveh Israel Emmanuel Synagogue** is the oldest temple still in use in the Western Hemisphere, founded in 1651. Twenty thousand visitors a year come to see the special floor of brilliant white sand, which signifies Moses' deliverance of his people to the Promised Land. Do visit the museum which displays Jewish artifacts from the centuries.

At the foot of the Pontoon Bridge is situated **Fort Amsterdam**, an 18th-century citadel that was once the center of the city. On the far side of the plaza stands the **Waterfort**, a 17th-century bastion which now houses, under the Waterfort Arches, one of the most delightful shopping malls on the Caribbean.

It will take a car to reach, but a visit to the **Curaçao Museum** will be worth it. On display are numerous Indian artifacts, as well as colonial and historical antiques. On the same road trip you can visit the **Landhuis Jan Rock**, a supposedly haunted house from the 17th century. Sunday mornings are the best time to come when the proprietor serves pancakes in the restaurant nearby.

A quick pass through the village of Soto in the northwest tip of the island is warranted. Past Soto a dry Arizona-type landscape is in evidence, with cacti and flamboyant dry bushes The road continues out to Westpunt Highway, curving back south to Boca Tabla, where the sea has carved a fine grotto. It's a lovely place just to lie back and listen to the waves crashing against the rocks.

On the eastern side of the island, the **Curaçao Seaquarium** is as fun as it is informative. Forty-six freshwater fish hold over 400 species of fish; nearby a man-made beach of white sand is good for young swimmers.

The **Senio Liqueur Factory** is the center of local production and distribution for the island's original Curaçao liqueur. The small open-air showroom is situated in a handsome landhouse. You can take a self-guided tour and read the story of the distillation process. Samples are offered and there is ample opportunity to stock up on your favorite flavors. A free tour of the Amstel Brewery is offered in nearby Salina—it's the only beer made from distilled seawater.

Craft demonstrations and folklore shows are held at **Landhuis Brivengat** on the last Sunday of each month. An Indonesian smorgasbord is served at the adjacent restaurant on Wednesdays. Dance bands play every Friday night for a party held on the veranda.

Historical Sites

Landhuis Brievengat ★★★

Brievengat, Willemstad.
This restored 18th-century plantation house has 18-inch-thick walls, watchtowers (where long-ago lovers met), and antiques of the era. The last Sunday of each month sees crafts demonstrations and folkloric shows, and there's live music on Wednesdays and Fridays. Located about 10 minutes out of Willemstad. General admission: $2.00.

Museums and Exhibits

Curaçao Museum ★★★

Van Leeuwenhoekstraat, Willemstad.
Housed in a former military quarantine hospital for those with yellow fever, this 1853 building displays art and Indian artifacts of historical significance. There's also a garden with specimens of all the plants and trees of Curaçao, and the small Children's Museum of Science, where kids are asked to please touch. General admission: $2.00.

Curaçao Seaquarium

Bapur Kibra, Willemstad.
More than 400 species of fish and marine life—in fact, EVERY species native to the area—is on display at this excellent aquarium. You can touch some of the creatures and take a glass-bottom boat ride—the truly daring can enjoy the "Animal Encounters" in which divers and snorkelers feed sharks by hand through a thick (let's hope so) mesh fence. You can also swim with sting rays, angelfish and grouper—or just watch the fun from a 46-foot-deep underwater observatory. General admission: $6.00.

Jewish Cultural Historical Museum

Kuiperstraat, Willemstad.
Located in two buildings constructed in 1728, this fine museum exhibits ceremonial and cultural objects from the 17th and 18th centuries used by one of the oldest Jewish communities in this hemisphere. General admission: $2.00.

Octagon House ★★

Penstraat, Willemstad.
This small museum houses antiques and personal items of Venezuelan liberator Simon Bolivar. Free admission.

Parks and Gardens

Christoffel National Park ★★★★★

Savonet, West Point.
Hours Open: 8:00 a.m.–4:00 p.m.
This 4500-acre nature preserve is located on the island's highest point, crowned by 1230-foot-high St. Christoffelberg, the highest point in all the Dutch Leewards. Well worth a visit, but come early to avoid the overwhelming late-afternoon heat. The park includes 20 miles of one-way roads, hiking trails, a small museum, rare orchids, cacti, divi-divi trees, palms, lots of birds and wild goats, Curaçao deer and donkeys. General admission: $5.00.

Curaçao Underwater Marine Park ★★★★★

Princess Hotel, East Point.
A wonderful spot for divers and snorkelers, this 3000 acre unspoiled reef is a protected national park. Sights include two well-preserved shipwrecks and an 875-foot underwater nature trail. On a clear day, you can see almost forever—or up to 150 feet, anyway.

Tours

Curaçao Liqueur Distillery ★★

Salinja, Willemstad.
The orange-flavored liquor *chobolobo* is produced here in a 17th-century *landhuis* (land house). Witness the process and sample the results. While in the area, head over to the Amstel Brewery, where beer is made from distilled seawater. Tours are conducted only on Tuesdays and Thursdays at 10:00 a.m., after which you can drink all you want for free (designate a driver!). ☎ *612944* for information. Free admission.

Hato Caves ★★★★★

F. D. Rooseveltweg, Willemstad.
Hours Open: 10:00 a.m.–5:00 p.m.

Just recently opened to the public, these limestone caves are imbedded with fossil coral formations. An hour-long guided tour takes you into several caverns and past Indian petroglyphs, active stalagmites and stalactites, and underwater pools. Neat! General admission: $4.30.

Old City Tours ★★★

De Ruyterkade 53, Willemstad.

Interesting walking tours of Willemstad and its wonderful architecture are sometimes led by owner Anko van der Woude, a local expert on the island's history. The two- to three-tour trek costs $15. Old City also conducts harbor tours on a small fishing bark. Prices range from $10–$17.00.

BEST VIEW:

A spectacular view of the sunset is available at Fort Nassau, on one of the highest hills in the city.

Sports

Windsurfing is one of the most popular sports here, given a tremendous boost by the constant trade winds that cool the island and blow the divi-divi trees into shape. The Curaçao Open international Pro-Am Windsurfing Championship, attracting masters from around the world, is held annually here. The best windsurfing spot is on the southeast coast between Jan Thiel and Princess beaches, the site of the annual competitions. Novices should begin at the more protected lagoon Spanish Water. Sports fishing has become extremely fashionable in Curaçao, with anglers hoping to catch tuna, dolphin, marlin, wahoo, sailfish and others. Boats may be chartered, with half or full-day trips, and can be arranged through most hotels, or at the marinas in Spanish Water. Only hook-and-line fishing is permitted in the Curaçao Underwater Park. Yachting is popular, and regattas are held frequently, but little sailing is commercially developed for visitors. Small crafts such as Sunfish are available through hotels.

Cruises

Various locations, Willemstad.

Take to the high seas aboard a variety of crafts. **Tabor Tours** (☎ *376637*) offers sunset cruises with wine and munchies, snorkel trips to Point Marine, and excursions aboard the *Seaworld Explorer*, a "semi-submarine" that cruises five feet below the water's surface. The 120-foot *Insulinde* (☎ *601340*), a rigged sail logger, offers sunset and afternoon sails. Finally, **Sail Curaçao** (☎ *676003*) has day and evening sails and snorkel trips. Bon voyage!

Curaçao Golf & Squash Club

Wilhelminalaan, Emmastad.

Tourists and other nonmembers can golf on this nine-hole course only from 8:00 a.m.–noon Fridays through Wednesdays, and Thursdays from 10 a.m. to dusk. Greens fees are $15.

Watersports

Various locations, Willemstad.

Lots of outfits offer all kinds of watersports; chances are good your hotel also has facilities. Try one of the following: **Coral Cliff Diving** (☎ *642822*) for dive and snorkel excursions and one-week courses on scuba, sailing and windsurfing; **Underwater Curaçao** (☎ *618131*), a PADI-accredited dive shop; **Seascape Dive and Watersports** (☎ *625000*) for snorkel and scuba trips and lessons, deep-sea fishing, water-skiing and glass-bottom boat rides; **Peter Hughes Diving** (☎ *367888*) for diving, snorkeling and deep-sea fishing; and **Curaçao High Wind Center** (☎ *614944*) at the Princess Beach Hotel for windsurfing lessons and rentals.

Where to Stay

Highest Rated Hotels in Curaçao

★★★★★	Avila Beach Hotel
★★★★★	Lions Dive Hotel & Marina
★★★★	Curaçao Caribbean Hotel
★★★★	Holland Hotel
★★★★	Princess Beach Resort
★★★★	Sonesta Beach Hotel
★★★★	Van der Valk Plaza Hotel
★★★	Ortabanda Hotel & Casino

Most Exclusive Hotels in Curacao

★★★★★	Avila Beach Hotel	$90–$415
★★★★	Curacao Caribbean Hotel	$140–$210
★★★★	Van der Valk Plaza Hotel	$105–$210

Fielding's Best Value Hotels in Curacao

★★★★★	Avila Beach Hotel	$90–$415
★★★★	Curaçao Caribbean Hotel	$140–$210
★★★★	Van der Valk Plaza Hotel	$105–$210
★★★★	Sonesta Beach Hotel	$160–$220
★★★	Ortabanda Hotel & Casino	$80–$140

Curaçao has a variety of accommodations that range from sprawling hotels with casinos to small, family-style inns. Many of the hotels have been renovated and expanded in recent years. You can choose to stay either in the suburbs (10 minutes from the shopping center) or in Willemstad. Unfortunately, none of the hotels are situated on notable beaches. The Hilton and Holiday Inn chains are now owned by the government, as is the Intercontinental and a number of other hotels, and the seeming indifference of some of the staff may be attributed to the fact that they are civil servants. Hotels charge a five percent government tax and at least a 10 percent service charge. There are a number of self-catering possibilities and a couple of inns.

Hotels and Resorts

Resorts in Curaçao run from the intimate, cliff-hugging kind (**Coral Cliff Resort**) to the deluxe beachfront extravaganza (**Curaçao Caribbean Hotel & Casino**), where there's no lack of nighttime entertainment. Serious divers tend to head for the **Lions Dive Hotel & Marina**. One of the best locations is the **Van der Calk Plaza Hotel & Casino**, which is tucked into an ancient fort at the mouth of Willemstad's harbor. Nearby the ancient arches have been renovated into a charming enclave of shops.

Avila Beach Hotel $90–$415   ★ ★ ★ ★ ★

Netherlands, Penstraat 130-134, Willemstad, ☎ *599-9-614377.*
Single: $90–$135. Double: $145–$415.
History buffs revel in this hotel, which comprises the former Governor's Mansion dating back to 1780; a modern extension was added in 1991. This is Willemstad's only beachfront hotel and the spot where the royal family of Holland stays when in town. Guest rooms in the original mansion are small and simple; those looking for more luxurious digs should book the newer section, which has modern amenities and 18 one- and two-bedroom apartments, some with kitchenette. The small beach is private and quite pretty. A lovely spot. 90 rooms. Credit Cards: V, MC, DC, A.

Coral Cliff Hotel $85–$150   ★

Santa Marta Bay, Willemstad, ☎ *599-9-641610.*
Single: $85–$130. Double: $90–$150.
Lots of Europeans stay at this beachfront enclave of bungalows situated on a bluff overlooking Spain Main. Guest rooms are quite spartan and could use an overhaul, but the rates are reasonable and the beach is gorgeous. There's lots to do here, including tennis, watersports, a slot casino and miniature golf. A daily shuttle transports guests to the restaurants and shopping of Willemstad, some 25 minutes away. 35 rooms. Credit Cards: V, MC, DC, A.

Curaçao Caribbean Hotel $140–$210   ★ ★ ★ ★

John F. Kennedy Boulevard, ☎ *599-9-625000.*
Single: $140. Double: $150–$210.
Located at the site of historic Fort Piscadera, just outside of Willemstad, this five-story hotel overlooks a tiny beach. Guest rooms are adequate but cry out for renovation; even the nicest rooms, on the top Executive Floor have seen better days. Nonetheless, there's a lot happening here, with organized parties, theme nights and dance lessons. A free bus takes you into town. Facilities include a dive shop, two tennis courts, pool and casino. 200 rooms. Credit Cards: V, MC, DC, A.

Holiday Beach Hotel $95–$115   ★ ★

Nether Angelus, Pater Euwensweg, ☎ *599-9-625400.*
Single: $95–$105. Double: $110–$115.

Though it's located on one of the island's better beaches and has a large, happening casino, this former Holiday Inn still brings to mind, well, a Holiday Inn. Still, this is a good middle-market property for those seeking all the amenities without sacrificing a year's salary. Recently renovated guest rooms are decent but only a few have ocean views. There's lots to do here: two tennis courts, watersports and scuba, supervised children's activities, a lively beach bar, organized tours and a large pool. 200 rooms. Credit Cards: V, MC, DC, A.

Holland Hotel   **$70–$130**   ★ ★ ★ ★

Roosevelt Weg, FDR weg 524, Willemstad, ☎ *599-9-688044.*
Single: $70. Double: $80–$130.
The air-conditioned guest rooms are basic but comfortable at this small hotel near the airport. Though it's not on the beach, they do offer scuba packages, and have a pool and small casino to keep guests busy. 40 rooms. Credit Cards: V, MC, DC, A.

Las Palmas Hotel   **$93–$140**   ★ ★

Piscadera Bay, ☎ *599.*
Single: $93–$140. Double: $93–$140.
Located two miles out of Willemstad on a hillside near a private beach, this sprawling complex—its full name is Las Palmas Hotel Villas Casino Beach Club—is a decent choice for those watching the purse strings. Accommodations are in air-conditioned guest rooms and two-bedroom villas with kitchens. All the expected recreational facilities, from watersports to pool to tennis to casino. 184 rooms. Credit Cards: V, MC, DC, A.

Lions Dive Hotel & Marina   **$105–$120**   ★ ★ ★ ★ ★

Bapor Kibra Street, Willemstad, ☎ *599-9-618100.*
Single: $105–$115. Double: $115–$120.
Located next to Willemstad's Seaquarium on the island's largest beach, this spot specializes in the scuba diving trade. Their PADI dive center is superb, and offers everything from resort courses to excursions to sunset sails. There's also an excellent fitness center with all the latest equipment for whipping that body into shape. The air-conditioned guest rooms are standard but fine. Guests get to visit the aquarium for free; the shuttle that runs back and forth to town is also complimentary. 72 rooms. Credit Cards: V, MC, DC, A.

Ortabanda Hotel & Casino   **$80–$140**   ★ ★ ★

Hoek Breedesstraat, Willemstad, ☎ *599-9-627400.*
Single: $80–$90. Double: $95–$140.
Located in the heart of Willemstad's business and shopping district next to Queen Emma Bridge, some air-conditioned guest rooms have great harbor views. There's a restaurant and casino on-site, but little else in the way of extras. Reasonable rates make this a good value. 45 rooms. Credit Cards: V, MC, DC, A.

Porto Paseo Hotel   **$95–$125**   ★ ★

De Rouvilleweg 47 Street, Willemstad, ☎ *599-9-627878.*
Single: $95. Double: $95–$125.
A peaceful oasis right in city center, this newer (1993) hotel has basic but comfortable air-conditioned rooms. The ubiquitous pool, casino and restaurant cater to rec-

reational needs, and the gardens are splendid. A good in-town choice. 44 rooms. Credit Cards: V, MC, DC, A.

Princess Beach Resort $140–$185   ★★★★

Dr. Martin Luther King Blvd., Willemstad, ☎ *(800)327-3286, 599-9-367888.*
Single: $140–$145. Double: $180–$185.

Despite the name, this hotel is a Holiday Inn Crowne Plaza property, and is not affiliated with the cruise line. Located directly in front of Curaçao's Underwater Park on a lovely but small beach, the hotel offers spacious guest rooms with all the modern comforts. The grounds are nicely landscaped and include two restaurants, four bars, a happening casino, pool and tennis court and all watersports. This lively spot leaves visitors satisfied. 341 rooms. Credit Cards: V, MC, DC, A.

Sonesta Beach Hotel $160–$220   ★★★★

Piscadera Bay, ☎ *(800)766-3782, 599-9-368800.*
Single: $160–$220. Double: $160–$220.

Set on the beach and built in Dutch Colonial style, this newer (1992) resort receives raves for its luxurious appointments, beautiful landscaping and attractive guest rooms, all with a patio or balcony and at least a partial ocean view. Parents like the fact that two of their kids (up to age 12) can stay with them free, and that complimentary activities keep the little ones busy. Lots of nice artwork scattered about—a Sonesta trademark—and gracious service help make this place tops. Health club, full casino, pool, tennis and watersports as well. 248 rooms. Credit Cards: V, MC, DC, A.

Van der Valk Plaza Hotel $105–$210   ★★★★

Plaza Piar, Willemstad, ☎ *599-9-612500.*
Single: $105–$180. Double: $105–$210.

Its 12-story tower sticks out like a sore thumb in quaint Willemstad, and the nearest beach is a 15-minute drive away. But nice harbor views make this hotel, built in the walls of a 17th-century fort, a pleasant choice. The central city location attracts lots of working travelers who are catered to with secretarial and business services. Guest rooms are merely adequate, but the great views of passing ships make a lot forgivable. There's a full casino and pool on-site. 350 rooms. Credit Cards: V, MC, A.

Apartments and Condominiums

Options range from the elegant at **La Belle Alliance** and **Las Palmas** to uninspiring apartment buildings which have basic kitchenettes.

Inns

One of the most atmospheric of all Curaçao's accommodations is the **Landhuis Hotel**. If you can get one of their few charming bedrooms, you'll feel as if you've been transported back 100 years (☎ *599-9-648-400*). Porta Paseo is more run-of-the-mill, though the restaurant attracts a lot of movement.

Low Cost Lodging

Best bet is to arrive in town and ask around for rooms in private homes. The tourist office can direct you to possibilities. In the off-season Coral Cliff Resort's rooms drop down to 450, and a free shuttle bus will take you to Willemstad. Cheap rooms with kitchen privileges are also available, though they take a young, adventurous constitution to enjoy them.

Trupial Inn Hotel **$65–$100**

5, Groot Davelaarweg, Willemstad.
Single: $65–$100. Double: $75–$100.

This bungalow-style motel is located in a residential neighborhood and has no beach, though a free shuttle will take you to the sea. Rooms are basic but comfortable and have air conditioning; there are also eight suites with kitchenettes. There's a restaurant, pool and tennis court, with additional eateries and shops within walking distance. 74 rooms. Credit Cards: V, MC, DC, A.

Where to Eat

Highest Rated Restaurants in Curaçao

★★★★★	**De Taveerne**
★★★★★	**L'Alouette**
★★★★	**Bistro Le Clochard**
★★★★	**Fort Nassau**
★★★★	**Rijstaffel Restaurant**
★★★★	**Seaview**
★★★	**Belle Terrace**
★★★	**Golden Star**
★★★	**La Pergola**
★★★	**Pirates**

Most Exclusive Restaurants in Curacao

★★★★★	**L'Alouette**	$30–$40
★★★	**Wine Cellar**	$20–$35
★★★★★	**De Taveerne**	$18–$32
★★★★	**Fort Nassau**	$20–$28
★★★	**Belle Terrace**	$14–$24

Fielding's Best Value Restaurants in Curaçao

★★★	**Pirates**	$15–$35
★★★	**Belle Terrace**	$14–$24
★★★	**Golden Star**	$8–$26
★★★★★	**De Taveerne**	$18–$32
★★	**Playa Forti**	$6–$16

Dining in Curaçao is an international smorgasbord of delights, from French, Swiss and Italian, to Danish, Dutch, Indonesian, Creole, South American and junk-food American-style. Excellent food isn't cheap here, but when combined with some of the most romantic atmospheres in the islands, you'll feel the bill was worth it. Ensconced in a wine cellar in one of the old landhouse estates, **De Taveerne** is a must for anyone on a honeymoon who wants the soap-opera-dinner-by-candlelight-on-a-tropical-isle experience. **Bistro Le Clochard** also rates high for romance, with its cozy, candlelit rooms tucked into an old fort overlooking the sea. For local dishes at bargain prices, prepare to trek a bit to **Golden Star**, on the coast road leading southeast from St. Anna Bay. Surroundings are humble, but such Curaçao delicacies as *kiwa* (criollo shrimp), *bestia chiki* (goat-meat stew) and *bakijauw* (salted cod) are superb. One of the best views of the island is at **Playa Forti**, in the extreme northwest of the island. Snorkel before lunch or dinner, then order a brimming plate of *ayaca*, a chicken-beef combo, stuffed with nuts, raisins, spices and olives, rolled up in a corn dough tortilla. *Funchi*, the local cornmeal staple, comes with everything.

'T Kokkeltje   **$$$**   ★★

F. D. Rooseveltweg 524,
International cuisine. Specialties: Split-pea soup, herring, Caribbean chicken.
Lunch: entrees $12–$27.
Dinner: entrees $12–$27.
Sample Dutch fare by the pool at the Hotel Holland located on the highway to the airport. The hard-to-pronounce name means cockles and this cozy restaurant serves marinated mussels when available. Other specialties to savor are split-pea soup, pickled herring and salads. There is also a dimly lit dining room for those who prefer it. Food is served from 7 a.m. to 10:30 p.m. Associated Hotel: Hotel Holland. Credit Cards: V, MC, A.

Belle Terrace   **$$$**   ★★★

Penstraat 130, ☎ *(599) 961-4377.*
Scandinavian cuisine. Specialties: Danish smorgasbord, keshi yena, barracuda.
Lunch: 12:00 a.m.– 3:00 p.m., entrees $10–$15.
Dinner: 7:00 p.m.–10:00 p.m., entrees $14–$24.
Eating out in Willemstad is very often a historic experience—one day it's breakfast high above the sea (never far away here) on a hilltop in a converted 18th-century fort, or, in the case of the Belle Terrace, right on the beach (albeit a rocky one) in a 200-year-old mansion, the former home of the island's governor. Sometimes the cuisine, which includes a smorgasbord at lunch, featuring salmon and other fish smoked on the premises, can be less than stellar, but with a setting like this, who cares? Breads and ice creams are homemade. Associated Hotel: Avila Beach Hotel. Reservations required. Credit Cards: V, MC, DC, A.

Bistro Le Clochard   **$$$**   ★★★★

Rif Fort, ☎ *(599) 962-5666.*
French cuisine. Specialties: Bouillabaisse, raclette, fondue.

Lunch: 12:00 a.m.–2:00 p.m., entrees $20–$30.
Dinner: 6:30 p.m.–11:00 p.m., entrees $20–$30.
Dine in this traditional French/Swiss bistro, one of a number of restaurants built in the vaults of what is left of the old (early 19th century) Rif Fort near the harbor. As with many Willemstad restaurants, you may dine indoors or on the open-air Harborside Terrace. Various fondues reflect the tastes of the owner's wife (who is Swiss), and they include raclette with potatoes, pickles and onions, and bourguignone. There's also fresh fish, veal and lobster. The outdoor terrace is only open for dinner, and there's no lunch served on weekends. Closed: Sun. Reservations required. Credit Cards: V, MC, DC, A.

Cactus Club   **$$**   ★★
6 van Staverenweg, ☎ (599) 937-1600.
American cuisine. Specialties: Fajitas, buffalo wings, cajun snapper.
Lunch: 11:30 a.m.– 3:00 p.m., entrees $4–$15.
Dinner: 5:00 p.m.– 11:30 p.m., entrees $7–$15.
A transplanted, stateside-style after-work restaurant and bar, the Cactus Club doles out tasty burgers, shakes, nachos, pastas and fajitas to homesick Americans and locals who love the place, which is always full. Decor is Southwest-desert, but it's nice and cool inside. Credit Cards: V, MC, DC.

De Taveerne   **$$$**
Landhuis Groot Davelaar, Salina, ☎ (599) 937-0669.
French cuisine. Specialties: Salmon carpaccio, chateaubriand stroganoff for two.
Lunch: 12:00 a.m.–2:00 p.m., entrees $18–$32.
Dinner: 7:00 p.m.–11:00 p.m., entrees $18–$32.
The owners of this innovative and highly regarded French restaurant in the Salina residential area have renovated a traditional old octagonal country mansion—the Landhuis Groot Davelaar, built in the early 18th century by a South American revolutionary—into an antique-filled mini-museum. Once the main house of a cattle-producing estate, it is one of many scattered throughout the arid countryside. Prime beef shows up on its tables in the form of platter-size steaks and chateaubriand for two. Closed for lunch on Saturdays. Closed: Sun. Reservations required. Credit Cards: V, MC, DC, A.

Fort Nassau   **$$$**   ★★★★
Fort Nassau, ☎ (599) 961-3086.
International cuisine. Specialties: Smoked salmon, shrimp with red linguine in a spicy sauce.
Lunch: 12:00 a.m.–3:00 p.m., entrees $20–$28.
Dinner: 7:00 p.m.–10:00 p.m., entrees $20–$28.
If you never dine anywhere else in Curaçao, don't miss Fort Nassau, which sings with history even though some dishes may be overambitious and miss the mark at times. Perched like an eagle's nest above Willemstad and overlooking Santa Anna Bay, diners can see forever from here. Used as a fort by the Dutch in the late 18th century and by Americans in World War II, it became a restaurant in the 1950s. Cuisine runs the gamut from Asian to Italian, utilizing fresh fish, pasta and game in combination with local tropical fruits. No lunch served on weekends. Reservations recommended. Credit Cards: V, MC, DC, A.

Fort Waakzaamheid Bistro   **$$$**   ★★

Seru di Domi, ☎ *(599) 962-3633.*
Seafood cuisine. Specialties: Veal curry, barbecued steaks.
Dinner: 5:00 p.m.–11:00 p.m., entrees $17–$26.
An alternative to the often-crowded Fort Nassau, which gets inundated with cruise-ship passengers, this hilltop aerie in the Otrabanda was held captive many moons ago by the notorious Captain Bligh, probably in part because he was spellbound by the view. There is no need to dress up for this American-style tavern and bar, which is open for dinner only. There is a fresh fish and salad special daily, as well as barbecued steaks, scampi and veal curry. Closed: Tue. Credit Cards: V, MC, A.

Golden Star   **$$$**   ★★★

Socratesstraat 2, ☎ *(599) 965-4795.*
Latin American cuisine. Specialties: Carni stoba, stoba de Carco, grilled conch.
Lunch: 11:00 a.m.–1:00 p.m., entrees $8–$26.
Dinner: 11:00 p.m.–1:00p.m., entrees $8–$26.
Go local in this deliberately tacky restaurant dive, which has the best authentic Antillean food in town. There may be no better place for *carni stoba* (meat stew), conch served lightly grilled or with vegetables, goat and criollo shrimp, accompanied with plenty of starchy and filling (and good) rice, fried bananas and *funchi* (cornmeal pancakes). Beer, especially locally brewed Amstel, is the preferred beverage with this food. Golden Star is open until 1:00 a.m. Credit Cards: V, MC, DC, A.

L'Alouette   **$$$**   ★★★★★

Orionweig 12, Salina, ☎ *(599) 961-8222.*
International cuisine. Specialties: Cheese flan, seafood sausage.
Lunch: 12:00 a.m.–2:30 p.m., entrees $18–$30.
Dinner: 6:00 p.m.–9:00 p.m., entrees $30–$40.
Amid beautiful, sleek surroundings, you can eat creative French cuisine and still keep your weight down at this sophisticated eatery specializing in the best ingredients available, embellished with light and springlike herbs and spices. Chef Maria Eugenia Saban pays close attention to detail in this restored house in a residential area on the east side of the harbor. Specials that never change are her cheese flan duet with mushroom and basil sauces. Cuisine may be light, but portions are substantial and worth the high tariff. Closed: Sun. Reservations required. Credit Cards: V, MC, DC, A.

La Pergola   **$$$**   ★★★

Waterfort Arches, ☎ *(599) 961-3482.*
Italian cuisine. Specialties: Smoked salmon with olive oil and cloves, grouper siciliana.
Lunch: 12:00 a.m.–2:00 p.m., entrees $25–$35.
Dinner: 6:30 p.m.–10:30 p.m., entrees $30–$35.
A seaside Italian eatery in the trendy Waterfort Arches shopping center, La Pergola serves pizzas, fresh fish and desserts with a light hand—no heavy tomato or gloppy cream sauces here. Take your seat on the lovely terrace facing wraparound windows and watch the wavy action below, and feast on the likes of grouper Sicilian-style with a puttanesca sauce and conclude with an airy, angelic Zuppa Inglese. Closed for Sunday lunch. Closed: Sun. Reservations recommended. Credit Cards: D, V, MC, DC, A.

Pirates   **SSS**   ★★★

Piscadera Bay, ☎ (599) 962-5000.
Latin American cuisine. Specialties: Paella, red snapper almendrado, ceviche.
Lunch: entrees $15–$35.
Dinner: entrees $15–$35.
In addition to an Indonesian restaurant, La Garuda, and bountiful buffets served on
the Pisca Terrace bar facing a spectacular swimming pool, this newcomer to the
Curaçao Caribbean Hotel and Casino's dining scene might assure that its guests
needn't leave this minicity-within-a-city resort on Piscadera Bay. Famous for theme-
night parties, the hotel's latest successful scheme is Pirates, specializing in tasty
Latin-style seafood, including paella and ceviche, served by a charming wait staff in
nautical garb. Associated Hotel: Curaçao Caribbean Hotel. Reservations recommended. Credit Cards: V, MC, DC, A.

Playa Forti   **SS**   ★★

Westpunt, ☎ (599) 964-0273.
Latin American cuisine. Specialties: Cabrito, fish soup, keshi yena.
Lunch: entrees $5–$16.
Dinner: entrees $6–$16.
If you find yourself in the northwest point of the island, dine at this clifftop retreat
overlooking Playa Forti beach. It's a hangout for tasty criollo food, and a good place
to try keshi yena, an island specialty of meats cooked with Creole sauce and covered
with Edam or Gouda cheese. Other specialties to try are cabrito or goat stew, and
funchi, or local cornbread. Sunsets are gorgeous here as well. Meals are served from
10 a.m. to 6 p.m. Credit Cards: V, MC, A.

Rijstaffel Restaurant   **SSS**   ★★★★

Mercuriusstraat 13, Salina, ☎ (599) 961-2999.
Asian cuisine. Specialties: Rijstaffel, bami goreng, jumbo shrimp in garlic sauce.
Lunch: 12:00 a.m.–2:00 p.m., prix fixe $9–$17.
Dinner: 6:00 p.m.–9:30 p.m., prix fixe $13–$20.
A carryover of Dutch colonial days, rijstaffel is a banquet of up to 25 spicy and
savory Indonesian-Javanese dishes surrounded by a mound of steaming rice. A
delightful change from the usual steaks and surf and turf awaits at this restaurant in
the Salina area, known for its nightlife. To eat here, get a group together and book
a table several days ahead for a 16-to-25 dish feast that includes bami goreng (fried
noodles, shrimp, meat and vegetables) and krupuk (gigantic shrimp chips). Vegetarian and a la carte dishes are also available. Reservations recommended. Credit Cards:
V, MC, DC, A.

Seaview   **SSS**   ★★★★

Waterfort Arches, ☎ (599) 961-6688.
Seafood cuisine. Specialties: Salpicon de mariscos, pepper filet.
Lunch: 12:00 a.m.–2:00 p.m., entrees $15–$30.
Dinner: 6:00 p.m.–10:00 p.m., entrees $15–$30.
An amiable surfside spot located right in the heart of the Waterfort Arches, one of
Willemstad's many converted old army posts and now a busy retail, nightlife and
culinary bazaar, Seaview offers up spectacular ocean and sunset vistas from a breezy
terrace or air-conditioned dining room. Its forte, naturally, is fresh-from-the-briny

fish and shellfish, as well as prime meats, fresh vegetables and international dishes. Closed: Sun. Reservations recommended. Credit Cards: A.

Wine Cellar $$$ ★ ★ ★

Concordiastraat, ☎ *(599) 961-2178.*
International cuisine. Specialties: Roast goose, lobster salad, red snapper.
Lunch: 12:00 a.m.–2:00 p.m., entrees $20–$35.
Dinner: 5:00 p.m.–11:00 p.m., entrees $20–$35.

Connoisseurs of fine wines repair here to master sommelier and rotisseur Nico Cornelisse's lair, a traditional, small (about eight tables) and comfortable Dutch home near the cathedral in downtown Willemstad. The voluminous wine list consists of vintages from the Alsace region of France, as well as Germany and Italy. To complement these refined labels are some hearty dishes to warm the blood, including filet of beef with goat cheese sauce, venison and roast goose. More delicate appetites will appreciate light seafood salads and red snapper. Service is attentive and personable. Closed: Mon. Reservations required. Credit Cards: V, MC, A.

Where to Shop

Curaçao is famed for its shopping, some of the best in the Caribbean, with over 200 shops. Three of the main shopping streets are pedestrian malls with no traffic or exhaust, making strolling a joy. Cruise ships dock at the downside terminal, which is a short walk to the shopping center; when ships dock, stores stay open on Sunday and holidays. Right in the heart of Willemstad is the Punda shopping district in a five-block square. Since everyone speaks three or four languages, you won't have any trouble understanding shop clerks. Best of all, Curaçao has a very low duty (3 percent) on imported tourist items and no sales tax. No import duty is charged on locally made jewelry, handcrafts, art and antiques. Good bargains can be found on German and Japanese cameras, Swiss watches, Dutch Delft blue souvenirs, and Curaçao liqueur. **Little Switzerland** is the premier watch store in the Caribbean. Designer clothes can be found at **Penha 7 Sons**. The **Yellow House** handles the best stock of perfume on the island.

The most charming shopping center is the **Waterfront Arches**, an historic waterfront remodeled into a cove of quaint boutiques with exotic imports from Paris, Indonesia and South America.

Curaçao Directory

ARRIVAL

American Airlines provides daily nonstop flights to Curaçao from Miami. American also offers flights to Aruba from New York, Miami, and San Juan, Puerto Rico, where you can make an easy transfer to Curaçao. American also offers discounts if their agent makes your hotel reservation at the same time as your air passage. ALM, the national carrier of Curaçao, also flies 13 times a week from Miami to Curaçao (three nonstop) and four times a week from Atlanta. Air Aruba also flies seven times a week to Aruba from Newark; easy transfers can be made to Curaçao.

CLIMATE

Like Bonaire and Aruba, its neighbors, Curaçao is to the south of the Hurricane Belt, making storms an extremely unusual occurrence. The island is constantly refreshed by trade winds blowing from 10–20 miles per hour and the temperature stays constant all-year-round, seldom fluctuating out of the mid-80s. Summer can be a few degrees hotter and winter a little cooler. Light, casual clothing is the rule. Hotels and casinos are air-conditioned so you may wish to bring fancier clothes, or a sweater.

DOCUMENTS

U.S. and Canadian citizens need to show proof of citizenship (passport, birth certificate, or voter's registration) plus a photo ID, and an ongoing or return ticket beyond the Netherlands Antilles.

ELECTRICITY

Current is 110–130 volts AC, 50 cycles. Outlets are American-style. Converters are not necessarily needed for American appliances, but hotels have supplies.

GETTING AROUND

Inquire whether your hotel has a free shuttle service to the shopping district of Willemstad. If not, yellow city buses stop at Wilhelmina Plein, near the shopping center, and travel to most parts of the city. Buses stop when you hail them.

Taxi rates are regulated by the government. Don't tip a driver unless he carries your luggage. Charges after 11 p.m. go up by 25 percent. You'll find lots of taxis waiting for passengers on the Otrabanda side of the floating bridge. If you want to make a tour by taxi, expect to pay about $20 per hour (up to four passengers allowed).

Rental cars are represented by **Avis** toll free ☎ *800-331-2112*, **Budget** toll free ☎ *800-527-0700* and **Hertz** toll free ☎ *800-654-3001*. Check your credit card to see if you can obtain insurance just by charging. To save money, reserve the car from the States before you arrive. Do note that all driving is on the right.

LANGUAGE

The native language is Papiamento, the official language Dutch, but most everybody speaks some form of English, as well as Spanish.

MEDICAL EMERGENCIES

The 550-bed St. Elizabeth Hospital is the main facility of the island.

MONEY

Official currency is guilder (Netherlands Antilles florin)., noted as NAf. U.S. dollars and credit cards are accepted unilaterally.

TELEPHONE

Country code is *5999*. From the States, dial *011* (international access code), *5999* (country code) + local number. If you are calling from another Caribbean island, check to see if the same code applies. Within Curaçao itself, use only the six-digit number.

TIME

Atlantic Standard Time all year long.

TIPPING AND TAXES

Ten percent service charge is added to restaurant bills, but waiters appreciate an extra five percent.

TOURIST INFORMATION

The **Curaçao Tourist Board** has offices in *Willemstad at the Waterfront Arches* ☎ *613397, closed weekends, and 19 Pietermaai* ☎ *661600.* At all offices you can obtain brochures, maps and have questions answered by English-speaking staff. An office is also at the airport ☎ *668678* (open daily till last flight arrives). In the U.S. call ☎ *(800) 270-3350.*

WATER

Tap water, distilled seawater, is safe to drink.

WHEN TO GO

Carnival takes place in January, an unrestrained revel complete with costumes, parades and street parties. Best time is the weekend right before Ash Wednesday. The International Sailing Regatta is held in March.

CURAÇAO HOTELS	RMS	RATES	PHONE	FAX
Willemstad				
★★★★★ Avila Beach Hotel	90	$90–$415	599-9-614377	599-9-614493
★★★★★ Lions Dive Hotel & Marina	72	$105–$120	599-9-618100	599-9-618200
★★★★ Curaçao Caribbean Hotel	200	$140–$210	599-9-625000	599-9-625846
★★★★ Holland Hotel	40	$70–$130	599-9-688044	599-9-688114
★★★★ Princess Beach Resort	341	$140–$185	(800) 327-3286	599-9-617205

CURAÇAO HOTELS		RMS	RATES	PHONE	FAX
★★★★	Sonesta Beach Hotel	248	$160–$220	(800) 766-3782	
★★★★	Van der Valk Plaza Hotel	350	$105–$210	599-9-612500	599-9-618347
★★★	Ortabanda Hotel & Casino	45	$80–$140	599-9-627400	599-9-627299
★★	Holiday Beach Hotel	200	$95–$115	599-9-625400	599-9-624973
★★	Las Palmas Hotel	184	$93–$140	599	
★★	Porto Paseo Hotel	44	$95–$125	599-9-627878	599-9-627969
★★	Trupial Inn Hotel	74	$65–$100		
★	Coral Cliff Hotel	35	$85–$150	599-9-641610	599-9-641781

CURAÇAO RESTAURANTS		LOCATION	PHONE	ENTREE

Willemstad

American

★★	Cactus Club	Willemstad	(599) 937-1600	$4–$15

Asian

★★★★	Rijstaffel Restaurant	Salina	(599) 961-2999	$9–$20

French

★★★★★	De Taveerne	Salina	(599) 937-0669	$18–$32
★★★★	Bistro Le Clochard	Willemstad	(599) 962-5666	$20–$30

International

★★★★★	L'Alouette	Salina	(599) 961-8222	$18–$40
★★★★	Fort Nassau	Willemstad	(599) 961-3086	$20–$28
★★★	Wine Cellar	Willemstad	(599) 961-2178	$20–$35
★★	'T Kokkeltje	Willemstad		$12–$27

Italian

★★★	La Pergola	Willemstad	(599) 961-3482	$25–$35

Latin American

★★★	Golden Star	Willemstad	(599) 965-4795	$8–$26
★★★	Pirates	Willemstad	(599) 962-5000	$15–$35
★★	Playa Forti	Willemstad	(599) 964-0273	$5–$16

Scandinavian

★★★	Belle Terrace	Willemstad	(599) 961-4377	$10–$24

CURAÇAO RESTAURANTS	LOCATION	PHONE	ENTREE
Seafood			
★★★★ **Seaview**	Willemstad	(599) 961-6688	$15–$30
★★ **Fort Waakzaamheid Bistro**	Willemstad	(599) 962-3633	$17–$26••

Note: • Lunch Only

•• Dinner Only

DOMINICA

Dominica's small Emerald Pool waterfall attracts hordes of tourists.

Home to one of the finest primal rainforests in the world, Dominica has changed little since Columbus set foot on its shore some 500 years ago. Just as it was in 1493, there are still no sugar-white beaches, no resorts, no McDonald's, no duty-free stores and little nightlife. What Dominica does have is one of the world's last ocean rainforests, a flooded fumarole said to be the largest in the world, a lake covered with purple hyacinths, and so many species of trees that one of them is even named "no-name." Here is an earth of boiling lakes and mountain cascades, of desolate lava-ravaged landscapes, of forests dense with bromeliads and lianas, chataigniers and gommiers, of landscapes so dazzlingly accented with helicnia and anthurium blossoms that you could easily believe you're in the Garden of Eden. (The island receives so much rain—400 inches a year—that it may be the only nation in the world that exports water, but there is so much mist from the morning and evening showers that rainbows are as predictable as the sun.) Days on Dominica simply take on a different dimension than on other Caribbean islands. The Dominica experience is about fighting your way up treacherous mountain paths, shading yourself beneath chatannyé and mang blanc trees, boiling your body in hot sulfur springs, and tracking the two-note song of the sifflé montang. Quite frankly, Dominica is not for the fainthearted or the out-of-shape tourist. Divers best know how to exploit a real surf-and-turf vacation—most take a two-hour tank dive in the morning, followed by some equally daunting land excursion in the afternoon. Simply, come to Dominica and expect yourself to be taxed to the max—you may need another Caribbean isle on which to recover.

 Note: *Wide Sargasso Sea*, a darkly romantic novel by Jean Rhyss, took place on a plantation in Dominica. Made into a fiercely erotic movie, it is now available on video.

Bird's Eye View

Not to be confused with the Dominican Republic, Dominica sprawls over a 29-mile by 16 mile rocky terrain, lying between Guadeloupe to the north and Martinique to the south. The island is part of the Caribbean Rim of Fire, those jagged terrains born of the violence of volcanic eruptions (Dominica was in fact formed by 15 such eruptions). Verdant-green mountains, some scaling up to 4700 feet, reach to the edge of the sea, as valleys actually dip under the sea, making for spectacular diving conditions as well as hot springs that provide natural spas. There is virgin rainforest with trees as straight as chimneys and tall as cathedrals growing in a tangle of ferns and epiphytes. Offshore, underwater pinnacles reflect the mountainous terrain above. A coral reef stretches along the south coast, attracting many species of tropical fish. In the interior, often cloaked by clouds of vapor, is **Boiling Lake**, near the Valley of Desolation in the 16,000-acre **Morne Trois Pitons National Park**. The lake is the second largest in the world, with temperatures that hover between 180-197 degrees F. In the lake basin, rainfall and water from two small streams seep through the lake's porous bottom to the lava, where it is heated to a boiling point. The small, beautiful Emerald Point and waterfall, in a for-

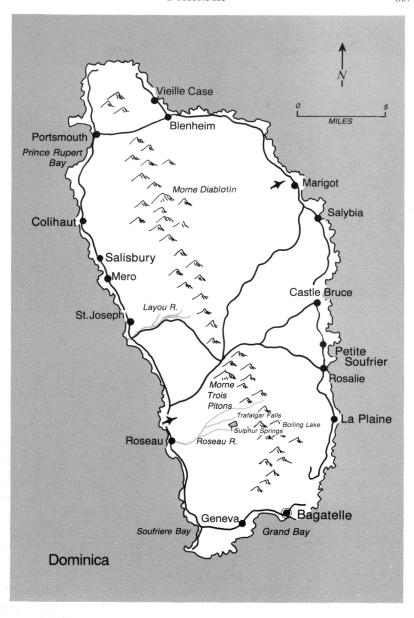

Dominica

est grotto about 45 minutes from Roseau, is a 10- or 15-minute walk from the main Castle Bruce road.

History

Dominica was first settled by Arawaks and then Carib Indians, the latter who dubbed the island "Tall Is Her Body." During the 17th and 18th centuries, control for the island was hotly contested between the British, the French and the native tribes. The British finally prevailed and Dominica formed part of the Leeward Islands federation until 1939. In 1940 it was transferred to the Windward Islands and remained attached to that group until the federal arrangement was ended in December 1959. Under a new constitution, effective from January 1960, Dominica achieved a separate status with its own administrator and an enlarged legislative council. In1967, it became one of the West Indies Associated States, gaining full autonomy in internal affairs with the United Kingdom retaining responsibility for defense and foreign relations. Following a decision in 1975 by the Associated States to seek independence separately, Dominica became an independent republic within the Commonwealth on November 3, 1978. A program instigated in August 1991, granting Dominican citizenship to foreigners in return for a minimum of U.S. $35,000 in the country, caused considerable controversy, but by July 1992, the amount had been reduced and a quota set, By mid-1993, 466 people had taken advantage of the program, however, mostly Taiwanese. In foreign policy, Dominica has close links both with France and the U.S. As a member of the Organization of the Eastern Caribbean States, it contributed assistance to the U.S. intervention in Grenada.

People

Almost all of the people on the island of Dominica profess Christianity, and about 80 percent are Roman Catholics. There is a small community of Carib Indians on the east coast. The tourist industry is small and farming is the principal industry, heavily dependent on the banana, which is very vulnerable to weather conditions. In 1989 the island and its residents suffered greatly from Hurricane Hugo, but have now recovered. Much effort in the last five years has made Dominica into one of the most active promoters of tourism in the Caribbean. As such, what hotels and restaurants may lack in efficiency is made up by a friendly, generous nature.

Beaches

Dominica has only a few beaches of any worth; the best bathing is done in rivers. The west coast does have some admirable strands, directly south of Prince Rupert Bay in the **Picard** area. On the Caribbean coast, the sand is black, as at Mero, where the Castaways Hotel is located. The closest beach to the city of Roseau is Scott's Head, a 20-minute bus ride away. White beaches best suited to swimming are located on the northeast coast, such as **Woodford Hill** (near Melville Hall airport) and **Hampstead**. The sand is a beautiful golden color at **Pointe Baptiste**. Most of the beaches, however, consist of black volcanic sand.

Treks

Most of Dominica's best attractions are to be found in the **Dominica National Park**, also called *Morne Trois Pitons National Park*, after its highest peak— actually a mountain with three peaks. The park's 16,000 acres are abundantly furnished with diverse plant and animal life, and five types of forest. The mountains, which are usually shrouded in mist, can be climbed, but you must have a guide. Trails are difficult or else disappear to nothing; some paths will require being cut down with a machete.

Waterfalls are serious goals in Dominica. There are several on the regular schedule of tour guides, including Middleham, Victoria, and Sari-Sari Falls, as well as others yet to be discovered. **Middleham Falls** makes for a semi-serious hike. It is somewhat strenuous, but approachable for someone in medium-good shape. Here you'll be able to stroll through a rainforest replete with the sounds of insects, birds and the fresh breeze. A delight on the trail is a 200-ft. waterfall that gushes straight down from a cleft in the cliff. **Titou Gorge** is an absolutely stunning site near Trafalgar, where a soft stream forms a deep gorge leading to the bush, meeting a hot spring at its opening. Be prepared to swim over the waterfall; you can't walk it. Once you get there, you'll be really happy if you remembered to bring along an inflatable float.

Trafalgar Falls, itself, is the most accessible, located on the western slope of Morne Micotrin. At the base of the cliff and the start of the trail is the **Papilotte Inn**, a wilderness and nature hotel with a stunning rainforest-type garden. Footpaths were created here over the years to reflect the slope's natural contours; following them around will take you past an incredible array of orchids, ferns, gingers, bromeliads, other exotic herbs, and plants. The hike to the main falls on a good trail takes about ten minutes through some of the lushest tropical landscapes you will ever see. At one point on the trail, the three waterfalls can be seen, but they are not that close. When you return to the inn, do take the opportunity to soak in the warm sulphur pools.

For those in excellent condition, there are two pinnacle hikes. Forestry officials recommend that any hiking to **Boiling Point** be done with a guide. The trek takes about three hours each direction and leads over narrow ridges with cliffs on either side and through the **Valley of Desolation**, an area rendered inhospitable owing to the thick fumes coming from subterranean volcanic activities. **Morne Diablotin**, the highest point of the island, also makes for a long and strenuous hike, since most of it is straight up. The reward, however, is a view few ever get to see.

Less adept hikers will enjoy the trip to **Emerald Falls** (don't forget to fuel up at the Emerald Bush Bar), as well as **Freshwater** and **Boeri Lakes**. Walking up the ridge to Boeri Lake renders wonderful panoramic views, and along the trail itself, the Antillean crested hummingbird can be sighted. The trail to Boeri Lake begins just before the village of Laudat with a steep one and a half-mile dirt road (too rough to negotiate except for a Land Rover truck or on foot) that rounds the south side of Micotrin Mountain on its way to Freshwater Lake. The hike by foot takes about a half hour.

The **Middleham Estate** on the northwest border of the Morne Trois Pitons National Park is considered one of the best examples of rainforest in Dominica. Access to the trails are from three sides—**Providence** (via Laudat), **Cochrane** on the west, and **Sylvania** on the north. Trails were recently improved and can be hiked most often without a guide. Do avoid them in the rainy season when they can become nearly washed out.

The easiest trek in Dominica is down the **Indian River**. Small row boats can be rented for a trip upriver through mangroves. After about a half hour, you depart and hike through the countryside with a guide who identifies the flora and fauna. To scale the upper reaches of the national parks you will definitely need a Land Rover and a guide. Escorted trips usually begin at sunup with half-hour rides by jeep or Land Rover to a base camp such as the village of Laudat. On the longest hikes, expect to be in the wilderness from breakfast to teatime—about 8–10 hours, plodding to and from the Valley of Desolation and the Boiling Lake. Good guides are Ivor or Helen Rolle, available through **Rainbow Rover Tours**, *P.O. Box 448, Roseau;* ☎*/FAX 448-8834, 24hr # (809) 448-8650.*

Insider Tip:

Dress right for trekking here: sturdy shoes with good ankle supports and loose-fitting, lightweight clothes. Take your own water supply and make sure you use sunscreen, even if there seems to be no light filtering through the treetops.

What Else to See

Roseau, Dominica's capital, has made Old Market Plaza a pedestrian area.

In Roseau, all the sights are within walking distance; don't miss the **Botanic Gardens** and especially the **Dawbiney Market Plaza**, which is chock full of art exhibits and local fruits and vegetable stands. You'll also find tourist information centers here. By the time you arrive, there may even be handicraft vendors.

Save a whole other day for a **circuit of the island**—north to Portsmouth and Fort Shirley, down the Atlantic coast, and through the Carib Indian reservation, with a stop for lunch at Calibishie or Castle Bruce. Many people visit the Carib reservation in the northeast of the island where some interesting woven handicrafts, like authentic native baskets, are for sale. Also interesting is **The Point Cabrits National Park**, a double-peaked peninsula defining the northern edge of Prince Rupert Bay and the southern edge of Douglas Bay. It's home to **Fort Shirley** (originally named Prince Rupert's Garrison), a British fort dating back to the mid-1700s. Most fascinating is the series of crisscrossing paths from the sentry post to the armory to the garrison.

Parks and Gardens

Cabrits National Park

> *Portsmouth,* ☎ *(809)448-2401.*
> Located on the northwestern coast, this gorgeous spot encompasses 1313 acres of tropical forests, swampland, beaches, coral reefs and various ruins. The best preserved is Fort Shirley, a 1770 military complex, which includes a small museum. Good for birding.

Morne Trios Pitons National Park

> *South-central region, Roseau,* ☎ *(809)448-2733.*
> The 25-square-mile slice of nature is a primordial rainforest complete with famous Trafalgar Falls, reached by an easy 15-minute hike. There are some other great sights to see here, including a lake nestled in the crater of an extinct volcano, and Boiling Lake, a bubbling mass of mud that's seen only by the hardy—it takes four strenuous hours to trek there. The Emerald Pool Nature Trail is for more moderate hikers.

Tours

Guided Tours

> *Various locations, Roseau.*
> A number of outfits will take you around Dominica, from the city sights of Roseau to the rainforest, Trafalgar Falls to Portsmouth: **Wilderness Adventure Tours** (☎ *448-2198*), **Rainbow Rover Tours** (☎ *448-8650*), **Dominica Tours** (☎ *448-2638*), **Emerald Safaris** (☎ *448-4545*), **Ken's Hinterland Adventures** (☎ *448-4850*), and **Sun Link Tours** (☎ *448-2552*), which also offers sea excursions. Prices are generally in the $20 to $30 range.

BEST VIEW:

Stop for a pick-me-up drink at the Picard Beach Cottages and enjoy a spectacular view of Prince Rupert's Bay.

Sports

Sailing, windsurfing and deep-sea fishing are popular pastimes in Dominica.

Although hiking predominates, Dominica also offers tennis, waterskiing, windsurfing and snorkeling. Scuba diving along walls plunging hundred of feet and even in hot springs is especially popular. Two dive shops are **Waitikubuli** (☎ *44-82638*) and **Dive Dominica** (☎ *44-82188*).

Scuba Diving

Various locations, Roseau.

If your hotel can't help you arrange a diving excursion, try one of these: **Castaways Hotel Dive Center** (☎ *449-6244*), **Dominica Dive Resorts** (☎ *448-2638*), and **Nature Island Dive** (☎ *449-8181*). All offer classes and dive trips. Prices are generally about $65 for a two-tank dive, $90 for a resort course. They also rent equipment to snorkelers.

Where to Stay

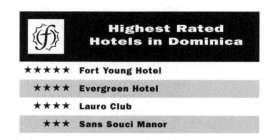

★★★★★ **Fort Young Hotel**

★★★★ **Evergreen Hotel**

★★★★ **Lauro Club**

★★★ **Sans Souci Manor**

	Most Exclusive Hotels in Dominica	
★★★★★	**Fort Young Hotel**	$105–$135
★★★★	**Lauro Club**	$73–$140

	Fielding's Best Value Hotels in Dominica	
★★	**Picard Beach Cottages**	$120–$145
★★	**Castaways Beach Hotel**	$75–$110
★★	**Castle Comfort Lodge**	$85–$120
★★★★	**Lauro Club**	$73–$140

The low price of hotels and guest houses will astound you on Dominica if you are used to inflated ones on other Caribbean islands. Most hotels are small (fewer than 40 rooms) and most are locally owned. You can choose to stay on the beach or on the hillsides, but since you're here in the middle of a volcano, why not immerse yourself in nature and stay 1000 feet up in the foliage at the **Papilotte Wilderness Retreat**, where the 10 simple rooms are decorated with handpainted representations of lianas and greenery and you wake up not knowing whether you are outdoors or in. For a complete list of hotels with the most recent prices, contact the **National Development Corporation**, *P.O. Box 73, Roseau, Dominica, West Indies;* ☎ *(809) 448-2351.*

Hotels and Resorts

Fort Young Hotel, on the site of the former fort, gets A-plus for historical value and civilized service. **Anchorage** is a companionable property run congenially by an entire family—from the reception to the dive facilities. **Layou River Hotel** is for those who can't get enough of the great outdoors.

Anchorage Hotel $65–$140 ★★

Castle Comfort, Roseau, ☎ *(809)448-2638.*
Single: $65–$80. Double: $85–$140.
Located about a mile south of Roseau, this casual hotel appeals mainly to divers. Accommodations are basic, and the older rooms need refurbishment, so be sure to book one of the newer units. There's a pool, good restaurant, dive center and watersports, which cost extra. Though it's located on the water, there is no beach to speak of, but this spot remains popular for its friendly, family-run service. 32 rooms. Credit Cards: V, MC, DC, A.

Castaways Beach Hotel $75–$110 ★★

Mero Beach, ☎ *(800)322-2223, (809)449-6244.*
Single: $75–$101. Double: $101–$110.
Situated between a rain forest and a long gray-sand beach, the Castaways is Dominica's major beach resort. Accommodations are in a two-story wing running along the beach; only a few have air conditioning, but all are pleasant and comfortable. Recreational pursuits include a dive shop, tennis, pool and watersports. A nice property, but if you're looking for a truly wonderful beach resort, pick another island. 26 rooms. Credit Cards: V, MC, A.

Evergreen Hotel $75–$165 ★★★★

Castle Comfort Street, ☎ *(809)448-3288.*
Single: $75–$85. Double: $100–$165.
Plenty of island character at this small, family-run hotel near Roseau. The converted two-story house is complemented by a lovely, lush garden that separates the property from a rocky beach. Accommodations are comfortable and bright and have air conditioning; the newer units are better, though the original rooms have more character. There's a pool and restaurant, and they'll help arrange watersports. 16 rooms. Credit Cards: V, MC, A.

Fort Young Hotel $105–$135 ★★★★★

Victoria Street, Roseau, ☎ *(809)448-5000.*
Single: $105–$115. Double: $125–$135.
Built within the ruins of old Fort Young, which dates back to the 1720s, this is Dominica's best property, though it draws mainly business travelers. Nicely accented with antique art, rooms are air-conditioned and look out over the harbor. The three suites are beautifully done, filled with antiques, and well worth the extra splurge. The pool is decent, too. A great in-town spot. 33 rooms. Credit Cards: V, MC, A.

Layou River Hotel $50–$100 ★★

Clark Hill Estate, ☎ *(800)776-7256, (809)449-6281.*
Single: $50–$70. Double: $60–$100.
Set beside a beautiful river that is cold but swimmable, this modern hotel houses guests in standard air-conditioned rooms. Futuristic structures house a restaurant (the Sunday buffet is popular) and a small boutique. There are two pools for cooling

off, and a free shuttle transports guests to the beach, about five minutes away. A neat spot for families. 36 rooms. Credit Cards: V, MC, A.

Portsmouth Beach Hotel $35–$145   ★

Picard/Portsmouth.
Single: $35–$145. Double: $45–$145.
Located near Cabrits National Park and on the beach, this casual spot has simple, motel-like rooms that rely on ceiling fans to keep things cool. There are also eight cottages that offer more room to spread out. There's a pool and watersports, and a dive center is nearby. Weekly entertainment is a plus. 104 rooms. Credit Cards: V, MC, A.

Reigate Hall Hotel $75–$180   ★★

Reigate Street, ☎ *(809)448-4031.*
Single: $75–$100. Double: $95–$180.
Set high on a hill overlooking Roseau, this stylish hotel is adorned with lots of antiques and artwork. Accommodations are nicely done with air conditioning, heavy wood furnishings, antique four-poster beds and balconies. The dining room chandelier hangs from the ceiling via a heavy chain. The beach is 2.5 miles away; a gym, sauna, pool and tennis court keep guests occupied. One of Dominica's better hotels. 25 rooms. Credit Cards: V, MC, A.

Reigate Waterfront Hotel $55–$95   ★

Castle Comfort, ☎ *(809)448-3111.*
Single: $55–$70. Double: $80–$95.
Located a mile south of Roseau and overlooking the sea, this motel-like property offers basic rooms that let you sleep in air-conditioned comfort. There's a pool, and diving and watersports can be arranged. Besides a weekly barbecue, not much happens here. 25 rooms. Credit Cards: V, MC, A.

Apartments and Condominiums

Dominica has a handful of places for rent, but don't expect to find modern shopping facilities, and if you have any favorites you can't live without, you better bring them from home. If you want to stay long-term, come to the island first and then snoop around for what you want. Prices could be negotiable, depending on the length of your stay.

Coconut Beach Hotel $60–$90   ★

Picard Beach, ☎ *(809)445-5393.*
Single: $60–$80. Double: $65–$90.
Located on one of the island's better beaches, this is an enclave of cottages and apartments that lack air conditioning but include kitchenettes; furnishings are simple and basic. There's also a restaurant on-site if you're not up to cooking. Activities include watersports, river tours and hiking; there's no pool. Populated mainly with European tourists. 22 rooms. Credit Cards: V, MC, A.

Lauro Club $73–$140   ★★★★

Salisbury, ☎ *(809)449-6602.*
Single: $73–$91. Double: $105–$140.
Situated on a cliff and bordered by two beaches, this rustic villa complex offers separate living rooms and kitchens on a large veranda—but no air conditioning. A long

staircase takes you to the beach; if you're feeling lazy, just hang by the pool. The restaurant is a nice spot to escape kitchen duties; a tennis court rounds out the facilities. You'll want to rent a car as this spot is rather remote. 10 rooms. Credit Cards: V, MC, DC, A.

Picard Beach Cottages   **$120–$145**   ★★

Prince Rupert Bay, ☎ *(809)445-5131.*
Single: $120–$125. Double: $140–$145.
Set on the northwest coast on a former coconut plantation at the foot of Morne Diablotin, the island's highest mountain, the cottages here are designed in 18th-century Dominican-style architecture. Each has a kitchenette and veranda; ceiling fans help cool things off. There's a bar and restaurant, and guests can use the pool at a hotel next door. Decent, but a tad pricey for what you get. 8 rooms. Credit Cards: V, MC, A.

Sans Souci Manor   **$110–$110**   ★★★

St. Aromet, Roseau, ☎ *(809)448-2306.*
Single: $110. Double: $110.
Set on a hill above Roseau, the choices here include one bungalow and three very nice two-bedroom apartments. All have full kitchens, and there's a restaurant and pool as well. An elegant spot, with lots of good artwork adding a touch of class. 4 rooms. Credit Cards: V, MC, A.

Inns

Papilotte has the best inn feel, but **Chez Ophelia,** with its five lovely cottages, and **Layou Valley Inn**, have their own distinct personalities. The latter is great for hikers who just want to find the trail outside their door.

Layou Valley Inn   **$55–$85**   ★

Layou Valley, ☎ *(809)449-6203.*
Single: $55–$85. Double: $65–$85.
Perfect for nature lovers, this appealing inn is situated in the foothills of Morne Trios Pitos, seven miles from the beach. Overlooking a primordial forest with great views, the inn has comfortable rooms with private baths but no air. A good jumping-off spot for hiking and rafting. 8 rooms. Credit Cards: V, MC, DC, A.

Papilotte Retreat   **$50–$125**   ★

Trafalgar Falls Road, ☎ *(809)448-2287.*
Single: $50–$125. Double: $55–$125.
This small family-owned inn is set right in the rain forest, some 20 minutes from Roseau, in a lush valley amid mineral pools, gardens and waterfalls. Standard rooms are simple and basic and lack air conditioning; there's also a two-bedroom, two-bath cottage with a kitchen. Meals are served outdoors with lots of fresh fruits and vegetables. Come prepared for the eventuality of rain—this is, after all, the rain forest, but if you don't mind that, this is a very special place far removed from city life. 8 rooms. Credit Cards: V, MC, A.

Springfield Plantation   **$45–$90**   ★★

Springfield, ☎ *(809)449-1401.*
Single: $45–$70. Double: $65–$90.

This mountain inn dates back to 1940. Accommodations are beautifully done with antique four-poster beds complete with mosquito netting, huge wooden armoires and other antiques. There are also several cottages available for monthly rental. There's a protected river pool for splashing about, nature trails for hiking and safari tours for exploring. Nature lovers love it here, but those into a resort atmosphere will be happier at a more commercial establishment. 12 rooms.

Low Cost Lodging

Since rates are not expensive on Dominica, budget opportunities are easy to find. You do sacrifice any hope of furnishings other than West-Indian basic. You will be lucky to find air-conditioning (Continental Inn has it).

Castle Comfort Lodge $85–$120   ★★

Castle Comfort Street, ☎ *(800)544-7631, (809)448-2188.*
Single: $85. Double: $120.
Located three miles from the beach, this small lodge attracts primarily divers. The rooms are basic but at least air-conditioned. The owners arrange dive trips and nature walks. There's a restaurant, but little else in the way of amenities. 11 rooms.
Credit Cards: V, MC, A.

Continental Inn $45–$55   ★

37 Queen Mary Street, Roseau, ☎ *(809)448-2215.*
Single: $45. Double: $50–$55.
This small hotel in the heart of Roseau has air-conditioned rooms, but only some have a private bath. The restaurant serves Creole dishes. Mainly used by business travelers. 11 rooms. Credit Cards: V, MC, A.

Where to Eat

Highest Rated Restaurants in Dominica

★★★★★ **La Robe Creole**

★★★★ **Evergreen**

★★★★ **Guiyave**

★★★★ **World of Food**

★★★ **Almond Beach Restaurant**

★★★ **Balisier**

★★★ **Callaloo Restaurant**

★★★ **Coconut Beach**

★★★ **De Bouille**

★★★ **Floral Gardens**

Most Exclusive Restaurants in Dominica

★★★ **De Bouille**	$14–$30
★★★★ **Evergreen**	$20–$20
★★★ **Balisier**	$13–$22
★★★ **Almond Beach Restaurant**	$8–$15
★★★ **Orchard Restaurant**	$4–$17

Fielding's Best Value Restaurants in Dominica

★★★ **Callaloo Restaurant**	$6–$14
★★★★ **Evergreen**	$20–$20
★★★ **Coconut Beach**	$10–$25
★★★ **Orchard Restaurant**	$4–$17
★★★★ **World of Food**	$2–$15

Although Dominica is sandwiched between Guadeloupe and Martinique, a French style of cooking has not invaded the island. Flavors tend to lean toward the English (meaning basic and sometimes boring). Most people are too tired after hiking to care about anything but quantity. The best place to find a good meal is at a hotel; the tastiest are the ones at **Papilotte** and **Springfield Plantation**. Freshly caught fish is the smartest way to go, as well as local fruits and vegetables; the local pawpaw (or papaya) and christophine (Caribbean squash) are delicious. Do beware when you see mountain chicken on the menu—here in Dominica, it isn't chicken at all, but the legs of huge frogs that burrow into the woods.

Almond Beach Restaurant $$ ★★★

Calibishi, Roseau, ☎ *(809) 445-7783.*
Latin American cuisine. Specialties: Callaloo, chicken palau.
Lunch: 12:00 a.m.– 2:00 p.m., entrees $8–$15.
Dinner: 6:00 p.m.– 8:00 p.m., entrees $8–$15.
A convenient village restaurant on the east coast, Almond Beach is a cool spot to stop for refreshing and exotic fruit and spice beverages made with anise or ginger. The view of the sea is just ahead, and meals include a savory chicken and rice dish, lobster or *callaloo* (dasheen) soup. Closed: Sun. Credit Cards: Not Accepted. Credit Cards: D, V, MC.

Balisier $$$ ★★★

Place Heritage, Roseau,
International cuisine. Specialties: Chicken garraway.
Lunch: 12:30 p.m.–3:00 p.m., prix fixe $9–$17.
Dinner: 7:00 p.m.–10:30 p.m., entrees $13–$22.
Located in a modern, newish hotel on the oceanfront in Roseau, the Balisier is a view restaurant on the first floor, serving competently prepared local fish, curries and a specialty, Chicken Garraway, a moist breast rolled around a local banana and exotic spices. Pies are home-baked and tasty. Associated Hotel: Garraway Hotel. Reservations recommended. Credit Cards: V, MC.

Callaloo Restaurant $$ ★★★

63 King George Street, Roseau, ☎ *(809) 448-3386.*
Latin American cuisine. Specialties: Curried conch, callaloo.
Lunch: 11:30 a.m.– 2:30 p.m., entrees $6–$14.
Dinner: 6:30 p.m.– 10:30 p.m., entrees $6–$14.
Chefs at Callaloo present home-style cooking on a terrace overlooking downtown Roseau. Like its namesake, the hearty soup made from the omnipresent *dasheen* (a spinach-like green) is made from scratch daily. There are daily specials, which often include conch prepared in a number of different ways. Credit Cards: Not Accepted.

Castaways Beach Hotel $$ ★★

Mero Beach, Mero, ☎ *(809) 449-6244.*
Latin American cuisine.
Lunch: 12:00 a.m.–2:00 p.m., entrees $12–$18.
Dinner: 7:00 p.m.–9:00 p.m., entrees $12–$18.

Dine informally by the ocean at this hotel restaurant popular for good breakfasts, tropical rum punches and the ubiquitous national dish of *crapaud*, or frog legs. Sometimes there is crab and conch, and although most of the food is freshly prepared, it varies in quality. Associated Hotel: Castaways Beach Hotel. Credit Cards: V, MC.

Coconut Beach $$$ ★★★

Picard Beach, Portsmouth, ☎ *(809) 445-5393.*
Seafood cuisine.
Lunch: 12:00 a.m.– 2:30 p.m., entrees $10–$15.
Dinner: 6:30 p.m.– 10:30 p.m., entrees $10–$25.
A casual sandwich and seafood foodery right on the beach located south of Portsmouth, the Coconut Beach serves as a yacht and boat stop as well as a watering hole for daytrippers passing through the island's second-largest town. It's also a good place to try *rotis*, or flatbread rolled around curried meat or vegetables. Associated Hotel: Coconut Beach Hotel. Credit Cards: V, MC, DC, A.

De Bouille $$$ ★★★

Victoria Street, Roseau, ☎ *(809) 448-5000.*
International cuisine. Specialties: Pumpkin soup, lobster.
Lunch: 12:00 a.m.– 2:30 p.m., entrees $5–$14.
Dinner: 7:00 p.m.– 10:00 p.m., entrees $14–$30.
A baronial and stately restaurant serving a varied cuisine, De Bouille is ensconced in an old fort, now one of Roseau's finest hotels. Diners can feel history in the stone walls, which add plenty of atmosphere to go along with the pumpkin soup, seafood and steaks served here. A good place to spot local movers and shakers. Associated Hotel: Fort Young Hotel. Reservations required. Credit Cards: V, MC, A.

Evergreen $$$ ★★★★

Castle Comfort, Roseau, ☎ *(809) 448-3288.*
International cuisine. Specialties: Frogs' legs, crab.
Lunch: 1:00 p.m.– 2:00 p.m., prix fixe $17.
Dinner: 6:00 p.m.– 10:00 p.m., prix fixe $20.
One of the island's most convivial spots, the Evergreen Hotel's dining room is open to non-guests for a prix-fixe five-course meal with a choice of soup and salad; entrees of chicken, frogs' legs and lamb; side dishes, relishes and homemade desserts. The owners, the Winston family, run a very tight ship, with excellent service all around. Associated Hotel: Evergreen Hotel. Reservations recommended. Credit Cards: V, MC, A.

Floral Gardens $$$ ★★★

Concord Valley, Concord, ☎ *(809) 445-7636.*
Latin American cuisine.
Lunch: 11:00 a.m.– 3:00 p.m., entrees $14–$25.
Dinner: 7:00 p.m.– 12:00 p.m., entrees $14–$25.
The name of this restaurant near the Carib Territory couldn't be more apt—the grounds are surrounded by amazingly fertile plants and flowers. Owned by a former prime minister and his wife, Floral Gardens serves Creole and international specialties in a room overlooking the Pagwa River. Tour groups often stop here for

refreshments, so service can be slow. Associated Hotel: Floral Gardens Hotel. Credit
Cards: D, V, MC, DC, A.

Guiyave $$ ★★★★

15 Cork Street, Roseau, ☎ (809) 448-2930.
Latin American cuisine. Specialties: Goat water, rotis.
Lunch: 8:00 a.m.–2:00 p.m., entrees $8–$19.
Dinner: 2:00 p.m.–5:00 p.m., entrees $8–$19.
This informal eatery is a popular breakfast and lunch spot serving ham and eggs,
French toast, and sandwiches during the week. Saturday's home-cooked creole food
is a tradition, and that may involve goat water (a spicy meat stew), blood pudding,
calalloo, pumpkin soup, and rotis. Guiyave is also THE local juice bar, squeezing
out whatever's fresh that day, including tamarind, mango, or soursop, a tangy citrus
fruit. Closed: Sun. Credit Cards: V, MC, A.

La Robe Creole $$$ ★★★★★

3 Victoria Street, Roseau, ☎ (809) 448-2896.
Latin American cuisine. Specialties: Mountain chicken, calalloo.
Lunch: 10:00 a.m.–3:30 p.m., entrees $7–$27.
Dinner: 3:30 p.m.–9:30 p.m., entrees $7–$27.
Regarded as Dominica's fanciest restaurant, La Robe Creole, named after the native
madras costume, serves a sublime calalloo soup with coconut and crab and an unfor-
gettable rum punch. There's also pizza and chicken and tropical fruit and coconut
pies. Patrons are prominent citizens who come to see and be seen in air-conditioned
luxury, but as sometimes happens on this relaxed isle, service can be very slow.
Closed: Sun. Reservations required. Credit Cards: D, V, MC.

Le Flambeau $$ ★★

Prince Rupert Bay, Portsmouth, ☎ (809) 449-5131.
International cuisine. Specialties: Creole pork chops, homemade ice cream.
Lunch: 7:00 a.m.–4:00 p.m., entrees $4–$6.
Dinner: 4:00 p.m.–11:00 p.m., entrees $9–$13.
A pleasing change from exotic Creole specialties, Le Flambeau, located on the sand
at the Picard Beach Cottage Resort, flips omelettes, pancakes and French toast to an
appreciative crowd at breakfast. The rest of the day and well into the evening, pork
chops and vegetarian specialties are available, and the fresh fruit ice creams are
delightful. Associated Hotel: Picard Beach Resort. Credit Cards: V, MC, DC, A.

Orchard Restaurant $$ ★★★

31 King George Street, Roseau, ☎ (809) 448-3051.
Latin American cuisine. Specialties: Callaloo, conch.
Lunch: 11:30 a.m.–4:00 p.m., prix fixe $4–$17.
Dinner: 7:00 p.m.–9:00 p.m., prix fixe $4–$17.
Hearty, complete meals for under $20 draw patrons to this informal downtown eat-
ery, which also has a popular bar. Entrees like conch (called *lambi* here) are served
with trimmings, which in this case involve rice, relishes, salads and whatever the chef
has on hand. Those wishing to eat lighter can order a la carte sandwiches and soups,
or get food to go. No dinner is served on Saturdays. Closed: Sun. Reservations
required. Credit Cards: V, MC, A.

Papilotte $$ ★★★

Trafalgar Falls Road, Trafalgar, ☎ *(809) 448-2287.*
Latin American cuisine. Specialties: Flying fish, callaloo soup.
Lunch: 12:00 a.m.–3:00 p.m., entrees $8–$19.
Paradise awaits in this garden of Eden near Trafalgar Falls, a haven for nature lovers; amateur botanists will be in seventh heaven. The Retreat's restaurant is only open to nonguests for lunch, but some selections from the small menu, like river shrimp and flying fish, are rarely available elsewhere. There's a hot springs pool on the premises where daytrippers can dip before or after meals. Associated Hotel: Papilotte Retreat. Closed: Sat. Reservations recommended. Credit Cards: V, MC, A.

Reigate Hall $$ ★★

Mountain Road, Reigate, ☎ *(809) 448-4031.*
French cuisine. Specialties: Mountain Chicken.
Lunch: 12:30 p.m.–2:30 p.m., entrees $7–$12.
Dinner: 7:00 p.m.–10:00 p.m., entrees $7–$15.
High up on King's Hill near Trafalgar Falls is the Reigate Hall Hotel, a refurbished plantation home with an attached restaurant serving French and Creole specialties. Not unlike eating in a castle, guests enjoy coq au vin, scampi or mountain chicken in a formal atmosphere, but the wait staff can be less than alert on occasion. Associated Hotel: Reigate Hall Hotel. Reservations required. Credit Cards: V, MC, A.

The Mouse Hole $ ★★

3 Victoria Street, Roseau, ☎ *(809) 448-2896.*
Latin American cuisine. Specialties: Rotis, pastries.
Lunch: 10:00 a.m.–2:30 p.m., entrees $6–$10.
Dinner: 2:30 p.m.–9:30 p.m., entrees $6–$10.
The cutely monikered Mouse Hole serves as the takeout-short order adjunct to its big sister, La Robe Creole, which holds court upstairs. There is a counter for sit-down service, but most patrons order rotis of curried chicken, sandwiches, pastries and small meals to go. Closed: Sun. Credit Cards: V, MC, A.

World of Food $ ★★★★

48 Cork Street, Roseau, ☎ *(809) 448-3286.*
Latin American cuisine. Specialties: Fresh fish, lambi (conch).
Lunch: 12:00 a.m.–3:00 p.m., entrees $2–$15.
Dinner: 6:00 p.m.–10:30 p.m., entrees $2–$15.
Literary lions will delight in the fact that this restaurant is located at the site of author Jean Rhyss' birthplace. Owner Vena McDougal has turned it into a patio restaurant that brims with office workers at cocktail hour. Diners can sit under a spreading fruit tree and partake of local fish cakes, souse (black pudding) or reasonably priced sandwiches and soups. Associated Hotel: Vena's Guest House. Credit Cards: Not Accepted.

Where to Shop

Martinique—Dominica isn't. There are no fancy imports or duty-free stores. Instead, you will have to scope out handicraft shops which, ironically enough, will render you some of the most fantastic souvenirs of your days in the Caribbean.

Dominica Directory

ARRIVAL AND DEPARTURE

Dominica cannot be reached directly by air from the United States but through such island gateways as Antigua, Puerto Rico, St. Maarten, Guadeloupe, Martinique, St. Lucia and Barbados. From those islands, passengers have to switch to a small regional plane like those on Air Guadeloupe, LIAT, or WINAIR, all of which fly into Dominica. There are two small airports on the island: Melville Hall is almost a one-hour drive from Roseau, where most hotels are situated. Canefield is about five minutes from the capital.

CLIMATE

Climate is tropical, though tempered by the sea winds which sometimes reach hurricane force, especially from July-September. Average temperature is 80 degrees F., with little seasonal variation. Rainfall is heavy especially in the mountainous areas, where the annual average is 250 inches compared with 70 inches along the coast.

DOCUMENTS

Visitors will need a passport or proof of citizenship in conjunction with a photo ID as well as a return or ongoing ticket.

ELECTRICITY

The current is 220 volts/50 cycles, which means you must have a transformer with the proper plug adapters. Rechargeable strobes and lights should be charged on the stabilized lines most dive operators have available for his purpose.

GETTING AROUND

Taxis and buses are inexpensive and plentiful. Car rentals are available, but driving is on the left and the roads are narrow and twisting, often with a steep drop on one side and a steep rain gutter on the other.

LANGUAGE

English is the official language, but a local French patois, or Creole is widely spoken. In part of the Northeast, an English dialect known as Cocoy, is spoken by the descendants of the Antiguan settlers.

MEDICAL EMERGENCIES

There are two main hospitals at Roseau and Portsmouth, with 242 and 50 beds respectively.

MONEY

The official currency is the Eastern Caribbean dollar, but the U.S. dollar is accepted virtually everywhere.

TELEPHONE

The area code is *809*. To call Dominica from the U.S., dial *011* (international code)+*809* (country Code)+*44* (local access) +five-digit number. If you want to save money, head for the Cable & Wireless (West Indies) Ltd. company where you can make international calls, send faxes, telexes, teletypes and telegrams. You can also purchase phone cards here which can be used in pay phones. You can make both local and international calls from pay phones. (Do avoid making long-distance calls from your room —if your room indeed even has a phone—as hotel surcharges and operator assistance can raise the bill even higher than the room rate.)

TIME

Atlantic Standard Time, one hour later than New York.

TIPPING AND TAXES

Hotels collect a five percent government tax; restaurants a three percent charge. A 10 percent service charge is added to your bill by most hotels and restaurants. In addition, there is another three percent sales tax. If you feel inclined to leave more for service, do so.

TOURIST INFORMATION

For more information write to the **Dominica Division of Tourism** *(Box 293, Roseau, Dominica, WI;* ☎ *(809) 448-2186, FAX (809) 448-5840).* Mail from the States takes about two weeks to arrive.

WHEN TO GO

Carnival takes place the Monday and Tuesday preceding Ash Wednesday.

Labor Day is May 1. Independence Day is November 1.

DOMINICA HOTELS	RMS	RATES	PHONE	FAX
Bagatelle				
★★★★★ **Fort Young Hotel**	33	$105–$135	(809) 448-5000	(809) 448-5006
★★★★ **Evergreen Hotel**	16	$75–$165	(809) 448-3288	(809) 448-6800
★★★★ **Lauro Club**	10	$73–$140	(809) 449-6602	(809) 449-6603

DOMINICA HOTELS	RMS	RATES	PHONE	FAX
★★★ Sans Souci Manor	4	$110	(809) 448-2306	
★★ Anchorage Hotel	32	$65–$140	(809) 448-2638	
★★ Castaways Beach Hotel	26	$75–$110	(800) 322-2223	(809) 449-6246
★★ Castle Comfort Lodge	11	$85–$120	(800) 544-7631	(809) 448-6088
★★ Layou River Hotel	36	$50–$100	(800) 776-7256	(809) 449-6713
★★ Picard Beach Cottages	8	$120–$145	(809) 445-5131	(809) 445-5599
★★ Reigate Hall Hotel	25	$75–$180	(809) 448-4031	(809) 448-4034
★★ Springfield Plantation	12	$45–$90	(809) 449-1401	(809) 449-2160
★ Coconut Beach Hotel	22	$60–$90	(809) 445-5393	(809) 445-5693
★ Continental Inn	11	$45–$55	(809) 448-2215	(809) 448-7022
★ Layou Valley Inn	8	$55–$85	(809) 449-6203	
★ Papilotte Retreat	8	$50–$125	(809) 448-2287	(809) 448-2285
★ Portsmouth Beach Hotel	104	$35–$145		
★ Reigate Waterfront Hotel	25	$55–$95	(809) 448-3111	(809) 448-3112

DOMINICA RESTAURANTS	LOCATION	PHONE	ENTREE
Bagatelle			
French			
★★ Reigate Hall	Reigate	(809) 448-4031	$7–$15
International			
★★★★ Evergreen	Roseau	(809) 448-3288	$17–$20
★★★ Balisier	Roseau		$9–$22
★★★ De Bouille	Roseau	(809) 448-5000	$5–$30
★★ Le Flambeau	Portsmouth	(809) 449-5131	$4–$13
Latin American			
★★★★★ La Robe Creole	Roseau	(809) 448-2896	$7–$27
★★★★ Guiyave	Roseau	(809) 448-2930	$8–$19
★★★★ World of Food	Roseau	(809) 448-3286	$2–$15
★★★ Almond Beach Restaurant	Roseau	(809) 445-7783	$8–$15
★★★ Callaloo Restaurant	Roseau	(809) 448-3386	$6–$14
★★★ Floral Gardens	Concord	(809) 445-7636	$14–$25
★★★ Orchard Restaurant	Roseau	(809) 448-3051	$4–$17

DOMINICA RESTAURANTS	LOCATION	PHONE	ENTREE
★★★ **Papilotte**	Trafalgar	(809) 448-2287	$8–$19•
★★ **Castaways Beach Hotel**	Mero	(809) 449-6244	$12–$18
★★ **The Mouse Hole**	Roseau	(809) 448-2896	$6–$10
Seafood			
★★★ **Coconut Beach**	Portsmouth	(809) 445-5393	$10–$25

Note: • Lunch Only

•• Dinner Only

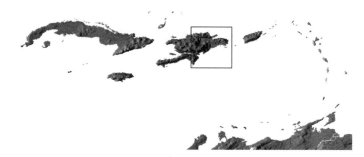

DOMINICAN REPUBLIC

The Dominican Republic is known for its beautiful beaches.

The Dominican Republic is the granddaddy of the Caribbean. It can claim age rank over any other island in the region in nearly every category. It has the oldest city, Santo Domingo, in the New World; the oldest street, the oldest cathedral, the oldest university, and even the remains of the oldest hospital. Despite its intense historical interest, the country has lagged behind in tourism for decades due to the negative influence of Generalissimo Rafael

Leónidas Trujillo, the former ruthless dictator who controlled the government for more than 30 years till 1961. His regime and the purposes of tourism were at cross-purposes, despite the building of several casinos; the presence of paramilitary troops on the streets didn't attract tourists in any case. Not until the mid-70s did interest in the island return, as the government poured millions into renovating and building a viable touristic infrastructure. The American firm, Gulf & Western, also contributed to the building of a famous resort in the south as well as other hotels, expanding the number of available rooms and offering new luxury accommodations. These days annual tourists have swelled to over two million, seeking many of the comforts of other islands—and at a fraction of the cost. The island is being heavily promoted today by tourist officials under the fantasy name "Dominicana," suggesting a calmer, less frantic paradise—not exactly the picture of bustling Santo Domingo where the crime rate has risen and tourists must travel with a big eye to caution. Electricity failures are common, which might be why many people head straight for outdoor treks—considered to be spectacular here. What the Dominican Republic excels in are beaches, a thousand miles worth, anywhere from mountainous backdrops to powdery coves.

Bird's Eye View

The Dominican Republic, which shares the island of Hispaniola with Haiti, is situated between Cuba and Puerto Rico in the Caribbean Sea. An ecological wonder, the island harbors 14 national parks and seven reserves. Beyond the beaches are tropical forests and mountains sprinkled with more than 300 varieties of orchids, and 5600 other plant species, 36 percent of which are endemic. The highest peak is **Pico Duarte** at 10,400 feet, which ranks as the highest mountain in the Caribbean. **Lago Enriquillo**, an unusual salt water lake 144 feet below sea-level, is home to a large reserve of American crocodiles. *Isla Cabrito*, **Goat Island**, which lies in the lake, has a research center where scientists collaborate with the National Zoo to increase the crocodile population. The capital and chief seaport is **Santo Domingo**, whose 12-block historical center, brings great charm to the island. The road from Santo Domingo leads through lush banana plantations and rice and tobacco fields to the groves of royal poinciana trees in the Cibao Valley, where the island's oldest settlement, **La Vega**, is located. A hundred miles north of the capital is

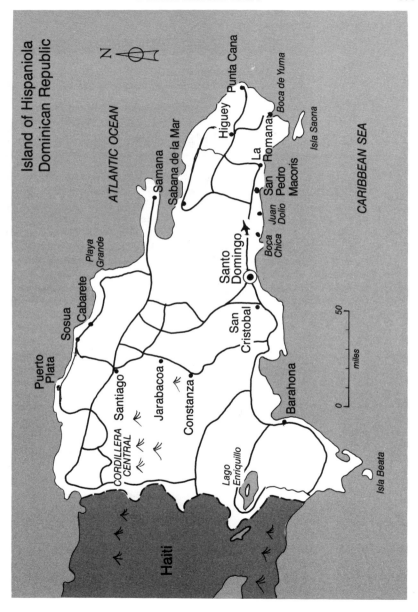

Island of Hispaniola
Dominican Republic

N

ATLANTIC OCEAN

CARIBBEAN SEA

Punta Cana
Higuey
Boca de Yuma
La Romana
Isla Saona
San Pedro Macoris
Sabana de la Mar
Samana
Juan Dolio
Boca Chica
Playa Grande
Santo Domingo
Cabarete
Sosua
San Cristobal
Puerto Plata
Santiago
Jarabacoa
Constanza
Barahona
CORDILLERA CENTRAL
Lago Enriquillo
Isla Beata
Haiti

0   50
miles

the industrial city of **Santiago los Caballeros**, currently a center for tobacco leaf production. Once a dynamic town now turned sleepy, **Puerto Plata** in the northern coast is home to many of the island's most luxurious resorts.

History

One could say that the Dominican Republic is really a family affair. The great Christopher Columbus dropped anchor in the Dominican Republic on his first voyage in 1492; four years later, his brother Bartolomeo founded the colony of Santo Domingo; 13 years after that, Christopher's son became the colony's governor, serving as viceroy when the Dominican Republic, then the colony of Santo Domingo, was the provisioning port and jump-off place for some of Spain's greatest expeditions to the New World. The list of explorers who sailed from this port is as impressive as a Hollywood A-list: Juan Ponce de Léon to Puerto Rico, Velasquez to Cuba, Cortés to Mexico. Even Sir Francis Drake put his mark on the port, attacking it, ransacking it, and then setting fire to it in 1586.

Over the next 300 years, the island changed hands between France, Spain, and Cuba, and for a time it was even self-ruled in a phase called "Ephemeral Independence." Since winning its independence from Spain in 1821 and from Haiti in 1844, the Dominican Republic has been plagued by recurrent domestic conflicts and foreign intervention; between 1916 and 1924 it was occupied by American forces. In 1930 the country entered into a 30-year dictatorship led by General Rafael Leónidas Trujillo Molina, who ruled personally until 1947 and indirectly thereafter until his assassination in 1961. His death gave rise to renewed political turmoil, and an election in December 1962 led to the inauguration of Juan Bosch Gaviño, a left-of-center democrat, as president in February 1963. In the same year, Bosch was overthrown by a military coup; subsequently the military installed a civilian triumvirate which ruled until April 1965, when civil war erupted. Military forces intervened on April 28, 1965 and imposed a truce while arrangements were made to establish a provisional government and prepare for new elections. For the next twelve years the country was run by a moderate, Dr. Joaquin Balaguer, who then returned after one term for another two consecutive ones. Presently there are at least ten different political parties representing diverse ideological viewpoints, including the Social Christian Reformed Party of 80-year-old Dr. Balaguer to the Dominican Revolutionary Party, a left-democratic grouping, to the right-wing Quisqueyan Democratic Party, the Dominican Communist Party (a traditionally pro-Moscow party), and the Dominican Popular Movement, which is pro-Peking.

People

The population of the island (over 3 million) is a mixture of black, white and mestizo, but each of those terms come with a special island definition. *Blanco* (or white) refers to anybody who is white, white/Indian mestizo, or substantially white with either or both Indian and African mixture. *Indio claro* is anybody who is white/black mixed mulatto or a mestizo; *indio oscuro* is anyone who is not 100 percent black; *negro* is 100 percent African. The African and Afro-Cuban influence is deeply present in the song and dance of the island, with merengue the dominant beat, typically played by a three-man group. There are festivals throughout the year, and international merengue celebrations that attract music lovers from all over. Due to political unrest and an unstable economy (not to mention high unemployment) there is, sad to say, a level of violence that underscores society here; in the last few years, unruly demonstrations and strikes have marred the island's equilibrium. Because of the hard economic conditions, great care should be taken with one's valuables (from luggage to camera to purse) at all times. Crime is quite prevalent, and tourists are often conned into various compromising situations (big and small). About a quarter of the population is employed in agriculture, and the further you go from the main city, the more simple and less harried will be the people you meet. Almost all profess Christianity and 80 percent are Roman Catholics. There are small Protestant and Jewish communities.

Beaches

A whopping one thousand miles of beaches await visitors, who often have a hard time just deciding which beach to pick for the day. Unfortunately, the beach closest to the city—**Boca Chica** (about 21 miles from the capital)—is also the most crowded, a veritable zoo on the weekends as locals and tourists alike invade the vanilla white strands. In the last five years the fine white sands have gone from nearly deserted to a clutter of pizza huts, plastic beach tables, and lounge chairs, and rental cottages full of screaming babies. The one thing that has remained protected here are the coral reefs, which serve to keep dangerous marine life from getting too close. As such, feel free to walk out in to the sea. Twenty minutes east of Boca Chica is **Juan Dolio**, with its powdery white beach. Here you'll find the Villas del Mar Hotel and the Punta Garza Beach Club. Other excellent beaches are the thumbprint-sized **Minitas** beach and lagoon, and the palm-fringed **Bayahibe**, only accessible by boat. This area, called **La Romana**, also houses the Casa de Campo Resort, which means it is usually crowded. The island's pride and joy is **Punta Cana**, a 20-mile sprawl (though it seems longer for its beauty), lined with shady trees and coconut palms. Here is located Club Med, the Melia Punta Cara, and the Bavaro Beach Resort. Primitive is the only description for **Las Terrenas**, tucked into the north coast of the Samaná peninsula. You'll be hard pressed to find anything here other than tall palms, sea, mountains and sand. **Sosuá** could be pleasant since the waves are gentle and the sand white and soft, but the scene is marred by camping tents and hawkers selling cheap trinkets. The beach of the future is **Puerto Plata**, on the north Amber Coast, where there are excellent reefs for snorkeling and the horizon hasn't yet been marred by too much civilization. Windsurfers and waterskiers particularly love the conditions, and many fishing expeditions take off from here. Windsurfing conditions on **Cabarete Beach** are excellent; between June and October wind speeds at 20–25 knots and 3–15-foot waves attract some of the best windsurfers in the Caribbean.

Dive Sites

The Dominican Republic is bordered on all three coast by reefs, but the sport of scuba is only in its beginning stages, dependent on resort facilities. Some attention is being directed toward the north coast, where there are several wrecks and a good supply of reefs, but strong northerly winds from December to March make the area unsuitable. Most divers head for the mouth of the **Smanaea Bay**, north of Miches, home to the 17th-century Spanish galleon wrecks *Tolosa* and *Guadeloupe*. Snorkelers will enjoy the area on the east coast from the Sananá Bay to Punta Caná, where the waves from the Atlantic are calmer.

On the southeast coast, a primary target for divers is **Catalina Island**, with a wall on its northern coast starting at 40 feet. Boats leave from the marina at La Romana to the island daily. Camping may even be accomplished on the island (given permission from the Naval Station at La Romana), but you will have to take your own water supply and there are no bathrooms.

In the immediate vicinity of Santo Domingo, the wreck of the *Hickory* was sunk here to artificially create a reef that would attract fish and restock the population. The area is a protected park now and has no facilities or equipment, so you must bring your own gear and make arrangements through your hotel. **La Caleta**, as the marine park is called, offers calm, clear Caribbean water, which makes it ideal for underwater photography. A similar artificial reed was created in **Bahía de Ocoa**, west of Santo Domingo.

Treks

The National Park of the East, 90 miles east of Santo Domingo and 22 miles east of La Romana, is popular and easy to reach on the country's major southern seaside highway. The park begins on the mainland in a heavily wooded area and ends in what UNESCO experts once described as possibly the world's best beaches, where dolphins and manatees sometimes find their way to the canals. The National Park of the East is also home to 11 island species of birds, including the popular little crown pigeon, and has the country's best-preserved system of prehistoric caves, lined with pre-Columbian petroglyphs. Visitors can enter most caves with the help of guides from the Parks Department. The department offers daily guided tours for an entrance fee of less than $6.

Lago Enriquillo, an unusual salt water lake, 144 feet below sea-level, is home to a large reserve of American crocodiles. A boat ride can be taken to **Isla Cabrito**, **Goat Island**, which lies in the middle of the lake and takes about a half hour. No unguided visits are allowed. The crocodiles can be seen from the mainland shore, the island and the boat ride. Pink flamingos and other waterfowl live along the lake, which is 144 miles west of Santo Domingo, the capital, a drive of about three hours, on a new highway. **Ecoturisa** ☎ *(809) 221-4101, FAX (809) 685-1544*, in Santo Domingo is a company which specializes in nature trips and offers a two-day tour of Lago Enriquillo region with an overnight stay in a riverside mountain resort for $160 a person

Most native orchids and birds are found in the mountain chain of **Cordillera Central**, and many migratory birds visit annually. The five-day trip climbing **Pico Duarte** (see below under "Best View") includes a visit to the **Bao Valley**, a stretch of beautiful terrain with waterfalls and cool, clear rivers. The cost of the tour depends on the number of people in the group and will be about $100 a person in groups of 10. In smaller groups, the price is higher ($150–$175).

On the road between La Vega and Jarabacoa, you'll discover the **Jimenoa Waterfalls**, about three miles from the town of La Confluencia. They're worth the vigorous trek up, but you'll need a guide (or a car if you're going it alone; the guards at the control post will look after it) The handsome cascade drops over 100 feet from the upper part of the river into a pool which makes for the most sensuous bathing you will ever come across. To reach the falls, drive south of Jarabacoa en route to Constanza for about six miles to El Salto, a village of only a few houses by the side of the road. A trail can be found at the edge of the road that heads to the falls. No signs mark the trail entrance, keep asking whoever you run into for directions. (Spanish will probably be necessary.) The descent is easy and not dangerous, but the return hike up is very rigorous. Closer to town, off the Constanza road, are the **Baiguate Falls**, an easy 1-1/2 mile walk. Just follow the signpost to the falls, second turn on the right, after Pinar Dorado. The scenery beyond Jarabacoa, near Constanza, is even more spectacular, crisscrossed with rivers, forests and more waterfalls that will leave a permanent dent in your pleasure memory.

El Morro National Park, near the Haitian border, is an enormous land-and-sea park northeast of the town of Monte Christi. The prominent feature of the park is the mesa, **El Morro**, which rises steeply at the edge of the sea. There are no nature trails here, but there are several goat paths which are walkable, providing you watch where you walk. Also, a road at the base of the mesa runs eastward through a dry forest to another beach area. Birdwatchers will delight in the fine national parks offering some excellent birding opportunities, and there are several waterfalls tucked into mountainous coves that make a great reason to exercise your hiking muscles. You'll spot frigate birds, American ketrels, ruddy turnstones, willets, gulls, brown noddy, and five species of terns.

On the road to the airport are the **Tres Ojos de Agua**, two water-filled caves and a sunken lake, which are well worth a peak. To reach the lake, you must take the raft across the second cave; it's supposedly the home to two crocodiles that were put there to mate; unfortunately no one bothered to check their sex.) At the entrance to the airport is a fine museum collection, **La Cale-**

ta Archaeological Museum, which display amazing Taino and Arawak ceramics and a Taino burial site. Entrance is free.

FIELDING'S CHOICE:

From January to late February, whales can be seen at the mouth of the Samaná Bay. There are no organized excursions, but local boatmen will arrange trips, though permission must be obtained from the Naval Station in advance. From late December to early March, 3000 migrating humpback whales come to mate in Silver Bank, a marine sanctuary located 50 miles off the coast, directly north of Cabrera. Occasional expeditions by scientists are taken to the site, which runs about 7–12 hours. To join an expedition, contact the National Parks Office in Santo Domingo.

BEST VIEW:

The panoramic sweep of the island, seen from the top of the Pico Duarte mountain, is spectacular. At almost 11,000 feet, it's a climb only the truly fit should attempt. It's best to go with a guide. Beginning in late fall 1994, Ecoturisa, in partnership with Occidental Hotels, will offer five-day packages, blankets, flashlights, guides, mules and meals. Part of the climb is covered on muleback, the rest on foot. During December and January, frost glazes the tropical landscape and intensifies the grandeur of the view.

What Else to See

The twelve-block area known as the **Colonial Zone** is a must-see on any itinerary. The area today bristles with feverish activity, as people and cars jostle their way through the narrow cobbled streets, home to some of the finest restaurants, shops and galleries on the island. Strange how all the noise and confusion of the modern cityscape takes one immediately back centuries, when the city was yet a colony and a home port for pirates, colonists and great explorers. Most recently, the island has invested millions of dollars to renovate this area, and numerous sights are well worth the time to visit. Top on the list should be the **Alcázar de Cólon**, an imposing Renaissance castle, once the home of Don Diego Colon (aka Columbus). The antiques and tapestries did not all belong to Columbus, who lived here with his bride, (some are even of the wrong century), but the total effect gives the feeling of life with the great explorers. Built in 1514, it was reconstructed and restored in 1957.

Across the street is the **La Ataranza**, the Royal Mooring Docks, once the colonial commercial district, and now home to several crafts stores, restaurants, and galleries. The **Museu de las Casas Reales** (Museum of the Royal House) presents exhibits that include replicas of Columbus' famous three ships, ancient maps, coats of arms, coaches and a royal courtroom, as well as Indian artifacts. The **Casa de Bastidas** (south on Calle Las Damas and cross Calle El Conde) boasts a beautiful courtyard full of tropical plants and temporary art exhibits that show unusually excellent pieces.

Do make time to step inside the most wondrous **Catedral Santa Maria la Meno**, **Primada de America**, the first cathedral in America. In the nave are four baroque columns, carved to resemble royal palms, which for more than four centuries guarded the magnificent bronze and marble sarcophagus containing (some Dominican historians claim) the final remains of Christopher Columbus. Started in 1514, the church was finally finished in 1540, its facade a heady mixture of late Gothic to Plateresque styles. The sarcophagus has been moved of late to the **Columbus Memorial Lighthouse**. (Actually, it was Columbus' last wish that he be buried in Santo Domingo.) After the French occupation, the Spaniards stole his remains from the cathedral and sent them to Cuba. Later, both Spain and Cuba claimed to have confiscated the bones of someone named Columbus, but nobody really knows whether it was Christopher (or even *the* Christopher) or one of his grandsons.

If you have time, stop by the Columbus Lighthouse, a newly constructed memorial that includes six museums, a laser-beam lighthouse, and a chapel (one more place that claims to hold the dear old bones of Columbus.) and the **Parque Zoological Nacional**, a lake for water-bound birds and an open plains park where animals roam freely. Children particularly love the children's section and the caves that are perfect for prowling and hooting up a storm. One of the most romantic things to do on the island is to take the horse carriage ride through the **Jardin Botanico Nacional Dr. Rafael M. Moscoso**. Other excellent museums are the Museum of Fine Arts, the Museum of Natural History, and the Public Library. The Museu del Hombre Dominicano is an excellent way to absorb the main points of Caribbean history, but a working knowledge of Spanish would seriously help. On the fourth floor is a fantastic exhibit of masks and costumes that feature the various carnivals around the country.

Historical Sites

Alcazar de Colon   ★★★

Calle Las Damas, Santo Domingo, ☎ *(809)687-5361.*
Hours Open: 9:00 a.m.–5:00 p.m.

Situated on the bluffs of the Ozama River, this is the castle of Don Diego Colon, Christopher Columbus' son, who was the colony's governor in 1509. Built in 1514 and reconstructed, after decades of neglect, in 1957, the 22-room house has 40-inch-thick limestone walls and 22 rooms filled with antiques from the 16th century. General admission: $1.00.

Capilla de los Remedios

Calle Las Damas, Santo Domingo.
Hours Open: 9:00 a.m.–6:00 p.m.
The Chapel of Our Lady of Remedies was built in the 17th century in the Castilian-Romanesque style. Sunday masses begin at 6:00 a.m. Free admission.

Cathedral Santa Maria la Menor

Calle Arzobispo Merino, Santo Domingo.
Hours Open: 9:00 a.m.–4:00 p.m.
This is the first cathedral built in the Americas, begun in 1514 and completed three decades later. The Spanish Renaissance-style building has a gold coral limestone facade and houses an impressive art collection and a high altar of beaten silver. Sunday masses begin at 6:00 a.m. Free admission.

El Faro a Colon

Av Espana, Santo Domingo.
Hours Open: 9:00 a.m.–4:00 p.m.
The Columbus Memorial Lighthouse was completed in 1992 to celebrate the 500th anniversary of his "discovery" of the Dominican Republic. The impressive pyramid cross-shaped monument houses six museums on the explorer and the early days of the New World. It also reportedly contains the remains of Columbus. Several institutions around the world make similar claims. At night, the monument projects a huge cross on the clouds above that can be seen as far away as Puerto Rico.

Fort San Felipe

Puerto Plata.
This, the oldest fort in the New World, dates back to 1564. You can explore its small rooms and eight-inch-thick walls and be glad you weren't a prisoner here during Trujillo's rule. Lots of sidewalk vendors lend a tawdry air. General admission: $0.80.

National Pantheon

Calle Las Damas, Santo Domingo.
Hours Open: 10:00 a.m.–5:00 p.m.
This Spanish-American colonial-style building dates back to 1714 and was once a Jesuit monastery. A mural of Trujillo's assassination is on the ceiling above the altar, and the ashes of martyrs who tried to oust him in 1959 are preserved here. Free admission.

Santa Barbara Church

Av Mella, Santo Domingo.
Hours Open: 8:00 a.m.–12:00 p.m.

This combination church and fortress, unique to the city, was built in 1562 and is worth a gander if you're in the neighborhood. Sunday masses begin at 6:00 a.m. Free admission.

Torre del Homenaje

Paseo Presidente Belini, Santo Domingo.
Hours Open: 8:00 a.m.–7:00 p.m.
The Tower of Homage in Fort Ozama was built in 1503, and was the place where condemned prisoners awaited execution. General admission: $0.80.

Museums and Exhibits

Museo de la Familia Dominicana

Calle Padre Bellini, Santo Domingo, ☎ *(809)689-5057.*
See how the other (richer) half lived during the 19th century at this Museum of the Dominican Family. General admission: $0.80.

Museo de las Casas Reales

Calle Las Damas, Santo Domingo, ☎ *(809)682-4202.*
Hours Open: 9:00 a.m.–5:00 p.m.
Two 16th-century palaces house the Museum of the Royal Houses, which spotlights Dominican history from 1492–1821. Exhibits include antiques and artwork, Indian artifacts, relics from two galleons sunk in 1724, pre-Columbian artwork, and replicas of Columbus' ships. General admission: $1.00.

Museum of Dominican Amber

Calle Duante 61, Puerto Plata, ☎ *(809)586-2848.*
Hours Open: 9:00 a.m.–5:00 p.m.
A beautiful mansion houses exhibits on amber, the country's national stone, which is found only in the Dominican Republic, Germany and the former Soviet Union. You can buy amber pieces and jewelry at the gift shop. Guided tours are conducted in English daily. General admission: $1.20.

Plaza de la Cultura ★★★★

Av Maximo Gomez, Santo Domingo.
This large, modern complex includes a theater, the national library and museums of Dominican man, natural history and modern art—each well worth a look. Guided tours of the complex are offered in English on Tuesday and Saturday afternoons at 2:30 p.m.

Parks and Gardens

Jardin Botanico Nacional

Arroyo Hondo, Santo Domingo.
Hours Open: 10:00 a.m.–6:00 p.m.
This is the largest botanical garden in the entire Caribbean, with 445 acres of orchids, Japanese plants and trees, colorful flowers and 200 varieties of palms. You can tour it via foot, boat, train or horse-drawn carriage. General admission: $0.40.

Los Haitises National Park ★★★★★

Samana, Santo Domingo.
A natural rainforest, pristine and primitive, with mangrove swamps, lakes and caves with Indian petroglyphs.

Tours

Acuario Nacional

Av de las Americas, Santo Domingo.
Hours Open: 10:00 a.m.–6:00 p.m.

This is the Caribbean's largest aquarium, with lots of tropical fishes and dolphins swimming about. General admission: $0.80.

Parque Zoologico Nacional ★★★

Av Maximo Gomez, Santo Domingo, ☎ *(809)562-2080.*
Hours Open: 10:00 a.m.–6:00 p.m.

Lions and tigers and bears roam in relative freedom at this 320-acre national zoo. There's also an aquatic bird lake, a pond teeming with crocodiles, a snake pit and a large aviary. General admission: $1.50.

FIELDING TIP:

Dress in the Dominican Republic is strangely conservative. Avoid wearing shorts, short skirts, or halters to churches; you may not even be allowed in. Businessmen wear suits, and female tourists should dress with decorum. Wearing shorts to dinner is frowned upon, even along the beach.

Sports

Although there is a plethora of sports activities on the island, most of the island's resorts have monopolized the organized programs. Even if you aren't staying at these resorts, you can still make use of their services, although some hotels offer their all-inclusive activities only to their own guests. Tennis is omnipresent (nets almost seem to be a national symbol); if your hotel is lacking one, make a reservation at one of the big hotels. Windsurfing between June and October is delightful, particularly on Cabarete Beach. Bicycling is a passion on the island, and you can choose your destination according to your own skill and endurance—from pancake-flat beaches to steep hill and mountain roads. Small-boat sailing is limited, though most resorts can hunt up at least one ragtag vessel for rent. The golf courses on the island are among the best on the Caribbean, especially the 18-hole Peter Dye wonders at **Casa De Campo**. Two new 18-holers are being planned for the Punta Cana Beach Resort and the Bávaro Beach. The Playa Dorada hotels also boast their own 18-hole courses designed by Robert Trent Jones. If you're staying in Santo Domingo, you'll be allowed to use the Santo Domingo Country Club course on weekdays—after members have teed off.

Canodromo el Coco

Av Monumental, Santo Domingo, ☎ *(809)560-6968.*
Greyhounds race at this track about 15 minutes from Santo Domingo. Post times are Monday, Wednesday and Friday at 7:30 p.m. and Sunday at 4:00 p.m. General admission: $0.30.

Golf

Various locations, Santo Domingo.
The best place to tee off is at one of the courses at Casa de Campo in La Romana; ☎ *523-3333* for details. Over at Puerto Plata, the Robert Trent Jones, Jr. - designed links are also good; ☎ *320-4340.* Santo Domingo's only course is private, but if you're staying at one of the better hotels, they can arrange to get you in on weekdays.

Hipodromo Perla Antillana

Av San Cristobel, Santo Domingo, ☎ *(809)565-2353.*
You can wager on a horse year-round at this racetrack. Post times are Tuesday, Thursday and Saturday at 3:00 p.m. Free admission.

Watersports

Various locations, Santo Domingo.
Your hotel will probably offer all you need in the way of aqua activity. If not, try one of these: Deep-sea fishing: **Andres Boca Chica Club** *(Boca Chica,* ☎ *685-4950),* and **Casa de Campo** *(La Romana,* ☎ *682-2111).* Scuba diving: **Mundo Submarino** *(Santo Domingo,* ☎ *566-0344).* Boat rentals: **Heavens** *(Playa Dorada,* ☎ *568-5250),* and **Casa de Campo** *(La Romana,* ☎ *682-2111).* Windsurfing: **CaribBIC Windsurfing Center** *(Caberete Beach,* ☎ *635-1155).*

Where to Stay

Highest Rated Hotels in Dominican Republic

★★★★★ **Club Mediterranee**

★★★★★ **Hotel Gran Bahia**

★★★★★ **Hotel Santo Domingo**

★★★★★ **Hotel V Centenario Global**

★★★★★ **Jaragua**

★★★★ **Bavaro Beach Resort**

★★★★ **Capella Beach Resort**

★★★★ **Casa de Campo**

★★★★ **Dominican Fiesta Hotel**

★★★★ **Dorado Naco Suite Resort**

Most Exclusive Hotels in Dominican Republic

★★★★★ **Hotel V Centenario Global**	$195–$255
★★★★ **Hotel Rio Taino**	$80–$305
★★★★★ **Hotel Santo Domingo**	$150–$150
★★★★ **Bavaro Beach Resort**	$80–$220
★★★★ **Capella Beach Resort**	$120–$160

Fielding's Best Value Hotels in Dominican Republic

★★★★ **Hotel Rio Taino**	$80–$305
★★★ **Jack Tar Village**	$90–$160
★★★ **Villas Doradas Beach**	$115–$270
★★ **Talanquera**	$70–$130
★★★★ **Bavaro Beach Resort**	$80–$220

The Dominican Republic has—flat out—more available lodging rooms than any other island in the Caribbean—6000 units. Most of the luxury resorts are located on the finest beaches on the island. One enclave is centered at Punta Cana on the east coast; another at Playa Juan Dolloa, Boca Chica, and La Romana on the south coast, and Puerto Plata on the far north coast. As such, most of these hotels offer fine watersports packages which will serve your every need. More European-style hotels with first-class amenities can be found in the city of Santo Domingo, complete with tennis courts and casinos. Most hotels are high-rises and extremely modern but with a Spanish/Dominican flair. Sometimes visitors stay in several hotels to vary the landscape of their vacation, from city to beach to forest to mountain, but it's just as easy to hunker down into an all-inclusive and not miss a thing. Resorts have found a way to link their walls to each other so that finding your way home may require a map and some creative signposts. Though charming decor is not a national attribute here, the low prices more than make up for any deficiencies. Even the larger resorts and all-inclusive hotels offer programs that won't break the budget. Since few restaurants are not within walking distance of most hotels, an easy way to save time and money is to buy the MAP or all-inclusive plan, where you take your meals at the hotel. (Most visitors tend to end up doing that anyway.)

Hotels and Resorts

The trend among resorts today is toward the all-inclusive program. Always check your contract to make sure what your particular program includes, but most include all meals and sports activities. The hotels in Santo Domingo, at least 30 minutes by car from any acceptable beach for swimming, often provide excellent views of the sea. (In contrast, hotels in Playa Dorado that are not situated on a beach offer a shuttle bus service that takes you to a suitable strand.) Among the top hotels in Santo Domingo are the **Ramada Renaissance Jaragua** resort, with its splashy Vegas-type casino, luxurious bedrooms, and bathrooms that belong on a Hollywood set. **Gran Hotel Lima** is known island-wide for its excellent restaurant and the nearby casino, which can be happening if you pick the right day (depends on the traffic). Hotel Santo Domingo retains both the elegance and the tropical feel of the island, and its views of the sea from many of the rooms are stellar.

Puerto Plata

Bayside Hill Resort   **$180–$350**   ★★

Costambar, Puerto Plata, ☎ *(800)877-3648, (809)523-3333.*
Single: $180–$185. Double: $180–$350.

Leave the kids at home—only adults are welcome at this resort set on a hill, with nice views of the Caribbean. All watersports are available, and there are also two pools, a gym, tennis and a handful of bars and restaurants. 150 rooms. Credit Cards: V, MC, A.

Boca Chica Resort   **$150–$390**   ★★

Juan Bautista Vicini, Puerto Plata, ☎ *(809)523-4522.*
Single: $150. Double: $240–$390.

Located near but not on the beach, this property offers decent accommodations and resort amenities like watersports and tennis. The all-inclusive rates cover all activities, meals and drinks. 273 rooms. Credit Cards: V, MC, A.

Caribbean Village Club $120–$330   ★★

Playa Dorada, Puerto Plata, ☎ *(809)320-1111.*
Single: $120. Double: $190–$330.
What is it with swim-up bars? Does anyone really use them? In any event, you'll find another one at this all-inclusive resort with accommodations in two-story buildings in a landscaped garden setting. The health club is excellent, and there are 18 holes of golf and seven tennis courts for the active set. Guests can choose from three restaurants, and there's nightly entertainment. The beach is a good 10-minute walk, or you can catch the free shuttle. 336 rooms. Credit Cards: V, MC, A.

Club Mediterranee $110–$230   ★★★★★

Alta Gracia, Puerto Plata, ☎ *(800)258-2633, (809)687-2606.*
Single: $110–$230. Double: $110–$230.
This all-inclusive vacation village appeals to singles and fun lovers who spend beads in lieu of cash. Accommodations are in bungalows clustered above the beach; nothing fancy, but the idea is to spend lots of time out and about among your fellow guests. There's tons going on at all hours—tennis, watersports, circus workshops—and the disco is lively. Nice, if you like Club Meds. Note that the company charges a one-time $30 initiation fee plus a $50 per year membership fee, on top of the rates. 339 rooms. Credit Cards: V, A.

Flamengo Beach Resort $110–$150   ★★

Playa Dorada, Puerto Plata, ☎ *(809)320-5084.*
Single: $110. Double: $110–$150.
Spanish-style in appearance, this resort is on a nice stretch of beach and has lushly landscaped grounds and a pretty lagoon. Accommodations, scattered about the property, are spacious and nicely decorated. All the standard resort diversions, including a pool, two tennis courts, watersports and nightly entertainment. Not bad. 310 rooms. Credit Cards: MC, DC, A.

Heavens $65–$150   ★★

Playa Dorada, Puerto Plata, ☎ *(809)586-5250.*
Single: $65–$120. Double: $75–$150.
This all-inclusive resort has a casual environment and tons of activities to keep guests busy. Rooms are pleasant and all have air conditioning, but the ones closest to the disco—which hops—can be noisy. You can choose to eat at a few restaurants, and for an added fee, dine at a steak house. 150 rooms. Credit Cards: V, MC, A.

Hotel Confresi $100–$120   ★

Puerto Plata, ☎ *(809)586-2898.*
Single: $100–$120. Double: $100–$120.
Situated on a rocky promontory over the Caribbean Sea, this all-inclusive resort appeals to those who crave a casual getaway. Rooms are air-conditioned, though you probably won't be spending much time in them, as the rates include tennis, watersports, scuba and the gym. There are also two pools, and for nightlife, live shows and a disco. 200 rooms. Credit Cards: V, MC, A.

Hotel Rio Taino $80–$305 ★★★★

Playa de Arena Gorda, Puerto Plata, ☎ *(809)221-2290.*
Single: $80–$305. Double: $115–$305.

Sitting right on a lovely beach, this newer (1991) hotel has pretty tropical gardens surrounding Dominican-style white two-story bungalows; inside are pleasant, air-conditioned rooms. The usual pool, tennis courts and watersports are on hand; those looking to dance head to the disco at sister property Riu Naiboa next door. If you're torn between the two, choose this one—it's nicer all around. 360 rooms.
Credit Cards: V, MC, DC, A.

Hotel Rui Naiboa $101–$277 ★★★★

Playa de Arena Gorda, Puerto Plata, ☎ *(809)221-7515.*
Single: $101–$277. Double: $101–$277.

It's a five-minute walk to the beach—no big deal, but all the other hotels in the area are right on the sand. This property has pretty guest rooms done up in pink and gray. The lagoon-style pool has a sandy area for those who don't feel like hoofing it to the real thing. There's also tennis and a disco, and lots of activities for children, making this primarily a family resort. 372 rooms. Credit Cards: V, MC, DC, A.

Hotel Sousa $35–$65 ★★

El Batey, Puerto Plata, ☎ *(809)571-2683.*
Single: $35–$50. Double: $50–$65.

Set five minutes from the beach in a suburban neighborhood, this budget, three-story hotel has basic but clean rooms that rely on ceiling fans to keep things cool. Three apartments offer kitchenettes. There's a pool and restaurant, but not much else in the way of extras. Good value for the money, though. 39 rooms. Credit Cards: V, MC, A.

Jack Tar Village $90–$160 ★★★

Playa Dorada, Puerto Plata, ☎ *(800)999-9182, (809)586-3800.*
Single: $90–$110. Double: $150–$160.

Situated on extensive grounds, this all-inclusive resort offers accommodations in Mediterranean-style villas with one to three bedrooms. Rates include all meals and most activities, but you'll pay extra for golf. Those into organized activity love this place; you get points for joining the fun, then redeem them for prizes at the end. Corny perhaps, but no one's complaining. All the usual amenities: tennis, pool, watersports, horseback riding and 18 holes of golf. 283 rooms. Credit Cards: V, MC, DC, A.

La Esplanada $90–$225 ★★

Pedro Clisante Street, Puerto Plata, ☎ *(809)571-3333.*
Single: $90. Double: $150–$225.

Located 10 minutes from downtown Sousa, as well as the beach, this newer (1991) resort has light and airy air-conditioned guest rooms, some with minibar and balcony. There are also 12 apartments for those who like to spread out. The grounds include a few restaurants and bars, a pool and two tennis courts. Decent. 210 rooms. Credit Cards: V, MC, DC, A.

Melia Bavaro Resort $90–$225 ★★★★

Playas de Bavaro, Puerto Plata, ☎ *(800)336-3542, (809)221-2311.*

Single: $90–$200. Double: $150–$225.
This resort houses guests in split-level suites with high-quality furnishings and impressive touches or bungalows with kitchenettes and platform beds. Fountains and ponds dotted throughout the grounds lend a nice touch. A shuttle takes guests back and forth to the beach, where there is also a large free-form pool with that inescapable swim-up bar. Tennis, horseback riding and watersports keep the doldrums away. 776 rooms. Credit Cards: V, MC, DC, A.

Paradise Beach Club $110–$330 ★★
Playa Dorada, Puerto Plata, ☎ *(800)752-9236, (809)586-3663.*
Single: $110–$150. Double: $220–$330.
Another of the area's many all-inclusive resorts, Paradise is stylish, with pretty architecture lending an elegant touch. Accommodations run the gamut from standard rooms to two-bedroom suites on two levels; all are pleasant and comfortable. Guests can dine in five restaurants and toss some back in another five bars. The lushly landscaped grounds include a cute artificial river, large pool, two tennis courts, watersports and a disco. Nice. 436 rooms. Credit Cards: V, MC, A.

Playa Dorada Hotel $95–$155 ★★
Playa Dorada, Puerto Plata, ☎ *(800)423-6902.*
Single: $95–$155. Double: $95–$155.
This contemporary beach resort, located two minutes out of Puerto Plata, has nice accommodations, most with balconies. Like many of the other properties in the area, the pool has a swim-up bar, and there are three tennis courts for working up a sweat. Watersports and 18 holes of golf complete the scene. 254 rooms. Credit Cards: V, MC.

Puerto Plata Beach Resort $130–$210 ★★★
Malecon Avenue, Puerto Plata, ☎ *(809)586-4243.*
Single: $130–$175. Double: $210.
Victorian-style in design, all accommodations are in suites with limited kitchenettes. All the typical resort amenities, including a pool, three tennis courts, sauna and watersports. The tiny beach is across the road and not especially good for swimming, but the restaurants and casino are nice. Generally a good choice. 216 rooms. Credit Cards: V, MC, DC, A.

Punta Cana Beach Resort $105–$200 ★★★
Punta Cana, Puerto Plata, ☎ *(809)686-84.*
Single: $105–$195. Double: $160–$200.
Located on a long, sandy beach, this well-run resort has nicely landscaped grounds. Accommodations are in studios, suites and villas, all with air conditioning, kitchenettes and balconies. The grounds include five restaurants, eight bars, a pool, four tennis courts, watersports, horseback riding and, for kids, supervised activities. Guests are mainly from Europe. 340 rooms. Credit Cards: V, MC, DC, A.

Victoria Resort $100–$120 ★★★★
Playa Dorada, Puerto Plata, ☎ *(809)586-1200.*
Single: $100–$120. Double: $100–$120.
Surrounded by a golf course on two sides, this family-run hotel has nice country and mountain views. The large guest rooms are well furnished. The beach is a bit of a

stroll; if you're feeling lazy they'll shuttle you there, or you can hang by the pool. All watersports, tennis and even horseback riding is complimentary. Peaceful and elegant. 120 rooms. Credit Cards: V, MC, A.

Villas Doradas Beach $115–$270   ★ ★ ★

Playa Dorada, Puerto Plata, ☎ *(809)320-3000.*
Single: $115–$185. Double: $180–$270.

Situated in a lush tropical setting, all accommodations at this resort have kitchenettes. A short walk leads to the private beach, which provides plenty of shade and has 24-hour security, a nice touch. Eighteen holes of golf, three tennis courts, horseback riding and organized tours keep folks active. An inviting spot. 207 rooms. Credit Cards: V, MC, A.

Santo Domingo

Bavaro Beach Resort $80–$220   ★ ★ ★ ★

Playa Bavaro, Santo Domingo.
Single: $80–$220. Double: $105–$220.

Located on its own private beach, this sprawling resort consists of several low-rise properties. Accommodations vary from standard guest rooms to apartments; all are air-conditioned and pleasant. The facilities are varied and ample, with nine restaurants, 16 bars, a disco, live entertainment, 18 holes of golf, six tennis courts, horseback riding, watersports and organized tours. Supervised programs keep kids out of harm's way. Tight security, too. A fun and very busy complex. 1295 rooms. Credit Cards: V, MC, A.

Capella Beach Resort $120–$160   ★ ★ ★ ★

Villas del Mar Beach, Santo Domingo, ☎ *(800)228-9898, (809)562-4010.*
Single: $120–$160. Double: $120–$160.

This beachfront resort, opened in spring 1994, offers all the luxury amenities resort guests expect, including watersports, tennis, two pools and an excellent health club. Rooms are nicely done; those opting to spend extra for the "Renaissance Club" units get VIP treatment, special amenities and complimentary Continental breakfast. The 17-acre site is lushly landscaped; city center is 45 minutes away. 283 rooms. Credit Cards: V, MC, DC, A.

Casa de Campo $180–$240   ★ ★ ★ ★

La Romana Street, Santo Domingo, ☎ *(800)773-6437, (809)523-3333.*
Single: $180–$240. Double: $180–$240.

A true mega-resort, set on 7000 acres, this is the country's best resort—in fact, it's one of the best in the entire Caribbean. The resort is essentially its own town—you can even fly directly into their own airstrip—with 16 bars and restaurants, seven pools, 13 tennis courts, 36 holes of golf, beaches, etc., etc. Guests get around on electric carts. Despite its sheer size, they do everything right here. The accommodations, designed by Oscar de la Renta, are in two-story villas with plush furnishings and kitchenettes. You'll hate to leave. 750 rooms. Credit Cards: V, MC, A.

Decameron Super Club $100–$300   ★ ★

Juan Dolio Beach, Santo Domingo, ☎ *(809)526-2009.*
Single: $100–$200. Double: $200–$300.

The name makes it sound like a restaurant, but in fact this is an all-inclusive resort with one- and two-bedroom suites. There's lots happening, from horseback riding to disco dancing to tennis to bike rides to the casino, and this place appeals mostly to a young crowd. Those with refined tastes will be put off by the gaudy decor, and the service is nothing to brag about. 292 rooms. Credit Cards: V, MC, A.

Dominican Fiesta Hotel $100–$200 ★★★★

Avna Anacaona, Santo Domingo, ☎ *(809)562-8222.*
Single: $100–$200. Double: $110–$200.
Located opposite Paseo de los Indios Park, this full-service resort and convention hotel has nice guest rooms with original artwork, refrigerators and balconies. The extensive grounds include a huge pool with swim-up bar, eight tennis courts, basketball, volleyball, a gym and casino. A great spot for those seeking all the bells and whistles of a large resort, as long as they don't mind sharing the facilities with a bunch of name tag-wearing business travelers. 337 rooms. Credit Cards: V, MC, DC, A.

El Embajador Hotel $105–$115 ★★★★

Ave Sarasota 65, Santo Domingo, ☎ *(800)457-67, (809)221-2131.*
Single: $105–$115. Double: $105–$115.
One of the island's original resorts, dating back to 1956, this hotel was built as dictator Rafael Trujillo's showplace. Guest rooms are oversized and done in French provincial style; each has a large balcony with sea or city views but could use an overhaul. There are all kinds of things to keep you busy here: Olympic-size pool, four tennis courts, wonderful restaurants (especially the Chinese one), casino, even a Turkish bath. 300 rooms. Credit Cards: V, MC, DC, A.

El Portillo Beach Club $95–$145 ★

Las Terrenas Beach, Santo Domingo, ☎ *(809)688-5715.*
Single: $95. Double: $145.
Set on a lovely beach, this all-inclusive resort houses guests in cottages or standard hotel rooms. A pool, two tennis courts, watersports and horseback riding supply recreation at this fairly isolated property. Nice, if you don't mind being far from other attractions. 159 rooms. Credit Cards: V, MC, A.

Gran Hotel Lina $105–$135 ★★★

Maximo Gomez Avenue, Santo Domingo, ☎ *(800)942-2461, (809)563-5000.*
Single: $105–$110. Double: $110–$135.
This Spanish-style high-rise is stylish, though guest rooms are disappointingly basic and only some have terraces. The public spaces are grand, though, with lots of colorful modern art and elegant touches. The gym is well equipped, and there's a large pool, boutiques, a casino and several restaurants and bars. Frequented by both tourists and business travelers. 217 rooms. Credit Cards: V, MC, DC, A.

Hotel Cayacoa Beach $105–$0 ★

Samana Bay, Santo Domingo.
Single: $105. Double: $155.
Surrounded by a park and near the National Park of the Haitises, this all-inclusive resort has attractive, air-conditioned accommodations. All the typical recreational pursuits, including tennis and watersports. All meals are served in a single restaurant; two bars provide a little more variety. 70 rooms. Credit Cards: V, MC, DC, A.

Hotel Cayo Levantado   **$125–$200**   ★

Cayo Vigia, Santo Domingo, ☎ *(800)423-6902, (809)538-3426.*
Single: $125. Double: $200.
This all-inclusive hotel reopened in 1993 after extensive renovations. The grounds
are lush and green, with wonderful beaches—one that remains secluded and one
that is popular with locals and vendors. Accommodations are in standard guest
rooms or cabanas of two or three bedrooms; all have air conditioning and bright
artwork. No pool, but ample watersports on the beach. 37 rooms. Credit Cards: V, MC,
A.

Hotel Gran Bahia   **$105–$155**   ★★★★★

Samana Bay, Santo Domingo.
Single: $105–$120. Double: $130–$155.
Set on a bluff near a mountainside rain forest, this Victorian-style hotel appeals to
lovers of all ages. Wonderful views abound everywhere. Guest rooms are spacious
and comfortably done. The rocky shore below has sandy inlets for sunbathing, and
there's also a pool. A good spot for whalewatching. 96 rooms. Credit Cards: V, MC.

Hotel Hispaniola   **$80–$125**   ★★

Avenida Independencia, Santo Domingo, ☎ *(800)877-3643, (809)221-1511.*
Single: $80–$90. Double: $90–$125.
Located in the heart of the city and certainly one of its better bargains, this older
(1956) hotel has nicely appointed guest rooms with handcrafted pine furniture,
large walk-in closets and tiled balconies. There's a restaurant, bar, elegant casino
and disco on-site, and guests can use the tennis courts at sister property Hotel Santo
Domingo. The rates make this one worth a look. 165 rooms. Credit Cards: V, MC, A.

Hotel Santo Domingo   **$150–$150**   ★★★★★

Av Independencia, Santa Domingo, ☎ *(809)221-1511.*
Single: $150. Double: $150.
This elegant resort is appreciated especially by business travelers—the true jet set
can land right on their helipad and then check in. Accommodations are beautifully
done with handsome furnishings, large modern baths, and good views. Three tennis
courts and a pool offer recreational diversion. Located some 15 minutes from
downtown, tourists may be happier in the historic district, but either way, this place
is a winner. 220 rooms. Credit Cards: V, MC, DC, A.

Hotel V Centenario Global   **$195–$255**   ★★★★★

Avenue George Washington, Santo Domingo, ☎ *(800)221-0000, (809)221- 0.*
Single: $195–$255. Double: $210–$255.
This high-rise, opened in 1992, has spacious guestrooms with marble accents, orig-
inal art and minibars; only the suites, alas, have balconies. Facilities include four res-
taurants, four bars, a casino, pool, tennis, squash, racquetball and a health club.
Locals like the cellar tapas bar; you will too. 200 rooms. Credit Cards: V, MC, DC, A.

Jaragua   **$80–$125**   ★★★★★

367 George Washington Avenue, Santo Domingo, ☎ *(800)327-0200, (809)221-2222.*
Single: $80–$125. Double: $90–$125.
This elaborate resort complex, situated on 14 garden acres facing the Caribbean, is
a Ramada Renaissance property. The glittering resort includes a large and happen-

ing casino, a large pool, four tennis courts and very nice guest rooms with all kinds of amenities, like three phones. Six restaurants and five bars give you lots of evening options, and the upscale spa and health club will help you burn it back off. Resort lovers need look no further. 310 rooms. Credit Cards: V, MC, A.

Metro Hotel & Marina $75–$115 ★★

Juan Dolio Beach, Santo Domingo, ☎ *(809)526-2811.*
Single: $75–$115. Double: $75–$115.
Situated on a nice, palm-studded beach, this modern hotel houses guests in adequate, if unexciting, standard rooms. Two restaurants and two bars keep people sated, and the activities range from watersports to a lively disco. There's also two pools and a pair of tennis courts. 180 rooms. Credit Cards: V, MC, DC, A.

Naco Hotel and Casino $40–$80 ★

Av Tiradentes 22, Santo Domingo, ☎ *(809)562-3100.*
Single: $40–$80. Double: $45–$80.
Near a large shopping mall in a mixed commercial and residential area, this budget property is 10 minutes from downtown. Rooms are clean and comfortable and come with kitchenettes. Reflecting the rates, the casino draws mainly low-rollers. The pool, set in a pleasant garden, is small. Nothing too exciting, but rates are extremely reasonable. 107 rooms. Credit Cards: V, MC, DC, A.

Punta Goleta Beach Resort $85–$100 ★★

Punta Goleta, Santo Domingo, ☎ *(809)571- 700.*
Single: $85–$90. Double: $85–$100.
Set on 100 acres across the street from a beach known for good windsurfing, this resort has large rooms with air conditioning and Victorian-style balconies. All the typical amenities, including a pool and tennis, at this all-inclusive resort, as well as three restaurants and four bars to keep things interesting. 130 rooms. Credit Cards: V, MC, DC, A.

Sand Castle Beach Resort $80–$125 ★★★★

Puerto Chiquito, Santo Domingo, ☎ *(809)571-2420.*
Single: $80–$120. Double: $85–$125.
Set on a bluff between the ocean and a saltwater pond, this isolated spot offers dramatic views and prettily furnished rooms; 80 suites offer up kitchenettes and very large baths as well. Everything is really nicely done here, with lots of marble, stained glass and finished stone. The beach below, reached via a stairway, is decent. Five restaurants, another five bars, two tennis courts and two pools keep folks busy. 240 rooms. Credit Cards: V, MC, DC, A.

Sheraton Santo Domingo $110–$130 ★★★★

Av George Washington, Santo Domingo, ☎ *(800)325-3535, (809)221-6666.*
Single: $110–$130. Double: $120–$130.
This high-rise, overlooking the sea, offers stylish rooms with the typical extras. A casino, two restaurants, disco and a few bars provide nightlife. By day, there's a large pool and two tennis courts. Nice, but not terribly noteworthy. 258 rooms. Credit Cards: V, MC, DC, A.

Talanquera $70–$130   ★★

Juan Dolio Beach, Santo Domingo, ☎ (809)541-1166.
Single: $70–$130. Double: $70–$130.
The well-landscaped grounds here lead to a nice beach, where all the usual watersports take place. There are also three pools and atypical activities like shooting and
archery. Accommodations run the gamut from standard rooms to junior suites in
cabanas; only some have balconies. Four bars and a disco keep things interesting
once the sun goes down. 250 rooms. Credit Cards: V, MC, A.

Tropics Club $115–$165   ★★

Juan Dolio Beach, Santo Domingo, ☎ (809)529-8531.
Single: $115–$165. Double: $145–$165.
This small resort offers all-inclusive packages, but lacks many of the facilities you'll
find at its larger competitors. Rooms are air-conditioned, and those wishing to cook
in can rent a suite with kitchen. There's the standard handful of restaurants and
bars, but you'll have to indulge in watersports and gambling next door at the
Decameron Super Club. 77 rooms. Credit Cards: A.

Yaroa Hotel $45–$55   ★

El Batey, Santo Domingo, ☎ (809)571-2651.
Single: $45–$55. Double: $45–$55.
Located on a quiet street five minutes from the beach, the comfortable hotel is in a
U shape surrounding a small pool. Guest rooms are nicely appointed, with air con-
ditioning and screened balconies. Pleasant. 24 rooms. Credit Cards: V, MC, A.

Apartments and Condominiums

In general, few of the self-catering units available in the Dominican Republic are anything to write home about, except for the luxury villas at Casa de Campo. If you don't
speak good English, you will have a real adventure trying to communicate your needs to
the management. Boca Chica and Juan Dolio boast more modern apartments; kitchens
are usually fully furnished. For units in the cityscape, contact **ARAH** (*194 Avenida 27 de
Febrero, Santo Domingo, R.D.* Another source is the **Villa, Condo and Apartment Rental
Service**, Box 30076, Pedro Henriques Urena 37, Santo Domingo, R.D., ☎ (809) 686-
0608.

Puerto Plata

Dorado Naco Suite Resort $80–$145   ★★★★

Playa Dorada, Puerto Plata, ☎ (800)322-2388, (809)586-2019.
Single: $80–$145. Double: $80–$145.
All accommodations are in one- and two-bedroom suites with full kitchens and bal-
conies at this Spanish Caribbean-style hotel. The beach is a short stroll away.
There's live entertainment nightly around the pool and two restaurants and three
bars for after-dark diversions. Kids are kept occupied in supervised programs year-
round. Guests can also use the facilities at the adjacent Playa Naco. 150 rooms.
Credit Cards: V, MC, DC, A.

Plaza Nico Hotel $85–$85   ★

Plaza Nico Mall, Puerto Plata, ☎ (809)541-6226.
Single: $85. Double: $85.

Every room at this 12-story twin tower is a suite with kitchenette. Handy, but could use a redo. There's a disco, fitness center and cafe on-site, as well as lots of shopping and eating options in the adjacent shopping center, but this spot doesn't offer much of a resort feel for tourists. Decent for business travelers, though. 220 rooms. Credit Cards: CB, V, MC, DC, A.

Inns

Inns have not found their identity in the Dominican Republic, but the following property comes closest to that old congenial feel, tucked into the historical section of the old city.

Low Cost Lodging

In a country where hotel rates start low (comparatively for the Caribbean), the cheapest rooms are not going to be impressive, or even acceptable according to some Western standards of cleanliness. However, deals can be found, especially among hotels geared to Dominican businessmen and Dominican tourists, which are always lower than the European and American-owned hotels and resorts. Do figure out beforehand if you are really saving any money, since you will no doubt have to rent a car to get around. Also be careful you have not stumbled upon a front for a brothel or pay-by-the-hour-room-rate.

Puerto Plata

Hotel Montemar　　　　　　$45–$120　　　　　　★★

Av Hermanas Mirabel, Puerto Plata, ☎ *(809)586-2800.*
Single: $45. Double: $90–$120.
This is the nation's hotel-training school, so you can be assured of perky, attentive service. Guest rooms are decent but lack balconies. There's no beach at this in-town spot, but guests can use the one at sister property Villas Doradas in Playa Dorada. Two tennis courts and a pool help make up for the off-sea location. Good value. 95 rooms. Credit Cards: V, MC, A.

Santo Domingo

Continental Hotel　　　　　　$60–$65　　　　　　★★

Maximo Gomex 16, Santo Domingo, ☎ *(809)689-1151.*
Single: $60–$65. Double: $65.
Located opposite the Palace of Fine Arts, this modern hotel is a block from the beach. Guest rooms are adequate; don't bother upgrading to a "deluxe" unless you really want that refrigerator. There's a disco, restaurant and small pool, but not much else to justify the rates. You can do better elsewhere in the same price range. 100 rooms. Credit Cards: V, MC, DC, A.

El Napolitano　　　　　　$50–$75　　　　　　★

51 George Washington Avenue, Santo Domingo, ☎ *(809)687-1131.*
Single: $50. Double: $55–$75.
It's bare bones here, but the rates appeal to those on a tight budget. Rooms are air-conditioned and have sea views. There's a pool and restaurant, but not much else, though plenty to do within an easy walk. This hotel does big business with Dominicans, and the atmosphere can be lively. 73 rooms. Credit Cards: V, MC, DC, A.

Hostal Nicolas de Ovando　　　　　　$45–$75　　　　　　★

53 Calle las Damas, Santo Domingo.

Single: $45–$75. Double: $45–$75.

Originally the palace of the first Spanish governor, dating from the 16th century, this hotel has old-fashioned, Spanish-style guest rooms with antique or reproduction furniture but little else of note. One courtyard houses a pool; the other three have patios and fountains. A restaurant and two bars round out the facilities. History buffs will like it here, but it has a way to go to reach its true potential. 107 rooms. Credit Cards: V, MC, DC, A.

San Geronimo Hotel   **$35–$40**   ★

1067 Av Independencia, Santo Domingo, ☎ *(809)533-1000.*
Single: $35. Double: $40.

Located near the sea and five minutes from downtown, this budget choice has small, air-conditioned rooms, some with kitchenettes. There's a restaurant, two bars, a pool and the inescapable casino. 72 rooms. Credit Cards: V, MC, DC, A.

South Coast Resorts

The majority of the beach resorts on the southern coast are located along a strip that includes Boca Chica, near the Las Américas International Airport, Playa Juan Dolio, a little further east on the south coast, and La Romana, even further east. Most of these resorts have all-inclusive plans and a full line of watersports activities. **Hamaca Beach Hotel**, only three years old, is the hub of Euro trash and jetsetters who adore the health club and sauna as well as the wonderfully air-conditioned bedrooms. **Don Juan Resort** is located near a wonderful beach with talcum-smooth sand that can now be truly appreciated since the hawking vendors have been evicted.

Playa Juan Dolio

About twenty minutes east of Boca Chica is the beach of Juan Dolio—dazzling white. Euro babes and dudes have found their way to this strand, joining the well-to-do Dominicans who openly ogle the gal (and gus sometimes!). You won't have any trouble finding a place to stay here—there are many. Some of the best include the **Ramada Capella Beach** resort, a fully modern low-rise with two pools and two tennis courts and spa; **Talanquera**, with three pools (who needs so many with the beach?) as well as horseback riding facilities; and **Decameron Resort**, whose casino and disco attracts a wild scene at night.

Where to Eat

★★★★★	Highest Rated Restaurants in Dominican Republic	
★★★★★	Casa del Rio	
★★★★★	De Armando	
★★★★★	Lina Restaurant	
★★★★	La Bahia	
★★★★	Restaurant Montparnasse	
★★★	El Alcazar	
★★★	El Conuco	
★★★	Pez Dorado	

	Most Exclusive Restaurants in Dominican Republic	
★★★	Pez Dorado	$18–$30
★★★	El Alcazar	$10–$25
★★★★	Restaurant Montparnasse	$11–$20

	Fielding's Best Value Restaurants in Dominican Republic	
★★	Reina de Espana	$8–$20
★★	Cafe del Sol	$8–$10
★★★★★	Lina Restaurant	$15–$30
★★★★★	De Armando	$10–$22
★★★	El Conuco	$8–$15

Dining out is a special event in the Dominican Republic—best done in elegant clothes (at the very least, don't go out dressed like a beach bum, unless you're on the beach); the rule is smart casual at lunch and dressier at dinner). The normal local time for dinner (Spanish style) is about nine or ten o'clock, but most American-style visitors cave in much earlier; luckily, restaurants usually open around 6:00 p.m.(as such, it will be easier to get a table in a popular restaurant if you eat early). Local dishes are spiked with Latin zest, especially the omnipresent paella, which is uniformly excellent. *Sancocho* is one of the most filling dishes, a thick stew made from five to seven different meats; if you eat it for lunch, you may be inclined to take a very long siesta. *Arroz con pollo* (chicken with rice) is a staple on every menu. *Plátanos*, or plantains, are cooked in a million different ways. A light delicious lunch might be a *tortilla de jamón* (spicy ham omelet). One of the most favored desserts is a hearty cornmeal custard called *majarete*. For to-die-for snacks that will ruin your diet and your cholesterol for many weeks, try *chicharrones* (fried pork rinds) or the less dangerous *galletas* (flat, biscuit crackers). The local beers are Bohemia, Quisqueya, and Presidente, and the local rums are Brugal and Bermúdez. It's always a Dominican delight to salute the end of a good meal with a dark brown aged rum over ice, called *añejo*.

Among the resort hotels, the best chefs are at Dominican Fiesta (La Casa), the Sheraton (Antoine) and Embajador (Manhattan Grill). After 10 p.m. is when the nightowls, dressed to kill, turn out for the post-supper stroll down the Malecón. Another delicious tidbit is the *bollito de yucca*, a postage-stamp-sized hors d'oeuvre made of ground yucca root and cheese—much tastier than it sounds. If you get homesick for American-style fixings, head for the hotel coffeeshops, where a steak sandwich, hamburger, or simple fruit salad will soothe the aching palate. Remember to peel and/or wash any fruit you may pick up in the local markets.

Puerto Plata

De Armando $$$ ★ ★ ★ ★ ★

Avenida Antera Mota 23, Puerto Plata, ☎ *(809) 586-3418.*
International cuisine. Specialties: Fresh fish, lamb in wine sauce.
Lunch: 11:00 a.m.–3:00 p.m., entrees $10–$22.
Dinner: 3:00 p.m.–11:00 p.m., entrees $10–$22.

The pride of North Coast dining is this top-rated restaurant in a Victorian building, where guests are served international cuisine serenaded by a guitar and string trio. Specialties have included fresh sea bass prepared with shellfish or mushroom sauces, lamb marinated in red wine, steaks and lobster. The menu also features Dominican specialties like lentils and rice and green plantains. Reservations recommended.
Credit Cards: V, MC, DC, A.

Roma II $$ ★ ★

Calle Beller, Puerto Plata, ☎ *(809) 586-3904.*
International cuisine. Specialties: Pizza, octopus.
Lunch: 11:00 a.m.–2:00 p.m., entrees $6–$15.
Dinner: 2:00 p.m.–12:00 p.m., entrees $6–$15.

This plain but comfortably air-conditioned bistro with charming service serves an excellent array of pizzas, plain or fancy—cheese or perhaps shrimp, made on dough baked fresh daily. More challenging appetites might go for the octopus, a specialty here, served with a vinaigrette sauce, or with fresh tomatoes, or on pasta. Steaks and filets are also on the menu. Credit Cards: V, MC, A.

Santo Domingo

Cafe del Sol $ ★★

Altos de Chavon Village, Altos de Chavon, ☎ *(809) 523-3333.*
Italian cuisine.
Lunch: 11:00 a.m.–4:00 p.m., entrees $8–$10.
Dinner: 6:00 p.m.–11:00 p.m., entrees $8–$10.
This pretty rooftop cafe in the artists' colony of Altos de Chavon is a perfect stop for a light repast of pizza or salad. Credit Cards: V, MC, A.

Caribae $$$ ★★

Camino Libre 70, Sosua,
International cuisine.
Dinner: entrees $20–$30.
Pick your own lobster or shrimp from myriad tanks in this unpretentious little restaurant in the gorgeous beach resort town of Sosua. The crustaceans you choose are all raised at the restaurant's private shrimp farm nearby. For accompaniment, a plate of organic vegetables from the same farm round out a healthy meal. Credit Cards: V, MC.

Casa del Rio $$$ ★★★★★

Altos de Chavon Village, Altos de Chavon, ☎ *(809) 523-3333.*
French cuisine.
Lunch: 11:00 a.m.– 4:00 p.m., entrees $14.
Dinner: 6:30 p.m.–11:00 p.m., entrees $18–$26.
Possibly the most expensive restaurant in the Dominican Republic (and the choicest), Casa del Rio is just the place for resort dwellers at the nearby Casa de Campo to go for a night on the town, but many fans have no compunction about driving the 100 miles from Santo Domingo to eat here. Any why not—it's hard to resist dining in a tower room glowing with candlelight, overlooking the Chavon River. French chef Philippe Mongereau likes a challenge, and constantly experiments with Asian and Caribbean spices to dress up shellfish, meats and poultry. Reservations required. Credit Cards: V, MC, A.

Che Bandoneon $$$ ★★

El Conde, ☎ *(809) 687-0023.*
Latin American cuisine. Specialties: Argentinian churrasco.
Dinner: 6:00 p.m.–12:00 p.m., entrees $15–$30.
Tango to this Argentinian charmer that nests in a restored home in the Old City area of Santo Domingo. Specialties include huge, choice cuts of ranch-style beef fillets or steaks. Seating is indoors or out on a pretty terrace, serenaded by troubadours playing the bandoneon (Argentinian accordion) for you. Desserts are rich and very French. Reservations recommended. Credit Cards: V, MC.

El Alcazar $$$ ★★★

Avenida Independencia, ☎ *(809) 221-1511.*
International cuisine.
Lunch: 12:00 a.m.–3:00 p.m., prix fixe $9.
Dinner: 6:00 p.m.– 11:00 p.m., entrees $10–$25.

The noonday lunch buffet at the El Alcazar is an exotic and very reasonable dining adventure, with a bevy of international dishes and succulent seafood items available daily. World-renowned couturier (and local hero) Oscar de la Renta designed the interiors of the chic hotel-restaurant on a grand North African theme, with gorgeous fabrics, shells and mirrors for accents. Associated Hotel: Hotel Santo Domingo. Reservations recommended. Credit Cards: V, MC, DC, A.

El Conuco $$ ★★★

Calle Casimiro de Moya, ☎ *(809) 686-0129.*
Latin American cuisine. Specialties: Sancocho, chicharrones de pollo.
Lunch: 11:00 a.m.– 4:00 p.m., entrees $8–$15.
Dinner: 6:00 p.m.– 11:00 p.m., entrees $8–$15.
This comically hokey but fun restaurant is situated in an ersatz thatched-roof house, where hanging artifacts from former diners provide a running commentary along with the hearty country cooking (*conuco*). Fill up on rice and kidney beans, stews, cod and crunchy fried chicken bits while hammy waiters turn into musicians and/or dancers at the drop of a sombrero. Reservations recommended. Credit Cards: V, MC.

Fonda La Aterazana $$ ★★

Calle Aterazana 5, ☎ *(809) 689-2900.*
Latin American cuisine. Specialties: Chicharrones de pollo.
Lunch: 10:00 a.m.–4:00 p.m., entrees $5–$20.
Dinner: 4:00 p.m.–1:00 a.m., entrees $5–$20.
Feel like a Spanish grandee in this whitewashed-stone building in the Aterazana section of the Colonial Zone, sharing seafood or crunchy fried Dominican chicken strips (more delicious than it sounds) with someone special. This bright and festive spot is often jumping with musical groups and dancers performing to a merengue beat. Closed: Sun. Credit Cards: V, MC, DC, A.

Jade Garden $$$ ★★

Avenida Sarasota 65, ☎ *(809) 221-2131.*
Chinese cuisine. Specialties: Peking chicken and duck.
Lunch: 12:00 a.m.–3:00 p.m., entrees $12–$22.
Dinner: 7:30 p.m.–11:30 p.m., entrees $12–$30.
Considered one of the best Chinese restaurants in town, Jade Garden boasts Hong-Kong trained chefs who prepare Peking duck or chicken in a beautifully decorated room in the imposing Hotel Embajador. Associated Hotel: Hotel Embajador. Reservations recommended. Credit Cards: V, MC, DC, A.

La Bahia $$$ ★★★★

Avenida George Washington, ☎ *(809) 682-4022.*
Seafood cuisine. Specialties: Kingfish in coconut sauce, conch.
Lunch: 9:00 a.m.–2:30 p.m., entrees $10–$18.
Dinner: 2:30 p.m.–11:30 p.m., entrees $12–$20.
Completely unpretentious and a very popular local hangout, La Bahia sits quietly on Santo Domingo's wide seafront and park, surrounded by towering luxury hotels and convivial cafes. It's very difficult to choose from a huge variety of luscious sea creatures served here, but you can't go wrong with a fish and shellfish soup loaded with shrimp and lobster, or kingfish with a tropical coconut sauce. The prices are so reasonable for what you're served, it's almost beyond belief. Credit Cards: V, MC, A.

Lago Grill   **$$**   ★★

Casa de Campo, La Romana, ☎ *(809) 523-3333.*
American cuisine.
Lunch: 12:00 a.m.–4:00 p.m., entrees $5–$15.

Terrific breakfasts and lunches are served at this view spot on the golf course of the Casa de Campo resort. Happily for the many top stateside executives who stay here, they (and you) can have cooked-to-order eggs and omelets any style or an array of freshly squeezed juices from an exotic fruit bar. Dominican and Caribbean entrees, delicious burgers and sandwiches, and a copious salad bar are top choices for lunch. Associated Hotel: Casa de Campo Resort. Credit Cards: V, MC, DC, A.

Lina Restaurant   **$$$**   ★★★★★

Avenida Maximo Gomez, ☎ *(809) 685-5000.*
Spanish cuisine. Specialties: Zarzuela de mariscos, paella.
Lunch: 11:00 a.m.–4:30 p.m., entrees $15–$24.
Dinner: 6:00 p.m.–12:00 p.m., entrees $15–$30.

Before the Dominican Republic became a popular tourist destination, Chef Lina Aguado was already a legend; after serving as personal chef to long-reigning president Rafael Trujillo, she opened a small eatery which grew like Topsy into a hotel/restaurant that bears her name. Today, others with equal skill and passion have inherited the great cucinera's recipes for *paella valenciana* or *cazuela de mariscos* with Pernod, and interpret them with aplomb. Associated Hotel: Gran Hotel Lina. Reservations required. Credit Cards: V, MC, DC, A.

Meson de la Cava   **$$$**   ★★

Avenida Mirador del Sur, ☎ *(809) 533-2818.*
International cuisine.
Lunch: 11:00 a.m.–3:30 p.m., entrees $25–$30.
Dinner: 6:00 p.m.–12:00 p.m., entrees $25–$40.

In order to eat here, diners must descend to a cavern way below ground (some 50 feet), reached via a scary staircase. What's down under is some rollicking entertainment from a live band (contemporary and merengue) and simply prepared, unsurprising, but delicious food. Some people might find this sort of thing silly, but kudos must be given to whomever thought up this clever idea, which seems to be working. Reserve way in advance, and dress fashionably. Reservations required. Credit Cards: V, MC, DC, A.

Neptuno's Club   **$$$**   ★★

Boca Chica Beach, Boca Chica, ☎ *(809) 523-4703.*
Seafood cuisine.
Lunch: 9:00 a.m.–2:00 p.m., entrees $10–$20.
Dinner: 2:00 p.m.–10:00 p.m., entrees $10–$25.

Calm and warm waters and a short (about 45 minute) drive from the capital make Boca Chica Beach, where this little hut is located, popular with daytrippers. Neptuno's has a good reputation for fish stews and sauteed kingfish, although international meals are served as well. Closed: Mon. Reservations recommended. Credit Cards: V, MC.

Pez Dorado   **$$$**   ★★★

43 Calle el Sol, Santiago Caballeros, ☎ *(809) 582-2518.*

Chinese cuisine. Specialties: Chinese seafood.
Lunch: 11:00 a.m.– 3:00 p.m., entrees $18–$30.
Dinner: 6:00 p.m.– 11:30 p.m., entrees $18–$30.

If you find yourself visiting the historical city of Santiago de los Caballeros, about two hours away from Santo Domingo, this restaurant serving seafood Chinese-style in a posh, comfortable room is one of the best dining choices in town. Perhaps afterwards, you can wend your way to a local dance club—after all, this is the birthplace of the merengue. Reservations recommended. Credit Cards: V, MC.

Reina de Espana $$ ★★

Avenida Cervantes 103, ☎ *(809) 685-2588.*
Spanish cuisine.
Lunch: 12:00 a.m.– 4:00 p.m., entrees $8–$20.
Dinner: 4:00 p.m.–11:00 p.m., entrees $8–$20.

In a city where Spanish food is treated with respect, Reina de Espana, located in a restored home not far from the sea, manages to present more than just the average paella or seafood stew for discriminating diners. The menu traverses each region of Spain, with roast quail or suckling pig prepared as specials from time to time. But the old favorites like gazpacho are all represented and rarely disappoint. Reservations required. Credit Cards: V, MC, A.

Restaurant Montparnasse $$$ ★★★★

Avenida Lope de Vega 24, ☎ *(809) 562-4141.*
Latin American cuisine.
Lunch: 12:00 a.m.–2:00 p.m., entrees $5–$18.
Dinner: 2:00 p.m.–12:00 p.m., entrees $11–$20.

Prominent local folk like to eat here, especially for lunch, making this creative Franco-Caribbean bistro a good place to observe them. But those not inclined to eavesdropping or voyeurism will still enjoy the unusual combinations of native vegetables like pumpkin and plantain pureed into creamy bisques or a vichyssoise. Decadent desserts like chocolate souffle are served all day and night—in true Dominican fashion, the place stays open late. Reservations recommended. Credit Cards: V, MC, DC, A.

Vesuvio I $$ ★★

Avenida G. Washington, ☎ *(809) 221-3333.*
Italian cuisine.
Lunch: 11:00 a.m.–2:00 p.m., entrees $8–$18.
Dinner: 2:00 p.m.–12:00 p.m., entrees $8–$20.

The Bonarelli family from Naples has been running this boisterous family restaurant on the Malecon since the 1950s. As they are not content to rest on past laurels, every visit brings a new specialty or improvements on old favorites. The voluminous menu features seafood and plenty of it, including crayfish with garlic, although veal scaloppine with fresh herbs is worth noting. Decor is contemporary, with plenty of colorful marine life painted on the walls. Credit Cards: V, MC, DC, A.

Where to Shop

Bargaining is as second nature as breathing in the Dominican Republic. If you don't bargain, you aren't respected; shopkeepers enjoy the cat-and-mouse game and even look forward to it. Don't disappoint them. At the same time, don't give in to a vendor's first, second, or third price—they can be hard-nosed because they know your time is precious and your wallet is on vacation. Before you go, bone up on a few choice phrases in Spanish, including the well-understood "Non!"

Everyone comes to the Dominican Republic hot on the trail of jewelry made from amber. The island boasts one of the world's largest deposits, and the prices for this translucent, semiprecious stone will make your jaw drop. (Don't succumb to the tourist disease called "souvenir overkill" when you see too many displays of them; they are lovely and will look special by the time you get your piece home.) A type of petrified resin taken from coniferous forests that disappeared from the Earth over 50 million years ago, amber comes in many colors ranging from pale lemon to dark brown. Best buys are those which have a tiny insect or small leaves embedded inside. (Remember that childhood novel *Bug in Amber*?)

Santo Domingo's main covered market is called **El Mercado Modelo**. Located in the Colonial Zone bordering Calle Mella, it has lots of shops, eateries, bars, and boutiques located in the restored buildings of La Ataranza, across from the Alcázar. It's lovely to walk down the Calle El Conde, Santo Domingo's main shopping street in the Colonial Zone, now sectioned off for pedestrians only. Some of the best shops are here are far north of the Colonial Zone between Calle Mella and Av. Las Américas. Fine art galleries are located in the **Altos de Chavón**, with stores grouped around the main square. The **Tourist Bazaar** *(Calle Duarte 61)* in Puerto Plata boasts seven showrooms in a finely renovated old mansion. For good souvenirs and local jewelry, try **Calle Beller** (in the Plaza Shopping Center *at Calle Duarte and Av. 30 de Marzo.*) Do avoid buying tortoise shell since a U.S. customs official will confiscate it if he finds it in your bag.

Fine art galleries are located in the Altos de Chavón, with stores grouped around the main square. Among the best names are **Arawak Gallery**, and **Novo Atarazana**.Other great home-crafted buys are hand-carved wood rocking chairs; they are sold unassembled and boxed for transport, so make sure you are handy with a screw. For other wood crafts, check out the stalls at the El Mercado Modelo. Macrame, baskets and pottery figurines are all reminiscent of the island's crafts.

Dominican Republic Directory

ARRIVAL AND DEPARTURE

Travelers to the Dominican Republic use two major international airports: Las Américas International Airport, about 20 miles outside Santo Domingo, and La Unión International Airport, about 25 miles east of Puérto Plata on the north coast. (Both airports have been undergoing extensive renovation; a major fire in the old terminal at Las Americas has caused congestion in a new terminal that was meant to solve the problem.) American Airlines offers the most flights to the island, with nonstops from New York to Santo Domingo. American, Continental, and Dominica also fly nonstop from New York to Puerto Plata. Continental Airlines offers connecting service to both Santo Domingo and Puerto Plata from San Juan, Puerto Rico; and American Eagle has two flights a day from San Juan to La Romana.

For interisland service, ALM flies from Santo Domingo to St. Maarten and Curacao. There is also limited domestic service available from La Herrera Airport in Santo Domingo to smaller airfields in La Romana, Samana and Santiago.

Do be cautious in both airports with regard to your luggage and personal valuables. Luggage theft is a common occurrence, and the general confusion can often lead to "lost" luggage. Try to carry your own luggage as you will be royally hassled for service by porters. The island is famous for buscones, who offer you assistance and then disappear with your belongings. If you have arranged for transport by your hotel, the representative should be awaiting you in the immigration hall.

CLIMATE

The climate is subtropical; with an average annual temperature of 80 degrees in Santo Domingo, temperatures are generally between 66 degrees F and 88 degrees F. The west and southwest of the country are arid. Hispaniola lis in the path of tropical cyclones.

DOCUMENTS

In order to purchase a $10 tourist card, good for 90 days, visitors must present a valid passport or other proof of citizenship (birth certificate, voter's registration card, with an official photo ID such as driver's license). Cards may be purchased upon arrival, or through the consulate.

ELECTRICITY

Current is 100 volts, 60 cycles, as in the United States.

GETTING AROUND

Taxis are available at the airport, and the 25-minute ride into Santo Domingo averages about U.S.$20. There is no bus service, but fellow travelers are usually open to sharing a taxi.

Buses in Santo Domingo are called *públicos*, small blue-and-white or blue-and-red cars that run regular routes, stopping to let passengers on and off. The fare is two pesos. There are also *conchos* or *coléctivos* (privately owned buses) whose drivers tool around the major thoroughfares, leaning out the window and trying to seduce passengers onboard. (For this inconvenience you get to pay a peso less.) Privately owned air-conditioned buses make regular runs to Santiago, Puerto Plata and other destinations. Avoid night travel because the country is rife with potholes. Reservations can be made by calling **Metro Buses** *(Av. Winston Churchill;* ☎ *(809) 586-6063* in Puerto Plata).

Cars can be rented in the airports and at many hotels. The top names are **Budget** ☎ *(809) 562-6812*; and **Hertz** ☎ *(809) 688-2277*. Driving is on the right side of the street, but drivers here are maniacs, often driving down the middle of the road and passing dangerously whenever they feel like it. They are nice enough, however, to flash their light on when they know the highway patrol is lurking about—the 50 m.p.h. (80 kph) limit is strictly enforced. (Police have been known to stop drivers on the pretext of some violation and insinuate the need for a bribe. If you must drive around the unilluminated mountain roads at night, drive with utmost caution since many cars do not have headlights or taillights, cows stand in the middle of the road, and bicycles are rarely well lit. Gas stations are few and far between.

Motorbikes, called *motoconchos*, are a popular and inexpensive way to tool around the island, especially in such places as Puerto Plata, Sasúa, and Jarabacoa. Bikes can be flagged down in road and town.

LANGUAGE

The official language is Spanish, so do as much as you can to bone up on Spanish before you go. Officially, nearly everyone involved in tourism speaks English, but it is sometimes a quizzical version and many people have trouble understanding English. Waitresses in coffeeshops may simply drop their jaws when you speak to them in English. In the outlying areas, it is absolutely necessary to speak Spanish. Do bring along a phrase book and keep it handy in your purse.

MEDICAL EMERGENCIES

The island has numerous hospitals and clinics; that is not say that you should pursue any medical attention with enthusiasm. The biggest and most revered is José Maria Cabral y Baez; ☎ *(809) 583-4311* on Central, near the church in the town of Santiago. You'll find a number of American medical students working here since the national medical school uses the facilities. Hospitals in Santiago tend to be crowded and harassed. Hospital Marion in Santo Domingo is known for its cardio-vascular center. Do bring your Spanish phrase book, particularly if you get stuck in a hospital for any length of time. Do your best to fly home to the States. Remember to bring any medications you need from home, with a copy of the prescription and a letter from your doctor that you have been medically directed to take them.

MONEY

Official currency is the Dominican peso. Most hotels and shops welcome American dollars as well as major credit cards and traveler's checks. Try to spend your pesos rather than having to exchange them back into dollars before you leave.

TELEPHONE

The country code is *809*. To call the Dominican Republic from the United States, dial *011* (international access), the country code *(809)* and the local number. Connections are generally made with ease and are clear. Calling from the Dominican Republic can become a head-ache—fast. There is a direct-dial system, but you should feel extraordinarily blessed to have it work right. Try dialing 1, then the area code, followed by the number.

TIME

Atlantic Standard Time year round.

TIPPING

Hotels and restaurants add a whopping 21 percent government tax (which includes a 10 percent service charge) to all bills. It is customary to leave a dollar per day for the maid; if you balk, just imagine her income status in such a poor country. In restaurants and nightclubs, an extra 5–10 percent above the service charge included on the bill will be greatly appreciated by the waiters and waitresses. Taxi drivers expect a 10 percent tip; tip more if you arrive alive. Skycaps and hotel porters expect at least five pesos per bag.

TOURIST INFORMATION

The **Dominican Tourist Information Center** is located at the corner of *Avs. México an d30 de Marzo;* ☎ *221-4660* or *00-752-1151.* There are also information booths in Santiago (City Hall Av. Duarte; ☎ *582-5885* and in Puerto Plata Av. Hermanas Mirabel ☎ *586-3676.* You can also find a booth at the airport open daily. In the U.S. call ☎ *(212) 768-2481.*

WHEN TO GO

Merengue Week explodes in late July, the island's biggest rum-filled festival dedicated to the national dance. Carnival is held on February 27.

DOMINICAN REPUBLIC HOTELS		RMS	RATES	PHONE	FAX

Puerto Plata

★★★★★	Club Mediterranee	339	$110–$230	(800) 258-2633	
★★★★	Dorado Naco Suite Resort	150	$80–$145	(800) 322-2388	
★★★★	Hotel Rio Taino	360	$80–$305	(809) 221-2290	(809) 685-9537
★★★★	Hotel Rui Naiboa	372	$101–$277	(809) 221-7515	(809) 658-6806
★★★★	Melia Bavaro Resort	776	$90–$225	(800) 336-3542	(809) 686-5427
★★★★	Victoria Resort	120	$100–$120	(809) 586-1200	(809) 320-4862
★★★	Jack Tar Village	283	$90–$160	(800) 999-9182	(809) 809-4161
★★★	Punta Cana Beach Resort	340	$105–$200	(809) 686-0084	(809) 687-8745
★★★	Villas Doradas Beach	207	$115–$270	(809) 320-3000	(809) 320-4790
★★	Bayside Hill Resort	150	$180–$350	(800) 877-3648	(809) 523-8548
★★	Boca Chica Resort	273	$150–$390	(809) 523-4522	(809) 523-4438
★★	Caribbean Village Club	336	$120–$330	(809) 320-1111	
★★	Flamengo Beach Resort	310	$110–$150	(809) 320-5084	(809) 320-6319
★★	Heavens	150	$65–$150	(809) 586-5250	(809) 320-4733
★★	Hotel Montemar	95	$45–$120	(809) 586-2800	(809) 586-2009
★★	Hotel Sousa	39	$35–$65	(809) 571-2683	(809) 571-2180
★★	La Esplanada	210	$90–$225	(809) 571-3333	(809) 571-3922
★★	Paradise Beach Club	436	$110–$330	(800) 752-9236	(809) 320-4858
★★	Playa Dorada Hotel	254	$95–$155	(800) 423-6902	
★★	Puerto Plata Beach Resort	216	$130–$210	(809) 586-4243	(809) 568-4377
★	Hotel Confresi	200	$100–$120	(809) 586-2898	(809) 658-6806
★	Plaza Nico Hotel	220	$85	(809) 541-6226	(809) 541-7251

Santo Domingo

★★★★★	Hotel Gran Bahia	96	$105–$155		
★★★★★	Hotel Santo Domingo	220	$150	(809) 221-1511	(809) 535-4050
★★★★★	Hotel V Centenario Global	200	$195–$255	(800) 221-0000	(809) 221-2020
★★★★★	Jaragua	310	$80–$125	(800) 327-0200	(809) 535-4050
★★★★	Bavaro Beach Resort	1295	$80–$220		
★★★★	Capella Beach Resort	283	$120–$160	(800) 228-9898	

DOMINICAN REPUBLIC HOTELS		RMS	RATES	PHONE	FAX
★★★★	Casa de Campo	750	$180–$240	(800) 773-6437	(809) 523-8541
★★★★	Dominican Fiesta Hotel	337	$100–$200	(809) 562-8222	(809) 562-8938
★★★★	El Embajador Hotel	300	$105–$115	(800) 457-0067	(809) 532-9444
★★★★	Sand Castle Beach Resort	240	$80–$125	(809) 571-2420	
★★★★	Sheraton Santo Domingo	258	$110–$130	(800) 325-3535	(809) 687-8150
★★★	Gran Hotel Lina	217	$105–$135	(800) 942-2461	(809) 686-5521
★★	Continental Hotel	100	$60–$65	(809) 689-1151	(809) 687-8397
★★	Decameron Super Club	292	$100–$300	(809) 526-2009	(809) 526-1430
★★	Hotel Hispaniola	165	$80–$125	(800) 877-3643	(809) 535-4050
★★	Metro Hotel & Marina	180	$75–$115	(809) 526-2811	(809) 526-1808
★★	Punta Goleta Beach Resort	130	$85–$100	(809) 571-0700	(809) 571-0707
★★	Talanquera	250	$70–$130	(809) 541-1166	
★★	Tropics Club	77	$115–$165	(809) 529-8531	
★	El Napolitano	73	$50–$75	(809) 687-1131	(809) 387-6814
★	El Portillo Beach Club	159	$95–$145	(809) 688-5715	
★	Hostal Nicolas de Ovando	107	$45–$75		
★	Hotel Cayacoa Beach	70	$105		
★	Hotel Cayo Levantado	37	$125–$200	(800) 423-6902	
★	Naco Hotel and Casino	107	$40–$80	(809) 562-3100	(809) 544-0957
★	San Geronimo Hotel	72	$35–$40	(809) 533-1000	
★	Yaroa Hotel	24	$45–$55	(809) 571-2651	(809) 571-2651

DOMINICAN REPUBLIC RESTAURANTS		LOCATION	PHONE	ENTREE
Puerto Plata				
	International			
★★★★★	De Armando	Puerto Plata	(809) 586-3418	$10–$22
★★	Roma II	Puerto Plata	(809) 586-3904	$6–$15
Santo Domingo				
	American			
★★	Lago Grill	La Romana	(809) 523-3333	$5–$15•

DOMINICAN REPUBLIC RESTAURANTS	LOCATION	PHONE	ENTREE
Chinese			
★★★ **Pez Dorado**	Santiago Caballeros	(809) 582-2518	$18–$30
★★ **Jade Garden**	Santo Domingo	(809) 221-2131	$12–$30
French			
★★★★★ **Casa del Rio**	Altos de Chavon	(809) 523-3333	$14–$26
International			
★★★ **El Alcazar**	Santo Domingo	(809) 221-1511	$9–$25
★★ **Caribae**	Sosua		$20–$30••
★★ **Meson de la Cava**	Santo Domingo	(809) 533-2818	$25–$40
Italian			
★★ **Cafe del Sol**	Altos de Chavon	(809) 523-3333	$8–$10
★★ **Vesuvio I**	Santo Domingo	(809) 221-3333	$8–$20
Latin American			
★★★★ **Restaurant Montparnasse**	Santo Domingo	(809) 562-4141	$5–$20
★★★ **El Conuco**	Santo Domingo	(809) 686-0129	$8–$15
★★ **Che Bandoneon**	Santo Domingo	(809) 687-0023	$15–$30••
★★ **Fonda La Aterazana**	Santo Domingo	(809) 689-2900	$5–$20
Seafood			
★★★★ **La Bahia**	Santo Domingo	(809) 682-4022	$10–$20
★★ **Neptuno's Club**	Boca Chica	(809) 523-4703	$10–$25
Spanish			
★★★★★ **Lina Restaurant**	Santo Domingo	(809) 685-5000	$15–$30
★★ **Reina de Espana**	Santo Domingo	(809) 685-2588	$8–$20

Note: • Lunch Only

•• Dinner Only

GRENADA

In Grand Anse, no development may be taller than a coconut palm.

Grenada isn't called The Spice Island for nothing. Walk along The Carenage, the island's bustling waterfront, and you'll see dozens of turbaned black ladies selling their fragrant cloves, allspice, cinnamon and nutmeg with a merry song and a spiel. Aroma, it seems, takes on a seductive, almost musical quality on this tiny island, whose stunning natural wonders—-lush mountain forests, cascading waterfalls, and secret beaches—complete a delightful package that tourists are now discovering twelve years after U.S. troops quelled the Marxist-based coup. From rum shop to fishing village to market square, Grenada preserves the Caribbean the way it *was*, long before the American cultural intervention of Big Macs and Coke; best of all, tourist development, though viable, has been kept to a reasonable scale. It's here on

Grenada that you can still glimpse women scrubbing laundry in the streets, goats and chickens vying with traffic and old native ladies wearing baskets of bananas on their heads. Beyond Grenada's 45-plus beaches, travelers can hike rainforest trails riddled with cascading rivers, seek out more than 450 flowering plant species and 150 varieties of birds, or just discover a new dive site. For refreshment, there's elegant dining in old plantation houses, where the delicious callaloo soup can be sampled in a hundred different ways, and for adventure, a few hours lost in the ramparts and tunnels of forts that the French and British built during their 100-year-old custody battle.

Bird's Eye View

Sixty miles southwest of St. Vincent and ninety miles north of Trinidad, Grenada lies in the southernmost part of the Windward Islands, the smallest independent nation in the Western hemisphere. Egg-shaped, the island is 12 by 21 miles, volcanic in origin, with vegetation so thickly clad that it looks as if it is upholstered in deep green velvet. Its fertile volcanic soil springs forth a bounty of tropical fruits and vegetables and grows more species per square mile than anywhere else on the planet. In fact, the landscape is so lush that Grenada's residents regularly carry machetes as if the path they cleared today will be overgrown with green tangles tomorrow. The capital of St. George is one of the prettiest harbors in the Caribbean, with a pedestrian walk, The Carenage, which hugs the horseshoe-shaped harbor, inviting you for a stroll beside the sea. Several lofty lookouts—Fort George with cannons aimed seaward, Fort Frederick and Cemetery Hill—present splendid views of the town clambering up the slopes from the waterfront. The island, once a British Crown Colony, but now independent, also includes two other islands—Carriacou, with a very slight infrastructure, and Petite Martinique, famous as a pirate's haunt.

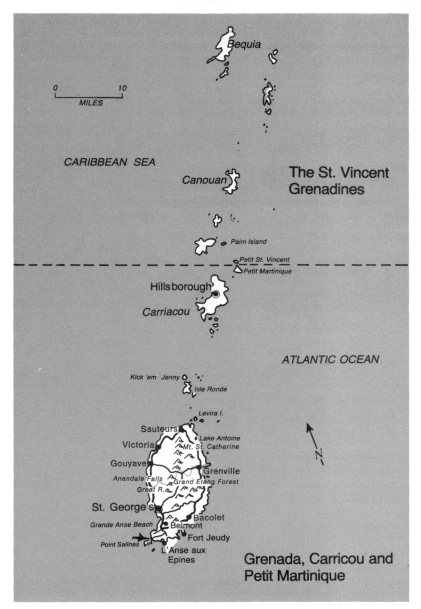

Bequia

0   10
MILES

CARIBBEAN SEA

Canouan

The St. Vincent
Grenadines

Palm Island

Petit St. Vincent
Petit Martinique

Hillsborough

Carriacou

ATLANTIC OCEAN

Kick 'em Jenny
Isle Ronde

Levira I.

Sauteurs
Lake Antoine
Victoria
Mt. St. Catherine

Gouyave
Grenville
Anandale Falls
Grand Etang Forest
Great R.

St. George's
Bacolet
Grande Anse Beach
Belmont
Point Salines
Fort Jeudy
L'Anse aux
Epines

Grenada, Carricou and
Petit Martinique

History

Grenada was discovered by Columbus on his third voyage in 1498. The French built Grenada's first settlement, first appeasing and then battling the native Carib Indians, the last of whom leaped to their death from Morne de Sauteurs, a rock promontory in the island's north coast, in 1651. Over the next century, Grenada was a battlefield between the French and British until the island was declared British under the Treaty of Versailles in 1783. Soon after, the island experienced the first rebellion led by a French plantocrat, Julien Fedon, resulting in the murder of 51 British colonists. (Fedon, who was never captured, remains a legend today in Grenada.) In 1838, the Emancipation Act freed Grenada's African slaves, forcing plantation owners to import indentured laborers from India, Malta and Madera. The descendants of this cultural stew live on today in the multi-ethnic cuisine, the French-African lilt to the language, and the British and French village names. Until 1958, the island remained a British colony, when it joined the abortive Federation of the West Indies. In 1967 it became a member of the West Indies Associated States, with Britain retaining responsibility. Many Grenadians were opposed to self-rule under Eric Gairy, the first Prime Minister, who was often compared to Haiti's Papa Doc Duvalier. Nevertheless, Gairy became a champion of the poor overnight, though he gained an irreverent reputation for some strange actions—for example, marching a steel band through an opponent's meeting and lecturing the U.N. about UFOs. In the early 70s, Maurice Bishop, a charismatic lawyer, just back from his studies in England, earned popular support as a human-rights activist when his New Jewel Movement convicted Gairy of twenty-seven crimes in a mock trial that called for his resignation. Bishop, along with other members of his party, was mercilessly beaten by Gairy's police, and thrown into jail for the night.

Such was the climate when Grenada (and its two dependencies, Carriacou and Petite Martinique) gained its independence from the British Commonwealth on Feb. 7, 1974. That very day management of the Holiday Inn pulled out, leaving an entire independence banquet in the hands of one pastry chef. By the late 70s, Gairy's economy was a shambles and his support diminished, even among the poor. On March 13,1979, Bishop staged the first modern coup in the English-speaking Caribbean while Gairy was off-island.

The economy improved early in his tenure and countries around the world accepted Bishop and the new Jewel Movement as a governing force. Still, free elections were never held. Bishop fostered ties with Cuba and the Eastern Bloc countries and as his friend Fidel Castro, granted Grenada aid and labor to build a larger airport at Port Salines in the south, U.S. ties began to unravel. In 1983 Bishop was ousted by a more Marxist/Leninist member of his own party, Bernard Coard, who placed Bishop under house arrest and imprisoned some of his followers. At a rally to support the release of Bishop, members of the People's Revolutionary Army fired into the throng; today no one is sure how many men, women and children were killed. The U.S. government, using the subsequent brutal execution of Bishop as pretext, landed 7000 troops on October 26, 1983, on the shores of Grenada, accompanied by the military forces of other neighboring islands—ostensibly to protect democracy and defend the lives of some 1000 Americans residing there, mostly medical students at St. George's University. Surprisingly, the American troops were welcomed with open arms by most Grenadians who called the mission not an invasion, but an "intervention."

The aftermath of what has been considered a bad dream by Grenadians has been a stars-and stripes p.r. blitz, new bridges, a retrained police force, and a renewed sense of democracy. The Americans put the finishing touches on the airport, and in 1990 American Airlines began its daily run. Today Grenada holds democratic elections every five years, with five major political parties vying for votes. Among these are the Maurice Bishop Patriotic movement and Gairy's GULP. The once-exiled Gairy, well into his 70s, and virtually blind, promises that if he's elected, the Almighty will restore his vision.

People

Like other recently created Caribbean countries freed from colonial ties, Grenada must constantly test the political waters—a fact which explains why Grenadians seem so politically aware and fascinated by foreigners. Warm and witty, Grenadians are insatiably curious, often quizzing tourists on Clintonomics or the latest word on Michael Jackson. About 75 percent of residents are black, the balance being largely mulatto. Although most of the 91,000 residents live off the land, unemployment is a huge problem (estimated to be about 30 percent in 1990). As a result, crime, especially in the lagoon area between St. George's and Grand Anse beach, has increased; hoteliers warn guests not to walk on that beach after dark, but to take the lighted service road instead.Grenadians are very pro-American, however, and still grateful to the U.S. for the military invention 13 years ago. In fact graffiti on the island still sings praises and thank-you's to "our saviour Ronald Reagan." Although there are no longer American troops on Grenada, you will run into lots of American students studying under palm trees at St. George's Medical School on the Grand Anse campus.

Beaches

Grenada claims 45 beaches, all free of charge to the public. All have fine white sand. The most famous is long and stunning **Grand Anse**, home to many of the island's resorts and hotels. Also in the south are **Calabash** and **Horseshoe**. If you are looking to pack a picnic lunch, head for **Levera Beach** on the northeastern shore, where you find swaying palms and deserted stretches. Other good beaches are near Lance aux Epines. This is where the Atlantic and the Caribbean meet. The best beaches in Carriacou are **Paradise** and **Sandy Island**.

Dive Sites

Dive sites in Grenada are some of the last great places to be discovered. Grenada's divers and snorkelers can take advantage of the submerged coral reef which lines most of the western coast as well as the 594-ft wreck, the *Bianca* cruiseliner that went up in flames and sank in 1961, just offshore. There are said to be about 40 different species of coral. Good snorkeling is found at offshore reefs within swimming distance south of Grand Anse beach and the nearby Morne Rouge Bay. The coral has not been maintained well and the fish are small. There are, however, numerous sea fans of enormous size, some of the largest in the Caribbean. Many divers sail around the reefs of Carriacou and Petit Martinique and simply use their own honing instincts where to anchor.

Treks

Your first stop before setting out on a trek should be to the **Grand Etang Forest Center** to pick up brochures and information for the self-guided walker. The Grand Etang Forest Reserve includes the spine of mountains that make up most of Grenada's interior. Hikes from the Forest Center range from 15 minutes to three hours. Anyone who intends to climb volcanic peaks or do serious hiking in remote areas must have a guide.

The trails in the Forest Reserve are quite good. Rainforest flora, such as rare orchids and heliconias are present; among the animals to be seen are mongoose, many species of frogs, lizard, and birds, armadillo and opossum. The 15-minute **LaBaye Trail** begins by the visitor's center and features twelve interesting points that end up in a lookout point over the east coast. **Mt. Qua Qua**, a one and a half-hour trail, leads over well-defined tracks with little slope as far as the Grand Etang Lake trail junction. From here, the trail gets steeper and often becomes slippery. Sometimes the trail becomes so narrow that it can become dangerous. Perhaps the finest trail here is the **Seven Sisters Trail**, that leads to an unbelievable seven waterfalls and pools, with a profuse collection of animals and flora. The trail can get difficult as it crosses dense bush; good balance is needed along the steep ridges. It's recommended to take along a guide.

Advanced hikers should consider a trek to **Concord Falls**, a triple-tiered cascade deep in the central mountains. Above Concord Village, the road stops directly in front of the first stage of the falls, where you will find a bathouse and concrete steps down to a swimming area. Lots of scout troops and groups of children often stop here on excursion, but real hikers should proceed on the footpath along the river, where large boulders have been placed in the riverbed to make crossing the river easier to reach the second cascade. Here the terrain can get a bit treacherous, especially during the rainy season. After about 45 minutes, you will reach a tremendous fall dropping 40 feet through jungle-dense vegetation to a pool where you can have a sensuous dip. (The trip back takes only about 25 minutes.) The last cascade, about a three-hour climb, should only be attempted by the most experienced hikers in need of a memorable challenge.

Fedon's Camp is the name of a trek on **Mount Fedon**, a five-hour arduous climb, which takes you along an ancient Indian path into the heart of the rainforest in the **Grand Etang National Park**. It was the outpost where Julian Fedon, a Grenadian of French birth, led a rebellion against the British in 1795. At the **Lake Antoine National Landmark**, south of Levera Park, there's a crater formed by volcanic eruption. A circular trail around the crater makes an excellent hike to see the large variety of birdlife, which includes snail kite, whistling duck, gray kingbird and large-billed seed-finch.

A new national park at Levera Bay east of Sauteurs in St. Patrick's encompasses 450 acres including a beach, pond, boiling springs and hill, where dozens of tropical birds make their nests. The area is one of the most scenic in Grenada, with white sand beaches fringed with palms. Hiking in the lagoon area can be done on a trail that circles the lagoon. A guide might be needed if the trail has not been improved upon of late. Ask first, otherwise you will be alone, cutting through the forest with a machete.

On the far southeastern coast, **La Sagesse Nature Center**, a four-room guesthouse and restaurant, lures nature-loving escapists and locals who come to veg out on weekends and beat the crowd on the busier beaches. After hiking one of the nearby trails through a cactus-strewn woodlands, you arrive at beaches even more secluded than Sagesse itself. Finally you return to the center's restaurant for fresh fruit smoothies and a delicious seafood lunch. If you want to spend the day at **La Sagesse** (☎ *809-444-6458*), you can pay $26 plus a ten percent service charge per person for roundtrip transportation from your hotel, a guided nature tour, lunch and a bout of beach bumming.

FIELDING'S CHOICE:

Prepare yourself first for dodging chickens, bikes and pedestrians, but rent a car and take the north along the coastline, turning inward at Halifax Harbour toward the central mountain range, leading to Grand Etang Lake, a 36-acre volcanic crater whose glassy waters shimmer in the shadow of 2373-ft. Mount Qua Qua. Add to that a boisterous hike around the lake or a heroic trek along a five-hour trail from Concord Falls deep in the central mountains, where the Concord River plummets down a series of rocky ravines.

What Else to See

Grenada is full of natural wonders, but a stroll through the narrow streets and cobbled alleys of **St. George's**, the capital, should be a priority on your itinerary. There are centuries-old churches to explore and the **National Museum**, once a French garrison, where an antique rum still, wildlife specimens, and even the personal effects of Josephine Bonaparte—including the marble tub she used as a child—are kept. The ramparts of Fort George tower over the Carenage and look out to sea—today it is the police headquarters. On Richmond Hill, marvel at the 18th-century military construction of Fort Frederick and drink in the view of the capital with a rum punch at the nearby Hotel Balisier. The best day to visit St. George's Market Square is on Saturday, when the plaza bustles with the brightest aromas and colors of the Caribbean. For a few dollars you can come home leaden with baskets of cocoa balls (to make coca tea), sorrel, tannia, yams, limes, mangoes, and luscious papayas. A tour of the **Doug Laldston Estate** near Gouyave will give you a glimpse into the secrets of nutmeg cultivation. Afterwards, a dollar will get you into the Nutmeg Processing Station, where nuts and mace are separated and graded by hand, then stored in huge burlap bags.

Historical Sites

Fort George ★★★

Church Street, St. George's.
Built by the French in 1705 on a promontory to guard the entrance to the harbor, this old fort has lots of small rooms and four-inch-thick walls. Free admission.

Museums and Exhibits

Grenada National Museum ★★★

Monckton Street, St. George's, ☎ *(809)440-3725.*
Hours Open: 9:00a.m.–4:30 p.m.
Set in the foundations of an old French army barracks and prison dating back to 1704, this small museum has some interesting exhibits on the island's natural and historical past. Don't miss Josephine Bonaparte's marble bathtub! General admission: $1.00.

Parks and Gardens

Annandale Falls ★★★★★

Main Interior Road, St. George's, ☎ *(809)440-2452.*
Hours Open: 8:00 a.m.–4:00 p.m.
Bring a picnic and your swimsuit (changing rooms are available) to this pretty spot, where water cascades down some 50 feet into a pool perfect for dips. There's a good gift shop on site with handicrafts and species native to the island. Free admission.

Grand Etang National Park ★★★★★

Main Interior Road, St. George's, ☎ *(809)442-7425.*
Hours Open: 8:30a.m.–4:00 p.m.
This rainforest and bird sanctuary, located in the island's interior between St. George's and Grenville, has lots of gorgeous, unspoiled scenery. Several trails wind throughout for easy to difficult treks. Don't miss Grand Etang Lake, whose 13 acres of cobalt blue waters are nestled in the crater of an extinct volcano. General admission: $1.00.

Tours

Nutmeg Processing Plant

Gouyave.

You'll never again take this little spice for granted after a half-hour tour of the processing plant. Nutmeg is Grenada's largest export and smells sweet, too. General admission: $1.00.

FIELDING'S CHOICE:

The Tower was a fabulous plantation house built in 1917 by a Grenadian lawyer to please his bride. Today, the owners, Paul Slinger and his wife Victoria, open their historic home to visitors for a $10 tour every Thursday. The Tower is full of antiques, including Hogarth prints collected by Paul's grandfather (who commanded the West Indian regiment in World War I). Situated on nine acres of land, the property is a veritable plantation of tropical fruits, samples of which are served during your tour along with a fruit punch.

Sports

Sailing is the premier sport on Grenada, particularly through the islands of the Grenadines, where the conditions are said to be some of the best in the world. Seagoing travelers always come back with great tales of derring-do, hidden coves, and an occasional disaster. St. George has excellent equipment for rent, including Hobie Cats, Sailfish, and Sunfish for short excursions. Numerous charter operations can arrange programs for any length or vessel (rates are about 20 percent lower in off-season). Sometimes the easiest thing is to hop a fishingboat to the nearby Hog Island or Calivigny. The Carriacou's Regatta, held in the first weekend of August, attracts classic seamen from all over the world who thrive on the ferocious competition.

Sportfishing is excellent November -May; several operators offer four-hour or longer charters. Several hotels have tennis courts, including Calabash, Coral Cove, Secret Harbor, Spice Island Inn, and the Grenada Renaissance.

Grenada Golf Club

Frand Anse, St. George's, ☎ *(809)444-4128.*

Not the greatest golf in the world, but since it's the only one on the island, it'll do. The nine-hole course has some nice views. Greens fees are a reasonable $20.

Watersports

Various locations, St. George's.

Your hotel will probably offer watersports for free or a nominal fee, or check out one of these outfits. Scuba diving and snorkeling: **Grenada Aquatics** (☎ *444-4129*), and **Dive Grenada** (☎ *444-4371*). Boating: **Seabreeze Yacht Charters** (☎ *444-4924*), and **The Moorings** (☎ *444-4548*). Cruises: **Best of Grenada** (☎ *440-2198*). Deep-sea fishing: **Dive Grenada** (☎ *444-4371*), and the **Best of Grenada** (☎ *440-2198*). A major fishing tournament is held each January. On Carriacou, contact **Dive Paradise** at the Silver Beach Resort (☎ *443-7337*) for watersports.

FIELDING"S CHOICE:

Every other Saturday a bunch of Grenadians known as the Hash House Harriers get together, split into teams, and set off on chases through glorious countryside on trails that always end up at Rudolf's, a bar right next to the Carenage in St. George's. It's a great way to meet and mingle with those Grenadians not in good enough shape for the triathlon.

Where to Stay

Highest Rated Hotels in Grenada

★★★★★	Calabash Hotel
★★★★★	La Source
★★★★★	Spice Island Inn
★★★★	Rex Grenadian
★★★★	Secret Harbour Hotel
★★★	Blue Horizons Cottages
★★★	Coyaba Beach Resort
★★★	Grenada Renaissance Hotel
★★★	Twelve Degrees North

Most Exclusive Hotels in Grenada

★★★★★	La Source	$250–$590
★★★★★	Calabash Hotel	$170–$495
★★★	Twelve Degrees North	$130–$285
★★★	Grenada Renaissance Hotel	$120–$170
★★★	Blue Horizons Cottages	$100–$165

Fielding's Best Value Hotels in Grenada

★★	Cinnamon Hill Hotel	$85–$153
★★★★	Rex Grenadian	$115–$360
★★★★★	La Source	$250–$590
★★	No Problem Apartments	$55–$85
★★★	Blue Horizons Cottages	$100–$165

More than 85 percent of Grenada's hotels are owned by Grenadians; their stake in tourism accounts for the pride they show in personal touches that make their guests feel very special. A doubling of hotels is expected in 1996, but a happy medium in new construction is being pursued to appease ecologists. Many of the island's finest resorts are located on the idyllic strip of sand called **Grand Anse Beach**; these are not high-rise hotels but small intimate inns and guesthouses. (By law no hotel in Grenada can be higher than a palm tree or more than three stories tall.) Other options on Grenada include apartments, yachts, or the proverbial cottage.

Hotels and Resorts

Not only new construction but renovations and additions have kept the hotel trade busy in the last year. At the **Calabash Hotel** six of the eight existing suites have been replaced by new units, complete with whirlpools, lounge areas and minibars, as well as a new fitness center, new boutique, and beach kitchen for hot lunches.At **Magonay Run**, a multi-million-dollar restaurant, bar, and 36 superior rooms with gardens will be completed by June 1995. **Spice Island Inn**, the romantic 36-room property on Grand Anse, has totally renovated eight whirlpool beach suites and extended both bathrooms and bedrooms. The newest addition is **La Source**, an all-inclusive 100-room resort with a spa and nine-hole golf course, and the **Rex Grenadian**, the island's largest hotel on a three-acre lake; both hotels are situated on expansive white sand beaches on the southwest coast.

Calabash Hotel　　　　　**$170–$495**　　　　　★★★★★

L'Anse aux Epines, St. George's, ☎ *(800)528-5835, (809)444-4334.*
Single: $170–$465. Double: $205–$495.
Set among coconut groves and gardens on an eight-acre estate, all accommodations are suites housed in stone and wood cottages at this very fine resort. Some have private pools, others kitchens, others Jacuzzis and all are bright and cheery. There are three bars and a restaurant, watersports and tennis, frequent live entertainment and wonderful, attentive service. A great choice. 28 rooms. Credit Cards: V, MC, A.

Coyaba Beach Resort　　　　　**$75–$165**　　　　　★★★

Grand Anse, St. George's, ☎ *(809)444-4129.*
Single: $75–$115. Double: $95–$165.
Set on the site of an ancient Arawak Indian village, this family-run resort puts guests up in tropically decorated rooms with bright island artwork. The pool has a swim-up bar, perfect for cooling off after a set or two on the tennis court. The restaurant and cafe are open-air. The beach is a short stroll from the rooms. 40 rooms. Credit Cards: V, MC, DC, A.

Flamboyant Hotel　　　　　**$70–$220**　　　　　★★

Grand Anse Beach, St. George's, ☎ *(800)223-9815, (809)444-4247.*
Single: $70–$215. Double: $85–$220.
Set on a hillside that slopes gently to the beach, this complex offers standard guest rooms and 23 suites with kitchenettes, most with sweeping views. The good location makes this a relative bargain, and the friendly staff keeps guests happy. There's a restaurant, pool and free snorkel equipment. 39 rooms. Credit Cards: V, MC, DC, A.

Grenada Renaissance Hotel   **$120–$170**   ★★★

Grande Anse Beach, St. George's, ☎ *(800)228-9898, (809)444-4371.*
Single: $120–$170. Double: $120–$170.

This handsome complex has a nice location—right on the beach and across from a
good shopping complex—but lacks island flavor. Accommodations are comfortable
but on the small side, and the motel-like furnishings are generic. On the plus side,
the hotel offers a complete range of amenities, from watersports to tennis courts to
yacht charters, and attracts families with its supervised children's programs (on holidays). A lively night scene, too. 186 rooms. Credit Cards: V, MC, DC, A.

Hibiscus Hotel   **$60–$125**   ★

Grand Anse, St. George's, ☎ *(809)444-4233.*
Single: $60–$125. Double: $80–$125.

This small hotel is 300 yards from Grand Anse Beach. Accommodations are in air-
conditioned duplex cottages with patios. There's a restaurant and pool on-site. 10
rooms. Credit Cards: V, MC, A.

Horse Shoe Beach Hotel   **$70–$155**   ★★

L'Anne Aux Epines, St. George's, ☎ *(809)444-4244.*
Single: $70–$130. Double: $80–$155.

Set on a hillside overlooking the bay, this hotel puts up guests in cottages with air
conditioning, period furnishings and patios; some also have four-poster beds. Each
two units share a kitchen. The six suites in the main building are the best choice.
Nicely landscaped grounds hold a pool and beach, with watersports nearby. 22
rooms. Credit Cards: V, MC, A.

Hotel Balisier   **$53–$109**   ★

Richmond Hill, St. George's, ☎ *(809)440-2346.*
Single: $53–$77. Double: $77–$109.

Standing on the site of an ancient fort and overlooking St. George's, this small hotel
has comfortable, basic rooms; only five are air-conditioned. There's a pool and restaurant, but the beach is out of walking distance. 15 rooms. Credit Cards: V, MC, A.

La Source   **$250–$590**   ★★★★★

Pink Gin Beach, St. George's, ☎ *(800)544-2883, (809)444-2556.*
Single: $250–$345. Double: $420–$590.

Just opened in late 1993, this all-inclusive resort is situated on two beaches on
Grenada's southwest tip. The price is steep, but includes all meals, drinks, watersports and—best of all—pampering treatments in the excellent spa. Accommodations are simply gorgeous, with Persian rugs, mahogany furniture, four-poster beds
and Asian artwork. When you're not being spoiled in the spa, you can play tennis or
nine holes of golf, swim in the two-level pool or enjoy a good array of watersports.
Simply fabulous. 100 rooms. Credit Cards: V, MC, A.

Rex Grenadian   **$115–$360**   ★★★★

Magazine Beach, St. George's, ☎ *(800)255-5859, (809)444-3333.*
Single: $115–$360. Double: $115–$360.

New in December 1993, this large property offers all the bells and whistles resort
lovers expect. Set on 12 acres that open onto two beaches, the hotel houses guests
in nicely done standard rooms; you'll pay a bit extra for air conditioning and a big-

ger bathroom. A couple of neat restaurants give guests dining choices, and the typical watersports, fitness center and tennis prevail. There's even a man-made lake stretching over two acres. Nice, but expect a lot of business groups. 212 rooms. Credit Cards: V, MC, A.

Secret Harbour Hotel   **$100–$225**   ★ ★ ★ ★

L'Anse aux Epines, St. George's, ☎ *(800)334-2435, (809)444-4548.*
Single: $100–$213. Double: $130–$225.
Overlooking Mount Hartman Bay on Grenada's southernmost tip, this elegant property consists of Mediterranean-style villas in which each unit is a suite. They're nicely decorated with four-poster beds, local art, trouser presses, large balconies and baths with Roman tubs. The grounds are lovely and the views breathtaking. The small beach offers all the usual watersports. Special packages allow guests to spend a few nights aboard one of their many yachts. Nice! 20 rooms. Credit Cards: V, MC, A.

Siesta Hotel   **$55–$140**   ★ ★

Grand Anse, St. George's, ☎ *(809)444-4645.*
Single: $55–$110. Double: $60–$140.
Located slightly inland from the beach, this small hotel has air-conditioned rooms with comfortable furnishings; some have kitchens. There's a restaurant and pool, but not much else in the way of extras. 37 rooms. Credit Cards: V, MC, A.

Spice Island Inn   **$270–$475**   ★ ★ ★ ★ ★

Grand Anse Beach, St. George's, ☎ *(809)444-4258.*
Single: $270–$425. Double: $320–$475.
Set on eight tropical acres on a gorgeous stretch of Grand Anse Beach, all accommodations at this very fine resort are in suites. Some have whirlpools (and even private dip pools), and all are simply but comfortably furnished with huge, pampering bathrooms. The grounds are nicely done with lots of flowers, and there's a gym and tennis court for the active set. Others are happy just lounging on the picturesque beach. Great food and service, too. Simply charming. 56 rooms. Credit Cards: V, MC, DC, A.

Apartments and Condominiums

Grenadians are leaders in the Caribbean self-catering business. Don't be shy about bringing food from home, though fresh tropical fruits and vegetables can be easily bought at the markets. The best views are to be found at the **Cinnamon Hill**, which looks out onto the bay at Grand Anse Beach, but **Twelve Degrees North** also has excellent sea views. At Mahogany Run, Maffiken Apartments, Gem Holiday Beach resort, South Winds, and Villamar, you will need to rent a car.

Blue Horizons Cottages   **$100–$165**   ★ ★ ★

Grand Anse, St. George's, ☎ *(809)444-4592.*
Single: $100–$155. Double: $110–$165.
Set on a terraced hillside some 300 yards from Grand Anse Beach, accommodations are in one-bedroom cottages and duplex suites, each air-conditioned and sporting kitchens. There's a restaurant and two bars on hand, as well as a pool and Jacuzzi. Watersports take place at nearby sister property, the Spice Island Inn. Good value. 32 rooms. Credit Cards: V, MC, DC, A.

Cinnamon Hill Hotel   **$85–$153**

Grand Anse Beach, St. George's, ☎ *(809)444-4301.*
Single: $85–$130. Double: $114–$153.

This Spanish-style hotel village consists of several buildings scattered over a hillside overlooking Grand Anse Beach; it's steep going so those with mobility problems should look elsewhere. Accommodations are in one- and two-bedroom apartments with kitchens and balconies. There's a restaurant and pool on-site, with all water-sports available on the public beach. 20 rooms. Credit Cards: V, MC, A.

Coral Cove Cottages   **$65–$120**   ★

Coral Cove Beach, ☎ *(809)444-4422.*
Single: $65–$120. Double: $65–$120.

Situated on a peaceful cove with nice views six miles from St. George's, this complex offers Spanish-style apartments and cottages with kitchenettes and terraces. There's a tennis court and small pool, but no dining facilities. 11 rooms. Credit Cards: V, MC.

Gem Holiday Beach Resort   **$55–$140**   ★★

Morne Rouge Bay, ☎ *(800)223-9815, (809)444-1189.*
Single: $55–$120. Double: $65–$140.

Located on the beach some six miles from St. George's, this apartment hotel houses guests in one- and two-bedroom units that are air-conditioned and have full kitchens. There's a restaurant and bar if you'd rather leave the cooking to someone else, and a lively disco. You'll probably want a rental car to get around. 23 rooms. Credit Cards: V, MC, DC, A.

Holiday Haven   **$60–$145**   ★

L'Anse aux Epines, St. George's, ☎ *(809)440-2606.*
Single: $60–$145. Double: $65–$145.

This basic complex offers one- to three-bedroom apartments with full kitchens and verandas; most have two bathrooms. Maids keep everything looking spiffy. Nothing extra in the way of facilities, so you'll have to venture out. 3 Cottages. 12 rooms.

La Sagesse Nature Center   **$40–$90**   ★

St. David's, ☎ *(809)444-6458.*
Single: $40–$75. Double: $65–$90.

Located in a remote setting 10 miles from the airport, this small, family-run operation has six apartments in a guesthouse with full kitchens and ceiling fans to keep things cool. The surrounding grounds are really pretty, with lots of hiking and bird-watching opportunities. Really appealing for nature lovers. 6 rooms. Credit Cards: V, MC, A.

Maffiken Apartments   **$60–$85**   ★

Grand Anse, St. George's, ☎ *(809)444-4255.*
Single: $60–$70. Double: $70–$85.

Set on a hillside overlooking Grand Anse Beach a short stroll away, this small stucco hotel houses one- and two-bedroom apartments with air conditioning, kitchenettes and maid service. No recreational facilities, but restaurants and shopping are nearby. 12 rooms. Credit Cards: V, MC, A.

No Problem Apartments   **$55–$85**

True Blue, St. George's, ☎ *(809)444-4634.*

Single: $55–$75. Double: $65–$85.

Located near the airport on the outskirts of town, this Mediterranean-style complex has air-conditioned suites with full kitchens. A free shuttle takes you to town and Grand Anse Beach, so you won't need a rental car as with most other apartment hotels. There's a restaurant and pool, and a fleet of bicycles for the asking. Decent. 20 rooms. Credit Cards: V, MC, A.

South Winds Holiday   **$40–$80**   ★

Grand Anse, St. George's, *(809)444-4310.*
Single: $40–$80. Double: $40–$80.

Grand Anse Beach is about 500 yards from this complex of cottages and apartments, all with kitchens and most with air conditioning. Popular with families, there's maid service, but little else in the way of extras. Good rates for the location, though. 19 rooms. Credit Cards: V, MC, DC, A.

True Blue Inn   **$65–$110**   ★★

St. George's, *(800)742-4276, (809)444-2000.*
Single: $65–$95. Double: $75–$110.

Accommodations at this south coast property are in one-bedroom apartments and two-bedroom cottages, all with air conditioning and full kitchens. There's maid service, a sailing school for both adults and children, a pool and bicycles for tooling about. A nice, friendly atmosphere. 7 rooms. Credit Cards: V, MC, DC, A.

Twelve Degrees North   **$130–$285**   ★★★

St. George's, ☎ *(800)322-1753, (809)444-4580.*
Single: $130–$285. Double: $130–$285.

Located on the southeast coast and facing the sea, this small property has one- and two-bedroom apartments with kitchens and—what a plus!— a housekeeper who cooks, cleans and even does laundry. No air conditioning, but ceiling fans do the job nicely. The grounds include a lot for an apartment complex, with a pool, tennis court, private beach and watersports. No kids under 12. 8 rooms. Credit Cards: Not Accepted.

Villamar Holiday Resort   **$42–$62**   ★

L'anse aux Epines, St. George's, ☎ *(809)444-1614.*
Single: $42–$52. Double: $52–$62.

Located in a remote spot two minutes from Grand Anse Beach, this complex has one- and two-bedroom suites with air conditioning, kitchens and private balconies. There's a bar, restaurant and pool, and they'll help arrange watersports and golf. 20 rooms. Credit Cards: V, MC, A.

Wave Crest Holiday Apts.   **$75–$95**   ★

Grand Anse, St. George's, ☎ *(809)444-4116.*
Single: $75–$95. Double: $75–$95.

Grand Anse Beach is a five-minute walk from this small property, where you can choose from standard guest rooms and one- and two-bedroom apartments with air conditioning, verandas and kitchens. There's a bar, but not much else. 20 rooms. Credit Cards: V, MC, A.

Inns

Grenada's inns are run and owned by devoted families who make their unique personalities known in every detail. Peace and quiet relaxation is the business at **Morne Fendue**, the private home of a longtime resident still full of her family antiques. **Hibiscus Hotel** gives the feeling of a tiny village with its five small cottages situated near a common pool. **True Blue Inn** is commendable for its modern kitchen facilities in the one-bedroom apartments and cottages, and the attractive seaside restaurant.

Low Cost Lodging

To save lots of money on Grenada, you will either have to share a bathroom, stuff a lot of people into an apartment or cottage, or go in off-season. You might also ask the tourist board if anyone rents rooms in private homes. The following are very inexpensive, but very basic small guesthouses. Don't expect any air conditioning.

Where to Eat

Highest Rated Restaurants in Grenada

★★★★★ La Belle Creole
★★★★★ Morne Fendue
★★★★ Canbouley
★★★★ Coconut's Beach
★★★★ Nutmeg, The

Most Exclusive Restaurants in Grenada

★★★★ Canbouley	$20–$36
★★★★ Coconut's Beach	$13–$26

Fielding's Best Value Restaurants in Grenada

★★ Le Karacoli	$8–$25
★★★★ Coconut's Beach	$13–$26
★★★★ Nutmeg, The	$9–$20

Few West Indians have mastered the art of adapting local fruits, vegetables, seafood, and spices to Continental-style recipes as well as Grenadians have. The restaurant scene in Grenada, which traditionally centered around the major hotels, now includes newcomers that have added not only spice but variety, to the island cuisine. The national dish, "Oil down," concocted with breadfruit and salt pork wrapped in dasheen leaves and steamed in coconut milk, is delicious, but also don't miss tasting callaloo soup (made with the spinachlike leaves of the dasheen), christophine au gratni, pepperpot stew, and nutmeg ice cream (nutmeg is the main spice import of Grenada). All dining options are available, however, whether you choose to dine on possum and armadillo at the tin-roofed **Mama's** or eat international cuisine in the elegant **Canboulay**, overlooking the Grand Anse beach. American medical students from St. George's Medical School hang at **Red Crab**, a legendary fish-and-chips, beer-belly pub just outside the gates of the Calabash Hotel. Don't miss sampling a proper Grenadian rum punch, or a local candy called nutmeg cheese.

Bird's Nest — $$$ ★

Grand Anse Beach, Grand Anse, ☎ (809) 444-4264.
Chinese cuisine.
Lunch: 10:30 a.m.–2:00 p.m., entrees $11–$24.
Dinner: 2:00 p.m.–11:00 p.m., entrees $11–$24.

A no-surprises, pleasant Chinese restaurant that also serves good sandwiches for lunch, Bird's Nest roosts near the airport and several hotels in Grand Anse. Specialties include sweet and sour chicken or fish, served with tasty fried rice. The restaurant is open on Sunday for dinner only, from 6 p.m. to 11 p.m. Reservations recommended. Credit Cards: D, V, MC, A.

Canbouley — $$$ ★★★★

Morne Rouge, ☎ (809) 444-4401.
International cuisine.
Lunch: 11:30 a.m.– 2:30 p.m., entrees $10–$20.
Dinner: 7:00 p.m.–10:00 p.m., entrees $20–$36.

For a grand night out in exotic surroundings, most visitors choose this festive restaurant with a view of the lights of the capital across the bay. The decor and the tropical-Asian cuisine reflect the heritage of Trinidad-born owners Erik and Gina Lee-Johnson, where spices, heady scents and Carnival are a way of life. The Johnsons really shine with shrimp prepared in interesting ways, including an Indonesian peanut and fruit satay. Desserts are memorable, especially a chocolate-orange mousse. Closed: Sun. Reservations recommended. Credit Cards: V, MC, A.

Coconut's Beach — $$$ ★★★★

Grand Anse Beach, ☎ (809) 444-4644.
French cuisine. Specialties: Lobster, conch.
Lunch: 10:00 a.m.–6:00 p.m., entrees $6–$13.
Dinner: 7:00 p.m.–10:00 p.m., entrees $13–$26.

As the name implies, guests can eat right on the beach in high style under palm-frond shelters, or in the dining room of a spiffy, native house with an open kitchen where the chefs deftly saute the catch of the day in gleaming cookware. Lobster with various butter sauces or *lambi* (conch) curry are mouth-watering choices, as are ribs, chicken or steak. A good lunch menu of crepes, salads or sandwiches offers most dishes for under $10. Closed: Tue. Reservations recommended. Credit Cards: V, MC.

Cot Bam — $$$ ★

Grand Anse Beach, Grand Anse, ☎ (809) 444-2050.
American cuisine.
Lunch: 9:00 a.m.–2:00 p.m., entrees $6–$30.
Dinner: 2:00 p.m.–11:00 p.m., entrees $6–$30.

Savory, quick meals and a cold brew draw guests to this convivial bar and grill after a hard day at the beach. Since it's within strolling distance of all hotels on Grand Anse, why settle for room service? Snacks and plate meals include West Indian rotis, salads, shrimp and chips, etc. Credit Cards: D, V, MC, A.

Delicious Landing $$$ ★

The Carenage,
Seafood cuisine.
Lunch: 10:30 a.m.–2:00 p.m., entrees $17–$24.
Dinner: 6:30 p.m.–11:30 p.m., entrees $17–$24.

Although many eating establishments on this island boast enviable views, Delicious Landing may have the best one of all, situated right on the water's edge near St. George's Harbor. Decently prepared seafood and fish is featured, but the sea vistas, breezes and excellent tropical drinks are the main reason to linger here. Credit Cards: Not Accepted.

La Belle Creole $$$ ★★★★★

Grand Anse Beach, Grand Anse, ☎ *(809) 444-4316.*
Seafood cuisine. Specialties: Callaloo quiche.
Lunch: 12:30 p.m.– 2:30 p.m., entrees $22–$28.
Dinner: 7:00 p.m.–9:00 p.m., entrees $25–$30.

Some of the most creative West Indian food is served in this airy terrace restaurant on the grounds of the Blue Horizons Cottages. For many years "Mama" Audrey Hopkin earned a deserved reputation as the best Creole home chef in town, and now her sons have carried the torch with admirable results. Real men (and women) eat quiche here, which is an unusual combo of callaloo (dasheen leaf) and lobster or shrimp; there's also a veal roulade with crab. An ever-changing fixed-price dinner of up to five courses, including dessert, is available nightly for $40. Associated Hotel: Blue Horizons. Reservations required. Credit Cards: D, V, MC, DC, A.

La Sagesse $$ ★

Eastern Main Road, St. David, ☎ *(809) 444-6458.*
American cuisine.
Lunch: 11:00 a.m.–3:30 p.m., entrees $6–$11.
Dinner: 6:30 p.m.–9:00 p.m., entrees $8–$12.

This small restaurant by the sea is part of the La Sagesse Nature Center, formerly the home of a cousin of Queen Elizabeth, now an inn and banana plantation. Fittingly, patrons can get a nice organic vegetarian platter or blended tropical fruit drinks. Other dishes include seafood, sandwiches and burgers. The calm waters here are only eight minutes away from the capital. Associated Hotel: La Sagesse Nature Center. Credit Cards: V, MC, A.

Le Karacoli $$$ ★★

Grande-Anse Beach, Grand-Anse, ☎ *590-28-41-17.*
French cuisine.
Dinner: entrees $8–$25.

This bustling beachfront restaurant with an unlikely name (the snail) offers reasonably priced Creole dishes (mostly seafood) to locals and the numerous tourists who have discovered the place. Try the crab backs stuffed with shrimp or enjoy a full-course meal with yams and vegetable accompaniments for $14. Service is gracious even during peak times. Reservations recommended. Credit Cards: V, MC.

Mama's $$$ ★★

Lagoon Road, ☎ *(809) 440-1459.*
Latin American cuisine. Specialties: Oil down, exotic small game.

Lunch: 8:00 a.m.–1:30 p.m., prix fixe $19.
Dinner: 7:30 p.m.–11:00 p.m., prix fixe $19.

Yes, eating here is like Sunday dinner at Mama's—if she was West Indian. But no one has to wait until the end of the week to dine here; Mama's daughter Cleo and other family members set out a groaning buffet of some 20 local dishes in a friendly, boardinghouse atmosphere every day of the week. The menu features the overwhelming bounty of this verdant isle, including the pear-shaped christophine vegetable stuffed with crab, oil down (breadfruit, meats, callaloo in coconut milk) and curries. The daring can call ahead for a taste of stewed armadillo or iguana. Reservations required. Credit Cards: Not Accepted.

Morne Fendue $$$ ★ ★ ★ ★ ★
St. Patrick's, St. Patrick's Parish, ☎ *(809) 442-9330.*
Latin American cuisine. Specialties: Pepper pot.
Lunch: 12:30 p.m.– 3:00 p.m., prix fixe $17.

Lunch at this history-laden plantation house may soon be a thing of the past, as owner Betty Mascoll, who has been holding court here for many years, is well into her 80s. So while you can, reserve a place at this traditional West Indian buffet and make friends with the repeat visitors and a faithful staff that prepares a mean pepper pot stew, peas and rice, stewed chicken and island vegetables every afternoon except Sunday. The house itself, built of native stone and decorated with family keepsakes, is a national treasure. Closed: Sun. Reservations required. Credit Cards: Not Accepted.

Nutmeg, The $$ ★ ★ ★ ★
The Carenage, ☎ *(809) 440-2539.*
Seafood cuisine. Specialties: Nutmeg ice cream, conch.
Lunch: 9:00 a.m.– 4:00 p.m., entrees $5–$15.
Dinner: 4:00 p.m.–11:00 p.m., entrees $9–$20.

This well-known and widely visited restaurant with a view of seagoing vessels in St. George's Harbor features its heady namesake spice in a few specialties, including a nutmeg ice cream and rum punch. Otherwise, for a few dollars, sample local dishes like callaloo soup, lambi curry or fish sandwiches and fries, washed down with the locally brewed Carib beer. Credit Cards: D, V, MC, A.

Portofino $$ ★
The Carenage, ☎ *(809) 440-3986.*
Italian cuisine. Specialties: Pizza, Pastas.
Lunch: 11:00 a.m.–2:00 p.m., entrees $6–$22.
Dinner: 2:00 p.m.–11:00 p.m., entrees $6–$22.

A comforting plate of pasta plus a harbor view make this upper-level Italian charmer an unbeatable draw. Jazz often plays in the background, putting everyone in a relaxed mood. It's also a good place for the kids, who can choose from a wide variety of their favorite food: pizza. Lobster and veal dishes are also available. Reservations recommended. Credit Cards: V, MC, A.

Red Crab, The $$$ ★
L'Anse aux Epines, Grand Anse, ☎ *(809) 444-4424.*
International cuisine. Specialties: Steak.
Lunch: 11:00 a.m.–2:00 p.m., entrees $10–$31.
Dinner: 6:00 p.m.–11:00 p.m., entrees $10–$31.

This place should have been named the Plush Cow, because although it serves sea-food, old-timers roll in here for the beefsteaks, which are the best on the island. It's located in the posh southern point of the island, in one of Grenada's original tourist developments. Travelers staying in the Grand Anse area can get here by car in five minutes. Closed: Sun. Reservations recommended. Credit Cards: D, V, MC, A.

Rudolf's   **$$**   ★

The Carenage, ☎ *(809) 440-2241.*
International cuisine. Specialties: Conch.
Lunch: 10:00 a.m.–2:00 p.m., entrees $8–$15.
Dinner: 2:00 p.m.–12:00 p.m., entrees $8–$15.

Although it's got a humming bar scene, Rudolf's features a large selection of sea-food and steak dishes for those who want to eat here. It also helps that this pub eatery with a harbor view has some of the best prices in town—many dishes are under $10. There are daily specials, usually lobster or conch (highly recommended), as well as sandwiches, salads and fish and chips. Closed: Sun. Credit Cards: Not Accepted. Credit Cards: V, MC.

Where to Shop

Shopping isn't duty free on Grenada, but sometimes bargains can get you very close. Special buys to bring home are spice baskets full of native-grown nutmeg, cinnamon, cloves, ground coriander, and others—perfect for Christmas gifts or for spiking the eggnog. At the **Grand Anse Shopping Center** (closest to the hotels) there are even spice vendors who stroll up and down the streets barking their prices (don't be shy about bargaining). Imported china can be found at prices 60 percent cheaper than in the States. You can find other shopping centers on the **Esplanade side of Fort George** and on **Melville Street**, facing the harbor. A good bakery and coffee shop is located in the **Le Marquis Complex**, in the Grand Anse district. Grenada shops open and close with their own schedules, but usually cater hours to cruise ships. Best time to visit the Granby Street food market on Market Square is Saturday.

CARRIACOU

Carriacou (Carry-a-COO) is a 14 -sq. mile island lying 40 miles northeast of St. George's, reachable by daily 10-minute flights in very small planes. Al-though administered by its own staff, the island is under the government of Grenada. The capital is Hillsborough and home to 4600. A postage-stamp paradise untouched by large-scale development, it boasts only 11 inns and guesthouses with no more than 20 rooms in the largest. **Gramma's Place** on Main Street, an unofficial meeting place, serves breakfast and snacks. For dinner the **Callaloo Restaurant** is a find. The tiny museum was once a cotton ginnery, and the hillside cemetery is notable as a place where young girls tend their goats. The Scottish influence can be seen in the wooden schooners of local white cedar, while strong African roots vibrate in the drum song and dance unique to the island.

To get there, take a small plane from Port Salines International Airport in Grenada on inter-island flights from St. Vincent or from Barbados. You can also catch a ride on the mailboat or fishing boat or charter a private yacht. Everyone on Carriacou will be clamoring for American dollars, so don't worry about exchanging any.

Where to Stay

Lodging is humble on Carriacou, but not without grace. The best are the cottages at the Caribbee Inn, easy accessible to the shore, and the seaview rooms at Silver Beach. More properties will be opening up in the future, so check with the tourist board.

Hotels and Resorts

Cassada Bay Resort   **$80–$125**   ★★

Belmont, Hillsborough, ☎ *(809)443-7494.*
Single: $80–$95. Double: $95–$125.

Accommodations are in simple cabins with ceiling fans set on a hillside sloping down to the beach. Wonderful views and lots of watersports, plus free ferry rides to neighboring islands. Good bird-watching possibilities. 16 rooms. Credit Cards: V, MC, A.

Silver Beach Resort   **$80–$95**   ★★★

Hillsborough, ☎ *(809)443-7337.*
Single: $80–$90. Double: $85–$95.

Set on a quiet beach, this family-run hotel has comfortable rooms with ceiling fans; eight cottages offer more room to spread out and full kitchens. Activities include fishing and boating to nearby islands, and all the usual watersports, including good scuba. 16 rooms. Credit Cards: V, MC, DC, A.

Inns

Caribbee Inn   **$95–$135**

Prospect, Hillsborough, ☎ *(809)443-8142.*
Single: $95–$135. Double: $95–$135.

All accommodations are in cottages on a hillside, with the beach a short stroll away. Ceiling fans keep things cool. Tasty dinners are served from a price-fixed menu. Great views of neighboring islands at this pleasant spot. 10 rooms. Credit Cards: A.

PETITE MARTINIQUE

A tiny burp in the sea is this third island in Grenada's troika. Fishermen know exactly where it is. To get here, best to hop a ride on a mail boat.

Grenada Directory

ARRIVAL

American Airlines provides daily service to Grenada from its San Juan hub while BWIA offers two direct flights a week from New York and connections from Miami and Toronto via Trinidad and other Caribbean islands. LIAT also serves Grenada several times a day from Barbados, Trinidad and Venezuela.

If you feel comfortable driving on the left and sharing the island's twisting roads with goats and peds, rent a car. A standard car at **Spice Island Retreats** which represent Avis *(☎ 809-440-3926)* and MCR Car Rentals *(☎ 809-440-2832)* or pager *411-8235* is about $50–60 a day. Alternately, taxi companies and tour operators excel at showing off Grenada's greatest assets.

CLIMATE

A dry and rainy season dominate Grenada's climate. April–December is the dry season; May–January the rainy, though showers are brief. Temperatures hover around 80 degrees F. There is blissfully little humidity because of the constant trade winds.

DOCUMENTS

U.S. citizens must present a valid passport or proof of citizenship (birth certificate or voter's registration card), plus a photo ID) and an ongoing or return ticket. All visitors pay a departure tax of $14.

ELECTRICITY

The official current is 230 volts, 50 cycles AC, so you must bring an adapter.

GETTING AROUND

Driving on the left, but risky for the twisting and sometimes poor roads over rough terrain. Instead, do as residents do, and get around on so-called buses, really vans that accommodate up to 14 in very cozy quarters. To make a sightseeing tour, hire a taxi and driver for a day, and head out to the forest reserve, waterfalls, small fishing village and great views.

Grenada's sister island of Carriacou is now accessible by air after dark with the addition of night landing facilities to the island's Lauriston Airport.

LANGUAGE

Since Grenada was formerly under the British throne, natives speak English with a beautiful lilt. A local dialect mixes French with African slang.

MEDICAL EMERGENCIES

The General Hospital in St. George has limited facilities; you might find better advice at the Grenada University School of medicine ☎ *809-444-4271*, a privately owned, U.S.-managed school on Grand Anse Beach.

MONEY

The official currency is the Eastern Caribbean dollar (EC). Make sure you know which dollar is being quoted to you by a shopkeeper or taxi driver. Traveler's checks and major credits are also widely accepted. If you exchange at the local bank, you may end up in endless lines. If you pay big bills in dollars, the exchange rate will probably not be calculated in your favor.

TELEPHONE

Area code is *809*. To save money, head for the Grenada Telecommunications, Ltd., in St. George or use a special phone card on other telephones. Cellular phone service can be purchased through Boatphone ☎ *800-567-8336*.

TIME

Atlantic Standard time, which is one hour later than New York time.

TIPPING

Expect a 10 percent service charge; no need to tip help further. At eateries not connected to your hotel, leave a 10–15 percent tip. Only tip a taxi driver if he carries your bags.

TOURIST INFORMATION

Grenada Board of Tourism is located at The Carenage, St. George's ☎ *440-2001* and will answer questions, offer brochures and maps. Stop here if you are traveling on to other Grenadine islands. **Grenada Hotel Association Ross Point Inn, Lagoon Road, St. George's** ☎ *444-1353*. In the U.S. call ☎ *(800) 927-9554*.

WHEN TO GO

Don't miss Grenada's Carnival in early August, a four-day-to-night blowout of calypso songs and steel bands, and the traditional "jump-up" parades. Carriacou comes alive in early August for their annual Regatta. Also check out the ninth annual International Triathlon, usually held in January. Competitors come from as far away as Australia and Norway and it takes place along and near Grand Anse Beach.

GRENADA HOTELS	RMS	RATES	PHONE	FAX

Carriacou

Hillsborough

		RMS	RATES	PHONE	FAX
★★	Silver Beach Resort	16	$80–$95	(809) 443-7337	(809) 443-7165
★	Caribbee Inn	10	$95–$135	(809) 443-8142	
★	Cassada Bay Resort	16	$80–$125	(809) 443-7494	

Grenada

St. George's

		RMS	RATES	PHONE	FAX
★★★★★	Calabash Hotel	28	$170–$495	(800) 528-5835	(809) 444-5050
★★★★★	La Source	100	$250–$590	(800) 544-2883	(809) 444-2561
★★★★★	Spice Island Inn	56	$270–$475	(809) 444-4258	(809) 444-4807
★★★★	Rex Grenadian	212	$115–$360	(800) 255-5859	(809) 444-1111
★★★★	Secret Harbour Hotel	20	$100–$225	(800) 334-2435	(813) 530-9747
★★★	Blue Horizons Cottages	32	$100–$165	(809) 444-4592	(809) 444-2815
★★★	Coyaba Beach Resort	40	$75–$165	(809) 444-4129	(809) 444-4808
★★★	Grenada Renaissance Hotel	186	$120–$170	(800) 228-9898	(809) 444-4800
★★★	Twelve Degrees North	8	$130–$285	(800) 322-1753	
★★	Cinnamon Hill Hotel	20	$85–$153	(809) 444-4301	(809) 444-2874
★★	Flamboyant Hotel	39	$70–$220	(800) 223-9815	(809) 444-1234
★★	Gem Holiday Beach Resort	23	$55–$140	(800) 223-9815	
★★	Horse Shoe Beach Hotel	22	$70–$155	(809) 444-4244	(809) 444-4844
★★	No Problem Apartments	20	$55–$85	(809) 444-4634	(809) 444-2803
★★	Siesta Hotel	37	$55–$140	(809) 444-4645	(809) 444-4647
★★	True Blue Inn	7	$65–$110	(800) 742-4276	(809) 444-1247
★	Coral Cove Cottages	11	$65–$120	(809) 444-4422	(809) 444-4718
★	Hibiscus Hotel	10	$60–$125	(809) 444-4233	(809) 444-2873
★	Hotel Balisier	15	$53–$109	(809) 440-2346	
★	Holiday Haven	12	$60–$145	(809) 440-2606	
★	La Sagesse Nature Center	6	$40–$90	(809) 444-6458	(809) 444-6458
★	Maffiken Apartments	12	$60–$85	(809) 444-4255	(809) 444-2832
★	South Winds Holiday	19	$40–$80	(809) 444-4310	(800) 233-9815

GRENADA HOTELS	RMS	RATES	PHONE	FAX
★ Villamar Holiday Resort	20	$42–$62	(809) 444-1614	(809) 444-1341
★ Wave Crest Holiday Apts.	20	$75–$95	(809) 444-4116	

GRENADA RESTAURANTS	LOCATION	PHONE	ENTREE

Grenada

St. George's

American

★ Cot Bam	Grand Anse	(809) 444-2050	$6–$30
★ La Sagesse	St. David	(809) 444-6458	$6–$12

Chinese

★ Bird's Nest	Grand Anse	(809) 444-4264	$11–$24

French

★★★★ Coconut's Beach	St. George's	(809) 444-4644	$6–$26
★★ Le Karacoli	Grand-Anse	590-28-41-17	$8–$25••

International

★★★★ Canbouley	St. George's	(809) 444-4401	$10–$36
★ Red Crab, The	Grand Anse	(809) 444-4424	$10–$31
★ Rudolf's	St. George's	(809) 440-2241	$8–$15

Italian

★ Portofino	St. George's	(809) 440-3986	$6–$22

Latin American

★★★★★ Morne Fendue	St. Patrick's Parish	(809) 442-9330	$17–$17•
★★ Mamma's	St. George's	(809) 440-1459	$19–$19

Seafood

★★★★★ La Belle Creole	Grand Anse	(809) 444-4316	$22–$30
★★★★ Nutmeg, The	St. George's	(809) 440-2539	$5–$20
★ Delicious Landing	St. George's		$17–$24

Note: • Lunch Only

        •• Dinner Only

GUADELOUPE

Bananas are the largest export for Guadeloupe.

Guadeloupe is an island with split personalities. Beaches wash up against volcanoes, sugarcane sprouts next to mangrove swamps; the most luxurious hotels vie for competition with mere wooden huts. Even its population is divided between French apologists and African militants, plus a growing new sector clamoring for a united Carib identity. Typically, Guadeloupe's terrain is shaped like a two-winged butterfly, one side verdant mountains, the other rocky and ringed with white beaches. These days Guadeloupe is a paradise for those eco-adventurers who want to challenge themselves to the max. Diving is a matter of fierce honor among the French-operated industry, and certification courses are considered to be some of the toughest in the world. An entire vacation could be spent trekking over 6000 acres within the national park. But the latest craze in Guadeloupe—a sport for which you need stamina, grit—and a big dose of humor—is cycling. The island terrain is perfect for the two-wheeler activity, which not only lets you see the countryside close up but permits the opportunity to compete with crazy French drivers—an experience that will leave you thankful to be alive.

Bird's Eye View

Guadeloupe is the most northerly of the Windward Islands group in the West Indies. Dominica lies to the south and Antigua and Montserrat to the northwest. A 659-square-mile archipelago, Guadeloupe is formed by two large islands, Grande-Terre and Basse-Terre, separated by the Riviere Salé, a narrow four-mile sea channel (but linked by a bridge) with a smaller island, Marie Galante, to the southeast, and another La Désirade, to the east. At 312 square miles, Basse-Terre (which means lowland) lies on the leeward side of the island, where the winds are calmer. The smaller, less mountainous Grande-Terre received the more dramatic waves and air currents typical to the windward side. There are also a number of small dependencies, mainly Saint Bart and the northern half of St. Martin.

History

Christopher Columbus stumbled upon Guadeloupe during his 1493 excursions, dubbing it Santa Maria de Guadeloupe de Estremadura in honor of a Spanish monastery with which he had close ties. Some 143 years later, the French landed, peopling the island with settlers who had to work in indentured conditions for three years to pay off their sea passage from France. Unfortunately, many proved to be unskilled and unacquainted with tropical farming, and the island soon fell into disrepair while nearby Martinique continued to prosper. The French Revolution inspired the settlers to revolt; they eventually declared themselves independent and even solicited the help of the British enemy. In response, the French government sent a troop of over a thousand men to whip the settlers into shape, expelling the British and exe-

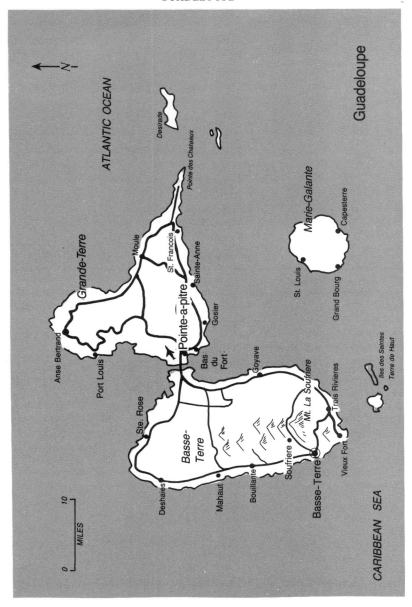

cuting over 4000 Guadeloupian rebels on guillotines set up in the main squares. Under the Napoleonic reign, slavery was reinstated. In 1810 the British successfully reinvaded the island, handing it over to Louis XVIII during the Restoration, and returning when Napoleon came to power; the Brits finally surrendered the island for the last time when the French emperor was exiled to St. Helena in 1815. Since then, Guadeloupe has retained its distinct French flavor combined with a spicy West Indian allure. In September 1989, Hurricane Hugo struck the islands, causing widespread devastation and leaving about 12,000 people homeless. But by the 1990s the banana industry and the tourist industry had recovered and the majority are looking forward to a thriving decade.

People

The proximity of rugged natural resources has bred a spiritual people highly attuned to nature. The medicinal uses of plants and their spiritual properties is common knowledge, particularly among the older residents, but it takes some convincing to induce them to part with the secrets. What most characterizes the people of Guadeloupe, however, is a love of music. In recent years, beats born in Guadeloupe have taken flight onto the international scene, bringing forth a new generation of musicians who are being recognized on the world market. Influenced by black American radicalism in the 1960s, Guadeloupe artists began to redefine their relationship to *gqoka*, or slave music, thus transcending any negative connotations. Infusing the beat with a new political message, a new African-based identity was affirmed. For years a struggle between two musical factions divided musical techniques; one favoring heavy Afro-oriented drum beat while the other favored beguines played on European instruments. The group Kassav suddenly bolted into prominence in the 80s, uniting the two factions by using all matters of instruments and rocking the dance clubs of New York, Paris and Amsterdam. In their wake, many younger groups have been inspired. (For more information about the music of Guadeloupe, see the chapter "Caribbean Culture.")

Most of the locals of Guadeloupe profess Christianity and many are Roman Catholics. There is a segment of the population which is East Indian, but like their fellow islanders from Africa, they have lost the use of their language and speak only Creole. Most women don't even know how to tie a sari anymore.

But Hindu worship still continues in the privacy of their homes. Offsetting the multiracial mixture is a small but significant group of whites called Blancs-Matignons, who steadfastly cling to racist attitudes.

Beaches

Most of Guadeloupe's beaches are lovely white strand open to the public at no extra charge. Hotels sometimes charge minimal fees for nonguests to utilize the resources of their changing facilities, including beach chairs and towels. Some of the best beaches, with long white stretches, are to be found in Grande-Terre. Gray volcanic sand characterizes the beaches in the southern tip of Basse-Terre; the color is gloriously golden as you move toward the northwest coast. Beaches on the windward (Atlantic side) are simply too rough for swimming; divers who use the water should be exceptionally skilled in maneuvering strong currents. Beaches are generally accessible by roads, paved and otherwise. The exception is Islet du Gosier, which is a blip off the shore of Gosier which welcomes nude bathers. It's a great place to plop yourself for a daylong picnic, and arrangements for watersports can be made through the Creole Beach hotel in Gosier.

Caravelle Beach probably wins the award for the most stunning in Guadeloupe—tropical beauty with an immense strand. The sand is exceedingly powdery. Reefs surrounding the beach make excellent conditions for snorkeling. **Club Med** makes use of one end of the beach, but the **Hotel La Toubana** in the hills above has snorkeling equipment for rent. Le Meridien Hotel also sports a fine beach at Raisin-Clairs, where equipment for water sports can be hired. Most popular with the weekend crowd—best to go during the week if you want seclusion—is **Anse de la Gourde**; you will find a restaurant and snack bar there. Lots of nude bathers head for **Tarare**, a private strand just before the tip of Pointe des Châteaux Another popular nude beach is **Place Crawen**, Les'Saintes' placid half-mile strand on Terre-de-Haut. Changing facilities are available a five-minute walk away at **Bois Joli Hotel**. A lovely "feet in the water" restaurant can be found on **La Grande Anse**, just outside of Dashaies, on the northwest coast of Basse-Terre. the Creole cuisine is excellent here at the **Karacoli Restaurant**. Along the western shore, you'll find lots of beaches in miniature, including the gray sands of **Pigeon Beach** and the blackish ones farther south. **Petit-Anse**, on Marie-Galante is a beautiful large beach with gleaming gold sand which fills up fast on the weekends.

Dive Sites

Diving was pioneered by the French and you will find their fierce pride still in tow throughout Guadeloupe. The CMAS, the national scuba association, has the most rigorous certification tests in the world. Even certified divers will be checked on their skills, and French dive tables and apparatus can differ enormously from what you are used to. Most of the dive operators are located in **Pigeon Island**; Jacques Cousteau has called this site one of the ten best diving places in the world. Other suitable sites in Basse-Terre are Grand Anse and Ile a Kahouanne on the northwest coast, and Goyave and Ste. Marie on the east coast. Open water diving is available at Grand Cul-de-Sac Marin, where there are enormous areas of coral gardens. Ilet a Fajou is the most important site, which is easily accessible in a day trip from the resorts in Grande-Terre. All arrangements can be made through operators connected with resorts or hotels.

Treks

There are almost 200 miles of marked trail within Basse-Terre's national park, with all levels of expertise represented. Before you head out, pick up brochures and maps from the Tourist Office in Pointe-a-Pitre.

Superb trails run through Basse-Terre's mountains, running through lush rainforests and elfin woodland, along rugged gorges, rivers, and some of the highest waterfalls in the Caribbean.

In the **Natural Park of Guadeloupe**, a 74,100-acre reserve runs the full length of Basse-Terre. The highlight of the park for nearly everybody is **La Soufriere**, a fire-and-brimstone volcano, still active. The rainforest here is also magical, with lush green foliage and blooming flowers. Easily accessible from the road are well maintained trails with good signs—you can choose the length of trail you desire by following the appropriate sign. In the park are numerous *gîtes*, or inns, that are of modest means. A mile from the entrance is **Crayfish**

Falls, a very popular hike along the banks of the Corossol River through dense and lush vegetation. The falls drop into a large pool below, which offers excellent bathing. Caution, however, should be taken in this area not to hike alone (groups of at least three are better), and avoid carrying valuable or cash. Cameras should never be left unattended.

Soufriere Volcano erupted for the first time in 1975 after centuries of threatening to do so. A visit to the top of this volcano is a rare opportunity to be close to the devastating forces of Mother Nature. There are four well-defined trails, which, total up to 3 1/2 hours if hiked together. All trails end at the peak where there is a witch's scene of boiling mud and steaming craters, piles of strangely shaped rocks, and hot gas spewing from giant, craggy fumaroles and chasms. The odor of sulphur can be overwhelming, and you will wish you have a multidimensional camera that could record sight, sound, taste and smell. Always wear sturdy shoes here as well as rain and wind protection; great care must be taken close to the fuming pits. If the sky is misty, wait a few minutes and it will probably clear. The clearest days are likely to be from December to April. If you're not up to the intense hike, there are several walks near Savane a Mulets that give the feel of the volcano without the effort needed to climb—especially west of the parking lot at Pic Tarade.

Ideal for a day trip are two tiny deserted islands east of the Pointe des Châteaux, called **Iles de la Petit Terre**. Terre-de-Haut is a bit difficult for hiking, but there is a path that runs across the island from a small beach in the north. Terre-de-Bas boasts a lighthouse and a path that runs the length of the island

The two longest and most treacherous trails in the park connect the central areas with the southern region of La Soufriere. In earlier days, slaves escaped over these trails on their way to hide in the mountains. Daring tradesmen who wanted to avoid disease-ridden coasts and also natives on the warpath trod over these trails, considered dangerous even then. The Victor Hugues Trail takes about 8-10 hours, crossing the high mountain plains between Matouba and Montebello on the east coast. Also 8-10 hours long, the Merwart trail follows the same trail to Matouba, then leads off to Matéliane for the final stretch along Morne Merwart to Vernou. If you are anything but advanced, be forewarned aplenty, since there will no assistance in any form anywhere near you, and the weather can change instantly from intense heat to cold mist. Only the most experienced hikers should try them, and only with a guide.

Other guided excursions can be arranged by the **Organization des Guides de Mantage** (☎ *(590) 81-45-75*). The **Organisation des Guides de Montagne de la Cariaibe** (☎ *(590) 81-45-79*) offers treks through the Caraibe Mountains.

Cycling

Cycling has become the latest craze in Guadeloupe. Roads are generally good, and its twin islands are large enough to be interesting terrain. As you bike, you may have French drivers yelling out *Courage* or *Alley-z. Alley-z*, which really means, if you hear the tone behind it, "get out the way, sucker before I run you over!" The sanest way to bike Guadeloupe may be group travel with one member transporting the gear in a rental car with roof racks for the bikes. The group can switch between car and bike according to which terrain suits you. The **Tour de la Guadeloupe** race takes place in August, a highly competitive contest that brings out the fiercest cyclists in the world.

Alternatively you can confine your cycling to flatter Grande-Terre. Rent a bike for day loops through cane country, followed by the rewards of a rum punch and Guadeloupe's superb cuisine, which, after a sweaty ride and cool shower, you can indulge in without guilt. But even on Grande Terre, you want to be road savvy before starting out. This is no island to learn the basics. Don't expect bike paths, though a short one with its own bridge across the Riviere Salé connects Grand-Terre and Basse-Terre. Shoulders, if they exist, tend to be choppy and gravel strewn. Skids happen. Local roads on Grand-Terre are roughened by cane haulers and great potholes on downhills can hide in the shade of tall tulip trees. Also you're fighting traffic, from oxen to Renault 16-wheelers.

A one-week itinerary could start in the main city of **Pointe-a-Pitre**, with a population of 26,000 on the southwest coast of Grand-Terre. The city is a mix of angular glass and masonry, narrow, one-way colonial streets, open-air markets full of straw bags and madras shopping bags. Color runs everywhere here.After crossing the bridge into Basse-Terre, head north. Just past Petit Boourg, begin the five-mile climb up the Route de la traversé, which crosses the mountainous National Park to the far coast. Nearby is the Auberberge de la Distillerie, a small inn. Then travel on to St. Franois, Le Moule, through Morne-a-l'Eau, the shortest route back to Pointe-a-Pointe.

Bike repairs can be checked into at **Elle Rollé** (☎ *590-831574, rue Frévault in Pointe-a-Pitre*), which provides reliable service. It's a good idea to check in with them before leaving town and establish rapport that will let you call in for advice on the road if necessary. On the other hand, every town of any size at all has a bike shop, quite possibly easier to find than public phone.

Do get supplied with good maps before you kick off.

What Else to See

Point-a-Pitre is the Caribbean in double time. The city of some 100,000 people moves at a faster peace than probably any other Caribbean city, a maze of narrow streets, traffic pileups and honking horns. The city has paid its dues over the years, a victim of various hurricanes, earthquakes and other natural disasters, the last being Hurricane Hugo in 1989. Some French colonial structures still remain, but downtown has been recently renovated, and the new cruise terminal called Centre St. John Perse has brought a lively commercial feel with its numerous boutiques and restaurants.

First stop in the city should be at the Tourist Office in Place de la Victire, to pick up maps and brochures. Even outside the door you'll find lots of lively locals hawking anything from pots and pans to underwear. Fruits and vegetables can be bought from a bevy of women dressed in brightly colored costumes near the port. The local Marketplace, between the streets of St.John Perse, Freebault, Schoelchen and Peynier, is a beehive of activity for the purchase of the latest crops from the fields. Take time to meet the ladies of the market, whose beautiful smiles could light up anybody's day. Due to the presence of crowds, give attention to your handbag as you stroll through.

Two museums are worth a look. The **Musee St. John Perse** in a restored colonial house is a tribute to the 1990 Nobel Prize winner in Literature, where you can read works of his poetry. Also check out the **Musée Schoelcher**, a memorial to Victor Schoelcher, a 19th-century Alsataon freedomfighter who was responsible for emancipation in the French West Indies.

The capital of the island, **Basse-Terre** is significant for its port and its market, both situated along boulevard General de Gaulle. A fine colonial square houses several old structures at Champ d'Arbaud. A few beautiful hours can be spent strolling the gardens at **Jardin Pichon**. A short stop can be made to the 17th-century fort St. Charles and the Cathedral of our Lady of Guadeloupe. A look at the volcano in this area can be made from any number of picnic tables in the suburb of **St. Clade**. (For information on how to scale the mountain, see under "Treks" above.) Near the ferry landing for Les Saintes, the **Parc Archéologique des Roches Gravees** contains a collection of pre-Columbian rock engravings. Exhibits explain the engravings of folk and fauna symbols on the petroglyphs. The park, inside a handsome botanical garden, is a quiet haven for tourists who need to escape the bustle of Pointe-a-Pitre.

Do take time to visit the islands lying directly offshore the mainland. Ferries run regularly to Marie-Galante, Desirade, and Terre-Haut (see below for more information, after "Where to Shop"). Ferry schedules, however, can never be counted on, but check with the tourist office to find out the latest pseudo-itinerary. If you plan to spend time on some of these outposts, a good handle on French is necessary because you will be hard put to find anyone who speaks English. Most of your simple needs can be met with a finger pointed to your mouth or the word "toilette" (pronounced twa-lette). There's no need to carry much with you; in fact you can wear your bathing suit under your outer clothes, but you should bring a towel. The island of Dominica is just a short hop away on an airplane. The trip can be done in a day and excursions can be arranged ahead of time to save you wasting time on the island itself.

Historical Sites

Parc Archeologique des Roches   ★★★

Trois-Rivieres.
Hours Open: 9:00 a.m.–5:00 p.m.
At this peaceful spot near the wharf, displays interpret the rock engravings by Carib Indians that date back to A.D. 300.

Museums and Exhibits

Edgar Clerc Archaeological Museum   ★★★

La Rosete, Moule.
This small museum displays artifacts from the Carib and Arawak Indians found on the islands of the Eastern Caribbean. Closed Wednesday afternoons and Tuesdays. Free admission.

Musee Schoelcher   ★★

24 Rue Peynier, Pointe-a-Pitre.
Displays highlight the personal papers and belongings of Victor Schoelcher, who, in the 19th century, worked to abolish slavery in the French West Indies.

Musee St. John Perse   ★★

Achille Rene-Boisneuf Rue, Pointe-a-Pitre.
Hours Open: 9:00 a.m.–5:00 p.m.
This museum in a restored colonial house contains the works of St. John Perse, a local boy made good who won the Nobel Prize in Literature in 1960.

Parks and Gardens

Parc Naturel de la Guadeloupe   ★★★★★

Route de la Traversee.
Covering 74,000 acres with 200 miles of trails, this national park has something for everyone: waterfalls, thick vegetation, nature walks and the centerpiece, La Soufriere, a smoldering volcano that last erupted in 1975. Stop by the Maison de la Foret for a look at the park's history (only, alas, in French) and a booklet on hiking trails.

Wear rain gear, as this area gets some 250 inches per year. If you're interested in a guided hike tailored to your level, contact the Organisation des Guides de Montagne de Caraibe at ☎ *80-05-79.*

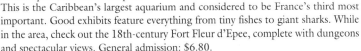

Tours

Aquarium de la Guadeloupe   ★ ★ ★ ★ ★

Place Creole, Marina Bas-du-Fort.
Hours Open: 9:00 a.m.–7:00 p.m.
This is the Caribbean's largest aquarium and considered to be France's third most important. Good exhibits feature everything from tiny fishes to giant sharks. While in the area, check out the 18th-century Fort Fleur d'Epee, complete with dungeons and spectacular views. General admission: $6.80.

Sports

Strong currents and good winds make yachting a popular sport in Guadeloupe. Safe anchorages can be found at the offshore isles of Marie-Galante and Les Saintes—many people go here on day excursions. In the harbor are yachts of all shapes and sizes, which can be hired, chartered, crewed or bareboat, for any length of time. You can, through the services of **Le Boat**, a unique service, take one boat to an island and leave it there (ask the Tourist Office for more information). Windsurfing is also popular and lessons and equipment can be arranged through all the seaside hotels. Hotels also assist in arrangements for deep-sea fishing from boats based at the **Port de Plaisance Marina in Bas du Fort** *(☎ 590-82-74-94).* Marlin and tuna are profuse in the waters off the west coast of Basse-Terre at Pigeon Island. The season for barracuda and kingfish is January to May. Horsebackriding can also be arranged through **Le Criolo**, a riding school at St. ƒélix near Gosier. (For diving, trekking, and cycling, see under the appropriate sections above.

Golf Municipal Saint-Francois

St.-Francois.
The island's only golf course features 18 holes designed by Robert Trent Jones and an English-speaking pro. Greens fees for the par-71 course are $45.

Holywind

Pointe de la Verdure, Gosier.
Feeling daring? Fly along the coastline in an Ultra Leger Motorise, a lightweight seaplane.

Watersports

Various locations, Pointe-a-Pitre.

Your hotel probably has enough watersports to keep you happy. If not, check out one of the following. Scuba diving: **Chez Guy et Christian** *(☎ 98-82-43)*, **Aqua-Fari** *(☎ 84-26-26)*, and **Nauticase** *(☎ 84-22-22)*. On Isle des Saintes, **Centre Nautique des Saintes** *(☎ 99-54-25)*. Windsurfing: **Callinago** *(☎ 84-25-25)* and **UCPA Hotel Club** *(☎ 88-64-80)*. Deep-sea fishing: **Caraibe Peche** *(☎ 90-97-51)*, **La Rocher de Malendere** *(☎ 98-70-84)*, **Evasion Exotic** *(☎ 90-94-17)*, and **Fishing Club Antilles** *(☎ 86-73-77)*. Boat rentals: **Soleil et Voile** *(☎ 90-81-81)*, **Vacances Yachting Antilles** *(☎ 90-82-95)*, and **Locaraibes** *(☎ 90-82-80)*.

Where to Stay

Highest Rated Hotels in Guadeloupe

★★★★★ Auberge de la Vieille Tour

★★★★★ Le Meridien St. Francois

★★★★★ Le Meridien la Cocoteraie

★★★★ Canella Beach Residence

★★★★ Club Med Caravelle

★★★★ Fleur d'Epee Novotel

★★★★ Hotel Hamak Beach

★★★★ La Creole Beach Hotel

★★★★ PLM Azur Marissol Hotel

★★★★ Villa Creole Hotel

Most Exclusive Hotels in Guadeloupe

★★★★★	Le Meridien la Cocoteraie	$160–$680
★★★★★	Le Meridien St. Francois	$199–$285
★★★★	Hotel Hamak Beach	$175–$255
★★★★★	Auberge de la Vieille Tour	$118–$231
★★★★	Fleur d'Epee Novotel	$123–$213

Fielding's Best Value Hotels in Guadeloupe

★★★	Plantation Ste. Marthe	$157–$315
★★★★	PLM Azur Marissol Hotel	$94–$185
★★★★★	Auberge de la Vieille Tour	$118–$231
★★★★	Hotel Hamak Beach	$175–$255
★★★	L'Auberge de Distillerie	$105–$125

Most of Guadeloupe's hotels and resorts predictably hug the coast and the sandy coves. Despite the French presence on the island, service is not the best in the Caribbean, but it is generally friendly. Simply, stiff formalities are not practiced here, and you are more likely to have to wait a while for a request to be fulfilled; enjoy the time relaxing. **Gosier**, once a sleepy town, is now the hub of tourism; there are several resorts to pick from as well as more intimate guest houses. **L'Anse Bertrans** on the northern coast of Grande-Terre is just now becoming developed. One of the most attractive newer areas is **Bas du Fort**, between Pointe-a-Pitre and Gosier; the apartments here are particularly serviceable and restaurants are conveniently located. About a half-hour drive from Pointe-a-Pitre is **Saint François**, where you can choose among several sailing options at the harbor.

Hotels and Resorts

It's hard to believe, but on Guadeloupe room service is hard to obtain, even in the finest hotels. **Club Med** remains a winner on Guadeloupe, the all-inclusive regime attracting a lot of French and Americans.

Basse-Terre

Villa Creole Hotel   **$71–$115**   ★★★★

Petionville, Soufriere, ☎ *509-45-62-41.*
Single: $71–$115. Double: $83–$115.

Set high on the hills and surrounded by a forest, this comfortable, family-run hotel has a loyal following. The spacious guest rooms are air-conditioned and accented with Haitian furniture. There's a free-form pool in a nicely landscaped garden and lots of interesting local art in the public areas. Two tennis courts await the strenuous set. A nice property with lots of island flavor. 72 rooms. Credit Cards: V, MC, A.

Grande-Terre

Auberge de la Vieille Tour   **$118–$231**   ★★★★★

Point a Pitre, Gosier, ☎ *(800) 221-4542, 590-84-23-23.*
Single: $118–$208. Double: $128–$231.

Set on a 15-acre estate overlooking the Caribbean Sea, this posh property includes the tower of an 18th-century sugar mill. Accommodations are nicely done with expensive furnishings and lots of amenities; request one of the newer ones, added a few years ago and situated in townhouses. There's two tennis courts and a pool, with watersports available nearby. The small beach can get crowded. 153 rooms. Credit Cards: V, MC, A.

Callinago Hotel & Village   **$102–$216**   ★

Pointe de la Verdure, Gosier, ☎ *590-84-25-25.*
Single: $102–$166. Double: $121–$216.

This complex comprises a 40-room hotel on a hill and a 115-unit apartment building on the beach. All units are nicely done with European baths; the apartments have kitchens, too. There are two restaurants, a pool and watersports, with a casino adjacent. A popular spot, especially with families. 110 rooms. Credit Cards: V, MC, DC, A.

Canella Beach Residence   **$87–$230**   ★★★★

Pointe de la Verdure, Gosier, ☎ *590-90-44-00.*
Single: $87–$230. Double: $109–$230.
Set in the heart of Gosier's hotel scene, this beachfront hotel has small but attractive air-conditioned guest rooms and suites with kitchenettes. All the usual resort diversions, and lots to do within an easy walk. Parents can stash the kids in supervised programs during high season. 146 rooms. Credit Cards: V, MC, DC, A.

Club Med Caravelle   ★★★★

Ste. Anne, ☎ *(800) 258-2633, 590-88-21-00.*
Encompassing 45 acres with a wonderful mile-long private beach, this Club Med appeals mainly to tourists from France, so much so that many activities are held in French. (A good chance to learn the language, and they have labs to help you do just that.) The all-inclusive rates cover just about everything. All the resort amenities are here, from tennis to watersports to a lively night scene—but while nice, this is not one of the better Club Meds. 310 rooms. Credit Cards: A.

Ecotel Guadeloupe   **$60–$130**   ★★

Montauban, Gosier, ☎ *590-90-60-00.*
Single: $60–$95. Double: $85–$130.
Located less than half a mile from the beach and a mile from Gosier Village, this motel-like operation is a hotel school, so you can count on professional, enthusiastic service. Rooms are comfortable and air-conditioned, but nothing too exciting. There are two restaurant and a pool, but not much else. A good bargain though, with a mostly European clientele. 44 rooms. Credit Cards: V, MC, DC, A.

Fleur d'Epee Novotel   **$123–$213**   ★★★★

Bas du Fort, ☎ *(800) 221-4542, 590-90-40-00.*
Single: $123–$182. Double: $142–$213.
Set on a peninsula near a fine sandy beach, this Y-shaped hotel is informal and friendly, attracting laid-back types who enjoy a range of activities from watersports to tennis to bridge. Guest rooms are air-conditioned and most have sea views from the balconies. Supervised programs keep kids busy while their parents laze at the pool or beach. Lots of young Europeans like this spot. 190 rooms. Credit Cards: V, MC, DC, A.

Hotel Arawak   **$130–$240**   ★★

Pointe de la Verdure, Gosier, ☎ *590-84-24-24.*
Single: $130–$200. Double: $150–$240.
Catering to a mostly European and Canadian clientele, this 10-story complex has bright and comfortable guest rooms, most with a nice ocean view and balcony. Three tennis courts, a pool, casino, watersports and a fitness center keep guests busy. The top-floor suites are enormous and worth the splurge. The beach is lively and topless. 154 rooms. Credit Cards: V, MC, DC, A.

Hotel Hamak Beach   **$175–$255**   ★★★★

St. Francois, ☎ *590-88-59-59.*
Single: $175–$225. Double: $205–$255.
Set on 200 secluded acres bordering a reef-protected lagoon, this lushly landscaped property is elegant and exclusive. Accommodations are in air-conditioned bunga-

lows with one or two bedrooms, kitchenettes and outdoor showers. There's an 18-hole golf course across the street, and tennis, air-charter tours (they have their own landing strip) and three small private beaches on site. Excellent service and a well-heeled atmosphere make this one of Guadeloupe's finest resorts. 56 rooms. Credit Cards: CB, MC, A.

Kaliko Beach Club $80–$99   ★

La Gonave Bay, Montrouis, ☎ *509-22-80-40.*
Single: $80. Double: $99.
Situated on 15 acres in the Arcahaie beach area, this complex houses guests in circular stone bungalows nicely furnished and air-conditioned. The beach is quite nice and affords all the usual watersports, plus a good diving center. There's also a pool and tennis on two courts. 40 rooms. Credit Cards: V, MC, A.

La Creole Beach Hotel $60–$550   ★★★★

Point de la Verdure, Gosier, ☎ *590-90-46-46.*
Single: $60–$550. Double: $151–$550.
Located on a 10-acre estate on Pointe de la Verdure Beach, this resort offers large and modern air-conditioned guest rooms. Entertainment nightly under the stars is a nice touch. The wide beach offers up all watersports, including free scuba lessons, and there are also a pool, two tennis courts, and a gym. The casino is nearby. 321 rooms. Credit Cards: V, MC, DC, A.

Le Meridien St. Francois $199–$285   ★★★★★

St. Francois, ☎ *(800) 543-4300, 590-88-51-00.*
Single: $199–$285. Double: $199–$285.
Located on the southern shore of Grand Terre, this contemporary resort sits on 150 acres fronting one of the best beaches in the country. The European-style resort is self-contained, with lots going on in the protected lagoon and on the tennis courts, in the marina and on the archery range. Guest rooms are on the plain side, but have comfortable tropical furnishings and English-language stations on the TV. A casino and the municipal golf course are nearby. Tres chic, and one of the few resorts where North Americans won't feel out of place. 265 rooms. Credit Cards: V, MC, DC, A.

Le Meridien la Cocoteraie $160–$680   ★★★★★

Avenue de L'Europe, Saint Francois, ☎ *590-88-79-81.*
Single: $160–$335. Double: $335–$680.
Mostly well-heeled Europeans visit this resort, where every room is a nicely furnished suite. The beach is quite small and there are two tennis courts and a restaurant. All other facilities are found next door, at the Meridien St. Francois, including a marina and watersports. Elegant, but English speakers may feel out of place (and out of touch). 50 rooms. Credit Cards: V, MC, A.

PLM Azur Marissol Hotel $94–$185   ★★★★

Bas du Fort, ☎ *590-90-84-44.*
Single: $94–$139. Double: $111–$185.
Facing the bay of Point-a-Pitre, this resort complex shares its fine beach with the Fleur d'Epee Novotel. Accommodations range from standard guest rooms to bungalows, all air-conditioned and sporting balconies. Pampering treatments await in

the spa. A few restaurants, large pool and watersports provide other diversions. There's also tennis on-site and a marina nearby. Like many of its competitors, this one attracts mostly young and casual Europeans. 200 rooms. Credit Cards: V, MC, DC, A.

Plantation Ste. Marthe   **$157–$315**   ★★★

St. Francois, ☎ *590-88-72-46.*
Single: $157–$315. Double: $181–$315.
Sitting high on a hill with sweeping views and surrounded by 15 acres of fields and gardens, this great choice puts up guests in Louisiana-style buildings housing very nice guest rooms and duplexes. Shuttles transport beach lovers to the sand. There's a pool, 18 holes of golf, and a fitness center; the French Creole restaurant is highly regarded. Very pleasant, if you don't mind the off-beach location. 120 rooms. Credit Cards: V, MC.

Apartments and Condominiums

Since eating out is an art in Guadeloupe, cooking on the island in your own facilities may seem superfluous or beside the point. However, it's nice to know you can whip up your own breakfast, and maybe picnic lunch, then apply the savings to fabulous dinners. Many French ex-pats rent out their fashionable villas and apartments during high season, however, some of the digs don't even have hot running water. Do your best to find out all facts before shacking up with a rental; some clients have been shocked at the results. Most rental operators don't speak English, so your French should be superb, particularly to verify any "small print" on your contract. Rentals can be arranged for one week (usually the minimum) to longer stays. Some beautiful seaside homes are among the prize of the lot. Do specify your exact needs (location, sea view, distance to the beach, proximity to shopping, restaurants, etc.).

Grande-Terre

Relais du Moulin   **$105–$156**

Chateaubrun, Ste. Anne, ☎ *590-88-23-96.*
Single: $105–$129. Double: $128–$156.
Located on an old sugar plantation amid tropical gardens, this complex is somewhat isolated, set in the remote, though scenic, countryside. Accommodations are in air-conditioned bungalows with kitchenettes and patios complete with hammocks. Tennis, archery and a swimming pool await. The beach is not too far a walk. Great views reward those who climb the windmill. 40 rooms. Credit Cards: V, MC, DC, A.

Inns

Inns on Guadeloupe are often defined as a lodging with less than 50 rooms. Such accommodations are handled through a local association of hotels called **Relais Créoles**. Membership in the association does not insure quality, so make sure you acquire as much information as possible. The best inns, like **Relais de Grand Soufriere**, combine the elegance of high ceilings and mansion like elegance with the tropical breeziness. The smaller the hotel, the more necessary it is to speak French well; although hosts can be congenial, don't expect too much in the way of room service. **Auberge du Grand Large** boasts excellent Creole food for both lunch and dinner.

Basse-Terre

L'Auberge de Distillerie   **$105–$125**   ★ ★ ★

Route de Versailles, Deshaies, ☎ *590-94-25-91.*
Single: $105–$125. Double: $105–$125.
This French-style country inn in a residential area near the national park appeals to nature lovers. Guest rooms are simple but comfortable with air conditioning and television sets. The Creole restaurant and bar are popular with locals. There's also a pool on-site. You may feel left out if vous ne parlez pas francais. 15 rooms. Credit Cards: V, MC, DC, A.

Relais Grand Soufriere   **$49–$93**   ★ ★ ★

St. Claude, Deshaies.
Single: $49–$76. Double: $49–$93.
This historic inn dates back to 1859 and reopened in 1986 after extensive renovations. The lovely hillside grounds include a pool. Accommodations are in a mansion, once a private residence, and are elegant and quite comfortable. 21 rooms. Credit Cards: V, MC, DC, A.

Grande-Terre

Auberge du Grand Large   **$100–$105**   ★ ★

Route de la Plage, Ste. Anne, ☎ *590-88-20-06.*
Single: $100–$105. Double: $100–$105.
Located on Ste. Anne Beach, a nice stretch frequented by locals, this casual spot places guests in air-conditioned bungalows. Besides a bar and Creole restaurant, there's not much in the way of extras, but the rates are reasonable. 10 rooms. Credit Cards: V, MC, A.

Grande-Terre

Hotel Toubana   **$105–$230**   ★ ★

Ste. Anne, ☎ *590-88-25-78.*
Single: $105–$170. Double: $130–$230.
Set on a hill overlooking the south shore of Grande Terre, this charming complex boasts magnificent views. Guests stay in air-conditioned bungalows with kitchenettes and private gardens. The grounds include a pool, tennis court, bar and restaurant. The beach is a short stroll down the hill, where watersports await. Not bad. 32 rooms. Credit Cards: V, MC, DC, A.

Low Cost Lodging

Considerable discounts can be arranged from mid-April to November, when the season moves into low status. Rates may vary with current fluctuations. **Relais Bleus de Raizet** is a motel whose chief virtue is that it is a 10-minute ride from the airport. Rooms are minuscule and the air-conditioning could keep you up all night, but it's cheap.

Where to Eat

Highest Rated Restaurants in Guadeloupe

★★★★★ Auberge de la Vieille Tour

★★★★★ La Canne A Sucre

★★★★★ La Plantation

★★★★★ Le Chateau de Feuilles

★★★★ La Rocher de Malendure

★★★ Chez Clara

★★★ Chez Paul de Matouba

★★★ Chez Violetta

★★★ La Louisiane

★★★ Le Poisson d'Or

Most Exclusive Restaurants in Guadeloupe

★★★★★ La Plantation	$14–$54
★★★★★ Auberge de la Vieille Tour	$23–$39
★★★★★ La Canne A Sucre	$18–$32
★★★ Les Oiseaux	$14–$29
★★★ Chez Clara	$9–$27

Fielding's Best Value Restaurants in Guadeloupe

★★★ Le Poisson d'Or	$14–$27
★★★ La Louisiane	$22–$30
★★★★★ Auberge de la Vieille Tour	$23–$39
★★★★★ La Canne A Sucre	$18–$32
★★★ Chez Clara	$9–$27

Guadeloupe boasts some of the best creole cuisine in the Caribbean, and chefs care for their food with pride and love. Trust places that specialize in local foods—typically they'll say *cuisine créole*—and they reflect the obvious pride in creole style, the way a place would look in the French countryside if France were the Caribbean—which is precisely the case in Guadeloupe. Court bouillon is a lively fish soup, which makes a good starter. Rice and beans are often prepared in coconut water. Of the more than two dozen creole restaurants that thrive on the islands, there are a few that are considered out of this world. Among the best are **La Canne a Sucre**, in an elegant new location in the modern Centre St.-John Perse at the edge of the water (the brasserie down below is cheaper than the restaurant which features red snapper with passion fruit mousse). **La Créole Chez Violetta** is also highly recommended. A voluptuous beachside lunch can be had at **Le Karacolo** restaurant in Deshaies (For more information, see the chapter "Caribbean Culture" under the heading Culinary Arts.

Basse-Terre

Chez Clara $$$ ★★★

Ste. Rose, Ste. Rose, ☎ *590-28-72-99.*
Latin American cuisine.
Lunch: 12:00 p.m.–2:30 p.m., entrees $9–$27.
Dinner: 7:00 p.m.–10:00 p.m., entrees $9–$27.
Like the jazz she once danced to, native chef Clara Lesueur's culinary improvisations are realized by years of perfecting basic techniques. Guests that patronize Clara's chez on Ste. Rose's seafront are fans of long-standing, guaranteeing a bit of a wait, but the refreshing rum drinks at the bar help ease the pain. Go easy on the cocktails so you can enjoy the Creole specials of lambi with lime and peppers, crayfish and crab backs. No dinner is served Sundays. Closed: Wed. Reservations recommended. Credit Cards: V, MC.

Chez Paul de Matouba $$ ★★★

Riviere Rouge, ☎ *590-80-29-20.*
International cuisine.
Dinner: entrees $12–$18.
Enjoy a refreshing country lunch in this Creole restaurant in Matouba, formerly a Hindu settlement, in the mountains above Basse-Terre. The ambience here is similar to a fishing lodge, where diners enjoy a veritable marketplace of local greens and fresh seafood while a river runs outside. Specialties include accras (codfish fritters) with an incendiary sauce, or grilled ouassous (crayfish). Fixed-price meals under $20 are available. Closed: Mon. Credit Cards: V, MC.

La Rocher de Malendure $$ ★★★★

Malendure Beach, Brillante, ☎ *590-98-70-84.*
French cuisine.
Dinner: entrees $8–$18.
The vista from this upscale eatery perched on a bluff above Malendure Beach is Pigeon Island, a top diving locale and underwater reserve. If you can keep your eyes

from the scenery, you'll be drawn to the delectable Creole treats on the fixed-price lunch that runs under $20—accras, barbecued chicken, crayfish in sauce and a beverage. Dinners are served Fridays and Saturdays only. Closed: Sun. Reservations recommended. Credit Cards: V, MC, DC.

Grande-Terre

Auberge de la Vielle Tour $$$ ★★★★★

Montauban, Gosier, ☎ *590-84-23-23.*
French cuisine.
Dinner: 7:00 p.m.–10:00 p.m., entrees $23–$39.

Possibly the finest cuisine in Gosier can be found in the main dining room of the Pullman Auberge de la Vielle Tour. The view alone, of the Ilet du Gosier and its lighthouse in the distance, is worth the high tariff. Tables facing the wraparound windows are, naturally, the most sought after, so request one way in advance. A la carte offerings include red snapper or catch of the day served with exotic fruit butters, or lamb loin roasted with herbs. A prix-fixe menu ($45) is also available. Associated Hotel: Pullman Vielle Tour Hotel. Reservations recommended. Credit Cards: V, MC, DC, A.

Chez Violetta $$$ ★★★

Perinette Gosier, Gosier Village, ☎ *509-84-10-34.*
French cuisine.
Lunch: 12:00 a.m.–3:30 p.m., entrees $11–$25.
Dinner: 7:30 p.m.–11:00 p.m., entrees $11–$25.

One of the best-known tourist establishments in the islands is this restaurant serving traditional Creole specials in a room resplendent with baroque trappings. This mecca for delicacies like accra (cod fritters) and lambi (conch) is still going strong, even after the death of its creator Violetta Chaville. Service is by women in traditional dress. This is an excellent visual and culinary experience for first-time visitors. Credit Cards: V, MC, DC, A.

Folie Plage $$$ ★★

Anse Laborde, Anse Laborde, ☎ *590-22-11-17.*
French cuisine.
Lunch: 12:00 a.m.–3:00 p.m., entrees $14–$18.
Dinner: 7:00 p.m.–10:00 p.m., entrees $14–$18.

Local families flock to this restaurant/guesthouse in Anse Laborde on the north coast of Grand-Terre, especially on weekends, for a combination of beachcombing and grilled fish, court bouillon and chicken curry. If you're so inclined, rent a simple room from Madame Marcelin for under $50. Associated Hotel: Chez Prudence. Reservations recommended. Credit Cards: V, DC, A.

La Canne A Sucre $$$ ★★★★★

Quai No. 1, Point-a-Pitre, ☎ *590-82-10-19.*
French cuisine.
Lunch: 12:00 a.m.–2:30 p.m., entrees $18–$32.
Dinner: 7:30 p.m.–10:00 p.m., entrees $18–$32.

This fine restaurant in Pointe-a-Pitre's port of Centre Saint-John Perse has a seagull's eye view of arriving ships, with a location on the quay. Patrons have a choice of dining in a ground floor brasserie on grilled lamb and mixed seafood platters, or upstairs in a tony, rose-hued chamber. Chef Gerard Virginius is fond of enhancing the finest seafood and poultry available locally with soursop and starfruit-infused vinegars and wine sauces. Closed: Sun. Reservations recommended. Credit Cards: V, MC, A.

La Louisiane $$$ ★★★

Quartier Ste. Marthe, St. Francois, ☎ *590-88-44-34.*
French cuisine.
Lunch: 12:00 a.m.–2:00 p.m., entrees $22–$30.
Dinner: 7:00 p.m.–10:00 p.m., entrees $22–$30.

Located a few miles from the chic resort of St. Francois in Sainte Marthe, this bloom-filled hillside house has an established reputation for creative French-Antillean cuisine. Dinner for two can get pricey, but the experience is worth the splurge—specialties include shark prepared in a saffron sauce and pate of sea urchin roe. Closed: Mon. Credit Cards: V, MC.

La Plantation $$$ ★★★★★

Galerie Commerciale, Bas du Fort, ☎ *590-90-84-83.*
French cuisine.
Lunch: 12:00 a.m.–2:30 p.m., entrees $14–$54.
Dinner: 7:00 p.m.–10:30 p.m., entrees $14–$54.

Guadeloupe's largest marina also boasts this well-known four-star establishment housed in two rosy, intimate dining rooms. La Plantation presents French classic cuisine with an emphasis on natural ingredients. Crayfish is a specialty, prepared in myriad ways—sometimes in a salad with foie gras, an unusual combination that works. Closed: Sun. Reservations required. Credit Cards: V, MC, DC, A.

Le Chateau de Feuilles $$$ ★★★★★

Campeche, Anse Bertrand, ☎ *590-22-30-30.*
French cuisine.
Lunch: 11:00 a.m.–3:00 p.m., entrees $18–$29.
Dinner: entrees $18–$29.

If you pass the remains of a crumbling old sugar mill in off-the-beaten-path Anse Bertrand, you're close to your goal—a four-star culinary landmark in an unlikely location—of a farm owned by chef-hosts Jean-Pierre and Martine Dubost. The atmosphere is like a house party, with a pool to swim in after lunch and a breathtaking choice of 20 flavors of rum, like a sophisticated Baskin-Robbins for adults. If you had a hard time finding the restaurant, don't indulge too much or you may never make it home. Dinner is served on Fridays and Saturdays, for a minimum of 10 people. Closed: Mon. Reservations required. Credit Cards: V, MC.

Le Poisson d'Or $$$ ★★★

Rue Sadi-Carnot 2, Port Louis, ☎ *590-22-88-63.*
Latin American cuisine.
Lunch: 9:30 a.m.–4:30 p.m., entrees $14–$27.
Dinner: 6:00 p.m.–9:00 p.m., entrees $14–$27.

The pride of the quiet fishing town of St. Louis is this cozy spot serving Creole specialties and seafood in a homey atmosphere. Specials change frequently, but usually feature crab farcis with spicy stuffing and homemade ice cream. Reservations required. Credit Cards: V, MC.

Le Restaurant $$$ ★★★

Chateaubrun, Ste. Anne, ☎ *590-88-23-96.*
French cuisine.
Lunch: 12:30 a.m.–2:30 p.m., entrees $25–$40.
Dinner: 7:30 p.m.–9:30 p.m., entrees $25–$40.
Le Restaurant at the tropical village-style Le Relais du Moulin serves the usual Antillean-French dishes with some flair in an elegant dining room facing the resort's pool. Fixed price meals for $40 and a la carte offerings include grilled langoustes with herbs, *blaff* (fresh seafood in a spicy infusion) and lobster. After dinner, stroll the grounds; an old mill *(moulin)* dating back to the inn's plantation days makes a picturesque photo opportunity. Associated Hotel: Relais du Moulin. Reservations recommended. Credit Cards: V, MC, DC, A.

Les Oiseaux $$$ ★★★

Anse des Rochers, St. Francois,
French cuisine.
Lunch: 12:00 a.m.–3:00 p.m., entrees $14–$29.
Dinner: 5:00 p.m.–10:30 p.m., entrees $14–$29.
It's easy to imagine that you're in the South of France while dining on the terrace of this stone structure facing the sea, located a few miles south of St. Francois. The talented chef is a whiz with seafood, attesting to the popularity of his cassoulet de fruits de mer, and a cheeseless fondue of various fish and shellfish cooked with aromatic oils. Closed: Mon. Reservations required. Credit Cards: V.

Where to Shop

Guadeloupe is not a shopper's paradise—better to go to Martinique. What Guadeloupe lacks in merchandise, it more than makes up for in fun, however. Head for the street stalls around the harbor quay, in front of the tourist office and at the open-air market. The **Juan Perse Cruise Terminal** caters to the more sophisticated, and expensive tastes of cruise passengers; here you'll find a spanking new mall with about 24 shops. Avoid days when cruise ships are in port and start shopping early in the morning, before the noonday sun gets too hot.

Paying with traveler's checks and/or credit cards can sometimes reap you a 20 percent discount. French products, from crystal to cosmetic, perfume and fashions, are often less expensive than stateside, but if you are interested in brand names, do check the prices at home before coming. Native craftwork can run from the junky to the intriguing; the best buys are salako hats made of split bamboo, straw baskets and hats, and wood carvings. Table linens made from madras are particularly fine. Even if you don't drink, bring back at least one bottle of Guadeloupe rum; there's sure to be someone back home who will love it. Best shops for rum are **Delice Shop** in Pointe-a-Pitre and **Ets Azincourt**.

The market at Pointe-a-Pitre, Guadeloupe, is a bonanza of straw hats.

In Pointe-a-Pitre, the main shopping streets are **rue Frébault**, **rue de Nozieres**, and **rue Schoelcher**. Bas-du-Fort's two shopping districts are the **Mammoth Shopping Center** and the **Marina**, where you will find a good supply of both boutiques and restaurants. This is the place to come if you are in need of resort wear fast. Duty-free shops can be found at the **Raizet Airport**.

Terre de Haut

The sailing school at Petite Anse, Terre-de-Haut, offers half or full day windsurfing courses.

Terre-de-Haut is the largest island in an archipelago of eight islands called Les Saintes, off the south coast of Guadeloupe. The 35-minute ferry ride to reach there from Trois-Rivieres or 60-minute ride from Pointe-a-Pitre can be torturous due to choppy waves; do take motion sickness pills if you are susceptible. Terre-de-Haut has but 1500 residents on its five-square-mile terrain; its largest city is Bourg with seerla boutiques, restaurants and gingerbread houses hugging the hillsides. Daring explorers can scope out secluded coves; there's even a nude beach at Anse Crawen, which has been compared to Rio de Janeiro for its beauty. A third of the island's economy is dedicated to tourism, so expect locals to be generous and friendly. Try to avoid driving here since roads are disastrous, at times hardly big enough for one car. Among the most important sites (there really aren't that many) is **Fort Napoléon**, leftover from the days when the English warred with the native population and a nearby museum which houses a modern collection of paintings.

What to See

Fort Napoleon　　　　　　　　　　★★★

Bourg, Lles des Saintes.

This old French fort, wherein you can survey barracks and prison cells, comes complete with modern-day touches like an art museum, botanical gardens and sweeping views.

Where to Stay

Hotels are small here, with the general atmosphere of a West Indian inn. Service is congenial, and at times so familiar you'll feel as if you are renting from your own family. Now is the time to visit the island before it succumbs to more commercial enterprises.

Hotels and Resorts

Hotel Bois Joli　　　　　　**$98–$233**　　　　　★★

Lles des Saintes, ☎ *590-99-52-53.*
Single: $98–$123. Double: $164–$233.

Set in a rustic setting on this hilly island, this modest hotel has simply furnished rooms, only some with air conditioning and private baths. The two bungalows sleep up to four people. There's a restaurant and bar, but not much else, though watersports can be arranged at the beach. 29 rooms. Credit Cards: V, MC.

Where to Eat

La Saladerie　　　　　　**$$**　　　　　★★

Anse Marie, Terre de Haute, ☎ *590-99-50-92.*
International cuisine.
Lunch: entrees $8–$10.
Dinner: entrees $10–$18.

As the name implies, guests can get a good green salad as well as seafood lightly grilled with fresh vegetables on the side at this patio restaurant near the ferry dock in Bourg des Saintes. Prices are very reasonable for the view, the quality of the food and the gracious service. Closed: Tue. Credit Cards: V, MC.

Le Amandiers　　　　　　**$$**　　　　　★★

Place de la Mairie, Terre de Haute, ☎ *590-99-50-06.*
Latin American cuisine.
Lunch: 11:00 a.m.–2:30 p.m., entrees $12–$16.
Dinner: 7:00 p.m.–11:00 p.m., entrees $12–$16.

This casual bistro is a superb base from which to while away the hours in the quaint Norman-flavored town of Bourg de Saintes, with its location right on the central square. A set-price lunch of local vegetables, salads, cod fritters and dessert is a bargain at $10. At dinner, sea-fresh selections like conch and crayfish keeps visitors coming back for more. Reservations recommended. Credit Cards: V, MC, A.

La Désirade

La Désirade, five miles east of Guadeloupe, was coveted by Columbus when he spotted the island on November 3, 1493. The name he chose, which means "desired land" showed his true feelings about the exotic nature of the terrain. Ironically, the island became a leper colony for several years. Today it is a perfect place to escape with a picnic to one of the more beautiful beaches of **Souffleur** and **Baie Mahault**. Presently, the island is nearly pristine. In the main village of Grand Anse, there is a charming old church to visit and a hotel called **La Guitone**, where you can get a fine fish meal.

Marie-Galante

At 60 square miles, Marie-Galante is the largest of Guadeloupe's islands. The Caribs retreated here when they were driven form the mainland by the French; centuries later it's become a favorite haven for tourists, both local and foreign, who find the beach at Petit-Anse particularly charming. The island is the epitome of laid-back, though back in the 1800s it had a thriving sugar plantation industry. Ruins of sugar mills can be found all over the island. To get here, take the ferry from Pointe-a-Pitre, which drops you off at Grand Bourg, its biggest city with a population of 8000.

Where to Eat

L'Auberge L'Arbre a Pain $$$ ★★

Rue Jeanne d'Arc, Marie-Galante, ☎ *590-97-73-69.*
International cuisine.
Lunch: entrees $10–$30.
Dinner: entrees $10–$30.

It may help if you have a working knowledge of French in order to stay or eat at this small (seven room) inn located in Grand-Bourg, the civic center of Marie-Galante. But most visitors to this rural outpost are drawn to the simple country ways and lack of development that make this destination choice. Guests who fly down for the day can enjoy unique seafood dishes here, like octopus, or a more familiar grilled conch or seafood platter. There's also a five-course meal for $30. Associated Hotel: L'Auberge L'Arbre a Pain. Closed: Sun. Reservations recommended. Credit Cards: V.

Guadeloupe Directory

ARRIVAL AND DEPARTURE

American Airlines makes year-round flights to Guadeloupe from more than 100 cities direct to San Juan, with nonstop connections to Guadeloupe via American Eagle. Minerve Airlines, a French charter carrier, has flights Friday-Sunday from New York during December-March peak season. Air Canada flies nonstop from Paris and Fort-de-France and has direct service from Miami, San Juan and Port-au-Prince. Air Guadeloupe flies daily from St. Martin and St. Maarten, St. Barts, Marie-Galante, La Desirade, and Les Saintes. LIAT flies from St. Croix, Antigua, and St. Maarten n the north.

All flights arrive at La Raizet International Airport, 2 1/2 miles from Pointe-a-Pitre. It's easy to hire a cab, from the many lined up at the airport. Cars can be rented at the airport.

CLIMATE

The climate is tropical with an average temperature of 79 degrees F. The more humid and wet season runs between June and November.

DOCUMENTS

If you're only staying up to three weeks, you need show only a current or expired passport (5 years old) or proof of citizenship (voter's registration, birth certificate and official photo ID), as well as an ongoing or return ticket. Longer stays require a valid passport.

ELECTRICITY

Current is 220 volts, AC, 50 cycles. Adapters for American appliances are needed.

GETTING AROUND

Taxis are plentiful and fares are set by the government. Between 9 p.m. and 7 a.m., fares increase 40 percent. You will have to be able to speak French to hire radio cabs.

Buses throughout the island run from 5:30 a.m.–7:30 p.m., and connect the island's major towns to Pointe-a-Pitre. Conditions are modern. Bus stops are included along the road and in shelters marked arrêtbus, but buses will often stop if you flag them down. Fares are inexpensive but the schedules are not reliable and they are often too crowded for comfort. Avoid riding them before and after school.

Since biking is a major sport here, you won't feel alone if you rent one. Bike rentals average about $10 a day, somewhat more for mountain bikes. Vespas are also good vehicles to rent, costing about $40 a day, plus a $200 deposit or a major credit card.

Cars are easy to rent on Guadeloupe. You may use your own driver's license up to 20 days; after that you need to obtain an international driver's permit. Roads are excellent here (over 1225 miles), though the hairpins on Basse-Terre will take some careful negotiating. Natives drive well but fast so be aware of passers. Stick with the top names like Hertz, Budget, and Avis, in case there is trouble with your bill once you return home. in general, rentals here, about $60, are a bit higher than on other islands. Do check with your travel agent to see if prearranged rentals will save you money.

Ferry service is available to and from Marie-Galante, Les Saintes, and La Desirade. One-day excursions are readily available through **Multi Marine Charter** (☎ *(590) 83-32-67)*. The *Princess Caroline* leaves Trois Rivieres for the 30-minute trip to Les Saintes Monday-Saturday at 8:30 a.m, Sundays at 7:30 a.m.

LANGUAGE

The official language is French. The African-influenced Creole is spoken by nearly everyone. Only some people speak English, so bring a French phrase book.

MEDICAL EMERGENCIES

There are five hospitals and 23 clinics in Guadeloupe. Your hotel or the tourist office can assist you in finding an English-speaking physician.

MONEY

The official currency is the French franc. The best exchange rate is to be found at banks or bureau de change; to convert francs back to dollars, you must go to a bank. For some reason, paying for purchases with dollar-denomination traveler's checks or credit cards may get you the best exchange rate.

TELEPHONE

The area code is *590*. To phone from Guadeloupe, buy a "telecarte," a plastic credit card sold at post offices and other outlets marked "Teleporte en Vente Ici." Use these cards on phones marked "Telecom." Operator-assisted calls and those made from your hotel room are much more expensive.

TIME

Guadeloupe is one hour later than Eastern Standard Time.

TIPPING

Restaurants and bars are required by law to add a 15 percent service charge. Most taxi drivers don't expect tips, especially if they own their own cars. Room maids should be tipped $1–2, bellboys 50 cents-$1 a bag.

TOURIST INFORMATION

Brochures, maps and advice can be found at the Office Départemental du Tourisme de la Guadeloupe located near the waterfront in *Pointe-á-Pitre at 5 Pl. de la Banque;* ☎ *820930.* The office is open Monday–Saturday. In the U.S. call ☎ *(213) 658-7462.*

WHEN TO GO

Between December and May. June–November is the humid and wet season.

GUADELOUPE HOTELS	RMS	RATES	PHONE	FAX
Basse-Terre				
Basse-Terre				
★★★★ **Villa Creole Hotel**	72	$71–$115	509-45-62-41	
★★★ **L'Auberge de Distillerie**	15	$105–$125	590-94-25-91	590-9-41191
★★★ **Relais Grand Soufriere**	21	$49–$93		

GUADELOUPE HOTELS	RMS	RATES	PHONE	FAX
Grande-Terre				

Pointe-a-pitre

		RMS	RATES	PHONE	FAX
★★★★★	Auberge de la Vieille Tour	153	$118–$231	(800) 221-4542	590-8-43343
★★★★★	Le Meridien St. Francois	265	$199–$285	(800) 543-4300	590-88-40-71
★★★★★	Le Meridien la Cocoteraie	50	$160–$680	590-88-79-81	590-88-78-33
★★★★	Canella Beach Residence	146	$87–$230	590-90-44-00	
★★★★	Club Med Caravelle	310		(800) 258-2633	
★★★★	Fleur d'Epee Novotel	190	$123–$213	(800) 221-4542	590-9-09907
★★★★	Hotel Hamak Beach	56	$175–$255	590-88-59-59	
★★★★	La Creole Beach Hotel	321	$60–$550	590-90-46-46	590-90-46-00
★★★★	PLM Azur Marissol Hotel	200	$94–$185	590-90-84-44	590-9-08332
★★★	Plantation Ste. Marthe	120	$157–$315	590-88-72-46	
★★	Auberge du Grand Large	10	$100–$105	590-88-20-06	
★★	Ecotel Guadeloupe	44	$60–$130	590-90-60-00	590-90-60-60
★★	Hotel Arawak	154	$130–$240	590-84-24-24	590-84-38-45
★★	Hotel Toubana	32	$105–$230	590-88-25-78	590-88-38-90
★	Callinago Hotel & Village	110	$102–$216	590-84-25-25	590-84-24-90
★	Kaliko Beach Club	40	$80–$99	509-22-80-40	
★	Relais du Moulin	40	$105–$156	590-88-23-96	590-88-03-92

Terre de Haut

Terre de Haut

		RMS	RATES	PHONE	FAX
★★	Hotel Bois Joli	29	$98–$233	590-99-52-53	590-99-55-05

GUADELOUPE RESTAURANTS	LOCATION	PHONE	ENTREE
Basse-Terre			

Basse-Terre

		LOCATION	PHONE	ENTREE
French				
★★★★	La Rocher de Malendure	Bouillante	590-98-70-84	$8–$18●●
International				
★★★	Chez Paul de Matouba	Basse-Terre	590-80-29-20	$12–$18●●

GUADELOUPE RESTAURANTS	LOCATION	PHONE	ENTREE
Latin American			
★★★ **Chez Clara**	Ste. Rose	590-28-72-99	$9–$27

Grande-Terre

Pointe-a-Pitre

French			
★★★★★ **Auberge de la Vielle Tour**	Gosier	590-84-23-23	$23–$39••
★★★★★ **La Canne A Sucre**	Point-a-Pitre	590-82-10-19	$18–$32
★★★★★ **La Plantation**	Bas du Fort	590-90-84-83	$14–$54
★★★★★ **Le Chateau de Feuilles**	Anse Bertrand	590-22-30-30	$18–$29
★★★ **Chez Violetta**	Gosier Village	509-84-10-34	$11–$25
★★★ **La Louisiane**	St. Francois	590-88-44-34	$22–$30
★★★ **Le Restaurant**	Ste. Anne	590-88-23-96	$25–$40
★★★ **Les Oiseaux**	St. Francois		$14–$29
★★ **Folie Plage**	Anse Laborde	590-22-11-17	$14–$18
Latin American			
★★★ **Le Poisson d'Or**	Port Louis	590-22-88-63	$14–$27

Terre de Haute

Terre de Haute

International			
★★ **La Saladerie**	Terre de Haute	590-99-50-92	$8–$18
Latin American			
★★ **Le Amandiers**	Terre de Haute	590-99-50-06	$12–$16

Marie-Galante

Marie-Galante

International			
★★ **L'Auberge L'Arbre a Pain**	Marie-Galante	590-97-73-69	$10–$30

Note: • Lunch Only;

•• Dinner Only

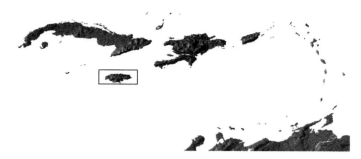

JAMAICA

Bamboo rafts on the Rio Grande River take tourists past magnificent scenery.

Rastas and reggae, jerk pork and ginger beer, cool mountains, hot beaches, damp jungles, and the cold refreshing water of streams and rivers—Jamaica is a continuous dance of the senses. The island can be so stimulating, in fact, that when Ian Fleming created his immortal character James Bond here in 1952, he insisted on facing a white wall in order to avoid the distracting beauty of both women and landscape. Midwife to the great all-inclusive-resorts which have given immediate pleasure a new definition, Jamaica today is fostering the growth of a new, less traditional style of resort—small, private places away from the beaches which allow intimate glimpses of island life and culture. In a back-to-the-future gesture, many of the great houses of century-old sugar plantations are being renovated today with artistic aplomb, and a pioneer in this work is Chris Blackwell, the rock entrepreneur who made Bob Marley an international superstar; his luxurious 10-room Good Hope Great House, a 45-minute drive from Montego Bay, high in Jamaica's lush green hills, gives you the opportunity to relax in the gentile atmosphere of a British country home, six miles from the beach. Ecologically, Jamaica is still a treasurehouse—rainforests, rivers, waterfalls, wetlands, coral reefs and caves are found in every corner of the island, and hundreds of miles of well-marked trails can run from the easy to the daredevilish. From Montego Bay to Ocho Rios, around the perimeter of the island, excellent conditions for all watersports make for exciting adventures, though one of the best is still the rafting sojourn down the Rio Grande River on a banana boat (a favorite pastime of Errol Flynn). These days, with a rising crime rate, you do need to take precautions in Jamaica, but once you sit down to a cold local brew and a big plate of Jamaican-style barbecue, shaded by a palm and served with the most gracious smile you can imagine, every care you've ever had will disappear in a wink.

Bird's Eye View

Located 700 miles southeast of Miami, 110 miles west of Haiti, and 90 miles south of Cuba, Jamaica sprawls over 4400 square miles, making it the third largest island in the Caribbean. Like other West Indian islands, it was formed from the outcropping of a submerged mountain range. A mountain range, reaching over 7402 feet at the Blue Mountain Peak, crosses the island in the east and descends westward; a series of gullies and spurs cross north to south. The north and west coasts harbor the majority of beaches, though a few good ones can be found in the south. The cultural and social pulse of the island, Kingston, the capital, is located in the southeast coast—one of the largest and best natural harbors in the world. Montego Bay, another landmark name in Jamaican tourism, lies in the northwest part of the island.

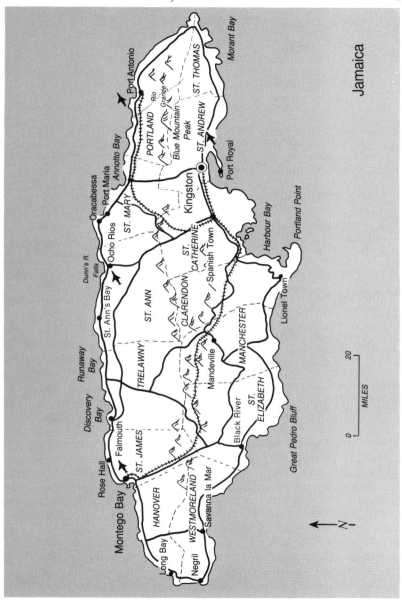

Jamaica

History

Columbus first glimpsed the north coast of the island in May 1494, landing in Montego Bay before he went back to Cuba. When he returned nine years later, stormy weather crippled two of his ships and he was forced to anchor at St. Ann's Bay, where he and his men were shipwrecked until the Governor of Hispaniola retrieved them. In 1510, a permanent Spanish settlement was finally established under the orders of Don Diego, the son of Columbus, who was then Governor of the West Indies, based in Santo Domingo. A new capital was erected in 1935 at Villa de la Vega (the Town on the Plain), now known as Spanish Town. In 1655, Britain, under Oliver Cromwell, challenged Spain's claim on the island, ultimately triumphing and establishing a head base at Port Royal, across the harbor from what is now Kingston. (The Spaniards fled to Windsor Cave, the home even today of many of their descendants.) The new headquarters at Port Royal became the hub of some of the most nefarious activities on the high seas, under the direction of the buccaneer Henry Morgan, whose sacking of the Spanish colony in Panama clinched England's claim to Jamaica. A massive earthquake in 1692 actually shook half the town—like Sodom and Gomorrah—-into the sea. The multi-ethnic, though black-based, population of Jamaica began to be born in the next centuries as sugarcane farming took root, and the need for imported labor in the form of black slaves became imperative. After Jamaica's slave population rose to 300,000 at the end of the 18th century, the ratio of blacks to whites was a staggering 15 to one. Included in the mix were free coloureds, the offspring of white men and slave women, and Maroons, descendants of free slaves. (For more information about the Maroons, see below under "People.") Slave revolts became a common occurrence in Jamaica, the largest, bloodiest conflict led by "Daddy" Sam Sharpe, a Baptist preacher whose oratory and convictions led the way to the abolishment of slavery in Jamaica in 1838. Emancipation, however, led directly to the fall of the sugarcane industry since there was a decided lack of labor. The condition of the freed blacks was further worsened by drought and unsteady economic conditions, leading to another revolt in 1865, which resulted in the murder of a government official. As a result, the island was designated a British Crown Colony in 1866, which it remained until 1944, when full adult suffrage was granted.

A British colony from 1655–1962, Jamaica developed a two-part system before World War II. A considerable measure of self-government was introduced in 1944, but full independence was delayed by attempts to set up a wider federation embracing all or most of the Caribbean Commonwealth territories. Jamaica joined the now-defunct West Indies Federation in 1958 but withdrew in 1961 because of disagreements over taxation, voting rights, and location of the federal capital. Sir Alexander Bustaments, one of the original founders of the two-party system, became the nation's first prime minister at independence in 1962. Under the 1962 constitution the queen is the titular head of state. Her representative, a governor general, is advised in areas bearing on the royal perogative, by a six-member privy council. Jamaica is divided into 13 parishes and the Kingston and St. Andrew Corporation, a special administrative entity encompassing the principal urban areas.

People

Like Brazil, Jamaica is a wonderful place to visit—if you don't get robbed. Jamaicans are a cheerful, generous bunch, full of an earthy humor and deeply inspired by the natural beauty of their island. As a society, they are inherently musical, with great artistic gifts—some of the finest craftwork in the Caribbean is done by untrained Jamaican artisans. And Jamaican people are deeply spiritual—it's said there are more churches per square mile than anywhere else in the world. Most are Protestant, though there are some Roman Catholics, Jews, Seventh Day Adventists, and Pentecostals, but the most apparent are the dreadlocked **Rastafarians**, a local minority cult best recognized by their long braided hair which resembles a rat's nest (Rastas take a religious vow not to wash their hair). Though they can often look a bit intimidating (their hairdos can look voluminous when they pull off their caps), they are nonviolent and do not eat pork; they believe the late Emperor Haile Selassie was a divine being, whose call for the end of racial superiority was connected to the belief that God would lead the blacks out of oppression and back to the Promised Land. Marcus Garvey, the ideologist born in St. Anne's Bay in 1887, is considered a prophet by the Rastas and is today a national hero.

The soul of Rastafarianism lives in the musical genre called reggae, Jamaica's most popular export known throughout the world. Over the years, such musical greats as Bob Marley, Peter Tosh, Jimmy Cliff and others, have used reggae as political and spiritual inspiration through strong lyrics often disguised in meaning. Recently in Jamaica reggae has been supplanted by a newer genre called Dance Hall, which sports a heavier beat, and like American rap, tends to focus on urban violence and sex. Both musical forms can be heard throughout the island; beaches cannot be considered Jamaican if there isn't at least one jam session going on close by.

In the heart of the mysterious and rugged Cockpit country live the Maroons, descendants of escaped slaves who through incredible courage and cunning managed to evade capture for a century. The attitude toward this community is diverse—they have been called anything from the world's most successful revolutionaries to desperate villains and rogues. The peace treaty they eventually signed with the British still exists, like their culture, 250 years later. Hidden deeply inside the hills along a barely passable road, their isolated, self-governing enclaves are only slightly more accessible today. In the past there have been stories reported by travelers of being stopped along the road to Moore Town by Maroons armed with machetes demanding a payment of a road tax. (Being self-ruled, the Maroons can do anything—only in the event of murder are they subject to Jamaican jurisdiction). Their resistance has been buoyed by strong African religious beliefs and rites, and modern Maroon leaders are thought to be imbued with supernatural powers aligned not only to religion but to military prowess. Obeah, the ashanti-inspired system of belief, plays a major part in the Maroon tradition in Jamaica. The January Accompong Festival celebrates the victory of the Maroons over the English. To get to their enclaves is difficult and can often end in a futile search. (For more information see below under the section "Porto Antonio—Treks")

There are many excellent Jamaican novelists whose fiction gives an excellent glimpse into the heart and soul of the people. *Abeng*, a novel by Michelle Cliff, explores the sensitive issues of race and class as seen through the eyes of a young girl. *Jamaica Farewell*, by Morris Cargill, is an honest portrait of the country and its people by a native newspaper columnist. Other fine writers include Olive Senior, H. Orlando Patterson and the poets Mervynn Morris and Dennis Scott.

INSIDER TIP

Note:. Illegal under Jamaican law, the "herb" locally called ganja (marihuana) is known to be a major source of income in the highlands. Officials, however, claim that ganja does not grow anywhere in the residential areas, adding that if it grows "anywhere" it is in the wilderness.

Beaches

The best way to acquaint yourself with the beaches of Jamaica—before even buying a ticket—is to rent a video of the first James Bond film, *Dr. No*—it's practically a travel promotional for the island's most beautiful strands. Then look for more specific information under the individual areas—Kingston, Montego Bay, Port Antonio—below.

Dive Sites (Overview)

Diving in Jamaica can be spectacular. Reefs are very close to shore, minimizing long boat rides. Most operations use island-made, open fisherman-style wooden V-hull boats. Reefs on the north side of the island take the form of a patch or banking reefs rather than the more familiar spur and groove formations. Quality tends to be good, with emphasis on large invertebrate growth. You'll see good sponge formations, though there is a lack of fish and algae overgrowth, but this is compensated by numerous multicolored tropical fish. Water is in the mid 80s degrees F during summer, dropping to mid-70s in the winter. A coverup in the form of a Lycra or Polartec suit is welcome protection. Visibility averages 60–100 feet. Current or proposed marine parks are found in or planned for Negril, Runaway Bay, Montego Bay, and Ocho Rios. For more specific information, see "Dive Sites" under the individual sections.

Treks (Overview)

Jamaica's natural wonders—mountains, rainforests, rivers, waterfalls, wetlands, caves and coral reefs—are found in every corner of the island. Between Port Antonio in the north and Kingston in the south, the **Blue Mountain-John Crow Mountain National Park** covers 192,000 acres and offers spectacular vistas, hiking trails, forests, rare wildflowers, and the Blue Mountain Peak at 7402 feet above sea level. In the west, the karst limestone terrain of the Cockpit Country features forested, conical hills, and countless caves—a hiking district best described by place names like "Land of Look Behind" and "Rest and Be Thankful."

Ever since Errol Flynn's days in Jamaica tourists have enjoyed drifting in the calm lower reaches of Jamaica's rivers on bamboo rafts. The rafts were originally used to float bananas downstream to port until Flynn began organizing raft races on the **Rio Grande**. Eventually, floating down Jamaican rivers, with a raftsman poling a bamboo raft, became a major tourist attraction. But many of the island's whitewater streams in the wild heart of the country still await discovery by paddlers. Today you can find streams that are both serene and suicidal. Jamaica's vast array of waterways gives rise to various vehicular adventures. At least 120 rivers and streams gush from mountain ravines, carving watery gashes into the earth as they tumble into the sea. These are the essential arteries of Jamaica, providing the abundant fresh water that is often so precious on an island. So prevalent are these rivers that the indigenous people called the island *Xamayca*, or "land of wood and water." A great adventure is to rent an inflatable raft down one of these rivers. Drivers Rivers is a good choice for a three-mile sojourn—you'll go through calm spots, challenging rapids, mangroves with flapping herons, and even run into locals bathing in the stream, as well as the waves of the Caribbean breaking on the rocks at the river mouth. Because Jamaica is comparatively small and mountainous, its streams are short and narrow and change character quickly as they charge down the mountainsides toward the sea. This is a country that's more willing to call a mountain a hill and a creek a river.

The **Martha Brae River** is the island's largest at 64 miles. It springs from the caverns in northwestern Jamaica's rugged Cockpit Country, where limestone hills erupt as rough and warty as a toad's back. After running underground, the Martha Brae emerges as milky green from the concentration of minerals and runs through classes two and three rapids before dropping into a big pool. On such a trip, you might run into fishermen who will show you how to cast bait for mullet using a juice can as a reel to hold the line. You can also paddle from here easily over swift rapids almost right up to the doorstep of Good Hope, a 240-year-old greathouse and now a country inn, perched in Georgian grandeur on a hill overlooking the river valley.

Another fantastic raft trip begins at the base of **Y.S. Falls**, a spectacular stair-step, three-tiered cascade of about 125 feet in the hills southwest of Maggot-ty. Though not as well known as **Dunn's River Falls** (famous for tourists walking hand-in-hand up the ledges), Y.S. is still a popular stop (there are many legends as to how the falls got its name). The falls make a great photo op, and kids love to swing out on ropes and dive into the main plunge pool. Starting the trip at below the falls and shooting down the Y.S. river several miles through class two and three rapids, you'll finally reach the point where the river slows in its winding course to Jamaica's southwest coast.

Other exciting and difficult runs are found on the White River near Ocho Rios, Rio Grande near Port Antonio, Wag Water River north of Kingston, and Rio Cobre north of Spanish Town. The Rio Grande in Portland and its tributaries offer "soft" rapids, magnificent scenery, and many swimming holes, mini-waterfalls and a few mineral springs.

Another fascinating trip has no white water at all. The 44-mile long Black River runs to the southwest coast, nearing the town of the same name, and entering the Black River Morass, a sprawling swamp forest and marsh that is the largest remaining crocodile refuge in Jamaica. Here you'll see shrimpers working the channels and women at the roadside selling fresh shrimp, boiled in peppers and salted. The fact that a bamboo raft will make no noise (except for your own yelps) will allow you a better chance to glimpse the crocodiles, osprey, tarpon, and snook in the mangrove roots. On the down side, you'll discover your raft is not much bigger than a good-sized croc. Further upstream, near Maggotty, the stream runs through a spectacular gorge, with an awesome 10-foot falls and roaring cascades.

Sense Adventures, based at Maya Lodge and Hiking Center at 1750 feet above Kingston at the start of the Blue Mountains *(c/o Peter Bentley, Box 216, Kingston, 7, Jamaica;* ☎ *and fax (809) 927-2097)* offers these bamboo raft tours. They inform us that due to the variety of Jamaica's streams, anyone can raft these rivers, no matter what their level of expertise. Flat-water sections on the Martha Brae and Black River make for relaxed exploration if you have never paddled a canoe. Intermediate runs, like the Drivers River, pose no problem and are lots of fun for paddlers with past experience on lakes and quiet streams. The wilder portions of some streams, however, especially when the water runs high and furious, require previous whitewater experience. The best paddling is to be had when the water is fairly high during the fall rainy season. Rainfall varies around the island, so be prepared to change plans in order to find streams with better water levels. Without rain, canoeing can involve tough hikes.

Most of Sense Adventures' rafting trips range from a few hours to all-day affairs, depending on the time you wish to spend. You can adjust the time by changing the put-in and take-out points. Overnight trips are also available.The company provides canoes, paddles, life vests, helmets and lunch. Bring a swimsuit, sunscreen and hat. Wear shoes while canoeing so you can wade in the rocky stream—either old tennis shoes or sandals made for kayaking. Also handy is a waterproof bag in which to stow your gear. Many country inns are available. Cost of river trips, with transport from your hotel, run $55-$90 a day, depending on the location and the number of people in your party. Guided raft and hiking tours range from two hours long to three days, all inclusive, and costing from $55–$90 and up a person a day, depending on the number of people and type of accommodation requested.

Sense Adventures also designs other special-interest tours—birding, cave exploring, etc., to any part of the island. Rates depend on the requirements. Accommodations range from a $5 campsite to a $250-a-night room in a great house in the Blue Mountains.

Mountain trips by **Sunventure Tours** ☎ *(809) 929-5694* include "High Blue," a day tour to Blue Mountain for $45 a person and "Blue Mountain Sunrise," an overnight tour of $140 per person which goes to the peak. A four-wheel drive vehicle takes trekkers to 4000 feet. The rest of the way is on foot. Overnight accommodations are in a hostel. A.Y.S. Falls and Black River Safari Tour from Ocho Rios, including drinks, breakfast, lunch, boat ride, and admissions is offered by **Tourwise** ☎ *(809) 974-2323,* at $79 a person. Sunventure Tours offers a similar tour from Kingston for $65 a person.

Hiking through caves and getting your shoes dirtied with unseen bat dung is a major thrill in Jamaica. The island has more than 380 mapped caves. The **Nonsuch Cave** ☎ *(809) 993-3740,* five miles east of Port Antonio, has lights, guides, fascinating formations and marine fossils. It's open daily from 9 a.m.–5 p.m., admission is $5, $2.50 for children 3 to 11, under 3 free. **Windsor Rock**, bordering Cockpit Country, is a nearly impenetrable area of sheer limestone outbursts. Full of stalagmites and stalactites with rooms ranging from cavernous to tight, it meanders for about two miles through deep lake and treacherous pitches. Most just want an hour's tour. No entry fee, but remember to tip the guide who lights your way with bamboo torches.

Sports (Island-Wide)

Every imaginable water sport is available in Jamaica; the all-inclusive resorts are masters at accommodating guests to arrange any and all levels of expertise. With such luxurious countryside, however, the latest trends are to pursue challenging treks (see the "Treks" section, above)—from floating lazily down the White River (near Ocho Rios) or tooling down the Martha Brae River on an inflatable raft.

KINGSTON

For many tourists, Kingston on first sight is everything they don't want in a Caribbean isle—grimy, traffic-clogged, polluted, noisy, crime-ridden and irrespressibly raucous, but it is, nevertheless, the soul and spirit of most native islanders whose eyes wax over when they remember their childhood memories. This is where the ethnic melting pot first produced the crossbreeding that makes up the present heady spice called Jamaican society. What Kingston truly is today is Bob Marley turf, the undisputed (albeit deceased) king of reggae whose 1974 song "Lively Up Yourself" became the cry of the masses. Today you can't go anywhere in Kingston without making homage to his name; indeed, some travelers come to Kingston *only* for that. His dreadlocked statue stands in the middle of the square across from the National Arena and his records can be found in every store on the island. The **Bob Marley Museum**, ensconced into a 19th-century home on Hope Road, is a visual testimony to his life, struggles and musical influence.

To see the full variety of sights in Kingston, you will probably need to rent a car, or hire a taxi for the day. At the top of the itinerary should be the **Devon House**, a restored 19th-century mansion that first belonged to one of the Caribbean's first black millionaires, George Steibel. The **National Gallery of Jamaica** is a fine place to appreciate the island's art, from 17th-century portraits to impressionist paintings and sculptures. **Hope Botanical Gardens** is a lovely pace to stroll and enjoy the exotic flora of the island; Sundays are crowded but give you a chance to see Jamaican families in action. Across the harbor is **Port Royal**, or what is left of Port Royal, once the island's premier city in the 17th century when buccaneers ruled the waves. Henry Morgan, the British pirate, called the city his home, before it toppled, in 1692, into the harbor by an earthquake and subsequent tidal wave. There's still quite a lot left to see, including the cockeyed **Giddy House**, which has been tilting off-center since a 1907 earthquake, as well as **St. Peter's Church**, **Fort Charles**, and the old **Naval Hospital**. At **Morgan's Harbor** marina you'll find a few restaurants, bar and small hotel.

West of Kingston is **Spanish Town,** Jamaica's old capital, with a few historical sites still standing. On the south coast, **Madeville** represents a quieter, calmer Jamaica. Bird-watchers will enjoy **Marshal's Pen**, an 18th-century greathouse set on a 300-acre wildlife sanctuary. Two of the best places to see the sunset are **Yardley Chase** and **South St. Elizabeth**. For touring the area as an ecologist, contact **South Coast Safaris** (on the Black Rover); ☎ *965-2513* for a 1-1/2 hour excursion covering 10 miles round-trip where you can photograph a variety of birds, crocodile and other wildlife. Special fishing tours can also be arranged.

Beaches in Kingston

Gunboat Beach is one of the most popular beaches around Kingston. A rare black sand beach is found at **Fort Clarence**, tucked into the Hellshire Hills southwest of the city. There you'll find changing facilities and live entertainment. Locals think nothing of driving the 30-odd miles for the special surroundings at **Lyssons Beach** at Morant Bay, whose golden sands gleam in the sun.

A delightful excursion is to hire a boat at the Morgan's Harbor Marina at Port Royal to cruise to **Lime Cay**, an island just beyond Kingston Harbor. Here is an ideal place to picnic, swim and sunbathe.

Treks Near Kingston

Great **hiking** (and free!) can be found at **The Gap**, a Blue Mountain retreat 42000 feet above sea level. Just follow the marked trails (you can choose among many) in the nearby **Hollywell National Park**. Don't miss lunching in the "rooftop" restaurant, which is surrounded by cloud formations—like dining in heaven.

Don't hesitate to ask the tourist board to suggest local guides who can take you to off-the-beaten tracks in the mountains. A full day should be set aside for hiking expeditions to **Mandeville** in the south coast. Boat trips to nearby islands can be arranged through your hotel; plan to stay for the day and pack a picnic. Remember to arm yourself with a strong suntan lotion.(Also see "Treks" above.)

What Else to See

City Celebrations

Reggae Sunsplash   ★★★★★

Jam World, Kingston.
The annual week-long party of all parties takes place each summer, usually in July. Lots of top-name reggae bands and groovin' folks. Book your hotel way in advance or you'll never get in.

Historical Sites

Devon House   ★★★★

26 Hope Road, Kingston, ☎ (809) 929-7029.
Hours Open: 10:00 a.m.–5:00 p.m.
This 1881 mansion is filled with period furnishings but the best reason to come is for the excellent crafts shops on the grounds. There are two restaurants and a great ice cream shop. General admission: $2.00.

Museums and Exhibits

Bob Marley Museum   ★★★

56 Hope Road, Kingston, ☎ (809) 927-9152.
Hours Open: 9:30 a.m.–4:30 p.m.
The national hero's clapboard house was his home and recording studio for many years. Reggae fans will appreciate the collection of Marley memorabilia and consider this a five-star attraction. Those not into Marley's brand of music can pass. General admission: $3.00.

Institute of Jamaica   ★★★

12 East Street, Kingston, ☎ (809) 922- 620.
Hours Open: 8:30 a.m.–5:00 p.m.
This museum has excellent exhibits on the island's history, with some impressive old charts and almanacs. It also houses the National Library.

National Gallery   ★★★★

12 Ocean Blvd., Kingston, ☎ (809) 922-1561.
This waterfront gallery displays paintings, sculpture and other works of art by Jamaica's most famous artist, Kapo. Other artists' works include Edna Manley, Alvin Marriott, Isaac Belisari and Augustin Brunias.

Parks and Gardens

Royal Botanical Gardens   ★★★

Hope Road, Kingston, ☎ (809) 927-1257.
A peaceful refuge from city life, these gardens encompass 50 acres. Most plants and trees are marked for identification.

Theatre

Little Theatre   ★★★

4 Tom Redcam Road, Kingston, ☎ *(809) 926-6129.*

This theater presents a variety of dramas, musical and special performances. Each December 26-April they produce the LTM Pantomime, a variety show with song, dance and stories.

Theme/Amusement Parks

Anancy Family Fun   ★★★

Negril, Kingston, ☎ *(809) 957-4100.*

This newer attraction consists of three acres of miniature golf, a fishing pond, go-carts and a nature trail. Geared toward kids.

Tours

Cruises

Various locations, Kingston.

Lots of choices for cruising the ocean blue. Montego Bay: **Paco Rabanne** *(*☎ *951-5020)*, the **Mary-Ann** *(*☎ *953-2231)*, the **Calico** *(*☎ *952-5860)*, and the **Rhapsody** *(*☎ *979-0104)*. Port Antonio: **Lady Jamaica** *(*☎ *993-3318)*. Ocho Rios: **Heave-Ho Charters** *(*☎ *974-5367)* and **Red Stripe** *(*☎ *974-2446)*. Negril: **Aqua Nova Water Sports** *(*☎ *957-4323)* and the **Lollypop** *(*☎ *952-4121)*. Excursions range from snorkel trips to catamaran sails to booze cruises with live bands.

Port Royal

Near Kingston ☎ *(809) 924-8706.*
Hours Open: 9:00 a.m.–5:00 p.m.

Now it's more touristy than anything, but this port used to be known as the "most wicked city in the world" because of its buccaneering past and frequent visits by Blackbeard. That all changed in 1692, when it was destroyed by an earthquake. There's lots to see in the complex, including **St. Peter's Church**, which dates back to 1725; the **Archaeological and Historical Museum**; a small maritime museum housed in the former British navel headquarters; **Fort Charles**, which dates back to 1656 and is the port's only remaining fort; and the **Giddy House**, permanently tilted after an earthquake.

River Rafting   ★★★★★

Various locations, Kingston.

Jamaica's many rivers make for great float trips, usually in a bamboo raft that holds just two and is piloted by a character who spins tales of local lore. Several outfits offer trips that last an hour or so and cost about $40 per couple. Highly recommended! In the Montego Bay area, try **Martha Brae's Rafting Village** *(*☎ *952-0889)* or **Mountain Valley Rafting** *(*☎ *952-0527)*. Near Port Antonio, try the **Rio Grande** *(*☎ *993-2778)*. In Ocho Rios, call **Calypso Rafting** *(*☎ *974-2527)*. "An Evening on the Great River" is a touristy but fun boat ride down the river lined with torchlights, followed by dinner and a folkloric show.

Sports in Kingston

Yachting is one of the major activities in Kingston since there are so many attractive offshore islets in the area. A well-attended regatta is sponsored in August by the Morgans Harbor Hotel. If you belong to a yacht club at home, inquire whether you have privileges to participate. Inquire at the Morgans Harbour Hotel regarding cruises around the harbor.

Many resorts have tennis courts. Public courts are available at the Ligunea Club across the road from the hotels in New Kingston. Squash can also be played at the Ligunea Club. Eighteen-hole golf courses can be found at the Caymanas Golf Club and the Constant Spring Golf Club.

Jamaica has a passion for **polo**. In the Kingston area, the Kingston Polo Club on the Caymanas Estates holds regular matches. For more information about activities at Chukka Cove, see "North Coast" below.

Golf

Various locations, Kingston.
Jamaica has lots of golf courses. The best by far are the links at Tryall, a PGA tour-approved, par-71 course that is considered one of the world's best. (☎ *952-5110*) Also in the Montego Bay area are the **Half Moon Golf Club** (☎ *953-2280*), a spacious, par-72 course designed by Robert Trent Jones; **Ironshore Golf and Country Club** (☎ *953-2800*), par 72 and known for its many blind holes; and **Wyndham Rose Hall Country Club** (☎ *953-2650*), a par-72 course on the historic Rose Hall estate with an imaginative layout. In Kingston, try **Caymanas Golf Club**, (☎ *926-8144*), a par 72 known for its very challenging 12th hole; and **Constant Springs** (☎ *924-1610*), a par-70 course.

Horseback Riding

Various locations, Kingston.
Several operations offer horseback riding. Ocho Rios: **Chukka Cove Farm** (☎ *972-2506*), $20 per hour; and **Prospect Plantation** (☎ *974-2373*), $18 per hour. Montego Bay: **Rocky Point Stables** (☎ *953-2212*), where 1.5-hour rides start at $38. Negril: **Horseman Riding Sables** (☎ *957-4474*), $25 for two hours.

Watersports

Various locations, Kingston.
Most hotels offer a variety of watersports, or check out one of the following operations. For scuba and snorkel, try **Fisherman's Inn** (*Falmouth, ☎ 247-0475*). Runaway Bay: **Jamaican Watersports** (☎ *973-4845*) and **Sun Divers Jamaica** (☎ *973-2346*). Negril: **Negril Scuba Centre** (☎ *957-4425*) and **Sun Divers Jamaica**

(☎ *957-4069*). Ocho Rios: **Sea and Dive Jamaica** (☎ *947-5762*). Montego Bay: **Seaworld** (☎ *953-2180*) and **Sandals Beach Watersports** (☎ *949-0104*). Port Antonio: **Lady Godiva** (☎ *993-3281*) and **Aqua Action** (☎ *993-3318*). In addition to the above, **Resort Divers** (☎ *974-0577*) has six locations around the island. For deep-sea fishing, check out **Seaworld Resorts** (☎ *993-3086*) and **Sans Souci** (☎ *974-2353*).

Where to Stay

Highest Rated Hotels in Jamaica

★★★★★	Grand Lido
★★★★★	Half Moon Beach Club
★★★★★	Round Hill Hotel & Villas
★★★★★	Sans Souci Lido
★★★★★	Trident Villas & Hotel
★★★★	Boscobel Beach Hotel
★★★★	Ciboney Ocho Rios
★★★★	Couples Jamaica
★★★★	Franklyn D. Resort
★★★★	Jamaica Grande

Most Exclusive Hotels in Jamaica

★★★★★	Sans Souci Lido	$465–$945
★★★★★	Trident Villas & Hotel	$255–$755
★★★★	Boscobel Beach Hotel	$415–$995
★★★★	Ciboney Ocho Rios	$175–$690
★★★★	Jamaica Pegasus Hotel	$180–$564

Fielding's Best Value Hotels in Jamaica

★★★	Braco Village Resort	$235–$260
★★★★	Trident Villas & Hotel	$255–$755
★★★	Jamaica Palace Hotel	$115–$285
★★★	Comfort Suites	$105–$205
★★★★	Sans Souci Lido	$465–$945

Hotels and Resorts

Braco Village Resort $235–$260 ★★★

Rio Bueno, ☎ *(800) 654-1337, (809) 973-4882.*
Single: $235–$335. Double: $160–$260.

This all-inclusive village is located 38 miles east of Montego Bay. The village reflects Jamaica's various architectural styles, from Georgian to gingerbread. The center-piece is the Town Square, with several restaurants, bars and artists in residence cre-ating and exhibiting their work. The idea is to make the village as authentically Jamaican as possible, while still spoiling guests with the amenities of a resort. Rec-reational facilities include an Olympic-size pool, a nine-hole golf course, four tennis courts, a soccer field, 85 acres of jogging and hiking trails, a fitness center, and all watersports, including scuba and kayaking. Each guest room has a unique feature such as a gazebo, balcony, or love seat. The 2000-foot beach has a clothing-optional section. Not open by press time, but it sounds like a winner. 180 rooms.

Courtleigh House & Hotel $79–$195 ★★

31 Trafalgar Road, ☎ *(800) 526-2400, (809) 926-8174.*
Single: $79–$195. Double: $83–$195.

This traditional garden-style property accommodates guests in large hotel rooms and suites and apartments with one to three bedrooms and kitchens. There are two pools, a few restaurants and a very popular disco on-site. Friendly service, but this spot could really use a renovation. Still, this is good value for the rates. 80 rooms.
Credit Cards: MC, A.

Four Seasons $71–$83 ★

18 Ruthven Road, ☎ *(809) 929-7655.*
Single: $71–$83. Double: $71–$83.

Obviously (if you noticed the rates) not affiliated with the luxury hotel chain of the same name, this small hotel in New Kingston is housed in an old mansion. Guest rooms are simple but adequate. No pool, but you can use the one at the very nice Pegasus, a five-minute stroll away. 39 rooms. Credit Cards: V, MC, DC, A.

Jamaica Pegasus Hotel $185–$569 ★★★★

81 Knutsford Blvd., ☎ *(809) 926-3690.*
Single: $185–$569. Double: $185–$569.

Located in New Kingston, three miles north of downtown, this high-rise hotel offers a sophisticated atmosphere that attracts lots of business travelers and conven-tioneers. Guest rooms are nice, with extras like coffeemakers and large balconies. There's a large pool, two tennis courts, and a jogging track, and guests can work out at a nearby fitness club. The top five floors of the 17-story building, the Executive Club, have added amenities. An excellent choice for the business traveler, though tourists may feel out of place. 350 rooms. Credit Cards: V, MC, A.

Medallion Hall Hotel $79–$83 ★★

53 Hope Road, ☎ *(809) 927-5721.*
Single: $79–$83. Double: $79–$83.

This small hotel, a former private residence, has an inn-like feel. Accommodations are simple but pleasant with traditional decor and dark woods. There's a small restaurant and bar, but nothing else in the way of diversions; you'll have to venture out for excitement. Good value, though. 16 rooms. Credit Cards: V, MC, DC, A.

Morgan's Harbour Hotel   **$98–$255**   ★ ★ ★

Port Royal, ☎ *(809) 924-8464.*
Single: $98–$255. Double: $216–$255.
Downtown Kingston is 20 minutes away from this colonial-style hotel. Completely rebuilt after devastating Hurricane Gilbert, it houses guests in extra-nice rooms with luxurious furnishings, good artwork, and wet bars. The pleasantly landscaped grounds include a saltwater pool, a marina that attracts lots of yachters, a disco and watersports. Perfect for those who need to be near Kingston but want the resort feel of a waterfront property. 45 rooms. Credit Cards: V, MC, A.

Terra Nova Hotel   **$120–$150**   ★ ★ ★

17 Waterloo Road, ☎ *(809) 926-2211.*
Single: $120–$150. Double: $120–$150.
Set on five acres near a commercial area, this motel-style property has an excellent restaurant, but rather drab guest rooms. Still, this is a popular spot for business travelers not looking to spend an arm or leg on a room. Resort amenities are in short supply, save for the pool, oddly set out front in full view of passersby. 33 rooms. Credit Cards: V, MC, DC, A.

Wyndham Kingston   **$165–$505**   ★ ★ ★

77 Knutsford Blvd., ☎ *(800) 322-4200, (809) 926-5511.*
Single: $165–$505. Double: $165–$505.
Situated in the business center on 7.5 acres, this towering hotel was recently redone, with good results. Primarily appealing to business travelers and conventioneers, it offers modern accommodations in the 16-story tower or older and funkier cabana units. There are two tennis courts, a pool and a fully equipped health club, as well as several bars and restaurants. Quite decent, but the Pegasus remains superior. 384 rooms. Credit Cards: V, MC, DC, A.

Low Cost Lodging

Indies Hotel   **$35–$62**   ★

5 Holborn Road, ☎ *(809) 926-2952.*
Single: $35–$58. Double: $58–$62.
This small guesthouse offers incredible rates, but not much else besides a popular restaurant. 15 rooms. Credit Cards: V, MC, A.

Where to Eat

Highest Rated Restaurants in Jamaica

★★★★★ **Reading Reef Club**

★★★★★ **Temple Hall**

★★★★★ **Trident Hotel Restaurant**

★★★★ **Almond Tree**

★★★★ **Blue Mountain Inn**

★★★★ **Norma's at the Wharfhouse**

★★★★ **Sugar Mill**

★★★ **De Montevin Lodge**

★★★ **Pork Pit**

Most Exclusive Restaurants in Jamaica

★★★★★	**Trident Hotel Restaurant**	$50–$50
★★★★	**Norma's at the Wharfhouse**	$26–$34
★★★★	**Blue Mountain Inn**	$12–$24
★★★★★	**Reading Reef Club**	$10–$24
★★★	**De Montevin Lodge**	$11–$18

Fielding's Best Value Restaurants in Jamaica

★★★★★	**Trident Hotel Restaurant**	$50–$50
★★	**Parkway Restaurant**	$6–$25
★★★★	**Norma's at the Wharfhouse**	$26–$34
★★	**Devon House Restaurants**	$6–$16
★★★★★	**Temple Hall**	$25–$25

Blue Mountain Inn $$$ ★★★★

Gordon Town Road, ☎ *(809) 927-1700.*
International cuisine.
Dinner: 7:00 p.m.–9:00 p.m., entrees $12–$24.

This is probably one of Jamaica's most elegant dining experiences, set in an old coffee plantation house overlooking the Mammae River, located about half an hour from Kingston. It's a good excuse for women to air out a little black dress and men a jacket (ties are not required) while sampling continental cuisine that's impeccably prepared and served by a gracious staff. Steak and lobster thermidor and flambeed desserts are some of the old fashioned but delicious choices frequently on the menu. Reservations required. Credit Cards: V, MC, DC, A.

Chelsea Jerk Centre $ ★

9 Chelsea Avenue, ☎ *(809) 926-6322.*
Latin American cuisine. Specialties: Jerk Chicken and Pork.
Lunch: 12:00 a.m.–3:30 p.m., entrees $3–$5.
Dinner: 3:30 p.m.–10:00 p.m., entrees $3–$5.

No, this isn't a self-improvement workshop for nerds on Chelsea Avenue—the Jerk Centre proffers blazingly hot barbecued chicken or pork that's been marinating for hours in a medley of incendiary spices that are a closely-guarded secret. Most dishes here are under $5 and come with sides of rice and peas (white rice with red beans). A half-chicken or pork slab can be packaged to go. Credit Cards: Not Accepted. Credit Cards: V, MC, A.

Devon House Restaurants $$ ★★

Devon House, ☎ *(809) 929-6602.*
Latin American cuisine.
Lunch: 10:00 a.m.–4:00 p.m., entrees $6–$16.
Dinner: 4:00 p.m.–12:00 p.m., entrees $6–$16.

This former colonial mansion turned restaurant/coffee house/craft emporium is one of Kingston's most visited tourist sites. An incredible Jamaican breakfast is served on the breezy Coffee Terrace every day except Sunday. Diners saunter to a long table topped with red-checked country cloths for a buffet of beautifully carved fresh fruit, ackee and saltfish, cod fish balls and breads. Blue Mountain coffee and exotic juices are included. If you have room, pop into the adjoining I-Scream for a frozen concoction of soursop or mango. Closed: Sun. Reservations recommended. Credit Cards: V, MC, A.

El Dorado Room $$ ★

17 Waterloo Road, ☎ *(809) 926-9334.*
International cuisine.
Lunch: 12:00 a.m.–2:30 p.m., entrees $7–$20.
Dinner: 7:30 p.m.–11:00 p.m., entrees $7–$20.

The main dining room of the Terra Nova Hotel, a boutique style hostelry, provides a gracious ambience for local residents taking a breather from the vibrant Kingston restaurant scene. Picture windows look out onto the spacious grounds of the former private estate built in the early 20s. Seafood shines here, whether it's freshly-caught grilled lobster or red snapper in ginger sauce. Associated Hotel: Terra Nova Hotel. Reservations recommended. Credit Cards: V, MC, DC, A.

Gap Cafe, The　　　　　　　**$$$**　　　　　　　★ ★

Hardwar Gap, Blue Mountain, ☎ *(809) 923-7055.*
International cuisine.
Lunch: entrees $12–$15.
Dinner: entrees $17–$22.

A visit to the Gap Cafe is a journey to another Jamaica—one where a fireplace may be glowing all year round, understandable at a height of 4200 feet. Gloria Palomino welcomes guests to sip Blue Mountain coffee and savor some of the best pastries on the island, served all day and at high tea on Sundays. Native guavas are used in the cheesecake, as well as soursop and passion fruit for the cakes and mousses. The Cafe, once an old fixer-upper, is now a cozy, flower-filled charmer decked out in tones of maroon and blue. There's a gift shop on the premises. Reservations recommended. Credit Cards: V, MC, A.

Hot Pot, The　　　　　　　**$**　　　　　　　★ ★

2 Altamont Terrace, ☎ *(809) 929-3906.*
Latin American cuisine. Specialties: Fricassee Chicken, Saltfish and Ackee.
Lunch: 8:00 a.m.–4:00 p.m., entrees $3–$4.
Dinner: 4:00 p.m.–10:00 p.m., entrees $3–$4.

A dandy place to try Jamaican specialties is this informal joint behind the Wyndham Hotel. The decor isn't much, but the authentic dishes are cheap and filling. The Hot Pot serves three meals a day, including the legendary saltfish and ackee (a vegetable brought over by Captain Bligh of *Bounty* fame) for breakfast. Credit Cards: V.

Indies Pub and Grill　　　　　　　**$**　　　　　　　★

8 Holborn Road, ☎ *(809) 926-5050.*
Latin American cuisine.
Lunch: entrees $4–$12.
Dinner: entrees $4–$12.

This is the Jamaican version of a local pub—roosting companionably in a New Kingston neighborhood. The fare is nothing fancy: just burgers, fish and chips or pizza, but sometimes there's nothing better than rubbing elbows with office workers on a comfortable alfresco terrace. The Indies is a popular late night spot as well—it serves food and drink until 1:30 a.m. on weekends and until midnight the rest of the week. Credit Cards: V, MC, A.

Ivor Guest House　　　　　　　**$$$**　　　　　　　★

Jack's Hill, ☎ *(809) 977-33.*
International cuisine.
Lunch: entrees $18–$22.
Dinner: entrees $22–$30.

This cozy guest house/dining room on a hill high above Kingston boasts a million dollar view (at 2000 feet) and the chef prepares reasonably-priced lunches and dinners with a Jamaican flair. The terrace of this small colonial inn is a popular spot for high tea and cocktails on the open terrace. On a clear night, the lights of the city in the distance make strong men (and women) swoon. Associated Hotel: Ivor Guest House. Reservations required. Credit Cards: V, MC, A.

Le Pavilion　　　　　　　**$$$**　　　　　　　★ ★

81 Knutsford Boulevard, ☎ *(809) 926-3690.*

International cuisine.
Lunch: 12:30 p.m.–3:00 p.m., prix fixe $16.
Dinner: 7:00 p.m.–11:00 p.m., entrees $16–$26.
As hotel dining rooms go, Le Pavilion just might be the most popular downtown meeting spot. Sophisticated city dwellers flock here for high tea on weekdays while others like the seafood buffets on Fridays and the reasonably-priced three-course lunches with a variety of Caribbean and Continental meat and fish concoctions. No lunch is served on Saturday. Associated Hotel: Jamaica Pegasus Hotel. Closed: Sun. Reservations recommended. Credit Cards: V, MC, DC, A.

Minnie's Ethiopian $$ ★

176 Old Hope Road, ☎ *(809) 927-9207.*
Latin American cuisine. Specialties: Gungo-Pea Stew, Festival Bread, Juices.
Lunch: entrees $10–$20.
Dinner: entrees $10–$20.
After a pilgrimage to reggae icon Bob Marley's Museum and Tuff Gong Recording Studio nearby, fans can repair to his former chef's eating establishment for some Rasta Ital food (mostly vegetarian, utilizing local bounty) prepared by Chef Minnie. The full name of this round wooden restaurant is Minnie's Ethiopian Herbal Health Food, and after a few freshly-squeezed juices and her signature gungo (pigeon pea stew, you'll feel truly cleansed. Reservations recommended. Credit Cards: Not Accepted.

Norma's at the Wharfhouse $$$ ★★★★

Reading Road, Reading, ☎ *(809) 979-2745.*
Latin American cuisine.
Lunch: 12:00 a.m.–2:30 p.m., entrees $26–$34.
Dinner: 7:30 p.m.–10:30 p.m., entrees $26–$34.
The finest restaurant on the island may be this historical dockside beauty created by Norma Shirley, Jamaica's most famous chef. Dine with influential Jamaicans and visiting celebrities while watching the action at a table set on the wharf of this 300-year-old warehouse, or in an antique-filled salon. Shirley, who owned a restaurant in New York, utilizes the rich bounty of the region to spectacular effect; the menu, which changes daily, often includes succulent smoked marlin with papaya or grilled deviled crab backs. The elegantly-dressed plates are a treat. Associated Hotel: The Wharfhouse. Closed: Mon, Tue, Wed. Reservations recommended. Credit Cards: V, MC.

Temple Hall $$$ ★★★★★

Temple Hall Estate, ☎ *(809) 942-2340.*
Latin American cuisine. Specialties: Fettucine Boston Jerk.
Dinner: 6:30 p.m.–11:30 p.m., entrees $25.
Of the handful of gracious plantation homes on the outskirts of Kingston, The Restaurant at Temple Hall Estate is probably on most gourmet lists of "don't miss" experiences. For the most part the vast property is self-sustaining, growing most of the herbs and vegetables and raising the livestock for the scrumptious meals. Guests are provided with complimentary transportation by the owners, who like to put on a light show at night by illuminating the long driveway with torches. Reservations required. Reservations required. Credit Cards: MC, DC, A.

MONTEGO BAY

Known to locals as Mo' Bay, Montego Bay is the primary port of entry by air for Jamaica. It's here, along the shoreline, where Jamaican tourism was born. Once a sleepy town, it's burgeoned into the apotheosis of what some tourists feel is the Caribbean nightmare, but for others it's a town that epitomizes the bustling, sweaty, crowded charm of a third-world port. Downtown is a joggerhead of traffic, people, vendors and markets, and if you want to stay in the middle of all that, you'll be able to find some small (but noisy, count on it) hotels. The Montego Bay experience starts even on arrival, at the Donald Sangster International Airport, where you will have to jostle your way past crowds, walk long hot distances to your luggage, and nearly kill your fellow travelers to get a porter's attention. In order to minimize the discomfort, arrange for your hotel to pick you up (many all-inclusives include airport transfer in the package). There's nothing like seeing a sign with your name on it and a helpful assistant when you are hot, tired and cranky after an international flight. (For more taxi information, see the directory under "Getting Around" at the end of the chapter.)

Beaches in Montego Bay

Cornwall Beach is a man-made phenomenon to provide tourists with an alternative to the postage-stamp patch called Doctor's Cave Beach—once the hub of Montego Bay's social scene during its heyday in the 60s. The scene is still happening at Cornwall, but with so many locals and tourists, that if you're the kind of person who needs to see the color of the sand beneath your feet, stay away. These days Doctor's Cave itself is just too reminiscent of Florida to get our vote for exotica, but the five-mile stretch of vanilla-colored sand still has its charm, though its overexposure in the press has brought every loud obnoxious tourist out of the woodwork. On the plus side, the changing facilities can be useful and there is a large variety of junk food to choose from.**Walter Fletch Beach**, on the bay near the center of town, is very good for swimming, since it is well protected from the strong winds.

Dive Sites Near Montego Bay

Montego Bay was the site of Jamaica's first marine park. The dive sites of Mo' Bay are typically close to shore and highly dramatic, with walls, big sponges and frequent dolphin encounters. **Basket Reef** starts in 50 feet of water, drops over the edge of the wall to 150 feet. At The Arena/Spanish Anchors, named for two anchors which are thoroughly embedded in the wall, boasts two tunnels leading to the face of the wall. **Canyon 1 and 2** is immediately adjacent to the The Arsenal. Canyon 1 is a tunnel entering the reef at 30 feet and exiting at 70. Canyon 2 offers Spiny Lobsters and occasional Nurse sharks. Try the Point for some serious high energy diving.

Treks Near Montego Bay

One of the greatest pleasures in Jamaica can be had **rafting** down the Martha Brae River. The river is said to be haunted by the duppy (ghost) of one Martha Brae, an Arawak Indian who was captured by the Spanish and forced to lead them to a gold mine. Legend has it that upon reaching the river, she enchanted the flow of the water to change course and then drowned herself, along with the greedy Spaniards, in a great tidal wave. Most hotel tour desks book the excursion, which takes about 1-1/2 hours and costs about $32 per raft. The river is located about 28 miles from the hotel drag in Montego Bay. At the top of the river, where you buy the tickets, there are boutiques, a bar/restaurant, and a pool for swimming. For more information contact ☎ *(809) 952-0889*. Other rafting opportunities are offered by **Mountain Valley Rafting** at Lethe, which includes a one-hour donkey ride (obviously on the land). (For more information on rafting, see "Treks" above.)

A fabulous full day can be spent trekking the mountain cockpit country of **Marron Bay**, the home of the first freed Jamaican slaves who courageously fought off the British more than a hundred years ago. The **Maroon Tourist Attraction Co.** ☎ *952-4546* offers guided historical tours from Montego Bay to Accompong Town, a Maroon village high up in the mountains. Here you'll be able to explore a variety of caves and climb hilly terrain. Some physical fitness is required.

Birdwatchers should flock to **Rocklands Bird Sanctuary**, a feeding station in Anchovy (turn left on Route B8 south of town). The brainchild of artist-naturalist-writer Lisa Salmon, the reserve began when she was forced to take care of the birdlife that congregated on her hillside home. Public feeding of the bird population takes place around 3:30 in the afternoon and visitors are invited to stay till sundown; if you're lucky, a rare hummingbird might even eat out of your hand. It's open daily, but it is best to call in advance.

Visiting some of the great houses, reminders of the old days when sugarcane ruled the island, is a relaxing and educational way to spend the day. The **Rose Hall Great House** is perhaps the most famous, less for its architecture and more for the eerie legend of its second owner, Annie Palmer who was thought to have killed not only her three husbands but her lover, who was the plantation overseer, as well. **Greenwood** (which houses the family heirlooms of the poet Elizabeth Barrett Browning) and **Good Hope** are also elegant structures, though very different in furnishings. **Sign Great House**, with its tangle of vines and moss, gives off the ambiance of a near-ruin.

One way to beat the heat in Montego Bay is to take a cruise around the north coast. Day and night cruises are as different as day and night; if you're looking for romance, the *Paco Rabann* ☎ *(809)951-5020* is unparalleled; during the day you'll see the scope of the entire north coast. Though the ship is only 167 feet, the presence of a live show and slot machines will make you think you're on a a real cruise—though in miniature.

What Else to See

Historical Sites

Greenwood Great House ★★★★
Highway A1, Montego Bay.
Hours Open: 9:00 a.m.–6:00 p.m.
One of Jamaica's greatest great houses, this one belonged to the Barrett family, of which Elizabeth Barrett Browning is a descendant. The early 19th-century mansion is nice to tour, filled with antiques, unusual musical instruments, rare books, custom-made china, and portraits of the family. General admission: $8.00.

Rose Hall Great House ★★★★
Rose Hall Highway, Montego Bay, ☎ *(809) 953-2323.*
Hours Open: 9:00 a.m.–6:00 p.m.

Not as architecturally impressive as Greenwood, but this great house from the 1700s is filled with tales of murder and intrigue. It seems that mistress Annie Palmer seduced slaves and then killed them, as well as murdering three husbands. Her story has been fictionalized in several books, which you'll find in the gift shop. There's also a neat pub in the basement. General admission: $10.00.

Parks and Gardens

Columbus Park Museum ★★★

Queens Highway, Discovery Bay, *(809) 973-2135.*
Hours Open: 9:00 a.m.–5:00 p.m.
This outdoor park, studded with pimento trees, has some interesting and eclectic exhibits. There are 18th-century cannons, a stone cross, a large mural of Columbus' landing in 1494, and displays on the history of sugarcane. Stop by if you're in the area, but don't bother making a special trip. Free admission.

Rocklands Wildlife Station ★★★

Anchovy, St. James, ☎ *(809) 952-2009.*
Hours Open: 2:00 p.m.–5:00 p.m.
This privately owned reserve is a must for birders (the rest can probably live without it). Doves, finches and other feathered creatures eat right off your hands. General admission: $4.00.

Tours

Appelton Estate Express ★★★★

Appelton Estate Station, Montego Bay, *(809) 952-6606.*
All aboard the Appelton Express, an air-conditioned diesel railcar that chugs some 40 miles into the mountains. Along the way you'll pass Jamaican villages, coffee and fruit plantations, and wonderful scenery. You'll also tour a rum factory and get to taste the goods. The fee includes transportation from your hotel, continental breakfast, buffet lunch, and an open bar. The train departs at 8:50 a.m. on Monday, Thursday and Friday, and returns about 5:00 p.m. General admission: $40.00.

JUTA Tour Company ★★★★

Claude Clarke Avenue, Montego Bay, ☎ *(809) 952- 813.*
This well-established tour company has offices all over Jamaica. They'll take you river rafting, on sea cruises, through great houses, and into Kingston.

Where to Stay

Hotels and Resorts

Coral Cliff Hotel **$54–$64** ★★

Gloucester Avenue, *(809) 952-4130.*
Single: $54–$63. Double: $58–$64.
This older hotel consists of a former mansion and a newer addition, perched on a hillside about five minutes from Doctor's Cave Beach. Rooms are pleasant and comfortable, but lack extras like TV. There's a bar and restaurant, pool, and entertainment during high season. A good budget hotel. 32 rooms. Credit Cards: MC, A.

Doctor's Cave Beach Hotel   **$85–$135**   ★★★

Gloucester Avenue, ☎ *(800) 223-6510, (809) 952-4355.*
Single: $85–$135. Double: $105–$135.

Set on four acres of tropical gardens in the heart of the resort district, this informal hotel is across the street from Doctor's Cave Beach. Guest rooms, decorated in rattan and air-conditioned, are comfortable. Facilities include a pool, two restaurants, watersports across the street and a small gym. The atmosphere is lively, with lots of special events like crab races and rum parties. 90 rooms. Credit Cards: V, MC, A.

Fantasy Resort   **$55–$85**   ★★

2 Kent Avenue, ☎ *(800) 237-3421, (809) 952-4150.*
Single: $55–$85. Double: $55–$85.

Located across the street from Doctor's Cave Beach, this high-rise property is only the fantasy of someone with low self-esteem. Everything is quite dated here and in real need of renovation. There's tennis on two courts, a fitness center, pool and Jacuzzi. Guest rooms are small but do have nice ocean views. Decent value, but not too exciting. 119 rooms. Credit Cards: MC, A.

Gloucestershire, The   **$60–$80**   ★★

Gloucester Avenue, ☎ *(800) 423-4095, (809) 952-4420.*
Single: $60–$80. Double: $60–$80.

Doctor's Cave Beach is across the street from this modern hotel. Guest rooms are adequate with cable TV and air conditioning. Besides the Jacuzzi, there's not much in the way of resort amenities. 88 rooms. Credit Cards: MC, A.

Half Moon Beach Club   **$255–$805**   ★★★★★

Rose Hall, ☎ *(800) 626- 592, (809) 953-2211.*
Single: $255–$505. Double: $305–$805.

Located on 400 acres with its own one-mile private beach, this resort is simply outstanding in every way. Accommodations are in standard rooms, cottages, and villas. All are luxurious, with tropical furnishings, antique reproductions, sitting areas, and patios or balconies with sea views. One-bedroom suites have full kitchens and spacious living areas, while the villas offer lots of space on two levels. There are two main swimming pools, plus 17 other pools shared among the villas, an equestrian center, 13 tennis courts, four squash courts, all kinds of watersports, and a children's center. There's also 18 holes of golf on a Robert Trent Jones-designed course. Aerobics classes are available in the fitness center, as well as sauna and massage for working out the kinks. Eating choices are varied and fine. This is one of Jamaica's best resorts, well worth the high rates. 213 rooms. Credit Cards: MC, A.

Holiday Inn Montego Bay   **$160–$205**   ★★

Rosehall, ☎ *(800) 465-4329, (809) 953-2485.*
Single: $160–$205. Double: $160–$205.

Located on a private beach and part of the historic Rosehall Sugar Plantation Estate, this large resort complex lives up to the dependable, if unexciting, Holiday Inn name. Accommodations are acceptable but many lack water views. There's lots going on, from organized activities and entertainment (crab races, anyone?) to a large pool, health club, four tennis courts, watersports and organized activities for the kids. Good security keeps non-guests at bay. Decent. 516 rooms. Credit Cards: V, MC, A.

Jack Tar Village   **$155–$205**   ★★

Gloucester Avenue, ☎ *(800) 999-9182, (809) 952-4340.*
Single: $155–$205. Double: $134–$205.
Located a mile from downtown Montego Bay, this all-inclusive resort is perched right on the beach, albeit, a narrow one. Guest rooms are comfortable and modern. The rates include all meals, drinks and activities, and there's lots to do, including four tennis courts, volleyball, watersports, and nightly entertainment. (You'll pay extra for scuba and jet skiing.) Those who book far in advance are rewarded with lower rates. 128 rooms. Credit Cards: MC, A.

Montego Bay Racquet Club   **$50–$155**   ★★

Sewell Avenue, ☎ *(809) 952- 200.*
Single: $50–$155. Double: $55–$155.
Located in the Red Hills area overlooking the harbor, three minutes from Doctor's Cave Beach (they'll shuttle you over for free), this informal resort lures tennis lovers with excellent facilities, including seven courts and two pros on hand to offer tips. Choose from simple and not especially pleasing villas or traditional guest rooms, which are a bit nicer. Besides the restaurant and pool, not much happens here other than tennis, tennis and tennis. Unless you're into that racquet, stay elsewhere. 51 rooms. Credit Cards: V, MC, A.

Reading Reef Club   **$65–$370**   ★★★

Bogue Lagoon, ☎ *(800) 223-6510, (809) 952-5909.*
Single: $65–$370. Double: $80–$370.
Located some 15 minutes west of Montego Bay, this small resort sets on 2.5 acres with its own small beach. Air-conditioned accommodations include rooms and suites. There's a few restaurants, a pool, and watersports, and, best of all, a lack of hustlers on the beach. A nice, quiet spot. 26 rooms. Credit Cards: MC, A.

Round Hill Hotel & Villas   **$305–$454**

Highway A1, ☎ *(800) 223-6510, (809) 952-2505.*
Single: $305–$615. Double: $285–$454.
Set on a lush green peninsula with a private beach eight miles from Montego Bay, this exclusive resort encompasses nearly 100 acres. Accommodations are in the main building (most with twin beds) or luxurious villas, some with their own private pools and all with the pampering of a maid, gardener and cook. Lots of rich and famous types stay here; keep your gawking to a minimum, please. Activities include five tennis courts, morning exercise classes, a pool, watersports, and glass-bottom boat rides. Tres chic—if you can afford it. 110 rooms. Credit Cards: V, MC, A.

Royal Court Hotel   **$45–$85**   ★

Sewell Avenue, ☎ *(809) 952-4531.*
Single: $45–$100. Double: $55–$85.
Located on a hillside with nice views, this simple hotel is a half-mile from the beach (they'll shuttle you there). Rooms are nicely done, and some sport kitchenettes. Two restaurants, a pool and disco complete the scene. Decent for the rates. 25 rooms. Credit Cards: MC, A.

Sandals Inn   **$290–$348**   ★★★

Kent Avenue, ☎ *(800) 726-3257, (809) 952-4140.*
Single: $290–$348. Double: $290–$348.
Open only to heterosexual couples, this small all-inclusive resort is hampered by its
location across from, not on, the beach. Guest rooms are colonial-themed and
large, but the sea is only visible from the more expensive units. There's lots to keep
busy couples happy, including a pool, tennis, a gym and watersports. Guests can
hop a free shuttle to the area's other two larger Sandals. This is the most inexpensive
one of the trio. 52 rooms. Credit Cards: MC, A.

Sandals Montego Bay   **$2375–$2835**   ★★★★

Kent Avenue, ☎ *(800) 726-3257, (809) 952-5510.*
The largest of the area's three Sandals couples-only resorts, this one sits right on its
own private beach. Guest rooms are quite nice, but avoid the few over the dining
room if you can help it. The all-inclusive rates cover all meals, drinks, entertainment
and facilities. Diversions include two pools, two tennis courts, a gym, all watersports, exercise classes, and several Jacuzzis. Dining options range from Jamaican to
Asian to Continental. Decent, but the noise from the nearby airport can be a drag.
$2375 to $2835 per couple per week. 243 rooms. Credit Cards: MC, A.

Sandals Royal Caribbean   **$2465–$2920**   ★★★★

Kent Avenue, ☎ *(800) 726-3257, (809) 953-2231.*
The most expensive of the three Sandals in the area, this couples-only (heterosexual
please) resort operates on an all-inclusive plan. Many guest rooms open right onto
the beach. All the bells and whistles associated with the chain are here, including
four restaurants and four bars, three pools, three tennis courts, a good health club,
all watersports, and lots of organized activities and entertainment. Those wanting to
tan sans suits have their own private island. A bit more sophisticated than its siblings. $2465 to $2920 per couple per week. 190 rooms. Credit Cards: MC, A.

Sea Garden Beach Hotel   **$297–$357**   ★★

Kent Avenue, ☎ *(800) 545-9001, (809) 952-4780.*
Single: $297–$357. Double: $297–$357.
Located across the street from the beach, this all-inclusive resort suffers from some
airport noise. Guest rooms are dated and could use spiffing up. The rates include all
meals, drinks and activities, including tennis, volleyball and watersports. There's
nightly entertainment and a disco. Service is not the greatest, and Sandals remains a
superior choice. 104 rooms. Credit Cards: MC, A.

Seawind Beach Resort   **$75–$120**   ★★★

Montego Freeport, ☎ *(800) 526-2422, (809) 979-8070.*
Single: $75–$120. Double: $90–$120.
Situated on a private 100-acre peninsula, this complex includes two 10-story towers
and two two-story wings. The towers house most of the guest rooms and are local
landmarks with their colorful bands. There are also studios and one-bedroom apartments with kitchen facilities. Lots going on at this lively spot, including four tennis
courts, two pools, watersports and horseback riding. Several restaurants and five
bars, including a popular disco. The locale, near the busy port, is a bit removed from
the action. 468 rooms. Credit Cards: V, MC, A.

Tryall Resort   **$235–$465**   ★★★★

Sandy Bay, ☎ *(800) 742- 498, (809) 965-5660.*
Single: $235–$415. Double: $285–$465.

Set on 2200 acres of a former sugar plantation estate some 30 minutes out of Montego Bay, this deluxe resort has a true country club feel. Guest rooms are located in the 1834 Great House and are beautifully done; luxurious villas with maid and cook service are also available. The resort's centerpiece is the 18-hole PGA championship golf course, but there are also nine tennis courts, a pool, a private beach, and all watersports. Lovely and grand. 52 rooms. Credit Cards: V, MC, A.

Wexford, The   **$85–$130**   ★★

Gloucester Avenue, ☎ *(800) 237-3421, (809) 952-3679.*
Single: $85–$120. Double: $95–$130.

This small hotel is across the street from Doctor's Cave Beach, and it's a bit of a walk to the sand. Accommodations are simple but adequate, and one-bedroom apartments with kitchenettes are available. The pool is small and uninspired. You can do better at comparable rates elsewhere. 61 rooms. Credit Cards: MC, A.

Winged Victory   **$95–$230**   ★★

5 Queens Drive, ☎ *(800) 223-9815, (809) 952-3891.*
Single: $95–$230. Double: $95–$230.

Situated on a hill overlooking the bay, five minutes from Doctor's Cave Beach, this is a peaceful, off-the-beaten-track spot. Guest rooms are comfortable and most face the ocean. There's a small pool, and the restaurant is good. 27 rooms. Credit Cards: MC, A.

Wyndham Rose Hall Resort   **$165–$705**   ★★★

Rose Hall, ☎ *(809) 631-4200, (809) 953-2650.*
Single: $165–$705. Double: $165–$705.

Set on 400 acres fronting a beach, this stylish property has large guestrooms accented by nice artwork and quality furnishings. Guests can choose from 18 holes of golf, six tennis courts with a pro on hand, a fitness center, three interconnected swimming pools and all watersports. Lots in the way of dining options, too. Parents can stash the little ones in the supervised Kid's Klub, and there are also lots of organized activities for adults. Very nice, but lacks any Jamaican mood. 500 rooms. Credit Cards: V, MC, A.

Apartments and Condominiums

Seacastles   **$75–$155**   ★★★

Rose Hall, ☎ *(800) 526-2422, (809) 953-3259.*
Single: $75–$155. Double: $75–$155.

Located on a 14-acre estate, this modern complex has one- to three-bedroom apartments, all with nice tropical furnishings and kitchenettes. Combining the convenience of apartment living with the amenities of a hotel, it offers turndown service and limited room service. There's a pool, two tennis courts, a playground for the kids, watersports, and a private, though small, beach. Nice, especially for families who don't mind the somewhat remote location. 198 rooms. Credit Cards: V, MC, A.

Inns

Richmond Hill Inn   **$78–$112**   ★★

Union Street, ☎ *(809) 952-3859.*
Single: $78. Double: $112.
Set high on a hill with stunning views, the main building of this casual inn dates from the 1700s. Guest rooms are simple but comfortable, and a few suites with kitchenettes are available for those who prefer to cook in. A pool and games room offer daytime diversions; the piano bar and open-air restaurant help fill evening hours. Not the greatest, especially since lots of tour groups troop through to check out the view. The beach is a 10-minute drive. 20 rooms. Credit Cards: MC, A.

Toby Inn   **$45–$80**   ★★

1 Kent Avenue, ☎ *(809) 952-4370.*
Single: $45–$55. Double: $70–$80.
Located in a few acres of tropical gardens one block from Doctor's Cave Beach, this relatively peaceful inn houses guests in simple but attractive rooms that lack telephones and TV. There are two pools, one with a waterfall, a restaurant, and two bars, one built to resemble a treehouse. Shopping, restaurants and nightlife are within an easy walk. Excellent value. 60 rooms. Credit Cards: MC, A.

Low Cost Lodging

Belvedere Beach Hotel   **$50–$80**   ★

33 Gloucester Avenue, ☎ *(809) 952- 593.*
Single: $50–$75. Double: $55–$80.
This small hotel is across the street from Walter Fletcher Beach and within walking distance of city center. There's a pool, restaurant and bar, but not much else, and it gets noisy here. Not especially recommended. 27 rooms. Credit Cards: CB, V, MC, A.

Blue Harbour Hotel   **$35–$105**   ★★

Sewell Avenue, ☎ *(809) 952-5445.*
Single: $35–$105. Double: $47–$105.
Set on a hill on the site of an old Spanish fort, this small hotel has adequate accommodations for the rates. Besides the pool, there's not much here to keep visitors occupied. 24 rooms. Credit Cards: V, MC, A.

Buccaneer Beach Hotel   **$83–$175**   ★

7 Kent Avenue, ☎ *(809) 952-6489.*
Single: $83–$175. Double: $83–$175.
Located near the airport and across the street from a public beach, this budget choice offers bland but functional rooms. Appealing mainly to college students hellbent on having a good time, it is best avoided by anyone over 25 during spring break. Typical hotel amenities include a restaurant, bar, nightclub and pool. 72 rooms. Credit Cards: MC, A.

Where to Eat

Georgian House   **$$$**   ★

2 Orange Street, ☎ *(809) 952-3353.*
International cuisine. Specialties: Pan-Barbecued Shrimp, Coconut Pie.

Lunch: 12:00 a.m.–2:30 p.m., entrees $22–$32.
Dinner: 6:00 p.m.–10:30 p.m., entrees $22–$32.

This restaurant's private van will pick you up from your hotel to dine in an 18th century townhouse and art gallery. Once there, you can eat outdoors on the patio if you prefer a more casual atmosphere—in any case feel free to dress resort-casual. Specialties are from the sea; usually shrimp or spiny lobster, barbecued, or sauteed with vegetables, or in a wine sauce. Steaks and filets are also marvelous, the coconut pie is deadly, and the wine list is well-chosen. Reservations recommended. Credit Cards: V, MC, DC, A.

Julia's   **$$$**   ★

Bogue Hill, ☎ *(809) 952-632.*
International cuisine.
Dinner: 6:00 p.m.–10:30 p.m., prix fixe $35.

It's highly advisable to take this mountaintop restaurant's offer of a private van to pick you up at your door. Negotiating the steep road that leads to this estate above MoBay (800 feet or thereabouts) can be hazardous. Once ensconced in your seat, relax and enjoy a four-course dinner served by an attentive staff, while the lights of the bay and the city glow below. The mostly-Italian entrees of veal (usually parmesan), chicken, or fish will include a salad, pasta, dessert and choice of beverage. Reservations required. Credit Cards: V, MC, DC, A.

Pier I   **$$$**   ★

Howard Cooke Boulevard, ☎ *(809) 952-2452.*
Seafood cuisine.
Lunch: 11:00 a.m.–4:00 p.m., entrees $16–$25.
Dinner: 4:00 p.m.–12:00 p.m., entrees $16–$25.

The cocktails and punches are fruity and potent, and the burgers are juicy; but even if kibble was served, the view from the waterfront bar would still be stellar. There's a tony dining room within where you can dine on well-prepared seafood and some hearty soups, chicken and steaks. Credit Cards: V, MC, A.

Pork Pit   **$**   ★ ★ ★

Gloucester Avenue, corner, ☎ *(809) 952-1046.*
Latin American cuisine.
Lunch: 11:00 a.m.–4:30 p.m., entrees $2–$9.
Dinner: 4:30 p.m.–11:30 p.m., entrees $2–$9.

Eat fiery jerk pork, chicken or spare ribs picnic-style on benches or tables open to the sea breeze. Common accompaniments include local cornbread *(festival)* and Red Stripe beer. Location is close to Cornwall Beach and the airport. Credit Cards: Not Accepted.

Reading Reef Club   **$$$**   ★ ★ ★ ★ ★

Bogue Lagoon, ☎ *(809) 952-5909.*
Italian cuisine.
Lunch: 12:00 a.m.–3:00 p.m., entrees $10–$24.
Dinner: 7:00 p.m.–10:00 p.m., entrees $10–$24.

Located in a discreet, small (21-room) hotel situated halfway between Montego Bay and the Round Hill Resort, this Caribbean-influenced Italian restaurant reflects the tastes of the hotel's owner, JoAnne Rowe, a New York-born expatriate. These include a strange combination of pasta served with ginger that works quite well, judging by its popularity. Crayfish, seafood and steaks are other standards paired with local produce. Associated Hotel: Reading Reef Club. Reservations required. Credit Cards: V, MC, DC, A.

Sugar Mill $$$ ★ ★ ★ ★
Rose Hall, *(809) 953-2228.*
International cuisine. Specialties: Bouillabaise, Smoked Marlin.
Lunch: 12:00 a.m.–2:30 p.m., entrees $14–$31.
Dinner: 7:00 p.m.–10:00 p.m., entrees $14–$31.
Swiss chef Hans Schenck creates Jamaican-Continental specialties at this restaurant in a historical house with a terrace that overlooks the ocean and the golf course of the Half Moon Club. Marlin, a specialty catch of the area, is often smoked and served with pasta; bouillabaisse is spiced with local pepper and citrus sauces. Even if you're just passing through, come for a look at the remains of the old sugar plantation that have been incorporated into the grounds of this soigne resort. Associated Hotel: Half Moon Club. Reservations required. Credit Cards: V, MC, A.

Town House $$$ ★ ★
16 Church Street, ☎ *(809) 952-2660.*
Latin American cuisine. Specialties: Red Snapper Baked in Parchment.
Lunch: 11:30 a.m.–2:30 p.m., entrees $13–$30.
Dinner: 6:00 p.m.–10:00 p.m., entrees $13–$30.
This grand, 300-year-old Georgian building is a fun place to eat, especially in an art-filled, brick-walled cellar room, which is a novel change from the favored practice of dining alfresco. But that can also be achieved here on an outdoor terrace. Specialties include a signature fresh red snapper baked in parchment with a cheese and seafood sauce. Reservations recommended. Credit Cards: V, MC, DC, A.

NEGRIL

Negril became known to the world at large in the early 70s when it was a mecca for hippies, escapists, artists and visionaries who spent most of the day bonged out on the local weed. Located on the extreme northwestern point of the island, it has grown from a sleepy bohemian town to one of Jamaica's finest resort areas—some of the best all-inclusives are situated right on the beach here. There are also campsites at the **Negril Lighthouse Park** and at **Roots Bamboo** (both off West End). The seven-mile stretch of pure white, powder-fine beach dotted with sea grape and coconut palms has inspired many a fantasy, and numerous fashion shoots have been conducted here. For some un-explained reason, the sunsets here are extraordinarily spectacular, bursts of neon color across the horizon. Although there's little sightseeing available, most visitors are just happy to relax and soak in the atmosphere. For the ac-tive, there are numerous watersports, superb scuba diving (see below), and fine snorkeling.

If you get to Negril, you must make an extra excursion to **Booby Cay**, a small island across from Rutland Point that attracts an inordinate number of nude bathers. Also spectacular is the sunset cruise on the *Sunsplash*, a 155-foot catamaran which can be booked through Sandals Negril. After you pass through town and head west to Negril Point, the resorts tend to get smaller and more quaint. Here the beach gives way to high limestone cliffs. At **Xtabi**, the sea caves cut into the cliffs to create a romantic setting that is ideal for sunset viewing. Everyone heads for **Rick's Cafe** —a terrific place to watch divers jump off from the cliff below and a perfect place to celebrate the glo-rious sunset, but if you don't like crowds, you won't love Rick's. If you're a night prowler, you'll find some of the biggest reggae stars in Jamaica per-forming throughout Negril until late into the wee hours. Recently, Negril, through the efforts of the Coral Reef Preservation Society, has instituted a very active mooring and education program. At present, 35 separate moor-ings virtually eliminate the need for anchoring.

Beaches in Negril

Negril Beach is seven long miles of heaven—everyone's idea of Eden. Un-fortunately, much of it is fenced off today, especially the nude area. Fortu-nately, some resorts have had the foresight to build their properties overlooking the nude areas. The famous (infamous) singles-only club **Hedonism II** is located on this beach. If you saw the movie *Exit to Eden* and fantasized about being at a resort like *that*, you will probably love Hedonism II.

Divers enjoy the beautiful cliffs and caves at the west end of Negril, Jamaica.

Dive Sites in Negril

The coral reef fringing Negril stretches more than 10 miles parallel to the beach and has more than **40 dive sites** with dropoffs ranging from 65 to 100 feet and deeper. The reef skirts Long Bay, veering up to a mile out to sea and enclosing Booby Cay, where a dive site known as the Gallery offers canyons, overhangs and caves. Reefs range from shallow and easily accessible to well beyond sport diving limits. The earmarks are huge coral heads (locally called "cottages") and massive sponge formations. Other marine life includes sea anemones, crabs, octopuses, scorpion fish and tiny fiery-like spotted rums. **The Throne Room** is a favorite, where there is a reef with a 65-foot drop; great sponge formations can be found at **Deep Plane**. **The Arches** site is marked by a 60-ft sunken plane filled with a large school of Blackbar Soldierfish. Coral gardens, one of the prettier sites, is the site of a regular fish feed. At night, tiny phosphorescent marine microorganisms create flashes and streamers of light in tropical waters. These marine fireflies are often seen near mangroves, creating luminous lagoons such as Oyster Bay just beyond Falmouth, where the underwater fireworks shine brighter from **Fisherman's Inn** ☎ *(809) 954-3427*, for $7 a person and **Glistening Waters Inn** ☎ *(809) 954-3229*, for $9. Diving in Negril is handled by a half-dozen pros. Karen McCarthy, of the **Negril Scuba Center** ☎ *(809) 957-4425*, offers guided dives with a staff of 10. Cost is $30 for a dive of 45 to 55 minutes, which includes round-trip transportation from Negril hotels; equipment rental is $20 a day. Night dives, costing $40 per person, are a specialty.

Where to Stay

Hotels and Resorts

Chuckles   **$75–$260**   ★★

Negril Square, ☎ *(809) 957-4277.*
Single: $75–$260. Double: $90–$260.
Located on a hill above the commercial center, this Mediterranean-style resort is peaceful and quiet. Guest rooms are nicely done and very clean; two-bedroom villas have kitchens. On-site facilities include two tennis courts, a large pool, volleyball and a disco. The public beach is down the hill. 78 rooms. Credit Cards: MC, A.

Drumville Cove Resort   **$40–$100**   ★★

West End, ☎ *(800) 423-4095, (809) 957-4369.*

Single: $40–$100. Double: $45–$100.

Set on the side of a cliff overlooking the sea, this complex is 2.5 miles from town. Accommodations are in cottages, some with kitchenettes. There's nightly entertainment, a weekly barbecue, restaurant and bar. 20 rooms. Credit Cards: V, MC, A.

Foote Prints on the Sands $55–$105 ★★★

Norman Manley Blvd., ☎ *(809) 957-4300.*
Single: $55–$105. Double: $55–$105.

This family-run hotel sits right on Seven Mile Beach. Guest rooms are nice and comfortable, and a few have whirlpool tubs. Four kitchenette suites are also available. There's no TV in the rooms, though you can watch the tube in the lounge. No pool. 33 rooms. Credit Cards: MC, A.

Grand Lido $250–$390 ★★★★★

Norman Manley Blvd., ☎ *(800) 423-4095, (809) 957-4010.*
Single: $250–$290. Double: $350–$390.

Very glamorous and elegant, this all-inclusive resort is open only to adults, though it's a lot less of a meat market than its neighbor, Hedonism II. Set on 22 acres, the Mediterranean-style property wows guests with a dramatic entrance, personalized check-in, and the *M.Y. Zein*, a yacht given by Ari Onassis as a wedding gift to Princess Grace and Prince Rainier. Accommodations are in wings that run parallel to the beach, all with sea views. They are beautifully done with tasteful decor, large baths, sitting areas, and such niceties as stereos. Four restaurants, six bars, two pools, four tennis courts, a full health club, cruises aboard the yacht, a beauty salon, and on and on and on. The large beach is divided in two for those who wear suits and those who don't. Service, of course, is superb. This place is really special for those who like to splurge and be in the company of equally monied people. 200 rooms. Credit Cards: MC, A.

Hedonism II $205–$376 ★★★

Norman Manley Blvd., ☎ *(800) 423-4095, (809) 957-4200.*
Single: $205–$260. Double: $305–$376.

This all-inclusive resort, open only to those over 18, is aptly named, as it is dedicated to the pursuit of pleasure—and partying. Lots of singles are mixed in with the couples, and depending on the clientele, this can be a bit of a meat market. Set on 22 acres at the northern end of Seven Mile Beach, it houses guests in comfortable though uninspired rooms; the whole point is to be out frolicking, anyway. The rates include all meals, drinks (drinking is a big pastime), and activities, and tips are forbidden. Two restaurants, five bars, a pool and two Jacuzzis, six tennis courts, all watersports, a gym, and nightly entertainment in the disco. The beach is divided for "prudes" and "nudes." Not for the conservative by any stretch, but lively and fun for young party animals. 280 rooms. Credit Cards: MC, A.

Negril Beach Club Hotel $77–$185 ★★

Negril Main Road, ☎ *(800) 526-2422, (809) 957-4220.*
Single: $77–$185. Double: $65–$185.

Very, very casual and informal, this complex includes traditional rooms, studios, and one-bedroom suites with kitchens. There's a small pool, health club and two tennis courts, but most activity centers around the beach, where watersports await and most bathers are topless. 85 rooms. Credit Cards: MC, A.

Negril Cabins $40–$55 ★★

Bloody Bay, ☎ *(809) 957-4350.*
Single: $40–$55. Double: $40–$55.

Set in a forest across from Bloody Bay beach, this complex of log cabins offers true bargain rates and rustic accommodations. Each unit has a balcony and simple furnishings, but only some are air-conditioned. There's a restaurant and occasional live entertainment, but not much else in the way of amenities. A nice alternative to the cookie-cutter beach hotels. 50 rooms. Credit Cards: MC, A.

Negril Inn $115–$145 ★★

Negril Beach, ☎ *(800) 634-7456, (809) 957-4209.*
Single: $115–$145. Double: $115–$145.

A nice alternative to the larger and livelier all-inclusives, this small resort offers everything for one price in a more peaceful setting. Guestrooms are simple but pleasant. Most meals are served buffet style, and there are two bars and nightly entertainment for dessert. Recreational facilities include two tennis courts, bicycles, horseshoes, a pool and gym. No kids under 16. 46 rooms. Credit Cards: MC, A.

Negril Tree House $85–$275 ★★★★

Norman Manley Blvd., ☎ *(800) 423-4095, (809) 957-4288.*
Single: $85–$275. Double: $85–$275.

Set right on Seven Mile Beach, this unusual spot accommodates guests in two-story octagonal "tree house" cottages. They are generally nicely done, but some could use repairs. Ask for a room on the second floor; they have better views and more atmosphere. Twelve suites offer one or two bedrooms and full kitchens. There's a pool, watersports, a handful of bars and restaurants, a Monday night beach party, and twice-weekly island picnics. Nice, if you don't mind rustic. 70 rooms. Credit Cards: MC, A.

Paradise View $75–$135 ★★

Norman Manley Blvd., ☎ *(809) 957-4375.*
Single: $75–$95. Double: $100–$135.

Modest in most ways, this hotel's real asset is its location on a gorgeous beach. Guest rooms are comfortable but on the small side. Watersports on the beach, but no pool. 17 rooms. Credit Cards: MC, A.

Poinciana Beach Hotel $168–$281 ★★★

Norman Manley Blvd., ☎ *(800) 468-6728, (809) 957-4100.*
Single: $168–$281. Double: $168–$281.

Set on six tropical acres fronting Seven Mile Beach, this resort houses guests in a varied mix of standard guest rooms, studios, and one- and two-bedroom apartments in villas. All are nicely done, with Murphy beds in the studios and kitchens, as well as cooks in the apartments. All kinds of watersports await, including PADI certification for divers. Two tennis courts, miniature golf, a weight room, rental bikes, two pools and a disco. Good for the active set. 130 rooms. Credit Cards: MC, A.

Sandals Negril $2890–$3995 ★★★★

Rutland Point, *(800) 726-3257, (809) 957-4216.*
Another of the chain's couples-only resorts, this operation is set on a narrow beach, with a boat shuttling guests to a small island where they can tan in the buff. Rooms are comfortable, but only the more expensive units have balconies and sea views. All kinds of activities (plus meals and drinks) are covered in the rate, including three tennis courts, watersports, a gym, two pools, and the usual resort diversions. A few bars and a disco provide nighttime fun. Appeals mainly to the young and in love, and a bit more subdued than Hedonism II. Rates are $2890 to $3995 per couple per week. Partying couples may be happier at Hedonism II, which is cheaper. 199 rooms. Credit Cards: MC, A.

Swept Away Resort $2770–$3785 ★★★★

Long Bay, *(800) 545-7937, (809) 957-4040.*
Yet another all-inclusive resort open only to couples, this special spot puts an emphasis on sports and fitness. Accommodations are in two-story villas near the beach and are beautifully decorated with large verandas. The centerpiece is the fitness center, an excellent facility with a gym, lap pool, ten tennis courts, and squash and racquetball. There's also all the usual watersports and a lagoon-style pool. You're welcome to booze, but the emphasis is on juice and veggie bars. Dedicated party animals look elsewhere! $2770 to $3785 per couple per week. 134 rooms. Credit Cards: V, MC, A.

T-Water Beach Hotel $125–$155 ★★

Norman Manley Blvd., *(800) 654-1592, (809) 957-4270.*
Single: $125–$155. Double: $125–$155.
Set on Seven Mile Beach, this resort accommodates guests in a varied mix of traditional rooms, studios with kitchens, and suites. Popular with families (kids under 12 stay free), it offers a pool, watersports, and constant volleyball games. Not too exciting, but the rates are relatively reasonable. 70 rooms. Credit Cards: MC, A.

Apartments and Condominiums

Beachcomber Club $105–$185 ★★★

Norman Manley Blvd., *(800) 423-4095, (809) 957-4171.*
Single: $105–$135. Double: $155–$185.
Set right on Seven Mile Beach, this Georgian-style condominium complex has one- and two-bedroom units with attractive furnishings, large verandas and full kitchens. Some also sport four-poster beds. Hotel-like touches include room service and nightly turndowns. Two restaurants, tennis, watersports, a pool, and supervised programs for children year-round. 46 rooms. Credit Cards: MC, A.

Crystal Waters Villas $85–$110 ★★

Negril, ☎ *(800) 443-3020, (809) 957-4889.*
Single: $85–$110. Double: $85–$110.
Located right on the beach, this complex offers villas with full kitchens, porches, one to three bedrooms, and the services of a personal maid and cook. No restaurant on-site, but many are nearby. Reasonable rates. 10 rooms. Credit Cards: MC, A.

Point Village   **$100–$155**   ★★★

Rutland Point, ☎ *(809) 957-4351.*
Single: $100–$145. Double: $115–$155.

Set on Rutland Point on the northern coastline among lush foliage, this village-style resort has tropically decorated studios and suites with kitchens and one to three bedrooms. A house band entertains six nights a week, and there are also occasional theme parties and a few bars for nighttime recreation. By day, there's a pool, private beach with watersports, and tennis. Parents can stash the kids in supervised programs. 130 rooms. Credit Cards: MC, A.

Xtabi Club Resort   **$50–$145**   ★★

West End, ☎ *(809) 957-4336.*
Single: $50–$145. Double: $50–$145.

Perfect for nature lovers and just plain lovers, this resort houses guests in octagonal cottages set on rugged cliffs or across the road in a garden setting. All are simply furnished and have small kitchens and enclosed outdoor showers, but no air conditioning. The grounds are lovely and natural, with dense foliage, sea caves reached via a spiral staircase and nice views. No beach to speak of, but great snorkeling, and there is a pool for cooling off. Lots of nude sunbathers here. 16 rooms. Credit Cards: MC, A.

Inns

Charela Inn   **$55–$165**   ★★★

Norman Manley Blvd., ☎ *(800) 423-4095, (809) 957-4648.*
Single: $55–$165. Double: $55–$165.

This small Spanish hacienda-style inn has lush inner gardens and is set right on Seven Mile Beach. Guest rooms have plenty of character with four-poster beds and balconies. Request one on the upper floor for the best views. There's a pool and free watersports, and a decent restaurant. Peaceful and friendly. 39 rooms. Credit Cards: MC, A.

Low Cost Lodging

Hotel Samsara   **$40–$115**   ★★

Light House Road, ☎ *(809) 957-4395.*
Single: $40–$115. Double: $40–$115.

Perched on low cliffs overlooking the sea, this small hotel has no beach, but a waterslide will dunk you right into the ocean, if you so desire. Accommodations are in cottages and quite spacious, but decorated with a minimal of fuss. Only some are air-conditioned. Relaxed and informal, the place hops during the Monday night reggae concerts. There's also a pool and tennis court. 50 rooms. Credit Cards: MC, A.

Negril Gardens   **$105–$140**   ★★

Norman Manley Blvd., ☎ *(800) 423-4095, (809) 957-4408.*
Single: $105–$140. Double: $105–$140.

Located on Seven Mile Beach, this two-story hotel puts up guests on the beach or across the road near the pool. There's entertainment four nights a week, and by day, a pool, tennis and watersports on the public beach. Informal and friendly. 54 rooms. Credit Cards: MC, A.

Rock Cliff Resort   **$55–$100**   ★★★

Light House Road, ☎ *(809) 957-4331.*

Single: $55–$100. Double: $55–$100.

This complex of two-story colonial-style buildings appeals mainly to divers with its excellent PADI center. There's no beach, but a free shuttle will take you to one. Guest rooms are modestly decorated but of good size. There's a pool, volleyball, basketball, and two restaurants. Unless you're into diving, you'll probably be happier at a beach property. 33 rooms. Credit Cards: MC, A.

Where to Eat

Cafe au Lait $$$ ★★

Lighthouse Road, ☎ (809) 957-4471.
French cuisine.
Lunch: 12:00 a.m.–3:00 p.m., entrees $9–$29.
Dinner: 5:00 p.m.–10:00 p.m., entrees $9–$29.
Located in a cottage resort on the West End, this authentic bistro (for Jamaica) features island-influenced, light French meals, including pizza and crepes (some made with callaloo), French bread, local seafood and French wines. A pleasant spot if you are passing through the area. Associated Hotel: Mirage Resort. Credit Cards: V, MC.

Chicken Lavish $ ★★

West End Road, ☎ (809) 957-4410.
Latin American cuisine.
Lunch: 9:00 a.m.–4:00 p.m., entrees $3–$5.
Dinner: 4:00 p.m.–10:00 p.m., entrees $3–$5.
Super informal, super cheap, and super delicious—with a juicy name like that what else can you expect? Once a local hangout jealously guarded by those in the know, the word is out about this unpretentious little spot on the beach renowned for toothsome fried chicken and curried goat. Credit Cards: V, MC.

Cosmo's $ ★★

Norman Manley Boulevard, ☎ (809) 957-4330.
Seafood cuisine. Specialties: Curried Conch.
Lunch: 11:00 a.m.–4:00 p.m., entrees $5–$12.
Dinner: 4:00 p.m.–10:00 p.m., entrees $5–$12.
Seafood is pretty much IT here, but what seafood! Owner-character Cosmo Brown specializes in conch, either stewed, curried or in a generous vat of soup. Since this chewy gastropod appears more often in other Caribbean islands, this is a good spot to try it. Otherwise, a grilled or baked escovitch (well-marinated in spices) whole fish is a popular choice. Cosmo's is situated in an informal, thatched-roof hut on a sparsely-populated East End beach. Credit Cards: V, MC.

Hungry Lion $$$ ★★

West End Road,
Latin American cuisine.
Lunch: entrees $18–$30.
Dinner: entrees $18–$30.
The setting at this small and popular restaurant is as verdant and colorful as the Rastafarian Ital cuisine served here. Ital, which is based on local vegetarian ingredients, often features foods that display the Rasta colors of green, red and gold. At the

Hungry Lion, if you dine outside by a fountain, you'll be surrounded by a greenhouse of flowering plants. Inside, the dining room is a living canvas of sophisticated tie-dye hues. A plate consisting of a marinated whole fish will be dressed with a hibiscus flower. It's that kind of place. Credit Cards: V, MC.

Paradise Yard $$ ★★

Gas Station Road, ☎ *(809) 957-4006.*
Latin American cuisine. Specialties: Rasta Pasta.
Lunch: 8:00 a.m.–4:00 p.m., entrees $6–$15.
Dinner: 4:00 p.m.–10:00 p.m., entrees $6–$15.

Life is fine at this relaxing open-air restaurant with a tin roof situated on the road to the port city of Savannah-del-Mar. You can get here early for a full-on Jamaican breakfast of saltfish and ackee, juicy local fruits and *bammies* (cassava bread). At lunch and dinner, ackee appears again in the Rasta Pasta—the golden vegetable (which tastes like scrambled eggs) is teamed with a thick tomato sauce and green peppers over fettuccine. There's also curried goat, pumpkin soup and enchiladas. This is a very authentic experience. Credit Cards: Not Accepted.

Rick's Cafe $$$ ★

West End Road, ☎ *(809) 957-4335.*
Seafood cuisine. Specialties: Grilled Lobster, Fresh-Fruit Daiquiris.
Lunch: 12:00 a.m.–4:00 p.m., entrees $11–$28.
Dinner: 4:00 p.m.–10:00 p.m., entrees $11–$28.

This famous (circa 1974) bar-restaurant-hangout is a scene and a place to be seen. One of the many draws here is a concept imitated from the La Quebrada divers in Acapulco—locals and visitors plunge some 25 feet into the sea from the cliffs at Rick's before emerging (it's hoped) for a papaya daiquiri. A tamer ritual takes place just before sunset when crowds of tanned and buffed young people pack the rock-encrusted, palm-fronded terrace for fun and frolic and a last glimpse of old sol. You can also come here for lunch or brunch, but for that you can go anywhere. Credit Cards: Not Accepted.

Tan-ya's $$$ ★

Norman Manley Boulevard, ☎ *(809) 957-4041.*
Latin American cuisine.
Lunch: 11:00 a.m.–3:00 p.m., entrees $5–$8.
Dinner: 6:30 p.m.–10:00 p.m., entrees $8–$25.

This oceanside restaurant at the quietly elegant Seasplash Resort is where guests and others go to dress up (just a little) for French-inspired seafood and a creative way with lobster. Associated Hotel: Seasplash Resort. Reservations recommended. Credit Cards: V, MC, A.

NORTH COAST

About 30 miles east from Montego Bay, **Falmouth** gives you the feeling of being a fairly quiet area while still maintaining proximity to the cities of Mo' Bay or Ocho Rios. This small 18th-century port town takes about a half-hour to explore on foot. There are a number of historical buildings that are interesting to see, such as the courthouse, a reconstruction of the 19th-century building, the customs office, the William Knubb Memorial Church, at George and King Street, and the 1796 parish church. Nearby is the **Good Hope** greathouse (leaving town, turn south), the 18th-century estate of John Thorpe, one of the richest Jamaican planters. The restoration of the main house and several outbuildings is exquisite, and it now stands as a fine hotel. Save time for a magnificent horseback ride through the countryside, over the estate's 6000 acres. (Make reservations in advance; ☎ *954-3289*). Near here, you will find the turnoff to **Rafter's Village**, where you can take a bamboo raft down the Martha Brae River (for information about river rafting and other river treks, see the section "Treks" above). Two miles east of Falmouth is the **Caribatik factory**, which is the artwork of a fine Jamaican artist, Muriel Chandler. At **Glistening Waters Marina**, east of Caribatik, you'll discover Oyster Bay that glows with bioluminescence caused by microorganisms in the water.

Dive Sites in the North Coast

The area of Falmouth shares the same wall that runs adjacent to Mo'Bay, though here it is a bit shallower and closer to shore. Try Wonderland, one of the nicer shallow reefs, usually used as a second dive or night dive. **Chub Castle** offers invertebrates and schools of Bermuda Chub. Split Rock is a 30-ft spur and groove formation with schools of squid and steeping nurse sharks.

There are numerous dive sites in **Runaway Bay**, which is east of Falmouth on the north coast. The Canyon has a pair of walls just 20 feet apart that maintain a top depth of 30 feet while the bottom drops off from 40-130 feet. Pocket's Reef features huge stands of black coral trees, huge purple tube sponges, and masses of rope sponges. Ganga Planes are two planes formerly used for the illegal transportation of marihuana that now rest in 75 feet of water. **Rackey's Reef** is one of the best known sites, with a wall dropping at a slope of 60–80 feet before dropping vertically to a sand shelf at about 130 feet.

Where to Stay

Hotels and Resorts

Ambiance Hotel $90–$215 ★★

Runaway Bay, ☎ (800) 523-6504, (809) 973-4606.
Single: $90–$215. Double: $97–$215.

Set on a small private beach, this casual hotel offers adequate accommodations and services. There's a pool, gym and two restaurants, but not much else to write home about. You can probably do better in the price range. 80 rooms. Credit Cards: MC, A.

Caribbean Isle Hotel $55–$65 ★

Runaway Bay, ☎ (809) 973-2364.
Single: $55–$60. Double: $60–$65.

This small, casual hotel offers budget accommodations and not much else, though there is a pool. The beach comes and goes, depending on the tides. 24 rooms. Credit Cards: MC, A.

Club Caribbean $125–$295 ★★

Runaway Bay, ☎ (800) 647-2740, (809) 973-4702.
Single: $125–$395. Double: $215–$295.

This resort offers all-inclusive resort amenities with self-serve accommodations. Guests are put up in octagonal cottages with ceiling fans (no air conditioning) and kitchenettes. There's lots happening in the activities department, with organized crab races, volleyball games and the like. Watersports, two tennis courts, a swim-up bar in the pool, and a disco. Just about everything but lunch is included in the rates. 128 rooms. Credit Cards: V, MC, A.

Eaton Hall Beach Hotel $135–$299 ★★★

Runaway Bay, ☎ (809) 973-3503.
Single: $135–$299. Double: $185–$299.

This former 18th-century Georgian-style slave station is an all-inclusive resort that caters to a predominantly young crowd. Guests stay in standard rooms, suites, or villas with kitchenettes; all comfortable, but showing their age. No beach to speak of, but there are two pools, as well as tennis, watersports, glass-bottom boat rides, and organized activities. 52 rooms. Credit Cards: CB, V, MC, A.

H.E.A.R.T. Country Club $55–$75 ★★★

Runaway Bay, ☎ (809) 973-2671.
Single: $55. Double: $75.

This plantation-style country club is staffed by people learning the hotel business (it stands for Human Employment and Resource Training), so you can count on enthusiastic service. Set on a hillside with nice views, guest rooms are nice and bright. There's a decent restaurant and pool, golf next door, and they'll shuttle you to a small private beach. Really good for the rates. 20 rooms. Credit Cards: MC, A.

Jamaica Jamaica $167–$240 ★★★★

Runaway Bay, ☎ (800) 423-4095, (809) 973-2436.
Single: $167–$240. Double: $167–$240.

Encompassing 214 acres opening onto a wide, sandy beach, this all-inclusive resort does just about everything right. Not only do the rates include all meals, drinks and activities, they even throw in free cigarettes! Accommodations are bare-bones, but everyone's too busy with organized activities to notice. There's an excellent golf course, four tennis courts, classes in Jamaican handicrafts, all watersports, horseback riding, and a full health club with aerobics classes. The disco hops and the snorkeling offshore is great. No kids under 16 at this generally singles resort. 242 rooms. Credit Cards: MC, A.

Apartments and Condominiums

Franklyn D. Resort ★★★★

Runaway Bay, ☎ *(800) 423-4095, (809) 973-4591.*

This Georgian-style resort is especially suited to families. Accommodations are in suites with one to three bedrooms, kitchens, and a "Girl Friday" to cook clean and look after the kids by day (there's an extra charge for nighttime babysitting). Kids under 16 stay free, so you'll see a lot of them here; romantic couples will be happier elsewhere. The beach is small, but there are two pools (one for kids), tennis, exercise room, and tons of organized activities for both kids and their parents. Rates are $3205 to $7205 weekly per couple. 76 rooms. Credit Cards: MC, A.

Portside Villas & Condos $85–$280 ★★

Highway A-1, ☎ *(809) 973-2007.*
Single: $85–$280. Double: $85–$280.

Located 20 minutes outside of Ocho Rios at Discovery Bay, this complex has studios and suites of one to three bedrooms, all with kitchens and cooks for an extra fee. The beach is small, and there are also two pools and nonmotorized watersports. You're on your own for meals. 15 rooms. Credit Cards: MC, A.

OCHO RIOS

Over the past 15 years, Ocho Rios has become one of the busiest, if most elite, tourism sites in Jamaica. Cruise ships dock nearly daily and a number of fine resorts are located here. Five outstanding beaches, excellent restaurants, abundant nightlife, and lots of sports make the area ideal for those who want to escape the third-world chaos of Kingston and Montego Bay. The town has fiercely hung onto its charm despite the massive development. The most exciting natural phenomenon near here is **Dunn's River Falls**, the internationally renowned stair-stepped falls that rush under the road and reappear to join the sea on the white beach to the left. Even if you don't throw yourself to the wetness in a fun tour of the falls, you must come to see its dramatic descent over the mountainside. Other natural attractions are plenty, from the Shaw Park Botanical Garden, where you can wile away a few hours studying the exotic tropical plants of the island.

If you're still feeling athletic, a terrific horseback riding jaunt can be arranged at the **Prospect Plantation**, which will take you through trails of citrus groves and coffee trees, and down by the banks of the White River. Jitney tours of the estate are free of charge. Rafting tours on the nearby White River are also available (see the section under "Treks.") Out on Annotto Bay, you'll find the 250-acre **Crystal Springs**, a natural garden replete with hundreds of birds, a myriad of tropical orchids, fierce waterfalls, rivers and a restaurant.

Beaches in Ocho Rios

Ocho Rios beach is giving Mo'Bay a run for its money these days in terms of traffic. Mallard's attracts the most crowds, somewhat due to the presence of the Jamaica Grande hotel, which caters to the convention crowd. (Don't write us if you find yourself on the beach sitting next to someone with elks' ears.) Turtle Beach is the adjacent strand, which has a very good reputation for swimming.

Dive Sites in Ocho Rios

Most dive sites are centered here in the east of the town to avoid detrimental effects of runoff from the rivers. **Devil's Reef** is one of the most popular, an elongated pinnacle offering depths of 60 feet to more than 100 feet. **Caverns** is an area riddled with caves, tunnels and swim-throughs. **Kathym** is a 140-feet minesweeper that was scuttled to form an artificial reef in February of 1991.

Treks near Ocho Rios

FIELDING'S CHOICE:

Chukka Cove, just outside Ocho Rios, is where English aristocrats go to keep their polo technique up to snuff during their winter sojourns in the former colony. Others go there to watch the polo matches; still others hire horses for canters along the cliffs and beaches. The very lucky few mount up for a three-day trek into the neighboring foothills. On these extended, escorted rides, base camp is 2000 feet above Chukka Cove, in a handsome 18th-century great house called Lillyfields, newly restored with 14 rooms filled with Jamaican artifacts. From there, riders make morning and afternoon expeditions through backwater villages, through sugar and banana plantations, along paths overhung with ferns and bamboo, stopping off now and again for dips to cool mountain streams. Although each evening brings the relief of hot baths and sundowners on the veranda, this is serious riding. Don't even think about the Chukka Cove trek unless you're in good enough physical shape to handle 60 miles of riding in three days and can show the guides that you know how to handle a horse on rough terrain. For more information contact Chukka Cove Farm P.O. Box 160, Ocho Rios, St. Ann, Jamaica ☎ 809-972-0814). Rates are $500 per rider for the three-day trek, which includes two nights' lodging and all meals.

What Else to See

Historical Sites

Firefly　　　　　　　　　　　　　　　　　　★ ★ ★

> *Grants Pen, St. Mary.*
> *Hours Open: 9:00 a.m.–5:00 p.m.*
> This is the home of Sir Noel Coward, who spent the last 25 years of his life in
> Jamaica. Donated to the Jamaican government upon his death in 1973, the man-
> sion remains unchanged since the actor and author lived there. Guided tours take
> you through the house to gawk at his bedroom, closets filled with clothes, antique
> furnishings and paintings by the man himself. His grave is also on the site, as well as
> a cafe and gift shop. General admission: $10.00.

Museums and Exhibits

Harmony Hall　　　　　　　　　　　　　　★ ★ ★

> *Highway A3, Tower Isle,* *(809) 460-4120.*
> *Hours Open: 10:00 a.m.–6:00 p.m.*
> This late 19th-century great house is now a gallery displaying high-quality paintings
> and arts and crafts by Jamaican artists. Free admission.

Parks and Gardens

Coyaba River Garden and Museum　　　　★ ★ ★

> *Shaw Park, Ocho Rios,* *(809) 974-6235.*
> This former plantation is now a private estate with lovely gardens, waterfalls, a river
> and fish ponds. The small museum displays relics from pre-Columbian days. *Coyaba*
> is the Arawak word for paradise and this spot is certainly a small slice of it. General
> admission: $5.00.

Tours

Dunn's River Falls　　　　　　　　　　　★ ★ ★ ★

> *Highway A3, Ocho Rios,* *(809) 974-2857.*
> *Hours Open: 9:00 a.m.–5:00 p.m.*
> These much-photographed falls cascade down some 600 feet into the sea. The best
> way to experience them is to hire a guide and make a human chain that climbs right
> up the slippery rocks. Wear sneakers, and don't forget to tip your guide. You can
> stop along the way to dip in pools and be massaged by the tumbling water. There's
> a path on dry land for the less daring. General admission: $3.00.

Prospect Plantation　　　　　　　　　　　★ ★ ★

> *Highway A3, St. Ann,* *(809) 974-2058.*
> Located just east of Ocho Rios, this working plantation can be toured via jitney.
> Among the highlights are sweeping views, gorgeous scenery, and lots of trees

planted by famous folks, including Noel Coward and Charlie Chaplin. General admission: $10.00.

Where to Stay

Hotels and Resorts

Boscobel Beach Hotel $415–$995 ★★★★

Ocho Rios, ☎ *(800) 423-4095, (809) 975-3330.*
Double: $415–$995.

Set on the beach, this all-inclusive resort caters to families. Accommodations range from spacious guestrooms to suites, all nicely done and some with sunken tubs. The grounds include a large playground, two theaters showing films, a disco, and two pools, one in the adults-only section. Four tennis courts, watersports and a health club. Kids are kept busy with supervised programs. Great for families, but those without kids should look elsewhere. 228 rooms. Credit Cards: MC, A.

Ciboney Ocho Rios $175–$690 ★★★★

Main Street, ☎ *(800) 777-7800, (809) 974-1036.*
Single: $175–$345. Double: $350–$690.

Set just outside of town on 45 hillside acres, this all-inclusive resort is impressive and stylish. Most accommodations are in villas with full kitchens, semiprivate pools, and personal attendants. You can work out and be pampered in the European-style spa, play golf on six courts, swim in two pools, and partake in all watersports. Very nice. 300 rooms. Credit Cards: MC, A.

Club Jamaica Beach Resort $180–$235 ★★

Main Street, ☎ *(800) 423-4095, (809) 974-6642.*
Single: $180–$235. Double: $115–$235.

Located on Turtle Beach near the crafts market, the all-inclusive property has comfortable guestrooms. As with other all-inclusives, there's lots to do, including themed buffets at poolside, nightly entertainment, a disco, and organized activities. No kids under 12. 95 rooms. Credit Cards: V, MC, A.

Couples Jamaica $365–$520 ★★★★

Autoroute 3, ☎ *(800) 423-4095, (809) 975-4271.*
Double: $365–$520.

Like the name applies, this all-inclusive resort is open to couples only—their logo is two lions copulating, in case you don't get the message. Guest rooms are modern and comfortable, with king beds. The beach is great and there's always something happening, from nightly entertainment to five tennis courts to all watersports (there's even a windsurfing school). If you get carried away by romance, they'll marry you for free. There's a spot for nudists on the beach, as well as nude cruises and snorkeling. You'll be making like lions in no time. 172 rooms. Credit Cards: MC, A.

Enchanted Garden $95–$555 ★★★

Main Road, ☎ *(800) 323-5655, (809) 974-1400.*
Single: $95–$555. Double: $95–$555.

It really is rather enchanting at this all-inclusive resort set in the foothills and surrounded by jungle greenery. The many gardens and waterfalls lend a truly exotic feel. Accommodations range from standard rooms to villas with kitchens and one to three bedrooms, all nicely done. You can swim in the pool or natural ponds with waterfalls. Dining is quite varied, with lots of ethnic choices. Two tennis courts, a fully equipped health spa, and an aviary. They'll take you to the beach or into town for free. 112 rooms. Credit Cards: V, MC, A.

Jamaica Grande $135–$195 ★★★★

Ocho Rios, ☎ *(800) 228-9898, (809) 974-2201.*
Single: $135–$195. Double: $135–$195.
Ocho Rios' largest hotel is a modern high-rise known for its fantasy pool, a large and fanciful body of water with grottos, waterfalls, a swinging bridge, and a swim-up bar. Accommodations are found in two towers and are generally nicely done. Facilities include a fitness center, four tennis courts, all watersports, activities for children, and a large and happening disco. Nightly entertainment and lots of theme parties. Nice, but the sheer size can be a bit overwhelming, and there's not much in the way of authentic Jamaican style. 720 rooms. Credit Cards: CB, V, MC, A.

Jamaica Inn $225–$250 ★★★★

Ocho Rios, ☎ *(809) 974-2516.*
Single: $225–$250. Double: $225–$250.
Located in a tropical setting on a private beach, this intimate resort requires guests to dress up in the evening. Most accommodations are in junior or full suites beautifully decorated with antiques, local artwork and large lanais. There's a pool and watersports, and guests can play tennis for free at a nearby resort. No kids under 14 at this very affluent and rather conservative property. If you're looking for riotous action, look elsewhere. 45 rooms. Credit Cards: MC, A.

Plantation Inn $300–$999 ★★★★★

Ocho Rios, ☎ *(800) 423-4095, (809) 974-5601.*
Double: $300–$999.
Located on a lush hillside, this colonial-style hotel has a country club atmosphere that draws a predominantly conservative (and rich) crowd. Rooms are quite nicely done with pampering amenities. The grounds include two beaches (reached via a steep walk down the hill), two tennis courts, a small pool, watersports, a gym and massage services. Not as nice as its neighbor, the Jamaica Inn, but a bit more casual, though you're still required to dress up at night. 78 rooms. Credit Cards: V, MC, A.

Sandals Dunn's River $2295–$4200 ★★★★

Main Street, ☎ *(800) 726-3257, (809) 972-1610.*
Set on 10 tropical acres fronting a beach, this couples-only resort is among the chain's best. Guest rooms come in a variety of configurations and are generally pleasant and comfortable. There's lots happening at all hours: 18 holes of golf (included in the rates), four restaurants and seven bars, frequent live entertainment, a huge pool and another smaller one, four tennis courts, a gym, all watersports, a free trip to Dunn's River Falls, and a 20-minute massage. A bit more sophisticated

than its siblings. $2295 to $4200 per couple per week. 256 rooms. Credit Cards: MC, A.

Sandals Ocho Rios   **$355–$455**   ★★★★

Main Street, ☎ *(800) 726-3257, (809) 974-5691.*
Double: $355–$455.
Set among lush beachfront gardens, this couples-only resort boasts immaculate grounds and excellent service. The all-inclusive rates cover all meals, drinks and activities, including nightly entertainment, all watersports, a gym with exercise classes, two tennis courts and nearby golf on 18 holes. Accommodations are nice and open onto furnished balconies, most with sea views. Dining is varied with three restaurants; afterwards, there are four bars and a disco in which to unwind. Very professional and well run. 237 rooms. Credit Cards: MC, A.

Sans Souci Lido   **$465–$945**   ★★★★★

Ocho Rios, ☎ *(800) 203-7450, (809) 974-2353.*
Single: $465–$945. Double: $465–$945.
This elegant all-inclusive resort is tops in any book. It is best known for its rejuvenating spa program, where guests are pampered and treated like royalty. Accommodations are quite smashing and range from standard rooms to suites with one or two bedrooms, some with Jacuzzis and kitchens. Set on a steep hillside overlooking the sea, the small beach is reached via elevator or steep walkways. There are three tennis courts, two outdoor pools, mineral baths, and watersports. Really special. 111 rooms. Credit Cards: V, MC, A.

Shaw Park Beach Hotel   **$165–$436**   ★★★

Cutlass Bay, ☎ *(800) 243-9420, (809) 974-2552.*
Single: $165–$436. Double: $179–$436.
Set on a private though narrow beach, this Georgian-style resort has adequate but quite simple guest rooms; the two-bedroom suites with kitchens are much nicer, but also much pricier. Standard recreational activities include two tennis courts, a pool, watersports, and exercise classes. Nights are kept busy with three bars, a lively disco and organized entertainment. Decent, but aging in a not particularly graceful fashion. 118 rooms. Credit Cards: V, MC, A.

Apartments and Condominiums

Comfort Suites   **$105–$205**   ★★★

17 DeCosta Drive, ☎ *(800) 423-4095, (809) 974-7084.*
Single: $105–$180. Double: $125–$205.
Brand-new in March 1994, this downtown hotel accommodates guests in suites with kitchenettes and patios. There's a pool, tennis and year-round supervised kids' programs, as well as maid service and a restaurant. Beaches are found within walking distance. 137 rooms. Credit Cards: CB, V, MC, A.

Sea Palms   **$145–$145**   ★★★

61 Main Street, ☎ *(080) 423-4095, (809) 974-4400.*
Single: $145. Double: $145.
A casual complex of apartments with a pool, but no other facilities. Units are comfortable and range from one to three bedrooms, all with patios or balconies and kitchens. 45 rooms. Credit Cards: MC, A.

Inns

Hibiscus Lodge $65–$93 ★★

Main Street, ☎ (800) 526-2422, (809) 974-2676.
Single: $65–$93. Double: $65–$93.

Situated in a quiet topical garden fronting the sea, this intimate Jamaican-style inn has no beach, but there is a pool for cooling off. Guest rooms are comfortable, but only a few have air conditioning. There's tennis and a well-regarded restaurant on site, as well as a bar built into the cliffs. Lots of atmosphere here. 26 rooms. Credit Cards: CB, V, MC, A.

Low Cost Lodging

Fisherman's Point $95–$135 ★★

Turtle Beach, ☎ (800) 423-4095, (809) 974-5317.
Single: $95–$103. Double: $125–$135.

This complex on Turtle Beach has one-, two-, and three-bedroom apartments with kitchenettes and maid and cook services. There's also a bar and restaurant if you can't face your own cooking. The modest grounds include a pool. The Ocean Village Shopping Centre is within walking distance. 64 rooms. Credit Cards: MC, A.

Turtle Beach Towers $87–$225 ★★

Ocean Village, ☎ (809) 974-2801.
Single: $87–$225. Double: $93–$225.

Their modern high-rises are on the beach and next to the Ocean Village Shopping Centre. Units are nicely done and run the gamut from studios to apartments with one to three bedrooms. Most have balconies and all have maid service. The grounds include a coffee shop, pool, two tennis courts, and watersports. 218 rooms. Credit Cards: MC, A.

Where to Eat

Almond Tree $$$ ★★★★

87 Main Street, ☎ (809) 974-2813.
Latin American cuisine. Specialties: Roast Suckling Pig, Pumpkin Soup.
Lunch: 12:00 a.m.–2:30 p.m., entrees $12–$26.
Dinner: 6:00 p.m.–9:30 p.m., entrees $12–$26.

If you can stop swinging in the unique chairs suspended from the ceiling in the bar of this small inn on a cliff overlooking the sea, you'll find the food in the restaurant to be quite good. The Almond Tree has a real tree growing through its roof, a diverse clientele (famous rock stars have been known to swing in) and roast suckling pig on the menu. Soups are divine, especially the pumpkin. Drop in at the piano bar on the hotel grounds for some good tunes to accompany after-dinner drinks in a more subdued atmosphere. Associated Hotel: Hibiscus Lodge. Reservations recommended. Credit Cards: V, MC, DC, A.

Evita's $$ ★★★★★

Eden Bower Road, ☎ (809) 974-2333.
Italian cuisine. Specialties: Homemade Pasta.
Lunch: 11:00 a.m.–4:00 p.m., entrees $7–$19.
Dinner: 4:00 p.m.–11:00 p.m., entrees $7–$19.

Don't cry for Evita—in this instance, restaurateur Eva Myers—who has no trouble drawing in pasta lovers and others to this 1860s-era gingerbread house perched over Ocho Rios Bay. Many guests prefer eating on the terrace as the sun sets over the deep blue Caribbean waters. Some of the seemingly endless parade of pastas include a lasagne rastafari with bell peppers, tomatoes and ackee—the Rastafarian (and Italian) colors. Fresh and delicious fish, especially red snapper, steaks and ribs are also available. Reservations recommended. Credit Cards: V, MC, A.

Parkway Restaurant   **$$$**   ★★

60 Da Costa Drive, *(809) 974-2667.*
Latin American cuisine.
Lunch: 7:30 a.m.–4:00 p.m., entrees $6–$25.
Dinner: 4:00 p.m.–11:00 p.m., entrees $6–$25.
This tropical diner-roadhouse in downtown Ocho Rios serves up some very reasonably priced and tasty Jamaican specialties to simple folk as well as prime movers and shakers. You can join them too, while watching local programming from the ever-present TV. Spicy Jamaican chicken or curries and banana cake or pie are popular choices. Credit Cards: V, MC, A.

Ruins Restaurant   **$$$**   ★

Da Costa Drive, *(809) 974-2442.*
Chinese cuisine.
Lunch: 12:00 a.m.–2:30 p.m., entrees $12–$33.
Dinner: 6:00 p.m.–9:30 p.m., entrees $12–$33.
The cuisine is mostly American-Chinese (chop suey, chow mein, etc.), but the scene is the thing at this refreshing alfresco restaurant named after the ruins of an old sugar mill that once occupied the site. Expect a lot of fellow revelers marveling at the surrounding waterfalls and pools that are softly lit at night. Dress is casual, and there is a cocktail lounge in an adjoining building. Specialties include shellfish and lobster; but you can also order a steak. No lunch is served on Sunday. Reservations required. Credit Cards: V, MC, DC, A.

PORT ANTONIO

Port Antonio is a miniature island port built around two **picturesque harbors** that could have served well as a Hollywood set. Indeed, Port Antonio *was* nearly a Hollywood set, at least the winter stomping ground, for such luminaries as Ginger Rodgers, Bette Davis, Clara Bow and such financial magnates as J.P. Morgan and William Randolph Hearst, who in the 20s, 30s, and 40s were drawn to the tropical exoticism and serene beauty of the bay. Port Antonio's biggest fan was actor Errol Flynn, who often could be seen prowling the bars at night. Strange architectural fantasies took shape in this town: the dream castle of architect Earl Levy, complete with turrets, over the shoreline east of the Trident Hotel, and the sprawling concrete mansion built by a Connecticut tycoon, now in crumbling remains. Ecologists won't want to miss the 282-ft.deep lagoon called **Blue Hole** off Route 44, or **Somerset Falls**, in the gorge of the Daniel River, above Hope Bay (you can't find a more romantic trip than the gondola ride under the falls). Hiking up to the **Blue Mountains** is spectacular and offers a terrific vista (for more information, see under "Treks"). Only the hardiest climbers will make it to the top of **Reach Falls** at Machioneal (no wonder the name!) but the effort will be worth it since the falls are considered to be the most beautiful in Jamaica. Nonsuch Cave is a few miles to the southeast where there are fossils and other hieroglypic signs of the Arawak tribes. There is no public transportation available so you will have to take a taxi and ask the driver to wait (about $10 round trip). The entrance fee is $5.

Beaches in Port Antonio

The best beaches in Port Antonio are **Boston Bay** and **San San Beach**. A delicacy of the area is the eye-watering peppery jerk pork, which will drive you to down a beer in as fast a time as possible. Just follow your nose and eyes to the smoke-spewing shacks, where local chefs cook them right on the beach. Cave Beach is a notable place to plop east of the town. **Navy Island** is located in the harbor and boasts two nude beaches—take the jetty on West Street near Musgrave Market. The island, one-time owned by Errol Flynn, has a memorial gallery to his life and career, where you can view movie stills and screenings of his old films. Snorkeling is available for a small fee, but the currents are strong and the fish are few. A complete wedding ceremony can be conducted in the chapel (for more information contact ☎ *993-2667*).

Treks in Port Antonio

A fabulous trip down the Rio Grande River can be accomplished in one of the former **banana rafts** designed to bring the fruits to market. (Years earlier, Errol Flynn envisioned the trip as a potential tourist gold mine.) The starting point is **Navy Island**, in the harbor (see above under "Beaches"). Each raft takes two people (what could be more romantic, especially if you've just gotten married in the resort chapel) Depending on the flow of the river, the trip takes about two hours, floating through spectacular lush scenery and with the chance to stop whenever you want to. A driver even takes your car from the embarkation point to the point of arrival, called **Rafter's Rest**, where you can also have a relaxing lunch after the hard work of floating downriver. (For more information, contact Keith Allen at the Huntress Marina in person, or just negotiate with raft owners when you arrive. Fee is $40 per trip from the ticket office, which opens at 8:00 a.m.) If you've come this far, and you are very adventurous (let us emphasize *very* again), try and visit the Maroon community (descendants of escaped slaves who have been self-governing their own people for centuries.) A Colonel Harris, said to be the leader of the Maroons, knows how to direct you (just ask about for him—we said you had to be adventurous) and then be prepared for anything. If you go looking like you have money, you will probably be asked to pay for taking photos or receiving interviews, etc., but if you have the ability to get suspicious strangers to trust you, you might hear some wonderful stories. There are no hotels or restaurants, so be prepared to return the same night, and take your own food.(For more information on the Maroons, see under the "People" section above.)

What Else to See

Parks and Gardens

Athenry Gardens and Cave of Nu   ★★★

Portland, Port Antonio, ☎ *(809) 993-3740.*
Hours Open: 9:00 a.m.–5:30 p.m.

The Nonsuch Cave dates back some 1.5 million years give or take a century or two, and can be toured to see its stalagmites and stalactites. Back on ground level there are great views at the pretty flowering gardens. Port Antonio is about 20 minutes away. General admission: $5.00.

Crystal Springs   ★★★

Highway A2, Port Antonio, ☎ *(809) 993-2609.*

This former sugar plantation is a privately owned estate that covers 158 acres. A peaceful spot to while away the hours, it has more than 15,000 orchids and lots of hummingbirds and other feathered friends. Bring binoculars. General admission: $1.00.

Where to Stay

Hotels and Resorts

Bonnie View Plantation $49–$83   ★★

Port Antonio, ☎ *(800) 448-5398, (809) 993-2752.*
Single: $49–$63. Double: $71–$83.

Sweeping views from this small hotel perched atop a hill and set on a farm. Guest rooms are quite simple, fitting in with the bargain rates. There's a pool, restaurant and bar, but not much else in the way of extras. They'll shuttle you down to the beach. 20 rooms. Credit Cards: V, MC, A.

Dragon Bay $101–$161   ★★

Port Antonio, ☎ *(800) 423-4095, (809) 993-3281.*
Single: $101–$161. Double: $101–$161.

Set on 55 acres with its own private cove, this villa-style resort is adjacent to Blue Lagoon. Accommodations are pleasant and run the gamut from single rooms to two-bedroom villas. Two restaurants and bars, weekly reggae concerts, a pair of pools and tennis courts, and all the usual resort amenities. A bit off the beaten track, so you'll want a rental car. 86 rooms. Credit Cards: MC, A.

Fern Hill Club   ★★★

Port Antonio, ☎ *(800) 263-4354, (809) 993-3222.*
Double: $215–$385.

Set on a hillside and encompassing 40 acres, this is an all-inclusive resort with wonderful views and a predominantly Canadian clientele. Accommodations vary from standard guest rooms to villas with kitchens; none are air-conditioned. The grounds include four pools, a restaurant and two bars, tennis, and an exercise room. The beach is down a steep hill; a shuttle bus will take you there if you're not up to the hike. Lots of honeymooners. 36 rooms. Credit Cards: MC, A.

Jamaica Palace Hotel $115–$285 ★★★

Port Antonio, ☎ *(800) 423-4095, (809) 993-2020.*
Single: $115–$285. Double: $115–$285.

Set on well-manicured grounds, this colonial-style mansion draws mainly European guests. Guest rooms are quite nice with antiques, Oriental rugs, and marble floors. There's no beach nearby, but you can dip in the pool, which is shaped like Jamaica. Elegant and refined, but a bit too out of the way for some folks. 80 rooms. Credit Cards: MC, A.

Navy Island Resort/Marina $75–$185 ★★

Port Antonio Harbour, ☎ *(809) 993-2667.*
Single: $75–$185. Double: $135–$185.

Comprising 64 acres on a 17th-century British naval station, this secluded resort later acted as Errol Flynn's personal hideaway. Like the name implies, it is located on its own small island a quarter-mile off the coast. Accommodations are in oceanfront villas with sun decks and kitchens, but no air conditioning. One of the three beaches is clothes optional. There's also a pool, tennis and watersports. 21 rooms. Credit Cards: MC, A.

Trident Villas & Hotel $255–$755 ★★★★★

Port Antonio, ☎ *(800) 237-3237, (809) 993-2705.*
Single: $255–$480. Double: $305–$755.

This is one of Jamaica's most luxurious resorts, set on 14 lush acres fronting the sea, two miles east of town. Guest rooms and villa suites are exquisitely furnished with antiques, plush decor, and ocean views. Only some are air-conditioned, but constant breezes keep everything cool. The lovely grounds include a small private beach, flowering gardens, pretty walkways, and two pools. Dinner is a formal affair that includes white-glove service; you'll have to dress up for the occasion. Service, of course, is outstanding. Truly elegant. 28 rooms. Credit Cards: MC, A.

Apartments and Condominiums

Goblin Hill Villas $1760–$2135 ★★★

Port Antonio, ☎ *(800) 423-4095, (809) 925-8108.*

Situated on 12 tropical acres of a hill above San San Beach, this complex has Georgian-style villas perfect for families. All are very nicely done, with locally made furniture and artwork, kitchens, and air-conditioned bedrooms. Each comes with a maid and cook. There are two lighted tennis courts, the beach down the hill, a pool and watersports. There's also a bar and restaurant, but besides occasional entertainment, not much of a nightlife. Rates, which range from $1760 to $2135 per couple weekly, include a rental car. 28 rooms. Credit Cards: MC, A.

Where to Eat

De Montevin Lodge   **$$**   ★★★

21 Fort George Street, ☎ *(809) 993-2604.*
Latin American cuisine.
Lunch: 12:30 p.m.–2:00 p.m., prix fixe $11–$18.
Dinner: 7:00 p.m.–9:00 p.m., prix fixe $11–$18.

Errol Flynn's chef used to rule the kitchen at this veddy British Victorian-style inn on Titchfield Hill (I don't think he paid much attention to what he was eating) but the food served here now is unadulterated Jamaican, prepared home-style; the number of courses that arrive depends on what you paid—the cheaper menus are just a tad over $10. Dishes include pumpkin soup, fricassee chicken, dessert and coffee. Associated Hotel: De Montevin Lodge. Reservations recommended. Credit Cards: Not Accepted.

Front Line, The   **$**   ★★

Boston Bay,
Latin American cuisine.
Lunch: entrees $5–$8.
Dinner: entrees $5–$8.

After leaving the chic resorts of Port Antonio (a town bereft of inexpensive eateries) travelers eagerly stop at Boston Bay beach for a soak and the best jerk barbecue on the islands. Of course, nothing is fancy, just a series of roadside stands vying for your attention—but the best one may be The Front Line, with the grills presided over by colorful pit men. Marinated chicken, pork or sausage swathed with a top secret sauce (lots of hot pepper and cayenne) is perfect with Red Stripe beer or rum. Credit Cards: Not Accepted.

Trident Hotel Restaurant   **$$$**   ★★★★★

Route A4, ☎ *(809) 993-2602.*
International cuisine.
Lunch: 12:00 a.m.–2:30 p.m., entrees $25–$35.
Dinner: 8:00-10:00, prix fixe $50.

Even if you aren't staying at this bastion of subdued luxury, it's a memorable experience to dine in the high-ceilinged restaurant of this 14-acre hotel. Here five course dinners are served on the terrace or in the main dining room by white-gloved waiters; the only sounds you hear are gentle murmurings from fellow guests and the softly-whirring ceiling fans above. Once in a while the stillness is broken by the shrill cries of the tame peacocks that live on the property. Associated Hotel: Trident Villas & Hotel. Reservations required. Credit Cards: V, MC, A.

SOUTH COAST

The south coast is Jamaica's ecological haven—the place where Jamaicans long to visit when they go on holiday. Here you'll find some truly "undiscovered" beaches, though you'll have to do a bit of driving to get there. The South Coast is also known as the best place for **deep-sea fishing**, and boat trips sail out from Belmont to the offshore banks and reefs. The bay is so calm here that **snorkeling** is often an exciting experience. Southeast of Bluefield are simply some of the most pristine, unspoiled strands in all Jamaica, but unfortunately, a new Sandals resort is moving in soon. Transport from Montego Bay is easily arranged. If you take the A2 road past Scotts Cove, proceed to the town of **Black River**, one of the oldest on the island, once a thriving port during the 18th century for logwood dyes. Along the coast are some handsome colonial mansions presently being restored. The longest river in Jamaica, the Black River is perfect for canoe and **rafting** trips. If you stay on A2 instead of turning off at Black River, proceed past Middle Quarters to the left turn which takes you to the **Y.S. Falls**, a glorious unspoiled area in the middle of a plantation—be prepared for a 15-minute hike from where you park your car.(For more information on Black River and Y.S. Falls excursions, see above under "Treks").

Mandeville is a lovely, peaceful upland town with what locals feel is the best climate on the island. For some reason, there are no slums among the population of 50,000—its present prosperity is due to the production of bauxite/alumina. The village green is reminiscent of New England, with its Georgian courthouse and parish church; do visit on Mondays, Wednesdays and Friday, if you want to see the market in full swing. Horseback riding, tennis, and golf on an 18-hole course are available.The Seventh Day Adventists run the Westici Health Foods store and also a vegetarian restaurant behind the church in the center of town. A craft center is located on Manchester Road.

Beaches

Bluefield Beach, near Savanna-la-Mer south of Negril, is the easiest to get to. Further out, another gem is Crane Beach at Black River. Most secluded is Treasure Beach (a strand that truly lives up to its name), 20 miles along the coast beyond Crane. To the east of Treasure Beach is **Lovers Leap**, a gorgeous view, where legend has it that a plantation owner's daughter and her love, a slave, leaped to their death.

What Else to See

Museums and Exhibits

Arawak Museum   ★★★

> *White Marl, Spanish Town,* ☎ *(809) 922-0620.*
> *Hours Open: 10:00 a.m.–5:00 p.m.*
> Located on the site of a large Arawak settlement, this small museum houses relics and artifacts from that era. Free admission.

Jamaica People's Museum   ★★★

> *Constitution Square, Spanish Town,* ☎ *(809) 922- 620.*
> *Hours Open: 9:00 a.m.–5:00 p.m.*
> This museum of native craft and technology houses farm implements, a sugar mill, an old fire engine and a hearse, as well as vintage prints, models and maps.

Tours

Milk River Mineral Baths   ★★★

> *Milk River, Clarendon,* ☎ *(809) 924-9544.*
> Arthritis acting up? Rheumatism got you down? Liver ailing? Come for a half-hour soak in what is reportedly the world's most radioactive mineral waters, said to help all those conditions—and more. The baths are private and tepid at 90 degrees. General admission: $2.00.

Somerset Falls   ★★★

> *Highway A4, Hope Bay,* ☎ *(809) 926-2950.*
> *Hours Open: 9:00 a.m.–5:00 p.m.*
> Ride in a gondola to these scenic falls, located in a deep grove and surrounded by tropical rainforest. Wear your swimsuit so you can take a dip in the refreshing pools. General admission: $2.00.

Where to Stay

The tourism infrastructure is so well developed that there are many housing options in Jamaica. Many hotels are dedicated on-the-property dive services, from villas (Villa Draybar at Ocho Rios) to smaller dive resorts such as Fisherman's Inn in Falmouth to small hotels such as Seaworld's Cariblue (Montego Bay) and Rock Cliff (Negril), the larger all-inclusive resorts. The all-inclusive has become one of Jamaica's most popular resort options—in fact, winter occupancies have risen back to the 80–90 percent range because of their popularity. One prepaid fee covers everything from food to alcohol to water and land sports and some island excursions. Resorts can be luxurious with long beaches, superb dining, sports facilities and entertainment, etc., like Hedonism in Negril (though it is a dedicated singles resort). Others are geared for couples or families, and some have an open policy. The focus of activities at these all-inclusive resorts vary. Some like Swept Away in Negril or Jamaica, Jamaica in Runaway Bay are very sports and health-oriented. While some resorts have dedicated dive operations, others will offer only a single tank per day. Do research and contact the resort to ask questions before you go. Many a misunderstanding that might have been diverted with some careful questioning has resulted in near-disaster vacations. (For more information, see "Where to Stay" under the individual sections.)

Apartments and Condominiums

Not too long ago you'd see flights to Jamaica filled with tourists toting their own food and staples. Not any more, not with the rise in quality imported foods, but you will find the cost of such "necessities" of life back home quite high, but not higher than at any other island.

Inns

If you are not athletic, don't care about a big social scene, and are adventurous enough to experience come what may, you'll save a lot of money staying in smaller inns—the majority have beachfront locations, or at the very least, provide a free shuttle to the nearest strand.

Astra Country Inn   **$60–$115**   ★ ★

62 Ward Avenue, Mandevile, ☎ (809) 962-3265.
Single: $60–$115. Double: $60–$115.
Set high up, some 2000 feet above sea level in the mid-island hills, this informal hotel is in a former home. Guest rooms are comfortable though not air-conditioned. There's a pool and sauna on site, as well as horseback riding. Great for birders and nature lovers. 22 rooms. Credit Cards: MC, A.

Mandeville Hotel   **$60–$200**   ★

4 Hotel Street, Mandeville, ☎ (809) 962-2460.
Single: $60–$200. Double: $60–$200.
This mountain hotel has traditional guest rooms, some with air conditioning, as well as apartments with kitchen facilities. Two restaurants, three bars, a disco, and, for recreation, a pool and horseback riding. Guests can golf at the nearby Manchester Club. 60 rooms. Credit Cards: MC, A.

Low Cost Lodging

If you're going to Jamaica for the wild outdoors, camping may be your best bet for saving money. There are extensive camping facilities in attractive locations that allow you immediate access to the wilderness. Because of the variety of fine local restaurants, you won't be losing any taste buds by not eating in the big fancy hotel restaurants; in fact you're more likely to find delightful surprises—like at "jerk centers" on the beach—that will whet your palate for years to come.

Where to Eat

The motto "Out of many, one People" goes as much for politics as it does for cuisine in Jamaica—for the influences that have gone into the dutchie, or cast-iron cooking pot, to create Jamaican menus, are many—the barbecuing techniques of the Arawaks, the African meat-preserving techniques in the country's best known dish jerk pork, Spanish marinades meet New World vegetables in two -cooked escovitched fish. British **cornish pastries**, which are meat-and-potato-filled pastries, have become Jamaican spicy beef patties. And the spices of Asia and the Levant come together in dishes like curried goat. Today nouvelle cuisine is also dressing up traditional ingredients in trendy resort restaurants along the North Coast. Rastafarianism—Jamaica's contribution to 20th-century religion—has created a cuisine all its own, one that places the accent on nature's bounty. Rastas don't drink alcohol, or eat meat, but their vegetarian cooking is delicious, including hearty vegetable stews with ingredients like *calllallo* (a spinach-like vegetable), *chocho* (a pear-shaped squash), pumpkin, and yams. Johnnycakes—flat, dense, unleavened breads—were a slave adaptation of British breads, while *bammie* was the Amerindian cassava bread that Columbus wrote about in his journals. Another newer addition is the popular Rasta Pasta, which features the Rastafarian colors in the red of tomatoes, the green of bell peppers, and the gold of ackee, all served over pasta. One of the bases of Jamaican cooking is "poor folk's food," like codfish, stew peas and roast breadfruit. It takes some experience to learn to like boiled green bananas as a breakfast dish.

Other Jamaican delicacies include: *bun* (a dark fruitcake served with cheese usually at Easter time); *cowfoot soup* (spicy soup of cow trotters and vegetables, claimed by Jamaican men to be an aphrodisiac); *dunkanoo* (a dessert of grated corn, flavored with sugar, cinnamon, ginger, and coconut milk, and steamed in a banana leaf); *pepper rum* (a mixture of fiery Scotch bonnet chiles and dark rum, used as a seasoning); *matrimony* (a dessert that blends orange segments with star apple pulp in cream); *mannish water* (a heavy goatmeat and vegetable soup, flavored with white rum and hot peppers, and reputed to be an aphrodisiac); *rundown* (mackerel or codfish boiled in coconut milk and eaten with ashed onions and peppers); *Solomon gundy* (pungent spiced pickled herring); and *stamp-and-go* (batter-fried saltfish fritters, usually eaten as a finger snack).

In Kingston, Sunday brunch is special at Devon House, a restored historic home dear to many Jamaicans for its food and ice cream. Seated on the wide veranda of mansions like The Coffee Terrace, with whirling fans overhead, you can indulge in fluffy yellow ackee, a Jamaican-grown tree vegetable, whose custardy flesh tastes and looks somewhat like scrambled eggs. This mixture of the savory ackee and salt fish—harks back to the days of slavery when feeding the slaves was a major concern for plantation owners. **Jerked cooking** is a method of barbecue using well-seasoned meat, said to have originated with the Maroons, the fierce escaped slaves who retreated to the mountains of Cockpit Country and kept the British at bay for more than a century. They would roast pork over hot coals in earthen pits that were covered with branches of green pimento, or allspice, wood. The smoking wood is what provides the unique seasoning. At Boston Beach today, pit men like Vasco "Kojak" Allen at Front Line #1, is famous for his grillwork, which includes jerked chicken, (pork, the classic dish), jerked sausage, and jerked fish.

In Ocho Rios, the **Ciboney Beach Resort** has some of the best options for dining: head for Orchid's, for pork chops filled with bread and chutney, or the al fresco **Casa Nina**, for ackee and callaloo. The **Ciboney Grill and Market Place** is designed like a Jamaican outdoor market with colorful food stalls.

In Montego Bay, the restaurant at the four-bedroom hostelry called **Norma's** at the Warehouse is a treasurehouse of delicacies, from smoked marlin with papaya salsa to roast loin pork with prunes. Desserts run the course between plantain turnover with brandied whipped cream or a vine-ripened papaya, with a drizzle of island grown ortanique (cross between an orange and a tangerine). Less fancy digs on the North Coast include the **Rite Stuff Café** and Caterers in Montego Bay's Westgate Plaza, where you can dig into curried goat, stew bee, or a steaming bowl of pumpkin soup. Meatpatties, flaky turnovers stuffed with a savory chopped meat and herb mixture, are a favorite snack on this island of nibblers.

You won't know the cuisine of Jamaica until you make a stop at the island's hub of hedonism, Negril. Head for the **Hungry Lion**, one of the best spots on the North Coast to try Ital food, and at **Paradise Yard**, where you can indulge in a special Jamaican breakfast feast.

FIELDING'S CHOICE:

Want a home-cooked meal while you're in Jamaica? Sign up with the "Meet the People" program and one of some 400 volunteer Jamaican families will spend the day showing you their island and taking you back to the house for dinner. Call the Jamaican Tourist Board at ☎ *800-233-4582 before you leave home to contact their local office when you arrive.*

Where to Shop

Jamaica has some wonderful opportunities for committed shoppers; you may find yourself wishing you had brought an extra piece of luggage to handle the overflow. Duty-free shopping is available in the cosmopolitan areas, with good buys on perfumes, crystals and china. Stop at the crafts markets or roadside stands for more authentic goods. Excellent wood carvings sell generally for a modest sum.

Kingston is the New York City of Jamaica—nearly anything you can buy in Jamaica can be found here. You can choose from a luxury list of duty-free items or concentrate on local crafts made by well-skilled artisans. Despite a 10 percent General Consumption tax that has been added to all goods and services, **duty-free bargains** will generally reap you significant savings from back home in the States. (Of course, if you are vulnerable to such bargains, you should figure in the cost of buying things you probably wouldn't buy at home.) This duty-free wish-list in Kingston includes: Swiss watches, gold jewelry, camera, electronic equipment, liquor, cigarettes, fine European crystal, china, French perfume and British woolens. You must carry proof of identity with you to receive the duty-free discount. Best liquors to pick up include the Jamaican rums, Rumona (a rum liqueur), and the coffee-flavored Tia Maria. Royal Jamaican **cigars** are a connoisseur's delight, purchasable at the airport as well as the pier. **Blue Mountain coffee** is the native brew, and will make one of the finest cups you have ever drunk. If you plan to do serious duty-free shopping, do bring a list of comparative prices in the States, so that you don't go home and want to shoot yourself in the head.

Local artists do excellent work in various mediums, but especially wood carvings, usually using *lignum vitae*, a rosy native hardwood. All kinds of objects are carved—from bookends to statues of saints (and Bob Marley) to furniture. You can pick up the best pieces in the crafts markets as well as at roadside stands on the north shore between Montego Bay and Falmouth. Straw work is also native to Jamaica, and good finds can also be found in basketry and batiks. Some of the best crafts at the best prices can be found at **Things Jamaica** at the Devon House (as well as at the airport); special buys are carved wood bowls and trays to reproduction of silver and brass historical pieces. Jamaican designers have quite a flair with resort wear, particularly using colorful fabrics silk-screened on the island. Silk batiks, sold by the yard, and so beautiful they can be used as wall art, can be found at **Caribatik**, the studio of the late Muriel Chandler, two miles east of Falmouth. Search through the shopping malls for fashionable clothes, like the New Kingston Shopping Mall, not far from the Pegasus hotel. If you need a new pair of sandals, try Lee's New Kingston in this mall.

You can't—don't even think about—leave Jamaica without buying a few reggae tapes. Records by some of reggae's greats like Bob Marley, his son Ziggy Marley, Peter Tosh and Burning Spear can be found at **Randy's Record Mart** at *17 N. Parade*—a legendary store where you can be directed to records by some of the new crop of up-and-coming stars.

Another shopping center for more mundane necessities is Lane's Shopping Mall (just one of half a dozen along Constant Spring Road). Hotel boutiques may have some cosmetics and toiletries, but they will be highly overpriced.Do discover the pleasure of aloe-based Jamaican skin creams. They also make excellent gifts.

Jamaica Directory

ARRIVAL AND DEPARTURE

American Airlines and Air Jamaica both fly nonstop from New York; Air Jamaica also flies nonstop from Miami and has service from Atlanta, Baltimore, Orlando and Philadelphia. BWIA flies form San Juan. Continental flies in daily from Newark. Northwest Airlines flies in daily from Minneapolis and Tampa and Aeroflot flies in from Havana. Air Canada offers service from Toronto and Montreal in conjunction with Air Jamaica, and both British Airways and Air Jamaica fly to London.

Donald Sangester International Airport in Montego Bay is the best place to arrive if you are headed for Montego Bay, Round Hill-Tyrall, Ocho Rios, Runaway Bay and Negril. If you are staying in Port Antonio or Kingston, the capital, it's best to land at Norman Manley Airport in Kingston. Trans-Jamaican Airlines ☎ *(809) 923-8680* offers a shuttle service.

In general, there is no public transportation to and from the airports. Taxi rates are not fixed, but sample fares to popular destinations are usually posted in public places. Do negotiate beforehand. All-inclusive resorts provide free transfers from the airport, as do many small hotels when you are using their package. Sometimes a hotel will throw it in for free if you ask in advance. If transfers are included in your package, you will normally be given a voucher with the name of the operator, and a company representative will meet you at the airport. If not, it's a good idea to ask your travel agent to reserve space in advance. JUTA (Jamaica Union of Travellers Association) offers taxis that hold up to five people (total price $80) that run from the nearest airports to hotels in Negril,

Ocho Rios, and Port Antonio. Runs to Montego Bay and Kingston, which are much closer, are much cheaper. If you are heading beyond Montego Bay (and you have time to spare), you'll save lots of money if you book one of Tropical Tours' air-conditioned minibuses at their desk just outside the luggage area of Sangster Airport ☎ *953-1111.* They run to Ocho Rios and Negril and charge a per-person fare. Unfortunately, you won't be able to leave right away until the bus is at least half full.

CLIMATE

Jamaica has a tropical climate with considerable variation. High temperatures on the coast are usually mitigated by sea breezes, while upland areas enjoy cooler and less humid conditions. Jamaica lies in the hurricane zone, so always check weather reports before you come (even before you book). Rainfall falls plentifully throughout Jamaica; the heaviest season is in May and from August-November. In Kingston temperatures range from 6 degrees F in January to 81 degrees F in July.

DOCUMENTS

U.S. citizens need either a passport or other proof of citizenship (birth certificate, voter's registration) and a photo ID. All others need a passport. Departure tax is U.S$5.

ELECTRICITY

Current is not consistent throughout the island. Some hotels feature 110, some 220. Adapters and converters are supplied by hotels who need them for foreign visitors.

GETTING AROUND

Taxis are best taken for short trips in Jamaica. At the airport you can always find a JUTA taxi and coach, as well as at most resorts. If you are planning an out-of-the-way excursion, particularly for dinner, arrange for the driver to pick you up afterwards and negotiate a good round-trip fare. Most taxis are unmetered; if you seem to be having trouble with the driver, enlist the help of your hotel's concierge or doorman, though you can never be sure if they are in cahoots with each other. When in doubt, ask to see the rate sheet, which all cabs are supposed to carry. After midnight, a 25 percent surcharge is added, though that is often negotiable, particularly if you have negotiated a round-trip deal or if your destination is especially far away.

Buses prove to be a cheap way to toot around the Kingston and Montego Bay areas; they do run often but they are often unbearably overcrowded, hot and dirty. (Moreover, a tourist on a crowded local bus is often a sitting duck for crime; if you are wearing your camera and an I Love Jamaica t-shirt, you might as well just hand over your valuables before being asked for them.) Kingston bus fares range from $3JDS to $7.50 JDS (about 15 cents to 35 cents in American currency) at press time). The fee depends on the distance traveled. You can tour the island on a bus, but here you will have to share aisle space with the local riff-raff—meaning chickens on their way to getting their heads slogged off at market. Minibus jitneys also travel around the island, but they are un-scheduled and you may have to flag them down in the street—not a re-liable way to get somewhere on time. As a result, most people cave in and rent cars or hire a cab.

Car rentals are a good idea on Jamaica since the roads are well paved and your own car will allow you to conduct your sightseeing at your own pace. You must be able, however, to handle that "British thing" of driving on the left; it takes getting used to, so be careful the first few days (the moment you "space out," a common occurrence on long trips or in new lands, you may find yourself veering to the right, which will be disastrous in the face of oncoming traffic. If you're driving with a companion, let them be a front-seat driver for a while and spot for you.) About a dozen agencies on the island offer rentals; among the best are **Avis** ☎ *926-1560*; **Budget** ☎ *952-1943*; and **National** ☎ *924-8344*. In Ocho Rios you'll find **Sunshine Car Rental** ☎ *974-2980*. In Port Antonio try **Eastern Car Rental** ☎ *993-3624*. Major international chains accept bookings through stateside toll-free *(800)* numbers. (Al-ways ask for a written confirmation a fax will do) and be sure you bring it along. There have been numerous cases of lost reservations, and sup-ply often runs low, despite the presence of over 2800 rental cars on the island. Also remember to add the cost of gas to your expenses (no free gas) and a 10 percent government tax. Valid U.S. and Canadian licenses are acceptable, but many agencies have a 25-and-over age limit (ask be-fore you book). Do beware of Jamaican drivers who suddenly and un-expectedly turn macho and wipe the road with the tar of their tires. In such cases, it is always best to yield. **Vacation Network**, an agency in Chicago ☎ *800-423-4095* offers a special "Fly Drive Jamaica/The Great Escape Package," which combines a rental car with air transpor-tation and overnight accommodations. Vouchers that come with the package allow you to use them at 45 participating small hotels and inns; the package comes with a guidebook geared for drivers as well as road maps.

LANGUAGE

The official language is English. The unique Jamaican dialect, used by natives, is English with African and native words and a British inflection and tropical rhythm.

MEDICAL EMERGENCIES

The most efficient and advance medical facilities are in Kingston, where you will find the country's largest hospital.

MONEY

The official currency is the Jamaican dollar, which has proven to be quite unstable in relation to the American dollar. American dollars are accepted in most establishments, but exchange rates will vary (also make sure when you are quoted a price, that you know which "Dollar" is being used. All airports have exchange houses; best rates are found at banks. Major credit cards are accepted by most hotels and many restaurants, as are traveler's checks. When changing money, be sure you keep the receipt so you can change the money back before you leave.

SECURITY

Crime in Jamaica is lower per capita than in most large U.S. cities, but the city of Kingston is rife with incidents. Downtown Kingston is particularly bad, and you should never walk in the street after dark. Don't even think about going to West Kingston, even in a car with the doors locked. Don't ever leave money, wallets, purses, or valuables like cameras unattended at the beach. Police foot patrols are present in all the major tourist areas, so head directly for one if you sense trouble approaching. Also avoid standing in the middle of a street to hail a taxi; it's best to head for a shopping center or ask your hotel to arrange one ahead of time.

TELEPHONE

The area code is *809*. Direct telephone, telegraph, telefax and telex services are all available.

TIME

Eastern Standard Time throughout the year.

TIPPING

Most Jamaican hotels and restaurants add a service charge of ten percent; always check first to see if it's included. If not, tip waiters 10–15 percent (depending on the service). Hotel maids should receive about $1–2 per person per day. Airport porters and hotel bellhops should be tipped 50 cents per bag (but not less than a $1). It's not necessary to tip taxi drivers, although 10 percent of the fare is usually appreciated.

TOURIST INFORMATION

The main office of the Jamaica Tourist Board is in Kingston *(Tourism Centre Building, New Kingston, Box 360, Kingston 5;* ☎ *(809) 929-9200).* There are also JTB desks at both Montego Bay and Kingston airports and in all resort areas. In the U.S. ☎ *(213) 384-1123.*

WHEN TO GO

Carnival is a recent addition to Jamaica, held oddly at Easter time. The annual reggae festival called Sun Splash is usually held in the middle of August, in Montego Bay, at the Bob Marley Centre. The Independence celebrations, also held for a week in August, are colorful blowout bashes (usually on Independence Day, August 1). In October the annual International Marlin Tournament at Port Antonio attracts fishermen from all over the world and includes festivals other than fishing. Contact the

Tourist Board for a twice yearly calendar of events covering a wide spectrum of sports and arts festivals.

JAMAICA HOTELS		RMS	RATES	PHONE	FAX
Kingston					
★★★★	Jamaica Pegasus Hotel	350	$180–$564	(809) 926-3690	(809) 929-5850
★★★	Braco Village Resort	180	$235–$260	(800) 654-1337	
★★★	Morgan's Harbour Hotel	45	$98–$255	(809) 924-8464	
★★★	Terra Nova Hotel	33	$120–$150	(809) 926-2211	(809) 929-4933
★★★	Wyndham Kingston	384	$165–$505	(800) 322-4200	(809) 929-7439
★★	Courtleigh House & Hotel	80	$79–$195	(800) 526-2400	(809) 926-7801
★★	Medallion Hall Hotel	16	$79–$83	(809) 927-5721	
★	Four Seasons	39	$71–$83	(809) 929-7655	(809) 929-5964
★	Indies Hotel	15	$35–$62	(809) 926-2952	(809) 926-2879
Montego Bay					
★★★★★	Half Moon Beach Club	213	$255–$805	(800) 626-0592	
★★★★★	Round Hill Hotel & Villas	110	$305–$454	(800) 223-6510	
★★★★	Sandals Montego Bay	243	$2375–$2835	(800) 726-3257	
★★★★	Sandals Royal Caribbean	190	$2465–$2920	(800) 726-3257	
★★★★	Tryall Resort	52	$235–$465	(800) 742-0498	
★★★	Doctor's Cave Beach Hotel	90	$85–$135	(800) 223-6510	
★★★	Reading Reef Club	26	$65–$370	(800) 223-6510	
★★★	Sandals Inn	52	$290–$348	(800) 726-3257	
★★★	Seacastles	198	$75–$155	(800) 526-2422	
★★★	Seawind Beach Resort	468	$75–$120	(800) 526-2422	
★★★	Wyndham Rose Hall Resort	500	$165–$705	(809) 631-4200	
★★	Blue Harbour Hotel	24	$35–$105	(809) 952-5445	
★★	Coral Cliff Hotel	32	$54–$64	(809) 952-4130	
★★	Fantasy Resort	119	$55–$85	(800) 237-3421	
★★	Gloucestershire, The	88	$60–$80	(800) 423-4095	
★★	Holiday Inn Montego Bay	516	$160–$205	(800) 465-4329	
★★	Jack Tar Village	128	$155–$205	(800) 999-9182	

JAMAICA HOTELS	RMS	RATES	PHONE	FAX
★★ Montego Bay Racquet Club	51	$50–$155	(809) 952-0200	
★★ Richmond Hill Inn	20	$78–$112	(809) 952-3859	
★★ Sea Garden Beach Hotel	104	$297–$357	(800) 545-9001	
★★ Toby Inn	60	$45–$80	(809) 952-4370	
★★ Wexford, The	61	$85–$130	(800) 237-3421	
★★ Winged Victory	27	$95–$230	(800) 223-9815	
★ Belvedere Beach Hotel	27	$50–$80	(809) 952-0593	
★ Buccaneer Beach Hotel	72	$83–$175	(809) 952-6489	
★ Royal Court Hotel	25	$45–$85	(809) 952-4531	

Negril

	RMS	RATES	PHONE	FAX
★★★★★ Grand Lido	200	$350	(800) 423-4095	
★★★★ Negril Tree House	70	$85–$275	(800) 423-4095	
★★★★ Sandals Negril	199	$2890–$3995	(800) 726-3257	
★★★★ Swept Away Resort	134	$2770–$3785	(800) 545-7937	
★★★ Beachcomber Club	46	$105–$185	(800) 423-4095	
★★★ Charela Inn	39	$55–$165	(800) 423-4095	
★★★ Foote Prints on the Sands	33	$55–$105	(809) 957-4300	
★★★ Hedonism II	280	$205–$376	(800) 423-4095	
★★★ Poinciana Beach Hotel	130	$168–$281	(800) 468-6728	
★★★ Point Village	130	$100–$155	(809) 957-4351	
★★★ Rock Cliff Resort	33	$55–$100	(809) 957-4331	
★★ Chuckles	78	$75–$260	(809) 957-4277	
★★ Crystal Waters Villas	10	$85–$110	(800) 443-3020	
★★ Drumville Cove Resort	20	$40–$100	(800) 423-4095	
★★ Hotel Samsara	50	$40–$115	(809) 957-4395	
★★ Negril Beach Club Hotel	85	$77–$185	(800) 526-2422	
★★ Negril Cabins	50	$40–$55	(809) 957-4350	
★★ Negril Gardens	54	$105–$140	(800) 423-4095	
★★ Negril Inn	46	$115–$145	(800) 634-7456	
★★ Paradise View	17	$75–$135	(809) 957-4375	
★★ T-Water Beach Hotel	70	$125–$155	(800) 654-1592	

JAMAICA HOTELS		RMS	RATES	PHONE	FAX
★★	Xtabi Club Resort	16	$50–$145	(809) 957-4336	

Ocho Rios

★★★★★	Sans Souci Lido	111	$465–$945	(800) 203-7450	
★★★★	Boscobel Beach Hotel	228	$415–$995	(800) 423-4095	
★★★★	Ciboney Ocho Rios	300	$175–$690	(800) 777-7800	
★★★★	Couples Jamaica	172	$365–$520	(800) 423-4095	
★★★★	Jamaica Grande	720	$135–$195	(800) 228-9898	
★★★★	Jamaica Inn	45	$225–$250	(809) 974-2516	
★★★★	Plantation Inn	78	$300–$999	(800) 423-4095	
★★★★	Sandals Dunn's River	256	$2295–$4200	(800) 726-3257	
★★★★	Sandals Ocho Rios	237	$355–$455	(800) 726-3257	
★★★	Comfort Suites	137	$105–$205	(800) 423-4095	
★★★	Enchanted Garden	112	$95–$555	(800) 323-5655	
★★★	Sea Palms	45	$145	(080) 423-4095	
★★★	Shaw Park Beach Hotel	118	$165–$436	(800) 243-9420	
★★	Club Jamaica Beach Resort	95	$180–$235	(800) 423-4095	
★★	Fisherman's Point	64	$95–$135	(800) 423-4095	
★★	Hibiscus Lodge	26	$65–$93	(800) 526-2422	
★★	Turtle Beach Towers	218	$87–$225	(809) 974-2801	

Port Antonio

★★★★★	Trident Villas & Hotel	28	$255–$755	(800) 237-3237	
★★★	Fern Hill Club	36	$215–$385	(800) 263-4354	
★★★	Goblin Hill Villas	28	$1760–$2135	(800) 423-4095	
★★★	Jamaica Palace Hotel	80	$115–$285	(800) 423-4095	
★★	Bonnie View Plantation	20	$49–$83	(800) 448-5398	
★★	Dragon Bay	86	$101–$161	(800) 423-4095	
★★	Navy Island Resort/ Marina	21	$75–$185	(809) 993-2667	

North Coast

★★★★	Franklyn D. Resort	76	$3205–$7205	(800) 423-4095	
★★★★	Jamaica Jamaica	242	$167–$240	(800) 423-4095	
★★★	Eaton Hall Beach Hotel	52	$135–$299	(809) 973-3503	

JAMAICA HOTELS	RMS	RATES	PHONE	FAX
★★★ H.E.A.R.T. Country Club	20	$55–$75	(809) 973-2671	
★★ Ambiance Hotel	80	$90–$215	(800) 523-6504	
★★ Club Caribbean	128	$125–$295	(800) 647-2740	
★★ Portside Villas & Condos	15	$85–$280	(809) 973-2007	
★ Caribbean Isle Hotel	24	$55–$65	(809) 973-2364	

South Coast

	RMS	RATES	PHONE	FAX
★★ Astra Country Inn	22	$60–$115	(809) 962-3265	
★ Mandeville Hotel	60	$60–$200	(809) 962-2460	

JAMAICA RESTAURANTS	LOCATION	PHONE	ENTREE

Kingston

International			
★★★★ Blue Mountain Inn	Kingston	(809) 927-1700	$12–$24••
★★ Gap Cafe, The	Blue Mountain	(809) 923-7055	$12–$22
★★ Le Pavilion	Kingston	(809) 926-3690	$16–$26
★ El Dorado Room	Kingston	(809) 926-9334	$7–$20
★ Ivor Guest House	Kingston	(809) 977-33	$18–$30
Latin American			
★★★★★ Temple Hall	Kingston	(809) 942-2340	$25–$25••
★★★★ Norma's at the Wharfhouse	Reading	(809) 979-2745	$26–$34
★★ Devon House Restaurants	Kingston	(809) 929-6602	$6–$16
★★ Hot Pot, The	Kingston	(809) 929-3906	$3–$4
★ Chelsea Jerk Centre	Kingston	(809) 926-6322	$3–$5
★ Indies Pub and Grill	Kingston	(809) 926-5050	$4–$12
★ Minnie's Ethiopian	Kingston	(809) 927-9207	$10–$20

Montego Bay

International			
★★★★ Sugar Mill	Montego Bay	(809) 953-2228	$14–$31
★ Georgian House	Montego Bay	(809) 952-3353	$22–$32
★ Julia's	Montego Bay	(809) 952-632	$35–$35••

JAMAICA RESTAURANTS	LOCATION	PHONE	ENTREE
Italian			
★★★★★ Reading Reef Club	Montego Bay	(809) 952-5909	$10–$24
Latin American			
★★★ Pork Pit	Montego Bay	(809) 952-1046	$2–$9
★★ Town House	Montego Bay	(809) 952-2660	$13–$30
Seafood			
★ Pier I	Montego Bay	(809) 952-2452	$16–$25

Negril

French			
★★ Cafe au Lait	Negril	(809) 957-4471	$9–$29
Latin American			
★★ Chicken Lavish	Negril	(809) 957-4410	$3–$5
★★ Hungry Lion	Negril		$18–$30
★★ Paradise Yard	Negril	(809) 957-4006	$6–$15
★ Tan-ya's	Negril	(809) 957-4041	$5–$25
Seafood			
★★ Cosmo's	Negril	(809) 957-4330	$5–$12
★ Rick's Cafe	Negril	(809) 957-4335	$11–$28

Ocho Rios

Chinese			
★ Ruins Restaurant	Ocho Rios	(809) 974-2442	$12–$33
Italian			
★★★★★ Evita's	Ocho Rios	(809) 974-2333	$7–$19
Latin American			
★★★★ Almond Tree	Ocho Rios	(809) 974-2813	$12–$26
★★ Parkway Restaurant	Ocho Rios	(809) 974-2667	$6–$25

Port Antonio

International			
★★★★★ Trident Hotel Restaurant	Port Antonio	(809) 993-2602	$25–$50
Latin American			
★★★ De Montevin Lodge	Port Antonio	(809) 993-2604	$11–$18

JAMAICA RESTAURANTS	LOCATION	PHONE	ENTREE
★★ Front Line, The	Port Antonio		$5–$8

Note: • Lunch Only

•• Dinner Only

MARTINIQUE

The Fort de France market in Martinique has a plethora of fruits.

Martinique is a little bit of foie gras in the middle of the Caribbean. From the cuisine to the chic style of the women, to the lilt of the language, Martinique exudes the charm of its mother country—France. But add to that a decidedly West Indian cachet and shopping values that would make a Parisian's jaw drop open, and you have a tiny island nation waiting to be loved. Rising from beaches to rainforest to the heights of a volcanic mountain that wiped out an entire city in 1903, Martinique is rife with opportunities to dive, trek, sail, surf, parasail, and about any other sport imaginable—from mountain biking to deep-sea fishing in some of the clearest waters in the Caribbean. The island has stayed ecologically pure enough to still boast good sightings of many birds in the mangroves, including the yellow-breasted sandbird, a symbol of the island. Best of all, tourism is just beginning to snap at the heels of this nearly forgotten island and locals are still green enough—business-wise—to have escaped becoming jaded. Of course, on an island such as this one, there will always be a few cases of French snoots, but try to ignore them and concentrate on the natural beauties.

Bird's Eye View

Fifty miles long and 22 miles long, Martinique covers 425 square miles. Of its neighboring islands, Dominica lies to the north and St. Lucia to the south; Miami is 1470 miles away. Martinique comes from volcanic origins, and today the 4575-ft. Mount Pelé in the Parc Naturel Regional de la Martinique, is the only active volcano, situated in the northwest island. Most of the island is mountainous. In the center of the island lie the Pitons de Carbet and the Montagne du Vauclin is in the south. These mountains are linked by hills, and the airport is situated in the central plains area. The north of the island is covered by an enormous rainforest; banana and pineapples are cultivated there, while sugarcane dominates the rest of the island. Black sandy coves are found throughout the south and along the rugged coast open to the Atlantic, white and gray sands characterize the beaches facing the Caribbean and in the south. On the east coast, the peninsula of Caravelle, the oldest volcanic formation of the island, stretches into the rough Atlantic, boasting a mangrove swamp lined with a coral reef. The capital, Fort-de-France, is situated on the Baie des Flamandes on the western coast, while the burgeoning town of Lamentin is slightly more inland.

History

Columbus was stunned when he chanced upon Martinique—historians can't decide whether it was 1493 or 1502—but phrases like "the most fertile, the softest...the most charming place in the world" leave no doubt regarding his true feelings. Carib Indians were the resident locals on Martinique when Columbus happened by. Martinica was the name Colum-

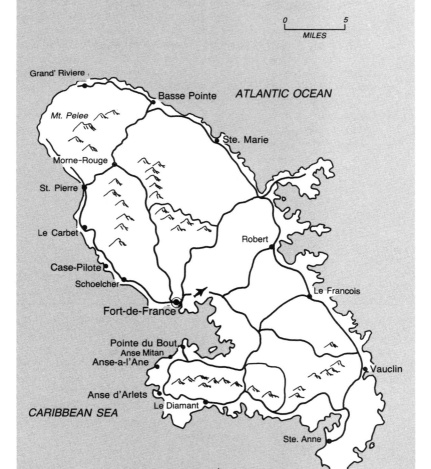

Martinique

bus bestowed on the volcanic island, in honor of St. Martin. The Caribs called it Madinina, meaning "island of flowers." The Caribs proved too hostile for the Spaniards who moved on to other shores, but they continued to fight the French who settled on the island in 1635. Twenty-five years later the French signed a treaty with the Caribs who agreed to stay on the Atlantic side of the island; nevertheless, they were soon exterminated. The next 200 years was a struggle between the Brits and the French. In 1762 the Brits took control, only to pass it over in exchange for Canada, Senegal, the Grenadines, St. Vincent and Tobago. France remained with Guadeloupe and Martinique because they were knee-deep in the sugarcane. The English took over again between 1794-1802, at the request of plantation owners who needed assistance in the face of growing dissent among slaves. Slavery was abolished in 1848 by the French but not before a major slave rebellion occurred in 1879, encouraged by the French Revolution. Eventually, a new wave of immigrant workers from India began to change the dominant color of skin in the island's population. Martinique finally became a French Department in 1946 and a region in 1974.

People

There are about 369,000 people in Martinique, about half of which are living in the capital of Fort-de-France. A racially mixed batch of Africans, East Indians, whites and others, they are all considered citizens of France, and governed by a Prefect, appointed by the French Government. Unemployment is quite high, about a third of the people have no jobs. About a quarter of those employed are in tourism. To get a good glimpse of social life, hang out in the Savane, a 12-acre park of lawn, shade trees, footpaths and benches where families relax and children play and old men play serious games of dominoes. Locals are called Martiniquaises.

Beaches

You can find a magnificent beach at **Grand Anse** in South Martinique. It is less visited by tourists than the beaches at Pointe du Bout, although it can get more crowded on weekends. Nearby is the petite pretty village of **Anse d'Arlets**. **Diamant Beach**, just south of Ande d'Arlets, is a paradisiacal stretch of 2-1/2 miles along the south coast dominated by the **Diamond Rock**, a famous volcanic rock that stands about a mile out to sea where the English stationed cannons in the 18th century (British ships still passing it salute her Majesty's "Ship Diamond Rock"). The beach is nearly deserted and fringed with coconut palms and almond trees. It is not advised for swimming since the currents are strong. From the town of Le Marin south, you'll find long white sand beaches fringed with palms trees and calm, clear seas. **Ste. Anne**, where the Club Med is, has its own fine beach, adjacent to the public one, where you can see a terrific view of the southwest coast. There are many places for shade on Ste. Anne under trees that sometimes overhang into the sea. There are lots of bars and restaurants here. There's a family beach on the road heading east from Marin called Cap Chevalier.

Dive Sites

Martinique has some of the most unusual and fascinating dive sites in the Caribbean. Marine life is abundant and water temperatures are ideal. Memorable dive sites include **Ilet la Perke** and the shipwrecks of **St. Pierre** in the north. Other excellent ones to check out are **Anses d'Arlets** and **Cap Salomon**, and **Diamond Rock** on the southwest coast. The UCPA is installed at Anse Coré, just north of St. Pierre on the northwestern coast; and Tropicasub operates at Anse Latouche, north of Carbet ☎ *78-38-03*. One solo dive averages about $40, but your best bargain is to inquire about dive packages at various agencies. You'll find excellent facilities and licensed instructors at the **Méridien's Scuba Club** ☎ *66-00-00* and **Bleue Passion** at Le Bakoua ☎ *66-02-02*.

Treks

The **Regional Natural Park of Martinique** (PNRM) and the National Forestry (ONF) with Le Club des Roandonneurs (Hiking Club) have marked 31 trails and written an excellent guide book—albeit in French—to assist trekkers. (the book is available from the government tourist office in Fort-de-France). The trails were chosen in such a way that hikers can venture forth alone with some safety, except for those trails specifically marked "guide needed" (guides trained by the PNRM are rigorously tested and spend five years as apprentices). Before you take off, you should always call the PNRM (☎ *73-19-30*) to ask about trail conditions. PNRM also organized special hikes for botanists and offers group hikes on Sundays.

A great way to meet people and see the terrain is to join one of the inexpensive guided hikes organized weekly through **Air Martinique** ☎ *51-09-09.* Serious hikers should head for the fantastic two-hour climb up **Mont Pelé**, fighting your way through dense foliage and overgrown trails. Less challenging, but still hearty is the trek through a dense coastal rainforest between **Grand'Riviere** and **Le Precheur**. Beginner's hikes can be found along the trails of the **Gorges de la Falaise** and **Les Ombrages**, a nature trail at Ajoupa Bouillon. The **Prequ'ile de la Caravelle**, a peninsula jutting into the Atlantic, has safe beaches and well-marked paths to historic **Chateau Dubuc's** ruins ☎ *51-09-09.* For off-the-beaten-track tours, using bus transportation to the departure point and including guide, lunch and insurance, you can't beat the services of **Cariballad** ☎ *54-26-00.* Prices range from $62–66, depending on the itinerary. The **Village des Z'Amandnines** also offers one-week packages with four days of hiking, at St. Laurent ☎ *69-89-49.*

What Else to See

The capital of Martinique, **Fort-De-France**, is one of the most charming cities in the Caribbean to see on foot. Among the first sites to check out is the city's architectural pride and joy, the **Bibliotheque Schoelcher**, or Schoelcher

Library, a Romanesque Byzantine treasure constructed a century ago for the Paris Exposition of 1889, then dismantled and shipped to Martinique piece by piece. It sits close to **Savane**, the city's central park, full of exotic flora; it's a lovely place to stroll and eavesdrop on locals. Narrow streets with beautiful balconies overhanging sidewalks filled with shops and restaurants lead you to another must-see: the **Cathedral of Saint-Louis**. Nearby is the Palais de Justice with its statue of Victor Schoelcher. The Musée Departemental de la Martinique presents archaeological finds from prehistoric Martinique. The **Jardin de Balata** (Balata gardens) is a tropical botanical park around a restored Creole house. It's a lovely place for browsing and relaxing. By the Riviere Madame (Madame River) you'll find the bustling fish markets. If you want a guided tour, you can find excellent ones offered by **Azimut** ☎ *60-16-59*.

Time should also be carved out on your itinerary for travels outside the city of Martinique.

North along the coast, you'll discover **St. Pierre**, considered the "Paris of the West Indies" until 1902 when Mount Pelé Volcano erupted and flowed lava Pompeii-style all over it. You can see the full extent of the tragedy in the exhibits of the museum there. To get here with style, take the little train called **Cyparis Express**, which presents one-hour tours during the week and half-hour tours on the weekend. The drive from Fort-de-France is less than an hour, but make time to stop at such atmospheric fishing villages as **Case-Pilote** and **Bellefontaine**, as well as **Carbet**, where Columbus landed in 1502; Gauguin lived and painted here in 1887. A museum featuring his work is found here.

In the north, a dazzling route through the rainforest, called **La Trace**, is lush with banana and pineapple plantations, avocado groves, cane fields and lovely inns like **Leyritz**, and **Habitation Lagrange**. Le Précheur, the last village along the northern Caribbean coast, is known for hot springs of volcanic origin as well as the **Tomb of the Carib Indians**. Ajoupa Bouillon is an enchanting flower-lined town with a nature trail called **Les Ombrages**.

Rum is king on Martinique and most visitors enjoy sampling the island-brewed wares at distilleries. The St. James Distillery at Sainte-Marie in the north operates the **Musée du Rhum**. Nearby is a straw-weaving center called **Horne des Esses**. The **Fonds Saint Jacques**, a historically important 17th-century sugar estate in the north, attracts visitors with its museum, Musée du Pere Labat. A modern museum devoted to sugar and rum, called **Maison de la Canne**, is just outside Trois Ilets. Also near Trois Ilets is Joséphone Bonaparte's birthplace, **La Pagerie**, which has a museum chock full of her mementos.

Martinique is often known as the "Ilse of Flowers" and there are numerous floral gardens that are lovely to visit. Nearby La Pagerie is **Parc des Floralies**, a peaceful and pretty botanical park. One of the most beautiful is the **Jardin de Balata** on the Route de La Trace in the suburbs north of the capital. A short drive from here is the Sacré Coeur de Balata, a replica of the well-known basilica which dominates Montmarte in Paris. Other attractions south of Martinique include the H.M.S. *Diamond Rock*, a kind of Rock of Gibralter Caribbean-style rising 600 feet from the sea as used by the British in 1804 as a sloop of war. Anyone not venturing into the depths of the sea with a dive tank should really take a ride on the thrilling **Aquascope**, a semi-submersible craft that makes about an hour tour. One is located at the Marina Pointe du Bout and the other at Le Marin.

Museums and Exhibits

Maison de la Canne ★★★

Trois-Ilets, Fort-de-France.
Hours Open: 9:00 a.m.–5:30 p.m.
You've probably always taken sugar for granted, but won't anymore after touring this museum dedicated to the history and production of sugarcane. Signage is in both French and English. Really quite interesting General admission: $15.00.

Musee Departementale de Martin ★★★

9 Rue de la Liberte, Fort-de-France.
Decent exhibits on the history of slavery, clothing and furniture from the colonial period and artifacts from the pre-Columbian eras of the Arawak and the Carib Indians. General admission: $15.00.

Musee Paul Gauguin ★★★

Anse-Turin, Le Carbet.
Hours Open: 10:00 a.m.–5:00 p.m.
Famed artist Paul Gauguin lived in Martinique in 1887. This museum pays homage to that period, with reproductions of works he created while here, letters and other memorabilia pertaining to his life. The museum also displays the works of other noted artists and changing displays by local artists. General admission: $10.00.

Musee Vulcanologique ★★★★

St. Pierre, Fort-de-France.
Hours Open: 9:00 a.m.–5:00 p.m.
American Frank Perrot established this museum in 1932, an homage to St. Pierre, the island's oldest city and a bustling one at that, until a devastating eruption of volcano Mt. Pelee on May 8, 1902. The entire town was buried in minutes and some 30,000 residents perished, all except for a prisoner whose underground cell saved him. (He later joined Barnum and Bailey's circus as a sideshow oddity.) Residents had been warned of the imminent danger but city fathers played it down because of an upcoming election. St. Pierre today is a modest village, but you can get a feel for its former glory days at the museum, which exhibits photographs and documents from the period. General admission: $10.00.

Musee de Poupees Vegetables ★★★

Leyritz Plantation, Basse-Pointe.
Hours Open: 7:00 a.m.–5:30 p.m.

Certainly the only one of its kind in Martinique (or possibly the world for that matter), this small museum displays sculptures made entirely of leaves and plants, designed to look like famous women in French history. It is located at the scenic Leyritz Plantation, which is detailed in the lodging section. General admission: $15.00.

Musee du Rhum

Ste. Matie, Fort-de-France.
Hours Open: 9:00 a.m.–6:00 p.m.

The St. James Distillery owns this monument to rum, located on a sugar plantation in an old creole house. After a guided tour showing the history and production of rum, you can taste-test the product yourself. Free admission.

Musee le la Pagerie

Trois-Ilets, Fort-de-France.
Hours Open: 9:00 a.m.–5:00 p.m.

Located on the grounds of the birthplace of Josephine, Napoleon's wife and empress of France from 1804-1809, this museum is housed in a stone building that was formerly the kitchen (the rest of the estate was destroyed by hurricane). Memorabilia of her life, her childhood bed, and a passionate love letter by Napoleon are among the interesting exhibits. General admission: $15.00.

Parks and Gardens

Jardin de Balata ★★★

Rte de Balata, Balata.
Hours Open: 9:00 a.m.–5:00 p.m.

This tropical park, located on a hillside some 1475 feet above sea level, has stunning views and more than a thousand varieties of trees, flowers and plants. A lovely spot to while away the afternoon exploring winding walkways, lily pond, and breathtaking overlooks. General admission: $30.00.

Tours

Martinique Aquarium

Blvd. de Marne, Fort-de-France.
Hours Open: 9:00 a.m.–7:00 p.m.

This large aquarium has more than 2000 fish and sea creatures representing some 250 species. Of special interest are the shark tank and piranha pool. General admission: $38.00.

Zoo de Carbet

Le Coin, Le Carbet.
Hours Open: 9:00 a.m.–6:00 p.m.

Also called the Amazona Zoo, this park showcases 70 species from the Amazon Basin, including birds and big cats. General admission: $15.00.

Sports

Sailing, scuba, snorkeling, golf, deep-sea fishing, windsurfing, horseback-riding, squash, tennis, cycling and motorbiking, hiking —the list of sports on Martinique is endless and depends only on your skill, passion, and time. Do consider touring the island by bike. For more information contact the **Parc Naturel Régional**; ☎ *73103*, which has designed highly unusual itineraries. You can even rent your own plane (have a license from back home in order to get the French equivalent at the Lamentin Airport. Then contact local plane owners through the **Aero Club de la Martinique** ☎ *55-01-84*. As for sailing, an enormous combination of excursions can be made to neighboring islands, among them Antigua, Dominica, Barbados, St. Lucia, St. Vincent and the Grenadines, and Mystique among others. Do look for the comprehensive bilingual yachting manual "Guide Trois Rivieres: A Cruising Guide to Martinique" available in local bookstores, about $35 or from *Edition Trois Riviere, B.P. 566, 97242 Fort-de-France* ☎ *(596) 75-0707*. Spectator sports on the island are weird but exciting if you have a taste for blood: mongoose and snake fights, and cockfights seem to be national pasttimes and can be seen December to the beginning of August at Pitt Ducos, **Quartier Brac** ☎ *56-05-60* and **Pitt Marceny**. Horseracing can be found at the Carere racetrack in Lamentin ☎ *51-25-09*.

Golf

Trois-Ilets, near Pointe du Bont.
Martinique's only course, the Golf de Imperatrice Josephine, was designed by Robert Trent Jones. The 18-hole, par-71 course covers 150 acres and is quite scenic. The grounds include a pro shop (with an English-speaking pro) restaurant, and three tennis courts. Greens fees are about $45; guests in some hotels receive a discount, so be sure to ask.

Horseback Riding

Various locations, Martinique.
Several outfits offer trail rides: **La Cavale** ☎ *(76-22-94)*, **Ranch Jack** *(*☎ *68-37-67)*, **Black Horse Ranch** *(*☎ *68-37-80)*, and **Ranch Val d'Or** *(*☎ *76-70-58)*.

Watersports

Various locations, Fort-de-France.
Most hotels offer watersports. If not, try one of following. Scuba diving: **Bathy's Club** *(Pointe du Bont, ☎ 66-00-00)*, **Sud Diamant Rock** *(Le Diamant, ☎ 76-42-42)* **Cressmal** *(Fort-de-France, ☎ 61-34-36)*, **Planete Bleue** *(Trois-Ilets, ☎ 66-*

08-79), **Oxygene Bleu** *(Lamentin, ☎ 50-25-78)*, and **Tropic Alizes** *(Le Bateliere, ☎ 61-49-49)*. Boating and sailing: **Soleil et Voile** *(Pointe du Bont, ☎ 66-09-14)*, **Captains Shop** *(Pointe du Bont, ☎ 66-06-77)*, **Ship Shop** *(Fort-de-France, ☎ 71-43-40)*, **Carib Charter** *(Schoelcher, ☎ 73-08-80)*, **Caraibes Nautique** *(Trois-Ilets, ☎ 66-06-06)*, and **Cercle Nautique** *(Schoelcher, ☎ 61-15-21)*. **Snorkeling: Aquarium** *(Fort-de-France, ☎ 61-49-49)*.

Where to Stay

Highest Rated Hotels in Martinique	
★★★★★	**Sofitel Bakoua Hotel**
★★★★	**Meridien Martinique**
★★★	**Anchorage Hotel**
★★★	**Diamant Novotel**
★★★	**Habitation Lagrange**
★★★	**La Bateliere Hotel**
★★★	**Leyritz Plantation**

Most Exclusive Hotels in Martinique		
★★★★	**Meridien Martinique**	$253–$779
★★★	**Diamant Novotel**	$167–$342
★★★	**La Bateliere Hotel**	$115–$275
★★★	**Leyritz Plantation**	$87–$147

Fielding's Best Value Hotels in Martinique		
★★	**Martinique Cottages**	$60–$65
★★	**St. Aubin Hotel**	$58–$86
★★★	**Habitation Lagrange**	$325–$355
★★★	**Diamant Novotel**	$167–$342
★★★	**La Bateliere Hotel**	$115–$275

Accommodations on Martinique run from the 300-room resort to the inn with ten rooms. You can choose between resorts happily ensconced on the seashore to guesthouses run by congenial families, part of the "Relais Creoles" organization. Prices range from expensive to modest. All of the larger hotels have sports facilities, a choice of restaurants and evening entertainment. All beachfront hotels offer a full watersports program. Some hotels even have kitchenette studios.

Hotels and Resorts

Sofitel Bakoua Hotel, perched on a hillside, is the leading resort, retaining a distinct local feel in the historical plantation-style surroundings. **La Bateliere Hotel**, with its recent renovations, comes in a close second for style, service and location.

Alamanda   **$69–$115**   ★★

Anse Mitan, ☎ *596-66-13-72.*
Single: $69–$87. Double: $89–$115.
Located right in the heart of the tourist region and within walking distance to the beach, this small hotel accommodates guests in studios, some with kitchens. There's not much here in the way of diversions, but you'll find watersports, shopping and restaurants nearby. 30 rooms. Credit Cards: MC.

Diamant Novotel   **$167–$342**   ★★

Diamant, ☎ *(800) 221-4542, 596-76-42-42.*
Single: $167–$252. Double: $195–$342.
Bordered by white sand beaches near a fishing village, this hotel houses guests in comfortable rooms in three-story buildings. Most rooms have nice views of the sea. There's a pool, table tennis, a floating barge on which to sun, two tennis courts and supervised programs for children. A handful of bars and restaurants complete the scene. Popular with families. 181 rooms. Credit Cards: V, MC, A.

Diamant les Bains Hotel   **$60–$120**   ★★

Diamant, ☎ *596-76-40-14.*
Single: $60–$95. Double: $73–$120.
Set on a sandy beach overlooking Diamond Rock, this small family-run property accommodates guests in the main house or in small, rustic bungalows with refrigerators. There's a pool and restaurant on-site, with watersports nearby. Service is cheerful and caring. 26 rooms. Credit Cards: V, MC.

L'Imperatrice Village   **$78–$123**   ★★

Anse Mitan, ☎ *596-66-08-09.*
Single: $78–$103. Double: $98–$123.
Set on tropical grounds across the bay from Fort-de-France, this resort houses guests in standard rooms, studios, and bungalows with kitchens. All are on the modest side, but pleasant enough. A bit off the beaten path, so you'll want to rent a car. On-site features include a restaurant and bar, pool and games like billiards and ping-pong. 59 rooms. Credit Cards: MC, A.

La Bateliere Hotel   **$115–$275**   ★★★

Schoelcher, ☎ *596-61-49-49.*
Single: $115–$185. Double: $200–$275.
Located on 6.5 acres on a bluff overlooking the sea, this five-story hotel opened as a Hilton. Guest rooms are spacious, with all the modern amenities. For recreation, there are eight lighted tennis courts and a pro, all watersports, a pool, excursions in a cabin cruiser, and a fine, sandy beach. Several restaurants, a disco, and the island's first casino. Dependable service. 199 rooms. Credit Cards: V, MC, A.

La Dunette　　　　　　　　　　**$100–$125**　　　　　　　　★

Ste. Anne, ☎ *596-76-73-90.*
Single: $100. Double: $120–$125.
Located in a fishing village, this three-story hotel offers simple rooms, some with balconies. Besides the bar and dining room, there is little in the way of extras. 18 rooms. Credit Cards: V, MC.

Meridien Martinique　　　　　**$253–$779**　　　　　　

Point du Bont, ☎ *(800) 543-4300, 596-66-00-00.*
Single: $253–$779. Double: $305–$779.
Located across the harbor from Fort-de-France, this seven-story property shows its age, and attracts mainly convention groups. Rooms are small but comfortable. There's lots to do at this busy resort, including complimentary watersports, a pool, health club, two tennis courts and a 100-slip marina. The man-made beach is small and gets crowded. There's also a casino and nightly entertainment during high season. A ferry transports passengers to Fort-de-France. Decent for its wide range of facilities, but best suited to the group market. 295 rooms. Credit Cards: CB, V, A.

PLM Azur Carayou Hotel　　　**$125–$243**　　　　　　★★

Pointe de Bout, ☎ *(800) 221-4542, 596-66-04-04.*
Single: $125–$243. Double: $130–$243.
Located on Fort-de-France Bay, this hotel caters mainly to groups. Accommodations are quite nice, with large, modern baths that include bidets. All units have a balcony. The small beach is found in a sheltered cove. There's also a large pool, two tennis courts, archery, a driving range and watersports. The disco is popular during high season. 197 rooms. Credit Cards: V, DC, A.

PLM Azur Squash Hotel　　　**$77–$141**　　　　　　★★

3 Blvd. de la Marne, ☎ *596-63-00-01.*
Single: $77–$141. Double: $92–$141.
Located in a residential neighborhood close to the center of town, this modern hotel is frequented by business travelers. Accommodations are clean, comfortable and tastefully decorated. There's live entertainment in the bar twice weekly. The well-equipped health club includes an exercise room, sauna, Jacuzzi and Turkish bath. There's also a pool and three squash courts. The beach is nearby. 108 rooms. Credit Cards: V, MC, A.

PLM Azur la Pagerie　　　　**$126–$175**　　　　　　★★

Pointe du Bout, ☎ *(800) 221-4542, 596-66-05-30.*
Single: $126–$136. Double: $155–$175.
This informal hotel faces the marina across the bay from Fort-de-France. Guest rooms are spacious with bidets in the bathrooms; some have kitchenettes while others have only refrigerators. Located in a high-density hotel area, there is a pool but little else on-site. Guests can use the facilities at the nearby PLM Azur Carayou, where they have restaurants, tennis and watersports. 98 rooms. Credit Cards: V, MC, A.

Sofitel Bakoua Hotel　　　　**$135–$270**　　　　★★★★★

Pointe du Bout, ☎ *(800) 221-4542, 596-66-02-02.*
Single: $135–$270. Double: $135–$270.

Located in a garden setting on a bluff above a private beach, this deluxe hotel is one of Martinique's best. Accommodations are on the hillside or the beach; all quite nice but on the small side. There are two lighted tennis courts, a lovely pool, all watersports and a nearby golf course. The service is among the island's best, and most of the French staff speaks at least some English. The beach is fine. Worth the splurge. 138 rooms. Credit Cards: CB, V, MC, A.

le Balisier   **$56–$77**   ★

21 Victor Hugo Street, ☎ *596-71-46-54.*
Single: $56–$77. Double: $67–$77.
Set in the heart of Fort-de-France, this budget property offers small and simple rooms. There are also three apartments with kitchenettes. There are no dining or recreation facilities on-site, but many within walking distance. 27 rooms. Credit Cards: MC, A.

Apartments and Condominiums

The **Villa Rental Service** of the Martinique Tourist Office ☎ *596-63-79-60* can arrange vacation home rentals. Among the choices are apartments, studios, or villas. Most of the properties are located in the southern sector, near good beaches. Rentals can be arranged for the week or month.

Les Ilets de l'Impératrice are two tiny islands off Le François on the windward coast, each with a 19th-century vacation house, beach, watersports, full-time maid and cook. Ilet Thierry's house has six double bedrooms; Ilet Oscar's has five. All-inclusive rates (airport pickup, lodging, food and drink, and sports, etc.) runs $200 per person per day year round. Contact Jean-Louis de Lucy ☎ *65-82-30,* FAX *(596) 63-18-22.*

Martinique Cottages   **$60–$65**   ★ ★

Jean d'Arc, ☎ *596-50-16-08.*
Single: $60. Double: $65.
Located in a residential area 15 minutes from Fort-de-France, this small operation is popular, especially with business travelers. Accommodations are in bungalows nestled among the trees. Each is nicely done with small kitchens and verandas. The beach is 15 minutes away; if that's too far, you can relax by the free-form pool. There's also a restaurant and bar. This family-owned spot is peaceful and pleasant. 8 rooms. Credit Cards: CB, V, MC, DC, A.

Residence Grand Large   **$325–$395**   ★ ★

Ste. Luce.
Off on its own on the south shore of Ste. Luce, a fishing village, this small complex offers fully furnished studios with kitchens and ocean views. There's nothing on-site, so you'll need a car to get around. The rates are quite reasonable: $325 to 395 per week. 18 rooms. Credit Cards: CB, V, MC, A.

Rivage Hotel   **$75–$75**   ★ ★

Anse Mitan, ☎ *596-66-00-53.*
Single: $75. Double: $75.
This small, family-run operation is near the beach. All rooms have a kitchenette and balcony; if you want a TV, you'll pay extra. There's a bar and pool, and lots of diversions within walking distance. 20 rooms. Credit Cards: V, MC.

Inns

Fregate Bleue Inn   ★ ★ ★

> *Le Francois,* ☎ *(800) 633-7411, 596-54-54-66.*
> *Double: $125–$230.*

Set on a hillside overlooking the sea, this gingerbread-trimmed inn is positively charming. All accommodations are in spacious studios with kitchenettes, armoires, antiques and four-poster beds. Breakfast is complimentary each morning, but you'll have to cook in or venture off-site for other meals. There's a pool for those too relaxed to walk three minutes to the beach. Very elegant and gracious, this lovely inn is best suited to those not seeking a lot of action. 7 rooms. Credit Cards: MC, A.

Habitation Lagrange   **$325–$355**   ★ ★ ★ ★

> *Marigot,* ☎ *596-53-60-60.*
> *Single: $325–$355. Double: $325–$355.*

This 18th-century creole mansion was refurbished and opened as an inn in 1991. Some guest rooms are in the great house, the former headquarters of a sugar and rum factory. Others are found in new two-story buildings. All are elegantly decorated with canopy beds, antique furnishings, VCRs and minibars, plus modern comforts like air conditioning. For recreation, there's a putting green, pool and tennis courts, plus exploring the ruins of the former plant. Charming and romantic. 17 rooms. Credit Cards: MC, A.

Leyritz Plantation   **$87–$147**   ★ ★ ★ ★

> *Basse-Point,* ☎ *596-78-53-92.*
> *Single: $87–$121. Double: $117–$147.*

This inn is another charmer, though its remote location isn't for everyone. Set on the grounds of a 230-acre banana plantation, it accommodates guests in a converted 18th-century great house and in the former guardhouse and slave quarters, as well as in bamboo and stone cottages. All are air conditioned, antique filled, have four-poster beds and loads of charm. The most atmospheric rooms are in the main house with its high ceilings, dormer windows, and thick walls. The beach is a full half-hour away, but there's a pool on-site for whiling away the hours. There's also a tennis court, and you can spend hours exploring the ruins of the former plant. A major drawback are the hordes of tourists trouping through on organized tours. Nonetheless, this picturesque spot is hard to leave. 70 rooms. Credit Cards: MC, A.

Low Cost Lodging

Martinique has more than 200 **Gites de France** ☎ *73-67-92*, which are apartments, studios, and guest rooms in private homes. **Logis Vacances Antilles** ☎ *63-12-91* also offers rooms in private homes, as well as holiday studios and houses. Camping can be done almost anywhere—in the mountains, forest, and on many beaches, although indiscriminate camping is not permitted. **Tropicamp** at Gros Raisins Plage, Ste. Luce ☎ *62-49-66* is one of several companies with full services, including hot showers. Other comfortable camps with showers and toilets are **Nid Tropical** at Anse-a-l'Ane near Trois Ilets ☎ *68-31-30*; one at **Vauclin** on the southeast Atlantic coast ☎ *74-45-88*; an another at **Pointe Marin** near the public beach of Ste. Anne ☎ *76-72-79*. A nominal fee is charged for facilities. For details, contact the **Office National des Dorês**, 3.5 km, route de Mouette, Fort-de-France; ☎ *(596) 71-34-50.*

The trend these days is to rent a camping car, which allows you opportunity to discover many of the treasures along Martinique's 300-mile roadway. One recommended camping-car operation is **West Indies Tours**, whose campers are outfitted with beds for four, refrigerator, shower, sink, 430-gallon water tank, dining table, stove, and radio/cassette player. Contact **Michel Yula, West Indies Tours, Le François**; ☎ *(596) 54-50-71*; or **Wind Martinique, Anse Mitan**; ☎ *66-02-22.*

It's also possible to rent rooms in private houses, apartments, and houses in all price ranges with weekly or monthly rates.To rent a gîte as they as called, contact **Gîtes de France**, *Martinique, Maison du Tourisme Vert, 9 BD du Général-de-Gaulle, BP 1122, 97248 Fort-De-France;* ☎ *73-67-92.*

Auberge de l'Anse Mitan $65–$95   ★

Anse Mitan, ☎ *596-66-01-12.*
Single: $65–$75. Double: $85–$95.
This casual French-style inn is within walking distance of the beach in Anse Mitan. Accommodations include standard rooms in the three-story main building and six studios with kitchenettes. All are air-conditioned and have private baths and telephones. There's a bar and restaurant serving French and creole fare, but little else in the way of extras. Friendly and cheerful service at this family-run establishment. 20 rooms. Credit Cards: V, MC, DC, A.

Caraibe Auberge $51–$110   ★

Anse Mitan, ☎ *596-66-03-19.*
Single: $51–$82. Double: $70–$110.
This small beachfront hotel is in the center of the hotel resort action. Rooms are simple and fairly spartan, as reflected by the rates. There's a small pool on-site, but little else. 31 rooms. Credit Cards: MC, A.

Victoria Hotel $65–$76   ★★

Rte de Didier, ☎ *596-60-56-78.*
Single: $65–$70. Double: $70–$76.
Located on a hillside in a residential neighborhood with nice views, this colonial-style hotel offers good value for its reasonable rates, and attracts mainly business travelers. Accommodations are in comfortable rooms, some with TVs and others with kitchenettes. There's a French restaurant and a pool on site. 32 rooms. Credit Cards: V, MC.

What to Eat

Highest Rated Restaurants in Martinique

★★★★	La Fontane
★★★★	Leyritz Plantation
★★★	Athanor
★★★	Aux Filets Bleus
★★★	Chez Mally Edjam
★★★	La Mouina
★★★	Le Coq Hardi

Most Exclusive Restaurants in Martinique

★★★★	Leyritz Plantation	$36–$50
★★★★	Le Fontane	$30–$50
★★★	Le Coq Hardi	$18–$36
★★★	La Mouina	$15–$30
★★★	Athanor	$11–$30

Fielding's Best Value Restaurants in Martinique

★★★★	Leyritz Plantation	$36–$50
★★★	Chez Mally Edjam	$11–$29
★★★	La Mouina	$15–$30

Perhaps it's the irrepressible French dedication to cuisine, but chefs in Martinique seem to take special care with their menus, overseeing both the preparation and the service. Throughout the island you will generally find one of two cuisines: traditional French or island Creole; many restaurants combine the two on their menus. Fresh seafood dishes are omnipresent, among the tastiest are *chatrou* (octopus), *langouste* (small clawless lobster), *lambi* (conch), and *cribiches* (large river shrimp). Red snapper is served in a variety of ways. *Coquille de lambi* (minced conch in creamy sauce served in a shell) is an island must; the *blaff de poisson* (steamed fish in local spices) is excellent at Le Mareyeur. Another island specialty, *pâté en pot*, is a thick creole soup made with mutton. A good afternoon drink to cool you off is *les planteurs*—a planter's punch in a sweet fruit juice base. Heart islanders tend to chug down *décollage*—aged herbal rum with a fruit juice chaser. Most restaurants have excellent selections of French wines. Prices per person for a three-course meal without wine range from $30–$45 and up. The French & English booklet *Ti Gourmet*, available from the Tourist Office, will give out more information about where and what to eat.

Fort-de-France

La Fontane **$$$** ★★★★

Km. 4 Rue de Balata,
French cuisine.
Lunch: entrees $30–$50.
Dinner: entrees $30–$50.
A highly-regarded French-creole restaurant, La Fontane is located in a restored gingerbread house surrounded by fruit trees. The service is formal, the interior is antique-filled and tasteful, with exotic carpets on the floors. Dishes have included crayfish salad with fruit, lamb and mango and red-snapper with a citrus sauce. Closed: Mon, Sun. Reservations required. Credit Cards: A.

La Mouina **$$$** ★★★

route de Redoute, Redoute,
French cuisine. Specialties: Crab Farcis.
Lunch: 12:00 a.m.–4:00 p.m., entrees $15–$30.
Dinner: 7:30 p.m.–9:30 p.m., entrees $15–$30.
This is suburbia Fort-de-France style—fine dining in a typical upper-class home in Redoute, high above the capital below. Guests are made welcome in a dining salon on a balcony with a garden view. The smart set likes to make La Mouina a regular stop for luncheons of stuffed crab backs, tournedos and crayfish. Dinners are served by candlelight. Closed: Sat, Sun. Reservations required. Credit Cards: V, MC.

Le Coq Hardi **$$$** ★★★

Rue Martin Luther King,
International cuisine. Specialties: Tournedos Rossini, Prime Rib.
Lunch: 12:00 a.m.–2:00 p.m., entrees $18–$36.
Dinner: 7:00 p.m.–11:00 p.m., entrees $18–$36.
Red meat is god here, prepared *au bleu* (very rare) which is the French way. Master charcutier Alphonse Sintive regularly imports the choice cuts of T-Bone, filet mignon and entrecote from France. After you choose your own steak, it's cooked over an open wood fire. An old-fashioned tournedos rossini is prepared with foie gras and truffles, and is a favorite here. If you still have room after the huge portions served, there's still a wide selection of scrumptious desserts and sorbets. Closed: Wed. Reservations recommended. Credit Cards: V, MC, A.

Le Second Souffle   **$$**   ★ ★ ★

27 Rue Blenac,
Latin American cuisine.
Lunch: 12:00 a.m.–3:00 p.m., entrees $8–$12.
Dinner: 7:30 p.m.–10:00 p.m., entrees $8–$12.

A treat for the body and soul is a cleansing visit to this pleasant vegetarian restaurant after a tour of the Byzantine Saint Louis Cathedral nearby. Le Second Souffle (is there a first?) dishes up a salad of seasonal fruits with honey sauce, or a meatless plat du jour, which may include a christophene or callaloo souffle. Closed: Sat, Sun. Credit Cards: V, MC.

Leyritz Plantation   **$$$**   ★ ★ ★ ★

Basse Pointe 97218, Leyritz,
Latin American cuisine.
Lunch: 12:30 p.m.–2:00 p.m., entrees $27–$40.
Dinner: 7:30 p.m.–9:00 p.m., entrees $36–$50.

Dining at one of Martinique's prime tourist attractions sounds like a recipe for disaster, but surprisingly, the Creole cuisine remains first rate. Guests also get a lot of food for their francs, especially a set luncheon of stuffed crab, blood pudding, an entree (sometimes conch), rice and vegetables and dessert. The million-dollar setting amidst an 18th century sugar plantation is a fond postcard memory. Although lunch is the preferred time, come for dinner when the tour bus pandemonium becomes practically nonexistent. Associated Hotel: Plantation de Leyritz. Reservations required. Credit Cards: V, MC.

Basse Pointe

Athanor   **$$$**   ★ ★ ★

Rue de Bord de Mer, Ste. Anne,
French cuisine. Specialties: Grilled Lobster.
Dinner: 7:00 p.m.–10:00 p.m., entrees $11–$30.

This informal eatery located one block from the beach in Ste. Anne prepares tasty pizzas, salads and other casual meals from a large menu. Diners can choose a few fancier items including the specialty, grilled lobster, which is delicious. There's a choice of seating in a pretty garden behind the restaurant or in a greenery-draped dining room indoors. Reservations recommended. Credit Cards: V, MC.

Aux Filets Bleus   **$$$**   ★ ★ ★

Point Marin, Ste. Anne,
Latin American cuisine. Specialties: Delices de la Mer, Turtle Soup, Court Bouillon.
Lunch: 12:30 p.m.–2:30 p.m., entrees $13–$30.
Dinner: 7:30 p.m.–9:30 p.m., entrees $13–$30.

A restaurant of many contrasts—although Aux Filets Bleus charges haute cuisine prices, the place is so casual you can come here in a beach cover-up after a swim in the briny which is in full view of the tables. Also, dishes are mostly hearty West Indian dishes like *chatrous* (octopus) with red beans and rice, hardly justifying the stiff tab. Still, what you're served is usually very good, and the ambience is friendly and intimate. Closed: Mon. Reservations required. Credit Cards: V, MC.

Chez Mally Edjam   **$$$**   ★ ★ ★

Route de la Cote,

French cuisine. Specialties: Fruit Confitures, Colombo de Porc.
Dinner: entrees $11–$29.

It's a very pleasant drive to get to this home-style restaurant run by stellar cuisiniere Mally Edjam and her family. The surrounding landscape en route is dotted with pineapple plantations, and trees hung heavily with boughs of green bananas. That's just a prelude to the symphony of flavors on the fixed-price lunches served here, which may include pork colombo (local curry), conch and fabulous desserts. Don't miss the homemade preserves made from local fruits. Dinners may be arranged by appointment. Reservations required. Credit Cards: V, MC, A.

La Dunette   **$$**   ★★

Sainte Anne, 97227, Ste. Anne,
Seafood cuisine.
Lunch: entrees $6–$20.
Dinner: entrees $6–$20.

La Dunette is like a lot of pleasant seaside restaurants on the island that serves seafood specialties. Dine inside or out in a tropical garden facing the sea on poached sea urchins, curries or grilled fish. Connected to a pleasant, intimate hotel where you might consider staying if you're in the area, which is noted for gorgeous beaches and fine weather. Associated Hotel: La Dunette. Credit Cards: V, MC.

Yva Chez Vava   **$$$**   ★★

Boulevard de Gaulle, Grand Riviere,
French cuisine.
Dinner: entrees $18–$27.

This chez on the northern tip of the island is the domain of local legend Vava and her daughter Yva, who now continues the tradition of cooking family-style creole meals in their own residence near a river. As Grand Riviere is a fishing village, seafood appears prominently on the menu. Specialties include *accras* (cod fritters), chicken colombo and *z'habitants* (crayfish prepared Martinique style). After lunch, you might want to visit the fish market where your food originated, or stroll on the black sand beach. Reservations recommended. Credit Cards: Not Accepted.

Where to Shop

"Go French" is the password when trying to decode what to buy in Martinique—a place where you can find the best bargains among French imports—perfumes, cosmetics, clothes, china, and crystal—at prices 25-40 percent lower than in the U.S. If you pay in traveler's checks, you'll receive an additional 20 percent discount. You will never find these prices in France. Don't miss picking up a few bottles of Martinique-brewed rum. Craft buys range from folk-styled applique wall hangings to the Martiniquais doll dressed in the national costume, which can be seen in nearly every store and in every size imaginable. A conical bakoua straw hat does nicely as a sunstopper. If you're interested in the bright gold Creole jewelry that seems to be around many women's necks, ears and wrists, you will be joining a longstanding cultural tradition. The special "convict's chain" called *chaîne forçat*, and the *tremblants*, gold brooches with special adornment, can be found in several stores, where you should be able to judge authenticity by the price. Among the most reputable are **Cadet Daniel**, **Bijouterie Onyx**, and **Emile Mothie's** workshop in Trenelle. (The latter are for serious fans who want to observe his work.) For delicious French delicacies, wines, foie gras and chocolates, head for **Boutique Michel Montignac**. To pick up the latest in island music, try Hit Parade on Rue Lamartine. The latest Parisian fashions can be found at **l'Univers**.

Martinique Directory

ARRIVAL AND DEPARTURE

Direct flights are available from New York/JFK every Saturday on North American Airlines. You can also catch one of many regular flights American Airlines offers to San Juan (via many gateways in the U.S. and a Sunday flight on Air France from Miami. Interisland connections to Martinique, from St. Martin, Antigua, Dominica, St. Lucia, Barbados, St. Vincent, Mustique, and Union Island can be made on Air Martinique. LIAT flies to and from neighboring islands. From Guadeloupe, you can catch frequent daily flights on Réseau Aérien Francais des Caraibes, a French Caribbean airline consortium which includes Air Martinique, Air Guadeloupe and Air France.

Martinique can also be reached from other islands by the ultra-modern catamaran Emeraude Express. Contact **Caribbean Express** ☎ *(596) 63-12-11*, FAX *(596) 63-34-47*.

Many cruise ships pull into Martinique as a port of call. Some dock at the attractive Passenger Terminal located at the harbor port a few minutes' drive from the center of the city; others anchor in Fort-de-France Bay and transfer passengers by tender, a 10-minute ride.

There is no departure tax charged for visitors, except charter flights only.

CLIMATE

Martinique's temperatures stay temperate year-long, hovering around 79 degrees F, with only a five degree difference between seasons. The air is cooled by constant wind currents (east and northeast); trade winds are called *les alizés*.

DOCUMENTS

For stays up to three weeks, U.S. and Canadian citizens traveling as tourists must show proof of citizenship in the form of a valid passport, or a passport that expired no more than five years ago, or other proof in the form of a birth certificate or voter's registration card with a government-authorized photo ID. For stays over three weeks, or for nontourist visas, a valid passport is necessary. Resident aliens of the U.S. and Canada, and other foreign nationals other than those in the Common Market must have a valid passport and visa. All passengers must show an ongoing or return ticket.

ELECTRICITY

Current is 220 AC, 50 cycles. American and Canadian appliances require a French plug, converter and transformers.

GETTING AROUND

Taxi stands are located at the airport, in downtown Fort-de-France, and at major hotels. Rates rise 60 percent between 8 p.m. and 6 a.m. Eighty percent of the taxis are Mercedes Benz. There are also collective taxis (eight-passenger limousines bearing the sign TC).

Car rentals are available at Lamentin Airport, though hours are dependent on international flights. A valid driver's license is required, the minimum age is 21. Other agencies can be found in Fort-de-France. Among the best are **Avis**, *4 rue Ernest Deproge* ☎ *70-11-60*; **Budget**, *12 rue Félix Eboué, Fort-de-France* ☎ *63-69-00*; and **Hertz**, *24 rue Ernest Deproge, Fort-de-France* ☎ *60-64-54.*

Ferries, called vedettes, link Fort-de-France with Pointe du Bout daily from early morning until after midnight, and with Anse Mitan, Anse-a-l'Ane, Grand Anse d'Arlet from early morning til late afternoon. All ferries leave and arrive at Quai d'Esnambuc.

LANGUAGE

The languages of the isle are French and Creole. You'll find English spoken in most hotels, restaurants and tourist facilities, but you'll be happy if you remember to bring along a French phase book and pocket dictionary.

MEDICAL EMERGENCIES

There are 20 hospitals and clinics on the island, many well equipped; the best is **La Meynard** ☎ *55-20-00.* Ask the Tourist Office to assist you in securing an English-speaking physician.

MONEY

The official currency is the French franc, but U.S. and Canadian dollars are accepted almost everywhere. The rate of exchange, approximately 5 francs to the dollar, can change due to currency fluctuation.

TELEPHONE

The area code is *596.* To direct-dial from the U.S., dial ☎ *011-596,* plus the local Martinique number for station to station, or *01-596* plus local number for person to person. The best way to make international calls in Martinique is to purchase a "Telecarte" (a one-minute call to the U.S. is about $2.10 These credit cards can be purchased at all post offices and other outlets marked "Telécarte en vente Ici."; the booths you use them in are marked "Telécom." To use the assistance of an operator or to make a call from a hotel room will raise the price enormously.

TIME

Martinique is one hour later than New York (Eastern Standard Time). Time is related on the 24-hour hour schedule; i.e., 1 p.m. is 13 hours.

TIPPING AND TAXES

Some hotels add a 10 percent service charge and/or 5 percent government tax to the bill. Check your bill carefully and avoid adding on an extra service charge. if there is no charge added, a 10–15 percent charge would be appreciated by waiters and waitresses.

TOURIST INFORMATION

The Martinique Tourist Office ☎ *63-79-60* is located in handsome quarters on the Boulevard Alfassa, which borders on the waterfront in Fort-de-France Hours are Monday-Friday 7:30 a.m.–12:30 p.m. and 2:30 p.m.–5:30 p.m., and Saturday 8 a.m.–noon. Do pick up complimentary maps, magazines and information bulletins; the English-speaking staff is quite helpful. A tourist office information desk at Lamentin Airport is open daily until the last flight comes in. In the U.S. ☎ *(213) 658-7462.*

WHEN TO GO

Carnival begins on January 7 for five days, a total-island experience with parties and parades. Ash Wednesday is a blowout affair on March 1, with jammed streets, flowing rum, wild dancing and a funeral cortege at La Savane, Fort-de-France. The Aqua Festival du Robert on April 15–22 is a sea extravaganza in this Atlantic coastal town with yawl races, regattas, and concerts. Jazz a la Plantation on June 2, for two weeks at Basse Pointe, is a New Orleans-meets-French Antilles affair, with concert jams, street bands, Creole nights, and jazz lectures and workshops. Images Caraibes, on June 2 for two weeks, is the 5th Caribbean Film Festival in Fort-de-France. Tour de la Martinique is July 7–16, a week-long bicycle race throughout the island. The tenth Tour des Yoles Rondes on July 30–August 6, a race of rawls used by Martinique fishermen. The Semi-Marathon, on November 19, is a large race contest. Christmas Eve is celebrated with a midnight mass followed by a sumptuous supper, called Le Réveillon. New Year's Eve is another huge bash celebrated at hotels and restaurants.

MARTINIQUE HOTELS	RMS	RATES	PHONE	FAX
Fort-de-France				
★★★★★ **Sofitel Bakoua Hotel**	138	$135–$270	(800) 221-4542	
★★★★ **Meridien Martinique**	295	$253–$779	(800) 543-4300	
★★★ **Diamant Novotel**	181	$167–$342	(800) 221-4542	
★★★ **Fregate Bleue Inn**	7	$125–$230	(800) 633-7411	
★★★ **Habitation Lagrange**	17	$325–$355	596-53-60-60	
★★★ **La Bateliere Hotel**	199	$115–$275	596-61-49-49	
★★★ **Leyritz Plantation**	70	$87–$147	596-78-53-92	
★★ **Alamanda**	30	$69–$115	596-66-13-72	
★★ **L'Imperatrice Village**	59	$78–$123	596-66-08-09	
★★ **PLM Azur Carayou Hotel**	197	$125–$243	(800) 221-4542	
★★ **PLM Azur Squash Hotel**	108	$77–$141	596-63-00-01	
★★ **PLM Azur la Pagerie**	98	$126–$175	(800) 221-4542	
★★ **Victoria Hotel**	32	$65–$76	596-60-56-78	596-60-00-24
★ **Auberge de l'Anse Mitan**	20	$65–$95	596-66-01-12	
★ **Caraibe Auberge**	31	$51–$110	596-66-03-19	
★ **Diamant les Bains Hotel**	26	$60–$120	596-76-40-14	
★ **La Dunette**	18	$100–$125	596-76-73-90	
★ **Residence Grand Large**	18	$325–$395		
★ **Rivage Hotel**	20	$75	596-66-00-53	
★ **le Balisier**	27	$56–$77	596-71-46-54	
Lamentin				
★★ **Martinique Cottages**	8	$60–$65	596-50-16-08	596-50-26-83
Ste. Anne				
★★★ **Anchorage Hotel**	187	$135	596-76-92-32	
Trinite				
★★ **St. Aubin Hotel**	15	$58–$86	596-69-34-77	

MARTINIQUE RESTAURANTS	LOCATION	PHONE	ENTREE
Basse Pointe			
French			
★★★ **Athanor**	Ste. Anne		$11–$30••
★★★ **Chez Mally Edjam**	Basse Pointe		$11–$29••
★★ **Yva Chez Vava**	Grand Riviere		$18–$27••
Latin American			
★★★ **Aux Filets Bleus**	Ste. Anne		$13–$30
Seafood			
★★ **La Dunette**	Ste. Anne		$6–$20
Fort-de-France			
French			
★★★★ **La Fontane**	Fort-de-France		$30–$50
★★★ **La Mouina**	Redoute		$15–$30
International			
★★★ **Le Coq Hardi**	Fort-de-France		$18–$36
Latin American			
★★★★ **Leyritz Plantation**	Leyritz		$27–$50
★★★ **Le Second Souffle**	Fort-de-France		$8–$12
Pointe du Bout			
Chinese			
★★ **Le Cantonnais**	Pointe du Bout		$14–$20••
Note: • Lunch Only			
•• Dinner Only			

MONTSERRAT

Montserrat is lushly green with beaches ranging from white to brown.

Montserrat is about the closest thing to a Caribbean moonwalk. A volcanic blip that burst out of the sea four million years ago, the island has been called one of the last perfect ecosystems in the world—its nickname is "Emerald Isle of the Caribbean." Propelled by tremendous planetary shifts, volcanic surges of lava have left the island so fertile that everyone from people to fish, to birds, to plants and cattle, have plenty to eat. Exuberant flora, like yellow hibiscus, blood-red canna, and gold allamanda snake up the cliffs and beside the winding roads. Craggy rock walls, stained with eons-old mineral deposits, glimmer with colors as luminescent as those of a rainbow. Beneath the rocks lie beaches so black that the one white beach, Rendezvous Bay, seems like a miracle when you finally cruise onto its shores. Simply, Montserrat is an island to lay back and admire. And yet despite what's been called "the fatal beauty of Montserrat," the island is brimming with culture, mainly in the form of a vibrant musicality. Especially during Carnival, but also all year round, some of the most talented stars of reggae, soca and calypso in the Caribbean can be found in Montserrat's bars. A few years back, thanks to the efforts of George Martin, the former manager of the Beatles, you might have even gotten the chance to rub shoulders with Sting, Paul McCartney and others international rockers, who piled into Montserrat to take advantage of the world-class recording studio Martin built a few years ago. Unfortunately, in 1989 Hurricane Hugo blew away the remains of Air Studios, but some Montserratians claim they they're happy to see their island return to some sleepy normalcy after its celeb rock invasion. Today the washed-away wharf is being built up again and homes have been restored, though a few are still standing as skeletons, a reminder of the devastation Mother Nature can wreak in the Caribbean. These days most of the income on the island is in the form of moneys sent from overseas relatives, and the only things locally made are sea-island cotton, ceramics, tapestries and postage stamps. Montserrat never set out to attract mass tourism, which is exactly why you should go now, before the inevitable commercial takeovers occur. Thankfully, these days Montserrat is still an island where you can find a storefront sign proudly announcing: "We Sell Brake Fluid, Pig Snout and Pig Tail."

Note: The national bird, the Montserrat oriole, can be found on no other place on earth except here. Although it lost half its 1200 population to Hurricane Hugo, the puffed up, yellow-breasted bird has managed to survive every single cataclysm that has hit the island.

Bird's Eye View

The British Crown Colony of Montserrat is a lushly landscaped, 39.5-sq. mile island, some 27 miles southeast of Antigua. The island is compact, only 11 miles long by 7 miles across; it takes almost twenty minutes to drive from the mid-island Anglo community of Woodlands to Plymouth. Near the airport, the land is flat and scrubby, but soon turns into a brilliant green terrain. Three mountain ranges cross the island; the highest, **Soufriere Hills**, rises to 3002 feet at the summit of **Mount Chance**. Volcanic in origin, Montserrat boasts several active fumaroles and bubbling hot springs;. an inactive volcano and sulphur spring. Most of the villages lie on the west coast, where they are

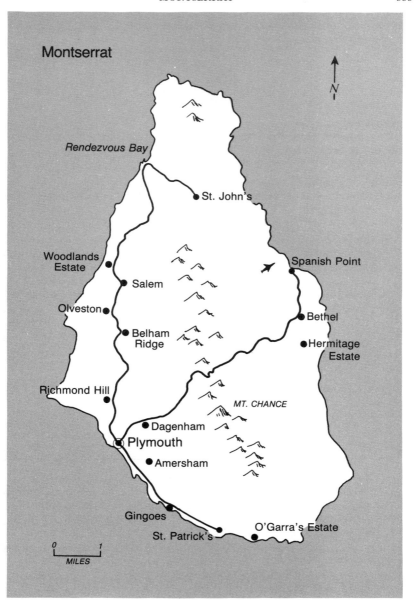

Montserrat

connected by solid roads. **Plymouth**, the capital of the island, is compact but complete, with an excellent harbor, court, banks and government offices.

History

Ciboney Indians were the first inhabitants of Montserrat some 1500 years ago, later replaced by Arawaks and cannibalistic Caribs, the latter who dubbed the island "Alliouagana," which means either "island of the aloe plant" or "island of the prickly bush." In 1943, it was Christopher Columbus who gave the name Montserrat because of the island's resemblance to the luscious terrain near the Montserrat Monastery in Spain. Irish roots were laid in 1623 when Sir Thomas Warner, in St. Kitts, commanded rebellious Catholics to colonize the island. Today St. Patrick's Day is celebrated with glee and you'll still find lots of Irish names in the phonebook. After the slave trade began to support a sugarcane industry, the ratio between blacks and whites soared—10,000 blacks to 1300 whites in 1678. Emancipation arrived in 1834. Today, Montserrat remains a British Crown Colony, with a resident governor appointed by and representing Queen Elizabeth. At present, the island seems completely at peace with its protectorate relationship, and shows no signs of rebelling,

People

Most of the towns and place names and even human names on Montserrat are of Irish origin, dating back to the mid-1600s when there were 1000 Irish families living here. Today, only a handful of full-blooded Irishmen still exist. The remaining are those of West African descent, whose ancestors were imported as plantation slaves from the 1660s to 1834. With such a small population (12,000), expect everyone in Montserrat to know each other (at least they make you think they do, so friendly are they). Also, everyone seems to know whenever and wherever a party is happening. Perhaps because of the devastating beauty of the island, locals tend to feel an intense connection to their land, and it's not surprising they have discovered numerous healing properties for native plants. Superstitions and belief in other-worldly things still run high, and many native-born carry not only their birth name but a "jumby" name as well—a magical name that protects them from spirits. Obeah, a voodoo-type religion with African roots, has been outlawed on the island, but expect to find a few hidden devotees amid the more Catholic masses. Most of the population is of African descent, but in recent years numerous wealthy Americans, Canadians and Britons, nicknamed "snowbirds," have bought retirement homes here. Consequently, much of the cultural life today in Montserrat, including the fine museum, is run by expats who have improved the quality of service, though a bit of genuine contact to folklore has been lost in the process.

Beaches

Montserrat is known for its black volcanic beaches, which in reality tends to mean sand that is a dark golden brown or silvery gray. Most of the "black" beaches are located in the northern tip of the island. Beaches with a bit whiter cast are located on the northwest coast; the most popular ones are **Rendezvous Bay**, **Little Bay**, and **Carr's Bay**. The finest beach is **Woodlands**, with very limited facilities, where a delightful activity is swimming through caves. A rocky beach full of pebbles is Fox's Bay. Most beaches are reachable only by sailing, which can be arranged by the Vue Pointe Hotel.

Dive Sites

Diving in Montserrat is excellent for both beginners and pros. One of the best sites for all levels is **O'Garros**, off the southern shores, where a short shallow shelf separates the Guadeloupe trench from the shore. Corals, barracudas, and sharks, as well as turtles and rays congregate around the abrupt dropoff. Another fine dive site is **Colbys**, large enough to accommodate several dives. Its rare elkhorn corals and pillar corals are said to be fantastic. Only the best divers should head for **Pinnacle**, whose depths range from 65-300 feet. Since spearfishing is banned, plenty of marine life, as well as brightly colored sponges and enormous basket sponges as big as a human, can be seen.

Treks

Montserrat is a wonderful island to hike—don't miss the opportunity. New hiking trails are presently being prepared by the Tourist Board in Plymouth; before you set out, inquire for more information. Many hotels have walking and hiking maps and can provide local guides.

The **Fox's Bay Bird Sanctuary**, three miles northwest of Plymouth on the coast, offers an interesting trail around the reserve, ending at the beach where good swimming and picnic sites can be found. This mangrove swamp is a primary nesting site for herons, cuckoos, kingfishers and gallinules, but caution must be taken to avoid the poisonous manchineel tree whose sap can burn the living daylights out of you (the little green fruit should never ever be put in your mouth).

The **Soufriere Hills** dominate the southern third of Montserrat, the youngest of the island's three volcanic formations. The majority of hikers make their first excursions here, since the rainforest covering the peaks are wonderfully dense rainforest. Trails range from the easy to the most challenging, which last all day.

South of Plymouth, on a thirty-minute drive over a paved road is **Galway's Soufriere**. The crater is a boil-boil-toil-and-trouble type, active enough for a great photograph. A fifteen-minute (slightly treacherous) walk from the road will take you through a deep green forest as the sickening-sweet smell of sulphur spurs you forward. Not a few hikers have burned themselves on the bubbling water because they ventured too close, so watch out, and make sure you are wearing sturdy hiking shoes. Nearby, a look back can be found at the Galway's Plantation, an 18th-century sugar mill and boiling house now under the auspices of the National Trust. Organized hikes to Galway's Soufriere are arranged through tour companies in Plymouth and guides can be hired at the police station in St. Patrick's Village.

On the south side of Galway's Soufriere, a foot path leads to **Roche's Estate** on the windward side, leading through a bamboo forest with 80-ft. high canes. Descending from the crater, the trail reaches a level area that runs along the forested slopes of the South Soufriere Hill to Roche's Estate (about 2-1/2 hours). If you continue on the path, you'll reach some of the most isolated, primitive areas in Montserrat, reachable only by foot. If you climb the other side of the *ghaut* (the Amerindian term for "ravine"), you'll be heading for **Bamboo Forest**, a protected reserve where you can hear the rare call of the Montserrat oriole, the national bird. The hike to **Long Ground** requires enormous effort and takes 5 hours one way, even for experienced hikers. You must arrange transportation back from Long Island to Plymouth.

A fantastic natural phenomenon is the 70-ft. high **Great Alps Waterfall**, where the sun splays into a million rainbow colors as it burns away the morning mist. The falls are only a fifteen-minute drive from Plymouth, but you will have to trek an hour from the road through a foresty landscape. From the canyon of the final approach, you can already begin to feel the cool wind from the falls. Don't hesitate to take a shower under the heavy hydro-massage of the cascade. (Boy George, Sting and Paul McCartney have all done the same, and sang, to boot, at the top of their lungs.) Bird-watchers will be delighted with the variety of herons, egrets, cuckoos and kingfishers that can be glimpsed in the **Foxes Bay Bird Sanctuary**, north of Plymouth.

One of the best hikes in Montserrat leads to **Chance Peak**, as you pass through rain and montane forests. You can complete the trail in one morning. The last leg of the hike follows a steep and narrow trail through what is considered the best elfin vegetation in the Caribbean.

What Else to See

The first compelling sights on Montserrat are the natural ones, and you should schedule most of your vacation time around those. The city of Plymouth holds some very interesting old wooden buildings of various sizes and styles, and fortunately, they were not much destroyed by Hurricane Hugo. The grounds of the Victorian Government House may be toured weekdays, except Wednesday, on a green hill above Wapping Village. Historical buffs will enjoy the **Montserrat Museum**, ensconced in an old sugar mill at Richmond Hill in Plymouth. Some artifacts date back to the original native inhabitants, as far back as pre-Columbian history. Devoted philatelists should ask for the huge collection of stamps hidden in the bank vault. The harbor is somewhat quiet, but do stop by the local market on Friday and Saturday when all the local vendors turn out. The Christmas season is the only time when nightlife in Plymouth can be described as anything beyond plebeian.

Historical Sites

Galways Estate   ★★★

Near Plymouth, Plymouth.

A thriving sugar plantation for some 250 years, this estate dates back to the 1700s. It's now in ruins, but has been selected for renovation by the Smithsonian Institute under the auspices of the Montserrat National Trust. You can inspect the impressive sugar mill, great house, windmill tower and other structures.

Museums and Exhibits

Montserrat Museum   ★★★

Richmond Hill, Plymouth, ☎ *(809) 491-5443.*

Located in an old sugar mill, the country's national museum tells its history from pre-Columbian times to the present. On display are old photographs, maps, natural history exhibits and ancient artifacts. Donations are welcome. Free admission.

Tours

Fox's Bay Bird Sanctuary   ★★★

Grove Road, Richmond Estate.

This mangrove swamp and bog encompasses 15 acres and is home to lots of feathered friends, including egrets and cuckoos. The nature trail leads to the beach.

Galway's Soufriere   ★★★

Near Upper Galway, south-central Montserrat.

A hike of 20 minutes or so up in the hills some 1700 feet above sea level takes you to this volcanic field, complete with a bubbling crater and the overpowering stench of sulfur.

Great Alps Waterfall   ★★★★

Shooters Hill Village, near St. Patrick's.

Stop in Shooters Hill Village to hire a guide for this quite strenuous hike through verdant rainforest that takes at least 45 minutes. Your reward is the awesome falls, which come from the White River and cascade down 70 feet into a shallow pool.

BEST VIEW:

Panoramic seascapes are compelling from the top of the 18th century Fort St. George, 1184 feet above sea level. It's a fifteen-minute drive from Plymouth.

Sports

Most of the island's activities are centered on scuba, snorkeling and sunbathing. (For diving sites, see above). Three tennis courts are available, asphalt ones at the Vue Pointe Hotel and the Montserrat Golf Club, and a floodlit court at the Montserrat Springs Hotel. The Montserrat Golf Club's 18-hole course, carries a tremendous reputation in the Caribbean. Day sails to Redonda, an island 16 miles northwest of Montserrat, can be arranged. Other boat trips along the coast can be arranged through your hotel or directly with boat captains and dive operators in Plymouth. Horseback riding is available at Sanford Farms for riders of all expertise and ages—over the beach, through the countryside and on all-day picnic rides. Overnight expeditions for two or more riders can also be arranged in advance.

Montserrat Golf club

Old Town, Belham Valley.
This very hilly (and therefore rather challenging) course encompasses 100 acres. It has just 11 holes, but by playing some twice, you get a full 18. There's a bar and clubhouse in a converted cotton gin. Greens fees are about $23.

Watersports

Various locations, Plymouth.
Try these outfits for watersports: **Vue Point Hotel** *(☎ 491-5210)* for general equipment, **Danny Water Sports** *(☎ 491-5645)* for windsurfing and other equipment, **Sea Wolf Diving School** *(☎ 491-7807)* for scuba excursions and instruction, and **Captain Martin** *(☎ 491-5738)* for sailing and snorkel trips.

Where to Stay

Highest Rated Hotels in Montserrat

★★★★ **ClubMed Buccaneer's Creek**

★★★ **Montserrat Springs Hotel**

★★★ **Villas of Montserrat**

★★★ **Vue Pointe Hotel**

Most Exclusive Hotels in Montserrat

★★★ **Montserrat Springs Hotel** $85–$165

Fielding's Best Value Hotels in Montserrat

★★ **Providence Guest House** $45–$85

★★★ **Montserrat Springs Hotel** $85–$165

★★★★ **ClubMed Buccaneer's Creek** $700–$1550

The lodging options on Montserrat could fit into the palm of your hand. Take your pick from two resort hotels, one standard hotel, rental condos, or guest house. Count on the trade winds to keep you cool, not air-conditioning. Check your bill for any extra charges that you didn't make, but expect the 7–10 percent room tax to be added to the final tab.

Hotels and Resorts

Vue Pointe is the hub of island life, congenial owned and run by an island family—the West Indian barbecue on Wednesday nights attracts everyone around. Views are not great at the Flora Fountain, but its West Indian buffet breakfast is the only place to be on Saturday morning. If you want to indulge in local delicacies. Montserrat Springs is 25 minutes by taxi from the airport and contains a pair of hot and cold baths since it is located in the site of natural springs.

ClubMed Buccaneer's Creek   ★★★★

Pointe Marine, Ste. Anne, ☎ *(800) 258-2633, 596-76-72-72.*
One of the Club Meds that still does the lion's share with singles, this village doesn't allow kids under 12. Very nicely designed, the resort covers 48 acres with lots of

coconut groves and winding footpaths. The beach is one of Martinique's best, and there you'll find all the watersports anyone could hope for, though scuba diving costs extra. Other activities include golfing on a Robert Trent Jones course 45 minutes away (they'll take you there, and you will pay greens fees), seven tennis courts, exercise classes, softball, billiards, ping-pong, and organized picnics and boat rides. Geared toward those who like group activity, this all-inclusive resort is best for singles looking for love (or at least lust) and outgoing couples. Accommodations are similar to other Club Meds: very simple and spartan, but also comfortable and clean. This year, the 4th Annual Club Med Bowl takes place here from April 1-8, with former Super Bowl champs on hand to sign autographs and conduct workshops. Rates are $700 to $1550 per week, double occupancy, plus $30 initiation fee and $50 annual fee. 300 rooms. Credit Cards: A.

Flora Fountain Hotel $50–$80 ★★

Lower Dagenham Road, ☎ *(809) 491-6092.*
Single: $50–$65. Double: $65–$80.
This hotel in city center attracts mostly business travelers. Built around a circular courtyard with an impressive fountain, it offers basic rooms with twin beds and balconies. Good for those who want to be in the center of town, but sun lovers will be happier at a beach property, or at least a hotel with a pool. 16 rooms. Credit Cards: V, MC, A.

Montserrat Springs Hotel $85–$165 ★★★

Richmond Hill, ☎ *(800) 253-2134, (809) 491-2481.*
Single: $85–$145. Double: $115–$165.
Set on a hillside with pretty sea views, this hotel has its own hot mineral springs, and guests can while away the hours soaking in a hot or cold whirlpool. Guest rooms, located in villas, are generally spacious and nicely done. There are also six suites with full kitchens. The steeply sloping grounds include a restaurant, two bars, a pool, two tennis courts, and the beach, where watersports await. 46 rooms. Credit Cards: V, MC, A.

Vue Pointe Hotel $80–$160 ★★★

Isles Bay Beach, ☎ *(800) 235-0709, (809) 491-5210.*
Single: $80–$150. Double: $105–$160.
Situated on a secluded hill above the beach, four miles from Plymouth, this property is Montserrat's best bet. Accommodations are housed in stucco buildings or hexagonal villas, all with Danish teak and rattan furnishings, twin beds and sitting areas. No air conditioning, but breezes help keep things cool. The grounds, which slope down to a black sand beach, include a pool, two tennis courts, a dining room with great food and two bars. Service is excellent. 40 rooms. Credit Cards: V, MC, A.

Apartments and Condominiums

Lots of Americans and Canadians are building second homes in Montserrat, contributing to the building boom of condos and apartments. If you want to save money, you'll have to be satisfied with an out-of-the-way location, a bad view, or small rooms. You can find luxurious apartments, but you'll have to add the cost of a car to your final bill. If you stay in a house around Vue Pointe, you'll be close to the supermarkets in Plymouth and the local vegetable market. Some of the best villas, rented in the owner's absence are the ones at Villas of Montserrat.

Belham Valley Hotel $255–$480   ★

Old Towne, ☎ *(809) 491-5553.*

This small complex sits on a hill overlooking Belham Valley (hence the name) and its river, near the Montserrat Golf Course. The complex includes one studio apartment, one two-bedroom apartment and a studio cottage, all with fully equipped kitchens and stereos, but no air conditioning. The restaurant is highly regarded, but there's nothing else on-site. The beach can be walked to in under 10 minutes. Rates are $255 to $480 per week. 3 rooms. Credit Cards: MC, A.

Lime Court Apartments $30–$50   ★

☎ *(809) 491-5069.*
Single: $30–$50. Double: $30–$50.

Located in the center of town, this small apartment building sells out fast due to its very reasonable rates. Units range from studios to two-bedroom apartments, all with full kitchenettes and maid service. The penthouse unit is by far the best and well worth the few extra dollars. There's nothing on-site in the way of recreation or dining, but lots within walking distance, including the beach. 8 rooms. Credit Cards: MC, A.

Shamrock Villas $630–$2000   ★★

☎ *(809) 491-4660.*

Located on a hillside near the Montserrat Springs Hotel, this complex consists of condominiums rented out in their owners' absence. Each is individually decorated and has a full kitchen and nice views. No air conditioning, though, and maid service costs extra. There's a pool on-site but little else. Shamrock also rents out villas located around the island, many with their own pool. Condos cost $430 to $670 per week, while villas run $630 to $2000. 20 rooms. Credit Cards: Not Accepted.

Villas of Montserrat $1400–$2000

☎ *(809) 491-5513.*

Located on a mountainside overlooking Isle Bay north of Plymouth, these three villas are quite luxurious, as they should be, since they cost a small fortune. Each has three bedrooms, three bathrooms (one with Jacuzzi), a living room, dining room, stereo, TV, and full kitchens with microwaves and dishwashers. Each also has maid service (only on weekdays) and their own pool. The services of a cook can be arranged. Rates are $1400 to $2000 per week; each villa sleeps six. 3 rooms. Credit Cards: Not Accepted.

Inns

Providence Guest House $45–$85

St. Peter's, ☎ *(809) 491-6476.*
Single: $45–$55. Double: $65–$85.

Located about 20 minutes from Plymouth in a country setting, this guesthouse has hosted the likes of Paul McCartney and Stevie Wonder. (Obviously, they rented out the whole house.) The old plantation house has been beautifully restored and has just two rooms for guests, both on the ground floor and very nicely decorated.

Wonderful views from the pool deck. There's a communal kitchenette, or you can arrange for the owners to make you dinner. Lovely, but a bit too off on its own for some tourists. You'll definitely want a car. 2 rooms. Credit Cards: Not Accepted.

Low Cost Lodging

Do ask around for rooms in private homes—someone always knows someone. Moose's Guest House is for the young at heart who don't mind sharing a bathroom. Lots of West Indian businessman stay at the Oriole Plaza hotel in the center of town.

Marie's Guest House   **$35–$35**   ★

   ☎ *(809) 419-2745.*
Single: $35. Double: $35.
This small inn in a garden setting near Plymouth offers simple but comfortable non-air-conditioned rooms at a price that's hard to beat. Guests share the kitchen, while each room has its own bath. 4 rooms. Credit Cards: Not Accepted.

Oriole Plaza Hotel   **$70–$70**   ★

   Parliament Street.
Single: $70. Double: $70.
Appealing mainly to business travelers, this modest hotel is right in the center of town, about a five-minute walk to the beach. Rooms are simple and basic, and rely on ceiling fans to keep things cool. There's a bar and restaurant on-site, but little else. 12 rooms. Credit Cards: MC, A.

Where to Eat

Highest Rated Restaurants in Montserrat

★★★★★ **Belham Valley Restaurant**

★★★ **Blue Dolphin**

★★★ **Emerald Cafe**

★★★ **Montserrat Springs Hotel**

★★★ **Mrs. Morgan's**

★★★ **Niggy's Bistro**

★★★ **Vue Pointe Restaurant**

Most Exclusive Restaurants in Montserrat

★★★★★ **Belham Valley Restaurant**	$14–$23
★★★ **Montserrat Springs Hotel**	$11–$19
★★★ **Niggy's Bistro**	$7–$17

Fielding's Best Value Restaurants in Montserrat

★★★ **Montserrat Springs Hotel**	$11–$19
★★★ **Emerald Cafe**	$4–$20
★★★ **Niggy's Bistro**	$7–$17
★★★★★ **Belham Valley Restaurant**	$14–$23

The volcanic lava on the island allows an enormous variety of vegetables to grow with gusto, from cucumbers, to breadfruit, tomatoes, pumpkin, cabbages, and the less familiar West Indian squashlike Christophene. The two national dishes are goat-water, made of goat meat and flavored with scallions and thyme, called "herbs and chile," and mountain chicken, which is actually gigantic frog legs cooked in a variety of ways. Don't miss biting down into a Montserrat *pawpaw*(papaya); it's a memory most never forget. Great food and great island music can be had at **Niggy's**, in an old clapboard house in

Kinsale, south of Plymouth. For elegance and top-class cuisine, try the **Vue Pointe Restaurant** at the hotel. **Emerald Cafe** is now considered an institution on the island since it was opened in 1988; recognizable food at a good price makes the floral ambiance even more pleasant. The **Blue Dolphin** restaurant is the prime spot to be initiated into the delicacy called "mountain chicken"— actually a large meaty frog that lives on the flanks of Mount Chance and is hunted after dark. Here it's served marinated in a spicy red sauce then deep-fried in batter. Don't miss tasting *Ting*, a popular carbonated grapefruit drink which has migrated from St. Kitts.

Belham Valley Restaurant $$$ ★ ★ ★ ★ ★

Old Towne, Belham Valley, ☎ (809) 491-5553.
International cuisine. Specialties: Conch Fritters, Seafood Delight.
Lunch: 12:00 a.m.–2:00 p.m., entrees $14–$23.
Dinner: 6:30 p.m.–11:00 p.m., entrees $14–$23.

This hotel dining room in a posh residential section of the island draws everyone in sooner or later for the serene views from an outdoor terrace and the chef's creative ways with fine local ingredients. The Seafood Delight, a trio of piscatorial pleasures (often including lobster) is blanketed with an herbed Vermouth sauce. The moderately-priced dinners often include a salad and fresh vegetables. When available, try the mango mousse or coconut cheesecake. Lunch is a viable option during the week in season. Associated Hotel: Belham Valley Hotel. Reservations recommended.
Credit Cards: V, MC, A.

Blue Dolphin $$ ★ ★ ★

Amersham ☎ (809) 491-3263.
International cuisine. Specialties: Mountain Chicken.
Lunch: 12:00 a.m.–2:00 p.m., entrees $9–$20.
Dinner: 6:00 p.m.–12:00 p.m., entrees $9–$20.

The interior of this West Indian restaurant in the Plymouth hills is nothing to brag about, but the mountain chicken (frog's legs) is the best in town, often prepared with a garlic sauce. Vegetarians won't feel slighted either, with a wide variety of fresh greens and starches available, including peas and rice and pumpkin soup. Closed: Sun. Reservations required.

Emerald Cafe $$ ★ ★ ★

Wapping Road, ☎ (809) 491-3821.
International cuisine.
Lunch: 8:00 a.m.–4:00 p.m., entrees $4–$20.
Dinner: 4:00 p.m.–12:00 p.m., entrees $4–$20.

There's something for everyone at this indoor-outdoor eatery located in a Plymouth suburb—burgers, crepes and West Indian blue plate specials. That often means mountain chicken, or fresh seafood served with rice and local vegetables. If you don't rate a table on the terrace under umbrellas, join a companionable group inside. This is also a good spot for a drink. Reservations recommended.

Evergreen Cafe $ ★ ★

Upper Marine Drive,
American cuisine.

Lunch: 7:00 a.m.–4:00 p.m., entrees $2–$12.
Dinner: 4:00 p.m.–8:00 p.m., entrees $2–$12.

Folks needing a fast-food hit head on up to this no-frills cafe with a bakery attached. The burgers, pizzas and fried chicken dishes are relatively expensive for the surroundings ($5-12), but the quality is pretty good, and there's always a crowd. It might be a better idea to pick up a pastry here for breakfast or a tea time snack. Credit Cards: Not Accepted.

Golden Apple $ ★★

Cook Hill, Cook Hill, ☎ (809) 491-2187.
Latin American cuisine. Specialties: Goat Water.
Lunch: entrees $5–$10.
Dinner: entrees $5–$10.

This spacious local eatery is one of a growing number of weekend-only goat water pit stops. The bizarrely-named national dish of Montserrat is a heady brew of goat meat cooked until tender, with an infusion of cloves, spices, and vegetables. Portions served are pretty hefty. Chicken and rice, conch and fish dishes are also available. Closed: Sun. Credit Cards: Not Accepted.

Montserrat Springs Hotel $$ ★★★

Richmond Hill, ☎ (809) 491-2481.
Latin American cuisine.
Lunch: 8:00 a.m.–3:00 p.m., entrees $4–$7.
Dinner: 3:00 p.m.–11:00 p.m., entrees $11–$19.

The vista from the poolside restaurant of this upscale hotel is spectacular, encompassing Chance's Peak (the highest on the island) and the Caribbean Sea. Unfortunately, the cuisine is nothing to write home about, with sandwiches and such for lunch and surf and turf for dinner. A better bet is the Sunday barbecue served from noon to 3 p.m.—for under $25, you get grilled chicken, fish or meat, served with island veggies, a plethora of salads, and a choice of two homemade desserts. Associated Hotel: Montserrat Springs Hotel. Reservations recommended. Credit Cards: D, V, MC, A.

Mrs. Morgan's $ ★★★

Airport Road, St. John's, ☎ (809) 491-5419.
Latin American cuisine. Specialties: Goat Water.
Dinner: entrees $4–$5.

Visitors and residents return time and time again for Mrs. Morgan's homemade goat water stew served only on Friday and Saturday. The humble hut, which serves as a bar the rest of the week, is located between the airport and Carr's Bay, a tiny fishing port. At these prices, a few bowls (bet you can eat only one) could feed a crowd. Call ahead to see what else she's preparing—it's a very informal operation. Usually open from 11:30 until the food runs out. Closed: Mon, Tue, Wed, Thur, Sun. Credit Cards: Not Accepted.

Niggy's Bistro $$ ★★★

Kinsale, ☎ (809) 491-7489.
International cuisine. Specialties: Beef Tenderloin with Bordelaise Sauce, Scampi.
Dinner: 6:00 p.m.–10:30 p.m., entrees $7–$17.

Local politicos chew the fat (but not on the food) at this pension and restaurant in a pretty cottage in the suburb of Kinsale. The place is often abuzz with Hollywood talk (ex-actor Anthony Overman is the owner), music and fun. Diners eat outside on picnic benches, and the fare is often a melange of West Indian and international specialties served with pasta and salad. The bar, a converted boat, is a great gimmick. Associated Hotel: Niggy's Guest House. Closed: Sun. Reservations recommended. Credit Cards: V, MC.

Oasis   **$$**   ★★

Wapping, ☎ *(809) 491-2328.*
International cuisine.
Lunch: 12:00 a.m.–1:30 p.m., entrees $5–$10.
Dinner: 6:30 p.m.–10:00 p.m., entrees $5–$16.
This place, located in an old stone structure, has plenty of atmosphere, and is a cool spot on warm days. But most patrons opt for the airy patio to nosh on fish and chips and such—the owners are English. If you don't fancy fish, there's chicken, steak, red snapper, pizza and vegetarian platters; the possibilities are endless. Closed: Mon, Wed. Credit Cards: Not Accepted.

The Attic   **$**   ★★

Upper Marine Drive, ☎ *(809) 491-2008.*
Latin American cuisine.
Lunch: 8:00 a.m.–3:00 p.m., entrees $2–$10.
Dinner: 6:00 p.m.–9:30 p.m., entrees $2–$10.
It's not really in an attic, located on the second level of a nondescript building in Plymouth. But the small size and bustle give this place a cozy feel. The menu is basically a list of tasty West Indian and American dishes like rotis, burgers, fish and sometimes lobster and goat water. Tends to get crowded at times, but the line moves quickly. Closed: Sun. Credit Cards: Not Accepted.

The Village Place   **$$**   ★★

Salem, north of Plymouth, ☎ *(809) 491-5202.*
American cuisine.
Dinner: 6:00 p.m.–12:00 p.m., entrees $5–$16.
This bar and restaurant (with an emphasis on bar) used to be the hangout of Jagger, Clapton and other visiting British rock greats when George Martin's Air Studios was up and running in the pre-Hurricane Hugo era. The Place is still popular with locals and other scenemakers who like the loud party atmosphere, the rum drinks and some of owner Andy Lawrence's thyme-marinated fried chicken. Since there's not much nightlife on this peaceful island, the Place, which stays open until at least midnight, should keep night owls pacified. Closed: Tue. Credit Cards: Not Accepted.

Vue Pointe Restaurant   **$$$**   ★★★

Old Towne, north of, Belham Valley, ☎ *(809) 491-5211.*
Latin American cuisine.
Lunch: 12:30 p.m.–2:00 p.m., entrees $13–$23.
Dinner: 7:00 p.m.–9:30 p.m., entrees $13–$23.
Few people can resist the charms of this place—welcoming proprietors, a jumping Wednesday evening barbecue, stupendous views of a black sand beach below, and

simple, but tasty cuisine. You can visit it for a simple lunch of seasonal fruit salads or sandwiches, a fixed-price ($25) dinner of mountain chicken and all the trimmings, or the aforementioned barbecue. If you opt for this event, get here early; it's popular. Otherwise, a more sedate barbecue is offered on Sundays around noon in the winter. Associated Hotel: Vue Pointe Hotel. Reservations recommended. Credit Cards: V, MC, A.

Where to Shop

Montserrat has a surprising number of crafts for a tiny island. Handwoven tapestries make excellent gifts, available from Montserrat Tapestries. Many island craftsmen work with wood, carving out fabulous furniture—chairs, beds, and tables can even be made custom-ordered. (Do inquire first about shipping charges.) To see leather workers creating highly original designs, check out the studios at **Cultural Frontier** or **Productions Tannery**. Fine leather jewelry made by local artists can be found at **Carol's Corner**, as well as the Montserrat cookbook *Goatwater*. Locally handwoven cotton products are best bought at the **Montserrat Sea island Cotton Company**.

Montserrat Directory

ARRIVAL AND DEPARTURE

LIAT provides several daily (18-minute) flights from Antigua, where you can catch a variety of other direct connections to the states (BWIA, Air Canada, British Airway, and American). LIAT also flies from St. Thomas, via Sint Maarten St. Kitts. WINAIR now provides two daily flights from Sint Maarten.

The departure tax is U.S.$6 for those over twelve years of age.

CLIMATE

Temperate and tropical, temperatures average 73.5 degrees F to 86.5 degrees F., with very little variation from season to season Humidity is blissfully low. Rain is most frequent in April and May, and July-September.

DOCUMENTS

U.S. and Canadian visitors need to show proof of citizenship (passport, birth certificate with photo ID), for stays up to six months. Those who do not show an ongoing or return ticket may be required to deposit a sum of money equivalent to that needed for repatriation.

ELECTRICITY

Current runs 22–230 volts AC, 60 cycles, so you will need an electrical transformer and an adapter.

GETTING AROUND

Taxi drivers are omnipresent whenever a flight arrives. Expect to pay about $11 from the airport to the town of Plymouth. Buses, another easy way to travel, cost about $1–2 one day.

Car rental agencies are only local outfits. Toyotas, Jeeps and Daihatsus are available at the reliable **Pauline's Car Rentals**, on Church Road *(P.O. Box 171) in Plymouth* ☎ *2345*. Cars can be delivered to the airport or your hotel. Cards are accepted. To rent a car, you need to show a valid driver's license and pay a $12. Ask the police officers at the Immigration Department at the airport for assistance.

LANGUAGE

Most everyone speaks English, though the lilt resembles a strong Irish brogue.

MEDICAL EMERGENCIES

Glendon Hospital in Plymouth ☎ *2552* has 68 beds and can provide adequate care for short-term cases. Serious emergencies should be flown to larger islands. Ask your hotel to suggest a doctor on call.

MONEY

The official currency is the Eastern Caribbean dollar. Some of the best exchange rates can be found at the Royal Bank of Canada.

TELEPHONE

The area code is *809*. Local numbers are four digits.

For international calls, skip calling from your room and head for the Cable and Wireless Ltd. on Houston Street, ☎ *2112*, open Monday-Thursday 7:30 a.m.–6:00 p.m., Friday 7:30 a.m.–10:00 p.m., and Saturday 7:30 a.m.–6:00 p.m. You'll find a new digital telephone system, faxes, telegraph, telex and data facilities. Phone cards (purchased there) and credit cards, toll-free service, and cellular phones can be used.

TIME

Atlantic Standard Time, one hour later than New York City.

TIPPING AND TAXES

Expect a ten percent service charge to be added to all bills. Tipping a taxi driver will make him (or her) happy, but there is no expectation.

TOURIST INFORMATION

The Montserrat Tourist Board is located on Church Road in the Government Headquarters building. The mailing address is *P.O. Box 7, Plymouth;* ☎ *2230*, FAX *7430*. The office has produced a new brochure delineating a cross-section of restaurants and bars on the island.

MONTSERRAT HOTELS		RMS	RATES	PHONE	FAX
Plymouth					
★★★★	ClubMed Buccaneer's Creek	300	$700–$1550	(800) 258-2633	
★★★	Montserrat Springs Hotel	46	$85–$165	(800) 253-2134	(809) 491-4070
★★★	Villas of Montserrat	3	$1400–$2000	(809) 491-5513	
★★★	Vue Pointe Hotel	40	$80–$160	(800) 235-0709	(809) 491-4813
★★	Flora Fountain Hotel	16	$50–$80	(809) 491-6092	(809) 491-2568
★★	Providence Guest House	2	$45–$85	(809) 491-6476	
★★	Shamrock Villas	20	$530–$2000	(809) 491-4660	
★	Belham Valley Hotel	3	$255–$480	(809) 491-5553	(809) 491-5283
★	Lime Court Apartments	8	$30–$50	(809) 491-5069	
★	Marie's Guest House	4	$35	(809) 419-2745	
★	Oriole Plaza Hotel	12	$70		

MONTSERRAT RESTAURANTS		LOCATION	PHONE	ENTREE
Plymouth				
American				
★★	Evergreen Cafe	Plymouth		$2–$12
★★	The Village Place	Plymouth	(809) 491-5202	$5–$16••
International				
★★★★★	Belham Valley Restaurant	Belham Valley	(809) 491-5553	$14–$23
★★★	Blue Dolphin	Amersham	(809) 491-3263	$9–$20
★★★	Emerald Cafe	Plymouth	(809) 491-3821	$4–$20
★★★	Niggy's Bistro	Kinsale	(809) 491-7489	$7–$17••
★★	Oasis	Plymouth	(809) 491-2328	$5–$16
Latin American				
★★★	Montserrat Springs Hotel	Plymouth	(809) 491-2481	$4–$19
★★★	Mrs. Morgan's	St. John's	(809) 491-5419	$4–$5••
★★★	Vue Pointe Restaurant	Belham Valley	(809) 491-5211	$13–$23
★★	Golden Apple	Cook Hill	(809) 491-2187	$5–$10
★★	The Attic	Plymouth	(809) 491-2008	$2–$10

Note: • Lunch Only

           •• Dinner Only

NEVIS

St. John's Fig Tree Church in Nevis contains interesting memorials to Admiral Nelson and his wife Fanny Nesbit.

With genteel plantations and scenic pastoral vistas, Nevis offers a taste of the old Caribbean. Sister to St. Kitts, Nevis is the quiet child, shunning the extravagant Kittian casinos for the leisure of a quiet drink on the veranda of a 200-year-old inn. To tell the truth, Nevis is no savvy island; sugar is sold for less than it costs to produce, and with the exception of the recent unfolding of the Four Seasons Resort on Pinney's Beach—one of the most beautiful strands in the Caribbean—nothing aggressive is much being done about tourism. Instead, what you find on Nevis are genuinely hospitable people, willing to share the quiet charm of their tiny island and the seemingly unlimited bank of their natural resources. No one seems to move faster than a ceiling fan in Nevis, and the dreams you might have, after a dinner of "hubcap chicken" (yes, that's right, deep-fried in hubcaps) will be about the luscious array of tropical fruits that will grace your breakfast buffet in the morning. Despite the laid-back nature of the island, however, locals have not remained lax in regard to ecology; in fact, Nevis boasts some of the strictest ecological laws in the world. For that reason, the hundred cruiseliners who stopped in Nevis last year did little to upset the island's perfect ecological balance and the island continues today to be a pristine environment.

Bird's Eye View

Six miles across and 18 miles around, Nevis is a little gumdrop-shaped volcanic island separated from St. Kitts by the two-mile Narrows Channel. Ecologically wilder than St. Kitts, Nevis has an exuberant rampage of trees, creepers and giant ferns that appear the moment you creep out of the sleepy capital of Charlestown on the single round-island road. The highest point, Nevis Peak, is usually shrouded in clouds and mist, which inspired Columbus to name the island "Las Nieves." What were once huge plantations have now returned to scrub punctuated by gardens lovingly cultivated by islanders on the slopes of Mount Nevis.

Charlestown, the capital (population 1200) is a laconic sprawl of pastel walls, tin roofs and shady gardens, one of the most well preserved in the Caribbean. As on St. Kitts, regulations prohibit any building taller than a palm tree. One reason the island has remained so virginal is that the Brimstone Hill Fortress of St. Kitts, perched like a sentinel high above the sea, was so intimidating that ship captains often changed course rather than fall within the range of its guns. Today the proverbial cannons have been replaced by the residential community's commitment to ecological preservation—so strong that the federal government has been inspired to initiate some of the strictest building and marine regulations in the world. Hurricane Hugo damaged Nevis badly, but today, most of the island has recovered. One of the strangest, but most wonderful facts about St. Kitts-Nevis is that there are more monkeys than people on St. Kitts and Nevis combined (125,000 monkeys vs. 46,000 humans).

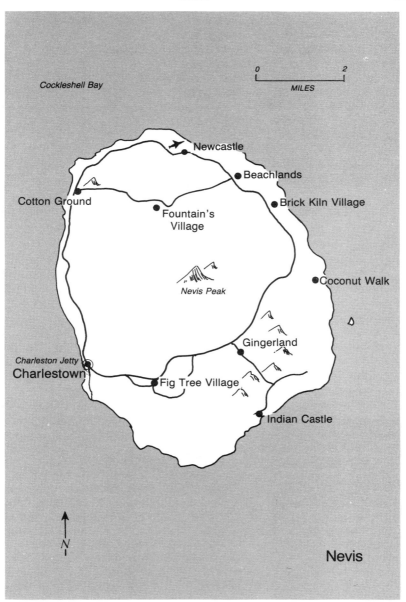

Nevis

History

Nevis has had a long history for such a short island. After spotting an island and naming it St.Christopher (later nicknamed St. Kitts) for his patron saint, Columbus spied a cloud-covered conic island rising out of the water during his second voyage, dubbing it "Nuestra Señora de las Nieves" or Our lady of the Snows—since it reminded him of the snow-capped Pyrenees—and promptly went on his way. British troops arrived in 1623, first joining forces with the French to conquer the Spanish and decimate the resident Carib Indian tribes, then later duking it out with the Gallic forces for the next 150 years. The British used St. Kitts as a base to colonize Nevis, Antigua, Barbuda, Tortola and Montserrat, while the French managed to dominate Martinique, St. Martin, Guadeloupe, St. Barts, La Désirade and Les Saintes. The Treaty of Versailles in 1783 ceded the islands to Britain. Known as the "Queen of the Carribbees" in the late 18th century for its thriving sugar trade, Nevis later saw its fortunes decline with the abolition of slavery in 1834. Almost 150 years later in 1983, Nevis, with St. Kitts, would become the Caribbean's newest independent country with the establishment of the federation of St. Kitts-Nevis in 1983.

People

The rhythm of life in Nevis is gentle and noninvasive, much quieter than St. Kitts. The local people are still imbued with age-old superstitions; door frames are painted blue to keep "jumby" spirits out in accordance with ancient obeah voodoo customs. Many still use herbal cures and some Nevisians retain their respect for the mystical powers of big fat toads called *crappos*. One of the most beguiling aromas you will smell throughout the island is that of souse, or pork stew. The local drink is *mauby*, made from the bark of a tree. A local phrase used commonly is "pocket o' mumps," which roughly means "in a good-spirited goof-off mood."

Nelson Spring on Nevis is one of the beautiful lagoons author James Michener visited while researching his novel **Caribbean.**

Beaches

Almost six miles of white sand, swaying palms and whispering surf makes **Pinney's Beach** (on the leeward side) the longest. It's also the location of the **Four Seasons Resort**, which boasts 196 luxurious rooms and suites, fine cuisine, myriad activities and an abundance of watersports. There are several beach bars here. **Booby Island** in the middle of Narrows Channel is mostly inhabited by pelicans; the waters around there are good for diving. **White Bay Beach**, down Hanleys Road on the Atlantic coast side, can get dangerous on windy days, but generally is a lively alternative to the calmer surf at Pinney's. A reef farther out from here usually renders good fishing. A smaller beach can be found at **Mosquito Bay** (live music and partying on Sunday afternoons) and the waters under **Hurricane Hill** support good snorkeling. Snorkeling is good at a small beach called **Mosquito Bay**.

Do consider chartered boat excursions to the beaches at St. Kitts. Depending on the wind, some windsurfers just let themselves drift from one island to the other.

Dive Sites

Nearly 400 ships sank in the Kitts-Nevis waters between 1492 and 1815. At present, only a mere dozen have been located by three full-time divemasters operating on the two islands. The largest reef is the **Grid Iron**, a long barrier reef that stretches over 6 miles from Conaree on the east coast of St. Kitts to Newcastle Bay on Nevis. These reefs help to protect The Narrows between St. Kitts and Nevis where there is a large, circular reef that spreads over an area about a half-mile in diameter at depths ranging from 18–50 ft. Schools of angelfish are prominent here. On the south side of the reef, called **Monkey Shoals**, thick black coral can be sighted at depths of 35 feet. (For more information on dive sites, see "Dive Sites" in the St. Kitts chapter.)

Treks

Nevis is ideal for those who love to amble down unmarked, unpaved country roads, and along footpaths well trod by locals. With maps in hand, you can go about anywhere here. Hiking through the lush rainforest can be geared to tourists of all villages and athletic inclination. Interesting walks can be arranged over old sugar plantations as well. A special "eco ramble" over the 18th-century **Coconut Walk** and **New River Estates** is held on Sunday-Wednesday.

A spectacular view of St. Kitts and the Caribbean Sea can be found at the **Cliffdwellers Resort**; it will take a hearty hiker to climb the steep hill to the main house perched high above the sea. If you stay till the late afternoon, a fantastic sight is the arrival of cattle egrets on the north end of Pinney's Beach at Nelson's Spring, a freshwater pond where they roost.

Another good hike takes you from **Fountain to Newcastle** on a track that runs along the east side of **Round Hill**. You can ascend part of the way to the summit by car or jeep, but the last half-mile must be done on foot—the sweeping view of **Newcastle** to **Charleston**—will be well worth the effort. North of the main road after Morning Star, on the south coast, there is an area locally known as **Gingerland**, the site of five former plantations whose sugar mills or great houses have been restored into inns. All are situated at about 1000 feet elevation on the southern slope of **Nevis Peak**. It's possible to hike on footpaths between the estate, taking a drink at each, and surveying the panoramic views. The inns can also arrange for you to visit some of the awesome private gardens.

Anyone who wants to escape the "limin'" attitude which seems to descend on nearly everyone should rev up their energy and head for the top of Nevis Peak. The cloud-capped volcano last erupted in 1692, today it still emits odorous gases with temperatures up to 392 degrees F from the vents. Only experienced hikers will make it up the treacherous trail, which is as difficult as any in the Caribbean. In some places, the climb is nearly vertical and you can proceed only by hanging onto vines and roots. Anyone with a shade of vertigo should not even start. The hike takes at least five hours round trip, and a guide can be arranged through your hotel (extremely necessary).

Less challenging, but just as rewarding is the rainforest trail, which starts at **Stoney Hill** at the top of Rawlins Road above Golden Rock Estate and winds north through groves of breadfruit, cocoa and nutmeg trees. From there you traipse through cedar forests to rainforest thick with hummingbirds, thrashers and tremblers. Monkeys can also be seen. A map is available through Golden Rock Estate, which can also arrange a guide. The hike takes three hour round trip.

What Else to See

The history of Nevis is buried behind the shutters and porches of its six great plantation houses, many of them now hotels. A taste of the leisure elegance of these times can still be experienced, especially if you head for one of them, like the Nisbet Plantation Inn, for an afternoon drink on the veranda. **Charleston**, the capital of Nevis (pop.1200) is a tropical rainbow of pastel storefronts, tin roofs and palm-shaded gardens—good for strolling and lingering. Anyone with a nautical interest should look into the new **Nelson Museum**, which offers fascinating displays of Nelsonia in the form of maps, model ships, mildweed prints, ornate costumes and other paraphernalia. You can also visit where Admiral Nelson married his bride, Fannie Nesbit in 1787—the St. John Fig Tree Church; his certificated of marriage is recorded there. In the city proper, a stop at the **Nevis Handicraft Coop** is *de rigeur*—particularly to pick up a few bottles of local fruit wines sold in old soda bottles; among the delicious flavors are sorrel, pawpaw, genip, gooseberry, and homemade pepper sauce. Around the corner is the **Nevis Philatelic Bureau**, which does a brisk business selling first-edition Nevis stamps (different from St. Kitts). Saturday, the market of Charleston along the waterfront, brims with excitement as local farmers and vendors lay out their latest crops and crafts.

The **Eva Wilkin Gallery** on the Clay Ghaut Estate (an old stone plantation) commemorated the work of a now-deceased elderly lady artist whose evocative pastels and watercolors of Nevis life were beloved by the island. Today the gallery, which also shows contemporary Nevis art, is run by a Canadian couple and open to the public. Most will be surprised to discover that a Jewish community once thrived on Nevis, and you can see the restored cemetery and synagogue remains that date back to 1650 (perhaps the oldest in the Caribbean). In the last year a *mikvah*, or ritual bath used in Jewish practices, was also said to be discovered by historians.

Historical Sites

Eden Brown Estate ★★★

Near Huggins Bay, Charlestown.
This government-owned estate house was built in 1740. It is said to be haunted by the ghost of Julia Huggins, who was all set to get married in 1822. But the night before the wedding, the groom and best man got drunk, argued and ended up killing each other in a duel. Poor Julia became a recluse and is said to still hang around the house. The estate also includes ruins from other buildings on the plantation.

Museums and Exhibits

Alexander Hamilton Birthplace ★★★

Low Street, Charlestown.
Hours Open: 8:00 a.m.–4:00 p.m.
This Georgian-style house on the waterfront is actually a replica of Hamilton's childhood home, which was built in 1680 and destroyed by hurricane in the 19th century. Hamilton was born on Nevis in 1755, later emigrated to the fledgling United States, and was appointed by George Washington as the first secretary of the U.S. Treasury. He died in a duel with Aaron Burr. The building contains memorabilia of his life, as well as photographs and exhibits on the island's history. The Nevis House of Assembly is on the second floor. Free admission.

Horatio Nelson Museum ★★★

Bath Road, Charlestown, ☎ (809) 469- 408.
Hours Open: 8:00 a.m.–4:30 p.m.
This small museum commemorates the life of Admiral Nelson, who married local girl Frances Nesbet in the 1787. General admission: $2.00.

Tours

Bath Springs ★★★★

Near Grove Park, Charlestown.
You can soak in a tub of these mineral hot springs for $2 for 15 minutes (longer is not recommended). They are on the site of the once-glamorous Bath Hotel, built in 1778, closed about a century later, and now in ruins. In its heyday, the hotel attracted wealthy guests the world over, who came to soak in its rejuvenating waters and gamble in its casino.

Sports

Waterskiing, windsurfing, snorkeling and scuba are all prime activities on Nevis, and if your hotel can't arrange it, there are several agencies who will. Sport fishing takes advantage of a good supply of wahoo, tuna, kingfish and dorado. A new 18-hole, Robert Trent Jones designed course has now been built at the Four Seasons resort, though some complain that it straddles the island road with its electric carts. Several hotels have tennis courts, the Jack Tar has four (two lighted) and a pro. The Pro-Divers shops, which is the first PADI instruction center on the island, operates fully certified resort diving facilities out of the Turtle Beach and from the Ocean Terrace Inn's Fisherman Wharf's restaurant, located not far from the hotel at water's edge in Pelican Cove. Half-day and full-day charters for cruising to other islands can be arranged through your hotel. (For more information on hiking, see "Treks" above.

The latest craze on Nevis is **horseracing**. Races are sponsored by the Nevis Turf & Jockey Club at the ramshackle track near White Bay at various times throughout the year. Races are generally held on holidays such as Boxing Day, New Year's Day, Tourism Week Sunday in February, Easter Monday, Culturama (the first Monday in August), Labor Day, and Independence Day. Admission is generally $4. The course follows the contour of the land, which means that it's a downhill race to the finish, tails and ears flying; the jockeys are often hard-put to stay astride. The setting is first-class, facing the sea on a rural tract known as Indian castle on the southeastern corner of the island, flanked by palm trees and volcanic mounds. To get to the racetrack, follow Hanley's Road south from Gingerland for two miles down to the sea. For more information call the Hermitage Inn ☎ *(809) 469-3477*.

For more information about diving and snorkeling, see "Dive Sites" above. Also see the chapter of St. Kitts for other activities.

Four Seasons Golf Course

Four Seasons Resort, Pinney's Beach, ☎ *(809) 469-1111.*
Designed by Robert Trent Jones, Jr., this is one of the Caribbean's most scenic and challenging courses. It encompasses 18 holes with tremendous views that made concentrating on your game a tad difficult. Greens fees are $95 for 18 holes if you are staying at the hotel otherwise it is $110. Celebrate the 19th hole at one of this posh resort's watering holes.

Horseback Riding

Various locations, Charlestown.
You can hop on a horse and ride into the sunset at one of three outfits: **Nisbet Plantation** *(*☎ *469-9325* ($45 for two hours)), **Cane Gardens** *(*☎ *469-5648)*, and **Gardner's Estate** *(*☎ *469-5528* ($35 for two hours)).

Watersports

Various locations, Charlestown.
A number of companies offer aqua activity. For general watersports equipment and boating, try **Newcastle Bay Marina** *(*☎ *469-9373)* and **Oualie Beach** *(*☎ *469-9518)*. For deep-sea fishing, contact **The Lady James** *(*☎ *469-1989)* or **Jans Travel Agency** *(*☎ *469-5578)*. For diving, try **Scuba Safaris** *(*☎ *468-9518)* or **Montpelier Plantation** *(*☎ *469-5462)*. Windsurfing can be arranged through **Winston Cooke** *(*☎ *469-9615).)*

Where to Stay

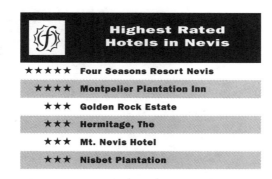

Highest Rated Hotels in Nevis

★★★★★	Four Seasons Resort Nevis
★★★★	Montpelier Plantation Inn
★★★	Golden Rock Estate
★★★	Hermitage, The
★★★	Mt. Nevis Hotel
★★★	Nisbet Plantation

Most Exclusive Hotels in Nevis

★★★	Hermitage, The	$85–$690
★★★	Mt. Nevis Hotel	$170–$440
★★★	Golden Rock Estate	$170–$245

Fielding's Best Value Hotels in Nevis

★★★★	Montpelier Plantation Inn	$150–$280
★★★	Mt. Nevis Hotel	$170–$440
★★★	Hermitage, The	$85–$690
★★★	Nisbet Plantation	$180–$340
★★★	Golden Rock Estate	$170–$245

Until the recent opening of the 350-acre Four Seasons Resort, considered one of the premier lodgings in the Caribbean and the Mt. Nevis Hotel and Beach Club, the island was known primarily for its intimate old plantation inns, most of which still flourish today despite the 1989 rampage of Hurricane Hugo. In general, the standards of rooms are as high as the cuisine, although at the inns, air-conditioning is usually not available. Inn meal prices are usually about $10 per breakfast, $10 for lunch, and $30 for dinner (in American currency). Many of the inns offer free shuttles to beaches and recreational activities and have all their own swimming pools. Rates do not include a seven percent government tax or service charge, usually 10 percent.

The Bath Hotel, with its soothing hot springs, still draws more visitors than any other attraction on Nevis.

Hotels and Resorts

Pinney's Beach Hotel and the **Four Seasons Resort** are the only two properties located on the coconut palm-lined Pinney's Beach overlooking the narrow of St. Kitts.

Four Seasons Resort Nevis   **$180–$555**   ★ ★ ★ ★ ★

Pinney's Beach, ☎ *(800) 332-3442, (809) 469-1111.*
Single: $180–$555. Double: $180–$555.

You can always count on a Four Seasons property for the utmost in style and luxury, and this resort is no exception—in fact, it is one of the Caribbean's best hotels. Scattered over 350 acres opening right onto Nevis' best beach, low-rise buildings house two restaurants, three bars, a well-equipped health club, and air-conditioned guest rooms. Accommodations are lovely, with high-quality furnishings, Persian rugs, large baths, robes, and fresh plants and flowers. The grounds include a championship 18-hole golf course, 10 tennis courts, a large pool, and a health club. All watersports can be found on the very fine beach. Parents can relax after putting their kids in varied supervised programs. Simply fantastic in every aspect. 196 rooms. Credit Cards: CB, V, MC, A.

Mt. Nevis Hotel   **$170–$440**   ★ ★ ★

Shaws Road, Newcastle, ☎ *(809) 469-9373.*
Single: $170–$195. Double: $240–$440.

Located on the slopes of Mt. Nevis, this family-run property includes air-conditioned rooms with VCRs (videos are available to rent) and private patios with great views of St. Kitts. Studio units also have full kitchens. Facilities include a restaurant, bar, pool, and their own beach club on the sand, where watersports await. The hotel owns a ferry that takes guests on moonlight cruises. 32 rooms. Credit Cards: V, MC.

Nisbet Plantation $180–$340 ★★★

Newcastle Beach, ☎ *(800) 344-2049, (809) 469-9325.*
Single: $180–$205. Double: $255–$340.

This well-run property combines the charm of an 18th-century coconut plantation with the amenities of a resort. Set on 35 acres fronting a mile-long beach, one of the island's best, this is the former home of Frances Nisbet, who married Lord Nelson. Accommodations are in air-conditioned cottages, all individually decorated and nicely done with screened-in porches. Facilities include two restaurants, two bars, a tennis court, a large pool, a small library, croquet and watersports. Complimentary laundry service and evening turndown are nice perks. The management will help arrange horseback riding and mountain climbing for the active set. A winner. 38 rooms. Credit Cards: V, MC.

Oualie Beach Hotel $100–$205 ★★

Oualie Beach, ☎ *(800) 255-9684, (809) 469-9735.*
Single: $100–$155. Double: $130–$205.

Located right on the beach, this small property accommodates guests in ginger-bread-style duplex cottages that are pleasant and comfortable. Only some have air conditioning and kitchens, but all sport screened porches with nice views of St. Kitts. There's a dive shop on-site that also handles most watersports. The restaurant is highly regarded. This is one of the few hotels without a pool if that's important to you. 22 rooms. Credit Cards: V, MC, A.

Pinney's Beach Hotel $60–$185 ★

Pinney's Beach, ☎ *(800) 742-4276, (809) 469-5207.*
Single: $60–$70. Double: $75–$185.

This budget property sits right on the beach, which is just about all it has going for it. Rooms are air-conditioned but quite basic. The grounds include a pool, several bars and restaurants, and two tennis courts. Nothing to write home about. 48 rooms. Credit Cards: Not Accepted. Credit Cards: V, MC, A.

Apartments and Condominiums

For grocery household needs, stop by the **Sunshine Shoppers** on Newcastle Airport Road, a one-stop mini-mart. **Nevis Bakery** on Happy Hill Drive in Charlestown features fresh breads, buns, pastries and cakes.

Hurricane Cove Bungalows $95–$400 ★★

Hurricane Bay, ☎ *(809) 469-9462.*
Single: $95–$145. Double: $155–$400.

Set on a steep hill with glorious views, this small complex consists of one- to three-bedroom bungalows with ceiling fans, complete kitchens and covered porches. There's a pool on-site, but little else. The beach is at the foot of the hill. 10 rooms. Credit Cards: MC, A.

Meadville Cottages $50–$80 ★

Meadville Lane, ☎ *(809) 469-5235.*
Single: $50–$80. Double: $50–$80.

Located five minutes from Pinney's Beach, this small complex consists of modest cottages with one or two bedrooms, living/dining rooms, kitchenettes, and verandas. Maid service is available, but that's it for extras. You'll have to cook in or venture out for meals. 10 rooms. Credit Cards: V, MC.

Inns

Croney's Old Manor Hotel $85–$175   ★★

Gingerland, ☎ *(809) 469-3445.*
Single: $85–$135. Double: $135–$175.

Perched high in the hills, this converted plantation house dates back to 1832. Many of the Georgian buildings on-site were made from lava rock. Guest rooms are nicely done and spacious, with marble floors, high ceilings, canopied king beds or twins with mosquito netting, verandas and ceiling fans (no air conditioning). Facilities include a bar, restaurant and pool. They'll shuttle you back and forth to the beach. Nice, but showing its age. 17 rooms. Credit Cards: V, MC, A.

Golden Rock Estate $170–$245   ★★★

Gingerland, ☎ *(809) 469-3346.*
Single: $170–$200. Double: $185–$245.

This 18th-century sugar estate, set high up in the hills, encompasses some 100 acres. Run by the great-great-great granddaughter of the man who built the main house in 1815, it practically oozes charm. Accommodations are in a converted sugar mill or in cottages, all with antiques, island art, canopied king beds, large verandas and ceiling fans in lieu of air conditioning. The estate is surrounded by lush rain forest, with a good hiking trail starting at the property. The grounds include a spring-fed pool, tropical gardens, a tennis court, and free transportation to two beaches or into town. Really wonderful. 15 rooms. Credit Cards: MC, A.

Hermitage, The $85–$690   ★★★

St. John's Parish, ☎ *(809) 469-3177.*
Single: $85–$640. Double: $120–$690.

Set on a 250-year-old plantation up in the hills, this property accommodates guests in restored cottages that are nicely done with Oriental rugs, pitched ceilings, canopied four-poster beds or twin beds, large verandas with hammocks and antiques. Some also have full kitchens. A gorgeous two-bedroom house with its own pool is also available, but quite expensive. The terraced grounds include stables for horseback riding, a pool, tennis and a plantation-style restaurant in an antique-filled room. Nice. 14 rooms. Credit Cards: V, MC, A.

Montpelier Plantation Inn $150–$280   ★★★★

St. John's Parish, ☎ *(800) 243-9420, (809) 469-3462.*
Single: $150–$225. Double: $180–$280.

Set on the slope of Mt. Nevis, this former sugar plantation encompasses 100 lovingly landscaped acres, including an organic garden and orchard that supplies ingredients for much of the excellent food. Accommodations are in cottages and of good size; all are nicely done with large private patios. Ceiling fans keep things cool. There's a pool and tennis court on-site, and they'll shuttle you to the beach, about 10 minutes away, where you can play with their speedboat. 17 rooms. Credit Cards: V, MC.

Where to Eat

★★★★★ Cooperage

★★★★★ Miss June's

★★★ Callaloo

| ★★★★★ | Miss June's | $63–$63 |

Fielding's Best Value Restaurants in Nevis

★★★★★	Miss June's	$63–$63
★★	Cla-Cha-Del	$9–$15
★★★★★	Cooperage	$12–$20

Nevisian cuisine takes shape with such West Indian delicacies as jerked chicken, curried goat, salt-fish casserole, johnnycakes, breadfruit salad and piles of steamed squash and rice 'n' peas. While most guests tend to dine at their hotel—sometimes because the meals are included in the rates, most times because the cuisine is excellent—do take the time to check out other locations. At the **Golden Rock Estate**, you can eat delicious West Indian buffet to the music of the Honey Bees String Band on Saturday nights. A sumptuous afternoon tea is served in the great house of the **Nisbet Plantation Beach Club**. For hearty breakfasts and light snacks, **Sea Spawn**, across from Pinney's Beach, is conveniently located and reasonably priced. Most dress is casual, but the atmosphere in the plantation great houses should inspire romantic dressing.

Callaloo   **$**   ★★★

Main Street, ☎ *(809) 469-5389.*
Latin American cuisine. Specialties: Grilled Kingfish, Burgers, French Pastries, Broasted Chicken.
Lunch: 10:00 a.m.–4:00 p.m., entrees $5–$7.

Dinner: 4:00 p.m.–10:00 p.m., entrees $5–$7.
This unprepossessing place on Main Street in Charlestown is the place to come for fabulous, charbroiled burgers. West Indian specialties abound also, and you have a choice of seating either squeezed in at little tables on a sidewalk patio or in an air-conditioned dining room. Callaloo offers a wide variety of dishes from pizza to pastries. Closed: Sun. Credit Cards: V, MC, A.

Caribbean Confections $$$ ★★

Main Street, ☎ *(809) 469-5685.*
International cuisine. Specialties: Pumpkin Bread, Lamb Curry.
Lunch: 8:00 a.m.–3:00 p.m., entrees $4–$10.
Dinner: 5:00 p.m.–11:00 p.m., entrees $12–$20.
As the name suggests, this popular downtown spot is known for fresh-from-the-oven pumpkin or ginger-infused sweets. Ferry passengers who alight near here come for the hearty breakfasts; others might drop in for lunch or dinner when the menu is either burgers, salads, curries or seafood specials. Dine indoors or in the tree-shaded garden restaurant known as the Courtyard Cafe. Closed: Sun. Credit Cards: V, MC, A.

Cla-Cha-Del $$ ★★

Shaw's Road, Newcastle, ☎ *(809) 469-9640.*
Latin American cuisine. Specialties: Goat Water, Conch, Lobster, Mutton.
Lunch: 9:00-11:00, entrees $5–$9.
Dinner: 9:00-11:00, entrees $9–$15.
Newcastle, on the north coast of Nevis, boasts broad, white-sand beaches, roadside stands with tasteful handicrafts, and the Pinney family's authentic eatery, Cla-Cha-Del. Named after siblings Claudina, Charlie and Delroy, this West Indian dining spot showcases the family's ties to the local fishing industry. Try parrotfish, conch or lobster, or drop in on a weekend for goat water. Burgers, soups and sandwiches are also available. Closed: Mon, Sun. Reservations recommended. Credit Cards: V, MC, A.

Cooperage $$$ ★★★★★

Gingerland, ☎ *(809) 469-3445.*
International cuisine. Specialties: Provimi Veal, Jerk Pork or Chicken, Filet Mignon.
Dinner: 7:00 p.m.–9:30 p.m., entrees $12–$20.
The historical setting and solidly good food help make a meal here well worth making a reservation for. Located in a restored, 17th-century plantation inn, the stone-walled dining room once reverberated with the sounds of coopers making barrels for the sugar mill. The cuisine, which is heavy on imported beef, veal or lamb, reflects the solid midwestern background of owner-hostess Vicki Knorr. For under $20 you can have filet mignon or veal scallopini. For a splurge, the green-pepper soup served with complete meals ($11 extra, includes dessert) is delicious. Associated Hotel: Croney's Old Manor Estate. Reservations recommended. Credit Cards: V, MC, A.

Eddy's $$ ★★

Main Street, ☎ *(809) 469-5958.*
Latin American cuisine. Specialties: Flying Fish, Conch Fritters.

Lunch: 12:00 p.m.–3:00 p.m., entrees $2–$7.
Dinner: 7:30 p.m.–9:30 p.m., entrees $9–$12.

Ever had a flying fish sandwich? Don't let it get away from you at this informal, second-story patio restaurant that's an ideal vantage point for tourist-watching. Inside the warmly decorated old wood townhouse, the crowd tends to be dominated by repeat visitors and permanent residents. Eddy's has a jumpin' bar with potent drinks and a well-attended Wednesday happy hour. Closed: Thur, Sun. Credit Cards: V, MC, A.

Miss June's $$$ ★ ★ ★ ★ ★

Stony Grove Plantation, ☎ (809) 469-5330.
Latin American cuisine. Specialties: All Inclusive West Indian Buffet.
Dinner: prix fixe $63.

Trinidadian Miss June Mestier serves a bountiful buffet groaning with delectable dishes (some 26 in all) several evenings a week, at one seating only, and strictly by reservation. Promptly at 7:30, guests assemble for a cocktail hour. Dinner begins at 8:30 with soup and fish, and then everyone is let loose at the buffet tables. After dinner, everyone adjourns to a parlor for aperitifs and anecdotes. Even if you have to eat dry toast and tea all week, this is a "don't miss" experience. Inquire about serving times when you make your reservation. Reservations required. Credit Cards: V, MC.

Muriel's Cuisine $$ ★ ★

Upper Happy Hill Drive, ☎ (809) 469-5920.
Latin American cuisine. Specialties: Curries, Seafood Rotis, Johnny Cakes.
Lunch: 8:00 a.m.–4:00 p.m., entrees $5–$7.
Dinner: 4:00 p.m.–10:00 p.m., entrees $12–$16.

Miss Muriel's establishment is fast becoming a choice spot to dine in Charlestown, especially for her substantial Wednesday West Indian buffet lunches. This talented lady can't offer a sea view, but the food is rib stickin', especially the variety of curries (chicken, goat, sometimes seafood) served with local vegetables, which may include christophene *(chayote)*, plantain and rice and peas. Closed: Sun. Reservations recommended. Credit Cards: V, MC, A.

Unella's $$ ★ ★

The Waterfront, ☎ (809) 469-5574.
Latin American cuisine.
Lunch: entrees $4–$10.
Dinner: entrees $5–$21.

If Eddy's nearby gets too crowded, give Unella's a try—it also has a second-floor patio, a more subdued atmosphere and luscious fresh lobster. Other fare includes scampi or conch, and Caribbean-style plate meals, although most of it is unexceptional. It's open from 9 a.m. Credit Cards: D, V, MC.

Where to Shop

Shopping is better in St. Kitts but Nevis need not be ignored. Island Hopper carries the full line of Caribelle Batik fashions. Swimsuits and cotton handmade dresses can be picked up at **Amanda's Fashions**. An excellent array of souvenirs, crafts, guava jelly, soursop jam, banana chutney and gooseberry jam are available at **Nevis Handicraft Co-op**, a must stop. Stamp collectors will be delighted to know that the two islands are famous throughout the world for their issued stamps, and a philatelic bureau on each island issues totally different stamps. The commemorative stamps of September 19,1993, which celebrate the tenth anniversary of the Federation's independence, are considered instant collectibles. All photo needs can be served at **Rawlins Photo Color Lab & Studio**, located on Main Street in Charlestown, with one-hour processing.

Nevis Directory

ARRIVAL

American Eagle ☎ *(800-43307300)* offers daily connections to St. Kitts from the hub in San Juan, LIAT ☎ *(809-465-2511)* serves St. Kitts from either San Juan, Antigua or St. Maarten.

Short-hop flight on local airlines—like Air St. Kitts-Nevis ☎ *(809-465-8571)*, Nevis Express ☎ *(809-469-3346)* and St. Croix-based Coastal Air Transport ☎ *(809-773-6862)* provide regular on demand service to Nevis from St. Kitts and other islands. For a more unusual experience, take a 45-minute ferry from Basse-Terre, capital of St. Kitts to Charlestown (about $8 roundtrip); ☎ *809-469-5521*. Complimentary transportation is provided from St. Kitts for guests of the Four Season Resort Nevis.

Modestly priced taxis fares are available for all island destinations and three-hour island tours can be arranged from about $40. Try All Seasons Streamline Tours ☎ *(809-469-1138)*, which has comfortable air-conditioned minibuses. Fares will usually be quoted in EC dollars.

Rental cars on Nevis start at $35 per day. Be sure to obtain a $12 driver's license and don't forget to drive on the left side of the road.

CLIMATE

As on St. Kitts, average temperatures hover between 78 and 85 degrees F, during the day; nighttime temperatures can drop to 68 degrees F. Trade winds keep it breezy, though the humidity can rise to uncomfortable levels during the summer. Downpours are quick but heavy between mid-June through mid-November, considered the rainy season.

DOCUMENTS

U.S. citizens need to present proof of citizenship (passport, voter's registration card, or birth certificate), along with a return or ongoing ticket. There is a departure tax of $10.

ELECTRICITY

The current is 230 volts, though some hotels have 110 volts. Bring a transformer and adapter just in case.

GETTING AROUND

Inter-island flights are now available with Nevis Express, a locally owned and operated airline, which uses 15-passenger Lyslander Tristars. The cost for the 6-minute flight between St. Kitts and Nevis is $20 U.S.

Carib Queen, the inter-island commuter ferry which links the two islands, makes multiple crossings every day. Other private ferries are operated by the Four Seasons Resort and Mt. Nevis hotel.

LANGUAGE

English is the official language, spoken with a rhythmic lilt. Natives also speak a local patois.

MEDICAL EMERGENCIES

Alexandra Hospital in Charlestown (☎ *469-5473*) operates a 24-hour emergency room service.

MONEY

Currency on both islands is the Eastern Caribbean dollar. In a pinch, shopkeepers and businesses will accept American and Canadian currency, but they have a hard time exchanging it.

TELEPHONE

The area code is *809*, for both St. Kitts and Nevis. Telegrams and telexess can be sent from the **Cable & Wireless office** on Main Street in Charlestown (☎ *469-5000*). You can also make international telephone calls from this office, which will save you a lot of money (do what you can to avoid making any international calls from your hotel room (if, indeed, your room even has a phone) since hotel surcharges will make the final bill outrageously expensive. The Cable & Wireless office is open from Monday-Friday 8 a.m.–6 p.m., and on Saturday from 8 a.m.–noon. It is closed on Sunday and on public holidays.

TIME

Atlantic standard time, which is one hour later than New York time, except during Daylight Saving Time, when it is the same.

TIPPING AND TAXES

Expect your hotel to add a 10 percent service charge. Check restaurant bills before adding your own 10–15 percent service tip. If a taxi driver hasn't added the tip himself, do so (10–15 percent).

TOURIST INFORMATION

The Nevis Tourist Office is located on Main Street in Charlestown ☎ 469-1042, FAX 469-1066. You can pick up brochures, magazines, and a current list of hotel prices. It's open only Monday–Friday. In the U.S. ☎ (212) 535-1234.

WHEN TO GO

December is the month of Carnival, celebrated with blowout parties, costumed parades, and general merrymaking for days. Alexander Hamilton's Birthday is celebrated on January 11. St. Kitts Horticultural Society holds an annual show usually in the last week of May featuring the work of local gardeners and nurserymen. The St. Kitts and Nevis Regatta of windsurfing and sunfish, an 11-mile race from Frigate Bay, is usually held in June. Culturama, a popular and festive event celebrates the island's history, folklore and arts with presentations, talent shows, beauty pageants, calypso contests and West Indian delicacies.

NEVIS HOTELS		RMS	RATES	PHONE	FAX
Charlestown					
★★★★★	**Four Seasons Resort Nevis**	196	$180–$555	(800) 332-3442	(809) 469-1112
★★★★	**Montpelier Plantation Inn**	17	$150–$280	(800) 243-9420	(809) 469-2932
★★★	**Golden Rock Estate**	15	$170–$245	(809) 469-3346	(809) 469-2113
★★★	**Hermitage, The**	14	$85–$690	(809) 469-3177	(809) 469-2481
★★★	**Mt. Nevis Hotel**	32	$170–$440	(809) 469-9373	(809) 469-9375
★★★	**Nisbet Plantation**	38	$180–$340	(800) 344-2049	(809) 469-9864
★★	**Croney's Old Manor Hotel**	17	$85–$175	(809) 469-3445	(809) 469-3388
★★	**Hurricane Cove Bungalows**	10	$95–$400	(809) 469-9462	(809) 469-9462
★★	**Oualie Beach Hotel**	22	$100–$205	(800) 255-9684	(809) 469-9176
★	**Meadville Cottages**	10	$50–$80	(809) 469-5235	
★	**Pinney's Beach Hotel**	48	$60–$185	(800) 742-4276	(809) 469-1088

NEVIS RESTAURANTS	LOCATION	PHONE	ENTREE
Charlestown			
International			
★★★★★ Cooperage	Charlestown	(809) 469-3445	$12–$20●●
★★ Caribbean Confections	Charlestown	(809) 469-5685	$4–$20
Latin American			
★★★★★ Miss June's	Charlestown	(809) 469-5330	$63–$63●●
★★★ Callaloo	Charlestown	(809) 469-5389	$5–$7
★★ Cla-Cha-Del	Newcastle	(809) 469-9640	$5–$15
★★ Eddy's	Charlestown	(809) 469-5958	$2–$12
★★ Muriel's Cuisine	Charlestown	(809) 469-5920	$5–$16
★★ Unella's	Charlestown	(809) 469-5574	$4–$21
Note: • Lunch Only			
•• Dinner Only			

PUERTO RICO

The best beaches near San Juan, are at Isla Verde in front of the major hotels.

Puerto Rico is probably the best kept secret in the Caribbean. Few people are aware that visitors from the U.S., Asia and South America reached a record four million for 1993–4, registering a 12.2 percent increase in hotel bookings. More than half of that four million were from the U.S.

The year 1994 was key for other reasons. A wet September enabled Puerto Rico officials to lift the drought restrictions in key tourist areas of the island following four months of such barriers. The surrounding areas of Old San Juan, Isla Verde and Condado—where many of the largest hotels are located—have returned to normal water service. Old San Juan, refurbished with a $41 million budget and another $41 million waterfront renewal project, is on a roll, though still a bit reeling from the 500th anniversary of Columbus' first sighting of Puerto Rico on November 19, 1493. There are 16 historic blocks that comprise this World Heritage site. Known as El Viejo, San Juan, embodies the spiritual heart of the island's nearly four million inhabitants. With centuries-old architecture, it symbolizes Puerto Rico's fight for identity in the face of 400 years of foreign assault and occupation.

A lovely way to visit Puerto Rico is to take a week to travel down the Ruta Panorâmica, (the island's Panoramic Route) which twists and turns from one end of the island to another across the Cordilleria Central—staying at a different parador, or country inn, every night.

Bird's Eye View

The farthest east of the four major islands that form the Greater Antilles, Puerto Rico is 110 miles by 35 miles in size. To the north lies the Atlantic Ocean, to the south the Caribbean. Three islands are situated off the coast of Puerto Rico: Vieques and Culebra to the east and Mona to the west. The island's terrain ranges from palm-lined beaches on four coastlines to rugged mountain ranges, gently rolling hills, and dry desert-like areas. The island boasts 20 designated forest reserves and an additional six are in proposal. The most notable are the 28,000-acre El Yunque rainforest near San Juan, part of the Caribbean National Forest and the only tropical rainforest in the U.S. Forest Service; the Guajataca Forest with 25 miles of trails through karst reserves; and the Guanica Forest Reserve, a dry forest with the largest number of bird species on the island. There are also two Phosphorescent Bays, one off the southwest coast and one off the island of Vieques.

History

In 1493,Columbus arrived on the island of Puerto Rico in the company of one Ponce de León, who named the island for his patron saint, San Juan. The island, however, already had a name—Borinquen—a Taino Indian nomenclature and one that is still lovingly used today by native Puerto Ricans. Caparra, inland and across the bay, was the first choice for a capital in 1508

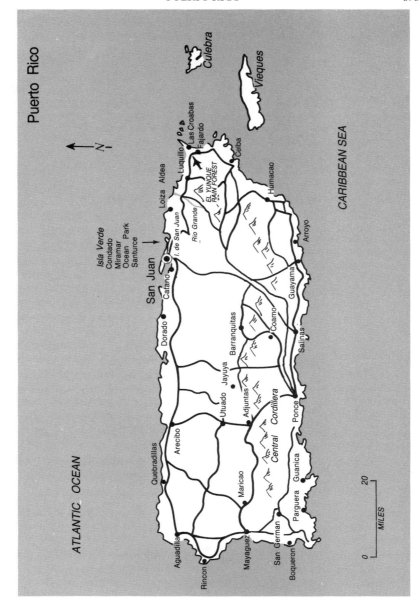

when Juan Ponce de León (the island's first governor) and his men with the permission of supreme cacique Agueybana, first scouted the island of San Juan Bautista. Eventually de León set off on his journey to discover eternal youth and never actually resided in the handsome home, Casa Blanca, that had been built for him. Thirteen years later, settlers decamped for the drier, windier islet fronting the Atlantic, where they permanently settled. During early years of colonization, the city repelled the British, French and Dutch corsairs. La Fortaleza, now the governor's mansion and El Morro and San Cristóbal forts, were built during those times with the specific aim of keeping marauders at bay.

By the early 1800s, the era of Caribbean piracy was finally brought to a halt. At the same time, Spain threw open her doors to immigration; subsequent increase in economic prosperity coupled with new aesthetic influences from abroad were soon reflected in the island's architectural styles. It was during this period that Old San Juan developed the colonial/neoclassic look that predominates today—all within the urban grid pattern envisioned by the original Spanish planners. In 1897 the island gained independence from Spanish rule in 1897. On July 25, 1898, however, Spanish troops landed in Guánica, in the middle of the Spanish-American War, and disturbed whatever modicum of peace had been achieved. The Treaty of Paris of 1899 handed the island over to the U.S. In 1917, Puerto Ricans were granted American citizenship; in 1952, the island achieved unique status by becoming the only member of the commonwealth to receive its own constitution and government. Although there have been several movements geared toward achieving complete independence, the 1993 vote to remain a U.S. possession has ensured a a long-standing and stable future with the mother country.

During the early 20th century a burgeoning population brought growth beyond the Old City gates and soon after, the destruction of substantial sections of its massive walls. Today Old San Juan boasts only 5000 residents; no longer the financial hub, it still pulls 5000 workers to offices and government buildings, eateries and shops. A seven-block enclave which boasts a large number of art studios, florists, doctor's offices, galleries, etc., is considered one of the more desirable spots to live in island.

People

Puerto Ricans consider themselves American but have a fierce pride about their island and their special Caribbean identity. American products are ubiquitous; in fact, Puerto Rico is considered among the top ten overseas markets for American goods manufactured on the mainland. Through such media as American cable TV, music, dance and fashion from the mainland have also invaded the culture, though tempered for tropical climes. Salsa, the music, is the biggest dance bet on the island, although it is often mixed with American rock 'n roll. Immense precautions, however, should be taken in regards to crime and petty thievery. Don't walk around with an ostentatious show of valuables, keep cameras tucked away in inexpensive-looking bags, and avoid wearing jewelry in the streets. Take special care when strolling through large cities like San Juan, and in targeted tourist areas, like Old San Juan.

Beaches

All the beaches on the island are public with one exception—the artificial beach at the Caribe Hilton in San Juan. Many hotels are situated right on the beach; if they aren't, they are but a short walk away. Hotels who do not enjoy such proximity usually provide a shuttle to the beach free of charge. **Luquillo Beach** is probably the best beach on the island for swimming. The waters are calm, and the coral reefs protect the pristine lagoon from the stronger waves of the Atlantic. Picnic tables are available as well as camp facilities. Also suitable for swimming is **Seven Seas**, a long strand with compacted sand. Trailers may be parked nearby as well as tents pitched. Water sports of all kinds can be arranged at **Sun Bay**, a sugar-white beach on Vieques. Vessels for sailing may be rented here. One of the most famous beaches is **Condado Beach**, along Ashford Avenue in San Juan. It's a beauty-watcher's delight, especially for those who want to see the latest trend in swimwear and the prettiest island girls. Within walking distance are the long beaches of **Rincón**, **Cabo Rojo**, and **Paguera**. Surfers claim that the best waves are along the Atlantic coastline from Borinquén Point south to Rincón. The surf is best from October through April. In summer, La Concha and Aviones give the best hang-dogs. All these beaches have board rentals nearby.

Dive Sites

Most divers think of Puerto Rico only as a place to change planes on the way to Bonaire, but the southwest corner of this volcanic island is a rare find. On a good day, the diving is stupendous, with 150 feet of visibility and the wall at **La Parguera** looks as good as Bloody Bay in the Caymans. The lush coral development at about 70 feet contains an abundance of black coral, which is seldom found in the Caribbean above 150 feet. Solid reef citizens include nurse sharks, moray and the occasional big groupers.

There are more than 50 dive sites off La Parguera. Boats are small and service is personal; on a typical day you might head out to the reef with four other divers. A half-hour boat ride takes you to the long wall, which starts at 60 feet and plunges to 6000. Closer to shore are the Pinnacles, huge mushroomlike coral formations riddled with caves. On a night dive on **Enrique Reef**, you'll want to splash around in the phosphorescence.

The town of La Parguera is reminiscent of Cozumel a decade ago with a few hotels and bars, a church and not much else.

Adventure Express Travel has a four-night San Juan Getaway package that include two inside reef dives (or one resort SCUBA course for nondivers), casino chips, discounts on some meals, seven percent hotel tax and more. Another one-week package at **Palmas del Mar** includes transfers from San Juan, seven nights accommodations, two tank boat dives daily, hotel taxes, and gratuities. There is a dive package for families. For more information call ☎ *(800) 443-0799*. **Parguera Divers** ☎ *809-899-4171* provides a complete roster of dive services, including several packages. A week's lodging at the **Parador Posada Porlamar Hotel**, steps away from the Parguera Divers docks, costs $433 and includes ten dives a day. Up the price to $550 and move next door to the larger, more resortlike **Parador Villa Parguera**, where you can spend your surface interval on the terrace of a waterfront room. Call for reservations ☎ *800-359-0747*.

Treks

Puerto Rico has some of the finest and most accessible trails in the Caribbean. Within easy reach of cosmopolitan San Juan is a scenic countryside, superb natural wonders, and centuries-old towns. Many trekking excursions can be made during the day and have you back in time for an elegant dinner in San Juan. In addition to El Yunque's trails there are 14 Commonwealth Forest Reserves *(Natural Resources Department, Box 5887, San Juan 00906;* ☎ *(809) 722-1726)*, which boast trails ranging from birding in the Guánica mangroves to those for high mountain trekking in the Cordillera Central.

Just 35 miles east of San Juan lies **El Yunque**, the only tropical rainforest in the U.S. National Park System—ever since Teddy Roosevelt claimed it for the U.S. in 1903. Named by the Spanish for its anvil-shaped peak, El Yunque receives more than 100 billion gallons of annual rainfall. Waterfalls, orchids, giant ferns, towering tabonuco trees and sierra palms make El Yunque a photographer's paradise. La Coca Fall and an observation tower with a souvenir shop are just off Route 191. Pick up a map and choose from dozens of trails graded by difficulty, up to the rugged six-mile-long El Toro trail to the peak at 3523 feet. El Yunque Trail leads to three of the area's most spectacular lookouts. Big Tree Trail is an easy walk to breathtaking **La Mina Falls**. Just off the main road is **La Coca Falls**, a sheet of water cascading down mossy cliffs. Don't hesitate to combine a morning trip to El Yunque with an afternoon of swimming and sunning on tranquil **Luquillo Beach**. *Luquillo* is a Spanish adaptation of Yukiyu, the god believed by the Tainos to inhabit El Yunque. Soft white sand shaded by majestic coconut palms and the crystal blue seas make this the Caribbean Eden. Take a picnic or sample local specialties from the kiosks. Many hotels arrange guided tours.

An hour and a half from San Juan, on the northeast coast near Fajardo, is **La Cabezas Nature Reserve**, with seven ecological systems and a restored 19th-century Spanish colonial lighthouse. From the lighthouse observation deck, majestic views extend to islands as far off as St. Thomas. Boardwalk trails wind through island-building mangroves, dry forest and a bioluminescent lagoon. Ospreys, sea turtles and an occasional manatee are seen from the windswept promontories and rocky beach. Under the tutelage of La Cabezas' guides, every visitor becomes a naturalist for a few absorbing hours.

Admission is by reservation only, Friday–Sunday. For more information: ☎ *(809) 722-5882.*

West of San Juan near Arecibo in the primeval karst limestone region, the **Camuy Cave System**, carved out by the world's third largest underground river, has been hailed by speleologists the world over as one of the most beautiful ever seen. Miles of natural waterways are surrounded by mammoth stalagmite and stalactite formations, with canyons, caverns and sinkholes sometimes reaching several hundred feet in depth. The site of the 300-acre **Rio Camuy Cave Park** was probably inhabited by the Tainos long before Christopher Columbus discovered Puerto Rico in 1493. Visitors and guides take trains to the mouth of **Clara Cave**, where a footpath winds through the 170-ft. high cave to a deeper sinkhole and spectacular views down into the Camuy River. A side trip by tram leads to the 650-ft.-wide **Tres Pueblos** sinkhole, where platforms are suspended over the Camuy River 400 feet below. The park includes a cafeteria, picnic area and small gift shop. It's located on Route 129, km. 18.9. **Tropix Wellness** Tours offers the Caveman Tour, which includes an expedition through the Camuy Cave Park, which costs $275 and includes 4 days/3 nights at the **Costa Dorado Hotel** in Isabella.

If you want to combine a dry forest hike with mangrove kayaking at sunset, try the **Wet & Dry Tour**, offered by the Tropix Wellness Tours. Included is an exploration of the world's largest remaining tract of tropical dry forest, located in the southwestern part of the island. The 4 days/3 nights package runs $275.

The **Guánica Reserve** is a paradise for bird-watchers. It's best to start out on the dirt roads in early morning to hunt for such Puerto Rican natives as the tody, bullfinch, nightjar, and emerald hummingbird. Road 334 northeast of the town of Guanica leads straight into the forest, where there is a ranger station and a primitive picnic area. Several dirt roads begin here, open only to hikers, where some of the best bird-watching can be found. Road 333 runs the southern perimeter of the forest, and a trail connects it to the ranger station.

Vieques, Puerto Rico's offshore island, is the site of the **Phosphorescent Bay Tour**, which includes an expedition to the Isla Nena, home to one of the most spectacular phosphorescent bays in the world. Additional natural attractions on Vieques include magnificent reefs, bird sanctuaries and deserted beaches. Tropix Wellness Tours (see information below) offers a 4 days/3 nights package for $320 with accommodations at the Casa del France.

Culebra, one of Puerto Rico's offshore islands, is ideally situated off the southeastern coast of the mainland. Boasting magnificent snorkeling, Culebra is home to the National Wildlife Refuge, which protects the habitats of the island's wildlife. The **Happy Turtle Tour**, offered by Tropix Wellness Tours, combines a half-day kayaking/snorkeling expedition and a visit to the sea turtles' nesting sites during the spring and summer season. The 4 days/3 nights package runs $315.

Tropix Wellness Tours will customize an itinerary for solo travelers or for groups of six or more depending on their individual needs. "Add-ons" to the fixed tours, such as body rafting expeditions through underground cave river systems, bird-watching and hiking excursions to the different rain forests, can also be arranged. Pre- and post-Wellness Tour hotel packages and car rental programs are available. Airfare to Puerto Rico is usually not included in the package. For more information contact **Tropix Wellness Tours** ☎ *(800) 582-0613* or *(809) 268-2173*.

OLD SAN JUAN

Known as El Viejo, San Juan, with its priceless architectural treasures, embodies the spiritual heart of the island's 4 million inhabitants. Caparra, inland and cross the bay, was the first choice for a capital back in 1508 when Juan Poncé de Leon the island's first governor, first scouted the island of San Juan Bautista.

Quincentennial Plaza, overlooking the Atlantic Ocean from atop the highest point in old San Juan, usually serves as the kickoff for visitors seeking the history and heritage of the rich Spanish colonial era in Puerto Rico. A symbolic feature of the Plaza, which was constructed as part of the celebration of the 500th anniversary of the discovery of the New World, is a sculpture which rises 40 feet from the top level of the Plaza. The monumental totemic sculpture in black granite and ceramics symbolizes the earthen and clay roots of American history and is the work of Jaime Suarez, one of Puerto Rico's foremost artists. From its southern end, two needle-shaped columns point skyward to the North Star, which traditionally has guided explorers. Placed among the Plaza are fountains, other columns and sculpted steps that represent various periods in the 500-year history. The Plaza is at the hub of a group of some of the most significant and impressive structures dating back from colonial times. Clear and sweeping views extend from the Plaza to El Morro Fortress at the headland of San Juan Bay and to the Dominican Convent and San Jose Church, a rare New World example of true Gothic architecture. The Asilo de Beneficencia, dating from 1832 as an indigents' hospital, occupies a corner of El Morro's entrance and is now the new home of the **Institute of Puerto Rican Culture**. Adjacent to the Plaza stands the **Cuartel de Ballaja**, built in the mid-19th century as Spanish army headquarters and still the largest edifice in the Americas constructed by Spanish engineers. It was declared a national historic monument in 1954 and now houses the Museum of the Americas.

The **Paseo de La Princesa**, a 19th-century esplanade where Spanish colonial gentry once strolled and inhaled the balmy Caribbean air, is a special thoroughfare—something akin to the Piazza San Marco in Venice or the Promenade des Anglais in Nice. The Paseo sweeps from the piers which welcome cruise ships past La Princesa, a restored former 19th-century prison housing the Puerto Rico Tourism Company, around the old city walls beneath **Casa Blanca**, the ancestral home of the Ponce de León family and continuing to the entrance of the famed 16th-century El Morro fortress. A charming gazebo serves light seafood, dishes, salads and the island's famed coffee. Outdoor tables with umbrellas, and the shade of more than 20 trees, makes a lovely place to roost, especially since delicious *criollo* dishes are dispensed from specially designed food carts with gaily colored awnings.

Among other things to see is the **Puerto Rico Tourism Company**, inaugurated last year. It's located in the La Princesa Building, the site of a 19th-century jail, on a promenade that skirts the Old City's southern walls. Here visitors can shop for t-shirts, handicrafts, sample foods, coffee, and take a leisurely stroll. A small art museum features the works of some of the island's finest artists. **La Casa Bianca**, an exquisite property renovated at a cost of $275,000 following heavy damage by Hurricane Hugo, houses two small museums, one dedicated to the Taino Indians who inhabited Puerto Rico at the time of European colonization. The **Museu de las America**, a museum of art and anthropology, presents exhibits on cultures from Alaska and Patagonia to Spain and Portugal. The **Museu Pablo Casals** is a beautiful memorial to the life and work of the world-renowned cellist, perhaps the island's greatest artist. Although Casals was Spanish, he spent the last twenty years of his life in Puerto Rico and left a marvelous legacy, the **Casals Festival**, which is held annually in June featuring the finest musicians in the world. Visitors can listen to recordings of past festival concerts as well as peruse documents of his life. His famous cello can be viewed in a special display upstairs.

What Else to See Around the Island

The world's largest rum distillery is the famed **Bacardi Distillery**, a short hop across the San Juan Bay by ferry. Daily tours are offered through its 127 acres and plant, where 100,000 gallons can be distilled daily. Complimentary rum drinks are offered at the beginning of the tour, so by the time you've finished, you're bonkered enough to want to stock up at the gift shop. The prices of Bacardi rums are better here than in the U.S. and some rums not sold on the mainland are excellent presents for the "exclusive" sort.

The **Arecibo Observatory** (two hours west of San Juan) is the site of the world's largest radar/radio telescope, operated by Cornell University and the National Science Foundation. Here scientists monitor radio emissions from distant galaxies, pulsars, mysterious quasars, and perhaps, even more mysterious sources. This is also home base for **SETI**, the Search for Extraterrestrial Intelligence, and rumor has it that great strides has been made in that direction, although the results of research still remains difficult to obtain. A 600-ton suspended platform hovers over a 20-acre dish set in a sinkhole 565 feet below.

After thirty years of silence, the **Hacienda Buena Vista**, an early 19th-century coffee plantation, has been reopened to the public following a massive restoration. Located along the Canas River just north of Ponce, the hacienda is a step back in time, and visitors are invited to explore the plantation's mills and two-story estate house, observe original machinery in action, and enjoy a sensory feast—coffee drying in the trays, and pineapples and bananas growing on the hillsides. The ground floor of the manor estate, now a museum, contains old maps, photographs, bills of sale, and other memorabilia of hacienda life. The rooms have been furnished with authentic period pieces from the 1850s, right down to the chamber pots, armoires, bathtubs and family portraits. Experts have considered the machinery—dating from the early days of the industrial revolution—of international importance because such machines rarely survived on the U.S. mainland. The entire estate resembles a hamlet of bygone days, including the manor house, the coffee and corn mills, a masonry storage shed that doubles as a hurricane shelter, and the former slave quarters which became a coffee storage and drying shed. Feel free to take a leisurely stroll on paths over which wagons once traveled carrying sacks of just harvested coffee beans or newly milled corn meal. The hills surrounding Buena Vista (aptly named "beautiful view") are rich with gurgling streams, cascading waterfalls and a variety of plant and animal life. Ducks wander freely over the grounds. Also available for sighting are the Puerto Rican screech owl, the mangrove cuckoo and the hummingbird.

Historical Sites

Capilla de Cristo ★★★

Calle del Cristo, Old San Juan, (809) 721-2400.
The Christ Chapel was built in 1753 after a horse rider's life was supposedly spared after a tragic accident. (Supposedly, because historical records say the youth did, indeed, die.) In any event, the small silver altar is dedicated to the Christ of Miracles. Free admission.

Casa de los Contrafuertes ★★★★

Calle San Sebastian 101, Old San Juan, (809) 724-5477.

Hours Open: 9:00 a.m.–4:30 p.m.

Called the House of Buttresses (for obvious reasons once you see it), this is believed to be the oldest residence left in Old San Juan, dating back to the early 18th century. Inside are two museums, one devoted to graphic arts, the other displaying a 19th-century pharmacy. Free admission.

Cathedral de San Juan

Calle del Cristo 151, Old San Juan, ☎ *(809) 722- 861.*
Hours Open: 8:30 a.m.–4:30 p.m.

The San Juan Cathedral was built in 1540, destroyed by hurricane in 1529, looted in 1598, and damaged by another hurricane in 1615. Today it holds the remains of Ponce de Leon and the relic of San Pio, a Roman martyr. Sunday masses begin at 9:00 a.m. Free admission.

Convento de los Dominicos

Plaza de San Jose, Old San Juan, ☎ *(809) 724-5949.*

This was Puerto Rico's first convent, started in 1523. It was home to Dominican friars until 1838, when it became barracks for the United States Army. Today, it is headquarters for the Institute of Puerto Rican Culture. Inside you'll find the old chapel, art exhibits and a fine gift shop. Free admission.

Fort San Cristobel   ★★★★

Calle Norzagaray, Old San Juan, ☎ *(809) 729-6960.*
Hours Open: 9:00 a.m.–5:00 p.m.

This massive fort dates back to 1634. Its walls rise 150 feet above sea level, and it covers 27 acres. Now run under the auspices of the National Park Service, the site includes a replica of 18th-century Spanish troop barracks. Free tours are given daily from 10:00 a.m.–4:00 p.m. Free admission.

Fort San Jeronimo

Next to the Caribe Hilton, Cordado Bay, ☎ *(809) 724-5949.*

This tiny fort was attacked by the British in 1797, 11 years after it was built. Now run by the Institute of Puerto Rican Culture, it houses a small military museum. Free admission.

Fuerte San Felipe del Morro

Calle Norzagaray, Old San Juan, ☎ *(809) 729-6960.*
Hours Open: 9:00 a.m.–5:00 p.m.

This fort, commonly known as El Morro, guards the entrance to San Juan Bay. The Spaniards started construction in 1540, but it wasn't until 1787 that the fort was deemed complete. Now run under the auspices of the National Park Service, the six-level fort can be explored via guided tours (free, from 10:00 to 4:00) or on your own. The dramatic fort contains dungeons, lookouts, barracks and vaults, as well as a small museum on its history. Free admission.

Governor Mansion

Recito Oeste Street, Old San Juan, ☎ *(809) 721-2400.*
Hours Open: 9:00 a.m.–4:00 p.m.

Puerto Rico boasts a lot of "oldest in the Western Hemisphere" —here's the oldest executive mansion in continuous use. It started as a fortress in 1553 and is the office and residence of Puerto Rico's governor. Now a U.S. National Historic Site, the mansion can be toured in the mornings, with tours of the gardens running all day. Free admission.

Inglesia de San Jose ★★★

Plaza de San Jose, Old San Juan, ☎ *(809) 725-7501.*
Hours Open: 8:30 a.m.–4:00 p.m.

The San Jose Church is the second-oldest in the Western Hemisphere, dating back to 1532. It was originally a Dominican chapel and was the family church of Ponce de Leon's descendants, many of whom are buried here. Among the highlights are a crucifix that belonged to the explorer, oil paintings by Jose Campeche and Francisco Oller, and ornate processional floats. Sunday mass is at 12:15. Free admission.

Museums and Exhibits

Casa Blanca

Calle San Sebastian 1, San Juan, ☎ *(809) 724-4102.*

The land on which the "White House" sits was given to explorer Ponce de Leon by the Spanish Crown. He died before the house was built in 1521, but his descendants lived there for some 250 years. In 1779, it was taken over by the Spanish military, then used later by the United States as a residence for military commanders. Today the mansion is restored to its former glory and is a National Historic Monument. It houses two museums, one on the Taino Indians (believed to be Puerto Rico's first inhabitants) and one on the house's history, with emphasis on life in the 16th and 18th centuries. Casa Blanca is the oldest continuously occupied residence in the Western Hemisphere.

La Casa del Libro ★★★

Calle del Cristo, Old San Juan, ☎ *(809) 723- 354.*
Hours Open: 11:00 a.m.–4:30 p.m.

Exhibits on printing and bookmaking are displayed at this 19th-century house. Noteworthy are pages from the Gutenberg Bible, a decree signed by Ferdinand and Isabella concerning Columbus' second voyage, and other pre-16th century examples of the art. Free admission.

Museo de Arte y Historia ★★★

Calle Norzagaray, Old San Juan, ☎ *(809) 724-1875.*

This center for Puerto Rican arts and crafts displays works by local artists. It was a marketplace in the 1850s in a previous incarnation. Audio-visual shows in English on the city's history are shown daily at 11:00 and 1:15. Free admission.

Museo de Pablo Casals ★★★

Calle San Sebastian 101, Old San Juan, ☎ *(809) 723-9185.*
Hours Open: 9:30 a.m.–5:30 p.m.

The famed Spanish cellist spent his last years in Puerto Rico, leaving behind a collection of memorabilia from his long and distinguished career. The 18th-century house displays his cello, manuscripts and photos from his life, as well as videotaped performances, shown on request. General admission: $1.00.

Theatre

Centro de Ballas Artes

De Diego and Ponce de Leon avs, San Juan, ☎ *(809) 721- 0.*
This fine arts center is the largest in the Caribbean. Call the box office or inquire at
your hotel about events—from operas to plays—while you're in town

Teatro Tapia

Ave. Ponce de Leon, San Juan, ☎ *(809) 722- 407.*
Dating back to 1832, this is one of the Western Hemisphere's oldest theaters. It is
named after Puerto Rican playwright Alejandro Tapia y Rivera. Check with the box
office for a schedule for upcoming plays and cultural events.

Tours

Bacardi Rum Plant ★★★

Poute 888, Catano, ☎ *(809) 788-1500.*
Located across the bay from San Juan (a short hop ferry), this plant offers 45-
minute tours at 9:00, 10:30, 12:00, and 4:00. You'll see the distillery and bottling
plant, and get to judge the results yourself. Free admission.

Caribbean National Forest ★★★★★

Near Luquillo Beach, Puerto Rico, ☎ *(809) 887-2875.*
Known simply as El Yunque, this pristine spot encompasses 28,000 acres of virgin
rainforest, with some 240 species of tropical trees, flowers and wildlife. It is home
to rare creatures like the Puerto Rican boa, which grows to seven feet, the colorful
Puerto Rican parrot, and 26 other species found nowhere else. There are more than
20 kinds of orchids, 50 varieties of ferns, and millions of tiny tree frogs, who serenade visitors with their tiny croaks. Stop at the Sierra Palm Visitor Center on Route
191 to peruse the interesting exhibits and pick up a map. Numerous trails traverse
the park, leading to waterfalls, natural pools and the peak of El Toro.

Rio Camuy Cave Park

Route 129, near Arecibo, ☎ *(809) 898-3100.*
Hours Open: 8:00 a.m.–4:00 p.m.
Located in Northwest Puerto Rico, 2.5 hours from San Juan, is one of the world's
largest cave networks. Sixteen entrances have been found and seven miles of pas-
sages explored so far. A tram takes you to the cave, where you get out and walk
through, passing sinkholes, one of the world's largest underground rivers, and giant
stalagmites and stalactites. The Taino Indians, believed to be Puerto Rico's first
inhabitants, also explored the cave. Reservations are essential, as this place is understandably popular. General admission: $10.00.

Sports

Every water sport imaginable is played on Puerto Rico's 272 miles of beachfront. *Balnearios* (public beaches) offer lockers, showers and parking at nominal rates, though they are closed on Mondays, Election Day and Good Friday. For information about overnight stays call ☎ *(809)722-1551* or *721-2800.* The Puerto Rico Water Sport Federation sets standards and guidelines for members specializing in scuba diving, snorkeling, sailing, deep-sea fishing, windsurfing and other aquatic activities. Members, including the Caribbean School of Aquatics, Coral Head Divers, and many others, can make arrangements for surfing (the 1988 World Cup Surfing Championship was held in Aguadilla), scuba diving, sailing, etc. Arrangements can also be made at the island's many resort hotels.

Puerto Rico hosts many deep-sea fishing tournaments, in which 30 world records have been broken. The **Annual Billfish Tournament** is the world's largest consecutively held tournament of its kind. Deep-sea fishing boats can be chartered in San Juan, Fajardo, Humaco, Mayaguez and other towns. Lake fishing for largemouth bass, peacock bass, sunfish, catfish, and tilapia is also popular. For more details, contact the **Department of Natural Resources** ☎ *(809) 722-5938.*

Horseback riding is tremendous on Puerto Rico—the island's palm-lined beaches are romantic settings. Riding and/or trail riding can be arranged through the Palmas del Mar Equestrian Center or the Hacienda Carabali.

Tennis is omnipresent here—there are over 100 tennis courts throughout the island, including 17 in San Juan's Central Park. A total of nine **golf championships** take place on Puerto Rico (public as well as at major resorts). The Hyatt Regency Cerromar and the Hyatt Dorado Beach resorts have two 18-hole Robert Trent Jones courses each. The newest 18-hole is east of San Juan at the Bahia Beach Plantation. The Berwind Country Club near Rio Grande has an 18-hole course open to the public on Tuesday, Thursdays and Fridays (except holidays). Ramey Golf Club, an 18-hole course, is located on the former Ramey Air Force Base in Aguadilla, in the northwestern part of the island. Greens fees and prices of equipment rentals vary with the season.

Cockfighting is a popular native spectator sport in Puerto Rico, particularly in the Cordillera Central.

Boating and Cruising

Various locations, Puerto Rico.

Lots of firms will take you out on the high seas for a simple sail or snorkel trip. Most charge about $45 per person. Try: **Fondo de Cristal** (☎ *889-5891*), **Island Safari** (☎ *728-6606*), **Spread Eagle** (☎ *863-1905*), **Erin Go Braugh** (☎ *860-4401*), **East Wind Catamaran** (☎ *863-2821*), **Captain Jack Becker** (☎ *860-0861*), and **Land and Sea Excursions** (☎ *382-4877*).

Golf

Various locations, Puerto Rico.

Unlike most of the Caribbean islands, which have just one or two golf courses (if any), Puerto Rico has a wealth of greens. All are 18-hole courses unless otherwise noted. Rio Grande: **Bahia Beach Plantation** (☎ *256-5600*), **Berwind Country Club** (☎ *876-3056*), **Club Riomar** (☎ *887-3964*). Fajardo: **Conquistador Resort** (☎ *863-1000*). Dorado: **Dorado del Mar Country Club** (nine holes, ☎ *796-2030*), **Hyatts Dorado and Cerromar** (38 holes, ☎ *796-1234*). Humacao: **Palmas del Mar Resort** (☎ *852-6000*) Aguadilla: **Punta Borinquen** (☎ *890-2987*). Check at your hotel or call **Luiz Ortiz** (☎ *786-3859*) for access to courses in metropolitan San Juan.

Horseback Riding

Various locations, Puerto Rico.

Just hop on a horse and ride off into the sunset (or along the beach or through the rainforest) at **Hacienda Carabali** (☎ *889-5820*) or **Palmas del Mar's** Equestrian Center (☎ *852-6000*).

Watersports

Various locations, Puerto Rico.

If your hotel doesn't offer watersports, try one of these. For general watersport equipment rentals, **Carib Aquatic Adventures in Miramar** (☎ *724-1882*) does everything from boat rentals to deep-sea fishing excursions. For scuba diving, call: *Adventure by the Sea (Cerro Gordo, ☎ 251-4923)*, **Caribbean Divers** (☎ *722-7393*), **Caribbean School of Aquatics** *(Condado, ☎ 728-6606)*, **Coral Head Divers** *(Humacao, ☎ 850-7208)*, **Dorado Marine Center** (☎ *796-4645*), and **Mundo Submarino** *(Isla Verde, ☎ 791-5764)*. For deep-sea fishing, try: **Benitez** *(San Juan, ☎ 723-2292)*, **Makaira Hunter** *(Miramar, ☎ 397-8028)*, **Southern Witch** *(Miramar, ☎ 731-9252)*, **Western Tourist Services** (☎ *834-4008*).

Where to Stay

Highest Rated Hotels in Puerto Rico

★★★★★ **El Conquistador Resort**

★★★★★ **El San Juan Hotel/Casino**

★★★★★ **Horned Dorset Primavera**

★★★★★ **Hyatt Dorado Beach**

★★★★★ **Hyatt Regency Cerromar**

★★★★★ **Sands Hotel & Casino**

★★★★ **Caribe Hilton & Casino**

★★★★ **Condado Plaza Hotel**

★★★★ **Palmas del Mar Humacao**

★★★★ **Radisson Ambassador Plaza**

Most Exclusive Hotels in Puerto Rico

★★★★	**Caribe Hilton & Casino**	$200–$1200
★★★★	**Palmas del Mar Humacao**	$145–$715
★★★★★	**Sands Hotel & Casino**	$290–$305
★★★★★	**El Conquistador Resort**	$170–$420
★★★	**Holiday Inn Crowne Plaza**	$185–$390

Fielding's Best Value Hotels in Puerto Rico

★★	**Sea Gate Guest House**	$40–$85
★★★★	**Horned Dorset Primavera**	$150–$440
★★	**Parador Banos de Coamo**	$55–$65
★★★	**Ponce Hilton and Casino**	$170–$375
★★	**Days Inn**	$80–$140

Accommodations in Puerto Rico rank among the finest in the world for the value. The top-class resorts and hotels offer all the amenities of sophistication, from casinos to spas, to some of the most glorious pool complexes in the world. Hotel spas on Puerto Rico have simply raised the facility to an art. The **Caribe Spa** at the Caribe Hilton offers both Universal and Nautilus weight machines, aerobic and yoga classes, aerobicycles, massages, herbal wraps, loofah body polish and facials. The **Penthouse Spa** at the El San Juan Hotel & Casino offers fitness evaluations, supervised weight-loss program, aerobics classes, sauna, steam room and massage. The fitness center at the **Palmas del Mar Resort** in Humacao features hydra-fitness exercise equipment, exercise program, free-weight training and computerized evaluations. The **Plaza Spa** at the Condado Plaza Hotel & Casino features Universal weight training machines, video exercycles, sauna, whirlpool, facials and massages. In contrast, moderate-priced hotels are rather anonymous and make it tempting either to splurge or economize. But budget accommodations can offer some wonderful treasures, especially if you look among the government-sponsored inns called *paradores*, which can turn a tropical vacation into a most memorable and intimate experience.

IN SAN JUAN AND CONDADO AREA

Today the Condado area, which runs around the Atlantic between Ocean Park and Miramar, is one of the main areas for hotels and resorts, now returning to its glitzy rep of years gone by. The **Condado Plaza Hotel & Casino** is practically a planet unto itself, with a full range of eateries, casinos, Vegas-type shows, its own shopping mall, and top American furnishings. One of the closest to the airport is **El San Juan Hotel & Casino**, also a luxury property of top proportions, including an enormous pool that inspires a lot of social climbing. A good moderate option is **Carib Inn**, near the airport, but a mere short walk to the beach. In Isla Verde, east of San Juan/ Santurce, is the U.S.-run **TraveLodge**, with comfortably large beds, modernized bathrooms, and an acceptable pool.

Hotels and Resorts

Best Western Pierre   **$97–$145**   ★★★

105 de Diego Avenue, ☎ *(800) 528-1234, (809) 721-1200.*
Single: $97–$135. Double: $107–$145.
Located in the heart of the Santurce business district, four blocks from Condado, this Best Western appeals to business travelers on a budget. Facilities are limited to a restaurant, bar, and pool. 184 rooms. Credit Cards: CB, V, MC, DC, A.

Carib Inn Tennis Club   **$105–$320**   ★★

Isla Verde, ☎ *(800) 548-8217, (809) 791-3535.*
Single: $105–$120. Double: $110–$320.
Located near the airport and a few minutes from the beach, this resort caters to tennis players, with eight courts, a ball machine, and video playback. Oddly enough, guests must pay extra to use the courts, and even more still for night play, which gives the feeling of being nickeled and dimed. The tennis theme continues with a pool shaped like a racquet. Accommodations are adequate but cry out for renova-

tion. There are a few restaurants and bars on-site, and the salsa bands on Friday and Saturday nights are popular. 225 rooms. Credit Cards: CB, V, MC, DC, A.

Caribe Hilton & Casino $200–$1200 ★★★★

Fort San Jeronimo, ☎ *(800) 468-8585.*
Single: $200–$755. Double: $225–$1200.

This behemoth does a huge business with meetings and conventions, so you'll be sharing facilities with lots of folks wearing name tags. Nevertheless, this is a smashing resort, with lots going on all the time. There's a putting green, six tennis courts, a health club with air-conditioned racquetball and squash courts, supervised programs for kids, six restaurants, and several bars, one with live entertainment. Snorkel and scuba equipment can be found on the small beach. Guest rooms are housed in two towers, one 10 stories, the other 20. All are quite decent, and most have ocean views. Business travelers are catered to on three executive levels. Fort San Jeronimo, which dates back to the 16th century, is footsteps away. The $40 million that Hilton poured into the resort a few years back really shows, but individual travelers may be happier at a smaller property, away from conventioneers. 670 rooms. Credit Cards: CB, V, MC, A.

Condado Beach Trio $140–$195 ★★★

Ashford Avenue, ☎ *(800) 468-2775, (809) 721-6090.*
Single: $140–$195. Double: $140–$195.

This government-owned complex consists of two hotels and the El Centro Convention Center, all greatly renovated with great results. The Spanish Colonial-style Hotel Condado Beach dates back to 1919. Guestrooms are elegant and tastefully done with nice furnishings and original art. The grounds include a few restaurants and bars, a casino and a pool. The nearby La Concha Hotel is oriented more toward families, with facilities like two tennis courts and a pool. Guest rooms there are not as nice as at Condado Beach, but they are cheaper. There's also a disco, two restaurants, and live entertainment in one of the two bars. The disco is quite upscale and shaped like a conch shell. Guests can use the facilities at both hotels; Condado Beach has better service. The "beach" in the title is quite narrow. Lots of conventioneers meet and stay at this complex. 481 rooms. Credit Cards: CB, V, MC, DC, A.

Condado Plaza Hotel $195–$355 ★★★★

999 Ashford Avenue, ☎ *(800) 468-8588, (809) 721-1000.*
Single: $195–$335. Double: $225–$355.

This full-service resort has a small beach, but most guests hang out at one of the five pools. The five-acre property was renovated in 1993, with good results. Accommodations are housed in two towers and are quite nice, though only some have sea views. Those shelling out extra for a Plaza Club room enjoy added amenities and the use of a lounge. The grounds include two tennis courts, a fitness center, air-conditioned squash and racquetball courts, a business center, and Puerto Rico's largest casino. There's also several eateries, bars and a hopping disco. 575 rooms. Credit Cards: CB, V, MC, A.

El Canario by the Lagoon $65–$110 ★★

4 Calle Clemenceau, ☎ *(809) 722-5058.*

Single: $65–$85. Double: $75–$110.

Located in the heart of Condado, this small European-style hotel is just a block from the beach. Rooms are basic but comfortable. Besides a tour desk, there are few facilities on-site, but many within walking distance. Not bad for the rates. 40 rooms. Credit Cards: V, MC, A.

El Canario by the Sea $80–$125 ★

4 Condado Avenue, ☎ *(800) 533-2649, (809) 722-8640.*
Single: $80. Double: $95–$125.

Located just off the beach, this small hotel is family-run. Rooms are modest but comfortable and air-conditioned. Each morning, a complimentary continental breakfast is served in the courtyard. There's a bar and tour desk, but little else in the way of extras. Good value, though. 25 rooms. Credit Cards: V, MC, DC, A.

El San Juan Hotel/Casino $250–$995 ★★★★★

Isla Verde Avenue, ☎ *(800) 468-2818, (809) 791-1000.*
Single: $250–$430. Double: $305–$995.

Opulence dominates at this well-known resort, one of the Caribbean's best and certainly among the most lavish. Accommodations are luxurious, with VCRs, stereos, TVs in the bathroom, minibars and modern art. Some have lanais and sitting areas, while others have sunken baths, whirlpools, or private garden spas. Facilities are quite extensive, and the service is excellent. The grounds include seven restaurants ranging from the formal Dar Tiffany to casual snackbars, eight bars, a disco, a casino, and three lighted tennis courts. There's also a Chinese restaurant housed in a pavilion from the 1964 New York World's Fair, all watersports including diving and waterskiing, a modern health club, and a pool for the kiddies. Staying here is an experience you won't soon forget. 390 rooms. Credit Cards: CB, V, MC, A.

Grande Hotel El Convento $85–$200 ★★

55 Condado Avenue, Cristo Street, ☎ *(800) 468-2779, (809) 721- 810.*
Single: $85–$175. Double: $95–$200.

This high-rise hotel consists of two linked towers. Accommodations range from standard guest rooms to suites with kitchenettes. The modest grounds include a casino, two restaurants, a bar and two pools, one for kids. Decent for the rates, but nothing special. 150 rooms. Credit Cards: CB, V, MC, DC, A.

Holiday Inn Crowne Plaza $185–$390 ★★★

Highway 187, ☎ *(800) 468-4578, (809) 253-2929.*
Single: $185. Double: $205–$390.

Located on Isla Verde Beach, close to the airport, this highrise is just a few years old. Accommodations are modern and comfortable, and most have sea views off the balcony. Facilities include a pretty casino, business center, gym, a pool, and two restaurants and three bars. All quite acceptable, but this hotel is so generic you'd hardly know you're in the Caribbean, and airport noise, particularly low-flying jets, can be obnoxious. 254 rooms. Credit Cards: CB, V, MC, DC, A.

Hotel Portal Del Condado $95–$125 ★★

76 Condado Avenue, ☎ *(809) 721-9010.*
Single: $95. Double: $115–$125.

Located in Condado within walking distance of the beach, this modest hotel offers clean and comfortable rooms for reasonable rates. There's no pool but guests can work on their tans on a rooftop deck. 48 rooms. Credit Cards: CB, V, MC, DC, A.

Radisson Ambassador Plaza　　　　**$170–$320**　　　　★ ★ ★ ★

1369 Ashford Avenue, ☎ (800) 333-3333, (809) 721-7300.
Single: $170–$310. Double: $180–$320.
Set in the heart of the Condado district, this glitzy hotel consists of an older hotel and an all-suite tower. Accommodations vary, but all are pleasant, though only some have ocean views. As expected, the suites offer the plushest digs and are well-suited to business travelers. Facilities include a rooftop swimming pool, business services center, health club, supervised children's programs, casino, and several restaurants and bars, one with entertainment nightly. This place has come a long way from its Howard Johnson roots. 233 rooms. Credit Cards: CB, V, MC, A.

Radisson Normandie　　　　**$160–$240**　　　　★ ★ ★

Munoz Rivera Avenue, ☎ (800) 333-3333, (809) 729-2929.
Single: $160–$200. Double: $240.
Housed in a landmark art deco building that dates back to 1940, this hotel is on the outskirts of Old San Juan. The hotel is shaped like a ship, and the staff wears nautical garb. Guest rooms are spacious and nicely decorated with art deco touches. Those on the Concierge Level enjoy extra amenities. Facilities include a few bars and restaurants and a pool. There's also a small beach. 177 rooms. Credit Cards: CB, V, MC, DC, A.

Ramada Hotel Condado　　　　**$130–$300**　　　　★ ★

1045 Ashford Avenue, ☎ (800) 468-2040, (809) 723-8000.
Single: $130–$160. Double: $160–$300.
Located adjacent to the San Juan Convention Center and on the beach, this high-rise offers adequate yet uninspired guest rooms and public areas. Facilities are limited to a bar, restaurant and pool. You can do better at these rates. 96 rooms. Credit Cards: V, MC, DC, A.

Regency Hotel　　　　**$140–$225**　　　　★ ★

1005 Ashford Avenue, ☎ (800) 468-2823, (809) 721- 505.
Single: $140–$225. Double: $140–$225.
This modest operation offers spacious guest rooms, studios with kitchenettes, and suites with full kitchens. All have balconies but not necessarily ocean views. Facilities are limited to a restaurant, pool and Jacuzzi. The beach is reached through an underground parking garage, an odd arrangement. Continental breakfast is included in the rates, and while this is nothing to write home about, it offers comfortable housing at a decent price. 127 rooms. Credit Cards: CB, V, MC, A.

San Juan Travelodge　　　　**$125–$175**　　　　★ ★

1313 Isla Verde Avenue, ☎ (800) 428-2028, (809) 728-1300.
Single: $125. Double: $140–$175.
Located near the airport, this budget choice offers acceptable rooms, some with balconies. There's a restaurant, deli and lounge on-site, as well as limited room service and a pool. 88 rooms. Credit Cards: CB, V, MC, A.

Sands Hotel & Casino   **$290–$305**   ★ ★ ★ ★ ★

Isla Verde Road, ☎ *(809) 791-6100.*
Single: $290. Double: $305.

Situated on five acres fronting three miles of sandy beach, this luxurious property is next door to the splashier El San Juan. Accommodations are generally plush with extras like minibars and floor to ceiling windows. All have balconies but not all have an ocean view. The extensive grounds include five restaurants, three lounges, a huge casino, daily activities, and a large free-form pool with a waterfall and swim-up bar. Nice, but the El San Juan is better, and the rates are comparable. 410 rooms. Credit Cards: CB, V, MC, DC, A.

Apartments and Condominiums

Local Puerto Ricans with luxury apartments or villas often rent their homes during high season, especially those located near the Hyatt Dorado Beach resort. Condominiums in high-rise buildings are also popular for tourist rentals; even rooms in hotels that have kitchenettes can be rented. Among the latter are ESJ Towers, the Regency, and the Excelsior. Shopping is easy since supermarkets tend to boast traditional mainland products along with more Latin-flavored spices, vegetables and fruits, etc.

Inns

Puerto Rico is famous for its network of charming country inns called *paradores puertorriqueños* (established in 1973), which offer superb accommodations and the ideal location for exploring the island's diverse attractions. Several privately owned and operated guest houses also serve as quiet and quaint accommodations far from the maddening crowds. What makes the paradores so special is they are each situated in a historic place or site of unusual scenic beauty. Prices range from $38–$96 per night, double occupancy, and are located from mountains to sea. Most have swimming pools and all offer the island's tantalizing cuisine. Many are even within driving distance from San Juan. Perhaps one of the most special sites is that of the **Parador Baõs de Coamo**, situated on the site of America's oldest thermal springs, once believed to be Ponce de Leon's "fountain of youth." Even FDR took advantage of the medicinal waters, praised by the Indians for over three centuries. Just a half-hour away is Ponce, the island's second largest city and home to the Caribbean's most extensive art museum.

Casa San Jose   **$205–$315**   ★ ★ ★

159 San Jose Street, Old San Juan, ☎ *(800) 223-6510, (809) 723-1212.*
Single: $205–$225. Double: $245–$315.

Set in Old San Juan, this charmer is housed in a converted 17th-century mansion. Each room and suite in the four-story Spanish Colonial house is decorated differently, and all are lovely, furnished with antiques, Persian rugs, Roman tubs, exquisite artworks, and ceiling fans. Suites have one or two bedrooms and even more opulent trappings. The rates include continental breakfast, afternoon tea and evening cocktails. The interior courtyard is accented by a fountain; its pleasant trickling can be heard in every room. Marvelous! 10 rooms. Credit Cards: V, MC, DC, A.

El Canario Inn   **$80–$125**   ★ ★

1317 Ashford Avenue, Condado, ☎ *(809) 722-3861.*
Single: $80. Double: $95–$125.

This modest inn is located a block from the beach. Rooms are air-conditioned and also have ceiling fans and private baths. They'll feed you breakfast, and there's a communal kitchen for self caterers, as well as lots within walking distance. The very reasonable rates make this a real bargain. 25 rooms. Credit Cards: CB, V, MC, DC, A.

Parador Hacienda Gripinas $64–$107   ★ ★

6a Ocean Drive, Jayuya, ☎ *(800) 443- 266, (809) 721-2884.*
Single: $64–$74. Double: $64–$107.

Located on a 20-acre plantation that in the 18th century produced coffee, this small country inn in the mountains is loaded with character. Guest rooms are simple but attractive; most have ceiling fans in lieu of air conditioning. There's little in the way of recreational facilities save a pool and basketball court; note that this area gets a lot of rain. The dining room serves up three tasty squares a day; Sunday brunch is especially popular. Not for those seeking a partying holiday, but perfect for relaxing and enjoying the scenery. 11 rooms. Credit Cards: V, MC.

Low Cost Lodging

During low season, mid-April through December expect to find the most expensive hotels dropping their rates down to a moderate range. Other hotels give special packages for low season. It doesn't hurt to sniff out the possibility of bargaining; just do it tactfully. The Puerto Rico Tourism Company currently recognizes 35 camping areas throughout the island, from El Yunque National Forest to Luquillo Beach and many of the public beaches around the island. Camping facilities in Puerto Rico come with a broad definition, including cottages, pup tents, huts, lean-tos and even trailer homes. Fees range from $5-$12. Don't always count on finding hot water or toilets. Be prepared to go rustic, if necessary.

Arcade Inn $40–$90   ★

8 Taft Street, ☎ *(809) 728-7524.*
Single: $40–$90. Double: $50–$90.

This guesthouse is within walking distance to the beach. Rooms are modest but air-conditioned and with private baths; a few efficiencies are also available. There's a bar on the premises, but you'll have to venture out for meals. That's easily done, as there is much within an easy walk. 19 rooms. Credit Cards: MC, A.

Atlantic Beach Hotel $60–$140   ★ ★

1 Calle Vendig, ☎ *(809) 721-6900.*
Single: $60–$110. Double: $75–$140.

This modest hotel caters mostly to gays, though anyone is welcome (except for children)—but check your homophobia at the door. Rooms are spartan but comfortable and air-conditioned; not all have private baths, so be sure to request one if that's important to you. The beach is footsteps away. There's no pool but the Jacuzzi offers pleasant soaking. The restaurant serves only breakfast and lunch, with lots of dinner options within walking distance. 37 rooms. Credit Cards: V, MC, A.

Green Isle Inn $43–$73   ★

Villamar Street, ☎ *(800) 677-8860, (809) 726-4330.*
Single: $43–$73. Double: $43–$73.

This small hotel has basic air-conditioned rooms, many with kitchenettes. There's a bar and restaurant, and two pools. Limited room service is available. The beach is an easy walk. 44 rooms. Credit Cards: V, MC, A.

International Airport $80–$90

Isla Verde, ☎ *(809) 791-1700.*
Single: $80. Double: $90.

Located right in the airport, on the third floor of the terminal building, this budget choice is adequate, but unless you're between flights, there's really no reason to stay here. More atmospheric lodging can be found at similar rates. 57 rooms. Credit Cards: CB, V, MC, A.

Where to Eat

Highest Rated Restaurants in Puerto Rico

★★★★★ Horned Dorset Primavera

★★★★★ La Compostela

★★★★★ Ramiro's

★★★★ Amadeus

★★★★ La Chaumiere

★★★ Ajilli-Mojili

★★★ Back Street Hong Kong

★★★ El Ancla

★★★ El Patio de Sam

★★★ La Bombonera

Most Exclusive Restaurants in Puerto Rico

★★★★★ Horned Dorset Primavera	$45–$45
★★★★★ Ramiro's	$22–$33
★★★ Back Street Hong Kong	$15–$32
★★★★★ La Compostela	$15–$29
★★★ Ajilli-Mojili	$15–$25

Fielding's Best Value Restaurants in Puerto Rico

★★★ La Mallorquina	$14–$30
★★★★★ Horned Dorset Primavera	$45–$45
★★★ El Patio de Sam	$9–$25
★★★ El Ancla	$3–$28
★★★★★ Ramiro's	$22–$33

The first thing you must learn before sitting down to dinner in Puerto Rico is the lively island equivalent to Bon Appetit—*Ibuen provecho!* The phrase becomes easily prophetic here where traditional island fare as well as contemporary cuisine is lovingly and expertly prepared. Puerto Rican cuisine is a delicious blend of Spanish, African and Taíno Indian cooking. Each of these traditions have contributed in terms of seasonings, cooking methods, and basic ingredients. *Cocina criolla* or creole cuisine, began with the Taínos, the indigenous tribe of the island. The Taínos cultivated many crops, notably *yuca* (yucca), corn, yam, and *yautía* (taniers). Yuca was used to prepare *casabe*, a flatbread that was eaten daily and is still enjoyed today. Taínos also used yuca to make vinegar, which was an important seasoning since salt was not used in cooking. Foods introduced by the Spaniards include wheat, chick-peas, cilantro, eggplant, onions, coconut, garlic and rum. The African slave trade also brought important foods and techniques to the island, including pidgin peas, plantains and okra. The African population is also credited with developing many coconut dishes that remain popular today. Their favorite technique was frying, which quickly became the most common way of cooking on the island. The blending of flavors and ingredients evolved from generation to generation, combining to form the Puerto Rican cuisine today.

As for noshing, the island has no lack of things on which to while away your calories. Fritters are the favorite finger food, and are sold at fritter stands and even incorporated into the daily menus in most homes. The most famous fritters are *tostones* (fried green plantains), which are used as well as a side dish with rice and beans, onion steak, or fried pork chops. Other favorites include *alcapurrias*, made from grated yautia, and green bananas, stuffed with *picadillo* (cooked ground meat), crabmeat or chicken, *empanadillas*, small deep-fried flour turnovers with cheddar or swiss cheese, ground meat or shredded chicken; *bacalaítos*, flour fritters made from salt codfish; *surrullos de maíz* or *surrullitos*, made of cornmeal, shaped like a cigar and served with a sauce made of mayonnaise and ketchup, and *rellenos de papa*, mashed potato balls stuffed with almost any filling and deep-fried to a crispy texture. Other traditional appetizers are chicken nuggets and marinated green bananas. The latter are now combined with the new ingredients like flavored vinegars to create interesting variations found even in elegant restaurants.

Get used to the fact that side dishes are often as hearty as the main dish in Puerto Rico. In fact, if you are dieting and/or trying to save money, eating side dishes can be your vacation saver. Nearly standard for every meal in Puerto Rico is *arroz blanco* (white rice boiled in water and oil), and *habichuelas* (beans stewed in sofrito (piré of onions, peppers, cilantro, garlic, and salt pork), and a tomato and coriander sauce. *Mofongo* is also popular—fried green plantains mashed with garlic, salt and fried pork rinds and rolled into a ball. It's usually served with beef or chicken broth or *carne frita* (pork meat, diced and fried).

The national soup of Puerto Rico is *asopao*, a hearty chicken and rice gumbo-like soup which can serve as an entree. Sometimes it's made with lobster and shrimp. Roast suckling pig is a national dish, especially for holidays. Steak and onions is an everyday dish, as are pork ribs stewed or prepared with yellow rice and green pigeon peas. With such exquisite access to the sea, fish dishes are supremely fresh and display the island's Spanish heritage, as they are mostly prepared in a sofrito-based sauce or *escabeche* (marinated) style. Escabeche is a combination of olive oil, white vinegar and spices. *Bacalho* (salt cod) has been a menu staple for centuries; other seafood to look for are red snapper, shrimp, langostinos (saltwater crayfish), mussels, and the spiny lobster characteristic of the Caribbean. The national dessert is flan, a condensed milk and vanilla custard, variations of which can be made by adding any one of the following ingredients: cream cheese, coconut milk, mashed pumpkin, or breadfruit. Puerto Ricans also prepare bread pudding: *tembleqque*, a gelatin-like coconut milk and cornstarch custard often eaten sprinkled with cinnamon, *arroz con dulce*, rice pudding cooked with condensed coconut milk, ginger, and raisins, and fruit sherbets made with tamarins and soursop. Other favorite desserts are green papaya or guava shells simmered in heavy syrup and served with white or cottage cheese.

Puerto Rican coffee is exquisitely aromatic, served either black or with frothy boiled milk. Since Puerto Rico is the leading producer of rum, you'll find the piña coladas on the island some of the tastiest you've ever had.

Ajilli-Mojili $$$ ★★★

Calle Clemenceau,
Latin American cuisine. Specialties: Mofongo.
Lunch: entrees $15–$25.
Dinner: entrees $15–$25.

This is probably one of the most popular eateries for tipico Puerto Rican food. A specialty is Mofongo, fried plantain stuffed with seafood, beef or chicken (here it's usually shrimp), a dish you probably won't find outside of these isles. Although it's located in a Condado hotel, many local families make this a regular gathering spot, so the ambience is cheerful and festive. Associated Hotel: Condado Lagoon Hotel. Reservations recommended. Credit Cards: V, MC, A.

Al Dente $$ ★★

Calle Recinto Sur, Old San Juan, ☎ (809) 723-7303.
Italian cuisine. Specialties: Fresh Pasta.
Lunch: 12:00 a.m.–4:00 p.m., entrees $10–$15.
Dinner: 4:00 p.m.–10:00 p.m., entrees $10–$15.

This restaurant is a touch of old Palermo in Old San Juan. Located in a historical building in the heart of the colonial city, the dining room features fresh pasta, chicken and fish in light sauces, utilizing fresh herbs and spices. The atmosphere is as unstuffy as the food. Closed: Sun. Reservations recommended. Credit Cards: V, MC, A.

Amadeus $$ ★★★★

Calle San Sebastian, Old San Juan, ☎ *(809) 722-8635.*
Latin American cuisine.
Lunch: entrees $8–$16.
Dinner: entrees $8–$16.

A name like Amadeus connotes glittering candelabra, spinets and powdered wigs. Contrary to that idea, this restaurant and cafe is as modern as can be—the clever chef adds a dash of French flair to native dishes; for example, a combination of caviar and sour cream with green plantain. A version of cassoulet is made here with chorizo and black beans. Some people could make a whole meal from a plate of some very creative appetizers that a group of four or more can share; a sort of Puerto Rican dim sum. Call in advance to reserve space in the back room. It's open from noon to midnight. Closed: Mon. Reservations recommended. Credit Cards: V, MC, A.

Anchor's Inn $$$ ★★

Route 987, Km. 2.7, Fajardo, ☎ *(809) 863-7200.*
Latin American cuisine.
Lunch: 11:00 a.m.–4:00 p.m., entrees $8–$15.
Dinner: 4:00 p.m.–11:00 p.m., entrees $15–$20.

This unpretentious spot by the sea offers a scrumptious plate of paella and an equally appealing vista of the Fajardo harbor. It's an ideal stopping point for people driving around the island, with a location near one of Puerto Rico's prime boating and watersports areas. If you tire of the nine restaurants at the posh El Conquistador resort nearby, give this place a try; it stays open late. Reservations recommended. Credit Cards: V, MC, A.

Back Street Hong Kong $$$ ★★★

Avenida de Isla Verde, Isla Verde, ☎ *(809) 791-1000.*
Chinese cuisine.
Dinner: 6:00 p.m.–12:00 p.m., entrees $15–$32.

This isn't your typical greasy spoon chop-suey, in fact, people like to dress up a bit to eat the savory Chinese food in a restaurant that recreates a Hong Kong back alley. The eclectic dining room was transported piecemeal from a Seattle World's Fair exhibition; it also contains a tropical aquarium that delights young children. Associated Hotel: El San Juan Hotel/Casino. Reservations recommended. Credit Cards: V, MC, A.

Butterfly People $ ★★

152 Calle Fortaleza, Old San Juan, ☎ *(809) 723-2432.*
International cuisine.
Lunch: 10:00 a.m.–6:00 p.m., entrees $5–$9.

Notice to lepidopterists—you will be dazzled at this restaurant and gallery that sells butterflies under glass from one of the most extensive private collections in the world. While the prices for these winged beauties range from moderate to stratospheric, the mostly-Puerto Rican dishes here are fairly reasonable. You can also have a soup (gazpacho is good), or salad in a plant-filled patio. Closed: Sun. Credit Cards: V, MC, DC, A.

El Patio de Sam $$$ ★★★

102 Calle San Sebastian, Old San Juan, ☎ (809) 723-1149.
International cuisine.
Lunch: entrees $9–$25.
Dinner: entrees $9–$25.
This oft-visited eatery is remarkable for serving the juiciest burgers in town in the oldest building in town. Of course, there's a well-balanced menu of lobster tail, soups, desserts and tropical fruit libations. The late-night crowd likes to party here; it stays open till the wee hours on weekends. Credit Cards: V, MC, DC, A.

La Bombonera $ ★★★

Calle San Francisco, Old San Juan, ☎ (809) 722-0658.
Latin American cuisine.
Lunch: entrees $5–$8.
Dinner: entrees $5–$8.
Like its name says, this old-fashioned eatery proffers a plethora of bonbons both sweet and savory. You can have a plate of calamares en su tinta (squid in its own ink served with rice), while your youngster sips hot chocolate. This place serves as the corner malt shop and tryst spot for locals who have been flocking to it since 1902. It's great for breakfast, very crowded at lunch, and ideal for tea and snacks. Takeout available. It's open from 7:30 am to 8:30 p.m. Reservations recommended. Credit Cards: V, MC, A.

La Casona de Serafin $$$ ★★★

Hwy 102, Km. 9, Cabo Rojo, ☎ (809) 851-0066.
Latin American cuisine. Specialties: Lobster.
Lunch: entrees $10–$20.
Dinner: entrees $21–$31.
Some people think the best seafood in Puerto Rico is served in this area of Joyuda Beach. Certainly the atmosphere at La Casona is great for eating peel-it-yourself shrimp or its specialty, lobster. Steaks and Puerto Rican dishes are also available, and there's a full bar and lounge. This restaurant is popular with local families who flock here on weekends, when the sleepy town wakes up to a noisy string of craft shops and oyster bars along the beach. Reservations recommended. Credit Cards: V, MC, A.

La Chaumiere $$$ ★★★★

367 Tetuan Street, Old San Juan, ☎ (809) 722-3330.
French cuisine.
Dinner: 6:00 p.m.–12:00 p.m., entrees $22–$37.
This restaurant serves classic French cuisine to a faithful clientele in surroundings that transport guests to the Gallic countryside. It's the kind of place where you can order rarely-found specialties like floating island (merengues in a sauce of creme anglaise) or oysters Rockefeller. Perfect for a pre-show supper; it's located behind the famous Tapia Theater. Closed: Sun. Reservations recommended. Credit Cards: V, MC, DC, A.

La Compostela $$$ ★★★★★

Avenida Condado, Santurce, ☎ *(809) 724-6088.*
Spanish cuisine.
Lunch: 12:00 a.m.–3:00 p.m., entrees $15–$29.
Dinner: 6:30 p.m.–10:30 p.m., entrees $15–$29.

Many repeat visitors recommend this Spanish restaurant with a French touch in a commercial suburb of San Juan. The owner has spent time laboring in the kitchens in both countries; he blends the styles effortlessly. The wine cellar is amazing: close to 10,000 bottles! Closed: Sun. Reservations recommended. Credit Cards: V, MC, DC, A.

La Mallorquina $$$ ★★★

Calle San Justo 207, Old San Juan, ☎ *(809) 722-3261.*
Latin American cuisine.
Lunch: 11:30 a.m.–3:00 p.m., entrees $14–$30.
Dinner: 4:00 p.m.–10:00 p.m., entrees $14–$30.

This restaurant may be a bit of a tourist trap, but it's still worth visiting for the house special *asopao*, the Puerto Rican version of risotto, served with a choice of seafood or chicken. It's one of the oldest restaurants in town, founded in 1848. Service is gracious and attentive. Closed: Sun. Credit Cards: V, MC, DC, A.

Parador Villa Parguera $$ ★★★

Route 307, Lajas, ☎ *(809) 899-7777.*
Latin American cuisine. Specialties: Red Snapper Stuffed with Seafood.
Lunch: 7:30 a.m.–4:00 p.m., entrees $5–$20.
Dinner: 4:00 p.m.–9:30 p.m., entrees $5–$20.

Simply prepared but very fresh seafood is a specialty at this seaside inn (one of the island's touted "paradores") surrounded by coconut palms on Phosphorescent Bay, on the West Coast. The Parador is an excellent base for viewing the local phenomenon—on moonlit nights, the bay is "lit" by thousands of tiny organisms called dinoflagellates. Come during the week, as hordes of families crowd the area on weekends. Associated Hotel: Parador Villa Parguera. Reservations recommended. Credit Cards: D, CB, V, MC, DC, A.

Ramiro's $$$ ★★★★★

Avenida Magdalena 1106, Condado, ☎ *(809) 721-9049.*
Spanish cuisine. Specialties: Lamb, Homemade Desserts.
Lunch: 12:00 a.m.–3:00 p.m., entrees $24–$33.
Dinner: 6:30 p.m.–10:30 p.m., prix fixe $22–$33.

Patrons dress up to dine at this plush salon of *cocina fantastica*; owner Jesus Ramiro may be the island's most creative chef. Although he uses local produce and ingredients, his technique is distinctly French, especially in the elaborate constructions of his sinful desserts. Lamb is one of his favorite meats to work with, on the menu you will find it in ravioli or paired with buffalo or venison in a spicy sauce, or a perfectly roasted rack. Closed: Mon. Reservations recommended. Credit Cards: V, MC, DC, A.

The Chart House $$$ ★★

1214 Ashford Avenue, Condado, ☎ *(809) 728-0110.*
American cuisine. Specialties: Prime Rib, Mud Pie.
Dinner: 6:00 p.m.–11:00 p.m., entrees $16–$25.

If the food here seems familiar to mainland guests, it is. The Chart House is a local link in the California-based steak and lobster chain, but what a link! The setting is in a historic turn-of-the-century homestead, which belonged to the Rauschenplat family. The property is surrounded by well-tended gardens and a treehouse. The all-American food is very popular with locals as well. Reservations required. Credit Cards: V, MC, DC, A.

Where to Shop

Puerto Rico has duty-free shopping at the Luis Munoz Marin International Airport and several factory outlets in Old San Juan. Both traditional and contemporary items can be bought in Old San Juan and out on the island, and you shouldn't go home without at least some representative of local craft. A day's excursion in a car could be spent touring the island to visit various craftsmen in their studios. (When you meet an artist and then buy his work, his personality and your memory of him or her always become indelibly entwined with the object itself—one of the true meanings of art.) The **Puerto Rico Tourism Company** ☎ *(809) 721-2400* offers a researched list of studios to visit along with a map to help you get there. Some studios are only open to the public at specific times, so make sure your itinerary fits the schedules. Possible workshops range from wood carvers to hammock-makers, to jewelry and furniture makers. It is always fascinating to visit the studio of an artisan who makes *santos* (saints); they are usually very spiritual people and the atmosphere of the saints themselves often pervades the workshop.

Even without the Biennial, Old San Juan has a remarkably lively arts scene. Walking along Cristo and San Jose Streets, you could lose count of the galleries. One of the best known is the **Galeria Botello** at *208 Cristo* with works by local artists as well as the Spanish artist Angel Botello and a fine collection of santos (small carved wooden figures of saints).

You'll find modern santos, carnival masks, pottery and the like at **Puerto Rican Arts and Crafts** at *204 Fortaleza*, old San Juan. And you can still get a Panama hat ($30–$50) at the **Casa Mendez Suarez**, which has been at *251 San Justo* since 1886, and elaborate flowered Spanish fans ($3.95 and up) at **La Nueva Opera**, *254 Fortaleza*. Another good place to check out is **La Piazoleta**, a Puerto Rican Craft Center, at *Pier 3, at the Customs House in Old San Juan.*

Old San Juan is also thick with antique stores, like **El Alcazar** at *103 San Jose* and *109 Sol.* both locations concentrate on 17th- and 18th-century Spanish art and 19th- and 20th-century French bibelots and brocante, and can ship home anything you buy.

The Book Store at *255 San Jose, Old San Juan,* has a good selection of English-language books as well as books on Puerto Rico, and CDs of Puerto Rican danza and salsa music.

Calle Fortaleza in Old San Juan is a treasurehouse of boutiques and stores. If you're in need of brightly colored resort wear made of special batiks and tie-dyes, stop by **La Casita**. On **Calle San Francisco**, the finest of the island's handmade lace can be found at **Aguadilla en San Juan**, including tablecloths and dresses.

THE NORTHWEST COAST

Dorado

Dorado, about twenty miles from San Juan off Route 693, is the closest town to the Hyatt Regency Cerromar Beach and the Hyatt Dorado Beach hotels. (If you're cruising the area, these are two fine resorts to plunk yourself down for a lunch or a drink.) The town has remained stuck in time despite the construction of the hotels. A few distracting hours can be wiled away at the shopping center and the handful of arts and crafts stores on the main streets. If you are staying at the resorts, a limousine will be sent to pick you up at San Juan's International Airport, about a three-quarters-of-an-hour-drive. The hotels also use a small airstrip a few minutes away from their front doors.

There are numerous mountain treks that can be taken in this area, especially through the **Parque de las Cavernas del Rio Camuy**, a 268-acre reserve featuring caves with an amazing array of stalactites and stalagmites. (For more information, see the section called "Treks" above.) The **Arecibo Observatory** also makes a fascinating excursion (For more information see "What Else to See on the Island," above.) Excursions from Dorado can easily be made to see the historic center of Old San Juan (45 minutes by car), as well as day trips down the southern coast at La Parguera and Cabo Rojo.

Where to Stay

The **Hyatt Dorado** is a no-holds-barred resort set on lushly landscaped grounds that caters to families as well as conventioneers. That might mean you forsake a bit of honeymoon-type privacy for the all-inclusive touch which makes some vacationers feel at home and others overwhelmed by overenthusiastic social directors. The **Hyatt Regency Cerromar Beach** is a bit less tropical, ensconced in a tall high-rise, with an absolutely spectacular pool that includes a waterfall, hydromassage and other playtoys.

Hotels and Resorts

Days Inn $80–$140 ★★

Route 1, Mercedita, ☎ *(800) 325-2525, (809) 841-1000.*
Single: $80. Double: $90–$140.
Located near the Intra-American University, this budget choice offers typical Days Inn accommodations and facilities. Rooms are on the basic side, but provide modern conveniences like TV and air conditioning. The premises include a pool, Jacuzzi, restaurant, nightclub and a games room. 121 rooms. Credit Cards: CB, V, MC, DC, A.

Hyatt Dorado Beach $160–$490 ★★★★★

Dorado, ☎ *(800) 233-1234, (809) 796-1234.*
Single: $160–$490. Double: $160–$490.

Located on a 1000-acre estate shared with its sister property, the Hyatt Regency Cerromar, this deluxe operation aims to please—and succeeds. Superior to its sibling, it has extensive facilities, all of the highest quality. Accommodations are in 14 two-story buildings and quite plush, with lots of room in which to move, rattan furnishings, balconies or terraces, minibars, and marble baths. There are also cottages of two or three bedrooms that line the fairway. Recreational options are the best on the island, with two 18-hole golf courses designed by Robert Trent Jones, a club house, two pools, one Olympic sized, a health club with aerobics classes, eight tennis courts, a windsurfing school, and a private beach with watersports. Dining options range from formal restaurants to the casual beach bar to theme night dinners; the food is high priced, but if you can afford the rates, you probably can afford the meals, too. A shuttle bus takes you to the casino and other facilities at the Hyatt Regency Cerromar. 298 rooms. Credit Cards: CB, V, MC, A.

Hyatt Regency Cerromar $165–$420 ★★★★★

Dorado, ☎ *(800) 233-1234, (809) 796-1234.*
Single: $165–$420. Double: $165–$420.

Sister property to the above-mentioned Hyatt Dorado and sharing its 1000 acres, this plush resort centers around a seven-story Y-shaped hotel. Guest rooms are decorated in an island theme and have minibars, spacious baths and balconies. The hotel boasts of having the world's largest pool, which comes in at 1776 feet, complete with whirlpools, a Jacuzzi grotto, a swim-up bar, 14 waterfalls, five separate swimming areas, and an impressive water slide. There's also an Olympic-size pool for the more sedate crowd. Health club, 14 tennis courts, a fine beach, supervised children's activities, all watersports, bicycle and jogging trails, and 36 holes of golf on Robert Trent Jones-designed courses. Guests can choose from four restaurants—one serving sushi, a rarity in Puerto Rico—or hop the shuttle to try the food at the Hyatt Dorado. For nightlife, try the casino, disco, or several bars. Excellent all the way, though expect to see a fair amount of business travelers. 504 rooms. Credit Cards: CB, V, MC, A.

Parador El Guajataca $77–$95 ★★

Route 2, Quebradjlas, Quebradillas, ☎ *(800) 964-3065, (809) 895-3070.*
Single: $77–$83. Double: $83–$95.

Set on a bluff overlooking the beach, this small hotel has many resort amenities at an unbeatable price. Accommodations are comfortable and modern. Guests can enjoy the nice beach, play tennis on two courts, or swim in the Olympic-size pool. The restaurant serves creole cuisine, and there's entertainment in the bar on weekends. 38 rooms. Credit Cards: CB, MC, DC, A.

Inns

Puerto Rico is famous for its network of charming country inns called *paradores puertorriqueños* (established in 1973), which offer superb accommodations and the ideal location for exploring the island's diverse attractions. Several privately owned and operated guest houses also serve as quiet and quaint accommodations far from the madding crowds. What makes the paradores so special is they are each situated in a historic place or site of unusual scenic beauty. Prices range from $38–$96 per night, double occupancy, and are located from mountains to sea. Most have swimming pools and all offer the island's tantalizing cuisine. Many are even within driving distance from San Juan.

Parador Vistamar   **$60–$75**   ★★

Highway 113, Quebradillas, ☎ *(800) 443- 266, (809) 895-2065.*
Single: $60–$75. Double: $60–$75.

Fine views of the sea from this hilltop inn, which offers air-conditioned rooms that are comfortable but on the plain side. There's a large pool, Jacuzzi, tennis court, and game room on-site, as well as a few dining outlets and three bars, one with music and dancing on the weekends. 55 rooms. Credit Cards: CB, V, MC, A.

Low Cost Lodging

Ask the Tourist Board about the possibility of renting rooms in the houses of local families. Also locals tend to know out-of-way places that do not appear in more established publications. Do note that you may not find standards of cleanliness at the level to which you are accustomed.

Where to Eat

Best international cuisine is found at the two Hyatt resorts, where you can be assured of cleanliness and safety. True Puerto Rican delicacies, with a Spanish twist can be found at **Los Naborias**. You will probably run into a strong local family scene at **La Famillia**, a warm, inviting, if simple place, particularly lively on Sundays.

EAST AND SOUTHEAST COAST

Fajardo and Humacao

Full of small-town spirit, the seaport of Fajardo lies but five miles south of Las Cabezas on Route 3. The lifestyle is slower-paced than in San Juan, and you can take morning and afternoon ferries to Culebra and Vieques. Treks can be made to the **Caribbean National Forest**, of which El Yunque Mountain is a part (see "Treks" above) and Losquillo Beach. Special expeditions can be arranged through Las Cabezas Nature Reserve (see "Trek" above) which could last all day, especially if you are interested in birdwatching. Native sloops set sail for Iacos where you will find fine snorkeling and swimming conditions. Deep-sea fishing and other watersports can be arranged at the **Puerto del Rey Marina**. The region has a fine 18-hole golf course and myriads of opportunities for scuba (see "Dive Sites" above.) Also see "Sports" above for more information.

This part of the island can be reached by taxis (expensive from the international airport), by small planes that land at the airport of Palmas del Mar, near Humacao; or by ferry boat (the cheapest at $2.50).

What Else to See

Parks and Gardens

Cabezas de San Juan Nature Res   ★★★★

Route 987, near Fajardo, ☎ *(809) 722-5882.*
Located on a peninsula, this nature reserve encompasses 316 acres and 124 acres of lagoons. It contains all of Puerto Rico's ecosystems except for the rainforest. A two-hour guided tour (reservations essential) will take you through a half-mile-long coral reef, mangrove swamps, beaches, a dry forest, and beds of turtle grass *(thalassia)*. A highlight is El Faro, a lighthouse built in 1880 and still used by the U.S. Coast Guard. The small nature center in the lighthouse, which is a designated National Historic Place, has touch tanks, aquariums, and an observation deck. Bilingual tours are at 9:30, 10:00, 10:30; the one at 2:00 is in English only. Well worth a visit. General admission: $5.00.

Where to Stay

Two hotels/resorts command the region with their enormous facilities. The patron saint of resorts, **El Conquistador**, has an amazing 16 restaurants and lounges—if you want to avoid the conventioneer crush, you should probably stay elsewhere. **Candelero**, near the beach at Palmas in the south, is more intimate, and less demanding socially, with activities geared for the athletic, including fine horseback riding, golf, tennis and artistic performances.

Also in this area are the Puerto Rican paradores, intimate inns that reflect the congeniality of the owner/host, and cheaper guesthouses.

Hotels and Resorts

El Conquistador Resort $170–$420 ★★★★★

Las Crobas, ☎ *(800) 468-8365, (809) 863-1000.*
Single: $170–$420. Double: $170–$420.

This is the mega-resort of mega-resorts, a huge enclave perched atop a cliff, overlooking the Caribbean on one side and the Atlantic on the other. The complex consists of five hotels, each a self-contained unit. Guest rooms are quite spiffy, with three phones, two TVs, VCRs, stereos, and refrigerators. There's also 88 suites and 176 casitas with more room and special amenities. The resort's 500 acres include a casino, six pools, eight tennis courts, pro shops, a health spa, 16 restaurants and bars, and watersports. There's also an 18-hole golf course, with another one planned at a future date. It's easy to see that the owners plucked down a cool $250 million to create this resort, which just opened in 1993. Among the gee-whiz attractions is an art collection worth a million dollars, a private island where you can spend the day, a 55-slip marina, and tons of shops. Despite its sheer size, service is efficient and cheerful. 926 rooms. Credit Cards: CB, V, MC, A.

Palmas del Mar Humacao $145–$715 ★★★★

Palmas del Mar, Humacao, ☎ *(800) 468-3331, (809) 852-6000.*
Single: $145–$715. Double: $145–$715.

This resort community, still under development in some areas, encompasses 2750 acres and fronts three miles of beach. Guests have a number of lodging options. The 100-room Candelero Hotel has spacious rooms with high ceilings and tropical decor, and offers the most affordable accommodations. The Palmas Inn has 23 suites with large living rooms, combination baths with bidets, and opulent furnishings. You can also book a two- or three-bedroom villa complete with kitchen. The well-tended grounds include an equestrian center, casino, marina, watersports, seven pools, 20 tennis courts (six lighted), 18 holes of golf, a fitness center with exercise classes, and supervised children's programs year-round. Dining outlets include a formal French restaurant, a casual Oriental eatery, and lots more. There's nightly entertainment at the Candelero. A free shuttle takes you to and from the action. Inquire about golf and tennis packages that can save you bucks. 298 rooms. Credit Cards: V, MC, A.

Apartments and Condominiums

Accommodations with fully equipped kitchens are available in any range of luxury, from the bareback simple near the seashore to the more luxurious privately owned condo rented in the owner's absence, usually during high season.

Inns

Paradores, or small inns, are for the more adventurous-minded who like to take chances on quality and ambiance. The best are true gems, and usually come complete with a very congenial host.

Parador La Familia $50–$70 ★

Route 987, Las Croabas, ☎ *(800) 443- 266, (809) 869-5345.*

Single: $50–$61. Double: $61–$70.

Located near Las Cabezas de San Juan Nature Preserve, this guesthouse is three miles from town; you'll definitely want a car for mobility. Rooms are basic but air-conditioned and comfortable. There's a good restaurant and pool on the premises. 28 rooms. Credit Cards: V, MC, A.

Parador Martorell   **$50–$85**   ★

Ocean Drive 6-A, Luquillo, ☎ *(800) 443- 266, (809) 889-2710.*
Single: $50–$85. Double: $70–$85.

This small family-run inn is located in Puerto Rico's northeast section. Rooms are small but comfortable; three share a bath and rely on ceiling fans to keep cool. The other seven have private baths and air conditioning, well worth the small bump in rates. There's a restaurant and pool on-site, and the beach is just two minutes away. 10 rooms. Credit Cards: MC, A.

Where to Eat

Best cuisine is found at the resorts; with so many facilities at **El Conquistador**, you may never have to leave the premises (that's their goal). Snacks can be found beachside (a cheap way to get through lunch on your way to a more expensive dinner). The best Italian food (if the most expensive) is at the **Azzuro** at the Palamas Mar Marriott hotel.

THE SOUTH COAST

Ponce

Ponce is Puerto Rico's second largest city, located about 70 miles south and west of San Juan. It dates back to 1692 when Ponce de Léon's great-grandson founded the small community. A high-speed road connects the two cities, which takes only about 90 minutes to traverse; you can also reach the area by plane from San Juan's International Airport. Many historical buildings, such as the stunning Cathedral of Our Lady of Guadeloupe are masterpieces of construction; as are some one thousand colonial houses designated national historic sites in a 40-by-80-block area. Nineteenth-century gas lamps illuminate the marble-edged streets glimmering with a pink glow; at night the stroll is extremely romantic. A fine collection of Latin American artists and international masters can be found in the **Museu de Arte de Ponce**, a light, airy place to stroll and relax out of the sun. Particularly fine are the works by Rubens and Rodin as well as many pre-Raphaelite paintings and sculptures. Anyone interested in sugarcane production and plantations will find an interesting exhibit at the **Castillo Serralles**, a restored 19th-century mansion, which has been refurbished to its 1930s furnishings. On Route 10, you'll discover the **Hacienda Buena Vista**, a restored coffee plantation which is open to visitors. (For more information, see under "What Else to See on the Island" above.)

Trekkers should head straightaway to the **Toro State Forest**, a 7000-acre preserve with waterfalls, the island's tallest peak, and an observation tour. (For more information, see under "Treks" above).

BEST VIEW:

A terrific perspective of the surrounding countryside and town can be seen from the 100-ft. tall El Vigia, an observatory tower, next to Castillo Serrallés.

What Else to See

Historical Sites

Hacienda Buena Vista ★★★

Route 10, near Ponce, ☎ *(809) 848-7020.*
From 1833 to the 1950s, this thriving plantation produced corn, citrus fruits and coffee. Today, under the auspices of Puerto Rico's Conservation Trust, it is a reconstructed farm from the late 19th century. Reservations are required for 1.5-hour tours, which are conducted Friday through Sunday; call 722-5882. The grounds include the estate house, former slave quarters, a 60-foot water slide, and working corn and coffee mills. General admission: $5.00.

Tibes Indian Ceremonial Center

Route 503, near Ponce, ☎ *(809) 840-2255.*
Hours Open: 9:00 a.m.–4:30 p.m.
This is the oldest cemetery in the Antilles, with some 200 skeletons unearthed from A.D. 300 and ballcourts and dance grounds from A.D. 700. The site also includes a recreated Taino village and a museum. General admission: $2.00.

Museums and Exhibits

El Museo Castillo Serralles

El Virgia 17, Ponce, ☎ *(809) 259-1774.*
Hours Open: 10:00 a.m.–5:00 p.m.
This Spanish-Revival mansion, Ponce's largest building, dates back to the 1930s. It is the former home of the Serralles family, producers of Don Q rum. Today it is a museum exhibiting elegant furnishings, the history of the local rum industry and a cafe. The lavishly landscaped grounds are a treat, and the views up here are breathtaking. General admission: $3.00.

Museo de Arte de Ponce   ★★★★

Ave. las Americas 25, Ponce, ☎ *(809) 848- 505.*
Designed by Edward Durell Stone, this fanciful museum exhibits traditional and modern art from the Americas and Europe, as well as contemporary works by Puerto Ricans. General admission: $3.00.

Ponce History Museum   ★★★

Calle Isabel, Ponce, ☎ *(809) 844-7071.*
Hours Open: 10:00 a.m.–5:00 p.m.
The name says it all: the history of Ponce detailed in two wooden houses dating back to the turn of the century. Closed Tuesday. General admission: $3.00.

Where to Stay

The Copamarine is a beach resort, located at least a 30-minute drive from the city—mostly characterized by its intimate, escapist ambiance. On the south shore of Ponce, the Hilton is making waves among southern resorts, but it's high-rise modernity takes a bit away from the tropical feel. It does have, however, an extensive water sports program and can make any arrangement for treks, etc. Other hotels in the middle of town give you easy access to the historic part of the city, especially at night when it is most atmospheric.

Hotels and Resorts

Melia Hotel $70–$90

2 Cristina Street, Ponce, ☎ *(800) 742-4276, (809) 842- 260.*
Single: $70–$80. Double: $75–$90.
This hotel in the historic district is pretty historic itself, dating back to 1914. The Spanish-colonial building includes interesting touches such as antiques and old chandeliers. Guest rooms are small and the furnishings dated—not antiques, just old. There's a decent restaurant on-site, but no other extras. Not a top choice by any means, but those who like historic hotels will be satisfied. Light sleeps should

request a room in the back, as street noises can be loud. Note that this hotel is not affiliated with the upscale Melia chain. 77 rooms. Credit Cards: V, MC, A.

Parador Boquemar   **$65–$70**   ★

Route 101, Cabo Rojo, Boquemar, ☎ *(800) 443- 266, (809) 851-2158.*
Single: $65–$70. Double: $65–$70.
This three-story hotel is near the beach. All the guest rooms, which are quite basic, have air conditioning, but some share baths. There's a restaurant and bar on-site, as well as a pool. 63 rooms. Credit Cards: CB, V, MC, DC, A.

Parador Villa Parguera   **$80–$90**   ★

Route 304, Lajas, La Parguera, ☎ *(800) 443- 266, (809) 899-3975.*
Single: $80–$90. Double: $80–$90.
Located near the beach on the southwestern shore, this parador offers rooms in an older guest house and in more modern wings, all with air conditioning, private baths, and balconies or patios. They have a restaurant and nightclub on the premises. The pool is filled with saltwater. 63 rooms. Credit Cards: CB, V, MC, DC, A.

Ponce Hilton and Casino   **$170–$375**   ★ ★ ★

P.R. 14 Avenue, Santiado de los Caballeros, Ponce, ☎ *(800) 445-8667, (809) 259-7676.*
Single: $170–$190. Double: $190–$375.
By far the area's nicest hotel, this Hilton sits on 80 acres of beachfront. Accommodations are stylish, with high-quality furniture, minibars, bidets, and balconies or patios. Nice public spaces and lots of recreational facilities, including a large lagoon-style pool, Jacuzzi, four tennis courts, gym, games room, and watersports on the private beach. There's also five restaurants, several watering holes and a casino. This well-run property does a lot of business with the meetings and convention markets. 153 rooms. Credit Cards: CB, V, MC, DC, A.

Ponce Holiday Inn   **$97–$145**   ★ ★

Highway 2, Ponce, ☎ *(800) 465-4329, (809) 844-1200.*
Single: $97–$120. Double: $99–$145.
Perched on a hillside one mile from the ocean, this commercial hotel has wonderful views of the surrounding area. Guest rooms are comfortable and pleasant; all have balconies with nice views. For an extra charge, they'll throw in a refrigerator. There's nightly entertainment in the lounge, as well as a disco, games room, pool and restaurant. You can count on the reliability that comes with a Holiday Inn, but you won't be writing home about it. Good especially for business travelers. 119 rooms. Credit Cards: CB, V, MC, DC, A.

Apartments and Condominiums

Harbour View Villas   **$50–$95**   ★

Borrio Melones, ☎ *(809) 742-3855.*
Single: $50–$75. Double: $75–$95.
This small enclave of villas is a quarter-mile from town and the beach. All are air-conditioned, have kitchens for do-it-yourselfers, and sleep up to six. You'll want a car to get around, as there's not much else on-site. 8 rooms. Credit Cards: V, MC.

Inns

Some of the nicest paradores, or government-sponsored inns, are located in this area; the **Parador Baõs de Coamo** is famous for its hot springs, and its most celebrated guest, Franklin Delano Roosevelt, who came to be healed. Many locals flock to the spring even today, which are rumored to cure a lot of illnesses. Do find a map of the panoramic route of this area; many of the paradores make good stops for atmospheric lunch or dinner.

Parador Banos de Coamo $55–$65   ★★

Route 546, Coamo, ☎ *(809) 825-2239.*
Single: $55. Double: $65.

Situated on the south coast on plains at the base of the mountains, this guest house dates back to 1847 and was once visited by Franklin Roosevelt. Guests can soak in natural hot springs that are said to be the most radioactive in the world—a dubious claim to fame. Guest rooms are large and comfortable, though minimally furnished. Besides the hot springs, there's a regular swimming pool and a tennis court. 48 rooms. Credit Cards: CB, V, MC, DC, A.

Parador Posada Porlamar $45–$90   ★

La Parguera Road, La Parguera, ☎ *(800) 443- 266, (809) 899-4015.*
Single: $45. Double: $60–$90.

This modest inn is right in the heart of this picturesque fishing village. Rooms are simple but comfortable and air-conditioned; all have private baths. There's no restaurant on-site, but guests have free use of a common kitchen, or can walk to nearby eateries. No pool, either. 18 rooms. Credit Cards: V, MC, A.

Where to Eat

The Hilton and the Copamarina Beach resort have fine dining facilities, and you can always be assured of safe cooking techniques. Seafood is a specialty along the south coast. As you head west, along route 2, you'll run across several possibilities.

El Ancla $$$ ★★★

9 Hostos Avenue, Ponce, ☎ *(809) 840-2450.*
Seafood cuisine.
Lunch: 11:00 a.m.– 4:00 p.m., entrees $3–$28.
Dinner: 4:00 p.m.– 12:00 p.m., entrees $3–$28.

This is an established family-owned restaurant perched over the water in Ponce Beach. Although it's long been popular with Poncenos and visitors, the welcome is always warm. That's probably what sets it apart from other restaurants serving seafood, which is the specialty of this eatery. Enjoy red snapper stuffed with lobster and shrimp served on a plate heaped with plenty of starchy side dishes. Credit Cards: V, MC, DC, A.

Lupita's Mexican $$$ ★★

Calle Isabel 60, Ponce, ☎ *(809) 848-8808.*
Mexican cuisine.
Lunch: 11:00 a.m.–4:00 p.m., entrees $7–$26.
Dinner: 4:00 p.m.–11:00 p.m., entrees $7–$26.

The better-than-average Mexican fare served here is blended with local specialties— lobster is grilled and served with green plantain, but you can also have tacos and nachos. Entertainment is provided several times a week by mariachis. It's located in a historic building near Plaza las Delicias, Ponce's main square. Lupita's stays open until 2 a.m. on Saturdays and until midnight on Sundays. Reservations required. Credit Cards: V, MC, DC, A.

THE WEST COAST

Mayaguez

Mayaguez is the island's third largest town, located about ten miles from Rinceon on Route 2. Baroque and Victorian buildings make this pretty, bustling port even more charming. It's the launching pad for treks into the western and southwestern interior; routes into the mountains lead to some spectacular climbs (see "Treks" above) and can be easily reached by car. Long a center of fine needlepoint, intrepid shoppers can still find some wonderful samples of fine island artistry in some of the older shops downtown. The island's only zoo is located behind the University of Puerto Rico's campus. The city itself is centered around the impressive Spanish-style **Plaza Colón**, a tribute to Christopher Columbus, whose statue stands in the middle of the square. The **Cathédrale de la Virgen de la Candelaria** is also a fine structure, dating back for centuries.

About 50 miles west of Mayaguez, stands Mona Island, a rugged uninhabited island whose only residents are large colonies of seabirds and enormous iguanas. The stunning cliffs make excellent photo ops; years ago it was said they held the booty of pirates who combed these waters. Rustic adventurers can find perfect places for camping overlooking the sea. Permission to visit must be granted by the tourist office. Twenty miles south of Malagues is **Boqueón Beach**, a stunning mile-long beach which boasts balneario facilities and excellent low prices for lodging. The small cottages are owned by the government and must be applied for four months in advance through the **Recreation and Sports Department**, *Box 2923, San Juan, PR 00903;* ☎ *722-1551.* Avoid weekends when local families with noisy teenagers carrying boom boxes disrupt the peacefulness of the area. Excellent seafood restaurants can be found a bit further north at **Joyuda Beach**. Along Route 301 can be found the **Cabo Rojo Wildlife Refuge** (see "Treks" above). If you would like a guide, check at the visitor's desk, where you can also get maps and individual assistance. BEST VIEW: At the southwesternmost top of the island, the best place to watch sunsets is at the **Cabo Rojo Lighthouse** at El Faro. The lighthouse is not open to the public, but the promontory overlooking red cliffs and ocean makes for a spectacular lookout.

What Else to See

Parks and Gardens

Puerto Rico Zoological Gardens ★★★

Route 108, Mayaguez, ☎ *(809) 834-8110.*
Hours Open: 9:00 a.m.–5:00 p.m.
Check out the birds and beasts—500 in all—at this tropical zoo spread over 45 acres. General admission: $1.00.

Where to Stay

Hotels and Resorts

Holiday Inn Mayaguez   **$120–$240**   ★ ★ ★

2701 Highway 2, Mayaguez, ☎ *(800) 465-4329, (809) 833-1100.*
Single: $120–$130. Double: $130–$240.

The beach is eight miles away from this typical Holiday Inn. Guest rooms fit the standard HI formula, which means clean, comfortable, air-conditioned, and on the bland side. One nice touch is a signal alert system for the hearing impaired. The hotel has a restaurant, lounge with live music, gym, sauna, and pool. Not exactly bursting with local flavor, but a safe choice. 152 rooms. Credit Cards: MC, A.

Horned Dorset Primavera   **$150–$440**   ★ ★ ★ ★ ★

Route 429, Rincon, ☎ *(809) 823-4030.*
Single: $150–$245. Double: $325–$440.

The name may be odd, but everything else is nearly perfect at this small and exclusive enclave. Guests are housed in plush suites with Persian rugs, armoires, four-poster beds, sitting areas, furnished balconies, and large baths. There are not a lot of facilities on-site, as the idea is to rest, relax and be pampered by the excellent staff. There is a pool and library, but that's about it. The grounds are exquisitely landscaped and open onto the sea, but there's really no beach to speak of. Dinner is a memorable affair with six courses nightly. No kids under 12 permitted. 30 rooms. Credit Cards: V, MC, A.

Mayaguez Hilton   **$135–$180**   ★ ★ ★

Route 104, Mayaguez, ☎ *(800) 445-8667, (809) 831-7575.*
Single: $135–$170. Double: $155–$180.

Set on 20 landscaped acres overlooking the harbor, this Hilton has a country club feel. Rooms are very comfortable and nicely furnished with all the amenities expected from Hilton. The grounds include a casino, nightclub, Olympic-size pool, three tennis courts, and a putting green. Children's activities are scheduled during high season. Very nice, but as the beach is 20 minutes away, this hotel caters mainly to a business clientele. 141 rooms. Credit Cards: MC, A.

Inns

The paradores system works well in this region; however, there is no real standard of quality and there may be big differences in service and surroundings. **Parador Hacienda Gripinas** is perhaps one of the most natural, replete with the sounds of nature. The **Parador Villa Antonio** tends to caters to the older; younger travelers might enjoy the **Parador Perichi** more. Businessmen tend to tuck in at the **El Sol**.

Parador Oasis   **$107–$107**   ★ ★

72 Luna Street, San German, ☎ *(800) 223-9815, (809) 892-1175.*
Single: $107. Double: $107.

This Spanish-style mansion, which dates back to 1896, is three blocks from the Inter-American University. Rooms are in the mansion (the least desirable ones, in fact) and a newer annex; all are air-conditioned and most are comfortable, though on the basic side. Facilities include a pool in a pretty courtyard, gym, sauna, restaurant, and bar. 53 rooms. Credit Cards: CB, V, MC, A.

Where to Eat

Horned Dorset Primavera   **$$$**   ★ ★ ★ ★ ★

Route 429, Km. 3, Rincon, ☎ *(809) 823-4030.*
Seafood cuisine.
Lunch: 12:00 a.m.– 2:30 p.m., entrees $15–$25.
Dinner: 7:00 p.m.–9:00 p.m., prix fixe $45.

This plush, whitewashed hotel/restaurant stands quite alone in its glory in a frontier location catering to surfers and daytrippers. That isn't to say the area isn't sublimely beautiful; it is. Many visitors make a special trip to eat here; it's quiet, it's right on the beach and the $40 fixed-price, six-course dinner is served with great ceremony. Although it's named after a breed of English sheep, seafood is a specialty. Location is six miles northwest of Mayaguez. Lunch hours vary, call for information. Associated Hotel: Horned Dorset Primavera. Reservations recommended. Credit Cards: V, MC, A.

San Germán

About 25 miles beyond the Cabo Rojo Lighthouse is San Germán, the island's second oldest city,

It takes about three hours to drive from San Juan, and a mere one hour from Mayaguez. The colonial atmosphere still pervades, despite the presence of a new highway; small-town customs still linger. A stroll around the town should reveal fine architecture including shops with gingerbread trim and turrets. The **Porta Coeli** Cathedral is considered to be the New World's oldest, dating back to 1606. Today the old church houses a fine museum with impressive sacred and secular art that dates back even a hundred years earlier than the building itself. The restoration of the former monastery and church is a model of perfection, and is considered one of the island's finest possessions.

PUERTO RICO'S ISLANDS

Culebra

Culebra is one of several islands located off the east coast between Puerto Rico and the U.S. Virgin Islands, which is rich in natural resources but not yet developed for tourism. The five mile-long island of Culebra is actually an archipelago of one main island and twenty surrounding cays. Most of the cays are part of the Culebra National Wildlife Refuge, which offers fine opportunities for bird-watching. Over 86 bird species are represented, including several nearly extinct ones. Four endangered sea turtles are also protected—green, loggerhead, hawksbill and leatherback. From April to July, the ecological organization Earthwatch sends teams of volunteers to the island for scientific studies, particularly along the beaches of Resaca and Brava.

Families run watersports businesses here, and boats can be chartered for a day-sailing around the islands. Windsurfing and limited deep-sea fishing can also be arranged from Dewey, the island's sole community. There are also excellent snorkeling sites here, especially at Punta Molines and Punta del Soldado.

To get to Culebra, you have two options. Ferryboats sail from Fajardo, which takes about one hour (the fee is extremely cheap). Getting to Fajardo, though, will tax your imagination, as taxi drivers charge exorbitant amounts for the ride. A small plane can be taken from Isla Grande airport aboard Flamenco Airways (though other local airlines also fly). The landing on the tiny strip can cause fibrillation, but it's best just to shut your eyes and keep breathing.

Where to Stay

Accommodations in this region run toward the simple, unpretentious and cheap.

Hotels and Resorts

Club Seabourne   **$65–$125**   ★★

Culebra Island, ☎ (809) 742-3169.
Single: $65–$115. Double: $70–$125.
Overlooking Fullodosa Bay, this small complex consists of air-conditioned rooms, villas and cottages, with refrigerators in the larger accommodations. Morning coffee and juice is on the house. The grounds include a pool, bar and restaurant that is closed on Mondays. 10 rooms. Credit Cards: V, MC, A.

Self-catering

Several options are available for self-catering, the best being the **Culebra Island Villas**, situated near enough to sea to make sports activities a cinch. Six people can pile into one of two houses that make up the **Harbor View Villas**, a perfect option for a small group of friends or a family who want to do their own thing.

Budget Bunks

You get what you pay for, and anything cheap in this region tends to run toward the dilapidated and unclean. An exception is the **Coral Island Guest House** which is mostly used by divers.

Vieques

Vieques is larger and a bit more cosmopolitan than Culebra, though the difference may be negligible. The port, **Isabel Segunda**, holds the distinction of having the last fort built by the Spaniards in the New World. Indian settlements date back to 200 B.C., a source of great interest to archaeologists who are presently studying them with passion. Two-thirds of the present land of Vieques is used by the U.S. Navy, some for military maneuvers, and some for the grazing of livestock. Some of the greatest primitive, unspoiled beaches are located on Navy land, which you can enter when there are no military maneuvers taking place. A fine beach is Sun Bay, which has bathing facilities and camping grounds. From Esperanza, you can make a nightly visit on a boat to the nearby bioluminescent bay, more spectacular than the better-known Phosphorescent Bay near La Parguera. With three protected sites called "hurricane holes," diving options can be arranged, along with other watersports, including windsurfing, at **Vieques Divers** at Esperanza. Certification courses are also available. There are also opportunities for horseback riding.

As a shopping hub, Isabel Segunda is best described as lethargic until a few handsful of tourists arrive in the ferry. Taxis and rental cars (Suzuki jeeps are best) available though local agencies, are the way to get around the island. To get to the island, you can either take a small plane from San Juan's Isla Grande airport, or a ferry boat from Fajardo—a two-hour sojourn. (As said above, getting to Fajardo is the difficulty here, since taxi rides from San Juan and its airports can be enormously expensive.)

Where to Stay

Don't expect any fancy resort here; most accommodations run the gamut from simple to simpler. The most atmospheric is La Casa del Frances, a restored Victorian house which gives off the ambiance of a country inn.

Hotels and Resorts

Villa Esperanza $65–$101 ★

    Calle Flamboyan.

Single: $65–$101. Double: $65–$101.

Most rooms at this beachfront hotel have air conditioning, but five do not, so be sure to ask. Located on the site of a former sugar mill, this hotel offers basic rooms in a villa complex. The grounds include a good deal of recreation for the rates, with a pool, two tennis courts, watersports, volleyball, and nine holes of miniature golf. There's also a restaurant and two bars. 25 rooms. Credit Cards: MC, A.

Apartments and Condominiums

Kitchen facilities can be found at the **Sea Gate** ☎ *(809) 741-4661* and **La Lanchita** ☎ *(809) 741-8449.*

Inns

Sea Gate Guest House **$40–$85** ★★

Vieques Island, ☎ *(809) 741-4661.*
Single: $40–$85. Double: $45–$85.

This small property is up on a hill overlooking the harbor town of Isabel Segunda and the sea beyond. Most rooms are efficiencies with kitchenettes. There's a very small pool on the premises, and the friendly owners will take you to the beach and arrange watersports. 17 rooms. Credit Cards: Not Accepted.

Low Cost Lodging

Very cheap accommodations can be found in guesthouses and a few apartment blocks. You'll be lucky if the furnishings are anything but basic.

Where to Eat

Fresh seafood is the way to go on this island. Anything else is probably shipped in. The best local cooking can be found at **Cerromar** in Puerto Real; you can tell it's good because most of the locals congregate there and you can enjoy watching how they interact. A plate of land crabs at the **Cayo Blanco** in Isabella Segunda is considered a must-do before you leave. In Esperanza, most of the local traffic ends up at the casual, laid-back **La Central Café**— ask anybody where it is.

Puerto Rico Directory

ARRIVAL

There are three airports in Puerto Rico, all undergoing extensive and expensive renovation. The Luis Munoz Marin in San Juan is the major hub for international travel. Since 1988 American Airlines has spent $260 million tripling the size of its San Juan hub, including the reservation center. The Mercedita Airport is located in Ponce, and the Rafael Hernandez is in Aguadilla. Major airlines including American, Delta, TWA, Tower, United and USAir fly into San Juan from most major U.S. cities. Carnival Airlines operates service to Aguadilla and Ponce from New York and Newark. American has made San Juan its hub for all flights from Puerto Rico to other Caribbean destinations, the U.S., Europe and Latin America. American Airlines also operates nonstop service from Miami and New York's JFK to Aguadilla and from Miami to Ponce. International carriers include British Airways, Iberia, and Lufthansa.Continental Airlines will begin nonstop service to San Juan. Starting Dec. 15, the airline will offer three flights a day from Newark. Packages start at $468 per person for four days including air fare and hotel accommodations.

The airport departure tax is included in the price of the airline ticket.

CLIMATE

Coastal weather in Puerto Rico is warm and sunny year-round. During the summer, temperatures average in the mid 80s; during the winter, they hover in the low 70s to the low 80s. The rainiest months are May to December, generally heavier on the north than the south coast. Temperatures in the mountains tend to be 5–10 degrees cooler.

DOCUMENTS

Since Puerto Rico is a commonwealth of the United States, no passports are required for U.S. citizens. Visitors do need a valid driver's license to rent a car. If you are a citizen of any other country, a visa is required. Vaccinations are not necessary. U.S. citizens do not need to clear customs or immigration (other citizens do). On departure, luggage must be inspected by the U.S. Agriculture Department, as law prohibits the taking of certain fruits and plants in the U.S. Dogs and cats may be brought to Puerto Rico from the U.S. with two documents: a health certificate dated not more than 10 days prior to departure showing that the animal is certified disease-free by an official or registered veterinarian, a certificate of rabies vaccination, dated not more than 30 days prior to departure, authenticated by the proper authorities.

ELECTRICITY

Current runs A.C. 60 cycles, 100 volts, single phase or 220 volts, three phase.

GETTING AROUND

Taxis, buses and rental cars are available at the airport and major hotels. All taxicabs are metered, but they may be rented unmetered for an hourly rate. There's an additional charge of 50 cents for every suitcase. *Publicos* (public cars) run on frequent schedules to all island towns (usually during daytime hours) and depart from main squares. They run on fixed rates. The *Ruta Panoramica* is a scenic road meandering across the island offering stunning vistas.

San Juan is the largest home-based cruise port in the world. Twenty-eight vessels use San Juan as their home port and each year new cruise ships either originate or call at the port.

Ferries shuttle passengers to and from Culebra and Vieques at reasonable rates. Car transport is also available. San Juan's harbor can also be crossed by the Catana ferry (50 cents) to the Bacardi Rum plant's free tours.

LANGUAGE

Spanish and English are both official languages of Puerto Rico. Many speak English—and many people don't, especially older people in outlying rural areas. In San Juan however, English is taught from kindergarten to high school as part of the school curriculum.

MEDICAL EMERGENCIES

Officially, the medical community of Puerto Rico meets the same standards as those required on the U.S. mainland (just explain why most rich Puerto Ricans come to the States for medical attention). Most physicians on the island are based in San Juan with almost all medical specializations represented. San Juan has 14 hospitals, most districts have at least one. Ask your hotel to recommend a physician on call.

MONEY

The official currency is the U.S. dollar and credit cards are widely accepted by hotels, restaurants and shops. Several foreign exchange offices are available in San Juan and at the airport.

TELEPHONE

The area code is *809*. Postage stamps are equivalent to those in the U.S. as are mail costs. You can dial direct to the mainland.

TIME

Atlantic Standard Time, year-round, which is one hour earlier than New York. During Daylight Saving Time, it is the same.

TIPPING AND TAXES

All hotels include a 6 percent government tax on the bill. Gratuities on restaurant bills are not included, but a usual 15 percent tip is expected.

TOURIST INFORMATION

For more information about the island, contact the **Puerto Rico Tourism Company**, *La Princesa Building, Old San Juan, PR 00901;* ☎ *(809) 721-2400*. There are offices in New York, Los Angeles, Coral Gables, London, Madrid, Mexico City, Milan, Paris, Stockholm, Toronto, and Weisbaden, Germany. In the U.S. ☎ *(213) 874-5991*.

WHEN TO GO

January-May the Puerto Rico Symphony Orchestra conducts its 36th season with performances through May. January 6 is traditional gift-giving day in Puerto Rico, celebrated by island-wide festivals with music, dance, parades, puppet shows, and caroling troubadours. January 1–19 is the International Folklore Festival, featuring dance groups from around the world. February (usually 3rd weekend) is the Coffee Harvest Festival. Carnival usually happens the second week in February. The Sugar Harvest Festival takes place in May. The Festival Casals takes place in early June, honoring the late cellist. San Juan Bautista Day is

June 23, celebrating the island's patron saint, as sanjuaneros walk backward into the sea three times at midnight for good luck. The Albonito Flower Festival takes place in July. The Barranquitas Artisans Fair is held July 16–18, the island's oldest crafts fair with 130 local artisans. The 42nd International Billfish Tournament takes place in September. The Inter-American Festival of the Arts takes place in September. The National Plantain Festival occurs in late October. The Baseball season begins in October. The Festival of Typical Dishes lasts from November-December. Old San Juan's White Christmas Festival takes place December-January. Island-wide Christmas festivities with life-size nativity scenes are held December–January. The Bacardi Arts Festival featuring more than 200 craftsmen is in December. Lighting of the Town of Bethlehem occurs for three days in mid-December.

In general, spring is always a good time to visit San Juan. Old San Juan is less crowded with cruise ship day trippers than during the winter, hotels rates begin to drop, and many hotels offer inexpensive summer packages to lure visitors during the slowest months. Puerto Rico doesn't have extreme seasonal changes so you may see that quintessential Christmas flower, the poinsettia blooming and mangoes ripening in the same gardens. San Juan shuts down for much of Holy Week, but there are Easter celebrations. An annual sunrise Easter service is usually held at **El Morro**. For more information call Rev. Martha McCracken ☎ *(809) 722-5372.*

PUERTO RICO HOTELS	RMS	RATES	PHONE	FAX
Culebra				
★★ **Club Seabourne**	10	$65–$125	(809) 742-3169	(809) 742-3176
Puerto Rico				
East and Southeast Coast				
★★★★★ **El Conquistador Resort**	926	$170–$420	(800) 468-8365	(809) 253-4387
★★★★ **Palmas del Mar Humacao**	298	$145–$715	(800) 468-3331	(809) 852-6320
★ **Parador La Familia**	28	$50–$70	(800) 443-0266	
★ **Parador Martorell**	10	$50–$85	(800) 443-0266	
Northwest Coast				
★★ **Days Inn**	121	$80–$140	(800) 325-2525	(809) 841-2560
★★ **Parador El Guajataca**	38	$77–$95	(800) 964-3065	(809) 895-3589
★★ **Parador Vistamar**	55	$60–$75	(800) 443-0266	(809) 895-2294
San Juan				
★★★★★ **El San Juan Hotel/Casino**	390	$250–$995	(800) 468-2818	(809) 263-0178

PUERTO RICO HOTELS	RMS	RATES	PHONE	FAX
★★★★★ Hyatt Dorado Beach	298	$160–$490	(800) 233-1234	
★★★★★ Hyatt Regency Cerromar	504	$165–$420	(800) 233-1234	
★★★★★ Sands Hotel & Casino	410	$290–$305	(809) 791-6100	(809) 791-8525
★★★★ Caribe Hilton & Casino	670	$200–$1200	(800) 468-8585	(809) 724-6992
★★★★ Condado Plaza Hotel	575	$195–$355	(800) 468-8588	(809) 722-4613
★★★★ Radisson Ambassador Plaza	233	$170–$320	(800) 333-3333	(809) 723-6151
★★★ Best Western Pierre	184	$97–$145	(800) 528-1234	(809) 721-3118
★★★ Casa San Jose	10	$205–$315	(800) 223-6510	(809) 723-7620
★★★ Condado Beach Trio	481	$140–$195	(800) 468-2775	
★★★ Holiday Inn Crowne Plaza	254	$185–$390	(800) 468-4578	(809) 253-0079
★★★ Radisson Normandie	177	$160–$240	(800) 333-3333	(809) 729-3083
★★ Atlantic Beach Hotel	37	$60–$140	(809) 721-6900	(809) 721-6917
★★ Carib Inn Tennis Club	225	$105–$320	(800) 548-8217	(809) 791-0104
★★ El Canario Inn	25	$80–$125	(809) 722-3861	(809) 722-0391
★★ El Canario by the Lagoon	40	$65–$110	(809) 722-5058	(809) 723-8590
★★ Grande Hotel El Convento	150	$85–$200	(800) 468-2779	(809) 725-7895
★★ Hotel Portal Del Condado	48	$95–$125	(809) 721-9010	(809) 724-3714
★★ International Airport	57	$80–$90	(809) 791-1700	(809) 291-4050
★★ Parador Hacienda Gripinas	11	$64–$107	(800) 443-0266	(809) 889-4520
★★ Ramada Hotel Condado	96	$130–$300	(800) 468-2040	(809) 722-8230
★★ Regency Hotel	127	$140–$225	(800) 468-2823	(809) 722-2909
★★ San Juan Travelodge	88	$125–$175	(800) 428-2028	(809) 268-0637
★ Arcade Inn	19	$40–$90	(809) 728-7524	
★ El Canario by the Sea	25	$80–$125	(800) 533-2649	(809) 725-4921
★ Green Isle Inn	44	$43–$73	(800) 677-8860	(809) 268-2415

South Coast

★★★ Ponce Hilton and Casino	153	$170–$375	(800) 445-8667	(809) 259-7674
★★ Melia Hotel	77	$70–$90	(800) 742-4276	(809) 841-3602
★★ Parador Banos de Coamo	48	$55–$65	(809) 825-2239	(809) 825-4739
★★ Ponce Holiday Inn	119	$97–$145	(800) 465-4329	(809) 841-8683
★ Harbour View Villas	8	$50–$95	(809) 742-3855	

PUERTO RICO HOTELS	RMS	RATES	PHONE	FAX
★ **Parador Boquemar**	63	$65–$70	(800) 443-0266	(809) 851-7600
★ **Parador Posada Porlamar**	18	$45–$90	(800) 443-0266	(809) 899-6082
★ **Parador Villa Parguera**	63	$80–$90	(800) 443-0266	(809) 899-6040

West Coast

	RMS	RATES	PHONE	FAX
★★★★★ **Horned Dorset Primavera**	30	$150–$440	(809) 823-4030	(809) 823-5580
★★★ **Holiday Inn Mayaguez**	152	$120–$240	(800) 465-4329	(809) 833-1300
★★★ **Mayaguez Hilton**	141	$135–$180	(800) 445-8667	(809) 834-3475
★★ **Parador Oasis**	53	$107	(800) 223-9815	(809) 892-1175

Vieques				
★★ **Sea Gate Guest House**	17	$40–$85	(809) 741-4661	
★ **Villa Esperanza**	25	$65–$101		

PUERTO RICO RESTAURANTS	LOCATION	PHONE	ENTREE

San Juan

American			
★★ **The Chart House**	Condado	(809) 728-0110	$16–$25••
Chinese			
★★★ **Back Street Hong Kong**	Isla Verde	(809) 791-1000	$15–$32••
French			
★★★★ **La Chaumiere**	Old San Juan	(809) 722-3330	$22–$37••
International			
★★★ **El Patio de Sam**	Old San Juan	(809) 723-1149	$9–$25
★★ **Butterfly People**	Old San Juan	(809) 723-2432	•$5–$9
Italian			
★★ **Al Dente**	Old San Juan	(809) 723-7303	$10–$15
Latin American			
★★★★ **Amadeus**	Old San Juan	(809) 722-8635	$8–$16
★★★ **Ajilli-Mojili**	San Juan		$15–$25
★★★ **La Bombonera**	Old San Juan	(809) 722-0658	$5–$8
★★★ **La Casona de Serafin**	Cabo Rojo	(809) 851-0066	$10–$31
★★★ **La Mallorquina**	Old San Juan	(809) 722-3261	$14–$30

PUERTO RICO RESTAURANTS	LOCATION	PHONE	ENTREE
★★★ Parador Villa Parguera	Lajas	(809) 899-7777	$5–$20
★★ Anchor's Inn	Fajardo	(809) 863-7200	$8–$20
Spanish			
★★★★★ La Compostela	Santurce	(809) 724-6088	$15–$29
★★★★★ Ramiro's	Condado	(809) 721-9049	$24–$33

South Coast

Mexican			
★★ Lupita's Mexican	Ponce	(809) 848-8808	$7–$26
Seafood			
★★★ El Ancla	Ponce	(809) 840-2450	$3–$28

West Coast

Seafood			
★★★★★ Horned Dorset Primavera	Rincon	(809) 823-4030	$15–$45
Note: • Lunch Only			

•• Dinner Only

SABA

Most of the houses on Saba are painted white with red roofs and green shutters.

An isolated outpost of only 1200 islanders, Saba (pronounced Say-buh) sticks out of the water like a green gumdrop in the middle of the sea, its 2850-ft. volcanic spiral clearly visible to neighboring isles. Until recently, this lava-encrusted Bali Hai was strictly for escapists contented with a well-thumbed paperback from their inn's library and their daily hike up the 1064 steps to the peak of Mount Scenery. But since divers started trickling in a few years ago, Saba has become a great little underwater destination. Encrusted with colorful coral and decorated with dramatic fingers of cooled lava that drop off 90–300 feet, Saba's sites are teeming with blue chromides, barracuda and marbled grouper. Today there are three dive shops (and a hyperbaric chamber donated by the Royal Netherlands Navy) to give you all the help you need to reach the 26 unspoiled dive sites along the flanks of the volcano—an area which the islanders had the foresight to protect as a marine park back in 1967. So precipitously do the red-roofed gingerbread-trimmed houses perch on the rocky hillside 1000 feet and more above the sea, that if you have vertigo, you should probably stay home. There is only one road, hand-built by islanders, and by the time you leave, you may have passed by everyone on the island. Cool breezes and a crime-free life (what's there to steal on a volcano?) have attracted some long-term visitors to Saba, but the majority (save serious divers) stay only a few days. Committed divers, however, thrill over the challenging dive sites, whose atmospheric names like Shark Shoal, Twilight Zone, and Outer Limits should scare off the dilettantes. If you're looking for one of the last frontiers in the Caribbean, you better get here before Winair increases its flights to twelve a day.

Bird's Eye View

The baby of the Netherlands Antilles, Saba lies 28 miles south of St. Maarten/St. Martin and 17 miles northwest of St. Eustatius. With virtually no flat ground, the island is literally an extinct volcano which protrudes out of the sea, lush with tropical vegetation. The capital, ironically called The Bottom, is halfway up the mountain. One tiny inlet acts as a dock, and until 1943 there wasn't even one road, since the terrain was so rugged. (Today that serpentine road connects the pier, the airport and four villages.) Another town, Windwardside, is highly picturesque, a neat and tidy toy town of red-iron roofs and white clapboard walls. Most visitors base themselves here, where you can find most natural air-conditioning in the world. The 1200-ft. airport runway is half the length of many aircraft carriers, and takeoff, if anything, is hairier than landing. Because the runway ends in midair (a crushing descent off a cliff to the sea down below), most people feel as if they are still on it when the plane abruptly lifts up.

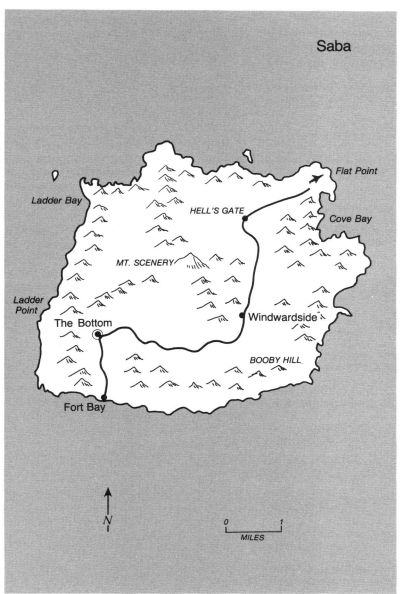

History

Columbus sighted the volcanic island in 1493, but it took another 129 years for some unlucky Englishman to shipwreck against the rocky coast. In 1665 the English privateer Thomas Morgan captured the island and threw out the original Dutch settlers. Morgan's men stayed behind when he left, a fact that some locals use to claim their ancestors were pirates. Some historians purport that Saba's original British settlers were actually Scottish refugees or exiles from the British civil wars in the 17th century. Until a pier was constructed in 1972, ships had to anchor in Fort Bay, where wooden longboats would transfer people and products to shore in a very wet ride.

People

There are about 1200 Sabans living on the island today, equally split between black and white. The blacks are descended from slaves who were imported to work the island's small farms and carry products up and down the mountain. The whites claim various ancestry, many look Irish, and strangely half the islanders, no matter which race, bear the Irish name Hassell (in 1699 seven Hassells were listed in the census). There's one Chinese family on the island, and they own the one Chinese restaurant. More than 100 Sabans served in the U.S. Navy during the first world war. A number of Sabans (particularly with the name Hassell) have distinguished themselves internationally. After World War I there was a desperate need to seek work abroad and the male-female ratio became disastrously unbalanced. Today the men have returned, growing their own food and exporting fish to St. Martin. For centuries, Saban men have plied their trade on the sea, transporting prisoners from one island to the other, carrying all manner of cargo. For some yet-to-be-explained reason, the national greeting is "Howzzit? Howzzit?"

Beaches

Saba has only one fat sandy beach, accessible only by a hilly walk or a drive guaranteed to cause fibrillation. If you want to swim, it's best done in a hotel pool—Queens Gardens, Captain's Quarters, Willard's of Saba, Juliana's Scout's Place (small,) and Cranston's Antique Inn.

Dive Sites

The **Saba Marine Park** surrounds the island to a depth of 200 feet. Shore diving is out because of the island's rugged coastline, but once offshore you'll discover steep walls, submerged pinnacles, and virtual forests of elk horn coral. Currents vary nutrients that attract colorful reef dwellers such as parrot fish, blue tanga and small hawkbill turtles at depths as shallow as 30 feet. In deeper water, 80–100 feet you'll run into large groupers, sharks and eagle rays. In summer the water is a bathtub warm at 86 degrees F, up from a winter low of 78 degrees F. Visibility is best in winter, when it approaches 125 feet. There are 27 permanent dive sites. Rent a laminated trail map to follow the **Edward S. Arnold Snorkel Trail at Torrens Point**. The $2 per tank fee helps to establish new moorings.

Treks

"The Road" on Saba (a highly descriptive name typical of Saban humor) is 19 miles long and crosses the island from the airport on the northeast to Fort Bay on the southwest, as it passes through four of the island's villages. Hiking the length of the road, which rises to 1800 feet, can be challenging but enjoyable; a rest comes as it drops into the sea on the southwest coast. Do pace yourself and rest at intervals. From The Road, others trails are accessible.

From the tiny village of English Quarter, a trail on the south leads to **Old Booby Hill** via **Spring Bay Gut**, two of the island's main sites for bird-watching. From **Upper Hell's Gaye**, another trail leads northwest to Sandy Cruz. It passes through land that was once farmed and is now returning to forest, through rainforest, and to the perimeter of a ravine known as **Deep Gut**. **Sandy Cruz Track**, one of the trails here, takes about 40 minutes to complete

The hike to the 2652-ft. high summit of **Mt. Scenery** starts at **Windwardside**, where the tourist bureau is. This peak is the main goal of hikers who come to Saba. The trail, which consists of 1065 hand-made steps, begins in front of a sign at the west end of Windwardside and climbs up through the rain forest and into the clouds of elfin forest at the peak. Year-round it's possible to pick wild raspberries to fortify yourself along the way, and an experienced guide can point out the rare orchids and heliconia blooms during the winter. A separate trail found at the summit leads through virgin vegetation in a forest rich with ferns and bromeliads. The hike takes a half-hour round trip, but do avoid going after a rain because the trail becomes extremely slippery and impassable. The hike itself, even on a good day, is very challenging, and hikers should be in the best of shape. Also dress appropriately for the summit which can get cool and damp.

At The Bottom, the main road turns south to Fort Bay by the sea; west of The Bottom at the end of the Ladder Bay Road, called The Gap, a series of 500 steps, lead to Ladder Bay. Today these steps belong to a scenic trail that arrives at a fine picnicking site overlooking Ladder Bay.

What Else to See

Places worth visiting, other than the great natural wonders, are minuscule, limited to one charming museum and a small library. Ensconced in a sea captain's house, the Saba Museum offers a look at the island's traditional furnishings, giving you a genuine feel of ye olden days. Queen Wilhelmina Library holds a special collection of studies on the flora and fauna of the island, as well as a special section on West Indian science and history.

Museums and Exhibits

Saba Museum ★ ★ ★

Behind the Captain's Quarters, Windwardside.

This small museum is found in the 19th-century home of a sea captain. It exhibits antiques from that era and pre-Columbian artifacts found around the island. Croquet matches are held the first Sunday of each month, a good chance to meet and greet the locals. Wear all white for that outing. General admission: $1.00.

Tours

Mount Scenery ★ ★ ★ ★

Mt. Scenery.

Pack a picnic lunch, catch your breath, then head up the 1064 steps that lead up 2855 feet to the top of Mount Scenery. Along the way you'll pass through gorgeous scenery, six ecosystems, all kinds of interesting flora and fauna (signs tell you what's what), and, the higher you climb, cooler temperatures. The summit has a mahogany grove and incredible views.

Sports

Sports on Saba are divided between trekking and diving. One of the greatest little hikes in the world is the ascent up to Mount Scenery which takes you through the secondary rainforest to the mountain's peak. The most spectacular version is probably the one starting from Windwardside up to thousand-or-so steps to the crest, best done on a clear day or you will feel as if you are disappearing in a cloud. No guide is needed; most people make it up to the 3000-ft. crest in two hours. Another hearty trek is the climb down from The Bottom to Ladder Bay, the island's former "dock" for arriving boats before the advent of the Fort Bay pier.

If you are a committed diver, buying a package deal saves you money and the time it takes to make arrangements. **Wilson's Dive Shop** (Windwardside, ☎ *599-46-2544*) offers a 7-night, 10-dive package that begins at $1490 for two divers, including hotel and breakfast. Lodgings are in simple inns up the hills, and two more were scheduled to open in 1995. The **Sea Saba Dive Center** (☎ *599-46-2246*) offers ten dives and a week's stay at Juliana's, a white gingerbread compound high above the sea for $745. (For more information about diving, see "Dive Sites" above.)

There is also a tennis court at the Sun Valley Youth Centre in The Bottom, open to the public.

Watersports

Various locations, The Bottom.

Scuba diving is very good in Saba, which is dedicated to preserving its underwater treasures. The Saba Marine Park circles the entire island and has various zoned sections, including five recreational dive sites, where you'll see towering pinnacles, colorful coral and sponges, and tons of sea creatures. The Harbor Office *(☎ 63295)* in Fort Bay provides literature and offers occasional slide shows. The Marine Park also includes Saba's only harbor and its only beach, a tiny stretch of sand only existing in the late spring and summer, submerged by the tides in winter. The park charges $2 per person per dive, in addition to the fees charged by dive centers.

Where to Stay

★★★ **Captain's Quarters**

★★★ **Captain's Quarters** $85–$130

★★ **Juliana's** $65–$130

Lodging in Saba might be called a hotel, but they all tend to look and feel like inns. One of the most charming is Captain's Quarters, in two houses (100 and 175 years old respectively) with antique furniture and views from the terrace. **Scout's Place** is cheap, unpretentious, and friendly, and the view is spectacular. **Queens Garden**, a premier luxury resort on Troy Hill may be open by the time you read this. Do give them a call (☎ *63339*, FAX *62450*). You can find wood cottages that rent by the day, week, or month. Contact the Tourist Board for information about kitchen-equipped apartments and furnished villas.

Hotels and Resorts

Juliana's $65–$130   ★★

Windwardside, ☎ (599) 4-62389.

Single: $65. Double: $80–$130.

Guests can choose from a variety of accommodations at this small property. There are standard guestrooms, an apartment with a kitchenette, and a nearly 90-year-old cottage with two bedrooms, a kitchen and a porch. All are quite decent, and the daily fresh flowers are a nice touch. The rec room has a TV, VCR, games and books for whiling away the hours. There's also a pool and restaurant. 10 rooms. Credit Cards: V, MC, A.

Apartments and Condominiums

Cottage rentals are a steal—$200–$300—compared to prices on other islands in the Caribbean. The charming small, wooden Saban variety will make you feel all tucked in and cozy. The tourist office will have more complete listings.

Inns

Captain's Quarters   **$85–$130**   ★★★

Windwardside, ☎ *(599)4-62377.*
Single: $85–$100. Double: $100–$130.
This charming inn is Saba's best bet—not that there are a lot of choices, but this place would get high marks anywhere. Set high on a hill with spectacular ocean views, this inn centers around an old wooden home, built by a sea captain in 1832. Four rooms are in this house, the rest in a newer wing. All are spacious and bright and have private baths; some also boast antique four-poster beds. The grounds are nicely landscaped with citrus trees and tropical blooms. The site includes a library, swimming pool and a very good restaurant. Divine! 10 rooms. Credit Cards: MC, A.

Cranston's Antique Inn   **$40–$75**   ★

The Bottom, ☎ *(599) 4-63203.*
Single: $40–$60. Double: $63–$75.
This former government guest house dates back to 1830. Only one room has a private bath, but all have antiques and four-poster beds. Some of the decor borders on the tacky and the whole place could use a redo. There's a pool and decent dining room on the premises, and the open-air bar is a locals' favorite. Ladder Bay is within walking distance. 6 rooms. Credit Cards: A.

Scout's Place   **$40–$105**   ★

Windwardside, ☎ *(599) 4-62388.*
Single: $40–$105. Double: $60–$105.
Great views from this casual inn, located some 1300 feet above the sea. Unless you're really into roughing it (or saving some bucks), reserve one of the newer rooms, which have private baths and hot water. (The original rooms have neither.) There's also an apartment with kitchenette that sleeps five. Known locally for its very good food, this spot also has a small pool and a bar. 15 rooms. Credit Cards: MC, A.

Low Cost Lodging

Rooms in private homes might be secured if you come in person and ask about. Cottages listed above, especially packed with several people, can be quite reasonable.

Where to Eat

Highest Rated Restaurants in Saba

★★ **Brigadoon**

★★ **Captain's Quarters**

★★ **Corner Deli**

★★ **Guido's**

★★ **Lollipop's**

★★ **Saba Chinese Restaurant**

★★ **Scout's Place**

★★ **Tea House**

★★ **Tropics Cafe**

Most Exclusive Restaurants in Saba

★★ **Lollipop's**	$26–$26
★★ **Captain's Quarters**	$13–$22
★★ **Saba Chinese Restaurant**	$13–$19
★★ **Tropics Cafe**	$4–$10
★★ **Tea House**	$2–$7

Fielding's Best Value Restaurants in Saba

★★ **Tropics Cafe**	$4–$10
★★ **Scout's Place**	$17–$25
★★ **Lollipop's**	$26–$26
★★ **Corner Deli**	$4–$10
★★ **Brigadoon**	$14–$17

Most guests don't travel much further than their own accommodations when the urge to eat strikes. When they do, they seem to congregate at **Scout's Place**, where you can get Caribbean fare like stewed mutton or more appetizing dishes from the sea; the view is spectacular. Good pizza can be had at **Guido's**.

Brigadoon $$$ ★★

Windwardside, ☎ *(599) 4-62380.*
International cuisine. Specialties: Saba fish pot, lobster, peanut chicken.
Dinner: entrees $14–$17.
One of the newer eating establishments on the island, Brigadoon is developing a reputation for innovative seafood cuisine. Grilled fish with tomato sauce or a spicy local bouillabaisse are standouts. There's also plenty of chicken and beef dishes served with fresh vegetables. Lighter fare is also featured. Reservations recommended. Credit Cards: V, MC, DC, A.

Captain's Quarters $$$ ★★

Windwardside, ☎ *599-4-62201.*
International cuisine. Specialties: Grouper, lobster bisque.
Lunch: 12:00 a.m.–2:00 p.m., entrees $13–$22.
Dinner: 6:30 p.m.–9:00 p.m., entrees $13–$22.
Guests dine comfortably in this pretty outdoor terrace restaurant on the grounds of the historical Captain's Quarters hotel. There's plenty of greenery and fruit trees providing shade. If you're staying here it's a nice spot for breakfast, but most non-guests come for lunch or hearty dinners. The menu changes often, but the chef is known for her way with lobster. Associated Hotel: Captain's Quarters. Credit Cards: V, MC.

Corner Deli $ ★★

Windwardside,
American cuisine.
Dinner: 2:00 p.m.–6:00 p.m., entrees $4–$10.
Homesick New Yorkers and others can pick up a thick sandwich on homemade bread at this deli-market owned by a seasoned restaurateur. Specialty coffees, pastries, and desserts can be sampled here or packaged for takeout. Stop by for picnic fixings on the way to Mt. Scenery. Closed: Sun. Credit Cards: V, MC, A.

Guido's $ ★★

Windwardside,
Italian cuisine. Specialties: Pizza.
Dinner: entrees $4–$10.
Yes, there is nightlife on Saba, contrary to the rumors. It's here at Guido's, which masquerades as a burger and pizza joint during the week and dons a few sequins as Mountain High Club and Disco on Saturday evenings. The food is okay, but it's better for pool or darts and informal socializing. Credit Cards: V, MC, A.

Lollipop's $$$ ★★

St. John's, ☎ *(599) 4-63330.*
Seafood cuisine. Specialties: Stuffed crab.
Lunch: entrees $10–$15.

Dinner: prix fixe $26.

Lollipop, or Carmen Hassell (everyone in town is either a Hassell or a Johnson) offers free pickup to and from her outdoor eatery—and you're in good hands, because she moonlights as a cab driver. Located in the suburb of St. John's, above The Bottom, the dining area is on a patio with a view, and the food is basically West Indian—curries, fish cakes, seafood, and goat. Reservations recommended. Credit Cards: Not Accepted.

Saba Chinese Restaurant $$$ ★★

Windwardside, ☎ (599) 4-62268.
Chinese cuisine. Specialties: Conch chop suey, lobster cantonese.
Lunch: 11:00 a.m.–4:00 p.m., entrees $13–$19.
Dinner: 4:00 p.m.–12:00 p.m., entrees $13–$19.

This Chinese restaurant on the north side of Windwardside offers rather pricey Cantonese and Indonesian dishes. It seems to satisfy a lot of locals, who patronize it often. There's a wide variety of choices, including an old favorite, sweet and sour pork, and a more unusual conch chop suey. Closed: Mon. Credit Cards: Not Accepted.

Scout's Place $$$ ★

Windwardside, ☎ (599) 4-62295.
International cuisine. Specialties: Curried goat.
Lunch: 12:30 p.m.–2:00 p.m., prix fixe $12.
Dinner: 7:30 p.m.–10:00 p.m., prix fixe $17–$25.

Scout's is the creation of Ohioan Scout Thirlkield, who also turned the Captain's Quarters into a hotel-restaurant. He is still around, but has passed the mantle onto chef Dianna Medero. The outdoor restaurant, attached to the hotel of the same name, is a beloved local hangout. The fixed-price menu features fresh seafood, and a delicious curried goat often appears. There's also a bar and a snack shop in front for short-order meals, snacks and ice cream. Associated Hotel: Scout's Place. Reservations required. Credit Cards: V, MC.

Tea House $ ★★

Windwardside,
American cuisine. Specialties: Pastries.
Dinner: 9:30 p.m.–6:00 p.m., entrees $2–$7.

After picking up some tips and brochures at the tourist office, stop at the Tea House right behind it for homemade, old-fashioned pastry treats like sticky cinnamon and raisin buns. There's a selection of soft drinks, coffees, teas and sandwiches. Closed: Sun. Credit Cards: Not Accepted.

Tropics Cafe $ ★★

Windwardside, ☎ (599) 4-63203.
American cuisine.
Dinner: entrees $4–$10.

The Tropics is a no-frills eatery attached to Juliana's Apartments, located near Captain's Quarters. It's good to know about for the decently priced breakfasts, burgers and sandwiches for under $10. Get them to pack up a picnic basket for you. Associated Hotel: Juliana's Apartments. Closed: Sun. Credit Cards: V, MC.

Where to Shop

Saba lace is an extraordinary 125-year-old art that was introduced to the island by Mary Gertrude Johnson, who learned it at a convent school in Venezuela. Fine work can be purchased at the Community Center (in Hell's Gate; lace-worked blouses, napkins and tablespreads are especially great buys). Silk-screening has also found a niche in Saba; try the Saba Artisans Foundation, which offers finely worked scarves, t-shirts, and beautiful dresses—they are not cheap.

Don't miss (or at least taste) the local brew called **Saba Spice**, a secret concoction unique to each brewer that's made with 151-proof cask rum, cinnamon, brown sugar and other spices.According to Queenie Simmons, who runs the Serving Spoon restaurant and offers her own highly regarded blend for sale, the final step of the brewing process is to "set a bit" and then "scratch a match and let it blaze off." You can enjoy the drink as a hot cider, mixed with eggnog, or in any drink that has Kahluá. As a summer drink, it's refreshing in a colada blended with cream and shaved ice, served like a milk shake. Bottling traditions are quaint, and if made at home, the brew is usually put into whatever bottle is hanging around.

If you're interested in local art, stop by the **Breadfruit Gallery** in the Lambert Hassell Building in Windwardside.

Saba Directory

ARRIVAL

Because the runway is short, large planes cannot fly to Saba, nor can any plane land or take off in bad weather. Winair ☎ *62255*, the only scheduled airline, makes up to five daily 20-seater flights from St. Maarten, 20 minutes away ($62 round trip). One or two flights are made from Eustatius. Flights with a stopover in St. Barts can be arranged ahead of time. Saba can sometimes be reached by boat, contact the Great Bay Marina in Sint Maarten ☎ *22167*.Cruise ships can call at a deep-water pier at Fort Bay.

The airport departure tax is U.S.$2 to the Netherland Antilles, U.S. $5 elsewhere.

CLIMATE

Temperatures average about 85 degrees F, but can dip as low as 65 degrees F on a cool night.

DOCUMENTS

U.S. and Canadian citizens need to show a current passport or one that expired less than five years ago, or other proof of citizenship (birth certificate or voter's registration plus a photo ID), as well as an ongoing or return ticket.

ELECTRICITY

The current is 100 volts, 60 cycles, the same as in the U.S.

GETTING AROUND

Numerous taxis are awaiting flights when they arrive, and drivers are usually the best guides on the island. Don't hesitate to ask one for a half-day tour or to stay with you the whole day until your flight leaves. If you want to join a group and save money, minibuses at the airport usually will make a 1-1/2 hour tour.

There are numerous agencies who will rent cars, although be forewarned; The Road, as it is called, is extremely difficult to navigate and the parking possibilities are limited. Hitchhiking is relatively safe.

LANGUAGE

The official language is English, though public signs are written in Dutch. English is the spoken language.

MEDICAL EMERGENCIES

Try not to get sick in Saba. Emergencies are flown to Sint Maarten; the clinic at The Bottom is limited in facilities.In cases of extreme illness, a chartered flight (one hour) should be arranged to San Juan, Puerto Rico. Saba does have a decompression chamber, located at the Marine Park Hyperbaric Facility in Fort Bay ☎ *63205.*

MONEY

The official currency is the Netherlands Antilles florin, also called the guilder and abbreviated NAf. U.S. dollars are accepted by most businesses.

TELEPHONE

The country code is *5994.* If you are calling from another Caribbean country, the code might differ, so check with the operator. For the U.S. dial direct *011* (international access code)-*5994*-local number.

TIME

Atlantic standard time, one hour ahead of eastern standard time, and the same as eastern daylight saving time.

TIPPING AND TAXES

Most hotels, restaurants and bars add a 10–15 percent service charge; if they don't that's what you should leave. No porters at the airport to carry your bags, but taxi drivers expect $1 or $2 as tip.

TOURIST INFORMATION

The Saba Tourist Bureau is located in Windwardside, in the renovated Lambert Hassell Building ☎ *62231*, FAX *62350*). It's open only Monday-Friday.

WHEN TO GO

The Queen's birthday on April 30 celebrates the life of Beatrix of Holland with festive fireworks, parades and sports competitions. The Saba Summer Festival takes place in late July (10 days) with much merrymaking, music (steel bands), dancing and games. Saba Days in December is a festival featuring maypole dancing, spearfishing and other games.

SABA HOTELS		RMS	RATES	PHONE	FAX
The Bottom					
★★★	**Captain's Quarters**	10	$85–$130	(599)4-62377	
★★	**Juliana's**	10	$65–$130	(599) 4-62389	
★	**Cranston's Antique Inn**	6	$40–$75	(599) 4-63203	599-4-63469
★	**Scout's Place**	15	$40–$105	(599) 4-62388	

SABA RESTAURANTS		LOCATION	PHONE	ENTREE
The Bottom				
	American			
★★	**Corner Deli**	The Bottom		$4–$10••
★★	**Tea House**	The Bottom		$2–$7••
★★	**Tropics Cafe**	The Bottom	(599) 4-63203	$4–$10••
	Chinese			
★★	**Saba Chinese Restaurant**	The Bottom	(599) 4-62268	$13–$19
	International			
★★	**Brigadoon**	The Bottom	(599) 4-62380	$14–$17••
★★	**Captain's Quarters**	The Bottom	599-4-62201	$13–$22
★★	**Scout's Place**	The Bottom	(599) 4-62295	$12–$25
	Italian			
★★	**Guido's**	The Bottom		$4–$10••
	Seafood			
★★	**Lollipop's**	St. John's	(599) 4-63330	$10–$26
Note:	• Lunch Only			
	•• Dinner Only			

ST. BARTHÉLÉMY

St. Barts boasts white sandy beaches surrounded by lush, volcanic hillsides.

One local island guide says it all: No bums allowed on St. Barts. And strangely enough, there isn't even one. Once known by its long nomenclature, St. Barthélémy, this thumbprint-sized isle is simply the antithesis of the ramshackle outpost. In fact, it could be easily considered one of *the* hoitiest-toitiest places alive on the planet. Try as you might, you won't find the seedy smells of West Indian life or the frenzied street markets that define Carib life. Instead, on St. Barts what you'll discover is a subculture of wealth superimposed on a native lore that is slowly but surely sinking into the sea. Even though there exists gorgeous scenery, pristine beaches and a sea-worthy harbor, St. Barts remains a place to snooze, to "cruise," to pick new husbands and discard old ones—in high season the island makes L.A. look limp. If you're the kind of person who feels happy paying for social comeuppance, then St. Barts will be your biggest fantasy isle.

Bird's Eye View

Shaped like a soprano sax or a backwards check mark, St. Barts covers only 9-1/2 square miles, making it half the size of Manhattan. A ten-minute flight from St. Martin, it is 125 miles from Guadeloupe, of which it is a dependency. There are six large lagoons scattered over the island, and no hill rising over the 920 ft. Morne Vitet. More than 20 tiny isles dot the surrounding water, the largest of which is Fourchue.

The harbor town of Gustavia puts the word quaint in the dictionary—a storybook setting for a fairytale. The eerily romantic streets are a mix of French, Colonial Creole, and Swedish style, so pristine that there's not even one piece of garbage sighted. Taking a road marked Lurin you can head out in a southeasterly direction and find achingly beautiful landscape. Latanier palms, imported for the straw hat industry, line the road, along with so many flowers—hibiscus, bougainvillea, dwarf poincianas, shell ginger flowers, baby orchids, flowering African tulips, frangipani—that you may feel overwhelmed. With trees bent permanently out of shape by the strong trade winds, the eastern side of the island, known as Grand Fond, resembles something out of *Wuthering Heights,* as tall grass waves hypnotically and stone walls that were constructed over a century ago by French immigrants continue to crumble. It's on this side of the island, nearly deserted, that you'll find one lone house perched on the rocks at ocean's edge—once owned by Rudolph Nureyev. At Lorient, on the east, local fishermen work as they have for centuries. As you travel northward, more buildings appear, though it is still largely residential housing around the northeastern tip at Petit Cul-de-Sac. The larger Grand Cul-de-Sac is a tourist enclave right out of *Lifestyles of the Rich and Famous.* An enclave of million-dollar villas dot the rocky tip of Pointe Milou, where it's rumored some of Prince Andrew's clan has nested.

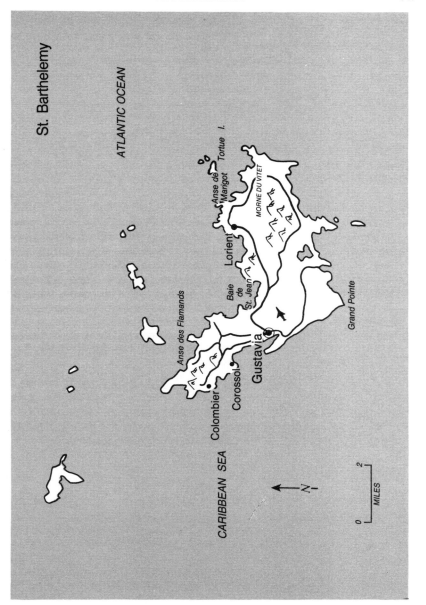

St. Barthelemy

ATLANTIC OCEAN

CARIBBEAN SEA

Anse des Flamands

Colombier

Corossol

Gustavia

Baie de St. Jean

Lorient

Anse de Marigot

Tortue I.

MORNE DU VITET

Grand Pointe

N

0   2
MILES

History

Some people believe Columbus discovered St. Barts, naming it after his brother, but the island didn't appear on any map until 1523, when a speck of dirt was labeled San Bartoleme by a Spanish cartographer. After being summarily ignored by both Carib Indians and European pirates, St. Barts was finally explored in 1637, eight years after St. Kitts was colonized, though some of the first Norman and British settlers were scalped by Carib Indians. Over time the island became a secret hiding place for pirates, while the island itself became tenaciously French. When Louis XVI traded the flagging island to the Swedes for some warehouse in Goteborg, the island magically flourished with new management (Thomas Jefferson himself declared the port free of all duties). By 1847, the island had been ravaged by hurricanes, trade competition, fires and piracy, leaving Gustavia, the capital, dirt poor—a fact that convinced the Swedes in 1878 to dump the island back in the lap of the French. Not until 1946 did the French government declare St. Barts a commune in the department of Guadeloupe in 1946. In 1947, aviator/hotelier Rémy de Haenen landed the first airplane here on the short, grassy pasture of St. Jean. With the construction of the airport and the island's first runway (called a STOL, i.e., short takeoff and landing), the floodgates of tourism were opened, with most visitors flocking to St. Jean, on the central point of the island.

People

As the actress Ann Magnuson once wrote, everybody on St. Barts looks related—to Olive Oyl. In truth, there are less than a hundred blacks on St. Barts since the island was too small to support a large import of slaves. Moreover, the rocky terrain of St. Barts was so inhospitable to growing sugarcane that the slave ships simply passed the island by, leaving the northern French farmers who settled here to follow their own Breton way of life. Today, the most traditional sect of the population are the fiercely independent grandmothers (or *grandmeres*)—tough old ladies, thoroughly Caucasian, West Indian by birth and French by heritage, who single-handedly raised their huge families in the absence of husbands who had to frequently leave the island to make ends meet. (Today you can see them wearing their straw *caleches* pulled low over their brows, a type of peasant bonnet that served to shield their faces not only from the sun but from the staring eyes of passing sailors.) Sadly, with the influx of more than a 1000 ex-pats (many of them French) and thousands of high-class international tourists, the old traditions are slowly dying out as the middle-aged generation is caught in transition while their children are looking solidly into a modernized future.

Anyone looking for political struggles or racial tension simply won't find them on St. Barts. An uncommon feeling of unity exists here among locals. Crime is unheard of (unless you call land developers thieves), simply because the cost of living is too high to support a petty thief. Instead, everyone seems to be gainfully employed, from fishermen, to builders, to shopkeepers to hoteliers and restaurateurs; even the dogs look well fed. As such, many visitors hitchhike around to see the island, which is said to be a completely safe way of passage, not to mention a great way to make friends. Between the native Bartians and the Euro babes and dudes who arrive during high season, rumor has it that there are ten men to every woman on St. Barts—and most of them are straight and very handsome. One word of warning: although the "genuine" locals are polite, if not unduly humble, the French ex-pats who run many of the hotels have an attitude that simply should be shipped home to Paris. Come armed with ammunition.

Beaches

St. Barts is famous for its pristine, white beaches—at present count, fourteen. Even during high season, they never become unbearably crowded, despite being public and free of charge. The Grand Saline is the only official nude beach, though stages of all levels of undress are seen throughout the island. (Grand Saline has been dubbed Indochine Beach, after the Manhattan restaurant frequented by the terminally fabulous. The unstated seating rule: hip and/or gay to the right side of the beach, conservative flanks to the left.) Both Grand Cul de Sac and St. Jean are the most developed beaches, with several hotels, restaurants, and water sports activities readily available; the two beaches are separated by the Eden Rock promontory. There is also a smattering of small hotels and restaurants at Flamanda to the west, a classic stretch of white sand fringed with lantana palms. For quiet seclusion, head for Marigot and Lorient on the north shore, where you'll see many island families on Sunday. Total privacy can be found at Gouverneur in the south. If you're walking, Shell Beach can be reached from Gustavia on foot; on the other side of town. The public beach is near the commercial pier but is good for a swim. The most difficult beach to reach is Colombier, a boat ride from Gustavia. If you're driving, go as far as the village of Colombier; from there, you'll have a half-hour hike down a scenic path.

Dive Sites

Shallow water reefs surrounding most of St. Barts make highly attractive conditions for divers and snorkelers. A dozen or more sites can be reached by merely swimming to them. The best dives can be found on the west coast, in the vicinity of Gustavia, in 5–60 feet of water (visibility ranges up to 100 feet). Outside the harbor the 75 -ft.-high rock called **Gros Ilet** surges out of the sea, attracting schools of snappers, groupers, lobsters, morays and barracudas. To the south, the three tiny Saintes are pieces of reefs where numerous fish swim and hide. **Pain du Sucre**, at the edge of the reef in open water, attracts some of the heartiest divers. Here you'll find elkhorn in abundance as well as colorful sponges, caverns and tunnels. Only experienced divers should venture into the windward coast at Toiny since sharks have been sighted and the strong currents make the waters extremely choppy.

At St. Jean Bay, the most accessible reefs lie northwest of Eden Rock, where there is a great variety of fish. Do take precautions, however, since you may run into hundreds of sea urchins. Ile Tortue is particularly suitable for the more advanced snorkeler, with its long narrow reef running southwest toward Marigot Bay. Snorkeling equipment may be rented in Gustavia and at watersports facilities around the island.

Treks

Many people choose to walk instead of drive on St. Barts because of its small size and the presence of lovely country roads and goat paths that cater to strolling. Just beyond the **Eden Rock Resort**, there is a road inland that crosses the island to **Grande Saline** where salt was once mined. From here a footpath leads over a low hill, to **Anse de Grande Saline**, a cove with no hotels and a mile-long beach. Near Grand Cul de Sac, the adjacent bay called Petit Cul de Sac harbors a footpath which head to the beach where a bed of oolitic rock—a granular form or limestone cemented together—is thought to be a geological anomaly in the Caribbean. A fascinating walk is the path between Grand Cul de Sac and Anse a Toiny, over the mountain where the slopes with patchwork fields outlined by low stone fences descend to the arid, rock windward shores of Grand Fond and Toiny. Two miles off the north coast you'll find **Ile Fourchue**, sometimes called the Five Fingers. The lunar landscape is eery and stark, with five peaks linked by steep ridges, forming a horseshoe and sheltering a bay with a small beach on the southwest. Although the island gets very hot, a day's excursion could be spent hiking over the strange terrain. The only creatures you will run into will be a few wild goats and seabirds. Boats can easily be hired from Gustavia on day charters, or you can seek an already existing trip.

The beach at **Colombier**, on the northwest coast, is only accessible by foot or boat. Take the main road to its end, then follow a path that meanders through tropical vegetation down to **Anse de Colombier**. There is a charming cove in the wooded slopes which day-chartered boats from Gustavia visit, particularly at sunset, which is a spectacular array of color. From April to August, the sight of female sea turtles coming on shore to lay their eggs is a sight you will never forget.

What Else to See

St. Barts is blissfully free of tourist traps and boring museums. Anything worth finding will be your own special discovery, but a few hints will get you started. To find one of the last threads of traditional life, go to the once-isolated fishing village of Corossol on the southwestern coast, where you can still find old St. Bartian women weaving handicrafts from latanier palms. The wide-brimmed hats they're wearing, called *caleches,* may be hard to find, but you will find stalls of straw hats and baskets for sale. Second hint: Head for the northwest tip of the island, where the road dead-ends at Petite Anse. There's a goat path here that leads to **Anse de Colombier**. This rugged mountain trail is the sole land access to a beach that can otherwise only be enjoyed by island-hopping yachtsmen. A lizard-laden trail winds through the towering torch cacti and along the edge of a spectacular shoreline, ending up a paradise beach that is beyond description.

Museums and Exhibits

Municipal Museum ★ ★ ★

Le Pointe, Gustavia.

This winsome little museum tells the island's history through costumes, antiques, documents and artwork. It also has exhibits on St. Barth's vegetation and sea creatures.

Sports

If you are interested in deep-sea fishing, head for the harbor at Gustavia, where boat charters with fishing gear can be hired; hotels also will usually make arrangements for you (you should expect them to, especially if you are paying a mint for the room). As opposed to other Caribbean islands, spearfishing is permitted, as long as the spearfisher is fully equipped in scuba gear. Both diving and snorkeling equipment can be purchased in Gustavia. Among the most popular fish anglers seek in St. Barts are dorado, bonito, tuna, marlin, barracuda, amberjack, grouper and moray eel. Do take time to talk to local fishermen and discover what are the best fish for the season and exactly what fish are edible—St. Barts has its own variety of edible fish. Local fishermen can also be the source of fascinating yarns that go on for hours, especially if they are inspired by a few beers.

Boating is more than a passion in St. Barts—it's a way of life, and sailors are often judged socially by the make of their boat. The ideal location of St. Barts—between Antigua and the Virgin Islands—gives sailors here a wide selection of destinations to choose from. In Gustavia, there are docking facilities and moorings for at least 40 vessels at one time. Other fine anchorages include Colombier, Public and Corossol bays. The calm winds of St. Jean and Grand Cul de Sac particularly take well to Sunfish; rentals are available there. It's very easy to pick up a full-day picnic excursion, leaving from Gustavia and headed to nearby beaches and islets (up to six passengers, usually). Full day sail to Ile Fourchue leaves the harbor at Gustavia at 9:30 a.m.

Surfing is terrific at Lorient. Always check the water conditions before you go; it will save you time and money, and sometimes your life, if the waves are too choppy. Most watersports facilities have boards for rent. Windsurfing equipment is also available at most facilities. Waterskiing is only authorized in Colombier Bay between 8:30 a.m. and 3 p.m.

Horseback Riding

Ranch des Flamands, Anse des Flamands.
Laure Nicolas is the person to see for trail rides and other excursions.

Watersports

Various locations, Gustavia.
La Marine Service *(☎ 27-70-34)* offers the island's most complete watersports center, with PADI-certified scuba diving, deep-sea fishing, snorkel excursions, and boat rides in the Aquascope from which you espy colorful coral, sea creatures, and a submerged yacht wreck. Also available are: **St. Barth Wind School** *(☎ 27-71-22)* and **Wind Wave Power** *(☎ 27-62-73)* for windsurfing instruction and rentals; **Club La Bulle** *(☎ 27-68-93)* and **Dive with Dan** *(☎ 27-64-78)* for scuba; and **La Maison de la Mer** *(☎ 27-81-00)* for deep-sea fishing.

Where to Stay

Highest Rated Hotels in St. Barthélémy

★★★★	Carl Gustaf Resort
★★★★	Castelets
★★★★	Guanahani
★★★★	Hotel le Toiny
★★★	Christopher Hotel
★★★	Club la Banane
★★★	El Sereno Beach Hotel & Villas
★★★	Filao Beach Hotel
★★★	Hostellerie Trois Forces
★★★	Hotel St. Barth

Most Exclusive Hotels in St. Barthélémy

★★★★	Hotel le Toiny	$394–$760
★★★	Hotel St. Barth	$380–$705
★★★★	Castelets	$100–$700
★★★	Filao Beach Hotel	$210–$420
★★★	Christopher Hotel	$195–$295

Fielding's Best Value Hotels in St. Barthélémy

★★★	Tropical Hotel	$97–$281
★★★	El Sereno Beach Hotel & Villas	$120–$340
★★★	Club la Banane	$130–$440
★★★★	Hotel le Toiny	$394–$760
★★★	Les Jardins de St. Jean	$60–$355

You don't come to St. Bart's without a gold card. Accommodations will be your biggest payout, unless you go crazy in the duty-free port. The trend in Bartian lodging leans toward the small, intimate and atmospheric—you won't see a high rise anywhere on the island. If you're intent on air-conditioning, ask in advance, because many properties depend on ceiling fans and the trade winds. Many people return to the same villa or inn year after year, having established a warm relationship with the owner. That's why reservations for the most popular properties should be made a year in advance, especially the villas, which go fast.

Hotels and Resorts

You'll find few big resorts on St. Barts. Most hotels have a homey feel; the final bill you receive will feel like nothing at home. Most of these hotels are environment-friendly, and take advantage of their luscious natural surroundings. The **Christopher Hotel** (a member of the Sofitel chain), and the **Grand Cul de Sac** are most typical of big hotels complete with modern facilities. More atmospheric are the villas of **Manapany**, tucked into a West Indian-type village, and the **St. Barth Isle de France**, where elegance prevails over efficiency. Namedroppers who want to run into other namedroppers tend to congregate at the **Guanahani**.

Baie des Agnes Hotel $175–$230 ★★

Baie des Flamands, ☎ *(590) 27-63-61.*
Single: $175–$200. Double: $175–$230.
Located on a picturesque beach, this small hotel has air-conditioned rooms with private bath and terrace, as well as bungalows with kitchenettes. The restaurant serves breakfast only, but other eateries are nearby. No pool or other facilities at this basic spot. 9 rooms. Credit Cards: CB, V, MC, A.

Castelets $100–$700 ★★★★★

Mount Lurin, ☎ *(590) 27-61-73.*
Single: $100–$700. Double: $100–$700.
This exclusive villa resort is perched high on a mountain, with stunning views. Formerly called the Sapore Di Mare, it is now back to its original owner. Two rooms are in the main house, the rest in two-bedroom duplex villas furnished with fine antiques, very luxurious accoutrements, spacious living rooms, terraces and kitchens. The atmosphere is sophisticated and discreet, attracting many celebrities. The grounds include a small pool and excellent French restaurant. You'll want a car to get around; the beach is five minutes' driving time. 10 rooms. Credit Cards: Not Accepted.

Christopher Hotel $195–$295 ★★★★

Pointe Milou, ☎ *(590) 27-63-63.*
Single: $195–$270. Double: $220–$295.
French Colonial in design, this is St. Barth's newest hotel, opened in 1993 on the island's northern tip. The 40 rooms are stylish and quite comfortable, with high-quality furnishings, minibars, and great views from the terrace or balcony. The beach is 10 minutes away, so most guests hang by the enormous pool—the island's largest. The site also includes a full-service health spa (each guest gets a free mas-

sage!), two restaurants, three bars, and a concierge to arrange off-premises activities. Service at this Sofitel-managed hotel is fine. 40 rooms. Credit Cards: V, MC, A.

Club la Banane $130–$440 ★★★★

Quartier Lorient, ☎ *(590) 27-68-25.*
Single: $130–$440. Double: $164–$440.
Located two miles from Gustavia, this small complex consists of nine inviting bungalows, each individually decorated. All are quite nice, with antiques, local artwork, TVs with VCRs, private terraces, and ceiling fans in lieu of air conditioners. Lush gardens surround the place. The restaurant is open only in the evenings. There's a pool on the premises and the beach is within walking distance. Nice. 9 rooms. Credit Cards: V, MC, A.

El Sereno Beach Hotel & Villas $120–$340 ★★★

Grand Cul de Sac, ☎ *(590) 27-64-80.*
Single: $120–$275. Double: $120–$340.
Located on the beach five minutes from Gustavia, this small operation consists of a hotel and gingerbread-trimmed villas, each housing three one-bedroom suites with full kitchens and lots of room. The standard hotel rooms are not as nice, but comfortable enough. There's a small pool on the premises, as well as two restaurants, two bars and lush gardens. Watersports await nearby. 29 rooms. Credit Cards: V, MC, A.

Filao Beach Hotel $210–$420 ★★★

Baie de St. Jean, ☎ *(590) 27-64-84.*
Single: $210–$420. Double: $210–$420.
Located right near the airport and on one of the island's better (and topless) beaches, this is a well-run operation. Guest rooms are in air-conditioned bungalows with all the modern comforts. They are quite private, but most don't have ocean views. Lovely perfumed gardens abound. There's also a large pool, windsurfing and snorkeling, and a good bar and restaurant. Excellent service, too. 30 rooms. Credit Cards: CB, V, MC, DC, A.

Francois Plantation $158–$405 ★★★

Colombier, ☎ *(590) 27-78-82.*
Single: $158–$404. Double: $205–$405.
Set on a hillside overlooking Baie des Flamands amid tropical gardens, this elegant spot consists of 12 bungalows scattered about. All are very nicely done, with mahogany furniture, four-poster beds, minibars, air conditioning, TVs, and terraces with views of the ocean or gardens. The views everywhere are simply astounding, especially from the pool terrace, and the restaurant is quite good. The beach is a five-minute drive. 12 rooms. Credit Cards: MC, A.

Grand Cul de Sac Hotel $110–$335 ★★

Grand Cul de Sac, ☎ *(590) 27-60-70.*
Single: $110–$185. Double: $195–$335.
Half the rooms at this bungalow complex have beach views and kitchenettes, while the other half have mountain views and refrigerators. All are air-conditioned and basic but comfortable. There's a bar and restaurant on the premises, as well as a salt-

water pool and gym. Guests can play tennis at sister property St. Barth's Beach Hotel and Tennis Club. 36 rooms. Credit Cards: MC, A.

Guanahani $110–$785   ★ ★ ★ ★ ★

Grand Cul de Sac, ☎ *(590) 27-66-60.*
Single: $110–$785. Double: $185–$785.
Located on seven beachfront acres at Cul de Sac, the romantic spot is especially popular with couples. Accommodations, in gingerbread-trimmed cottages, are deluxe. The higher-priced studios and one-bedroom suites have full kitchens, as well as whirlpools in the studios and plunge pools with the suites. The grounds include two restaurants, two tennis courts, a pool and watersports at the two beaches. Prepare for a lot of walking up and down the hillside. Nice. 80 rooms. Credit Cards: V, MC, A.

Hostellerie Trois Forces $80–$175   ★ ★ ★

Vitet, ☎ *(590) 27-61-25.*
Single: $80–$175. Double: $80–$175.
When someone asks "what's your sign?" here it's not just the old come on—each cottage is individually decorated and designed to compliment the astrological sign after which it's named. Located up in the mountains, three miles from Gustavia, this peaceful retreat is run by the island's leading astrologer, who also happens to be a quite decent chef. The gingerbread-trimmed cottages are tiny but nicely done with hand-made wooden furnishings and large terraces. Only four are air-conditioned, and none have phones or TV. There's a pool on-site, and this is probably the only hotel in the Caribbean where you can take yoga lessons, have your tarot cards read, and get your chart done. Very pleasant. 8 rooms. Credit Cards: MC, A.

Hotel Baie des Flamands $95–$135   ★ ★ ★

Anse de Flamands, ☎ *(590) 27-64-85.*
Single: $95–$105. Double: $105–$135.
Set on a half-mile stretch of beach, one of the island's best, this small motel-like property is fairly isolated, so you'll want a rental car to get around. Accommodations are clean and basic, with the more expensive rooms offering a kitchenette on the patio. (The others come with a refrigerator.) The grounds include a very fine French restaurant, bar and saltwater pool. Good service at this family-run operation. 24 rooms. Credit Cards: MC, A.

Hotel St. Barth $380–$705   ★ ★ ★ ★

Anse des Flamands, ☎ *(590) 27-61-81.*
Single: $380–$705. Double: $380–$705.
Set along one of the island's best beaches, this newer property houses guests in cottages or a plantation-style house. All guest rooms are spacious and furnished with antiques, locally made pieces, expensive linens, large baths (some with whirlpool tubs), refrigerators, and patios or balconies. Facilities include an air-conditioned squash court, tennis court, two pools, and a fitness center. Very nice! 28 rooms. Credit Cards: V, MC, A.

Manapany Cottages $125–$990   ★ ★ ★ ★

Anse des Cayes, ☎ *(590) 27-66-65.*

Single: $125–$990. Double: $205–$990.

Set in a small cove on the north shore, this property consists of a complex of cottages along a hillside or the beach. Accommodations vary from standard guestrooms to suites with one or two bedrooms and full kitchens. All are fine, but not as luxurious as the rates suggest. The site incudes two restaurants, an exercise room, pool and tennis court. The beach is pretty but tiny, and constantly windy. This operation is quite chic, but on the small side compared to other luxury resorts. 52 rooms. Credit Cards: MC, A.

Normandie $65–$80   ★★

Loriet, Loriet, ☎ *(590) 27-61-66.*
Single: $65–$80. Double: $65–$80.

This basic, family-run place offers some of St. Barth's cheapest accommodations. The rooms are decent for the rates—obviously quite basic, but clean and comfortable. Only two (the most expensive) have air conditioners; the rest rely on ceiling fans. There's a small pool but nothing else, so you'll want a car. 8 rooms. Credit Cards: Not Accepted.

St. Barth's Beach Club $68–$115   ★★★

Grand Cul de Sac, ☎ *(590) 27-60-70.*
Single: $68–$83. Double: $93–$115.

This two-story hotel is right on the beach. Though it calls itself a hotel and tennis club, it has only one court. Other facilities include a saltwater pool, gym and a windsurfing school. Accommodations are modern; all have a balcony or patio, while some boast minibars and kitchens. You'll want a rental car, as this spot is fairly isolated. 52 rooms. Credit Cards: MC, A.

Taiwana Hotel $955–$999   ★★★

Anse des Flamands, ☎ *(590) 27-65-01.*
Single: $955–$999. Double: $955–$999.

Located on a secluded beach, this incredibly expensive spot houses its well-heeled guests in beautifully furnished and quite large suites loaded with antiques, modern furniture, hand-painted tiles and enormous bathrooms, many with whirlpools. There are two pools (one for kids), tennis, and a restaurant. Watersports are available on the beach. The service can be sullen—not exactly what one has in mind when forking over $1000 for a night's stay. Unless you're turned on by paying exorbitant prices, try someplace else. 9 rooms. Credit Cards: Not Accepted.

Tropical Hotel $97–$281   ★★★

Baie de St. Jean, Baie de St. Jean, ☎ *(590) 27-64-87.*
Single: $97–$207. Double: $125–$281.

Set some 25 yards from the beach on a hill overlooking St. Jean Bay, this small hotel centers around a gingerbread-trimmed building that houses the reception area, a lounge and bar. Guestrooms are light and airy, with comfortable trappings and furnished patios overlooking the ocean or lush gardens. There's also a restaurant and pool on-site. Pleasant. 22 rooms. Credit Cards: MC, A.

Apartments and Condominiums

Self-catering in St. Barts is not "roughing it." Prices on villas with fully equipped kitchens can be exorbitant, but the surroundings are often worth it, such as the **Hotel Carl Gustaf** near Shell Beach. Rental agencies are your best bet to secure the perfect accommodation for your needs. Do decide ahead of time if you want to rent a car or whether you need a live-in staff. Snob-weary Americans should contact Sibarth, a real estate agency in Gustavia, run by Brook and Roger Lacour, a former U.S. citizen who married into the St. Barts life. Sibarth rents out villas that range from the modest to the luxurious. It also arranges sailing, snorkeling, diving, horseback riding, as well as transportation and restaurant reservations. Call ☎ *800-932-3222*; villas start at $900 per week. One of the most spectacular and celebrity-oozing rentals is dancer Mikhail Baryshnikov's two Mexican-style villas superbly decorated by Billy du Mesnil, available December–April, for about $4000 a week (each). (Contact ☎ *011-590-278-672* for more information.) For villa renters whose phone is restricted to local calls, a world-wide phone service, Liaisons Mondiales, allows off-island calls by dialing ☎ *27-79-91*. Do find a copy of the *Vendôm Guide*, an elegant, four-color publication which details villa rentals, hotels, restaurants and a variety of island sports. It's in English and on sale through Sibarth on the island or through WIMCO in Newport, RI.

Carl Gustaf Resort   **$500–$1000**   ★★★★

Rue des Normands, ☎ *(800) 948-7823, (590) 27-82-83.*
Single: $500–$1000. Double: $500–$1000.
Named in honor of the king of Sweden, this all-suite hotel is situated on a hilltop overlooking Gustavia harbor. Guests are housed in cottages of one or two bedrooms with wooden sundecks and tiny private plunge pools. The units are quite stylishly done, with high ceilings, marble floors, luxurious furnishings, fax machines (!), stereos, VCRs, and fully equipped kitchens. Two-bedroom suites have bunk beds for kids. Facilities include a gourmet French restaurant, two bars, a fitness center, a private cabin cruiser for sea and fishing excursions, and a botanical garden. Wonderful views abound everywhere at this sophisticated French-style resort. If you can afford the rates, you won't be disappointed. 14 rooms. Credit Cards: MC, A.

Emeraude Plage Hotel   **$208–$500**   ★★★

Baie St. Jean, ☎ *(590) 27-64-78.*
Single: $208–$500. Double: $208–$500.
Situated right on the beach, this popular spot does a lot of repeat business, so book early. Accommodations are in simple yet comfortable bungalows with all the modern conveniences, plus kitchenettes on the patios. Three units have two bedrooms, and there's a beachside villa with two bedrooms, two baths and great views. All is kept in tip-top shape by the very friendly staff. There's little in the way of extras, but no one seems to mind. Guests get a discount on watersports at the nearby concession. 30 rooms. Credit Cards: V, MC.

Hotel le Toiny   **$394–$760**   ★★★★

Anse de Toiny, ☎ *(590) 27-88-88.*
Single: $394–$623. Double: $349–$760.
Set on a remote hillside on the southeastern coast, this newer hotel is set in a grove of trees. Accommodations are lovely, consisting of suites in individual cottages with

quality furnishing and linens, four-poster beds, full kitchens, and TVs with VCRs—plus a private pool for each. Spectacular views abound. There's an open-air French restaurant and a large communal pool as well. The beach is a five-minute walk, but you'll need a car to do any other exploring. Elegant. 12 rooms. Credit Cards: V, MC, A.

Les Islets Fleuris Hotel Residence $70–$220 ★★

Hauts de Lorient, ☎ *(590) 27-64-22.*
Single: $70–$220. Double: $100–$220.
This small complex has eight cottages set on the hillside. All are studios with full kitchens and large terraces that rely on ceiling fans for comfort. There's a pool on-site, with restaurants nearby. 8 rooms. Credit Cards: Not Accepted.

Les Jardins de St. Jean $60–$355 ★★★★

Rue Victor Maurasse, Baie de St. Jean, ☎ *(590) 27-70-19.*
Single: $60–$255. Double: $88–$355.
This condominium hotel is located on a hillside, some 300 yards from the beach. Accommodations are in a cluster of two-story bungalows and run the gamut from studios to units with one or two bedrooms. All have full kitchens, private terraces and air conditioning. TV and radio are available for an extra charge. There's a large pool on the premises and much within walking distance. 22 rooms. Credit Cards: MC, A.

Marigot Bay Club $80–$185 ★★★

Marigot Bay, ☎ *(590) 27-75-45.*
Single: $80–$185. Double: $80–$185.
This small apartment hotel offers clean and basic units at a fair price. Set on a hillside overlooking the Atlantic, units are simply furnished and include full kitchens, private terraces, TVs and living rooms. Maids keep things tidy. There's a French restaurant on-site, but not much else. The beach is walkable. 6 rooms. Credit Cards: MC, A.

Village St. Jean Hotel ★★★

Baie de St. Jean, ☎ *(590) 27-61-39.*
Double: $85–$300.
Set on a hillside close to the beach, this property consists of 20 cottages with one or two bedrooms. Each is simply furnished but pleasant enough, with kitchens and private terraces. There are also standard hotel rooms with twin beds and small refrigerators. A restaurant, pool and Jacuzzi are on the premises, with lots within walking distance. This friendly, family-run operation is a good buy. 20 rooms. Credit Cards: MC, A.

White Sand Beach Cottages $55–$205 ★★

Baie de Flamands, ☎ *(590) 27-82-08.*
Single: $55–$145. Double: $85–$205.
This casual spot has eight cottages within walking distance of the beach and nearby resorts. The accommodations are simple yet pleasant, with kitchens and air conditioning. No facilities on-site. 4 rooms. Credit Cards: MC, A.

Yuana Hotel $150–$355 ★★★

Quartier du Roy, ☎ *(590) 27-80-84.*

Single: $150–$305. Double: $150–$355.

Set in a lush garden, this hillside hotel has great views. Guests are put up in spacious studios with full kitchenettes, TVs with VCRs, and comfortable furnishings. The restaurant serves breakfast only; you'll have to cook in or rent a car for other meals. There's a small pool for cooling off. 12 rooms. Credit Cards: MC, A.

le P'tit Morne   **$67–$120**   ★ ★

Colombier ☎ *(590) 27-62-64.*
Single: $67–$120. Double: $67–$120.

Set high up in the hills far from the madding crowds, this apartment hotel's rates are quite reasonable for expensive St. Barts. Units are air-conditioned studios with cable TV, minibars, fully equipped kitchens and decks. The premises include a pool and snack bar, which serves breakfast only. The beach is a five-minute drive down a twisting road. 14 rooms. Credit Cards: MC, A.

Inns

For more intimate lodgings, many tourists are flocking to the "inn scene," where the personal service and often remote locations create the profile of perfect hideaways. One of the grandest places, **Le Filao**, is a member of the Relais & Chateau clan, always a top name in lush surroundings and elegant cuisine. **Hotel Baie des Anges** is one of the few that offer kitchenettes in some rooms.

Low Cost Lodging

There are very few cheap lodgings on St. Barts, because frankly tourists without money are generally treated like lepers. You can save money by coming off-season, cramming a party the size of a small fraternity into a cottage or villa, and cooking your own food. At Presqui'ile, you should probably be able to speak French well, particularly since you will most likely have to share the bathroom. Hotel Le P'tit Morne is in the middle of nowhere, so you should have a car to get to the beach, unless you want to spend your St. Bart days near a pool. The best location is **Les Mouettes**, on the beach at Lorient.

Where to Eat

Highest Rated Restaurants in St. Barthélémy

★★★★★ **Le Toque Lyonnaise**

★★★★ **Ballahou**

★★★★ **Francois Plantation**

★★★★ **La Fregate**

★★★★ **Le Gaiac**

★★★★ **Le Sapotillier**

★★★ **Au Port**

★★★ **Castelets**

★★★ **Eddy's Ghetto**

★★★ **Hostellerie Trois Forces**

Most Exclusive Restaurants in St. Barthélémy

★★★★ **Le Sapotillier**	$45–$60
★★★ **Marigot Bay Club & Art Gallery**	$40–$50
★★★ **Wall House**	$30–$45
★★★★ **Francois Plantation**	$16–$50
★★★ **Castelets**	$25–$35

Fielding's Best Value Restaurants in St. Barthélémy

★★★ **Wall House**	$30–$45
★★★ **Pasta Paradise**	$10–$25
★★★ **Marigot Bay Club & Art Gallery**	$40–$50
★★★ **Le Select**	$5–$10
★★★ **La Langouste**	$23–$42

The food in St. Barts has to be good enough to suit the persnickety jetsetters who arrive, plus locals have to have the attitude to endure them. Cuisine usually runs to the French, often using the spoils of the sea, such as *langouste* (lobster) and redfish, but you can find a few West Indian kitchens, like the casual Topolino, on the road to Salines. The harborside **Chez Maya** is the hippest celebrity hangout, where the atmosphere is relaxed and the exotic cuisine—from French to Creole to Vietnamese—is superb. Best dining can be found at la Cuisine de Michel, a tiny roadside takeout place on the Grand Fond road; many locals stop by to pick up their Sunday meals here from the French chef Michel Brunet. **Eddy's Ghetto**, in Gustavia, is an open-air restaurant where everyone fits in, a funky lively joint where great meals come with good prices. When wallets get low, the village of Lorient proffers good hamburgers at **Chez Jo Jo**. Do your best to seek out the fresh-baked bread that a little old lady sells near the cemetery.

The club scene has slumped since the infamous club Au Tour de Rocher mysteriously burned down two years ago. Weekend nights at **Le Pélican** in St. Jean seem like a frat party. Every night except Wednesday is cabaret at **Club La Banane**, run by the French lady whose Parisian cabaret inspired "La Cage Aux Folles." Two of the favorite local bar hangouts—**Bar de l'Oubli** and **Le Sélect**—sit kitty-corner from each other on rue du Général de Gaulle in Gustavia, the busiest thoroughfare of the town, and are the places where you're most likely to meet new friends. If you are a young, drunken poet wannabe, drop in at **Chez Ginette S.O.S.**, and try the famous Punch Coco (a rum concoction whose ingredients are known only to owner Ginette). Wannabe sailors should try to get invited to dinner on one of the impressive yachts anchored in the match-box-size harbor—one even has the name *Octopussy*.

Adam   **$$$**   ★★

Village St. Jean, St. Jean, ☎ *(590) 27-84-56.*
French cuisine.
Dinner: prix fixe $35.

On an island where fabulous eateries come and go, Adam prevails by proffering a seemingly infinite variety of three-course, prix-fixe dinners at a reasonable tariff. Entrees like filet mignon, lobster, or filet of pork with a coconut sauce are capped off with creme brulee or other heavenly desserts. The setting is also paradisiacal, high on a hillside with garden and lagoon views; there's art on the walls as well as on the plates. Closed: Tue. Reservations recommended. Credit Cards: A.

Au Port   **$$$**   ★★★

Rue Sadi-Carnot, ☎ *(590) 27-62-36.*
French cuisine.
Dinner: 6:30 p.m.–10:00 p.m., entrees $19–$27.

Guests navigate a steep staircase to get to the second-floor dining room of this charming old house above the port of Gustavia. Cuisine is a fanciful blend of traditional French and creole—witness the popular *colombo* (Creole curry) of prawns or lamb served with seasoned rice. Ambience is understandably nautical. Reservations recommended. Credit Cards: A.

Ballahou $$$ ★★★★

Anse des Cayes, Anse des Cayes, ☎ *(590) 27-66-55.*
French cuisine.
Lunch: 12:30 p.m.– 4:00 p.m., entrees $15–$30.
Dinner: 7:30 p.m.–9:30 p.m., entrees $27–$45.
There's a lot of understandable ballyhoo (and hip-hooray) about this gorgeous restaurant in the sleek Hotel Manapany—architecturally, it seems to blend as one with the rim of the swimming pool. Specialties usually include seafood, but the menu changes often. Guests of the hotel and others dine here by candlelight only five months out of the year; it's closed in the warmer months. Manapany's Italian restaurant, Ouanalao, serves lunch and dinner all year round; try the gazpacho and risotto with prawns. Associated Hotel: Hotel Manapany. Reservations required. Credit Cards: V, MC, DC, A.

Castelets $$$ ★★★★

Morne Lurin, ☎ *(590) 27-6173.*
French cuisine.
Dinner: 7:00 p.m.–9:00 p.m., entrees $25–$35.
This long-established hotel went through a brief Italian phase as Sapore de Mare. Manager Genevieve Jouany returned and brought everything back to normal, including the chic dining salon presided over by two under-30s chefs (aren't they all?). These young wizards eschew heavy cream sauces in favor of fresh herbs and virgin olive oils. They also exhibit a propensity for wild morel and boletus mushrooms that show up frequently in pasta and seafood dishes. Associated Hotel: Castelets. Closed: Tue. Reservations required. Credit Cards: V, MC, A.

Eddy's Ghetto $$$ ★★★

Rue du General de Gaulle,
French cuisine.
Dinner: 7:00 p.m.–10:00 p.m., entrees $15–$18.
When locals go slumming they go to Eddy's for simple grills, salads, ribs, beef ragouts and island music. The yacht crowd often fills the wicker and plant-filled restaurant the moment it opens at 7 p.m., if the locals haven't gotten there first. The place fills the need for light meals and casual ambience not found in some of the pricier establishments in town. The owner is Eddy Stakelborough (a member of the clan that founded Le Select across the street), who oversees the action from a perch behind the bar. Closed: Sun. Credit Cards: Not Accepted.

Francois Plantation $$$ ★★★★

Colombier ☎ *(590) 27-7882.*
French cuisine.
Dinner: 6:30 p.m.–10:00 p.m., entrees $16–$50.
No one doubts the serene beauty of this place—for exotic plantings, greenery and an interior boasting highly polished woods. But the food (lighter versions of traditional French favorites) and service have been slipping somewhat. It's hoped things

will improve, as the innovativeness of the cuisine can't often be faulted. Associated Hotel: Francois Plantation. Closed: Sun. Reservations required. Credit Cards: V, MC, A.

Hostellerie Trois Forces $$$ ★ ★ ★

Vitet ☎ *(590) 27-6125.*
French cuisine.
Lunch: 12.00 a.m.–3.00 p.m., entrees $10–$50.
Dinner: 7:00 p.m.–9:45 p.m., entrees $10–$50.
Tarot readings and fine food commingle nicely at this surprisingly unpretentious holistic, new age resort-restaurant in the small town of Vitet, east of Lorient. Chef and chief astrologer Hubert Delemotte and family serve creole/French meals with a nod to organic and vegetarian diners, although there is red meat on the menu. There's a three-course, prix-fixe dinner offering nightly. Ambience is low-key and pleasant. Associated Hotel: Hostellerie Trois Forces. Reservations required. Credit Cards: V, MC, A.

L'Entrepont $$$ ★ ★

La Pointe, ☎ *(590) 27-9060.*
Italian cuisine.
Lunch: entrees $17–$25.
Dinner: entrees $25–$33.
Located in a newly fashionable area on the west side of Gustavia's harbor, this Italian restaurant owned by a Neapolitan family is renowned for unusual pizzas. Guests eat well in a garden setting that's open to the breezes. Other choices include beef carpaccio, pastas and veal. Reservations recommended. Credit Cards: V, MC.

L'Escale $$$ ★ ★ ★

La Pointe, ☎ *(590) 27-8106.*
Italian cuisine.
Dinner: 7:00 p.m.–12.00 p.m., entrees $14–$29.
This mostly Italian trattoria on the west side of the harbor has many faithful followers who clamor for the wide variety of pizzas (some say it's the best in town), or lasagna and seafood. Lately it's been facing some competition from other eateries in the area serving similar cuisine, although it swings at night, especially in the hip bar. Closed: Tue. Reservations required. Credit Cards: V, MC.

La Fregate $$ ★ ★ ★ ★

Flamandes Beach, Flamandes, ☎ *(590) 27-6651.*
French cuisine.
Lunch: 12:00 a.m.–3:00 p.m., entrees $10–$19.
Dinner: 7:00 p.m.–9:00 p.m., entrees $10–$19.
Aim for an outside patio table at this excellent restaurant—if you still can. The word is out about the incredible edibles emerging from Jean-Pierre Crouzet's kitchen in a somewhat tacky beachfront motel in Baie des Flamandes. Island regulars know him from his past successes at Gustavia's La Sapotillier, where he was chef de cuisine. Here he continues to unleash a plethora of dishes utilizing the freshest local ingredients possible with a tried and true technique—although he is not yet 30, he has already worked his way through quite a few three-star establishments in France.

Associated Hotel: Baie des Flamandes. Closed: Mon. Reservations required. Credit Cards: V, MC, A.

La Langouste $$$ ★★★

rue Bord-de-la-Mer, ☎ *(590) 27-69-47.*
Latin American cuisine. Specialties: Langouste.
Lunch: 12:00 a.m.–2:00 p.m., entrees $23–$42.
Dinner: 7:00 p.m.–10:00 p.m., entrees $23–$42.

The island's national crustacean (a clawless lobster) is the star at this pleasant creole/French eatery owned by Annie Ange, a member of a St. Barts landowning family (St. Barth Beach Hotel). The delectable seafood is dependably fresh, and other finny offerings include stuffed crabs and *accra de morue* (cod fritters). It's located is a traditional Swedish-style dwelling near several public offices. Reservations required. Credit Cards: V, MC.

Le Gaiac $$$ ★★★★

Anse de Toiny, Anse de Toiny, ☎ *(590) 27-8888.*
French cuisine.
Lunch: entrees $30–$60.
Dinner: entrees $30–$60.

Nowadays, few great chefs stay in one place for long—Manapany's Jean Christophe Perrin has turned his talents to this small, very in spot at Le Toiny, a resort on a hilltop above a windward beach. It's very difficult to secure a seat in the 28-table outdoor restaurant (book way in advance) where such delights as conch cannelloni and rabbit with figs and pine nuts continue to dazzle guests. Associated Hotel: Le Toiny. Reservations required. Credit Cards: V, MC, A.

Le Pelican $$$ ★★

Plage de St. Jean, Plage de St. Jean, ☎ *(590) 27-6464.*
Latin American cuisine.
Lunch: 11:30 a.m.–3:00 p.m., entrees $20–$40.
Dinner: 6:30 p.m.–1:00 p.m., entrees $20–$40.

This pleasant restaurant located a few steps from St. Barth's most popular beach satisfies on many counts. At lunch it's perfect for casual meals and ocean and people watching from a vast, covered terrace. Later, for dinner, the large dining rooms are awash in candlelight while sounds of piano music grace the background. Cuisine is a melange of creole and French favorites. Closed for dinner on Sundays. Reservations recommended. Credit Cards: V, A.

Le Sapotillier $$$ ★★★★

rue Sadi-Carnot, ☎ *(590) 27-6028.*
French cuisine. Specialties: Couscous with shrimp creole, fish mousse.
Dinner: prix fixe $45–$60.

Some fine chefs have emerged with an appreciative following from the kitchens of this memorable restaurant in a traditional old stone structure in Gustavia, including Le Fregate's Jean-Pierre Crouzette. La Sapotillier's reputation is still stellar, with classic French cuisine served with finesse in a small dining room or alfresco under the branches of a vast sapodilla tree. Closed: Sun. Reservations required. Credit Cards: V, MC.

Le Select $ ★★★

rue de la France, ☎ *(590) 27-86-87.*
International cuisine. Specialties: Burgers.
Lunch: 10:00 a.m.–4:00 p.m., entrees $5–$10.
Dinner: 4:00 p.m.–11:00 p.m., entrees $5–$10.
This old favorite (circa 1950) provides a safe haven for ordinary folk seeking refuge
from the high prices and sometimes overstuffed, precious atmosphere of some
island dining establishments. Besides serving what is probably the best cheeseburger
in town (it's called cheeseburger in paradise), the scruffy, poster-festooned old
warehouse is great for loud reggae, zouk, or soca music. Newcomers can't possibly
miss it—just walk around Gustavia during the day and you'll bump into it; at night
you hear it before you see it. Closed: Sun. Credit Cards: Not Accepted.

Le Toque Lyonnaise $$$ ★★★★★

Grand Cul-de-Sac, Grand Cul-de-Sac, ☎ *(590) 27-6480.*
French cuisine. Specialties: Grilled lobster with vanilla bean.
Dinner: 7:00 p.m.–10:00 p.m., prix fixe $43–$61.
It's hard not to have a good meal here—chefs are from Lyon, which is the gourmet
capital of France. This modern, oceanfront eatery, located a few miles out of Gusta-
via, boasts chefs who have trained with Paul Bocuse. Grilled seafood is the specialty,
and the wine list is extensive and well-chosen. Closed June through October. Asso-
ciated Hotel: El Sereno Beach Hotel. Reservations recommended. Credit Cards: V,
MC, DC, A.

Marigot Bay Club & Art Gallery $$$ ★★★

Marigot Bay, Marigot, ☎ *(590) 27-7545.*
French cuisine.
Lunch: entrees $40–$50.
Dinner: entrees $40–$50.
Two giant grilled langoustines appear on your plate here like creatures from Mars—
yet they were freshly caught only this morning by a family of fisherfolk who own this
popular restaurant at an intimate resort in the small bayside village of Marigot. You
can have your crustacean plain or with a variety of sauces. Specialties rarely change,
which is how most people who eat here like it. Closed for lunch on Monday and on
Sundays from September through October. Reservations required. Credit Cards: V, A.

Maya's $$$ ★★

Public Beach, Public, ☎ *(590) 27-7361.*
Latin American cuisine.
Dinner: 6:00 p.m.–11:00 p.m., entrees $27–$35.
Maya from Martinique serves savory creole cuisine with some spicy touches to an
appreciative crowd; it's one of the more popular eateries on the island. The restau-
rant has a waterfront location in Public (west of Gustavia) with tables on a plant-
filled patio. The menu changes frequently, but the salads are a standout. Closed:
Sun. Reservations required. Credit Cards: V, MC, A.

Pasta Paradise $$$ ★★★

Rue de Roi, ☎ *(590) 27-8078.*
French cuisine.
Lunch: entrees $10–$25.

Dinner: entrees $10–$25.

French-inspired Italian food is served at this very popular restaurant in a traditional, historic building in Gustavia. Formerly the site of La Citronelle, the jolly exterior features gingerbread trim, white shutters, tangerine and white railings and a tropical mural. Guests can dine on several different daily pasta offerings in air-conditioned insularity or in a breeze-cooled patio. The menu also features lobster in saffron oil and beef filets. Closed for lunch on Sunday. Reservations recommended. Credit Cards: V, MC.

Santa Fe $$$ ★★

Morne Lurin,
American cuisine. Specialties: Burgers, steaks.
Lunch: 12:00 a.m.–2:00 p.m., entrees $10–$21.
Dinner: 5:00 p.m.–10:00 p.m., entrees $10–$21.

Although the name evokes the American Southwest, the food served here is basically burgers (excellent), steak, and barbecue at American prices (reasonable). It's also a hangout for Anglais-speakers and sports fans of any stripe who come to watch their favorite teams play on wide-screen television, especially on Sundays. Located just a few miles east of Gustavia, it seems worlds away in atmosphere and in its isolation on a lofty hilltop. There's no ocean view; but that's not really necessary here. Closed for lunch on Sundays. Closed: Wed. Credit Cards: Not Accepted.

Wall House $$$ ★★★

Gustavia Harbor, ☎ *(590) 27-71-33.*
French cuisine.
Lunch: entrees $30–$45.
Dinner: entrees $30–$45.

Almost every table in this whitewashed restaurant in the harbor has a lovely view; the wide picture windows in the dining room offer a panorama of swaying palms, small craft, azure waters, and a row of red tile-roofed, gingerbread-trimmed buildings. Diners can also sit outside to be closer to the action. The menu features lobster, rare lamb, duck breast, fabulous pates, and sinful desserts. Reservations recommended. Credit Cards: V, MC.

Where to Shop

To find one of the last threads of traditional life, go to the once-isolated fishing village of Corossol on the southwestern coast, where you can still find old St. Bartian women weaving handicrafts from latanier palms. The wide-brimmed hats called *caleches* may be hard to find atop their heads, but you will find stalls of straw hats and baskets.

Duty-free reigns in St. Barts, so if you're in the market for fine perfumes, china, crystal and liquor, you can find some of the best bargains in the Caribbean. Some French perfumes, like Chanel, are cheaper than they are in Paris. Due to the jetset crowd, a number of local crafts have found their way into international fashion magazines. Check around the small shops in Gustavia and in some of the outlying villages. **The Shell Shop** features unique jewelry, shells and coral found on the island. Yacht-owners and wannabes tend to congregate at **Loulou's Marine** in Gustavia, where everything you ever needed for a cruise is available—from clothes to rigs.

St. Barthélémy Directory

ARRIVAL

From the States, the principal gateway is Sint Maarten where you can make connections via inter-island carriers to St. Barts. Many flights are available daily. **Windward Islands Airways** offers a ten-minute flight from Juliana Airport on Sint Maarten ☎ *(590) 27-61-01* or **Air St. Barthélémy** ☎ *(590) 27-71-90*, which also has flights from San Juan, Guadeloupe, and Espérance Airport on French St. Martin. **Air Guadeloupe** ☎ *(590) 27-61-90* makes the flight from Espérance in 10 minutes and from Guadeloupe in one hour. Air Guadeloupe also flies from St. Thomas a few times a week. (To get to St. Thomas, take the 30-minute flight from San Juan, Puerto Rico, where **Air St. Thomas** ☎ *(590) 27-71-76* has connecting flights to St. Barts, a 45-minute ride.) If you have trouble making connections, you can always charter a flight through Windward Island Airways and Air St. Barthélémy.

St. Barts' airport has a short landing strip that can handle planes no larger than a 20-seat STOL aircraft. It is not equipped for night landing. Boutiques, bar and car rental agencies can be found at the airport, and a pharmacy and food market across the road in La Savane Commercial Center.

There is an airport departure tax of 10 francs (about $2) to the French side of St. Martin or Guadeloupe, and 15 francs ($3) to other destinations.

CLIMATE

St. Barts has an ideal dry climate and an average temperature of 72–86 degrees F.

DOCUMENTS

For stays of up to three weeks, U.S. and Canadian citizens traveling as tourists must have proof of citizenship in the form of a valid passport or that has expired not more than five years ago, or a birth certificate (original or copy) or voter's registration accompanied by a government authorized ID with photo.

For stays over three weeks, or for nontourist visits, a valid passport is necessary. Resident aliens of the U.S. and Canada, and visitors from countries other than those in the Common Market (E.E.C.) and Japan, must have a valid passport and visa. A return or onward ticket is also required of all visitors.

ELECTRICITY

Current runs at 220 AC, 60 cycles. American-made appliances require French plug converters and transformers.

GETTING AROUND

Car rentals are easy to secure on the island, but it is best to ask your hotel to reserve one for you in advance, especially during the winter season. Roads are hilly, steep, narrow and winding, and drivers must know how to use a stick shift; your best options are VW Beetles, little open Gurgels, and Mini-Mokes. You'll save money if you rent by the week — daily rates go as high as $60 a day, which includes unlimited mileage, collision damage insurance (first $500 deductible) and free delivery. Gas costs about $3.25 a gallon. None of the two gas stations (near the airport and in Lorient) is open on Sunday. St. Barts' first all-night automatic gas station recently opened near the airport, requiring magnetically sensitized cards on sale at the station.

Some reliable agencies are: **Avis** at the airport ☎ *27-71-43*; **Budget** airport and town ☎ *27-67-43*; **Hertz** at the airport ☎ *27-71-14* or *27-60-21*. A few hotels have their own fleet of rentals, and may ask you to book through them because of limited parking.

Taxis stations (two) are located at the airport and one in Gustavia on rue de la République. To call a **taxi**, dial ☎ *27-66-31* on a local phone. For night taxis, call **Jean-Paul Janin** ☎ *27-61-86*, **Raymond Gréaux** ☎ *27-66-32*, or **Mathilde Laplace** ☎ *27-60-59*.

Motorbikes, mopeds, and scooters are easy to rent, but you must wear a helmet, required by law. You must also have a motorbike or driver's license. Rentals can be found at: **Denis Dufau's Rent Some Fun** ☎ *27-70-59*, which also carries 18-speed mountain bikes or **Fredéric Supligeau** ☎ *27-67-89*.

Sleek catamarans leave the marina on Dutch St. Maarten between 9:00 and 9:30 a.m. daily, arriving in Gustavia harbor less than 90 minutes later. One-way trips are possible, but the usual fare is one day round trips.

You can also arrive on St. Barts by ferryboats from St. Martin, like the *St. Barth Express III*, which leaves at 7:30 a.m. and returns from Marina Porte La Royale in Mariot at 3:30 p.m. and Bobby's Marina in Philipsburg at 4:15 p.m., arriving in Gustavia 45 minutes later. To reserve, ☎ *(590) 27-77-24*, FAX *(590) 27-7723*. Two other ferryboats are the *Dauphin II* and the *Bateau Dakar*.

Private boat charters can be arranged through Sibarth in Gustavia ☎ *(590) 27-62-38* or its American affiliate WIMGO, Newport RI ☎ *(800) 932-3222* or *(410) 849-8012*.

LANGUAGE

French is the official language, spoken with a quaint Norman dialect. Most people speak English, but do plan to come loaded with an attitude to match that of the French employees at many hotels.

MEDICAL EMERGENCIES

Gustavia has a **hospital** ☎ *27-60-35*, eight resident doctors, three dentists, one gynecologist, and specialists in opthalmology, dermatology, etc. There are pharmacies at **La Savane Commercial Center** ☎ *27-66-61* and in Gustavia ☎ *27-61-82*.

MONEY

The official currency is the French franc; the official exchange rate (on October 1994) was approximately 5 francs to the American dollar. The rate is subject to change due to currency fluctuations. Dollars are accepted everywhere and prices are often quoted in dollars.

TELEPHONE

The area code for St. Barts is *590*. To call from the U.S. dial *011* (international access code), then *590* plus the local number in St. Barts. To call St. Barts from Dutch St. Maarten, dial 6 plus St. Barts's local six-digit number. To call St. Barts from other F.W.I (Martinique, Guadeloupe, and French St. Martin), you can dial direct.

Public phones require the use of "Telecartes" that look like credit cards and can be easily purchased at the Gustavia, St. Jean and Lorient post offices and at the gas station near the airport. Both local and international calls can be made from these phones using the card.

TIME

St. Barts is one hour ahead of Eastern Standard Time. When it is nine o'clock in St. Barts, it is eight o'clock in New York. During daylight saving time, there is no time difference.

TIPPING AND TAXES

Most hotels include tax and service in their quoted room rates; others add 5–15 percent to the bill.

TOURIST INFORMATION

The Tourist Board, called the Office de Tourisme, is located in attractive quarters on the Quai Général de Gaulle, across from the Capitainerie in Gustavia, open Monday–Friday 8:30 a.m.–6:00 p.m., and Saturday 8:30 a.m.–noon. From May to November, hours are a bit shorter. When writing to the **St. Barts Tourist Office**, use the address: *B.P. 113, Gustavia, 97098 Cedex, St. Barthélémy, F.W.I.* In the U.S. ☎ *(213) 658-7462*.

For what's happening weekly, pick up a current issue of *St. Barth Magazine*, distributed throughout the island. There's also an English program at noon on Mondays and Thursdays called "This Week in St. Barts."

WHEN TO GO

Three Kings Day on January 8 is celebrated with special ephinany cakes served at festivals. The 11th Anniversary of the S. Barts Music Festival is held Jan. 8–22, with jazz, chamber music and guests from the Metropolitan Opera. Carnival is celebrated Feb. 24, with a school parade, Mardi Gras pageant and parade, and the burning of Vaval, King of Carnival at Shell Beach.The award-winning cookbook author and instructor Steven Raichlen presents a one-week class on Caribbean cuisine at Hotel Yuana. The Festival of Gustavia is celebrated on August 20, with dragnet fishing contests, dances and parties.The Festival of St. Barthélémy is a feast day of the island's patron saint, celebrated with the pealing of church bells, a regatta, public ball, fireworks and the blessing of boats. The Fête du Vent on August 26–27 is honored with dragnet fishing contests, dances, fireworks and a lottery in the village of Lorient. The Swedish Marathon Race is held in December 6. The Réveillon de la Saint Sylvestre, on New Year's Eve, is a grand gala at the island's hotels and restaurants.

ST. BARTHÉLÉMY HOTELS	RMS	RATES	PHONE	FAX
Gustavia				
★★★★ Carl Gustaf Resort	14	$500–$1000	(800) 948-7823	590-27-82-37
★★★★ Castelets	10	$100–$700	(590) 27-61-73	
★★★★ Guanahani	80	$110–$785	(590) 27-66-60	590-27-70-70
★★★★ Hotel le Toiny	12	$394–$760	(590) 27-88-88	590-27-89-30
★★★ Christopher Hotel	40	$195–$295	(590) 27-63-63	590-27-92-92
★★★ Club la Banane	9	$130–$440	(590) 27-68-25	590-27-68-44
★★★ El Sereno Beach Hotel & Villas	29	$120–$340	(590) 27-64-80	509-27-75-47
★★★ Filao Beach Hotel	30	$210–$420	(590) 27-64-84	590-27-62-24
★★★ Hostellerie Trois Forces	8	$80–$175	(590) 27-61-25	590 27 81 38
★★★ Hotel St. Barth	28	$380–$705	(590) 27-61-81	590-27-86-83
★★★ Les Jardins de St. Jean	22	$60–$355	(590) 27-70-19	590-27-84-40
★★★ Manapany Cottages	52	$125–$990	(590) 27-66-65	590-27-75-28
★★★ Tropical Hotel	22	$97–$281	(590) 27-64-87	

ST. BARTHÉLÉMY HOTELS		RMS	RATES	PHONE	FAX
★★★	Village St. Jean Hotel	20		(590) 27-61-39	590 27 77 96
★★	Emeraude Plage Hotel	30	$208–$500	(590) 27-64-78	590-27-83-08
★★	Francois Plantation	12	$158–$405	(590) 27-78-82	590 27 61 26
★★	Grand Cul de Sac Hotel	36	$110–$335	(590) 27-60-70	590-27-75-57
★★	Hotel Baie des Flamands	24	$95–$135	(590) 27-64-85	
★★	Marigot Bay Club	6	$80–$185	(590) 27-75-45	590-27-90-04
★★	St. Barth's Beach Club	52	$68–$115	(590) 27-60-70	590-27-75-57
★★	Taiwana Hotel	9	$955–$999	(590) 27-65-01	590 27 68 82
★★	White Sand Beach Cottages	4	$55–$205	(590) 27-82-08	590 27 70 69
★★	Yuana Hotel	12	$150–$355	(590) 27-80-84	590-27-78-45
★	Baie des Agnes Hotel	9	$175–$230	(590) 27-63-61	590-27-83-44
★	Les Islets Fleuris Hotel Residence	8	$70–$220	(590) 27-64-22	590-27-69-72
★	Normandie	8	$65–$80	(590) 27-61-66	590 27 98 83
★	le P'tit Morne	14	$67–$120	(590) 27-62-64	590 27 84 63

ST. BARTHÉLÉMY RESTAURANTS		LOCATION	PHONE	ENTREE
Gustavia				
American				
★★	Santa Fe	Morne Lurin		$10–$21
French				
★★★★★	Le Toque Lyonnaise	Grand Cul-de-Sac	(590) 27-6480	$43–$61••
★★★★	Ballahou	Anse des Cayes	(590) 27-66-55	$15–$45
★★★★	Francois Plantation	Colombier	(590) 27-7882	$16–$50••
★★★★	La Fregate	Flamandes	(590) 27-6651	$10–$19
★★★★	Le Gaiac	Anse de Toiny	(590) 27-8888	$30–$60
★★★★	Le Sapotillier	Gustavia	(590) 27-6028	$45–$60••
★★★	Au Port	Gustavia	(590) 27-62-36	$19–$27••
★★★	Castelets	Gustavia	(590) 27-6173	$25–$35••
★★★	Eddy's Ghetto	Gustavia		$15–$18••

ST. BARTHÉLÉMY RESTAURANTS	LOCATION	PHONE	ENTREE
★★★ **Hostellerie Trois Forces**	Vitet	(590) 27-6125	$10–$50
★★★ **Marigot Bay Club & Art Gallery**	Marigot	(590) 27-7545	$40–$50
★★★ **Pasta Paradise**	Gustavia	(590) 27-8078	$10–$25
★★★ **Wall House**	Gustavia	(590) 27-71-33	$30–$45
★★ **Adam**	St. Jean	(590) 27-84-56	$35–$35••
International			
★★★ **Le Select**	Gustavia	(590) 27-86-87	$5–$10
Italian			
★★★ **L'Escale**	Gustavia	(590) 27-8106	$14–$29••
★★ **L'Entrepont**	Gustavia	(590) 27-9060	$17–$33
Latin American			
★★★ **La Langouste**	Gustavia	(590) 27-69-47	$23–$42
★★ **Le Pelican**	Plage de St. Jean	(590) 27-6464	$20–$40
★★ **Maya's**	Public	(590) 27-7361	$27–$35••

Note: • Lunch Only

•• Dinner Only

ST. CROIX

Buck Island, St. Croix offers guided tours of underwater snorkeling trails.

If St. Thomas is the sophisticated cosmopolitan island of the United States Virgins Islands, and St. John is the nature island, then St. Croix is a cross between the two, a rustic environment with tinges of elegance. Columbus thought St. Croix looked like a lush garden when he first saw it. Today, the island is a combination of graceful Danish architecture, modern development and natural beauty. There are two main towns, Christiansted on the northeast coast and Frederiksted on the west. Christiansted, designed by the Dutch West Indies Company as a planned community, shows its Dutch influence plainly, but it is more than just historic buildings. There is modern shopping, excellent dining, wonderful little bars and numerous outstanding resort hotels. Guarded by Fort Frederik, Frederiksted is a very quiet commu-

675

nity on the west seashore, differing substantially from Christiansted because many of the original buildings were destroyed by a hurricane and high waves in 1867 and the fire of 1878. The real pleasure in Frederiksted is its bustling, colorful port, attracting freighters, cruiseships and navy vessels, vying for sleeping quarters in the well-kept harbor. For years, divers and macrophotography buffs around the world have known the famous **Frederiksted Pier** as one of the Caribbean's premier dives for all kinds of marine life. By January, 1995 the port of Frederiksted will have endured a major expansion, with vendor kiosks in Victorian gingerbread style lining the waterfront and two shaded bus stops installed in General Buddhoe Park. The old pump station has been converted into a hospitality lounge for tourists, a police substation, and a VITRAN bus token station. The best place to watch the glorious sunsets of St. Croix is now an old clock tower adjacent to the park which has been renovated to include a second-story observatory.

WARNING:

In 1993, an Italian visitor was shot to death in an apparent robbery attempt in downtown Christiansted, though overall crimes against tourists in the Virgin Islands are infrequent, with only one hundredth of 1 percent of the two million people who visited the Virgin Islands in 1993 reporting they were victims. Most cruise lines give extensive safety precautions before passengers alight on shore, as well as providing escort shore tours with local tour operators.

Bird's Eye View

Lying 75 miles east of Puerto Rico and 40 miles south of St. Thomas, St. Croix (rhymes with "boy"), is the largest of the U.S. Virgin Islands (which also includes St. John and St. Thomas)—in fact more than two times larger than St. Thomas, but only 50,000 people live there. With a landmass 29 miles long by 7 miles (82.2 square miles), St. Croix is separated from St. Thomas and St. John by 32 miles and a 12,000-ft. oceanic trench. Rocky terrain fills the eastern sector, while the west end has higher elevation and more forests. Salt River on the north coast has now been approved as a National Park, including not only the sight where Columbus first landed, but also the underwater Salt River drop-off and canyon. Among the many natural attractions are wildlife refuges for birds and leatherback turtles, rain for-

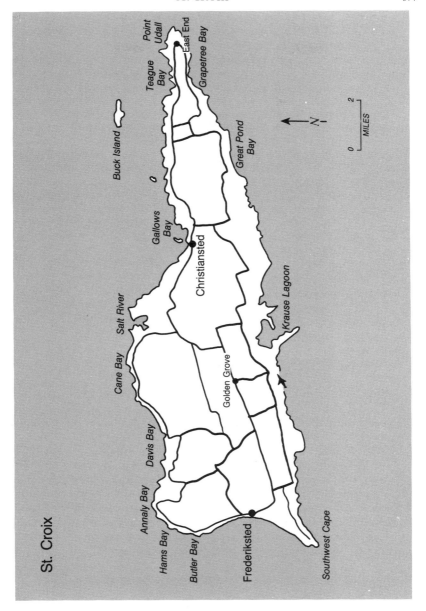

St. Croix

est, botanic gardens, three nature preserves, and three parks—one under the sea.

History

Columbus and his crew first came ashore at St. Croix's Salt River in 1493, but native Caribs did their best to fight them off. In haste he named the island Santa Cruz (Holy Cross) and sailed on to lay claim to St. John and St. Thomas. Eventually he renamed the entire group—including the British Virgin Islands at the time—for the legendary 11,000 virgin followers of St. Ursula. Today, we know that he unknowingly wildly exaggerated the number of islands in the area. Soon after Columbus' departure, British, Dutch, and French colonists began to establish farms on St. Croix, and in 1653, the island was awarded the crusaders' Order of St. John, better known as the Knights of Malta. France took control a few years later, and for the next 50 or so years, possession alternated between the French and the Spanish. As St. John and St. Thomas became acquired by the Danish West India Company and Guinea Company, St. Croix remained in the background. In 1773 the Danes also purchased St. Croix, attracted by its already burgeoning slave population and sugarcane fields. Planters and pirates mingled together during this golden age; some secluded coves are still said to harbor buried treasure. As the sugar beet was introduced to Europe, and the uprisings of slaves threatened the status quo, commercial interest in the island began to flag. Over the last 250 years, seven different conquerors took control of the island, though the Danish influence has remained the most lasting. During World War I, the Danes, sensing the sugarcane industry had all but dissolved, looked for buyers, finding the U.S. who was seeking a Caribbean base from which it could protect the Panama Canal. Eventually a great deal was struck between the two powers—$25 million dollars for three islands. The opening of the Carambola Beach Resort and Golf Club attracted a new wave of visitors to St. Croix starting in 1986. Though St. Croix was hard hit by Hurricane Hugo in 1989, islanders were not daunted and threw themselves body and soul into renovating the tourist facilities.

People

People born on St. Croix are called Crucians. The majority are of African descent, with a cultural mix from many other Caribbean islands. There is even a community of people from the island of Vieques (Puerto Rico). Lots of ex-pats from the U.S. also settle here. As well, there is a smattering of French, Germans and Italians who create their own small enclaves. A few Danes, stemming back to the original owners of the island, can even be found here.

Beaches

All beaches on St. Croix are public and free of charge, but if you go to a beach which is maintained by the resident hotel, you may have to pay a small fee for facilities. Lying 1.5 miles off northeast St. Croix, **Buck Island**, an 850-acre national monument has some of the best beaches in the St. Croix area, reachable by boat from Christiansted; the six-mile trip takes 45 minutes to an hour. Some concessionaires who offer sail or motorboat tours also include a picnic lunch and an overland hike to the island's 400-ft. summit with terrific views. Turtles also lay their eggs here. Cane Bay also has a stunning beach on the island's north side. Other fine beaches can be found at **Cane Bay**, **Protestant Cay**, **Davis Bay**, **Cramer Park** on the east shore, and **Frederiksted Beach** to the north of town. The last two have changing facilities and showers. Surfing is best on the north coast, and you'll find great shells on the northwest coast, from **Northside Beach** to **Ham's Bay**, as well as on **Sprat Hall Beach**.

Dive Sites

One of St. Croix's best snorkeling and diving sites is found along **Cane Bay** on the island north's shore. On clear days, you can swim out 150 yards to the drop-off and see a "wall" that drops off dramatically. Various fish and coral are in abundance here. Salt River Drop-off at the mouth of the Salt River is a prime dive location encompassing actually two sites—the east and west walls of a submerged canyon. The east wall is gently sloping and attracts a huge variety of marine life; the west wall starts at 30 ft. and plunges to a shelf at 90 ft., where it takes a vertical nose-dive to more than 1000 ft. The wall's caves and deep crevices are covered with corals and tube sponges and forests of black coral. Fully equipped dive operators can be found at the **Salt River Marina**, on the western shore of the bay, and boats can be chartered for trips into the mangrove area.

More than 250 species of fish have been recorded at the spectacular 850-acre island-and-reef system of Buck Island Reef National Monument, two miles off St. Croix's north shore, as well as a variety of sponges, corals and crustaceans. You might even see a few sea turtles gliding by. The park is famed for its underwater, marked snorkeling trail (about 30 minutes), which lies along the shallow reef (average 12 feet) fringing the north and south shores, and converging at this eastern point. You'll discover such species as yellowtail, red snapper, spadefish, star and brain coral, elkhorn coral and a variety of sponges. The island itself is a rookery for endangered brown pelicans, and a feeding habitat for leatherback, hawksbill and green sea turtles. Most dive operators conduct half-and full-day trips to Buck Island, which is part of the U.S. National Park system. **Frederiksted Pier** has the reputation for being one of the most interesting pier dives in the Caribbean; its pilings have become an underwater forest at about 35 ft. depth with sponges, plume worms and great numbers of tiny yellow, orange, and red sea horses. Snorkeling is also said to be good. Many hotel properties offer splendid snorkeling sites, as well as snorkeling equipment For information on special hotel packages, contact the **St.Croix Hotel Association** ☎ *(800) 524-2026.*

Treks

St. Croix boasts a remarkable array of natural resources which can be scaled, dived and trekked in all manner of excursions. Most of the arranged excursions are those involving watersports or sailing; trekkers should obtain more information (and in some cases, permission) from the tourist board before setting off on their own.

It's a good idea at the beginning of your stay to acquaint yourself with the flora of the island by visiting the St. George Village Botanical Gardens east of Frederiksted. The gardens surround the ruins of a worker's village on an 18th-century sugar plantation. Over the years Arawak artifacts have been discovered on the grounds by farmers, and in 1976 historians established that it had been the site of the largest of 96 Indian communities that had existed on St. Croix. Today the gardens are profuse with bright poinsettias, hibiscus, bougainvillea and numerous flowering bushes and trees, some endemic to the region.

A volcanic islet of 300 acres, **Buck Island** lies 3.5 miles offshore from St. Croix. Divers know the area for its fine shallow reef snorkeling and underwater coral gardens. But the island itself is fine for trekking since it boasts untouched white sand beaches on the west and southwest coasts. Turtles can also be seen hatching eggs here. The land slopes gently, embraced by a dry forest of red birch, frangipani, scrub and cactus. A well-marked 1.4-mile trail starts from the pier and picnic area in the south (where you'll also find a salt pond with black mangroves), then loops over the island's highest point marked by an observation tower to another picnic area on the west coast. Here you'll find the poisonous manchineel trees, and also the endemic touch-me-not, whose yellow needles on its underbelly can easily and painfully get lodged in the skin. The best way to see Buck Island is to take a glass-bottom boat or motorboat cruise offered by the four major companies and four individual operators authorized by the Park Service. They depart twice daily from the **Kings Wharf** in Christiansted; thirty minutes each way. Do ask for the pamphlet published by the Park Service featuring the fish of the area; it will help snorkelers feel as if they're meeting old friends. Outer reef diving is also available; you can even sail here on half or full-day cruises. Do insist that your trip includes lunch; not all do and you can get easily famished without a restaurant in sight. One of the best boats is **Captain Heinz's** comfortable

42-ft. trimaran, which leaves from **Green Cay Marina**. For more information, ☎ *(809) 773-3161.*

South of Frederiksted, along three miles of sandy beach, is situated one of the island's main birding reserves called **Westend Saltpond**, as well as Sandy Point, the site of the **National Wildlife Refuge**, a nesting ground for leatherback and hawksbill turtles, protected by the U.S. Fish and Wildlife Service. A spectacular excursion is to come witness the turtles waddling ashore, digging nests and laying their eggs in the sand. Prime time to watch is between April and early July (sometimes March-June), and approximately two months after hatching, the hatchlings emerge from the hidden sandpits and dash to the sea. Visitors are welcome to come when the refuge is open, only on weekends from 6 a.m.–6 p.m. For reservations call the **Sandy Point Refuge Manager** ☎ *(809) 773-4554*

Two parks located on the far east of the island are seldom visited by tourists, only because of lack of publicity. At the end of Route 83 is a fine picnic area at **Cramer Park**, alongside the seashore. There are camping facilities, but no shade, so be prepared to protect yourself against the sun. A solid trek will take you across the hilly, airy landscape of the **Farleigh Dickinson Territorial Park**, covered with scrub and cacti; a wild variety called Turk's head cacti, looks like Siamese twins with its two bulbous heads. A dirt road goes up the 672-ft. **Sugar Loaf Hill**, but you must obtain permission from the park (or tourist board) to climb it. A variety of other footpaths lead to fine beaches good for snorkeling. From the top of 226-ft. **Point Udall**, you can enjoy a fabulous view of the island of Saba, knowing you are on the easternmost point of the United States. A risky path descends the slope to the end of the Point, but only the best hikers should attempt it.

North of Frederiksted is a hilly terrain covered with dense woods, commonly called the **Rain Forest**. The area actually doesn't receive enough rain to be officially designated as such, but it seems to suit the islanders' needs. An intriguing road trip can be taken down **Mahogany Road** (Routes 76,76,765) which leads through groves of enormous kapok, gumbo limbo, and red birch trees, as well as loads of tropical fruit trees, such as apple, mango, hog plum and mammee apple. Most easily traveled by jeep are the more northern roads—the **Creque Dam Road**, the **Western Scenic Road**, and the **Scenic Road**—all narrow winding trails, often unpaved. The best hiking, birding and horseback riding are found in the west because traffic is light. Footpaths which are rarely marked on maps tend to veer off into dry beds and guts that become pools, streams and waterfalls, after a heavy rain. A delightful waterfall is located along an inland track from Butler Bay (on Route 63), which is a popular birding area with huge trees and dangling vines. From the Scenic Road, there are hearty tracks to the summit of both the 1096-ft. **Blue Mountain** and the flat-topped 1165-ft. **Mount Eagle**, both the highest points on the island.

To tour the island by bus, including the rainforest, take **Sweeney Toussaint's Safari Tour** ☎ *(809) 773-6700*. The tour runs Monday to Saturday from 10 a.m.–3:30 p.m., departing from near the gazebo at Fort Christiansted in Christiansted. Price is about $25 per person.

What Else to See

There are two major towns to see in St. Croix, the largest which is **Christiansted**, and the place most ships dock, **Frederiksted**. Christiansted is a homey and culturally stimulating urban center, full of attractive 18th century buildings, many considered U.S. national historic sites. Covered walkways, mortar arches, colonnades lend an 18th century tropical ambiance. Do take a look at the 17th-century French fortress, **Fort Chritiansvaern**, full of dungeons and cannons, from which there are excellent views of the harbor. A block away is the **Steeple Building**, today a historical museum with a small collection of Carib and Arawak relics and photos of the city from the 1800s. Also historically intriguing is the old **Scalehouse**, which was built in 1856 to house the huge scale used to weigh merchandise being shipped abroad, and the **Government House**, now home to the U.S. District Court, but still one of the most beautiful Danish colonial buildings in the islands. Saturday morning is the best time to visit the outdoor markets at **"Shan" Hendricks Square**, chock full of tropical fruits and vegetables for sale, including the island's favorite—green genips. The harbor itself is a joy to contemplate; nearby, on the waterfront and **Company Street**, you'll find lots of stores.

On the western end of the island is Frederiksted, usually asleep until a cruise liner docks at port. In contrast to the colonial Danish style of Christiansted, Frederiksted is more Victorian gingerbread. Pick up a free walking tour guide from the visitor's bureau at the end of the pier. Fort Frederiks, on the far side of Lagoon Street, was the site of the 1848 proclamation freeing the slaves. **The Market Place** is two blocks south and one block east of the fort. Feel free to browse up and down streets and alleys here—the best way to glimpse the stunning architecture. One especially pretty building is on Strand Street (along the waterfront) is the **Old Customs House** from the 18th century, now the headquarters of the Energy Commission., and the gingerbread-trimmed **Victorian House**. Not far from Christiansted is the **Cruzan Rum Factory**, which offers guided tour and drink samples.

North of Frederiksted, the shore road north will take you past **Sprat Hall**, an old plantation home turned guesthouse, all the way to the rainforest, and the **Scenic Drive**. Heading down Centerline Road you'll arrive at the fully restored **Estate Whim Plantation Museum**, dating back to the 17th century, and including a main house, and a half-dozen other structures like a windmill and cookhouse. Other places outside the urban areas include the rainforest at **St. Croix Leap**, where you will find a talented group of woodcarvers who create pieces carved in native mahogany. They practice a form of forest management, using wood from trees culled for specific purposes only. This is a truly lovely place to stroll and inspect the remains of a greathouse and a spectacular historical garden hosting some of the original crops of the native Indian tribes. Also worth a visit is the **St. Croix Aquarium**, notable for its ecological approach for staffing its tanks and fresh-food feeding its "staff" daily, by recycling marine life after they have "performed" for a time in the aquariums. The aquarium houses about 40 species of marine animals and more than 100 species of invertebrates.

City Celebrations

Crucian Christmas Fiesta

Various locations, Frederiksted.
This annual two-week festival celebrates the Christmas season with arts and crafts exhibits, food fairs, parades (one for children, the other for adults), the selection of Miss St. Croix, and the coronation of the festival's Prince and Princess. Most events take place in Christiansted and Frederiksted. Each town has a Festival Village complete with amusement rides and nightly entertainment.

Historical Sites

Fort Christiansvaern ★★★★

 Downtown, Christiansted, ☎ *(809) 773-1460.*
Hours Open: 8:00 a.m.–5:00 p.m.
This fort was built by the Danes in 1738 and rebuilt after hurricane damage in 1772. Its five rooms are decorated as they were in the 1840s. The admission charge (free for those under 16) includes entry to the Steeple Building. The fort's newest attraction is the St. Croix Police Museum, just opened in 1994. Created by Lt. Elton Lewis a 20-year veteran of the St. Croix Police Department, the idea behind the museum is to "promote high morale" and esprit de corps among police officers. Exhibits include weapons, photos, artifacts, and an old police motorcycle from St. Croix's past. General admission: $2.00.

Fort Frederik ★★★

Emancipation Park, Frederiksted, ☎ *(809) 772-2021.*
Hours Open: 8:30 a.m.–4:30 p.m.
This fort dates back to 1760, and is now an art gallery and museum. It is best known as the site where on July 3, 1848, Governor General Peter Von Scholten freed the Danish West Indies slaves. Free admission.

Steeple Building ★★★★

Downtown, Christiansted, ☎ *(809) 773-1460.*

Built by the Danish in 1754, this was their first Lutheran church, called the Church of Lord God of Sabaoth. Deconsecrated in 1831, it served as everything from a bakery to a school, and is now under the auspices of the U.S. National Park Service. Interesting exhibits tell the island's history, with emphasis on Native Americans and African Americans. The entry fee includes admission to Fort Christiansvaern. General admission: $2.00.

Museums and Exhibits

Aquarium ★★★

On the waterfront, Frederiksted, ☎ *(809) 772-1345.*
Hours Open: 11:00 a.m.–4:00 p.m.

Opened in 1990 by marine biologist Lonnie Kaczmarsky, this aquarium displays some 40 species of marine animals and more than 100 species of invertebrates. What makes it really unique is its "recycling" of sea life—after doing a stint in the tanks, creatures are released back to the open seas. Kaczmarsky is passionate on preserving the ocean environment; this a good place to pick up hints before diving and snorkeling on how to minimize your impact. General admission: $3.00.

Estate Whim Plantation Museum ★★★★

Centerline Road, Frederiksted, ☎ *(809) 772- 598.*
Hours Open: 10:00 a.m.–4:00 p.m.

This partially restored sugar plantation gives a good look at what life was like in St. Croix in the 1800s. The handsome great house, built of lime, stone and coral and boasting walls three feet thick, is beautifully restored and filled with antiques. The grounds also include the cookhouse (where you can feast on Johnny cakes), a woodworking shop, a windmill, and an apothecary. $1 for children. General admission: $5.00.

Parks and Gardens

St. George Village Botanical Gardens ★★★★★

St. George Estate, Kingshill, ☎ *(809) 772-3874.*
Hours Open: 9:00 a.m.–4:00 p.m.

Built among the ruins of a 19th-century sugarcane plantation workers' village, this little slice of paradise is not to be missed. The 17 acres were the site of an Arawak settlement dating to A.D. 100. Stop by the Great Hall to pick up a brochure for a self-guided walking tour, then feast your senses on the lovely gardens, which include 850 species of trees and plants. Each ecosystem of St. Croix is represented, from rainforest to desert. The grounds also include restored buildings from the plantation era, including workers' cottages, storehouses and a blacksmith shop. General admission: $4.00.

Tours

Buck Island Reef ★★★★★

Buck Island.

This national monument island, located three miles northeast of the mainland, is a volcanic rock comprising some 300 acres with hiking trails and an observation tower. The real attraction, however, is its surrounding 550 acres of underwater coral gardens, home to more than 250 species of fish. This is a true snorkelers' paradise, with an underwater trail and visibility of more than 100 feet. Several operators will take you there and set you up with snorkel equipment: Big Beard's Adventure Tours (☎ *773-4482*), Diva (☎ *778-3161*), Llewellyn's Charter (☎ *773-9027*), Teroro II (☎ *773-3161*), and Mile Mark Water Sports (☎ *773-2628*). Not to be missed!

Cruzan Rum Factory ★★★

West Airport Road, Frederiksted, ☎ *(809) 772- 799.*
Tours of the rum distillery and bottling plant are offered Monday-Friday from 9:00-11:30 a.m. and 1:00-4:15 p.m. You get to sample the product at the conclusion.

Estate Mount Washington ★★★

West coast, Frederiksted, ☎ *(809) 772-1026.*
Take a self-guided walking tour through the excavated ruins of a sugar plantation.

Guided Tours ★★★

Various locations, Frederiksted.
If you choose to leave the driving to someone else, these companies are happy to oblige with guided tours of St. Croix's highlights: **Eagle Tours** (☎ *778-3313*), **St. Croix Safari Tours** (☎ *773-6700*), and **Travellers Tours** (☎ *778-1636*). Take-a-Hike offers walking tours and hikes; ☎ *778-6997.* For a birds-eye view of the island, call **St. Croix Aviation** (☎ *778-0090*), which offers sightseeing flights.

Salt River Bay National History ★★★★

Route 80 near Route 75, Frederiksted.
These 912 tropical acres were added to the national park system under the Bush Administration. The park remains in a pristine condition and is home to many threatened and endangered plant and animal species. It is the largest remaining mangrove forest in the Virgin Islands and a great spot for birdwatching. The site includes an old earthen fort, an Indian ceremonial ball court, and burial grounds. This is also the only documented site on U.S. soil on which Christopher Columbus landed. His ill-fated "discovery" in 1493 led to a skirmish with Carib Indians, with fatalities on both sides.

Sports

Sports on St. Croix run the tropical gamut of water games to golf, horseback riding, sailing, and sportsfishing.(For diving information, see "Dive Sites" above.) Many visitors charter a sailboat to Buck Island or to other neighboring islands. Prices on charters and boats-for-hire are controlled by the National Park Service, but they may change, so do your best to negotiate. Scuba packages, which include hotel, often can save you loads of dollars.

Golf

Various locations, Christiansted.
Duffers have three choices on St. Croix. **Carambol Golf Club** (☎ *778-5638*) is a gorgeous, par-72 course designed by Robert Trent Jones. Located in St. Croix's northwest part, golfing on scenic 18 holes costs $50 per person per day (you can go around as many as you want), plus $18 mandatory cart rental for 18 holes. Near Christiansted, the Buccaneer course is a challenging 18 holes. Greens fees are about $25. ☎ *773-2100*. **The Reef Club** at Tegue Bay (☎ *773-8844*) is a nine-hole course. Greens fees are $8 for nine holes, $12 for 18.

Paul and Jill's Equestrian Stable

Sprat Hall, near Frederiksted, ☎ *(809) 772-2880.*
Well-regarded for their high-quality horses, this stable takes folks out for two-hour trail rides through the rainforest and past Danish ruins. Jill's family has lived on St. Croix for some 200 years. Two-hour rides are about $50, and reservations are essential. Closed Sundays.

Watersports

Various locations, Frederiksted.
For scuba diving, try: **Dive Experience** (☎ *773-3307*), **Virgin Island Divers** (☎ *773-6045*), **Anchor Dive Center** (☎ *772-1522*), **Blue Dolphin Divers** (☎ *773-8634*), **Cruzan Divers** (☎ *772-3701*), **Cane Bay Dive Shop** (☎ *773-9913*), and **Dive St. Croix** (☎ *773-3434*). For deep-sea fishing: **St. Croix Marin** (☎ *773-7165*), **Captain Pete's Sportfishing** (☎ *773-1123*), and **Cruzan Divers** (☎ *772-3701*). For cruises and boating, try **Sundance** (☎ *778-9650*), **Llwewellyn's Charter** (☎ *773-9027*), **Bilinda Charters** (☎ *773-1641*), and **Junie Bomba's** (☎ *772-2482*). For windsurfing: **Lisa Neuburger Windsurfing Center** (☎ *778-8312*) and **Minstral School** (☎ *773-4810*).

Where to Stay

Highest Rated Hotels in St. Croix

★★★★★	**Buccaneer Hotel**
★★★★	**Villa Madeleine**
★★★	**Cane Bay Reef Club**
★★★	**Carambola Beach Resort**
★★★	**Cormorant Beach Club**
★★★	**Cormorant Cove**
★★★	**Hibiscus Beach Hotel**
★★★	**Hilty House Inn**
★★★	**Hotel on the Cay**
★★★	**St. Croix by the Sea**

Most Exclusive Hotels in St. Croix

★★★★	**Villa Madeleine**	$305–$425
★★★★	**Buccaneer Hotel**	$155–$340
★★★	**Cormorant Beach Club**	$110–$265
★★★	**Cormorant Cove**	$105–$230
★★★	**Hibiscus Beach Hotel**	$95–$190

Fielding's Best Value Hotels in St. Croix

★★	**Sprat Hall Plantation**	$95–$220
★★	**King Christian Hotel**	$80–$135
★★★	**St. Croix by the Sea**	$90–$145
★★★	**Hibiscus Beach Hotel**	$95–$190

St. Croix's roster of accommodations are varied. Some are intimate properties downtown while others are sprawling complexes including beaches and golf courses. While the accommodations on this island shy away from the cookie-cutter familiarity of typical chain motels, there is no shortage of amenities. The best will have air-conditioning, direct-dial telephones, cable color television, and likely will have their own in-house dive service or a close working relationship with a shop to facilitate their diving clients' convenience. If you want to be near the beach, don't stay in Christiansted, where none of the hotels have beachfront property. (The exception is Hotel on the Cay, with its postage-stamp strand.) Restoration since Hurricane Hugo finds most properties in shipshape form. Most of the restaurants are in Christiansted, so you will probably need a car to dine out if you are staying along the coast.

Hotels and Resorts

The premier property on most anybody's list (not to mention the most expensive) is the **Buccaneer**, which sprawls down a hillside. It simply boasts the best facilities on the island—with three beaches, 18-hole golf course, jogging trail, spa, shops and a full watersports program. In any property on the beach, ask for rooms above the first floor, so you will feel safe leaving the window open to the breeze at night.

Christiansted

Buccaneer Hotel   **$155–$340**   ★ ★ ★ ★ ★

Gallows Bay, ☎ *(800) 223-1108, (809) 773-2100.*
Single: $155–$325. Double: $165–$340.

Set on a landscaped peninsula and encompassing 240 acres with three beaches, this deluxe property is located two miles east of Christiansted. A former sugar plantation has been transformed into a well-polished resort that the same family has run since its inception in 1946. Accommodations vary widely, through all are comfortable and include refrigerators and patios or balconies. The best rooms are right on the beach, and there are also beautifully decorated suites, rooms atop the hillside, and one-bedroom, two-bath cottages, also on the hill. Guests are kept busy with lots of recreational facilities, including an 18-hole championship golf course, eight tennis courts, two pools, a health club with sauna, and a shopping arcade. There are also lots of organized activities and watersports. Four restaurants, four bars and nightly entertainment round out the action. Resort lovers are kept happy. 149 rooms. Credit Cards: CB, V, MC, A.

Carambola Beach Resort   **$160–$330**   ★ ★ ★

Kings Hill, ☎ *(800) 333-3333, (809) 778-3800.*
Single: $160–$240. Double: $160–$330.

Situated on 26 acres on the north shore of Davis Bay, this property reopened in the summer of 1993 after renovations and joining the Radisson hotel family. Rooms and suites are found in villa-style, red-roofed buildings surrounded by lush landscaping. All are quite nice, with sitting areas, coffeemakers, minibars, screened porches, large baths and English country furnishings. Facilities include 18 holes of golf, a pool, four tennis courts, three restaurants, two bars and watersports, including a dive shop. Very fine. 151 rooms. Credit Cards: V, MC, A.

Club Comanche $35–$126 ★

1 Strand Street, ☎ *(800) 524-2066, (809) 773-0210.*
Single: $35–$126. Double: $45–$126.
This hotel dates back to 1948 and it shows—not necessarily because of historical charm, but because it would really benefit from an overhaul. Guest rooms are small and simple; most have TV sets. The premises include two good restaurants and a pool. There's nothing special about this budget choice except the fine food, but the rates are quite reasonable. 42 rooms. Credit Cards: MC, A.

Cormorant Beach Club $110–$265 ★★★

4126 La Grande Princesse, ☎ *(800) 548-4460, (809) 778-8920.*
Single: $110–$265. Double: $125–$265.
Located three miles west of Christiansted on the north shore, this intimate resort makes for a great getaway. Guest rooms are in three-story beachfront villas, tastefully decorated with rattan furniture, bright fabrics, island artwork, and luxurious touches like bathrobes and fresh flowers. The grounds include a large free-form pool, two tennis courts, croquet, and a library. Guests can choose from several plans that include meals and drinks. The beach is excellent, and this spot gets high marks for service. No kids under five during the winter. 38 rooms. Credit Cards: V, MC, A.

Hibiscus Beach Hotel $95–$190 ★★★

4131 La Grande Princesse, ☎ *(800) 442- 121, (809) 773-4042.*
Single: $95–$170. Double: $105–$190.
Located three miles outside of Christiansted, this hotel opened in 1992. Accommodations are in two-story buildings that line the palm-studded beach. All have ocean views off the balcony or patio, and are nicely done, though the baths are on the small side. There's a pool on-site, as well as a beachfront restaurant and lounge. Snorkel equipment is included in the rates, and other watersports (which cost extra) are found nearby. Nice and small, with the feel of a resort but not the cost of one. 38 rooms. Credit Cards: V, MC, A.

Hotel Caravelle $79–$255 ★★

44A Queen Cross Street, ☎ *(800) 524- 410, (809) 773- 687.*
Single: $79–$255. Double: $89–$255.
This waterfront hotel is in Christiansted's downtown historic district, overlooking the bay. Guestrooms are comfortable and pleasant, with modern furnishings and colorful fabrics. There's a pool on-site and watersports nearby. The waterfront restaurant and bar are lively and popular with boaters. A good in-town choice, and the rates are reasonable. 43 rooms. Credit Cards: CB, V, MC, A.

Hotel on the Cay $95–$198 ★★★

Protestant Cay, ☎ *(800) 524-2035, (809) 773-2035.*
Single: $95–$188. Double: $95–$198.
Located on a small cay in Christiansted Harbor, a two-minute ferry ride from the mainland, this imaginatively landscaped hotel offers great seclusion, though boat service to Christiansted is frequent. Guest rooms are comfortable and pleasing, with extras like coffeemakers, VCRs, and private terraces with water views. The grounds

are dotted with waterfalls, canals, and bridges, lending a welcome tropical feel. Recreational options include a pool, tennis court and watersports on the small beach. Nice, if you don't mind the isolated location. 55 rooms. Credit Cards: V, MC, A.

King Christian Hotel $80–$135 ★★

59 King's Wharf, ☎ (800) 524-2012, (809) 773-2285.
Single: $80–$105. Double: $95–$135.

Located in the heart of town overlooking Christiansted Harbor, this hotel opened in 1940, though the building it is housed in is some 200 years old. Guest rooms are spacious and air-conditioned; the best ones have large furnished balconies with harbor views. Those counting every penny can stay in one of the 15 budget rooms which have no views but are clean and comfortable. There's a restaurant and coffeeshop on the premises, as well as a pool and dive center. Boats to Buck Island leave right from their dock. A great in-town choice. 39 rooms. Credit Cards: CB, V, MC, A.

St. Croix by the Sea $90–$145 ★★★

St. John's Estate, ☎ (800) 524-5006, (809) 778-8600.
Single: $90–$145. Double: $90–$145.

This family-run resort is located three miles west of Christiansted. Guestrooms are contemporary and comfortable enough, but not particularly special. The grounds include a large saltwater pool, (the site of scuba lessons), four tennis courts, two restaurants and a bar. A European plan is available for an extra $10 per person per day. 65 rooms. Credit Cards: V, MC, A.

Frederiksted

On the Beach Resort $55–$110 ★★

☎ (800) 524-2018, (809) 772-1205.
Single: $55–$90. Double: $65–$110.

No kids under 14 at this small hotel, which draws a largely gay clientele. Accommodations are spacious and tropically furnished; most have kitchens but only some have balconies. The premises includes a good beach for snorkeling, a pool, a bar and a bistro open for breakfast and lunch. You'll want a car to get around, though downtown Frederiksted can be walked to in about 10 minutes. 13 rooms. Credit Cards: CB, V, MC, A.

Sprat Hall Plantation $95–$220 ★★

Route 63N, ☎ (809) 772- 305.
Single: $95–$215. Double: $110–$220.

This family-run hotel is structured around the island's oldest great house, which dates back to 1670. Located just north of Frederiksted, accommodations range from nonsmoking, antique-filled rooms in the great house to air-conditioned contemporary seaview units, some with TV. There are also several one-bedroom cottages with kitchenettes for rent. The grounds are lush and inviting, and dinner is a somewhat formal affair. No kids under 16 in the great house rooms. You'll be needing a car. 16 rooms.

Apartments and Condominiums

Self-catering is easy, and most properties—from private homes to condos—can come with maid service. Supermarkets are modern and well stocked, and fresh local fruits and vegetables can be bought at market. You will probably need to count the cost of a car rental into most choices.

Christiansted

Cane Bay Reef Club   **$85–$165**   ★★★

1407 Kingshill Street, Kingshill, ☎ *(800) 253-8534, (809) 778-2966.*
Single: $85–$165. Double: $85–$165.
Located about 20 minutes from both Christiansted and Frederiksted, this property was rebuilt after Hurricane Hugo's extensive damage. All units are one-bedroom apartments with modern kitchens, tiled balconies and ceiling fans. The best choices are the two condominium units—the only ones that are air-conditioned—which are much more nicely furnished. There's a restaurant, bar, and saltwater pool on-site; the beach is a three-minute walk. You'll definitely want a rental car, as this place is fairly remote. 9 rooms. Credit Cards: MC, A.

Caribbean View All-Suites   **$80–$120**   ★

66 La Grande Princesse, ☎ *(809) 773-3335.*
Single: $80–$120. Double: $80–$120.
Located a half-mile from the sea and 10 minutes from downtown Christiansted, this complex consists of two-story apartment buildings. Each has four one-bedroom units with VCRs, kitchens, terraces and maid service. Facilities are limited to a pool and shuffleboard court; you'll need a car to get around. Decent for the rates. 18 rooms. Credit Cards: CB, V, MC, A.

Club St. Croix   **$120–$194**   ★★

3280 Golden Rock, ☎ *(800) 635-1533, (809) 773-4800.*
Single: $120–$194. Double: $120–$194.
This beachfront condominium resort is one mile out of Christiansted. Accommodations include studios, a penthouse, and one- and two-bedroom apartments, all with full kitchens, cable TV, private balconies, ceiling fans and air conditioning. Recreational choices are good for a condo operation, with three tennis courts, a large pool, Jacuzzi, and a catamaran for cruising the high seas. Inquire about special packages. 54 rooms. Credit Cards: CB, V, MC, A.

Colony Cove   **$130–$290**   ★★

3221A Golden Rock, ☎ *(800) 524-2025, (809) 773-1965.*
Single: $130–$290. Double: $130–$290.
Set on the beach two miles from Christiansted, this condominium complex offers two-bedroom, two-bath units with full kitchens, laundry facilities, private balconies and ocean views. Each is individually owned and decorated, but all can be counted on for clean, comfortable living. The premises includes a restaurant, two tennis courts, a business center and a pool. Watersports await on the wide beach. 60 rooms. Credit Cards: MC, A.

Cormorant Cove   **$105–$230**   ★★★

4126 La Grande Princesse, ☎ *(800) 548-4460, (809) 778-8920.*
Single: $105–$230. Double: $105–$230.
Set right on the beach near its sister property, the Cormorant Beach Club, this condo complex has 16 units of one to three bedrooms. All are luxuriously furnished, air-conditioned, and have fully equipped kitchens, private terraces, maid ser-

vice, washers and dryers and Jacuzzis. The grounds include a large pool and two tennis courts. Guests can use all the facilities at the Cormorant Beach Club, so it works out as the best of both: apartment living and hotel amenities. 38 rooms. Credit Cards: V, MC, A.

Gentle Winds Resort   **$230–$305**   ★ ★

9003 Gentle Winds, ☎ *(809) 773-3400.*
Single: $230–$305. Double: $230–$305.
Set on the beach some eight miles northwest of Christiansted, this contemporary condo complex offers two- and three-bedroom units. All are air-conditioned, have two or three baths, full kitchens, VCRs, telephones, and nice sea views. There's a pool, two tennis courts, games room, and a beach bar, but you're on your own for meals. Guests can get reduced rates at the Carambola Beach Golf Course, eight miles away. Ideal for families. 66 rooms. Credit Cards: Not Accepted.

Schooner Bay Resort   **$145–$295**   ★ ★

5002 Gallows Bay, ☎ *(800) 524-2025, (809) 773-9150.*
Single: $145–$295. Double: $145–$295.
You can walk to downtown Christiansted from this three-story condominium resort, which overlooks the harbor. Two- and three-bedroom units are plush, with full kitchens, nice decor, living and dining areas, VCRs, radios, telephones, washer/dryers, and private balconies. The three-bedroom condos have an upstairs and downstairs. There's a pool, Jacuzzi, and tennis court on-site, but you'll have to look elsewhere for meals. 62 rooms. Credit Cards: MC, A.

Sugar Beach Condominiums   **$110–$250**   ★ ★

3245 Estate Golden Riock, ☎ *(800) 524-2049, (809) 773-5345.*
Single: $110–$250. Double: $110–$250.
Situated on a reef-protected beach beside a historic sugar mill in a residential neighborhood two miles out of Christiansted, this condo complex has studios and apartments with one to three bedrooms. All have full kitchens, seaview balconies, and modern, comfortable appointments. You'll pay extra for maid service. There are two tennis courts, a pool, and the private beach, but no restaurant. 46 rooms. Credit Cards: V, MC, A.

Villa Madeleine   **$305–$425**   ★ ★ ★ ★

19A Teague Bay, ☎ *(800) 548-4461, (809) 778-7377.*
Single: $305–$425. Double: $305–$425.
This deluxe operation is set on a hill between two beaches, some 15 minutes from Christiansted. Accommodations are in two-bedroom villas beautifully done and including sitting rooms, modern, full kitchens, four-poster beds and chaise lounges in the bedrooms, two full baths, and—best of all—private pools. Really luxurious! The Italian restaurant draws raves for its gorgeous decor and smashing food, and there's also a bar, billiards room, and tennis court. This is one of St. Croix's best properties, and all is quite sophisticated and elegant. Wonderful! 20 rooms. Credit Cards: MC, A.

Waves at Cane Bay   **$85–$195**   ★ ★

Kingshill ☎ *(800) 545- 603, (809) 778-1805.*

Single: $85–$195. Double: $85–$195.
Located on the north shore a short walk from Cane Bay Beach, this operation offers large studios with kitchens, screened porches, ceiling fans and TVs. Only some are air-conditioned, but all are quite comfortable. Maids tidy up six days a week. The pool is a natural sea-fed grotto and the snorkeling is great off the small beach. There's a bar but no restaurant, and you'll definitely need a car, as this spot is somewhat remote. 12 rooms. Credit Cards: MC, A.

Frederiksted

Chenay Bay Beach Resort   **$125–$210**   ★★

Estate Green Cay, ☎ *(800) 548-4457, (809) 773-2918.*
Single: $125–$180. Double: $125–$210.
This cottage colony is located on 30 acres three miles from Christiansted. The West Indian-style cottages are scattered about well-landscaped grounds; all have kitchenettes and patios, and most are air-conditioned. The grounds, surrounded by a 14-acre wildlife preserve, include a pool, two tennis courts, watersports (snorkeling and kayaking are free), the beach, and a casual restaurant and bar. Nice and relaxing, but you'll want a car to get around. 50 rooms. Credit Cards: MC, A.

Cottages by the Sea   **$70–$110**   ★

127A Smithfield, ☎ *(800) 323-7252, (809) 772- 495.*
Single: $70–$110. Double: $70–$110.
Located on the western end of the island just outside of Frederiksted, this basic complex is right on the beach. The 20 wood and fieldstone cottages are simply furnished and have kitchenettes, patios, and air conditioning. Maids tidy things up daily. Three large patios are situated on the beach for sunning and barbecuing. No children under eight at this agreeable spot. 20 rooms. Credit Cards: MC, A.

Inns

Most of the inns on St.Croix are located in historic buildings in Christiansted, rife with Danish colonial architecture. A few are situated on the shores. All exude the personality of the owners who tend to be extremely personable.

Christiansted

Anchor Inn of St. Croix   **$80–$150**   ★★

58 King Street, ☎ *(800) 524-2030, (809) 773-4000.*
Single: $80–$130. Double: $95–$150.
This friendly little spot is located in downtown Christiansted in a courtyard at the harbor's edge. Due to motel-like furnishings and tinted windows that keep the sun out, rooms are on the drab side. There's a pool, restaurant, coffeeshop, and bar on-site, as well as extensive watersports—everything from scuba to deep-sea fishing. Popular despite its uninspired accommodations. 31 rooms. Credit Cards: CB, V, MC, A.

Hilty House Inn   **$65–$130**   ★★★

2 Hermon Hill, ☎ *(800) 524-2026, (809) 773-2594.*
Single: $65–$160. Double: $85–$130.
This bed and breakfast was built on the ruins of an 18th-century rum distillery, 1.5 miles from the beach. Guest rooms are individually decorated and have private baths, but no air conditioning. There's also two one-bedroom cottages with kitch-

enettes. TV can be watched in the library, and there's a large pool on-site. Most rooms at this pleasant spot are under $100. 6 rooms. Credit Cards: Not Accepted.

Pink Fancy Hotel $70–$120 ★★

27 Prince Street, ☎ *(800) 524-2045, (809) 773-8460.*
Single: $70–$120. Double: $80–$120.
It is indeed pink (the shutters, anyway) and it is indeed somewhat fancy at this popular inn, which comprises four buildings, the oldest dating to 1780. Located downtown within walking distance of shops and restaurants, this intimate inn is loaded with charm. Guest rooms are immaculate, and each boasts West Indian decor, air conditioning, and a kitchenette. The grounds are lush with lots of plants, and include a nice pool and hammocks for lazy afternoons. The rates include continental breakfast and free drinks. 13 rooms. Credit Cards: MC, A.

Low Cost Lodging

Since lodging is based on the scale of the American dollar, not much is to be found in the category of cheap, unless you can bear very small rooms and basic furnishings. Make sure the property is close enough to a beach or stores/restaurants if you can't afford to rent a car. **Danish Manor** takes advantage of its location in the center of Christiansted, although you'll need to take a bus to the beach.

Christiansted

Danish Manor $225–$305 ★

43A Queen Cross Street, ☎ *(809) 773-1377.*
Single: $225–$305. Double: $225–$305.
This two-story hotel is a charmer, and attracts lots of young people and those who like nightlife. The bar is popular with both locals and tourists, and frequently offers entertainment. Guest rooms have private baths, tropical furnishings, TVs, and small refrigerators. There's no pool or restaurant on-site, but the loyal hordes who stay here don't seem to mind. If you're looking for a peaceful island oasis, look elsewhere! Note that the quoted rates are for a week's stay. 12 rooms. Credit Cards: V, MC, A.

Danish Manor Hotel $54–$99 ★

2 Company Street, ☎ *(800) 524-2069, (809) 773-1377.*
Single: $54–$99. Double: $54–$99.
This downtown inn consists of an old West Indian-style manor house and a newer addition. Guestrooms are small and simply furnished, but do have private baths, air conditioners, and television sets. There's a pool, Italian restaurant, and bar on the premises. Good value for the rates, and lots (including the beach) within walking distance. 35 rooms. Credit Cards: V, MC, A.

Frederiksted

Frederiksted Hotel $80–$110 ★★

20 Strand Street, ☎ *(800) 524-2025, (809) 772- 500.*
Single: $80–$100. Double: $90–$110.
This small hotel overlooks the harbor at the edge of town. The air-conditioned guest rooms are comfortable enough, but lack phones and are somewhat dark. Ask for a seaview room, by far the best accommodations. There's a pool and pool bar,

the site of entertainment on the weekends. The restaurant serves breakfast only. A free shuttle transports guests to the beach and nearby tennis courts. 40 rooms. Credit Cards: V, MC, A.

Where to Eat

Highest Rated Restaurants in St. Croix

★★★★	Great House
★★★★	Kendrick's
★★★	Blue Moon
★★★	Harvey's
★★★	Le St. Tropez
★★★	Top Hat

Most Exclusive Restaurants in St. Croix

★★★★	Great House	$25–$35
★★★	Top Hat	$14–$28
★★★★	Kendrick's	$14–$26
★★★	Le St. Tropez	$10–$25
★★★	Harvey's	$8–$20

Fielding's Best Value Restaurants in St. Croix

★★★	Top Hat	$14–$28
★★★★	Kendrick's	$14–$26
★★★★	Great House	$25–$35
★★★	Blue Moon	$10–$20

The best restaurants are in Christiansted, though you can find a handful of good ones in Frederiksted. New ones sprout up all the time; it's best to ask your hotel to recommend the latest trend-setters. Prices are not cheap and could run you up to $100 for two (without wine) for the top-class options. It's always safer to make a reservation than not to; on the weekends it's essential, particularly if you are headed for a show afterwards. Grilled fish are the specialty of the island, particularly **Comanche Restaurant**, which adds extremely exotic sauces. **Chart House** has a terrific view of the boat-filled harbor.

Christiansted

Antoine's   **$$$**   ★★

58A King Street, ☎ *(809) 773-0263.*
International cuisine. Specialties: Omelets, goulash, wienerschnitzel, lobster.
Lunch: 11:00 a.m.–2:30 p.m., entrees $14–$32.
Dinner: 6:30 p.m.–9:30 p.m., entrees $14–$32.

Many visitors get their wakeup javas at this second-floor charmer in the Anchor Inn. The breakfast menu boasts at least a dozen omelets loaded with interesting combinations. But that's not all that's here—bartenders proffer tropical concoctions and a huge selection of beer to a lively crowd. At dinner, hearty and tasty German and Middle-European food appears on the generous plates—despite the restaurant's French name. From the terrace, there's a great view of seagoing vessels on the wharf below. Associated Hotel: Anchor Inn. Reservations required. Credit Cards: V, MC, A.

Banana Bay Club   **$$$**   ★★

44A Queen Cross St., ☎ *(809) 778-9110.*
Seafood cuisine.
Lunch: 7:00 a.m.–4:00 p.m., entrees $15–$25.
Dinner: 4:00 p.m.–11:00 p.m., entrees $15–$25.

Sit surrounded by 18th-century buildings and 20th-century businessfolk who gather for gossip and low-key deal-making in this open-air eatery known for fresh seafood, burgers and steaks. The Banana Bay Club is located in the Caravelle Hotel, one of downtown's lodging bargains. You don't have to pay high prices for unsurprising, well-prepared food and a great view of the Christiansted harbor. Associated Hotel: Caravelle Hotel. Reservations recommended. Credit Cards: V, MC, A.

Chart House   **$$$**   ★★

59 King's Wharf, ☎ *(809) 773-7718.*
American cuisine. Specialties: Prime rib, mud pie.
Dinner: 6:00 p.m.–10:00 p.m., entrees $14–$26.

Most stateside visitors are familiar with this chain restaurant based in California. Christiansted's version does not disappoint—the wait staff is perky, the prime rib is cut the way you like it, the copious salad bar is one of the best on the island, and it's constantly mobbed. There's no outdoor dining, but the decor is nautical and it's so close to the water that it really doesn't matter, especially when you're lucky to get a seat with a harbor view. Reservations recommended. Credit Cards: V, MC, DC, A.

Comanche   **$$**   ★★

1 Strand Street, ☎ *(809) 773-2665.*
International cuisine.
Lunch: 11:30 a.m.–2:30 p.m., entrees $9–$21.
Dinner: 6:00 p.m.–9:00 p.m., entrees $9–$21.

A pianist tickles the ivories nightly at this intimate and consistently reliable terrace restaurant in the Comanche Inn. Decor is south-seas style, with wicker chairs and fans, and the cuisine runs the gamut from Chinese specialties to conch chowder. Serving three meals a day, the Comanche is also known for a filling West Indian lunch. Associated Hotel: Club Comanche. Reservations recommended. Credit Cards: V, MC, A.

Dino's $$$ ★★

4-C Hospital Street, ☎ *(809) 778-8005.*
Mediterranean cuisine. Specialties: Fresh pasta.
Dinner: entrees $14–$20.

After a tour of the nearby 17th-century Fort Christiansvaern, repair to this historical house serving thoroughly modern Italian fare. Chef Dwight deLude makes his pasta fresh every day, and he likes to experiment; sometimes there's ravioli made with sweet potatoes or other interesting vegetables. Sauces are always intensely flavored and made with fresh garden herbs. Reservations recommended. Credit Cards: Not Accepted.

Harvey's $$ ★★★

11 Company Street, ☎ *(809) 773-3433.*
Latin American cuisine.
Lunch: entrees $8–$20.
Dinner: entrees $8–$20.

Motherly Sarah Harvey is the chef-owner of this small West Indian dinner house and local hangout. Timid diners won't remain so for long, because Harvey likes to visit at every table, and since there's no real menu, she'll discuss what's cookin' for the evening. Sometimes there's goat water or local seafood in butter sauce, and a mountain of island-grown veggies and starches. The decor could be described best as thrift-shop modern: plastic tableware and folding chairs. Closed: Sun. Reservations recommended. Credit Cards: Not Accepted.

Kendrick's $$$ ★★★★

52 King Street, ☎ *(809) 773-9199.*
International cuisine.
Dinner: 6:00 p.m.–10:00 p.m., entrees $14–$26.

Dine among the antiques in yet another restored old Danish home that's one of the island's toniest (and priciest) eating establishments. The nattily attired and well-trained wait staff keeps wineglasses full and dishes cleared deftly between courses. Chef David prepares island-inspired French cuisine and his specialties often include a luscious pork loin with a roasted pecan crust or rack of lamb marinated with crushed herbs and served with roasted garlic and thyme sauce. There are three dining rooms, and you'll be equally well-treated no matter which one you end up in. Closed: Sun. Reservations recommended. Credit Cards: V, MC, A.

Picnic in Paradise $$ ★★

Cane Bay, ☎ *(809) 778-1212.*
Italian cuisine.
Dinner: entrees $10–$20.

It's worth a drive up the north coast to dine at this lovely indoor-outdoor restaurant in a protected coral cove near Cane Bay. Whether on the deck or in a breeze-filled dining room, meals are generally well-prepared and often include conch fritters, filet mignon and other West Indian-Continental specialties. If not quite paradise, it comes pretty close, if only for an hour. Reservations recommended. Credit Cards: V, MC, A.

Tivoli Gardens $$$ ★★

39 Strand, ☎ *(809) 773-6782.*
International cuisine.
Lunch: 11:15 a.m.–2:30 p.m., entrees $6–$15.
Dinner: 6:00 p.m.–9:30 p.m., entrees $11–$20.

There's a fairyland of lights and greenery on the spacious porch of this popular saloon facing Christiansted harbor. A surprising carnival of eclectic treats are prepared with aplomb—witness Hungarian goulash and a Thai curry on the same menu. The frequently served chocolate velvet cake is wicked on the waistline and heaven on the tastebuds. Reservations recommended. Credit Cards: V, MC, A.

Top Hat $$$ ★★★

52 Company Street, ☎ *(809) 773-2346.*
Seafood cuisine. Specialties: Herring appetizers, frikadeller with red cabbage, gravlax.
Dinner: 6:00 p.m.–10:00 p.m., entrees $14–$28.

Probably the only Danish restaurant on the island, Top Hat has consistently pleased visitors and residents for 20 years. The Danish owners—chef Bent Rasmussen and his wife Hanne—run a spic-and-span operation on the top floor of a charming gingerbread trimmed-house. Located above a shopping center, it's painted in muted, tasteful tones. Closed: Sun. Reservations recommended. Credit Cards: V, MC, A.

Frederiksted

Blue Moon $$ ★★★

17 Strand St., ☎ *(809) 772-2222.*
International cuisine.
Dinner: entrees $10–$20.

Hot jazz and hot food draw folks to this restaurant and club in a quaint Victorian building in the heart of funky, laid-back Fredericksted. The place bustles Friday night for live jazz concerts and at Sunday brunch, and this bistro's creative chefs are always experimenting with different cooking styles. Some nights, specials could be Cajun, or at other times French-influenced Asian temptations. Usually there are one or more chocolate delights on the dessert menu. Closed July-September. Closed: Mon. Reservations recommended. Credit Cards: A.

Great House $$$ ★★★★

Estate Teague Bay, Teague Bay, ☎ *(809) 773-8141.*
Italian cuisine.
Dinner: entrees $25–$35.

The crowning glory of the Villa Madeleine, the honeymoon haven on the east coast of the island, the Great House recalls a posh plantation house of bygone days. It's all dolled up in butter-yellow paint, and a patio bursts with bright blooms. The primarily Italian-continental cuisine is some of the finest on the island. There's lively entertainment on weekends. Reservations required. Credit Cards: V, MC, DC, A.

Le St. Tropez $$$ ★★★

67 King Street, ☎ *(809) 772-3000.*
French cuisine.

Lunch: entrees $10–$25.
Dinner: entrees $10–$25.

This amiable bistro is a corner of Gallic charm in the center of the West Indian town of Fredericksted. Familiar favorites like quiche, roast duck and frog legs are served on a terrace or in a romantic dining room. The woodsy bar is a little dark, but that's how many people like it. Closed: Sun. Reservations recommended. Credit Cards: V, MC, A.

Where to Shop

Shopping only seems to get better on this island, though the brick or stone sidewalks and some hefty flights up may make it difficult for those with knee problems or the elderly. If you're healthy and able, pray that your ship docks at Christiansted's **Gallows Bay** (where there are more stores than at Fredericksted). Some new complexes near the water (**Pan Am Pavilion** and **Caravelle Arcade**) are more walker-friendly. If you are turned on by low prices, look for substantial savings on fine china and crystal (30–50 percent), perfume, liquor (60 percent cheaper), cigarettes (40 percent cheaper), watches, gold jewelry, and imported cosmetics. If you're in need of resort wear and Indonesian style sarongs, head for **Java Wraps** in the Pan Am Pavilion. **Wayne James Boutique**, a famous native designer, offers excellent ladies' fashions. For an excellent selection of crafts, try the **Mongoose Junction**, a complex of wood and brick studios featuring original pottery, hand-painted garments, batiks and silk screens, jewelry, and seaworthy knickknacks. U.S. citizens are allowed to bring home $1200 worth of goods tax-free and five-fifths of liquor (six, if one is locally produced., plus up to $100 in gifts.

St. Croix Directory

ARRIVAL

American Airlines offers nonstop service to St. Croix from Miami, with connecting service from NYC, Newark and Raleigh/Durham via Miami on San Juan. (Flights into San Juan connect into St. Croix on convenient commuter airlines.) Carnival Airlines flies nonstop from Miami, NYC, Orlando and Newark to San Juan with connecting flights on commuters. Continental flies direct from Newark to St. Croix, with connecting service from Boston, Chicago, Detroit and Philadelphia via Newark. Delta flies direct from Atlanta to St. Croix, nonstop from Atlanta to San Juan. Trans World Airways flies nonstop from NYC, St. Louis, and Miami to San Juan,. United Airlines flies nonstop from Dulles International (WashingtonD.C.) to San Juan. USAir flies nonstop from Baltimore, Charlotte and Philadelphia to San Juan. Once you're in the Caribbean you might consider Air Anguilla, which flies direct from Anguilla to St. Croix, and returns via St. Thomas. American Eagle flies daily from San Juan to St. Croix and back. LIAT flies from St. Croix to other Caribbean islands to the south and return. Sunaire Express offers frequent jet-prop and daily service between St. Croix and St. Thomas, and San Juan to St. Thomas and St. Croix and return. Virgin Air makes passenger/freight service between San Juan and St. Croix and islands to the south. It also has a charter ambulance.

One of the joys of the USVI is the ability to island hop. Inexpensive transportation via ferry is available among the USVI and the BVI as well, opening up other possibilities for day trips. Year-round Caribbean cruises from San Juan, Miami and other stateside ports go to St. Croix and return.

CLIMATE

Temperatures during the summer, cooled by eastern trade winds, keep the temperature around 82 degrees F. Brief showers also keep things cool. Winter temperatures rise to 77 degrees F. Rainiest months are September–January, and about 40 inches of rain fall per year. A light sweater is needed in winter.

DOCUMENTS

U.S. citizens need not carry a passport, although some proof of identity will be required upon leaving the islands. A passport is a good idea since the nearby British Virgin Islands are so accessible from St. John and St. Thomas. If you wish to dive the Rhone or snorkel amid the fantastic granite boulders at the baths on Virgin Gorda, you'll need to first clear BVI Customs with a passport and an $8 entry fee.

ELECTRICITY

Current runs at 110 volts at 60 cycles.

GETTING AROUND

Transportation on the islands is handled either by taxi or rental cars. Remember, that driving is on the left side of the road. Many rental companies in Cuz Bay offer competitive rates. Expect to pay roughly $60 per day, plus gas and insurance for a Suzuki Sidekick (with four-wheel drive to accommodate the blind switchbacks and extreme mountain inclines).

LANGUAGE

The official language is English, but the special lilt to the accent is called cruzan. Some locals speak a musical patois called English Creole—a blend of English, African and Spanish. Many people also speak good Spanish.

MEDICAL EMERGENCIES

St. Croix has a 250-bed **hospital** ☎ *778-6311*, with 24-hour emergency service. Ask your hotel about doctors on call when you check-in.

MONEY

The official currency is the U.S. dollar.

TELEPHONE

The area code is *809*. Since USVI is an incorporated territory, toll-free numbers that operate in the U.S. work here. You can also dial direct to the mainland. Normal postage rates apply.

TIME

Atlantic Standard Time, one hour later than New York City; during daylight saving time, it is the same as New York.

TIPPING AND TAXES

Some hotels include a 10–15 percent service charge; this should include all tips for both restaurant and room service, unless the attention was extraordinary. If no service is added, leave a 15 percent tip for the waitress, $1–2 a day to the maid; bartenders and wine stewards should be tipped always. Tip the bellboy and porter at least 50 cents a bag. Taxi drivers should receive a 15 percent tip if you are satisfied with the service.

TOURIST INFORMATION

The **St. Croix Tourist Office** ☎ *773-0495* is located at the Christiansted Wharf. It is open daily.

WHEN TO GO

The Fiesta Food Fair is held on January 5 at the Agriculture Fair Grounds in Estate Lower Love, featuring native cooks and their cuisine, arts and crafts, and steel and quelbe bands. Organic Act Day is June 21. October is one of the busiest months. The Champagne Mumm's Cup Regatta sets sail on October 8–10. Columbus Day/Puerto Rican Friendship Day is celebrated on October 6–10, a week-long celebration featuring parade, horse racing and native foods and music. The St. Croix Jazz & Caribbean Music & Arts Festival takes place October 14–23, featuring Patti Austin, George Benson, Stanley Jordan and others. The Golden Hook Challenge is slated for October 21–23, a sportsfishing contest. Veterans Day is celebrated on November 11, with island-style parades of steel bands, calypso and partying. The Crucian Christmas Fiesta, the traditional two-week event that features parades, pageants, food and music starts December 11–January 7. The Crucian Christmas Festival Food Fairs in Christiansted and Frederiksted is held in the third week of December. The Festival Village in Christiansted takes place on December 29. Frederiksted's Village opens on December 30, with nightly reggae, calypso and Latin music. A Carnival-like Christmas celebration takes place from several days before Christmas to about a week after New Year's.

ST. CROIX HOTELS	RMS	RATES	PHONE	FAX
Christiansted				
★★★★★ Buccaneer Hotel	149	$155–$340	(800) 223-1108	
★★★★ Villa Madeleine	20	$305–$425	(800) 548-4461	(809) 773-7518
★★★ Cane Bay Reef Club	9	$85–$165	(800) 253-8534	(809) 778-2966
★★★ Carambola Beach Resort	151	$160–$330	(800) 333-3333	(809) 778-1682
★★★ Cormorant Beach Club	38	$110–$265	(800) 548-4460	(809) 778-9218
★★★ Cormorant Cove	38	$105–$230	(800) 548-4460	(809) 778-9218
★★★ Hibiscus Beach Hotel	38	$95–$190	(800) 442-0121	(809) 773-7668
★★★ Hilty House Inn	6	$65–$130	(800) 524-2026	809 773 2594
★★★ Hotel on the Cay	55	$95–$198	(800) 524-2035	(809) 773-7046
★★★ St. Croix by the Sea	65	$90–$145	(800) 524-5006	
★★ Anchor Inn of St. Croix	31	$80–$150	(800) 524-2030	809 773 4408
★★ Club St. Croix	54	$120–$194	(800) 635-1533	(809) 778-4009
★★ Colony Cove	60	$130–$290	(800) 524-2025	(809) 778-4009
★★ Gentle Winds Resort	66	$230–$305	(809) 773-3400	809 778 3400
★★ Hotel Caravelle	43	$79–$255	(800) 524-0410	(809) 778-7004
★★ King Christian Hotel	39	$80–$135	(800) 524-2012	809 773 9411
★★ Pink Fancy Hotel	13	$70–$120	(800) 524-2045	(809) 773-6448
★★ Schooner Bay Resort	62	$145–$295	(800) 524-2025	(809) 778-4009
★★ Sugar Beach Condominiums	46	$110–$250	(800) 524-2049	(809) 773-1359
★★ Waves at Cane Bay	12	$85–$195	(800) 545-0603	(809) 778-4945
★ Caribbean View All-Suites	18	$80–$120	(809) 773-3335	(809) 773-1596
★ Club Comanche	42	$35–$126	(800) 524-2066	809 773 0210
★ Danish Manor	12	$225–$305	(809) 773-1377	809 773 1913
★ Danish Manor Hotel	35	$54–$99	(800) 524-2069	(809) 773-1913
Frederiksted				
★★ Chenay Bay Beach Resort	50	$125–$210	(800) 548-4457	(809) 773-2918
★★ Frederiksted Hotel	40	$80–$110	(800) 524-2025	(809) 772-0500
★★ On the Beach Resort	13	$55–$110	(800) 524-2018	(809) 772-1757

ST. CROIX HOTELS		RMS	RATES	PHONE	FAX
★★	Sprat Hall Plantation	16	$95–$220	(809) 772-0305	
★	Cottages by the Sea	20	$70–$110	(800) 323-7252	809 772 0495

ST. CROIX RESTAURANTS		LOCATION	PHONE	ENTREE
Christiansted				
American				
★★	Chart House	Christiansted	(809) 773-7718	$14–$26••
International				
★★★★	Kendrick's	Christiansted	(809) 773-9199	$14–$26••
★★	Antoine's	Christiansted	(809) 773-0263	$14–$32
★★	Comanche	Christiansted	(809) 773-2665	$9–$21
★★	Tivoli Gardens	Christiansted	(809) 773-6782	$6–$20
Italian				
★★	Picnic in Paradise	Christiansted	(809) 778-1212	$10–$20••
Latin American				
★★★	Harvey's	Christiansted	(809) 773-3433	$8–$20
Mediterranean				
★★	Dino's	Christiansted	(809) 778-8005	$14–$20••
Seafood				
★★★	Top Hat	Christiansted	(809) 773-2346	$14–$28••
★★	Banana Bay Club	Christiansted	(809) 778-9110	$15–$25
Frederiksted				
French				
★★★	Le St. Tropez	Fredericksted	(809) 772-3000	$10–$25
International				
★★★	Blue Moon	Frederiksted	(809) 772-2222	$10–$20••
Italian				
★★★★	Great House	Teague Bay	(809) 773-8141	$25–$35••

Note: • Lunch Only

•• Dinner Only

SINT EUSTATIUS

St. Eustatius is a diver's dream with coral reefs, marine life and many shipwrecks to explore.

St. Eustatius is the least touristic of the Leewards Islands with mediocre beaches, an oil refinery, and an unprepossessing landscape. What is marvelous about St. Eustatius is that it is relatively cheap—the same salad that goes for $25 on St. Barts is a mere $6 here. And it's a must for history buffs. Forever hymned in the United States s as the first place to salute the rebel stars and stripes in 1776, the free port of Oranjestad was a constant thorn in the side of the British until Admiral George Brydges Rodney was sent to raze it, making his base in what is now the excellent museum in the beautiful old Gin House Hotel on the water's edge. Often called Statia, the island today is also a paradise for hikers, even if there are no parks, picnic tables, or water fountains. Instead you can find at least 17 different kinds of orchids, iguanas, huge land crabs and pristine coral reefs teeming with fish. Self-reliant and rugged adventurers will also find the trails underwater exciting—and gloriously deserted. Simply, Statia is a place where you make your own schedule and nobody cares whether you follow it or not. Best of all, packing for Statia is a cinch since there is absolutely no reason to dress up for any occasion anywhere on the island.

Bird's Eye View

St. Eustatius lies 35 miles south of St. Martin and 17 miles southeast of Saba. The island is eight sq. miles with a population of 1800. The highest point of the island, at its southern end, is the 2000-ft. high Quill, a geologically young volcano that is already extinct. The classic volcanic cone harbors a beautiful crater filled with dense tropical rainforest (where towering kapok trees grow and at least 15 types of wild orchids). Statians once cultivated cocoa, cinnamon and coffee here in the crater's fertile soil; today bananas are the solitary crop. At night locals hunt for land crabs inside the crater. Contorted cloud forests carpet the summit of Mazinga Peak, where on a clear day, you can see St. Kitts, Nevis and Anguilla. The Panorama track rewards with glorious views of St. Eustatius, Saba, St. Martin and St. Barts. There are five wildly diverse trail options for climbing to the rim, around it and into the bowl-shaped crater.

History

Columbus discovered St. Eustatius on his second voyage, but a Spanish settlement never followed. The Dutch founded the first settlement in 1636, building Fort Orange but the Dutch claim it was never finalized until 1816, after the island changed hands 22 times. During the 18th century, the island became extraordinarily prosperous, as over 8000 swarmed to the island, half of which were slaves. Trade became the most profitable way to make a living, and the island gained the nickname "The Golden Rock."

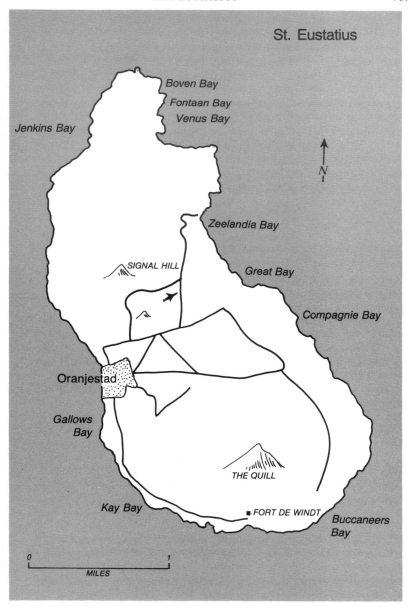

St. Eustatius

Boven Bay

Fontaan Bay

Venus Bay

Jenkins Bay

N

Zeelandia Bay

SIGNAL HILL

Great Bay

Compagnie Bay

Oranjestad

Gallows Bay

THE QUILL

Kay Bay

■ FORT DE WINDT

Buccaneers Bay

0   1

MILES

Statia has a long and unique relationship with the United States. At the time of the War for Independence, Statia was a major port from which arms were shipped to General Washington's troops via Boston, New York and Charleston. On November 16, 1776, the island unknowingly fired the first initial salute to the just-declared nation, but the British retaliated, the port being taken in 1781 by Admiral George Brydges Rodney, who captured 150 merchant ships and 5 million pounds before the French expelled him the next year.

After that, the economy began to decline as control of the island changed power numerous times, and merchants were banished by changing rules. The Emancipation Act of 1863 significantly squashed any hope for a plantation industry. Most natives were reduced to subsistence farming and receiving monetary assistance from relatives abroad.

People

There are numerous nationalities represented on St. Eustatius since the island has changed hands over two times. Most people are involved in farming, fishing, trading and a small oil industry. Locals are extraordinarily friendly and there is great hope that tourism will be the wave of the future. At present there is no crime.

Beaches

One of the loveliest beaches is **Oranje Baai**, stretching for a mile along the coast away from the Lower Town. The strand is perfectly safe for swimming, with a large expanse of sand appearing January-July. Other times the beach narrows and even disappears. Avoid **Zeelandia** for swimming, but you can see interesting geological formations in the cliff and even nesting sea birds. (A dangerous undertow here can be deadly and there is no lifeguard to save you.) After a rain, you can find lots of shells and driftwood on the beach— hikers love it. The beach itself, however, is especially lovely and two miles long. **Lynch Beach**, also on the Windward side, is a bit safer for swimming if you do not venture far out into the surf.

Dive Sites

Untouched corals cover much of Statia's reeds and are full of marine life. Between 1463 and 1700, political rivalries and exchange of power were so intense and frequent that the bottom of the leeward coast is filled with at least 200 shipwrecks and other ruins. To this day, divers still find antique bottles. Around this underwater litter has grown massive corals and a great variety of fish and marine life. Most diving takes place in 20–80 feet of water, with visibility over 200 feet. Snorkeling conditions are excellent. Sixteen dive sites have been designated in the area, the most popular being the Supermarket, situated a half-mile off the coast from Lower Town, in 60 feet of water. Red tub sponges lay at 100 feet here. Off the southwest coast, elkhorn corals, large sea fans and pillar corals can be found at **Croos Reef**. At **The Crack in the Wall**, you'll find walls of pinnacle coral shooting up front from the ocean depths. Blacktip sharks, eagle rays and large ocean fish burrow into the coves. **Barracuda Reef** gets its name from the enormous number of barracuda who like the environs. On the northwest coast, the shallow coral gardens at Jenkins Bay make for excellent snorkeling and beginning dive sites.

Treks

St. Eustatius is a paradise for trekkers. Twelve trails using old donkey or farm tracks are marked and numbered. (Ask the tourist office for a guidebook delineating them.) The main trail not to be missed is called the **Track**. It starts at the end of the **Behind the Mountain Road** (Statia's place names are nothing if not descriptive). The hike will demand about four hours of your time, and you should be physically prepared. The time will probably be extended, however, if you go to the top to look at the amazing orchids or have a picnic overlooking the fabulous views of St.Kitts. The **Venus Bay Track**, characterized by intricate rock formations, crosses a rocky seashore.

From Lower Town (in Oranjestad), you can take a 20-minute hike north along the beach (**White Bird Track/XII**) passing beneath the cliffs of **Powder Hill** (also called Fort Royal Hill) which is a favored nesting ground for tropic-birds.

The **De Boven Track** begins at Venus Bay and will give you a stupendous glimpse of the Atlantic Ocean and the Caribbean, not to mention neighboring islands. Truly hearty hikers can attack the **Quill Track** up the 2000-ft. mountain to the crater, which takes about a half hour to 45 minutes up and a half hour down, starting from **Welfare Road**. It can become slippery in places, particularly after a rain. The trail begins on the south side of Oranjestad on Welfare Road at a telephone pole marked "Quill Track" and proceeds up the western part of the crater's rim at 1415-ft. elevation. At sign no. 5, follows the gut, or gully, on a straight shoot for the rim. There is no trail marked into the crater. If you want to get closer, follow a fluorescent orange and white ribbon. Then you climb down the rocks to the bottom, where the trail is clearly defined.

Track Around the Mountain/VI is a trail for inexperienced hikers, easily meandering along the south and west slopes of **The Quill**. After a short ascent through dry forest, it bends to the west and continues on rather flat terrain to the summit of **White Wall**. The hike, which takes about 90 minutes, finally ends up on **Rosemary Lane** on the outskirts of Oranjestad. A side trail leads to a lookout over the southern coast. **Panorama Track V** is an up-and-down drama on the northeast rim of the crater. Most of the trail passes through dense rainforest. Beyond no. 11, the trail simply becomes too steep and dangerous to proceed.

Note: Start your hike at dawn, when the air is cooler. Birds are more plentiful then and you might find a large iguana sunning in the morning's first rays. Always take water, no matter how long the hike is, since anything can happen.

What Else to See

Upper Town the main urban center, can be seen in an eyeblink. There is **Fort Oranje**, the government center and where you go to hear the latest gossip. (On an island as small as this, gossip ranks high on the list of entertainment options.) The island museum is the **Doncker-De Graf House**, where you can see relics from Statia's history. Archeological digs are often underway so check with the tourist board about possible sites. One site recently discovered was a synagogue built in 1738. For trekking expeditions, see above under "Treks."

Historical Sites

Fort Oranje ★★★

Upper Town, Oranjestad.

This fort dates back to 1636. It was restored in honor of the U.S. Bicentennial in 1976. St. Eustatius was the first foreign entity to support the United States in the Revolutionary War, and a plaque here, presented by Franklin D. Roosevelt, gives thanks. The British retaliated by sacking the then-rich town and its harbor, and much of the rebuilding was done with U.S. funds. The tourist office out front is a good place to pick up brochures and maps and hire a guide.

Museums and Exhibits

St. Eustatius Historical Museum ★★★

Wilhelmina Way, Oranjestad.
Hours Open: 9:00 a.m.–5:00 p.m.

This museum is housed in a beautifully restored 18th-century building once lived in by British Admiral Rodney during the American Revolution. (Not a popular man, as he's the one who ordered the town destroyed after it acknowledged the fledgling United States as an independent country.) The museum's eclectic exhibits focus on sugar production, slave trading, 18th-century antiques, and pre-Columbian artifacts. General admission: $2.00.

Tours

The Quill ★★★★

Southern portion, Oranjestad.

The island's highest point at 1968 feet, the Quill is an extinct volcano with a lush rainforest in its crater. Twelve marked trails offer all level of hikes, from simple treks to strenuous trips to the summit. Pick up a brochure at the tourist office, or hire a guide to take you for about $20. Excellent birdwatching. Locals come at night to catch the large crabs that live in the crater. You can accompany them and get your hotel to cook your quarry. Inquire at the tourist office for details.

Sports

Sports on the island are limited to hiking, climbing, diving and swimming. Softball, basketball and volleyball can be played at the Community Centre on Rosemary Lane.

Tennis

Rosemary Lane, Oranjestad.

St. Eustatius is not the place to come to play tennis—there's one lone court on the entire island. The concrete court at the Community Center is open every day and lit for night play, but you'll have to bring your own racquet and balls, though they do have changing rooms. The fee is about $5.

Watersports

Lower Toen, Oranjestad.

Dive Statia is the island's most complete (and virtually only) watersports center. They offer deep-sea fishing trips, snorkeling equipment, and scuba instruction and excursions. St. Eustatius is a diver's paradise, with all sorts of interesting undersea items to explore, including myriad sunken ships and their booty. Snorkelers can see a lot too, as the depths are often only about 10 feet.

Where to Stay

★ ★ ★   **Old Gin House**

★ ★ ★   **Old Gin House** $125–$225

★ ★ ★   **Old Gin House** $125–$225

Forget about big fancy resorts on St. Eustatius. It's just not that kind of island. There are four small hotels and a number of apartments and rooms to rent. Little is to be expected in regards of style. Basic comfort is the most prevailing feature. The French-inspired **Maison Sur La Plage** is located on a lovely beach but the **Old Gin House** ranks as the most stylish, erected amid the ruins of an old cotton gin.

Hotels and Resorts

Golden Era   **$75–$93**   ★ ★

Lower Town, ☎ *(599) 3-82445.*
Single: $75. Double: $93.
This small hotel sits right at the water's edge, but you'll have to travel a half-mile for the beach, as the shoreline here is rocky. Guest rooms are quite basic, but comfortable with air conditioning, phones and tiny private balconies. The restaurant serves decent Caribbean cuisine. The saltwater pool is the only other facility. Acceptable for the rates, but nothing too exciting. 20 rooms. Credit Cards: MC, A.

Maison sur la Plage   **$60–$95**   ★ ★

Zeelandia, ☎ *(599) 3-82256.*
Single: $60–$80. Double: $60–$95.
Located on the northeastern coast, this small property took a real pummeling during Hurricane Hugo, and has yet to return to its predestruction days. That's not to say that all is in ruins, but some repairs have a slapdash quality. Accommodations are in cottages with basic furnishings, private terraces and bright artwork. Facilities include a gourmet French restaurant, a bar, a TV lounge (you won't find one in

your room), a small library and a pool. The beach stretches for two miles, but the sea is too rough for most swimmers. 10 rooms. Credit Cards: MC, A.

Talk of the Town   **$54–$81**   ★★

Oranjestad, ☎ *(599) 3-82236.*
Single: $54–$65. Double: $68–$81.

This small hotel is set off the beach, but does have a pool. Rooms are quite basic but nice, with air conditioning, locally made furnishings, telephones, and cable TV. The downstairs restaurant is fine. Though frills are few, this is still one of the better choices on this tiny island. 18 rooms. Credit Cards: MC, A.

Apartments and Condominiums

Ask the tourist board for help in finding just the right house or apartment for your needs. Bring your own staples from home.

Airport View Apartments   **$60–$75**   ★★

Golden Rock, ☎ *(599) 3-82474.*
Single: $60. Double: $75.

Like the name implies, these units are indeed near the airport. Each unit is a studio with just the basics—refrigerator, coffeemaker, cable TV—but not complete kitchens, though there is a barbecue area where you can grill meals. There's also a bar and restaurant on the premises, but not much else, not even a pool. 9 rooms. Credit Cards: MC, A.

Inns

Old Gin House   **$125–$225**   ★★★

Lower Town, ☎ *(599) 3-82319.*
Single: $125–$150. Double: $175–$225.

This elegant inn is by far the nicest place to stay on St. Eustatius, and also by far the most expensive. Housed in a restored 18th-century cotton gin factory, rooms are spacious and individually decorated with good artwork, antique furnishings and ceiling fans (no air conditioning). Request one of the rooms in the original inn as they have the most character, though the ones in the newer building across the street are also quite pleasant. There's a restaurant, small pool and library on the premises, and the beach is steps away. No children under 10 permitted. 20 rooms. Credit Cards: CB, V, MC, A.

Low Cost Lodging

There are a few guesthouses in Oranjestad in which you can rent rooms. Rather than reserve from afar, it's best to see in person the situation before you part with your money. The tourist office, which you should contact upon arrival, will also help you find a suitable room.

Where to Eat

★★★ **La Maison Sur La Plage**

★★★ **Old Gin House**

★★★ **Talk of the Town**

| ★★★ La Maison Sur La Plage | $15–$25 |
| ★★★ Talk of the Town | $5–$20 |

| ★★★ Talk of the Town | $5–$20 |
| ★★★ Old Gin House | $10–$22 |

Don't expect to eat cordon bleu here. No one's heard of it. Even credit cards are looked at with quizzical looks; do everybody a favor and pay in cash. The best restaurants are the **Old Gin House** (for atmosphere and cuisine); **Maison Sur La Plage** (for the windswept view of the beach); **Talk of the Town** (for sandwiches Dutch style); **Kim Cheng's Chinese Restaurant** (for the expected fare), and **L'Etoile** (for home-cooked meals).

Cool Corner $ ★★

Fort Oranjestraat, ☎ *(599) 38-2523.*
International cuisine.
Lunch: 10:00 a.m.–4:00 p.m., entrees $8–$10.
Dinner: 4:00 p.m.–12:00 p.m., entrees $8–$10.
This hot spot (for Statia) beckons with a prime location near the local tourist office. A good place to meet the friendly townspeople, Cool Corner stays open late to serve the needs of the few night owls who may be prowling. Fare is Caribbean-Chinese, with curry plates and Cantonese specialties available. Credit Cards: Not Accepted.

Kim Cheng's Chinese $ ★★

Prinsesweg, Upper Town, ☎ *(599) 30-2389.*

Chinese cuisine.
Lunch: entrees $5–$10.
Dinner: entrees $5–$10.

Sometimes called The Chinese Restaurant this tiny eatery manages to produce plates heaped with hearty food in rather cramped surroundings. The fare is actually a potpourri of dishes encompassing West Indian, creole and Chinese. Closed: Sun. Credit Cards: Not Accepted.

L'Etoile $$ ★★

6 Van Rheeweg, ☎ *(599) 38-2299.*
Latin American cuisine.
Lunch: 12:00 a.m.–4:00 p.m., entrees $7–$20.
Dinner: 4:00 p.m.–10:00 p.m., entrees $7–$20.

What appears to be a roadhouse is really a warm, welcoming room proffering tasty island specialties prepared by the amiable Caren Henriquez. Its location on a hillside is a little out of the way for the average tourist, so it's mainly frequented by a crowd of regulars. Along with hamburgers, tasty spareribs and hotdogs, Henriquez prepares goat stew or stuffed crab. Reservations required. Credit Cards: Not Accepted.

La Maison Sur La Plage $$$ ★★★

Zeelandia Beach, Zeelandia, ☎ *(599) 38-2256.*
French cuisine.
Lunch: entrees $15–$25.
Dinner: entrees $15–$25.

In what's considered to be an out-of-the-way location for Statia, La Maison sur Plage is the only fine French restaurant on Zeelandia beach, which is only a few miles from Oranjestad. Meals are served on a breezy, trellised terrace overlooking windswept sands and the Quill. Expect traditional Gallic specialties like duck breast or beef fillets with green peppercorn sauce, and crepes for dessert. Associated Hotel: La Maison Sur La Plage. Reservations required. Credit Cards: V, MC.

Old Gin House $$$ ★★★

Lower Town, ☎ *(599) 38-2319.*
American cuisine.
Lunch: 12.00 a.m.–2:00 p.m., entrees $10–$22.
Dinner: 6:30 p.m.–8:00 p.m., prix fixe $10–$22.

Dinner at the Mooshay Bay Dining Room of this venerable hotel is one of the best deals in town. A delicious four-course meal that often includes chateaubriand or lobster and two kinds of wine is available for $22 per person. The 18th-century tavern room is spiffily decorated with burnished pewter and gleaming crystal, and it faces the pool. Across the street, the Terrace Restaurant, which has an ocean view, is a nice place for burgers or steak and chicken plates. Associated Hotel: Old Gin House. Reservations recommended. Credit Cards: V, MC, DC, A.

Stone Oven $$ ★★

16A Feaschweg, Upper Town, ☎ *(599) 38-2247.*
Latin American cuisine.
Lunch: entrees $10–$15.
Dinner: entrees $10–$15.

This cozy, coconut-palm fringed bar and danceteria serves as a West Indian eatery depending on who's available to cook. When the burners are going, it's a good spot for goat water or conch. Check out the wild party animals swinging on Friday nights when it stays open until the last guest moseys on home. Reservations required. Credit Cards: Not Accepted.

Talk of the Town   **$$**   ★ ★ ★

L.E. Saddlerweg, Upper Town, ☎ *(599) 38-2236.*
International cuisine.
Lunch: 11:30 a.m.–2:00 p.m., entrees $5–$20.
Dinner: 7:00 p.m.–10:00 p.m., entrees $5–$20.

A Dutch family owns and operates this plant-filled, indoor-outdoor restaurant near the airport. It has a reputation for the best creole meals in town, but the cuisine jumps often from one exotic clime to the next. Specialties include lobster stew, which can be ordered in advance. Good deals include the Dutch-style breakfast buffet with some American standards thrown in—all for under $10. Associated Hotel: Talk of the Town. Reservations recommended. Credit Cards: V, MC, A.

Where to Shop

Statia is no St. Thomas. You'll find a few items imported from Holland, including cosmetics, perfumes, liquors, cigarettes and jewelry at the **Mazinga Gift Shop** in Upper Town (Fort Oranjestraat). One good native buy is **Masinga Mist** (schnapps made from soursop) which you can pick up at **Dive Statia's boutique** near the Old Gin House. The museum at Fort Oranje has a small selection of books and postcards.

Sint Eustatius Directory

ARRIVAL AND DEPARTURE

You can reach St. Eustatius several times a day on 20-minute flights from St. Maarten on WINAIR. WINAIR also flies to the island from St. Kitts, which takes only 10 minutes. WINAIR also offers flights from St. Eustatius to Saba from WINAIR. All flights are in small planes, but be sure you look out the window when you land and takeoff to get a great view of The Quill, the island's volcano. There is a departure tax of $3 if you are going to the U.S., $3 if you are going on to any other Caribbean island.

CLIMATE

Daytime temperatures hover in the mid-80s during the day and drop to the 70s during the evening, year-round. Only 45 inches of rain fall a year.

DOCUMENTS

U. S and Canadian citizens need to show only proof of citizenship (current passport or one that expired less than five years ago, or voter's registration card or birth certificate with raised seal and a photo ID), plus an ongoing or return ticket.

ELECTRICITY

Current runs 110 volts, 60 cycles, same as in the U.S. No converter or transformer necessary.

GETTING AROUND

Most destinations are within walking distance, but several taxi drivers make excellent guides. A tour around the island runs about $35. Cars can be hired at the airport, but you must show your own driver's license or an international driver's license. Driving on the right, but the cows and sheep and goats who casually graze over the roadways don't seem to know. You should drive slowly to avoid hitting them.

LANGUAGE

The official language is Dutch (most of the signs are written so), but everyone speaks English. if you meet someone on the street, use the national greeting; "Awright, ok-a-a-y."

MEDICAL EMERGENCIES

Most emergencies are immediately flown to Sint Maarten (though you may want to charter a flight to San Juan, Puerto Rico), but there is a small hospital on the outskirts of Oranjestad.

MONEY

The official currency is the Netherlands Antilles florin (abbreviated NAf), also called the guilder. American dollars are generally accepted everywhere, but Canadians should change their money into florins (Barclays Bank in Wilhelminaweg) or in St. Maarten before coming. Only hotels and a few restaurants will accept credit cards. Imagine you are out in the middle of nowhere.

TELEPHONE

The country code is *599*. To call from the States, dial *011* (international access code), plus *599* (country code) plus *38* (city code) plus 4-digit local number. You may need to use a different code when calling from another Caribbean island.

TIME

Atlantic Standard Time, one hour ahead of New York, except during daylight saving time, when it is the same.

TIPPING AND TAXES

Restaurants, hotels and bars all add a 15 percent service charge. You don't need to tip anyone on top of this. Taxi drivers should get $1–2. No porters to worry about, so be prepared to carry our own luggage.

TOURIST INFORMATION

There are three tourist offices on the island: at the airport, in Lower Town opposite Roro Pier, operated by the St. Eustatius Historical Society, and in the village center. For more information, call ☎ *82433*. In the U.S. ☎ *(800) 344-4606*.

WHEN TO GO

The Queen's Coronation Day on April 30 is a big island bash with fireworks. music, dancing and sports events. Carnival is celebrated in July. Statia-America Day is commemorated on November 16, honoring the first salute to the American flag by a foreign government. Boxing Day is celebrated the day after Christmas on December 26.

SINT EUSTATIUS HOTELS		RMS	RATES	PHONE	FAX
Oranjestad					
★★★	**Old Gin House**	20	$125–$225	(599) 3-82319	599 3 82555
★★	**Airport View Apartments**	9	$60–$75	(599) 3-82474	
★★	**Golden Era**	20	$75–$93	(599) 3-82445	599-3-82445
★★	**La Maison sur la Plage**	10	$60–$95	(599) 3-82256	599-3-82831
★★	**Talk of the Town**	18	$54–$81	(599) 3-82236	599-3-82640

SINT EUSTATIUS RESTAURANTS		LOCATION	PHONE	ENTREE
Oranjestad				
	American			
★★★ **Old Gin House**		Oranjestad	(599) 38-2319	$10–$22
	Chinese			
★★ **Kim Cheng's Chinese**		Upper Town	(599) 30-2389	$5–$10
	French			
★★★ **La Maison Sur La Plage**		Zeelandia	(599) 38-2256	$15–$25
	International			
★★ **Cool Corner**		Oranjestaad	(599) 38-2523	$8–$10
★★★ **Talk of the Town**		Upper Town	(599) 38-2236	$5–$20

SINT EUSTATIUS RESTAURANTS	LOCATION	PHONE	ENTREE
Latin American			
★★ **L'Etoile**	Oranjestad	(599) 38-2299	$7–$20
★★ **Stone Oven**	Upper Town	(599) 38-2247	$10–$15
Note: • Lunch Only			
•• Dinner Only			

ST. JOHN

Tourists enjoy the exotic greenery and fresh air of St. John.

For many die-hard ecotourists, St. John is one of the greatest natural wonders of the three U.S. Virgin Islands. In fact, the two major diversions here are climbing and "limin" (that is, "laying back," Caribbean style)—the latter preferably done before *and* after the former. Unlike so many other flat, arid Caribbean isles, the U.S. Virgin Islands (which also includes St. Croix and St. Thomas), are beautifully sculpted and vividly green, and St. Thomas has more than its fair share of emerald green bays, snow-white beaches, and lushly carpeted mountain peaks; in fact, almost two-thirds of the island's land area, plus another 5600 acres underwater, comprise the U.S. Virgin Islands National Park, donated to the U.S. by Laurence Rockefeller. As such, there are terrific adventures both above and under water, so untrod that many visitors come for weeks and never get beyond the gorgeous **Cinnamon Bay Beach**. All it takes is a good pair of boots and a little guidance to mash one's way through densely packed rainforest or hike over well-marked nature trails that lead past 200-year-old plantation houses. Underwater the views are just as spectacular, with rock formations, grottoes and wrecks that rate as some of the best in the Caribbean. The absence of sales tax here has been known to drive some visitors to frenzy, but once the shopper's dust settles, they find that the most pleasant thing to do on St. Thomas is just to lay back, drink in hand, shades in place, and learn the recipe for sugar molasses and rum mortar.

Bird's Eye View

The U.S. Virgin Islands lie 1500 miles southeast of New York and about 1000 miles south of Miami. A mere 18 degrees above the equator, they are bounded to the north by the Atlantic Ocean and the south by the Caribbean Sea, except for St. Croix, which is surrounded by the Caribbean. St. John, is just two miles east of St. Thomas (and a mere 20-minute ferry ride away) is the laid-back little island (19 square miles) of St. John. A three-mile expanse called Pillsbury Sound separates St. John from St. Thomas, and between the two islands lie a few, smaller, mostly uninhabited ones, or so Christopher Columbus fantasized when he named the group St. Ursula and her 11,000 virgins. The highest peak is **Bordeaux Mountain** at 1277 feet. Most of St. John's 2500 residents live in the area surrounding **Cruz Bay**, a tiny ramshackle town, where ferries and cruise-ship tenders dock, tourists shop, and islanders go about their very laid-back business. Scenic overlooks provide a glimpse of broad expanses of white sand lapped by a turquoise sea. Closer inspection reveals a sugary white sand and interesting snorkeling offshore. When the ferry landing was built in Cruz Bay, opening a gateway to St. Thomas and her airport, the closest to St. John, Coral Bay sank slowly into seclusion. It's a pass-through for those on their way to Salt Pond Beach or Don Carlos Mexican Seafood Cantina. The new eateries like Skinny Legs and Shipwreck Landing are beginning to lure crowds to Coral Bay.

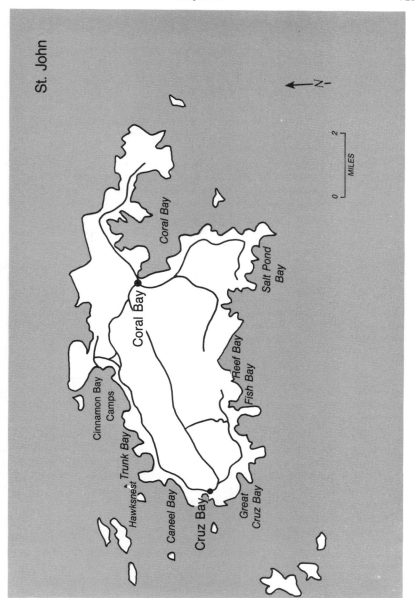

History

Archaeologists have yet to decide whether the Arawaks or Caribs (the island's first pre-Columbian inhabitants), African slaves, or a combination thereof were responsible for the primitive etchings along the Reef Bay trail. In 1493, Columbus discovered the islands of St. Croix, St. John and St. Thomas, and then shoved off to Puerto Rico. A hundred years later saw the arrival in St. John of Sir Francis Drake as he prepared to confront the Spanish troops in San Juan. While St. Croix changed hands between the French and Spanish, St. John (along with St. Thomas) was appropriated by the Danish West India Company, becoming a hub of business (St. Thomas), and a magnet for sugarcane, tobacco and cotton plantations (St. John). In 1717, the Danes established St. John's Coral Bay as a permanent port. In 1733, a great slave rebellion devastated the country, when a large mass of slaves, ostensibly carrying bundles of wood, were admitted to Fort Berg in Coral Bay. Once inside, they brandished cane knives and massacred hundreds of settlers and the entire Danish garrison. The rebels held the fort for nine months until the Danes, with the support of two French warships and an army from Martinique, recaptured the island and rebuilt the factories. In 1848, slavery was abolished, though planters tried to hold onto their crops until the advent of the European sugar-beet soured their profits. When the planters eventually left the island, the former slaves divided up their properties and relied on the land and the sea to provide their sustenance. In 1917, with a view to protect its interest in the Panama Canal, the U.S.bought the Virgin Islands package—St. John, St. Thomas and St. Croix—from the Danes for a mere $25 million. Starting in the 50s, tourism began to strategically raise the standard of living. In 1956, Laurence Rockefeller took a shine to the island and erected his Caneel Bay resort, which gave visitors full opportunity to enjoy the pleasures of the park. With the advent of the Maho Bay resort in 1976, more ecologically-oriented travelers arrived on St. John's shores, ready to scale and sail the challenging resources. Luxury entered with the opening of the Virgin Grand, now the Hyatt Regency, with a slew of high-class condos following in its wake.

People

There are only about 3500 people who live on St. John, many of them not quite sure they want their small island overrun with tourists. That may be the reason why visitors are sometimes treated with a measure of distance. Locals take time to warm to conversation, and while they stop traffic talking among themselves, few may laugh with you. (To be fair, just one look at how American cruise passengers sometimes treat islanders—with an air of patronization leftover from the master-slave dynamic—should fully explain their coolness.) Reggae is a major passion, as is the Rastafarianism influence, and belief in the supernatural runs high: natives still believe the jumbies (spirits) caused the closing of the Reef Bay Sugar Factory in 1916. You'll find a number of American ex-pats here, who, keen to the laid-back lifestyle, spend their days casually selling wares in Cruz Bay. If you can leave your cellular phone and datebook at home, it will take only a few days to understand the Virgin vibe called "limin"—a kind of wrinkle in time phenomenon that makes it impossible to do anything else but lounge, sip cool drinks and daydream.

Hawk's Nest Bay on St. John has two good reefs offshore with elkhorn coral.

Beaches

The island's best beach, **Trunk Bay** is the most photographed spot in the Caribbean, but underwater it's beginning to show wear and tear. Non-divers can use a unique snorkeling scuba system that involves an air-support raft attached to a 20-ft. line allowing the snorkeler the thrill of diving. There are also snorkel rentals and lockers for hire, as well as snack bars. The beach, however, should be well avoided on days when cruise ships pull into port. **Hawks Nest Bay Beach**, a rollercoaster ride from Cancel, is a favorite beach. It's a 15-minute walk from the reception area of the **Caneel Bay** resort, and is usually very deserted. **Cinnamon Bay** is long and powdery, and the national park maintains a little historical museum. Difficult to reach over a torturous road, **Maho Bay** is beautiful and calm, full of turtles, and well worth the effort. Coves unreachable by car are **Solomon** and **Honeymoon** behind the Cruz Bay Center. The short hike will fill a morning (nudists prefer it, even if there is an official law against taking it all off). Palm trees fringe both coves and a rocky outcropping separates them, providing excellent snorkeling. **Reef Bay**, in the south, is reached by a 2 1/2- mile trail descending through a shady moist rainforest, after which comes a dry scrub forest. **Salt Pond** is also especially good for snorkeling and features a hearty climb to **Ram's Head**.

Dive Sites

A favorite snorkeling spot among residents of St. John, the small **Haulover Bay**, although usually rougher than **Leinster**, is often deserted. The snorkeling is dramatic, with ledges, walls, nooks and sandy areas located close together; it's best visited only by confident swimmers because of choppy waters. Other snorkeling "hotspots" on St. John include: Hawks Nest Bay, Salt Pond, Chocolate Hole and Honeymoon Beach. With easy access from land and sea, Leinster Bay is a particularly interesting place to snorkel. The water is usually calm and uncrowded, offering an abundance of sea life. The underwater trail at **Trunk Bay** within the **Virgin Islands National Park** on St.

John is a popular snorkeling spot, especially for beginners, but it's beginning to show signs of wear. The self-guided, 225-yard-long trail has large underwater signs which clearly identify species of coral and other items of interest. There are changing rooms, freshwater showers, equipment rentals, a snack bar, off-street parking and a lifeguard on duty. Cinnamon Bay, near Trunk Bay, has a fine outlying coral reef rife with angelfish, triggerfish and others. Changing rooms and showers are available. Hawks Nest Bay boasts two good patch reefs offshore and some admirable stands of elkhorn coral. Salt Pond Bay has no facilities but the mile-long Ram Head Trail leads to a spectacular overlook above the water. **The Baths** is a remarkable system of underwater coves and secluded beaches along the southwest coast. Note: Many hotel properties offer splendid snorkeling sites, as well as snorkeling equipment; For information on special hotel packages, contact the **St. John Hotel Association** ☎ *809-774-6835.*

Treks

Of all the U.S. Virgin Islands, hiking and trekking is best on St. John. The **Virgin Islands National Park** has superb trails. Do make your first stop at the Visitor Center which offers tours by park rangers, hikes, wildlife lectures, and films; there is even a boating tour around the island. Rangers here are extraordinarily informative and give vital information during the treks about flora, fauna and history. During the winter months, do make reservations ahead of time because the hikes are popular. An essential booklet to ask for is "Trail Guide for Safe Hiking." There are 21 marked hiking trails in the park, accessible from the North Shore Road or from Centerline Road. Some of the easiest trails are only 10 minutes long, though they can range up to two hours (two treks for couch potatoes are Cruz Bay and Hawknest). If you want to get to know intimately the flora of the park, take the trail from Cinnamon Bay to Mary Point, which takes an hour if you linger. It goes through a tropical rainforest and an old sugar factory site. The park's most comprehensive hike, **The Reef Bay Trail**, three miles from 1100 feet above sea level to three feet below, passes through both rainforest and scrub, and is one of eight trails on the southern coast, the steepest being the **Bordeaux Mountain Trail** (1000 ft. above sea level) whose views are stupendous. **The Ram Head Trail** begins at the south end of Salt Pond Bay beach and leads to a unique pebble beach, then follows the sides of a hill to a plateau 200 feet above the sea. The view, here, is also gorgeous, but climbers should be careful of the footing near the edge of the cliff. Along the north shore there are 13 different trails; some are dubbed "self-guided" by the National Park service, meaning they are easy to traverse and are well marked, while others require more skill and caution. The 1.5 mile **Lind Point Trail**, linking the National Park Visitor Center at Cruz Bay with Caneel Bay Plantation, offers a scenic overlook before descending to Caneel Bay through dry forest and scrub cactus. The **Annaberg Forest Trail** goes close to a mangrove forest, with land crabs, pelicans, and wading birds visible. From the top of the **Annaberg Sugar Mill Plantation** you'll see an excellent perspective of the entire British Virgin Islands.

FIELDING'S CHOICE:

Do sign up for the National Park Service tour, whose guided adventure hikes acquaint you with native wildlife, including rippled tail man lizards, black spiny sea urchins, and peely barked "tourist trees."

What Else to See

Most of your time on St. John will want to be spent hiking, climbing and limin', but a few historical sites are worth the effort (some are even located on trails). Among the most interesting is the **Annaberg Sugar Mill Ruins**, operated by the National Park Service, which gives living history demonstrations of how islanders managed to survive in the post-slavery years. The **Elaine Spauve Library** and the **Museum of Cultural Arts** in Cruz Bay occupy an 18th-century plantation house which contains photos and artifacts illustrating the survival of island arts. A trip to **Caneel Bay**, the resort launched by Laurence Rockefeller, is worth a visit, even if you aren't staying there, to enjoy the dazzling view of the Bay from the North Shore road. **Catherineberg Plantation** down Centerline Road, approachable from a rocky road, also has stupendous views, as well as a now crumbling windmill, full of stupendous views.

Museums and Exhibits

Elaine Ione Sprauve Museum   ★★★

> *Cruz Bay,* ☎ *(809) 776-6359.*
> *Hours Open: 9:00 a.m.–5:00 p.m.*

This small museum has exhibits on St. John's Danish West Indian history, as well as displays of locally created artwork. Free admission.

Parks and Gardens

Virgin Islands National Park ★ ★ ★ ★ ★

Cruz Bay, ☎ *(809) 776-6201.*

No visit to St. John—or any of the U.S. Virgins—would be complete without at least a day spent at the breathtaking national park. It encompasses 12,624 acres and has 20 miles of trails to explore. Stop by the Visitors Center (open daily from 8:00 a.m. to 4:30 p.m.) to peruse the exhibits, pick up a map, and get details of special ranger-led events. Highlights on the park include the Annaberg Ruins, a sugar plantation and mill from the 1780s; the Reef Bay Trail, which passes plantation ruins and petroglyphs); and Trunk Bay, a picture-postcard beach and the start of a marked underwater trail well-loved by snorkelers.

Tours

Guided Tours

Various locations, Cruz Bay.

The **St. John Taxi Association** will show you around the island for about $30 for one or two people, $13 per person for three or more. The **St. John Island Tour** (☎ *774-4550*) lasts two hours and costs $12 per person. Ranger-led tours are popular at **Virgin Islands National Park**; call ☎ *776-6201* for details. Finally, local personality **Miss Lucy** (☎ *776-6804*) tailors private tours to individual interests.

BEST VIEW:

Le Chateal de Bordeaux clings to the edge of a mountain top along Centerline Road which gives spectacular views of Bordeaux Mountain, St. John's highest peak, and the serpentine Sir Francis Drake Channel, with the British Virgin Islands scattered below. And the cuisine of New Zealand red deer venison and arugula is superb.

Sports

Watersports are an integral part of the St. John lifestyle. At Trunk Bay, a new sport called SNUBA has become very popular—a combination of snorkeling and scuba diving that doesn't require lengthy certification courses. Both campgrounds offer extensive sports packages, including scuba and trekking. The Virgin Islands are famous for spectacular deep-sea fishing for blue marlin, with many world records to prove it. Anglers from all over the world head here for the **Blue Marlin Fishing Tournament** in August. No deep-sea fishing is allowed in the National Park, but you can rod-and-reel fish from the beaches in St. John's. Excellent sea conditions with balmy weather and numerous covers and sheltered anchors create unparalleled conditions for sailing. Every type of vessel, from sailfish to oceangoing yachts can be hired. Boats may be chartered with a full crew or bareback, but do know what you are doing if you choose to leave the crew behind. There are many half-day and full-day boat excursions; check first with your hotel, who probably has a full list and can recommend what will best suit your needs. Operators in St. John are based in Cruz Bay and Coral Bay. Because of the constant trade winds, windsurfing also finds a large group of fans. The winds, whipping down the **Sir Francis Drake Channel** north of St. John, are funneled by two hills through the Narrows to the Windward Passage. About five miles north of Trunk Bay, on the north side of **Johnson's Reef**, the conditions are simply perfect. Windsurfers can also sail cross **Pillsbury Sound** to St. Thomas. (See trails for hiking under "Treks" above. For more information on diving, see "Dive Sites" above.)

Watersports

Various locations, Cruz Bay.

St. John's two lavish resorts, the Hyatt Regency and Caneel Bay, have their own watersports facilities. Otherwise you're probably on your own. For general equipment rentals, try: **Coral Bay Watersports** (☎ *776-6850*), **Paradise Watersports** (☎ *693-8690*), **Low Key Watersports** (☎ *693-8999*), **Cinnam Bay Watersports Center** (☎ *776-6330*), and **Cruz Bay Watersports** (☎ *776-6234*). The latter four also offer diving instruction and excursions. For deep-sea fishing, try **Gone Ketchin** (☎ *693-8657*), **World Class Anglers** (☎ *779-4281*), and **Low Key Watersports** (☎ *693-8999*). For kayaking and windsurfing, in addition to other rentals, call **Paradise Aqua Tour** (☎ *776-6226*).

FIELDING'S CHOICE:

No other sport will bring you closer to the spirit of the original Arawaks and Caribs than sea kayaking, and the best Caribbean waters for it are found among the sheltered cays and coves of the British and the U.S. Virgin Islands. Arawak Expeditions offers a challenging trip of 3- hours paddling a day, 5–6 miles a day, 5- days in a row. The tour begins in St. John, where you're briefed and supplied with rows, sleeping bag, tents and sleeping pad. Then you and your two-person 20-foot long kayak are taken by launch to Virgin Gorda, so you'll be paddling downwind back to St. John. Itineraries vary, depending on weather and tides, but can include stops at Ginger, Peter, Norman, and Jost Van Dyke islands. To avoid the afternoon breezes and blustery seas, you do most of the traveling before lunch, then pitch camp on a deserted beach. You don't even have to know which way to point the kayaks. The company gives you full instructions how to slip in, button up, manage the paddles, and get back in when you flip. First-timers from 14–73 have returned. Arawak Expeditions, P.O. Box 853, Cruz Bay, St. John, USVI 00831, ☎ 800-238-8687. Five-night cruises cost $750 per person, seven days $925 year-round, including kayaks, camping equipment, meals and drinks, minimum four guests per tour.

Insider Tip:

Wednesday is cruise day, so hunker down and stay clear away from Cruz Bay.

Where to Stay

Highest Rated Hotels in St. John

★★★★	**Caneel Bay Resort**
★★★★	**Hyatt Regency St. John**
★★★	**Cinnamon Bay Campground**
★★★	**Gallows Point Suites**
★★★	**Maho Bay Camp Resort**

Most Exclusive Hotels in St. John

★★★★	**Caneel Bay Resort**	$225–$695
★★★	**Gallows Point Suites**	$140–$360
★★★	**Maho Bay Camp Resort**	$60–$90

Fielding's Best Value Hotels in St. John

★★★	**Cinnamon Bay Campground**	$15–$95
★★	**Inn at Tamarind Court**	$40–$110
★★★	**Maho Bay Camp Resort**	$60–$90
★★★★	**Hyatt Regency St. John**	$195–$515

On St. John, you can choose from the super-luxurious, the ecologically sound, or the charmingly simple. Demand in some cases is excessive, so expect unreasonably high prices. Many people choose to camp because it's cheaper, and because they've come to brave the great outdoors anyway. The camping properties at Cinnamon Bay and Maho Bay are more than agreeable for those used to roughing it. Do make reservations far in advance.

Hotels and Resorts

You have two resorts to choose from. **Caneel Bay**, the heart child of Laurence Rockefeller and the premier property on St. John, has been spruced up for the 90s but still retains an ideal serenity at the same time providing the services of an all-inclusive: 7

beaches, 7 tennis courts, and it's actually in the park. (The most published line about Caneel Bay is "for the newly wed and the nearly dead.") The **Hyatt Regency** is modern, luxurious, with a huge pool, but only 6 courts!

Caneel Bay Resort $225–$695 ★★★★★

Caneel Bay, ☎ *(800) 928-8889, (809) 776-6111.*
Single: $225–$695. Double: $225–$695.

Set on a 170-acre estate, this distinguished resort continues to do everything right, as it has since Laurence Rockefeller bought it in 1956, when it was already in operation for 20 years. Accommodations are scattered about in spacious cottages. All are very nice and include patios, minibars and coffeemakers, but lack air conditioning, TV and telephones. The extensive grounds offer up 11 tennis courts, three restaurants, a lounge with nightly entertainment and a pool. There are seven beaches from which to choose, with all the watersports one could want. The grounds, which abut Virgin Islands National Park, are kept in gorgeous condition year-round. This is truly one of the Caribbean's finest resorts, but it's not for everyone. You're required to dress for dinner, there's not much of a nightlife, and the rates keep out most young folks. No children under five. 171 rooms. Credit Cards: V, MC, DC, A.

Hyatt Regency St. John $195–$515 ★★★★★

Great Cruz Bay, ☎ *(800) 233-1234, (809) 693-8000.*
Single: $195–$360. Double: $240–$515.

This glamorous resort attracts a younger set than at the Caneel Bay, but it too is quite expensive. Set on 34 landscaped acres opening onto a lovely beach, the Hyatt puts guests up in plush guestrooms near the beach and pool. All have modern comforts, but only some have balconies. There are also seven one-bedroom suites and 14 two-bedroom townhouses. Dining options range from Chinese to Italian to West Indian specialties. Recreational facilities include six tennis courts, a large pool, gym, watersports (there's a charge for scuba, sailing and fishing), and organized activities for the kids at "Camp Hyatt." Very very fun and very very nice but this is the kind of crowded, busy resort that turns some people off. If you're looking for true island flavor, stay elsewhere, but if you're a luxurious resort lover, look no further. 285 rooms. Credit Cards: CB, V, MC, A.

Apartments and Condominiums

Rental properties have become extremely popular here for their affordable prices. First-class private homes and villas and plush condos outnumber traditional vacation accommodations on the island. Most villas or beachfront homes offer fully equipped kitchens, plus VCRs, stereos, patio grills, and beach toys. Maid and chef service are often available. Choices range from massive, multi-room resort homes that hug the hillside overlooking Cruz Bay to simply decorated one-bedroom condos with a bay view. Villa rentals year-round average $1200–$2000 per week. Condos run $105–$360 per nit per unit. For more information, call ☎ *800-USVI-INFO* or contact your nearest USVI tourist board. Do check with several rental agencies before you settle on something. Prices range greatly, and you can choose between simple one-room apartments or more elaborate private homes. Food in supermarkets runs high in St. John; better to stock up in St. Thomas or bring staples from home.

Gallows Point Suites   **$140–$360**   ★★★

Cruz Bay, ☎ *(800) 323-7229, (809) 776-6434.*
Single: $140–$325. Double: $170–$360.

All accommodations at this oceanfront resort are suites. Garden units have sunken living rooms, while the larger upper suites have loft bedrooms and two baths. All are spacious, with quality furnishings, fully equipped kitchens, living and dining rooms, and ceiling fans (no air conditioning, but breezes generally do the job.) There's a restaurant and two bars on the premises, and they'll shuttle you into town (a five-minute walk) for free. The beach is quite small, but the free-form pool is large and inviting. Very nice. No kinds under five. 60 rooms. Credit Cards: V, MC, DC, A.

Lavender Hill Estates   **$135–$265**   ★★

Cruz Bay, ☎ *(800) 562-1901, (809) 776-6969.*
Single: $135–$210. Double: $160–$265.

Set on a hillside within walking distance of Cruz Bay shops and restaurants, this complex offers condominium living. Each of the 12 units have full kitchens, nice views, spacious living rooms, and one or two bedrooms. All are quite nice and have TVs and phones, but rely on ceiling fans instead of air conditioners. There's a large pool on the premises. Credit Cards: V, MC, A.

Serendip Condominiums   **$90–$145**   ★

Cruz Bay.
Single: $90–$145. Double: $90–$145.

This secluded mountainside resort consists of eight one-bedroom units and two studios, each with kitchens, limited maid service, and dining areas. Furnishings are simple but adequate. There are no facilities on-site, but beaches and watersports can be found nearby at the national park. 10 rooms. Credit Cards: MC, A.

Inns

Two inns are available on the island; for a tad more sophistication (some private bathrooms), try the Inn at Tamarind Court, which comes with a complimentary breakfast.

Cruz Inn   **$55–$90**   ★

Cruz Bay, ☎ *(800) 666-7688, (809) 776-7688.*
Single: $55–$90. Double: $55–$90.

Accommodations at this basic guesthouse range from simple guest rooms with shared baths to efficiencies with private baths and kitchen facilities. You'll pay extra for air conditioning. Continental breakfast is served daily, and there is entertainment three times a week in the busy bar. Okay for the rates. 14 rooms. Credit Cards: MC, A.

Inn at Tamarind Court   **$40–$110**   ★★

Cruz Bay, ☎ *(809) 776-6378.*
Single: $40–$110. Double: $70–$110.

Most rooms for two at this simple spot are around $75, making it one of St. John's least-expensive properties. Most share baths and seem to be decorated with garage sale specials. There are also a few suites and a one-bedroom apartment. Despite its somewhat rundown accommodations, the Tamarind Court does a brisk business with penny-watching young people, and the atmosphere is friendly and fun. A bar and restaurant are on the premises. 20 rooms. Credit Cards: MC, A.

Raintree Inn   **$60–$115**   ★ ★

Cruz Bay, ☎ *(800) 666-7449, (809) 693-8590.*
Single: $60–$100. Double: $70–$115.

The rooms here are as simple as the rates suggest, but very comfortable and with private baths. No air conditioning, but each room has a ceiling fan. There are also loft bedrooms and kitchens in three of the units. Smoking is forbidden. The restaurant serves dinner only. Not bad for the price. 11 rooms. Credit Cards: CB, V, MC, A.

Low Cost Lodging

Camping is a popular alternative on St. John, since the park is so conducive to nights under (or at least near) the stars. Both Cinnamon Bay and Maho Bay campgrounds feature tent-type dwellings (Cinnamon Bay has a few cottages), cafeteria, communal bathrooms, and sports activities. Maho Bay even hosts marriages and offers massage facilities and a great view. Reserve both far in advance (in some cases, a year). Rooms in private rooms might be available, but check with the tourist office on arrival.

Cinnamon Bay Campground   **$15–$95**   ★ ★ ★

Cinnamon Beach, ☎ *(809) 776-6330.*
Single: $15–$95. Double: $30–$95.

Set in the woods in beautiful Virgin Islands National Park, this park-run campground offers everything from bare sites on which to pitch a tent to cottages with electricity, simple cooking facilities, and two trundle beds. There are also small tents with wooden floors that lack electricity but do have gas lanterns and stoves. Four bath houses provide toilets and showers. Meals can be had in the cafeteria. There's no pool, but the nearby beach is grand, and many watersports are complimentary. Two-week maximum stay. 113 rooms. Credit Cards: MC, A.

Campgrounds

Maho Bay Camp Resort   **$60–$90**   ★ ★ ★

Maho Bay.
Single: $60–$90. Double: $60–$90.

Set on 14 forested acres in the Virgin Islands National Park, this gorgeous spot is for nature lovers who like to camp without sacrificing too many creature comforts. Accommodations are in three-room tent-style cottages, with kitchenettes, a screened dining area, sofabeds, twin beds, living areas, private decks and electricity. Five communal bath houses have toilets and showers. The grounds include a sandy beach, simple restaurant and watersports. Each site is limited to two adults and two kids. Quite comfortable and nice, and very popular. 113 rooms. Credit Cards: Not Accepted.

Where to Eat

Highest Rated Restaurants in St. John

★★★★	Le Chateau de Bordeaux
★★★★	Paradiso
★★★	Chow Mein
★★★	Don Carlos
★★★	Ellington's
★★★	Garden of Luscious Licks
★★★	Mongoose
★★★	Morgan's Mango
★★★	Pussers
★★★	Sugar Mill

Most Exclusive Restaurants in St. John

★★★	Mongoose	$10–$50
★★★★	Le Chateau de Bordeaux	$18–$28
★★★	Ellington's	$17–$25
★★★	Chow Mein	$11–$24

Fielding's Best Value Restaurants in St. John

★★★	Vie's Snack Shack	$0–$0
★★★	Sugar Mill	$26–$32
★★★★	Paradiso	$17–$25
★★★	Mongoose	$10–$50
★★★	Garden of Luscious Licks	$5–$10

Restaurants in St. John favor American, British, West Indian and Italian cuisines. Atmosphere can range from an outdoor patio with neighborhood strays, a West Indian gingerbread house, the peak of a mountain, or the ruins of a sugar mill—almost all are open to the wind. The best selection is in Cruz Bay, where you can also find elegant dining. Outside Cruz Bay is **Le Chateaux de Bordeau**, the island's most ambitious restaurant, a comfortable low-ceiling room set atop the 1277-ft. **Bordeaux Mountain**, St. John's highest point; the menu ranges from scrumptious pumpkin soup to West Indian curry to Peking duck. Etta, at the Inn at Tamarind Court, is perfect for callaloo soup—a delicious, thick seafood porridge with okra and spinach—-and other West Indian delights. Remember **Morgan's Mango** for creative neo-Caribbean cuisine in a gingerbread setting. One of the most romantic settings on the island is Caneel Bay's **Sugar Mill**, a pretty stone building open to the fresh air. Their pan-fried flying fish makes a memory. For a quick, agreeable pub lunch in Cruz Bay, try **Pusser's** waterfront balcony.

Cafe Roma $$ ★★

Cruz Bay, ☎ *(809) 776-6524.*
Italian cuisine. Specialties: Pizza, shrimp with garlic sauce.
Dinner: 5:00 p.m.–10:00 p.m., entrees $11–$16.
A touch of Italy in the tropics, this pretty trattoria overlooks the sights and sounds of Cruz Bay from a second-floor perch. No slouch on gustatory or olfactory senses either, the place is noted for dynamite pizza—there's a choice of a white or traditional tomato sauce as a base for several tasty toppings. Seafood is also a standout, especially shrimp with garlic sauce. An excellent choice for a varied selection of tropical drinks. Credit Cards: V, MC.

Chow Mein $$$ ★★★

Great Cruz Bay, ☎ *(809) 693-8000.*
International cuisine.
Dinner: 6:00 p.m.–9:30 p.m., entrees $11–$24.
This restaurant's name has changed a few times since its inception (it used to be called Ciao Mein), but the cuisine atop the sprawling, atrium-style Hyatt Regency St. John has remained a successful melange of Asian and Italian culinary concoctions. Guests can watch the lobby action below while dining on wok-stirred seafood, pot stickers, or pasta with vegetables. Associated Hotel: Hyatt Regency. Closed: Sun. Reservations recommended. Credit Cards: V, MC, DC, A.

Don Carlos $$ ★★★

10-19 Estate Carolina, ☎ *(809) 776-6866.*
Mexican cuisine.
Lunch: 11:00 a.m.–4:00 p.m., entrees $9–$17.
Dinner: 4:00 p.m.–9:00 p.m., entrees $9–$17.
This upscale cantina buzzes with zingy waiters delivering foaming margaritas and zippy fajitas (this stateside chain is famous for them) to happy customers. Don Carlos also features lots of lively entertainment three nights a week. You might see

island favorites like conch fritters slipped in here and there on the menu along with south of the border staples. Credit Cards: V, MC, A.

Ellington's $$$ ★★★

Gallows' Point, ☎ *(809) 693-8490.*
International cuisine.
Dinner: 6:00 p.m.–10:00 p.m., entrees $17–$25.

Some of the best seafood on the island is prepared here at this view spot positioned near the ferry dock. On a clear day, you can see St. Thomas from a front-row seat on the terrace. After a tasty drink, dine on hearty seafood chowder followed by the daily special, which could be blackened something, or shrimp in an exotic fruit sauce. A light breakfast is also served from 8 to 10 a.m. Associated Hotel: Gallows Point Resort. Reservations required. Credit Cards: V, MC, A.

Garden of Luscious Licks $ ★★★

Main Street, Cruz Bay, ☎ *(809) 776-6070.*
American cuisine.
Lunch: entrees $5–$10.
Dinner: entrees $5–$10.

It's named after the ice cream—specifically the many flavors of Ben and Jerry's cones and sundaes offered here. Serving mainly vegetarian specialties, Licks resembles a funky big-city coffeehouse. It's a welcome haven for folks who want to read the paper and munch on a dairy-free muffin or a meatless burger. Surroundings are a little cramped, so you may want to consider it for takeout. Credit Cards: Not Accepted.

Le Chateau de Bordeaux $$$ ★★★★

Junction 10, Centerline Road, Bordeaux Mountain, ☎ *(809) 779-4078.*
French cuisine. Specialties: Banana, papaya and conch fritters, saffron pasta.
Lunch: 11:00 a.m.–4:00 p.m., entrees $6–$8.
Dinner: 5:30 p.m.–8:45 p.m., entrees $18–$28.

This petite dazzler clings to the cliffs of Bordeaux Mountain in the center of the islands, and its terrace commands an unparalleled view of the last rays of the setting sun. Despite its unprepossessing exterior, within are tables laid with hand-crocheted cloths, and the cozy room is illuminated by oil lanterns. It's no surprise many honeymooners end up here. Cuisine is island-inspired and creative, and fresh seafood is delivered daily to the kitchen door. Reservations required. Credit Cards: V, MC, DC.

Mongoose $$$ ★★★

Mongoose Junction, Mongoose Junction, ☎ *(809) 693-8677.*
International cuisine.
Lunch: 11:30 a.m.–5:00 p.m., entrees $6–$10.
Dinner: 5:00 p.m.–10:00 p.m., entrees $10–$50.

A pleasant refueling spot for tired shoppers souvenir hunting at the Tony Mongoose Junction arcade, this eatery and bar offers a bevy of cooling fruity alcoholic drinks and plates of fresh seafood. Patrons poise themselves on a tree-shaded wooden deck or at the bar, which serves light meals until midnight. Reservations recommended. Credit Cards: V, MC, DC, A.

Morgan's Mango $$ ★★★

Cruz Bay, ☎ *(809) 693-8141.*

Latin American cuisine.
Dinner: 6:00 p.m.– 10:00 p.m., entrees $7–$22.
There's often a crowd at this very popular dining spot in a gingerbread trimmed-house painted in pastels. One reason is an excellent bar and unusual Argentinian specialties interspersed with local seafood and chicken. Another is the woodsy patio where guests sit surrounded by trees and greenery. A plate-crowding hunk of prime beef comes accompanied by the piquant Pampas-style chimmichurri sauce—a spicy melding of oregano, peppers, lots of garlic and olive oil. Reservations recommended. Credit Cards: Not Accepted. Credit Cards: V, MC, A.

Paradiso **$$$** ★ ★ ★ ★

Mongoose Junction, Mongoose Junction, ☎ (809) 693-8899.
Italian cuisine. Specialties: Lobster fra diavolo.
Dinner: 6:00 p.m.–10:00 p.m., entrees $17–$25.
The words "suave" and "chic" appropriately describe this Italian restaurant all dolled up in burnished woods and marble. Dine in air-conditioned comfort on lobster or a daily seafood special prepared with their signature fra diavolo sauce. Paradiso also has an impressive wine list and well-mixed drinks. Reservations recommended. Credit Cards: V, MC, A.

Pussers **$$$** ★ ★ ★

Wharfside Village, ☎ (809) 693-9080.
International cuisine. Specialties: Mud pie.
Lunch: 11:00 a.m.–6:00 p.m., entrees $6–$10.
Dinner: 6:00 p.m.–10:00 p.m., entrees $15–$25.
The purveyors of the British Royal Navy's favorite rum have been successful in expanding their small chain of souvenir shops/pub establishments into U.S. Virgin territory with this open-air crowd pleaser. Offering special meal deals that should satisfy all but the very fussy, there are all-you-can-eat Alaskan king crab nights on Friday and Caribbean specials on Thursdays. Sandwiches, seafood plates, and gooey desserts are also available, including the famous mud pie. Reservations recommended. Credit Cards: V, MC, A.

Sugar Mill **$$$** ★ ★ ★

Caneel Bay, ☎ (809) 776-6111.
International cuisine.
Dinner: 6:30 p.m.–9:00 p.m., entrees $26–$32.
Dine in a restored horse-powered sugar mill located on the Caneel Bay Resort grounds. It's a cavernous round room with a large terrace where many patrons begin their meals with a luscious peach daiquiri. The seafood served here nightly is very well-regarded, and non-guests can also enjoy a West-Indian buffet lunch. Associated Hotel: Caneel Bay Hotel. Closed: Mon. Reservations recommended. Credit Cards: V, MC, DC, A.

The Lime Inn **$$** ★ ★

Cruz Bay, ☎ (809) 776-6425.
International cuisine. Specialties: All-you-can-eat shrimp.
Lunch: 11:30 a.m.– 3:00 p.m., entrees $3–$10.
Dinner: 5:30 p.m.– 10:00 p.m., entrees $3–$20.

The local practice of *limin'* is strictly adhered to here (it means "hanging out") and the congenial group of limers include veteran travelers" as well as residents. Settle for a terrace seat to while away the hours with a bowl of goat water, seafood, or a sandwich. Hungry bargain hunters crowd the place Wednesday nights for the well-regarded, all-you-can-eat shrimp extravaganza, but no reservations are taken, so line up early. Closed: Sun. Reservations required. Credit Cards: V, MC, A.

Vie's Snack Shack $ ★ ★ ★

East End, ☎ *(809) 693-5033.*
Latin American cuisine.
Lunch: 10:00 a.m.–5:00 p.m., entrees $2–$6.
This is probably the best local cooking in town—but it's only open four days a week, and only for lunch. But if you're in town when Vie's at the stove, don't miss it for fritters both sweet and savory, homemade fruit drinks and spicy chicken. Closed: Mon, Fri, Sun. Credit Cards: Not Accepted.

Where to Shop

Duty-free shopping is the major incentive to pull out your wallet here, and aside from attractive pricing on watches, china, gems, electronics and jewelry, there is no sales tax and a $1200 per person exemption from duty when returning to the U.S. Liquor is also a bargain and anyone over 21 years of age can return to the States with five bottles duty-free (or six, if one is produced in the USVI). Island clothing and t-shirts are also good buys. Stop by Bamboula in Mongoose Junction for ethnic folk art and artifacts.

St. John Directory

ARRIVAL

For North America, the major carriers are American, Continental, Delta, and U.S. Air, with Tower Air scheduled several times each week out of New York's JFK Airport, and TWA connecting via Puerto Rico. Some arrivals will first stop at St. Thomas and some will stop first on St. Croix, but with only 32 miles separating the two islands, both are included on most itineraries. Virtually any North American gateway provides easy access to the USVI. In addition to these air arrivals, about one-half of the 1.8 million visitors to these islands arrive via cruise ships, most of which dock in St. Thomas Harbor at Charlotte Amalie.

For interisland air transport, both Sunaire and American Eagle fly between St. Croix and St. Thomas offering hourly departures all day long. There is no airstrip on St. John but ferryboat rides from downtown and Red Hook on St. Thomas operate on an hourly basis until 11:00 p.m. Schedules are subject to change and not every carrier operates every day, so for more complete and current information, on USVI travel connection, call ☎ *800-USVI-INFO*.

CLIMATE

Temperatures during the summer, cooled by eastern trade winds, keep the temperature around 82 degrees F. Brief showers also keep things cool. Winter temperatures rise to 77 degrees F. Rainiest months are September-January, and about 40 inches of rainfall per year. April-August are the calmest sea conditions with the best visibility, although days of stunning clarity in excess of 100 feet are not unusual in winter.

DOCUMENTS

U.S. citizens need not carry a passport, although some proof of identity will be required upon leaving the islands. A passport is a good idea since the nearby British Virgin Islands are so accessible from St. John and St. Thomas. If you wish to dive the Rhone or snorkel amid the fantastic granite boulders at the baths on Virgin Gorda, you'll need to first clear BVI Customs with a passport and an $8 entry fee.

ELECTRICITY

Current runs at 110 volts at 60 cycles.

GETTING AROUND

Many rental companies in Cruz Bay offer competitive rates. Expect to pay roughly $60 per day, plus gas and insurance, for a Suzuki Sidekick (with four-wheel drive to accommodate blind switchbacks and extreme mountain inclines). And be prepared to drive on the left.

LANGUAGE

The official language is English. Some locals speak a musical patois called English Creole—a blend of English, African and Spanish. Many people also speak good Spanish.

MEDICAL EMERGENCIES

Police ext. *915*, fire ext. *921*, ambulance ext. *922*.

MONEY

The official currency is the U.S. dollar.

TELEPHONE

The area code is 809. Since USVI is an incorporated territory, toll-free numbers that operate in the U.S. work here, normal postage rates apply. You can also direct dial to the mainland.

TIME

Atlantic Standard Time, one hour later than New York City; during daylight saving time, it is the same as New York.

TIPPING AND TAXES

Some hotels include a 10–15 percent service charge; this should include all tips for both restaurant and room service, unless the attention was extraordinary. If no service is added, leave a 15 percent tip for the waitress, $1–2 a day to the maid; bartenders and wine stewards should be tipped always. Tip the bellboy and porter at least 50 cents a bag. Taxi drivers should receive a 15 percent tip if you are satisfied with the service.

TOURIST INFORMATION

The St. John Tourist Office ☎ *724-3816* is located around the corner from the Cruz Bay ferry dock by the post office. It is open daily.

WHEN TO GO

St. John's Carnival events take place from June 18-July 4, including a food fair, boat races, and the recreation of a carnival village. The St. John Carnival Parade takes place on July 4.

The area code is *809*. Since USVI is an incorporated territory, toll-free numbers that operate in the U.S. work here, normal postage rates apply. You can also direct dial to the mainland.

ST. JOHN HOTELS		RMS	RATES	PHONE	FAX
Coral Bay					
★★★★★	**Caneel Bay Resort**	171	$225–$695	(800) 928-8889	809 693 8280
★★★★★	**Hyatt Regency St. John**	285	$195–$515	(800) 233-1234	809 693 8888
★★★	**Cinnamon Bay Campground**	113	$15–$95	(809) 776-6330	(809) 776-6458
★★★	**Gallows Point Suites**	60	$140–$360	(800) 323-7229	809 776 6520
★★★	**Maho Bay Camp Resort**	113	$60–$90		809 776 6504
★★	**Inn at Tamarind Court**	20	$40–$110	(809) 776-6378	
★★	**Lavender Hill Estates**		$135–$265	(800) 562-1901	(809) 776-6969
★★	**Raintree Inn**	11	$60–$115	(800) 666-7449	(809) 693-8590
★	**Cruz Inn**	14	$55–$90	(800) 666-7688	
★	**Serendip Condominiums**	10	$90–$145		

ST. JOHN RESTAURANTS		LOCATION	PHONE	ENTREE
Coral Bay				
American				
★★★	**Garden of Luscious Licks**	Cruz Bay	(809) 776-6070	$5–$10

ST. JOHN RESTAURANTS	LOCATION	PHONE	ENTREE
French			
★★★★ Le Chateau de Bordeaux	Bordeaux Mountain	(809) 779-4078	$6–$28
International			
★★★ Chow Mein	Coral Bay	(809) 693-8000	$11–$24••
★★★ Ellington's	Coral Bay	(809) 693-8490	$17–$25••
★★★ Mongoose	Mongoose Junction	(809) 693-8677	$6–$50
★★★ Pussers	Coral Bay	(809) 693-9080	$6–$25
★★★ Sugar Mill	Coral Bay	(809) 776-6111	$26–$32••
★★ The Lime Inn	Coral Bay	(809) 776-6425	$3–$20
Italian			
★★★★ Paradiso	Mongoose Junction	(809) 693-8899	$17–$25••
★★ Cafe Roma	Coral Bay	(809) 776-6524	$11–$16••
Latin American			
★★★ Morgan's Mango	Coral Bay	(809) 693-8141	$7–$22••
★★★ Vie's Snack Shack	Coral Bay	(809) 693-5033	•$2–$6
Mexican			
★★★ Don Carlos	Coral Bay	(809) 776-6866	$9–$17

Note: • Lunch Only

       •• Dinner Only

ST. KITTS

Untrammeled by tourism, St. Kitts is a stunning combination of volcanic mountains, rain forest and golden beaches.

Imagine empty beaches, the lushest of flora, dark, humid rainforests, spectacular dive sites, and even fat black ladies sashaying down country roads with pumpkin-sized washing atop their proud heads—St. Kitts has a little something for everybody. With its sister island Nevis, St. Kitts forms a Caribbean nation that just declared its first decade of independence, but the pace of life hasn't changed here in centuries. The epitome of the "limin' life," Kittian culture is still propelled by that "stop for a beer anytime" attitude—an almost ecological spirit, since, despite a lot of dream schemes, the coastline hasn't yet been marred by too much construction. Simply, unhampered tranquility reigns in St. Kitts, and the noisiest thing you'll ever hear will be the gentle skittering of the surf across the black and blonde sands. At one time, St. Kitts was distinguished only by its array of small inns fashioned from old plantations. Today, after the once-pristine Frigate Bay has been developed into an enclave of condos and package-tour hotels, Kittians are understandably nervous about change, even as the island struggles to recover from losses incurred from the demise of Pan Am, the Iraqi War and 1989's Hurricane Hugo, which did serious damage. Nevertheless, there's an unmistakable stir in the breezy Kitts air, and new luxury hotels are not the only signs of resurgence. A waterfront warehouse has been restyled into a lively duty-free mall, and concerned citizens are busily recycling fine old buildings in the capital city into boutiques, restaurants and offices. With just a few more trendy stores and cafes added to its vast array of water activities, St. Kitts could easily become the next Caribbean nexus.

Bird's Eye View

Part of the northern chain of the Leeward Islands in the Eastern Caribbean St. Kitts covers an area of 68 square miles, divided by three volcanic mountains split by deep ravines and a low-lying peninsula in the southeast. From the air, both St. Kitts and Nevis look like two green blips floating between St. Martin and Montserrat. St.Kitt's curious layout—three islands in one—recalls the shape over an oversized tennis racket. The "head" to the northwest is dominated by the 3793-ft. **Mount Liamuiga** and a rainforest ringed by sugarcane plantations and a rugged shoreline; the neck is a low-lying isthmus known as **Frigate Bay;** and the "grip" is the hilly southwest peninsula, until 1992 reachable only by boat or four-wheel-drive buggy. For many years the Southeast Peninsula was considered the "Caribbean Shangri-La," blessed with palm-fringed coves that resemble lagoons, rugged, lush topography and a large salt pond. Today the peninsula is also a reserve for many of the green vervet monkeys and white-tailed deer that roam about.

The "last frontier of the Caribbean" was considered to be the beach of Sir Timothy Hill, once approachable only by a rugged stony trail that led to the southernmost tip of St. Kitts. The massive natural barrier, covered with steep slopes, thorn bushes and spiky acacia trees has daunted many a bather in search of the 23 beautiful peninsula beaches that had nearly become legend. Today the seven-mile Dr. Kennedy Simmonds Highway allows motorists to

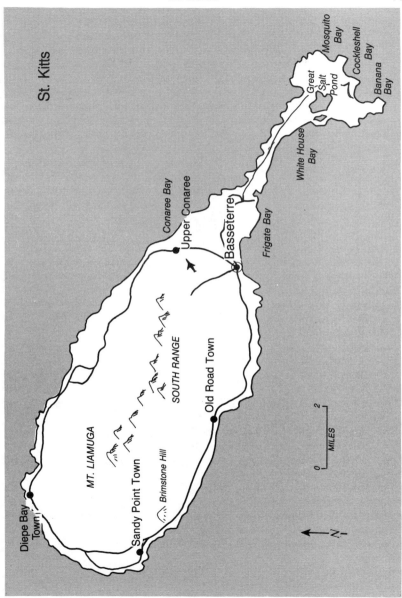

St. Kitts

traverse the hill in minutes. To preserve the pristine beaches, only a few select hotels have been allowed to build on the site.

St.Kitt's capital of **Basseterre** (pop. 20,000) seems to boom with an irrepressible West Indian vigor. The traffic police are crisply dressed, reggae blasts from music stores and cafes. Already being built is a $16.23-million deep-water cruiseship facility, which will include an expanded shopping area and sailing; the position allows debarking passengers to step off their ships and find themselves less than a block away from the Berkeley Memorial Clock.

History

Columbus first sighted the island of St. Kitts, dubbing it —with a touch of self-aggrandizement—St. Christopher. (The title was later shortened to St. Kitts by British tobacco planters, who ignored Spanish claims and moved in with their African slaves.) For years the island remained lost in obscurity, inhabited by cohiba-smoking Carib Indians who found nourishment from the island in the form of turtles, iguanas and mawby liquor. In 1623, a daring group of settlers led by Sir Thomas Warner, plopped themselves on the island, soon having to share the beach uneasily with some French colonists. On June 20, 1690, during a French occupation, the Englishman Sir Thomas Thornhill led a party of soldiers in the dead of night through Friars Bay and over a rocky hill full of thorn bushes and spiky acacia trees to catch the French sentries off guard, who thought the British could only attack from the sea. After taking Basseterre, the island's main city, the English troops spiked the fortress cannons so that other English troops could land in safety. (The hill was later named Sir Timothy in honor of Thornhill, but remains a daunting natural barrier, stretching from steep cliffs on the Atlantic to even steeper cliffs on the Caribbean. (The 1783 Treaty of Versailles finally awarded sovereignty to the Brits.) Independent from Britain since 1983, St. Kitts is dealing peacefully with the challenges of economy, but still maintain affectionate ties with the mother country. In fact, Queen Elizabeth II visited St. Kitts in 1985 and her portrait continues to grace island bank notes.

Jewish communities on both islands can be traced back to the 17th century.The earliest date on the nineteen tombstones in the Jewish cemetery on Nevis goes back to the 1680s, and records in England suggest that the Nevis synagogue is older than the 1732 synagogue in Curaçao. Recently, a "mikvah," or ritual bath, was discovered by an island historian. When large populations of Jews fled to the islands to escape the Spanish Inquisition, the majority of those who came to Nevis were from Brazil.

People

Friendly and cricket-loving, Kittians are still living the remains of British gentility at the same time catering to the Caribbean rhythm of life. A little fishing, a little gardening, long pauses to chat—that's the pattern of a day's dally. Kittians were delighted with Queen Elizabeth's comments about the unspoiled beauty, an opinion shared by Christopher Columbus. The beauty, however, seems to have dazzled residents into a slumber that doesn't inspire too much art. A few are notable like the sculptor Valentine Brown, who lives in Dieppe Bay and is known for his finely crafted sculptures of faces and figures out of cedar. Style in St. Kitts is casual, but tourists are advised not to wear short shorts, bikinis, or bare chests in public places. Today, the British are still aground, running many of the inns and hotels on the island.

Beaches

Most of the Kittian beaches are a dramatic black, born from rich volcanic sand, although the beaches at Frigate Bay and Salt Pond, on the southern peninsula, are brilliantly white. The best beaches are generally located in the south—**Major's Bay**. **Banana Bay**, **Cockleshell Bay**, and **Mosquito Bay**—connected today by a new road that makes them fully accessible. Talcum white beaches can also be found in the southeast peninsula. Most of the watersports activities are centered around Frigate Bay, and swimming is especially good, as is snorkeling. Banana Bay and Cockleshell Bay are twin beaches, where conditions are also excellent for swimming, and there are cottage beach resorts with watersports facilities operated by Ocean Terrace Inn in Basseterre. Conaree Beach, two miles from Basseterre, and Friar's Bay, a peninsula where you can see the Atlantic and the Caribbean meet, are also considered user-friendly. Although all beaches are public, you may have to pay a small fee to use the facilities of a hotel located on the beach you choose. (For beaches in Nevis, see the chapter on Nevis.)

The southern beaches of St. Kitts, Frigate Bay and Salt Pond, have long been considered the "Caribbean Shangri-La."

Dive Sites

The western (or Caribbean) side of St. Kitts and Nevis is more protected and offers huge sections of reef that begin in shallow water and fall off to depths of 100 feet or more. A quick boat ride is all that's needed to reach most sites. However, rain runoff from the volcanic mountains tends to make water near the shore murky, so your best bet is to dive a mile or further offshore. **Black Coral Reef** is a great opportunity to witness the rare black coral, which is made into stunning jewelry in the Caribbean. The reef begins at 40 feet and descends to 70 feet. **Bloody Bay Reef** is laced with small caves filled with purple anemones, yellow sea fans, and rust-colored bristle worms. The reef ranges from 60–80 feet. The area is also good for catching snapper. **Booby Island**, in the channel, sports numerous marine life, with large schools of jacks and snappers. **Monkey Reef**, situated off the western coast of St. Kitts' Southeast Peninsula, gives roost to lobster, rays, lizard fish, and a nurse shark or two. Only experienced divers should dive in **Nags Head**, a meeting place of the Caribbean and the Atlantic, where the currents are strong and the reef plunges to 80 feet. New divers would enjoy **Coconut Tree Reef**, one of the largest reefs in the area, ranging from 20–200 feet in depth.

The largest reef is **Grid Iron**, a long barrier reef that stretches over six miles from Conaree on the east coast of St. Kitts to Newcastle Bay on Nevis at depths varying from 6–50 feet. The waters here are chock full of angelfish and other species common to the area. Thick black coral predominates in the southern side of the reef, known as **Monkey Shoals**.

History has shown that at least 300 ships have sunk in the neighboring water, although only about eight have been discovered. Of the four marked wrecks, **Brassball** is particularly good for snorkeling and photography

The Pro-Divers shop, which is the first PADI instruction center on the island, operates fully certified resort diving facilities out of Turtle Beach and from the Ocean Terrace Inn's Fisherman Wharf's restaurant, located not far from the hotel at water's edge in Pelican Cove.

Treks

Walking is a major form of transport on St. Kitts, so with a map tightly held in your hands, you shouldn't have any trouble navigating the ups and downs of the highlands and lowlands. (Contact the tourist board for a good one.) Fabulous treks can be made straight into the rainforest and around the sides of the volcano, but in the mountains, however, you should never hike without a guide because some trails have become dangerous, overgrown with vegetation and slippery after a rainfall.

The macho hiker's dream is to scale the heights of the famous **Mt. Liamuiga**, formerly (and for good reason) known as Mount Misery. The actual peak is located to the rest of the volcanic crater, surrounded in elfin woodland. To reach the lip of the crater, you must hike through dense rainforest, though the coastal views are terrific. To scale the peak of Mt. Liamuiga, you must begin from the north end of the island at Belmont Estate, where a dirt road leads eventually to the trail that continues through rainforest and along deep ravines—about a 2 1/2-hour hike. Expect a real jungle experience—wildlife encounters, steep ascents, slopes where you will have to hang onto vines for dear life. Always inquire about conditions before you start out, and if you go without a guide (not suggested for beginning hikers), you must arrange transportation for your return from Belmont Estate to your starting base. Clearest conditions usually occur in February, March, and June, when the views of St. Kitts, Saba and St. Eustatius, can be miraculous. Dress for both rain and cold, and make sure you are wearing sturdy (preferably) lightweight hiking boots. There are a number of organized walking tours which are, in general, much safer than going on your own.

Northern St. Kitts is dominated by Mount Liamuiga and a rugged shoreline.

Hikers also head to **Dos d'Anse Pond** at Verchilds Mountain, accessible from the Wingfield, Molineaux and Lambert estates. The hike on an unmarked trail leads up steep mountain slopes through seasonal evergreen forest on the lower slopes and tropical rain forest in the higher ones. Beyond the pool is a half-mile, truly treacherous hike through tangled vines and elfin woodland to the summit of the mountain. A local guide is required for these treks since the lack of clear demarcation can lead to trouble.

There are six salt ponds that grace the island, the largest, **Great Salt Pond**, located in the south between Sand Bank Bay and Major's Bay. Ornithologists are beginning to identify the numerous birds which alight here, which include Wilson's plover, black-necked stilts, purple-throated caribs, and red knots. Excellent trails for observing nature can be found in the southwest peninsula, where you might glimpse a Kittian green monkey and deer.

What Else to See

St.Kitt's capital of Basseterre (pop. 20,00) is in the midst of a booming revival. Decimated by fire in 1867 and rebuilt in the Franco-British colonial style, Basseterre today boasts such delightful Caribbean nuances as high-pitched, no-awning roofs (to lessen their vulnerability in storms); shutters (to reduce sun glare but retain the essential movement of air through the hot interior spaces); and occasional outbursts of carpenter Gothic trim. Many of the renovations are due to the efforts of the "Basseterre Beautiful" organization which is working hard to restore sections of the old town, opening up new stores and courtyard cafes, and keeping the frilly, high-roofed architecture. A bit of the old St. Kitts can be seen in **St. George's Anglican Church**; its wood pews and dusty gravestones in the unruly cemetery point to another era. History buffs interested in the archaeological dig undertaken on the supposed site of a 17th century synagogue in Nevis should contact the historian **Dr. Vincent K. Hubbard in St. Kitts** ☎ *(809) 469-1817*, FAX *(809) 469-1794.*

Brimstone Hill Fortress, the most photographed tourist attraction on St. Kitts is considered one of the most magnificent fortresses in the West Indies—the second largest of its kind in the hemisphere. Set on a mountainous ridge of volcanic origin, the fortress was adapted to the existing geological conditions of the hill, giving it a maximum potential for defense. Walking around the ruins, only partially restored and deep in weeds, you can easily imagine the violent struggles waged here between the British and the French, the latter who thought they captured the "Gilbralter of the West Indies" in 1782, only to be ejected for the final time a year later. If you climb the hefty staircase, you'll discover a small museum that gives an overview of the island, and you'll be able to inspect the cannon; if you're lucky, you might even be visited by a local Vervet monkey. The view from here gives a marvelous panorama of the ocean and the two cone-shaped islands of Saba and St. Eustatius.

Old Carib rock drawings can be found in **Old Road Town Village** and the ravine at **Bloody Point**, where over 2000 Indians died in a massacre in 1626.

Twenty minutes north of Basseterre, along the west coast, stands the **Romney Manor**, home of **Caribelle Batik**, where island craftswomen use Indonesian techniques to create a dazzling array of fabrics and clothes unique to the

Caribbean. Also, make a tour of the sugar refinery and taste the pride and joy of Baron Edmund de Rothschild, who distills his own subtle brand of CSR (Cane Spirits Rothschild).

For trekking possibilities, see the section under "Treks" above.

Historical Sites

Brimstone ★★★★★

Main Street, Basseterre.
Hours Open: 9:30 a.m.–5:00 p.m.
This national park houses one of the Caribbean's largest and best-preserved fortresses, called the "Gilbralter of the West Indies" due to its sheer size. It dates back to 1690, covers 38 acres, and saw several skirmishes between the French and the British, who alternated in their control of the fort. Today it is quite nicely restored, and you can see the officer's quarters, barracks, hospital and kitchen. A museum is devoted to military history. The park also includes numerous nature trails through its dense vegetation and stunning views of neighboring islands. General admission: $5.00.

Romney Manor ★★★★

Old Road, Basseterre, ☎ *(809) 465-6253.*
Hours Open: 8:30 a.m.–4:00 p.m.
Romney Manor is a beautifully restored 17th-century plantation great house, and is home to Caribelle Batik. You can watch local artists produce batik clothing and wall hangings in the same way it's been done for more than 2000 years. Prepare to drop a bundle in the duty-free shop. One of the best reasons to come is to stroll the ground's five acres of colorful gardens. The highlight is a saman tree said to be 350 years old. Free admission.

Sports

Watersports activities on St. Kitts are focused on Frigate Bay, where you find options from sailing to scuba to windsurfing. Facilities for nearly any sport can be found at the **Jack Tar Village**; the 18-hole Trent Jones-designed golf course is particularly popular. The best locations for windsurfing are **Banana Bay** and **Frigate Bay** and equipment may be rented from watersports operators at hotels and resorts. The coast from Cades Bay and Oualie Beach to Newcastle is also excellent for windsurfing due to strong winds. Tennis courts can also be found there, as well as a few other resorts. Chartering a one-day cruise on a sailboat (picnic included) to Nevis is a wonderful way to spend the day. Horseback riding on St. Kitts can take the form of half-day outings available in Conaree from **The Stable at Trinity Inn**. Inquire whether the sport has been taken up again in the southeastern peninsula, temporarily stopped due to construction in the area.

Horseback Riding

Various locations, Basseterre.
Several outfits offer trail rides along the beach or through the rainforest: **Royal Stables** *(☎ 465-2222)* and **Trinity Stable** *(☎ 465-3226).*

Royal St. Kitts Golf Club

Adjacent to Jack Tar Village, Frigate Bay, ☎ *(809) 465-8339.*
Hours Open: 7:00 a.m.–6:00 p.m.
St. Kitts' lone golf outlet is an 18-hole championship course designed by Robert Trent Jones. Greens fee are about $30. General admission: $35.00.

Watersports

Various locations, Basseterre.
General watersports equipment and instruction can be found at **R.G. Watersports** *(☎ 465-8050)* and **Pro-Divers** *(☎ 465-3223).* **Tropical Tours** *(☎ 465-4167)* and **Pelican Cove Marina** *(☎ 465-2754)* offer deep-sea fishing excursions. For scuba diving, try **Kenneth's Dive Center** *(☎ 465-7043)* and **Pro-Divers** *(☎ 465-3223).* For boating and cruising, call **Kantours** *(☎ 465-2098),* **Leeward Island Charters** *(☎ 465-7474),* and **Tropical Tours** *(☎ 465-4039).*

Where to Stay

Highest Rated Hotels in St. Kitts

★★★★ **Ottley's Plantation Inn**

★★★★ **Rawlins Plantation**

★★★ **Frigate Bay Beach Hotel**

★★★ **Golden Lemon Inn & Villas**

★★★ **Jack Tar Village**

★★★ **Ocean Terrace Inn**

★★★ **St. Christopher Club**

★★★ **White House**

Most Exclusive Hotels in St. Kitts

★★★ **Golden Lemon Inn & Villas**	$175–$950
★★★★ **Ottley's Plantation Inn**	$155–$460
★★★★ **Rawlins Plantation**	$175–$380
★★★ **Jack Tar Village**	$110–$340

Fielding's Best Value Hotels in St. Kitts

★★★ **White House**	$270–$375
★★★★ **Ottley's Plantation Inn**	$155–$460
★★★ **Golden Lemon Inn & Villas**	$175–$950
★★★ **Jack Tar Village**	$110–$340

While the inns of St. Kitts offer unique and intimate vacation experiences, diversified accommodations are increasing, from the familiar hotels of Basseterre (**The Ocean Terrace Inn** and **Fort Thomas Hotel**) to the burgeoning condo resorts along the vast beach of Frigate Bay (where the **Jack Tar Village Beach Resort and Casino** typifies the luxury of the Carib's all-inclusives) to the major complexes like **Hyatt Regency** and the couples-only **FDR Resort** in the Southwest Peninsula, recently linked to the rest of the island by an ambitiously engineered, but scenic new "highway of progress." In general, standards of rooms and cuisine are generally high, although air-conditioning is not always available, particularly in the old plantation inns. A few of the 35 sugar mill ruins have been converted to guest accommodations, such as the honeymoon suites of **Olden Rock Estate** on Nevis and **Rawlins Plantation** on St. Kitts. In Nevis, **Pinney's Beach Hotel** and the **Four Seasons Resort** are the only two properties located on the coconut palm-lined Pinney's Beach overlooking the narrow of St. Kitts.

Hotels and Resorts

The **Jack Tar Village at Frigate Bay** is the island's premier all-inclusive, about twenty minutes from the airport. Because of the private country club atmosphere, most clients stay a week, or even longer. Nearby, the Colony's **Timothy** beach resort, on one of the finest beaches on St. Kitts, is also near the golf course. **Ocean Terrace Inn** has a marvelous honeymoon package which includes seven nights with an ocean view, a romantic Saturday evening gourmet dinner, a bottle of wine, welcoming cocktail, champagne served in the Jacuzzi, local fruit basket, a hard-day rainforest tour, and airport transfers. You can also receive a $375 "Get Married on St. Kitts" supplement that includes legal documents, a minister, bouquet and boutonniere. Resorts in the Southeast Peninsula, Casablanca, and Sandals (the 275-room Kittian cousin of Jamaica's highly successful couples-only resorts) should open sometime in 1995.

Bird Rock Beach Hotel   **$75–$310**   ★★

Basseterre, ☎ *(809) 465-8914.*
Single: $75–$180. Double: $85–$310.

This small hotel is located on a bluff near the sea, one mile from town. Accommodations are in one- or two-room units with air conditioning, balconies and cable TV; some have kitchens. Two restaurants serve continental and local cuisine, and there are also two bars a pool and a tennis court on the premises. The beach is especially good for snorkeling. 38 rooms. Credit Cards: V, MC, A.

Casablanca Resort   **$240–$355**   ★★

Cockleshell Bay, ☎ *(800) 231-1945, (809) 497-6999.*
Single: $240–$355. Double: $240–$355.

This new resort is on the island's southeast peninsula, facing a white sand beach. Accommodations are in air-conditioned suites or villas, all with living rooms, minibars, VCRs, refrigerators and balconies. On-site facilities include three restaurants, two bars, a stylish lobby, pool, fitness center, and six tennis courts. 66 rooms. Credit Cards: MC, A.

Fort Thomas Hotel   **$75–$115**   ★★

Basseterre, ☎ *(800) 851-7818, (809) 465-2695.*
Single: $75–$90. Double: $90–$115.

Built on the site of an old fort, this hotel reopened in 1993 after extensive renovations. It caters mainly to business travelers who don't mind the fact that the beach is four miles away (they'll shuttle you over for free). Guest rooms are spacious but nothing special, though you can count on modern amenities and good housekeeping. The dining room serves West Indian and international dishes. There's also a few bars and a pool. 64 rooms. Credit Cards: V, MC, A.

Jack Tar Village   **$110–$340**   ★★★

Frigate Bay, ☎ *(800) 999-9182, (809) 465-8651.*
Single: $110–$185. Double: $100–$340.

Set on 20 acres overlooking Lake Zuliani on the isthmus between the Caribbean and Atlantic, this is a popular all-inclusive resort. Guest rooms and suites are scattered about the grounds in two-story buildings. Rooms are simple but comfortable and have modern conveniences; the more expensive suites provide a higher level of pampering. Just about everything is included in the rates, from scuba lessons to tennis on four courts to nightly entertainment. Even the greens fees at a nearby golf course are covered—but you'll need your own cash in the casino. 244 rooms. Credit Cards: V, MC, A.

St. Christopher Club   **$100–$235**   ★★★

Frigate Bay, ☎ *(809) 465-4854.*
Single: $100–$175. Double: $135–$235.

This oceanfront hotel is located just outside of town. Accommodations range from traditional guest rooms to spacious studios to one- and two-bedroom suites with kitchenettes. All are pleasant and comfortable and have air conditioners, phones and TV. There's a restaurant, bar and pool on the premises. 32 rooms. Credit Cards: V, MC.

Timothy Beach Resort   **$105–$380**   ★★

Frigate Beach, ☎ *(800) 777-1700, (809) 465-8597.*
Single: $105–$190. Double: $105–$380.

This basic condominium complex is just off the beach. Accommodations range from standard guest rooms to one- and two-bedroom suites, some with full kitchens. All have air conditioning, phones, private balconies, and coffeemakers. There's a cafe and bar on-site, as well as an inviting pool and tennis court. Watersports await at the beach. Good value for the rates. 36 rooms. Credit Cards: V, MC, A.

Apartments and Condominiums

The recent trend in St. Kitts is to set up housekeeping along **Frigate Bay**, a fantastic beach area, in one of the many newly built apartment complexes. Some clusters have their own grocery, but food is never cheap on these islands, so bring your own necessities from home. Among the most elegantly furnished are the **Golden Lemon Villas**, created by the famous New York interior designer Arthur Leaman. Both the **Sun 'n Sand Beach** and **St. Christopher Beach Hotel** can take advantage of being near the facilities of the Jack Tar resort.

Frigate Bay Beach Hotel   **$75–$200**   ★★★

Frigate Bay, ☎ *(809) 465-8935.*
Single: $75–$150. Double: $100–$200.

Set right on the beach as the name implies, the condominium hotel consists of four three-story buildings that face either the pool or the hills. Accommodations are air conditioned and nicely done; many, but not all, have kitchens. There's a swim-up bar in the Olympic-size pool and a bar and restaurant on the premises. Watersports and an 18-hole golf course are within an easy walk. 64 rooms. Credit Cards: V, MC, A.

Island Paradise Village **$98–$285**

Frigate Bay, ☎ (809) 465-8035.
Single: $98–$170. Double: $155–$285.
This condominium complex on the beach consists of one- to three-bedroom units, all with fully equipped kitchens, living/dining areas, and balconies or patios. Some have TV and air conditioning, but not all, so be sure to make your reservations accordingly. There's a pool and Italian restaurant on the premises, while golf, tennis and a casino are within walking distance. 62 rooms. Credit Cards: Not Accepted.

Leeward Cove Condominiums **$50–$275**

Frigate Bay, ☎ (809) 465-8030.
Single: $50–$80. Double: $60–$275.
This condominium complex occupies five acres in the Frigate Bay area. All units are air-conditioned and have one or two bedrooms, full kitchens, living and dining areas, and patios or balconies. Some also have TVs and phones. Standard guest rooms are also available, for about $80 to $110 per couple. Guests who stay a week get a free rented car—not a bad deal. All can golf for free at the municipal course. There are no facilities on the premises, but many within an easy walk. 10 rooms. Credit Cards: V, MC, A.

Sun 'n Sand Beach Resort **$120–$250**

Frigate Bay, ☎ (809) 465-8037.
Single: $120–$150. Double: $120–$250.
Adjacent to Jack Tar Village, this complex consists of air-conditioned cottages that house studios or two-bedroom, two-bath units. All have phones, cable TV, kitchens and patios. There are two pools on-site (one for kids), two tennis courts, and a beach bar and restaurant. The golf course is just across the street, and restaurants and shops are within walking distance. A nice combination of self-catering and resort amenities. 68 rooms. Credit Cards: V, MC, DC, A.

Inns

A true "backwards in time" experience can be had in a number of great plantation houses now beautifully restored and converted into inns. American designer Arthur Leaman has worked his magic into the antique restoration at **Golden Lemon Inn**, though it remains an adults-only complex. A true West Indian feeling, congenial and without attitude, prevails at the **Rawlins Plantation**, also known for its excellent authentic cuisine. Only twelve rooms are available at **The White House**, giving an extra-intimate ambiance.

Fairview Inn **$75–$145** ★★

Base of Ottley's Mountain, ☎ (080) 223-9815, (809) 465-2472.
Single: $75–$145. Double: $75–$145.
Located some ten minutes from Basseterre, this complex consists of cottages set around an 18th-century great house. Guest rooms, housed in the cottages, are quite small and motel-like, but decent enough. Only some are air-conditioned, and not all have ceiling fans, so be sure to make your requests accordingly. The site includes

a pool, West Indian restaurant and a bar. You'll need a car to get around. 27 rooms.
Credit Cards: V, MC, A.

Golden Lemon Inn & Villas $175–$950   ★★★

Dieppe Bay, ☎ *(800) 633-7411, (809) 465-7260.*
Single: $175–$435. Double: $175–$950.
One of the best inns in all the Caribbean, the Golden Lemon is located on a black-
sand beach at St. Kitts' northwestern tip. Each of the 24 guest rooms are located in
the 18th-century great house, beautifully restored with lots of fine antiques. Each
room is individually furnished, all with smashing results, sporting antiques, Oriental
rugs, West Indian art, raised four-poster beds, ceiling fans (no air), and verandas.
The site also includes 14 villas, each with a private pool. Complementary afternoon
tea is a refined treat. Creole, American, and continental fare. There's also a pool and
tennis court. No kids under 18 allowed at this very tony operation. Those who
enjoy life's finer things will not be disappointed. 32 rooms. Credit Cards: V, MC, A.

Ocean Terrace Inn $76–$350   ★★★

Basseterre, ☎ *(800) 524- 512, (809) 465-2754.*
Single: $76–$175. Double: $100–$350.
This informal inn, set on lushly landscaped hilltop grounds, overlooks the bay.
Great sea views from all the air-conditioned rooms, which are modern and tasteful.
There's also several one- and two-bedroom apartments and six suites. Two restau-
rants and three bars keep guests sated. Facilities include two pools, a business center
and free transportation to the nearby beach at Turtle Bay, a 20-minute ride. Popular
especially with business travelers. 53 rooms. Credit Cards: V, MC, DC, A.

Ottley's Plantation Inn $155–$460   ★★★★

Basseterre, ☎ *(800) 772-3039, (809) 465-7234.*
Single: $155–$360. Double: $190–$460.
This charming inn sits on a 35-acre estate at the foot of Mt. Liamuiga. Accommodations are in the 1832 great house or in cottages, all air-conditioned and sporting
antique and wicker furniture, ceiling fans, phones, combination baths and verandas.
The large pool is spring-fed and built into the ruins of a sugar mill, and there are
nature trails for exploring the adjacent rainforest. They'll shuttle you to the beach,
but it's so nice here you'll hate to leave. The restaurant is wonderful—as is everything here. 15 rooms. Credit Cards: V, MC, A.

Rawlins Plantation $175–$380   ★★★★

Mount Pleasant, ☎ *(809) 465-6221.*
Single: $175–$250. Double: $255–$380.
Located on 12 acres at the base of Mt. Misery, wonderful views abound everywhere
at this charming inn. It was built around the ruins of a 17th-century sugar mill on
well-landscaped grounds. Guest rooms are in cottages decorated with good local
artwork, nice fabrics, four-poster beds, and antiques. No air conditioning, but
breezes generally do the job. Guests can relax at the small spring-fed pool, play tennis on a grass court, enjoy croquet, or take advantage of the free transportation to
the beach. Afternoon tea, included in the rates, is a nice touch. The food in the West
Indian restaurant is really great. You'll want a rental car to get around, though it's

so peaceful and relaxing here you'll have to really motivate to move on. 9 rooms. Credit Cards: Not Accepted. Credit Cards: V, MC, A.

White House $270–$375

St. Peters, ☎ *(800) 223-1108, (809) 465-8162.*
Single: $270–$275. Double: $275–$375.
Located in the foothills above Basseterre, this inn centers around a gorgeous plantation great house that dates to 1738. Accommodations are in a converted stable, coach house and cottage. All are nicely done with four-poster beds, antiques, fine linens, ceiling fans (no air) and private baths. The dining room serves up island cuisine in high style. They'll take you to the beach for free, or you can enjoy the pool, grass tennis court and croquet lawn on the premises. The rates include afternoon tea and laundry service. 8 rooms. Credit Cards: V, MC, A.

Low Cost Lodging

Cheap rooms on St. Kitts offer the most basic of furnishings and facilities. **Conaree Beach Cottages** makes up for any lack of luxury by being right on the beach. Lots of back-to-basics Europeans tend to cram into the cottages at **Trade Winds**, also on Conaree Beach. You can ask around for rooms in private homes, but you should do so in person.

Where to Eat

Highest Rated Restaurants in St. Kitts

★★★★★ **The Royal Palm**

★★★★ **Golden Lemon**

★★★★ **Rawlins Plantation**

★★★ **Ballahoo**

★★★ **Chef's Place**

★★★ **Fisherman's Wharf**

★★★ **PJ's Pizza**

★★★ **The Georgian House**

★★★ **The Patio**

★★★ **Turtle Beach Bar & Grill**

Most Exclusive Restaurants in St. Kitts

★★★★★ **The Royal Palm**	$45–$45
★★★ **Ballahoo**	$25–$55
★★★★ **Rawlins Plantation**	$35–$35
★★★ **The Georgian House**	$14–$21
★★★ **PJ's Pizza**	$10–$20

Fielding's Best Value Restaurants in St. Kitts

★★★ **The Patio**	$26–$30
★★★★ **Rawlins Plantation**	$35–$35
★★★★ **Golden Lemon**	$35–$50
★★★ **Ballahoo**	$25–$55

For such a small island, St. Kitts has a wide spectrum of dining experiences, from gourmet delights in historical settings to the homey kitchens of casual local hangouts. Each of the four plantation inns have delightful outdoor patios for candlelit dinners. In Basseterre, dinner at the 400-year-old **Georgian House** is a leisurely elegant evening in a high-ceilinged salon, with aperitifs enjoyed in the walled garden beneath the big mango tree. At the **Ocean Terrace Inn**, the award-winning chef James Vanterpool makes a stunning Two-Flavor Soup (pumpkin and broccoli) and a carrot cake with local sugar cane sauce. Good West Indian food can be found at **The Ballahoo**, overlooking the town center. Some typical delicacies of the island include goat dishes, fried plaintains, Creole bean soup, boiled saltfish, goat water (actually, a rich lamb stew), conch chowder, and poached parrotfish with grilled yams. Don't miss an opportunity to try a swig of the island brew called **Royal Estra Stout**, or a glass of mauby, made from tree bark.

Ballahoo $$$ ★ ★ ★

Fort Street, at the Circus, ☎ *(809) 465-4197.*
Latin American cuisine.
Lunch: 8:00 a.m.–6:00 p.m., entrees $5–$55.
Dinner: 6:30 p.m.–10:00 p.m., entrees $25–$55.
This upper-level eatery overlooks the bustling downtown district that is Basseterre's version of Piccadilly Circus. The restaurant's customer base is a hodgepodge of cruise ship passengers, businesspeople and shoppers who are apt to find a wide variety of items to munch on, including fresh parrotfish fillets, rotis, burgers and yummy desserts. The place prides itself in presenting reasonably priced French wines. It's also a great location for West Indian or American-style breakfasts—be adventurous and have saltfish with your eggs instead of bacon. Closed: Sun. Reservations recommended. Credit Cards: V, MC, A.

Chef's Place $$ ★ ★ ★

Church Street, ☎ *(809) 465-6176.*
Latin American cuisine. Specialties: Souse, lamb stew.
Lunch: 8:00 a.m.–6:00 p.m., entrees $5–$10.
Dinner: 6:00 p.m.–11:00 p.m., entrees $5–$20.
Get friendly owner Oliver Peetes to describe the West Indian specialties on the daily blackboard—he'll probably oblige. Then settle down on picnic tables outdoors with a streetside view and await generous helpings of souse (pigs feet stew with a special sauce) or lamb stew. Main dishes will be rounded out with rice, a tasty salad and island vegetables. Beverages are also homemade and may include mauby, a bittersweet and spicy brew made from tree bark, or fresh ginger beer for the less adventurous. Closed: Sun. Credit Cards: Not Accepted.

Coconut Cafe $$$ ★ ★

Frigate Bay Beach, Frigate Bay, ☎ *(809) 465-3020.*
American cuisine.
Lunch: 7:30 a.m.–4:00 p.m., entrees $6–$45.
Dinner: 4:00 p.m.–11:00 p.m., entrees $25–$53.

Open to the sea breezes and steps away from the sand on the island's most popular swimming beach, this cafe dispenses three meals a day, but it's most popular for sunset cocktails and fresh seafood suppers to follow. There's steel band entertainment on Saturday evenings, and the bar stays open 'till the wee hours. Associated Hotel: Timothy Beach Resort. Credit Cards: V, MC, DC, A.

Fisherman's Wharf $$ ★★★

Fortlands, ☎ (809) 465-2754.
Seafood cuisine.
Dinner: 7:00 p.m.–12:00 p.m., entrees $8–$22.
Eating here is like a beach cookout, with diners choosing meat, fish, or chicken to be grilled to order, and serving themselves from a salad and condiments buffet. Orders are taken to long wooden tables facing the oceanfront. Everything is reliably good, but the fresh lobster and shrimp are standouts. A steel band entertains on Friday. Associated Hotel: Ocean Terrace Inn. Credit Cards: V, MC, A.

Golden Lemon $$$ ★★★★

Dieppe Bay Town, Dieppe Bay, ☎ (809) 465-7260.
International cuisine.
Lunch: 11:30 a.m.–3:00 p.m., entrees $7–$12.
Dinner: 7:00 p.m.–10:00 p.m., entrees $35–$50.
Some returning visitors would never dream of leaving the island without at least one visit to this exquisite boutique inn's fine restaurant. The three-course, prix-fixe dinners are rotated frequently; owner Arthur Leaman creates the internationally themed menus himself. Gleaming antiques and crystal chandeliers accentuate the dining room and a breezy patio is a gathering spot for Sunday brunch and cocktails. While touring by car, stop by for lunch, which features more informal offerings, including sandwiches, salads and fish dishes. Associated Hotel: Golden Lemon. Reservations required. Credit Cards: V, MC, DC, A.

PJ's Pizza $$ ★★★

North Frigate Bay, Frigate Bay, ☎ (809) 465-8373.
Italian cuisine. Specialties: Pizza, subs.
Lunch: 10:00 a.m.–6:00 p.m., entrees $5–$20.
Dinner: 6:00 p.m.–10:30 p.m., entrees $10–$20.
A reputation for some of the most creative pizza toppings in the Caribbean chain is putting this small place on the culinary map. Refried beans embellish the Mexican pizza and a Rastafarian Ital pie is capped with island veggies in the Rasta colors of gold, red and green. The rest of the offerings are basically Italian, with hero sandwiches made on home-baked bread. Dinner plates usually include lasagne and chili. Closed: Mon. Credit Cards: V, MC, A.

Rawlins Plantation $$$ ★★★★

Mt. Pleasant, Mt. Pleasant, ☎ (809) 465-6221.
International cuisine.
Lunch: 12:30 p.m.–2:00 p.m., prix fixe $23.
Dinner: 8:00 p.m. Seating, prix fixe $35.
Cap off a tour of the island with lunch or dinner at this splendidly restored estate on the northwest coast. A varied buffet of creole specialties is served to diners on the

terrace of the estate's great house, and offerings often include curries, fritters, salads, vegetables and several international specialties. Call before noon to make a reservation for a fixed-price dinner of four courses with soup, salad, entree and a tantalizing dessert—possibly chocolate terrine with passion fruit sauce. Closed mid-August-mid October. Associated Hotel: Rawlins Plantation. Reservations required. Credit Cards: Not Accepted. Credit Cards: V, MC, A.

The Georgian House $$$ ★ ★ ★

Independence Square, ☎ *(809) 465-4049.*
International cuisine.
Dinner: 6:00 p.m.–10:00 p.m., entrees $14–$21.
This beautifully restored home, decorated with Georgian-era reproductions, is a showcase for owner-chef Roger Doche, who prepares a continental menu of seafood, chicken, and steaks, prepared with West Indian flourishes. Peas and rice accompany some of the main courses. Dinner is served nightly on a patio behind the house. Reservations recommended. Credit Cards: V, MC, A.

The Patio $$$ ★ ★ ★

Frigate Bay Beach, Frigate Bay, ☎ *(809) 465-8666.*
Latin American cuisine.
Dinner: 7:00 p.m.–11:00 p.m., entrees $26–$30.
The father-daughter cooking team of Peter and Helen Mallalieu prepare island-inspired continental suppers served with a flourish on the patio of their Frigate Bay Beach home. Diners face one of the prettiest private gardens on the island while feasting on specialties like pepper pot stew, broiled fresh seafood, and tropical desserts. Wines and liquors are included with dinner. Closed: Sun. Reservations required. Credit Cards: V, MC.

The Royal Palm $$$ ★ ★ ★ ★ ★

Ottley's Estate, ☎ *(809) 465-7234.*
International cuisine.
Lunch: 12:00 a.m.–3:00 p.m., entrees $8–$18.
Dinner: 8:00 p.m. Seating, prix fixe $45.
Possibly the most creative food on the island is served at this restaurant located in Ottley's Plantation Inn. Chef Pam Yahn's new "island cuisine" has been glossied on the pages of national magazines, including *Food and Wine*. Her ever-changing menu has included delights like lobster quesadillas and sweet treats like mango mousse with raspberry sauce. Lunches, dinners and Sunday brunch with champagne are served in a location that couldn't be lovelier—the dining room skirts a nearby rainforest. Fixed-price brunch is $20, and served from 12 to 2 p.m. Associated Hotel: Ottley's Plantation. Reservations required. Credit Cards: V, MC, A.

Turtle Beach Bar & Grill $$$ ★ ★ ★

S.E. Peninsula Road, Turtle Beach, ☎ *(809) 469-9086.*
American cuisine.
Lunch: 8:00 a.m.– 6:00 p.m., entrees $16–$24.
Combine an afternoon of snorkeling (the preferred activity), scuba diving, or just plain loafing on the beach with a notable barbecue of chicken, fish, meat, or lobster prepared at this solar-powered eatery on the southeast coast. Operated by the

Ocean Terrace Inn in Fortlands, the Grill is also a cool place Sundays for a well-regarded West Indian buffet replete with live entertainment. Dinner is served only on Saturdays, from 7:30-10:00 p.m. Equipment for watersports can be rented here as well. Associated Hotel: Ocean Terrace Inn. Reservations recommended. Credit Cards: V, A.

Where to Shop

Shopping is mostly concentrated at several shops and boutiques in and around the traffic circus less than a block from the waterfront. There are at least 57 stores on the island, including the famous **Caribelle Batik**, the island's world-famous designs manufactured at Romney Manor. Also good buys can be found at **Pelican Mall**, a 26-shop arena which features traditional Kittian architecture and pastel colors that resemble a Caribbean market. Duty-free items are available at **A Slice of the Lemon Duty-Free Gift Shop**, on Fort Street, where you can browse through pottery, teas, spices, and condiments lower that those in St. Maarten or the USVI. **Splash** at the TDC Mall carries very attractive resort wear and colorful fabrics. Any groom in need of a tux can find one at **Valentino's Men's Wear** on Fort Street. **Windjammer & Caribbean Scents**, in the Pelican Mall, sells outstanding Caribbean resort wear and a fine selection of Caribbean perfumes, as well as **Jamaica's Blue Mountain coffee**. One gallery that shouldn't be missed is the **Plantation Picture House**, featuring the work of Kate Spencer, known for her portraits, landscapes and still lifes. Her designs are now available on stone-washed silk and may be worn as scarves.

St. Kitts Directory

ARRIVAL AND DEPARTURE

American Eagle offers daily connections to St. Kitts from American's hub in San Juan. LIAT and WInair serve St. Kitts from either San Juan, Antigua, or St. Maarten.

Apple Vacation operates a series of 28 Saturday charter departures from Chicago's O'Hare International Airport to St. Kitts and Nevis, available only through retail travel agents. It is the only direct link between the Chicago area and the two-island nation. For information call ☎ *800-365-2775.*

Modestly priced taxi fares are available for all island destinations and three-hour, round-island tours can be arranged for about U.S. $40. Fares are usually quoted in EC dollars.

Rental car rates start around $3 per day. Be sure to obtain a $12 island driving license at the police station on Canyon Street in Basseterre—drive on the left side.

A U.S $10 departure tax is charged all tourists leaving the Golden Rock International Airport and for non-St. Kitts flights departing from Newcastle Airport on Nevis.

CLIMATE

The climate is pleasant and moderate, with an average temperature of 79 degrees F. Humidity is low and constant northeast trade winds keep the islands cool. Although there is no rainy season, annual rainfall averages 55 inches.

DOCUMENTS

U.S. citizens must present proof of citizenship (passport, voter's registration, or birth certificate), along with return or ongoing tickets. There is a departure tax of $8.

ELECTRICITY

The current runs 230 volts, 60 cycles AC. While the electricity supply at some hotels is 110 volts, AC transformers and adapters are generally needed.

GETTING AROUND

Local transportation is available via minibuses and taxis. Automobiles may be rented from a variety of agencies; ask your hotel. A visitor's driver's license is required and can be obtained from the Police Traffic Department for a fee. Driving is on the left side of the street.

Among the agencies: Avis, located at South Independence Square ☎ *465-6507*, Choice Car Rental on Cayon Street in Basseterre ☎ *465-4422*.

The passenger ferry, *The Caribe Queen*, operates on a regular schedule between the two islands. The crossing takes about 45 minutes and costs $8 round trip.

LANGUAGE

The official language of both St. Kits and Nevis is English.

MEDICAL EMERGENCIES

There is a 24-hour emergency room at Joseph N. France General Hospital in Buckley ☎ *465-2551*. Also ask your hotel about physicians on call.

MONEY

The official currency is the Eastern Caribbean dollar. Make sure you understand which dollar is quoted on bills.

TELEPHONE

Area code is *809*. International calls, telexes, and telegrams can be made from Skantel, Cayon Street, Basseterre ☎ *465-2219*, Monday-Friday from 8 a.m.–6 p.m., on Saturday 8 a.m.–2 p.m., and on Sundays and holidays from 6:00 p.m.–8:00 p.m.

TIME

Atlantic Standard Time. That is to say, it's one hour ahead of New York time, except during daylight saving time, when it is the same.

TIPPING

Expect a ten percent service charge added to most hotel and restaurant bills. If it isn't, be prepared to tip 10–15 percent.

TOURIST INFORMATION

Good brochures and information can be found at the **St. Kitts Tourist Board**, Pelican Mall, P.O Box 132, Basseterre; ☎ *465-2620/4040*, FAX *465-8794*. In the U.S. ☎ *(212) 535-1234*.

WHEN TO GO

Carnival Celebrations take place in a week-long spectacle the last week of December, featuring calypso competitions, queen shows, street dancing and festivals. Tourism Week in Nevis is an annual fair in February. Museum Day is May 18, usually an open house at various museums. Culturama 20, in Nevis the last week of July, is a 20-year-old festival of native arts, crafts and music. Every other month the St. Kitts-Nevis Boating Club provides races and relays for residents and tourists alike. On the last Sunday of every month the Golden Rock Golf Club presents a day of fun golf played on a nine-hole fun course. The Nevis Jockey Club has scheduled nine race days throughout the year to coincide with national holidays.

ST. KITTS HOTELS		RMS	RATES	PHONE	FAX
Basseterre					
★★★★	Ottley's Plantation Inn	15	$155–$460	(800) 772-3039	(809) 465-4760
★★★★	Rawlins Plantation	9	$175–$380	(809) 465-6221	(809) 465-4954
★★★	Frigate Bay Beach Hotel	64	$75–$200	(809) 465-8935	(809) 465-7050
★★★	Golden Lemon Inn & Villas	32	$175–$950	(800) 633-7411	(809) 465-4019
★★★	Jack Tar Village	244	$110–$340	(800) 999-9182	(809) 465-1031
★★★	Ocean Terrace Inn	53	$76–$350	(800) 524-0512	(809) 465-1057
★★★	St. Christopher Club	32	$100–$235	(809) 465-4854	(809) 465-6466
★★★	White House	8	$270–$375	(800) 223-1108	(809) 465-8275
★★	Bird Rock Beach Hotel	38	$75–$310	(809) 465-8914	(809) 465-1675

ST. KITTS HOTELS		RMS	RATES	PHONE	FAX
★★	Casablanca Resort	66	$240–$355	(800) 231-1945	(809) 497-6899
★★	Fairview Inn	27	$75–$145	(080) 223-9815	(809) 465-1056
★★	Fort Thomas Hotel	64	$75–$115	(800) 851-7818	(809) 465-7518
★★	Island Paradise Village	62	$98–$285	(809) 465-8035	809 465 8236
★★	Leeward Cove Condominiums	10	$50–$275	(809) 465-8030	(809) 465-3476
★★	Sun 'n Sand Beach Resort	68	$120–$250	(809) 465-8037	(809) 465-6745
★★	Timothy Beach Resort	36	$105–$380	(800) 777-1700	(809) 465-7723

ST. KITTS RESTAURANTS		LOCATION	PHONE	ENTREE
Basseterre				
American				
★★★	Turtle Beach Bar & Grill	Turtle Beach	(809) 469-9086	$16–$24•
★★	Coconut Cafe	Frigate Bay	(809) 465-3020	$6–$53
International				
★★★★★	The Royal Palm	Basseterre	(809) 465-7234	$8–$45
★★★★	Golden Lemon	Dieppe Bay	(809) 465-7260	$7–$50
★★★★	Rawlins Plantation	Mt. Pleasant	(809) 465-6221	$23–$35
★★★	The Georgian House	Basseterre	(809) 465-4049	$14–$21••
Italian				
★★★	PJ's Pizza	Frigate Bay	(809) 465-8373	$5–$20
Latin American				
★★★	Ballahoo	at the Circus	(809) 465-4197	$5–$55
★★★	Chef's Place	Basseterre	(809) 465-6176	$5–$20
★★★	The Patio	Frigate Bay	(809) 465-8666	$26–$30••
Seafood				
★★★	Fisherman's Wharf	Basseterre	(809) 465-2754	$8–$22••

Note: • Lunch Only

   •• Dinner Only

ST. LUCIA

St. Lucia's dramatic countryside includes emerald hills, waterfalls, rainforest, volcanic mineral baths and pristine beaches.

Watching a local cook an egg in steamy sulphur pools might be cliche now on lovely St. Lucia, but the rest of the island's attractions are far from worn out. Bit by bit St. Lucians are getting the ecotourism bug, finally figuring out that this Caribbean island's biggest draw is its lush natural resources—from exclusive beaches fringed with forests to waterfalls that change color from yellow to purple. In fact, it should be made mandatory for every visitor to drive the steep roads that wind the emerald hills at the island's southern end, where jungle flowers scent the air and giggling children soap themselves under roadside water faucets. To get the full Lucian experience, however, you must get out and trod toe to heel over the dramatic countryside, breathe in the rainforest, and even bathe in the volcano's hot mineral baths. But the spirit of St. Lucia lies not only in the land but in the people as well—friendly, musical and forever ready to party. Festivals carve the rhythm of life here, and ones like the two flower festivals, La Rose and Marguerite, and Carnival—a calypso explosion two days before Ash Wednesday—shouldn't be missed.

Bird's Eye View

The second largest of the former West Indies Associated States, the avocado-shaped St. Lucia lies between Martinique and St. Vincent in the Windward Islands chain of the eastern Caribbean. It sprawls over a total area of 238 square miles, a majority of which is covered with dense tropical flora, such as hibiscus, frangipani, orchids, jasmine and poinciana Every visitor should drive the steep roads that wind up around the emerald hills at the southern end, where jungle flowers scent the air and giggling children soap themselves under roadside water faucets. By contrast, the northern end of the island seems positively cosmopolitan. Castries, the capital, is still in need of beautification, but marinas and resorts are filling in the coastline. (The proliferation of all-inclusive resorts is starting to rankle local businesspeople—especially struggling restaurateurs.) Though tourism has been growing rapidly, the principal sector is agriculture (especially bananas and coconut) along with manufacturing, with over 40 relatively diversified enterprises.

History

The first inhabitants of St. Lucia were surely Arawak Indians, and later Caribs, who did not appreciate the British invasion of their island in the early 17th century; for some time they managed to successfully fend off colonization. In 1650, the French overcame the resistance and settled a colony, completing a treaty with the Caribs in 1660. Over the next 164 years, the island exchanged hands fourteen times between the French and British in an almost comical seesaw play of power. It was not until the issue of the 1814

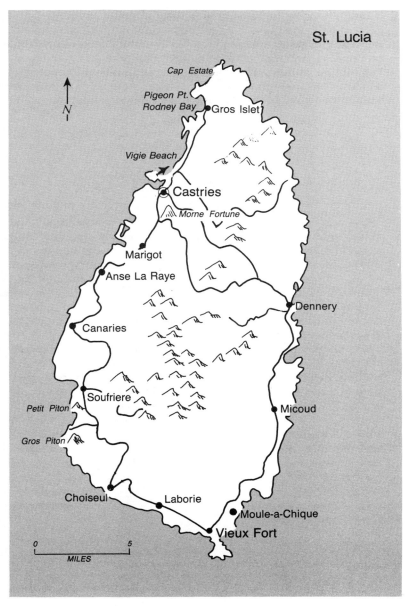

St. Lucia

N

Cap Estate

Pigeon Pt.
Rodney Bay • Gros Islet

Vigie Beach

• Castries

Morne Fortune

• Marigot

• Anse La Raye

• Dennery

• Canaries

• Soufriere

Petit Piton

Gros Piton

• Micoud

• Choiseul

• Laborie

• Moule-a-Chique

• Vieux Fort

0   5
MILES

Treaty of Paris that the British finally secured all rights. During this time, the Carib Indians were played as a pawn between the two powers until the British finally—and unceremoniously—exiled them to a still-existing reservation on Dominica. Although the island gained control of its own government on February 22, 1979, its official head of state still remains the British throne, represented by a Governor General, who appoints the eleven members of St. Lucia's Senate. The House of Assembly is elected by popular vote.

People

As in neighboring states, about 75 percent of the inhabitants of St. Lucia are descendants of African slaves who were imported as plantation laborers in the 17th and 18th centuries. (Two percent are descended from indentured servants brought from India and another two percent are of European origin.) The rich mixture has produced a highly musical local patois, a combination of French, English and Spanish words utilizing a French and African grammatical structure. Although tourism is conducted in English, most private conversations, jokes, street jibe and some court cases are conducted in patois. Friendly and helpful, they have retained a love of African and Caribbean rhythms; in fact, St. Lucians so love to party that dancing has practically become a national sport. Every small town and village holds dances regularly, propelled by a little beer, rum, smoking weed, and ear-splitting speakers. Friday block parties in the village of **Gros Islet** are especially welcoming to tourists; other neighborhoods are more closed. Despite all the spontaneous partying, about 80 percent of the population still remain self-acclaimed Roman Catholics. Most of the older island women continue to wear the Madras head-tie and a modern version of the panniered skirt. A blend of French and British cultures, islanders share a passion for both savory French-Creole cooking and their beloved sport of cricket. St. Lucia has also given birth to two Nobel Laureates: Sir W. Arthur Lewis won the Nobel Prize in Economics in 1979 and the poet Derek Walcott won the 1992 Nobel Prize in Literature.

Beaches

St. Lucia's prime goal is to keep beaches open to the public but as pristine as possible; therefore, you'll only find a few with restrooms, changing facilities and snack bars. The best way to find *your* beach is to hire a sailboat and scope around the dozens of nearly deserted possibilities. Because shade is not always available, make sure you always travel to the beach with hat or umbrella, towel and liquid refreshment. Among the best beaches is **Anse Chastanet**, just north of Soufriere which some claim offers the Windward Islands' only "perfect beach dive," with its steep dropoff, colorful fish, and variety of sponges (parts of *Superman II* film were shot here). Anse Couchon beaches feature black, volcanic sand, calm waters for swimming, and a tropical, romantic setting accessible only by boat. Lying at the foot of the Pitons, the crescent-shaped bay of Anse des Piton rates as one of St. Lucia's most dramatic beaches. Facilities are few at Anse LaRaye, a small village beach just beyond Marigot Bay, but there are plenty of shady palm trees. **Cas en Bas**, just opposite Gros Islet on the island's north end, is a windsurfer's dream, comparable to the excellent conditions of Silver Sands on Barbados. Some of the island's major hotels are located on the nearly perfect **Reduit Beach**, chock full of shady palms, white sand and a full range of watersports facilities. Swimmers should avoid the strong currents at **La Toc Bay**, south of Castries Harbor, where the majestic **Cunard La Toc Hotel** lies, though the view is lovely for lunch and sunbathing. One of the most popularly frequented beaches is **Choc Bay**, a long, sweeping stretch of sand and coconut palms, not far from Castries and the major hotels along the northeastern coast. At the southernmost tip of the island you'll find **Vieux Fort**, where the beach makes up for the lack of facilities with gloriously white sand and miles of shady coconut palms.

Dive Sites

Twenty-four miles of untouched reef make St. Lucia a stunning destination for diving and snorkeling. The quality and variety of sites on both Atlantic and Caribbean coasts are comparable to some of the best in the islands. Unfortunately, the rough waters on the Atlantic side tend to push away all but the most experienced divers. Visibility reaches up to 100 feet at most sites. Much of the coastline is yet to be explored. A wall of patch reefs defines the western coast, with coral gardens lying in shallow water near the shore. Species such as fairy basslet, squirrelfishes, French grunts, assorted butterflyfishes, damselfishes and gobies are profuse in these waters,. That many of the reefs lie so close to shore makes excellent conditions for snorkelers. The Anse la Raye and Anse Chastenet have proven highly favorable sites for both scuba and snorkeling.

The volcanic chain, known as the **Pitons**, reach far below sea level, and provide a spectacular environment for divers. Profuse varieties of sponges grow along the walls, and underwater caves are filled with thousands of fish. Currents, in particular, allow for some very interesting drift dives. In addition to the special experience of the Pitons, the more advanced diver can enjoy the deeper reefs, caves, walls and canyons, where large coral arches and basket sponges predominate. Numerous wrecks have been marked; two aircraft were sunk in the 1970s at Vieux Fort and were made into an artificial reef, for the very advanced diver only, due to extremely strong currents in the area. In 1983 the freighter *Wauwinet* was also added to the marine park, resting in 50 feet of water, with plenty of natural lighting—do ask if it is now available for dives. A well-known wreck, the *Lesleen M*, is a 165-ft. freighter lying upright in 60 feet of water near Anse Cochon. The fish here are said to be so tame they will even rub noses with divers. The famous **Key Hotel Pinnacles** are four underwater peaks, actually miniature pitons covered with brilliant corals and sponges called gorgonians four to six feet tall. Farther south, between the villages of Choiseul and Laborie, a two-mile stretch of narrow beaches and platform reefs are ideal for snorkeling. Extensive dive packages are available at the **Anse Chastet Hotel** and **Marigot Bay Resort** (listed below under Hotels/Resorts). Dive operators also rent custom dive boats and underwater camera equipment.

The road to St. Lucia's volcanic spikes, The Pitons, is surrounded by forest.

Treks

St. Lucia is a also a treasurehouse of resources for devoted trekkers. Some of the treks are easy, across lovely beaches and flat terrain; others are hand-to-heel over some of the toughest slopes in the Caribbean. The Forestry Reserve has extensive information and maps and will supply local guides on request. In some instances, local guides are required by the Forestry Reserve due to adverse or challenging conditions. Before you head off into the wild, always check about weather conditions and whether you will need transportation to return to your home base—sometimes local transportation is simply not available, forcing you to hike even further than expected, with the possibility of getting irrevocably lost. Organized expeditions usually are the easiest way to solve all these problems and tend to ensure your safety over unknown routes.

Among the most challenging sites are **The Pitons**—two ancient volcanic spikes (Petit Piton at 2438 feet and Gros Piton, 2619 feet) which mark two of the higher points of the island. The highest point of the island, the 3117-ft. **Mt. Gimie**, can be hiked only with a local mountain guide. From whatever vantage you view the two Pitons, they are awesomely beautiful, bracketing a steep dense forest whose hillside drops to a strikingly attractive deep-water bay. Unstable and severely steep, the Pitons have frequent landslides so hiking should be done only in dry weather. Both of the Pitons have trails, but check to see if both are open; one or the other close due to frequent rockfalls. To reach the top of Gros Piton takes about three hours, over rough, challenging, nearly perpendicular terrain.

St. Lucians claim to have the only drive-in volcano in the world. On the southeast side of **Soufriere**, here is indeed a volcanic crater into which a road runs—pools of hot muddy water still bubble and belch steam up to 50 feet in the air. At the entrance, you'll find a guide at the Government Tourist Office who must accompany you on the tour. Don't hesitate to squish your hands in the mud, but do ask about the temperature beforehand.

About 13 percent of St. Lucia's woodlands are rainforest, protected in a nature reserve of 19,044 acres of lush mountains and valleys in the interior highlands. Rain is frequent here and heavy mists are customary. On a clear day hikers can have the pleasure of extremely beautiful panoramic views from various lookouts. The Forestry Department has established a **Rain Forest**

Walk, about seven miles long, between the villages of Mahur in the east and Fond St. Jacques in the west—permission must be arranged in advance to be picked up at the far end, since no local transportation is available until one reaches the coast. To hike from the start of the **Edmund Forest Reserve** to **Quilesse Forest** in the east takes about 3 1/2 hours. Birdlife is abundant, particularly three rare species of hummingbirds. A Forestry Department guide can point out the many exotic flowers, fruits, trees and tropical birds (ask for Marial, who knows every plant and creature). Be on the lookout for the colorful St. Lucia parrot affectionately called "jacquot" by islanders. As a result of intense conservation efforts, the nearly extinct parrot has increased hundredfold in the last decade. They are most visible in the early morning and late afternoon, and can usually be seen flying in pairs (parrots mate for life and the female lays only two eggs a year). You may find them feeding at the edge of the forest, which is their customary haunt. (Do note, if you are staying in Castries, the easiest way to visit is through organized hiking expeditions arranged by the Forestry Department, which will pick you up at your hotel.)

Naturalists can also observe native wildlife at the **Maria Islands Interpretive Centre**, the habitat of two endemic reptiles, and at Frigate Island, a haven for frigate birds during the mating season. The highest point of the island, the 3117-ft. **Mt. Gimie**, can be hiked with a local mountain guide.

Hikers on St. Lucia have a choice of several beautiful panoramic views.

What Else to See

The best time to experience the hustle and bustle of West Indian port life in Castries, the island's capital, is on Saturday at the morning market, when small farmers and artisans lay out their tropical wares for serious barter. Not much else is of interest in the city which has been rebuilt and decimated by fire several times over, except perhaps for **Columbus Square**, where a 400-year-old samaan tree shades the Cathedral of the Immaculate Conception built in 1897. Afternoons are the best time to visit the tiny fishing villages of **Anse-la-Raye** and **Canaries**, where you can watch the boats arrive with their daily catch. North of Castries, the **Pigeon Island National Park** offers the opportunity to relive the days when France and England waged over St. Lucia. (George Rodney, the British admiral who defeated the French in the Dominica Passage, raised pigeons as a hobby—hence the name.) Friday nights, the fishing town of **Gros Islet**, is a wild "jump-up" scene, noisy with soca and reggae, traditional beats of the Caribbean. The new marketplace at Soufriere in the south is also exceptional, decorated with colorful murals and gingerbread trim; the shabby town itself still retains a Third World aura. The dormant "Drive-in Volcano" of nearby **Mt. Soufriere** presents a face akin to a B-movie horror movie, complete with open pits of boiling sulfur. (You'll need a guide, available at the entrance of the park.) If you want to linger under cascading waterfalls and bathe in natural and more aromatic springs, go to the nearby **Diamond Falls**, where the Diamond Mineral Baths are located on the Soufriere Estate. Legend has it that King Louis XVI himself partook of the healing waters here during a French occupation.

Pigeon Island is a 40-acre islet connected by causeway to St. Lucia's west coast near the Rodney Bay resort area. The site of St. Lucia's annual jazz festival, the area also boasts two beaches, restaurant, and the remnants of the 18th-century British naval garrison. The new Pigeon Island Museum and Interpretive Centre is housed in the elegant former British officers' mess building and provides a hands-on display of the island's natural and political history.

A startling panoramic view can be glimpsed from the Fort Charlotte fortress at the top of Morne Fortune, the same sight used by French and British troops alternately to defend the island. To the north is Pigeon Island, to the south the Pitons, and the entire scope of the capital's harbor and the Virgie Peninsula. While you're at the fort, notice the difference between the French architecture and the walls built by the British at different stages.

Historical Sites

Fort Charlotte ★ ★ ★

Morne Fortune, Castries, ☎ *(809) 456-1165.*

Set atop a hill 853 feet above sea level, this fortress was started by the French in 1764 and finished 20 years later by the British. Today it holds government and education offices, but it's worth a trip for the great views if nothing else. The grounds include a military cemetery that dates back to 1782 where French and British soldiers are buried as well as six former governors of the island.

Parks and Gardens

Maria Islands Nature Reserve ★ ★ ★

Half a mile offshore, Castries, ☎ *(809) 454-5014.*
Hours Open: 9:30 a.m.–5:00 p.m.

This reserve consists of two small islands in the Atlantic--one 25 acres, the other just four. It is home to a thriving population of birds and rare snakes and lizards. Great snorkeling off the larger island, Maria Major.

Pigeon Island National Park ★ ★ ★ ★

Pigeon Point, Castries, ☎ *(809) 452-5005.*
Hours Open: 9:00 a.m.–4:00 p.m.

This 40-acre island is connected to the mainland by a causeway. It has a long history and was used for all sorts of things before becoming a national park—pirates hid out here in the 1600s, the French and British militaries used it as a fort, and long before any of them, the Arawak Indians lived here. Ruins from some of these days still exist on the island, but this is primarily a place to picnic and hang out on its picturesque beaches. General admission: $1.00.

Tours

Diamond Falls and Mineral Bath ★ ★ ★ ★

Soufriere Estate, Soufriere.
Hours Open: 10:00 a.m.–5:00 p.m.

The water in these sulfuric mineral baths average a toasty 106 degrees Fahrenheit. Louis XVI ordered them built in 1784 so French soldiers stationed in the area could soak the supposedly curative waters. Bring your suit so you, too, can "take the waters." General admission: $2.00.

La Soufriere ★ ★ ★

Soufriere.
Hours Open: 9:00 a.m.–5:00 p.m.

Called the world's only drive-in volcano, this spot encompasses a seven-acre crater complete with pool of boiling mud and sulfurous waters.

The Pitons   ★★★★

Soufriere.

These dramatic twin cones are St. Lucia's most identifying landmark. Formed by a prehistoric volcano eruption, Petit Piton rises to 2619 ft., Gros Piton (the fatter of the two) to 2461 ft. Most folks just admire them from the land or sea, but the truly hardy can climb through their lush foliage to the top. You'll need a permit from the **Forestry Division** (☎ *452-3231*), and it's best to hire a guide for the very strenuous hike.

Sports

Most hotels boast tennis courts and watersports facilities, including windsurfing, water skiing, and small sailboats. Windsurfers all head for Anse de Sables, the bay on the southeastern tip of the island between Moule-a-Chique and the Maria Islands. Actually, conditions for windsurfing are ideal all along the entire south coast, on both the Atlantic and the Caribbean sides. Beginners normally like the calmer waters of the Caribbean while the more daring windsurfers take advantage of the rougher, choppy waters on the Atlantic coast. Golfers can enjoy two challenging golf courses. Half-day and full-day fishing charters are available and can be arranged through hotels and resorts, or at the marinas at Rodney Bay and Castries. The two main fishing seasons run between January to June (for tuna, kingfish and dolphin) and July to December (where the catch is closer to shore). As St. Lucians depend on fishing for their livelihood, the ways and means are many—you can join fishermen using lines and pots to catch snapper, lobsters and reef fish. Yachtsmen and day-trippers from Castries tend to congregate at Soufriere Bay. One of the region's major charters is **The Moorings**, which offers cruises for 4-6 passengers with lunch and drinks—bareboat or with crew. Other similar cruises can be found at Rodney Bay; **Stevens Yachts** is one of the foremost names in the region. Horseback riding through the forest is also available.

Golf

Two locations, Castries.

The choices for duffers are limited to two courses, both nine holes but set up so you can go around twice. **Cap Estate Golf Club** (☎ *452-8523*) is open to the public while the course at **Sandals St. Lucia** (☎ *452-3081*) is only available when not fully booked by guests at the island's two Sandals resorts.

Horseback riding

Various locations, Castries.
Three stables await the horseman (and woman): **North Point** (☎ *450-8853*), **Trim's** (☎ *452-8273*), and **Jalousie Plantation** (☎ *459-7666*).

Watersports

Various locations, Castries.
If your hotel doesn't offer the watersports you're seeking try one of these. Deep-sea fishing: **Mako Watersports** (☎ *452-0412*) and **Captain Mike's** (☎ *452-7044*). Scuba diving: **Dive Jalousie** (☎ *459-7666*), **Moorings Scuba** (☎ *451-4357*), **Scuba St. Lucia** (☎ *459-7355*), **Buddies Scuba** (☎ *452-5288*), and **Windjammer Diving** (☎ *452-0913*). **Mistral Windsurfing** (☎ *452-8351*) specializes in board rentals and instruction. For cruises and snorkel expeditions, call **Captain Mike's** (☎ *452-0216*), **Surf Queen** (☎ *452-8351*), **Brig Unicorn** (☎ *452-6811*), and **Cat Inc.** (☎ *450-8651*). Finally, **St. Lucian Watersports** (☎ *452-8351*) offers water-skiing and parasailing in addition to general equipment rentals.

Where to Stay

Highest Rated Hotels in St. Lucia

★★★★★ Le Sport

★★★★ Anse Chastanet Hotel

★★★★ Jalousie Plantation

★★★★ Sandals St. Lucia

★★★ Club Med St. Lucia

★★★ Club St. Lucia

★★★ Ladera Resort

★★★ Marigot Bay Resort

★★★ Rendezvous

★★★ Royal St. Lucian Hoel

Most Exclusive Hotels in St. Lucia

★★★★★ Le Sport	$245–$905
★★★ Ladera Resort	$180–$655
★★★ Wyndham Morgan Bay Resort	$250–$580
★★★ Royal St. Lucian Hotel	$215–$385
★★★ Marigot Bay Resort	$90–$220

Fielding's Best Value Hotels in St. Lucia

★★★★ Sandals St. Lucia	$0–$0
★★★★★ Le Sport	$245–$905
★★★ Rendezvous	$0–$0
★★★ Club St. Lucia	$175–$445

St.Lucia offers a full-range of lodging, from the very expensive all-inclusive resorts (some of the best in the Caribbean) and luxurious five-star hotels to intimate inns surrounded by lush greenery and talcum-soft beaches; there are also numerous self-catering options in villas and apartments. Throughout the entire island, there are 29 hotels, 23 guest houses, and 10 villas and apartment complexes. Many properties offer the optional Modified American Plan (MAP), which includes breakfast and dinner. You can get up to 50 percent discounts during the summer season. In most circumstances you will receive a 10 percent service charge on the hotel bill, plus an eight percent government tax. Families tend to do best at all-inclusive resorts since you don't have to run around trying to find an activity to please everybody (everything you need is right outside your doorstep). Properties not located on the south side (where the airport is located) will incur an extra fee for transfer.

Hotels and Resorts

Sandals, the St. Lucia version of the famous all-inclusive Caribbean resort, has winter rates starting at $1575, going up to $3000 (per week), the highest on the island. A second Sandals resort, **Sandals Halcyon**, opened last year on the site of the former Halcyon Beach Club at Choc Bay, offering breathtaking seaviews from its restaurant, **The Pier House**, which extends over a 150-ft. pier. Guests can use all the super sports facilities at the mother resort. It's been said that if you begin your stay at Ladera, you won't want to go anywhere else, so fabulous is the setting. Special spa facilities characterize **Le Sport**, where the beach, tennis courts, golf course and apartments are only steps from each other. The all-inclusive **Rendezvous** bans kids (couples only), and there are some packages that include airfare.

Anse Chastanet Hotel $95–$505   ★★★★

Anse Chastanet Beach, ☎ *(800) 223-1108, (809) 459-7000.*
Single: $95–$355. Double: $135–$505.
Situated on a 500-acre hillside beachfront plantation, this unique resort is located on the southwest coast, north of Soufriere. The grounds are wonderfully lush and steeply lead down to a black-sand beach. Accommodations are found on the hillside or on the beach. Each is large, individually decorated, and quite posh. The grounds include an excellent dive center (lots of scuba enthusiasts stay here), two good restaurants, two bars, and a tennis court. No pool or air conditioning, but no one's complaining. Best suited to the fit, as there are steep stairs everywhere. 48 rooms.
Credit Cards: V, MC, A.

Candyo Inn $75–$90   ★★

Rodney Bay, ☎ *(809) 452- 712.*
Single: $75–$90. Double: $75–$90.
You can walk to the beach in five minutes from this small hotel. The four guest rooms are standard and well-kept, with modern amenities like phones, TV, and clock radios. The eight apartments have kitchens and more room to spread out; all accommodations are air-conditioned. Facilities are limited to a snack bar, mini-mar-

ket and pool. There are many restaurants within walking distance, and this small operation is a good deal. 12 rooms. Credit Cards: MC, A.

Club Med St. Lucia   **$800–$1300**   ★★★

Vieux Fort, ☎ *(800) 258-2633, (809) 454-6546.*

This Club Med is set on 95 acres at Savannes Bay, on the southeast coast--a fairly remote region, so you'll have to depend on organized tours (or rent a car) to see the island. Many of the guests here are families with children; this is not a swinging singles Club Med. Accommodations are small, with air conditioning, twin beds and balconies. As with all Club Meds, there's always tons going on, and lots of activities for the youngsters, including an intensive English riding program for kids eight and above (which, like scuba and island tours, costs extra). Among the recreational options are tennis on eight courts, circus workshops, all watersports, a fitness center, exercise classes, archery, rollerblading, and on and on and on. Great for families; singles may want to look elsewhere. Rates are $800 to $1300 per week per adult, and $520 to $845 per week per children 2–11. They occasionally take small children (ages 2–5) free; ask for details. It also costs $30 for a one-time initiation fee (per family) and $50 per person annual dues. 265 rooms. Credit Cards: MC, A.

Club St. Lucia   **$175–$445**   ★★★

Cap Estate, ☎ *(809) 450- 551.*
Single: $175–$445. Double: $235–$445.

This all-inclusive resort appeals to romantics--they even have two wedding chapels for those who get so carried away they decide to tie the knot. Guest rooms and suites are large and nicely done; most, but not all, are air-conditioned (those without rely on ceiling fans). There are two pools, nine tennis courts, a health club, a disco, nightly entertainment, and supervised children's programs year-round. Watersports await on two beaches. The rates include all activities (including golf nearby), meals and drinks. A good deal for the price. 312 rooms. Credit Cards: CB, V, MC, A.

East Winds Inn   **$225–$465**   ★★

La Brelotte Bay, ☎ *(809) 452-8212.*
Single: $225–$345. Double: $345–$465.

This small all-inclusive resort accommodates guests in duplex cottages right on the beach. Each unit has a living area and kitchenette, and relies on ceiling fans to keep things cool. The beach bar and dining room are in a thatched hut, and there's also a library and pool on the premises. 10 rooms. Credit Cards: V, MC, A.

Hummingbird Beach Resort   **$80–$165**   ★★

Soufriere, ☎ *(809) 459-7232.*
Single: $80–$125. Double: $105–$165.

This small resort is private and secluded. Guest rooms have ceiling fans (no air), mosquito netting over the beds, and balconies. The grounds are very nicely landscaped and open onto a public black-sand beach. Facilities are limited to a fine restaurant and a pool. Decent for the rates, and don't miss the gift shop, which has a lovely array of batik articles created by the owner. 10 rooms. Credit Cards: MC, A.

Islander Hotel/Apartments $80–$135 ★★

Rodney Bay, ☎ (809) 452-8757.
Single: $80–$125. Double: $85–$135.
Guests at this resort can choose from standard rooms (nicely done and very comfortable) and one-bedroom apartments with fully equipped kitchens. All are air-conditioned and benefit from maid service. The grounds include a restaurant, terrace bar and pool. The beach is nearby, and there are lots of eateries within walking distance. Quite a bargain. 63 rooms. Credit Cards: V, MC, A.

Jalousie Plantation $345–$655 ★★★★

Soufriere, ☎ (800) 392-2007, (809) 459-7666.
Single: $345–$655. Double: $485–$655.
Environmentalists with a conscience probably wouldn't consider staying at this all-inclusive resort, as it was developed in a pristine area that many believe should have been left alone. The setting is gorgeous, perched on a hillside between the Pitons on beautifully landscaped grounds. Most accommodations are in one- and two-bedroom cottages with air conditioning, refrigerators, cable TV, verandas and plunge pools. Twelve suites are housed in a former sugar mill. The extensive grounds include many dining options, four tennis courts, a spa, and private beach. 115 rooms. Credit Cards: MC, A.

Ladera Resort $180–$655 ★★★

Soufriere, ☎ (800) 841-4145, (809) 459-7323.
Single: $180–$655. Double: $180–$655.
Set on a lush hillside 1000 feet above sea level, this resort offers great views of the Pitons and beyond. Accommodations are in nine villas and nine suites, all quite luxurious with four-poster beds and antiques. The best feature in each is the completely open wall that affords breathtaking views. Some units also have private plunge pools or Jacuzzis. The food in the restaurant is as fine as the views; a bar and communal pool round out the facilities. This unique spot is really special and very popular with those who like luxury combined with peace and privacy. 16 rooms. Credit Cards: MC, A.

Le Sport $245–$905 ★★★★★

Cap Estate, ☎ (800) 544-2883, (809) 450-8551.
Single: $245–$305. Double: $405–$905.
Prepare to be pampered, spoiled and primped at this all-inclusive resort situated at the island's northwestern tip and encompassing some 1500 acres. The health spa, called the Oasis, is a sterling facility with exercise classes, yoga programs, and wonderful treatments like massages, facials and body wraps. Guest rooms are as plush as everything else. Meals are wonderfully prepared, with lots of delicious dishes that are also low on calories and--could it be true?--good for you. There's also tennis, watersports, nightly entertainment and bicycles. Indulge! 102 rooms. Credit Cards: MC, A.

Rendezvous $2470–$3420 ★★★

Malabar Beach, ☎ (800) 544-2883, (809) 452-4211.
This all-inclusive resort used to be a Couples, but is now independent (though still open only to twosomes). Encompassing seven acres with two miles of beachfront, it

houses guests in garden or oceanfront rooms, all with air conditioning, modern amenities, and balconies or patios. The rates include all meals, drinks, and activities, and there's plenty to do: two pools, two tennis courts, all watersports, and exercise classes in the gym. There's daily entertainment in the Terrace Bar, and night owls appreciate the Piano Bar, which stays open until the last guest leaves. Rates range from $2470 to $3420 per couple per week. Tipping is not allowed. 100 rooms. Credit Cards: MC, A.

Royal St. Lucian Hotel $215–$385 ★★★

Reduit Beach, ☎ *(800) 255-5859, (809) 452-9999.*
Single: $215–$385. Double: $215–$385.
Located north of Castries on the beach, all accommodations at this hotel are suites with all modern conveniences. The hotel's centerpiece is the large pool, a series of interconnected waterholes complete with falls and a swim-up bar. Great food in the two restaurants, and guests can spend hours whiling away the time in the gorgeous marbled atrium lobby. Tennis and watersports await at the adjacent St. Lucian, the hotel's sister property. Very elegant. 98 rooms. Credit Cards: CB, V, MC, A.

Sandals Halcyon ★★★

Choc Beach, ☎ *(800) 726-3257, (809) 452-5331.*
This all-inclusive resort just joined the Sandals family in 1984 after a previous incarnation as the Halcyon Beach Club Hotel. Open only to opposite-sex couples, the resort is set on a nice beach four miles outside of Castries. The rates cover everything from soup to nuts, with three restaurants and seven bars from which to choose. Recreational facilities include two tennis courts, two pools, watersports, plenty of organized tours and activities, and nine holes of golf at Sandals St. Lucia. Rates are $810 to $1020 per person per three days, the minimum stay. 180 rooms. Credit Cards: MC, A.

Sandals St. Lucia $2775–$4650 ★★★★

La Toc, ☎ *(800) 726-3257, (809) 452-3081.*
This 155-are resort is set in a valley 10 minutes outside of Castries. Open only to heterosexual couples, it follows the all-inclusive plan that has made its resorts so popular in Jamaica. Guests are housed in standard rooms very nicely done with four-poster beds and modern amenities; there are also 54 suites with living rooms, VCRs, refrigerators, and terraces. Some even have private plunge pools. The rates ($2775–$4650 per couple weekly) include virtually everything, including tennis on five courts, nine holes of golf, watersports, fitness classes, and lots of activities. Fun. 209 rooms. Credit Cards: V, MC, A.

St. Lucian Hotel $59–$165 ★★★

Reduit Beach, ☎ *(800) 255-5859, (809) 452-8351.*
Single: $59–$165. Double: $59–$165.
Set on one of the island's best beaches, this sprawling resort houses guests in typical rooms that are air-conditioned and comfortable enough, but a bit on the worn side. The grounds include two restaurants, three bars, a very happening disco, a pool, two tennis courts, and all watersports, including a certified windsurfing school. Not

the most luxurious resort on St. Lucia by any means, but the rates are quite reasonable, and the active set is kept happy. 260 rooms. Credit Cards: V, MC, A.

Wyndham Morgan Bay Resort $250–$580 ★★★

Gros Islet, ☎ *(800) 822-4200, (809) 450-2511.*
Single: $250–$415. Double: $355–$580.

This all-inclusive resort is located a mile from Castries on a small beach. Guest rooms and suites are modern and attractive, with all the creature comforts associated with Wyndham. The rates include all meals, drinks and activities, and there's plenty to keep guests busy: four tennis courts, fitness center, watersports (scuba, snorkeling, and fishing costs extra), and nightly entertainment. Children are kept occupied in organized programs. 238 rooms. Credit Cards: CB, V, MC, A.

Apartments and Condominiums

You can rent either luxurious villas or more basic digs that come with kitchenettes. Decide whether you want to be closer to the tourist hub or away from it all; apartments in Soufriere and Gros Islet will seem more secluded. Fruits and vegetables can be picked up at the local market, and fish can be bought right off the boats.

Harmony Marina Suites $123–$291 ★★

Rodney Bay, ☎ *(809) 452- 336.*
Single: $123–$205. Double: $193–$291.

This all-suite hotel is set on Rodney Bay Lagoon, some 200 yards from the beach. Standard suites are air-conditioned and include coffeemakers and minibars; some also have kitchens. Deluxe units have four-poster beds and Jacuzzis. All are serviced by maids. The grounds include a pool, mini-market, and restaurant. Popular with families. 30 rooms. Credit Cards: MC, A.

Marigot Bay Resort $90–$220 ★★★

Marigot Bay, ☎ *(800) 334-2435, (809) 451-4357.*
Single: $90–$160. Double: $90–$220.

Located seven miles from Castries, this resort encompasses several buildings that offer everything from studios to two-bedroom cottages. Its marina attracts the yachting set, and the property is split in two by the lovely bay; water taxis provide transportation back and forth. Guests are put up in an inn, villas, and pretty cottages, all with nice decor and full kitchens. The grounds include two restaurants, two bars, a pool, and extensive watersports--this place is home to both a windsurfing school and a dive shop. You'll need a car to get around, as it's pretty isolated here. 40 rooms. Credit Cards: MC, A.

Inns

Green Parrot Inn $65–$115

Morne Fortune, ☎ *(809) 452-3399.*
Single: $65–$95. Double: $80–$115.

Located on a mountainside with nice views of Castries and the sea, this inn houses one of St. Lucia's best gourmet restaurants. Guest rooms are air-conditioned and have balconies, but won't win any prizes for decor or ambience. There's a large pool on the premises but no other facilities. You'll want a car to get around. Okay for the rates, but you're probably better off just eating here (that's a delight) than staying overnight. 60 rooms. Credit Cards: MC, A.

Low Cost Lodging

Depending how many people you can stuff into an apartment will determine how much you pay per person. Do ask the Tourist Board for other cheap rooms for rent, but don't always trust a description sight unseen. Don't expect much decor or air conditioning in inexpensive guesthouses.

Caribbees Hotel $50–$75   ★

La Pansee, ☎ *(809) 452-4767.*
Single: $50–$60. Double: $65–$75.
This small hotel offers low-cost rates for those who don't mind sacrificing a beach location. Guest rooms are air-conditioned and simple, with phones, TVs, and patios or balconies. There's a bar, restaurant and pool on the premises, but not much else. You'll want a car for mobility. 18 rooms. Credit Cards: A.

Where to Eat

Highest Rated Restaurants in St. Lucia

★★★★ **Dasheene Restaurant**

★★★★ **Jimmies**

★★★ **Bistro**

★★★ **Capones**

★★★ **Chart House**

★★★ **Chez Paul**

★★★ **Green Parrot**

★★★ **Hummingbird**

★★★ **Key Largo**

★★★ **Marina Steak House**

Most Exclusive Restaurants in St. Lucia

★★★★	**Dasheene Restaurant**	$35–$45
★★★	**Chez Paul**	$20–$35
★★★	**Chart House**	$11–$30
★★★	**Bistro**	$14–$24
★★★	**Hummingbird**	$9–$26

Fielding's Best Value Restaurants in St. Lucia

★★★	**San Antoine**	$15–$32
★★★★	**Jimmies**	$14–$28
★★★	**Green Parrot**	$33–$40
★★★	**Chez Paul**	$20–$35
★★★	**Capones**	$11–$24

Excellent international cuisine can be found on St. Lucia. The fertile volcanic soil supports a cornucopia of exotic fruits and vegetables; the six types of bananas are particularly delicious. Island chefs make inventive use of papayas, soursops, mangos, passionfruit and coconuts. Most restaurants try to take advantage of the unparalleled natural beauty, so beautiful views have become almost commonplace. One of the most atmospheric eateries is **San Antoine**, perched in the hills overlooking Castries, which incorporates the walls of a 19th-century greathouse, with antique tableware to match. Try the delicious swordfish at **Jammer's** at Windjammer Landing, a villa complex, with pole beams, table linens and bridal-white cane furniture. **Naked Virgin** in Castries is a good bet for traditional West Indian and creole specialties like callaloo, curries and pepperpot stew. Excellent jerk chicken, a Jamaican specialty, can be had at **Jimmie's**.

A-Pub $$$ ★★

The Waterfront, Rodney Bay, ☎ *(809) 452-8725.*
International cuisine.
Lunch: entrees $15–$30.
Dinner: entrees $15–$30.

A convivial yachtie hangout and local watering hole fronting Rodney Bay, the A-Pub serves up terrific steaks, fish and chips, West Indian specialties, and a few international dishes. Join the crowd for a friendly happy hour each evening. Closed: Sun.

Credit Cards: V, A.

Bistro $$$ ★★★

Waterfront, Rodney Bay, ☎ *(809) 452-9494.*
Seafood cuisine.
Dinner: 5:00 p.m.–10:30 p.m., entrees $14–$24.

The British owners provide pub offerings like steak and kidney and shepherd's pie along with a varied, extensive seafood menu. Dining is on a wide elevated deck perched on the waterfront. Nautical types and others like the 20 percent discount on food items before 6:30 p.m., sort of a Caribbean early bird special. Closed: Thur. Reservations recommended. Credit Cards: V, MC, A.

Capone's $$$ ★★★

Reduit Beach, Rodney Bay, ☎ *(809) 452-0284.*
Italian cuisine.
Lunch: 11:30 a.m.–4:30 p.m., entrees $11–$24.
Dinner: 4:30 p.m.–10:30 p.m., entrees $11–$24.

Patrons are served by wait staff dressed like 1930s mobsters who present the dinner check in a violin case. But it's all a lot of fun, and the Italian food is skillfully prepared. Dishes include fresh pasta, *osso bucco*, and juicy steaks. If the atmosphere is too heavy in the main dining room, there's a pizza parlor adjacent serving decent pies, burgers and sandwiches. Closed: Mon. Reservations recommended. Credit Cards: V, MC, A.

Chart House $$$ ★★★

Reduit Beach, Rodney Bay, ☎ *(809) 452-8115.*
American cuisine.

Dinner: 6:00 p.m.–10:30 p.m., entrees $11–$30.

The most popular dining room on the island could be this all-American chain steakhouse overlooking the yacht harbor. Guests like the attentive service by a loyal staff (very little turnover here) and the food, which is steak, lobster (in season), tangy baby back ribs, and some Caribbean specialties, all familiar and well-prepared. The restaurant is a fern-filled wood-frame house that exudes warmth. Closed: Sun. Reservations recommended. Credit Cards: V, MC, DC, A.

Chez Paul $$$ ★★★

Derek Walcott Square, Rodney Bay, ☎ (809) 452-3022.
International cuisine.
Lunch: 9:00 a.m.–4:00 p.m., entrees $20–$35.
Dinner: 4:00 p.m.–11:00 p.m., entrees $20–$35.

Chez Paul is a more streamlined version of Rain, the South Pacific-themed restaurant that has held court on this spot since 1885. The drinks are still heady and rum-based, but the food, which was never the real attraction, is now a more sophisticated melding of European, Asian and Caribbean influences. It's open for sandwiches and lighter meals all day long. The tin-roofed house overlooks Derek Walcott Square, which is named after St. Lucia's distinguished Nobel Prize winner. Reservations recommended. Credit Cards: V, MC, DC, A.

Dasheene Restaurant $$$ ★★★★

Ladera Resort, Soufriere, ☎ (809) 459-7850.
International cuisine.
Lunch: entrees $35–$45.
Dinner: entrees $35–$45.

The view from this hilltop aerie is unbeatable, nestled between the Pitons in Soufriere, an old French fishing community known for its sulphur springs. Located in a rustically chic villa resort, Dasheene is named after an exotic leaf used in cooking, and the menu, which changes often, incorporates locally grown produce, prime meats and seafood. The Austrian chef favors kingfish, which he likes to smoke and serve with mango or avocado and coconut sauces. Fish and shellfish are delivered to the restaurant daily. Associated Hotel: Ladera Resort. Reservations recommended. Credit Cards: V, MC, A.

Eagle's Inn $ ★★

Reduit Beach Road, Rodney Bay, ☎ (809) 452-0650.
Latin American cuisine.
Lunch: entrees $8–$10.
Dinner: entrees $8–$10.

This small funky spot, which is one of a friendly string of similar joints in Reduit Beach, serves French-inspired West Indian food. The atmosphere is very low-key and romantic, with an eagle-eye view of Gros Ilet in the distance. A good place for curry and fish dishes. Closed: Fri, Sat. Credit Cards: V, MC, A.

Ginger Lily $ ★★

Reduit Beach, Rodney Bay, ☎ (809) 452-8303.
Chinese cuisine.
Lunch: 11:30 a.m.–2:30 p.m., entrees $7–$11.
Dinner: 6:00 p.m.–11:00 p.m., entrees $7–$11.

Cantonese specialties are on hand at this popular restaurant near the tourist hotels in Reduit Beach. There's always a long list of familiar favorites, which pleases residents who flock here often when the urge hits. Lunch specials are available, with several courses for under $8. Closed: Mon. Credit Cards: V, MC, A.

Green Parrot $$$ ★★★

Red Tape Lane, Morne Fortune, ☎ *(809) 452-3399.*
International cuisine.
Lunch: 12:00 a.m.–3:00 p.m., entrees $33–$40.
Dinner: 7:00 p.m.–12:00 p.m., prix fixe $33–$40.
Chef Harry brought his years of culinary expertise learned at Claridge's in London home to St. Lucia, and now cooks and entertains nightly at this lively spot on a hilltop in Morne Fortune, overlooking Castries. His spiced pumpkin creation, "soup oh la la" will make you say just that when you taste it. Known for a scrumptious lunch buffet where you can heap your plate with West Indian goodies for under $8, Green Parrot is also a wild scene several nights a week when belly or limbo dancers (including Harry) reign. There's a well-chosen wine list. Associated Hotel: Green Parrot. Reservations recommended. Credit Cards: V, MC, A.

Hummingbird $$$ ★★★

Anse Chastenet Road, Soufriere, ☎ *(809) 459-7232.*
French cuisine.
Lunch: entrees $9–$26.
Dinner: entrees $9–$26.
Combine lunch with a plunge in the pool at this restaurant located in a rustic resort on the Soufriere waterfront. Visitors flock here when the house specialty, freshwater mountain crayfish, is in season. At other times, enjoy other seafood dishes, steaks, sandwiches and rich desserts. Associated Hotel: Hummingbird Resort. Credit Cards: V, MC.

Jimmies $$$ ★★★★

Vigie Cove Marina, Rodney Bay, ☎ *(809) 452-5142.*
Latin American cuisine.
Lunch: 11:00 a.m.–4:00 p.m., entrees $14–$28.
Dinner: 4:00 p.m.–11:00 p.m., entrees $14–$28.
Jimmies' bar has long been known as the place to meet and greet, but the cuisine, authentic West Indian specialties prepared by a local chef who trained in fine restaurants in England, is also worth noting. Jimmie cooks with a light touch, and his pancakes and crepes stuffed with vegetables and seafood are sublime. Closed: Sun. Credit Cards: V, MC, A.

Key Largo $$ ★★★

The Marina, Rodney Bay, ☎ *(809) 452-0282.*
Italian cuisine.
Lunch: 11:30 a.m.–4:00 p.m., entrees $6–$17.
Dinner: 4:00 p.m.–10:00 p.m., entrees $6–$17.
Sophisticated pizzas on a patio are served at this small restaurant with its own outdoor brick oven. All manner of Italian coffee drinks are dispensed here as well. Try the house specialty, a pizza made with artichokes and shrimp. Closed: Mon. Credit Cards: V, MC.

Kimlan's $ ★★

Micoud Street, Rodney Bay, *(809) 452-1136.*
Latin American cuisine.
Lunch: 7:00 a.m.–4:00 p.m., entrees $3–$5.
Dinner: 4:00 p.m.–11:00 p.m., entrees $3–$5.

A local family runs this upper-level West Indian restaurant with a terrace positioned directly across from Columbus Square. Steaming bowls of curry or fish stews are served with rice and salad. A good spot for people watching, and for lighter snacks and ice cream. Closed: Sun. Credit Cards: Not Accepted.

Marina Steak House $$$ ★★★

The Marina, Rodney Bay, *(809) 452-9800.*
Seafood cuisine.
Dinner: 5:00 p.m.–12:00 p.m., entrees $13–$19.

You'll find steak and seafood in a series of dim rooms with a bar where jazz piano can be heard playing on Friday nights. The restaurant, a converted private home in Rodney Bay Marina, is a reliable spot for American-style meals with vegetables and a baked potato served alongside. Closed: Sun. Reservations recommended. Credit Cards: V, MC, A.

Naked Virgin $$$ ★★

Marchand Road, Marchand, *(809) 452-5594.*
Latin American cuisine. Specialties: Flying fish.
Lunch: entrees $15–$25.
Dinner: entrees $15–$25.

This graceful West Indian building in the suburb of Marchand is the home of an excellent punch that gives the restaurant its provocative name. The brew is so potent, it might encourage you to take your clothes off. Be that as it may, the Virgin also has a loyal following of regulars who admire chef/owner John Paul's traditional creole cooking. Reservations recommended. Credit Cards: V, MC, A.

Paul's Place $ ★★★

Bridge St., Rodney Bay, *(809) 452-3398.*
International cuisine.
Lunch: 9:00 a.m.–4:00 p.m., entrees $7–$10.
Dinner: 4:00 p.m.–10:00 p.m., entrees $7–$10.

Paul's provides a tasty lunch buffet to office workers who crowd the place at noon. Those who don't want to brave the line can choose from a menu of rotis, sandwiches, and plate meals. Dinner is more subdued, with innovatively prepared fish, chicken, and steak dishes. It's not always up to par, but when it is, it shines brightly. Reservations recommended. Credit Cards: V, MC, A.

San Antoine $$$ ★★★

Old Morne Rd., Morne Fortune, *(809) 452-4660.*
International cuisine.
Lunch: 11:45 a.m.–2:15 p.m., entrees $15–$32.
Dinner: 6:15 p.m.–9:30 p.m., entrees $15–$32.

The surroundings are old fashioned and gracious, with meals served in the main house of the old San Antoine Hotel. The dining room, lit by candles at night, is run by an English couple who keep things purring along smoothly. Those looking for a special night out often choose this salon, which overlooks the twinkling lights of the harbor. The menu includes French and continental specialties, including seafood in parchment, pepper steak, or filet mignon with crayfish stuffing. Closed: Sun. Reservations recommended. Credit Cards: V, MC, A.

Where to Shop

St. Lucia's shopping won't disappoint. A new harborfront shopping complex called **Pointe Seraphine**, features a large variety of duty-free imports such as designer perfumes, crystal and china. You'll also find native crafts and resort wear there, but do try to avoid the complex when a cruise ship has docked. Market day (Saturday) at the Castries' 100-year-old market will give you a chance to kibitz with farmer's wives displaying luscious tropical fruits and vegetables, spices and local crafts; don't be shy about asking to sample a bite of tamarind, but keep a watch on your handbag and wallet. Good buys are woven fruit baskets for the kitchen back home; a good place to shop is the **government handicraft store** at the waterfront. A number of shops also sell locally made baskets, wood carvings and pottery. Hand-screened clothing and colorful batik apparel are featured buys, especially at the famous **Caribelle Batik** store. St. Lucia's artists tend to specialize in designs and portraits of the island's flora and fauna. If you want to see craftspeople working in their studios, stop by the **Arts &Crafts Development Centre**, near Choiseul, on the southwest coast; baskets, dishes, tapestries and woodcarvings are good buys. Some shops are being developed on the west coast, south of Castries. In general, prices at hotel and resort boutiques run much higher than elsewhere.

St. Lucia Directory

ARRIVAL AND DEPARTURE

American Airlines serves St. Lucia nonstop from New York/JFK every Sunday and daily from its San Juan, Puerto Rico hub, with connecting service to major U.S. cities. BWIA flies nonstop to the island twice a week from New York/JFK through September 14, and three times a week from Miami. St. Lucia is now directly accessible to six U.S markets, with charter programs beginning out of Boston (GWV), Chicago (Club Med), and Detroit (Keytours), in addition to those already available from Atlanta, Cincinnati and St.Louis.

The airport departure tax is US $11.

CLIMATE

Temperatures year-round average between 70 and 90 degrees F. Constant trade winds keep the air cool and the humidity form becoming oppressive.

DOCUMENTS

U.S. and Canadian citizens need to show a full and valid passport. British citizens need no passport if their stay does not exceed 6 months. French citizens must show an ID card. An ongoing or return ticket must also be shown.

ELECTRICITY

Current runs 220 volts, 50 cycles, with a square three-pin plug. A few hotels use 110 volts, 50 cycles. Bring an adapter and converter plug.

GETTING AROUND

Travel between Castries and other towns like Soufriere and Vieux Fort can be done in minibuses, usually overcrowded and stocked with local produce; you may have to share your seat with a carton of tomatoes. Buses leaving for Soufriere and Viewux Fort can be picked up in front of the department store on Bridge Street. To get to Cap Estate, take the bus near the market on Jeremy Street in Castries.

Taxis are omnipresent all over the island. They have excellent experience with the small, winding roads outside the capital. Many taxi drivers are guides and have been trained in showing tourists around the city and island. Cars are unmetered, but official rates have been set by the government. Before setting off for a destination, do verify the price in advance, and in what currency. When someone says dollar, you must specify whether it is the American dollar or the Eastern Caribbean dollar that is being talked about.

Rental cars are available in St. Lucia, but roads are difficult in the countryside and driving is on the left—always a bit hazardous for drivers used to the right side of the road. A driver's license is required and may be obtained from the Immigration Office upon arrival. It remains valid for three months. Stick with the top American names in agencies. You have assurance that you can use your credit card, arrangements can be easily made in advance before you leave, and if anything goes wrong, you can easily contact the head office back home. **Budget** ☎ *(809) 452-8021*; **Avis** ☎ *(809) 353-2046*; and **Hertz** ☎ *(809) 452-0679*. Of the three Hertz is the most expensive. It's best to get collision insurance; membership in auto clubs may lower the price in certain circumstances. Budget is the least expensive, about $300 per week for their least expensive car. All agencies can have cars waiting at the airport, or you can contact their office at the airport when you arrive. If it is the first time you are driving on the left-hand side of the road, it's a good idea to be traveling with a companion and allow them to spot the road for you. In foreign situations or one in which there are many distractions, or late at night, it is very easy to become forgetful and cross to the wrong side of the road, especially when you are turning or looking for directions.

LANGUAGE

The official language is English, though a local patois is spoken.

MEDICAL EMERGENCIES

A 24-hour emergency room is available a St. Jude's Hospital, Vieux Fort ☎ *454-6041* and Victoria Hospital, Hospital Road, Castries ☎ *452-2421*.

MONEY

The currency is the Eastern Caribbean dollar.

TELEPHONE

The area code is *809*. Local numbers have 7 digits, all of which should be dialed. International phone calls, as well as cables, can be made at the offices of the Cable & Wireless in the George Gordon Building on Bridge Street in Castries ☎ *452-3301*. Placing calls through your hotel or from your hotel room usually results in an enormous surcharge which is best avoided; some tourists have just been paralyzed by seeing the final bill tallying all their carefully monitored calls home.

TIME

Atlantic standard time, all year round, one hour earlier than New York time. During daylight saving time, however, it is the same hour.

TIPPING AND TAXES

The government imposes an 8 percent occupancy tax on hotel room rentals. Sometimes hotels and restaurants add a 15 percent service charge, but do check your bill carefully. In restaurants it is customary to tip waiters or waitresses 10–15 percent if it has not already been added to the bill. Airport porters usually receive about 75 cents a bag.

TOURIST INFORMATION

The **St. Lucia Tourist Board** is located at Point Seraphine in Castries ☎ *(809) 452-5968*. It's always worth stopping by to see if they have any brochures or suggestions for hikes, excursions, etc. It is also a source to find out what is happening in the community. In the U.S. call ☎ *(800) 456-3984*.

WHEN TO GO

January 1 and 2, which is the New Year's celebration, culminates in a two-day street fair offering local foods, island music, and dancing and games for children. Carnival is celebrated February 14 and 15 with elaborate costumes, dancing before dawn and national calypso contests. The annual St. Lucia Jazz Festival usually takes place in the middle of May. June 29 is the feast of St. Peter, a Fisherman's Day, where priests bless the fishermen's brightly decorated boats. August 30 is the Feast of

St. Rose of Lima, a spectacular flower festival dating back to the 18th century where members of the La Rose Flower Society sing and dance in the streets in costumes. September hosts an annual island-wide culinary competition. September 30–August 4 is an annual International Billfish tournament, with anglers from the region and North America participating. November 22 is St. Cecilia's Day, celebrated by musicians serenading the streets of Castries. Early December hosts the Atlantic Rally for Cruisers with the world's largest annual trans-ocean yacht race. Christmas, on December 25, is usually celebrated by early morning serenaders visiting homes and sampling holiday gourmet fare.

ST. LUCIA HOTELS	RMS	RATES	PHONE	FAX
Castries				
★★★★★ Le Sport	102	$245–$905	(800) 544-2883	809 450 0368
★★★★ Anse Chastanet Hotel	48	$95–$505	(800) 223-1108	809 459 7700
★★★★ Jalousie Plantation	115	$345–$655	(800) 392-2007	809 459 7667
★★★★ Sandals St. Lucia	209	$2775–$4650	(800) 726-3257	809 452 1012
★★★ Club Med St. Lucia	265		(800) 258-2633	809 454 6017
★★★ Club St. Lucia	312	$175–$445	(809) 450-0551	
★★★ Ladera Resort	16	$180–$655	(800) 841-4145	809 273 5302
★★★ Marigot Bay Resort	40	$90–$220	(800) 334-2435	809 451 4353
★★★ Rendezvous	100	$2470–$3420	(800) 544-2883	809 452 7419
★★★ Royal St. Lucian Hotel	98	$215–$385	(800) 255-5859	809 452 9639
★★★ Sandals Halcyon	180	$810–$1020	(800) 726-3257	809 452 5434
★★★ St. Lucian Hotel	260	$59–$165	(800) 255-5859	809 452 8331
★★★ Wyndham Morgan Bay Resort	238	$250–$580	(800) 822-4200	809 450 1050
★★ Candyo Inn	12	$75–$90	(809) 452-0712	
★★ East Winds Inn	10	$225–$465	(809) 452-8212	
★★ Harmony Marina Suites	30	$123–$291	(809) 452-0336	809 452 8677
★★ Hummingbird Beach Resort	10	$80–$165	(809) 459-7232	809 459 7033
★★ Islander Hotel/Apartments	63	$80–$135	(809) 452-8757	809 452 0958
★ Caribbees Hotel	18	$50–$75	(809) 452-4767	
★ Green Parrot Inn	60	$65–$115	(809) 452-3399	809 453 2272
★ Tapion Reef Hotel	30	$50–$80	(809) 452-7471	809 452 7552

ST. LUCIA RESTAURANTS	LOCATION	PHONE	ENTREE

Castries

American

| ★★★ Chart House | Rodney Bay | (809) 452-8115 | $11–$30•• |

Chinese

| ★★ Ginger Lily | Rodney Bay | (809) 452-8303 | $7–$11 |

International

★★★ Chez Paul	Rodney Bay	(809) 452-3022	$20–$35
★★★ Green Parrot	Morne Fortune	(809) 452-3399	$33–$40
★★★ Paul's Place	Rodney Bay	(809) 452-3398	$7–$10
★★★ San Antoine	Morne Fortune	(809) 452-4660	$15–$32
★★ A-Pub	Rodney Bay	(809) 452-8725	$15–$30

Italian

| ★★★ Capones | Rodney Bay | (809) 452-0284 | $11–$24 |
| ★★★ Key Largo | Rodney Bay | (809) 452-0282 | $6–$17 |

Latin American

★★★★ Jimmies	Rodney Bay	(809) 452-5142	$14–$28
★★ Eagle's Inn	Rodney Bay	(809) 452-0650	$8–$10
★★ Kimlan's	Rodney Bay	(809) 452-1136	$3–$5
★★ Naked Virgin	Marchand	(809) 452-5594	$15–$25

Seafood

| ★★★ Bistro | Rodney Bay | (809) 452-9494 | $14–$24•• |
| ★★★ Marina Steak House | Rodney Bay | (809) 452-9800 | $13–$19•• |

Soufriere

French

| ★★★ Hummingbird | Soufriere | (809) 459-7232 | $9–$26 |

International

| ★★★★ Dasheene Restaurant | Soufriere | (809) 459-7850 | $35–$45 |

Note: • Lunch Only

•• Dinner Only

SINT MAARTEN/ ST. MARTIN

Simpson's Bay lagoon is spectacular at sunset.

Half-Dutch, half-French, the island of Sint Maarten/St. Martin gives a bi-polar vacation for the price of one. Sint Maarten, the Dutch side, is part of the trio of islands that makes up the Dutch Windwards (including Sint Eustatius and Saba), while only a few steps away, St. Martin belongs to the French West Indies. A mere welcoming sign acts as the only border between the two sides—nary a customs officer in sight—but the contrasts are startling, if quite tantalizing. Not only are the native languages different (though most people speak English as a common dominator), the ambiance of each sovereign state nation bears its own unique personality. Quiet and

more refined, St. Martin's capital of Marigot is the place to go if you're looking for good (duty-free) shopping, fine Creole cooking, and French haute
cuisine; if you're looking to sail, frenzied Philipsburg, Sint Maarten's capital,
has the best port. Beaches are superb all away around the island, and scuba
divers and snorkelers will find very exciting conditions. Some of the Caribbean's most luxurious (and most expensive resorts) are situated on the island, but most tourists let themselves be lured to the sea at least for one day
(if not a week) to sail to some of the other glorious islands nearby.

Bird's Eye View

St. Martin/Sint Maarten lies at the top of the Guadeloupe archipelago,
144 miles east of Puerto Rico. The total land mass is 37 square miles. The
main airport and seaport are located on the Dutch side, which occupies the
southern part of the barely triangular island. The western coast is low-lying
and mostly comprised of Simpson Bay Lagoon, where small craft find a safe
harbor. The rest of the Dutch side is very hilly, almost conical scrubland,
though a good strong rain can turn it into a lush garden. Two ranges cross
the island, in-between which lies Great Bay and its Salt Pond, the valley of
Belle Plaine, and the smaller salt ponds at Le Galion. Dotting the coastline
are numerous bays that make for excellent beaches.

History

Columbus discovered and named St. Martin in 1493, and by the 1630s
both the Dutch and French had settled on the island. Pirates combed the
craggy shores and secret coves of the island, burying treasure and booty they
had won at sea. It was in St. Martin that Peter Stuyvesant (the last Dutch
governor of New York) lost his leg in a struggle with the Spanish in 1640.
According to legend, the bi-national division of St. Martin was determined
when a Dutchman and a Frenchman stood back to back, then circled the island until they encountered each other again, face to face. Since the French
side is somewhat bigger than the Dutch, leading devotees of this legend like

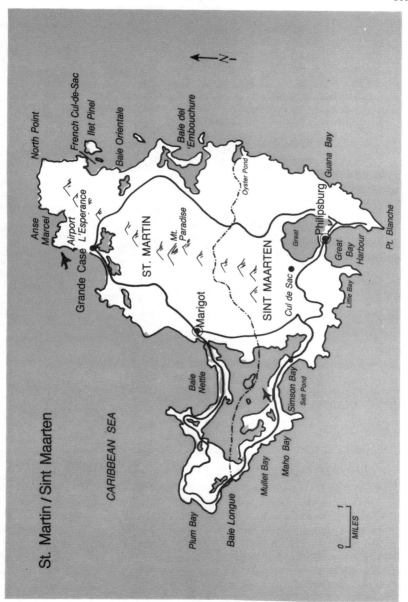

St. Martin / Sint Maarten

CARIBBEAN SEA

North Point

French Cul-de-Sac

Ilet Pinel

Baie Orientale

Baie del Embouchure

Anse Marcel

Airport

L'Esperance

Grande Case

ST. MARTIN

Mt. Paradise

Oyster Pond

Guana Bay

Philipsburg

Great

Pt. Blanche

Great Bay Harbour

Little Bay

Marigot

SINT MAARTEN

Cul de Sac

Simson Bay

Salt Pond

Baie Nettle

Mullet Bay

Maho Bay

Plum Bay

Baie Longue

0   1

MILES

—N—

to believe that the Dutchman was fatter and slower. More legitimate historians tend to suppose that a small group of French and Dutch prisoners escaped their Spanish captors and drew up an agreement to divide the island between them. In 1946, Guadeloupe, of which St. Martin is a dependency, became an Overseas Department of France and in 1974, an Overseas Region of France.

A cannon on St. Maarten is a reminder of days when pirates roamed the shores.

People

As of 1994, there were about 28,000 residents on the French side and 32,000 on the Dutch side, but ask residents what they want to be called and nobody knows. The confusion lies in the multilinguistical nature which divides the island as well as the genuine amiability which unites it. On the Dutch side, children in primary school study in English, while students on the French side don't learn English until secondary school. Still, there's no real overt competition, and the signs separating the Dutch from the French side are truly ones of welcome, rather than declarations of partisanship. To make matters even more confusing, there are many different accents among English speakers (one distinctly Jamaican) and even a lively street dialect called *papiamento*, a hefty Caribbean mix of English, Spanish, Portuguese, Dutch and African languages. There's enough interest in Papiamento to warrant its own newspaper.

With all the French sophistication and the Dutch gentility, superstition and backwoods lore are still strong and thriving in St. Martin, including the belief in *jumbies* (evil spirits) and *soucouyants*, a kind of vampire woman. The fetish for calypso is also pure Caribbean, though the lyrics lack the political bite known on more dissident islands, and contests and parties are held regularly throughout the year. The poet Lasana Sekou singularly upholds the literary tradition as the island's only published poet, rich in the local dialects and slang.

Beaches

St. Martin has 37 white sand beaches in excellent condition; many still wait to be discovered. Colors are dazzling, from deep blue to turquoise to emerald green. Take your pick from coastal crescent-shaped stretches noted for their seclusion to broad swatches of pristine virgin sand. Access to public beaches is easy, usually through little roads off the highway and even in high season, you won't find them uncomfortably crowded. In addition to the mile-long beach at **Great Bay** in Philipsburg, there is **Little Bay**, within a walking distance from town, with excellent watersports activities. At the west end of Cupecoy, you can bathe au naturel, but there are no facilities. Reachable more easily by boat are the more secluded beaches of **Plum Bay** and **Rouge Beach** (no facilities). You'll find a nudist beach (and clothes-optional hotel) at one end of **Orient Bay**. No roads go directly to the beach; rather, one must park on tracks off the main road at the north or south end of the beach and walk a few hundred feet to the water.

Dive Sites

Diving is excellent all year round in St. Martin, mostly done from boats, since wrecks tend to be some distance offshore. Among the different types of diving are reef, wreck, night, cave and drift; depths of dive range from 40-60 feet. Beginners will find excellent conditions for learning to snorkel or dive, with numerous sites accessible from shore and visibility averaging 150 feet. Basic can be taught in a day. Off the northeast coast, **Ilet Pinel** is extremely good for shallow diving. Also, **Green Key** makes a good barrier reef, and **Flat Island** (also known as Ile Tintamarre) is suitable for sheltered coves and sub-sea geological faults. To the north you'll find **Anse Marcel**, a good site, as well as the neighboring island of **Anguilla** (see the chapter on Anguilla for more information). Off the northeast coast, **Spanish Rock**, about one mile off North Point, is one of the best dive sites on the island, particularly for divers experienced with large swells. A small hill of rock and corals that starts at about two feet attracts lobsters, nurse sharks and large numbers of angelfish. On the Dutch side one of the best sites is **Proselyte Reef**, named for the British frigate, HMS *Proselyte*, which sank near Great Bay in 1801. Among the best dive shops are **Lou Scuba Club**, headed by PADI and CMAS instructor Lou Couture at the **Marine Hotel**. A reasonably priced packaged of 10 dives is offered by **Orient Bay Watersports**.

The calm waters ringing the shallow reefs and tiny coves make St. Martin exceptional for snorkelers. Most hotels rent equipment, and excursions are available to a shallow 15 ft.-coral reef. Some of the best sites are around Orient Bay, Green Kay, and Ilet Pinel; Flat Island (or Tintamarre) has been declared a regional underwater nature reserve. The use of harpoons is forbidden.

Treks

In general, there are no marked trails and there is no organized hiking on the island; you're on your own, so take along all the supplies you need. There are, however, numerous rural roads, where you are not likely to see much traffic, and which allow you to hike into the interior of the island with some safety. Trekkers should work on their thigh muscles before they come—most roads are very hilly.

Many hearty souls head for the restored ruins on the hill above Marigot, or the arid hills above Anse Marcel. Short hikes are excellent along the road from Marigot and Grande Case, the main town in the north. About halfway to Grand Case, a country road leads inland through peaceful green pastures that seem as if they are from another time and place. To see traditional homes with gardens profuse with poinsettias and bougainvillea, walk or drive the mile from Grand Case to **Colombier**. About two/tenths of a mile before the turnoff to Colombier, another country lane turns inland from the main road and winds up at **Paradise Peak**, the island's largest hill. You can either drive up the hill or take a pleasant hike. Since the area receives more rainfall than any other in St. Martin, the landscape is lush and verdant. At the parking area, you'll find a path leading to a lookout with spectacular panoramic views of the island.

Horses can be rented on St. Maarten/St. Martin for excursions over the hills of Anse Marcel to the beaches of Petite Cay or Cole Bay.

One of the best places to hike for a fabulous sunset is at the west end of the **Simpson Bay Lagoon**. Here the main road turns north, but secondary roads wind through the hilly peninsula westward. Traffic is light so walking can be quite pleasant, especially with superb coastal views. Start out in the late afternoon and witness a memorable color show in the sky.

Just offshore are the tiny islands of Petite Clef on the south and Ilet Pinel on the north—both have excellent beaches and good reefs for snorkeling. It takes about an hour to walk around Ilet Pinel, which is inhabited by wild goats that nibble on the scrub and cactus. To get there, contact a local fisherman in Cul de Sac, though boat excursions from Marigot and Philipsburg can be arranged through local operators

---

FIELDING'S CHOICE:

The Land-Sea Option—the newest craze in the Caribbean where for one price you get several nights in a room ashore and a few days of island hopping by boat—ideal for people who've thought that a yacht charter might be a great way to spend a vacation but didn't want to commit to an entire week. One of the best is the 32-room Biras Creek on Virgin Gorda, which lures you to its 140-acre nature preserve, with the promise of deluxe lodging with garden showers right beside the beach and the option of spending three days and two nights aboard a classy 445-foot Norseman 447 in a master stateroom with air-conditioning, kingsize bed, private shower, TV, radio, and stereo CD system. A crew of two who know these waters well take care of the sailing and cooking, and a high-speed tender puts you ashore on the beaches of the neighboring lakes. Contact Biras Creek, P.O. Box 54, Virgin Gorda, BVI; ☎ 809-494-3555 or 800-223-1108. Sailaway packages for two start at $3425 with five nights ashore, two nights on board.

What Else to See

Unless you have a fort fetish, there's not much to see in St. Martin; better stay on the beach, cruise to a neighboring island, or go shopping in **Marigot**, a kind of St. Tropez of the Caribbean which sports its own jet-set scene, nude beach, sidewalk cafes and fishing boats. The **Port La Royale Marina** makes an interesting pitstop (you may be there anyway, chartering a schooner), and the museum **On the Trail of the Arawaks** can be worth the trouble if you have any interest in Native American history. A good view of the French capital can be seen from the top of **Fort St. Louis** but be prepared for a hefty climb. To take your choice among the island's top restaurants, head for **Grand Case**, whose "Restaurant Row" has earned this tiny beachfront town the title "Gastronomic Center of St. Martin."

St. Maarten's shops at Simpson's Bay offer French fashions, batiks from St. Barts, jewelry, perfumes and quality gift items.

Don't miss the pastoral hamlet of **Orléans** (also known as the French Quarter), the oldest French settlement on the island. Here you'll find handsome small homes set among gardens alive with such tropical blossoms as bougainvillea, wisteria, flamboyant and hibiscus. **Roland Richardson**, a neighborhood artist, conservationist, and historian, welcomes visitors to his studio on Thursdays.

Philipsburg, the capital of the Dutch side, boasts **Great Beach Bay**, perhaps one of the cleanest city beaches in the world. You can find more about the history of the city at the **St. Martin Museum** at Museum Arcade on *119 Front Street*. Fauna and flora from the island can be glimpsed at the zoo, at **Madam Estate**, close to the New Amsterdam Shopping Center.

Museums and Exhibits

Simartn Museum   ★★★

111 Front Street, Philipsburg, Dutch Side.
Hours Open: 10:00 a.m.–6:00 p.m.
This small museum is housed in one of the few remaining 19th-century West Indian-style cottages on the island. Exhibits are on a changing basis, most focusing on the island's history and culture. There are some upscale specialty boutiques on the premises. Not worth a special trip, but a nice way to kill an hour or two if you're in the neighborhood. General admission: $1.00.

Tours

St. Maarten Zoo   ★★★

Madame Estate, Philipsburg, Dutch Side.

Hours Open: 9:00 a.m.–5:00 p.m.

This small zoo is especially suited to children (who get in for $2), with its playground and petting zoo. The grounds include botanical gardens, two walk-through aviaries, and caged animals from the Caribbean and South America. General admission: $4.00.

BEST VIEW:

At 1278-ft., Paradise Peak, called Pic du Paradis, offers a breathtaking view of both the French and Dutch capitals.

Sports

Almost every beachfront hotel has facilities for windsurfing and sunfish sailing; windsurfing lessons average about $20. Waterskiing and parasailing are offered by a few hotels.

Sailing is one spectacular sport in St. Martin. From bases in Marigot, as well as Anse Marcel and Oyster Pond near the French/Dutch border, you can find any number of yacht charters. Recommended moorings on the French side of St. Martin include: **Bai Rouge** (good anchorage), **Nettlé Bay** near Marigot, **Marigot Bay** (for shopping), **Friar's Bay** (calm), **Happy Bay** (beach-grazing), and **Grand Case Bay**, a charming fishing village with a dock grocery, pharmacy and excellent restaurants. A top-class marina can be found at **Port Louvilliers** at Anse Marcel, with docking space for 60 boats (29–73 ft.) and boutiques, grocery, cafe and **La Capitanerie**, a ship chandlery. At **Oyster Pond** you'll also find a large marina and **Captain Oliver's**, a popular restaurant and hotel, plus a small grocery and a ship chandlery. Sailing excursions from St. Martin to other islands (Anguilla is a favorite, but boats also go to St. Barts, Saba, St. Kitts, Nevis, and St. Eustatius) can be arranged by most hotels. Rates for a day trip with snorkeling, open bar and picnics run between $65–$70 per person.

Caid & Isa, a horseback riding facility located at Meridien L'Habitation at Anse Marcel, is operated by longtime pro Brigitte Sacaze. Paso Finas can be hired for 2 1/2-hour excursions over the hills of Anse Marcel to the private beach of **Petite Cayes**. Other facilities include the **OK Corral** at the Coralita Beach (including one pony for children) and **Crazy Acres** at Cole Bay (on the Dutch side).

Sport-fishing finds big fans on St. Martin. Half-and full-day charters with tackle, bait, and snacks are readily available at **Bobby's Marina**, **Great Bay**, **Simpson Bay**, and **Port La Royale Marina**. December to April is the season for kingfish, dolphin and barracuda; tuna is available year-round.

Boating is available on two types of vessels: large catamarans holding 25 or more passengers that sail to St. Barts for the day, or small sailboats that hold six to ten passengers for excursions to secluded beaches or deserted island. Boats depart from **Bobby's Marina** and **Great Bay Marina** in Philipsburg, **Simpson Bay Lagoon**, and **Port La Royale Marina** at Marigot Bay. A new marina is located at **Port Lonvilliers** at the north end of the French section.

There are numerous tennis courts on the island. **Le Privilege**, overlooking Meridien L'Habitation, has six lighted courses and **La Belle Créole** has four lighted Omni courts. **Laguna Beach** has three lighted hard-surface courts. Other hotels include **Nettlé Bay Beach Club**, **Mont Vernon**, **Simson Beach**, **Oyster Bay**, **Grand Case Beach Club**, **Coralita**, **Esmeralda Resort**, and **Green Cay Village**.

Golf

Mullet Bay Resort, Philipsburg, Dutch Side.

The island's only links are an 18-hole course designed by Joseph Lee. It is quite scenic and very challenging, but often open only to guests at the Mullet Bay Resort—if your heart is really set on golfing, play it safe and stay at this well-run resort. Greens fee for nonguests (when they are allowed) are about $100, and considerably less for guests—another reason to stay here.

Horseback Riding

Various locations, Philipsburg, Dutch Side.

On the Dutch Side, horses can be rented at **Crazy Acres** (☎ *5-42793*). On the French Side, try **Caid and Isa** (☎ *87-32-92*) and the **O.K. Corral** (☎ *87-40-72*). The going rate is about $40 for a two-hour trail ride.

Watersports

Various locations, Philipsburg, Dutch Side.

If your hotel doesn't offer the watersports you're seeking, a slew of companies are happy to help. Dutch Side: for boating and cruises, try **White Octopus** (☎ *5-23170*), **Caribbean Watersports** (☎ *5-42801*), **Bobby's Marina** (☎ *5-22366*), and **Lagoon Cruises** (☎ *5-52801*), which also offers parasailing. For deep-sea fishing, try **Wampum** (☎ *5-22366*), **Sea Brat** (☎ *5-24096*), and **Bobby's Marina** (☎ *5-22366*). Scuba divers can call **Leeward Island Divers** (☎ *5-242268*), **Tradewinds** (☎ *5-54387*), **St. Maarten Divers** (☎ *5-22446*), and **Ocean Explorers** (☎ *5-45252*), which also runs a unique underwater walk on which non-swimmers can stroll with the help of special helmets that supply oxygen.

Where to Stay

Highest Rated Hotels in Sint Maarten/ St. Martin

★★★★★ La Belle Creole

★★★★★ La Samanna Hotel

★★★★ Le Meridien l'Habitation

★★★★ Oyster Pond Hotel

★★★★ Point Pirouette Villas

★★★★ Sheraton Port Plaisance

★★★ Beachside Villas

★★★ Belair Beach Hotel

★★★ Captain Oliver's Hotel

★★★ Cupecoy Beach Club

Most Exclusive Hotels in Sint Maarten/St. Martin

★★★	Mullet Bay Resort	$270–$765
★★★★	Point Pirouette Villas	$161–$845
★★★★	Sheraton Port Plaisance	$225–$600
★★★	Pelican Resort & Casino	$125–$585
★★★	Maho Beach Hotel & Casino	$140–$460

Fielding's Best Value Hotels in Sint Maarten/St. Martin

★★★	Grand Case Beach Club	$95–$425
★★★★	Oyster Pond Hotel	$120–$310
★★★	Royal Islander Club	$180–$320
★★★	Pavillion Beach Hotel	$95–$255
★★★	Dawn Beach Hotel	$105–$290

Dream about it and you've got it in St.Martin, provided you can pay for it. Lodging runs from the fabulously chic resort to intimate inns tucked into beachside coves around the island. There are small, family-run establishments where you can make friends with the mom-and-pop owners, or time-share condos where you will never meet the owner. Even if you aren't in the Prince Charles tax bracket, you can still find digs worthy of your wallet. In 1995, the number of hotels totaled 50, with more than 3500 rooms. There are also apartment-hotels with cooking facilities, as well as privately staffed villas and homes for rent by the week or month. You could save money buying package deals. Do inquire when you are making your reservation whether you can pay by credit card.

Hotels and Resorts

Some fabulous resorts have been built during the boom that hit the French St. Martin in the last decade. **Le Meridien L'Habitation** is now integrated with **Le Domaine**, sporting a French attitude in service, but fortunately also in quality. **La Samanna** is nearly an intimate resort inn out of the Riviera; if you don't want twin beds, make sure you specify. La Belle Creole resembles a Mediterranean fishing village; the most special rooms are the three-story villas. Mont Vernon, built in 1990, boasts its own duty-free shopping mall, large swimming pool and full sports facilities.

Coralita Beach Hotel $115–$140   ★★

Marigot, ☎ (590) 87-31-81.
Single: $115. Double: $140.
This small hotel is family run. As the name implies, it's located right on the beach, about four miles from the center of town. Rooms are pleasant and air-conditioned, but could use a little work; some boast kitchenettes. Facilities include a bar, restaurant, pool and a tennis court. They'll arrange horseback riding, watersports and even yoga classes. 24 rooms. Credit Cards: CB, V, MC, A.

Divi Little Bay Resort $110–$350   ★★★

Philipsburg, ☎ (800) 801-5550, (599)-5-22333.
Single: $110–$350. Double: $110–$350.
Located a mile out of Philipsburg and set on a wide, sandy beach, this resort dates back to 1955, making it one of the island's oldest. Accommodations run the gamut from standard guest rooms to casitas to suites with one to three bedrooms. All are quite comfortable, air-conditioned, and feature refrigerators and balconies or patios. Guests can choose from two restaurants and two bars; other facilities include a pool on three levels, three tennis courts, shops and watersports. Busy and fun. 147 rooms. Credit Cards: V, MC, DC, A.

Esmeralda Resort $180–$300   ★★

Baie Orientale, ☎ (800) 622-7836, (590) 87-36-36.
Single: $180–$300. Double: $180–$300.
Situated on secluded grounds overlooking the bay, this property consists of 15 villas that can be rented in their entirety or partially as standard guest rooms. All are nicely decorated and have all the modern conveniences; some units have kitchenettes as well. Each villa has its own pool, but you may be sharing it, depending on how

much of the villa you rent. There are two restaurants, a bar, a large communal pool and three tennis courts. Watersports await on the mile-long beach, one of the island's best. 54 rooms. Credit Cards: V, MC, A.

Great Bay Beach Hotel $164–$285   ★★★

Philipsburg Bay, ☎ *(800) 223- 757, (599) 5-22446.*
Single: $164–$245. Double: $125–$285.

The Great Bay is one of the island's few all-inclusive resorts. Guest rooms are adequate, but nothing to write home about. The 10 junior suites have very large bathrooms with whirlpool tubs, but are not necessarily worth the bump in price. There are two restaurants and three bars, one with entertainment and shows nightly. The grounds also include two pools, a casino, a tennis court, gym, and all the usual watersports at the pleasant beach. 285 rooms. Credit Cards: V, MC, A.

Holland House Beach Hotel $69–$195   ★★

Philipsburg.
Single: $69–$180. Double: $84–$195.

This hotel is right in the center of Philipsburg on a small palm-dotted beach. Air-conditioned guest rooms have sitting areas, twin beds, TVs, and private balconies, though not all have views. The larger junior suites also have small kitchenettes. Be sure to book a room on the beach side, or you'll suffer from the din of the noisy street. There's a beachfront restaurant and bar, but no other facilities—much within walking distance, however. As many rooms can be had for just under $100 a night, this is a good in-town bet. 54 rooms. Credit Cards: V, MC, A.

Hotel Anse Margot $138–$261   ★★★

Baie Nettle, ☎ *(800) 742-4276, (590) 87-92-01.*
Single: $138–$247. Double: $169–$261.

Located a mile out of Marigot and fronting the lagoon, this hotel is a popular spot. Nine three-story buildings with pretty gingerbread trim house the guestrooms and suites, all quite pleasant with air conditioners, refrigerators, and private balconies. The restaurant is a beautiful spot for a romantic meal, and there's also a bar, two pools, and watersports on the beach. The clientele is predominantly European. 96 rooms. Credit Cards: V, MC, A.

Hotel Mont Vernon $105–$160   ★★★

Baie Orientale, ☎ *(800) 223- 888, (590) 87-62-00.*
Single: $105–$125. Double: $135–$160.

Situated on a mile-long beach, all accommodations here are in suites, all rather large, comfortable and pleasant. The free-form pool is the island's largest, and there are also two tennis courts and a fitness room for energetic types. The beach has all watersports and many topless bathers. Supervised programs keep little tykes busy during holidays and high season, and a free shuttle makes getting into Marigot and Philipsburg easy. Lots of conventioneers at this bustling resort. 394 rooms. Credit Cards: V, MC, A.

La Belle Creole $205–$455   ★★★★★

Marigot, ☎ *(590) 87-66-00.*
Single: $205–$455. Double: $205–$455.

Designed to resemble a Mediterranean village, this resort encompasses 25 acres and has two beaches. Guest rooms are found in villas linked by picturesque pathways. All are very spacious and luxuriously appointed. The 18 suites, which run from $900 to $1320 per night, are as posh as can be (at that rate, they'd better be!). The grounds include a lovely plaza, four tennis courts, a croquet lawn, pool, complete water-sports including a dive center, and exercise classes in the fitness center. Dining choices range from casual to elegant and there's frequent entertainment in one of the three bars. The beaches are not the greatest, but no one seems to mind at this lovely enclave. 160 rooms. Credit Cards: CB, V, MC, A.

La Residence $75–$98 ★★

Marigot, ☎ *(800) 365-8484, (590) 87-70-37.*
Single: $75–$80. Double: $92–$98.
This small hotel is in the heart of Marigot, one mile from the beach. Rooms are air-conditioned, modern, and comfortable, and a few accommodations offer kitchens. The French restaurant is quite good, and there's also a bar for unwinding. Popular with business travelers, as there is much within an easy walk. 21 rooms. Credit Cards: V, MC, A.

La Samanna Hotel $280–$995 ★★★★★

Baie Longue, ☎ *(590) 87-64-00.*
Single: $280–$825. Double: $280–$995.
This tony spot is set on 55 beachfront acres and is designed to resemble a Moorish Mediterranean village. Accommodations are in the main building and in villas scattered about the beach. All are on the small side but very elegant and spotless. Large patios, minibars, refrigerators, and air conditioning are standard throughout; massive renovations a few years ago did the job splendidly. The resort's well-heeled guests can play tennis on three courts, partake in all watersports, and splash about in the nice pool. The food is grand, and la Samanna gets high marks for seclusion and sophistication. Attentive service and extra touches like daily fresh flowers make this one of the Caribbean's finest resorts—and one blessedly free of pretensions. 80 rooms. Credit Cards: V, MC, A.

Laguna Beach Hotel $70–$185 ★★★

Baie Nettle, ☎ *(800) 333-1970, (590) 87-91-75.*
Single: $70–$180. Double: $80–$185.
This Victorian-style hotel overlooks the lagoon and its beach. Guests are housed in standard rooms to studios with two baths and kitchenettes. All are air-conditioned and have modern comforts like cable TV and hair dryers. The grounds include a large pool, restaurant and bar, and three tennis courts. Watersports can be rented on the public beach. Decent for the rates. 62 rooms. Credit Cards: V, MC, A.

Le Flamboyant $115–$364 ★★★

Baie Nettle, ☎ *(800) 221-5333, (590) 87-60-00.*
Single: $115–$364. Double: $115–$364.
This large beach hotel houses guests in tropically decorated standard rooms; the more expensive one- and two-bedroom suites have kitchenettes. Many resort amenities at this busy spot, including two pools, a tennis court, and watersports. Many on

the beach go topless. Two restaurants offer a choice of elegant or casual dining. 271 rooms. Credit Cards: CB, V, MC, DC, A.

Le Meridien l'Habitation $175–$655 ★★★★

l'Anse Macel, ☎ *(800) 543-4300, (590) 87-33-33.*
Single: $175–$655. Double: $175–$655.
Situated on 150 acres, this resort consists of the 251-room l'Habitation and the 145-room Le Domaine. All the guest rooms are nicely decorated and comfortable, though those in Le Domaine are larger, have oversized tubs, and are the better bet. Many rooms have kitchenettes; be sure to ask if this is important to you. The extensive grounds cater to resort lovers, with four restaurants, three bars, two pools, six tennis courts, racquetball and squash courts, and watersports at the beach. Most activities are included in the rates. 396 rooms. Credit Cards: CB, V, MC, A.

Maho Beach Hotel & Casino $140–$460 ★★★

Maho Bay, ☎ *(800) 223- 757, (599) 5-52115.*
Single: $140–$315. Double: $155–$460.
Set on a rocky bluff above the beach, this large resort is near the airport and can suffer from the roar of jets. Accommodations are quite nice and feature private balconies and large baths, all with bidets and some with whirlpool tubs. There are also 57 efficiency units with small kitchenettes. Facilities include nine restaurants, two cafes, a nightclub and several bars, a large casino, two pools, four tennis courts, a full-service health club, and all the usual watersports. This spot appeals to those who like busy resorts with all the accompanying activity. 600 rooms. Credit Cards: V, MC, A.

Mullet Bay Resort $270–$765 ★★★

Mullet Bay, ☎ *(800) 468-5538, (599) 5-52801.*
Single: $270–$515. Double: $270–$765.
Located seven miles from Philipsburg on 172 beachfront acres, this mega-resort is situated around the island's only 18-hole golf course. Accommodations include 300 guest rooms and 300 suites with kitchens. All are spacious and comfortable with refrigerators, modern conveniences, and views of the ocean, lake, or golf course. Guests can choose from six restaurants, eight bars, a casino, and a host of recreational options: 14 tennis courts, two pools, aerobics classes in the fitness center, all watersports, and lots of organized programs. There's also an arcade with more than a dozen tony boutiques, so bring lots of cash. The grounds are nicely landscaped and include a boardwalk and nature path for scenic strolls. Very nice for resort lovers, but lots of conventioneers can make things crowded. Those who like large and thriving resorts will not be disappointed. 570 rooms. Credit Cards: V, MC, DC, A.

Oyster Pond Hotel $120–$310 ★★★★

Oyster Pond, ☎ *(599) 5-22206.*
Single: $120–$310. Double: $120–$310.
This intimate hideaway is located in a secluded cove and surrounded on three sides by water. Accommodations are beautifully done in white wicker and pastel fabrics; each room is individually decorated and has ceiling fans, air conditioners, and seaview patios. The 20 suites are especially luxurious. The French restaurant is romantic and highly regarded, and there's also a comfortable lounge for quiet respites.

The mile-long beach is quite lovely but not the greatest for swimming; most guests prefer the saltwater pool. All is quite chic at this fine resort. 40 rooms. Credit Cards: CB, V, MC, DC, A.

Point at Burgeaux Bay $70–$395 ★ ★

Philipsburg, ☎ *(599) 5-54335.*
Single: $70–$395. Double: $70–$395.

This three-story hotel is located in a residential area, 15 minutes from downtown Philipsburg. It fronts the ocean, but the beach is a bit of a walk. Accommodations range from standard rooms to one- and two-bedroom suites with kitchens and terraces. Maids tidy up daily. Facilities are limited to a swimming pool and Jacuzzi. 14 rooms. Credit Cards: Not Accepted.

Royale Louisiana $49–$129 ★ ★

Marigot, ☎ *(590) 87-86-51.*
Single: $49–$129. Double: $67–$129.

Located in downtown Marigot above several shops, this hotel is a great bargain—if you don't mind the fact that a decent beach is a good 20-minute walk away. (There's a small one closer, but it's nothing to brag about.) Air-conditioned guest rooms are simple but comfortable, with telephones and VCRs. Facilities are limited to a restaurant and bar, but there's much within walking distance. Since the beach is not terribly convenient, it's unfortunate that this hotel does not have a pool. 75 rooms. Credit Cards: V, MC.

Sheraton Port Plaisance $225–$600 ★ ★ ★ ★

Simpson Bay, ☎ *(800) 732-9480, (599) 5-45222.*
Single: $225–$420. Double: $225–$600.

There's no beach at this large resort, but no one seems to mind. Perhaps they don't even notice—there's that much going on. The grounds include two pools (one made of rock with a large waterfall), seven tennis courts, a gym with exercise equipment, a marina, three restaurants and several bars, and a large and impressive casino. The accommodations are really quite special and run the gamut from studios to one- and two-bedroom suites with full kitchens. All are elegantly appointed with lots of marble and extras like VCRs. Future plans call for a golf course and many more rooms. 88 rooms. Credit Cards: V, MC, DC, A.

Summit Resort Hotel $55–$150 ★ ★

Simpson Bay Lagoon, ☎ *(599)5-52150.*
Single: $55–$135. Double: $65–$150.

Perched on a bluff and overlooking the lagoon, this complex consists of gingerbread-trimmed cottages clustered very closely (too closely) together. Accommodations are either studios or duplexes, all air-conditioned and boasting sitting areas and verandas. Some also have kitchens. There's a restaurant and bar on the premises, and the large saltwater pool is very nice. They'll shuttle you to the beach and Philipsburg, but you'll probably want a car so you can travel on your own schedule. 50 rooms. Credit Cards: V, MC, A.

Apartments and Condominiums

You can actually spend as much money on a fabulous villa as you would at a chic resort. Or you can find more modest digs and cook your own meals in a fully equipped kitchenette. The self-catering options in St. Martin are that vast. If you don't have a car, it will be important to be near the beach so you don't have to hire a taxi; the best on the shore are Dawn Beach Hotel, Belair Beach Hotel, Laguna Beach Hotel, and the Pavilion Beach Hotel. Do contact villa rental companies such as Carimo ☎ *87-57-58*, Immobilier St. Martin Caraibes ☎ *87-55-21*, and West Indies Immobilier ☎ *87-56-48*.

Beach House $53–$100   ★

Philipsburg.
Single: $53–$90. Double: $63–$100.
Located on Great Bay, a 10-minute walk from downtown Philipsburg, this guesthouse provides air-conditioned efficiencies with maid service. All have terraces and simple furnishings, as the rates suggest. You can cook in or saunter over to one of the many restaurants in the area. 10 rooms. Credit Cards: MC, A.

Beachside Villas $160–$405   ★★★

Simpson Bay.
Single: $160–$405. Double: $160–$405.
These Mediterranean-style villas are set on the beach and are quite elegant. All are individually owned but identically decorated, with two bedrooms, fully equipped kitchens, combination baths, living and dining areas, VCRs, and decks. Maids tidy up daily. Facilities are limited to a small pool, but there are many restaurants and shops in the area. The only downside is the proximity to the airport, which means loud roars when jets take off and land. 14 rooms. Credit Cards: MC, A.

Belair Beach Hotel $165–$375   ★★★

Little Bay Beach, ☎ *(800) 933-3264, (599) 5-23362.*
Single: $165–$300. Double: $190–$375.
This all-suite hotel is situated on the beach, next to the Divi Little Bay. The condos at this Mediterranean-style hotel are individually owned and rented out when the owners are elsewhere. Each unit has two bedrooms, two baths, full but small kitchens, living and dining rooms, VCRs, and private patios or balconies, and can sleep up to six. Facilities include a bar and restaurant and a tennis court—no pool, but the beach is right there, where watersports equipment can be rented. Request a unit on an upper floor for more privacy. Good for families. 72 rooms. Credit Cards: V, MC, A.

Captain Oliver's Hotel $100–$200   ★★★

Oyster Pond, ☎ *(590) 87-40-26.*
Single: $100–$165. Double: $110–$200.
Located on the French/Dutch border and fronting the lagoon, this charming complex gets high marks for its peaceful grounds and reasonable rates. Guests are housed in attached pink bungalows that hold junior suites with kitchenettes, rattan furnishings, air conditioners, and private balconies. The well-landscaped grounds feature two restaurants, a bar, a 100-slip marina, a dive center, and a pool. Watersports can be found at Dawn Beach, reached via water taxi. 50 rooms. Credit Cards: MC, A.

Club Orient Resort   **$120–$320**   ★ ★

Baie Orientale, ☎ *(800) 828-9356, (590) 87-33-85.*
Single: $120–$275. Double: $140–$320.
This resort has a "clothes-optional" policy which means that most (if not all) guests
are nudists. Located on a peninsula on the Atlantic side of the island, guests are
housed in rustic wooden chalets that have living rooms, full kitchens and large
porches. No air conditioners, but ceiling fans generally do the job. Facilities include
a casual beachside restaurant, a bar and two tennis courts. No pool, but you're right
on the beach. You'll need a car for mobility. 83 rooms. Credit Cards: CB, V, MC, A.

Cupecoy Beach Club   **$100–$650**   ★ ★ ★

Cupecoy Lowlands, ☎ *(215) 885-9008.*
Single: $100–$225. Double: $105–$650.
Situated on white sandstone cliffs that overlook Cupecoy Beach (whose size varies,
depending on the tides), this Mediterranean-style complex offers suites with one to
three bedrooms. All have full kitchens, nice decor, and spacious terraces. There's a
pool and bar on the premises, and they'll help arrange other activities and watersports. A restaurant and casino await across the street. They have no local phone;
the number shown is in Pennsylvania. 126 rooms. Credit Cards: Not Accepted.

Dawn Beach Hotel   **$105–$290**   ★ ★ ★

Oyster Pond, ☎ *(800) 351-5656, (599) 5-22929.*
Single: $105–$290. Double: $105–$290.
This resort is located three miles from Philipsburg in a relatively remote area. Guests
are accommodated in cottages on the hillside or beach, each holding studios with
rattan furnishings, living and dining areas, full kitchenettes, and private balconies or
patios. The pretty pool is accented by a waterfall. There are also two tennis courts,
a restaurant and watersports on the very nice beach. You'll need a car to get around.
155 rooms. Credit Cards: V, MC, A.

Grand Case Beach Club   **$95–$425**   ★ ★ ★

Grand Case, ☎ *(800) 447-7462, (590) 87-51-87.*
Single: $95–$260. Double: $95–$425.
Located on a crescent beach, this apartment complex consists of six white stucco
buildings that offer nice ocean views. Accommodations include studios and one-and
two-bedroom suites, all air conditioned and with rattan furnishings and fully
equipped kitchens. All have a private patio and are serviced daily by maids. Facilities
include a restaurant, bar, tennis court and complete watersports. No pool, but the
beach is fine for swimming. 71 rooms. Credit Cards: V, MC, DC, A.

Horny Toad Guesthouse   **$103–$185**   ★ ★

Simpson Bay, ☎ *(599) 5-53316.*
Single: $103–$185. Double: $103–$185.
This former governor's residence combines guesthouse ambience with apartment
living. It is located on a lovely beach that sometimes suffers from jet noise at the
nearby airport. Each one-bedroom apartment is individually decorated and quite
charming, with fully equipped kitchens, fresh flowers, and maid service. The friendly
owners, Earle and Betty Vaughn, treat renters like personal guests, providing a gracious touch lacking in the fancier resorts. There are no facilities on-site, but there's

plenty to do within walking distance. No kids under seven. 8 rooms. Credit Cards: Not Accepted.

Hotel le Belvedere $85–$120   ★★

Cul de Sac, ☎ *(800) 221-5333, (590) 87-37-89.*
Single: $85–$120. Double: $85–$120.
Located on the northeast coast, all accommodations at this property are suites that are on the small side but offer kitchenettes and all the creature comforts. There's a large free-form pool and a bar and restaurant on the premises, and guests are transported free of charge to Pinel island where watersports await. You'll want a car, as this place is fairly remote, but the rates are very reasonable for what you get. 130 rooms. Credit Cards: V, MC, A.

Le Pirate Beach Hotel $110–$180   ★★

Marigot Bay, ☎ *(800) 666-5756, (590) 87-78-37.*
Single: $110–$180. Double: $110–$180.
Set on the beach just outside of Marigot, this condominium hotel houses guests in air-conditioned studios with kitchenettes and terraces; each can sleep up to four. There's a bar and restaurant on the premises, as well as watersports and an activities desk for booking sightseeing excursions. Several restaurants are within walking distance, so renting a car is not as important as at some of the more remote resorts. 60 rooms. Credit Cards: V, MC, A.

Marine Hotel Simpson Beach $101–$230   ★★

Baie Nettle, ☎ *(800) 221-4542, (590) 87-68-68.*
Single: $101–$230. Double: $111–$230.
This property combines self-catering units with resort amenities. Accommodations are found in five-story creole-style buildings, each decorated with rattan furniture and sporting kitchenettes on the balcony. There are also 45 duplex units with two bedrooms and two baths. The premises include a restaurant, bar, pool, tennis court and watersports. Not bad for the rates. 165 rooms. Credit Cards: CB, V, MC, A.

Nettle Bay Beach Club $100–$450

Baie Nettle, ☎ *(800) 999-3543, (590)87-95-24.*
Single: $100–$450. Double: $140–$450.
Accommodations here range from villas to garden suites, all with full kitchens. Villas are large and bright though rather sparsely furnished, and come in one- and two-bedroom configurations. The garden suites are one-bedroom units with smaller kitchen areas. All are air-conditioned and have private terraces or patios. The grounds include three tennis courts, five pools, and a restaurant. 230 rooms. Credit Cards: MC, A.

Pavilion Beach Hotel $95–$255

Marigot, ☎ *(590) 87-96-46.*
Single: $95–$255. Double: $125–$255.
This small hotel is set right on the beach, with a sea view from each of its 16 rooms. Accommodations are either studios or suites, all large and inviting and boasting kitchenettes. Request an upper floor for more privacy. There are no on-site facilities, but the central location puts much within walking distance. 16 rooms. Credit Cards: MC, A.

Pelican Resort & Casino   **$125–$585**

Simpson Bay, ☎ (800) 626-9637, (599) 5-42503.
Single: $125–$345. Double: $125–$585.

This full-service resort combines the best of both worlds: condo living with full resort amenities. The air-conditioned accommodations range from studios to three-bedroom suites, all colorfully done in tropical decor and with fully equipped kitchens with dishwashers and microwaves. Facilities include three restaurants, a large casino, a full-service health spa, six pools—two with swim-up bars—six tennis courts, and a marina. Extensive watersports include cruises aboard the property's catamaran. There's even a doctor's office! With all that going on, this resort isn't for everyone—it's not exactly an idyllic escape, more like a teeming mini-city. Especially suited to families with its two kiddie pools, playground and poolside barbecue areas. 655 rooms. Credit Cards: CB, V, MC, A.

Point Pirouette Villas   **$161–$845**

Simpson Bay Lagoon, ☎ (599) 5-44207.
Single: $161–$700. Double: $161–$845.

This villa complex is situated on a private peninsula in the lowlands area. The Mediterranean-style villas have one or two bedrooms. All are air conditioned and have living and dining rooms, VCRs, stereos, full kitchens, and small private pools, and all are quite posh. Facilities include a tennis court and gym; restaurants, shops, and casinos are within walking distance. 85 rooms. Credit Cards: MC, A.

Royal Islander Club   **$180–$320**

Philipsburg, ☎ (599) 5-52388.
Single: $180–$250. Double: $180–$320.

This time-share property shares the beach and facilities with its sister property, the Maho Beach Hotel & Casino. Guests, therefore, have the convenience of condo living combined with the bells and whistles of a full resort. Accommodations range from studios to one- and two-bedroom suites, all very tastefully done with kitchens and all the modern comforts. There's an Olympic-size pool on the grounds, and guests can take advantage of the restaurants, bars, tennis courts, and other extensive facilities next door. Nice. 135 rooms. Credit Cards: V, MC, DC, A.

Town House Villas   **$130–$305**

Philipsburg, ☎ (599) 5-22898.
Single: $130–$305. Double: $130–$305.

Located on the outskirts of Philipsburg and right on the beach, this complex consists of 11 duplex villas. Each has two bedrooms, 1.5 baths, living and dining rooms, and full kitchens. Patios are set along a nice courtyard. Maids keep things tidy. No facilities on the premises, but lots of shops and restaurants are a short stroll away. Reasonable rates make this a popular choice. 12 rooms. Credit Cards: V, MC, A.

Tradewinds Beach Inn   **$61–$155**   ★

Simpson Bay, ☎ (599) 5-54206.
Single: $61–$115. Double: $61–$155.

This small inn is located on the beach at Simpson Bay. Guests can choose from studios and one- and two-bedroom apartments, all air-conditioned and with kitchenettes and maid service. Facilities are limited to a pool. 10 rooms.

Inns

Inns range in quality and cost. The smallest have now merged into a group called **Inns of Sint Maarten/St. Martin**; ask the Tourist office for more information. At Horny Toad, you may have to wave off landing planes at the nearby airstrip, but the beach is lovely and the management is family-friendly.

Mary's Boon   **$80–$155**   ★★★

Juliana Beach, ☎ *(599) 5-54235.*
Single: $80–$155. Double: $80–$155.

Located next to the airport, 15 minutes from Philipsburg, this is an authentic West Indian inn—not someone's idea of one. The beach is quite nice, but can disappear during high tide. Accommodations are in large studios with kitchenettes, patios, and ceiling fans in lieu of air conditioners. Public spaces are nicely accented with island art, tropical prints, and antiques. There's a restaurant and bar, but no other facilities. As with all the properties in this area, occasional airport noise is intrusive. 12 rooms. Credit Cards: Not Accepted.

Pasanggrahan Royal   **$73–$153**   ★★

Great Bay, ☎ *(599) 5-23588.*
Single: $73–$153. Double: $73–$153.

This inn, housed in a 19th-century governor's house, sits on a small strand of Great Bay Beach. Guest rooms are decorated in wicker and have balconies or patios; not all are air-conditioned and some are fairly run down. The studios are a better bet with their superior furnishings and kitchenettes. Guests forego modern amenities like phones and TV but are rewarded with a good dose of historical charm, especially noteworthy on this modern and developed island. The bar and restaurant are popular with locals. Lots within walking distance. 30 rooms. Credit Cards: MC, A.

Low Cost Lodging

The way to save money in St. Martin is stuff as many people as you can in an apartment or villa, go in off season, or cook your own food. Even small hotels can have big rates, so don't be misled by the size of the building. Cheap rooms usually mean noise, few furnishings and no tub. If you're savvy, you might be able to bargain down some prices.

Where to Eat

Highest Rated Restaurants in Sint Maarten/St. Martin

★★★★ **L'Auberge Gourmande**

★★★★ **Le Perroquet**

★★★★ **Saratoga**

★★★ **Antoine**

★★★ **Captain Oliver Restaurant**

★★★ **Cha Cha Cha's**

★★★ **Cheri's Cafe**

★★★ **Chesterfield's**

★★★ **Coco Beach Bar**

★★★ **David's**

Most Exclusive Restaurants in Sint Maarten/St. Martin

★★★	**Hevea**	$22–$38
★★★	**La Maison sur Le Port**	$17–$34
★★★	**La Nadaillac**	$16–$32
★★★	**Le Bec Fin**	$16–$31
★★★	**Coco Beach Bar**	$15–$30

Fielding's Best Value Restaurants in Sint Maarten/St. Martin

★★★	**The Wajang Doll**	$21–$30
★★★	**The Grill & Ribs Co.**	$5–$11
★★★★	**Le Perroquet**	$18–$26
★★★	**La Nadaillac**	$16–$32
★★★	**L'Escargot**	$18–$29

With its strong French influence, St. Martin almost has a legal obligation to serve world-class cuisine, and it doesn't disappoint. Out of 50 restaurants in Marigot, and another 20 in Grand Case and two dozen scattered throughout the island, many have top gourmet French kitchens; there are also fine Italian, Swiss, Vietnamese and Chinese eateries. American junk food is always within reach. Seafood is omnipresent, and French wines are in abundance. At some restaurants, you can dine to the tune of jazz, reggae, and pop, and bars stay busy until midnight. In Philipsburg, the best French restaurant is surely **Le Bec Fin**, where the Dutch royal family dines. In Philipsburg, good burgers and conch chowder for prices that won't break can be found at **The Greenhouse**, and cheap Chinese restaurants can be found on Back Street. Do reserve for most elegant dining, especially during high season. Prices for a three-course meal for two, without wine, can run from $60–$120 and upwards. Service charges are often added inconspicuously in the wrong place on credit card charges, so always peruse your slip carefully before signing or adding more tip. The legal age for drinking and gambling is 18.

Philipsburg

Antoine   **$$$**   ★★★

49 Front Street, Philipsburg, ☎ *(599)5-22964.*
French cuisine. Specialties: Fresh local crayfish.
Lunch: 11:30 a.m.–5:00 p.m., entrees $16–$32.
Dinner: 5:00 p.m.–10:00 p.m., entrees $16–$32.

A gorgeous setting on a breezy patio above Great Bay makes this restaurant a romantic choice for a celebration dinner. Cuisine is classic French with Italian touches. Some specialties offered bring back memories of an uncomplicated past; to wit, duck with cherries, lobster thermidor, and chocolate mousse. When in season, fresh local crayfish makes a welcome appearance. Closed: Sun. Reservations recommended. Credit Cards: V, MC, A.

Cheri's Cafe   **$$**   ★★★

Cinnamon Grove Center, Maho Beach, ☎ *(599) 55-3361.*
American cuisine. Specialties: Steaks, seafood.
Lunch: 11:00 a.m.–4:30 p.m., entrees $6–$12.
Dinner: 4:30 p.m.–1:30 p.m., entrees $12–$17.

Cheri Batson, owner of the legendary cafe and bar that bears her name, must share the honors for the success of her hugely popular eating establishment with her steak purveyor—customers are always raving about the quality and quantity of the grilled beef. A huge sirloin steak fills out a plate for a modest $10.95. A lot of customers think the place is just plain fun—nobody sits down for long when the house band, Ramon, starts to play. Great burgers are also on the menu, along with the inevitable grilled seafood. Credit Cards: Not Accepted.

Chesterfield's   **$$**   ★★★

Great Bay Marina, Pointe Blanche, ☎ *(559) 5-23484.*
American cuisine.

Lunch: 11:30 a.m.–2:30 p.m., entrees $7–$12.
Dinner: 5:30 p.m.–10:00 p.m., entrees $7–$20.

Rub epaulets with the boating crowd at this pierside restaurant with a casual, congenial ambience. The food is well-prepared, with a host of seafood, duckling and beef dishes served with flair at lunch and dinner. A companionable group often gathers for happy hour on a daily basis. Reservations recommended. Credit Cards: Not Accepted.

Greenhouse   **$$$**   ★★

Bobby's Marina, Philipsburg, ☎ *(599) 5-22941.*
American cuisine.
Lunch: 11:00 a.m.–5:00 p.m., entrees $6–$10.
Dinner: 5:00 p.m.–10:00 p.m., entrees $11–$25.

An all-purpose eatery that serves American favorites and exotic Indonesian specialties, the Greenhouse has a harbor location and a dining room lush with plant life. Guests can play pool, throw darts and dance as well as dine. It jumps daily at happy hour, which actually lasts a little longer; good for twofers and gratis hors d'oeuvres. Credit Cards: V, MC, A.

L'Escargot   **$$$**   ★★★

76 Front Street, Philipsburg, ☎ *(599) 5-22483.*
French cuisine.
Lunch: 11:00 a.m.– 3:00 p.m., entrees $8–$23.
Dinner: 6:30 p.m.– 11:00 p.m., entrees $18–$29.

Snail fanciers will enjoy a meal at this venerable grande dame of a restaurant, which has been in the same spot for over 20 years. The delectable delicacy is a specialty, and it shows up stuffed in mushrooms and in various other ways. The rest of the menu is largely French, encompassing duck, seafood, and meat dishes. Reservations required. Credit Cards: V, MC, A.

Le Bec Fin   **$$$**   ★★★

119 Front Street, Philipsburg, ☎ *(599) 5-22976.*
French cuisine.
Dinner: 6:00 p.m.–10:00 p.m., entrees $16–$31.

Ascend a flight of stairs to this second-floor dining salon in the courtyard of the St. Maarten Museum. At night, the ambience is candlelit and intimate, during the day try to snag a table overlooking the sea; there are only a few of them available. The kitchen really shines with its seafood preparations, especially lobster, served grilled or flamed in brandy. Reservations required. Credit Cards: V, MC, A.

Le Perroquet   **$$$**   ★★★★

72 Airport Road, Simpson Bay, ☎ *(599) 5-41339.*
French cuisine.
Dinner: 6:00 p.m.–10:00 p.m., entrees $18–$26.

This restaurant, situated in a typical West Indian house near the airport, serves very unique meals. Once seated, servers wheel a cart to your table with a choice of nightly specials—which often include filets of ostrich or boar steaks. Surprisingly, ostrich tastes more like beef, rather than the expected chicken. For less adventurous palates, fresh red snapper or beef dishes are usually available. Simpson Bay Lagoon

can be viewed from the plant-filled porch. Closed: Mon. Reservations required.
Credit Cards: V, MC, A.

Saratoga $$$ ★★★★

Simpson Bay Yacht Club, Simpson Bay, ☎ *(599) 5-42421.*
Seafood cuisine.
Dinner: 6:30 p.m.– 10:00 p.m., entrees $16–$26.

A perennial favorite, this yacht club restaurant in a mahogany-panelled dining room
features a changing menu of very fresh seafood offerings. Although pricey, its faithful following returns for specialties like scallops seviche or salmon in puff pastry with
spinach and mushrooms. Leafy salads feature at least two kinds of greens, served
with two homemade dressings. Steaks and beef dishes are also available. Closed:
Sun. Reservations recommended. Credit Cards: V, MC, A.

The Grill & Ribs Co. $ ★★★

Old Street Shopping Cntr., Philipsburg,
American cuisine.
Lunch: 11:00 a.m.–4:00 p.m., entrees $5–$11.
Dinner: 4:00 p.m.–10:00 p.m., entrees $5–$11.

This informal place is the island's best-known and best-loved ribarama. For a reasonable price of $12.95, diners can chow down on an unlimited amount of pork or
beef ribs. The Grill & Ribs Co. has two locations to choose from: a second story
alfresco terrace eatery at the Old St. Shopping Center, or the rib place behind Pizza
Hut on Simpson Bay Beach. Other offerings include chicken fajitas, burgers,
chicken and sandwiches heaped with a side of fries. Reservations required. Credit
Cards: Not Accepted.

The Seafood Galley $$ ★★★

Bobby's Marina, Philipsburg,
Seafood cuisine.
Lunch: 11:00 a.m.–3:00 p.m., entrees $7–$18.
Dinner: 6:00 p.m.–10:00 p.m., entrees $7–$18.

Although this pierside establishment has a clubby restaurant offering hot plates of
fresh fish and seafood, some people bypass it and head straight for the adjoining raw
bar. There they can graze all night from a generous menu of oyster shooters, clams
on the half shell, or crab claws. Lunchtime is popular for the view and the hearty
sandwiches and egg dishes. Closed: Sun. Reservations recommended. Credit Cards: V,
MC, A.

The Wajang Doll $$$ ★★★

134 Front Street, Philipsburg,
Asian cuisine. Specialties: Rijstaffel.
Dinner: 6:45 p.m.–10:00 p.m., entrees $21–$30.

It helps to come here with a big group and a healthy appetite for this restaurant's
20-item Javanese feasts. This cuisine, known as *rijstaffel* (rice table), originated in
the former Dutch colony of Indonesia. Seemingly endless plates of savory and spicy
seafood, meats and chicken are devoured over a mountain of fragrant rice. They can
be embellished with "try them if you dare" hot pepper sambals. Couples and singles

won't feel left out, as smaller and cheaper versions are available as well as a la carte dishes. Closed: Sun. Reservations recommended. Credit Cards: V, MC, A.

Marigot

Captain Oliver Restaurant   **$$$**   ★★★

Oyster Pond, Marigot, ☎ *(590) 87-30-00.*
Seafood cuisine.
Lunch: 12:00 a.m.–3:00 p.m., entrees $16–$24.
Dinner: 7:00 p.m.–11:00 p.m., entrees $16–$24.
A popular outdoor restaurant/snackbar/store on a pier facing the sea, Captain Oliver's sits across from its namesake resort. A thoroughly democratic place, the good Captain has provided a choice of eateries to fit every budget. There's a snack shack dispensing le chili dog and other light meals, with a grocery store attached. The centerpiece, though, is the oceanfront restaurant, where creative international cuisine, with an emphasis on seafood, is served for lunch and dinner. Soups are delicious and different, and the fresh tuna, when available, is stellar. Associated Hotel: Captain Oliver's. Reservations recommended. Credit Cards: V, MC, A.

Cha Cha Cha's   **$$$**   ★★★

Boulevard de Grand Case, Grand Case, ☎ *(590) 87-53-63.*
Latin American cuisine.
Dinner: 6:00 p.m.–11:00 p.m., entrees $11–$20.
This colorful cafe draws the au courant set who like to behave a little outre. The menu is a melting pot of piquant Latin and Gallic specialties that usually taste as good as they read. Skillfully grilled or steamed fresh seafood is served with tropical salsas. Some people never make it to the dining room, preferring to graze on a daring tapas menu while sipping a blender drink in a whimsical garden. Come before 7 p.m. to save a little money on a generous prix-fixe, three-course supper for under $20. Credit Cards: V, MC.

Coco Beach Bar   **$$$**   ★★★

Orient Beach, Marigot,
International cuisine.
Lunch: entrees $15–$30.
Dinner: entrees $15–$30.
By day Coco Beach bar is just one of five plain open-air eateries competing for the tourist dollar on clothing-optional Orient Beach. But at night, it becomes a quaint little candlelit restaurant, with tastefully set tables and a diverse menu, which includes caesar salad, filet mignon, and lobster with pasta. Softly lapping ocean waves provide atmospheric background music. Despite an often-full house, service is among the best on the island. Credit Cards: V, MC, A.

David's   **$$**   ★★★

Rue de la Liberte, Marigot, ☎ *(590) 87-51-58.*
English cuisine.
Lunch: 11:30 a.m.–2:30 p.m., entrees $6–$17.
Dinner: 6:00 p.m.–10:00 p.m., entrees $6–$17.
When it's crowded, David's can be a convivial place, with word games or darts providing the entertainment while waiting for light pub fare or full dinners. An inter-

esting menu of hearty soups, meat, and pasta dishes are all reasonably priced, and freshly caught seafood is a standout. The bar stays open until the witching hour and the scene can be boisterous or dull, depending upon who shows up. Reservations recommended. Credit Cards: V, MC, A.

Drew's Deli $ ★★★

French Cul-de-Sac, Marigot,
American cuisine. Specialties: Cheeseburgers, cheesecake.
Lunch: 11:00 a.m.–3:00 p.m., entrees $3–$15.
Dinner: 7:00 p.m.–9:30 p.m., entrees $3–$15.
North of Orient Bay lies the little community of French-Cul-de-Sac, where Drew from Wisconsin, a wonderful host, grills up some of the best bacon cheeseburgers around. Cole slaw and New York-style cheesecake with the burger provides a well-balanced vacation diet. The place is a little cramped, but the friendly reception might urge you to sit a spell. Full meals are also offered. Closed: Fri, Sat. Credit Cards: V, MC, A.

Hevea $$$ ★★★

Boulevard de Grand Case, Grand Case, ☎ *(590)-87-56-85.*
French cuisine.
Dinner: 6:30 p.m.–10:00 p.m., entrees $22–$38.
Only a few customers per night can dine at this small and formal yet friendly dining room in a Grand Case inn. The size of the dining room ensures the consistently fine quality of the French cuisine served here. The proprietors, who hail from Nice, use only the finest ingredients and believe that simplicity is key. Sauces made with fresh herbs, wine reductions, or wild mushrooms are often used to subtly accentuate, never overpower, lamb, duck breast, or a signature red snapper en papillote. Closed Mondays from April 15–December 14. Associated Hotel: Hevea. Reservations required. Credit Cards: V, MC.

L'Auberge Gourmande $$$ ★★★★

89 Boulevard Grand Case, Grand Case, ☎ *(590) 87-73-37.*
French cuisine.
Dinner: 6:30 p.m.–10:00 p.m., entrees $15–$31.
The setting is a quaint, converted residence sporting jalousied windows. Guests dine by candlelight in a comfortable room, although increased noise on the streets of Grand Case may affect a romantic tete-a-tete. Soups are a specialty and are interestingly prepared, including a brew of mussels with orange. Grilled fish is reliable, although the roast pork and roast lamb were only average on one occasion and the once-impeccable service has slipped of late. Closed: Wed. Reservations required. Credit Cards: V, MC, A.

La Maison sur Le Port $$$ ★★★

rue de Republique, Marigot, ☎ *(590) 87-56-38.*
French cuisine.
Lunch: 12:00 a.m.–2:30 p.m., entrees $11–$14.
Dinner: 6:00 p.m.–10:00 p.m., entrees $17–$34.
Chef Christian Verdeau presents impeccably prepared but rather small portions of duck, lobster and other prime meats and seafood on an outdoor patio with a harbor

view. Prices remain stable, though, for the excellent quality of the ingredients, and a warm welcome is reserved for all comers. Closed: Sun. Reservations recommended. Credit Cards: V, MC, A.

La Nadaillac   **$$$**   ★ ★ ★

Rue de la Liberte, Marigot, ☎ *(590) 87-53-77.*
French cuisine.
Lunch: 12:00 a.m.–2:30 p.m., entrees $16–$32.
Dinner: 6:30 p.m.–9:30 p.m., entrees $16–$32.

This intimate gem, albeit a very dear one (as in prices), is the province of Fernand Mallard, from the Perigord. Appropriately enough, most specialties involve products from that region of France, including preserved goose. The restaurant is on an attractive patio facing the harbor, nestled among the chic clothing stores in the Galerie Périgourdine. Reservations required. Credit Cards: V, MC, DC, A.

Mark's Place   **$**   ★ ★ ★

French-Cul-de-Sac, Marigot, ☎ *(590) 87-34-50.*
Latin American cuisine.
Lunch: 12:30 a.m.–2:30 p.m., entrees $3–$13.
Dinner: 6:30 p.m.–9:30 p.m., entrees $3–$13.

The West Indian food served here is hearty, plentiful, and varied—on a given night you could have lobster bisque with a curry of conch or goat, or a crab back appetizer and swordfish, but sometimes the quality is unexceptional. It's hard to quibble with the reasonable prices, but you get what you pay for. And the crowds keep coming—Mark's Place is usually jammed. Closed: Mon. Credit Cards: V, MC, A.

Mini-Club   **$$$**   ★ ★

Rue de la Liberte, Marigot, ☎ *(509) 87-50-69.*
French cuisine.
Lunch: 12:00 a.m.–3:00 p.m., prix fixe $32.
Dinner: 7:00 p.m.–10:30 p.m., entrees $18–$35.

Locals who like to stuff themselves silly with food as good as mother makes are grateful for the continuing success of the gargantuan French-creole buffet served here on Wednesdays and Saturday nights. The setting is lots of fun too: a junglelike, tropical terrace suspended over the water. The feast includes all the wine you can drink, so bring a friend who can help you down the stairs. On other days sample an unparalleled lobster souffle and other French specialties. The buffet is $40 per person. Reservations required. Credit Cards: V, MC, A.

FIELDING'S CHOICE:

Little known to the outside world is the special purple and bittersweet gua-vaberry liqueur produced on the island ever since Dutch colonists settled in the 18th century. During the Christmas holidays, it's customary to go from home to home serenading for samples. Every family makes a different brew, which is usually fully consumed by the end of the Christmas season. The Sint Maarten Guavaberry Company now makes the liqueur locally, and offers shade, seating, and a few samples at its midtown production area at the Gua-vaberry Shop on 10 Front Street. Try a guavaberry colada (blended with cream of coconut and pineapple juice), or a guavaberry screwdriver (mixed with orange juice). A bottle of guavaberry sells for less than $15 and is considered duty-free because it is an island craft.

Where to Shop

Philipsburg, capital of Dutch St. Maarten, is full of shops and markets.

St. Martin's duty-free port carries all the typical products one would expect to find at 25–50 percent discounts: china, jewelry, crystal, perfumes and fashions. Usually prices are quoted in American dollars and sales clerks speak

English. Local art shown in galleries and artist's studios make great buys; besides **Roland Richardson** in Orleans, seek out the work of **Genevieve Curt** ☎ *87-88-52*, at the **Tropical Gallery**. Other fine names are the painter Alexandre Minguet and the Lynn family (husband, wife, and two sons). Both the Dutch and French side have some of the most sophisticated fashion shops in the Caribbean, but be prepared to pay in francs on the French side if you want a good exchange. (Hours on the French side are iffy, but usually run Monday-Saturday 9 a.m.–12:30 p.m. and 3:00 p.m.–7:00 p.m. Some stores adjust their schedules to accommodate cruise ships on Sunday and holidays.

Philipsburg may seem more crowded and junk oriented than Marigot, but you can find highly memorable leather (**Domina**), clothes (**Maurella Senesi**), and jewelry (**Caribbean Gems**). Shopping on Grand Case is limited to narrow main street. Best shops in Marigot are at the **Marina Royale**. Don't miss the lively **early morning market in Marigot** where locals sell their spices, handicrafts and tropical fruits and vegetables. **Port La Royale** is a bee hive of activity after dawn; hang out here if you want to meet yachties and even local schooner captains cruising in from other islands with new goods. High-fashion designs can be found in the **Galerie Périgourdine** shopping complex, across from the post office.

Sint Maarten/St. Martin Directory

ARRIVAL AND DEPARTURE

American Airlines offers flights from New York, Miami, Dallas, Raleigh/Durham, and San Juan, Puerto Rico. Continental flies out of Newark. BWIA flies from Miami. Air St. Barthélémy flies daily to and from St. Barts, as does WINAIR (Windward Islands Airways). Inter-island service is provided by ALM, Air Martinique, LIAT, and WINAIR. All flights arrive at Juliana Airport on the Dutch side of the island as does Air Guadeloupe which offers daily flights to and from Guadeloupe. There is a $10 departure tax from Juliana Airport on the Dutch side.

For its daily 10-minute flights to St. Barts, Air Guadeloupe, and Air St. Barthélémy also use Espérance Airport, a small domestic terminal near Grand Case on the French side. There is a 15 French franc (about $3) departure tax from Espérance Airport on the French side. The latter is already calculated into tickets written and sold on St. Martin. If it is not shown on the ticket, then you will be expected to pay in cash at the departure gate—have the francs ready.

CLIMATE

Sunshine prevails on the island and it is warm year-round. Temperatures during the winter average 80 degrees F, in the summer, it gets a little warmer. Constant trade winds keep the climate pleasant.

DOCUMENTS

U.S. citizens entering via the Dutch side (Juliana Airport) for stays of up to three months need a valid passport, or one that has expired no longer than five years prior, or a notarized or original birth certificate with raised seal, or a voter's registration card. Canadian citizens must have a valid passport. U.S. residents and Canadians who are not citizens must have a green card or multiple re-entry stamp. Travelers must also show a return or onward ticket.

U.S. citizens and Canadians traveling as tourists and entering via the French side (Espérance Airport) for stays up to three weeks must have proof of citizenship in the form of a valid passport, a passport that has expired no more than five years prior, or other proof of citizenship, in the form of a birth certificate (original or official copy), or a voter's registration card, plus a government-authorized identification with photo. For stays over three weeks, or for nontourist visits, a valid passport is necessary. Resident aliens of the U.S. and Canada, and visitors from countries other than those of the Common Market (E.E.C.) and Japan must have a valid passport and visa. A return or onward ticket is also required for all visitors.

ELECTRICITY

Current runs 220 AC, 50 cycles. American and Canadian appliances require French plug converters and transformers.

GETTING AROUND

Taxis from Juliana Airport to Marigot run about $8, double that for Grand Case. Between 9 p.m. and midnight, rates rise 25 percent, after midnight 50 percent. The taxi center in Marigot is near the tourist office ☎ *87-56-54*; in Grand Case ☎ *87-75-79*. Car rentals can be made at Juliana Airport or delivered free to hotels. Most have automatic transmission, many are air-conditioned. All foreign driver's licenses are honored. Major credit cards are accepted, and a tank of gas should last a week. Cars cost about $25–$55 per day, depending on make, and unlimited mileage is offered.

Scooters rent for about $18–$23 per day from **Rent 2 Wheels** in Baie Nettlé ☎ *87-20-59*, or **Moto Caraibes** ☎ *87-25-91*. Given the hilly terrain of St. Martin, mopeds, scooters and motorbikes should only be rented by experienced riders.

Buses run from 6 a.m.–midnight, leaving from Grand Case, and can be flagged down anywhere. Buses run to Marigot, Cole Bay, Simson Bay, Mullet Bay, etc., as well as Marigot/Philipsburg, Orleans/Philipsburg, and French Quarter/Philipsburg.

LANGUAGE

French is the official language of St. Martin and Dutch is the official language of Sint Maarten, but English is spoken everywhere.

MEDICAL EMERGENCIES

There is a hospital in Marigot ☎ *87-50-07* and another in Philipsburg ☎ *31111*. Hotels can contact English-speaking physicians for you. There are about 18 doctors practicing general medicine, six dentists, and specialists in many varied fields. In addition, French St. Martin has about six pharmacies.

MONEY

The official currency is the French franc, but U.S. dollars are accepted everywhere. Prices are often quoted in U.S.; dollars. The rate of exchange is subject to change due to currency fluctuation.

TELEPHONE

The international country code for St. Martin is *590*. To call the Dutch side, dial the code *599-5*. French side numbers have 6 digits, the Dutch side 5. The cheapest way to make calls is with a telephone card on public phones (8 on the square in Marigot and 2 in Grand Case in front of the pier).

TIME

St. Martin is one hour ahead of East Standard Time in New York. French St. Martin uses the 24-hour system of telling time; hence, 1 p.m. in the afternoon is 13 hours.

TIPPING AND TAXES

Most hotels include tax and service quoted in room rates, which together add 10–15 percent to the bill. If no service charge is added, feel free to leave 10–15 percent on restaurant bills.

TOURIST INFORMATION

The St. Martin Tourist Office is located at the Waterfront in Marigot ☎ *87-57-21*, FAX *87-56-43*. A good source for history, architecture, and art on the island can be found in the beautiful four-color magazines called *Discover St. Martin*, available free at hotels and tourist sites. A slew of other free publications are available, including *What to Do*, *St. Maarten Nights*, *St. Martin's Week* and *Focus*, among others. Some of the larger hotels distribute to guests free of charge a daily *Times* FAX in conjunction with the *New York Times*. In the U.S. ☎ *(212) 989-0000*.

WHEN TO GO

Mardi Gras is held on February 28, a frenzied carnival with dancing filling the streets of Marigot and Grand Case. Another carnival, with calypso, "jump ups," floats, steel bands, and bright costumes takes place the last two weeks in April and early May, mostly on the Dutch side, but with some French participation. The Marlin Open de St. Martin on May 29–June 3 is an invitational organized by the Sailfish Caraibes Club. June 6 is the African Festival with arts, crafts, music, and dance lectures. Bastille Day on July 14 is celebrated with fireworks, parades, and sports contests. Schoelcher Day, on July 21, in honor of the French parliamentarian who led the campaign against slavery, is celebrated with boat and bike races. Concordia Day, on November 11, starts the season off with parades and ceremonies. New Year's Eve, called Réveillon de la Saint Sylvestre, is celebrated noisily with balloons, late-night dancing, and dining at hotels and restaurants.

SINT MAARTEN/ ST. MARTIN HOTELS	RMS	RATES	PHONE	FAX
Philipsburg				
★★★★★ La Belle Creole	160	$205–$455	(590) 87-66-00	590-8-75666
★★★★★ La Samanna Hotel	80	$28–$995	(590) 87-64-00	590 87 87 86
★★★★ Le Meridien l'Habitation	396	$175–$655	(800) 543-4300	590 87 30 38
★★★★ Oyster Pond Hotel	40	$120–$310	(599) 5-22206	599-5-25695
★★★★ Point Pirouette Villas	85	$161–$845	(599) 5-44207	599 5 42338
★★★★ Sheraton Port Plaisance	88	$225–$600	(800) 732-9480	599-5-42315
★★★ Beachside Villas	14	$160–$405		
★★★ Belair Beach Hotel	72	$165–$375	(800) 933-3264	599-5-25295
★★★ Captain Oliver's Hotel	50	$100–$200	(590) 87-40-26	
★★★ Cupecoy Beach Club	126	$100–$650	(215) 885-9008	(215) 572-7731
★★★ Dawn Beach Hotel	155	$105–$290	(800) 351-5656	599-5-24421
★★★ Divi Little Bay Resort	147	$110–$350	(800) 801-5550	599-5-23911
★★★ Grand Case Beach Club	71	$95–$425	(800) 447-7462	590-8-75993
★★★ Great Bay Beach Hotel	285	$164–$285	(800) 223-0757	599 5 23859
★★★ Hotel Anse Margot	96	$138–$261	(800) 742-4276	590-8-79213
★★★ Hotel Mont Vernon	394	$105–$160	(800) 223-0888	590-8-73727
★★★ Laguna Beach Hotel	62	$70–$185	(800) 333-1970	590-8-78165
★★★ Le Flamboyant	271	$115–$364	(800) 221-5333	590-8-79957
★★★ Maho Beach Hotel & Casino	600	$140–$460	(800) 223-0757	(212) 969-9227
★★★ Mary's Boon	12	$80–$155	(599) 5-54235	599-5-53403
★★★ Mullet Bay Resort	570	$270–$765	(800) 468-5538	599 -5-54281
★★★ Nettle Bay Beach Club	230	$100–$450	(800) 999-3543	590 87 21 51
★★★ Pavillion Beach Hotel	16	$95–$255	(590) 87-96-46	590 87 71 04
★★★ Pelican Resort & Casino	655	$125–$585	(800) 626-9637	599 5 42133
★★★ Royal Islander Club	135	$180–$320	(599) 5-52388	599-5-52585

SINT MAARTEN/ ST. MARTIN HOTELS		RMS	RATES	PHONE	FAX
★★	Club Orient Resort	83	$120–$320	(800) 828-9356	
★★	Coralita Beach Hotel	24	$115–$140	(590) 87-31-81	
★★	Esmeralda Resort	54	$180–$300	(800) 622-7836	590-8-73518
★★	Holland House Beach Hotel	54	$69–$195		599 5 24673
★★	Horny Toad Guesthouse	8	$103–$185	(599) 5-53316	599 5 53316
★★	Hotel le Belvedere	130	$85–$120	(800) 221-5333	590 87 30 52
★★	La Residence	21	$75–$98	(800) 365-8484	590-8-79044
★★	Le Pirate Beach Hotel	60	$110–$180	(800) 666-5756	590-8-79567
★★	Marine Hotel Simpson Beach	165	$101–$230	(800) 221-4542	590-8-72151
★★	Pasanggrahan Royal	30	$73–$153	(599) 5-23588	599 5 22855
★★	Point at Burgeaux Bay	14	$70–$395	(599) 5-54335	(516) 466-2359
★★	Royale Louisiana	75	$49–$129	(590) 87-86-51	590-8-79649
★★	Summit Resort Hotel	50	$55–$150	(599)5-52150	599 5 52150
★★	Town House Villas	12	$130–$305	(599) 5-22898	599-5-22418
★	Beach House	10	$53–$100		599-5-30308
★	Tradewinds Beach Inn	10	$61–$155	(599) 5-54206	

SINT MAARTEN/ST. MARTIN RESTAURANTS		LOCATION	PHONE	ENTREE
Philipsburg				
American				
★★★	Cheri's Cafe	Maho Beach	(599) 55-3361	$6–$17
★★★	Chesterfield's	Pointe Blanche	(559) 5-23484	$7–$20
★★★	The Grill & Ribs Co.	Philipsburg		$5–$11
★★	Greenhouse	Philipsburg	(599) 5-22941	$6–$25
Asian				
★★★	The Wajang Doll	Philipsburg		$21–$30••
French				
★★★★	Le Perroquet	Simpson Bay	(599) 5-41339	$18–$26••
★★★	Antoine	Philipsburg	(599)5-22964	$16–$32

SINT MAARTEN/ST. MARTIN RESTAURANTS	LOCATION	PHONE	ENTREE
★★★ L'Escargot	Philipsburg	(599) 5-22483	$8–$29
★★★ Le Bec Fin	Philipsburg	(599) 5-22976	$16–$31••
Seafood			
★★★★ Saratoga	Simpson Bay	(599) 5-42421	$16–$26••
★★★ The Seafood Galley	Philipsburg		$7–$18

Marigot

	LOCATION	PHONE	ENTREE
American			
★★★ Drew's Deli	Marigot		$3–$15
English			
★★★ David's	Marigot	(590) 87-51-58	$6–$17
French			
★★★★ L'Auberge Gourmande	Grand Case	(590) 87-73-37	$15–$31••
★★★ Hevea	Grand Case	(590)-87-56-85	$22–$38••
★★★ La Maison sur Le Port	Marigot	(590) 87-56-38	$11–$34
★★★ La Nadaillac	Marigot	(590) 87-53-77	$16–$32
★★ Mini-Club	Marigot	(509) 87-50-69	$32–$35
International			
★★★ Coco Beach Bar	Marigot		$15–$30
Latin American			
★★★ Cha Cha Cha's	Grand Case	(590) 87-53-63	$11–$20••
★★★ Mark's Place	Marigot	(590) 87-34-50	$3–$13
Seafood			
★★★ Captain Oliver Restaurant	Marigot	(590) 87-30-00	$16–$24

Note: • Lunch Only

•• Dinner Only

ST. THOMAS

Crown Mountain Road in Charlotte Amalie offers an excellent view of the grassy hills, white beaches and blue water of St. Thomas.

St. Thomas is one of the most cosmopolitan of the U.S. Virgin Islands, if not the most unabashedly commercial. Lots of Caribbean islands boast white sands, aquamarine seas and lush mountains, but few display luxury goods in such abundance. A commercial hub long before Blackbeard, the pirate prowled its waters, St. Thomas is now a prime destination for cruise ships, whose passengers rush ashore—not unlike the 19th century buccaneers—in hot pursuit of duty-free booty.

Others still come to get away from it all, even if the wave of development that followed Hurricane Hugo in 1989 gave a jolt to urban American reality. Along with new resorts and fast-food restaurants there is now a K-mart and a

Hard Rock Cafe, and luxurious homes have blossomed like frangipani on the northern and eastern hillsides. Gridlock in paradise today aptly describes the sidewalks and narrow alleyways of downtown Charlotte Amalie (pronounced ah-MAHL-ya), the territorial capital and St. Thomas's only real town. But beyond the city bustle, there lies another St. Thomas, with more than 40 beaches, submersible rises aboard an Atlantic submarine, golf, tennis, parasailing, boardsailing, big game fishing—the activities of an endless summer. Simply, St. Thomas is an ideal destination for the couple in which one shops and the other grumbles. Just one word of warning: whatever you do, avoid the cityscape when cruise ships dock in port (and if you're on a cruise ship yourself, duck!).

Warning: Following the 1994 killing of a San Diego tourist in a botched nighttime robbery, authorities in the USVI beefed up the police force, cracked down on juvenile crime, prepared a safety advisory, and took other measures to better protect visitors.

Bird's Eye View

The tram to Paradise Point gives a bird's eye view of the St. Thomas harbor.

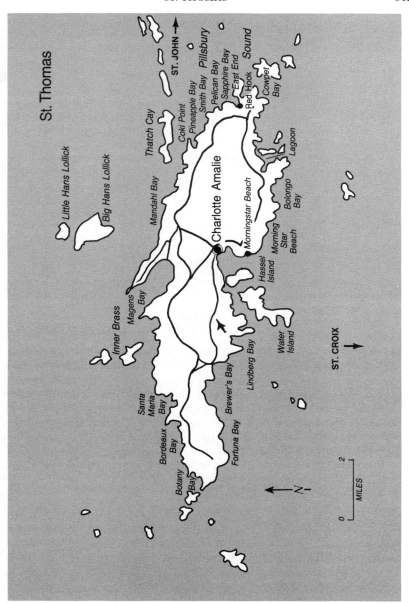

St. Thomas lies about 40 miles north of St. Croix and 75 miles east of Puerto Rico. Only 14 miles by 3 miles long, it is literally built on a mountain—the reason it's called "Rock City"—with its one main town, Charlotte Amalie, situated on the central south shore. At its highest peak, Crown Mountain, it measures 1550 feet high. A scenic road around the island, **Skyline Drive** (Route 40) allows a simultaneous view of both sides of the island. Beach resorts dot most of the coastline; private homes with bright red, roof of corrugated iron nestle into the hillside in the wooded interior. The island is easy to navigate by automobile, but there are the inevitable daily traffic jams that clog downtown Charlotte Amalie at rush hour. An excellent view of grassy hills, talcum-white beaches and blue waters can be glimpsed from the Crown Mountain Road, west off Harwood Highway. On the outskirts of town (follow Veterans Drive along the waterfront and turn left at the Villa Olga sign) you'll discover Frenchtown, a community of Swedish descendants from the time Sweden invaded St. Bart in the late 18th century. (Locals still speak a Norman French dialect.)

History

As with St. Croix and St. John, Columbus discovered these islands on his third voyage in 1493. A plan for colonizing St. Thomas was signed by Frederick III of Denmark, but the first settlement failed. Charlotte Amalie, St. Thomas's first permanent European settlement, dates back to 1671. Set on a grand circular harbor, the town was laid out by planners in Denmark who had never seen the mountainous 32-square mile island. Danish control of the Virgin Islands ended when the U.S. bought St. Croix, St. Thomas and St. John for $25 million in order to protect its interests in the Panama Canal. Today, the self-governing unincorporated territory has a nonvoting delegate to the U.S. House of Representatives.

Beaches

Though St. Thomas endures a lot of visitors, beaches have remained appealing, with fine white sand sloping into beautiful bays. The heart-shaped **Magen's Bay**, the largest bay along St. Thomas' rugged northeast coast, is often considered one of the prettiest beaches in the world. It's also the only beach with an admission charge (50 cents, 25 cents for children under 11 and under, $1 for parking), but it also has all the conveniences of civilization, including parking, lifeguards, equipment rental, changing rooms, restaurants and bars. The calm waters are good for swimming, first-time sailors, and a small craft can be rented on the beach (for about $20 hourly). On the northeast shores, **Coki Point** is sterling (stop by the 80,000-gallon aquarium at **Coral World** and the underwater observatory) as is **Sapphire Beach** on the east coast, pointing toward St. John and the **British Virgin Islands**. In the south, two excellent beaches are **Lindbergh Bay**, in front of a hotel near the airport, and **Morning Star**, in front of a resort just east of Charlotte Amalie. There are few deserted beaches here, which is just as well, because isolated areas tend to attract more crime here.

FIELDING'S CHOICE:

From January to April, pilot whales frequent the breeding grounds off the north end of the island. Inquire at your sports activity center about whale-watch tours.

Dive Sites

St. Thomas has 34 dive sites, with access only about a twenty-minute ride from shore. **Magella Bay** is a good site for snorkeling, but even better are two rocks, **Cow and Calf**, off the southeast coast in **Jersey Bay**, where they are impressive corals, caves and large schools of fish at 5025 feet of water. (Four minutes from Charlotte Amalie, the two sites also boast a coral tunnel network with reefs, caves and coral-encrusted boulders.) St. James Islands boast rocky shelves, sea whips and tiny caves, surrounded by a large coral garden. Further east of St. Thomas' north shore, **Coki Point** offers tremendous snorkeling, especially around the coral edges near the Marine Park and Underwater Observatory, but you may have to share water space with a lot of divers, who consider it a classic dive. Southeast from Coki is **Smith Bay**, located adjacent to Stouffer Grand Beach Resort. The most advanced divers head for St. Thomas' north coast, where the Atlantic and the Caribbean meet as rushing currents support the transport of thousands of fish. **Congo Cay** is known for its fascinating huge boulders and lava arches accessible in only 30 feet of water. Divers particularly love the swim-through tunnels at Thatch Cay. Elsewhere on St. Thomas, **Hull Bay** and **Long Point** offer impressive snorkeling. **Sapphire Beach** is known for its large, fish-rich reef. (The trenchlike coral formations near **Pretty Knip Point** are worth a peak, but beware of surges near the rocks.) Bay whales (also known as cowpets) sometime migrate past the beach at Cowpet Bay. Cow and Calf, 4 minutes from Charlotte Amalie, boasts a coral tunnel network with reefs, caves and coral-encrusted boulders. **Buck Island** features the coral-encrusted ruins of the *Cartenser*, a World War I cargo vessel. Night diving is considered the thing to do for intermediate and advanced divers. Spearfishing is forbidden in the National Park, and in some cases photography. On St. Thomas/St. John there is presently also a closed session for two years on the taking of a queen conch. For the latest regulations, contact the local Division of Fish and Wildlife office. Many hotel properties offer splendid snorkeling sites, as well as snorkeling equipment; there are about a dozen or so dive operators offering two or three dives per day as well as instruction for certification. Dive excursions can start from St. John and end up on the east side of St. Thomas—an interesting way to travel between islands. For information about special hotel packages, contact the **St. Thomas Hotel Association** ☎ *(809) 74-6835.*

Treks

Treks in St. Thomas are spontaneous and can be inspired simply by the rumor of a stunning vista or secluded beach; do talk to locals who often know the best country paths to follow. Just make sure you have the directions straight and that you know how to return to your starting base. If you go anywhere off the beaten track, do take your own water supply. Maps can be obtained from the tourist office, which can also suggest local guides. From Magen Beach, there is a wonderful walk along dry woodlands to the **Peterborg Peninsula**, on the northside of the bay. If you walk west along the Atlantic shore, you'll find tidal pools that have attracted scores of crabs and small fish, which are sought after by large shorebirds. Nearby Botany Bay is a nesting ground for sea turtles.

Sailboats leave Charlotte Amalie for excursions to St. John and the British Virgin Islands.

One of the most handsome spots in St. Thomas is Fairchild Park, an oasis atop a forested mountain some 1200 feet high; from here the views of the north and south coast are simply stunning. The 1500-ft. peak of **Mountain Top** is the highest point in the island, but it is usually overrun by tourists.

The Virgins Island National Park on St. Thomas has a few trails but no tourist facilities. On **Hassel Island**, hikers can explore nine different ruins of plantations and old fortresses; the only way to get here is to hire a boat from Charlotte Amalie, but negotiate for the captain to pick you up at a designated hour. You probably won't want more than two hours on the island; take your own food and water and a sun hat since there is no shade.

The ferry to St. John takes only twenty minutes. There you'll find some of the best hiking trails in the entire Virgin Islands.

What Else to See

A look around Charlotte Amalie can be done in less than a morning; choose a rainy day if you can find one. The Government House is a bit of a bore, as is the Virgin Islands Museum, though Fort Christian itself might harbor a few detectable ghosts since it was the center of social and political activity for the island over several hundred years. More captivating is the **Estate St. Peter Greathouse Botanical Gardens** sprawling over 11 lush acres high atop the volcanic peaks of the north side of the island. Opened in 1992, after a renovation that was completely destroyed by Hurricane Hugo (and then renovated again by a hearty New England couple, the meticulously landscaped gardens offer self-guided nature trails through such exotic flora as the umbrella plant from Madagascar, the cane orchid from China, and the bird of paradise from South Africa. You can also spend time here visiting an orchid jungle, rainforest, waterfalls and monkey habitat. Superb views from the outdoor observation deck renders 20 other Virgin Islands. Some visitors plant themselves on the deck's benches and sit for hours.

The second-oldest synagogue in the U.S. and its territories is located at St. Thomas in Charlotte Amalie, picturesquely situated on a narrow street high above the harbor. It was built in 1833 and is worth visiting for its architecture and its fittings. Its sand floor is said to commemorate the Exodus. Tourists are welcome not only during the religious services but also during the week. An international Bicentennial celebration slated for 1995–96 will commemorate 200 years of Jewish life in St. Thomas. Visitors of all faiths will travel to St. Thomas in honor of the St. Thomas Synagogues' proud history. For more information contact the St. Thomas Tourist Board.

Coral World has an underwater observatory ☎ *(809) 775-1555* which provides a 360-degree look at coral life. At 2 p.m. divers hand-feed sharks in the Predator Tank. Admission is \$14, \$9 for children 3 and over. Open daily from 9 a.m.–6 p.m.

Reinhold Center for the Arts at the University of the Virgin Islands, located on a hillside overlooking Brewers Bay, holds many cultural events. Don't miss folk dances performed by the **Caribbean Dance Company**. Contact ☎ *(809) 774-8475.*

Tillett Gardens in the Tutu area, the site of arts and crafts studios, often hosts classical concerts ☎ *(809) 775-1929*

Carnival follows Easter in the Virgin Islands, and it will take place April 18–22. The Carnival Food Fair offers a chance to sample dishes like kallaloo (a stew of meat, seafood and greens) and drinks prepared with sea moss and soursop, a local fruit. A predawn dance through the streets, called the J'Ouvert Morning Tramp, is followed by the Children's Parade that day. On April 30, the Adults' Parade is led by Mocko Jumbies, stilt dancers in extravagant, brightly covered costumes.

Most tourists make at least one excursion to St. John, two-thirds of which is the Virgin Islands National Park, where each uncrowded beach seems to surpass the one before ($3 one way for a 20-minute ferry that leaves every hour from Red Hook on the East End, $7 for the 45-minute ride from Charlotte Amalie.)

BEST VIEW:

From atop the 1500-ft. Mountain Top, on St. Peter's Mountain, you can see a panoramic view of both sides of the island as well as a multitude of islands stretching east to Virgin Gorda.

FIELDING'S CHOICE:

To experience the scuba thrill without getting wet, take a ride on the Atlantis Submarine, *a 46-passenger underwater craft that takes passengers for an hour-ride at depths of 50-90 feet. The sub's large windows give good views of corals reefs and a multitude of marine life. Hours are generally 10 a.m.-2 p.m., but call first for reservations. The boat ride leaves from the West Indies dock at Havensight Mall on the outskirts of Charlotte Amalie. For more information* ☎ (809) 775-1555.

Historical Sites

Fort Christian ★★★

At the harbor, ☎ *(809) 776-4566.*
Hours Open: 8:30 a.m.–4:30 p.m.
This brick fortress is the oldest building in the Virgin Islands and a U.S. national landmark, dating back to 1672. It has housed everything from the entire St. Thomas colony to a jail to a church over the years, and is now home to an art gallery, police station, book store, and, in the former dungeons, the Virgin Islands Museum, which traces the island's history. It's currently under renovation, so access may be limited. Free admission.

Historic Churches ★★★★

Various locations.
Charming Charlotte Amalie is home to several historic churches well worth a look. The Frederick Lutheran Church (Norre Gade) is the Western Hemisphere's second-oldest Lutheran church. All Saints Anglican Church on Garden Street was built in 1848 to celebrate the end of slavery. The Dutch Reformed Church on Nye Gade

was built in 1844, but actually dates back to 1744 (the original was destroyed by a fire in 1804). Finally, the Cathedral of St. Peter and St. Paul in Kronprindsens Alley was built in 1848 and is enhanced by murals done in 1899 by Belgian artists.

St. Thomas Synagogue ★★★★

Synagogue Hill, ☎ *(809) 774-4312.*
Hours Open: 9:00 a.m.–4:00 p.m.

This is the oldest synagogue in continuous use under the America flag, and the second-oldest in the Western Hemisphere. The floor is sand, symbolic of the desert through which Moses and the Israelis wandered for 40 years. A bicentennial celebration, commemorating 200 years of Jewish life on St. Thomas, takes place in 1995-96, with art shows, celebrity guests, special events, and Jewish cultural productions. Call for a schedule once on the island. Free admission.

Museums and Exhibits

Seven Arches Museum ★★★

Government Hill, ☎ *(809) 774-9259.*
Hours Open: 9:00 a.m.–3:00 p.m.

This Danish house was built in 1800 and is now a private home, but they'll let you in to see its historic furnishings and antiques. The grounds include a separate kitchen and a walled garden, the perfect spot to quaff the drink included in the admission fee. General admission: $7.50.

Tours

Coral World ★★★★

Coki Point, ☎ *(809) 775-1555.*
Hours Open: 9:00 a.m.–6:00 p.m.

Nonswimmers can see what all the fuss is about at this five-acre marine park, home to 21 aquariums, a touch tank, an 80,000-gallon tank showcasing the world's largest living man-made reef, an exotic bird habitat, and semi-submarine rides. The highlight is the underwater observatory, an air-conditioned room 20 feet below sea level through which you can observe all sorts of sea life, an especially exciting sight at feeding time. The grounds also include duty-free shops, a bar and restaurant, and a pretty beach where they rent snorkel and scuba equipment (showers and changing rooms are available). Kids get in for $10. General admission: $16.00.

Guided Tours

Various locations.

St. Thomas is easily explored on your own, but if you'd like to spare the expense of renting a car, take a guided tour. **Destination Virgin Islands** (☎ *776-2424*) offers walking tours, beach and shopping trips, and excursions to St. John and St. Croix. Prices vary. The **St. Thomas Islands Tour** (☎ *774-7668*) explores the island in two hours for $14 per person; another excursion takes in the many splendid views and costs $20. **Tropic Tours** (☎ *774-1855*) offers various shopping and scenic tours; call for prices.

Paradise Point Tramcom, Inc. ★★★

Havensight Area, ☎ *(809) 774-9809.*
Hours Open: 9:00 a.m.–9:00 p.m.

When this $2.8-million tramway opened in August 1994, it brought back a popular attraction that ceased to exist in the 1970s. The 3.5-minute ride—not recommended for those afraid of heights—gives a birds-eye view of the harbor and stops at 697-foot-high Paradise Point, where you can wander among the shops or try a banana daiquiri at the bar that lays claim to inventing the drink. General admission: $10.00.

Sports

All watersports activities are enjoyed on St. Thomas. Sportfishing, on St. Thomas is devoted primarily to the blue marlin. In March, April, May and June they can be found in the south in the Caribbean, north in the Atlantic in July-September. On the Atlantic side of the Virgins is the 100-fathom dropoff, bordering on the Puerto Rico Trench, the deepest hole in the Atlantic Ocean. Because the Virgin Islands lie in the Trade Winds Belt, fishing can always be done on the leeward side. **Redbook**, at the main center of St. Thomas, is the main center for boat operators. Many operators offer half and full-day boat excursions on any number and variety of craft; full-day fishing expeditions can come with equipment, picnic, ice and beer. The waters northeast of St. Thomas are prime fishing grounds, helping the Virgin Islands live up to their reputation as a superb site to catch blue marlin. Surfing attracts lots of fans during the winter since the sea huskily rolls in with a blast at Hull Bay on the north coast of St.Thomas. Windsurfing here is best at the eastern end where winds peak during noontime; the roughest conditions are at Hull Bay, the gentlest at Morningstar in the south. Even novices are invited for a two-hour lesson of windsurfing at the Windsurfing St. Thomas/ School of Boardsailing at St. Pleasant. Kayaking is popular, as is sportfishing. Horse racing is a party event on St. Thomas, involving thoroughbred horses, pan-mutuel, and daily double betting. Events are approximately monthly, usually on a local holiday or Sunday. English-style riding lessons are available at **Rosenthal Riding Ring**, which also offer trial rides. St. Thomas has a spectacular 18-hole championship course, designed by George and Tom Fazio, at **Mahogany Run**. There are six public tennis courts on St. Thomas, as well as private ones at many hotels. Do play early morning or late afternoon until you get used to the weather.

Mahogany Run Golf Course

Mahogany Run Road, North Shore, ☎ *(809) 775-5000.*

St. Thomas' only golf course is an especially scenic and challenging one, a par-70 known for its dramatic 13th and 14th holes, which hug cliffs overlooking the Atlantic Ocean. Designed by George and Tom Fazio, greens fees vary depending on the time of year, and range from a high of $85 for 18 holes to a low of $65, including carts.

Watersports

Various locations.

If your hotel doesn't offer the equipment you need, these companies are happy to help out. For boating, try: **Island Yachts** *(7☎ 75-6666 or 800-524-2019)*, **Avery's Marine** *(☎ 776-0113)*, **Coconut Charters** *(☎ 775-5959)*, **Nightwind** *(☎ 775-4110)*, and **New Horizons** *(☎ 775-1171)*. For scuba and snorkel instruction and excursions, try: **Seahorse Dive** *(☎ 774-2001)*, **Adventure Center** *(☎ 774-2990)*, **Dean Johnston's Diving** *(☎ 775-7610)*, **Hi-Tec Water Sports** *(☎ 774-5650)*, **Aqua Action** *(☎ 775-6285)*, **Underwater Safaris** *(☎ 774-1350 or 800-524-2090)*, and **Dive In** *(☎ 775-6100)*. Deep-sea fishers can call **Fish Hawk** *(☎ 775-9058)* and **St. Thomas Sportfishing Center** *(☎ 775-7990)*.

Where to Stay

Highest Rated Hotels in St. Thomas

★★★★★ **Marriott Frenchman's Reef**

★★★★ **Anchorage Beach Villas**

★★★★ **Bolongo Club Beach Resort**

★★★★ **Grand Palazzo**

★★★★ **Island Beachcomber**

★★★★ **Stouffer Grand Beach**

★★★★ **Sugar Bay Plantation**

★★★★ **Watergate Villas**

★★★ **Blackbeard's Castle**

★★★ **Bluebeard's Castle Hotel**

Most Exclusive Hotels in St. Thomas

★★★★	**Grand Palazzo**	$250–$865
★★★★	**Stouffer Grand Beach**	$220–$560
★★★	**Sapphire Beach Resort**	$190–$395
★★★★★	**Marriott Frenchman's Reef**	$160–$395
★★★	**Secret Harbourview Villas**	$140–$360

Fielding's Best Value Hotels in St. Thomas

★★★	**Blackbeard's Castle**	$75–$140
★★★	**Windward Passage**	$125–$235
★★★★	**Stouffer Grand Beach**	$220–$560
★★★	**Point Pleasant Resort**	$200–$380
★★★★	**Island Beachcomber**	$95–$150

Bluebeard's Castle gets high marks for retaining historic touches while providing modern amenities to hotel guests/visitors.

Accommodations can run wild in St. Thomas—from a posh resort that features live alligators in the moat to historical inns reputed to be haunted. In between are congenial inns, high-rise hotels and faux Italiante villas. Many big resorts offer the use of tennis courts, fitness center, and nonmotorized watersports equipment at no extra charge to guests. Not all lodgings are in the best of shape; ironically, some of the best ones today suffered the worst damage during Hurricane Hugo and now sport new faces and interiors.Most people head for the large congregations of lodgings on the south coast, near Charlotte Amalie. Other good locations include the Pineapple Beach curve of Water Bay, where the Stouffer's Grand Beach Hotel is located, and near Red Hook on the east coast.

With only $200 and a 250-word essay, you could also win the entire 15-room Danish Chalet Inn—forever. The owners are hoping to retire. Built in the 1940s, the Chalet features 4454 square feet of living area on an acre of landscaped grounds, and is valued at $600,000, with a 38 percent gross profit yearly. The deadline is September 15, 1995. For more information, write the Inn Foundation, *Box 2934, St. Thomas, USVI;* ☎ *800-635-1531.*

Hotels and Resorts

With over 14 resorts to choose from, you need to first set down your priorities. Do you want to be near shopping or near private coves? Do you want an all-inclusive, like the Bolongo Limetree, where you pay one price for everything, or would you rather take advantage of a special "Land and Sea" package that would get you close to the British Virgin islands (Windward Passage Hotel)?

Not all hotels have air-conditioning, not a necessity if you are on the windward side of the island, important if you need a refuge from the hot sun. If your hotel is on the beach, you can save considerable money by not taking a sea view, but if you stay in your room a lot, the lack of fresh breeze and view may not be worth it.

Bluebeard's Castle Hotel — $140–$235 — ★★★

P.O. Box 7480, Bluebeard's Hill, 801, *(800) 524-6599, (809) 774-1600.*
Single: $140–$235. Double: $140–$235.
Set high up on a hill with splendid views of the harbor and beyond, this venerable hotel is built around a 17th-century tower. Lodgings are found in villas and range from studios to one-bedroom suites, all air-conditioned, nicely decorated, and boasting balconies or terraces. There's nightly entertainment in the lounge, two well-regarded restaurants, a large pool, two tennis courts, and a fitness center. They'll shuttle you over to the beach for free. Nice, but group business dominates here, so individual travelers can feel lost in the shuffle. 170 rooms. Credit Cards: CB, V, MC, DC, A.

Bolongo Club Beach Resort — $195–$235 — ★★★★

#50 Estate Bolongo, Cowpet Bay, 802, *(800) 524-4746, (809) 779-2844.*
Single: $195–$235. Double: $195–$235.
This busy property offers full resort amenities and a variety of all-inclusive or semi-inclusive packages. Guests are accommodated in standard guestrooms, large efficiencies, or villas with full kitchens and one to three bedrooms, all quite nice with modern accoutrements. The extensive facilities include five restaurants, six bars, three pools, six tennis courts, a fitness center, complimentary watersports, year-round supervised children's activities, and boat rides. The palm-studded beach is quite fine. Resort lovers need look no further. 200 rooms. Credit Cards: V, MC, DC, A.

Bolongo Elysian Resort — $210–$690 — ★★★

6800 Estate Nazareth, Cowpet Bay, 802, ☎ *(800) 524-4746, (809) 779-2844.*
Single: $210–$500. Double: $210–$690.
This resort, set in a peaceful cove, houses guests in nicely done rooms or loft units that have full kitchens and one to three bedrooms. Sporting facilities include a large and elaborate pool, a tennis court, an excellent and well-equipped health club, and complimentary watersports. Dining choices range from the elegant Palm Court to the casual Oasis outdoor grill. This property is more luxurious than its sibling, the Bolongo Club Beach Resort, but there's also less going on--which is a plus or minus, depending upon your preferences. 118 rooms. Credit Cards: V, MC, DC, A.

Carib Beach Hotel — $79–$139 — ★

70-C Lindberg Bay, Lindbergh Beach, 802, ☎ *(800) 792-2742, (809) 774-2525.*
Single: $79–$129. Double: $89–$139.
This hotel just reopened in 1994 after damage from Hurricane Hugo forced it to close in 1989. Located on a small, palm-fringed beach, each cottage-style room is air-conditioned and has a private balcony and modern amenities like cable TV and telephones. The continental breakfast is on the house. Facilities include a restaurant, snack bar, pool and watersports. 69 rooms. Credit Cards: V, MC, A.

Emerald Beach Resort **$139–$239** ★ ★ ★

8070 Lindbergh Bay Beach, Lindbergh Beach, 802, ☎ (800) 233-4936, (809) 777-8800.
Single: $139–$200. Double: $149–$239.

Located just a mile from the airport, this smaller hotel has decent guestrooms that won't win any prizes for originality, but are quite modern and comfortable nonetheless. Facilities include a bar and restaurant, pool and tennis court. There's watersports for hire at the very nice public beach, just steps away. 90 rooms. Credit Cards: CB, V, MC, DC, A.

Grand Palazzo **$250–$865** ★ ★ ★ ★ ★

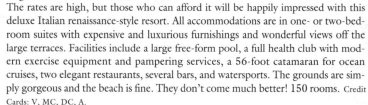

Great Bay, ☎ (800) 545-0509, (809) 775-3333.
Single: $250–$865. Double: $250–$865.

The rates are high, but those who can afford it will be happily impressed with this deluxe Italian renaissance-style resort. All accommodations are in one- or two-bedroom suites with expensive and luxurious furnishings and wonderful views off the large terraces. Facilities include a large free-form pool, a full health club with modern exercise equipment and pampering services, a 56-foot catamaran for ocean cruises, two elegant restaurants, several bars, and watersports. The grounds are simply gorgeous and the beach is fine. They don't come much better! 150 rooms. Credit Cards: V, MC, DC, A.

Island Beachcomber **$95–$150** ★ ★ ★ ★

P.O. Box 302579, Lindbergh Beach, 803, ☎ (800) 982-9898, (809) 774-5250.
Single: $95–$145. Double: $100–$150.

Set right on a fine beach, this hotel took a licking in Hurricane Hugo, but has been rebuilt to the joy of its faithful clientele. This casual spot houses guests in comfortable, air-conditioned rooms facing the lush garden or beach; all have cable TV, phones, refrigerators, and patios or porches. The restaurant is open-air and reasonably priced, and there's also a beach bar. No pool, but the sea is calm and good for swimming. Snorkeling equipment and water rafts are complimentary; other watersports cost extra. A pleasantly informal spot. 48 rooms. Credit Cards: CB, V, MC, DC, A.

Mafolie Hotel **$65–$97** ★ ★

P.O. Box 1506, Mafolie Hill, 804, ☎ (800) 225-7035, (809) 774-2790.
Single: $65–$87. Double: $80–$97.

Set high on a hill overlooking Charlotte Amalie, this Mediterranean-style villa hotel is only for those who can handle steep climbs. Guestrooms are simple and basic; only some have air conditioners and none sport TVs or phones. There's a pool and two restaurants on the grounds, and the views are stunning. They feed you breakfast for free, and the shuttle to Magen's Bay Beach is also gratis. The reasonable rates (most rooms are under $100) made Mafolie worth considering. 23 rooms. Credit Cards: V, MC, A.

Magens Point Hotel **$105–$305** ★ ★

Magens Bay, ☎ (800) 524-2031, (809) 775-5500.
Single: $105–$255. Double: $118–$305.

Set on a hillside next to the Mahogany Run Golf Course and overlooking the beach, this informal operation consists of motel-style guestrooms and 22 studio and one-

and two-bedroom suites with cooking facilities. There's a restaurant, bar, pool, and two tennis courts on-site, and they'll shuttle you to the beach (about a half mile away) at no charge. All here is quite casual, including, sometimes, the maintenance, but it's pleasant enough and the rates are relatively reasonable. 54 rooms. Credit Cards: CB, V, MC, DC, A.

Marriott Frenchman's Reef $160–$395 ★★★★★

#5 Estate Bakkaroe, ☎ *(800) 524-2000, (809) 776-8500.*
Single: $160–$395. Double: $160–$395.
This full-service resort complex, which incorporates the Morning Star Resort, has so much going at all hours that you'll never have to venture outside its boundaries. Guests are housed in accommodations right on the beach (Morning Star) or on a rocky promontory surrounded by water on three sides (Frenchman's Reef). Whichever you choose, you can count on modern and comfortable living, though the rooms on Morning Star are more luxurious (and expensive). Facilities include two pools, four tennis courts, watersports on the fine beach, a dinner theater, and six restaurants, several bars, and a disco. Live entertainment is frequently scheduled, as are all sorts of activities. A water taxi will whisk you into town—if you can tear yourself away from the happenings here. On the downside, the property hosts a lot of conventions, so you'll be sharing the facilities with name tag-wearing business folk. This is a grand spot for those who covet full resorts, but if you're looking for a laid-back tropical escape, look elsewhere. 520 rooms. Credit Cards: CB, V, MC, DC, A.

Point Pleasant Resort $200–$380 ★★★

Estate Smith Bay, ☎ *(800) 524-2300, (809) 775-7200.*
Single: $200–$275. Double: $260–$380.
This property takes up 15 acres on a lush hillside overlooking Smith Bay. Guests are put up in large standard rooms or spacious suites with full kitchens and living and dining areas. If you choose not to do your own cooking, two restaurants will do the job. Facilities include a small beach, tennis, three pools, and complimentary watersports. Guests also get free use of a car for four hours each day—a welcome idea we'd like to see more resorts follow. A better beach is found next door at the Stouffer Grand, which guests are welcome to use. Very nice. 134 rooms. Credit Cards: V, MC, A.

Ramada Yacht Haven Hotel $90–$225 ★★★

5400 Long Bay, 802, ☎ *(800) 228-9898, (809) 774-9700.*
Single: $90–$200. Double: $90–$225.
Guests sacrifice a beach for the relatively reasonable rates at this so-so hotel. Located on a large marina from which you can watch the cruise ships come in, accommodations are found in six low-rise buildings. Rooms have modern amenities like VCRs but are a bit run down. The grounds include two pools (one with a swim-up bar) and two restaurants and bars. They'll shuttle you over to the beach at the Marriott for free. 151 rooms. Credit Cards: CB, V, MC, DC, A.

Stouffer Grand Beach $220–$560 ★★★★

P.O. Box 8267, Water Bay, 801, ☎ *(800) 468-3571, (809) 775-1510.*
Single: $220–$560. Double: $220–$560.

Set on a lush hillside sloping to a beautiful beach, the Stouffer is another full-service resort that keeps guests pleasantly occupied. As with other large resorts, there's not a lot of true island flavor here, but no one seems to mind (or even notice). Guestrooms are quite plush; a few hundred dollars more buys a two-story townhouse suite or a one-bedroom unit with an indoor whirlpool. Recreational options include six tennis courts, two pools, an excellent health club, and watersports. There's also a sprinkling of restaurants and bars, and organized programs for the kids. 297 rooms. Credit Cards: V, MC, DC, A.

Sugar Bay Plantation $180–$370 ★★★★

Estate Smith Bay, ☎ *(800) 927-7100, (809) 777-7100.*
Single: $180–$370. Double: $180–$370.

Located on the island's east end, this resort just opened in 1992. A large complex of nine buildings, it has all the usual resort diversions and very pleasant guestrooms and suites, all with coffeemakers, refrigerators, and nice views off the balcony. The grounds include three interconnected pools complete with bar and waterfalls, seven tennis courts, a fitness room, two restaurants, four bars, and watersports at the small beach. Kids are kept busy (and parents relaxed) with supervised programs year-round. A good, all-around resort. 300 rooms. Credit Cards: V, MC, DC, A.

Windward Passage $125–$235 ★★★

P.O. Box 640, 804, ☎ *(800) 524-7389, (809) 774-5200.*
Single: $125–$230. Double: $135–$235.

The rates are fairly reasonable at this busy commercial hotel, located downtown and overlooking the harbor. Guestrooms are basic but fine, and the 11 more expensive suites offer sitting areas, hair dryers and refrigerators. There are a few restaurants and bars and a pool, but no other facilities. Most of the guests are business travelers, as the beach is beyond walking distance. 151 rooms. Credit Cards: CB, V, MC, DC, A.

Apartments and Condominiums

Apartments and villas are numerous in St. Thomas, and the common language and the familiar U.S-style supermarkets make self-catering a breeze. The one shock will be how high the prices for food are. You can always bring staples from home, especially frozen meats and soft packages of soup, etc., that can fit easily into the corners of a suitcase.

Anchorage Beach Villas $195–$235 ★★★★

Cowpet Bay Point, Bluebeard Hill, ☎ *(800) 524-6599, (809) 774-1600.*
Single: $195–$235. Double: $195–$235.

Located on the beach near the island's eastern tip, this complex consists of 30 villas that are large and modern. Each has two bedrooms, two baths, full kitchens, sky-lights, large decks, and washer/dryers. Most sleep up to four, while the loft units can accommodate six. Maids tidy up daily. Facilities include a pool, two tennis courts, and a fitness center. There's a restaurant for those who don't feel up to cooking in. The weekly manager's cocktail party is a nice opportunity to meet your fellow guests. The beach is small but decent, and they'll shuttle you about for a fee. 30 rooms. Credit Cards: V, MC, DC, A.

Cowpet Bay Village $247–$420 ★★★

6222 Estate Nazareth, Cowpet Bay, ☎ *(800) 524-2038, (809) 775-6220.*

Single: $247–$300. Double: $247–$420.

This complex, located on the beach at Cowpet Bay, consists of 30 two- and three-bedroom villas. All are spacious and airy, with fully equipped kitchens, living/dining areas, balconies, washer/dryers, and maid service. There's a restaurant on site, and guests can borrow snorkeling equipment for free. There's no pool, but the beach is right at hand. You'll need a car for mobility. 30 rooms. Credit Cards: V, MC, DC, A.

Crystal Cove $126–$273   ★ ★

Route 6, Sapphire Bay, 802, ☎ (800) 524-2038, (809) 775-6220.
Single: $126–$205. Double: $131–$273.

This 25-year-old complex shows its age, but the rates are reasonable for self-sufficient types who want kitchen facilities. Accommodations are in condominiums that range in size from studios to one- and two-bedroom units, all with complete kitchens, balconies, and basic furnishings. Maid service is available every day but Sunday. Facilities include a saltwater pool and two tennis courts. There's no restaurant on site, so you'll want a car. 50 rooms. Credit Cards: V, MC, DC, A.

Pavilions & Pools $180–$260   ★ ★ ★

Estate Smith Bay, ☎ (800) 524-2001, (809) 775-6110.
Single: $180–$260. Double: $180–$260.

This villa resort is located seven miles from Charlotte Amalie, near Sapphire Beach. Each of the 25 air-conditioned villas has one bedroom, living/dining areas, complete kitchens, VCRs, and private, decent-sized pools. Maids tidy up daily, and the rates are quite reasonable for self-sufficient types. There's a restaurant and open-air bar that occasionally hosts live entertainment. Guests can play tennis on the courts at the nearby Sapphire Bay Beach Resort for free; watersports equipment can be rented there as well. 25 rooms. Credit Cards: V, MC, A.

Sapphire Beach Resort $190–$395   ★ ★ ★

Sapphire Bay, 801, ☎ (800) 524-2090, (809) 775-6100.
Single: $190–$395. Double: $190–$395.

Located on one of St. Thomas' best beaches, this villa resort encompasses 35 picturesque acres. It's a bit out of the way, so you'll want to rent a car to get around. The accommodations are quite posh with large balconies, fresh flowers, and fully equipped kitchens. The largest units have two baths, two balconies, and two queen-size sofa beds in addition to the bedroom, so can sleep six. Maids tidy up daily, and room service is available. Watersports and supervised children's programs are free. There's also a restaurant, pool, two bars, and a 67-slip marina. 171 rooms. Credit Cards: V, MC, A.

Secret Harbor Resort $179–$310   ★ ★ ★

6280 Estate Nazareth, 801, ☎ (800) 524-2250, (809) 775-6550.
Single: $179–$310. Double: $199–$310.

All accommodations are in suites at this secluded resort set on a private beach. Lodging is in studios and one- and two-bedroom condos with kitchens and quality tropical furnishings. Facilities include an extensive watersports center, a pool, full-service health club, and two tennis courts. Two restaurants and a few bars complete the scene. The beach is lovely, and this operation combines the best of self-sufficient and resort living. 60 rooms. Credit Cards: V, MC, A.

Secret Harbourview Villas $140–$360   ★ ★ ★

P.O. Box 8529, Nazareth Beach, 801, ☎ *(800) 874-7897, (809) 775-2600.*
Single: $140–$281. Double: $140–$360.

Set on a cliff above the beach, this condominium resort offers studios and one- and two-bedroom units, all with complete kitchens, balconies, and maid service. Facilities include a restaurant, pool, and three tennis courts. Guests can use the beach and facilities at the nearby Secret Harbour Beach Resort. While they offer shuttle service into town (for a fee), you'll probably want to rent a car for independence. 30 rooms.
Credit Cards: V, MC, DC.

Watergate Villas $73–$375   ★ ★ ★ ★

Route 7, Estate Bolongo Bay, 803, ☎ *(800) 524-2038, (809) 775-6220.*
Single: $73–$247. Double: $142–$375.

Set on a hill on the south coast 15 minutes out of Charlotte Amalie, this complex offers individually decorated villas that are rented out in their owners' absence. Configurations range from studios to one-, two-, and three-bedroom units, all with complete kitchens, living/dining areas, maid service, balconies, and contemporary furnishings. There are three pools, two tennis courts, and a restaurant on the premises. Good for self-sufficient types, but you'll want to rent a car to get around. 100 rooms. Credit Cards: V, MC, DC, A.

Inns

Inns in St. Thomas are especially homey, and reminiscent of the days when a weary traveler could find sustenance and a room along the wayfaring highway. A number of colonial houses have been restored by owners who use the main area as a restaurant and rent out a few rooms in the back. (Imagine the wonderful cooking smells you can enjoy all day!) Some are located on hillsides; others, like **Island Beachcomber**, are situated on some of the best beaches around. **Pavilions and Pool** is perhaps the most romantic inn since you have to pass by a waterfall and several pools before you even get to your room.

Admiral's Inn $79–$149   ★ ★

Villa Olga, 802, ☎ *(800) 544- 493, (809) 774-1376.*
Single: $79–$149. Double: $79–$149.

This inn is not in one of St. Thomas' better neighborhoods, but on the other hand, the area is home to many fine restaurants. Guestrooms, located on the hillside, are air-conditioned and have private baths and cable TV, but the furnishings have seen better days. The inn's four acres include two restaurants, a pool, and a small man-made beach good for snorkeling. Continental breakfast is included in the rates. 16 rooms. Credit Cards: V, MC, A.

Blackbeard's Castle $75–$140   ★ ★ ★

Waterfront Veterens Drive, ☎ *(800) 344-5771, (809) 776-1234.*
Single: $75–$110. Double: $95–$140.

This inn, a national historic landmark, is built around a stone tower once reportedly used by pirates. Guestrooms are quite small but charming enough with simple furnishings, air conditioners, and tiny balconies. There are also several one-bedroom suites with more amenities. The grounds include a large pool, a highly regarded restaurant, and a bar with nightly jazz bands. Wonderful views abound everywhere.

The beach and downtown Charlotte Amalie are within walking distance. 25 rooms.
Credit Cards: V, MC, A.

Danish House   **$64–$124**   ★★

P.O. Box 6041, 804, ☎ *(809) 774-6952.*
Single: $64–$114. Double: $74–$124.
Located on a hill (nice views) in the historic district, this small inn is within walking
distance of shops and restaurants. All guestrooms are air-conditioned, but not all
have a private bath, so be sure to reserve accordingly. There's a pool on-site, but little else, although, as noted, you'll have no trouble finding things nearby. 14 rooms.
Credit Cards: V, MC, DC, A.

Hotel 1829   **$55–$285**   ★★★

P.O. Box 1567, 804, ☎ *(800) 524-2002, (809) 776-1829.*
Single: $55–$285. Double: $65–$285.
This atmospheric inn was built in (you guessed it) 1829 by a French sea captain for
his bride. Now a national historic site, it accommodates guests in charming rooms
enhanced with antiques, air conditioners, minibars and VCRs. The price you pay
depends on the size of your room, which varies widely. The continental restaurant
is well-regarded, and there's also a bar and tiny pool. Not especially suited to small
children or the physically challenged, as there are many steep stairs to negotiate. 15
rooms. Credit Cards: V, MC, A.

Low Cost Lodging

A budget consciousness does exist in St. Thomas, and there are several options under
$50 per double in small, unassuming hotels. Camping is becoming ever more popular on
the island. Checking out your room ahead of time is essential; insist on seeing the room
you will be renting since the conditions could vary from apartment to apartment. The
Tourist Office in Charlotte Amalie could also help you find arrangements; also peruse the
Virgin Island daily newspapers under the classified section.

Heritage Manor   **$50–$135**   ★★

P.O. Box 90, 1A Snegle Gada, 804, ☎ *(800) 828-0757, (809) 774-3003.*
Single: $50–$130. Double: $55–$135.
Located in the historical district, this small inn dates back to 1830 and was originally
the home of a Danish merchant. All rooms are air-conditioned and include such
niceties as ceiling fans, refrigerators and brass beds, but only the two apartments,
which boast kitchens, have private baths. There's a pool on-site but little else,
though you can walk to shops and restaurants. Most rooms are under $75, making
this one of St. Thomas' rare budget choices. 8 rooms. Credit Cards: V, MC, A.

Island View Guest House   **$60–$100**   ★

P.O. Box 1903, Constant Hill, ☎ *(800) 524-2023, (809) 774-4270.*
Single: $60–$94. Double: $65–$100.
This informal guest house is five minutes out of Charlotte Amalie and perched high
on a hill with great harbor views. Guestrooms are quite simple, as suggested by the
rates (most are under $100), but comfortable enough. Most, but not all, have pri-
vate baths, and those who want air conditioners will pay an extra fee. The high-
priced units have kitchenettes. There's a restaurant, honor bar and small pool on the

premises, and continental breakfast is complimentary. Ask about special packages. 15 rooms. Credit Cards: V, MC, A.

Where to Eat

Highest Rated Restaurants in St. Thomas

★★★★ **Cafe Normandie**

★★★★ **Craig and Sally's**

★★★★ **Fiddle Leaf**

★★★★ **Palm Terrace**

★★★ **Agave Terrace**

★★★ **Blackbeard's Castle**

★★★ **Chart House**

★★★ **Cuzzin's**

★★★ **Epernay Champagne Bar**

★★★ **Hard Rock Cafe**

Most Exclusive Restaurants in St. Thomas

★★★★	**Cafe Normandie**	$25–$39
★★★	**Hotel 1829**	$20–$32
★★★	**Blackbeard's Castle**	$18–$29
★★★★	**Fiddle Leaf**	$18–$27
★★★	**Agave Terrace**	$18–$24

Fielding's Best Value Restaurants in St. Thomas

★★★	**Victor's New Hide Out**	$11–$20
★★★	**Raffles**	$15–$29
★★★	**Piccola Marina Cafe**	$13–$24
★★★	**L'Escargot**	$15–$27
★★★	**Hook, Line and Sinker**	$6–$20

Locals dine out as frequently as visitors on St. Thomas, which accounts for the extraordinary range of dining options, with cuisines hailing from nearly every corner of the world. Splurging on Sunday brunch is a national pastime. Restaurants are generally informal and open-air, but prices can rival those of Manhattan's most elegant dining rooms. Casual dress, even shorts, generally pass muster, but reservations are advisable. Each of the big hotels have several restaurants and a few have gained renown. One of the newest, most elegant spots is the **Grand Palazzo Hotel's Palm Terrace**, where excellent spa-style "light" cuisine dubbed "Floribbean" (Florida meets Caribbean) is serenaded by a pianist in a white diner jacket. A taste of France can be found at **Provence**, in funky Frenchtown, where you can sample such delights as hearty soups, casseroles and a fine antipasto bar. One delicacy not to pass up are the liquer-flavored milkshakes like the one with Jamoco-chocolate ice cream, coconut ice cream and Kahlua which you can find at **Udder Delite Dairy Bar** near Magens Bay. ☎ *809-775-2501*. Sorry to say, but St. Thomas is one of only two Caribbean islands with a Hard Rock Cafe. Go only if you feel homesick.

Agave Terrace $$$ ★ ★ ★

6400 Estate Smith Bay, Water Bay, ☎ (809) 775-4142.
Seafood cuisine.
Lunch: 10:00 a.m.–6:30 p.m., entrees $18–$24.
Dinner: 6:30 p.m.–10:00 p.m., entrees $18–$24.
It may be a little hard to find, with a resort-hotel location on the northeastern end of the island. But even non-guests should try to make it here for a leisurely breakfast or dinner on the patio while the light is still good for an unparalleled view of the Caribbean sea in the distance. The cuisine is mostly Mediterranean style seafood, and the chef is delighted to create any dish (within reason) that a customer requests. Associated Hotel: Point Pleasant Resort. Reservations required. Credit Cards: V, MC, A.

Blackbeard's Castle $$$ ★ ★ ★

P.O. Box 6041, Blackbeard Hill, ☎ (809) 776-1234.
American cuisine.
Lunch: 11:30 a.m.–2:30 p.m., entrees $8–$13.
Dinner: 6:30 p.m.–9:30 p.m., entrees $18–$29.

Feel like Blackbeard the pirate surveying his domain from this stunning aerie with an eagle eye view of the harbor and the city. The international cuisine has won many awards from local publications several years in a row. It's hard to have a meal here without sampling from a varied array of house-made soups, salads or creative appetizers. Entrees include a choice of veal, excellent seafood, beef filets or a devilishly rich pasta. Lighter meals can be had in the lounge or by the pool, where non-guests can swim. There's a bountiful buffet Sundays from 11:00 to 3:00 pm. Associated Hotel: Blackbeard's Castle. Reservations recommended. Credit Cards: V, MC, A.

Cafe Normandie $$$ ★ ★ ★ ★

rue de St. Barthélémy, Frenchtown, ☎ (809) 774-1622.

French cuisine.
Dinner: 6:00 p.m.–10:00 p.m., entrees $25–$39.

In an informal survey, island residents anointed this cozy, elegant French restaurant with a bright yellow painted exterior as their favorite overall dining out spot a few years ago. Food, service and location are all exceptional, but I suspect people return again and again for the sinful chocolate fudge pie. There's a well regarded five-course, prix-fixe supper available nightly that includes a palate-cleansing sorbet. Make sure to reserve in season, as it is small and popular. Closed Mondays in summer. Closed: Mon. Reservations recommended. Credit Cards: V, MC, A.

Chart House $$$ ★ ★ ★

P.O. Box 3156, Villa Olga, ☎ (809) 774-4262.
American cuisine.
Dinner: 5:00 p.m.–10:00 p.m., entrees $13–$37.

Salad bar lovers flock here for a huge spread of many items, including passable caviar. Dinner specialties include sizzling steaks, juicy prime rib, chicken and lobster; the salad bar is included. All this bounty is consumed on a terrace overlooking the sea, situated in a 19th century building which was once home to Russian diplomats. Don't overlook the famous "mud pie" if you still have room. Associated Hotel: Admiral's Inn. Reservations recommended. Credit Cards: V, MC, DC, A.

Craig and Sally's $$$ ★ ★ ★ ★

22 Estate Honduras, Frenchtown, ☎ (809) 777-9949.
International cuisine.
Dinner: 6:00 p.m.–10:30 p.m., entrees $11–$26.

A talented husband and wife team combine his knowledge of fine wines and her culinary expertise in the operation of this muraled restaurant in Frenchtown. Although there are several dining areas, it's often crowded; the word is out on the creative Mediterranean and Asian specialties prepared here. Sun-kissed tomatoes, broiled peppers or salsas made with market picked fruits are used liberally on plump scallops, chicken or swordfish. Sally's desserts recall a childhood learning to bake at mother's elbow—there's key lime pie or a brown sugar pound cake. Reservations required. Credit Cards: V, MC, A.

Cuzzin's $$ ★ ★ ★

Back Street, Charlotte Amalie,
Latin American cuisine.
Lunch: entrees $10–$20.
Dinner: entrees $10–$20.

Half the fun while eating at this downtown hangout is deciphering the menu, which describes food items in island patois. But most of the specialties are familiar friends, including stewed conch, curried chicken, and a mountain of vegetables. The daring will like the homemade hot sauce that accompanies some meals. Reservations recommended. Credit Cards: V, MC, A.

Epernay Champagne Bar $ ★ ★ ★

24 B Honduras St., Frenchtown, ☎ (809) 774-5343.
International cuisine.
Dinner: 4:30 p.m.–1:00 a.m., entrees $6–$10.

Before or after a night on the prowl, nestle here for champagne by the glass; sample up to six different varieties. A grazing menu of sophisticated snacks covers the globe—there's sushi, caviar and goat cheese. Food is served from 5 p.m. to 12 a.m.; it's open later on weekends. Wine and desserts are also available. Closed: Sun. Credit Cards: V, MC, A.

Eunice's Terrace $$$ ★★

66-67 Smith Bay, Route. 38, Smith Bay, ☎ (809) 775-3975.
Latin American cuisine.
Lunch: 11:00 a.m.–4:00 p.m., entrees $6–$11.
Dinner: 6:00 p.m.–10:00 p.m., entrees $10–$28.

An island success story, Eunice's establishment grew like crazy from a simple food stand to a two-story building with a popular bar in Smith Bay. The West Indian cuisine that built her reputation is possibly the best on the island. There's a daily menu, but conch fritters and an incomparable tropical rum cake are usually available. Closed: Sun. Reservations recommended. Credit Cards: V, MC, A.

Fiddle Leaf $$$ ★★★★

31 Kongens Gade, Charlotte Amalie,
International cuisine.
Dinner: 6:00 p.m.–10:00 p.m., entrees $18–$27.

The well-travelled chef, who once lived in the South Pacific, has created a mouth-watering, tropically-inspired menu that relies on fruit chutneys, coconut, ginger and curry. Plates are garnished like a Carmen Miranda fruit-salad hat, and happily, everything tastes as good as it looks. The location is a winner too, high on a choice spot on Government Hill with a harbor vista from the terrace. Closed: Mon. Reservations recommended. Credit Cards: V, MC, A.

The Frigate $$$ ★★★

P.O. Box 1506, Mafolie Hill, ☎ (809) 774-2790, (800) 225-7035.
Seafood cuisine.
Dinner: entrees $15–$30.

An awe-inspiring ocean view and tender steaks hot off the charcoal broiler continue to please the regulars that ascend to this small, charming hotel dining room on Mafolie Hill. Non-red meat eaters will be pleased with fresh seafood, chicken and a salad bar. There's a smaller branch in Red Hook (No 18-8) near the Marina, 775-1829. Associated Hotel: Mafolie Hotel. Reservations recommended. Credit Cards: V, MC, A.

Hard Rock Cafe $$ ★★★

International Plaza, Charlotte Amalie,
American cuisine.
Lunch: 11:00 a.m.–4:00 p.m., entrees $7–$16.
Dinner: 4:00 p.m.–12:00 p.m., entrees $7–$16.

This memorabilia-laden retro-rock burger palace draws a more subdued crowd than those in mainland cities, but there's the requisite antique auto suspended over the entrance. Bob Marley mementoes are also included with the gold Beatle records behind glass frames. Among the wall exhibits is a red and gold neon sign proclaiming "No drugs or nuclear weapons allowed" inside. Good burgers barbecue ribs nachos and fajitas are served. Credit Cards: V, MC, A.

Hook, Line and Sinker $$ ★★★
#2 The Waterfront, Frenchtown, ☎ *(809) 776-9708.*
International cuisine.
Lunch: entrees $5–$10.
Dinner: entrees $6–$20.
Yachties tie up to this seaside eatery that's nothing special, but it's a good meet and greet place. There's a nice outdoor deck, and offerings are reasonably priced. It's a convenient stop if you're in the area, especially for a burger or steak lunch. Reservations recommended. Credit Cards: V, MC, A.

Hotel 1829 $$$ ★★★
30 Kongens Gade, Charlotte Amalie, ☎ *(809) 776-1829, (800) 524-2002.*
American cuisine.
Dinner: 5:30 p.m.–10:00 p.m., entrees $20–$32.
Streamlined service and stellar food are served in a restored Government Hill hotel. Tables on the terrace are well-sought after for the terrific views, but wherever you sit, the cuisine is pleasing. Specialties include a wilted spinach salad and dessert souffles; and the raspberry chocolate is especially toothsome. Associated Hotel: Hotel 1829. Closed: Sun. Reservations required. Credit Cards: V, MC, A.

L'Escargot $$$ ★★★
#12 Submarine Base, Charlotte Amalie, ☎ *(809) 774-6565.*
Seafood cuisine.
Lunch: 11:45 a.m.–2:30 p.m., entrees $7–$15.
Dinner: 6:00 p.m.–10:00 p.m., entrees $15–$27.
A long-established dining room, this classic French restaurant is one of a few eateries located at a submarine base west of Charlotte Amalie, near the airport. Meals are taken in a patio overlooking the ocean. Specialties are old favorites like rack of lamb or lobster thermidor; all simply and impeccably prepared. Closed: Sun. Reservations recommended. Credit Cards: V, MC, A.

Palm Terrace $$$ ★★★★
Great Bay, ☎ *(809) 775-3333, (800) 545-0509.*
International cuisine.
Dinner: 6:30 p.m.–10:00 p.m., entrees $22–$32.
A chef with a background in cooking for luxury health spas in California and Florida holds court at this, the Grand Palazzo resort's crown jewel. Weight watchers can delight in the fact that many of the delectable meals are prepared in natural juices and infusions, instead of heavy cream sauces. Alas, the calories await in the desserts, one of which is caramel ice cream encased in chocolate. Apparently, this ensures a return to the fat farm. The surroundings here are some of the most luxurious on the island—everything exudes a rosy glow—pink plaster walls, marble floors. Associated Hotel: Grand Palazzo. Reservations required. Credit Cards: V, MC, A.

Piccola Marina Cafe $$$ ★★★
6300 Smith Bay, Red Hook, ☎ *(809) 775-6350.*
American cuisine.

Lunch: 11:00 a.m.–5:30 p.m., entrees $5–$14.
Dinner: 5:30 p.m.–10:30 p.m., entrees $13–$24.

This alfresco restaurant on a Red Hook Marina dock is a fun place, with a selection of pastas for your dining pleasure. Sauces range from tomato marinara to a creamy alfredo. Others can order sandwiches, chicken, fresh seafood or quaff a brew or two. Sunday brunch is served in the winter from 10 a.m. to 3 p.m. Reservations recommended. Credit Cards: V, MC, A.

Provence $$$ ★★★

Honduras Street, Frenchtown, ☎ (809) 777-5600.
French cuisine. Specialties: Antipasto Table.
Dinner: 6:00 p.m.–10:30 p.m., entrees $15–$19.

Chef and restaurateur Patricia La Corte, who created the well-regarded Fiddle Leaf on Government Hill is now roosting at this country-French bistro on the second floor of a wooden building in funky Frenchtown. The warmly-decorated room, with arched doorways and potted palms, offers a wharf-side view. Specialties include lamb shank with hearty chakerny and rosemary sauce on a bed of mashed potatoes and oven roasted garlic chicken. Nibblers go into grazing heaven with La Corte's reasonably priced antipasto table, served daily until 11:00 p.m. Closed: Sun. Reservations recommended. Credit Cards: V, MC, A.

Raffles $$$ ★★★

The Marina, Compass Point, ☎ (809) 775-6004.
Seafood cuisine.
Dinner: 6:30 p.m.–10:30 p.m., entrees $15–$29.

This south-seas themed restaurant is a favorite with residents, who enjoy the steaks flambeed at tableside. Ladies especially like the high-backed peacock chairs in a salon cooled by ceiling fans and ocean breezes. Other specialties include fresh fish, and stuffed leg of lamb. Closed: Mon. Reservations required. Credit Cards: V, MC, A.

Victor's New Hide Out $$$ ★★★

103 Submarine Base, Charlotte Amalie, ☎ (809) 776-9379.
International cuisine.
Lunch: 11:30 a.m.–3:30 p.m., entrees $9–$11.
Dinner: 5:30 p.m.–10:00 p.m., entrees $11–$20.

Chef Victor left quiet Montserrat for more action, and he cooks his West Indian specialties for an appreciative crowd of locals, tourists, and the occasional celebrity. The ubiquitous conch and curried chicken dishes are available, as well as his signature dish, Lobster Montserrat, cooked with fruit and cream sauce. Newcomers should probably arrive by taxi, as the hilltop hideaway is a little hard to find. Reservations recommended. Credit Cards: V, MC, A.

Where to Shop

Since Charlotte Amalie was declared a free port in 1755, opening it for trade with the European powers and growing American colonies, the islands have moved to a mercantile beat. Jewelry, liquor and electronics stores, interspersed with shops offering china, linens, and perfume crowd Main Street. Jitneys take cruise ship passengers downtown; most stores also have outlets at the Havensight Mall near the dock.

United State residents may bring home $1200 in goods free of duty, with the next $1000 each subject to 5 percent duty. Members of a household may make a joint declaration, entitling a family of four to a $4800 duty-free allowance. There is no sales or luxury tax. Best buys include unmounted gems (duty-free for Americans, no matter the price), gold jewelry and watches. Before stepping into a store, know what you are looking for and what the price is back home. Finesse in bargaining goes a long way.

Reputable establishments offer dealer warranties and certificates of authenticity and generally avoid the sidewalk barker come-ons that grow more shrill as one moves west on Main Street. Most visitors leave toting at least one bottle of rum. Local brands like Cruzan cost less that $3 a fifth, and if you buy any spirits produced in the territory, you are allowed to take six bottles rather than the normal five bottles back to the States duty-free.

Must-see for shoppers are several specialty stores that showcase the impressive work of artisans from Jamaica, Haiti, Dominican Republic, Martinique, and others. Start with **Down Island Traders** next to Post Office Alley on the Waterfront, where you can choose everything from edible delicacies such as marmalades and jellies to sweet Caribbean rum balls, fiery mustards, tasty fruit chutneys, and exotic spices, as well as extensive Haitian and Jamaican wall hangings, handmade cloth and wooden dolls, including the legendary Caribbean worry doll. (According to an ancient island tale, these precious-looking figures will take away your troubles if you hand them over. The bigger the worry, the bigger the doll—one worry per doll.) Upstairs is **The Gallery**, a two-room studio featuring fine Caribbean folk art, including work from some of the island's top primitivists. The **Caribbean Marketplace** in Havensight Mall specializes in exotic condiments as well as "Sunsations," a new line of flower, fruit and herbal extracts for bath gels, body splashes and skin oils. Handmade steel-pan drums can also be found here. At **Mango Tango** in the Al Cohen Building (across the street from Havensight), you can stock up on wooden masks from Jamaica, wooden earrings from Trinidad, and original and print work from the Virgin Islands. **Tillet Gardens Craft Complex**, located in Tutu across from Four Winds Plaza, features the work of Jim Tillett's screen-painted maps of the Caribbean, cruising maps of the Virgin Islands, and also abstract paintings by himself and other local artists. Also in the same complex is **Okidanokh**, where goldsmith Abel Fabri's original jewelry includes such precious stones as tourmaline, sapphire, topaz and agate. The **Color of Joy** is a boutique that features watercolors and prints by St. Thomas painter Corinne Van Rensselaer, as well as varied gifts from the islands; the **Caribbean Enamel Guild**—a small annex—features handpainted jewelry, boxes, and various accessories. Also visit the **Virgin Island Stained Glass** store, which contains mesmerizing stained-glass gifts—sculptures, hangings, windows, and even doors. The best time to visit Tillett Gardens is during the popular Arts Alive arts and crafts fairs, held on-site three times a year. For more information call ☎ *(809) 775-1929* about the next festival.

St. Thomas Directory

ARRIVAL

American Airlines offers nonstop service from Miami, NYC and Raleigh-Durham to St. Thomas, connecting from all parts of the world via NYC. Carnival Airlines flies nonstop from Miami to San Juan, with connections on convenient carriers. Continental Airlines flies nonstop from Newark to St. Thomas, connecting from Boston, Chicago, Detroit, and Philadelphia via Newark. Delta Airlines flies nonstop from Atlanta to St. Thomas, continuing to St. Croix. Trans World Airways flies nonstop from NYC, St. Louis and Miami to San Juan, with connections to St. Thomas in convenient carriers. Virgin Island Paradise Airways flies direct from Newark to St. Thomas via St. Croix, connecting from Chicago, Dallas, Houston and Philadelphia.

Inter-island flights include daily service from St. Croix, St. Kitts-Nevis, and Anguilla to St. Thomas on Air Anguilla. Air Calypso offers daily service between St. Croix, St. Thomas and San Juan. American Eagle offers daily service from San Juan to St. Thomas/St. Croix, and between St. Croix and St. Thomas. Also check service on Sunaire Express, Windward Island Airways and Leeward Island Air Transport (LIAT).

CLIMATE

Summer temperatures, cooled by eastern trade winds, hover around 82 degrees F. Winter temperatures range from 77 degrees F., dipping to 69 degrees F. at night and rising as high as 84 degrees F. The rainy season runs September-January, though the sun shines nearly every day.

The average rainfall is about 40 inches per year, and showers are usually brief.

DOCUMENTS

U.S. citizens need no passport. But if you plan to visit the British Virgin Islands, you must show proof of citizenship (passport, or birth certificate with photo ID). Canadians must have a valid passport.

ELECTRICITY

Current runs at 110 volts, 60 cycles.

GETTING AROUND

Taxis at the airport usually stand at the far left end of the new terminal, not at all close to where inter-island flights land. Cabs are not metered but each driver must carry the most up-to-date list of fares. Rates quoted are for one passenger, extra passengers are charged more. If you decide to go to a destination not on the official list of rates, do negotiate firmly ahead of time.

There are public buses every 20 minutes from the terminal to the town (about $1).

Rental cars are widely available, including the large name agencies in the U.S. Rates are about $35 a day.

Ferry boats are an easy way to get around the islands. You can catch one from Red Hook to St. John (every hour from 8:00 a.m.- midnight); it takes 20 minutes one way, about $3. There's also a ferry at Charlotte Amalie to St. John (45 minutes, about $7), as well as one from downtown to Frenchman's Reef Hotel and Morningstar Beach ($3)—it's a cool way to get to the beach and only fifteen minutes long.

LANGUAGE

English is the official language. Locals also speak a native patois, a mixture of English, African and Spanish. Many people are bilingual in Spanish.

MEDICAL EMERGENCIES

Police ext. *915*, fire ext. *921*, ambulance ext. *922*.

MONEY

The official currency is the American dollar.

TELEPHONE

The area code is *809*. Since USVI is an incorporated territory, toll-free numbers that operate in the U.S. work here, normal postage rates apply. You can also direct dial to the mainland.

TIME

Atlantic Standard Time, which means an hour later than New York City, except during daylight saving time, when it is the same.

TIPPING AND TAXES

Some hotels include a 10–15 percent service charge; this should include all tips for both restaurant and room service, unless the attention was extraordinary. If no service is added, leave a 15 percent tip for the waitress, $1–$2 a day to the maid; bartenders and wine stewards should be tipped always. Tip the bellboy and porter at least 50 cents a bag. Taxi drivers should receive a 15 percent tip if you are satisfied with the service.

TOURIST INFORMATION

The **St. Thomas Tourist Office** has information booths at the airport ☎ *774-8784*, on the waterfront at Charlotte Amalie ☎ *774-8784*, ext. *147*; and in Havensight Mall near the cruise shipper ☎ *774-8784*. All the offices are open daily. You can also pick up brochures, rest your feet, and even check shopping bags at an island-sponsored hospitality lounge in the Old Customs House next to Little Switzerland.

WATER

There is ample water for showers and bathing, but you are asked to conserve water whenever possible.

WHEN TO GO

The Calypso Competition is held at the University of the Virgin Islands cafeteria on March 4. Arts Alive & Crafts Festival, where Caribbean vendors sell handmade crafts and arts, is held on March 17–19. The Caribbean Chorale, one of the most popular groups in the USVI, performs a blend of classical, West Indian, and native compositions on April 2. The Tenth annual Easter Bonnet Contest takes place on April 17. The Virgin Islands Carnival Events, with nightly competitions in music and costumes takes place on April 18–22. The 22nd Annual International Rolex Cup Regatta is April 21–23 (tentative). Virgin Islands Carnival Village features local foods, drink, and rides on April 24–29. STARfest 1995, a star-studded tribute to Caribbean talent, is May 13. The 8th Annual American Yacht Harbor Billfish tournament is July 13–18. Arts Alive Arts & Crafts Festival is August 11–13. The Hebrew Congregation of St. Thomas Bicentennial Celebration Gala Opening Weekend, featuring a celebration of Jewish History, is September 15-17. Hebrew Congregation of St. Thomas Bicentennial Celebration Interfaith Succot Service is October 6–8. The Hebrew Congregation of St. Thomas Bicentennial Celebration Jewish Musical Performance starts October 24 for four weeks. St. Thomas/St. John Agriculture Food Fair is November 18–19. Arts Alive Arts & Crafts Festival is November 24–26. The Hebrew Congregations of St. Thomas Bicentennial Celebration, featuring an authentic Sephardic Service and Chanukah Celebration is December 22.

ST. THOMAS HOTELS	RMS	RATES	PHONE	FAX
Charlotte Amalie				
★★★★★ **Marriott Frenchman's Reef**	520	$160–$395	(800) 524-2000	(809) 776-3054
★★★★ **Anchorage Beach Villas**	30	$195–$235	(800) 524-6599	(809) 774-5134
★★★★ **Grand Palazzo**	150	$250–$865	(800) 545-0509	(809) 775-5635
★★★★ **Island Beachcomber**	48	$95–$150	(800) 982-9898	(809) 774-5615
★★★★ **Stouffer Grand Beach**	297	$220–$560	(800) 468-3571	(809) 775-2185
★★★★ **Sugar Bay Plantation**	300	$180–$370	(800) 927-7100	809 777 7200
★★★★ **Watergate Villas**	100	$73–$375	(800) 524-2038	(809) 775-2298
★★★ **Blackbeard's Castle**	25	$75–$140	(800) 344-5771	(809) 776-4321
★★★ **Bluebeard's Castle Hotel**	170	$140–$235	(800) 524-6599	(809) 774-5134
★★★ **Emerald Beach Resort**	90	$139–$239	(800) 233-4936	(809) 776-3426
★★★ **Hotel 1829**	15	$55–$285	(800) 524-2002	(809) 776-4313
★★★ **Pavilions & Pools**	25	$180–$260	(800) 524-2001	(809) 775-6110
★★★ **Point Pleasant Resort**	134	$200–$380	(800) 524-2300	809 776 5694
★★★ **Ramada Yacht Haven Hotel**	151	$90–$225	(800) 228-9898	(809) 776-3410
★★★ **Sapphire Beach Resort**	171	$190–$395	(800) 524-2090	(809) 775-4024
★★★ **Secret Harbor Resort**	60	$179–$310	(800) 524-2250	(809) 775-1501
★★★ **Secret Harbourview Villas**	30	$140–$360	(800) 874-7897	(809) 775-5901
★★★ **Windward Passage**	151	$125–$235	(800) 524-7389	(809) 774-1231
★★ **Admiral's Inn**	16	$79–$149	(800) 544-0493	(809) 774-8010
★★ **Crystal Cove**	50	$126–$273	(800) 524-2038	(809) 775-4202
★★ **Danish House**	14	$64–$124	(809) 774-6952	(809) 774-6952
★★ **Heritage Manor**	8	$50–$135	(800) 828-0757	(809) 776-9585
★★ **Mafolie Hotel**	23	$65–$97	(800) 225-7035	(809) 774-4091
★★ **Magens Point Hotel**	54	$105–$305	(800) 524-2031	(809)776-5524
★ **Carib Beach Hotel**	69	$79–$139	(800) 792-2742	(809) 777-4131
★ **Island View Guest House**	15	$60–$100	(800) 524-2023	(809) 774-6167
Red Hook				
★★★★ **Bolongo Club Beach Resort**	200	$195–$235	(800) 524-4746	(809) 775-3208

ST. THOMAS HOTELS		RMS	RATES	PHONE	FAX
★★★	Bolongo Elysian Resort	118	$210–$690	(800) 524-4746	(809) 775-3208
★★★	Cowpet Bay Village	30	$247–$420	(800) 524-2038	(809) 775-4202

ST. THOMAS RESTAURANTS		LOCATION	PHONE	ENTREE
Charlotte Amalie				
American				
★★★	Blackbeard's Castle	Blackbeard Hill	(809) 776-1234	$8–$29
★★★	Chart House	Villa Olga	(809) 774-4262	$13–$37••
★★★	Hard Rock Cafe	Charlotte Amalie		$7–$16
★★★	Hotel 1829	Charlotte Amalie	(809) 776-1829	$20–$32••
French				
★★★★	Cafe Normandie	Frenchtown	(809) 774-1622	$25–$39••
★★★	Provence	Frenchtown	(809) 777-5600	$15–$19••
International				
★★★★	Craig and Sally's	Frenchtown	(809) 777-9949	$11–$26••
★★★★	Fiddle Leaf	Charlotte Amalie		$18–$27••
★★★	Epernay Champagne Bar	Frenchtown	(809) 774-5343	$6–$10••
★★★	Hook, Line and Sinker	Frenchtown	(809) 776-9708	$5–$20
★★★	Victor's New Hide Out	Charlotte Amalie	(809) 776-9379	$9–$20
Latin American				
★★★	Cuzzin's	Charlotte Amalie		$10–$20
Seafood				
★★★	L'Escargot	Charlotte Amalie	(809) 774-6565	$7–$27
★★★	The Frigate	Mafolie Hill	(809) 774-2790	$15–$30••
Red Hook				
American				
★★★	Piccola Marina Cafe	Red Hook	(809) 775-6350	$5–$24
International				
★★★★	Palm Terrace	Great Bay	(809) 775-3333	$22–$32••
Latin American				
★★	Eunice's Terrace	Smith Bay	(809) 775-3975	$6–$28

ST. THOMAS RESTAURANTS	LOCATION	PHONE	ENTREE
Seafood			
★★★ **Agave Terrace**	**Water Bay**	(809) 775-4142	$18—$24
★★★ **Raffles**	**Compass Point**	(809) 775-6004	$15—$29••

Note: • **Lunch Only**

•• **Dinner Only**

ST. VINCENT AND ITS GRENADINES

Picturesque St. Vincent's terrain ranges from rugged cliffs to lush valleys and beaches with golden and black sand.

The Grenadines is a small archipelago of islands a short boat hop south of St. Vincent which offers some of the best cruising possibilities in the Caribbean. Only a few of the islands have any touristic infrastructure, though many of them are so primitive and paradisiacal that most visitors arrive at least for the day to snorkel, trek and sunbathe in complete privacy. Collectively the islands total about 30 square miles of land mass, and while some are uninhabited, those which have residents are mostly populated by descendants of African slaves. The chain perhaps acquired its name from the French word for passionfruit, *grenadine*, of which there are many on the islands. Other historians believe that the chain was discovered at the same time Grenada was, hence "little grenada" or grenadine. The lifestyle in general is extremely laid-back and simple. Islands such as Mustique, Pal Island, Petit St. Vincent, and Young Island are privately owned, and have the most luxurious resorts. Others like Union, Bequia and St. Vincent are definitely for the vagabond on a budget.

St. Vincent and its Grenadines

Baleine Falls
La Soufriere

Georgetown

Chateaubelair
Troumaca
Barrouallie
Penniston
Layou
Ft. Charlotte

Sans Souci
Biabou
Mesopotamia
Ratho Mill
Calliaqua

Kingston

Indian   *Young Island*
Bay

CARIBBEAN SEA

Bequia

Mustique

Canouan

ATLANTIC OCEAN

Palm Island

Petit St. Vincent
Petit Martinique

Hillsborough

Carriacou

Grenada's Grenadines

Conference I.

0   10
MILES

N

Kick 'em Jenny
Isle Ronde

ST. VINCENT

Boat excursions and hiking trails lead to cascading waterfalls and mineral springs on St. Vincent.

Green and volcanic, St. Vincent is the main island of the Grenadines, more rugged than Grenada and offering a vast array of nature-oriented activities. From Bequia, motor vessels make the nine-mile run to St. Vincent (locally called the mainland here). Although the area is just now awakening to tourism, yachtsmen and sailors have long used the island as a jumping port for fabulous cruises through the surrounding islets; recently many visitors are staying on the island to experience the superb nature trails, stunning waterfalls, and the demanding hike to the crater of La Soufriere that last erupted in 1979. The western and eastern side of the island are wonderful areas to explore by bus; along the west, the coastline descends to beaches so golden they seem to glitter in the sun. At other times, the beaches turn coal black. In between are incredibly verdant landscapes flourishing with coconut, beadfruit, bananas, sweet potatoes and cocoa. Wild scenic excursions can be found along the rocky, rugged Atlantic coast, where, the farther you go, the more primitive the houses become; this is an island where you can see residents carrying their own water and pulling up arrowroot, a kind of skinny white radish which has become the island's major export (used for dressing wounds). The capital of Kingston can claim the oldest botanical garden in the Western hemisphere, begun in 1765; among its exotic specimens on the beautifully kept grounds is a breadfruit tree brought to the island in 1793 by

Captain Bligh of the Bounty. Endangered St. Vincent parrots can also be found here.

Bird's Eye View

Roughly 18 miles long by 11 miles wide, St. Vincent sprawls over 133 square miles while the Grenadines make a total of 17 more square miles. The highest peak on the island is **La Soufriere** on the leeward and windward coasts, an active volcano in the north rising to 4000 feet. It last erupted in 1979, when glowing avalanches rushed down the mountain and the sea boiled off the north coast, but careful monitoring succeeded in evacuating everybody before it blew. Today there is a dome of lava which extruded during this eruption and during an earlier disturbance in 1973. The steep mountain range of **Morne Garu** rises to 3500 feet and runs southward with spurs to the east and west coasts and the steep hills are forested. Most of the central mountain range and the steep hills are forested. Dominating the island are beaches of both golden and volcanic black with lush valleys and rugged cliffs.

The capital, **Kingstown**, is located on a sheltered bay, in the southern coast of the island.

History

Columbus marked the presence of St. Vincent on his third voyage in 1498, but luckily didn't go ashore since the resident Carib Indians might have cannibalized him. The native tribes here were more tenacious than other islands, keeping the European conquistadors at bay longer than any other island. In 1763 a treaty allowed the British to take control of the island. Sixteen years later, they found themselves battling the French, but the Treaty of Versailles in 1783 gave the power back to England.

Some years later, Captain Bligh took off for Tahiti from England with his crew of the *Bounty*, only to be mutinied by them and pushed out to sea. In

1793 he finally reached St. Vincent on his own, equipped with a canoeful of breadfruit seedlings, which became the progenitors of a crop that would eventually make the island famous. In 1795, the native population sided with the French and burned down British plantations during a ferocious battle; a year later the Brits triumphantly quelled the rebellion. At that time, the Brits decided to deport the rest of the native Indians to British Honduras (now known as Belize), where their ancestors live today. Until 1979 the island was under British rule at which time it received independent statehood, along with the other Grenadines, within the Commonwealth. It is governed by a governor-general appointed by the Crown on the advice of the prime minister. The Parliament's House of Assembly is elected every five years.

People

Locals of St. Vincent and the Grenadines are unusually generous and courteous people, who have a gift for making others feel at home. A British formality, however, still runs through their behavior, a type of gentility which is also expected of visitors. Any trace of Gallic influence is tempered by a West Indies flavor, which is heard in the lilt of the language as well as the spices in the food. Service at most hotels, which are generally small, is characterized by enormous personal attention and care. Little serious crime ever happens on the islands, though valuables should never be left unguarded or ostentatiously displayed. The further you travel into the interior, the more primitive the lifestyle.

Beaches

If you're looking for white-sand beaches, stay around Kingston; the black ones are located around the rest of the island. Beautiful white sands can be found at **Villa Beach**, on the calm western coast. Also fine for swimming is the black **Questelle's Bay** and the black **Buccament Bay**. Dive shops are located at Villa beach and the CSY Yacht Club. The exposed Atlantic Coast is considered too rough for swimming, but the view of the crashing waves can be very exciting. None of the beaches here sport lifeguards, so do take your own precautions; even experienced swimmers should have someone spotting them, particularly when the water is rough. No beach or changing facilities are located on the windward side.

Dive Sites

Those in the know consider St.Vincent the biggest dive secret in the business. At 25 feet of water here, you can discover the same marine and plant life that can be found at 80 feet in other waters. The amount and variety of fish life is also extraordinary, including such tropical reef fish as angelfish, sergeant majors, peacock flounders, trumpetfishes, and parrotfish. Some species are unique to St. Thomas and can only be found here, such as the rooster-tail conch, cones, cowries, music volutes, and hawking conch. Black coral walls are stunning here, as are the enormous patches of brain and pillar corals. Strong currents in some areas, however, require the most advanced of skills; beginning divers should carefully follow the advice of instructors and avoid these areas.

Since shallow reefs surround nearly every one of the Grenadines, the snorkeling conditions are simply perfect. (Good snorkeling can also be found at Young Island Cut and on the leeward coast.) As well, the archipelago hosts enormous schools of fish traveling through. Divers will find fewer competitors for water space if they head for the fringed reefs of the Grenadines.

Operators can be found on the southern shores in St. Vincent, on Bequia, Union, and the private resort islands. You will probably find that prices are lower than other islands.

Treks (St. Vincent)

Mountainous describes most of the terrain on St. Vincent, while hilly is the best word for the Grenadines. Locals hike out of habit and necessity, and are often the best source for tips and trails. Sometimes, particularly in the Grenadines, locals are so friendly they might even offer to accompany you or they may be going your way. Don't hesitate to ask. In St. Vincent the Forestry Division and the Government Tourist Board both offer guides; if you choose to forego assistance, do take the time to ask these offices for advice and maps, and particularly advice on weather and trail conditions.

The **Buccament Forest Nature Trail** is an excellent, well-marked loop trail improved recently by the Forestry Department with the help of Peace Corps foresters. The trail leads up the slopes of the **Grand Bonhomme Mountain** range (over 3000 feet), passing through evergreen forest to a tropical rainforest. Surprise visits along the trail might be made by quail dove or tremblers, as well as such tropical birds as the purple-throated Carib hummingbird and pearly thrasher. In the late afternoon, look for the beautiful St. Vincent parrot, the national bird of the islands. On the way to the Nature Trail, about a mile after the town of Vermont, a marked footpath on the right of the road, leads to **Table Rock**, a huge, long sheet of lava rock in a riverbed where a waterfall has carved channels and basins that allow for swimming.

The huge active volcano called **La Soufriere** is located in the northern third of St. Vincent.

Although the volcano erupted in 1812, it is now safe to scale, and the excursion to climb the volcano requires a day to drive from Kingstown, the capital, hike to the crater and return. A walk through coconut groves leads to a moist tropical forest. The path emerges onto a steep-sided ridge covered with waist-high wild begonia. Farther up the mountain, you cross a stream which has carved swirling channels through the old lava flow. Resting places have been built on the way to the summit. The plant cover thins almost to bare ash near the steep cliffs of the crater rim.

High on the windward side of Grand Bonhomme are the **Montreal Gardens**, a botanic garden and nursery with beds of wild tropical flowers as well as rainforest vegetation. There are numerous walkways for leisurely strolling, a swimming pool and a mineral spring. Magnificent views of the sea can be seen on the drive there.

The most ornate botanical gardens in the entire Caribbean are north of Kingston on 20 acres east of the Leeward Highway. You can also see the St. Vincent parrots in an aviary as well as such rare plants as African tulips and the national flower, Ixora.

What Else to See in Kingston

As St. Vincent's capital and commercial hub, Kingston bristles with the excitement of a busy port. A trip down to the waterfront is mandatory, to peruse all the island schooners and fishing boats delivering and exchanging goods with their colorful sails flapping in the wind. Do take a pilgrimage to the 19th-century **St. Mary's Catholic Church**, which presides in the center of town, a strange concoction of architectural styles designed by a rather eccentric Flemish monk, who loved to pit Romanesque against Baroque, Gothic and Moorish styles. On the north side of town stands the remains of **Fort Charlotte** (all cabs end up there, as does every cruise passenger, it seems). The winding road there passes through lush landscape, the view from the top, at 636 feet, is superb. "Charlotte" was the wife of King George III, whose countrymen built the fortress to defend themselves against French invaders. Driving east of the fort you'll discover one of the most placid places on the island—the **Botanical Gardens**, founded in 1765, and considered the oldest in the Western hemisphere. On the grounds is a breadfruit tree grown from the seedling originally brought to the island by Captain Bligh. Here you'll also find the **National Museum**, which contains ancient Indian artifacts.

Saturday mornings, take yourself down to the southern corner of town for the weekly market that draws farmers, vendors, and fishermen from all over the island to sell their exotic-looking fruits, fresh fish, and interesting crafts. If you are involved in self-catering accommodations, it's a good place to pick up your weekly rations.

Historical Sites

Fort Charlotte ★★★

Kingston, ☎ *(809) 456-1830.*
Hours Open: 6:00 a.m.–6:00 p.m.
Construction on this fort was started around 1791, and it was completed in 1812. It's mostly in ruins today, but well worth a visit for the stunning views from its perch some 650 feet above sea level of Kingston and the Grenadines. Check out the murals that tell the history of black Caribbeans. Free admission.

Parks and Gardens

Botanical Gardens ★★★★

Kingston, ☎ *(809) 457-1003.*
Hours Open: 7:00 a.m.–4:00 p.m.

Located on a hillside north of town, this 20-acre garden is the oldest in the Western Hemisphere, dating back to 1765. Among the teak, mahogany and cannonball trees and exotic plants and flowers are bread fruit trees descended from seedlings brought over by Captain Bligh in 1793. The lush grounds also include a pagoda, lily pond, and the Archeological Museum, located in a West Indian house and displaying artifacts from pre-Columbian days. Admission to the gardens is free, but once there, it's well worth a couple of dollars to hire a guide for an hour-long tour. Garden lovers should also checkout **Kingston's Montreal Gardens** *(☎ 458-5452)*, which are not as well-tended. Free admission.

Tours

Soufriere Volcano   ★★★★★

The north side.

St. Vincent's dominant feature is the Soufriere Mountains, home to a volcano that has been active for centuries. The most devastating eruption occurred in 1812 and claimed some 2000 lives. Another in 1902 created the mile-wide crater; in 1972, still another eruption created the lava rock island in the crater lake. The latest eruption, in 1979, caused thousands to evacuate but happily took no lives. Two trails climb through rainforest to the crater rim; the easiest (that's a relative term) starts 26 miles out at Kingston at Rabacca. It takes at least three hours to get to the top, though it's only a three-mile trek. Hiring a local guide is strongly advised.

Sports

Sport fishing is only in its early stages of development in these parts, though there are abundant marine life, both in the waters around St. Vincent and in the Grenadines. Deep-sea fishing, however, can be arranged through watersports operators. Better yet, talk to a local fisherman and convince him to let you go along for the day's ride. As for sailing, the Grenadines hold a world reputation for some of the best conditions in the Caribbean. Yachts can be easily chartered, holding up to 8–10 people. The **St. Vincent Tourist Board** has extensive information on how and from whom to charter. Most yachts come with food, drink and full facilities. If you don't know much about sailing, your best bet is to hire a yacht with crew; it's also easier and less troublesome and you can spend the time relaxing. Passengers are routinely briefed before leaving the harbor and you should be prepared to ask any questions you need to. A full week can be spent touring the islands, with the skipper doubling as chef and chambermaid. There is a windsurfing school on St. Vincent on the southern coast, and all islands in the

Grenadines with resorts have windsurfing equipment. Horseback riding is available only in Mustique, at the Carlton House Hotel.

Watersports of all kinds can be arranged through hotels. Scuba certification is available on St. Bequia and St. Vincent, utilizing the terrific marine sources in the region. (For more information, see under "Dive Sites" above.) Sport fishing is not yet formally organized, but dive shops can arrange a fishing boat; you should bring your own gear. (Spearfishing is not allowed here except by special permission). Tennis is available on several courts on St. Vincent (Prospect Racket Club, Emerald Valley Hotel, and Grand View Beach Hotel, among others. The Cotton House on Mustique also has one.) Windsurfing lessons are offered at the Young Island resort, as well as the Cotton House on Mustique. There is a squash court in Kingston at the Cyril Cyrus Squash Complex on St. James Place.

The region was made for sailing, and every effort should be made to take at least a one-day cruise. Crafts from Sunfish to Sailfish are available for hire; many hotels have their own fleet. Young Island, Palm Island and Petit St. Vincent regularly offer day sails. Bareboat and skippered yachts can be chartered as well on St. Vincent. An exciting sojourn would be a speedboat trip along the western coast to the **Falls of Baleine**, a 60-ft. waterfall. You can also sail on a 36-foot sloop, moving in slow motion, to the Falls of Baleine.

For trekking, see under "Treks" above.

Watersports

Various locations.

Most watersports can be found at your hotel, and those staying on the Grenadines should be amply outfitted at the exclusive resorts. Otherwise, try one of these. For boating and cruising, call **Barefoot Yacht Charters** *(☎ 456-9526)* or **Lagoon Marina** *(☎ 458-4308)*, both on St. Vincent. On Bequia, call **Frangipani Yacht Services** *(☎ 458-3255)*. For scuba, call **Dive St. Vincent** *(☎ 457-4714)* and **St. Vincent Dive Experience** *(☎ 456-9714)*, both on St. Vincent. On Bequia, call **Dive Bequia** *(☎ 458-3504)* or **Sunsports** *(☎ 458-3577)*. **Grenadines Dive** *(☎ 458-8138)* handles diving on Union Island, while **Dive Mustique** *(☎ 456-3486)* takes care of that island's needs.

Where to Stay

Highest Rated Hotels in St. Vincent and Its Grenadines

★★★★★	Young Island Resort
★★★★	Cotton House
★★★★	Petit St. Vinvent Resort
★★★	Canouan Beach Hotel
★★★	Friendship Bay Hotel
★★★	Grand View Beach Hotel
★★★	Mustique Villas
★★★	Palm Island Beach Club
★★★	Plantation House
★★★	Saltwhistle Bay Club

Most Exclusive Hotels in St. Vincent and Its Grenadines

★★★★	Cotton House	$225–$730
★★★★	Young Island Resort	$160–$555
★★★	Plantation House	$140–$330
★★★	Grand View Beach Hotel	$100–$335

Fielding's Best Value Hotels in St. Vincent and Its Grenadines

★★★	Spring on Bequia	$75–$195
★★★	Plantation House	$140–$330
★★★	Palm Island Beach Club	$140–$325
★★★	Grand View Beach Hotel	$100–$335
★★★★	Cotton House	$225–$730

Accommodations on St.Vincent can range anywhere from the most enchanting resorts on earth to the bare-bones primitive. You can shell out over
$600 for top-class luxury, a moderate $125–$150 for two during winter
(some with two meals), or a mere $450 for a bed, nightstand and place to
hang the clothes. A great bargain is the 30 percent discount you can usually
wrangle during the summer season. Most of the lodgings lie along the lovely
south coast, a few minutes from the center of downtown Kingston. Most do
not have air-conditioning and rely on the trade winds and a ceiling fan to
cool the heat, quite adequately, though mosquito screens are de rigeur.

Hotels and Resorts

St. Vincent simply hasn't gone the way of the high-rise resort. The closest is the property at Young Island, which covers the entire islet, but Sunset Shores gives off the ambiance of a enclosed conclave, fortunately air-conditioned, with a family ambiance running
through the management.

Beachcombers Hotel   **$50–$75**   ★

P.O. Box 126, Villa Beach, ☎ *(809) 458-4283.*
Single: $50–$55. Double: $75.
This basic property accommodates guests in five different buildings, with all rooms
air-conditioned and sporting TVs and private patios. Facilities are limited to a bar
and restaurant, with watersports available on the beach. 12 rooms. Credit Cards: V,
MC, A.

Grand View Beach Hotel   **$100–$335**   ★ ★ ★

P.O. Box 173, Villa Point, ☎ *(809) 458-4811.*
Single: $100–$215. Double: $125–$335.
A former plantation house is the focal point of this quiet property, located on a
promontory overlooking a small private beach. And, as the name suggests, the views
here are indeed grand. Lodgings are simple yet comfortable, and while all share the
splendid views, not all have air conditioners. The hotel's eight acres include tennis
and squash courts, a small pool, a health club, a reading room, and a restaurant serving West Indian fare. Don't come looking for nightlife, but do come for tranquil
surroundings and friendly, family-run service. 19 rooms. Credit Cards: V, MC, A.

Lagoon Marina & Hotel   **$80–$105**   ★

P.O. Box 133, Blue Lagoon, ☎ *(809) 458-4308.*
Single: $80–$105. Double: $85–$105.
This simple hotel overlooks Blue Lagoon and its marina, and is often filled with sea
folk. Rooms are basic and you'll pay a bit extra for air conditioning, but all have
large patios nice to while away the hours on. The bar and restaurant do a brisk business with marina customers, and there's also a pool and watersports center on the
black-sand beach. 19 rooms. Credit Cards: V, MC, A.

Sunset Shores Beach Hotel   **$115–$210**   ★ ★

849 Villa Street, Villa Beach, ☎ *(809) 458-4411.*
Single: $115. Double: $115–$210.
The name makes it sound something like a retirement community, but in fact this
motel-like property is one of St. Vincent's few commercial hotels. Guestrooms are

air-conditioned and comfortable enough; they form a horseshoe around an attractive courtyard. Facilities include a small pool, a bar and restaurant favored by locals, and nearby watersports on the beach. Kingston is some 10 minutes away. 32 rooms. Credit Cards: V, MC, A.

Villa Lodge Hotel $105–$185   ★★

P.O. Box 1191, Indian Bay, ☎ *(809) 458-4641.*
Single: $105–$140. Double: $115–$185.
Set on a hillside and overlooking the sea, this converted home is popular, friendly, and family run. Guestrooms are air-conditioned and simply furnished; most have balconies or patios. The restaurant serves West Indian fare, and the large pool is a nice alternative to the small beach, which is easily within walking distance. The occasional poolside barbecues attract a lot of locals and are great fun, especially when steel bands liven things up. 10 rooms. Credit Cards: V, MC, A.

Young Island Resort $160–$555   ★★★★★

Young Island, ☎ *(809) 458-4826.*
Single: $160–$555. Double: $250–$555.
Set on its own private island 200 yards offshore St. Vincent, this resort offers the kind of tropical pleasures most folks have in mind when they dream of a Caribbean vacation. In this case, the dream is restricted to those who can afford the high rates and honeymooners blowing the bank. Accommodations are scattered along a hillside or set on the beach, and while the pricing determines what you get, all are spacious, cooled by ceiling fans, tropically decorated, and have private patios. Most also have unique rock showers that are open-air but very private. There are no phones or TVs, the better to appreciate nature by. Facilities include a lagoon-style pool, a tennis court, two yachts that whisk guests over the Grenadines, a tiny, picturesque beach, a bar and restaurant, and most watersports. The lushly landscaped 25 acres include cages of exotic birds, a floating bar off the beach, and charming stone walkways and steps. Despite the high rates, the atmosphere is casual and informal—this is not so much luxurious as it is the ultimate escape. Everyone seems to be in love, so singles beware. 29 rooms. Credit Cards: V, MC, A.

Apartments and Condominiums

Options are easy to find, since self-catering has long been a tradition on the island. Food is readily available in the market at Kingston, as is fresh fish. Everyone seems to know someone who has a fishing boat—they might still be squiggling. Staples that are strictly American-made should be brought from home, as are any special delicacies you can't leave without.

Indian Bay Beach Hotel $55–$85   ★

Indian Bay, ☎ *(809) 458-4001.*
Single: $55–$60. Double: $70–$85.
This small apartment hotel offers one- and two-bedroom units with kitchens, patios, telephones, and living and dining areas. Furnishings are simple but adequate. Indian Bay's beach is small and rocky, but the snorkeling just off the coast is good. There's a restaurant and bar on the premises, and the rates are certainly reasonable. 14 rooms. Credit Cards: V, MC, A.

Umbrella Beach Hotel $38–$53 ★

Villa Beach, ☎ *(809) 458-4651.*
Single: $38–$43. Double: $48–$53.

The rates are incredibly low, and the lodgings prove that you get what you pay for, but if you're on a tight budget and want the convenience (and economy) of having a kitchenette, this may be just the spot. As noted, the rooms are very basic and rely on ceiling fans for sleeping comfort, but they are clean and the location is handy, right near the beach and several restaurants. 9 rooms. Credit Cards: V, MC, DC, A.

Inns

Most accommodations in St. Vincent come with an "inn" feeling about it. That's the nature of the St. Vincent life. Some can be found in Kingston, others in the highlands away from the hustle of city life.

Cobblestone Inn $60–$75 ★★

P.O. Box 867, ☎ *(809) 456-1937.*
Single: $60. Double: $75.

This harborside inn dates back to 1814 and was originally intended as a sugar warehouse. Guestrooms are cozy (read small) but comfortable and air-conditioned, and all have private combination baths. Request one in the back to avoid street noise, but be warned that all are rather dark. The bar and restaurant are popular with locals, and the in-town location attracts mostly business travelers. There's no pool, which is unfortunate since the beach is a 10-minute drive away. 19 rooms. Credit Cards: V, MC, A.

Kingston Park Guest House $25–$28 ★

☎ *(809) 456-1532.*
Single: $25. Double: $28.

This 18th-century plantation house, a private home, is set in a garden overlooking the town and, further out, the Grenadines. As can be expected by the rates (among the island's cheapest), the rooms are nothing too exciting, and many share baths. You'll need a car, which may offset the savings on your accommodations. 20 rooms. Credit Cards: Not Accepted.

Low Cost Lodging

It is possible to find cheap lodgings in simple hotels in the Kingston area. The style is usually West Indian, with very basic furnishings. Cleanliness is usually not a problem.

Heron Hotel $49–$65 ★

☎ *(809) 457-1631.*
Single: $49–$51. Double: $55–$65.

Located on the waterfront within walking distance of the town center, this is another of St. Vincent's economical and simple guesthouses. The rooms are very basic and quite old-fashioned, and lack modern amenities like TV but at least have air conditioners and private baths. The restaurant is similarly no-frills, but the reasonably priced meals are tasty enough. 15 rooms. Credit Cards: V, MC.

Campgrounds
Petit Byahut $125–$145 ★★

Petit Byahut Bay, ☎ *(809) 457-7008.*
Single: $125–$140. Double: $130–$145.

The rates are high for camping, but guests are pampered at this remote spot a bit more than at your typical tent site. Set in a 50-acre valley that's reached only by boat from Kingston (included in the rates), this isolated spot accepts only 14 people at a time, and kids are not allowed. Accommodations are in large tents with wooden floors, queen-size beds, decks, and sun-warmed showers. The rates include all meals and watersports off the black-sand beach. Inquire about weekly and scuba packages. Not for everyone, but well-loved by those seeking an offbeat alternative. Credit Cards: Not Accepted.

What to Eat

Highest Rated Restaurants in St. Vincent and Its Grenadines

★★★★★ Mac's Pizzeria

★★★★★ The French Restaurant

★★★★ Basil's Bar & Raft

★★★ Basil's Bar & Restaurant

★★★ Cobblestone Roof Top

★★★ Gingerbread Cafe

★★★ Heron Restaurant

Most Exclusive Restaurants in St. Vincent and Its Grenadines

★★★★★	Mac's Pizzeria	$7–$30
★★★★★	The French Restaurant	$8–$16
★★★	Basil's Bar & Restaurant	$3–$15
★★★	Cobblestone Roof Top	$5–$6

Fielding's Best Value Restaurants in St. Vincent and Its Grenadines

★★★★★	The French Restaurant	$8–$16
★★★	Heron Restaurant	$5–$10
★★★★	Basil's Bar & Raft	$4–$28

No one visits these islands in search of the last great chef; he's not hiding out here. There is almost a unilateral menu for the island's casual cafés: a handful of West Indian dishes (callaloo soup, local fish or lobster prepared creole style), fried chicken baskets with french fries, and hamburgers—what locals believe that tourists like. The most sophisticated food is found at the hotel restaurants. One island diversion is to visit as many bars as you can and make a serious study of the varieties of rum punch—each bartender takes great pride in his or her own unique recipe.

Basil's Bar & Restaurant $ ★★★

Bay Street, Kingston, ☎ *(809) 457-2713.*
International cuisine.
Lunch: 10:00 a.m.–4:00 p.m., prix fixe $11.
Dinner: 4:00 p.m.–12:00 p.m., entrees $3–$15.

Those who can't get to Basil Charles' Fantasy Island over-water bar in Mustique make the scene at his second namesake hangout with food on the ground floor of the Cobblestone Inn. Lunchtime buzzes with hungry diners going back and forth from a tasty all-you-can-eat buffet. The spread includes salads and desserts, and a la carte burgers, sandwiches, egg dishes, and seafood are also available. Nighttime is more romantic, with candlelit tables and simple grills on the menu, plus French wines at decent prices. There's a Chinese buffet on Friday evenings. Associated Hotel: Cobblestone Inn. Closed: Sun. Reservations recommended. Credit Cards: V, MC, A.

Cobblestone Roof Top $ ★★★

Bay Street, Kingston, ☎ *(809) 456-1937.*
Latin American cuisine.
Lunch: 7:30 a.m.–3:00 p.m., entrees $5–$6.

Whatever business is conducted on this leisurely island is usually done at breakfast or lunchtime from this eatery atop the Cobblestone Inn. Housed in a quaint, restored early 1800s-era warehouse, the restaurant serves substantial West Indian lunches along with good burgers and fish and chips. Associated Hotel: Cobblestone Inn. Credit Cards: V, MC, A.

Heron Restaurant $ ★★★

Upper Bay Street, Kingston, ☎ *(809) 457-1631.*
International cuisine.
Lunch: 12:00 a.m.–1:30 p.m., entrees $5–$10.
Dinner: 7:00 p.m.–10:00 p.m., prix fixe $5–$10.

A friendly local couple run this budget hotel and restaurant that's popular with residents for American bacon and eggs breakfasts. Lunch features soups, salads, and sandwiches, and a soup-to-nuts supper is served daily for a set price. Market fresh vegetables are a standout. There's always a lot of action here, and reservations are required for dinner. Associated Hotel: Heron Hotel. Reservations required. Credit Cards: Not Accepted.

The French Restaurant $$ ★★★★★

Villa Beach, Villa Beach, ☎ *(809) 458-4972.*
French cuisine. Specialties: Lobster.
Lunch: 7:00 a.m.–9:00 p.m., entrees $6–$14.
Dinner: 7:00 p.m.–9:30 p.m., entrees $8–$16.

Behind a homey white picket fence lies an excellent restaurant that dazzles with its simplicity. Guests sit on plain folding chairs, feet planted on rough wooden floors in a windowless structure open to salty breezes. Succulent lobster couldn't get much fresher, retrieved as they are live from an on-site pool. The Parisian chef serves the juicy crustaceans flambeed in brandy, sliced in crepes, or broiled. All dishes are prepared with island-grown herbs and spices. The dining room overlooks Villa Beach and Young Island. Associated Hotel: Umbrella Beach Hotel. Reservations recommended. Credit Cards: V, MC, A.

Where to Shop

St. Vincent and the Grenadines is simply not a paradise for shoppers—there is no duty-free sport— but there are some interesting handicrafts to be discovered. Batiks and tye-died fabrics are the province of **Batik Caribe**, a famous name in the Caribbean. The **St. Vincent Craftsman** is a cooperative featuring the work of local artisans; the quality rates among the best crafts in the Caribbean. Many of the crafts represented here are a revival of very ancient techniques, rejuvenated through an unusual program sponsored by the United Nations. If you're headed down the road leading from the banana-boat docks, stop at the shop on the **Old Cotton Ginnery**; while you're there, ask about how you can visit some of the artists in their own homes in the countryside.Other crafts can be found at **Noah's Arkade**, next to the Batik Caribe, where you can also pick up history books about the West Indies. Do drop by the local markets to pick up a few bottles of sun-dried peanuts (great for the beach) and local spices. West Indian hot sauce is infamous for making eyes run. Philatelists will adore picking up a bunch of colorful stamps of the islands, available at the post office.

THE GRENADINES
Bequia

Bequia (BECK-we), a three-hour schooner-run from Union, is a chain of islets between St. Vincent and Grenada attracting escapists of all kinds—from advertising execs who live in homes carved from caves to writers and painters in search of a last-ditch inspiration. It has a great natural beauty, a warm, small world flavor, and an endearing innocence; everyone here seems to have a cousin who works on a ship or tanker. (Every time a Bequia grandmother has to visit her offspring on the mainland of St. Vincent, she has to brave the choppy seas on the two islands.)Port Elizabeth's main street bordering Admiralty Bay is but a a few blocks of pavement, then turns into a footpath weaving past shops and small hotels and restaurants under the canopy of trees at the water's edge. Long a favorite of Caribbean insiders and yachties, the island was accessible only by boat until mid-1992 when an airport accommodating small planes was built. Some visitors, especially Americans, return to Bequia yearly. Local buses will get you around— actually, just pickup trucks with benches built into the truck bed with a canvas roof. On small islands, your hotel will probably give you a lift. Main beaches are **Friendship Bay**, **Lower Bay**, and **Spring Bay**, the latter graced by restless coconut palms. Each has a restaurant or snack bar and sometimes even beach chairs.

In general, Bequia is a place for shuffling between beach and bed, pool to beach, from bar to bar to dinner. The best way to sightsee is to stroll around, with your intuitive antennae out for a good round of spontaneous adventure. No major fortresses or historical plantations, but there are some interesting shops including the **Crab Hole Island** (artifacts); **Melinda's** (original handprints); **Maurice's Model Boat Shop** (model boat making is a renowned Bequia craft); and the **Bequia Sailing Club** (distinctive T-shirts; the **Wearable Art Shop**; and the **Bequia Bookstore**.

To get to Bequia, you can either arrive by small plane via LIAT, or by boat from Kingston, St. Vincent. The mail boat is an option as is any one of a number of motor launches or chartered yachts.

Treks in Bequia

In Bequia, hikes from Admiralty Bay lead over unpaved roads and footpaths, but are relatively easy, and arrive at such places as **Mt. Pleasant**, where there is a spectacular view of Bequia. A favored destination also is Hope Bay, where the waves are good for body surfing. The northern part of the island is covered with gentle hills good for hiking; in the central and southern sections, more mountainous areas give hikers a chance to view incredible vistas. There are no roads or cars on Mayreau, but from the bay you can take a track to the tiny hilltop village in the center of the island; here you can see a great view of **Tobago Cays**. Tobago Cays is considered one of the most serene paradises in the Caribbean—four uninhabited islets ringed by pure white beaches and clear blue waters. From a beach anywhere here, you can walk/paddle to see clusters of tropical fish swimming through the coral gardens. **Petit Rameau**, the northernmost cay, has a short trail through heavy mangroves along a sandy beach.

Sports in Bequia

The **Frangipani** and **Plantation House** hotels have fully equipped dive facilities. You can also find windsurfing and sunfish sailing in **Admiralty Bay** and snorkeling around **Spring** and **Friendship Bays**. To find a new beach, hop on a water taxi to **Lower Bay**. Or rent a bicycle at the **Almond Tree** boutique and toot over to Spring or Friendship Bay. Evening entertainment revolves around whichever hotel is sponsoring a jump-up, a beach barbecue with bamboo bands and vigorous, sexy dancing.

Where to Stay

Lodging in Bequia is geared for total relaxation. Nearly each property is unique and exudes a certain personal ambiance. Prices for rooms are not exorbitant and many are within an unbelievably reasonable range.

Hotels and Resorts

Accommodations range from the very expensive Plantation House, a series of 1, 2, and 3 bedroom cottages, to the still expensive Spring on Bequia, a 200-year-old working plantation house to relatively inexpensive Blue Tropic Apartments, with kitchens and balconies overlooking Friendship Bay.

Friendship Bay Hotel **$115–$200**

Friendship Bay, ☎ *(809) 458-3222.*
Single: $115–$130. Double: $130–$200.
Set on a palm-studded cove and a sandy beach, this casual complex provides motel-like lodging in stone buildings scattered around picturesque grounds. The rooms are basic but comfortable enough, with ceiling fans, private baths, and verandas. Facilities include a bar and restaurant popular with locals, a watersports center (some rentals are complimentary), and a tennis court. The weekly barbecues and jump-ups are not to be missed, and the beach is quite fine. 27 rooms. Credit Cards: V, MC, A.

Plantation House **$140–$330**

P.O. Box 16, Belmont Backway, Admiralty Bay, ☎ *(809) 458-3425.*
Single: $140–$245. Double: $185–$330.
Located on 10 handsome acres, this property's focal point is the pretty colonial-style main house with a wide veranda on three sides—a great place for people watching and gazing at the harbor. Accommodations are in the main house, cottages, and (relatively) deluxe cabanas. Those in the main house are air-conditioned, while the rest rely on ceiling fans and sea breezes. All are nicely done and quite comfortable.

There's a pool, tennis court, health club, restaurant and beach bar on the premises, and a dive shop and watersports center on the beach. Nice. 25 rooms. Credit Cards: V, MC, A.

Spring on Bequia $75–$195   ★★★

Spring Bay, ☎ *(809) 458-3414.*
Single: $75–$180. Double: $95–$195.

Set on a hillside of the grounds on a 200-year-old working plantation, this rather isolated spot practically oozes tranquillity. Don't come here for the beach life—the nearest one is 10 minutes away and nothing great—but do come if you're looking for a true escape in pastoral surroundings. Lodging is found in three stone and shingle buildings; all rooms are clean and comfortable, and kept cool by constant breezes. There's a tennis court and pool on-site, and the Sunday curry buffet is a popular hit. 10 rooms. Credit Cards: V, MC, A.

Apartments and Condominiums

It's always a good idea to fully check out a property before committing yourself to it. As such, it's best to save the self-catering option until your second visit to Bequia, or at least station yourself at a hotel and investigate the possibilities. There are numerous private homes which are rented in the owner's absence; some are quite luxurious; others simpler with adequate kitchen facilities.

Inns

Frangipani Hotel $30–$130   ★★

Frangipani Beckway, Admiralty Bay, ☎ *(809) 458-3255.*
Single: $30–$130. Double: $80–$130.

This small inn dates back to 1920 and was once the childhood home of the island's current prime minister. Guestrooms are found in the main building—a New England-style house—or in superior garden units in the rear. All are simply furnished and rely on fans to keep things cool and mosquito netting over the beds to keep the pests at bay. Not all have a private bath. The beach is a 10-minute walk and there's no pool, but you can swim in the harbor. Facilities are limited to a restaurant, bar, tennis court, and watersports center. Nice for casual types. 15 rooms. Credit Cards: V, MC, A.

Low Cost Lodging

The cheapest lodging is found in simple guesthouses. Ask the tourist board for assistance.

Julie & Isola Guesthouse $36–$59   ★

P.O. Box 12, Port Elizabeth, ☎ *(809) 458-3304.*
Single: $36. Double: $59.

It's as basic as basic can be, which explains the rates, but the rooms, located in two buildings, are clean, though they can be uncomfortably hot. Not all have private baths, and showers are not always hot. Facilities are limited to a bar and small restaurant serving up good West Indian fare. 20 rooms. Credit Cards: Not Accepted.

Where to Eat

No great claims to chefdom here, but do get ready for home-style island cooking with lots of fresh seafood. Most of the eating places are along the waterfront within walking distance of each other.

Gingerbread Cafe $$ ★★★

P.O. Box 1, Gingerbread Complex, Admiralty Bay, ☎ *(809) 458-3800.*
International cuisine.
Lunch: entrees $4–$10.
This cute Hansel and Gretelish stone cottage is the place to go for Italian coffees, puckery-fresh limeade and fruit juices, and the appropriate cakes and breads to go with them. Sit here at leisure all day at an outdoor table with a book and gaze out at the activity in the harbor. Next door, the Gingerbread Restaurant serves full meals and sandwiches, and is a nice spot for happy hour rum drinks and music. Credit Cards: V, MC, A.

Mac's Pizzeria $$$ ★★★★★

Box 23, Belmont Beach, Port Elizabeth, ☎ *(809) 458-3474.*
International cuisine. Specialties: Lobster Pizza.
Lunch: 11:00 a.m.–4:00 p.m., entrees $7–$30.
Dinner: 4:00 p.m.–10:00 p.m., entrees $7–$30.
Bequia veterans daydream about the 15-inch lobster pizzas that this terraced restaurant is famous for. Besides the dream pies, Mac's home-bakes all its scrumptious breads and bakery goods, and the banana bread, plump with raisins and flavored with rum, is especially toothsome. The menu also features East Indian *samosas* (fried pastries stuffed with curried vegetables or meats), crunchy conch nuggets, and chunky pita bread sandwiches. This place is a winner. Closed: Mon. Credit Cards: V, MC.

Where to Shop

Bequia isn't a shopper's fantasy, but you can discover a number of stores featuring various handicrafts and unusual clothing. Visit Crab Hole, next to the Plantation House, to watch cotton fabrics being silk-screened. Garden Boutique in Port Elizabeth features stunning batik dresses and hand-dyed blouses. Local artwork can be found at Made in the Shade in Port Elizabeth. At Mauvin's Model Boat Shop you can order a model made of your yacht.

Canouan

Where to Stay

Hotels and Resorts

Canouan Beach Hotel $108–$316 ★★★★

Canouan Beach, ☎ *(809) 458-8888.*
Single: $108–$316. Double: $249–$316.
This all-inclusive resort is located on a peninsula on the island's west side. Accommodations are in nicely furnished bungalows that have air conditioners and patios.

Facilities include a very good restaurant, large bar, tennis court, and watersports. The beach is really pretty and a catamaran takes guests to neighboring islands at no extra charge. The rates include all meals, drinks and activities, but those not speaking French may feel left out. Though it has only 43 rooms, this is St. Vincent's largest and most modern resort. 43 rooms. Credit Cards: CB, V, MC, DC, A.

Mustique

Where to Stay

Hotels and Resorts

Cotton House   **$225–$730**   ★★★★

☎ *(809) 456-4777.*
Single: $225–$730. Double: $225–$730.
Built on the remains of an old sugar plantation, this deluxe operation is Mustique's only hotel, and it's quite lovely (and pricey). Guests are accommodated in elegant cottages that house standard guestrooms, junior suites, or full suites, all nicely decorated and sporting balconies or patios. The grounds include a highly regarded restaurant, bar, two beaches, and most watersports at no extra charge. Horseback riding can be arranged, and there's also a pool, two tennis courts, and occasional live bands. This exclusive spot pampers guests and attracts the well-heeled set. 20 rooms. Credit Cards: V, MC, DC, A.

Apartments and Condominiums

Mustique Villas   **$2500–$15,000**   ★★★

☎ *(800) 225-4255, (809) 458-4621.*
These 38 privately owned villas are located on Mustique's northern end. Several were designed by Oliver Messel, the late architect and stage designer. Each is individually decorated and has from one to six bedrooms and full kitchens. Each is staffed with a maid, cook and gardener, and the rates include free use of a Land Rover. Rates are on a weekly basis and range from a low of $2500 to a high of $15,000 for the five- and six-bedroom mansions. One of the pools belongs to Princess Margaret! Credit Cards: V, MC, DC, A.

Where to Eat

Basil's Bar & Raft   **$$$**   ★★★★

Britannia Bay, Mustique, ☎ *(809) 458-4621.*
International cuisine.
Lunch: entrees $4–$26.
Dinner: entrees $4–$28.
Basil's is not just a bar—it's a way of life. Possibly the most beautiful watering hole in the world, this unique establishment is a thatch-roofed structure built over the turquoise waters of Britannia Bay in Mustique. Owner Basil Charles has a great thing going—this is the only nightlife spot on the island. Everyone ends up here sooner or later, including titled lords and ladies and *People* magazine cover girls and boys. There's good seafood served daily and a $28 barbecue on Wednesday nights.

It's open from 10:00 am until the last guest goes home. Reservations recommended. Credit Cards: V, MC, A.

Union Island

Union Island is 3520 acres in size and attracts many American and Europeans, especially French, who are ready to fish, dive, beachcomb, and sail. Many land at the airstrip and walk to the adjacent dock of the posh Anchorage Yacht Club, where they board their charter or private boats. Not much happens in tiny Clifton, so head outside town to deserted Big Sand Beach and to the crest of Fort Hill with its magnificent view. Trekkers are attracted to the jagged, slab-faced mountainous slopes, especially the 999-ft. high **Mt. Tabor**, the Grenadines' highest peak. A foot trail leading inland from Ashton around Rock Fall ends up in Chatham Bay.

St. Vincent Directory

ARRIVAL AND DEPARTURE

The departure tax from St. Vincent and the Grenadines is U.S.$6 (E.C.$15). A 5 percent government tax is added to all hotel and restaurant bills. Hotels regularly add a 10 percent service charge. If a 10 percent service charge is not added to your restaurant check, it would be very acceptable (and expected) for you to do so.

CLIMATE

Temperatures all year round fluctuate between 78–80 degrees F, cooled by gentle northeast trade window. Rain is heavier in the mountains of St. Vincent than in the Grenadines, which are generally flatter. Hurricanes can ravish the islands in the fall, while summers attract high humidity. Mosquito repellent is a must between July to November.

DOCUMENTS

U.S. and Canadian citizens must have a passport; all visitors must hold return or ongoing tickets. Visas are not required.

ELECTRICITY

Current runs 220/40 v. 50 cycles.

GETTING AROUND

Island roads are like roller coasters, so if you're not used to such challenging driving, you're probably better off hiring a taxi to get around. Potholes are everywhere and increase the possibility of accidents and car damage.

Taxis fares run about $3–$4 around Kingston, $8 from Kingston to Villa Beach. A good way to see the island is to hire a taxi by the hour (about $15). Rates are fixed by the government, but most drivers try to get twice as much.

Public buses in the form of minivans are the cheapest way to get around; they tend to be boisterous, noisy and crowded, and full of local color. All you need to do is wave at the driver and he will stop for you. The terminal is at Market Square in Kingstown.

Rental cars run about $45–$50 a day. Driving is on the left. Since roads are not well maintained, do get as many directions as possible before you get behind the wheel. You might even take a minibus tour of the island first to get acquainted with the potholes. To rent a car, you will need a Vincentian license, unless you already have an international license.

LANGUAGE

English is spoken everywhere, often with a Vincentian patois or dialect.

MEDICAL EMERGENCIES

The government hospital, called General Hospital ☎ *61185*, is located at the west end of Kingstown. There is also Bequia Casualty Hospital at Port Elizabeth ☎ *83294*.

MONEY

The official currency is the Eastern Caribbean dollar, although U.S. and Canadian dollars are accepted at all but the smallest shops. Most establishments would prefer to take the Eastern Caribbean dollar. When quoted a price, make sure you know what dollar is being referred to. You can get a slightly higher exchange rate at banks; hotels are notoriously low and sometimes charge a fee.

TELEPHONE

The area code for St. Vincent and the Grenadines is *809*. At press time, only AT&T offered direct dial to the area, but check with the Sprint and the MCI offices in your area to verify the latest service. Before dialing other countries from St. Vincent, do ask the operator; sometimes there are special codes. Also verify in advance the probable cost, surcharge and government tax; your hotel will probably also add another fee, which can send the bill sky-high. When dialing a local number from your hotel, you can drop the 45-prefix. Few hotels have phones in the rooms.

TIME

Atlantic Standard Time, one hour ahead of New York time, except during Daylight Saving Time, when it is the same.

TIPPING AND TAXES

Hotels tend to add 10–15 percent service charge. If so, you won't be expected to tip chambermaids as well, but the gesture is always appreciated. Restaurants usually charge 10 percent for service. Do tip taxi drivers 10 percent of the fare.

TOURIST INFORMATION

The St. Vincent Department of Tourism is located at Administrative Centre, Bay St., Kingstown, ☎ *457-1502*. Stop by and pick up brochures on lodging and sightseeing options. The St. Vincent and the Grenadines tourist guide called Escape contains useful tips and suggestions for excursions. The office is only open Monday–Friday.

Bequia has its own office on the waterfront in Port Elizabeth, ☎ *458-3286*, closed on Saturday afternoons. In the U.S. call ☎ *(212) 687-4981*.

WHEN TO GO

Carnival is a huge week-long celebration in early July, one of the most fantastic parties in the entire eastern Caribbean. Here you'll be able to witness and participate in calypso and steel-band competitions. Do be around when the queen and king of Carnival are crowned, a spectacular event.

ST. VINCENT AND ITS GRENADINES HOTELS	RMS	RATES	PHONE	FAX
Bequia				
★★★ **Friendship Bay Hotel**	27	$115–$200	(809) 458-3222	(809) 458-3840
★★★ **Plantation House**	25	$140–$330	(809) 458-3425	(809) 458-3612
★★★ **Spring on Bequia**	10	$75–$195	(809) 458-3414	(809) 457-3305
★★ **Frangipani Hotel**	15	$30–$130	(809) 458-3255	(805) 458-3824
★ **Julie & Isola Guesthouse**	20	$36–$59	(809) 458-3304	(809) 458-3812
Canouan				
★★★ **Canouan Beach Hotel**	43	$108–$316	(809) 458-8888	809 458 8875
Mustique				
★★★★ **Cotton House**	20	$225–$730	(809) 456-4777	(809) 456-5887
★★★ **Mustique Villas**			(800) 225-4255	(809) 456-4565
St. Vincent				
Kingston				
★★★★★ **Young Island Resort**	29	$160–$555	(809) 458-4826	(809) 457-4567
★★★ **Grand View Beach Hotel**	19	$100–$335	(809) 458-4811	(809) 457-4174
★★ **Cobblestone Inn**	19	$60–$75	(809) 456-1937	(809) 456-1938
★★ **Sunset Shores Beach Hotel**	32	$115–$210	(809) 458-4411	(809) 457-4800
★★ **Villa Lodge Hotel**	10	$105–$185	(809) 458-4641	(809) 457-4468
★ **Heron Hotel**	15	$49–$65	(809) 457-1631	(809) 457-1189

ST. VINCENT AND ITS GRENADINES HOTELS	RMS	RATES	PHONE	FAX
★ Indian Bay Beach Hotel	14	$55–$85	(809) 458-4001	(809) 457-4777
★ Lagoon Marina & Hotel	19	$80–$105	(809) 458-4308	(809) 457-4716
★ Petit Byahut		$125–$145	(809) 457-7008	(809) 457-7008
★ Umbrella Beach Hotel	9	$38–$53	(809) 458-4651	(809) 457-4930
★ Beachcombers Hotel	12	$50–$75	(809) 458-4283	(809) 458-4385
★ Kingston Park Guest House	20	$25–$28	(809) 456-1532	
The Grenadines				
★★★★ Petit St. Vinvent Resort	22	$210–$685	(809) 458-8801	
★★★ Palm Island Beach Club	24	$140–$325	(809) 458-8824	809 458 8804
★★★ Saltwhistle Bay Club	10	$200–$340	(809) 493-9609	
★★ Anchorage Yacht Club	10	$95–$165	(809) 458-8221	809 458 8365

ST. VINCENT AND ITS GRENADINES RESTAURANTS	LOCATION	PHONE	ENTREE $
Bequia			
International			
★★★★★ Mac's Pizzeria	Port Elizabeth	(809) 458-3474	$7–$30
★★★ Gingerbread Cafe	Admiralty Bay	(809) 458-3800	$4–$18
St. Vincent			
Kingston			
French			
★★★★★ The French Restaurant	Villa Beach	(809) 458-4972	$6–$16
International			
★★★ Basil's Bar & Restaurant	Kingston	(809) 457-2713	$11–$15
★★★ Heron Restaurant	Kingston	(809) 457-1631	$5–$10
Latin American			
★★★ Cobblestone Roof Top	Kingston	(809) 456-1937	$5–$6•
Mustique			
International			
★★★★ Basil's Bar & Raft	Mustique	(809) 458-4621	$4–$28

ST. VINCENT AND ITS GRENADINES RESTAURANTS	LOCATION	PHONE	ENTREE $

Note: • Lunch Only

•• Dinner Only

TOBAGO

The quiet turquoise waters of Tobago are great for swimming.

The sister island of nearby Trinidad, Tobago remains largely unknown, though its assets, cultural to ecological, are more than fantastic. Whereas Trinidad is emboldened by the rhythms and harmonies of steel pan bands, Tobago runs to the more subtle natural sounds of the jungle and country-side. The proximity to South America has given Tobago its Latin-based heritage that, combined with African, East Indian, Chinese and European influences, has created a rich cultural stew. And it's a heritage evident in every aspect of life, from the look of the people to the musical cadences of the language to the spicy flavors of the cuisine. A favored destination for South Americans and Europeans as well as Trinidadians, Tobago has remained somewhat a secret to North Americans, though that is beginning to change. What has saved Tobago from overdevelopment is 24,700 acres of rainforest set aside in 1765 by British growers, who intuitively realized over 200 years ago that there was a connection between the amount of available water for crops and the number of standing trees. As such, the natural resources of Tobago have been ably preserved, today embodying a kind of frozen Fujichrome beauty—from rolling fields of tall, stately coconut palms swaying in the wind to steep, thickly overgrown, emerald-green hills, to the bright hues of fishing boats anchored on beaches that range in color from pale vanilla to rich butterscotch. If you stay in Trinidad, don't hesitate to take the ferry to Tobago, which, incidentally, has the best beaches in the region. The proliferations of plant, animal and reptile life residing within the island's several nature reserves make marvelous opportunities for ornithologists and biologists who can indulge in miles and miles of trekking. Divers should not miss the stupendous experience of swimming with Atlantic manta rays, usually dangerous marine creatures that have been subtly trained by locals to carry humans on their backs.

Bird's Eye View

Tobago, 27 miles by 7 miles wide, lies in the extreme southeastern corner of the Caribbean, just 70 miles from Venezuela, on the northeastern shoulder of South America. It is separated from Trinidad by a narrow channel less than 20 miles wide; by plane the trip takes a mere twelve minutes. From the lowlands of the southwest end (home to Scarborough, Tobago's capital and center of population) the island slowly climbs in elevation until it reaches the northeast end. Here, the hills form steep, thickly jungled slopes populated by a wide variety of parrots and other birds. The end of this island is as popular with bird-watchers as it is with divers. Divers will be happy to know that the island is surrounded by fringing and patch reefs that take a broad variety of forms, including rolling fields of coral, sloping coral walls, huge blocks of invertebrate, and sponge-encrusted stone with offshore rock structures and pinnacles.

The island's development is concentrated in the southwestern corner, where visitors will find long, palm-lined stretches of beaches and a sea made for scuba, diving, waterskiing, wind surfing, and snorkeling, especially at the spectacular **Buccoo Reef**, a shallow-water spot about a half-mile offshore. But the remaining two-thirds of the island is relatively untouched. Mountains

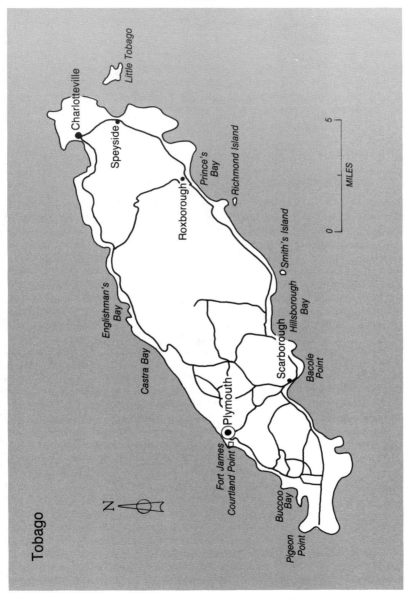

Tobago

rise to 1900 feet; hiking trails weave through stands of giant ferns, bamboo and calabash and saman trees. Farms and plantations of brilliant green dot the deeply indented coastlines. Fishing villages drowse in the sun, their brightly painted pirogues hauled up on beaches beneath coconut palms and sea grapes.

Several areas in Tobago have been designated as protected reserves or sanctuaries. The rainforest of the **Main Ridge** is the oldest forest reserve in the western hemisphere, dating back to 1764. Another important sanctuary is **Little Tobago Island**, which lies just offshore from the fishing village of Speyside. Here can be found important nesting grounds for an enormous number of species, including Audubon's shearwater, the red-footed booby, the sooty fern, the red-billed tropic-bird, and at least 600 species of butterflies—a lepidopterists's dream.

Renovations and new constructions in recent years have spruced up Tobago's tourist facilities. A monster runway now makes it simple for visitors to arrive from Trinidad. In July 1992, a \$20 million terminal for cruise ships was inaugurated in Scarborough.

History

Most historians believe Tobago was discovered by Columbus in 1498, who supposedly dubbed it "Bella Forma" (beautiful form). Its present name was derived from the word tobacco, which the native Caribs cultivated. In 1641 a Baltic duke received permission to settle a number of Courlanders on the north side of the island, but the Dutch took over in 1658, remaining in control until 1662. For the next few centuries the island changed hands at least a dozen times among world powers who considered the island a treasure worth fighting for. Not only the Dutch, but the French and English fought each other for control, not to mention pirate invasions and settlers from Latvia. Some of the conflicts had the stuff of legend about them. Bloody Bay, on the island's west coast, earned its name after a 17th-century clash between combined French and Dutch forces against a British fleet (the latter was the victor). History records that the battle was so "sanguinary" that the water became red with blood. In another ferocious struggle, over 1700 lives were lost in the battle of Roodklyn Bay, fought between the Dutch and the French. Eventually Tobago was declared neutral territory and promptly became a haven for pirates and treasure hunters. (In fact, rumors of treasure still buried on Pirate's Bay abound today.) During the early 19th century, Tobago was a leading contender in the British and French sugarcane industry, producing more sugar per square acre than any other island. When the sugar industry went bust, Tobago also went bankrupt, and in 1888 the island was tacked to nearby Trinidad by a British colonial government that didn't know what to do with it. In 1962, both islands gained independence from Britain and became a republic within the Commonwealth in 1976. Today Tobago has its own 12-seat House of Assembly, which runs many local services. (For more information, also read the history section in the Trinidad chapter.)

People

Tobago's population numbers about 51,000; about 90 percent of Tobagonians are of African descent, and their food, folklore, music and religion are all African based. Although the official language on both islands is English, Tobagonians speak with a more lilting, softer accent than Trinidadians. In general, locals on Tobago are extremely friendly and helpful, and perhaps because the island's economy depends on tourism, visitors seem to receive special attention. There is also much less crime on Tobago than on Trinidad. Linguistically original, Tobagonians have invented their own rich local idioms, among them: *beat pan* (play the steel pan); *free up* (relax); *dougla* (a person of mixed Indian and African parentage); *maco* (a person who minds other people's businesses); and *lime* (spend time talking, laughing and watching the girls or boys go by).

About two-fifths of Trinidad and Tobago's people are descended from India, and major Hindu and Muslim festivals are recognized as public holidays. "Eid mubarak!" is the official greeting for Eidul-Fitr on March 14, marking the end of the Ramadan during which Muslims observe a daytime fast. Muslims celebrate this day by fasting and going to the mosque to say prayers, as well as giving alms to the poor. During this time, there is much hospitality extended, even to foreigners, homes are cleaned and decorated, and lavish meals mark the end of the abstinence. In November thousands of tiny deyas (clay pots with oil-fueled wicks) appear in parks and sidewalks to mark the Hindu Festival of Divali, in honor of Lakshmi, the goddess of light and beauty. If you drive through the towns and villages at sunset, you will find them transformed into a gentle wonderland. One of the most beautiful festivals to witness takes place on March 27, marking the Hindu New Year in India and the arrival of spring. Singing groups gather in villages and temples to perform the festive choral songs, and bonfires are lit to mark the triumph of light over darkness. Festivities the following day feature Phagwah bands, tassa drumming and singing, and colored water is sprinkled over everyone in sight. Hardly traditional, Easter is an enormously festive occasion, celebrated with goat and crab races.

To really tap into the traditions of Tobago, try to attend the Tobago Heritage Festival in July, when you can witness old-time weddings, hear traditional local music played with fiddles and tambourines, and hear about the complex courting rituals and codes and dances of days gone by. Each village presents one aspect of the island's heritage, showing off its own versatility in music, dance, drama, cooking and costuming.

Beaches

By all accounts, the best beach on the island is **Pigeon Point**, called by some the "archetype of paradise." Its quiet turquoise waters are good for swimming and the sunsets along the coast are fantastic. The land, however, is privately owned, and a small fee is charged for use, but you'll find seaside bars, boutiques, boats for hire and most watersports. Near the airport, **Store Bay** is Tobago's most happening beach, where young rastas sell locals arts and crafts; expect the vibe to be lively, if not noisy. The land, however, is privately owned, and a small fee is charged for use. Turtle Bay is also a well-kept beach. **Buccoo Reef** is excellent for snorkeling. **Salybia Bay** is delightfully secluded and good for swimming. Leatherback turtles can be seen nesting at certain times of the year on Matura Beach (see below). Surfers should head to **Mt. Irvine Bay**, home of the famous "Irvine wave;" the occasional whale has been sighted in this area.

For those who like clambering over slippery rocks, head for the so-called **Crusoe's Cave**, on the lowlands coast behind Crown Point Airport. The cave, which is gouged on to the coral, was originally the mouth of the tunnel that was thought to have twisted inland for miles. Today fallen rocks have blocked any explorations further than a few feet into the cave. Access to the cave is through private property. Expect to pay a small fee.

FIELDING'S CHOICE:

Leatherback Turtles, by the hundreds, come out of the water to nest during the months of March-June. This is one of the few places in the Caribbean where this occurs. Organized turtle watches allow visitors to witness the awesome spectacle while also protecting the nesting sites. Watchers help their guide measure each turtle and gather relevant statistics, which are sent to the U.S. turtle research stations. The primary location is along the southwestern shore from Great Courland Bay to Turtle Beach. On one June night last year, 80 giant leatherbacks as much as six feet long came up on Grand Riviere beach, while tiny hatchlings, emerging from eggs laid in the sand, were making their way to the sea. For more information contact Thalia Moolochan of the Grande Riviere Environmental Trust ☎ (809) 670-8458, who is in charge of the program. Trinidad and Tobago Sightseeing Tours ☎ (809) 628-1051, FAX (809) 627-0856, has turtle-watching trips for $50, Caroni Swamp tours for $34, Buccoo Reef tours for $20, including hotel transport.

Dive Sites

Thirty years ago, Tobago was one of the first islands to be discovered by scuba fanatics. The diving, however, has remained rugged, and the lack of promotion has left the island a bit undiscovered. Fringe reefs completely surround the island, much of it close to shore (within swimming distance) on depths that range from 3–30 feet. There are sites for all levels of skill. Visibility ranges up to a spectacular 150 feet, which makes it a photographer's fantasy shoot. The reefs are uncommonly attractive and the color of the marine life is unusual and bright. On the leeward coast, the Caribbean waters are calm enough to serve beginners who are still learning to manage their equipment. At Grouper Ground, on the western coast opposite Pigeon Point, the currents are suitable for drift diving, but only advanced divers should attempt it and it is suggested you must be in very good physical shape.

FIELDING'S CHOICE:

The peak experience of diving in Tobago is the sighting of an Atlantic Manta Ray. In Tobago these mantas (about a dozen) seem to seek out and even enjoy the company of divers, who can swim with the manta and actually stroke their back (reports claim the mantas quiver with small waves of pleasure.) An exceptionally gentle diver might even be granted the honor of riding on this "Tobago Taxi." Though the activity is controversial among those who are proponents of the total hands-off policy with marine life, it's reported that when a diver finally drops off the back of a manta, the creature often returns, as if to say, "Just one more time, please!" Sightings tend to drop off in winter, and are more frequent in the spring and summer.

Treks

Before you even put on your hiking boots, get a copy of the guide showing the island's trails from the Lands and Survey Division on Richmond Street. Excellent birdwatching is found around Barcolet Bay, reachable first by taking a bus from Scarborough to Mount St. George, and then hiking (or hitching) to Hillsborough Dam, then continuing northeast through the forest to Castara or Mason Hall. (Don't even think about doing this without a map, compass, and water and food supplies.) If you continue on the road to Pembroke and Belle Garden, you'll stumble upon Richmond Great House, now a hotel. An exquisite quartet of waterfalls formed by the Argyll River near Roxborough is but a ten-minute walk upstream from the road. Just do your best to avoid the obnoxious guides who are waiting to point you there.

For an extended excursion, take the road from Roxborough to **Parlatuvier** and **Bloody Ray** rainforest. You won't have to share the road with traffic, and the singing of hundreds of forest birds is exciting. The most easily identified trail is **Gilpin Trace**, accessed from the Roxborough/Bloody Bay Road; the entrance is clearly marked by a sign on the main road. Starting in the mountain, the trail leads downhill past a small waterfall to Bloody Bay. It's a big hike, and you should consider having a car pick you up in Bloody Bay village.

One of the best sites for trekking is **Little Tobago Island** (a 450-acre bird preserve adjacent to Angel Reef), reachable from the fishing village of Speyside (where you can hire a boat, about TT$30 per person round trip). The island is extremely hot with no facilities for food or water, so make sure you bring your own. Here you can find wild fowl and 58 species of other birds, including the red-billed tropic in their large nesting colony in the North Atlantic. Crossing the islet is done in boats, but bargain beforehand for the price and make sure it includes the return trip and a guided tour of the islet. The leeward bar is a good site for snorkeling, and manta rays have been seen occasionally. Camping permission must be obtained from the Forestry Division at Studley Park ☎ *639-4468*. Another excellent trek is the **Main Ridge Rain Forest Trail** (ask the Forestry Division for more information).

Grafton Estate is a former estate house whose grounds have been turned into a nature reserve. A number of trails lead into the forest; bird feeders have been set up in the old cocoa house. After the hurricane of 1963, the owner of the estate took to feeding the forest birds, whose natural habitat had been destroyed; today most still arrive for a mouthful around teatime; they will even pick cheese from your hand.

The **Louis d'Or River Valley** is reached from the main Windward Road, between Roxborough and Delaford. Follow the river as far as the local road allows. Then splash your way upriver; the water is cool and clear, with small pools for bathing, and the canopy of trees offers a wealth of birdwatching.

Adventure Farm and Nature Reserve is a twelve-acre estate on the Arnos Vale Road which grows citrus, mangoes, bananas and papaya on a commercial scale. Sheep and goats are reared in the pasture. Two acres of "bush" have been retained to attract birds. Visit the Farm between 7 a.m.-9 a.m. and 5 p.m.-6 p.m. (when the birdwatching is best and a caretaker is available to act as guide). The Farm is closed on Saturdays. A wonderful afternoon can be had picking fruit (for which you will be charged market prices) and you can also observe different agricultural practices. At certain times of the year, butterflies are profuse. Admission is U.S.$3, guided tour U.S.$1.

Apart from its varied birdlife, Tobago is blessed with an abundance of plant, insect and reptile life. If you're interested in discovering the underbelly of Tobago's ecology, contact one of the tour operators who organize guided tours into the rainforest, such as **Little Tobago Island**, **Bon Accord Swamp**, etc. **Hew's Nature Tours** on Pigeon Point ☎ *639-9058* has a good rep; most hotels will assist in setting up an excursions.

Some tour operators also offer trips to No Man's Land, a sandspit that curves across the Buccoo Lagoon to form a smaller inner lagoon fringed with wetlands where wildfowl feed and turtles breed.

FIELDING'S CHOICE:

A great way to see Little Tobago is in a glass-bottom boat. They are found mostly on Store Bay, and trips run $15-$20 (a boat from Buccoo Village could be less expensive.) Wear your swimsuit; snorkeling equipment and special shoes are provided. Unfortunately, much of the reef has been destroyed by divers and snorkelers walking on it; do be careful, particularly since the area is now protected and it is against the law to damage coral. Visitors may swim at Nylon Pool, two miles out in the ocean, where the water is only waist high.

What Else to See

The star attractions on Tobago are mostly natural, but one of the main focuses of any excursion should be the delightful, though eccentric little town of **Scarborough**, Tobago's capital. Market days on Friday and Saturday are an explosion of sights, sounds and aromas as the turbaned vendors lay out their enormous piles of fresh vegetables and fruits. Bargaining is the joy of the day; but don't try so hard to get a good deal that you miss biting down on a delicious papaya or a ripe golden tomato. From here, you can start the trek up to **Fort King George**, the city's most significant historical monument. Built in the 1770s, it stands a towering 450 feet above the town; today it houses a small but fascinating museum collection of colonial and Indian artifacts. Just below is the **Centre of Fine Art**, where you can peruse the products of local talent.

Even if you don't hike, do take time to wander the island. Worthwhile is simply the joy of driving from Scarborough in the lowland to the fishing villages of **Charlotteville** and **Speyside** on the far side of the island. (While in Speyside, a visit to **Little Tobago**, the bird reserve, is highly recommended; see above.) As the road leaves the capital and enters the hills, it gradually narrows and becomes more and more convoluted until it becomes little more than a narrow, barely two-lane road, teetering along the edges of the seaside cliffs and plunging into palm-filled valleys, only to climb back again. The journey to the far side goes further back in time the further you go. The town soon takes on that true Caribbean look of small fishing villages, covered with zinc roofs and animals wandering onto the road. Most watersports, golf, fine eateries, and nightlife are all found in the southern region. If you want to stay in nature, stick to the "far side" of Tobago.

Not to be missed is **Charlotteville**, a picturesque fishing village embraced by high hills. Here, the bay is deep and sheltered; many head for a lively cove called **Pirate's Bay**, a twenty-minute hike through the national forest. Legend has it that pirate treasure is buried here, but not a single piece of gold has ever turned up.

If you have time, the drive on the **Northside Road** will show you an uncommonly rugged, but beautiful glimpse into rural Tobago. The starting point, where the ruins of the 17th-century **Fort James** are located, offers a wide-angle, windswept view of the west coast. This is the site of one of Tobago's earliest communities, settled by the Dutch in 1633. A requisite stop is the **Mystery Tombstone**, whose 18th-century epitaph for young Betty Stiven is as chilling as it is poetic: "A Mother without knowing it and a Wife without letting her husband know it except by her kind indulgence to him." Driving north from Plymouth, an excellent place to stop for a spot of tea is the charming **Arnos Vale Hotel**, an old estate house set in a beautifully lush tropical garden. A nature reserve is nearby (see above under "Treks."). As you continue north, you enter the heart of rural Tobago; the tiny mountain villages come alive with the rhythms of life. In **Golden Lane**, seek out the grave of Gang Gang Sara, an African woman rumored to be a witch who in olden days was said to have flown to Tobago, where she took up residence. When she tried to leave, it was said, she lost her power to fly because she had eaten salt while on the island.

BEST VIEW:

The view from the top of Fort King George is a panoramic sweep of the surrounding coastline, but for sunsets head for Flagstaff Hill on the island's northernmost tip, to watch the last golden rays penetrate the deep indigo sea. Deep-sea fishing is also available, as is horsebackriding, with equipment provided by the Palm Tree Village Beach Resort. The leading beachfront hotels have their own watersports facilities

Historical Sites

Fort King George ★★★

Scarborough.

Tobago's best-preserved historical building is this fort perched on a hill above Scarborough. English troops built it in 1779 and over the years it traded hands several times between the English and French. You can inspect its ruins and cannons, and on a clear day you can see forever—or at least to Trinidad. The Barrack Guard House is the site of the Tobago Museum (☎ *639-3970*), whose exhibits center on Amerindian pottery and relics, military artifacts, and documents from the slave era. It's open weekdays from 9:00 a.m. to 4:30 p.m. General admission: $1.00.

Tours

Adventure Farm and Nature Reserve ★★★

Anros Vale Road, Plymouth.

This 12-acre plantation grows mangoes, citrus, bananas and papaya, and rears sheep and goats in its pasture. You can come and pick your own fruit (they charge market prices) and for birdwatching. Open to the public every day but Saturday from 7:00 a.m.–9:00 a.m. and 5:00–6:00 p.m., when a caretaker acts as guide for an extra $1. General admission: $3.00.

Sports

The leading beachfront hotels boast their own watersports activities program. Deep-sea fishing is also available through the local **Gerard "Frothy" de Silva** ☎ *639-7108*. Other tour operators can be found in the vicinity of Pigeon Point/Crown Point; in the rural areas, arrangements can be made with local fisherman. The **Palm Tree Village Beach** resort also offers horsebackriding (equipment provided) ☎ *639-4347*; they maintain their own stables. There are several professional sports associations, where like-minded athletes can find each other, such as the **Surfing Association** ☎ *637-4533*; **Windsurfing Association** ☎ *659-2457*. Anyone interested in yachting should contact the **Viking Dive and Sail/Yacht Chartering Limited**, inside Pigeon Point Resort at Crown Point; ☎ *639-9209*, FAX *639-0414*.

Mount Irvine Golf Course

Mount Irvine Hotel, Scarborough, ☎ (809) 639-8871.
Hours Open: 6:30 a.m.–3:00 p.m.

This 18-hole, par-72 course is among the Caribbean's most scenic, covering 125 acres of rolling hills and overlooking the sea. Great views from the clubhouse, too. Greens fees are about $46.

Watersports

Various locations.

If your hotel can't supply the necessary aqua activity, try one of these. Scuba diving: **Tobago Marine Sports** (☎ *639-0291*), **Dive Tobago** (☎ *639-0202*), **Man Friday Diving** (☎ *660-4676*), and **Viking Dive** (☎ *639-9209*). Boating: **Viking Sail/Yacht Chartering Limited** (☎ *639-9209*). Deep-sea fishing: **Gerald deSilva** (☎ *639-7108*). Windsurfing: **Windsurfing Association of Trinidad and Tobago** (☎ *659-2457*). General watersports: **Blue Waters Inn** (☎ *660-4341*), and **Mt. Irvine Watersports** (☎ *639-9379*).

Where to Stay

Highest Rated Hotels in Tobago

★★★★	Grafton Beach Resort
★★★★	Richmond Great House
★★★	Arnos Vale Hotel
★★★	Kariwak Village Hotel
★★★	Mount Irvine Bay Hotel
★★★	Palm Tree Village
★★★	Turtle Beach Hotel

Most Exclusive Hotels in Tobago

★★★	Palm Tree Village	$80–$455
★★★★	Grafton Beach Resort	$160–$245
★★★★	Richmond Great House	$85–$125

Fielding's Best Value Hotels in Tobago

★★	Salt Raker Inn	$45–$130
★★	Blue Waters Inn	$60–$115
★★	Pelican Beach Hotel	$95–$230
★★★	Kariwak Village Hotel	$65–$95
★★★★	Richmond Great House	$85–$125

Accommodations run the gamut from the comfortable family feeling of small, inexpensive bed and breakfast guest homes to the luxury of opulent four-star hotels. Several hotels on the southwest/tourist end of the island are within walking distance of the airport. Most of the favorite vacation hangouts are near a long, palm-covered sandspit called Pigeon Point and adjacent to the snorkeling at Buccoo Reef. Five miles up the island's Caribbean side there are a few more hotels of ascending levels of luxury, found on a succession of bays along the scalloped coastline. Above the little hamlet of Speyside, the only bona fide hotel on this side of the island is the **Blue Waters Inn**, a walk away from **Jemma's** restaurant suspended mysteriously over the branches of an immense almond tree.

Hotels and Resorts

Renovations are on the upswing in Tobago. The **Grafton Grand**, an 88-room hotel, was completed in December 1994. This property is independent of the Grafton Beach Resort, but the two properties are connected by way of a bridge and the guests from either property have access to the other's facilities. The former **Crown Reef Hotel** has been given a $23 million facelift. If you want to be close to nesting turtles (in season), stay at the **Turtle Beach Hotel**. They won't be in your room, but the nearby beach will be close enough.

Arnos Vale Hotel $110–$240   ★★★

Arnos Vale Road, ☎ (809) 639-2881.
Single: $110–$160. Double: $160–$240.

This self-contained resort, located 20 minutes from Scarborough, attracts a mostly Italian clientele. The sloping grounds are nicely landscaped and include acres of fruit orchards—the bounty of which often enhance the creole, Italian and international meals. Accommodations are located on the hillside and near the beach; all are air-conditioned and decorated with wood and wicker furniture, and most have private balconies. Facilities include three bars, a disco, pool and watersports. 30 rooms. Credit Cards: V, MC, DC, A.

Grafton Beach Resort $160–$245   ★★★★

Black Rock, ☎ (809) 639- 30.
Single: $160–$245. Double: $160–$245.

This upscale resort, 15 minutes out of Scarborough, attracts a mostly European clientele. Guestrooms are very nicely appointed with teak furnishings, minibars, marble baths and all the modern comforts. The two suites, which go for $555–$600 per night, also have Jacuzzis. There's lots to do: a large pool, shuffleboard, two air-conditioned squash courts, a well-equipped gym, and two restaurants and three bars. A dive shop takes care of sporting needs on the nice beach, and there is frequent evening entertainment. One of Tobago's better choices. 112 rooms. Credit Cards: V, MC, DC, A.

Kariwak Village Hotel $65–$95   ★★★

Crown Point, ☎ (809) 639-8545.
Single: $65–$95. Double: $65–$95.

This authentic island getaway is nicely designed and quite popular with both tourists and locals. Accommodations are in 10 octagonal stucco cottages arranged around a swimming pool. Rooms are simple but comfortable. Couch potatoes can camp out in the TV lounge to get their fix. You can walk to the beach in five minutes or take the free shuttle. The restaurant is a local favorite, and on the weekends, this place is a popular spot to hear live music. They'll help arrange tours and watersports. 18 rooms. Credit Cards: V, MC, DC, A.

Mount Irvine Bay Hotel $125–$365 ★ ★ ★

Mount Irvine Bay, ☎ *(809) 639-8871.*
Single: $125–$365. Double: $145–$365.

This sprawling north shore resort is highlighted by its 18-hole golf course, the best on the island. There's plenty to keep travelers occupied off the greens, too, with two tennis courts, Tobago's largest pool, a health spa, and watersports on the private beach. There's also two restaurants and two bars, with frequent entertainment once the sun goes down. Lodging is in modern and well-appointed guestrooms and in 46 fairly plush cottages that fetch $330 to $432 per night. One restaurant, found in an 18th-century sugar mill, is especially atmospheric. 105 rooms. Credit Cards: V, MC, DC, A.

Pelican Beach Hotel $95–$230 ★ ★

Whitby, ☎ *(809) 946-7112.*
Single: $95–$130. Double: $130–$230.

This small hotel is situated on six miles of beach. The oceanview guestrooms have ceiling fans and balconies. The premises include a restaurant and bar, with watersports nearby. 14 rooms. Credit Cards: V, MC, DC, A.

Turtle Beach Hotel $110–$200 ★ ★ ★

Plymouth Local Road, Great Courland Bay, ☎ *(809) 639-2851.*
Single: $110–$200. Double: $110–$200.

If you're visiting this hotel between May and October, you'll get the chance to see leatherback turtles laying their eggs on the beach—hence the name. It's decent any time of the year here, though, with a lovely beach, full dive shop, two tennis courts, and pool to keep guests happy. Accommodations are comfortable, though central air would be a great improvement over the individual units. Additional facilities include two restaurants and two bars at this well-run spot. 125 rooms. Credit Cards: V, MC, DC, A.

Apartments and Condominiums

Enormous variety exists in the self-catering department; you can splurge on luxury homes and apartments (with a live-in chef and maid) or you can hole up in a cottage and do your own cooking. Several attractive villas are available for rent on the **Mount Irvine Beach Bay Estate**, some right next to the beach, others along the fairways. Opportunities also exist in extremely isolated coves, though you will surely need to rent a car. Most of your supplies will need to be met by the Friday and Saturday fruit and vegetable markets in Scarborough. Do bring what staples you will need because you will be hard put to find a supermarket that is sufficient. For more information and rates, contact the **Tobago Villas Agency**, Box 301, Scarborough; ☎ *809-639-8737,* FAX *809-639-8800.*

Crown Point Beach Hotel $55–$105 ★

Store Bay Beach, Crown Point, ☎ *(809) 639-8781.*
Single: $55–$105. Double: $55–$105.

Set on seven acres overlooking Store Bay Beach, this condominium resort is eight miles from Scarborough. Accommodations are in studios and one-bedroom units with air conditioning and kitchenettes; maids tidy up daily. There's a restaurant, bar, two tennis courts, and a supermarket on the premises. 100 rooms. Credit Cards: V, MC, DC, A.

Golden Thistle Hotel $40–$60   ★

Store Bay Road, Crown Point, ☎ *(809) 639-8521.*
Single: $40–$45. Double: $60.

This low-frills property is two minutes from the airport and houses guests in air-conditioned studios with kitchenettes, twin beds, and TV sets. The beach is walkable, but there's a pool on-site for those feeling especially lazy. A bar and restaurant complete the limited facilities. 36 rooms. Credit Cards: V, MC, DC, A.

Man-O-War Bay Cottages $55–$70   ★★

Charlotteville Estate, ☎ *(809) 660-4327.*
Single: $55–$70. Double: $60–$70.

Set on a 1000-acre cocoa plantation, these modest cottages are located right on the beach. Configurations vary from one to four bedrooms, all with kitchens, fans and verandas. Maid and cook service is available for an extra charge. This spot is especially popular with birdwatchers and those really looking to get away form it all. You'll want a car for mobility. 6 rooms. Credit Cards: Not Accepted.

Palm Tree Village $80–$455   ★★★

Milford Road, ☎ *(809) 639-4347.*
Single: $80–$455. Double: $80–$455.

This self-styled village is located five minutes from Scarborough and is across the street from a busy public beach. Guests can choose to stay in the hotel with its standard air-conditioned rooms, or in 40 villas with two to four bedrooms, large living areas, kitchens and patios. Maid service is available, as are cooks. Facilities include a restaurant, bar, Jacuzzi, steam room, pool, gym and tennis court. 60 rooms. Credit Cards: V, DC, A.

Sandy Point Beach Club $40–$75   ★★

Sandy Point Village, ☎ *(809) 639-8533.*
Single: $40–$70. Double: $50–$75.

This resort, located near the airport, sometimes suffers from the roar of jets. Accommodations are in studios and one-bedroom suites, all with air conditioners, kitchenettes, and pleasing decor. The beach is pretty but not good for swimming, so guests splash about in one of the two pools or take the free shuttle to the beach at Pigeon Point. The casual beachside restaurant serves varied fare for those not into cooking. This friendly spot is a great bargain. 50 rooms. Credit Cards: V, MC, DC.

Inns

The following inns are so-called because of their size, rather than any abiding congeniality. The **Blue Waters Inn** in Speyside may be in danger of losing its unofficial "inn" status since it is presently undergoing a 30-room expansion project.

Blue Waters Inn $60–$115   ★★

Batteaux Bay, Speyside, ☎ *(809) 660-4341.*
Single: $60–$100. Double: $70–$115.

Set in a protected cove along a small beach, this property is found 90 minutes from Scarborough. Guestrooms are basic and rely on sea breezes to keep cool. The surrounding rainforest attracts nature lovers and those who like seclusion—rent a car or you may suffer from too much isolation. There's a tennis court, restaurant, and bar on the grounds, but no pool. Birdwatching excursions are frequently offered, and watersports are nearby. 28 rooms. Credit Cards: V, MC, A.

Coral Reef Guest House $40–$70 ★

P.O. Box 316, Milford Road, Scarborough, ☎ *(809) 639-2536.*
Single: $40–$45. Double: $45–$70.
This basic guesthouse has simple air-conditioned rooms with private baths. Eight apartments have one to three bedrooms and kitchenettes. Facilities are limited to a dining room, bar, pool and games room. 24 rooms. Credit Cards: V, MC, DC, A.

Richmond Great House $85–$125 ★★★★

Belle Garden, ☎ *(809) 660-4467.*
Single: $85–$125. Double: $85–$125.

Located on the southern coast on a remote hillside, this unique spot brims with interesting African art and local antiques. The 200-year-old plantation house offers a handful of nicely decorated and colorful rooms, each individually done. The beach is a 10-minute drive. 10 rooms. Credit Cards: Not Accepted.

Salt Raker Inn $45–$130 ★★

P.O. Box 1, Duke Street, ☎ *(809) 946-2260.*
Single: $45–$125. Double: $70–$130.
This small inn dates back to 1835 and was originally a shipwright's home. Rooms are individually decorated and some have air conditioning; there are also three one-bedroom suites. The beach is across the street. Facilities include a charming eight-stool bar, an open-air restaurant, a dive shop and a library. The occasional live entertainment is appealingly informal. 12 rooms. Credit Cards: V, MC, A.

Low Cost Lodging

Bed and breakfasts are the cheapest way to go on Tobago, and are full of charming possibilities which are infused with the personality of the owner who is often the cook, maid and chief bottle washer.

Pentridge Lodge ☎ *(809)639-4129* is the island's consummate bed and breakfast featuring rooms the size of small apartments beneath vaulted ceilings. The home is mansion-like with three wings, and completely private. Bird-watchers will be delighted with the parakeet sightings. The owner is a successful dress designer with champagne sensibilities who loves to entertain. Following a good meal, the beach is a welcome ten-minute walk away.

Hillcrest ☎ *(809) 639-9263*. This is a whole house that sleeps 10, with three bedrooms of two double beds and two twin bedrooms. The living room opens onto a wide porch, though the bedrooms are small. It's very secluded up a dirt road. It's the place to be if you have a big family.

Arthur's-on-Sea $40–$75 ★

Crown Point, ☎ *(800) 742-4276, (809) 639- 196.*
Single: $40–$65. Double: $45–$75.
This small hotel is situated on a busy street a few minutes' walk from Store Bay Beach. The air-conditioned guestrooms are simple and basic, with private patios. TVs are available on request. There's a restaurant, bar and pool on the premises. 15 rooms. Credit Cards: V, MC, DC, A.

Where to Eat

Highest Rated Restaurants in Tobago

★★★★★	Blue Crab
★★★★★	La Tartaruga
★★★	Dillon's Seafood
★★★	Jemma's Sea View Kitchen
★★★	Miss Jean's
★★★	Old Donkey Cart House
★★★	Papillon

Most Exclusive Restaurants in Tobago

★★★	Old Donkey Cart House	$20–$25
★★★	Papillon	$15–$25
★★★	Jemma's Sea View Kitchen	$10–$27
★★★	Miss Jean's	$5–$6

Fielding's Best Value Restaurants in Tobago

★★★	Papillon	$15–$25
★★★	Miss Jean's	$10–$20
★★★★★	La Tartaruga	$18–$24
★★★	Dillon's Seafood	$12–$27

While most of the big hotels and resorts offer "continental" cuisine—that means food that's recognizable back home—local cuisine is a flavorful combination of Indian curries blended with the more traditional Caribbean fare. Favorites include curried crab and dumplings, served in a curry sauce with hard dumplings (be sure to bring a bib, this is a messy one), and *rotis*, chicken or beef and potatoes in a curry sauce wrapped in a thin, unleavened bread.

In the coastal areas, especially around festival times, indulge in a bit of *pacro*, a shellfish concoction that is reputed to have heady aphrodisiacal powers.

Down the street from the airport there are numerous stands advertising local food—**Miss Jean**, **Sylvia's**, **Alma's**, **Esme's**—that is some of T&T's most authentic cuisine. Here you'll be able to sample conch, crab and kingfish with roti, an especially Indian flat bread stuffed with ground chickpeas (a ubiquitous fast food in this country). At **Jemma's Seaview Kitchen** in Speyside, try the callaloo—a popular T&T "blue food" made from the leaves of the dasheen plant; her entrées of shrimp, kingfish, crab and chicken run a reasonable $10. Also unforgettable is the flying fish at the **Blue Crab** on Robinson and Main in the funky town of Scarborough ☎ *639-2737*, entrees from $10.

Blue Crab   **$$$**   ★ ★ ★ ★ ★
Robinson Street, Scarborough, ☎ *(809) 639-2737.*
Latin American cuisine.
Dinner: 6:00 p.m.–10:00 p.m., entrees $12–$20.
The hardworking family that runs this popular spot whips up tasty meals that combine the cuisines of East India, Portugal and Creole. Fresh vegetables and fruits from their own gardens are used in the preparation of such delights as pumpkin soup and homemade ice cream and fruit wines. Lunches are served on the wide terrace of the traditional West Indian building. Only fish caught that day is used in their seafood dishes. Treat an island friend to dinner here, which is available by advance reservation only from Wednesday through Friday. Closed: Sat, Sun. Reservations recommended. Credit Cards: V, MC, A.

Dillon's Seafood   **$$$**   ★ ★ ★
Airport Road, Crown Point, ☎ *(809) 639-8765.*
Seafood cuisine.
Dinner: 6:00 p.m.–10:00 p.m., entrees $12–$27.
A charter captain and fisherman runs this modern restaurant cooled by air-conditioning—which assures that all fish and seafood is so fresh it snaps back at you. There's lobster thermidor, or island kingfish in a tomato sauce, and fish soup. Some of the food though, could use a braver hand with the salt shaker or the spice rack. Closed: Mon. Reservations required. Credit Cards: V, MC, A.

Jemma's Sea View Kitchen   **$$$**   ★ ★ ★
Windward Road, Tyrell's Bay, ☎ *(809) 660-4066.*
Latin American cuisine.
Lunch: 9:00 a.m.–4:00 p.m., entrees $10–$20.
Dinner: 4:00 p.m.–9:00 p.m., entrees $10–$27.
The kids, big and small, will enjoy eating in a real treehouse overlooking Tyrell's Bay. They may have to fight for space though, as there are only 10 tables. The emphasis is on local dishes, served in generous portions by an amiable staff. Specialties include callaloo soup, grilled seafood, and crab and dumplings. It's a great place to stop on a circle-island tour or a day at the beach. Open Fridays from 8 a.m. to 5 p.m. only. Closed: Sat. Reservations required. Credit Cards: Not Accepted.

La Tartaruga $$$ ★★★★★

Buccoo Bay Beach, Buccoo Bay, ☎ *(809) 639-0940.*
Italian cuisine.
Dinner: 7:00 p.m.–11:00 p.m., entrees $18–$24.
Fresh is the key word at this intimate, friendly spot. The Italian owner and chef prepares delicious pasta that's homemade daily. Sauces are embellished with garden-grown herbs. Fish is delivered to his door from a reliable source. The service, by a well-trained staff, is as quick as it gets on the island. Recommended dishes include spaghetti with dorado in a sauce of olive oil and pepper, served with tomatoes. Stop by for a drink, an espresso, or some homemade ice cream. Closed: Mon, Sun. Reservations recommended. Credit Cards: V, MC, A.

Miss Jean's $ ★★★

Store Bay Beach, Store Bay, ☎ *(809) 639-0211.*
Latin American cuisine.
Lunch: 9:00 a.m.–4:00 p.m., entrees $4–$5.
Dinner: 4:00 p.m.–10:00 p.m., entrees $5–$6.
Miss Jean's motto is if you love good food we love to feed you and she means it. All manner of seafood, soups and stews, including the island favorite, crab and dumplings, emanate miraculously from a small shed on the island in the sand in Store Bay. If you like, sample a few things at Jean's and mosey on to Miss Esmie or Miss Trim's place next door. For a carbo load, try the macaroni pie, which is stewed chicken or beef with macaroni, if it's available. Credit Cards: Not Accepted.

Old Donkey Cart House $$$ ★★★

Bacolet Street, Scarborough, ☎ *(809) 639-3551.*
International cuisine.
Lunch: 12:00-3:00 p.m., entrees $3–$10.
Dinner: 6:30 p.m.–12:00 p.m., entrees $20–$25.
The Viennese owner of this charming restaurant is the island's only authority on German wines, which are a specialty of the place. These fine vintages accompany well-prepared local fish, steaks and pastas. Start your meal with some excellent cheese. At lunch, sandwiches are served on homebaked bread. Reservations recommended. Credit Cards: V, MC, A.

Papillon $$$ ★★★

Buccoo Bay Road, Mt. Irvine, ☎ *(809) 639-0275.*
Seafood cuisine.
Lunch: entrees $15–$25.
Dinner: entrees $15–$25.
Chef Jakob Straessle's cuisine may not be on the cutting edge of chic, but the Swiss restaurateur always delivers reliably tasty old favorites like lobster thermidor, served with a choice of soup, rice and salad. Also featured are conch in season, cooked in coconut milk. Dine in air-conditioned comfort in a rustic, out-of-the-way lodge. Closed for lunch on Sundays. Associated Hotel: Old Grange Inn. Reservations required. Credit Cards: V, MC, DC, A.

Where to Shop

Compared to the cascades of goods available in Trinidad, Tobago's share represents a mere trickle. Three malls cater to the obvious and uninspiring: **Scarborough Mall** in the center of town; **IDC Mall** at Sangster Hill; and **Breeze Mall** on Milford Road. (Breeze Hall is perhaps a tad more fashionable.) You'll find more original items in the designer boutiques such as **The Cotton House** on Bacolet Street (with smaller outlets at Sandy Point Hotel and Pigeon Point, where you can pick up unusually beautiful batiks and tie-dyes). Tobago's own fashion mavens head for **Nairobi**, above the Starting Gate Pub off Shirvan Road. As for arts and crafts, you can find some of them at the malls (Scarborough and IDC), but it's more fun to buy them from vendors hawking their own wares in the market. Good buys are leather sandals, carved gourds, hand-wrought jewelry. Most hotels have small gift shops, but expect the prices to be exaggerated. A couple of nice craft stores can be found on the road leading to Pigeon Point, a fine beach. The jeweler **Jose Andres** is especially revered for his unique jewelry made from indigenous woods, bone, coral and seedpods. The duty-free allowance covers one quart of liquor, 200 cigarettes/50 cigars, and gifts up to TT$50.

Tobago Directory

ARRIVAL AND DEPARTURE

Multiple flights daily depart from major North American gateways to Tobago. BWIA (British West Indian Airlines), familiarly known as Bee Wee because of its friendly, comfortable service. BWIA is the official airline of Trinidad and Tobago and has been providing dependable service to the Caribbean for more than 50 years. There are daily flights from Miami, New York and Toronto. The flight to Tobago from Miami is about 2-1/2 hours, with a short stop in Port of Spain, Trinidad, to clear customs.

Several companies rent well-maintained cars for about $50 a day, but since driving is on the left and the roads are narrow and hilly, most visitors prefer to hire a car and driver (about $60).

There is a departure tax of TT$75 (in local currency only-about U.S.$120 is collected at the airport.

CLIMATE

Weather conditions are very comfortable, with temperatures averaging 83 degrees F. The wet season runs June to December, with rainfall in mostly short sharp bursts. Tobago is slightly cooler and less humid than Trinidad. A scant 11 degrees above the equator, the climate is decidedly tropical.

DOCUMENTS

A passport is required for entry, as is a return or ongoing ticket. A departure tax of about $12 in U.S. currency is collected at the airport. An international driver's license is required for car rentals

ELECTRICITY

Current runs either 115 or 220 volts at 60 cycles. While many hotels have 115 volt current, it is advisable to travel with a small transformer just in case. These supplies are readily available at low cost.

GETTING AROUND

Although both Trinidad and Tobago are small, you'll need a car to get around. Get one at the airport, from Singh's or Amar. And ask for maps. Driving is on the left side of the street. A ferry service links Trinidad and Tobago, about a 2-1/2 hour journey.

Taxis charge fixed fares to the downtown area and major hotels from the airport. Fares from Crown Point International Airport to Crown Point run about $4, to Pigeon Point about $6 in U.S. currency. Taxis to Speyside run about $32, and Roxborough about $22.

Car rentals are mostly local agencies. Among the best are **Auto Rentals Crown Point Beach hotel** ☎/FAX *639-0644* and **Singh's Auto Rentals, Grafton Beach Hotel**; ☎ *639-0191.*

Bicycles, scooters and motorcycle rentals are available at **Blossom Enterprises**, *Milford Rd., Canaan;* ☎/FAX *639-8485.* **Toyota Rent a Car**, *177 Tragarete Rd.;* ☎ *628-5516;* and **Kalloo's Auto Rental** *32 Ariapita Ave., Woodbrook;* ☎ *622-9073.*

Among the best tour companies are **Pioneer Journeys**, *Man O'War Bay Cottages, Charlotteville;* ☎ *660-4327;* and **Bruce Ying Sightseeing Tours Around Trinidad and Tobago**, *Bacolet St., Scarborough;* ☎/FAX *639-4402.*

LANGUAGE

English is the official language and is spoken with a rich, melodious accent. The old French-based patois has almost died out; some Hindi is still used among the Indian community.

MEDICAL EMERGENCIES

There are hospitals in Port of Spain, Scarborough, Mount Hope (a large teaching hospital), and Fernando, and an extensive network of health centers and clinics, both public and private; both government and private doctors practice.

MONEY

The official currency is the Trinidad and Tobago dollar (written TT$), which floats against other currencies. Daily rates are listed in the newspapers. Credit cards are widely accepted in tourist areas, and by rental car companies, hotels, restaurants and major shops.

TELEPHONE

The country code is *809*. If dialing direct from the U.S. and Canada, and much of the Caribbean, dial "1" first; from other countries, including Haiti, Cuba and the Dutch and French Caribbean, dial "01." The phone system is digital, and international direct dialing and other standard services are available throughout the system.

TIME

Atlantic Standard Time, one hour ahead of New York City, except during Daylight Saving Time, when it is the same.

TIPPING

Many hotels add a 10–15 percent service charge. If the restaurant bill does not add a 10–15 percent service charge, feel free to do so.

TOURIST INFORMATION

Local information offices are at **Piarco Airport** ☎ *664-5196*; **Crown Point Airport**; ☎ *639-0509*; **Tobago: N.I.B. Mall**, Scarborough; ☎ *639-2125/3566*. In the U.S. call ☎ *(800) 232-0082*.

WATER

Tap water is safe to drink; bottled mineral waters are widely available and tasty.

WHEN TO GO

Carnival explodes in February with steel bands, parades and lots of local foods and drink. Tobago Arts Festival occurs March-April. The Round the Gulf Sailing Competition takes place in March. Goat and Crab races take place in April. The Indo-Caribbean Festival of Arts takes place in May. The Tobago Heritage Festival is in July. The Steelband Festival is in August and October. The Tobago Music Festival takes place in November and December. The Tobago Christmas Pageant, with local music and dance, is in December. For more information, contact the tourist board. Also check out "When To Go" at the end of the Trinidad chapter.

TOBAGO HOTELS	RMS	RATES	PHONE	FAX
Plymouth				
★★★★ **Grafton Beach Resort**	112	$160–$245	(809) 639-0030	
★★★★ **Richmond Great House**	10	$85–$125	(809) 660-4467	(809) 660-4467
★★★ **Arnos Vale Hotel**	30	$110–$240	(809) 639-2881	(809) 639-4629

TOBAGO HOTELS	RMS	RATES	PHONE	FAX
★★★ **Kariwak Village Hotel**	18	$65–$95	(809) 639-8545	(809) 639-8441
★★★ **Mount Irvine Bay Hotel**	105	$125–$365	(809) 639-8871	(809) 639-8800
★★★ **Palm Tree Village**	60	$80–$455	(809) 639-4347	(809) 639-4180
★★★ **Turtle Beach Hotel**	125	$110–$200	(809) 639-2851	(809) 639-1495
★★ **Blue Waters Inn**	28	$60–$115	(809) 660-4341	(809) 660-5195
★★ **Man-O-War Bay Cottages**	6	$55–$70	(809) 660-4327	
★★ **Pelican Beach Hotel**	14	$95–$230	(809) 946-7112	(809) 946-7139
★★ **Salt Raker Inn**	12	$45–$130	(809) 946-2260	(809) 946-2817
★★ **Sandy Point Beach Club**	50	$40–$75	(809) 639-8533	(809) 639-8495
★ **Arthur's-on-Sea**	15	$40–$75	(800) 742-4276	(809) 639-4122
★ **Coral Reef Guest House**	24	$40–$70	(809) 639-2536	(809) 639-0770
★ **Crown Point Beach Hotel**	100	$55–$105	(809) 639-8781	(809) 639-8731
★ **Golden Thistle Hotel**	36	$40–$60	(809) 639-8521	(809) 639-8521

TOBAGO RESTAURANTS	LOCATION	PHONE	ENTREE
Plymouth			
International			
★★★ **Old Donkey Cart House**	Scarborough	(809) 639-3551	$3–$25
Italian			
★★★★★ **La Tartaruga**	Buccoo Bay	(809) 639-0940	$18–$24••
Latin American			
★★★★★ **Blue Crab**	Scarborough	(809) 639-2737	$4–$20
★★★ **Jemma's Sea View Kitchen**	Tyrell's Bay	(809) 660-4066	$10–$27
★★★ **Miss Jean's**	Store Bay	(809) 639-0211	$4–$6
Seafood			
★★★ **Dillon's Seafood**	Crown Point	(809) 639-8765	$12–$27••
★★★ **Papillon**	Mt. Irvine	(809) 639-0275	$15–$25

Note: • Lunch Only

•• Dinner Only

TRINIDAD

Trinidad's Carnival is the Caribbean's most celebrated annual spectacle with islanders working all year on floats and costumes.

Trinidad is the largest of the Lesser Antilles Islands, home to calypso, steel pan bands, and some of the most spectacular aviary habitats in the Western World. Practically ringed with beaches, the island is a cultural smorgasbord of cuisines, festivals and religious rituals that draws tourists despite the almost studied indifference to their comfort. During the 70s, the two-island nation (which includes its sister island Tobago), became the wealthiest, if not the most cosmopolitan nation in the Caribbean, allowing it to eschew tourism as an unneeded intrusion. As finances plummet in the early 90s, Trinidad is now courting tourism with an attractive come-on, and a special amiability toward foreigners is being seriously cultivated. Even without such natural re-

sources as its fine rainforest, palm-fringed beaches, and exotic nature reserves, simple daily life alone in Trinidad makes a fascinating diversion. The
island's capital, Port-of-Spain is a vibrant, dizzying waterfront town of colorful gingerbread houses competing with ramshackle stalls and short high-
rises as at least seven distinct nationalities stream down the narrow, winding
alleyways intent on doing business somewhere between First World and
Third. Eco-treks are fabulous on the island, and especially on Tobago, which
is a short ferry ride away. Excellent accommodations are available on both islands, but the latest trend is to snuggle up in one of the many bed and break-
fast-type inns, where you can forge an intimate relationship with the host,
who usually doubles as chef, chambermaid and chauffeur. This is the real
way to experience these islands in order to forge memories you can take
home and cherish. Of course, Carnival in Trinidad is one of the most spectacular events in the Caribbean, an annual blowout affair whose efforts can
be seen year-round in the studious productions of floats, costumes and musical performances.

Bird's Eye View

Trinidad is situated in the Caribbean Sea about 12 kilometers off the
northeast coast of Venezuela. Tobago is 30.7 kilometers further to the
northeast. The entire land mass of Trinidad covers 1861 sq. miles while Tobago has a mere 117 miles. Almost all of Trinidad's hotels and restaurants
are confined to the foothills around Port of Spain, the capital city, which has
over 60,000 residents; the entire island has a population of over one million.
Below the Savanah Park, lined with gingerbread mansions, spreads the city, a
jumble of wooden houses and tiny stores whose wares often spill onto the
sidewalk.

Just an hour from the city is a primeval rainforest, arrived at by a coiled
spring of a road that leads to Arima Valley, where wildlife is so profuse that
the New York Zoological Society began its first tropical ecology center there
in 1949. This was later turned into a neighboring coffee and cocoa estate
turned into a hotel for birdlovers—the **Asa Wright Nature Centre and Lodge**.
The grotto here is the most accessible place in the world to see the rare cave-
dwelling oilbird, equipped with batlike sonar.

Trinidad

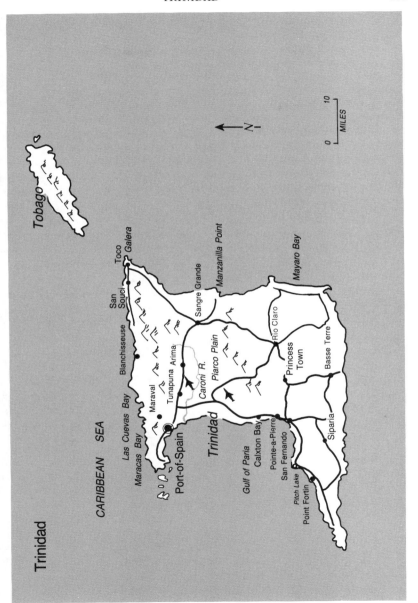

CARIBBEAN SEA

Tobago

Toco
Galera
San Souci
Blanchisseuse
Las Cuevas Bay
Maracas Bay
Maraval
Tunapuna Arima
Caroni R.
Port-of-Spain
Trinidad
Sangre Grande
Piarco Plain
Manzanilla Point
Rio Claro
Princess Town
Basse Terre
Mayaro Bay
Gulf of Paria
Calxton Bay
Pointe-a-Pierre
San Fernando
Pitch Lake
Point Fortin
Siparia

N

0   10
MILES

History

Columbus stumbled upon Trinidad and Tobago in 1498. Since then, the two islands have been a battlefield of contention between the French, Dutch, British and Spanish. Trinidad was long viewed as a source for Amerindian slaves, so the island was fiercely guarded, in contrast to Tobago which was nearly deserted by the Spanish. In 1592, an inland capital was erected at St. Joseph, stimulating interest in the cultivation of tobacco and cocoa. During the middle of the 18th century, plagues swept through the area, decimating the settlement and forcing the Spanish governor to move to a more coastal location, less vulnerable to jungle diseases and Indian raids. Port of Spain took its time to develop, attracting a slow stream of settlers followed by Christian missionaries intent on civilizing the Indians. Both tobacco and cocoa production soon fell into disfavor, the former a victim of competition among the northern islands, the latter a victim of blight. In 1776, the Spanish government offered land grants and tax incentives to Roman Catholic settlers; in response, numerous French planters from French Caribbean countries poured in to establish farms. By the end of the century, prosperous Frenchmen had gained control of the government, spreading the lilt of their patois and their tasty cuisine islandwide. During the Napoleonic Wars in 1797, the British sent a fleet to Trinidad, who swiftly overcame the resident Spaniards who had been too distracted fighting off Indians. In 1815, Tobago itself came under British control and was made a ward of Trinidad in 1897.

In the 1970s, offshore petroleum discoveries propelled Trinidad to the enviable status of the wealthiest nation in the Caribbean. Literacy rose to 90 percent, roads were paved, electricity installed. Signs of abject poverty, common among West Indian nations, nearly disappeared. In 1962, Sr. Eric Williams, the father of Trinidad and Tobago's new independence from British rule, vowed to avoid what he called the mistakes of his Caribbean neighbors, which in his mind, was servile catering to tourists. As such, tourism lay fallow for several decades. However, during the mid-80s, resources plummeted, and the challenge of the Trinidadian government in this decade will be to reestablish economic stability and ensure conservation of the island's natural resources.

People

Trinidad's population is well over one million people. Their facial features represent a mingling of characteristics from Africa, America, Europe, Asia and the Indian subcontinent. Calypso lyrics hold the soul of the people—often editorials which bemoan what the oil bust has done to the country. Yet by all standards, Trinidad and Tobago are prosperous nations; children are kept fed by plentiful fish and fruit, healthy by free medical care, and taught in schools responsible for a literacy rate higher than the United States. Today, the two-island nation is 40 percent black and 40 percent East Indian, plus Chinese, Arab, British and remnant Carib Amerindian stock—only with each passing generation are bloods mixing so much that you can't tell who's who. The cultural jetsam takes its biggest influence from the conquerors who stayed the longest—Spain, France and Holland. Important is the legacy left by the Africans who arrived as slaves, indentured servants from India brought to replace them after abolition, Chinese who proved unfit to harvest sugar but adept at everything else, Syrians bearing textiles, and former British estate owners whose descendants wouldn't leave for anything. Color is less an issue in this country where intercultural cooperation has received lots of elbow grease. Race relations here are considered a miracle of worked-at harmony

Music and Carnival are nearly year-round industries. A century ago, the British outlawed African drums in Trinidad, for allegedly inciting passions leading to violence. People switched to beating on bamboo, biscuit tins, hubcaps, and as local petroleum exploitation surged on, oil drums, which someone noticed tended to change pitch after much pounding, and particularly when dented. Pan music can now be heard everywhere from Sunday mass to jazz ensembles to 120-musician orchestras during Carnival's Panorama. Best of all is the ubiquitous pan yard, especially in the month preceding Carnival, where the neighborhoods gather to hear free rehearsals. Best jam is on Oxford Street. For more information, see the chapter called "Caribbean Culture" in the front of the book.

Beaches

On the subject of beaches, Tobago wins hands down over Trinidad. The latter, however, does have numerous ones—they are simply not as beautiful or as memorable as Tobago's. Most of Trinidad's beaches are on the Caribbean coast from Las Cuevas to Balata Bay, and on offshore islands such as Monos.

One of the most beautiful beaches is **Cyril Bay**, complete with a small waterfall and fantasy sites for picnics. The cove is made of pebbles and sand and can be reached only by foot. Surfers congregate at **Tyrico Bay**, but the beach is small for bathing. Swimmers who are not experienced should avoid the strong undertow. **Maracas Bay** is a favorite among locals who love the long stretch of sand and the ample parking spaces. You can also find food and changing facilities here. Along the north coast you'll find **Las Cuevas Bay**, a very pretty stretch of sand ringed by submerged and partially submerged caves. Some of the best fruit on the islands is sold across the street. Swimmers should avoid the waters because of a fierce current, but the beach is usually serene and uncrowded. **Blanchisseuse Bay** is located about eight miles east, with lovely palm trees for shade and no crowds. Lovers should enjoy the near absolute seclusion.

Northeast beaches take about an hour to reach by car. Bodysurfers particularly like the conditions at **Balandra Bay**. Good swimming can be found in the calm waters of **Salibea Bay**, just past Galera Point. A lovely drive can be had down **Cocal**, the road between Manzanilla Beach and Cocos Bay, lined as it is with towering palm trees who make an arch over the highway. The water at Manzanilla is sometimes polluted by the Atlantic overflow, so avoid swimming if the sea looks muddy.

Dive Sites

The word has been slowly getting out that Trinidad's underwater resources are as yet unspoiled. Coral reefs can be found around the entire perimeter in good shape and in every possible shape and variety; an enormous brain coral is off the coast of **Little Tobago**. Divers can choose from a variety of sites, from caves to walls, to canyons and coral gardens because of the strong Guyana current that flows around the southern and eastern shores of Tobago—the marine life is varied and profuse. Among the best sites are: **Batteaux Bay**, **Pirates Bay**, **Man O'War**, **Stone Bay** and **Arnos Vale**.

Treks

A good book to pick up before you even put on your hiking shoes is *The Nature Trails of Trinidad* by Richard French and Peter Bacon. You also might contact the Trinidad and Tobago Field Naturalist's Club, who sometimes offer hikes and know the conditions of tracks quite well.

One of the most favorite hikes is up the El Tucuche Peak, the island's second highest, along the Maracas Valley Road. It's a seven-mile track, but it makes complicated turns and bends, passing over riverbeds, abandoned roads and overgrown paths. The forest reserve is also a wildlife sanctuary and you may be lucky to spot some pacas, armadillos, deer and agoutis. From Ortinola, the hike takes about 4-5 hours for experienced hikers in good shape, but it's best to be accompanied by a guide who knows the route well.

The **Asa Wright Nature Centre** is an unusual institution in the Caribbean, a former cocoa-coffee-citrus plantation that was converted into a hotel, bird sanctuary, wildlife refuge and study for amateurs and professionals alike. Just sitting on the veranda, you can hear the symphony of the forest birds, and photography possibilities are endless and creative. There are five marked trails, ranging from easy half-hour strolls to challenging three-hour treks that take one through steep slopes and dense forests. All trails are designed to maximize the amount and quality of flora and fauna observed. During the summer, nature and painting seminars are given; during the winter, photography classes. Visitors are welcome for the day (you don't need to stay overnight at the hotel), and only a small fee is asked for use of the trails.

The **Caroni Swamp National Park and Bird Sanctuary** is a magical place. The best time to be there is just before sunset when hundreds upon hundreds of fire-engine-red ibis along with white snowy egrets and herons perch upon the trees, making the island glow like a fluorescent bulb. Local travel companies offer tours to the park daily from Port of Spain. From the boat, you can take any one of a number of walking trails along the mangrove marshes. The bird sanctuary can even be visited by boat; arrange an excursion with a local fisherman.

The **Pointe-a-Pierre Wild Fowl Trust** is a refuge designed to protect the island's endangered species. There are nature walks around the two lakes and at some points you can actually sit on park benches and watch waterfowl. An enormous variety of rare birds are visible in the treetops. The refuge is solely maintained by volunteers, so you must make a reservation to visit in advance.

Few people are aware that Trinidad is home to one of the most beautiful waterfalls in the Caribbean, **Maracas Falls**, deep in the heart of the Maracas Bay National Park, is a major hiking destination. The falls reach to 300 feet and are simply stunning, falling onto the Naraja River in the mountains above the valley. The road north from St. Joseph leads along the Maracas River to Maracas village where a signpost on the right leads to walking trails in about a mile. You can reach the base of the falls on an easy mile-walk through secondary forest. Only the most advanced hikers, accompanied by a guide, should attempt the rock-hopping climb up a steep, very narrow path. You arrive above the falls, and near a freezing pool (where some daring souls swim).

Trinidad is known for numerous caves, but few are developed for any commercial excursions. The most famous are the **Aripo Caves**, reached by a path designed by the Tourist Board. It is, however, considered dangerous. Oilbirds are rumored to live inside the sea caves on the northwest coast at **La Vache Point**. An enormous number of bats swarm through the **Tamana Caves** in the central range.

What Else to See

Drive Saddle Road north from the Savannah for 30 minutes to beautiful Maracas Bay; continue east to Las Cuevas Bay. In the northeast the nicest beaches are **Ma Tura**, **Salybia**, **Pajes**, **Toco** (take the lighthouse road), **Grand Riviere**, **Shark River**, and **Matelot**.

Nariva Swamp, the backdrop to Cocos Bay, is one of the world's great birding regions. **Canoni Swamp**, with its red ibis, four-eyed fish, and other wonders, is 20 minutes south of Port of Spain on the Butler Highway toward San Fernando. Call Winston Nanan at **Nanan's Bird Sanctuary Tours** ☎ *645-1305.*

A stroll in **Queen's Park Savannah** in Port of Spain is obligatory. You'll ramble alongside training thoroughbreds, admire gingerbread mansions, watch sandlot cricket matches, and buy fruit, corn, or barbecued fish from park vendors who also sell fresh coconut milk.

City Celebrations

Carnival ★★★★★

Port of Spain, ☎ *(809) 623-8867.*
Trinidad's famous carnival officially lasts just two days, from sunrise on Monday to midnight on Tuesday before Ash Wednesday. However, the unofficial season starts right after Christmas. Started by the French plantocracy 200 years ago, the festival was adopted by the island's blacks as a celebration of the end of slavery. Today, the joyous festival is eagerly anticipated by Trinidadians all year long. Most everyone dons elaborate costumes they've spent months making, then parades through the streets to the beat of steel bands. Tourists are welcome to join a troupe from a few hundred to literally thousands of costumed revelers.

Museums and Exhibits

National Museum ★★★★

117 Frederick Street, Port of Spain, ☎ *(809) 623-5941.*
Hours Open: 10:00 a.m.–6:00 p.m.
The museum's exhibits center on Trinidad's geography and history through the ages, with artifacts from pre-Columbian times. The highlight is a large art gallery with changing displays and a permanent exhibit on the works of famed 19th-century painter Michel Jean Cazabon. Free admission.

Parks and Gardens

Royal Botanical Gardens ★★★★★

Queen's Park Savannah, Port of Spain, ☎ *(809) 622-3530.*
Hours Open: 9:30 a.m.–5:30 p.m.

Located in the two-mile Queen's Park Savannah, these lush gardens cover 70 colorful acres on land that was once a sugar plantation. The grounds include the President's House, an 1875 Victorian mansion home to the president of Trinidad and Tobago, and the Emperor Valley Zoo (☎ 625-2264), named after the huge Emperor butterflies common in the area. The gardens, laid out in 1820, showcase specimens from around the world.

Tours

Asa Wright Nature Center   ★★★★★

Spring Hill Estate, Port of Spain, ☎ *(809) 667-4655.*
Hours Open: 9:00 a.m.–5:00 p.m.

This 191-acre estate turned wildlife sanctuary is a must for bird watchers, with more than 100 species waiting to be glimpsed. The grounds include eight trails, one leading to the world's most accessible colony of nocturnal oilbirds. Guided tours are offered daily at 10:30 a.m. and 1:30 p.m.; reservations are suggested. They also take in guests here; see the entry under lodging for more details. General admission: $6.00.

Caroni Bird Sanctuary   ★★★★★

Butler Highway, Port of Spain.
Hours Open: 4:00 p.m.–6:30 p.m.

This sanctuary comprises 40 square miles of mangrove swampland bisected by waterways. Come at sunset to see the national bird, the scarlet ibis, come home to roost—an amazing, colorful sight. Boat tours are conducted by **David Ramsahai** *(☎ 663-4767)* and **Winston Nanon** *(☎ 645-1305)*. General admission: $10.00.

Sports

Deep-sea fishing is available in the cliff-bound Boca Islands in the northwest where mackerel, kingfish, wahoo, yellowtail tuna, barracuda, red snapper, and groupers are in profuse abundance. Your hotel can make all arrangements. Much sailing is done on a private basis in Trinidad, though it is in its infant stage commercially. Weekly races are held by the Yachting Association, and you may be able to inquire about renting or hiring boats among the owners. There is also a great interest in power-boat racing; the major annual competition is the Great Race (90 miles) between Trinidad and Tobago which takes place in August. Over the last several years surfing has become a passion on Trinidad. The Surfing Association of Trinidad and Tobago is very warm to visitors and will offer all the assistance they can. There is no particular season for surfing; conditions are favorable year-round. Four surfing breaks are available. The biggest swells happen around Toco Point, on the northeast coast of Trinidad. Chaguaramas Bay is the prime spot for windsurfing.

Golf

Two locations, Port of Spain.
Trinidad has two courses for duffers. The island's only 18-hole course is at **St. Andrew's Golf Club** in Maravel; ☎ *629-2314.* The **Chaguaramas Golf Course** has nine holes; ☎ *634-4349.*

Watersports

Various locations, Port of Spain.
A variety of companies are happy to assist with watersports. Deep-sea fishing: **Bayshore Charters** *(☎ 637-8711)* and **Trinidad and Tobago Game Fishing Association** *(☎ 624-5304).* Boating and sailing: **Island Yacht Charters** *(☎ 637-7389).* Windsurfing: **Windsurfing Association of Trinidad and Tobago** *(☎ 659-2457).* General watersports equipment and instruction: **Ron's Watersports** *(☎ 622-0459)* and the **Surfing Association of Trinidad and Tobago** *(☎ 637-4355).*

Where to Stay

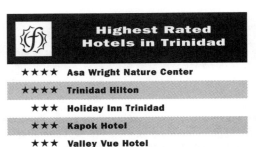

Highest Rated Hotels in Trinidad

★★★★ Asa Wright Nature Center
★★★★ Trinidad Hilton
★★★ Holiday Inn Trinidad
★★★ Kapok Hotel
★★★ Valley Vue Hotel

Most Exclusive Hotels in Trinidad

★★★★	Trinidad Hilton	$149–$460
★★★	Valley Vue Hotel	$80–$300
★★★	Kapok Hotel	$70–$140

Fielding's Best Value Hotels in Trinidad

★★	Monique's Guest House	$45–$50
★★★	Valley Vue Hotel	$80–$300
★★	Normandie Hotel	$60–$95
★★★	Holiday Inn Trinidad	$100–$300
★★	Chaconia Inn	$65–$95

Accommodations in Trinidad run from the traditional high-rise (with U.S. Connections) to the intimate bed and breakfast. Most lodgings are near the Savannah. No hotel in Port of Spain opens onto a beach; to get to the nearest beach you'll have to take a taxi and it's expensive. Anyone with a yen for the wild outdoors will have a memory of a lifetime at the **Asa Wright Nature Reserve**, where you'll feel as if you are sharing the room with the wildlife. During Carnival and culture fests, finding a hotel room on Trinidad can be tricky. On Tobago, it's downright impossible.

Hotels and Resorts

One of the premier hotels, the **Trinidad Hilton**, currently undergoing a multimillion dollar renovation, has unveiled an expanded conference center and refurbished grand ballroom; the second phase of the renovation has encompassed the addition of two new function rooms and executive business center. **The Kapok**, however, is actually more pleasant than the Hilton and less costly **The Normandie** is a charming work of sculpture in colored concrete, with shops, cafe and an art gallery.

Asa Wright Nature Center $103–$187 ★★★★

Spring Hill Estate, ☎ *(809) 667-4655.*
Single: $103–$127. Double: $147–$187.

This special spot is devoted to preserving nature. Located two hours out of Port of Spain some 1200 feet up, it is a former coffee estate converted into a 191-acre wildlife sanctuary. Two guestrooms are in the main house, which dates to 1908, and are quite romantic and furnished with antiques. The rest are located in cottages; all are very basic. The lush grounds and neighboring rainforest attract birders from around the world. The rates include afternoon tea and three meals a day—a good thing, since this spot is way off on its own. You'll need a car. 20 rooms. Credit Cards: Not Accepted.

Chaconia Inn $65–$95 ★★

106 Saddle Road, Maraval, ☎ *(809) 628-8603.*
Single: $65–$85. Double: $75–$95.

Located three miles form Port of Spain in a mountain valley, this hotel houses guests in air-conditioned rooms (most with TV). There are also four two-bedroom apartments with kitchenettes for self-catering types. Facilities include two restaurants, a pool and occasional entertainment in the bar. A decent and friendly spot, but a bit out of the way. 35 rooms. Credit Cards: V, MC, DC, A.

Farrell House Hotel $60–$140 ★★

P.O. Box 4185, Southern Main Road, ☎ *(809) 659-2230.*
Single: $60–$125. Double: $93–$140.

This government-owned hotel appeals primarily to business travelers. Located on a 15-acre estate in the Point Lisas area, it puts up guests in air-conditioned, motel-style rooms—nothing too exciting. Eleven suites have kitchenettes and small living rooms. There's a restaurant and pool, but not much else in the way of extras. Tourists will be happier elsewhere. 51 rooms. Credit Cards: V, MC, A.

Holiday Inn Trinidad $100–$300 ★★★

Wrightson Road and London Street, ☎ *(800) 465-4329, (809) 625-3361.*
Single: $100–$300. Double: $110–$300.

This downtown hotel overlooks the harbor and attracts mainly business travelers and conventioneers. Accommodations are standard tried-and-true Holiday Inn: modern, air-conditioned, cable TV, and balcony with nice views. Those staying on the executive floor pay extra for upgraded rooms and a private lounge. There's a revolving rooftop restaurant (another HI tradition), dancing in the lounge, a nice pool and a health club. 235 rooms. Credit Cards: V, MC, DC, A.

Kapok Hotel   **$70–$140**   ★★★

16-18 Cotton Street.
Single: $70–$125. Double: $85–$140.

This contemporary hotel is located five minutes from downtown, near Queen's Park Savannah. Guestrooms are spacious and modern, and the six suites have kitchenettes. The two restaurants offer a choice of Caribbean or Chinese/Polynesian fare, and there's also a cocktail lounge and pool. Quite decent for the rates; most rooms are under $85. 71 rooms. Credit Cards: V, MC, DC, A.

Normandie Hotel   **$60–$95**   ★★

10 Nook Avenue, ☎ *(809) 624-1181.*
Single: $60–$85. Double: $70–$95.

This two-story hotel is located in St. Ann's Valley, near the botanical gardens. Taking a cue from the gardens, its own grounds are nicely landscaped and include a restaurant, disco and pool. Guestrooms are air-conditioned and comfortable, but on the dark side. Many of the 12 two-story suites have kitchens and are well worth the bump in price. Right next door is an art gallery and shopping arcade with well-made local wares. 63 rooms. Credit Cards: CB, V, MC, DC, A.

Trinidad Hilton   **$149–$460**   ★★★★

Lady Young Road, Belmont Hill, ☎ *(800) 445-8667, (809) 624-3211.*
Single: $149–$460. Double: $161–$460.

This commercial hotel is located a mile from downtown. The air-conditioned guest rooms and suites have all the modern conveniences, and some include fax and computer hookups for business travelers. Facilities include two restaurants, three bars, a pool, and two tennis courts. Guests are mainly American business travelers who appreciate the nice trappings and attentive service. 394 rooms. Credit Cards: V, MC, DC, A.

Valley Vue Hotel   **$80–$300**   ★★★

67 Ariapita Road, P.O. Box 442, ☎ *(809) 624- 940.*
Single: $80–$300. Double: $80–$300.

Located 10 minutes from Port of Spain on a hillside overlooking the city, this modern hotel attracts mostly business travelers. Accommodations are in comfortable air-conditioned rooms; most are under $100. Facilities are plentiful for the number of guestrooms: a restaurant, two bars, disco, business center, a pair of tennis and squash courts, a pool, playground and gym. The Valley Vue also has a small waterpark with three 400-foot waterslides leading to a splash pool. 68 rooms. Credit Cards: V, MC, A.

Inns

Guest houses in Trinidad have a stylish way of approximating inns; the Trinidadian personality fills in any gaps with its natural congeniality. There's an elegant casualness to the best inns, where you will feel so at home you may never want to leave. The **Mount St. Benedict Guest House** is near-religious in its peaceful ambiance; spiritual seekers can escape to the nearby monastery for a shady refuge, but the views from some of the inn's apartments can be objects of profound contemplation.

Monique's Guest House $45–$50   ★ ★

114 Saddle Road, ☎ (809) 628-3334.
Single: $45. Double: $50.
This friendly guest house is located in the Maravel Valley and surrounded by lush hills. Rooms are nicely furnished, air-conditioned, and spotless. The small restaurant serves bargain fare, and guests can splash about in a nearby pool. One of Trinidad's better guest houses. 11 rooms. Credit Cards: V, MC, A.

Low Cost Lodging

The newest trend on Trinidad and Tobago is bed and breakfasts. There is an association for these kinds of places, but the communication is often informal; if one B&B is filled, the owner will call up her friends for you. Chances are a car will even be sent to pick you up and hot tea and pastries awaiting you on arrival. Best of all, you may find a South American family next to your room, or even Finns; the host could be Chinese, African, Indian or British. To go the B&B route, you need a sense of adventure and a passion for unexpected experiences. Sometimes you don't get all the privacy you are used to since B&B's treat you like family—whoever knows where that leads? Because accommodations and policies vary widely from home to home, it's best to ask specific questions about what you can expect before you go (i.e., how to get from the airport, children, pets, air-conditioning, and noise). Some houses are way out of the way, so get specifics.

La Maison Rustique is a B&B with a wonderful tearoom and garden. In the Arima Valley, the Asa Wright Nature Centre and Lodge is a fine accommodation, simple, but good local food and unbelievable birding. Meals are included.

Bel Air International $56–$89

Piarco, ☎ (809) 664-4771.
Single: $56–$89. Double: $75–$89.
This hotel is found three minutes from the airport, so attracts mainly travelers in transit. The air-conditioned guestrooms are rather simple and dated, and could use soundproofing to buffet airport noise. Facilities are limited to a pool and decent restaurant. There's no reason to stay here unless you're enroute to someplace else. 56 rooms. Credit Cards: V, MC, DC, A.

Where to Eat

Highest Rated Restaurants in Trinidad

★★★★★ **Veni Mange**

★★★ **Breakfast Shed**

★★★ **Cafe Savannah**

★★★ **Chaconia Inn**

★★★ **Hong Kong City**

★★★ **Michael's**

★★★ **Monsoon**

★★★ **Philip and Fraser's**

★★★ **Rafters**

★★★ **Singho**

Most Exclusive Restaurants in Trinidad

★★★ **Michael's**		$8–$25
★★★ **Rafters**		$6–$21
★★★ **Hong Kong City**		$8–$20
★★★ **Tiki Village**		$6–$13
★★★ **Monsoon**		$5–$5

Fielding's Best Value Restaurants in Trinidad

★★★★★ **Veni Mange**		$8–$10
★★★ **Singho**		$7–$12
★★★ **Philip and Fraser's**		$8–$20
★★★ **Michael's**		$8–$25
★★★ **Chaconia Inn**		$12–$19

No fewer than seven distinct cultures have influenced the cuisine of Trinidad, from the Spanish settlers who cooked up pastelles to the French who introduced herbs like broad-leaved thyme and basil. The British brought tamarind from the East Indies for sauces used still today in red snapper. A ten-alarm chile pepper called a *habañero* hails from Mexico. Spicy pastelles are a favorite snack—tamales concocted by placing meats, raisin, capers and fresh herbs atop grated corn or cornmeal and folded in bright green leaves instead of the usual corn husks. "Oil-down" is another local specialty, made from breadfruit, a round starchy yamlike fruit that makes a gooey thick stew when cooked. Before you go, check out the delicacies in *Callaloo, Calypso & Carnival*, a new cookbook from The Crossing Press in Freedom, California by Dae De Witt and Mary Jane Wilan. Most nights, calypso or pan music is heard at the exceedingly friendly **Mas Camp Pub** (*French St., at Ariapita Ave.,* ☎ *623-3745*, $2). There are also frequent concerts at **Spektakula Forum** (*Henry St.,* ☎ *623-2879*, about $5.)

Breakfast Shed $ ★★★

Waterfront, Wrightson Road, ☎ *(809) 627-2337.*
Latin American cuisine.
Breakfast/Lunch: 5:00 a.m.–3:00 p.m., entrees $5–$7.
Break bread with the wharf rats on huge platters of homestyle West Indian food near the cruise ship dock and the Holiday Inn. Fellow diners are working people and early risers who like the fish breakfasts served from 5 a.m. Lunch (the only other meal served) is accompanied by plantains, rice and peas and other plate stretchers. So down home, the hall-like room is called the "Holiday Out" by regulars. Closed: Sun. Credit Cards: Not Accepted.

Cafe Savannah $$ ★★★

16-18 Cotton Hill, St. Clair, ☎ *(809) 622-6441.*
Latin American cuisine.
Lunch: 11:45 a.m.–2:15 p.m., entrees $8–$9.
Dinner: 6:00 p.m.–10:15 p.m., entrees $8–$17.
Possibly the best callaloo soup on the islands is served at this intimate restaurant on the lower level of the Kapok Hotel. Prepared with a rich stock of dasheen (taro leaf) and okra, it's filled with pumpkin, coconut and crabmeat. Other specialties include lobster Soucouyant and pork steak in zippy mustard sauce. There's a prix fixe lunch of several courses, but sandwiches and salads are available. Associated Hotel: Kapok Hotel. Closed: Sun. Reservations recommended. Credit Cards: V, MC, DC, A.

Chaconia Inn $$$ ★★★

106 Saddle Road, Maraval, ☎ *(809) 628-8603.*
Latin American cuisine.
Lunch: 11:00 a.m.–2:00 p.m., entrees $12–$19.
Dinner: 7:00 p.m.–11:00 p.m., entrees $12–$19.
The dining rooms of this motel-like resort in a Port of Spain suburb serve a double purpose: at lunch in the Lounge, business folk gather for a no-frills lunch of fish, pasta, pork and some vegetarian offerings. Sandwiches are tasty and moderately priced. And once a week, a West Indian barbecue is the attraction at the modern,

plant-filled alfresco Roof Garden atop the hotel. A bar serves drinks until 2 p.m.
Associated Hotel: Chaconia Inn. Reservations recommended. Credit Cards: V, MC, DC,
A.

Hong Kong City   **$$**   ★★★

86 Tragarete Road, Newtown, ☎ (809) 622-3949.
Chinese cuisine.
Lunch: entrees $8–$20.
Dinner: entrees $8–$20.
Spicy, creative Tri-Chi food is served amidst gaudy red and gold trappings. Bright
Oriental lanterns hang from an intricately decorated ceiling. Chinese-food loving
Trinidadians favor pepper shrimp, pork with dasheen and other delights. Karaoke
nights sometimes, for those who enjoy that sort of thing. For more Chinese food
around town, try: **New Shay-Shay Ten**, *81 Cipriani Blvd.,* ☎ *627-8089*, and in San
Fernando area **Soong's Great Wall**, *97 Circular Road,* ☎ *652-2583.* Credit Cards: V,
MC, DC, A.

Michael's   **$$$**   ★★★

143 Long Circular Road, Maraval, ☎ (809) 628-0445.
International cuisine.
Dinner: 6:00 p.m.–10:30 p.m., entrees $8–$25.
Michael's offers toothsome Italian food livened with local produce. His version of
proscuitto is served with vividly-flavored fresh papaya instead of the more common
melon. Pastas are a standout; they're all homemade. Filet mignon, fish and chicken
are also served. Decor is modern, chairs are comfortable and hug the back, floors are
polished hardwood. Located in a townhouse in the suburb of Maraval, the service is
notably efficient. Reservations recommended. Credit Cards: V, MC, A.

Monsoon   **$**   ★★★

72 Tragarete Road, Port of Spain, ☎ (809) 628-7684.
Indian cuisine.
Lunch: 11:00 a.m.–4:00 p.m., entrees $5.
Dinner: 4:00 p.m.–10:00 p.m., entrees $5.
This brisk, but stylish East/West Indian restaurant is probably the most popular in
town for curries an the flatbread *(paratha)*. Lunch is a fast-paced affair, and very
busy; many people take advantage of the takeout service. Complete meals built
around shrimp, chicken, and fish include several veggies, lentils and rice. There are
great rotis, or dough wrapped around spiced conch or chicken, and fresh squeezed,
exotic drinks. The Wednesday night buffets are a good bet for a well-rounded feast
in quieter surroundings. Closed: Sun. Reservations recommended. Credit Cards: V,
MC, DC, A.

Philip and Fraser's   **$$**   ★★★

16 Phillips St., Port of Spain, ☎ (809) 623-7632.
International cuisine.
Lunch: 11:00 a.m.–4:00 p.m., entrees $8–$12.
Dinner: 4:00 p.m.–10:00 p.m., entrees $8–$20.
All meals are cooked to order at this bastion of new creole cuisine, which translates
into smaller, but intensely-flavored dishes. Thankfully, vegetables are very lightly

cooked, in the French style, rather than stewed out of all nutrients. Surroundings are tasteful and muted, with plenty of greenery and basketry. There's live jazz on Friday nights. Open Saturdays for dinner only, from 7 to 10 p.m. Closed: Sun. Reservations recommended. Credit Cards: V, MC, A.

Rafters
$$ ★★★

6A Warner Street, Newtown, ☎ *(809) 628-9258.*
Seafood cuisine.
Lunch: 11:30 a.m.–4:00 p.m., entrees $6–$21.
Dinner: 4:00 p.m.–11:00 p.m., entrees $6–$21.

Meat and potatoes people and seafood lovers all get their culinary kicks here: On Wednesday, a buffet of fresh local sea creatures is featured, Thursdays, Fridays and Saturdays chefs carve hunks of roast beef and other meats nonstop until it's all gone. In an adjacent lounge snacks and sandwiches are available for folks with more prudent appetites and pocketbooks. The restaurant resides in a lovely old restored dry goods store. Closed: Sun. Reservations recommended. Credit Cards: V, MC, DC, A.

Singho
$$ ★★★

Long Circular Mall, Port of Spain, ☎ *(809) 628-2077.*
Chinese cuisine.
Lunch: 11:30 a.m.–7:00 p.m., entrees $5–$7.
Dinner: 7:30 p.m.–11:00 p.m., entrees $7–$12.

Solidly good Cantonese food is the star at this tony eatery in the gargantuan Long Circular Mall. Decor features an aquarium, and meals run on the lines of cashew chicken, spareribs in black bean sauce, and curries. Regulars and tourists like to stop in Wednesday nights for the Chinese buffet. Credit Cards: V, MC, A.

Tiki Village
$$ ★★★

16-18 Cotton Hill, St. Clair, ☎ *(809) 622-6441.*
Chinese cuisine.
Lunch: 11:30 a.m.–7:00 p.m., entrees $6–$13.
Dinner: 7:30 p.m.–9:00 p.m., entrees $6–$13.

The island's version of Trader Vic's sits atop the plush Kapok Hotel, with a night vista of the glittering city lights; at lunch, Queens Park Savannah is spread out in all its glory. Food is good to average, with a dim sum lunch served from 11 a.m. to 3 p.m. on weekends and holidays. Management thoughtfully provides cards for diners to mark their choices on. The regular menu features Polynesian-style fish, steaks and chicken. Associated Hotel: Kapok Hotel. Reservations recommended. Credit Cards: V, MC, DC, A.

Veni Mange
$ ★★★★★

13 Lucknow Street, St. James, ☎ *(809) 622-7533.*
Latin American cuisine.
Dinner: entrees $8–$10.

Come and eat, say local media star Allyson Hennesey and co-owner and sister Rosemary Hezekiah, in the local lingo. A cross between Julia Child and Oprah Winfrey, Allyson manages to run the best West Indian lunch spot in town and host her own TV talk show. Specialties include tasty crab backs, hollowed out crab shells filled with peppered meat and a spicy mix of peppers and tomatoes. Hearty soups, including pumpkin and callaloo, are also recommended. Open for dinner on Wednesdays 7:30 to 10 p.m., and for drinks on Fridays, from 7 to 10 p.m. Closed: Sat, Sun. Reservations required. Credit Cards: Not Accepted.

Where to Shop

Fabrics on the island of Trinidad are simply fantastic—a true art in themselves. East Indian silks and cottons come in high-class quality; the best bargains are found in downtown Port-of-Spain on Frederick Street around Independence Square. Even if you don't drink, do stock up on local brews like Angostura Bitters and Old Oak or Vat 19 rum, all which can be bought duty-free and make excellent gifts at Christmas time.

Local artisanry is quite skilled, ranging from fine straw work to cane-inspired creations to miniature steel pans (the large ones, of course are too bulky to ship home, but if you must, shopkeepers will have some interesting suggestions how to lug them home). Island-designed fashions are spectacular at **The Village**, near the Hotel Normandie, and you can find a top-class gallery, **Art Creators**, just around the corner on St. Ann's Road. The latest designs in batik work and island-inspired jewelry can be picked up at The **Cotton House** on Bacolet and Windward Roads. Calypso records are also a favorite buy here. The assistants at **Rhyner's Record Shop** on Prince Street will help you find the latest releases; do ask to see some of the old classics. Soca music is also a great buy; many a traveler who just bought albums blindly has come away with great party music, only regretting he hadn't bought more at the time. **Metronome**, in Port-of-Spain, on Western Main Rd. is also a good source for music.

Trinidad Directory

ARRIVAL AND DEPARTURE

BWIA offers daily nonstop flights to Piarco Airport, about 30 miles east of Port-of-Spain, from New York and Miami as well as daily direct flights from Toronto. It also offers flights three times a week from London and serves Boston and Baltimore once a week. American Airlines and Air Canada also have regular nonstop flights. LIAT and BWIA offer inter-island flights, all lighting at Piarco Airport. Most round-trip flights includes airfare to Tobago, so be sure to verify before you pay for the ticket. To fly to Tobago from Trinidad takes about 15 minutes. Departures are available several times a day. LIAT also flies regularly to Trinidad from Barbados.

Taxis are generally plentiful at the airport; a ride to downtown Port-of-Spain runs about $19 in U.S. currency. Buses run on the hour from the airport to the South Quay Bus Terminal, but you will probably need to hire a taxi from there to get to your hotel.

Ferry service is available between Trinidad and Tobago, once a day except Saturdays. The trip takes about 6 hours. Tickets can be purchased in Port-of-Spain and at Scarborough in Tobago.

The airport departure tax is about U.S.$12.

CLIMATE

Trinidad has a tropical climate whose dry season runs from January - June, with a wet season the rest of the year. Temperatures are uniformly high the year round. In Port-of-Spain, average temperature in January is 78 degrees F, in July 79 degrees F. Annual rainfall is 1.556 meters.

DOCUMENTS

U.S. and Canadian citizens, as well as those of the United Kingdom, may enter the country with a valid passport if they only plan to stay less than two months. An ongoing or return ticket is also required. An immigration card is handed to you upon arrival (or on the plane) which must be filled out and handed in as you depart. Do not lose it. A visa is required for longer stays. Long delays in clearing customs have often been reported. Visitors may bring in 200 cigarettes or 50 cigars, plus one quart of "spirits." To facilitate matters, pack as lightly and unostentatiously as possible.

ELECTRICITY

Current runs 110 or 220 volts, AC 60 cycles. Always inquire of your hotel when you are making reservations what kind of transformer or adapter you will need.

GETTING AROUND

Port-of-Spain is full of crazy drivers who taunt each other into dangerous maneuvers. Do your best to avoid driving yourself around the city, or at least downtown; better conditions are available in the countryside. If you're staying in the suburbs, a car is probably necessary, since you will always be waiting for hired cabs to arrive. You can explore the northern coast by taxi, but a car is more feasible.

Taxis run on fixed rates according to the destination. There is a set route which they follow and will drop off passengers anywhere along that route. There are minibuses as well as regular sedans. Before getting in the car, determine whether you are entering a route taxi or a private one, which will take you anywhere. Even though fares are fixed, drivers are not necessarily honest, and unless you're knowledgeable, expect to be stiffed a few dollars.

Private taxis do not pick up any other passengers and they take you straight to your destination. Take one for longer trips or destinations not on the regular route. Rates are usually not observed during Carnival, when anything goes since the demand is so high. Adjust and go with the flow or you will drive yourself crazy arguing.

Buses are an inexpensive way to get around the island, but they are often too crowded and dilapidated for comfort. Buses depart from the South Quay Bus Terminal. Cars can be rented form several agencies including **Auto Rentals** ☎ *(809) 675-2258* and **Bachhus Taxi Service** ☎ *(809) 622-5588*. Roads are fairly well paved but turn narrow and tortuous in the backcountry. During the rainy season they may be dangerously washed out. Forget driving into downtown Port-of-Spain during rush hour—you'll never get out. Remember that all driving is on the left.

LANGUAGE

The official language is English, spiced with a rich slew of local idioms. There is also some facility in Chinese, Hindi, Spanish and French, due to the large amount of immigrants.

MEDICAL EMERGENCIES

There are several adequate hospitals in Port-of-Spain. Among them are the Tobago Country Hospital on Fort Street in Scarborough ☎ *(809) 639-2551*; and Port-of-Spain General Hospital on Charlotte Street ☎ *(809) 625-7869* Ask your hotel to suggest the nearest pharmacy, but bring your own prescription medicine (an extra dose) in case you lose your luggage. Medicine made in the U.S. is far superior to any you could buy in the islands. Severe medical emergencies should be flown to San Juan or back home stateside.

MONEY

The Trinidadian dollar (written as TT$) has been devalued twice in the past few years. You can exchange money in the major hotels in Port-of-Spain, which offer rates comparable to banks. Most shops, hotels and restaurants will accept American dollars if you run short of local money, but they would prefer their own currency.

TELEPHONE

The area code for the two islands is *809*. Telegraphs, telefax, teletype, and telex, can be sent through the textel office at *1 Edward St., Port-of-Spain;* ☎ *(809) 625-4431*. Cables can be sent from the Tourism office and major hotels. To place an intra-island call, dial the local 7-digit number. To reach the U.S., dial 1, the area code, then the local number.

TIME

Atlantic Standard TIme.

TIPPING AND TAXES

Restaurants and hotels add a 15 percent Value Added Tax (called VAT). Many hotels and restaurants add an additional 10–15 percent service charge; check your bill carefully. If they don't, do add your own tip, if you find the service satisfactory.

TOURIST INFORMATION

The **Trinidad & Tobago Tourism Development Authority** is located locally at *134-138 Frederick Street, Port-of-Spain;* ☎ *(809) 623-1932.* Stop by for brochures, maps, and advice and assistance in obtaining lodging, especially bed and breakfast situations. In the U.S. call ☎ *(800) 232-0082.*

WHEN TO GO

New Year's Day is January 1. Good Friday and Easter Monday are both holidays. Whit Monday is June 7. Corpus Christi is June 18. Labor Day is June 19. Emancipation Day is August 1. Independence Day is August 31. Republic Day is September 24. Christmas Day is December 25. Boxing Day is December 26.

Fielding's Choice:

Don't miss Divali, the Hindu Festival of Lights, usually celebrated in October. The beauty of Pan Music is epitomized by the world steel band festivals. The festival called Pan Is Beautiful, is held in the last week of October. Check with the tourist board for exact dates.

TRINIDAD HOTELS		RMS	RATES	PHONE	FAX
Port of Spain					
★★★★	**Asa Wright Nature Center**	20	$103–$187	(809) 667-4655	
★★★★	**Trinidad Hilton**	394	$149–$460	(800) 445-8667	
★★★	**Holiday Inn Trinidad**	235	$100–$300	(800) 465-4329	(809) 625-4166
★★★	**Kapok Hotel**	71	$70–$140		(809) 622-9677
★★★	**Valley Vue Hotel**	68	$80–$300	(809) 624-0940	(809) 627-8046
★★	**Chaconia Inn**	35	$65–$95	(809) 628-8603	(809) 628-3214
★★	**Farrell House Hotel**	51	$60–$140	(809) 659-2230	(809) 659-2204
★★	**Monique's Guest House**	11	$45–$50	(809) 628-3334	(809) 622-3232
★★	**Normandie Hotel**	63	$60–$95	(809) 624-1181	(809) 624-1181
★	**Bel Air International**	56	$56–$89	(809) 664-4771	(809) 664-4771

TRINIDAD RESTAURANTS   LOCATION   PHONE   ENTREE

Port of Spain

	Chinese		
★★★ **Hong Kong City**	Newtown	(809) 622-3949	$8–$20
★★★ **Singho**	Port of Spain	(809) 628-2077	$5–$12
★★★ **Tiki Village**	St. Clair	(809) 622-6441	$6–$13
	Indian		
★★★ **Monsoon**	Port of Spain	(809) 628-7684	$5–$5
	International		
★★★ **Michael's**	Maraval	(809) 628-0445	$8–$25••
★★★ **Philip and Fraser's**	Port of Spain	(809) 623-7632	$8–$20
	Latin American		
★★★★★ **Veni Mange**	St. James	(809) 622-7533	$8–$10•
★★★ **Breakfast Shed**	Wrightson Road	(809) 627-2337	$5–$7•
★★★ **Cafe Savannah**	St. Clair	(809) 622-6441	$8–$17
★★★ **Chaconia Inn**	Maraval	(809) 628-8603	$12–$19
	Seafood		
★★★ **Rafters**	Newtown	(809) 628-9258	$6–$21

Note: • Lunch Only

•• Dinner Only

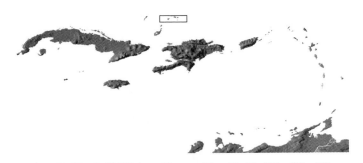

TURKS & CAICOS
ISLANDS

Divers in the Turks/Caicos Islands may run into the Spanish hogfish.

Turks & Caicos sound like something out of an Arabian fantasy, and indeed, most Americans have never heard of this archipelago of arid and rough-hewn islands lying 575 miles southeast of Miami. The beauty of this region is simply the pure interplay of earth and water, the contrast of sculpted limestone formations interspersed with sprawling, unspoiled beaches, groves of cactus and thickly entwined scrub bush, and acres of spreading mangroves and wetlands. As a result, these islands offer plenty of opportunities for the observation of natural behavior, particularly in the deserted cays etched along the shoreline. The entire chain of the large Caicos islands, from

953

uninhabited East Caicos to North Caicos, is cut through with extensive caverns and cave systems, many of which have offered up artifacts traced back to the Taino Indians. Besides excellent diving, the wetlands offer serious exploration to the intrepid, graced by the flaming pinks of flamingos which inhabit the islands of South Caicos, North Caicos and Grand Turk. Other great birdwatching is found along the shores of Lake Catherine on West Caicos.

Providencials (familiarly known as Provo), is one of the most popular roosting grounds for visitors, having led the Turks and Caicos into the modern age of tourism. Just 25 years ago, Provo had no roads other than foot or donkey paths connecting its three settlements; there was not even a single motorized vehicle, and most locals made their living by fishing, farming, or bartering. Today one of Provo's greatest assets is a broad, unbroken extent of beach stretching 12 miles along the shore of Grace Bay. Accommodations here can run from the small to the medium-sized hotel to luxury condos to resorts. There's a modern telecommunications system, and access to items generally unavailable elsewhere. There is also fine dining, nightclubs, casinos, a bit of shopping, tennis courts, and an 18-hole golf course. Virtually every type of watersports toy is available. But the best thing about the Turks & Caicos is that nobody cares who or what you are, as long as you pay the bill.

Bird's Eye View

Located 575 miles southeast of Miami and about 100 miles north of Hispaniola (the Dominican Republic and Haiti), the Turks and Caicos are an extension of the same geological structures that make up The Bahamas. In fact, they were part of the same country until 1874 when the two countries were divided by Great Britain to make governing them easier.

The 50-plus islands of the Turks and Caicos are arrayed around the edges of two large, limestone platforms. These platforms are not unlike the great mesas of the American southwest, huge-flat-topped structures surrounded by cliffs. The big difference is that the limestone platforms of the Turks and Caicos are awash in water that seldom exceeds a depth of 20 feet. The westernmost bank, Caicos, is the largest of the two by far. It serves as a the base for six primary islands—West Caicos, Providenciales (Provo), North Caicos, Middle Caicos, East Caicos and South Caicos—along with some 30 smaller

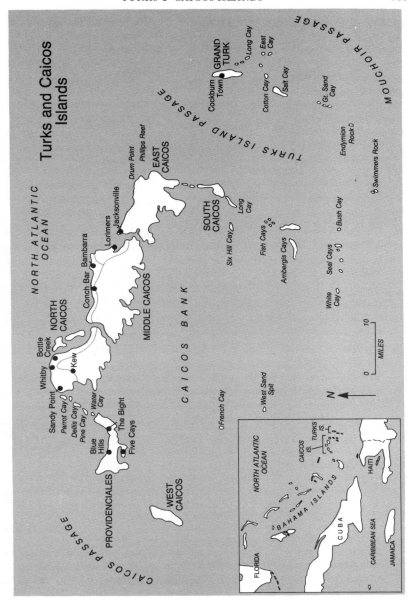

cays. The bulk of this landmass is clustered across the north of the bank, with just a few small (but significant) islands elsewhere.

The Caicos are encircled by a barrier reef lying from one to two miles offshore. Between the reef and the islands are scattered coral in calm, clear waters. The two groups of islands are separated by a deep channel between the Caribbean and the Atlantic.

History

Serious evidence suggests that Grand Turk was the first landfall made by Columbus in 1492. Since the islands had no riches, however, the fleet quickly moved on. For 900 years prior, the Taino and Lucayan Amerindians, had occupied these islands, having originated in the Orinocco region in South America—peace-loving tribes who had survived by fishing, farming and trading dried conch meat and conch pearls in Hispaniola to the south. Only 40 years later after their first European contact, the native tribes were totally wiped out by enslavement, disease and abuse. With the exception of an odd shipwrecked sailor, the islands remained uninhabited for over 200 years.

In the mid-1600s, Bermudian saltrakers arrived and their influence is still felt. They divided the tidal lakes on Salt Cay, Grand Turk and South Caicos into salt pans (called *slainas*), controlled the flooding and evaporating of the sea water and raked out the salt, creating an industry that was the mainstay of the economy for the next 275 years. Even today, broken windmills stand, ghostly sentinels over the salinas. Simultaneously, buccaneers hiding out in the Caicos preyed on treasure vessels passing through the Caicos Passage. Colorful legends still abound about Calico Jack Rackman and the two women pirates Bonnie Anne and Mary Reid. In the late 1700s, British patriots departing from the newly formed United States arrived taking up the role in the growing plantocracy of sisal and cotton—a valiant but frustrating attempt doomed to failure. The most extensive ruins of plantations may be seen at Yankeetown on West Caicos and Wade's Green on North Caicos.

Today with the exception of Provo, time stands still here. History is found in every cove on the Turks and Caicos. The outlines of wrecked vessels in the shallow sand, the Loyalist plantation homes and workhouses abandoned to weather, rust tools lying in ruins. The history is peppered with tales of explorers and adventurers, indentured servants, slaves, fishermen, pirates, saltrakers and shipbuilders.

Grand Turk

Six miles long by one mile across, Grand Turk is the seat of government for the Turks and Caicos. Accommodations here largely take the form of historic hotels dating from the early 1800s. This is an ideal place for divers who don't like places that cater to tourists. Activities here center around diving, or simply lying on the beach and taking it easy.

What to See

Turks and Caicos National Museum, a must-see under the direction of Brian Riggs, gives you a glimpse into the early days of the islands, reaching back to the tribal population. A special exhibit on the **Molasses Reef** wreck, found on the southern reaches of the Caicos Bank, is fascinating. The wreck, dating from the early days of the 16th century, is the first recorded European wreck in the New World.

Museums and Exhibits
Turks

Turks & Caicos National Museum ★★★

Guinep House, Cockburn Town, ☎ *(809) 946-2160.*
Hours Open: 9:00 a.m.–4:00 p.m.
This small museum, housed in an old stone building, centers on the nation's people and natural history. The highlight is the wreck of a caravel that sank on Molasses Reef in 1513, believed to be the earliest shipwreck found in the Americas. General admission: $5.00.

Providenciales

Island Sea Center ★★★

Blue Hills, ☎ *(809) 946-5330.*
Visitors can learn about the ocean and its creatures at this spot, highlighted by the Caicos Conch Farm, where the tasty critters are bred from tiny eggs. You can watch a video on their production and a touch tank allows for up-close inspections. The admission is $6.00 for Adults and $3.00 for Children.

Sports/Recreation
Turks

Watersports

Various locations, Cockburn Town.
These islands are especially known for their excellent beaches and wonderful scuba diving. If your hotel lacks the necessary equipment, try one of these. Grand Turk:

Blue Water Divers *(Fax: 946-2432)* and **Sea Divers** *(☎ 946-1407)*. Diving on Providenciales can be found at **Dive Provo** *(☎ 946-5040)*, **Provo Turtle Divers** *(☎ 946-4232)*, and **Flamingo Divers** *(☎ 946-4193)*. Boats can be rented at Provo at **Dive Provo** *(☎ 946-5040)*.

Providenciales

Provo Golf Club

Blue Hills, ☎ *(809) 946-5591.*
Hours Open: 7:00 a.m.–7:00 p.m.
This challenging course, designed by Karl Litten, just opened in 1991. It has 18 holes and a par of 72. There's a club house, driving range, and pro shop on the premises. Greens fees are about $80, cart included.

Salt Cay

Salt Cay is stuck in time. It's a monument to the days when salt ruled the island—for over three centuries, till it slowed in the mid 1900s. Today you can still see tools lying about, exactly as they were dropped on their final day of use—the great houses along the shoreline are still packed with high-quality sea salt, the final harvest that was never shipped. As a historical testimony to an era long gone, Salt Cay is considered so important it has been named a World Heritage site by UNESCO. The island has only 200 residents, a couple of small hotels, one guesthouse and a dozen motorized vehicles. There is one professional dive operator who not only specializes in the excellent shallow reef and wall sites along the island but also does whale watching in the winter months and runs to the isolated wreck of the *Endymion*.

FIELDING'S CHOICE:

Both Grand Turk and Salt Cay, down to the Mouchoir and Silver Banks off Hispaniola, are the southern terminus of the migrational route of the Atlantic herd of some 2500 humpback whales. Sightings happen daily from December -April and divers frequently have a chance encounter both in water and from the boat.

Dive Sites

On the island of Providenciales, known as Provo, the center of tourism, several excellent snorkeling spots can be reached from shore. **Smith's Reef**, a shallow system with lively marine life, lies just east of Turtle Cove, while the extensive **White House Reef** can be reached from Lower Right Highway down Penn's Road. The reefs, which lie off beautiful beaches, are within the **Princess Alexandra Land and Sea National Park**. Many boats make snorkeling, shelling and exploring trips to nearby deserted caves, where you'll be greeted by the rock iguana. A "plan your own trip" aboard the *Beluga*, a 37-ft. catamaran ☎ *(*09) 941-5196*, costs $250 for a half-day and $450 for a full day for up to six people. The full day trip includes a buffet lunch and drinks; the half-day trip, snack and drinks. If you're lucky, you'll see JoJo, a seven-foot-long Atlantic bottlenose dolphin, who has lived in island waters since 1989, mingling with people in the water, although he does not like to be touched. The islands are known among scuba divers for their underwater spectacles. A coral wall off the North shore of Provo starts at 56 feet below the surface and goes down about 6000 feet. Off the Wall Divers and Guanahani Beach hotel have offered dive packages at unbelievable prices in the past years. Contact owners Terry and Maria Hopkins on Grand Turk ☎ *809-946-2159* or to make reservations or information ☎ *800-332-7736*.

Treks

Dotted with hundreds of tiny cays, the striking azure of **Chalk Sound** makes it one of the island's most scenic waterways. To find it, drive down South Dock Road to the southernmost tip of Provo, turn right off on the gravel road at the Shell storage center, and drive northwest to the national park.

A four-wheel drive vehicle is needed to reach the western end of Providenciales and the **North West Point Marine National Park and Nature Reserve**, where there is a stretch of empty beach and to the south, a group of abandoned tiki huts good for picnicking and shade. Further south, rocky coves offer private sunbathing and swimming.

Pumpkin Bluff Pond Nature Reserve, on lush North Caicos, is home year round to a flock of flamingos, from several hundred to a thousand. **InterIsland Airways** ☎ *(800) 941-5481*, offers a daily guided tour of the rural island for $119 a person, including lunch.

Where to Stay

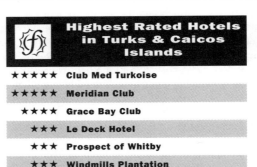

Highest Rated Hotels in Turks & Caicos Islands

★★★★★	**Club Med Turkoise**
★★★★★	**Meridian Club**
★★★★	**Grace Bay Club**
★★★	**Le Deck Hotel**
★★★	**Prospect of Whitby**
★★★	**Windmills Plantation**

Most Exclusive Hotels in Turks & Caicos Islands

★★★	**Windmills Plantation**	$440–$595
★★★★★	**Meridian Club**	$395–$575
★★★	**Prospect of Whitby**	$90–$460

Fielding's Best Value Hotels in Turks & Caicos Islands

★★★	**Windmills Plantation**	$440–$595
★★★	**Prospect of Whitby**	$90–$460
★★★	**Le Deck Hotel**	$95–$175
★★	**Guanahani Beach Hotel**	$120–$165
★★★★★	**Meridian Club**	$395–$575

Most of the rentals on the Turks and Caicos are in Provo, although you can find a few cottage rentals on the out islands. **Cockburn**, the capital of Grand Turk, caters to small hotels that are personally run by colorful locals. **Turks Head Inn** is an unusually atmospheric 19th-century dwelling with 6 rooms. Even the hotels/resorts in North Caicos hardly aspire to their name, but are serviceable to those who have come to experience the outdoors. Overlooking the south side of Providenciales are attractive, newly refurbished one and two bedroom apartments in **Casuarina**. The only property which can be faithfully called a resort is the **Meridian Club** in Pine Cay, a private island, where you will find 23 private homes and 15 hotel guest rooms. One of the loveliest places to stay is the **Windmills Plantation Salt Cay**, a 2-1/2-square mile isle which was the hub of the salt industry in the 60s. The colonial-style property is built around the plantation great house and is situated on a superb beach. For information about lodging in the Middle Caicos and South Caicos, contact the Tourist Board. Sometimes locals open up their homes.

Hotels and Resorts
Grand Turk

The best property here is **Turks Head Inn**, in Cockburn Town, formerly the Government Guest House turned American Consulate, housed in a 19th-century mansion, complete with hardwood floors and antique furnishings.

Guanahani Beach Hotel $120–$165 ★★

P.O. Box 178, Guanahani Beach, Cockburn Town, ☎ *(800) 468-8752, (809) 946-2135.*
Single: $120–$165. Double: $120–$165.
This small hotel is a 20-minute walk from Cockburn Town. Guestrooms are simple and rely on ceiling fans to keep cool. This property attracts mainly divers, and has an excellent dive shop and resident instructor. There's also great snorkeling right off the beach. Facilities include a restaurant, bar and pool at this casual spot. 16 rooms.
Credit Cards: V, MC, A.

Kittina Hotel $75–$220 ★★★

Duke Street, Cockburn Town, ☎ *(800) 548-8462, (809) 946-2232.*
Single: $75–$215. Double: $95–$220.
Located on the west side, five minutes from town, this family-owned hotel is across the street from the beach. Guestrooms are generally pleasant (but could use some refurbishing), with local art, ceiling fans, and balconies; most are air conditioned. The newer beachfront suites also have kitchenettes. The grounds include a dive shop, two bars, a restaurant, and scooter rentals. The Friday night barbecues, held around the pool, are great fun. 43 rooms. Credit Cards: V, MC, A.

Prospect of Whitby $90–$460 ★★★

North Beach, Cockburn Town, ☎ *(809) 946-7119.*
Single: $90–$195. Double: $145–$460.
Situated on seven miles of beach, this isolated hotel bills itself as perfect for escaping the outside world. Rooms are spacious and air conditioned, with basic but comfortable furnishings. There's a pool, tennis court, bar and restaurant on the premises, and they'll handle watersports requests. 28 rooms. Credit Cards: V, MC, A.

North Caicos

The finest property out of a small pool of unimpressive fish is the **Ocean Beach Club**, an apartment complex with units rented when the owner is absent. Kitchens are included. A swimming pool is on the premises.

Pine Cay

The Meridien is romantic and rustic.

Meridian Club $395–$575 ★★★★★

Pine Cay, Cockburn Town, ☎ *(800) 331-9154, (809) 946-5128.*
Single: $395–$520. Double: $400–$575.

This deluxe operation is located on its own 800-acre private island with a very spectacular beach. Accommodations are in colorful and quite pleasant beachfront rooms; 15 more expensive cottages supply sitting areas, screened porches, and kitchenettes. The idea here is pure escapism—no TV, newspapers, or radios to remind guests that there is a world out there. Ceiling fans and trade winds make up nicely for the lack of air conditioners. There's a bar and restaurant, and active types are kept happy with a pool, tennis court, watersports and nature trails. Nice. 28 rooms. Credit Cards: Not Accepted.

Providenciales

This is where some of the premier properties are located now in the region. **Club Med** is synonymous with great food (a challenge here) as well as unmitigated enthusiasm for all things sensuous. **Le Deck Hotel & Beach Club** comes in a close second, though the atmosphere is more inn-line.

The new **Grace Bay Club** has been elegantly designed as a Spanish village in stucco the color of the late-afternoon sun, with red-tiled roofs, terra-cotta floors, stone balustrades, wrought-iron balconies, umbrella-covered terraces and lush courtyards. The Canadian chef magically makes use of Caribbean ingredients, including the local spiny lobsters.

Club Med Turkoise $850–$1650 ★★★★★

Blue Hills, ☎ *(800) 258-2633, (809) 946-4491.*

This large Club Med is one of the best in the chain. It is set on 70 acres with a mile-long beach and attracts mainly couples and singles devoted to scuba diving—as well as the pleasures of a tropical vacation. Lodging is found in low-rise buildings lining the beach, all with two double beds and ceiling fans. The extensive facilities include three restaurants, a theater complex, a pool, eight tennis courts, a fitness center and a nightclub. The rates include all activities, meals and watersports, though you'll pay extra for diving and golf at a nearby course. Children from age 12 and teens are welcome, though unlike the family-oriented Club Meds, there are no special facilities for them. Rates range from $850 to $1650 per person per week, plus a one-time $30 membership fee and a $50 annual fee. 400 rooms. Credit Cards: V, MC, DC, A.

Grace Bay Club $255–$725 ★★★★

Grace Bay, ☎ *(800) 946-5758, (809) 946-5757.*
Single: $255–$555. Double: $355–$725.

Situated on a 12-mile sandy beach and designed to resemble a Mediterranean village, this deluxe choice pampers guests nicely. Lodging choices range from studios to one- and two-bedroom suites and penthouses, all air conditioned, elegantly appointed, and with kitchens and all the latest creature comforts. On-premise facilities include a gourmet restaurant, bar, pool, two tennis courts and most watersports. 22 rooms. Credit Cards: V, MC, A.

Le Deck Hotel $95–$175 ★★★

Grace Bay, ☎ *(809) 946-5547.*
Single: $95–$175. Double: $95–$175.

This two-story hotel is located on Grace Bay's lovely sandy beach. The air-conditioned guestrooms are clean and simple. Facilities include a pool, watersports and a popular bar and restaurant. Lots of young singles and couples at this informal and popular spot. 27 rooms. Credit Cards: V, MC, A.

Turtle Cove Inn $90–$180 ★★

Blue Hills, ☎ *(800) 633-7411, (809) 946-4203.*
Single: $90–$180. Double: $90–$180.
This hotel, located at the marina, houses guests in air-conditioned rooms with TV, VCRs, small refrigerators and phones. Sporting facilities include a pool, two clay tennis courts, bike rentals, and watersports, including diving. Snorkelers can take advantage of free boat service to a reef and beach. Ramada's casino is nearby and there's lots within walking distance. 30 rooms. Credit Cards: V, MC, A.

Salt Cay

Windmills Plantation is a five-minute flight from Grand Turk, hardly worth the time to buckle up your seat belt. You must like small planes.

Windmills Plantation $440–$595 ★★★

North Beach Road, Cockburn Town, ☎ *(800) 822-7715, (809) 946-6962.*
Single: $440–$595. Double: $440–$595.
This all-inclusive resort is located on Salt Cay, nine miles south of Grand Turk. Set on a 2.5-mile sandy beach, this recreated colonial plantation is a colorful and eclectic mix of architectural styles and facades that is as inviting as it is comfortable. Each lovely guestroom is uniquely decorated with four-poster beds, antiques, and porches or verandas. Dinner is served by candlelight in the fine restaurant, and three bars keep thirsty throats at bay. There's also a pool and watersports, included in the rates. Horseback riding and nature trails are nearby. Wonderful! 8 rooms. Credit Cards: V, A.

Apartments and Condominiums
Providenciales

Check with **Prestigious Properties** ☎ *(809) 946-4379* for villas and cottages that have kitchen facilities. Don't expect any to come with a maid, though you might ask around if a local is interested. Do audition first.

Ocean Club $125–$390 ★★

Grace Bay, ☎ *(809) 946-5880.*
Single: $125–$390. Double: $125–$390.
This deluxe condominium complex sits on nicely landscaped grounds fronting a gorgeous beach. Accommodations are found in five buildings housing studios and units of one to three bedrooms, all air conditioned and quite luxuriously appointed with modern amenities and full kitchens. There's a bar and grill on-site, as well as a pool and lighted tennis court. You can walk to the casino at the Ramada and area restaurants. Very nice. 32 rooms. Credit Cards: V, MC, A.

Grand Turk

Check with the agency Prestigious Properties, Ltd. ☎ *(809) 946-2463* for properties with kitchens. Supplies will be a problem as you are sure not to find what you are accustomed to in this region. Bring whatever you have to have from home, or be willing to make do.

Coral Reef Beach Club $65–$135   ★★

The Ridge, Cockburn Town, ☎ *(809) 946-2055.*
Single: $65–$135. Double: $65–$135.

This beachfront property accommodates guests in one- and two-bedroom apartments with motel-like furnishings and air conditioners. Recreational amenities include a dive shop, watersports, a pool and a tennis court. There's also a bar and restaurant for those not up to cooking in. A good combination of efficiency living and hotel facilities. 21 rooms. Credit Cards: V, MC, A.

Ocean Beach Hotel/Condos $94–$175   ★

Whitby, Cockburn Town, ☎ *(809) 946-7113.*
Single: $94–$145. Double: $105–$175.

This complex is set right on the beach. Guests can choose from standard rooms or apartments with kitchens, all done in rattan furnishings and with ocean views. Ceiling fans do the job in lieu of air conditioners. Facilities include a bar, restaurant and pool, and they'll help arrange watersports and island tours. 10 rooms. Credit Cards: V, MC.

Treasure Beach Villas $112–$175   ★

Bight, Turtle Cove, ☎ *(809) 946-4211.*
Single: $112–$175. Double: $112–$175.

This complex offers one- and two-bedroom villas sitting on the beach, each with living and dining areas, full kitchens, and ceiling fans in lieu of air conditioners. There's a pool and tennis court on the premises, and restaurants are within a five-minute walk—though you're best off renting a car for true mobility. They'll help arrange watersports and deep-sea fishing. 18 rooms. Credit Cards: V, MC, A.

Inns
Grand Turk

Erebus Inn $80–$150   ★★

Turtle Cove Marina, Turtle Cove, ☎ *(809) 946-4240.*
Single: $80–$150. Double: $80–$150.

Set on a cliff with wonderful views, this cheerful spot accommodates guests in comfortable rooms, bungalows and chalets. All have telephones and TV, and 22 are air-conditioned. There's a restaurant, bar, two pools and two tennis courts on the premises, and they'll shuttle you over to a nearby beach. Unless your heart is set on being right on the sea, this property fills most needs very nicely. 30 rooms. Credit Cards: V, MC, A.

Turks Head Inn $55–$80   ★

Cockburn Town, ☎ *(809) 946-2466.*
Single: $55. Double: $80.

This Bermuda-style inn dates back to 1849 and was a government guest house and American Consulate in prior years. Guestrooms are simple but very pleasant with antiques, air conditioners, and private baths. Facilities are limited to a bar and restaurant. 7 rooms. Credit Cards: V, MC, A.

Low Cost Lodging
Grand Turk

Anything considered inexpensive will be in the most basic of properties. For up-to-date options, contact the **Castaways Beach House** ☎ *(809) 946-6921*.

Provo

In a region where upscale tourists are courted to the demise of the hard-core backpacker, cheap digs are hard to come by. Contact the tourist board for suggestions. Hotel rates drop late April to November.

Pine Cay

Smith's Cottage is about the only place on Pine Cay that has any rates close to low-cost. Again, on these high-priced islands, it's all relative, but rest assured, the surroundings won't be Club Med.

Salt Cay

Contact the Tourist Office for your best help in finding low-cost lodging. **Mount Pleasant Guest House** ☎ *(809) 946-6927* has a story reputation, but reservations must be made in advance.

Where to Eat

Highest Rated Restaurants in Turks & Caicos Islands

★★★★★ **Anacaona**

★★★★ **Alfred's Place**

★★★★ **Hey, Jose**

★★★ **Dora's**

★★★ **Fast Eddie's**

★★★ **Top o' the Cove**

Most Exclusive Restaurants in Turks & Caicos Islands

| ★★★★★ **Anacaona** | $28–$32 |
| ★★★★ **Hey, Jose** | $8–$14 |

Fielding's Best Value Restaurants in Turks & Caicos Islands

| ★★★ **Fast Eddie's** | $10–$15 |
| ★★★★★ **Anacaona** | $28–$32 |

Providenciales

Alfred's Place $$$ ★★★★

Turtle Cove, ☎ (809) 946-4679.
International cuisine.
Lunch: 12:00 p.m.–4:00 p.m., entrees $12–$19.
Dinner: 4:00 p.m.–11:00 p.m., entrees $10–$25.

A French chef and Austrian owner dish out mostly American meals and stiff drinks to an appreciative crowd. Diners schmooze and munch on a deck set above Turtle Cove. Prime rib, swordfish, lobster, salads and sandwiches are on the bill of fare. Closed: Mon. Reservations required. Credit Cards: V, MC, A.

Anacaona $$$ ★★★★★

Grace Bay Club, ☎ (809) 946-5950.
International cuisine.
Lunch: entrees $10–$25.

Dinner: entrees $28–$32.
It's hard not to feel like a god or goddess while dining indolently under one of the stunningly decorated thatched roofed huts fronting the ocean. Each of the discreetly spaced tables within display pristine napery and gleaming glassware and a single candle encased in a hurricane lamp. Ceiling fans cool the air and torches enhance the glow from the star-filled night sky. Succulent seafood straight off the fishing boats are often served tasting redolently of the in-house smoker. Terrific wine list, homemade desserts and Italian coffee drinks. Associated Hotel: Grace Bay Club. Reservations required. Credit Cards: V, MC, A.

Dora's $$$ ★★★
Leeward Highway, ☎ (809) 946-4679.
Latin American cuisine.
Lunch: entrees $8–$10.
Dinner: prix fixe $20.
The abundant marine life in the area have made a goldmine out of this unprepossessing place that's always packed—four days a week there's an all-you-can-eat seafood buffet for $20. Those who shun our fishy friends can opt for hearty soups served with homemade bread, or pork chops and a side of vegetables. Free transportation to and from neighboring hotels is provided. Reservations recommended. Credit Cards: Not Accepted.

Fast Eddie's $$ ★★★
Airport Road, ☎ (809) 946-4075.
American cuisine.
Lunch: 8:00 a.m.–4:00 p.m., entrees $10–$15.
Dinner: 4:00 p.m.–11:00 p.m., entrees $10–$15.
Hungry tourists love the juicy prime rib, served on Fridays, and a bountiful seafood buffet on Wednesday evenings for $20. Other times there's locally caught turtle steak, chicken, conch, salads and burgers. It's also a good place to round up a friendly group for a game of darts. Live bands rock the place once a week. Reservations recommended. Credit Cards: V, MC.

Hey, Jose $$ ★★★★
Atlas House, Leeward, ☎ (809) 946-4812.
Mexican cuisine.
Lunch: 12:00 p.m.–3:00 p.m., entrees $8–$13.
Dinner: 6:00 p.m.–10:00 p.m., entrees $8–$14.
This airport area restaurant has a whiz behind the bar who makes the frothiest margaritas on the island. The chef keeps tasty platters of tacos and sizzling fajitas coming out of the kitchen at all hours of the day and night. Housed in a shopping center, it isn't very intimate, but that's not what the boisterous crowds come for. Pizza, burgers and chicken are also available. Closed: Sun. Reservations recommended. Credit Cards: V, MC, A.

Top o' the Cove $ ★★★
Leeward Highway, ☎ (809) 946-4694.
American cuisine.
Lunch: 6:30 a.m.–4:00 p.m., entrees $5–$12.

Homesick New Yorkers and other big city dwellers appreciate the bagels and deli fare provided by this cozy spot. The mean cups of eye-opening espressos and foamy cappuccinos wake everybody else out of a midday torpor. There's a nice atmosphere despite its location next to an auto parts store. Mostly takeout, but there are a few tables to park the body for an hour or two. Credit Cards: Not Accepted. Credit Cards: V, MC, A.

Turks and Caicos Directory

ARRIVAL

Travel to and from the Turks and Caicos is made easy by American Airlines, the country's primary carrier, which flies into Provo from Miami seven times a week. Transfers to Grand Turk are handled by Turks and Caicos Airways, with small, six passenger planes. TCA also flies a 19-passenger jet, offering alternative service from Nassau and Miami as well as other destinations. Air travel to all other inhabited islands is also offered by TC as well as several small carriers such as Interisland.

A departure tax of $15 is collected at the airport.

CLIMATE

Temperatures range from 75–85 degrees F. from November -May, spiraling up to the 90s in June through October. Constant tradewinds keep the heat bearable. There is no marked rainy season. Hurricane season runs June-October.

DOCUMENTS

Visitors are required to write a valid passport (or proof of citizenship in the form of a birth certificate, voter's registration card plus a photo ID).

ELECTRICITY

Current runs 100 volts, 60 cycles, the same as in the United States.

GETTING AROUND

Those who've come to the Turks and Caicos for watersports and trekking will find that a cab to and from the airport is probably the only transportation they will need. Major hotels are within walking distance of a beach; those which aren't offer a shuttle service. However, restaurants and most attractions to Provo are located about a $10 taxi trip from most hotels, making a scooter or rental car necessary.

Taxis are unmetered, and rates, posted in the taxis, are regulated by the government. A trip between Provo's airport and most major hotels runs $15. On Grand Turk, a trip from the airport to town is about $4.; from the airport to the hotels outside town $5–$10.

Rental cars are available on the island. On Provo, **Budget** ☎ *(809) 94-64079* and **Highway** ☎ *(809) 94-52623* offer the lowest rates, which average $40–$50 per day. Scooters are available at **The Honda Shop** ☎ *(809) 94-65585* and **Scooter Rental** ☎ *(809) 94-65585* and ☎ *(809) 94-64684* for $25 per 24-hour day.

Ferry service is available with the **Caicos Express** ☎ *(809) 94-67111* or *(809) 94-67258* with two scheduled interisland ferries between Provo, Pine Cay, Middle Caicos, Parrot Cay, and North Caicos daily except Sunday. Tickets cost $15 each way. Caicos Express also offers various guided tours to the out islands.

A bus runs into town from most hotels on Providenciales, running about $2–$4 one-way. A new public bus system on Grand Turk charges 50 cents one-way to any scheduled stop.

LANGUAGE

The official language of the Turks and Caicos is English.

MEDICAL EMERGENCIES

Emergency medical care is provided at the Provo Health Medical Centre downtown ☎ *946-4201*, including eye and dentalwork. The government Blue Hills Clinic has a doctor and midwife on call ☎ *946-4228*. Grand Turk has a hospital on the north side of town. Other islands organize emergency air service to the closest hospital available.

MONEY

The official currency of the Turks and Caicos is the U.S. dollar.

TELEPHONE

The area code is *809*. To dial direct from the U.S., dial *011* (international access) + *809* (country code) +local number. To make international calls from the Turks and Caicos, it's best to go to the Cable & Wireless office in Provo ☎ *(809) 94-64499* and Grand Turk *(809) 94-62200*. These offices are open Monday-Thursday 800 a.m.–4:30 p.m., Friday 8:00 a.m.–4 p.m. You can make calls from local phones with the use of a credit card purchased in increments of $5, $10, and $20.

TIME

Atlantic Standard Time, meaning one hour earlier than New York. During daylight saving time, it is the same time as New York.

TIPPING AND TAXES

Hotels charge a 7 percent government tax and add a 10–15 percent service charge to your bill. In a restaurant, it's appropriate to leave a 10–15 percent tip if it is not added already; do check so you don't duplicate efforts. Taxi drivers expect a small tip.

TOURIST INFORMATION

The **Turks and Caicos Islands Tourist Board** has a toll-free number on the islands ☎ *(800) 241-00824*. For hotel information, contact **The Turks & Caicos Resort Association** ☎ *(800) 2 TC-ISLES*.

WATER

Outside of Providenciales, where desalinators have transformed much of the island into a riot of flowers, water remains a precious commodity. Drink only from the decanter of fresh water provided by the hotel, but tap water is safe for brushing your teeth and other hygienic purposes.

WHEN TO GO

Late April to the end of November is off-season, when you can save 15–20 percent on hotel rates.

TURKS & CAICOS ISLANDS HOTELS	RMS	RATES	PHONE	FAX
Providenciales				
Blue Hills				
★★★★★ **Club Med Turkoise**	400	$850–$1650	(800) 258-2633	
★★ **Turtle Cove Inn**	30	$90–$180	(800) 633-7411	
Grace Bay				
★★★★ **Grace Bay Club**	22	$255–$725	(800) 946-5758	(809) 946-5758
★★★ **Le Deck Hotel**	27	$95–$175	(809) 946-5547	(809) 946-5547
★★ **Ocean Club**	32	$125–$390	(809) 946-5880	(809) 946-5845
Turks				
Cockburn Town				
★★★★★ **Meridian Club**	28	$395–$575	(800) 331-9154	(809) 946-5128
★★★ **Prospect of Whitby**	28	$90–$460	(809) 946-7119	(809) 946-7114
★★★ **Windmills Plantation**	8	$440–$595	(800) 822-7715	(410) 820-9179
★★ **Coral Reef Beach Club**	21	$65–$135	(809) 946-2055	(809) 946-2503
★★ **Erebus Inn**	30	$80–$150	(809) 946-4240	(809) 946-4704
★★ **Guanahani Beach Hotel**	16	$120–$165	(800) 468-8752	(809) 946-1460
★★ **Kittina Hotel**	43	$75–$220	(800) 548-8462	(809) 946-2877
★★ **Sunworshippers Pelican Beach Club**	25	$70–$120	(809) 946-4488	(809) 946-4488
★ **Ocean Beach Hotel/Condos**	10	$94–$175	(809) 946-7113	
★ **Treasure Beach Villas**	18	$112–$175	(809) 946-4211	(809) 946-4108
★ **Turks Head Inn**	7	$55–$80	(809) 946-2466	(809) 946 2825

TURKS & CAICOS ISLANDS RESTAURANTS	LOCATION	PHONE	ENTREE

Providenciales

lue Hills

	American			
★★★ **Fast Eddie's**	Blue Hills	(809) 946-4075	$10–$15
★★★ **Top o' the Cove**	Blue Hills	(809) 946-4694	$5–$12•
	International			
★★★★ **Anacaona**	Blue Hills	(809) 946-5950	$10–$32
★★★★ **Alfred's Place**	Blue Hills	(809) 946-4679	$12–$25
	Latin American			
★★★ **Dora's**	Blue Hills	(809) 946-4679	$8–$20
	Mexican			
★★★★ **Hey, Jose**	Leeward	(809) 946-4812	$8–$14

Note: • Lunch Only

•• Dinner Only

INDEX

Order Your Fielding Travel Guides Today

BOOKS	$ EA.
Amazon	$16.95
Australia	$12.95
Bahamas	$12.95
Belgium	$16.95
Bermuda	$12.95
Borneo	$16.95
Brazil	$16.95
Britain	$16.95
Budget Europe	$16.95
Caribbean	$18.95
Europe	$16.95
Far East	$19.95
Freewheeling RV Adventures	$19.95
Hawaii	$15.95
Holland	$15.95
Italy	$16.95
Kenya's Best Hotels, Lodges & Homestays	$16.95
London Agenda	$12.95
Los Angeles Agenda	$12.95
Malaysia and Singapore	$16.95
Mexico	$16.95
New York Agenda	$12.95
New Zealand	$12.95
Paris Agenda	$12.95
Portugal	$16.95
Scandinavia	$16.95
Seychelles	$12.95
Southeast Asia	$16.95
Southern Vietnam on Two Wheels	$16.95
Spain	$16.95
The World's Great Voyages	$16.95
The World's Most Dangerous Places	$19.95
The World's Most Romantic Places	$16.95
Vacation Places Rated	$19.95
Vietnam	$16.95
Worldwide Cruises	$17.95

To order by phone call toll-free
1-800-FW-2-GUIDE

(VISA, MasterCard and American Express accepted.)

*To order by mail send your check or money order,
including $2.00 per book for shipping and handling (sorry, no COD's) to:
Fielding Worldwide, Inc. 308 S. Catalina Avenue, Redondo Beach, CA 90277 U.S.A.*

*Get 10% off your order by saying "Fielding Discount"
or send in this page with your order*